Ethics Applied

Edition 3.0

Primary Authors

Paul De Vries, Ph.D.
Robert Veatch, Ph.D.
Lisa Newton, Ph.D.

Editors

Emily V. Baker
Michael L. Richardson

Pearson
Education

Boston • Menlo Park • New York
London • Ontario • Sydney • Mexico City • Madrid • Amsterdam • Paris

Cover Art by Jack Barrett
Cartoons by Donald G. Addis
Four-color art courtesy of the Leepa/Rattner Collection,
   St. Petersburg, Florida
Photographs of four-color art by Barton Gilmore
Signature design by Christian Stolte and Kristen Kiley
Book design by Peter Schiller and others

Library of Congress catalog card number: 94–12045
1. Ethics   2. Ethics-History   3. Business Ethics
4. Professional Ethics   5. Science and Ethics   6. Social Ethics

Printed in United States of America

10 9 8 7 6 5 4 3 2 1

Please visit our website at www.pearsoncustom.com

ISBN 0–536–60243–3

BA 990615

PEARSON EDUCATION
Boston • Menlo Park • New York
London • Ontario • Sydney • Mexico City • Madrid • Amsterdam • Paris

Text Copyright Acknowledgments

CD-ROM COPYRIGHT ACKNOWLEDGMENTS

DEDICATION

To the students, faculty, trustees,
alumni and staff of St. Petersburg Junior College

ACKNOWLEDGMENTS

The college especially appreciates the outstanding contributions of the authors, for their expertise, cooperation and enthusiasm in this very special, interdisciplinary project, designed for the use of students throughout their lives. As former student government president John Griffis stated: "I may not use calculus every day of my life, but I will use this ethics course every day for the rest of my life."

In the fall of 1982 Paul Ylvisaker, then dean of the Harvard School of Business, addressed the Association of Governing Boards of Colleges and Universities. He challenged postsecondary education to do more in the study of ethics. In the audience was Thomas H. Gregory, former chairman of the Florida Commission on Ethics who subsequently became chairman of the District Board of Trustees of St. Petersburg Junior College. Gregory accepted the challenge. The college's president shared it with the college faculty. By early 1985, after careful planning, the college established a required course in Applied Ethics for Associate in Arts degree students. The college is indebted to the memory of Dr. Ylvisaker, now deceased, for his inspiration and guidance. Without his encouragement this textbook would not have been attempted.

Among the many who played vital roles in the book's creation are Emily Baker M.S., J.D., director of the Applied Ethics Institute at the college; members of the Applied Ethics Faculty at the College; Dr. Carl M. Kuttler, Jr., SPJC president, whose vision and commitment made the project possible; trustees including W. Richard Johnston, Chairman; Evelyn Bilirakis, Kenneth P. Burke, Dr. Susan D. Jones, and Kenneth T. Welch. Also involved in the historic commissioning of this project were past Chairman Dr. Pamela Jo Davis, and former trustees Stanley A. Brandimore, Lacy Harwell, Ann Hines, Gary Megaloudis, Robert Young as well as Chairman Emeritus Joseph H. Lang; and deceased former trustees Demos A. Megaloudis and Mac J. Williams; and Karen K. White J.D., who guided the establishment of the department and the course and served as textbook project manager for the first edition.

The college also wishes to acknowledge David Daniels and Don Kilburn of Simon & Schuster and the professional services of publisher's senior editor Hal Hawkins, as well as the following individuals who assisted in various ways from simple encouragement to various levels of expertise and detailed editing: Barbara Barksdale, Chris Gill, Julie Froelich, Debbie Coniglio, JoAnne Weaver, Kristen Colman, Peter Schiller, Jim Moorhead, Dr. Carol Copenhaver, Dr. Robert Sullins, David Henniger, Kathy Federico, Shirley Hunter, William Martin, Barton Gilmore, Charles Lasater, Margaret Richardson and the telecommunications staff of the college.

FOREWORD

American society has functioned in large measure for 200 years on a glorious assumption: Basic moral choices and ethical values would be inculcated by the institutions of family, community and religious organizations. That assumption, though increasingly tenuous, has worked. Public education, for the most part, has operated on the same assumption and added another: The study of those values in higher education occurs primarily in liberal arts curricula and postgraduate education in the humanities. But the marketplace has been telling us for some time that many workers are not prepared for the *application* of these very values in the context of their daily work. Regularly, the news media parade before us an array of ethical failures in all walks of life.

This book is intended to meet that marketplace need. It is a bold initiative, deep into the practical application of ethics to life decisions, and wide in the range of issues it analyzes. It was commissioned because there simply are few textbooks in *applied* ethics and secondly, because seldom are so many issues presented — allowing the faculty to choose upon which topics sound moral reasoning may be applied by students.

I strongly commend this wonderful book to those institutions who are wrestling with the issue of values education. It is well past time higher education recognized that, in the world of work, at least, there, indeed, are some practices that are right and some that are wrong. The book, of course, skillfully avoids indoctrination, but it provides readers with a veritable banquet for ethical thought as well as appropriate instruction in how to apply one's beliefs to daily decisions. It leaps into electronically delivered learning in several exciting ways.

America's higher education community now has an advanced tool to stimulate teaching in critical thinking and ethical decision-making. They will find in *Ethics Applied* **e**dition *3.0* an instrument that will serve as a catalyst to begin their own efforts in this increasingly important field. I am well within the bounds to suggest that no college or university should tackle ethics instruction without this volume in its possession.

Dale Parnell
Retired Professor, University of Oregon
and of the Higher Education Program
University of South Florida
Past President and Chief Executive Officer
American Association of Community Colleges

CONTENTS

PART I: THE EXAMINED LIFE PAUL DE VRIES, PH.D.

Contributors: Roy Peter Clark, David Seiple, Allen F. Plunkett

PART II: MAJOR MORAL ISSUES ROBERT VEATCH, PH.D.

Contributors: Nancy Jecker, Susan Terkel, Emily Baker, Cindy Stark, David Seiple, Ric Machuga, F. Barbara Orlans, Holmes Rolston III, James W. Nickel

PART III: MORES IN THE MARKETPLACE
LISA NEWTON, PH.D.

Contributors: William F. Edmonson, Garland Thompson, Joanna Wragg,
Donald Pride, Michael Richardson, Keith Goree

ETHICS APPLIED
eDITION 3.0

MISSION STATEMENT:

The purpose of this book is to cause the reader to stop and think, reflectively, to use the powers of critical thinking and moral reasoning to apply ethical principles in the challenges of life. The chief outcome of understanding this textbook will be that students will have a grasp of theories of moral reasoning and be able to develop and apply their own approaches to ethical decision-making.

THE PRIMARY WRITING FACULTY

Paul De Vries, M.A. and Ph.D. University of Virginia, is the president of NYES Fund Inc., an educational program, and a partner in Leadership Excellence Inc. He also is president of the International Research Institute on Values Changes, based in New York and Moscow. He is co-author of two recent books, *Ambitious Dreams*, and *The Taming of the Shrewd*.

— *Part I: The Examined Life*

Robert Marlin Veatch, B.S. Purdue, B.D. Harvard, M.S. California at San Francisco, M.A. and Ph.D. Harvard University, professor of medical ethics at Georgetown University and former director of the Kennedy Institute of Ethics at Georgetown. He was a teaching fellow at Harvard and served as associate for medical ethics at Hastings-On-Hudson, N.Y. He is author of *Value-Freedom in Science and Technology; Death, Dying and the Biological Revolution; A Theory of Medical Ethics*; and *Case Studies in Medical Ethics*. Currently he is associate editor of *The Encyclopedia of Bioethics* and serves on the editorial boards of several journals including the *Journal of the American Medical Association* and the *Journal of Medicine and Philosophy*.

— *Part II: Major Moral Issues*

Lisa H. Newton, B.S. and Ph.D. Columbia University, is Professor of Philosophy and Director of the Program in Applied Ethics at Fairfield University in Fairfield, Connecticut. She is author or co-author of several textbooks in the fields of Ethics and Environmental Studies, including *Wake Up Calls: Classic Cases in Business Ethics* (1996), *Watersheds: Cases in Environmental Ethics* (2nd ed. 1997), and *Taking Sides: Controversial Issues in Business Ethics and Society* (5th ed. 1998); she also is author of more than 70 articles on ethics in politics, law, medicine and business, and was the writer and ethics consultant for Media and Society's 1990 series, *Ethics in America*, broadcast on public television. She consults on issues of health care ethics with several regional health care providers, and has a faculty appointment in the Department of Medicine at Yale Medical School for the teaching of medical ethics.

— *Part III: Mores in the Marketplace*

THE CONTRIBUTING WRITERS

Roy Peter Clark, M.A. Providence College, Ph.D. State University of New York at Stony Brook, is Dean of the Faculty at The Poynter Institute for Media Studies, which has centers on ethics, writing, graphics and broadcasting. The Long Island native teaches writing and has established a national newspaper writing center at Poynter to hold seminars and workshops for editors, reporters, students, and teachers from around the world. Among his publications is *Coaching Writers: Editors and Reporters Working Together*.

— *Introduction*

David I. Seiple, M.A. and Ph.D. Columbia University, M.T.S. *magna cum laude*, Drew University Theological School, is Adjunct Lecturer of Humanities at New York University. His most recent articles include contributions to *The Encyclopedia of Aesthetics* and *The Dictionary of Literary Biography*. He is co-editor of *Democracy and the Aesthetics of Intelligence: Essays in Deweyan Pragmatism* (forthcoming from SUNY Press) and is author and web editor of Philosophies Labyrinth.

— *Approaches, Punishment, War*

Allen F. Plunkett, Jr., M.R.E. Providence College, is Professor of Ethics at St. Petersburg Junior College where he teaches Applied Ethics, Logic and Philosophy and is sponsor of the Phi Theta Kappa Chapter at the Tarpon Springs Center.

— *Critical Thinking*

Nancy S. Jecker, M.A. Philosophy Stanford University, M.A. and Ph.D. University of Washington, is assistant professor at the University of Washington School of Medicine, Department of Medical History and Ethics. She is 1993 visiting fellow at the DeCamp Program in Ethics and the Life Sciences, Princeton University, and winner of the American Journal of Nursing 1992 Book of the Year as editor of *Aging and Ethics: Philosophical Problems in Gerontology*.

— *Abortion*

Susan Neiburg Terkel, B.S. Cornell University, is author of 12 books on social and medical issues, including *The Drug Laws: A Time for Change?, Finding Your Way: A Book About Sexual Ethics,* and *People Power: A Look at Nonviolent Action and Defense*. She was founder and director of Temple Beth Shalom School, Hudson, Ohio. She has appeared on radio and television to discuss ethics and moral education.

Emily Baker, M.S. Criminal Justice, University of Southern Mississippi, and J.D. Mississippi College School of Law, is Director of the Applied Ethics Institute at St. Petersburg Junior College. For 16 years she presided as County Court Judge in Jackson County, Miss., including eight years as senior judge. She also has served as a consultant to the National Resource Center on Child Sex Abuse and as a member of the Foundation for the National Council of Juvenile and Family Court Judges.

— *Pornography*

Ric S. Machuga, M.A. Philosophy, University of Oregon, M.A. History, California State University, Chico, is a tenured professor of philosophy, ethics and history at Butte College in Oroville, Calif. and is currently the President of the Academic Senate. He was a Regents Fellow in Philosophy at the University of California, Davis. His publications include numerous critical essays in Magill's Literary Annual, Books and Culture and elsewhere.

— *Economic Justice*

William Fred Edmonson, M.B.A. University of Southern Mississippi, Ed.D. University of Mississippi, is President of Panola Junior College, Carthage, Texas. Former Dean of Instructional Affairs at Itawamba Community College in Fulton, Miss., he was selected "Outstanding Educator in America" while at North Florida Junior College.

— *Employee Rights and Responsibilities*

Joanna DeCarlo Wragg, B.A. Florida State University, a Pulitzer Prize-winning editorial writer and former associate editor of the *Miami Herald*, is a partner in Wragg and Casas, a communications and advertising firm in Miami. Past president of the National Conference of Editorial Writers, she also served as chair of the Professional Standards Committee. Formerly editorial director of WPLG-TV (ABC) Miami, she is non-lawyer member of the Florida Bar Grievance Committee and the Miami-Dade Community College Committee of 100.

— *Communications in Commerce*

Garland Thompson, J.D. Temple University School of Law, is a member of the Editorial Board of the *Baltimore Sun*, executive editor of *The Crisis*, official publication of the National Association for the Advancement of Colored People, and a Gannett Fellow teaching at the University of Kansas. His interest and research contributed to a landmark Equal Employment Opportunity Commission case.

— *Employee Rights and Responsibilities*

Donald Pride, former press secretary for two-time Florida Governor and U.S. Senate candidate Reubin Askew, was director of investigations for the Chief Inspector General, Office of the Governor, State of Florida. Former editor of a New England weekly newspaper, editorial writer and political writer for the *St. Petersburg Times* and columnist with the *Tampa Tribune*, he also was a candidate for Florida Secretary of State.

— *Ethical Decision-Making in Public Service*

Keith Goree, B.A. Harding University, M.A. Abilene Christian University, is professor of Applied Ethics and Honors Applied Ethics at St. Petersburg Junior College and author of an ethics text for secondary students.

— *Codes of Ethics*

Donald G. Addis, B.A. University of Florida, is an editorial cartoonist for the *St. Petersburg Times*, and nationally recognized for his "Bent Offerings" distributed by Creators Syndicate Inc. His pungent wit has appeared in national publications for more than three decades. The prize-winning artist is a 1993 recipient of honors from the National Cartoonists Society.

— *Cartoons*

Cynthia A. Stark, Ph.D. University of North Carolina, is assistant professor of philosophy at the University of Utah. She specializes in feminist theory, political philosophy and ethical theory. Her publications on pornography are: "Pornography, Verbal Act and Viewpoint Discrimination," Public Affairs Quarterly, October, 1998 and "Is Pornography an Action?: The Causal vs. the Conceptual View of Pornography's Harm," Social Theory and Practice, Summer 1997. She has also published on Kant and on impartiality in ethics.

— *Pornography*

F. Barbara Orlans, Ph.D. is a Senior Research Fellow at the Kennedy Institute of Ethics, Georgetown University. A physiologist, she conducts research on the ethical and policy issues of animal experimentation. In previous years she conducted animal experiments on heart disease at the National Institutes of Health. She is the author of *In the Name of Science: Issues in Responsible Animal Experimentation*, published in 1993 by Oxford University Press.

— *Animal Well-Being*

Holmes Rolston III, Ph.D. University of Edinburgh, 1958, is University Distinguished Professor at Colorado State University where he is especially known as a leading scholar in environmental ethics having published *Philosophy Gone Wild* (1986), *Environmental Ethics* (1988) and *Conserving Natural Value* (1994). He is also a co-founder and associate editor of the Journal of Environmental Ethics and founding past-president of the International Society of Environmental Ethics. Rolston is also a backpacker, a field naturalist, and a biologist.

— *The Environment*

James W. Nickel, Ph.D. University of Kansas, is a professor of philosophy at the University of Colorado since 1982. Previously he taught at Wichita State University and in the Jurisprudence and Social Policy Program of the University of California at Berkley Law School. Nickel's fields of specialization are ethics, political philosophy, and the philosophy of law.

— *Human Rights*

Michael Richardson, award winning editor of editorials of the *St. Petersburg Evening Independent* and former member of the editorial board of the *St. Petersburg Times*, is executive assistant to the president of St. Petersburg Junior College. Author of a human rights documentary, *After Amin—The Bloody Pearl*, he is a past chairman of the professional standards committee of the National Conference of Editorial Writers (NCEW) and former president of the NCEW Foundation.

— *Decision-Making in Public Service*

EDITORS' NOTE

Perhaps, in this instance, you can tell a book by its cover. Artist Jack Barrett, whose work has graced galleries in the U.S. and Canada, captures in a glance the theme of this text with his portrayal of a stoplight emphasizing the yellow light. Those who conceived the textbook and those who commissioned and produced it have no desire to tell anyone which direction to turn. Their objective is to cause a thoughtful pause that will lead readers to look and listen with heightened awareness of the risks and rewards of ethical decisions made in life. And this second edition enters the interactive, electronic world in a modest but effective way:

* The inclusion of a CD-Rom of supplemental learning materials.
* Electronic "hot links" to research of key points covered in the text.
* Links to the web page of the Applied Ethics Institute.
* Each chapter's listing of Internet resources.
* Listings of motion pictures in which ethical issues have been depicted.

In addition, there is a unique, 16-page full-color section of related art from the Leepa/Rattner Collection, interspersed with timeless wisdom.

Ethics is a discipline related to what is good and bad including moral duty and obligation, values and beliefs used in critical thinking about human problems. In *Ethics Applied e*dition 3.0 the emphasis is on applying that thinking to daily decisions. The concept of teaching applied ethics, as has been noted in the Acknowledgments, was inspired by Dr. Paul Ylvisaker, former dean of the Harvard School of Education, who in 1982 urged colleges and universities to require courses in ethics to meet an emerging societal need. Creation of the book was affected also by the work of the Hastings Center Institute for Society, Ethics and the Life Sciences, which directed a two-year study on "The Teaching of Ethics in Higher Education."

The purpose of the text is to provide breadth and balance to ethical problems. Written with clarity by an amalgam of academicians and practicing professionals for the postsecondary student experiencing a first taste of ethics study, it emphasizes actual application of ethics to daily decision-making. Considerable effort has been made to avoid indoctrination. Eight approaches to moral reasoning are presented with the stipulation that the theories are only guideposts to assist students in recognizing and applying their own moral and ethical lights.

In 1959 a study jointly sponsored by the Ford Foundation and Carnegie Corporation urged training for managers to develop "a personal philosophy or ethical foundation." American society has been rocked on its heels many times before and since due to moral failure and ethical scandal. The need for ethics in the marketplace has never been more pronounced; so it is that approximately 40% of this text is devoted to marketplace ethics, but not to the exclusion of the classical ethical concerns of life-and-death decisions and social justice.

The book is a wake-up call to the array of conflicts of interest that pose ethical challenges in every walk of life. It meets students where they are, with no assumption that they have given much thought to the issues of ethics. It relies heavily on actual news stories of recent vintage that depict the ethical traps into which many have fallen, from Ivan Boesky to Janet Cooke, not to mention the scandal-a-day world of Washington, D.C. It also explores the ethical implications of such apparently mundane transactions as paying for roof repairs.

The Examined Life takes up Socrates' warning of the danger of thoughtless living and begins the self-examination process. Carefully, slowly, in an explanatory style, authors show students how to develop critical-thinking skills, to recognize behavior and to understand eight different approaches to moral reasoning — from classical to contemporary — and the accounts and stories from which they are drawn. Moral development itself is explained so that students can recognize stages of moral awareness in decision-making. *In fact, Chapters 4 and 5 comprise the fulcrum of the book as to ethical reasoning, and it is expected that students will want to read them more than once, in order to develop their own integrated worldview*.

Major Moral Issues features chapters on bioethics, abortion, death and dying, sexual ethics, pornography, the environment, animal well-being, punishment, war, human rights and economic justice. It is not expected that each of these topics would be covered in a single course. It is expected that faculty would exercise their judgment in the selection of those issues which would most benefit their students. These chapters are often heavily devoted to information peculiar to each subject. In this way the book practices what it has instructed in earlier chapters — that, often, the key to ethical decision-making is a complete examination of the details and implications of an issue. Students are challenged to apply general moral principles and critical thinking to the problems inherent in these issues and to draw their own conclusions.

Mores in the Marketplace is a six-chapter section full of information about the ethical implications of actions on the job — ranging from insider trading to sexual harassment to the actual communications of commerce. Here the student finds the grist of the business world — corporate culture, discrimination in the workplace, employee rights, the corporate social audit, unscrupulous advertising, employer and employee obligations, government regulation and public policy.

The wide margins belong to the reader as a place for dialogue with the writing faculty and the editors. The reader is urged to make notes throughout the text (pages are provided) but mainly in the margins. Especially pertinent notes of authors are emphasized in the margins (and cumulatively compiled at the end of each chapter). Also the margins are host to the poignant comments of others, asides, levity and critically placed icons emphasizing strategic elements of the text. Have fun in the margins!

The chapter sub-section "For Further Inquiry" establishes a baseline for student learning activity. This section, of course, is not intended to supplant the instructor's primary role in teaching and learning. Note also additional matter for inquiry included on the CD-ROM which is a part of this textbook. Instructions for its use may be found on the last page of the book. It includes references to Internet addresses, motion pictures related to the topic, additional readings, selections, notes and links to still other applicable information.

Uniquely, the text is illustrated with cartoons drawn by a prominent national cartoonist. The intent here obviously is not to suggest that the issues of life are frivolous but that a sense of humor goes a long way in promoting understanding and, even, reader endurance. Also, some have suggested life is too important to leave to philosophers!

An Appendix, Comprehensive Glossary and Index complete the text. These instruments are offered to assist instructor and student as they pursue the application of their own ethical standards in daily choices. A Study Guide, Instructor's Manual and test bank are available from Pearson Education.

It is important that students remember the purpose of the text is to equip them to recognize and use their own moral compasses — not to persuade them of any particular philosophical lifeview. The authors recognize that both faculty and students have rights in the classroom which may be invoked if they are subjected to ridicule or harassment for their beliefs, and that these grievances may be appealed to faculty and administration or to local, state and federal human relations agencies and to state and federal courts.

A final note: "If you could sum up what this book is about," authors are asked, "what would you say?" We would be remiss if we did not attempt an answer, and it goes like this: "There are general moral principles in life. And there are human problems. A person can build self-confidence in taking control of problems by understanding and applying general moral principles, making ethical judgments and reaching conclusions about the most appropriate action to take in the various situations of life. When you do that, you have practiced applied ethics." To that end, the book is dedicated.

— The Editors

INTRODUCTION

A fter a big storm, you discover that the roof of your house leaks. You are concerned because times are tough. You don't want to deplete your savings by having to pay for costly roof repairs. Someone recommends ACME roofers to you: "Good work at a fair price."

Mr. Johnson of ACME inspects your roof. "You've got some pretty extensive damage," he says. "It'll take three days to fix it."

"How much?" you ask.

"Well, we'd usually get about $3,000 for this. But I'd be willing to do it for $1,500 — if you pay me in cash."

You are surprised, and then relieved. What a good price! Much less than you expected. But suddenly you get a funny feeling in the pit of your stomach. "I wonder why he wants to be paid in cash?"

Welcome to the world of applied ethics!

Even if you have integrity, doing the right thing may not be a piece of cake.

DOING THE 'RIGHT THING'

Your roofer is a member, in good standing, of the underground economy. He lowers his price in exchange for cash payments. His goal is to avoid paying taxes. He is breaking the law, but he, and others like him, have been at this a long time, and there is little chance he will be caught.

People don't turn him in for one simple reason: self interest. He does provide good service at the best price in town. Americans appreciate a bargain, don't they?

Imagine that your roofer has offered you his best deal. Now consider these questions:

1. Is it wrong for you to pay him in cash?
2. Is it wrong for you to act in your family's self-interest? After all, times are hard.
3. What do you need to know about your roofer, his business, and his motives in order to make a good decision? How would you find out?
4. Is Mr. Johnson really doing any harm? Isn't he helping people by offering a low price?
5. Why is your stomach still hurting?

YOUR 'GUT INSTINCT'

We have several names for that pain in your stomach. Some call it your conscience. Some call it your sense of right and wrong. Others call it your gut reaction.

Whatever it is, maybe it resides in another part of your body. Perhaps you hear a "warning bell" or see a "flashing caution light." We say that something "smells fishy." We look at a person in conflict and wonder, "What's eating him?"

Our body wisdom sends us signals about what is right and wrong.

We may read volumes of philosophy or sit at the feet of a wise and ancient holy man. We may be young or old. Rich or poor. But for many of us, an ethical decision may begin not with an idea, but with a feeling in the gut.

But ethics cannot end there. It must move from the gut to the heart, mind, and soul. We grow as ethical people by moving from our instinct to rules and guidelines that light the way.

FOLLOWING 'THE RULES'

Let's return to the tough decision we need to make about the repairs on our roof. We're suspicious of the roofer's motives, but what next? Maybe there are some "rules" that would help. Is there a law against paying Mr. Johnson in cash? Probably not, but there are laws against evading your taxes. Am I, in some way, helping him break the law? Am I his accomplice? Aren't there some "rules" that say "a person should not lie or steal," or "people should respect the legitimate authority of government," that is, they should pay their taxes?

The world of law is smaller than the world of ethics. You can follow the law and still do something wrong. Perhaps you have every legal right to pay in cash and take the lower price. You may have heard someone say this before: "Just because it's legal, doesn't make it right."

FINDING A WAY THAT WORKS

When we talk about ethics, we say that acts have consequences. You go out drinking, you get behind the wheel of a car, you hit someone, she dies, her children are left without a mother, their lives are changed forever, and so is yours.

There's a problem: You can't always see how things will turn out. Sometimes good comes out of bad. Terry Anderson, an American reporter taken hostage for almost seven years in Lebanon, often talks passionately about the good things that have happened to him as a result of his painful captivity. He would not have chosen that path or wished it on others, but fate, destiny, providence, whatever name we give those mysterious forces that shape our lives have unforeseen consequences. Good comes out of bad. Or in the words of an old religious saying: "God writes straight with crooked lines."

TOOL 1: MORAL REASONING

When some people talk about ethics, about what is right and wrong, they want to go beyond their gut instinct and even beyond the rules that they know.

They want to follow a process of moral reasoning — moving from general moral principles to the facts of the matter — that ultimately leads them to a good conclusion. Learning to apply this process is central to the purpose of this book. The process often progresses through a series of questions. A news reporter, for example, working on a sensitive story may ask this series of questions:

1. What good will be accomplished by publishing this story?
2. How can I best fulfill my duty to inform citizens about this important issue?
3. Will anyone be hurt if I publish this?
4. Are there ways I can minimize that harm?

These questions often are best answered through consultation with others. The reporter who talks with editors, with sources, with other reporters, and with independent experts will benefit from the conversation. Good talk, especially with good people, often leads to good decisions.

Lucy Makes a Pitch, a Charles Schulz comic strip.

A meeting on the pitcher's mound:

Linus: "If you strike out this last guy, Charlie Brown, you're going to make him very very unhappy . . . "

Lucy: "That's right. Are you sure you want to bring unexpected grief into that poor kid's life?"

Charlie Brown: "Just what I need . . . Ninth-inning ethics."

TOOL 2: ETHICS SOURCES

Our sense of right and wrong comes from many places. We may learn our sense of fairness, how to share, from growing up with brothers and sisters. We may go to church or synagogue and learn the Ten Commandments or the Sermon on the Mount. Years of schooling can teach us values such as hard work, honesty, and tolerance. Films and literature also are among those influences that help to form us with their powerful messages.

Advancement within our profession may lead us to embrace a special set of values and duties, which is sometimes call the "ethos" of that profession. The word "ethics" comes from that Greek word. It refers to "the guiding beliefs, standards, or ideals" that define a group or set it apart.

But the forces that shape us, and the institutions that nurture us, are complex and contradictory. An abusive family warps the child into a life of abuse. The church may teach us intolerance for the beliefs of others. Schools may teach us narrow-mindedness and pressure us to cheat in our classes. Not all literature or film, of course, appeals to our better instincts. And the only thing some people learn about ethics in their profession, is how to avoid them.

AS THE STOPLIGHT TURNS . . .

When people first study ethics, they sometimes come into the class with this idea: There are so many gray areas in life, and so many different opinions, that decisions can only be made on a case by case basis. In the face of what is called "situational ethics," frustrated students throw up their hands and reject the hard work necessary to reach a good moral judgment.

It is true, there are few moral principles that apply without exception. Even the rule "thou shalt not kill" is not absolutely and universally enforced. We kill in self-defense. We kill in war. We electrocute heinous murderers. And many people think abortion, permitted by law, is the killing of a human being.

Many dilemmas are difficult to resolve because they involve the conflict of two competing good goals.

* It is good to deter people from murder.
* It is good not to kill.
* Capital punishment suggests it is difficult to do both.

* It is good for a journalist to inform the public about important social issues.
* It is good not to invade a person's privacy.
* In some cases it may be impossible for the journalist to carry out his public duty without harming others.

Consider the case of tennis star and social activist Arthur Ashe. He contracted the HIV virus through a blood transfusion during surgery. Years later, *USA Today* received a tip that Ashe had AIDS. Although the tip was reliable, the paper has a policy of not using unnamed sources, especially in important stories. A reporter went to Ashe about the story. Although Ashe wanted to retain his privacy, he announced in a news conference that he had AIDS and criticized the press for its pursuit of this story.

When they heard about this story, many people, including many journalists, had a gut reaction that something was wrong, that a good man, fighting a fatal illness, was harmed unnecessarily by an insensitive press. *USA Today* had its defenders. The argument went like this:

* Even a public figure like Ashe should be able to keep things to himself to protect his family.

* But Ashe built his reputation as an athlete and a social activist through publicity. He's a role model. The public cares about what happens to him.

* Yes, but shouldn't he have the right to decide the time and place to reveal his condition?

* Listen, AIDS is one of the great public health menaces of our lifetime. The press needs to help make people care about those with AIDS.

* Like it or not, there's still a stigma in our society about having the disease.

* We help remove the stigma by reporting fully on the nature of the illness, and we humanize its effects by showing lots of different people can get it.

* But you are hurting a person without good reason, just to sell newspapers. If you had ethics, you'd consider the consequences of your actions.

* You're wrong about us. And about the reaction. Most of the things that resulted from this report were good: people were informed that anyone can get the disease; Ashe was surrounded by sympathetic admirers; his role as a social activist was enhanced, not weakened. He was even selected Sportsman of the Year by *Sports Illustrated*. The story about his award was titled "The Eternal Example: Arthur Ashe epitomizes good works, devotion to family and unwavering grace under pressure." Ashe died early in 1993, and was widely eulogized as a great humanitarian and athlete.

The language we use often reflects whether we are taking a red light or green light point of view:

Red light: Thou shalt not kill.
Green light: Love thy neighbor.

Red light: Don't miss Mass on Sunday.
Green light: Love God and worship him.

Red light: Don't cheat on your exams.
Green light: Be an honest, hard-working student.

And the yellow light that often flickers caution as we approach decisions, if we honor it, can cause us to pause and ponder the implications, to weigh the conflicting interests, to start a process of moral reasoning that leads to a good decision.

SELF-INTEREST: NOW OR LATER?

Our society honors those who act against their obvious self-interest. We admire those who reject the easy road, who make difficult sacrifices for the cause of justice. Mother Teresa's followers reject material comforts and devote their lives to the service of the poor and dying in Calcutta, India. The struggle for racial justice led the Rev. Martin Luther King, Jr., to the jails of Birmingham, and finally to his death by an assassin's bullet.

We can trace the values of selflessness far back into our culture, to the story of Socrates, the Greek philosopher, who submitted to execution by drinking hemlock rather than compromise his principles; and to the story of Jesus, who Christians believe suffered and died by crucifixion so that humankind might find eternal life.

Dr. Stockmann, the hero of Henrik Ibsen's play, "An Enemy of the People," risks his personal fortune, his reputation in the community, his family, and his personal safety in an effort to tell the citizens of his community one unpopular and agonizing truth: that the waters of the town's therapeutic warm springs are poisoned. No matter that the town's tourist economy is in jeopardy. The doctor yells out the truth, even in the face of ostracism and death: "The children are poisoned! The people are poisoned!" (Adapted by Arthur Miller, New York: Penguin Books, 1979.)

A MATTER OF TRUST

You have studied hard in college and worked hard in your career and risen to a position of influence in your community as a successful corporate attorney. You enjoy donating your time and energy to non-profit and charitable organizations, one of which is the local community college.

You have accepted a position as a member of the Board of Trustees, and you influence the President of the college, the other board members, and the direction of the entire institution.

As a successful corporate lawyer, you have many important clients. A large construction company has retained your services for 10 years. You represent this company in many important business deals, and their success has contributed to your success.

The community college is about to undertake a 10-year project to expand the campus, a project that, when completed, will require the construction of three classroom buildings, a library expansion, and a student union. The construction company you work for plans to compete for this job. It will offer, along with six other contractors, a bid to do the work. You have a conflict of interest. Do you see it?

Consider and discuss the following alternatives:

1. Resign immediately from the Board of Trustees.

2. Tell your construction clients you can no longer represent them.

3. Don't bother to reveal the nature of your conflict. You know you are an honorable person, and you are experienced enough to choose what is right.

4. Disclose the nature of your conflict as quickly and as widely as possible.

5. Consult state law and the state bar association to find guidelines governing such conflicts.

6. Choose not to vote on any question in which you face a conflict.

Now imagine yourself as the President of the Construction Company. Consider and discuss the implications of these choices:

1. Fire your attorney.

2. Ask him to resign from the Board of Trustees.

3. Ask him to lobby hard so that your company can gain the contract.

4. Ask him to feed you information so that you can offer a bid that is lower than the rest, but high enough to maximize profits.

5. Ask for a meeting with the Board to discuss the potential conflicts.

6. Consult experts on business ethics.

In pondering your decisions, consider the following thoughts about the ethics of college trustees that come from the summer 1989 edition of the *Trustee Quarterly of the Association of Community College Trustees*. Read them as a guide to solving the problems in the above case studies. Do they shed any light?

* Refrain from even the appearance of impropriety.

* Be a catalyst for change in the meeting of community needs.

* Be a model of community values, encouraging the best practices agreed and carried out in the highest fashion.

* Never allow personal or family gain as a direct result of public action.

* Avoid nepotism (hiring or promoting family members) and personal influences of hiring practices.

* Declare real or potential conflicts of interest before voting; abstain when appropriate.

* Respect the "no-surprise rule." Give fellow trustees and administrators advance warning of new issues of concern.

* Emphasize education as the means for building ethical foundations and maintaining them.

NATIONAL AND GLOBAL INTERESTS

The word "incest" describes one of our most powerful taboos — the legal ban against sex among close relatives. By analogy, the word "incestuous" is often used to describe ethical conflicts that extend into the highest reaches of our government and influence global and international issues.

It works this way: For the last eight years you have worked in a high government position in the Department of Commerce. You were appointed by the President of the United States. You are an expert on international trade, and you have worked closely with the Congress, and have made many contacts in business and in government.

A new administration has been elected, and it is time for you to leave government service and take the next step in your career. What will you do? You are approached by a U.S. law firm that represents the interests of Japan on issues of international trade. You are offered $500,000 a year to use your knowledge of the system and your numerous personal contacts to lobby Congress on behalf of Japanese business interests.

Perhaps you see why people call such a system "incestuous." Working for the government one day, then lobbying the government the next, seems an unhealthy form of "influence peddling" filled with all sorts of opportunities for conflict of interest.

WHERE WE ARE

It is difficult for individuals to form a moral compass without the help of the sustaining institutions that form our society.

At the heart of the "good society" is the family, but no family can do its job of raising children alone. Parents need the support of neighborhoods, religious institutions, schools, businesses, labor unions, the media, and government at every level. Yet many people consider all these institutions to be in serious decay. As a result they feel adrift, heartsick, drawn back to self-interest and self-reliance as the only means of survival.

"If the well-being of its children is the proper measure of the health of a civilization," wrote *Fortune* magazine in 1992, "the United States is in grave danger. Of the 65 million Americans under 18, fully 20% live in poverty, 22% live in single-parent homes, and almost 3% live with no parent at all. Violence among the young is so rampant that the American Academy of Pediatrics calls it a public health emergency.

"The loss of childhood innocence is a recent phenomenon, affecting all income levels and all ethnic groups. Playground fights that formerly ended in bloody noses now end in death. Saturday-night cruising can end in drive-by shootings. Schools that once considered talking in class a capital offense are routinely frisking kids for weapons, questioning them about drugs. AIDS has turned youthful experimentation with sex into Russian roulette. And good public education, safe streets, and family dinners — with both mother and father present — seem like quaint memories of a far distant past. The bipartisan National Commission on Children wrote in *Beyond Rhetoric*, its 1991 report, that addressing the unmet needs of American youngsters 'is a national imperative as compelling as an armed attack or a natural disaster.'"

Cain, having killed his brother Abel, asks God, "Am I my brother's keeper?"

The Golden Rule tells us to "Do unto others, as you would have others do unto you."

Thomas Kochman, a scholar of cultural diversity, prefers: "Do unto others, as they would do unto themselves."

All of these imperatives derive from an ethic of connectedness and community — not only that we have individual rights, but that we have collective responsibilities. The study of ethics can lead us to an understanding of what those are.

We began this chapter with the case of you and your roofer. Would you pay him in cash for a lower price, knowing that he was trying to avoid paying taxes? Try to remember your first reactions, your gut instincts, when you read that case. Think about it again, in the light of these other cases, and any classroom discussions you have had in trying to figure out the right thing to do. Add the following story into your thinking.

In August of 1992, Hurricane Andrew hit the southeast coast of Florida. One of the most powerful storms on record became one of America's most terrible disasters. Thousands of homes were destroyed, resulting in billions of dollars worth of damage.

A storm need not have ethics, but the people who build houses do. An investigation of the storm damage revealed that the damage to houses was, in many cases, greater than it need have been. The problem, said investigators, was sub-standard construction. In some cases, flimsy staples, instead of sturdier nails, were used to attach roofs to houses.

Perhaps nothing in America symbolizes community more powerfully than a row of sturdy houses filled with families and surrounded by helpful neighbors. That image might be little more than Norman Rockwell mythology. But the people devastated by Hurricane Andrew believed that their homes would be constructed up to legal standards. So think, once more, about your deal with ACME roofers. Is your immediate self-interest identical to your long-term interests? How far are you willing to put your trust in someone who engages in shady business practices? And, when the next storm hits, will you be left without a roof over your head, in the literal and ethical sense?

PART I

The Examined Life

CHAPTER 1

ETHICS AND HUMAN CONFLICT

"Once you give up integrity, the rest is a piece of cake."
— **J.R. Ewing, of Dallas *fame*, bragging on his ethics**

"Integrity is the singleness of life, character and person that informs us at our best, that requires us always to act in accord with our moral principles, and thereby permits us to undertake courses of action that, if we waited for deep analysis, would scare us to death."
— **Lisa Newton, professor, author, Fairfield College**

Who knows when ethical concerns first start to affect us? They are definitely part of our daily experience and behavior no matter where we are, and regardless of what we are doing. We live, act and think within the context of the ethics environment.

When does the ethical environment start to affect us? Even in our mother's womb we are responsive to voices of love and expressions of care. Babies in the womb react to words of anger and rejection, too. And even rather soon after birth babies can detect certain emotions in people's facial expressions. Attitudes of love and acceptance are so very important to the earliest human development, it is important that body language expressing these things be understood by babies.

Nor are these ethical attitudes merely passive, infantile experiences. Babies themselves respond with love, while they also have ways of asserting their personal power, demanding the attention of others around them. Babies begin early to learn that parents and other adults are selective in the attention they give, often in some fair proportion to the specific needs of each situation.

Then, even as toddlers, in some way or another, ethical concerns were probably part of our conversation, almost from the time we were able to start talking. Very early in our childhood we learn to watch out for ourselves to be sure that we receive our fair share of the cookies or ice cream or attention. We also learn new ways of expressing and receiving love and care. Moreover, we begin in early childhood to learn elementary kinds of accountability: We must behave in certain ways, or else there are either penalties or missed rewards.

Paul De Vries, M.A. and Ph.D. University of Virginia, is the president of NYES Fund Inc., an educational program, and a partner in Leadership Excellence Inc. He also is president of the International Research Institute on Values Changes, based in New York and Moscow.

We learn to give **attentiveness** to our environment, and look for **fairness**, for **care**, and for **accountability**. We live in a world in which, if you do not watch out, others' unfairness, uncaring, or lack of accountability can hurt you.

WHAT IS ETHICS?

People's concepts of ethics depend upon a number of factors, both personal and cultural, so that it is impossible to design a clear definition that will please everyone. Some people think first of personal ethics, giving attention to cheating or sexual conduct. Others think first of ethical crises or dilemmas in business, government, community, and family. **Ethics** is a discipline related to what is good and bad including moral duty and obligation, values and beliefs used in critical thinking about human prob-

CHIEF LEARNING OUTCOME

I can recognize moral issues and understand the role of ethics in solving human conflicts.

lems. This book emphasizes **applied ethics,** which is the actual use of moral standards of behavior in making decisions about human problems.

In any case, the common thread is **"human problems."** Ethical concepts, concerns, reasoning processes, solutions, and resolutions are simply some of the resources for approaching those human problems. If you consider **"critical thinking"** to be informed and responsible human thought, then a good working definition of ethics is "critical thinking about human problems."

Of course, formulating and remembering a definition of ethics is not the point. Instead, we are trying to recognize and resolve ethical issues in a responsible manner. Nevertheless, with this definition in mind let us begin to clarify how ethics is similar to and different from other human enterprises.

The terms "ethics" and "morals" come from Greek and Latin terms having to do with behavior, culture, and habits. The words are often interchangeable. Sometimes "ethics" is used more to refer to conscious choices of principles and goals, and "morals" is then reserved for descriptions of actual behavior. However, this is a distinction that rarely holds, since we talk often of "moral reasoning" and "moral theory," and when we question someone's ethics we may be referring to some very specific, concrete behavior.

THE ROOTS OF ETHICS

Some of the earliest thorough writers on ethics in the "Western world," were Greek philosophers Plato and his student Aristotle, who made the ethics environment very inclusive. In Plato's writings, for example, the four ultimate virtues or moral standards of justice, wisdom, courage and temperance are ultimate principles for our universe, and they apply to every aspect of community and individual life. For this reason, ethics was to be the ultimate focus of the educational process. In Plato's concept of a well-run republic, only those who spend years studying ethics, and who have been recommended by their teachers — who then also prove themselves with years of excellent service — would be allowed to hold public office. The ethics environment was that important, from Plato's point of view.

Aristotle's concept of ethics was different from his teacher's, but for him the ethics environment was no less encompassing. A person's virtues and moral habits are still the most important aspect of his or her personal development, and the most essential element for success in life. The Aristotelian ethical environment is inclusive of every aspect of life, including our use of money and our cultivation of quality friendships. The objective is to obtain a good balance in our social behavior, between the extremes of being a buffoon or a bore. In the ethics environment one should seek a "golden mean" between extremes in most things. However, with respect to some things there is no good middle ground in the ethics environment. For example, even though he taught moderation in most things, Aristotle also taught that the extreme of *faithfulness in marriage* was always right, while the other extreme, adultery, was always wrong.

Although their ethical perspectives were very encompassing, neither Plato nor Aristotle connected their moral perspectives with Greek religion. They were either critical of the myths of the gods' immoralities, or they ignored the traditional deities. They hardly tolerated some of the festivals and prayers of traditional Greek religion. In sharp contrast, the ethical perspectives of the Near East and the Far East were almost always grounded in religion, in some way or another. As a result, when Aristotelian scholars first met with Jewish scholars in Alexandria, Egypt long before Jesus' birth, they saw that **Judaism** was very different from Greek religion. They saw that Judaism affected every

KEY CONCEPTS

Ethics is a discipline related to what is good and bad including moral duty and obligation, values and beliefs used in critical thinking about human problems.

Applied ethics is the actual use of moral standards of behavior in making decisions about human problems.

Critical thinking is informed, reasoned and responsible human thought about human problems.

Conflict of interest — the predicament arising when a person confronts two actions that cannot be ethically reconciled; competing loyalties and concerns with others, self-dealing, outside compensation; divided loyalties among, for example, public and-or professional duties and private and-or personal affairs.

Moral means capable of distinguishing right from wrong with a predilection for right; as an adjective, it describes a person or act or thing that conforms to agreed-upon standards of conduct; as a noun, it is a summation of truth from an incident or parable.

aspect of life, including the ethics environment. These Greek philosophers called Judaism a "philosophical religion."

They were right. An assumption of all the Hebrew scriptures is that God, who is the almighty, the creator and the redeemer, has the right to set some of the moral standards. Cultic worship and sacrifice are explicitly less important than obedience. One's relationship to God is commonly used as a standard for one's behavior.

When it comes to ethics, not much is changed from the Old to the New Testament. In the terms of Aristotle's followers, original **Christianity** also was a wholistic "philosophical religion." Jesus insisted that the basic law cannot change, while at the same time he increased the attention given to attitudes and personal relationships to God and each other. To make the central point that godly faith is not legalistic, Jesus openly violated the rigid interpretations of the law promoted by the main religious teachers of his time, while never actually violating the law. This tweaking of the moral legalists' noses contributed to their conspiracy to crucify him. Nevertheless, Jesus asks for an all-consuming ethical commitment to God that will shape every aspect of life. The other New Testament teachers reaffirm all these themes of Jesus' teaching.

In Far Eastern culture, ethics was closely tied to religion as well. Perhaps the Greeks would have called these "philosophical religions" as well. In India, for example, **Hinduism** focuses on individual spiritual disciplines that dominate one's behavior. There are four main disciplines, or yogas, and each one is wholistic. For example, if one is a male born in the priestly caste, he is expected to devote his whole life to either the meditation-discipline or the knowledge-discipline. In the meditation-discipline, devotees might spend 12 to 16 hours a day in quiet meditation, and others will come to watch them to be inspired by their concentration. In knowledge-discipline, followers will spend all their time studying, memorizing, and applying the Hindu scriptures. Those born in some other castes are required to pursue duty-discipline, completely and consistently fulfilling the moral and social duties assigned to people of that caste. Finally, all others are called upon to focus their whole lives through devotion-discipline, devoting

Figure 1. Hindu worshippers prepare to bathe in the sacred Pushkar Lake on the day of the full moon in India. Photograph—United Nations.

every thought and action to honoring the deity. Regardless of the particular yoga, the moral-spiritual discipline is all encompassing.

Buddhism borrows some of the disciplines of Hinduism. In addition, the Buddha taught the Five Precepts, which are actually five prohibitions: the taking of human or animal life, stealing, wrong sexual relations, wrong speech including malicious gossip and lying, and the consumption of drugs and alcohol. The precepts and the disciplines help people to be more aware of what is happening, and more able to control their desires in every situation. The ethical virtues of attentiveness and temperance (a form of self-accountability) are very central to Buddhism, in all its many forms.

In the Chinese religious-ethical traditions, the focus is more on the social dimensions of one's life, rather than individual spiritual discipline. For example, **Confucianism** has made ethics the central focus, to the point of sometimes being legalistic. There are thousands of rules that are supposed to guide proper behavior, for the purpose of healing social relations and developing the right kind of humanness. In particular, there are 300 rules for proper, respectful tea drinking. These rules embrace what westerners would view as both ethics and etiquette.

Taoism found the Confucianist rules to be stifling. Taoists taught that the very rules themselves created aberrant behavior: There are some bad things that people would generally not think of doing, except that they are told not to do them. As the old saying goes, "Forbidden fruit tastes better." Even when moral rules guide people to do what is right, the Taoists point out, the rules are only a thin patch covering over a spiritual brokenness that then only festers. Instead of rules, Taoists urged people to cultivate a natural humanity, with freedom and spontaneity, and without guilt or pretense. Moral lessons should be taught by human instinct and example, but never by rules or principles. Taoism attacked rule-based morality, but it was dominated by ethical values and personal behavior.

THE GROWTH OF MORALS

The ethics environment is so much a part of our lives that it also provides a measure of our own personal growth and maturity. Are we attentive to dangers and opportunities around us, or are we merely creatures of our own desires and hormones? Some adults are very clever at hiding how immature and unthinking they are, but their childish or inhumane behavior shows their unthinking condition for what it is.

Similarly, children are generally socialized into at least some minimal level of fair and caring behavior. This socialization occurs through parental respect and discipline, neighborhood games, group activities at school, exposure to good literature, the study of history, the professions and other subjects. Unfortunately, many people learn the appearance of fairness and caring, while they truly remain greedy and selfish. One of the most important challenges of life is figuring out what the true ethical stature is of the people with whom we work and live. An even more difficult challenge may be ourselves to live up to the good standards of fairness and caring we use in judging others' behavior.

Accountability and responsibility also describe a crucial measure of human maturity. **It is a very old human game to blame others for our mistakes. To say and mean "It was my fault" requires human growth.** Young children often have rather wild and laughable explanations for why things go wrong: why the lamp is broken, why the chocolate-chip cookies are missing, how the peanut butter got all over the carpet, how the money disappeared. Adult attempts at cover-up are sometimes equally laughable, although they are often quite tragic at the same time. When is the last time you believed a politician's explanation for a mistake? Taking responsibility and learning from mistakes are signs of maturity.

Children are not just little adults; they have much to learn, especially in terms of awareness, fairness, caring, and accountability. Most adults are not just big children, or big children with language skills and some knowledge of technology or business. Adults who function well and who positively contribute to society must be skilled in at least some levels of attentiveness, justice-thinking, care, and responsibility. In Chapter 2 we will examine some specific measures of human maturity in each of these four dimensions of the ethics environment.

MORAL MEDIA

Doubtless you have heard people decry the lack of good morals in the media. There is too much abusive sex and violence in sit-coms, talk shows, soap operas, and even in the news broadcasts and prime-time programming. Advertisers exploit sex appeal to sell everything from candy to cars and computers. Some movies draw crowds to theaters through gratuitous sex and violence. The gods of Eros (sex appeal) and Thanatos (death) seem to have undepletable resources for attracting human attention.

All this may be true, and such criticism of the media is often well-documented. Nevertheless, there is a deeper point to be made: There would be no media at all were it not for morals. All kinds of media depend on morality — they are parasites of propriety, they are exploiters of ethics. This dependence is true whether the particular morality of the specific media is good or bad.

Take news broadcasts, for example. The particular news stories are selected by the news editors because they have some moral import:

* people are being injured and killed in some war,
* the credibility of some politician is being questioned,
* children's lives are at risk because some school bus drivers are ill-trained and careless,
* new research reveals that a particular shampoo causes cancer,
* a deli owner prepares free sandwiches for hungry homeless people.

All of these stories touch on ethical issues in some way, and the news editors know that we are interested in these stories because morality matters to us. Even the stock market report is important to many people because it helps them to make responsible choices with the resources that they have. Maybe there are some important news stories that have no moral import, but most of them do.

Similar observations can be made for entertainment. It is no coincidence that most popular music has something to do with some kind of love, happy or unhappy, perverse or pure, sensual or sacred. Love matters to us, and popular music helps express our joys and disappointments. Music can also express devotion to God, patriotism, awe at the power and beauty of nature, and many other attitudes that have significant places in the ethical environment.

Drama on the stage or in movies grips our attention because it attends to the human issues of fairness, courage, love, and accountability, as well as injustice, weakness, carelessness, hate, and irresponsibility. There is no plot unless there are human crises to be resolved and some movement toward a good resolution or toward a tragic failure. Both the main plot and sub-plots deal with problems that call for critical thinking. As a result, ethics is the fabric of fine theater, on the stage or on the screen.

ETHICS AND EDUCATION

It is far from clear how some people mature into exemplary adults, and how others with similar backgrounds, education, and training become abusive, exploitive people with little or no integrity. Nevertheless, virtually every subject in school touches on the ethics environment in some way, for the purpose of helping boys and girls and men and women to be aware, fair, caring, and responsible.

One especially obvious educational area is gym classes and sports. Sports activities help people to be healthy, which is an ethical concern. They also teach self-discipline, obedience to rules, team cooperation and encouragement, attentiveness, courage, and so forth. Sports and other games — such as board games and card games — are also primary resources for teaching children the attitudes and concerns of fairness. Games can be an opportunity for both players and spectators to learn more of the ethics environment.

Elementary school arts and crafts, as well as high school and college technology courses and "shop" courses, are arenas for learning efficient use of resources, respect for other people's creativity, self-discipline, planning ahead, coping with failure, and other skills that are valuable throughout the ethics environment.

Business and economics courses help people to learn ethical behavior. They teach good work attitudes, accounting and accountability, resource management, motivation skills, understanding human needs, comprehending and utilizing the dynamic of social forces, and so forth. Knowledge of business and economics contributes to critical thinking about human problems. Moreover, business and economics students examine particular ethical issues, such as the unfairness of insider trading, the economic dependency of much of the clothing industry on sweatshops. In addition, business students study the liability of tobacco companies for the health of smoking Americans, and even the health of smokers in other countries, the uneven distribution of wealth, natural resources, ecological damage, and other critical issues. Awareness of these issues should help students to be more conscientious adults. Much of business is taught in terms of greed and self-interest, but keep in mind that those are forces in the ethics environment, too.

Also, the study of literature and other aspects of the humanities constantly raises ethical issues and sharpens ethical awareness, from whatever country or culture the literature originates. Literature contributes to a wholistic understanding of the ethics environment in at least four ways. **First,** through novels, short stories, biographies, drama, and poetry we are able to enter imaginatively into the experiences, activities, and attitudes of people who are quite different from ourselves. This helps us to build resources for sincere sympathy in our daily lives. **Second,** quality literature very often composes and develops difficult dilemmas involving tensions between ethical principles, and in our reading of this literature we can begin to comprehend more the force and relative importance of these very principles.

Third, in the reading of gripping stories, we are called upon to make decisions along with the key characters of the story, and we are also able to experience imaginatively the consequences of those decisions. In this way literature provides a veritable laboratory for developing personal moral judgment within the relatively safe environment of sitting in a chair and reading a book. This context for learning ethical decision-making and its consequences is much safer and less costly than in our daily lives where our reputations, fortunes and life itself may be at stake. **Fourth,** literature helps us understand aspects of human character, motivation, and meaning that might be nearly impossible to grasp without it. No wonder William Shakespeare's writings are used in some business management courses, and some corporations assign novels for their managers to read.

Need we mention also philosophy, sociology, anthropology, psychology, and religious studies? The ethics environment comes up both in the discussions of the methodologies of these disciplines and in the particular subjects that are analyzed and discussed.

Each of these school sources — as well as even the school bus conversations, notes passed between students, and the writing on restroom stall walls — for better or for worse, provides some material in the process of educating students to understand the ethics environment. Generally young adults have been exposed to a veritable wealth of human experiences, activities, and attitudes, both the bad and the good, both the evil and the exemplary. And here is the understatement of the week: Not everything learned in the educational system is worthwhile.

Keep in mind also that there is great probability that the pieces of information provided by these multiple sources do not fit neatly together like a well-designed, manufactured puzzle. Instead, some pieces have to be turned upside-down, or re-shaped, or even rejected. Additional pieces may have to be discovered or imagined in order to complete the puzzle picture of the ethics environment. Each person has the challenge of understanding and completing the whole picture. After all, ethics is critical thinking about human problems.

ETHICAL CONFLICT IN THE CLASSROOM

To make this more practical, let's talk about something you already know a lot about: the ethics of the classroom. Do you know someone who has:

* Looked on another student's test paper during an exam?

* Copied a term paper word for word from another source, an act we call "plagiarism"?

* Bought a term paper from a service and handed it in as her own?

* Ripped a page out of a research journal, depriving others of that information?

These acts would violate most people's gut feelings of right and wrong. They probably go against the rules of the college. And it would be hard to imagine a process of reasoning that would justify them. Yet these are common acts, done out of laziness, carelessness, panic, frustration, or jealousy.

Ideally, a person who studies ethics would become a better person, but "doing" ethics and "being" ethical are not the same thing. You can master the knowledge in this book — and then steal a car! You can learn a process of moral reasoning that should lead to a good choice — and then make a bad one. Making real-life decisions will be difficult, even if you can make an "A" in your college ethics course.

A NEW WAY OF THINKING

Let us look at three characteristics of this new way of thinking about human problems. First, this way is called critical thinking about human problems, but that does not imply that all the problems are solved. Nor does it imply that the task is ever complete. There are always more problems to consider, and more information and wisdom to bring to bear on the world of human problems.

Second, unlike most subjects, ethics is not limited to a specific range of information. As the activity of critical thinking it can bring to the table the very widest range of wisdom, insights, proverbs, principles, exemplars, revelation, knowledge, goals, and motivations. That is why much of what we learn inside of school and outside of school is relevant to the ethics environment. As with the rest of life, all that we learn is filtered and sorted out in our human critical thinking processes.

Third, critical thinking about human problems is never bound to the choices presented to us in the ethics environment. Instead, we are equipped as humans to discover or design additional alternatives. For example, rarely are circumstances in the ethics environment strictly "either/or." Often the best choice is "neither" or "both." Just like our responses to the question posed by the restaurant waitress: "Do you want ice cream or pie?" Some of us want to say "Both, thank you," and many of us should say "Neither one, thank you." Consider these:

* If you want to keep our friendship, you really must go to bed with me.
* I love you very much, but what you are asking is not appropriate.
* Your money or your life!
* Sorry, but neither one. There is a policeman standing right behind you.
* If you don't need a receipt, I'll do the $170 timer repair for $130 cash.

* Since you are here, fix it for $130, but I still need a receipt for the warranty.
* Help me with some answers on this test, and we will be best friends forever.
* I will help you study for this test, and we will be even better friends.

HAVE A SANDWICH!

Ethics, as critical thinking about human problems, always involves thinking on at least two levels at once. It is at least a two-level sandwich for the brain and for behavior. For starters, in the ethics environment we are aware of how things are in actuality, and also how we would like them to be. Moreover, we are often aware of two or more choices overtly presented to us, and sometimes also we are able to discover — or even design — additional options for our decisions. To do this, multiple levels of thinking are required.

Furthermore, we approach our decisions with the values that we have, and the circumstances themselves may challenge those values. By far, most of the time we apply the values that have guided our experience, activities, and attitudes in the ethics environment in the past. This use of our values structures is fairly automatic, a kind of "second nature." Nevertheless, the question of making adjustments to our own ethics value structures can arise. You see, we not only make choices; in some sense we also choose the values on which those choices are made.

> How can we be more alert to such dangers or opportunities? How can justice apply to such complex and deep-seated conflicts? What does proper care mean for nasty problems like this? Does this new situation call for a better understanding of accountability?

Consequently, ethics is always at least a double-decker sandwich:

> The way things are. The way things ought to be.

Sometimes in the ethics environment we are presented with a six-layer sandwich, such as:

> The way things are. The choices presented in the situation. Other choices that could be discovered or designed. The values that guide the way I think the world should be. Possible improvements on the values structure that I use. The way things ought to be.

Are there other possible layers? How much can we chew at once? Can we take the sandwich apart? Where should we start? These new questions themselves add at least a seventh layer to the ethics sandwich! *Bon Appetit!*

CAN ETHICS BE TAUGHT?

There is an ethics awareness to be learned, and there are skills we have all acquired from childhood which can be improved. In addition, knowledge and critical thinking are at the center of ethics, and education can improve these as well. Moreover, you are reading this textbook on ethics as part of many people's efforts to improve the ethical environment in our world.

Nevertheless, from ancient times people have raised the question of whether ethics can be taught. For one thing, they have observed that the children of very moral people often behave worse than other people's children. If ethics could be taught, certainly these exemplary men and women would raise exemplary children. There would be nothing they would want to teach their children that they valued more. So, why did the children from these homes turn out so bad? What is missing from this picture?

Perhaps you could supply your own examples of exemplary citizens whose children are delinquents, or ministers' children who reject much of what their parents teach. If you have thought about such examples, you are in good company. Plato observed this phenomenon many years ago, and it caused even him to raise doubts about the teachability of ethics. Even very moral parents who were wealthy enough to pay for the best of every kind of education for their children often had especially abusive children. The prospects for moral education seemed so dim to Plato, that at the end of the famous dialogue "The Meno," he concludes with this pronouncement in the mouth of *Endnote 1* Socrates:

> If all we have said in this discussion, and the questions we have asked, have been right, virtue will be acquired neither by nature nor by teaching. Whoever has it gets it by divine dispensation without taking thought, unless he be the kind of statesman who can create another like himself. Should there be such a man, he would be among the living practically what Homer said Tiresias was among the dead, when he described him as the only one in the underworld who kept his wits — the others are mere flitting shades. Where virtue is concerned such a man would be just like that, a solid reality among shadows. [Translated by W.K.C. Guthrie.]

There are also some cases in the Bible of very moral people with rather immoral children. For example, Eli's two sons were guilty of some terrible wrongs, so that Samuel became the main spiritual leader in their place. Nevertheless, Samuel's own children were dishonest, "took bribes, and perverted justice." Considering Samuel's own brilliance and moral commitments — and after the vivid example of Eli's children and what happened to them — why was Samuel unable to raise his own children better? Similar questions arise in other ancient traditions, including Confucianism.

Ethics can be taught. The real question is, "Will you *learn* ethics?" The answer to that question at least partly depends upon you.

THREE OTHER CHALLENGES:
PLURALISM, PROTOPLASM, AND PERVERSITY

In our effort to teach and learn ethics, there are at least three other potential challenges. First is the "**pluralism** problem." We are in a pluralistic society in which people with diverse views work and live together. What does it mean to teach ethics when people's value systems can be quite different? If we cannot agree on every question of right and wrong, can we learn ethics together?

In early research on so-called primitive societies, it seemed that every adult had basically the same perspective. This is in contrast to modern American society where varieties of values and differences of perspectives are expected, and even encouraged. More recent research has discovered that there are real differences of value and perspective even in "primitive" societies. Some level of pluralism seems simply to be part of the human condition—although freedom of expression for different perspectives is another issue. Nevertheless, diversity is not a problem for ethics, for two reasons. On the one hand, differences of ethical commitment help sharpen our awareness of the importance of fully developed decision-making when it comes to morals. In a world where everything is green, color does not matter, but in our pluralistic world choices are significant. On the other hand, the moral values held by responsible adults are not so diverse as one might think. Certainly the core values we keep coming across — attentiveness, fairness, caring, and accountability — are held in high regard by most responsible people, and by every major culture and civilization. In building a pluralistic society, people should be all the more conscious of their individual decisions. A pluralistic society itself cannot produce "pluralistic people" who hold any and every opinion. Failing to make a decision, in fact, is making a decision that affects others. Not to choose is to choose.

A second problem might be called the "**protoplasm** problem." Some people say that they believe that human beings are merely complex bundles of chemical compounds and energy states. That is, humans are simply samples of the present stage of a long strictly material process. If this picture of human nature were true, then "moral" behavior would be only complex chemical-mechanical responses to material stimuli. There would be no creativity, no conscience, and no choice. Neither would there be awareness, justice, caring, or accountability, as we understand these terms. All these moral realities would be the amazing illusions of the different varieties of protoplasm.

Perhaps no one truly believes such a vision of human nature, because the very suggestion that chemicals can have illusions implies that they are more than chemicals. Moreover, those who defend a

We do not know all the factors that affect our moral learning, but your positive attitude and commitment will certainly make a difference.

purely materialistic understanding of human nature take great pains to develop clever mental argument, and they treat themselves and their loved ones as little more than expensive machines. However, in a world of very refined robots would there develop behavior that intensely resembled human creativity, conscience, and choice — as well as moral awareness, fairness, caring, and accountability? That is a good science fiction question. However, for now humans program robots.

The third challenge has to do with evil: **perversity**, monstrous cruelty, sickening atrocity, malignant wickedness. Understanding and coping with our need for moral guidance in difficult circumstances is one thing. Understanding and coping with malignant wickedness is something else. Here are three examples:

1. Lyle and Erik Menendez claimed that they had killed their parents because their father had abused them in some way. Some people were sympathetic to this defense — until it was revealed that after they had emptied their shotguns into the bodies of their parents, and both parents were mortally wounded, Lyle went out of the house, reloaded his shotgun, and again attacked his mother.

2. There has been a great effort to guarantee that something good will come out of the Oklahoma City bombing that killed 168 innocent people, including many children. However, can we begin to comprehend the mentality of someone who would knowingly plan and pursue this multiple murder?

3. Susan Smith strapped her two young boys — three-year-old Michael and 14-month-old Alex — into their safety seats in her Mazda, and sent it rolling to their drowning deaths in John D. Long Lake in South Carolina. Then this Southern white woman played the race card, trying to blame an African-American for abducting her children. She even succeeded in getting the media to help her propagate the deceit nationwide. She eventually admitted that she had wanted herself to be more marriageable and her children to be in a "better place."

How does an ethics class deal with malignant wickedness? There is a reported rebirth of Satanic worship at the end of the twentieth century. Evil is again being personified and glorified in fiction. As many have said, even if there were no devil you would have to invent him to explain some of the irrational evil that occurs. The twentieth century has been the century of science and technology, but also of monstrous cruelty and sickening atrocities, with violent racism, ethnic "cleansing," and more people killed for their faith than have been martyred in all previous centuries combined.

Ethics can be taught, and it can even be learned. So can evil. This is illustrated in America's treatment of African-American slaves, in South Africa's apartheid doctrine and in U.S. Native American policies today. These problems need more than critical thinking. While the world would be a better place if most people learned and followed good ethics, huge problems would remain.

ETHICS ARENAS IN OUR LIVES

Arena	Self-directed	Other-directed
Personal values	■ Becoming the kind of person I want to be. ■ Being equipped for the kinds of achievements I want to make. ■ Cultivating the right kinds of expectations from others.	◆ Discerning moral character in others. ◆ Being slow to judge others. ◆ Learning skills of nurturing moral development in others.
Friendship values	■ Being the kind of person others will want to befriend. ■ Becoming able to shape friendships for positive purposes. ■ Having the moral fiber to be a faithful friend in difficult circumstances.	◆ Discerning the difference between good and bad peer pressure. ◆ Setting the "agenda" to protect relationships from abuse, and focus on good. ◆ Understanding strengths and limits in friendships.
Family values	■ Honoring parents in appropriate ways. ■ Having good relations with sisters/brothers. ■ Being responsible in family relations.	◆ Keeping the bonds strong, in good times and bad. ◆ Contributing to the good reputation of the family. ◆ Avoiding traps of family patterns.
Sexual values	■ Becoming a self-disciplined woman or man. ■ Differentiating between attraction and seduction. ■ Committing to a life of faithfulness.	◆ Understanding the motives and drives of others. ◆ Shaping and clarifying others' expectations. ◆ Nurturing faithfulness in others.
Consumer values	■ Budgeting and using financial resources well. ■ Reducing consumption of depletable resources. ■ Acquiring responsible knowledge of product safety, ecology, etc.	◆ Supporting enterprises that benefit the community. ◆ Encouraging ecologically wise policies. ◆ Informing retailers and others of ethical concerns.
Racial values	■ Respecting your own race and its heritage. ■ Learning about the harms of the past and being able to apologize and forgive. ■ Developing ways of expressing sincere care.	◆ Respecting others' races and racial heritage. ◆ Detecting and addressing racial discrimination. ◆ Coping positively with the sensitivities and feeling of others.
Employment values	■ Learning good work ethics and work habits. ■ Helping to shape a humane work environment. ■ Being responsible and trustworthy.	◆ Selecting a trustworthy and ethical employer. ◆ Discerning co-workers' positive and negative motives. ◆ Detecting and resolving human problems.

ARENAS OF ETHICS

Learning ethics is a very useful enterprise — both in working with individual situations and with groups. The benefits vary considerably from situation to situation, and from person to person. Of course, we think in terms of the ethics environment, because it is part of our human lives. No one "invents" the ethics environment because it is "useful;" it is not a matter of invention, anyway. Nevertheless, it has many positive uses, and those uses may depend on the different Arenas or circumstances of our lives.

For example, in business relations it is very important to know whom you can trust, and to know how to develop structures of accountability for all the people you work with. If you must work with some people who are not trustworthy, are there ways to help them to live up to their word, or to hold them to their obligations? Are there effective incentives and punishments? If not, should you work with other people instead?

In some kinds of business there is no real opportunity to formulate and enforce contracts. In these circumstances, the demonstrated trustworthiness of the people you work with is all the more important. For example, in the fresh produce business, agreements among farmers, truckers, wholesalers, and grocers must be made quickly. For this reason Produce Reporter, Inc. publishes a large Blue Book every few months rating the trustworthiness and integrity of each person and company in the fresh produce business. If someone lacks integrity, their business could be in jeopardy.

How many different ethical Arenas are there in our lives? There is no definitive number. The chart on page 17 outlines some of the common uses of ethics. What is missing in the chart? What else comes to your mind?

OTHER VALUES

Ethics is critical thinking about human problems. In this book we are looking at ethics in the "big picture" — ethics as an integral part of our lives and thought. We will see how ethical values affect every human interest and activity, so that there are important choices that we can make to help shape our own lives and influence society. We will look at specific moral issues as examples, and to increase our own abilities to be alert, fair, caring, and accountable. As in any good chemistry, business, or music course, if you do not have practice applying what you learn in ethics, the "knowledge" remains irrelevant. Studying specific examples helps stretch our imaginations and develop seasoned personal judgment. However, the goal of this book is not to convince you to take specific positions on one or two dozen issues. Instead, the goal is to become more alert, more fair, more caring, more accountable, and to learn critical thinking skills and how to apply them in order to reach your own ethical decisions.

Sometimes people think of morality only in terms of some "hot" issues, like sex, money, and power. However, the ethics environment is much broader and more inclusive than even these important areas of life. **Moral** means capable of distinguishing right from wrong with a predilection for right; as an adjective, it describes a person or act or thing that conforms to agreed-upon standards of conduct; as a noun, it is a summation of truth from an incident or parable. Generally, we will refer to moral or ethical issues interchangeably.

Even though the use of sex, money, and power are areas where we may feel envy or guilt especially, we would be distracted from the big picture of the ethics environment if we gave these areas all our attention.

Nevertheless, the ethics environment is not as big as the whole universe. There are probably many choices we make every day that have no *noticeable* ethical impact.

> Did you put Cheerios or Product 19 in your cereal bowl?
>
> Did you buy gasoline at Shell or Getty?
>
> Did you say "Good morning" or "How are you?" to the first person you met today?
>
> Did you take the bus or drive?
>
> Did you read the newspaper this morning or this evening?
>
> To which broadcast station is your radio alarm set?
>
> Which set of shoes did you put on?

These and many other choices we make at least *seem* to be **nonmoral**, because they do not affect the resolution of human problems. Of course, even for these cases there could be something else going on. For example, if there is a problem of shoe companies using slave labor to make the shoes, then the kind of shoes we wear is a moral issue. Also, if it is your responsibility to be informed by the morning news, or if you need religious music to help you with your attitudes, the radio station you listen to could be an ethics choice. After all, you do have responsibilities, even to yourself, to resolve human problems, including your own problems.

In contrast, the term **immoral** is used to describe attitudes, decisions, actions, and situations that are contrary to good moral thinking. Immoral attitudes, decision, actions, and consequences are ones that should be improved. They are a significant part of the ethics environment, and they need the attention of good ethics thinking and acting.

The word **amoral** is a stronger term for the absence of any moral sensitivity or concern for moral standards or decency. An amoral person may do immoral things, but with no feeling of guilt or bad con-

© 1988 Creators Syndicate, Inc.

FOOLS' ENTRANCE

WISE MEN'S ENTRANCE

EXPRESS LANE

6-25

science. An amoral person is to ethics what a completely tone-deaf person is to music. It is a kind of aspect-blindness that leads a person to completely miss the whole ethics environment in his or her perception, thought, and action. An amoral person is close to what psychologists call a "sociopath." Perhaps the study of ethics would help amoral people, but it is possible that the ethics environment would seem to be merely a fictitious world to them. Their problems may be diagnosed to be psychological and-or spiritual.

Law has a mixed relationship with the ethics environment. Many laws have been established in an effort to enforce ethical standards that we deem essential for society: laws that punish slander, stealing, murder, assault, and so forth. Even laws against jaywalking or spitting on the sidewalk have a moral base in care for human safety and health. These basic laws are rooted in moral thought, and they have been developed and modified through the ethics environment, **but ethics is larger than the law.**

Nevertheless, there are some laws that are properly non-moral — such as laws concerning which side of the street everyone must drive on, or how quickly the signal lights should change. These are matters of human cooperation that are at least initially morally neutral. However, once a law is established, there is a moral obligation to obey it.

While we have a moral obligation to obey laws, it is possible that some of our laws are themselves immoral or unjust, because they enforce or reward behavior that is contrary to good ethics. In the circumstance of immoral laws, people are faced with the dilemma of either being legal and obeying an immoral law, or being moral by disobeying the immoral law and following the higher ethical standard. These dilemmas are often intensely difficult to face, and bearing the consequences of disobeying the law can be costly. Thomas Jefferson and those who fought in the American Revolution were engaging in illegal activity because they perceived the laws to be immoral. Similarly, Rev. Martin Luther King, Jr. and those who fought for civil rights often suffered the consequences for breaking immoral legal regulations in order to obey a higher moral law. Those who engage in civil disobedience do so only because the cost to their conscience would be even greater if they obeyed immoral laws.

YOUR INTEREST, MY INTEREST

You may never become a billionaire or influence the future of great financial institutions, but, chances are, early in your professional life, you will confront one of the most common, and most serious kinds of ethical dilemmas: **conflict of interest.**

Remember this important term. A **conflict of interest is the predicament arising when a person confronts two actions that cannot be ethically reconciled;** competing loyalties and concerns with others, self-dealing, outside compensation, divided loyalties among, for example, public and-or professional duties and private and-or personal affairs.

If you work in journalism, in criminal justice, in medicine, in business, in government, in almost any job, you will encounter a conflict of interest. Most people fail to see these conflicts. Instead, they trip over them, bruising their reputations and damaging the integrity and credibility of their professions. In cases of conflict of interest, we often learn that *appearances* are as important as *reality*. If a judge plays golf with one of the lawyers before her in a case, even if they do not discuss the case, there is an appearance that the judge cannot be impartial. (In the courts, when such behaviors occur, judges "recuse" themselves from sitting on the case, thereby avoiding the appearance of a conflict of interest.)

CONFLICT OF INTEREST: LEGAL HISTORY, GUIDELINES

Although they were not called "conflicts of interest," controversial activities by high government officials were condemned from the earliest days of the American republic. People with government authority inevitably have opportunities to increase their personal wealth. That temptation toward corruption led, from as early as 1789, to some spot restrictions on those in government.

During the century from 1860 to 1960 the American government increased those restrictions significantly, but in sporadic ways, and with lots of exemptions. The problem for government is always to attract talented people to public service. Such people often are drawn from business or other professions, and opportunities for conflict of interest are inevitable.

Before 1960, confusing and incoherent regulations, filled with loopholes, attempted to set standards for government officials in such activities as self-dealing, aiding outsiders in dealing with the government, outside compensation, and post-employment activities. Enforcement of these regulations was far from adequate.

During the early 1960s, under the leadership of President John F. Kennedy, modern conflict of interest rules for government officials were created. A seminal report by the New York City Bar Association titled "Conflict of Interest and Federal Service and an Advisory Panel" on Ethics and Conflict of Interest in Government, created by the president, made recommendations which, in 1963, became law.

Endnote 2

Bayless Manning, a professor at Yale Law School and a key scholar of conflict of interest rules, wrote *Federal Conflict of Interest Law* (Harvard University Press, 1964). Quoting extensively from the earlier Bar Association report, Manning attempts to draw a narrow definition of conflict of interest in government:

Endnote 3

(From "Conflict of Interest and Federal Service," published by the Association of the Bar of the City of New York, 1960, and cited in companion volume *Federal Conflict of Interest Law*, by Bayless Manning, Cambridge, Mass.: Harvard University Press, 1964.)

"The term 'conflict of interest,' with related terms, has a limited meaning in this study. Any interest of an individual may conflict at times with any other of his interests. This book, however, is concerned with only two interests: One is the interest of the government official (and of the public) in the proper administration of his office; the other is the official's interest in his private economic affairs. A conflict of interest exists whenever these two interests clash, or appear to clash.

"A conflict of interest does not necessarily presuppose that action by the official favoring one of these interests will be prejudicial to the other, nor that the official will in fact resolve the conflict to his own personal advantage rather than the government's. If a man is in a position of conflicting interests, he is subject to temptation however he resolves the issue. Regulation of conflicts of interest seeks to prevent situations of temptation from arising. An Internal Revenue agent auditing his own tax return would offer a simple illustration of such a conflict of interest. Perhaps the agent's personal interest in the matter would not affect his discharge of his official duty; but the experience of centuries indicates that the contrary is more likely, and that affairs should be so arranged as to prevent a man from being put in such an equivocal position." (Bar pp. 3–4)

"But conflict of interest is a special concern, different from theft, bribery, or fraud, and the difference requires special attention and regulation.

"The mint worker who takes home part of the daily product is an example. In a rather elemental way he is involved in a conflict of interest, but we call him a thief, not an offender against conflict of interest principles. His offense is an act of commission. Its criminal character depends entirely on what he does, not who he is. And his act — the taking of the money — is itself the evil consequence that the law seeks to prevent.

"Similarly, the government contracting officer who accepts money from a contractor in exchange for granting him a contract puts himself in an extreme position of conflict between his official duty and personal economic interest. Again we have a specialized name for this offense . . . bribery. Unlike theft, it must involve an official. Its essential element is a payment to influence official action. It assumes a quid for a quo; the official is to do something in his official character in return for payment.

"But now assume that the same contracting officer simply receives a large gift from the contractor. There is no agreement or discussion about any contract, and the officer in fact does not give the contract to the donor. If this act is to be forbidden, it cannot be on a theory of theft or bribery. It must be on the theory that the conflict of interest set up by the gift is LIKELY to lead to a warping of the official's judgment, or is likely to create the appearance of improper influence. If the official were not an official, the gift would be unexceptionable under federal law. The wrong arises entirely out of the undesirably inconsistent position of the official, first in his relationship to the outside party, and second in his relationship to his federal employer . . .

"Regulation of conflicts of interest is regulation of evil before the event; it is regulation against potential harm. These regulations are in essence derived, or secondary — one remove away from the ultimate misconduct feared. The bribe is forbidden because it subverts the official's judgment; the gift is forbidden because it may have this effect. This potential or projective quality of conflict of interest rules is peculiar and important. We are not accustomed to dealing with law of this kind. It is as though we were to try to prevent people from acting in a manner that may lead them to rob a bank, or in a manner that looks to others like bank robbery." (Bar pp. 18–20)

Although these reports limited themselves to the executive branch of government, the experts who drafted them knew that rules controlling the actions of Congress would become necessary. They could almost foresee, three decades into the future, the explosion of special interests, armies of professional lobbyists, and the corrupting influence of PAC money for campaigns. Their early efforts at defining the problem of conflict of interest and drafting legislation to control it set the legal and ethical groundwork for all those who have concerned themselves with conflict of interest in government, at any level.

Because of the dangers of undue influence and conflict of interest, states now have laws that create standards of conduct for public officers and others employed by the state. For example, Florida law states: "No public officer, employee of an agency, or candidate for nomination or election shall solicit or accept anything of value to the recipient, including a gift, loan, reward, promise of future employment, favor, or service, based upon any understanding that the vote, official action, or judgment of the public officer, employee, or candidate would be influenced thereby." (Florida Statutes 112.313)

Many gray areas remain, and many opportunities for temptation. For example, the same law which prohibits "gifts" permits "Contributions or expenditures . . . campaign-related personal services provided without compensation by individuals volunteering their time, or any other contribution or expenditure by a political party."

BEST ANTIDOTE TO CONFLICT

One strategy, above all others, armors the professional against the most painful consequences of conflict of interest. The strategy? **Disclosure**.

In many conflict of interest cases, disclosure of the conflict is the antidote: The doctor discloses his personal interest in a therapy center, and offers you a list of other therapists, as well. The attorney immediately informs her fellow board members that she represents the bidding construction company.

Disclosure works in personal, everyday cases as well: "I'd be happy to give you a job recommendation for Angela, but you should know, she's my godchild."

Inevitably, secrecy makes conflicts of interest seem worse. To the common observer, your failure to disclose your conflict creates the suspicion that you have something to hide. Disclosure is the sunshine that slays that dragon and preserves credibility. It has one other beneficial effect. Disclosure inspires conversation, and begins the process of moral reasoning in a social setting that best insures a good resolution, and an ethical one.

FINAL COMMENTS

When decisions are difficult, when pursuing the subtle keys to positive outcomes seems hard, it is easy simply to back away from the struggle. But that itself becomes a decision, and often it is one that leads to the perception by someone, perhaps someone we value or someone in authority, that our behavior is unethical. Yet tough decisions can be made. Juries do it every day. Judges do it with human lives on the line. Newspaper editors make those hard ethical choices that float among personal, professional, corporate and societal interests. A doctor decides to operate. A lawyer decides to sue. A nation chooses to go to war or negotiate for peace.

The key point to remember is this: If we do not resolve human problems ourselves, with the best tools of ethics and critical thinking, someone else will make the decisions for us, and in ways that may contradict our best values. Choosing to be alert to conflicts of interest and other human problems can sharpen our decision-making skills. That gnawing in the stomach — or that mild sense that something is wrong — can be converted into critical thinking that produces ethical decisions. Being alert is the first and essential step. The information we pull together and the decisions we make should still be crafted with fairness and caring. Many people approach human problems with a sense of accountability, at least to ourselves, if not also to our families, friends, communities, humanity itself, nature, and, to borrow a phrase from the Declaration of Independence, "nature's God." Persisting in the struggle for well-reasoned decisions helps produce ethical lives; it may even be the foundation to a sound society.

FOR FURTHER INQUIRY

REVIEW QUESTIONS

1. Describe in detail the four dimensions of the ethics environment. Take a story from today's newspaper and reconstruct it in terms of these four dimensions — from the points of view of at least two people in the story.

2. Are the four dimensions of the ethics environment interconnected? How do they reinforce each other?

3. Do you know moral people who have immoral children? Why is morality so difficult to pass on to the next generation?

4. What is malignant wickedness? Do you know an example of it? Is this something that you have experienced? What accounts for it?

ENDNOTES

1. Plato, *The Collected Dialogues*, New York: Pantheon Books, 1961.

2. *Conflict of Interest and Federal Service. A Report of the Special Committee on the Federal Conflict of Interest Laws.* New York: The Association of the Bar of the City of New York, 1960.

3. Manning, Bayless. *Federal Conflict of Interest Law.* Cambridge, Mass.: Harvard University Press, 1964.

4. Bellah, Robert N. *The Good Society.* New York, N.Y.: Knopf, 1991.

5. _____. *Habits of the Heart: Individualism and Commitment in American Life.* New York: Harper & Row, 1986.

6. Bok, Sissela. *Lying: Moral Choice in Public and Private Life.* New York: Vintage Books, 1979.

7. _____. *Secrets: On the Ethics of Concealment and Revelation.* New York: Vintage Books, 1983.

8. How to Keep Out of Trouble: Ethical Conduct for Federal Employees, In Brief. Washington, D.C.: Office of Government Ethics, 1988.

9. Lambeth, Edmund B. *Committed Journalism: An Ethic for the Profession.* Bloomington, Ind.: Indiana University Press, 1986.

10. MacIntyre, Alasdair. *After Virtue.* South Bend, Ind.: Notre Dame University Press, 1981.

11. Pojman, Louis P. *Ethics: Discovering Right and Wrong.* Belmont, Cal.: Wadsworth Publishing, 1990.

12. de Vries, Paul, and Gardner, Barry, *The Taming of the Shrewd*, Nashville: Thomas Nelson, 1992.

13. Beauchamp, Tom L., and Terry P. Pinkard. *Ethics and Public Policy: An Introduction to Ethics.* Englewood Cliffs, N.J.: Prentice-Hall, 1983.

CHAPTER 2

DIMENSIONS OF MORAL DEVELOPMENT

"For this is the journey that people make: To find themselves. If they fail in this, it doesn't matter much what else they find."
— *James A. Michener,* **The Fires of Spring**

"If a man will begin with certainties, he shall end in doubts; but if he will be content to begin with doubts, he shall end in certainties."

— *Francis Bacon*

Thinking is a great exercise! It is an asset we humans have that gives us an edge in coping with nature and in working with each other. To make a decision — and even to decide not to decide — requires thought. When we do not like the situation we are in, and when we dream of a better day, we are thinking. Ethics, as critical thinking about human problems, always involves thought.

Nevertheless, we often do one more thing as well. We think about thinking; we reflect on our own thinking processes. Perhaps nothing is more natural, although we do not do it as young children. Gradually, however, as we grow up and become young adults, we develop the ability to think about our thinking. And right now we are thinking about thinking about thinking. You see, it is not so hard, even if it sounds complicated.

Years ago some scholars were concerned to establish a way to talk about language. They wanted to analyze the ways in which we use words to describe facts, express emotions and feelings, make commitments, convince other people to do things, and the like. And they wanted to express and analyze all these functions in ways that were not complicated by the ambiguities, prejudices, and connotations of the various "natural languages" — such as English, Spanish, Swahili. They sought to create a "meta-language" above ordinary language through which we could then analyze and critique ordinary language.

Paul De Vries, M.A. and Ph.D. University of Virginia, is the president of NYES Fund Inc., an educational program, and a partner in Leadership Excellence Inc. He also is president of the International Research Institute on Values Changes, based in New York and Moscow.

What they produced was, of course, another language — or perhaps a dialect of a "natural" language, especially English. They usually used English to introduce the other language and to define some of its terms. Of course, English could be critiqued in the new meta-language, but they found they could also critique the new meta-language in ordinary English. That is, English, or another "natural" language, could be a "meta-language" to the meta-language. This discovery reduced some of the attractiveness of an artificial meta-language. Why not simply use English to analyze and critique English? English could be its own meta-language! In the process we create new words within English to make it more powerful and useful as a language and as its own meta-language, but that is to be expected. After all, English and all other living languages are self-adjusting, developing languages.

The pattern is the same in ethics and critical thought. We as individuals, and in groups, adjust our ways of talking and thinking in order to solve our problems with greater awareness, fairness, care, and accountability. Let's look at a situation and evaluate people's behavior according to some of those factors.

CHIEF LEARNING OUTCOME

I understand the stages of human moral development as theorized primarily by Kohlberg and Gilligan.

CHRISSA AND THE WORLD

Chrissa: "Don't ask. My head is still spinning. You know how guilty I felt for being such a selfish American teenager. Not that I'm rich or privileged or anything, but so many others in the world have far less than I have. You know — all those pictures of starving children and mothers. So I raised the money and gave my whole vacation to the great cause — Save the World Foundation. 'Go to a Third World country and make a difference.'

"Ah, yes. Their slogans are great, but the organization stinks. It is so hard to explain. I knew that living conditions would be rough, with no running water or electricity. And with my long hair, what a pain! And I grumbled, of course, but the living conditions were okay. Really. And I didn't mind cleaning people's dirty, stinking bodies at the clinic. I had nightmares about that before I left, but I was prepared to give a lot. I had decided to reach beyond myself.

"But here's my point: Why the indignity? Why did the site director keep yelling at me? Why did he look at me as if I was dirt? Why did he keep haranguing about 'selfish Americans like you'? He never gave one compliment, not one word of encouragement the whole time. No warmth. And he treated the patients at the clinic even worse. He never looked into their eyes. He never really listened.

"Hundreds of times the words formed in my head: 'Hey, Mr. Big Guy, these people are important, and I'm important, too. It's not just the work we do that counts. It's dignity; it's human relationships.' But I never said those words. He knew I was angry and hurt — that's why he kept calling me selfish. No wonder that country's so depressed, with people like him 'helping.'"

Chrissa understands that she can be selfish and that she can provide help and care for others — including those who cannot help her or pay her back in some material way. But she still wants others to care about her, even if she does not want them to take care of her or coddle her. Is it okay for her to be angry if others do not treat her as an important person? Should she worry whether she is being selfish again?

In this example, the personal patterns of *awareness, justice, care,* and *accountability* are changing and developing. Chrissa is alive, learning, and growing — and engaged in a process that may continue the rest of her life. And her personal development is not limited to just one dimension.

For example, we read about Chrissa's growth in her understanding of care, but her own awareness of human problems around her — and her understanding of justice and accountability — are probably developing at the same time. Those changes could be either quite rapid or so slow that they are barely noticeable to her. Wherever we came from, and however mature we are physically, it still takes years of experience, reflection, pain, and accomplishment before we begin to fulfill our moral potential.

KEY CONCEPTS

Moral development is human growth in the awareness of rightness and wrongness of actions, often accompanying physical maturity but not necessarily.

Kohlberg's six stages of moral development are Stage 1: Obedience/Punishment; Stage 2: Instrument and Relativity; Stage 3: Interpersonal Concordance; Stage 4: Law and Social Order; Stage 5: Social Contract; Stage 6: Universal Ethical Principles.

Gilligan's Steps of moral development: (1) Care for self, (2) Care for others, (3) Balancing and Integrating self-interest and interests of others.

Kierkegaard's stages of life: (1) Aesthetic, (2) Ethical, (3) Religious.

Osgood's Attitudes: (1) Idealistic, (2) Frustrated, (3) Defiant, (4) Resigned, (5) Aware, (6) Decisive, (7) Committed.

MORAL DEVELOPMENT'S GROWING PAINS

As we develop in our awareness of problems or our comprehension and application of justice, care and accountability, we can think about our own thinking and behavior. We can recognize and sometimes choose those changes that happen to us. Certainly, these changes are consequential to us as well as to the people with whom we live and work. Is there anything more important to people around you than the development of your **moral character** and the patterns of your responses to problems around you?

We have a definite stake in our own development and in the growth of others around us. We can expect changes and recognize them when they come. When we understand these changes, we are less surprised or resistant, and we can even experience the pleasure of watching our own character grow and become more mature. While there may be few things we can do to actually hasten our own character development, we can at least avoid stunting it. By expecting certain positive changes toward maturity, we can nourish these developments when they begin.

However, there is a double role for pain in this maturing process. The changes, when they occur, take us out of established patterns of thought and behavior in which we have become comfortable. Personal stagnation may be boring, but it can be cozy.

Character building is rewarding, but it may require costly adjustments. Do you remember when you tried to get into last-year's snow boots or swim suit, after you had grown a size? If you have grown in a way that your family and friends have not, your relationships will "fit" a little differently.

Pain frequently plays another role as well. It is the most frequent and powerful stimulus for personal moral growth in any of the four dimensions of ethics. Of course, personal disappointment and failure can come our way with no positive effect; we can be numb to any benefit.

But when disappointment leads us to reflect on our lives and to consider changes in our own attitudes — or when tragedy leads us to take a new perspective on others' suffering — our own behavior may well become more sensitive, fair, caring, or accountable. Pain and difficulty make us wonder:

* Would we be genuinely aware of what is happening around us if there were no problems to solve?
* Could justice be an issue if there were unlimited resources available to all?
* Would we learn to be caring in a world without pain?
* Could accountability make sense in a world without temptations to evil?
* Are any of these reasons why we have pain?

Of course, **success and accomplishment** can help us grow as well. Pain is not the only stimulus for personal development. Moreover, simply by our being around other people and repeatedly solving little problems, our comprehension of these aspects of ethics can increase, even with very little pain. Our personal growth depends more on an openness to learn and on an eagerness to get our lives right than it does on the surrounding circumstances.

In any case, whether we are self-conscious of it or not, moral development occurs, and people can recognize themselves at different stages of that development. Humans, by definition, are neither born mature nor do they automatically grow into maturity. By our decisions and our reactions to experiences and problems, we take a hand in developing our own moral character. We influence the character development of others, and we often affect the moral character of our families, schools, businesses, communities, churches and synagogues, governments, and the world.

Look at it this way. You probably find that people around you often come up with answers to the problems of life that are quite different from your own answers. You may have found something your friend did to be shocking or puzzling. In the past you may have considered these only varieties of opinion or part of the differences between men and women, older and younger, of different ethnic backgrounds.

But these divergent responses to life situations could also be caused by disparities in people's moral development stages as well. With this awareness in our backgrounds, we should be more tolerant of children as well as of less-mature adults. We will also have an initial vision and understanding of what the more-mature adults around us are thinking and feeling.

MORAL DEVELOPMENTS OF THE AGES

Personal moral development has been a preeminent concern to some of the greatest intellects throughout the centuries — from Plato (427–347 B.C.) to Carol Gilligan in our own time. Psychologists and philosophers especially have given considerable thought to the way we think about our own thought and behavior. These scholars have developed numerous divergent theories about moral development — theories that often compete and conflict with one another. Unfortunately, intellectuals generally select one particular dimension of moral development — such as justice or accountability — and build a theory that gives attention almost exclusively to that dimension. They may be selecting the dimension that they consider to be the most important for problem-solving, and they may not have seriously considered or thought about the other dimensions. In fact, their own ideas may have seemed so powerful that their full attention was given to development and application of one basic theme. As ordinary mortals, however, we can read and integrate even these diverse theories within our own lives.

When these intellectuals describe the kind of people they consider mature, it is usually a given fact that children are a far cry from the ideal of maturity. Intellectuals then try to create theories about how people can be nurtured step by step into this preferred ideal.

Obviously, when these ideal patterns differ from one another, the maturing processes and stages vary as well.

The goal makes all the difference. As a result, exemplary behavior on one scale may be considered immature on another. For example, if the ideal person is one who makes detached, impartial decisions of justice, then the "baggage" of emotional involvement and personal commitment will be treated as symptoms of an immature level. However, if caring for yourself and others is the ideal pattern for human life, then detached, impartial decisions are understood as immature, if not positively pathological. It will be our task to see through these incompatible intellectual theories, and to discover even deeper congruences that each of them does not have.

SEQUENTIAL AND CUMULATIVE

Now, just before we look at different theoretical developmental scales, there are two very important general observations for you to consider. First, where development comes in a sequence of stages, it is possible for a person to make progress as well as to retreat. There is no "locked in" security in the success of a higher level. A person can achieve very mature thought and behavior, and yet prefer the "benefits" of less mature patterns, simpler choices, more selfish results, and the like. People can withdraw to less mature levels — immediately or later — because they feel more comfortable there, because they can achieve their personal goals better there, it takes less thought and information there, or for some other reason. In fact, for most of these theories, the higher levels involve mental and emotional concentration and difficult balances to maintain. Consistent upper-level behavior is almost impossible.

Endnote 1

Second, in spite of what some of the theorists argue, the stages of moral development appear to be generally cumulative. Ability to function on a higher level does not surgically remove one's ability to also function on lower levels — because we choose to or because we feel tired, threatened, angry, or whatever. We have achieved a higher level when we have acquired the ability to perform on that level, while the total collection of our present motives and our methods of thought and action may be quite a "mixed bag." Even the best saints and heroes can be quite self-centered and selfish at times.

In fact, people often are moved by a mixture of motives for the very same decision and action. For example, Chrissa (in a scenario opening this chapter) may have volunteered her vacation time to work in a Third World country because she truly cares about the health and happiness of fellow human beings. Fine. She may also have seen this as an opportunity to get some sun and surf, to get away from an unwanted "boyfriend" for a while, or to be able to say she had "seen the world." Does this take away from her genuine care for the people she wanted to serve?

"Mixed Motives"

This term is used in our language to describe insincere behavior. Does Chrissa have mixed motives? Probably so. Does the mixture of her motives take away from her genuine commitment to care or fairness? Do we have to assume that there is only one real reason for her behavior? That would be unfair to almost any human choice. If our care for others and our concerns for fairness to them is mixed with some self-centered motives, should we assume that the care and justice motives are only pretenses? Are the "real" motives always selfish? Not really. Of course, there is the old joke: *For everything we do there are two motives: a good motive . . . and the real motive.*

But is that joke true to life? It certainly is cynical. In fact, the good motives are often the real motives. Moreover, clusters of diverse good motives often work together — including motives of concern for oneself and others.

Here is a classic problem: Religiously aware people generally believe that they should be fair, caring, and accountable in their behavior, because this is how God asks them to believe and behave. The same ones are convinced that God rewards people whose consciousness and conduct demonstrate devotion to fairness, care, and accountability — with happiness and other benefits in this life and in life after death. Now, if they are "good," is it because they are just seeking these great rewards, or because they want to honor and obey God? What is the real reason? Can it not be both? In fact, what kind of world would it be if good behavior were not rewarded?

In a similar way, politicians can even have good motives. They propose and vote for good programs because they want to get re-elected. Nevertheless, their commitment to the good programs may be genuine, and their desire to be re-elected may be quite good and appropriate as well. Of course, there are also some hypocritical believers and manipulative politicians who have mixtures of dangerous and deceitful motives. But we should not attribute those to everyone.

For the same reason that interests, memories, and habits from our childhood and youth stay with us throughout our lives, some of our motivations and behavior patterns are cumulative as well. It would be frightening to meet people who had totally "outgrown" childhood. Are they human? Are they for real? When no one else is watching could they be a little selfish or a little playful? Who needs plastic saints?

The point is that the higher stages of personal development enable you to recognize more accurately what is going on, to engage broader information, to act with more conscious and consistent care, and to explain your behavior with greater reliability. The menu gets longer, but adults can still pick from the "children's selections" once in a while — for better or for worse.

THE DEVELOPING ROOM

Just think about how different the world appears to you now than it did when you were a child! Then words were indistinct sounds or markings on paper — without clear meaning. Now you converse with others with little effort, and you read whole phrases at a glance, immediately recognizing the meaning. Then, as a child, computers seemed to be weird boxes with TV screens. Now you recognize computers in a variety of uses at home, work, and school. Then, years ago, you may have even thought of matches, the kitchen stove, and household cleaning chemicals as toys for your amusement — or at least you were quite curious about them. Now you see them in terms of their risks, dangers, and positive uses.

Moreover, as a child you probably thought the world revolved around you. Objects were there for you to use; people were there to meet your needs. Now, hopefully, you have matured beyond that egocentric view of the world. There are other "selves" in addition to yourself, and these others have legitimate claims upon you for fair treatment, caring action, and accountability, while they are also responsible for you. The world indeed seems very different than it did to you as a child.

Of course, there are some people who really never do grow up. Some remain illiterate, computer naive, firebugs, or egocentric. When an adult is stuck in a child-like state we consider it abnormal, pathological, or criminal. An adult firebug is a pyromaniac or an arsonist. An adult who has no sense of moral responsibility to others — no conscience — is a sociopath, suffering from an anti-social, personality disorder. Even if a few sociopaths have managed to become kings, queens, senators, dictators, corporate bosses, police officers, or some of your neighbors, we can still recognize that the lack of a moral conscience is a tragic defect in personality.

STAGES OF AWARENESS

The first and often the most difficult developmental dimension is the ability to recognize the moral human problems around us. This is a challenge for child-raising, but it is also an enduring hurdle for adults in their own continuing development. For example, children usually need to be taught to share their own toys and to respect other people's property, including their toys. Being able to recognize and restrain their own possessiveness takes time and training for children to develop.

Adults may have difficulty recognizing the obvious as well. For example, some major corporations have had difficulty convincing their male managers to stop sexually harassing female employees. One corporation made tremendous progress when it created a video vignette and required all managers to watch it. In the vignette a female manager pressures one of her male employees for a "date," and the relationship is clearly as manipulative, degrading, and unprofessional as it is in the more common situation — where a male manager propositions a female employee. By turning the tables, the video aids male managers' imaginations, helps them to recognize how manipulative and degrading sexual harassment is. As a result, they are far more likely to recognize and avoid any sexual harassment of their employees in the future.

Acquiring the ability to recognize a kind of problem or a range of problems can sometimes have the form of a mystical realization. Suddenly you see clearly what is totally obvious to you now — and yet other people may remain insensitive or blind to it. For example, in the early history of the Massachusetts Colony, Roger Williams became convinced that American Indians were just as human as he or other white people. It was wrong to treat them differently, or to take their land without fair compensation. When he defended his perspective, he was forced by the authorities to leave Massachusetts, and so he founded Rhode Island with a deeper commitment to human rights. In a similar way, when Abraham Lincoln actually watched a slave auction, he became far more deeply convinced of the gross unfairness and the human degradation of slavery. Perhaps you have experienced a similar moral conversion on some other issue.

Figure 1. Slave auction in Virginia. The New-York Historical Society.

Whether in dramatic or in subtle ways, we can grow in our ability to recognize problems. The range of problems we are able to recognize, and the accuracy with which we identify them, varies from person to person on a broad continuum. Even our greatest saints and heroes who were intensely accurate in their perceptions of some major problems have sometimes been nearly blind on other weighty matters. For example, Thomas Jefferson recognized with great acuity the injustices of England's government in its dealings with the American Colonists. In our Declaration of Independence he was able to proclaim with brilliance and courage that:

> *"We hold these truths to be self-evident, that all men are created equal, that they are endowed by their Creator with certain unalienable Rights, that among these are Life, Liberty and the pursuit of Happiness . . ."*

Nevertheless, for a variety of possible reasons, Jefferson continued to hold slaves. Were these persons not human? Were they not equal? Was not their right to liberty inalienable? Even if we allow that Jefferson was probably a nicer-than-average slaveholder, or that he was protecting his slaves from even worse conditions elsewhere, the apparent inconsistency is definitely hard to explain. Nevertheless, we all know that no one is perfectly perceptive about everything. What kinds of moral blindness do you see in people around you? Are there areas of moral blindness you have uncovered in your own life? Can you explain them to others?

What is crucial is that our minds and imaginations have been stretched to include some concept for the problem before us, or we may not ever notice the problem. And how are our minds and imaginations stretched? There are at least five instruments for doing this, as we will see shortly. Each instrument can help open up our moral and intellectual pores. Without some such instruments our minds tend to trust completely the established patterns, continuing to overlook just the kinds of problems we have already recognized.

Endnote 2

We almost always *assimilate* new experiences into established categories of our thought and perception. This is the initial stage in any growth in awareness. Change in our perception occurs only as we are puzzled, stretched, or *awakened* by a new experience. We may stay in this middle stage briefly until we find or create improved categories. If we cannot find or create a sufficient change, we may simply return to the first stage of assimilation. This middle stage of awakening, however, may lead us successfully to *accommodate* our perception and thought by adding or creating some new categories of active awareness.

INSTRUMENTS OF AWARENESS DEVELOPMENT

What instruments help awaken us to additional problems around us? There are numerous tools that lead us to accommodate our thought and perception, but here is a brief list of five:

The first instrument is our own personal stake. We are far more alert to injustices and the lack of care or accountability when we are the real or potential victims. For example, products that manufacturers consider "good enough" are less likely to be deemed good enough by alert customers or consumer advocates. Similarly, women are more sensitive to patterns of sexual harassment and alert to recognize it because they are more likely than men to be its victims.

The second instrument we bring to bear is a substantial knowledge of various literatures and

stories. Good literature draws us into other people's perspectives and experiences — thereby stretching our own repertoires of concepts. For example, we do not have to live in a crime-ridden neighborhood — or be the victim of unsafe products, or have AIDS — to recognize the many problems associated with these situations. There are plenty of news reports and sensitive stories that help us perceive the issues more clearly.

Fiction can be tremendously valuable in this effort. Science fiction novels and movies — such as *Star Trek* episodes — can also help sensitize us to partly hidden problems before us here and now, not just in the distant future. An even more potent source is history, where we can investigate the actual results of people's decisions — not just the imagined consequences created by story-writers. Of course, reading itself is not essential; stories and episodes of history do not have to be read or even seen on videos. Illiterate peoples usually have huge repertoires of stories that help stretch their moral imaginations.

The third instrument is the awareness of potential solutions. Most of us tend to minimize problems that we think are unsolvable. But when there is a way to make a positive difference we are less pained giving full attention to the problems. A farmer is less apt to complain about plowing around rocks in the field if he thinks the rocks are very deep. When it is discovered that these big rocks are only two inches thick, the farmer is more apt to see them as a problem to be solved. Huge pot holes irritate us more than large rainstorms, and we are more likely to focus on others' bad habits than their permanent handicaps. The sweltering heat in some factories was not seen as much of a problem until air conditioning was available. In general, the problems that can be solved draw our attention more. Studies have shown that mere abstract or theoretical knowledge of how to handle problems does not increase awareness — but concrete hope for specific problems does.

The fourth instrument is perceived frequency. On the one hand, when spouse abuse, child abuse, and date rape were seen as rare, they received little attention. Few people discussed them, and victims were left largely on their own in dealing with these problems. Most people were not alert to watch for them. However, when we understand their frequency and danger, we are more alert to recognize symptoms of their presence. On the other hand, when some problems become over-whelmingly frequent, people can become numb to them as well; their hope that there will be a solution is diminished.

The fifth instrument is personal sensitivity and eagerness to learn from experience. We are created with a feedback system that allows us to learn from our own experience. Did I learn anything from those successes? Did I grow from those failures? As we said earlier, we can think about our thinking. We can see our blindness to problems as itself a problem, and then take steps to become more sensitive.

These five instruments can aid our awareness of human problems — our personal stake, stories, potential solutions, frequency, and personal openness to learn from experience. Are there any other instruments to make us morally aware that you can think of?

STAGES OF JUSTICE

Several scholars have given significant attention to the development of our ability to reason ethically. They have studied ways that children, youth, and adults engage information and recommend or resolve decisions. They have noticed that the very structures of thought change as we mature. Also, they have observed that when presented with a complicated story with a moral dilemma, people at different stages of development select out of the available information distinct sets of facts as relevant data for a good solution to the dilemma. These studies have concentrated especially on the second step of problem-solving outlined in Chapter 3 of this book — engaging information and reasoning. Not surprisingly, therefore, they have focused primarily on issues of justice and fairness in both patterns of thought and in sifting through information. After all, justice is the key value for the second stage of problem-solving.

Endnote 3

Jean Piaget was the first to provide such a study. He noticed that children faced with the same problems approach them differently as they mature. Their very perceptions of reality change, and this evolution moves in stages from less complex to more complex perceptions. In each successive stage, the child accommodates greater and greater complexity of reality in his or her experiences. For example, gradually as children approach adulthood they shift from responding primarily to rules or duties that are imposed by others — or assumed to be fixed — to understanding moral guidance based on cooperative arrangements and win-win agreements that are freely selected. The more mature children engage in "autonomous" thinking, deciding and problem-solving.

KOHLBERG'S THEORY

Lawrence Kohlberg became so impressed with Piaget's ground-breaking work that he devoted a lifetime of writing and research to this subject. In the process, he developed a theory much more detailed and complex than Piaget's view. In fact, he discovered *six stages in our development of moral judgment,* as well as fairly thorough means of recognizing whether a person is in one stage or another.

Kohlberg's vision is useful and profound; it has captured the imagination of many writers, and spawned a wealth of literature. In short, he sees our development in making fair moral decisions progressing through three levels: Pre-conventional (egocentric), conventional (social), and post-conventional (principled). Also, each of the three levels of development for Kohlberg is divided into two stages, so that there are six stages in all. Each stage represents a different approach to justice and fairness.

Primarily, Kohlberg theorized that persons move sequentially through the stages with no guarantee they will reach the higher stages. As one progresses, there may be some overlap among stages (and one may regress temporarily). Second, Kohlberg stated that our moral thinking at each stage is dominated by these structures of that stage. To him, each stage is a complete, wholistic unit. Let's look more closely at the stages.

At the first level, **pre-conventional (egocentric) people** make their decisions on personal bases — either in terms of obedience to a power figure or in terms of personal agreements with other individuals. On this level, the social structure is not really utilized. Straight obedience to some authority to avoid punishment or negative physical consequences is the main feature of *stage one*; pursuing self-interest and the satisfaction of others only for personal gain governs *stage two*.

At the second level, **conventional (social) people** make decisions on the basis of social patterns and rules — whether these patterns are informal or are explicitly stated. On this level, people use and fit the social and moral structure. This social structure is defined in terms of stable friendships and harmony in personal roles in *stage three*; more explicit legal and moral conventions for the good of society dominate *stage four*.

At the third level, **post-conventional (principled) people** seek to follow timeless principles — whether or not these principles will be articulated within the conventional structures. On this level, people see some of the limitations of the social structures, and they try to fix them or rise above them. In *stage five*, for example, various procedures are developed for the goal of protecting everyone's basic rights and improving the social conventions. In *stage six,* decisions are made on the basis of impartial, ideal, eternal principles that perfectly protect everyone's claim to fairness — regardless of the influence of social and moral conventions.

In short, people can have three attitudes to conventional social and ethical structures around them: They can act apart from them, in conformity to them, or in a role of mastery over them. Another way to make these developments clear is to compare the primary guidelines on each level and stage.

Level One: Pre-Conventional (Egocentric)

Stage 1: Do what you are told in order to avoid punishment or other negative physical consequences.

Stage 2: Seek your interests and the interests of others if meeting theirs will benefit you.

Level Two: Conventional (Social)

Stage 3: Develop lasting friendships that seek to understand and satisfy each person's interests.

Stage 4: Live up to the explicit agreements, laws, duties, and expectations that help define the groups in which you participate and allow them to function in harmonious order.

Level Three: Post-Conventional (Principled)

Stage 5: Develop fair ways of bringing the agreements, laws, duties, and expectations of your groups into *closer* harmony with broader basic human rights.

Stage 6: Follow and seek to advance the basic principles of human fairness and justice — regardless of your personal circumstances.

Please note that while people's *motives* may change, their actual *behavior* may not as they mature through the six stages. For example, students may abstain from cheating and plagiarism for various reasons — they are afraid of being caught, they see that everyone's real interests are served this way, they respect the rules, or they are devoted to the ultimate standards of fairness. They may move from one stage to another, while their behavior stays the same. What changes between stages is not necessarily the behavior but rather the motives and rationale that people use to define their problems and interpret their decisions. Of course people do change their behavior, too, but they can stay on the same stage and do that. *For Kohlberg, it is not what people do but* why *they do it that defines their stage of moral development at a given time.*

Let us look again at the example of Chrissa that we examined earlier in the chapter. Here's how Chrissa would look at her problem from the perspective of each of the six stages:

Level One: Pre-Conventional (Egocentric)

Stage 1: Oh well. To keep out of trouble with the site director, I'll do what he says.

Stage 2: Perhaps I should talk with the site director. Maybe if I butter up the jerk, I'll get a better report. At least I'll have more peace and quiet around here.

Level Two: Conventional (Social)

Stage 3: You know, I should really try to see things from the site director's perspective. Maybe he'll like me and see I'm a good person. He has so much to take care of, he does not have the time or energy to really care for people. I can be more patient with him — and maybe we can even become friends.

Stage 4: I should use my job description and the public literature and purpose statement of Save the World Foundation to improve our communication. If I work within the structures and guidelines of the organization I can help the level of cooperation and service. Those guidelines are there for that purpose.

Level Three: Post-Conventional (Principled)

Stage 5: However the organization is structured, something is missing, something is not working. There is no reason why people should feel so bad about doing good! Truly, the organization stinks. I'll fulfill my obligation to Save the World Foundation and to the people I promised to help during my vacation. But I'm also looking for a way to help this organization see what it is doing — and change so it will fulfill its mission.

Stage 6: Yes, Save the World Foundation needs restructuring, and working with its representatives has been difficult. I'll try to help them wake up and change, because theirs is a worthwhile cause even if they're a little weary now. Every human being has infinite and eternal value, and together what the organization and I do will help disadvantaged people see and feel their worth.

To summarize, Kohlberg's focus is on *why* people do things. His six stages have been described in brief with various terms. For easy reference, they may be restated in the shaded box to the left.

Let us now explore in some depth the six stages that Kohlberg has written so much about. His primary explanations revolve around a dilemma that a man named Heinz faces in the following story. Kohlberg and his colleagues might ask people how Heinz should approach his problem, and their answers help reveal the stage on which they are thinking. Think about what Heinz should do in this dilemma, a human problem that is used constantly in the literature of moral development, and a story that is not difficult to imagine.

Endnote 4

THE HEINZ DILEMMA

In Europe, a woman was near death from a very bad disease, a special kind of cancer. There was one drug that the doctors thought might save her. It was a form of radium that a druggist in the same town had recently discovered. The drug was expensive to make, but the druggist was charging 10 times what the drug cost him to make. He paid $200 for the radium and charged $2,000 for a small dose of the drug. The sick woman's husband, Heinz, went to everyone he knew to borrow the money, but he could get together only about $1,000, which was half of what it cost. He told the druggist that his wife was dying, and asked him to sell it cheaper or let him pay later. But the druggist said, "No, I discovered the drug and I'm going to make money from it." Heinz got desperate and broke into the man's store to steal the drug for his wife.

After reading or hearing this story, people are asked: "Should Heinz have done that? Was it wrong or right? Why?" At each stage children, youth, and adults can say that Heinz was right or wrong (Kohlberg says that). What differentiates the stages is more the answer to the "Why?" question.

PRE-CONVENTIONAL (EGOCENTRIC) PEOPLE

On the first stage people respond in terms of the superior power of authorities who provide fixed rules of behavior, or the threat of punishment. Morality, then, is a matter of obedience to explicit rules which others have passed on to us and enforced in some way. People on this stage are likely to say that Heinz is wrong because he stole something, and is likely to be punished for stealing by the law. This first stage involves an unquestioning acceptance of the power of law and authority — only because of the punishment and negative consequences it can inflict, without considering any other human interests or purposes that may be at the basis of the laws involved. On this stage the traditional *Golden Rule* might not apply, but the older Chinese tradition's version might: "Do not do unto others as you would not have them do unto you."

So, any time we slow down and drive within the speed limit only because a police officer is watching and we don't want to get fined — not at all because of the inherent safety benefits to ourselves and others — we are functioning on this stage. Moreover, any time we directly obey the leaders of a political group or party, corporate bosses, moral or religious authorities, without consciously considering the purposes of their rules or directives, we are thinking in this initial stage. Of course, our involvement in this stage can be very effective so long as the authorities providing the rules and meting the punishment are trustworthy.

Those in the second stage — still at the pre-conventional level — think in terms of the interests that each person brings to the problem, and they will try to "make a deal" to seek some level of cooperation or exchange for their own personal benefit. In a sense, each person is seen as an egocentric negotiator, not bound by others' rules or social commitments. Your own needs and interests are paramount, and the needs and interests of others are of concern only to the extent that meeting them helps you. Here the *Golden Rule* must be diminished to apply: Seek to fulfill others' interests and needs only when doing so helps to fulfill yours. The fear of negative consequences in Stage 1 is replaced here by a desire for personal reward.

In the Heinz story, then, both Heinz and the druggist have the right to do what they want to do — and take the risks and rewards that may follow. Obeying the law or not obeying the law is merely a matter of prudence. There is no deep desire to obey if detection and punishment are unlikely. As a result, Stage 2 people are concerned about obedience to authority if it somehow benefits them.

CONVENTIONAL (SOCIAL) PEOPLE

The third stage of Kohlberg's theory initiates the conventional (social) level. Here public roles, expectations, personal relationships and observations are crucial. Now shared feelings and interests are more important than the individual interests that dominated Stage 2. From this personal knowledge, you can imagine putting yourself in other people's shoes. On this third stage the *Golden Rule* is based upon concrete knowledge of other people's feelings and expectations: Do for others what you would want them to do for you, based upon your personal knowledge and relationships with them.

The driving force is one's self-image and peer-image as a "good person"; you want to be a good person in your own eyes and in the opinions of others. Essential is doing the right thing, having good motives, and maintaining concern for others, through trust, loyalty, respect, and gratitude. People in Stage 3 are additionally aware that they and their associates are actively looking out for each other within enduring friendships. While in Stage 2 they bargained for each favor, in Stage 3 they know each other — including the "inner selves" — well enough to accommodate needs and desires.

Moreover, the inner quality of being "a good person" is understood on this stage to be more important than particular acts of rule-obedience to avoid punishment that Stage 1 had portrayed. As a result, Stage 3 provides a level of stability and cooperation unachieved in Stages 1 and 2.

In Heinz's story, then, the most crucial factors in Stage 3 are Heinz's relationships — with his wife and with the druggist. His commitment to his wife is probably the deeper and more valued relationship, and it is her appraisal of him as a "good person" that will count the most. Nevertheless, Heinz still has some desire to be considered a "good person" by the druggist as well, and would relish receiving his approval, too, if possible.

Stage 3, however, fails to define morality outside the personal contacts with friends, relatives, or others in one's group. Fortunately, Stage 4 seeks to remedy that lack by institutionalizing expectations and services through a system of general laws and trained moral conscience. It is not interpersonal agreement and understanding that guides now, but the social system that defines both our roles and rules of behavior. The more personal touch of justice in Stages 1, 2 and 3 is now replaced by a matrix of fair laws, and our primary moral responsibility is to society and its institutions, rather than merely to the flesh-and-blood people we know. The *Golden Rule* is here stabilized and institutionalized: Fulfill your legal responsibilities to society while you expect that others will fulfill their legal responsibilities to society as well. As a result, Stage 4 seeks even more stability than was achieved in Stage 3, along with a broader knowledge and greater consistency of moral responsibility.

In Stage 4, therefore, justice is defined by general rules and shared expectations that are binding on everyone. This institution of law protects us from chaos and gives meaning to human life. No one is personally privileged or above the law; therefore, no one should make an exception of his or her own case. Because sets of social laws usually prohibit stealing but do not require saving lives, Heinz's theft is more likely to be criticized in Stage 4. If Heinz asked, "What if everybody did it?" he would realize that society would suffer if everyone committed theft. As a consequence, Heinz should realize that according to Stage 4, it would be wrong for him to steal regardless of punishment or reward, regardless of how others feel about him, but rather because it would be best for society.

POST-CONVENTIONAL (PRINCIPLED) PEOPLE

A higher level of stability, generality, and abstraction is reached in the fifth stage of Kohlberg's theory. Here existing legal structures are not as important as methods for selecting and improving systems of laws. The standard here is not concrete rules but rather individuals as equal contractors within the larger social system. These rational contractors select what is the most fair to all, and also what promotes the greatest good for the greatest number. The assumption of Stage 5 is that our own societies and their laws can gradually be reformed to live up to mutually agreed-upon standards. Informed citizens should then agree to abide by these rational dictates as a matter of contract they freely endorse — because that society continues to be subject to procedures of rational self-improvement.

What actually unites people is this law-making process, not the laws themselves that had provided the social glue in Stage 4. The *Golden Rule* for the fifth stage is then: With their cooperation, seek to create for others and for yourself the rational and impartial society you would want them to create.

Endnote 5

In short, the central feature of Stage 5 is a consensus-building procedure — whether or not that procedure is some version of democracy. Above the specific self-rewarding bargains of Stage 2, beyond the more stable personal relationships of Stage 3 — and even above the consistent legal structures and consciences of Stage 4 — Stage 5 hangs on people's general commitments to create and obey rational laws for the benefit and for the rights of every person. The procedure is the defining standard. What if the right procedure is followed, but you still disagree with the particular laws and rights that were established through that rational procedure? You are then obligated to try to change the laws, obeying them while you seek reform; otherwise the laws and rights would be a farce. They would not be laws and rights at all if people were always allowed to selectively obey them.

In the story, one could conclude in stage five that Heinz may or may not obey the laws against theft, depending on whether he viewed the purpose of the law as promoting justice for society. An escape loophole exists in Stage 5. Heinz could still justify his breaking the law if he is firmly convinced that the society's laws are not rational enough — if it does not build in sufficient safeguards, for example, for protecting human lives. Your "contract" with society certainly does not include standing by and watching your spouse die unnecessarily! Should the laws or courts justify or excuse such a theft to protect a life? If Heinz honestly thinks such a justification of theft is a rational standard, he can morally excuse his theft, even if he is still punished by the society. Stage 5's standard of rationality provides, then, some protection for human rights. As a result, Stage 5 provides principles for fair social cooperation, without violating the individual rights that should be rationally defended.

See Human Rights, Ch. 15

At Stage 6, according to Kohlberg, the ultimate stage in the development of moral reasoning and in the refining of the concepts of justice, we find another level of protection of individuals' rights. Stage 6 people seek to define not only the due processes for deriving people's obligations and rights within a society, but general positive principles for society as well. We should ask not only what procedures would rational people follow, but what great principles of general cooperation would they use to select or reject proposed social laws and human rights.

These general principles for Stage 6 may include standards of equality for human rights and the respect for the dignity and value of every human being. The general principle one selects must be consistently applied regardless of personal taste. The *Golden Rule* for Stage 6 is: Do for others what you would have them do for you — totally apart from any prejudice, inequality, or personal feelings, and independent of established punishments, mutual agreements, personal knowledge, structures of law, and so forth. Unlike the qualified versions we saw on other stages, this is the purest and simplest form of the Golden Rule. It is what Jesus and Confucius saw as the basis of all other obligations.

In the story, Heinz could appeal to universal respect for life. He could claim that the protection of human life is always more important than the protection of property. Of course, then Heinz would have to excuse another person's theft of property from him, if that would help save a life as well. With Heinz's now-established devotion to the protection of life, he would probably be willing to negotiate a gift or a loan to protect a life, rather than forcing the desperate people involved to steal from him. He must see every life as sacred, not only his or his wife's life.

His wife's fate would not merely be determined by due process, as in Stage 5, or by law, as in Stage 4, or by his personal commitment to her, as in Stage 3, or on the basis of a mutually beneficial agreement, as in Stage 2, or even on some other person's command that he should always protect his wife's life, as in Stage 1. Stage 6 recognizes the protection of life as a possible universal principle of justice whether or not it was created by due process, an established law, an implicit expectation in Heinz's marital relationship, a bargain he struck with her, or some authority's rule.

The chief advantage of the higher stages in the development of moral reasoning is the internalization of fair thought processes. Also, when the thought processes are more internalized they are more stable. On one extreme, in Stage 1, a person relies on others to provide rules and punishments to guide behavior. When authorities change their opinions, or new authorities come along, people in Stage 1 change without taking any responsibility. On the other extreme, in Stage 6, every law, human right, moral incentive, and punishment is subjected to the scrutiny of a universal criterion for rationality, impartiality, and equality. The word of no authority goes without challenge. Even the Golden Rule itself, which some might regard as a classic definition of justice, and which has its clearest formulation in Stage 6, must be scrutinized by itself: Apply the *Golden Rule* to others and yourself as you would have others apply it.

Apart from the internalization and stability that developed moral reasoning supplies, our talk of moral virtue will be superficial or hypocritical. In contrast, some of our greatest moral heroes, such as Socrates and Martin Luther King Jr., addressed the problems of their time in Stages 5 and 6. And Kohlberg himself, in later years, confessed he had stopped trying to differentiate between Stages 5 and 6. Here is a selection from Lawrence Kohlberg's *Education for Justice: A Modern Statement of the Socratic View.*

KOHLBERG ON KOHLBERG

The fact that there are no traits of character corresponding to the virtues and vices of conventional language should comfort us. Those who try to achieve the bag of virtues prescribed by the culture find themselves in the plight described by the theme song of the show, *You're a Good Man, Charlie Brown.*

You're a good man, Charlie Brown. You have humility, nobility and a sense of honor that is very rare indeed. You are kind to all the animals and every little bird. With a heart of gold, you believe what you're told, every single solitary word. You bravely face adversity; you're cheerful through the day; you're thoughtful, brave and courteous. You're a good man, Charlie Brown. You're a prince; could be a king. With a heart such as yours you could open any door if only you weren't so wishy-washy.

If we, like Charlie Brown, define our moral aims in terms of virtues and vices, we are defining them in terms of the praise and blame of others and are caught in the pull of being all things to all people and end up being wishy-washy. The attraction of the bag of virtues approach to moral education is that it encourages the assumption that everyone can be a moral educator. It assumes that any adult of middle-class respectability or virtue knows what virtue is and is qualified to teach it by dint of being adult and respectable. We must all make these assumptions as parents, but perhaps they are not sound. Socrates asked "whether good men have known how to hand on to someone else the goodness that was in themselves" and went on to cite one virtuous Greek leader after another who had nonvirtuous sons.

The delicate balance between social reform and moral education is clarified by the example of Martin Luther King. King was a moral leader, a moral educator of adults, not because he was a spokesperson for the welfare of blacks, not because he was against violence, not because he was a minister of religion, but because, as he himself said, he was a drum major for justice. His words and deeds were primarily designed to induce America to respond to racial problems in terms of a sense of justice, and any particular action he took had value for this reason, not just because of the concrete political end it might achieve.

I have used King as an example of a moral educator to indicate that the difference between the political reformer and the moral educator is not a difference in the content of their concern. Civil rights is as much a matter of morality as is honesty in financial matters. The distinctive feature of moral education as against ordinary political action is in the relation of means and ends. Black power politicians using unjust means in the name of civil rights are clearly not in the enterprise of teaching justice, any more than are policemen in the enterprise of teaching honesty when they shoot down rioters. King's acts of civil disobedience, however, flowed directly from a sense of principles of justice and thus were moral leadership, not just propaganda or protest.

Let me recapitulate my argument so far. I have criticized the "bag of virtues" concept of moral education on the grounds, first, that there are no such things and, second, if there were, they couldn't be taught or at least I don't know how or who could teach them. Like Socrates, I have claimed that ordinary people certainly don't know how to do it, and yet there are no expert teachers of virtue as there are for the other arts. Rather than turning to nihilism, I have pointed to an example of an effective moral educator at the adult social level, Martin Luther King. Since I cannot define moral virtue at the individual level, I tried it at the social and found it to be justice, and claimed that the central moral value of the school, like that of the society, was justice. Justice, in turn, is a matter of equal and universal human rights. I pointed to the cloud of virtue labels attributed to King and pointed out that only one meant anything. Justice was not just one more fine-sounding word in a eulogy; it was the essence of King's moral leadership.

My hope is to have stirred some feelings about the seriousness and the reality of that big word, that Platonic form, *justice*, because people like King were willing to die for it. I suppose there may have been people willing to die for honesty, responsibility, and the rest of the bag of virtues, but if so, I have no empathy with them. I am going to argue now, like Plato, that virtue is not many, but one, and its name is *justice*. Let me point out first that justice is not a character trait in the usual sense. You cannot make up behavior tests of justice, as Hartshore and May (1928–1930) did for honesty, service, and self-control. One cannot conceive of a little set of behavior tests that would indicate that Martin Luther King and Socrates were high on a trait of justice. The reason for this is that justice is not a concrete rule of action such as lies behind virtues like honesty.

To be honest means "Don't cheat, don't steal, don't lie." But justice is not a rule or a set of rules, it is a moral principle. By a moral principle, I mean a mode of choosing that is universal, a rule of choosing that we want all people to adopt always in all situations. We know it is all right to be dishonest and steal to save a life because it is just, because one person's right to life comes before another person's right to property. We know it is sometimes right to kill, because it is sometimes just. The Germans who tried to kill Hitler were doing right because respect for the equal values of lives demands that we kill someone who is murdering others, in order to save lives. There are exceptions to rules, then, but no exception to principles. A moral obligation is an obligation to respect the right of claim of another person. A moral principle is a principle for resolving competing claims: You versus me, you versus a third person. There is only one principled basis for resolving claims: Justice or equality. Treat every person's claim impartially regardless of the person. A moral principle is not only a rule of action but a reason for action. As a reason for action, justice is called *respect for* people.

Because morally mature people are governed by the principle of justice rather than by a set of rules, there are not many moral virtues, but one. Let me restate the argument in Plato's terms. Plato's argument is that what makes a virtuous action virtuous is that it is guided by knowledge of the good. A courageous action based on ignorance of danger is not courageous; a just act based on ignorance of justice is not just; and so on. If virtuous action is action based on knowledge of the good, then virtue is one, because knowledge of the good is one. I have already claimed that knowledge of the good is one because the good is justice. Let me briefly document these lofty claims by some lowly research findings. Using hypothetical moral situations, I and my colleagues have interviewed children and adults about right and wrong in the United States, Britain, Turkey, Taiwan, and Yucatan. In all cultures, we find the same forms of moral thinking. There are six forms of moral thought, and they constitute an invariant sequence of stages in each culture. These stages are summarized in the Appendix.

Why do I say that existence of culturally universal stages means that knowledge of the good is one? First, because it implies that concepts of the good are culturally universal. Second, because people at a given level are pretty much the same in their thinking regardless of the situation they are presented with and regardless of the particular aspect of morality being tapped. There is a general factor of maturity of moral judgment much like the general factor of intelligence in cognitive tasks. If they know one aspect of the good at a certain level, they know other aspects of the good at that level. Third, because at each stage there is a single principle of the good, which only approaches a moral principle at the higher levels, for instance, there is some reason for regard for the law and some reason for regard for rights. Only at the highest stage, however, is regard for universal human rights. At this point, both regard for law and regard for human rights are grounded on a clear criterion of justice that was present in confused and obscure form at earlier stages.

Let me describe the stages in terms of the civil disobedience issue in a way that may clarify the argument I have just made. Before the Civil War, we had laws that allowed slavery. According to the law, escaped slaves had to be returned to owners like runaway horses. Some people who didn't believe in slavery disobeyed the law, hid the runaway slaves, and helped them to escape. Were they doing right or wrong?

A bright, middle-class boy, Johnny, answers the question this way when he is 10: "They were doing wrong because the slave ran away himself. They're being just like slaves themselves trying to keep 'em away." Asked, "Is slavery right or wrong?" he answered, "Some wrong, but servants aren't so bad because they don't do all that heavy work."

Johnny's response is Stage 1, *punishment and obedience orientation*. Breaking the law makes it wrong; indeed, the badness of being slaves washes off on their rescuers.

Three years later, Johnny is asked the same question. His answer is mainly Stage 2, *instrumental relativism*. He says "They would help them escape because they were all against slavery. The South was for slavery because they had big plantations and the North was against it because they had big factories and they needed people to work and they'd pay. So the Northerners would think it was right but the Southerners wouldn't."

So early comes Marxist relativism. He goes on: "If a person is against slavery and maybe likes the slave or maybe dislikes the owner, it's OK for him to break the law if he likes, provided he doesn't get caught. If the slaves were in misery and one was a friend he'd do it. It would probably be right if it was someone you really loved."

At the end, his orientation to sympathy and love indicates the same Stage 3, *orientation to approval, affection and helpfulness*, better suggested by Charlie Brown.

At age 19, in college, Johnny is Stage 4, *orientation to maintaining a social order of rules and rights*. He says, "They were right, in my point of view. I hate the actual aspect of slavery, the imprisonment of one man ruling over another. They drive them too hard and they don't get anything in return. It's not right to disobey the law, no. Laws are made by the people. But you might do it because you feel it's wrong. If 50,000 people break the law, can you put them all in jail? Can 50,000 people be wrong?"

Johnny here is oriented to the rightness and wrongness of slavery itself and of obedience to law. He doesn't see the wrongness of slavery in terms of equal human rights but in terms of an unfair economic relation, working hard and getting nothing in return. The same view of rights in terms of getting what you worked for leads Johnny to say about school integration, "A lot of colored people are now just living off of civil rights. You only get education as far as you want to learn, as far as you work for it, not being placed with someone else, you don't get it from someone else."

Johnny illustrates for us the distinction between virtue as the development of principles of justice and virtue as being unprejudiced. In one sense, Johnny's development has involved increased recognition to the fellow-humanness of the slaves. From thinking of slaves as inferior and bad at age 10, he thinks of them as having some sort of rights at age 19. He is still not just, however, because his only notions of right are that you should get what you earn, a conception easily used to justify a segregated society. In spite of a high school and college education, he has no real grasp of the conceptions of rights underlying the Constitution or the Supreme Court decisions involved. Johnny's lack of virtue is not that he doesn't want to associate with blacks, it is that he is not capable of being a participating citizen of our society because he does not understand the principles on which our society is based. His failure to understand these principles cuts both ways. Not only does he fail to ground the rights of blacks on principles, but he also fails to ground respect for law on this base. Respect for law is respect for the majority. But if 50,000 people break the law, can 50,000 be wrong? Whether the 50,000 people are breaking the law in the name of rights or of the Ku Klux Klan makes no difference in this line of thought.

It is to be hoped that Johnny may reach our next stage, Stage 5, *social contract orientation*, by his mid-twenties, because some of our subjects continue to develop up until this time. Instead of taking one of our research subjects, however, let us take some statements by Socrates as an example of Stage 5. Socrates is explaining to Crito why he refuses to save his life by taking advantage of the escape arrangements Crito has made:

"Ought one to fulfill all one's agreements?" Socrates asks. "Then consider the consequences. Suppose the laws and constitution of Athens were to confront us and ask, Socrates, can you deny that by this act you intend, so far as you have power, to destroy us? Do you imagine that a city can continue to exist if the legal judgments which are pronounced by it are nullified and destroyed by private persons? At an earlier time, you made a noble show of indifference to the possibility of dying. Now you show no respect for your earlier professions and no regard for us, the laws, trying to run away in spite of the contracts by which you agreed to live as a member of our state. Are we not speaking the truth when we say that you have undertaken in deed, if not in word, to live your life as a citizen in obedience to us? It is a fact, then, that you are breaking covenants made with us under no compulsion or misunderstanding. You had seventy years in which you could have left the country if you were not satisfied with us or felt that the agreements were unfair."

As an example of Stage 6, *orientation to universal moral principles,* let me cite *Martin Luther King's "Letter from the Birmingham Jail" (1965):*

"There is a type of constructive nonviolent tension which is necessary for growth. Just as Socrates felt it was necessary to create a tension in the mind so that individuals could rise from the bondage of half-truths, so must we see the need for nonviolent gadflies to create the kind of tension in society that will help men rise from the dark depths of prejudice and racism.

"One may well ask, 'How can you advocate breaking some laws and obeying others?' The answer lies in the fact that there are two types of laws, just and unjust. One has not only a legal but a moral responsibility to obey just laws. One has a moral responsibility to disobey unjust laws. An

unjust law is a human law that is not rooted in eternal law and natural law. Any law that uplifts human personality is just, any law that degrades human personality is unjust. An unjust law is code that a numerical or power majority group compels a minority group to obey but does not make binding on itself. This is difference made legal.

"I do not advocate evading or defying the law, as would the rabid segregationist. That would lead to anarchy. One who breaks an unjust law must do so openly, lovingly, and with a willingness to accept the penalty. An individual who breaks a law that conscience tells him is unjust, and willingly accepts the penalty of imprisonment in order to arouse the conscience of the community over its injustice, is in reality expressing the highest respect for law."

King makes it clear that moral disobedience of the law must spring from the same root as moral obedience to law, out of respect for justice. We respect the law because it is based on rights both in the sense that the law is designed to protect the rights of all and because the law is made by the principle of equal political rights. If civil disobedience is to be Stage 6, it must recognize the contractual respect for law of Stage 5, even to accepting imprisonment. That is why Stage 5 is a way of thinking about the laws that are imposed on all, while a morality of justice that claims to judge the law can never be anything but a free, personal ideal.

PROBLEMS AT THE PEAK STAGE

As we observed before, Stage 6 makes the most sweeping claims for pursuing universal justice and engaging the broadest information — beyond even the proper processes of Stage 5. However, very rarely are people motivated by the concerns of Stage 6 alone. It takes a significant level of mental concentration and ability to abstract away the concerns for punishment, beneficial exchange, personal relationships, and stable society. Besides, what general principle or principles should rule Stage 6? The answer for Kohlberg is justice or fairness, for which he thinks we all have some understanding.

In addition, there may be very few humans in this world who are sufficiently rational and detached in their observations and decisions to maintain Stage 6 thought very long. Moreover, much that is attractive about the other stages is missing in Stage 6 — such as attention to personal interests and loyalties to lasting relationships. Someone totally oriented to such consistent universal justice may be our complete ideal — such as Socrates, Jesus, Gandhi, Lincoln, King, or any person whose life and values were so consistently lived for the highest and best for all that we would want to emulate him or her.

Would such a heightened sense of justice compromise or jeopardize some of the dimensions of the values we treasure within families and friendships?

BALANCING 'JUSTICE' AND 'CARE'

Moral reasoning and justice are intensely important, just as are moral human decisions, relationships, and care. They are poor substitutes for each other. Care always connotes closeness — shown especially in a hug, one of the most delightful expressions of care! Here personal interests and relationships play a big role. We seek to be near the people we care about. The Good Samaritan parable became the good "neighbor" first of all because he got close to the person in need. Caring about people who share no physical contact with us is more difficult. We care for the victims of a flood by sending resources and gifts. We care about customers through special attention to safety and quality — perhaps even going beyond what the industry standards require. The image of "arm's length" perceptions and attitudes are grossly out of place when it comes to genuine care.

In a similar way, we often think about decisions of what is fair coming from diligent, detached analysis of information. The higher stages of justice prize abstract, impartial, and impersonal reasoning. Personal, emotional considerations are not the primary focus. Meanwhile, actions that arise from care generally spring from some kind of attachment to people or to specific results. We care about how decisions affect others' welfare as well as our own. When others are hurt, we are hurt. When they are benefited, we feel good.

The highest levels of thinking about justice are impersonal; a just decision involves a careful and fair resolution of a problem, undistracted by — but not unconcerned with — any personal feelings or commitments. In contrast, a caring decision expresses personal feeling, concern, or commitment to other people involved. We also require just decisions to be impartial — without respect for elevated social positions or privilege. No favoritism is allowed. In contrast, one way of saying that we care for someone is to say that we are "partial to" that person.

Furthermore, justice is disinterested. We consider it immoral for a legislator or judge to make a decision on a matter in which he or she has a personal interest. We suspect that a decision would not be fair or just when the people in power have personal interest in the results of the decision. In contrast, a truly caring person takes an intense interest in both the content and the effects of the decisions he or she makes. Of course, people can be intensely "interested" in the sense of truly caring about the people and about good results, but still make an unbiased, disinterested decision — all at the same time.

A COMPARISON	
JUSTICE	**_CARE_**
Impersonal analysis	**Personal decision**
Impartial to	**Partial to (be fond of)**
Detached	**Attached**
Disinterested	**Interested**
Arm's length	**Close-up**
Blind	**Eyes wide open**

Finally, justice is blind. Our vivid symbol for justice is a blindfolded woman holding an analytical balance. This blindness is crucial to implementing the impartial and detached aspects of justice. Meanwhile, care requires an eagerness to learn more about the other. In care, the eyes are wide open! We sometimes say that love is blind, but what we mean is that care — or love — is willing to make allowances for weakness. These and other points of contrast between common symbols of justice and care are displayed in the chart to the left. Notice the impact of the terms we use to describe such basic concepts as "justice" and "care" on our understanding of personal moral development.

Endnote 6

ANOTHER VOICE

The requirements of justice by themselves, especially in Stages 5 and 6 of the development of reasoning, may seem to drain us of much of what is important to us as humans. We may be capable of thinking in these levels of abstraction, and can also imaginatively detach ourselves from our interests and relationships for brief periods of time. Our lives and friendship are too important to distort in reality.

Carol Gilligan uncovered this problem in her studies of the development of young men and women. It seemed that women were less comfortable detaching themselves from their friendships and personal relationships than men were. A larger percentage of women seemed to remain at Stage 3 of Kohlberg's scale of stages. Combining this discovery with the fact that Kohlberg did his initial studies with young men only, Gilligan became suspicious that there was a sex-based bias against women in Kohlberg's theory.

For example, Carol Gilligan contrasts the responses of two 11-year-old, bright and articulate sixth graders — Jake and Amy. Contrary to popular stereotypes, Amy loves mathematics and is planning to become a scientist, while Jake's favorite subject is English. Nevertheless, Jake approaches the Heinz dilemma discussed earlier as if it were an abstract, self-contained problem of logic or mathematics. At the same time, Amy has more of a feeling for the various interests and relationships involved.

Endnote 7

The following excerpt from her *In a Different Voice* is typical of the way Professor Gilligan describes the contrast between Jake and Amy — and in general between the ways men and women tend to think:

GILLIGAN'S EMPHASIS

The dilemma that these 11-year-olds were asked to resolve was one in the series devised by Kohlberg to measure moral development in adolescence by presenting a conflict between moral norms and exploring the logic of its resolution. In this particular dilemma, a man named Heinz considers whether or not to steal a drug which he cannot afford to buy in order to save the life of his wife. In the standard format of Kohlberg's interviewing procedure, the description of the dilemma itself — Heinz's predicament, the wife's disease, the druggist's refusal to lower his price — is followed by the question, "Should Heinz steal the drug?" The reasons for and against stealing are then explored through a series of questions that vary and extend the parameters of the dilemma in a way designed to reveal the underlying structure of moral thought.

Jake, at 11, is clear from the outset that Heinz should steal the drug. Constructing the dilemma, as Kohlberg did, as a conflict between the values of property and life, he discerns the logical priority of life and uses that logic to justify his choice:

For one thing, a human life is worth more than money, and if the druggist only makes $1,000, he is still going to live, but if Heinz doesn't steal the drug, his wife is going to die. (*Why is life worth more than money?*) Because the druggist can get a thousand dollars later from rich people with cancer, but Heinz can't get his wife again. (*Why not?*) Because people are all different and so you couldn't get Heinz's wife again.

Asked whether Heinz should steal the drug if he does not love his wife, Jake replied that he should, saying that not only is there "a difference between hating and killing," but also, if Heinz were caught, "The judge would probably think it was the right thing to do." Asked about the fact that, in stealing, Heinz would be breaking the law, he says that "the laws have mistakes, and you can't go writing up a law for everything that you can imagine."

Thus, while taking the law into account and recognizing its function in maintaining social order (the judge, Jake says, "should give Heinz the lightest possible sentence"), he also sees the law as man-made and therefore subject to error and change. Yet his judgment that Heinz should steal the drug, like his view of the law as having mistakes, rests on the assumption of agreement, a societal consensus around moral values that allows one to know and expect others to recognize what is "the right thing to do."

Fascinated by the power of logic, this 11-year-old boy locates truth in math, which he says, is "the only thing that is totally logical." Considering the moral dilemma to be "sort of like a math problem with humans," he sets it up as an equation and proceeds to work out the solution. Since his solution is rationally derived, he assumes that anyone following reason would arrive at the same conclusion and thus that a judge would also consider stealing to be the right thing of Heinz to do. Yet he is also aware of the limits of logic. Asked whether there is a right answer to moral problems, Jake replies that "there can only be right and wrong in judgment," since the parameters of action are variable and complex. Illustrating how actions undertaken with the best of intentions can eventuate in the most disastrous of consequences, he says, "like if you give an old lady your seat on the trolley, if you are in a trolley crash and that seat goes through the window, it might be that reason that the old lady dies."

Theories of developmental psychology illuminate well the position of this child, standing at the juncture of childhood and adolescence; at what Piaget describes as the pinnacle of childhood intelligence, and beginning through thought to discover a wider universe of possibility. The moment of preadolescence is caught by the conjunction of formal operational thought with a description of self still anchored in the factual parameters of his childhood world — his age, his town, his father's occupation, the substance of his likes, dislikes, and beliefs. Yet as his self-description radiates the self-confidence of a child who has arrived, in Erikson's terms, at a favorable balance of industry over inferiority — competent, sure of himself, and knowing well the rules of the game — so his emergent capacity for formal thought, his ability to think about thinking and to reason things out in a logical way, frees him from dependence on authority and allows him to find solutions to problems by himself.

This emergent autonomy follows the trajectory that Kohlberg's six stages of moral development trace, a three-level progression from an egocentric understanding of fairness based on individual need (Stages 1 and 2), to a conception of fairness anchored in the shared conventions of societal agreement (Stage 3 and 4), and finally to a principled understanding of fairness that rests on the free-standing logic of equality and reciprocity (Stages 5 and 6). While this boy's judgments at 11 are scored as conventional on Kohlberg's scale, a mixture of Stages 3 and 4, his ability to bring deductive logic to bear on the solution of moral dilemmas, to differentiate morality from law, and to see how laws can be considered to have mistakes points toward a principle conception of justice that Kohlberg equates with moral maturity.

In contrast, Amy's response to the dilemma conveys a very different impression, an image of development stunted by a failure of logic, an inability to think for herself. Asked if Heinz should steal the drug, she replies in a way that seems evasive and unsure:

Well, I don't think so. I think there might be other ways besides stealing it, like he could borrow the money or make a loan or something, but he really shouldn't steal the drug — but his wife shouldn't die either.

Asked why he should not steal the drug, she considers neither property nor law but rather the effect that theft could have on the relationship between Heinz and his wife:

If he stole the drug, he might save his wife then, but if he did, he might have to go to jail, and then his wife might get sicker again, and he couldn't get more of the drug, and it might not be good. So, they should really just talk it out and find some other way to make the money.

Seeing the dilemma as not a math problem with humans but a narrative of relationships that extends over time, Amy envisions the wife's continuing need for her husband and the husband's continuing concern for his wife and seeks to respond to the druggist's need in a way that would sustain rather than sever connection. Just as she ties the wife's survival to the preservation of relationships, so she considers the value of the wife's life in a context of relationships, saying that it would be wrong to let her die because, "if she died, it hurts a lot of people and it hurts her." Since Amy's moral judgment is grounded in the belief that "if somebody has something that would keep somebody alive, then it's not right not to give it to

them," she considers the problem in the dilemma to arise not from the druggist's assertion of rights but from his failure of response.

As the interviewer proceeds with the series of questions that follow from construction of the dilemma, Amy's answers remain essentially unchanged, the various probes serving neither to elucidate nor to modify her initial response. Whether or not Heinz loves his wife, he still shouldn't steal or let her die; if it were a stranger dying instead, Amy says that "if the stranger didn't have anybody near or anyone she knew," then Heinz should try to save her life, but should not steal the drug. But as the interviewer conveys through the repetition of questions that the answers she gave were not heard or not right, Amy's confidence begins to diminish, and her replies become more constrained and unsure. Asked again why Heinz should not steal the drug, she simply repeats, "Because it's not right." Asked again to explain why, she states again that theft would not be a good solution, adding lamely, "If he took it, he might not know how to give it to his wife, and so his wife might still die." Failing to see the dilemma as a self-contained problem in moral logic, she does not discern the internal structure of its resolution; as she constructs the problem differently herself, Kohlberg's conception completely evades her.

Instead, seeing a world comprised of relationships rather than of people standing alone, a world that coheres through human connection rather than through systems of rules, she finds the puzzle in the dilemma to lie in the failure of the druggist to respond to the wife. Saying that "it is not right for someone to die when their life could be saved," she assumes that if the druggist were to see the consequences of his refusal to lower his price, he would realize that "he should just give it to the wife and then have the husband pay back the money later." Thus she considers the solution to the dilemma to lie in making the wife's condition more salient to the druggist or, that failing, in appealing to others who are in a position to help.

Just as Jake is confident the judge would agree that stealing is the right thing for Heinz to do, so Amy is confident that "if Heinz and the druggist had talked it out long enough, they could reach something besides stealing." As he considers the law to "have mistakes," so she see this drama as a mistake, believing that "the world should just share things more and then people wouldn't have to steal." Both children thus recognize the need for agreement but see it as mediated in different ways — he impersonally through systems of logic and law, she personally through communication in relationship. Just as he relies on the conventions of logic to deduce the solution to this dilemma, assuming these conventions to be shared, so she relies on a process of communication, assuming connection and believing that her voice will be heard.

An analysis research with 27-year-olds produced similar results for Gilligan. The women identified themselves primarily in terms of care, intimacy, attachments, and personal relationships; men emphasized more the categories of fairness, logic, and separation. Gilligan concludes that these women and men may have quite different concepts of adulthood:

The participants in this study were an unequal number of men and women, representing the distribution of males and females in the class on moral and political choice. At age 27, the five women in the study all were actively pursuing careers — two in medicine, one in law, one in graduate study, and one as an organizer of labor unions. In the five years following their graduation from college, three had married and one had a child.

When they were asked at age 27, "How would you describe yourself to yourself?" one of the women refused to reply, but the other four gave as their responses to the interviewer's question:

"This sounds sort of strange, but I think maternal, with all its connotations. I see myself in a nurturing role, maybe not right now, but whenever that might be, as a physician, as a mother . . . It's hard for me to think of myself without thinking about other people around me that I'm giving to."
(Claire)

"I am fairly hard-working and fairly thorough and fairly responsible, and in terms of weakness, I am sometimes hesitant about making decisions and unsure of myself and afraid of doing things and taking responsibility, and I think maybe that is one of the biggest conflicts I have had . . . The other very important aspect of my life is my husband and trying to make his life easier and trying to help him out."
(Leslie)

"I am a hysteric. I am intense. I am warm. I am very smart about people . . . I have a lot more soft feelings than hard feeling. I am a lot easier to get to be kind than to get mad. If I had to say one word, and to me it incorporates a lot, *adopted*."
(Erica)

"I have sort of changed a lot. At the point of the last interview (age 22) I felt like I was the kind of person who was interested in growth and trying hard, and it seems to me that the last couple of years, the not trying is someone who is not growing, and I think that is the thing that bothers me the most, the thing that I keep thinking about, that I am not growing. It's not true, I am, but what seems to be failure partially is the way that Tom and I broke up. The thing with Tom feels to me like I am not growing . . . The thing I am running into lately is that the way I describe myself, my behavior doesn't sometimes come out that way. Like I hurt Tom a lot, and that bothers me. So I am thinking of myself as somebody who tried not to hurt people, but I ended up hurting him a lot, and so that is something that weighs on me, that I'm somebody who unintentionally hurts people. Or a feeling, lately, that it is simple to sit down and say what your principles are, what your values are, and what I think about myself, but the way it sort of works out in actuality is sometimes very different. You can say you try not to hurt people, but you might because of things about yourself, or you can say this is my principle, but when the situation comes up, you don't really behave the way you would like . . . So I consider myself contradictory and confused."
(Nan)

The fusion of identity and intimacy, noted repeatedly in women's development, is perhaps nowhere more clearly articulated than in these self-descriptions. In response to the request to describe themselves, all of the women describe a relationship, depicting their identity in the connection of future mother, present wife, adopted child, or past lover. Similarly, the standard of moral judgment that informs their assessment of self is a standard of relationship, an ethic of nurturance, responsibility, and care. Measuring their strength in the activity of attachment ("giving to," "helping out," "being kind," "not hurting"), these highly successful and achieving women do not mention their academic and professional distinction in the context of describing themselves. If anything, they regard their professional activities as jeopardizing their own sense of themselves, and the conflict they encounter between achievement and care leaves them either divided in judgment or feeling betrayed. Nan explains:

"When I first applied to medical school, my feeling was that I was a person who was concerned with other people and being able to care for them in some way or another, and I was running into problems the last few years as far as my being able to give of myself, my time, and what I am doing to other people. And medicine, even though it seemed that profession is set up to do exactly that, seems to more or less interfere with your doing it. To me it felt like I wasn't really growing, that I was just treading water, trying to cope with what I was doing that made me very angry in some ways because it wasn't the way that I wanted things to go."

Thus in all of the women's descriptions, identity is defined in a context of relationship and judged by a standard of responsibility and care. Similarly, morality is seen by these women as arising from the experience of connection and conceived as a problem of inclusion rather than one of balancing claims. The underlying assumption that morality stems from attachment is explicitly stated by Claire in her response to Heinz's dilemma of whether or not to steal an overpriced drug in order to save his wife.

Explaining why Heinz should steal, she elaborates the view of social reality on which her judgment is based:

"By yourself, there is little sense to things. It is like the sound of one hand clapping, the sound of one man or one woman; there is something lacking. It is the collective that is important to me, and that collective is based on certain guiding principles, one of which is that everybody belongs to it and that you all come from it. You have to love someone else, because while you may not like them, you are inseparable from them. In a way, it is like loving your right hand. *They are part of you*; that other person is part of that giant collection of people that you are connected to."

To this aspiring maternal physician, the sound of one hand clapping does not seem a miraculous transcendence but rather a human absurdity, the illusion of a person standing alone in a reality of interconnection.

For the men, the tone of identity is different, clearer, more direct, more distinct and sharp-edged. Even when disparaging the concept itself, they radiate the confidence of certain truth. Although the world of the self that men describe at times includes "people" and "deep attachments," no particular person or relationship is mentioned, nor is the activity of relationship portrayed in the context of self-description. Replacing the women's verbs of attachment are adjectives of separation "intelligent," "logical," "imaginative," "honest," sometimes even "arrogant" and "cocky." Thus the male "I" is defined in separation, although the men speak of having "real contacts" and "deep emotions" or otherwise wishing for them.

There seems at present to be only partial agreement between men and women about the adulthood they commonly share. In the absence of mutual understanding, relationships between the sexes continue in varying degrees of constraint, manifesting the "paradox of egocentrism" which Piaget describes, a mystical respect for rules combined with everyone playing more or less as he pleases and paying no attention to his neighbor. For a life-cycle understanding to address the development in adulthood of relationships characterized by cooperation, generosity, and care, that understanding must include the lives of women as well as men.

Among the most pressing items on the agenda for research on adult development is the need to delineate *in women's own terms* the experience of their adult life. My own work in that direction indicates that the inclusion of women's experience brings to developmental understanding a new perspective on relationships that changes the basic constructs of interpretation. The concept of identity expands to include the experience of interconnection. The moral domain is similarly enlarged by the inclusion of responsibility and care in relationships. And the underlying epistemology correspondingly shifts from the Greek ideal of knowledge as a correspondence between mind and form to the Biblical conception of knowing as a process of human relationship.

Given the evidence of different perspectives in the representation of adulthood by women and men, there is a need for research that elucidates the efforts of these differences in marriage, family, and work relationships. My research suggests that men and women may speak different languages that they assume are the same, using similar words to encode disparate experiences of self and social relationships. Because these languages share an overlapping moral vocabulary, they contain a propensity for systematic mistranslation, creating misunderstandings which impede communication and limit the potential for cooperation and care in relationships. At the same time, however, these languages articulate with one another in critical ways. Just as the language of responsibility provides a web-like imagery of relationships to replace a hierarchical ordering that dissolves with the coming of equality, so the language of rights underlines the importance of including in the network of care not only the other but also the self.

As we have listened for centuries to the voices of men and the theories of development that their experience informs, so we have come more recently to notice not only the silence of women but the difficulty in hearing what they say when they speak. Yet in the different voice of women lies the truth of an ethic of care, the tie between relationship and responsibility, and the origins of aggression in the failure of connection. The failure to see the different reality of women's lives and to hear the differences in their voices stems in part from the assumption that there is a single mode of social experience and interpretation. By positing instead two different modes, we arrive at a more complex rendition of human experience which sees the truth of separation and attachment in the lives of women and men and recognizes how these truths are carried by different modes of language and thought.

To understand how the tension between responsibilities and rights sustains the dialectic of human development is to see the integrity of two disparate modes of experience that are in the end connected. While an ethic of justice proceeds from the premise of equality that everyone should be treated the same, an ethic of care rests on the premise of nonviolence that no one should be hurt. In the realization that just as inequality adversely affects both parties in an unequal relationship, so too violence is destructive for everyone involved. This dialogue between fairness and care not only provides a better understanding of relations between the sexes but also gives rise to a more comprehensive portrayal of adult work and family relationships.

As Freud and Piaget call our attention to the differences in children's feelings and thought, enabling us to respond to children with greater care and respect, so a recognition of the differences in women's experience and understanding expands our vision of maturity and points to the contextual nature of developmental truths. Through this expansion in perspective, we can begin to envision how marriage between adult development as it is currently portrayed and women's development as it begins to be seen could lead to a changed understanding of human development and a more generative view of human life.

MAN IS MAN? WOMAN IS WOMAN?

Carol Gilligan's interpretation of her research has raised a number of controversies that are beyond the purposes of this book. Did she study enough cases to make such general conclusions about men and women? In *Development in Judging Moral Issues*, **James Rest** reports on more than 20 extensive independent studies of men and women in which people were classified into Kohlberg's six stages of development of moral reasoning. In each study, women's reasoning and justice concepts were rated, on an average, as high as or very slightly higher than men's.

However, even if Gilligan's conclusions had been broadly matched and accepted by others, would that mean that every man is more oriented to reasoning and fairness than women generally are? Of course not. Would it mean that every woman is more in tune with relationships and care than men generally are? Certainly not. No such

Endnote 8

stereotyping is ever either fair or caring to the individuals involved. Some women are far more skilled at detached impartial judgment than most men, and some men are more caring and sensitive to others than most women. In fact, the same person — man or woman — can score highly on both measures. Men and women can be very adept at reasoning and raising the justice issues from the perspective of Kohlberg's Stage 6 and still affirm their enduring relationships through caring decisions.

Endnote 9

To demonstrate this claim of the real compatibility of reasoning and relationships, and of justice and care, we can look for people who did or do embody both. Mother Teresa is a great example of one whose high-level reasoning on justice issues is well known but who also embodies a deep sense of care as well. Moreover, the father of modern economics, **Adam Smith**, argued for three driving values in society and personal life — prudence, justice, and care (which he called benevolence). Smith considered care the greatest of these values. In addition, Dr. **Martin Luther King Jr.** certainly had a well-developed ability to reason on justice issues. He is one of the few people Kohlberg himself clearly classified in Stage 6. Without contradiction, he lived and taught love and care at least as much as justice and rights.

Dr. King considered the self-giving love taught and lived by Jesus to be the most powerful instrument for change ("love your neighbor as yourself" and "love your enemies"). To this he added Augustine's advice to "love the sinner while you hate the sin" and Booker T. Washington's wisdom to "let no man pull you so low as to make you hate him." Only with such a relationship to others is a protest or an issue focused on what is just and fair, rather than on mere personal conflict. For Dr. King, the decision to love enhanced the cause of justice. Notice, for example, how Dr. King, as a young, unrenowned preacher in Montgomery, concluded his first public speech as a protest leader:

Endnote 10

> "If you will protest courageously, and yet with dignity and Christian love, when the history books are written in future generations, the historians will have to pause and say, 'There lived a great people — a black people — who injected new meaning and dignity into the veins of civilization.' This is our challenge and our overwhelming responsibility."

What other examples do you know about, of people who are intensely caring and who are also paragons of good reasoning and justice? Do you think of both men and women?

STEPS OF CARE

Whether or not women and men are statistically different in their maturity in justice and care — and whether or not any of us does very well with our lives without plenty of both detached reasoning and deep relationships — **Carol Gilligan's** most lasting contribution may be another dimension of her theory: **The steps of development she notices in people's understanding and expressions of care.** Perhaps understanding these steps will help people to be more understanding of changes in their own behavior, and more perceptive and tolerant of the shifts in others' conduct.

Briefly, Gilligan's theory describes three steps. The **first step** observes that people all seem to start out caring only for themselves. We seem to express selfish egoism quite easily. What motivates us in our decisions is our own desire for survival, at least, if not also greed and personal pride. Nevertheless, society often judges and restrains such behavior through peer pressure, laws, and psychological sanctions. The feeling of guilt for selfishness nudges many toward the second step.

Behavior on the **second step** is driven by responsibility to help others — especially our children and others who depend on us, but also others who seem to need special care. Both personal identity and survival are now understood in terms of the help we give to others, and how well they accept and benefit from that help. The need for other people's approval is a driving force for conduct on step two. Are we doing enough good to merit their acceptance?

Eventually people who remain on this second step are likely to encounter a number of problems. There are often completing claims for care, and our human needs for care are so insatiable — care for one's spouse, parents, children, neighbors, the disabled, the poorer children somewhere else in the city, the homeless, AIDS victims, orphans of war, the starving millions on another continent, and such like. The list could be endless, the burden of care overwhelming in size, and the opportunities to serve competing for our personal attention in innumerable directions. There is so much good that needs to be done for others! Can we give some attention to our own cares as well? These tensions of step two can be dissolved or ignored by retreating to step one, or maturely resolved in moving to step three.

On Gilligan's **third step** the former concern for producing large quantities of good for others is replaced by truth — honest awareness of our limits and the meaning of our mutual relationships. From step two to three there is also a shift in the source of approval. People on step three are not much affected by others' judgment — "You are selfish," "You are a great helper" — but have a more inner awareness and confidence in their goals and accomplishments.

On this step, according to Gilligan, we are also comfortable balancing and integrating our own interests with the interests of others. In the fourth short monologue at the beginning of this chapter, Chrissa is probably attempting to enter this third step. She seems honest about her own needs and the needs of others, but she remains disturbed by the accusations of her own "selfishness." Truth is the standard for this most mature step of care, but it is not truth in a wooden sense. Gilligan holds up as a good example the woman who comes before Solomon, the Jewish king, and seeks to save her child's

Endnote 11

Endnote 11

life by denying being its mother. The point is that if she no longer claims to be the mother, Solomon will call off his bluffing threat to cut the baby in half and divide the corpse between the two women who claimed to be the baby's mother. Because the other woman tells Solomon to go ahead and kill the baby, Solomon recognizes who is the true mother. According to Gilligan, the mother "verifies her motherhood by relinquishing truth in order to save the life of her child."

Endnote 12

The driving vision of the third level is the universal, self-chosen injunction of care that embraces care for others and for oneself. Self-assertion then can have a place in structuring care for others and in helping us feel better about ourselves. Moreover, "once obligation extends to include the self as well as others, the disparity between selfishness and responsibility dissolves." Consequently, the third step is a balanced and stable position.

Endnote 13

How do these steps of care that Gilligan has uncovered match up with the stages of the development of justice? That is not totally clear. Is it possible to reach high levels of reasoning about justice while still caring only about yourself? Consider the member of Congress who argues eloquently and rationally for a very just cause, knowing it will get him re-elected. Also, people with a mature sense of care for oneself and others may have developed only to Stage 3 on the justice scale, depending essentially on interpersonal relations.

INDEPENDENT SCALES

The moral content of our behavior is supplied by our own reasoning and choices, especially as these are informed by justice and care. The particular blend of fairness and care depends on the individual person, that person's degree of development, and the particular challenges at hand.

The stages of development of justice and the steps of development of care are partly independent. Especially as we look at particular cases of problems and decisions, we can easily imagine approaches to problem-solving that exemplify, at the same time, a "high" degree of maturity on one scale and a "low" degree of maturity on another scale. The same person, of course, may be capable of functioning on a "high" level on both scales, but in the particular problem-solving case does not use all the acquired abilities. Alternatively, another person may have matured tremendously on one scale, with only limited growth on another scale, and so high-level functioning on both scales together would be beyond that person's ability.

Do examples bear this out? Can you think of people who can reason in terms of universal principles of justice and who are articulate about the need for dignity for all human beings — Stage 6 of Kohlberg's scale — and yet who, nevertheless, act with consistent selfishness — on Gilligan's Step 1?

To take a concrete case, let us look again at Chrissa. She is quite alert to a human problem. While her personal ability to reason about justice is probably more advanced than this, her complaints about the site director focus on issues of Stage 3: the personal relationships and feelings of all those involved. Had she talked longer she may have made important observations on responsibilities to fulfill earlier fair agreements, or on how rational and impartial people would work together at the clinic — thus demonstrating some of her ability to reason in Stages 5 and 6. However, she might not use those abilities in solving every problem in which she finds herself. Finally, her sense of care is very advanced. Her concern for other people is genuine and strong, including physical and personal care for those who are neglected and ignored by nearly everyone else. Nevertheless, she is intensely aware and honest about her own need for care as well.

Chrissa honestly cares how the site director treats her — manipulating, exploiting — and it bothers her. However, the director's behavior does not at all detract from her mature "autonomy," including her own conviction of the value of her work and her personal dignity and worth. Of course, with more experience in life, she will probably be less angry when she again encounters people like the site director, but she may continue to care — honestly and deeply — about the ways others treat her. This sensitivity is completely consistent with the desire for truth and the care for self and others that characterizes step three.

DEVELOPMENT OF ACCOUNTABILITY

We have looked again at the aspects of ethics and critical thinking about human problems. We have also examined some of the personal development patterns — the development of awareness, fairness, and care. But we still must be able to explain the decision to ourselves and others. The working value for this explanation is accountability.

Is there a developmental scale for accountability? Not exactly. After all, accountability depends not only on our own development, but also on the structures around us. A very immature person who is constantly followed by police, FBI, IRS agents, and the like, will probably be more "accountable" — at least in one common use of that word. But this aspect of accountability depends very little on personal development.

Notice there is an aspect of accountability that depends on personal development: Commitment. This is the subjective or personal aspect of accountability. To what extent and with what maturity are you committed to the other values you profess to believe? On the one hand, are those values — including justice and care — only attractive window dressing and wonderful talk? Do those values honestly explain your behavior? On the other hand, are they the standards you use if you honestly vindicate your decisions to yourself, your friends, your family or your God? Since this is so important, developmental positions of commitment have been analyzed and described by a number of important scholars. Here we will look briefly at the insights of Soren Kierkegaard and Donald Osgood on the development of commitment.

KIERKEGAARD'S CATEGORIES

Danish philosopher **Soren Kierkegaard** (1813–1855), the father of existentialism, described three main positions in life's development. He called them **"stages of life,"** and they focused on one's definitive commitments. First, we all start out with no authentic or deep commitments. We do what feels good; we conform to peer pressure; we fit in to the roles and social patterns around us. In this position that Kierkegaard calls the **"aesthetic stage,"** people never actually choose their roles or patterns of life. In fact, people in this position rarely even think of these as choices they could make.

On the one hand, he found that some in this position are "sexually active" because their hormones are strong or because they have developed highly successful methods of seducing others. Mimicking this point of view, for example, Kierkegaard wrote a fascinating pseudonymous work, "The Diary of the Seducer." In this "Diary" — a popular book in Kierkegaard's own time — "Johanes de Seducer" is almost carried away with the success of his clever methods. Even though he is a little bored, and he wonders if there is more meaning to life, he never ventures out of his comfort zone of erotic exploitation.

On the other hand, very responsible adults who are faithful to their spouses, devoted to their children, reliable on their jobs, and ardent members of their church or synagogue are generally still in this "aesthetic" position as well, according to Kierkegaard. They are faithful — or generally faithful — to their spouses because that is the simplest, more comfortable way to go. They are devoted to their children because this is the role society assigns to them, and they do not want to be criticized. Also, they are reliable on the job because they are paid, and they like having a job. Moreover, they are ardent about their religious practice because it feels good, going to church is a nice way to start the week, the sanctuary is beautiful, the songs and scripture readings are uplifting. Again, commitment is based on good feeling and comfort, not explicit choice.

The people who have evaluated their lives, and made conscious choices about their life's directions, have already stepped into the second position of commitment — what Kierkegaard called the **"ethical stage."** Three attributes characterize people in this position. First, they have made an explicit choice and commitment to a set of values, quite conscious that they were thereby rejecting other sets of values. This commitment, therefore, requires some significant knowledge of alternative sets of values that were at least viable choices. According to Kierkegaard, one does not choose if there is only one believable choice. Second, the choice is always associated with a group. There is always a group of other people that provides mutual support and guidance for living out the chosen commitment. Third, the choices one makes on the basis of the commitment are always "rational" choices — choices that can be explained to others, especially those in the same "support" group.

Commitments in this second position can be very strong and meaningful. However, one's dependence on the "support" group for the definition of that moral commitment in the first place, and some continuing approval by the groups as well — these aspects can limit the depth of personal commitment. The third position allows us to go deeper and reduce these limitations. As in the second position, those in the third take responsibility for their choices, generally fit into a group, and are usually able rationally to explain their behavior to that group — but neither the group nor its approval is necessary for them. In fact, Kierkegaard thought that the group and its approval could well hinder sincere commitment.

What distinguishes the third position is the willingness to choose what you believe is right, even when there is no group that agrees with you, and no group to rationally understand and approve your choices. For Kierkegaard, this highest position of commitment is completely independent of peer pressure, herd instincts, and the comfort of others' praise. Our commitment is our choice alone — in total, unpretentious, naked honesty before our God. Because only we and God can be fully informed of our real thoughts and reasons — although we do deceive even ourselves sometimes — this level is far less open to hypocrisy and deceit than the "aesthetic" and "ethical" positions. Moreover, because this highest level of development forces the issue of "honest to God" sincerity, flexibility, and openness to keep learning, Kierkegaard chose to call it the **"religious stage."** Of course, by far most of what people in Kierkegaard's time, and our time, call "religion" merely feels right, on position one, or depends on the affirmation of the group, on position two. The sincerity, flexibility, and openness of this position of commitment are, in fact, the opposite of what many people mean by "religion." In Kierkegaard's vital sense of religion, it is the rare person whose moral commitments, standing by themselves, would endure the test of God's thorough inspection.

OSGOOD'S GOOD CURVE

Donald Osgood, an American business management wizard, has uncovered a curve of personal development toward commitment. His discovery is based on decades of work with IBM and other Fortune 500 corporations, and apart from any knowledge of Soren

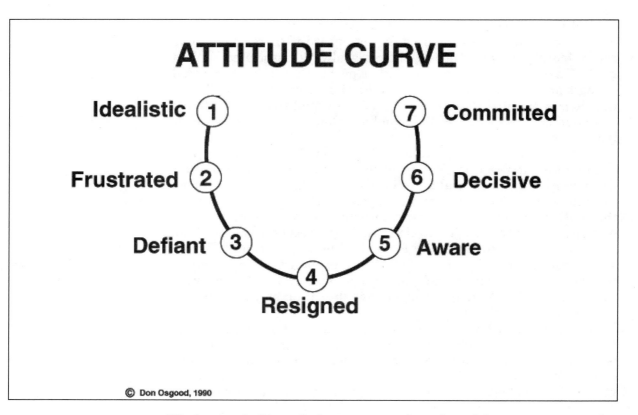

ATTITUDE CURVE

Idealistic ① ⑦ Committed

Frustrated ② ⑥ Decisive

Defiant ③ ⑤ Aware

④

Resigned

© Don Osgood, 1990

Kierkegaard. Nevertheless, progression along his curve is remarkably similar to development along Kierkegaard's positions.

First on Osgood's curve, we start off **"idealistic"** — confident of our values and our ability to succeed. High expectations and goals dominate our thought, but our confidence is naive. This attitude always leads us to the second position, being **"frustrated."** Present circumstances are always a far cry from our goals and desires. Our initial reaction is usually dominated by fear, indecision, and anxiety. After all, the world is not so simple as we had believed or hoped.

The third attitude is **"defiance."** Fear and indecision are overcome as we realize that we have to take some responsibility in our own hands. This attitude could signal the beginning of Kierkegaard's "ethical stage." However, defiance is usually negative and destructive, especially if it is covert, buried. Unfortunately, people can continue to "live" for years with covert resentments and defiance that pollute their relationships with parents, spouse, employer, society, country, and religious authorities. These people who harbor covert defiance slip into the fourth position, simply **"resigned"** to disappointment and aimlessness in their lives. In the words of the rock group Pink Floyd, they are "comfortably numb."

Hope is found in position five, being **"aware"** of the problem. Our development toward commitment shares this essential step of any

Endnote 14

problem-solving activity. In Osgood's terms, at this point we become aware of some of the damage of our defiance and resignation, and we realize that we must change. Acting upon that realization draws us into the sixth attitude, **"decisive."** We consciously do something different, consciously take responsibility for our lives.

While we may be hesitant at first, our initial decisions for change make our lives more vital, meaningful, creative. As these decisions become stronger we achieve the seventh and highest fulfillment on Osgood's attitude curve, **"committed."** In this position we do not expect perfection of ourselves, our plans, family, friends, job, school, community, society, or nation. Nevertheless, we are committed to attempt our best ideals, with our best ability, while remaining realistic about our results and talent. This is not the fragile idealism that can be easily shattered, but purposeful and prudent devotion — sincere, flexible, and open to learn and grow further.

These levels of commitment make us more accountable, whether others are watching and checking on us or not. The commitment that Kierkegaard and Osgood describe so well in their highest positions of development is our deepest and strongest human quality of accountability — sincere, flexible and open.

FINAL COMMENTS

However important commitment and accountability are, they are parasitic values. They have no intrinsic worth. We are never merely "committed"; we have to be committed to some additional value. We are never merely "accountable"; we must be accountable for some standard, some goal. These standards and goals that we use are derived from the more or less mature stages of fairness and justice, and the more or less high steps of care that we achieve. Could a person be committed to a set of simplistic concepts of justice alone — mere punishment-and-reward systems? Yes, but you can also be committed in any of the other stages as well — including universal principles of justice. Can a person be committed only to selfish goals? Unfortunately yes, but many treasure far more the mature, honest care for self and others that Gilligan describes. Clearly, the developmental positions of accountability must be matched with development in these other dimensions as well, so that our accountability will have especially valuable content.

As you ponder these various approaches to moral development, keep in mind that these developmental human stages also affect the classical and contemporary approaches to moral reasoning that we will explore in Chapters 4 and 5. In the meantime, in the next chapter, Chapter 3, you will be able to add certain skills of expression, argumentation, and problem-solving.

FOR FURTHER INQUIRY

DISCUSSION

Consider how Kohlberg would view the life of Marcus Junius Brutus (85–42 B.C.). Brutus was a noble Roman general, senator, and orator. He is especially well-known to us for having killed his best friend Julius Caesar in 44 B.C. Earlier, Caesar himself had pardoned Brutus from the accusation of treason — thereby saving his life. However, there was no win-win relationship between them, or even deep personal feeling. Instead of returning a favor, Brutus killed this friend in a futile effort to save the crumbling Roman Republic. He had become convinced that Caesar's power and ambition would transform the structure of Roman society. Considering this observed threat to be unjust and unfair, and a threat to the very values that make civility possible, Senator Brutus took his elevated concept of justice into his own hands and assassinated Caesar. For this extraordinary and devoted "justice" he is made into a kind of hero by Shakespeare and idealized by some as the last of the true Romans. Nevertheless, we all also stand warned against having friends like Brutus.

Even before this tragic incident with his friend Caesar, Senator Brutus was no stranger to placing justice above companionship and human kindness. It is reported that during an earlier period when he served as a judge, Brutus' own son was brought before him and accused of treason. Convinced of his own objective fairness, Brutus chose to try the case himself. Unfortunately, the information and evidence was convincing and convicting. Certainly not one to let personal feelings or care for others get in the way of justice, honorable Brutus condemned his own son to death! He received a pardon himself, from Caesar, from the accusation of treason, but he chose not to seek mercy for his own son.

REVIEW QUESTIONS

1. In what stage would Kohlberg have placed Brutus's conception of justice? Why?

2. At what step would Gilligan have placed his level of caring? Why?

3. How would you characterize Brutus's level of accountability or commitment? Why?

4. What advice would you give Brutus during the trial of his son? Why?

5. What advice would you give him on the way to meeting Julius Caesar that fateful day, March 15, 44 B.C.? Why?

ENDNOTES

1. James R. Rest, critique of other theorists, especially Lawrence Kohlberg, in *Development in Judging Moral Issues*, (Minneapolis: University of Minnesota Press), 1979, pages 48–74.

2. Jean Piaget (1896–1980) The terms "accommodate" and "assimilate" are borrowed from the description he gave to perceptual change. Piaget referred to the middle stage as a "disequilibrium."

3. Piaget, *The Moral Judgment of the Child*, 1932.

4. Lawrence Kohlberg, *The Philosophy of Moral Development* (New York: Harper and Row) 1981, p. 12.

5. See Jesus' comments in the Sermon on the Mount (St. Matthew, Chapters 5–7, especially 7:12) and Confucius' teaching in the *Analects*. Confucius uses the negative version: "Do not do to others what you would not want them do to you."

6. From Paul de Vries and Barry Gardner, *The Taming of the Shrewd* (Nashville: Thomas Nelson) 1992, p. 230.

7. Carol Gilligan, *In a Different Voice*, (Cambridge, Massachusetts: Harvard University Press), 1982, pages 25–29.

8. James R. Rest, *Development in Judging Moral Issues*, (Minneapolis: University of Minnesota Press), 1979, pages 120–124.

9. See Adam Smith, *The Theory of Moral Sentiments*, and also an analysis of this book in Paul de Vries' article "Resource X: Sirkin and Smith on a Neglected Economic Staple," *Business and Professional Ethics Journal,* Fall, 1989.

10. Martin Luther King, Jr., *Testament of Hope*, (Harper: San Francisco), 1986, page 436.

11. See Gilligan, pages 64–105.

12. Gilligan, pages 104 and 105. This comment is based on the Biblical story in I Kings 3:16–28.

13. Gilligan, pages 93 and 94.

14. See Pink Floyd, *The Wall*.

CHAPTER 3

CRITICAL THINKING

"It appears to me that in ethics, as in all other philosophical studies, the difficulties and disagreements, of which history is full, are mainly due to a very simple cause: namely, to attempt to answer questions, without first discovering precisely what question it is which you desire to answer."

— *George Edward Moore*, **Principa Ethica**

"We make a ladder of our vices, if we trample those same vices under foot."

— *St. Augustine*, **Sermons 3**

After an argument, we may ask: "How could I have expressed myself in a way that would have been more convincing?" In part, this chapter will help you express your statements with an awareness of the patterns of *critical thinking within the ethics environment*. First, we will examine critical thinking aspects, including how to recognize moral issues in human problems, engage information, reach a decision and be able to communicate and justify it. Later we will see the various elements of a statement, the parts of an argument, the dangers of fallacies, the tools of deductive and inductive reasoning, and the tests of validity and soundness. Perhaps this knowledge will help you be effective in your next argument!

An ethical person examines and exemplifies critical-thinking considering the issues of life. We call it **"critical thinking" because it is thinking that makes a difference: It has a critical edge and a critical mass. It includes the best imagination, analysis, synthesis, logic, comparison, knowledge, wisdom, deliberation and resolution applied to specific problems.** It is "critical thinking" because it is not mere personal reflection or day-dreaming but rather the finest of our thinking for the purpose of solving problems.

The chart of Key Concepts on page 71 shows where we are headed in this chapter; it is your map for our journey in thinking.

When we do it well, "critical thinking" is also self-critical and self-adjusting. Reflective experience helps improve the critical thinking process, and critical thinking itself helps the person who uses it to be

Paul De Vries, M.A. and Ph.D. University of Virginia, is the president of NYES Fund Inc., an educational program, and a partner in Leadership Excellence Inc. He also is president of the International Research Institute on Values Changes, based in New York and Moscow. Contributors were Emily Baker and Michael Richardson.

CHIEF LEARNING OUTCOME

I can apply critical thinking skills in making ethical arguments that avoid fallacious reasoning.

a better person. Critical thinking involves logic (a system of evaluating statements or arguments), but it is more than logic. It includes effective uses of stories, common sense, and perception as well. Critical thinking brings together our best skills and achievements. Ethics, utilizing critical thinking, brings the optimum resources each of us can bring to resolve human problems. Simply put, ethics is being smart about our problems.

CRITICAL THINKING: STEP BY STEP

This kind of critical thinking about human problems involves the four crucial steps in any critical thinking process. The steps are not always equally important, not all of them need to be emphasized specifically in each situation in which a human problem is resolved, and they are not always sequential. Nevertheless, each of the four steps is necessary, or else our critical thinking is incomplete.

1. **Recognizing a problem**
   Key Question: What is truly going on?
2. **Engaging all available information**
   Key Question: Is your information factual and fair?
3. **Deciding what to do and doing it**
   Key Question: What do you really care to achieve?
4. **Being able to explain the decision to yourself and others**
   Key Question: To whom, for what, are you accountable?

We will now examine each of these steps one at a time and consider some examples and explanations. We will also look for a standard of excellence for each step, a pattern that epitomizes our best hopes and efforts for that step. Finally, we will look at the difference between ethics and other problems. Next, we will discover how to draft syllogistic arguments, and how to recognize and avoid fallacies. Then, prepared to argue and justify our decisions, we will see that our arguments need to include powerful rationale, which meets the tests of consistency, accountability, law, rules and the benefits of moral choices.

First of all, however, we may want to review whether a problem even has moral dimensions. It may simply be *non-moral,* having no particular ethical value at all, beyond the place of moral consideration. For example, is it a moral issue whether I choose the right fork to eat my salad? Not at all! (It could become one, however, if I hear my mother's voice ordering me to use a certain fork and then I choose not to use that one!) A non-moral, or amoral, issue is simply devoid of moral account; a potted plant cannot be a prostitute. By contrast, *moral issues* — while not relying exclusively on some authority or tradition — nonetheless do address issues of conduct and societal import while offering some sense of being impartial. Meanwhile, *immoral* conduct is that which ignores standards and does as it pleases.

KEY CONCEPTS

Critical Thinking Steps: Recognizing a problem, engaging all available information, deciding what to do and doing it, being able to explain the decision to yourself and others. It makes use of arguments, reasoning and rationale.

Types of Arguments include deductive, inductive, valid and invalid, sound and unsound, cogent and uncogent.

Fallacious reasoning is an attempt to persuade emotionally or psychologically, not rationally, and involves statements that in one way or another deceive or mislead.

Ethical rationale correlates an argument with the standards of consistency, reasons, accountability, law, rules and the benefits of moral choices.

OUR VALUES ENVIRONMENT

What do we think is important to talk about? What conversation gets our attention? What are our most crucial thoughts? What makes us sincerely concerned, or angry?

Your answers to these questions may be a little different from what other people say, and your response today may be different from what you said yesterday and what you will say tomorrow. Nevertheless, the ever-present, familiar gap between the way we hope things might be and the way they are — this chronic gap accounts for a tremendous amount of our daily conversation, conceptualization, and concerns.

> You think or dream about what could be,
> You recognize how things really are, and
> You know the difference — you see the gap.

Trying to understand this gap drives our pursuit of information from education, science, philosophy, the news media, history and even gossip. Also, this gap provides both the motivation and the material for our favorite music and movies, as well as great world literature and philosophy. Obviously, we have all been aware of this gap in varying degrees since our first childhood disappointments.

This gap has a simple name: ***Human problems***.

Most of us have been complaining almost as long as we could talk. **"It is not fair," "It's not right," "Someone ought to do something"** — so we have often claimed and argued, ever since we were very small children. And what concerns have been more important to us? Not many. What issues provide better material for novels, movies, or television programs?

You probably do not remember the first time you felt ignored, the first time you saw that others were uncaring, or the first time you knew that someone got away with "murder." We make these observations daily in the experiences of our own lives, and when we are reading newspapers or fiction, watching movies or television programs. Is it possible for us even to imagine what the world would be like without this chronic gap we call human problems? How would our lives be? Would we be happy? Would we be bored?

As we approach problems, from a distance, we begin to ask good questions about ourselves and the situation at hand:

    ❋ Whom should I trust?

    ❋ When, if ever, is violence justified?

    ❋ Should I do what I want, even if someone is disappointed?

    ❋ It is so easy to cheat — why is it wrong?

    ❋ Has this product been tested enough to sell it to customers?

    ❋ Why should I treat people equally if they do not seem equal?

    ❋ Really, is there anything wrong with greed?

    ❋ Should I tell the truth even if it hurts someone else?

    ❋ Is there any cause worth living for — or dying for?

    ❋ Is it a good thing to disobey an unjust law?

    ❋ Should I put my seat belt on even for short trips?

    ❋ Do I report it when my boss breaks the law?

    ❋ Can anyone really love me?

    ❋ How do you recognize a love that will last until death?

From these anxious probes around the edges, we can move into what Aristotle tried to develop, a **systematic approach** to solving problems, ways of thinking that will make sense to ourselves and others after we have "thought our way through" the issues of life.

STEP ONE: RECOGNIZE THE PROBLEM

Without some vision or concept of what life could be, and without thoughtfully observing what is going on, even intelligent and educated people can blindly resign themselves to morally bankrupt policies, disgusting decisions and corrupt circumstances. Seeing the obvious may not be very simple to achieve, and talking about what is self-evident often takes courage in the face of substantial danger. Many leaders have sacrificed their lives for making such self-evident claims.

In Hans Christian Andersen's famous story, only the little child could recognize that the emperor had no clothes. The Massachusetts Bay Colony forced Roger Williams to leave because he insisted that American Indians were human beings with rights. In Nazi Germany, apparently few Germans asked themselves why multitudes of Jews were continually herded into cramped prison camps, with precious few of them occasionally leaving. In the 1980s, the former Soviet Union and other communist regimes were cruel and corrupt, but when Ronald Reagan said the obvious, calling the Soviet Union an "evil empire," he altered the world's perception — he made people look again, and thus, to see clearly.

Research has shown how difficult and important this step is. People can learn moral principles and study the cases in which they apply. They can write wonderful essays about these principles, engage in thoughtful discussion about them, and apply these principles within prepared cases and other assignments for college ethics classes. They can even earn an "A" in their ethics classes — but the ethical quality of their lives may still not be improved or affected. Even when they face real life cases very much like the ones they studied in their ethics course, they often miss the similarity and do not even see a problem. Precious few will recognize the simple fact that the principles they have studied might actually apply in their own daily lives. How can this be?

"We have faced the enemy and it is us." —Pogo

People can watch good and bad day in and day out on television. Go to church or synagogue or temple week after week. They can even listen carefully to the lessons and participate in thoughtful discussion. Right and wrong can be utterly clear. But the very next week the same people might cheat on their spouses or lie to the Internal Revenue Service — and never recognize that there was a problem. How can this be?

We can be far more blind than we realize. Years ago, a noted philosophy professor told the story about a conference of intelligent and responsible people who met to discuss ideas on how to become involved in reducing crime and violence in our society. These valuable deliberations were interrupted only by the desperate cries for help from a young woman. She was being beaten for several minutes right under the windows of their meeting room. *The conferees watched from the windows, but not one person moved to help the victim.* This true story is a sad parable of much of life. Was this the conduct these conference thinkers really wanted? Were they even aware of the huge gap between their aspirations and their actions? Did they see that their behavior belied their beliefs? Did their ethical deliberations make any difference for their actions?

RECOGNIZING THE PROBLEMS OF RECOGNIZING THE PROBLEM

Endnote 2

Recognition of facts depends on more than just being awake and having our eyes and ears open. What we see depends on so much more. In examining the history of science, author Thomas S. Kuhn observed that two people can look at the same phenomenon and examine the same data, and yet see quite different things — even if they are both highly intelligent and have trained minds. For example, a seasoned scientist may continue to apply an old and deeply flawed theory while, at the same time, a young scientist interprets the same phenomena and data according to a new theory. The new concepts allow the younger scientist to recognize facts that the older scientist might not even consider — let alone see.

In one case, two historic chemists, Joseph Priestly (1733–1804) and Antoine Lavoisier (1743–1794), both studied combustion quite thoroughly. On the one hand, Priestly used a number of ideas but never considered the role of oxygen in the combustion process — mainly because his theory failed to include the concept of oxygen. On the other hand, Lavoisier observed that oxygen played a major role in combustion. The big difference was that Lavoisier was using a new theory in which the concept of oxygen was introduced for the first time — a theory that *he* had developed. In a similar example, a science teacher, seasoned in the discipline, may immediately see the trajectories of subatomic particles in a cloud chamber. While the students see only the droplets, the trained eye of the teacher will recognize the equally obvious but more significant structures.

Is it possible to cultivate and expand our abilities to recognize human problems? Yes, and the two most important ingredients for enhancing our capacities to recognize a problem are these:

1. Familiarity with the problem's patterns.
2. Personal interest in addressing the problem.

We have acquired certain knowledge through thoughtful experience, the study of history and literature, the examination of religious traditions, an awareness of the checks and balances of our political and business structures, and so on. These help alert us to problems. Personal interest in our own improvement must also be cultivated.

Remember the story of the "Good Samaritan." It took an outsider, a veritable reject in the community, to recognize the problem and provide the help that was obviously needed. The people who were supposed to be community examples, including religious leaders, bypassed the wounded crime victim. **They had spent much of their lives *thinking* about righteous actions, but they did not *apply* that thought to the situation before them.** Why? They neither truly recognized nor understood the problem lying under their noses. Perhaps they were blind because they had neither studied nor *experienced* the ravages of crime, and remained unfamiliar with its real costs. Perhaps, also, they could not imagine being in the same need as the crime victim on the side of the road — so they lacked the *interest* to help such a needy person. They were probably blind to many other obvious problems and needs around them as well. In contrast, the Samaritan, as an outcast, had personally experienced at least some of the violence of society against himself. Whether or not he had been a victim of the same crimes, he had *personally identified* with the needy, seen such disaster before, and could easily imagine similar attacks against himself. Consequently, he could see what the others missed. Whom do we each resemble?

STEP TWO: ENGAGE ALL AVAILABLE INFORMATION

Ethical decisions are informed decisions; critical thinking about human problems requires knowledge. We need information about the problem, its history, possible solutions, and the consequences of various decisions. Rarely do we have time to acquire that amount of knowledge on the spot within the time we have to make a wise decision. Instead, our primary sources are the knowledge, experience, and understanding we can acquire over a period of time as we become intelligent, mature, and caring people. Then, occasionally additional facts of a new human problem are added to our veritable library of (1) knowledge, (2) experience, and (3) understanding that we carry around within us in our hearts and minds.

First, **knowledge** is essential. How else can we make decisions — for our lives, our time, our bodies, our families, our relationships, our careers, our governments, our community organizations — unless we know about purposes and possibilities, facts and fashions? This is one of the main reasons why you are in college, and this is one reason why some of the courses are mandated for graduation or for completion of a major.

Second, **experience** prepares us to cope with human problems as well — especially experience that is not passive but dynamic and responsive. Experienced people act and then digest the results of their actions in order to act more effectively and skillfully in the future. Such savvy people frequently re-evaluate both the intentions and consequences of their actions in order to make even more wise decisions.

Helix

The process of gaining experience and the basic structure of experience itself is shaped like the form of a spiral spring we call a helix, a circular spiral. It revolves round and around, each time coming back to a different place and on another level. At each turn there are new requirements and rewards. Experienced people actively expand their knowledge in order to extend their effective mastery of their living, working, and playing environment. The circularity of experience both demands and honors engaged thought. Experienced people are usually more open to new and surprising experiences, building upon the confidence that experience brings, sustaining the openness encouraged by experience itself. The benefits of this practiced openness are then evident to anyone who is thoughtful and sensitive.

Experience affects how we relate to theories in life. Our awareness of their limits forces us to use theories more cautiously and humbly. Our best theories are still only tools in our own hands, to be used by us, and interpreted or modified by our own perceptive experience.

Third, **understanding** is another essential resource for engaging all available information when coping with human problems. As with experience, the process of understanding follows helictical patterns. We cannot understand a part of a situation unless we have some understanding of the larger picture, and we cannot understand the larger picture unless we understand many of the parts.

Is this a frustrating vicious cycle, since we cannot understand either the problem or its greater context without some understanding of both? If we need to understand the problem in order to understand the context, and understand the context in order to understand the problem, where can we start? The answer is simple: *We start where we are, and with the understanding that we have.* Probing the problem more enriches our understanding of the larger picture, which in turn helps us to frame the problem better. The very interdependence of the problem and its context gives us resources of understanding.

The **Golden Rule** highlights two central features of our second step of ethics: Engaging all available information. "Do for others what you would want them to do for you." The assumption of this rule is that the other people involved in the problem are at least a little bit different than you are, and you need to understand their perceptions, hopes and ideals — from their point of view. As Stephen R. Covey in *The Seven Habits of Highly Effective People* (Simon & Schuster, 1989) puts it: Seek first to understand and then to be understood. Listening and observing, as well as drawing from your own resources of experience and understanding, will make all the difference.

As a result, this ancient standard of fairness, or justice, establishes the epitome of the second step of ethics. We engage all available information by bringing our knowledge, experience, and understanding into the problem-solving situation. And we do this in a way that the others involved in the problem should recognize as fair, because it is the approach we would want them to take if our roles were reversed. The standard is not what others want us to do, but *what we would want them to do if they were us*. And our primary resource for applying such a standard is the accumulated knowledge, experience, and understanding that we bring with us into every situation and problem.

STEP THREE: MAKE A DECISION AND DO IT

Our critical thinking about human problems necessarily includes our decisions, our problem-resolutions. "Thinking" that does not lead to a decision, that does not make a difference, is not "critical thinking," because it is not really engaged in life in the first place. Unlike abstract thought, critical thinking must make some impact, or it is no longer "critical," no longer significant. Critical thought reaches beyond the comfortable ranges of mental imagination and into our flesh-and-blood behavior, decisions, risks.

From recognition of the existence of a problem and research of its facts and our knowledge about such problems, we then begin **telling the story** of that problem. The story will change as we think about it. How we tell it each time makes a difference. It affects our own view of the story as we reinforce our understanding. It affects others' perceptions of the story and of us. Story problems, or word problems, are necessary for learning. The stories and problems of ethics are often more complicated than most of the others in life, and their telling and retellings help refine them for our understanding.

"That is the story of my life," we often say — especially when we are faced with major frustrations. Our responses, actions, and attitudes are some of the main methods by which we continue to write our flesh-and-blood autobiographies. It is here in the real story — where the "rubber meets the road," where what we eat and do affects our own health, where our present choices determine a future we will live with — that critical thinking about human problems must be tested.

The critical-thinking tools of decision making enable us to resolve the human problems we face. Even the "decision" not to decide is a decision. "Not choosing" is still a choice, a conclusion of thought, an attempt to resolve the problem for now. Giving someone else the responsibility, putting off a decision, passing the buck — these are all possible choices, and they are paragraphs in our personal stories that will continue to live with us. It is no coincidence that history is replete with leaders who gained prominence because they were skillful storytellers. Often their lives and their deaths were shaped by the way they chose to tell the stories they experienced. **How exactly do we want our story lines to go?**

Augustine (354–430 A.D.) was the first person to write and publish an autobiography, and his dramatic and revealing story is still

Figure 1. St. Augustine. City of St. Augustine and St. John's County Chamber of Commerce.

considered valuable literature, penetrating in its psychological and spiritual insights. He saw in his own life the way his own decisions revealed both his temporary wants and his long-term priorities and motivations. Augustine also wrote extensively about the frightening collapse of the Roman Empire that he observed occurring right before his eyes. The Vandals entered and plundered his city in northern Africa as he lay on his own deathbed.

On the basis of his discerning and sagacious observations of both individuals and empires, Augustine repeated one particular theme in dozens of his books: **The critical attribute of persons or organizations is what they care about the most.** What people and organizations love most will always be shown in the patterns of their lives and history, even if these cares and priorities are not evident in every individual decision. What we truly care about will keep cropping up and be utterly evident over a period of time in the tales of our lives.

For example, when students cheat on a paper or a test, it is evident that they care more for the appearance of knowledge and skill than actually having knowledge and skill. Similarly, when people are unfaithful in marriage, it is evident that they care more for the pleasure or excitement of the affair than working toward a stable and happy marriage. Any changes in our cares will be shown in our choices and conduct.

OBTAINING QUALITY THINKING MATERIAL

Stories that might help show us what can be done or what should be avoided we will call **exemplars** — time-tested stories of concrete problems and resolutions and the summation of the values in them. By studying these exemplars we can build our own ethical constructs. Exemplars should be recognized as essential tools for responsible decisions, and for critical ethical thought in general, for these contributions that they make:

1. Quality exemplars enable us to create moral **agreement** where such consensus otherwise eludes us.

2. Creative exemplars aid us tremendously in achieving **impartiality** in decisions.

3. Frequent use of exemplars uniquely facilitates the balanced **integration** of diverse personal and organizational values.

4. Using and rethinking exemplars helps cultivate **personal judgment** by exercising critical thinking about human problems.

5. Exemplars provide an irreplaceable resource for the **flexibility** so valuable for mature ethical decisions.

Before recorded history, these exemplars were the key stories of cultures passed from one generation to the next by oral telling and retelling. Many now have become written. Exemplars include a large variety of case studies, anecdotes, and even fables and myths that are used in various types of meetings and training seminars within college classes and clubs, business corporations, government offices. **Exemplars used in critical ethical thought can depict either** *admirable or objectionable* **concrete puzzles or resolutions for human problems.** In fact, exemplars often include in their rich texture a whole range of qualities of critical thought. However, they are never merely the run-of-the-mill, moderately good stories of concrete problem-resolution. Instead, they stand out as especially good or bad examples. They become exemplary models or paradigms of what a person should do or avoid. They open windows of understanding to possible decisions and experiences.

In short, exemplars help us to become impartial through expanding our moral imagination and knowledge, and through catching us off guard to see parallel problems and solutions where our prejudices are not quite as strong as in questions of our own personal decisions.

Agreement First, exemplars facilitate *agreement*, even where agreement on detailed moral rules or general moral policy eludes us. People only rarely share particular, detailed rules for ethical decisions, even within communities and corporations. Yet shared exemplars pervade internal community and corporate discussions. And even highly regulated industries and organizations have detailed rules only where there are special problems or particular legal xregulations.

Impartiality We not only want to come to agreement, we want those agreements to be *impartial*. Here exemplars are a great asset as well. It is not easy to rise above both personal wants and the desires of one's particular group. It takes effort, courage, and character to rise to the level of moral impartiality. It may be the greatest challenge of moral behavior. For example, applying the *Golden Rule* is difficult when we cannot imagine ourselves in someone else's shoes — for example, someone quite a bit older, of the opposite sex, with different cultural values, with marked differences of family obligation. How can I really know what it is "I would have them do for me" were I so different? It seems unrealistic actually to "walk a mile" in another's shoes. How can I forget who I am?

The difference between an example and an exemplar is that there are zillions of the former and a handful of the latter.

Integration of Diverse Values The third contribution of exemplars for critical ethical thought is that exemplars uniquely *integrate* and *balance* diverse sets of values. All of us have multiple priorities and values, all of which are important to us. For example, we want to be respected, loved, and trusted; we want to succeed, be comfortable or even rich; we want to have some enduring meaning and purpose. In fact, it is futile to try to list all our values. It would be even more difficult to create formulas for proportioning, balancing, or integrating them. And every human problem involves a number of things we care about.

For example, how would you rate the value of honesty in comparison with the value of helping someone feel good? In some circumstances these two values are almost entirely contradictory. And how should a business rate the values of service to customers, quality of product, commitment to integrity, monetary profit, personal growth of employees, and so forth? This is a complicated mix. Individual moral principles state important truths, but in a form that keeps them isolated from the competing principles. Autobiographies of great people, management stories of excellent corporations, religious narratives and parables, heroic family stories — these bring together multiple values in balanced, integrated, even interwoven fabric. What are some of the stories your family, business, community organization or religious group tells?

Personal Judgment The fourth contribution of exemplars in pursuing critical ethical thought is that they appropriately cultivate mature *personal judgment*, making detailed moral rules useful in exceptional cases only. There is a place for detailed rules only when exemplars seem too ambiguous or too weak. For example, in society at large, we legislate laws only when personal examples and tacit cultural patterns, regularly expressed in stories — such as religious traditions and case law — prove inadequate in important cases of personal judgment.

Endnote 3

In a similar way, Peters and Waterman, authors of *In Search of Excellence* (New York: Harper and Row, 1982), found that the stronger the culture — the richer the repertoire of exemplars — the less need there was "for policy manuals, organization charts, or detailed procedures and rules." Large organizations are much too complex to be run by detailed rule books. Instead, they need people who can make wise moral judgments that are consistent with the culture and purposes of the organization. Dee Hock of VISA, quoted by

Endnote 4

Peters and Waterman, correctly points out, "substituting rules for judgment starts a self-defeating cycle, since judgment can only be developed by using it." This is so obvious that it has to be stated. Like a muscle that needs exercise, personal judgment develops through use; otherwise it will atrophy. The only way to develop it is to use it. Good exemplars give us veritable ethical laboratories for exercising and cultivating moral judgment — especially when it comes to history, literature, and case studies. Conversely, the experience of watching television and movies is so passive that we rarely have the opportunity to reap any benefits of practiced moral judgments.

Flexibility Our fifth and last contribution of exemplars is this: Exemplars equip us with the irreplaceable *flexibility* necessary to make responsible decisions within the environment of continual change. The goal is to resolve concrete human problems and conflicts maturely. However, considerations weigh differently in each particular case, as we all know. Thus, even the best detailed moral rules will become quite arbitrary in a new situation. **Freshly applying general moral principles in each new case can be complicated and risky. By assigning exemplars an essential place in our toolbox for critical thinking about human problems, we can have both a community of deeply shared values on the one hand, and on the other the attention to detail that also demands individual, creative, critical ethical thought.**

STEP FOUR: EXPLAIN THE DECISION

Once you have recognized a human problem, engaged information, and made your decision, is everything wrapped up? Not quite. We must be able to explain our decision to ourselves and others — our higher power, teachers, bosses, IRS agents, family, friends and neighbors as well as, perhaps, the prying media.

Most of the time, no one directly asks us for an explanation. But the possibility that they might ask — and the honesty of our own conscience asking us anyway — helps make the other steps more serious. We are more likely to give them the critical attention they deserve instead of letting them slide. In a way, it is similar to target shooting. The whole process is silly if no one checks how close your aim was to the center of the target.

There are many other good analogies and examples for this fourth step of applied ethics. What examples could you add to this list?

READY— Recognize the problem.
AIM— Engage all available information.
FIRE— Make a decision and do it.
CHECK— Be able to explain your decision.

   ❋ tape-recording a song or speech to see how well it really sounds.

   ❋ completing regular sales and accounting reports to measure how well the business is actually doing.

   ❋ checking the results of an experiment to be sure it really did come out as it should.

   ❋ knowing that you will get a grade for an assignment, and thus trying to follow the teacher's instructions.

   ❋ the team watching the video of last night's football game to see what really happened — the good and the bad.

Critical thinking involves being accountable for the quality of our thinking and decision-making. The crucial value here is **accountability**. Unlike digestion and blood circulation, we have considerable

FOUR STEPS OF THE ETHICS CONSTRUCT: CRITICAL THINKING ABOUT HUMAN PROBLEMS

1. **Recognizing a problem**
   Key Question: What is truly going on?
   Working Value: Awareness—being awake, smart, vigilant, alert

2. **Engaging all available information**
   Key Question: Is your information factual and fair?
   Working Value: Fairness, justice

3. **Deciding what to do and doing it**
   Key Question: What do you really care to achieve?
   Working Value: Care, community

4. **Being able to explain the decision to yourself and others**
   Key Question: To whom, and for what, are you accountable?
   Working Value: Accountability

personal control over the character of our thought — both our general habits of thought and our particular problem-resolutions. Plant behavior we explain primarily in terms of genetic background and environmental influences. While genetics and environment deeply affect us as humans beings, we are also capable of evaluating, learning, choosing, and changing our behavior.

Our evaluation of our own and others' ethics — critical thought about human problems — involves two simple assumptions. First, human thought is not infallible. That is the understatement of this chapter! Even our most instantaneous thinking processes are open to error and can be corrected. Careful, ponderous thought also can go wrong in a variety of ways. Even seasoned critical thinkers can continue to make mistakes. Our thinking is exposed to the power of prejudice, limited by inexperience, blinded by self-conceit, and open to careless mistakes of many other sorts as well.

Second, we have reliable standards for evaluating ethical decisions. The vast majority of so-called ethical dilemmas — real ones, not the fictitious ones created in late-night bull sessions or by philosophers trying to demonstrate irresolvable conundrums — can be solved through the use of critical thinking, a sort of rigorous common sense. We have already noticed four general criteria for appraising critical thinking about human problems — each associated with one of the four steps of ethics. Am I truly aware of what is going on, of what is needed? Are my information and decisions fair to all concerned? Does this decision show what and who I genuinely believe are worth caring about? Can I actually defend this decision before others?

Ethics is much more, of course, than mere thinking, because it is thinking for action, for principles, for results, and for character development. That's why it may be the most important kind of thinking.

CRITICAL THINKING: ARGUMENTS

Because thinking is so central to ethics, quality thinking is an essential skill for the development of good ethics. There is an entire field of study for learning good thinking skills; it is called *logic*. In the discipline of logic we examine both the *grounds* and the *structures* of arguments — in order to evaluate whether the *conclusions* that are apparently strengthened or proven by those arguments are sufficiently supported by them. **These three parts of arguments are the essential ingredients — the grounds, structures, and conclusions.** Understanding their roles and the standards that apply to each of these three parts is the mandatory first step both to evaluating other people's arguments and to creating good ones ourselves.

The most important element of any argument is the conclusion. It is the point or the statement that the argument was designed to strengthen or support. An essential step is to be clear about what the conclusion is before any other parts of the argument are evaluated or even located, because the conclusion defines the argument. One must know *where the argument is going* before either of the other parts — the grounds and structures — makes sense at all. That is why both in conversation and in reading it is very important to ask, "Where is this going?" Or "What is the point?" The conclusion is often identified in our language by the beginning word "thus" or "therefore," or "finally." Only when the conclusion, the real point of the argument, is clear, can the other parts of the argument be identified and evaluated in light of their purpose in supporting the conclusion. However, if there is no conclusion, or if it cannot be identified, then there is no argument in the first place.

Sometimes the conclusion is not directly stated, but it is only implied. Nevertheless, an implied conclusion is good enough if the information that is given, along with the context, make the implied conclusion sufficiently obvious. Consider, for example, these cases of **implied conclusions:**

CHART A — DEPICTING CONCLUSIONS

---

1. *You are always thinking about what other people have and you want.*
   Just remember the old command, "Do not envy."
   [Unstated conclusion: You have been guilty of envying.]

---

2. *Daryl keeps misrepresenting facts and getting into trouble.*
   Everyone should know that "honesty is the best policy."
   [Unstated conclusion: Daryl should be more honest about the facts.]

---

3. *Christina says "No" even to the polite, smart, good-looking, rich guys!*
   No young woman does that unless she has something else in mind.
   [Unstated conclusion: Christina wants something besides popularity with the men.]

---

4. *I didn't see Jody pay for the necklace she was still "trying on" when she left.*
   Taking merchandise without paying for it is shoplifting!
   [Unstated conclusion: Jody is guilty of shoplifting.]

---

5. *Isaac copied whole paragraphs from library books to complete his paper easily.*
   The college rules make this kind of copying a case of plagiarism.
   [Unstated conclusion: Isaac has committed plagiarism.]

Are the conclusions obvious in the above cases? Probably, although some are more obvious than others, and some people might state them differently. In fact, in these kinds of arguments, especially in informal daily conversation, it may sometimes even seem awkward to have to state the conclusion. Nevertheless, when evaluating these and other arguments it is still necessary to be crystal clear about each conclusion.

The second part of an argument that should be identified is the grounds. The grounds include all the evidence that is cited, directly or indirectly, for the conclusion. The grounds could include facts, perceptions, opinions, principles, rules, proverbs, advice, precedents, traditions, and any other factors that could help strengthen people's confidence in an argument's conclusion. In the four arguments above, all the stated sentences are the grounds for the unstated conclusions. Clearly, a wide range of sentence subject matter can count as grounds.

CHART B — DEPICTING GROUNDS

1. "No, I am just admiring other people."
   "I am just motivated to do my best and get rewarded."

2. "Daryl is just exaggerating; he is not dishonest about anything."
   "Daryl is not getting in trouble now, because he is more clever."

3. "Peer pressure has worn her down. Christina is different now."
   "That is what you think. Boy are you blind! She has her ways."

4. "No, that is the necklace her brother gave her six months ago."
   "Don't worry about it. Jody is a special friend of the storekeeper."

5. "I'm sorry, but I am sure Isaac never did that."
   "You are just jealous because Isaac is so articulate as a writer."

In many cases the strength or usefulness of particular grounds will **depend on the intended audience** for the argument. People's accepted traditions and proverbs vary widely, for example. As a result, the appeal to a tradition or proverb that has been rejected by the intended audience would actually *weaken* the support for the conclusion. The same argument in a social environment that unquestioningly affirms that tradition or proverb would be considered much stronger. On the one hand, argument #1 above the saying "Do not envy" may be very important to some. For those people this argument would be strong. Others ignore this command, and would find the argument irrelevant and unimportant. On the other hand, in argument #4 above the standards for shoplifting are quite widely accepted. As a consequence, most people would evaluate this argument as relevant and strong.

Facts as grounds may seem the most secure, but even the facts may contribute virtually nothing if the people hearing or reading the argument seriously question or reject those facts. In all of the arguments above, for example, the conclusion may be rejected because the facts are in disputes — or the facts may be rejected because the conclusion is in dispute.

In the five examples above, the grounds could be in dispute in any of the arguments — whether the conclusions are explicit or not. People might reasonably say one or more of the statements from Chart B.

People may have questioned the facts in the first place, or they may doubt the facts because they want to reject the conclusion. Both are possible and legitimate approaches. People can question a conclusion because the factual evidence seems weak, and people can doubt the alleged "facts" because they seem to lead to a questionable conclusion.

The third part of an argument is the structure. Whole textbooks are written on the subject of argument structure, a subject that we cannot adequately explore here. There are, nevertheless, some general principles.

* Statements in the grounds should directly connect with one another. If the connection is loose between a "factual" statement and a "rule" statement, the argument is weak.

* The stronger the conclusion, the weaker the argument, because the conclusion may claim more than the grounds can support. (Thus, the weaker the conclusion, the stronger the argument.)

* One way to test the strength of an argument is to try to think of exceptions that could stand between the grounds and the conclusion. The more likely the exceptions, the weaker the argument.

* Another way to expose the weakness of an argument is to find another argument with the same structure, sound grounds, but an obviously false conclusion.

CHART C — Depicting Structures

1. Here the connection between the two statements in the grounds is rather weak, since "envy" is not part of the factual statement. Thus, the argument is weak.

2. The conclusion is quite weak, making the argument have moderate strength.

3. This is a strong argument because the conclusion itself claims so little. Yet, the little that it claims is supported by the facts.

4. This argument may seem strong at first, but there are a number of exceptions that one could make from the conclusion: Jody may be going to get cash; maybe this was not the necklace she was trying on; and such like.

5. The evidence seems to fulfill the definition of plagiarism — unless all this "copying" was part of the research assignment, but then the grounds would not say, "this kind of copying."

CRITICAL THINKING: TYPES OF ARGUMENTS

All arguments are either inductive or deductive. An inductive argument works like this: If one is **assuming the truth of the grounds, exceptions to the conclusion are still allowed — by the wording of the argument and its context; such an argument is *inductive*.** Inductive arguments reason from within and apply the conclusion generally, usually based on intuitively measuring the probability of its application.

Many arguments take the form suggested first by Aristotle, a syllogism or deductive argument, which he defined as inference or reasoning from "discourse in which certain things being posited, something else than what is posited necessarily follows merely from them." Therefore, a **syllogism consists of two statements followed by a third that is conclusionary.**

Among deductive arguments, two central distinctions are important:

❋ A deductive argument is **valid** if the grounds and the structure in fact guarantee the conclusion. If the grounds and structure do not guarantee the conclusion, the argument is **invalid**. "Validity" is not a matter of degree; deductive arguments are either valid or invalid.

❋ An argument is **sound** if the statements in the grounds are all true. If any of the grounds is false, the argument is **unsound**.

With these two distinctions in mind, there are four kinds of deductive arguments: valid sound arguments, invalid sound arguments,

CHART D—DEDUCTIVE ARGUMENTS

The shaded argument, by logic and reasoning, is "the best" because it alone passes both the tests of soundness and validity.

Type of Deductive Argument	Valid (form)	Invalid (form)
Sound (truth, or truthfulness of grounds, is known)	Slavery is evil. Lincoln hated evil. Therefore, Lincoln hated slavery.	Slavery is evil. Lincoln hated evil. Therefore, Lincoln is a hero.
Unsound (truth, or truthfulness of grounds, is unknown)	Slavery is evil. Lincoln liked slavery. Therefore, Lincoln was evil.	Slavery is evil. Lincoln had no evil thoughts. Therefore, Lincoln could not free the slaves.

valid unsound arguments, and invalid unsound arguments. Some examples are shown in Chart D. Notice that the conclusion can be true, even if the argument is invalid, unsound, or both.

INDUCTIVE ARGUMENTS AND COGENCY

There are two central distinctions among *inductive* arguments as well:

* An inductive argument is **cogent** if the grounds and the structure of the argument make the conclusion believable, otherwise the argument is **uncogent**. "Cogency" is a matter of degree; inductive arguments are more or less cogent.

* An argument is **sound** if the statements in the grounds are all true. If any of the grounds is false, the argument is **unsound**.

How cogent does an inductive argument have to be to satisfy? That depends upon the circumstances. On the one hand, an argument better be *very cogent* to convince you to invest your life savings — or your life — in some particular cause or purpose. On the other hand, the *slightest cogency* of an argument that a particular herb could lead to a cure for some kind of cancer would be cogency enough to give substantial attention to that herb. Also, the slightest chance that another person has AIDS is reason enough to act with great caution. In a hospital, boxing ring, or the NBA, for example, procedures presume that anyone could have AIDS, because the slightest cogency to the argument that a particular person has AIDS is cogency enough.

CHART E—INDUCTIVE ARGUMENTS

With these distinctions in mind, there are four kinds of inductive arguments. The shaded argument, by logic and reasoning, is "the best" because it alone passess both the tests of soundness and cogency.

Types of Inductive Arguments	Cogent (strong, probable)	Uncogent (weak, improbable)
Sound (truth, or truthfulness of grounds, is known)	I could lie on my tax return. Honesty is the best policy. Therefore, I will tell the truth on my tax return.	I could lie to this crazed terrorist. Honesty is the best policy. Therefore, I should tell the truth to this terrorist.
Unsound (falsity, or truthfulness of grounds, is unknown)	I could lie on my tax return. Truth is unimportant. Therefore, I can make strange claims on my IRS tax return.	I could lie to this crazed terrorist. Truth is unimportant. Therefore, I should tell the truth to this terrorist.

SYLLOGISM: MORAL ARGUMENTATION

A deductive argument is a moral reasoning process that frequently can progress from a general first premise to a more specific conclusion, although this is not so in every case. The structure, then, of a typical deductive moral argument is as follows:

1. General moral principle

2. Fact or non-moral premise

3. Specific moral judgment

An example of *applying* this would be as follows:

1. *All killing is wrong.*

2. *Capital punishment is killing.*

3. *Capital punishment is wrong.*

This argument (about capital punishment) begins with a **general statement** about killing being wrong, and concludes with a statement about a **specific example** of killing being wrong. Often when people make moral claims, they imply in those claims general moral principles. For example, if someone made the statement, "I believe abortion is wrong because it involves killing an innocent human being," they are implying that "it is wrong to kill an innocent human being." This is their **general moral principle**. Their *fact or non-moral premise* is "abortion involves killing an innocent human being." Their *specific moral judgment*, or **conclusion** is, then, "abortion is wrong."

It is helpful, in argumentation, to be able to dissect and separate the moral argument into (at least) these three distinct elements of it. In this way, the arguers can determine what general principles they are dealing with, and they can debate, initially, the merits of, and points of agreement concerning those general principles. Also, by introducing other issues that, if accepted, would seem to contradict those general moral principles, the arguers can determine whether or not the individual who makes a specific moral claim is consistent in opposing all (or other) specific examples that would violate their own implied general principle(s).

CRITICAL THINKING: FALLACIOUS REASONING

(Latin *fallere* — to deceive)

Sometimes arguments seem persuasive, even though the grounds provide little or no evidence for the conclusion. For example, weak arguments can so rely on common human emotions, expectations, and even prejudices, that they seem to be stronger than they are. A kind of deception occurs. There are frequent patterns of such mistakes that have been identified as common informal fallacies.

While a complete study of logic is far beyond the scope of this book, it is still helpful to examine some of the common informal fallacies that may mislead us in moral reasoning. To know what these **fallacies** look like helps us to be more *alert* to their use. There are more than one hundred different kinds of fallacies, but we will look at some of those that occur most frequently.

In the ethics environment it is important to recognize that while there is a logic to moral reasoning, there are also ethical standards to logic. We study the fallacies in order both to avoid committing them ourselves, and to be forewarned against them when others use them. Be aware of the temptation to use some of these deceptive fallacies intentionally to mislead people. Knowledge is power, power to be used responsibly.

Fallacious reasoning is an attempt to persuade emotionally or psychologically, not rationally and logically, and involves statements that in one way or another deceive or mislead. Informal fallacies are called such because of the *wording* of the argument, *not* the "form" or structure in which the arguments are constructed.

Detection of fallacies is done through analysis of the content of the argument. The fallacies are mistakes that arise in ordinary conversation, rendering the arguments unsound or uncogent.

1. AMBIGUITY — An argument is ambiguous if it shifts the meaning of a term or phrase in the middle of the argument. It occurs when we use a word or phrase in such a way that its meaning is not clear or can be taken in more than one way. Two ways in which an argument can be claimed to be ambiguous:

   a) equivocation — A play on words by the arguer when the conclusion of the argument depends on one or more words being used, either explicitly or implicitly, in two different senses in the argument.

   Example:

   ✳ I have a right to say what is necessary.
   What I am expressing I believe is right.
   Therefore, it is necessary that I express what I believe.

   The problem here is in the use of the word "right" because (1) in the first premise, it indicates a freedom, whereas in (2) the second premise, the word "right" is used to assert correctness. These uses of the term are not from the same context, and therefore the grounds do not connect together.

   b) amphiboly — The arguer misinterprets a statement that is ambiguous owing to some structural defect and *proceeds to draw a conclusion based on this faulty interpretation*. A grammarian might look upon this as a "dangling participle."

Example:

* The guide said standing in Tampa Bay, the Vinoy Hotel could be easily recognized.

* We can *only* conclude that the Vinoy Hotel must be in Tampa Bay.

Who's in Tampa Bay? The guide or the hotel? **The amphiboly occurred when the arguer drew a conclusion based on the vague and faultily constructed sentence.**

2. GENETIC FALLACY — This is an attempt to discredit a position by condemning its source or beginning, or to establish a position by condemning the source of an opposed viewpoint. Two types of genetic fallacy are common:

   a) *ad hominem* abusive (to the man) — This is an attempt to disparage the character of the person presenting the argument, to deny that person's intelligence, or to question his or her integrity, while not addressing the statements or arguments being presented. Sometimes this is known as character assassination.

   Example:

   * The Executive Board is making bad policy for the United Way.

   * But I suppose it should be expected because they're all radical, rabble-rousing dissidents.

   b) *ad hominem* circumstantial — This begins the same way as "abusive," but instead of using verbal abuse in attacking the opponent, the person attempts to discredit the arguer's statements by alluding to certain circumstances that affect the opponent. This forces the arguer into a mode that sides with the opponent's point of view. This charges that the arguer is so prejudiced that he or she cannot be objective in his or her views; i.e., you are wrong because of your circumstances.

   Example:

   * Those who supported the war wanted freedom.

   * Baloney, they owned weapons companies making sales to the government.

3. FAULTY CAUSATION — This occurs whenever the connection between the premises and the conclusion depends on some imagined causal connection that more than likely does not exist. Sometimes in a causation argument, the

cause can be valid, so examination of the facts is very important before "faulty" can be claimed. Three types of faulty causation are:

a) Post Hoc — (after the thing) — This states that because one event followed a previous event, the one following was a result caused by the first event and, therefore, similar events are likely to occur in the future.

Example:

❋ Allen had a beer and then got 100% on an Ethics exam.

❋ Therefore, Allen got 100% *because* he had a beer. While the premise here may be true, it did not necessarily cause the conclusion.

b) Slippery Slope — This occurs when the conclusion of an argument depends upon the claim that a certain event will set off a chain reaction, leading in the end to some undesirable consequence — yet there is not sufficient logical reason why the chain reaction should take place.

Example:

❋ Now it's mercy killing. Tomorrow it will be AIDS victims, then the infirm and elderly, then the mentally ill, and before you know it, anyone whose care costs "too much."

c) Statistical Correlation — This occurs when stating that because two phenomena are related by numbers, they must be related by *cause*. We can use statistics to help support an argument, but statistics only help; they do not of themselves prove anything.

Example:

❋ In 1985 the speed limit on the Penn turnpike was 55 m.p.h. And there were 25 fatalities. In 1986, the speed limit was raised to 65 m.p.h. And there were 50 fatalities. It is clear speed kills: increase the speed limit by 10 m.p.h., the U.S. fatality rate will double.

4. FALSE APPEAL TO AUTHORITY — This occurs when the stated authority is not qualified or where there is reason to believe the authority is wrong, biased, or lying. These arguers are resting their entire claim to the argument on the "reputation" of this person or group of persons. One must be careful here, because there can be times when the "authority" or "group" may in fact be an acknowledged expert in the field or subject matter in which the argument is being presented. An example of a reasonable appeal to authority is the Surgeon General's report on cigarette smoking as being a hazard to one's health.

Example:

❋ Michael Jackson drinks Pepsi. It must be better than Coca-Cola.

5. ARGUMENT TO THE PEOPLE (*arguments ad populum*). This also is known as the "appeal to emotion." This fallacy is used to replace reason and rationality as the norm and is calculated to excite through enthusiasm, excitement, love or hate. Very often the advertising media use it to entice, employing such terminology as " the best," "the most nutritious," *et cetera*. Instead of arguing the facts of an issue, a writer might play upon the readers' negative response to such words as "communism" and "fascism" or their positive response to words and concepts like "God," "country," and "liberty." The arguer avoids any discussion of the merits or weaknesses of the bill and merely substitutes an emotional appeal.

Example:

❋ If you are a true American, if you care about democracy, if you want a healthy economy and if you want to be able to protect your family, everybody you know should work for the Red-White-and-Blue Party's candidates.

6. INVINCIBLE IGNORANCE — Despite facts to the contrary, the arguer insists on propounding the proposition or argument as legitimate.

Example:

❋ I really don't care where you got your map because to travel to Chicago from Atlanta you must drive through Dallas.

7. IGNORANCE — The arguer insists that a statement is true until proved false or false until proved true. It presumes that what is unknown now would support its claim if revealed. This fallacy happens mostly in the developing sciences, psychic phenomena, and often in matters of religion.

Example:

❋ Scientists have been trying to prove for years that planet Earth was visited by alien beings eons ago. No proof exists. We can conclude that no alien being from outer space has ever visited planet Earth.

8. INCONSISTENCY — This amounts to believing two or more logically incompatible things at the same time. A contradiction occurs without presenting justification. It is perhaps the most important fallacy! Consistency requires that we work out a harmony between our *ethical* beliefs and the way we live.

Inconsistency occurs when we contradict ourselves in word or action *without the justification for the change.*

Note this fallacy is very common in parenting and politics and is often identified with the statement, "Do as I say, not as I do."

Example:

❉ On the first day a group is told, "I'll support stronger emission standards." Here the politician is talking to environmentalists. The next day he exclaims, "I'll do whatever I can to lower emission standards, if elected." On this day he is talking to industrialists.

9. STRAW MAN — This occurs when the arguer distorts the opponent's argument so that it might be more easily attacked, destroys the weakened argument, and then concludes that he or she (as the arguer) has won the argument. The term is derived from "setting up" an opponent as a straw man, or scarecrow, and then knocking him down.

Example:

❉ The newspaper editorial claims Libertarian government would lead to anarchy, elaborately demonstrates the dangers of anarchists to homes and families and businesses, then asserts that the two-party system *alone* is best for the nation, and therefore claims no Libertarian will ever be elected.

10. RED HERRING — This argument introduces an irrelevant point to divert the reader's attention from the main issue. This term originates from the tactic used by escaped prisoners of dragging a strong-smelling fish across their trail to confuse tracking dogs by making them follow the wrong scent.

Example:

❉ I appreciate your concerns about where I get the money for my gambling hobby, but have you noticed how worn-out your shoes look? You must have used those for a long time. There's a sale down at Shoeless! Let's go get you a pair.

11. EITHER/OR — The argument tries to suggest that there are only two sides to an issue — one right, one wrong. In most circumstances there are more than two possible choices, as we noted also earlier in this chapter. (See the section entitled "Ethical Critical Thinking.")

Example:

❉ "If you don't enlist for the war against Iceland, you don't love your country."

12. HASTY CONCLUSION (sometimes called Hasty Generalization) — This is caused by too much reliance upon inductive reasoning. Usually a hasty conclusion is reached with respect to an entire group of things or individuals based on premises from a small or an atypical sampling or isolated case. Polls sometimes can be included in this fallacy. Stereotypes are typical of this fallacy. It is when one goes from a specific case to a general rule as a result of the specific.

Example:

* This morning's newspaper had three stories about high school students from three sections of town who were involved in drug dealing. Therefore, America's high school students are obviously nothing but druggies and pushers.

13. TWO WRONGS MAKE A RIGHT

When someone tries to justify a wrong deed merely on the basis that another wrong deed had been done earlier, the "two wrongs make a right" fallacy has occurred. Just because other people break principles of ethics or etiquette is no reason for you to break those principles, too. Let the other person's wrong stand; you do not have to add your own. Besides, one more wrong does not make anything more right.

Example:

* George, did you see what that taxi did to me on that last intersection? I am going to cut him off on the next one! That'll teach him!

14. PROVINCIALISM

Whenever moral attention or change is resisted merely on the basis of established views of our own group, the fallacy of provincialism has occurred.

Example:

* The good men of Boston never wear sandals. It is beneath their dignity. They'll never accept shoeless job applicants as employees in their banks.

15. IS/OUGHT CONFUSION

If something is the case, reality or state of affairs, it should continue to be that way. "We've never done it that way before" is the theme song of the is/ought reasoner.

Example:

❋ The policy of this company has always been that you don't get a raise until you have been here one year. It applied to me, and it ought to apply to you and anybody else they hire, no matter how much technology training they have.

16. QUESTIONABLE CLAIM

This is a statement that is so broad it cannot withstand scrutiny.

Example:

❋ Cigarette ads are only pictures and words; they never hurt anybody!

USING REJOINDERS

A thoughtful discussion involving fallacies doesn't necessarily end with one party's claim that another party's statement was fallacious. There is the **rejoinder**, the thoughtful response, that may take several tacks: attempt to shed new light on the grounds of the statement, or to x-ray a weakness in the argument, or to call for rational and unemotional restatements, or to invoke another fallacy to rebut an argument. These are merely a few of the kinds of argumentation a person can develop. Below are two such responses based on one or more of the examples of fallacies listed above. Try to match the "thoughtful response" with the appropriate fallacy example.

Thoughtful Response:

The beer may have relaxed him after a tense schedule, but Allen got 100% on his Ethics exam only because he read his assignments and studied carefully. **Which Fallacy example does this counter?**

Thoughtful Response:

I appreciate your concern for those three high school students that were mentioned in the newspaper. But there is no reason to think that those three represent the more than 4,000 high school students in this town. **Which Fallacy example does this counter?**

PERSPECTIVE ON THE THINKING PROCESS

Thus far on our journey, we have learned about critical thinking, have discovered how to draft syllogistic arguments, and how to recognize and avoid fallacies. We're now prepared to argue and justify decisions, but there is more.

Next, we will see that our arguments need to include ethical rationale, which is the correlation of an argument with the tests of consistency, reasons, accountability, law, rules and the benefits of moral choices.

With these and an understanding of the approaches to moral reasoning found in Chapters 4 and 5, we will have a full toolbox to reason critically on moral issues.

CRITICAL THINKING: DEVELOPING RATIONALE

Justifying our decisions involves making and presenting strong arguments. This requires the development of **rationale**, which involves the correlation of statements, facts, data and arguments with certain standards in the ethics environment. A good rationale would correlate with the following six major standards:

1. CONSISTENCY

Consistency is a general standard for both ethics and logic: that means **applying the same values to ourselves as we seek in others.** This is why inconsistency is an important informal fallacy, as we saw above. We cannot arbitrarily change values when we shift between talking about others and ourselves.

Endnote 5

Endnote 6

Confucius said it well: "The faults I find in others I correct in myself." King David of Israel demonstrated this wisdom when Nathan confronted him. David recognized that the principle by which he convicted the rich man in Nathan's story applied to himself as well, and he had the courage and integrity to follow its implications.

A clever example of this standard of consistency is used in some business partnership agreements. When one partner wants to buy out the other partner, the first partner names the price for the second partner's shares. The second partner then has the option of turning down that purchase price and buying out the first partner instead for the same price per share. The incentive is on the first partner to name a fair, or even generous price, because the alternative — too low a valuation — could result in the second partner exercising the buy-out option on him. The simple standard of consistency is so profound. Can you give other examples of this power of consistency?

Consistency can never be our highest standard of critical thinking. The famous American philosopher Ralph Waldo Emerson wisely warned against elevating consistency as an ultimate virtue. "Foolish consistency is the hobgoblin of small minds," he said. First, foolish consistency would inhibit us from making reasonable exceptions to general rules and policies, even if these exceptions would be completely fair. Should you always tell the truth, even to the hateful henchmen of a racist government? Must you come to a full stop at every stop sign, even if you are rushing a dying person to the hospital?

Second, foolish consistency would limit our growth, improvement, maturing process — as individuals and as a society. The ability to learn from experience, and the skills of improving our relationships, behavior, character, and society — these are even more precious than consistency. With mere consistency we could all behave like children, slavery would be permitted, and racial and sexual discrimination could never be overcome.

2. Reasons: The Power of "Why?"

World-renowned psychologist Viktor Frankl used to ask patients preparing to leave the psychiatric hospital two questions. "Will you take your own life?" Invariably the answer was "No." "Why not?" he would immediately ask. If patients hesitated or could not come up with a convincing reason, he concluded that *they were not yet ready for normal human freedom*. We all need reasons to live, in order to keep on living. So Frankl believes.

We also need reasons to do what is right. The multiple checks and balances of accountability force each of us to come up with reasons for doing the right thing. And if we do not have good reasons for our decisions, they are probably not ethical. **The stronger our reasons for doing what is right, the more likely we will do it even when it seems that no one else is watching.** It has been well said that the true character of people is revealed by what they are willing to do in the dark when there are no human observers. [See the story of Gyges' Ring in Plato's *Republic, Book II*. A ring that would make us invisible would be almost too powerful for humans to handle, because the temptations for crime and evil would be so great. In *The Hobbit* and other novels, J.R.R. Tolkien (1892–1973) developed the same idea. Nevertheless, we can achieve mature character where our internal motivations are strong enough to resist temptation, without external pressure of other people and without the threat of being caught.]

Endnote 7

3. Accountability

Historically, accountability for our decisions in the ethics environment has embraced a whole range of different types of reasons — character, goals, results, traditions, duties, human rights, promises, commandments, and so forth. In modern times there has been a major split between two camps of intellectuals with mutually incompatible definitions of accountability — those who focus primarily on *rules* and principles, and those who give primary consideration to *results* and consequences. We will look at a variety of kinds of accountability as we examine classic and contemporary standards for moral reasoning in Chapters 4 and 5.

While a person can choose one approach to moral reasoning and accountability, one can also allow for a full range of explanations for our choices and behavior. In any case, people's moral reasoning still needs to be based upon **true awareness, actual fairness, authentic caring, and honest accountability.** A model for such human breadth is Dr. Martin Luther King, Jr. He had a clear sense of moral *rules* defined by what he understood as the biblical standards of fairness. To him, responsibility to God's laws and a commitment to his vision of justice established a duty no one should compromise.

At the same time, *results* were essential for Dr. King. It is important to contribute to real progress toward a more loving and fair community, and that progress is assured if our own behavior is guided by love — even love for those who hate us. Dr. King believed that Aristotle was right to say that our goals should define our means, and then those means are measured by the end result. Loving behavior will help produce a loving society.

Both duties and outcomes do matter, of course. Sometimes it makes sense to concentrate more on one than the other, but it is always a mistake to ignore either one.

4. LEGAL CONCERNS

"There ought to be a law!" people have often said, and then sometimes someone has gone on to write a law on the subject. The motivation is similar to ethics; laws have been written in an effort to solve human problems. And, like moral decisions, laws sometimes have the unfortunate effect of increasing or complicating human problems. Kings, queens, presidents, judges, and legislators have often been greedy, prejudiced, misinformed, and foolish, and so the laws they create and enforce can actually do more harm than good. In any case, like moral decisions, laws and those who write and enforce them can be evaluated in terms of how aware, fair, caring, and accountable they are. This is appropriate because these laws affect our problems, our lives, our hopes, and our futures.

Ethics includes the ways we use laws, too. For example, legal regulations can be used to deceive and exploit others, and they can be used to help give people respect, protection, and liberty. Whenever we try to solve one of our human problems, existing laws can function as part of the problem, or part of the solution, or both. In the civil rights cause, for example, the segregation laws were part of the problem, while civil rights laws helped to address the problem. How would people have behaved without the segregation laws in the first place? That is hard to say, but the segregation laws did add muscle to the terrors of racism.

When people think about the purposes of governments and their laws, they usually appeal to ethical intentions or goals — for the benefit of the rulers, citizens, or both. Plato (c. 427–347 B.C.), for example, claimed that all laws of society are rough approximations of an eternal standard of justice, although some laws are far closer to that standard than others. Paul (c. 5–67 A.D.) stated that government is established by God in order to approve what is good and to punish those who do evil. Thomas Jefferson (1743–1826 A.D.), the main author of the Declaration of Independence, asserted that governments derive "their just powers from the consent of the governed" for the purpose of producing "safety and happiness" for the citizens. Similar perspectives have been held by other people as well. Seeking justice, approving the good, punishing evil, creating safety and happiness — these are all explicitly ethical goals that help to solve human problems. In contrast, when personal power is the goal, governments and laws will take on selfish and egocentric methods and ambitions. In such cases human problems are multiplied and our fellow citizens are not served.

Nevertheless, **a legal responsibility is not the same as a moral responsibility.** Once a law is adopted by a government, that law has some authority over us, but the power behind the idea is no longer merely its moral quality. From then on, the substantial power of government and its enforcement tools are there to "persuade" people to behave according to the law. As a result, even when a person thinks that the law is bad, he or she still has some reason to live up to it.

People's obedience to the law — or their appearance of obeying the law — often follows without people even thinking about its *moral value*. Their main motivation is to avoid confrontations with any of the various courts or law enforcement agencies. Who wants the expense, hassle, and bad publicity this might involve? Is this why much of what corporate America does in the name of ethics seems so illusory? In many cases, the ethics department of a corporation employs a battery of lawyers merely to help it avoid or solve legal problems. The broader ethical issues are often completely missed or ignored, because in most cases the corporations and their lawyers are not even considering or asking those questions. What difference do they make?

Let us draw some lines. **Can a law be immoral?** Isn't that our primary motivation for reforming laws? **Can a law's enforcement be immoral?** Yes, that is why we have limited terms of office, political campaigns, investigative reporting, police review boards, and special prosecutors. Informed people assume that the laws they have and the people who enforce them will often fail to solve the problems they were supposed to solve — whether from weakness, ignorance, exploitation, or some other source.

Can a moral responsibility be illegal? Sometimes. Some of our greatest heroes engaged in "civil disobedience." The founders of the United States believed, on the basis of certain moral concerns, that they had a responsibility to rebel against the authority of England. This violated the English law that they were under — to say the least. In 1955, Ms. Rosa Parks believed she had a moral responsibility to defy the Montgomery laws that would take away her seat on the bus just because a white man wanted to sit on the same row of seats. She had already engaged in some serious critical thinking about discrimination in bus seating, and she broke the law for the sake of her own dignity, the self-respect of her children, and the dignity of many other people as well. The rest is history. Many expressions of civil disobedience have been less successful than the protest of Ms. Parks and the American War of Independence.

Can laws be amoral? Yes, in a way of speaking. In fact, laws can be neither especially good or bad solutions to human problems. There

We are drowning in data, smothered in information, yet famished for knowledge and dying for wisdom.

is no profound ethical reason why "stop" signs have to be red. They could just as well be green or pink — although red seems to catch our attention more than these colors. Would not "hot pink" stop signs catch our attention a little more, though? Also, there is often no major moral significance to the specific content of zoning laws. Nevertheless, zoning decisions can still be fair or unfair, and without zoning laws society itself would be much less fair, caring, and accountable. In any case, it is necessary to solve problems, like traffic safety and community planning, in ways that are at least not unfair or uncaring, and in ways that are consistent and accountable.

Can laws be a poor replacement for ethics? Yes, and far more often than we usually realize. Too often both corporations and private citizens are more concerned for what they can get away with — without peer rejection or punishment of the authorities — rather than for what is moral. And even when there is an appearance of legality, the moral problems the laws were written to solve do not really get solved. For example, there are many ways people discriminate on the basis of race. Legislators, law enforcement and the courts may not be capable of keeping up or finding sufficient evidence for all of them. In general, it often seems as if the introduction of laws to help solve human problems does not even increase our opportunities, nor decrease our responsibilities, for solving them. Or as Vietnam War-era comedian Pat Paulsen, erstwhile candidate for president, declared, "Solutions are the problem!"

5. THE ROLE OF RULES

Not only do laws not replace the opportunities and responsibilities of ethics, but much of ethics has very little to do with rules at all. We discovered this in our discussion of exemplars earlier in the chapter. Perhaps when we were children our most memorable encounters with ethics were the rules of our parents, teachers, or religion. However, as we grow up we find many other sources for wisdom and guidance — common sense, independent thinking, the examples of people we know, the stories we read and hear, as well as team or group decision-making.

History is rich with criticism of rule-based ethics — especially in the Taoist and Christian traditions. Taoists considered the rules taught by Confucianists and other moralists to be positively harmful to personal and public morality. The specific contents of the rules were not the problem; they thought the net effect of any moral rules to be negative. Similarly, Jesus criticized the religious leaders of his time for the way their rigid rules had blinded them and their followers. These moralists were well-practiced in applying the rules, but blind to the value of people and to people's needs.

What are the hazards of rule-based ethics? First, rules can merely cover up rather than solve our human problems. For example, you should not have to tell people how to respect their own parents. If they have so denied their natural impulses that they have no idea how they should honor their parents, the mere appearance of honor taught by the rules would be a farce. If we are really so lost, so morally degenerate, the Band-Aids of formal rules will neither cover nor heal our "values pathology." What is needed is the restoration of the person.

Second, moral discipline often backfires. The very behavior that the rules are supposed to reduce may become even more likely because of the rules. Do you remember when you were a child and your mother asked you not to eat the cookies? For a moment, think very seriously about this rule: "DO NOT THINK ABOUT MONKEYS." Chances are that you are now thinking of monkeys because the rule said not to. It's a joke. Without the rule you probably would not have thought about monkeys all day. The T-shirt saying "DON'T THINK ABOUT GOD" causes people to think about God. One of the best ways to get people to read a book is to censor it, because forbidden fruit tastes the sweetest. Speaking against a movie can quadruple the ticket sales. Detailed statements forbidding immoral business behavior can serve as an idea bank for the less creative, greedy mind.

Third, lists of detailed rules can be used to condemn the behavior of others, a problem that is related to the one above. With any substantial list, careful examination of another person's behavior will always uncover some flaw, some breaking of the code. No one can follow a detailed code with perfect consistency, especially in the ambiguous world in which we live. Disciplined rules are too often used as ammunition for attacking, condemning, ostracizing, rejecting, or firing people whom we do not like. What may be only a cultural difference, or a matter of choice, is then tragically used to abuse other people and to divide the human race. Even if this were not the original intent of the moral rules, it can be their net effect.

So rules can sometimes be harmful: (1) They can cover up problems rather than solve them. (2) They can backfire, since telling us not to do something often increases our interest in doing it. And (3) they can be used to hurt others rather than improve our selves and society. Rules can be useful, but as with anything powerful they have to be used with caution.

The T-shirt saying "DON'T THINK ABOUT GOD" causes people to think about God. One of the best ways to get people to read a book is to censor it, because forbidden fruit tastes the sweetest.

6. BENEFITS OF MORAL CHOICES

Ethics, critical thinking about human problems, provides numerous benefits to each of us — and to society. Frankly, these advantages are more numerous and intricate than we can explain here. But let us stretch our imaginations anyway.

First, **"not to decide is to decide."** When faced with human problems we can put off decisions, but that itself is a decision. We can also react badly, without using the critical thinking skills of perception, information, stories, and reasoning. But then we still are responsible — we will still live, or die, with the implications and consequences of those decisions. Why not use the abilities we have to make our decisions well?

© 1989 Creators Syndicate, Inc.   3-24

Second, **our decisions help make us who we become.** Even the simple decisions that each one of us makes help form our character and reputation. Is anything more important than character in our lives, families, and careers?

Third, **our commitments within communities make a difference.** What would the world be like without ethics? Ancient Chinese thinker Hsuntzu (298?–238? B.C.) pointed out that the necessity for ethics is obvious to the most elementary human intelligence. Here is his simple argument: We humans need to have guidelines that will help us work together. On the one hand, for us to work together successfully, our community's guidelines must be recognized as fair — at least to some measure of fairness. On the other hand, if we do not work together, our lives are destined for poverty and failure. We will be poor because as individuals we can do so little on our own.

> A single individual needs the support of the accomplishments of hundreds of workmen. Yet an able man cannot be skilled in more than one line, and one cannot hold two offices simultaneously. If people live all alone and do not serve one another, there will be poverty.

Also, we will even fail to harness natural resources for good:

> Man's strength is not equal to that of an ox; his running is not equal to that of a horse; and yet ox and horse are used by him. How is this? I say that it is because men are able to form social organizations whereas others are unable . . . When united, men have greater strength; having greater strength, they become more powerful; being more powerful, they can overcome other creatures.

That is, without some minimal level of fairness in society, all of us, and the human race in general, are in jeopardy. Our projects and our lives will fail. Moral community is our chief source of strength in a hazardous world. To Hsuntzu, this should be obvious to any human of minimal intelligence. Do even some of the worst communities and governments have at least some fairness? Is there honor among thieves?

Finally, there are levels of personal spiritual development that are possible only as we use some of the disciplines of ethics, critical thinking about human problems. The process of becoming a whole person seems to require cultivating certain personal skills. We will understand more about that in Chapters 4 and 5 of this book. Can you think of any other benefits to ethical thought?

FINAL COMMENTS

In this chapter we have uncovered the essential steps of ethical thinking — critical thinking about human problems — and we have compared ethics with some other types of thought. In today's problems and choices, and in today's decisions, can you recognize **the four steps and the four values of the ethics construct?**

We also have discovered how to draft **syllogistic arguments,** and how to recognize and **avoid fallacies.** We're now prepared to **argue and justify decisions.** We also saw that our arguments need to include powerful **rationale, which meet the tests of consistency, reasons, accountability, law, rules and the benefits of moral choices.** Next, in Chapters 4 and 5, we'll learn how to include various **approaches to moral reasoning** as part of excellent thinking.

FOR FURTHER INQUIRY

Please examine the story below. As you consider each part of this case study, try walking through the four steps of critical-ethical thought. Do all four steps for practice, and see what difference it makes.

PAPER JUSTICE

Click.

The nearly silent turnstile of the college library registered one more body. Kyle, a little bemused, glanced back at the "No Exit" sign now immediately behind him. The exit was a few feet away, next to the book check-out counter. It's good to know where the exit is, he thought with a chuckle.

Well, in Kyle's experience of two semesters, the library was not one of the more familiar parts of the college. He had been here a few times before, but only for a quiet place to study, or rest. This time he had to find a book, or even a few books. Kyle's research paper for ethics class was due the next Friday. It was certainly time to get started.

"Hey, hunk, you're right on time," Tricia whispered. She was in the same class. Tricia had agreed to help him use the computerized book search. "These computers will find what you're looking for in a minute. So, what topic did you choose for your paper?"

Kyle stroked his chin. "That's my first problem. You know I can do pretty well memorizing class notes for the tests, but this research stuff is something else. It's so new. My high school didn't prepare me for this at all. Would you believe, I've never written a research paper in my life."

"Oh, it's not so hard, Kyle," Tricia teased as she nudged her hand against his biceps. "I've written dozens of them."

"SSHHH!" Kyle warned firmly, and then started whispering again. "This is the library, Trish. I only told you one of my problems. Even if I knew how to do it, I really don't have any time. Chemistry reports, a project for management class, a big test in accounting — and I have to wait on tables at the restaurant every night. It's too much."

For several seconds they both silently stared at the blank computer screen in front of them.

"I have an idea," Tricia broke the silence with a very low voice, causing Kyle to lean a little closer to hear her better. "I have found so much material for my research I could easily write two papers. Really. Writing is such a breeze anyway. Then, when the restaurant closes Thursday night you can come over, look at what I've written for you, we could make some changes on my computer, and — *voila!* — your paper will be done. It's no problem." She grabbed his arm in a reassuring gesture.

QUESTIONS FOR THOUGHT AND DISCUSSION

1. Is there a problem here?

2. Does Kyle know what he is doing? Does Tricia know what she is doing? Is either one really alert to the real and potential problems involved?

3. Could Kyle have avoided his present crisis? Explain.

ENDNOTES

1. See Paul de Vries, "The Original Sin," *Christianity Today*, May 15, 1987.

2. See Thomas S. Kuhn, *The Structure of Scientific Revolutions*.

3. Thomas Peters and Robert Waterman, *In Search of Excellence* (New York: Harper and Row, 1982) p. 75.

4. Peters and Waterman, p. 278.

5. Confucius, *Analects*.

6. II Samuel 11 and 12, *The Holy Bible*.

7. See the story of Gyges' Ring in Plato's *Republic*, Book II. A ring that would make us invisible would be almost too powerful for humans to handle, because the temptations for crime and evil would be so great. In *The Hobbit* and other novels, J.R.R. Tolkien (1892–1973) developed the same idea. Nevertheless, we can achieve mature character where our internal motivations are strong enough to resist temptation, without external pressure of other people and without the threat of being caught.

CHAPTER 4

CLASSICAL APPROACHES TO MORAL REASONING

"Without civic morality communities perish; without personal morality their survival has no value."

— ***Bertrand Russell***

"Reason is a light that God hath kindled in the soul."

— ***Aristotle***

In Chapter 1 we examined some of the dimensions of the ethics environment in which all of us live, study, work, and play. We have seen how ethics is part of the very "fabric" of our reasoning, communication, creative work, critical thinking and problem-solving. Although the issues concerning how we learn ethical values are perhaps as complex as human life itself, the presence of ethical choices is a simple fact of our daily lives. In Chapter 2 we examined the results of some revealing contemporary research concerning every human's personal development with respect to the various useful moral skills or capacities. These moral skills included the abilities of ethical awareness, deftness for justice-thinking, competence at personal care for others and oneself, and capacities for responsibility and accountability. As we saw, people develop in these various abilities at different rates, so that each person's capacities in these different dimensions are a very individual matter. In Chapter 3 we examined critical thinking and moral reasoning. We uncovered some basic patterns of good logic as well as fallacious reasoning as they applied to ethics.

Now we will examine eight **approaches to moral reasoning** that have been designed and defended by individuals and groups, typically, over extended periods of time. Individuals identifying with one of these approaches to moral reasoning, in fact, may have achieved different levels of moral development in the distinct ethical dimensions of awareness, justice, care, and accountability. Nevertheless, diverse individuals have rallied around one or another of these

---

Paul De Vries, M.A. and Ph.D. University of Virginia, is the president of NYES Fund Inc., an educational program, and a partner in Leadership Excellence Inc. He also is president of the International Research Institute on Values Changes, based in New York and Moscow.

eight common conceptions of the essential nature of moral reasoning and ethical decision-making.

Each one of these eight different approaches is often called an **ethical theory**. Each approach involves a cluster of ethical concepts, in a coherent framework of meaning that is useful and applicable for understanding and resolving wide ranges of ethical issues. (For purposes of this study, the terms theory and approach will be used interchangeably.) The function of theories is quite congruent with the original meanings of the word "theory." The common English word "theory" comes from the ancient Greek word "theoria" which has the primary meaning of "a looking at, viewing, beholding, observing." For our purposes, then, a **theory is a systematic way of looking at or approaching a set of issues, facts, questions, or phenomena.** In particular, an ethical theory is a systematic way of looking at or approaching moral reasoning, issues, facts, questions, or phenomena.

Endnote 1

This use of an ethical theory is quite similar to how we use other kinds of theory. For example, the theories of the natural sciences and social sciences are known especially for their distinctive clusters of concepts in coherent frameworks of meaning. In a given theory, the concepts are defined and understood in relationship to one another, and the framework of the theory provides a context for describing and understanding a whole range of phenomena. For example, in geology almost all phenomena may be understood by using the concepts and framework of the theory of continental drift. Also, nearly the full range of phenomena in physics can be analyzed under the concepts of relativity and quantum theory.

CHIEF LEARNING OUTCOME

I am familiar with the five classical approaches to moral reasoning and I am developing my own particular worldview as a result.

Like these scientific theories, the central concepts and principles of an ethical theory provide unifying themes that are helpful for understanding a wide range of concerns. In addition, these theories or approaches enable clear communication and agreement among the people who share them. Let us illustrate: On the one hand, two "egoists" will generally understand each other rather quickly — as will two "natural rights" advocates — even if they disagree on particular points. On the other hand, an egoist and a natural rights advocate are likely to speak rather different languages — choose different words, and have different meanings for the same terms. As a result, they commonly will not communicate, but instead "talk past each other," unless they have also studied each other's "language" and values. In this illustration, egoists will talk primarily in terms of what each of them wants and has a right to claim, while the natural rights advocates will seek mainly to protect the basic rights of all the people affected in a particular decision or situation.

We could easily cite up to 50 examples of approaches to moral reasoning. We have chosen to focus on eight different approaches including egoism, divine command, virtue ethics, consequentialism, deontologism, natural law, contractarianism, and natural rights. We present them because they are an aggregation reflecting students' common views, as well as the dominant classical and contemporary approaches to moral reasoning. This chapter is a survey of the first five of these approaches.

In the next chapter we will look at three contemporary approaches and how to compose your own ethical theory. This study of ethical theories is somewhat oversimplified. Much more detail is available on each approach from many sources. Sorting them out and applying them in the issues we face can be a lifelong enterprise.

But first let's understand how these eight approaches or ethical theories will often function like scientific theories in other ways as well. For example, the mere acceptance of the general structure helps people to agree on answers to certain common questions. For more creative and adventuresome people, the accepted moral framework of these ethical theories can also be used as an avenue to reach their purposes of broadened and heightened ethical awareness.

As a contemporary model of this creative use of an ethical theory, Dr. Martin Luther King, Jr. often focused on the basic statement of rights found in the birth certificate of the United States, the Declaration of Independence — the statement that "we are endowed by our Creator with certain unalienable rights,

KEY CONCEPTS

The *Egoism* Approach emphasizes the aim of always acting for perceived self-interest, usually in the long term, even at the expense of the well-being of others.

The *Divine Command* Approach emphasizes that conduct is based on what is understood to be the will of God.

The *Virtue-Ethics* Approach emphasizes the aim of excellence by doing the right thing as a result of focusing on certain character values.

The *Natural Law* Approach emphasizes conduct based upon the perceived order inherent in the universe.

The *Deontology* Approach emphasizes basing conduct on a self-determined, innate sense of moral duty, with no regard for consequences.

that among these are life, liberty, and the pursuit of happiness." He then led many people consistently to apply these values into a broader environment, to a more complete set of circumstances than they had been applied before. Thomas Jefferson, for example, had used John Locke's popular moral theories as the scaffolding to reach an ethical perspective for American independence. As with these examples in moral theory, scientific theories are often also used as the bricks and mortar for constructing a person's expanded awareness within the spheres of the related sciences and technologies. This is one of the primary functions of theory in both ethics and science.

One other point of comparison with science is especially worthy of note here: Scientific theories often open up new ways of seeing familiar phenomena, in two senses of the word "seeing." On the one hand, a scientific revolution will lead people to think about a certain range of phenomena differently, and thus their mental "seeing" or thoughtful perception changes. On the other hand, people may perceptually experience some phenomenon in more complex and sophisticated ways. For example, after Hawksbee's revolutionary discovery of "electrostatic repulsion," those informed by his discovery began thinking about ("seeing") various electrical phenomena quite differently. Additionally, what people had formerly generally ignored — odd movements of dust particles or hair sticking up inexplicably — then became the expected events that were noticed, named and recognized in the context of Hawksbee's theory of electrostatic repulsion.

In a similar way, ethical theories can also help shape people's thinking, as well as their sensory perceptions. For example, for one who comes to believe in natural human rights, that person's thinking concerning the value of human beings will be affected. Also, attitudes about human practices such as slavery and racial discrimination will be challenged. In addition, people who believe in natural human rights may well literally see and hear others differently, perhaps as genuine brothers and sisters, and also as beings of tremendous value. Alternatively, one who devotes himself to egoism may interpret all of life as an intensely competitive milieu, with other people concretely perceived as personal threats and as objects to be exploited. It seems, therefore, that an ethical theory can help bring attention to — or twist or "color" — some events and some people's behaviors that are otherwise understood differently or ignored.

While theories can aid or enhance our perceptions, they can also create blinders, for better or for worse. In physics, for example, we learn that the mass of the weight at the end of a pendulum is irrelevant to the velocity with which the pendulum swings. Consequently, informed people learn to make helpful comparisons of pendulums without having to give attention to the mass of the weights. The perception of the mass of the weights is filtered out because it is irrelevant information. A similar phenomenon often occurs under the influence of one or another of the ethical theories, as we will see. An egoist, for example, will interpret any rhetoric about human rights as attempts to establish power positions, and will tend to ignore any appeals to objective bases for universal human rights. Similarly, a devoted deontologist will tell you to consider only the general ethical principles, while ignoring the results or consequences of people's behavior — come what may. In the meantime, a committed consequentialist will tell you that people's intentions and principles can be safely ignored if the results or consequences of the decisions can be thereby enhanced. Therefore, says the consequentialist, "only look at the results." There are those who would say a consequentialist preoccupation with the financial bottom line sometimes has harmed the long-term best interests of American companies. However, blind com-

"If we are facing the right direction, all we have to do is keep on walking."
— ancient Buddhist expression

mitment to principles without practical management can be disastrous, too. As Charlie Brown of the *Peanuts* world discovers over and over again, mere sincerity is not enough.

It is important to notice that some of the educated expectations of the roles of scientific theories do not apply to ethical theories. For example, in the sciences we reserve serious commentary about theories to those people who have been seasoned by years, if not decades, of professional labors in the particular scientific field. A seasoned chemist's opinion about geology's theory of continental drift would not be given much serious consideration. In contrast, ethical theories are investigated, defended, evaluated, attacked, and modified by people with a wide range of professional experience and training — or no particular training at all. Even people who have never read or heard of the classic articulations of any particular theory often have well-crafted views that are remarkably similar to one or another of the five classic ethical theories we will examine here. Without having taken a single ethics course, students and others have often already seriously thought about some of the major issues and defenses of an ethical theory that they may have unconsciously adopted.

THE 'SPAR' DIMENSIONS

In our examination of these approaches, we will discover that every ethical theory has at least four dimensions — most of which are accessible to every reflective adult. We will call these the **"SPAR dimensions"** — the Substance, Principles, Actions and Results of each theory. These will provide one simple basis for comparisons between and among ethical theories. As we examine each approach, these SPAR questions will unlock major points of understanding about that theory:

* **Substance:** What is the basic meaning of human existence? What is the primary concept of human nature?

* **Principles:** What are the essential guidelines for human life? What principles should people recognize for every situation?

* **Actions:** What behavior is worthy of praise and encouragement? What actions are exemplary of the way things should go?

* **Results:** What goals or purposes should people work toward? What results or consequences please us or are signs of moral success?

Almost every reflective adult has already had to apply some world-view or perspective on wide ranges of ethical questions day after day, month after month. And their perspectives shape people's answers to these four basic sets of questions. The most significant point of comparison is that each of these kinds of theories — scientific, sociological, philosophical, theological, or ethical — provides a perspective on the world. In short, each theory helps a person define a worldview, at least with respect to an important dimension of our world, such as ethics or morals.

As we carefully examine each of the eight approaches to moral reasoning, we will consider the personal background of the main proponents of each particular approach, its history, its focus, the SPAR dimensions, individual and group examples of the use of the approach, and a summary of its strengths and weaknesses. These elements will help us unpack the key issues, understand the perspectives, and give us a standard of comparison for the eight classic approaches we are studying.

Perhaps everyone can understand egoism, the view that praises self-centered actions as the ultimate model of moral behavior. Of course, we all know what self-centered actions are. Most people learn how to take care of themselves and look after their own needs as an integral part of normal human development. This is why every one of the eight theories of moral reasoning probably includes a place for actions that benefit oneself.

CHIEF LEARNING OUTCOME

The Egoism Approach emphasizes the aim of always acting for perceived self-interest, usually in the long term, even at the expense of the well-being of others.

It is good to take care of oneself, so what makes egoism different? Egoism treats self-centered behavior as the ideal for all circumstances and in all relationships. In the process, of course, egoism does not condemn all acts of "generosity" or "care" for others; it merely rejects those that have no net payoff for the self that would ultimately justify the acts of seeming generosity or care in some self-centered terms. Nor does egoism condemn all acts of "honesty" and "integrity" that may seem costly to the individual at first; it simply rejects what might be seen as "honesty" and "integrity" when there is no long-term benefit to the self. Ethical acts to the egoist are those acts which are in their best, long-term personal interest without regard to the well-being of others.

1. PERSONAL BACKGROUND

One of the most influential and articulate modern defenders of egoism is **Friedrich Nietzsche** (1844–1900), a German philologist, philosopher, and poet. As the foundation of his perspective, Nietzsche insisted that the most ultimate characteristic of a human being is the lust for power. The more consistently and effectively an individual pursued this lust for power, the more exemplary this person would be. An egoistic person could even be active in caring for others — as a teacher, rabbi, or public servant — and use those positions of respect to amass power, satisfying the inherent lust for power, and thus fulfilling Nietzsche's ideal. Usually, power is especially secure and effective if it is accumulated under some guise — such as education, religion, or the public good. As a result, Nietzsche's egoistic ideal is someone who can exploit these and other seemingly altruistic roles for personal advantage. Wolves in sheep's clothing can be especially successful.

Nietzsche believed that most people lacked either the intelligence or the inner strength (the guts) to pursue their own lust for power effectively and consistently. These "weaklings" (whom Nietzsche would call the sincere representatives of other moral theories) then create moral concepts that they use to disguise their botched condition — words like community, peace, forgiveness, love, patience. These are moral words that Nietzsche considered quite unnatural and harmful — unless they were deceitfully used to help protect and enhance one's self-centered, egoistic behavior. Note that for Nietzsche, such deceit and exploitation are necessary parts of what he considered the morally good life. Nietzsche believed that he was merely describing, with brutal honesty, how most people actually think and behave.

Those who sincerely defended a morality of community, forgiveness, patience, and compassion, Nietzsche considered "sub-human" and "slaves." In contrast, those who applied intelligence and strength to pursue their lust for power he called "supermen" and "masters." The fact that most people might be "slaves" was not a problem to him. In a manner of speaking, "masters" love "slaves," just as wolves love sheep. Within 30 years after Nietzsche's death, Adolph Hitler was writing *Mein Kampf* and found a ready audience in Germany willing to seek a "superior race" at the expense of humanity.

Endnote 1

Curiously, the egoist philosopher Nietzsche was reared in a home in which his father and both of his grandfathers were Christian ministers, although his father died when Friedrich Nietzsche was only five years old. One of the greatest influences on his life was Charles Darwin's *Origin of Species*, which Nietzsche read as soon as it was translated into German, and while he was still a teenager. Nietzsche took Darwin's biological theory and transformed it into something different — a theory of ethics. A speculative theory of human origins was then transformed into a perspective on how we should live. Darwin's explanations of natural selection became for Nietzsche the justification of self-centered, egoist behavior — the "survival of the fittest."

As a consequence of his extreme egoism, Nietzsche considered the ethical values that had become dominant in the Europe of his day to be especially degraded and sub-human. He especially deplored those values that can jeopardize the highly competitive survival of the fittest, as he understood it. In others words, he saw values such as love, forgiveness, patience, and community as weak and corrosive of egoism. Consequently, he came to believe that the most degraded nationality was the Jewish people, for they were the first to believe and to teach that God loves and forgives. Consistent with this stance, he saw the life of Jesus of Nazareth as despisable. While Nietzsche respected the Nazarene's remarkable intelligence and character strength, he thought Jesus was weak to let his love for others lead to his death, when He could have done much more for himself!

When's the last time you enjoyed an Epicurean delight?

There were other articulate defenders of this approach to moral reasoning in both ancient and modern times. **Epicurus** (341 B.C.–270 B.C.) was an influential egoist of the ancient Greek world; he campaigned for each person's pursuit of his or her own individual pleasure and happiness as the ultimate standard of moral behavior. In his understanding, people are primarily creatures of pleasure and pain.

Figure 1. Banquet scene. Stele di C. Giulio Materno. Museo Archeologico Nazionale, Naples, Italy. Alinari/Art Resource, NY.

Consequently, one's actions should be determined and evaluated by the total pleasure or pain they will produce just for oneself. The pleasures and pains of others are of no real concern for such an egoist except as they might impact one's own pleasures and pains. Moreover, in Epicurus' understanding, the pursuit of pleasure will be the most successful for a person when it is done prudently, and in moderation — in spite of the fact that Epicurus' name is now often associated with sumptuous living and eating.

He considered water to be better than wine for reducing thirst and for benefiting long-term health — even if what we would now call an "Epicurean" meal would now certainly include wine. For him, friendships are fine in moderation, too, as long as there are no attachment and no ongoing obligation to the friend. Consequently, marriage is not advised, and having children is much more to be avoided, because it is quite risky. As everyone knows, a spouse or a child can actually lead to some inconveniences, as they say, or even cause some pain or disappointment in the future! Finally, Epicureans do not think that they should worry about what the gods think of our human behavior, or how they might judge us. According to them, the gods are so busy pursuing and attending to their own fine pleasures that they have no time or interest in either observing or judging how humans behave. Later followers of Epicurus held to his pursuit of pleasure, but with less prudence and moderation.

Thrasymachus (thra-sim'-e-cuss) was another ancient defender of egoism, arguing that no one should pursue anything but what is in that person's own interest. So, whoever rules that society determines the standard of "justice" in that particular society. Thus, "Might makes right" becomes the law because the rulers define what justice means in the way that they write and administer the laws. He recognized no standard by which a government could be judged, other than by its mastery at benefiting its own interests. Consequently, for Thrasymachus individuals are "just" only if they successfully pursue their own interests, including avoiding punishment or censure by whoever are the rulers at the time. All other moral talk he considered to be mere pretense.

2. HISTORIC BACKGROUND

Whatever else one may say about egoists, they describe fairly vividly — as well as factually and accurately — much of the behavior of many people. In almost any period of time, and in almost any place, large numbers of people have been and are self-centered egoists in their behavior. Some people talk blatantly about looking out for "number one." There is no chance that they are talking about looking out for you, or even their spouse, or their children, or God as they may understand him or her to be.

Long before Darwin and his concept of competitive survival, people acted in self-centered ways that placed their own personal desires and benefits well above any other ethical value. As an overt perspective, egoism has thrived, especially during periods of time when there has been social unrest. When trust in community values wanes, egoism becomes more overt. In ancient Greece, for example, when the city-states were deteriorating, the Sophists openly taught the attitudes and skills of egoistic, self-centered advancement. Every world religion has treated some version of egoism as a serious alternative to its own perspective, from the earliest roots of religious thought and writings.

3. HOW DOES THIS WORLDVIEW AFFECT PERCEPTION?

STOP

a. **Focus:** Egoists give great attention to their individual rights, especially their rights to act in their own behalf and to do what they want. They also focus on each individual person's role as a decision-maker determining his or her own fate. They are quick to remind others of the diversity of tastes, and that each person sees the world from a unique perspective.

b. **Blind spots:** Egoists tend to deny, to ignore or to give little attention to any role of a "higher power." Egoists tend to ignore or deny the role of objective values for life. They also try to ignore or minimize the threat of objective consequences to behaviors that violate those values. For example, some egoists might ignore the impact of certain sexual practices on their partners.

4. SPAR DIMENSIONS

a. **Substance** — Egoists see the active individual person as the center of power, the master of his or her own fate. Egoists may even be altruistic if it is in their own long-term, best interests. However, ideal egoists include those who could exploit others in the pursuit of their own long-term goals and interests.

b. **Principles** — Egoists live by the principle that they should follow their own desires and best, long-term, personal interests in their own way. Values and decisions should be selected on a self-centered basis, without obligations to other people or to any "higher power."

c. **Actions** — Egoists prize actions that are self-centered, shaped for benefit to oneself, or at least shaped for the avoidance of personal harm or rejection, especially if this self-interest is pursued subtly, so that the individual self-interest is hidden from most people.

d. **Results** — Egoists seek to get their own way, for their own benefit, both in terms of short-term and long-term results and consequences.

5. INDIVIDUAL EXAMPLES

The examples of individual egoists are quite numerous. Perhaps, some aspect of most people's behavior is egoistic, in a sense. However, it is the lives of truly devoted egoists that are the most instructive for understanding this perspective, the egoist approach to moral reasoning.

Thomas Hobbes (1588–1679) seems to have believed that following moral prescriptions (be kind to others, be honest, *et cetera)* is the best way of attaining what each of us most wants — peaceful coexistence in an otherwise hostile social environment. Adam Smith (1723–1790) laid the basis for free enterprise economics by insisting that if people are allowed to use their money in whatever ways their economic self-interest dictates, the common good automatically will be enhanced, as if by the workings of some "invisible hand."

Nietzsche sought to live according to his own quite public teaching, attempting to fulfill his own lust for power without the conscience or the constraints associated with the categories of "good and evil." He achieved fame, influence, and popularity among intellectuals, but no deep friendships, no marriage, no family, and no place of worship. He was often sick, and for the last ten years of his life he was catatonic, a condition likely caused by syphilis. So it seems that following his self-centered desires was detrimental to Nietzsche's own health and life. There is an "egoistic paradox": sometimes the harder people pursue selfishness, the more they undermine their own happiness and status.

6. GROUP EXAMPLES

Self-centered behavior can also be seen as a social phenomenon, a group mentality. Of course, egoism is essentially individualistic, yet nations, businesses, gangs, organizations, and other clusters of individuals can act by egoistic standards, too. Aggressive nations and colonial powers are often egoistic in this sense. A type of self-centeredness can also be found in various kinds of racism, male chauvinism, and radical feminism. Similarly, dictatorial regimes and tyrannies actually embody egoistic values within the sphere of government. It is no coincidence that **Adolph Hitler's** favorite philosopher was Nietzsche. In short, people can be self-centered in ways that link them with whole groups of people.

7. STRENGTHS

Egoism is a popular approach to moral reasoning, in part, because there is much that can be said for it. First, egoism often produces accurate descriptions of the way people actually comport themselves. It does not "sugar-coat" typical human behavior, but "tells it like it is." Second, egoism often accurately describes the way many non-egoistic actions can be perceived. Even when people examine another person's caring and altruistic behavior, they frequently look for — or even invent — self-centered motives to explain what happens. We accept this approach because we at least "half-believe" that some subtle selfishness is really at the root of others' generous and loving actions.

Third, egoism can engender a refreshing honesty about motives. This ethical theory is willing to consider selfish purposes, without even pretending to have altruistic motivations. Fourth, there are obvious personal attractions — not to mention the elegant consistency — to being motivated by self-centered appeals for being self-centered! Everyone understands self-centered reasoning, and so everyone can identify with egoism. For these reasons it is common as a private standard of decision-making and occasionally useful for national public policy development.

8. WEAKNESSES

Nevertheless, there are serious dangers in the egoistic lifestyle. Not all other people are stupid, and once people figure out that a person's only motivations are self-centered, they are far less apt to be cooperative and trusting with that person. There may be a fresh honesty in egoism, but if one is too honest about his or her own egoism, there are serious negative consequences. The wolf has to stay in sheep's clothing, and not show off his or her sleek fur or sharp fangs. There is much in life that a self-centered person may give up — consciously or unconsciously: deep friendship, generosity, loyalty, integrity, trust, community.

In addition, self-centered behavior is at the root of wars, aggression, racial exploitation, and abuse in personal and business relationships. It neglects common respect for other people, professional standards, and other community values.

9. COUNTER ARGUMENTS

Egoists have developed their own defenses against these criticisms. First, they claim that they are essentially describing how everyone acts, if you peel away the mere pretenses of higher morality. Second, they say that their own self-centeredness is moderated by their long-term goals, so that there is a place for a little bit of respect for others, because it usually benefits "number one" more. Third, as long as there are punishments for the abuse of others, self-centered people will restrain themselves anyway. Fourth, they will try to remind us that egoism alone embodies the "survival of the fittest" values that, according to devoted egoists, made human life possible. Consistently, they argue that only egoism can sustain the continued human evolutionary process to "higher" forms of more intensely self-centered human life and resulting explorations of others. Therefore, they argue, we should affirm egoism although some of the immediate consequences are painful or unpleasant.

10. SUMMARY

Egoism is understandable, simple, and relatively easy to follow. It helps explain much of what we see and experience in individual and group behavior. However, its perspective may cut off much that is valuable in human life. Learning about egoism helps us to be more aware of the limitations of self-centered frameworks, which may inhibit moral growth and development of individuals and society.

The second perspective on moral reasoning that we are investigating defines what is morally right in terms of God's commands; i.e. God's expressed will in a matter. This is a broad view that can include anyone's religion, for example, as the basis for understanding the will of God. Specifically, this **divine-command theory** says that what is forbidden, or permitted, or required are just those things that are forbidden, or permitted, or required by God, according to their understanding. Also, nothing is forbidden unless God forbids it; nothing is permitted unless God permits it, and nothing is required unless God requires it. **God's will** becomes the total orientation of ethics for those subscribing to this ethical approach to moral reasoning.

Perhaps everyone who believes in a supernatural being also believes that some aspects of morality are determined by

The Divine-Command Approach emphasizes that conduct is based on what is understood to be the will of God.

their God. To believe that there is either a Superior Being or a Supreme Being is already to acknowledge that such a Being has some authority over human behavior. Others, however, who also believe in a God allow that some moral principles may come from other sources, too, such as customs, the needs of society, and individual human choices, for example. For these persons, whom we could call theists, as opposed to atheists, not all moral principles are divine commands, and you do not need a divine command to have a moral principle.

Also, it may be that not all divine commands are moral principles — for some commands from God may be practical principles or spiritual principles that do not satisfy the criteria for ethics that we described in Chapter 1. For the divine-command theory, however, there is an exact, one-to-one correspondence between divine commands and *justifiable* moral principles. **Whatever God does not prohibit is morally permitted, whatever God forbids is morally excluded, and whatever God commands is morally required.** It logically follows under this approach that if there were no God, there would be no divine commands, and so there would be no morality. That is, if there were no God, and if the divine-command theory were correct, then everything would be permitted, and nothing would be forbidden or required, as Dostoyevsky once claimed.

In the divine-command view, the character of ethics will resemble the character of God and His will. Alternatively, people may be drawn to affirming a God whose commands resemble their preferred principles for ethics. On the one hand, if God were to give *detailed* rules about every possible situation — so that there are thousands and thousands of divine commands — then ethics itself would be too rigid to practice. People who want such a rigid and elaborate ethic will therefore be drawn to religious groups that teach that there are thousands of rules coming from God, as, in fact, some religions do teach.

On the other hand, if God's commands are fairly *general* — such as "Do not murder" or "Love your neighbor as yourself" — then considerable amount of interpretation would still be left to the individ-

ual to seek the will of God. But how are we mortals to know the will of the Divine? The search for God's will can include human reason. It can rely on conscience. It can make use of prayer — of any word or thought addressed to God or gods for such purposes as petition, adoration, confession or thanksgiving. To pursue the will of God, the **monotheistic religions** — Judaism, Christianity, Islam and their variants — all turn to certain "sacred scriptures" for their journeys. God also could disclose His will through aspects of nature in addition to giving explicit verbal commands. The most widely published book in history is the Holy Bible, containing as it does the primary scriptures both for Judaism and for Christianity, itself an offshoot of Judaism. Its adherents claim it as a guide for faith and practice. Its detractors discredit its religious authority but some accord it literary value. The U.S. Supreme Court (1962) opined that study of it as literature was appropriate for public education, although a federal judge in Florida recently has ruled that only the Old Testament is suitable for public education. As H.L. Mencken, American critic and atheist, wrote:

> "It is full of lush and lovely poetry. The Bible is unquestionably the most beautiful book in the world. Allow everything you please for the barbaric history in the Old Testament and the silly Little Bethel theology in the New, and there remains a series of poems so overwhelmingly voluptuous and disarming that no other literature, old or new, can offer a match for it — No other religion is so beautiful in its very substance — none other can show anything to match the great strophes of flaming poetry which enter into every Christian gesture of ceremon(y) and give an august inner dignity to Christian sacred music. Nor does any other, not even the parent Judaism, rest upon so noble a mythology. The story of Jesus — is, indeed, the most lovely story that the human fancy has ever devised — Moreover, it has the power, like all truly great myths, of throwing off lesser ones, apparently in an endless stream." — H.L. Mencken, "The Poetry of Christianity," *The World's Best* (New York, The Dial Press, 1950), pp. 148–150,

Other considerations drawn from other theories may be necessary to increase the practical content of a god's commands. In this case, followers of the divine-command approach would be seeking contributions and insights also drawn from other approaches. For example, a person may believe that the best way to apply the Golden Rule — 'Do unto others as you would have them do unto you" — would be to develop a virtuous moral character, as an essential resource for discerning what is best for oneself and others.

In the next chapter we will look more carefully at other ways people have combined the insights of two or more of the classical or contemporary ethical theories. Eventually we will be challenged to see what approach or combination of approaches makes the most sense to us in meeting the issues of daily life. Perhaps each one within the whole range of ethical theories has something to contribute to our reasoning and conduct.

Similarly, another person might combine divine-command theory with consequentialism, under the belief that a god wants people to focus their attention upon producing good consequences for their behavior. In this case, the Golden Rule would require the moral person to help produce the greatest amount of happiness for the greatest number of people.

1. PERSONAL BACKGROUND

In almost every culture, the Ten Commandments would be recognized as examples of divine commands. They stand as a unique, historical monument of profound, elementary, moral guidance. There have been attempts to correlate the content of the Ten Commandments with that of other ancient codes — such as the Code of Hammurabi from about 1800 B.C., which has about 300 legal provisions.

The name we most associate with the Ten Commandments is Moses (about 1350–1230 B.C.) who led the nation of Israel out of slavery. According to the biblical account, the key events in Moses' personal life are defined by explicit divine commands. Moses, with the promised divine help, was successful at fulfilling such divine commands. A mere 50 days after escaping Egypt, the whole nation of Israel was standing near where Moses had heard the voice of his God, and they were preparing to meet that God themselves. Then something surprising happened. Moses' God indeed spoke to the whole nation of Israel, giving

Figure 2. Moses and God in the burning bush. Palazzo Vaticano, Rome. Copyright © 1991, Archivi Alinari. All rights reserved. Art Resource, NY.

the historic Ten Commandments, but the people did not listen. Rather, they immediately asked Moses to ask his God to shut up, and instead for Moses himself to find out what God wanted, and for him to communicate it back to them. The point was that the people were afraid to listen to this God's voice themselves.

Moses pled with them, stating that if they heard the commands directly from God they would be more motivated to obey them, but he was unpersuasive. As a result, Moses lived by his God's commands, but the people lived indirectly by God's commands as they were passed on through Moses. The Israeli people at that time chose to codify, interpret, and develop traditions around the commands, rather than deal directly with the divine source of the commands. Nevertheless, Moses did not give up, for in the last sentence of his final speech before the people, Moses urged them to "obey God's voice," and not merely to consider God's commands. Followers of Moses expanded on the Ten Commandments and developed the religion of Judaism based on their understanding of God's will.

There are many other examples of people who have lived by some version of the divine-command approach. Deists who rejected much of the teaching of the Bible nonetheless held a positive place for the moral teaching of the Bible — such as the Ten Commandments and Jesus' Golden Rule and love commandments — because they considered the core point of religion to be morality. Thomas Jefferson (1743–1826 A.D.), who was often called a deist, rejected the supernatural elements of the Bible and wrote his own, the *Jefferson Bible*. However, he considered the divine moral teachings of Jesus to be the best moral standard.

2. HISTORIC BACKGROUND

Those who follow the divine-command theory claim that their approach has "timeless" characteristics. For some, a defining characteristic of being human is our interest in the subject of beings superior to ourselves. In studies of pre-historic times, it seems that for as long as there has been evidence of humans making tools, there is also evidence of icons or symbols through which these pre-historic humans sought communication with deity.

A common tenet of Western Civilization is that a person has the **moral autonomy** to choose good or evil. In divine-command theory, that autonomy is used to pursue the Divine Will. The divine-command approach is also central to the *Koran of Islam* and to the Hindu scriptures such as the *Upanishads* and the *Bhagavad Gita*. In contrast, the core writings of Confucianism, Taoism, and Buddhism generally have little place for the commands of a deity.

Confucian ethics are based primarily on a negative version of the Golden Rule, sometimes called the **Silver Rule: Do not do for others what you would not want them to do for you.** The meaning of this venerable rule was developed by Confucius (551–479 B.C.) and his followers through their collecting and cataloging of hundreds of rules of propriety, or *li,* most of which predated them. These rules of ethics and etiquette helped embody the basic element of the Silver Rule: *shu* or mutual human respect and reciprocity. Confucius also advised his students not to concern themselves with prayer, an afterlife, or gods, because one's only responsibility is right human relations based on shu.

Similarly, **Buddhism** and **Taoism** have little or no place for divine commands. While versions of both Buddhism and Taoism have a place for nonhuman spirits, these are not supreme beings like Islam's "Allah," Hinduism's "Brahman," or the Judeo-Christian "Lord God." At its core, Buddhism advises human restrictions on our desires in order to achieve nirvana, a condition of spiritual peace undisturbed by passion or desire. The Buddha is not treated as God, but instead as a highly advanced human whose exemplary enlightenment and spirituality should provide both a personal model and effective encouragement to the rest of us. In Taoism it is the "natural" — never the supernatural — that is the guide. Simplicity and spontaneity are prized, and people are advised merely to be themselves and follow those instincts they may have that are uncontaminated by either moralism or other-worldly intrusion. The natural spirits can be honored, but they provide no divine commandments.

In contrast, **Islam** gives its major focus to Allah's commands; the very name "Islam" is Arabic for submission, as in submission to Allah, and "Moslem" is Arabic for one who submits. Muhammad (570–632 A.D.), the founder of Islam, preached that there was only one God, Allah, and that he, Muhammad, was Allah's messenger. Muhammad claimed that he spoke the words of Allah himself, and these teachings and commandments from Allah were recorded in the Muslim holy book, the Koran. The Koran outlines the basic perspective and duties that Allah requires of humans in submission to him. Commandments of Allah include explicit prohibitions against lying, stealing, adultery, and murder, while Allah requires honor to parents, patience, kindness, industry, courage, and generosity. Punishment is based on the concept of retaliation, as in "an eye for an eye and a tooth for a tooth" (as also advocated by Moses). The entire life of a Muslim, including the chief duties of prayer, almsgiving, fasting, and a pilgrimage to Mecca, is understood primarily in the context of Allah's commands.

In the Middle East many followers of Islam and of Judaism have rigid and detailed concepts of divine commands that vary broadly from one another. As a consequence, conflicts between those peoples are deep and not easily resolved, especially when both understand revenge ("eye for an eye") as a fundamental divine command. Frequently, critics of divine-command theory note that heinous wars and crimes have been committed in the name of religion. They often

Figure 3. Muslim pilgrims bow outside the Grand Mosque of Mecca. AP/Wide World Photos.

overlook that the cessation of those same wars was obtained by those who also thought they were obeying the will of God. Recently, there have been signs of hope, as Protestants and Catholics have begun to make peace in Northern Ireland. Moreover, some observers hold that the shared belief in divine commands was probably the catalyst for peace in South Africa.

In **Hinduism** the central focus is Brahman, the supreme spiritual essence, the power sustaining the whole cosmos. Those people in the highest Hindu caste, the priestly caste, have a special relationship to this supreme cosmic power. Consequently, the powerful priestly caste is also called Brahman, in a derivative sense. They are supposed to most closely represent and serve Brahman. It is the cosmic Brahman that represents itself in the multiple gods that are worshiped by different Hindus. These Hindu gods include especially Brahma, the creator god; Vishnu, the teaching and revealing god who occasionally takes on human form as Krishna; Siva, the brutal god of both sex and death; and Kali, the beautiful and fierce goddess of both sex and death. The most common image of Brahman is the *lingam*, a carved phallic symbol representing Siva's power. There is no Hindu temple without at least one such symbol; some temples have dozens for people to worship and touch.

For the most part the numerous duties taught in the Hindu scriptures are not strictly ethical duties, but divine self-disciplines (yoga) of meditation, study, and devotion. However, there is one area of the divine disciplines that does relate directly to moral reasoning: karma-yoga, the yoga of complete devotion to duty with no thought of consequences or results to oneself or others. The actual duties one must follow to fulfill karma-yoga are largely defined by one's circumstances, and these divine duties are especially defined by the caste in which one is born. However, the Hindu scriptures, especially the Bhagavad Gita, make clear that these apparently circumstantial duties are not a matter of choice or mere social expectation. They are the divine requirements for one's life. In the particular story of the Bhagavad Gita, Vishnu in the form of Krishna tells a warrior, Arjuna, that he must fight in an impending battle, for the simple reason that he was born into the warrior caste. Then he is required of Vishnu (and thus Brahman) to try his very best to kill and maim the "enemy," even though hundreds will suffer terrible pain and death, and thousands will be widowed and orphaned, including many of Arjuna's own relatives on both sides of the battlefield.

The modern Hindu hero, **Mahatma Gandhi** (1869–1948 A.D.), the successful leader for Indian independence, took the Bhagavad Gita to be a parable. The understanding of duty that Vishnu taught Arjuna, Gandhi took to be a pristine model of the godly duty that Gandhi believed he himself had to pursue non-violently, but still like a soldier without consideration of cost or consequences to himself or to others. He was a devoted soldier for the deity.

"Science without religion is lame; religion without science is blind."
— *Albert Einstein*

Although the divine-command perspective is arguably timeless, it has received renewed attention at many specific periods of history in various cultures. It may be that most people take for granted that moral standards come from God. However, in times of historic stress and conflict the moral leaders most often give special attention to the divine origins of ethical values and moral reasoning. This was true in the modern case of Gandhi.

Consider also **Socrates** (470–399 B.C.) an articulate stone-mason in another time of social and political unrest, who insisted that there was no higher personal standard than obeying the one he called "the God." He taught that "the God" should be obeyed regardless of the consequences.

Socrates, on trial for heresy, included these remarks in his defense:

> "That is why I still go about seeking and searching in obedience to the divine command. . . . (p. 52, Plato, *The Last Days of Socrates*, translated and with an introduction by Hugh Tredennick, Penguin Books, London, 1969).

> "I felt compelled to put my religious duty first." (p. 50.)

> "This duty I have accepted, as I said, in obedience to God's commands, given in oracles, and dreams and in every other way that any other divine dispensation has ever impressed a duty upon man." (p. 66)

Consistent with that devotion, Socrates was martyred for his belief in "the God."

Further, in United States history, the first "great awakening" (1730s to 1750s), led by New England philosopher and preacher Jonathan Edwards (1703–1758), made very vivid the awareness of divine commands. He influenced some of the American constitutional writers who feared the damage of absolute power. He thus painted a divine-command backdrop for the writing of a profound set of checks and balances on government powers. Also, the "second great awakening" was shaped largely by the New York educator Charles Finney (1792–1875 A.D.) and England's William Wilberforce. It dramatically helped people recognize during the 1830s to 1850s how abominable the stench of slavery and other social and personal sins were in light of the commands of the God they understood. Others, however, used biblical accounts of slavery to rationalize their own use of slaves.

3. How Does This Worldview Affect Perception?

a. Focus: The followers of the divine-command theory are especially attentive to the spiritual aspects of human life, and to evidence of what they understand to be God's communication. They also recognize objective reference points for value in divine-commands, something less subjective than individual human desires of egoism.

b. Blind spots: With their focus on God's commands, some people may be blinded to the subtle role of personal bias and distorting prejudice in interpreting divine commands. In addition, the power structures of religious communities can demand an arbitrary conformity to their own purposes, which may not often reflect actual divine commands. Also, whose God is the "right" one? This lack of human certainty plagues the divine-command theory.

4. SPAR Dimensions

a. Substance — Whatever God does not prohibit is morally permitted, whatever God forbids is morally excluded, whatever God commands is morally required.

b. Principles — The basic principle for the divine-command approach is to obey the will of God as one understands it in personal and societal commands.

c. Actions — Divine-command theorists especially praise actions that directly obey and honor the deity.

d. Results — The explicit expected result of obedience, from the divine-command perspective, is a relationship with God, personal wholeness, and spiritual peace in harmony with God's will, personally and societally.

5. Individual Examples

There are numerous accounts of people who have devoted their lives to obeying the God, of their understanding. From Judaism, we obtain the especially vivid account of Abraham, who lived in a society where the highest expression of devotion was for a father to sacrifice his first-born child to his God. Although he considered his son Isaac to be a special gift from God, he believed that God asked him to sacrifice this only child of his marriage with Sarah. Therefore, he went through all the steps to be obedient to this voice, even to the point of tying up his son and raising his knife to kill him. At that very second he heard God's voice telling him now to stop, and to sacrifice an animal that God provided as a substitute. Instantly Abraham believed and obeyed these new instructions.

Inspired by this story, the young, devout, Danish, philosopher **Soren Kierkegaard** (1813–1855 A.D.) came to believe that it was God's will for him to give up what was most precious to himself, his engagement with Regina Olsen. In an attempt to cause Olsen the least disappointment, he feigned insanity, offended her father, and then left town. Shortly after, he re-read the Abraham story and realized that he had made a big mistake breaking his engagement. After all, God had never asked him to dump Olsen in the first place, and so God did not stop him at the last second from destroying the engagement either! As a result, Abraham had kept Isaac, but Kierkegaard had lost Olsen. As Kierkegaard saw it, his own mistake was a failure of his weak faith in God, because he had acted upon an egoistic desire to make a sacrifice for God, rather than paying obedient attention to what God actually wanted. Some of Kierkegaard's thoughts about this personal failure are artfully immortalized in his clever book *Fear and Trembling* (1843), under the pseudonym "Johannes de Silentio."

As a result Abraham had kept Isaac, but Kierkegaard had lost Olsen.

Fortunately, most individual examples of the divine-command approach are less tragic than Kierkegaard's. **Mother Theresa** is a 20th-century example of someone who was a personal failure until she responded to what she took to be a specific call from God for her to help the poorest of the poor in Calcutta, India. Some extraordinary examples include Sir John Templeton in investments, R.G. Letourneau in construction equipment, Ambassador Robert Strauss in statecraft, Elie Wiesel in human rights, Jack Eckerd in pharmacies, and J.C. Penney in merchandising.

6. GROUP EXAMPLES

The largest single example of a group that follows some version of the divine-command theory, by population measure, is the Judeo-Christian basis of Western Civilization. Hinduism, and Islam, as we have seen above, also are large group examples. In contrast, Confucianism, Buddhism and Taoism put no stock in the commands of God. Nevertheless, the concept and possible personhood of God remains a perennial topic of ethical reasoning and discussion, as in the rest of human life.

Some nations have obvious illustrations of divine-command in their culture. One of the most obvious examples is the United States with its motto: In God We Trust. Other countries such as Israel, Iran, and South Africa also have deeply divine-command cultures that predicate much of what is done in social relationships, government, business, and education upon God's will. In Indonesia and Pakistan, for example, the Islamic command not to charge interest on loans (*sharia*) is governmental law, although companies dealing in money still find ways to make profits!

7. STRENGTHS

Many people describe an awareness of a Supreme Being who issues commands, and there is an authentic, deep human desire both to know and to please the Supreme Being. This desire is acknowledged as a central human element in the divine-command approach to human reasoning. Most humans seek an inner peace or a spiritual serenity, and for them that goal is nurtured by coming to terms with the commands and will of God. Furthermore, knowledge of God's "calling" for one's life frequently is the basis for a genuine passion for one's work and service to others. This common understanding is reflected in our daily language, for "vocation" is based on the Latin *vocare*, to call — as in what God calls us to do.

8. WEAKNESSES

Discerning what God has actually commanded is frequently complex if not impossible. Some of the reported divine commands are ambiguous. In other cases people are at least sometimes self-deceived when they claim that they have heard God's voice. Moreover, deceitful religious leaders have often exploited people's sincere spiritual interest by falsely representing God's commands to them. Sometimes, too, excessive interest in searching for divine commands can lead people to neglect ordinary human needs and moral responsibilities, such as the care of one's family. A stop sign goes up when religious sects advocate the violation of basic societal laws protecting against murder, for example.

9. COUNTER ARGUMENTS

There are a number of factors that may cause God's commands to seem ambiguous, and these causes can be understood to include immaturity and personal rebellion against the concept of a single God's authority. Self-deception and the deception of others can also be reduced through wise counsel and a stable spiritual community. The very fact that divine commands can be distorted is evidence that they still are important and real. In addition, genuine divine commands from a *loving* God might lead one to be all the more intensely aware of genuine human needs and responsibilities.

10. SUMMARY

Human interest in the commands of a distant Supreme Being or a personal God can be genuine, deep and enduring. Moreover, some of the greatest human accomplishments have been achieved by people deeply transformed and moved by applying the divine-command approach to moral reasoning in their lives — Moses, Esther, Socrates, Mary, Jesus, Muhammad, Mother Theresa, Isaac Newton, George Washington, Lincoln, Mahatma Gandhi, Martin Luther King, Jr., and countless others. On the other hand, Roman Emperor Nero thought he was pleasing the gods when he sacked his own city and murdered thousands. The Ayatollah Khomeini sent nearly one-million Iranian Muslims to their deaths in a war with Iraq. Two factors seem to matter to mere mortals about their gods: the character of the god served and what is involved in mediating the commands of the god.

Figure 4. Mother Theresa. Hulton Getty.

In the **virtue-ethics approach** to moral reasoning, the primary focus is one's **character**, especially the personal disposi-

The Virtue-Ethics Approach emphasizes the aim of excellence by doing the right thing as a result of focusing on certain character values.

tion to act well in various circumstances. According to this theory, what really guides our behavior as humans is not ultimately self-centeredness or obedience to God — or explicit commitments to moral rules or results — but rather the deep patterns of each of our personalities and behaviors. **The primary concern of virtue ethics is being the right kind of people, so that we will do the right thing.** The central issue is: Do we have the personal propensity — the self-control, courage, wisdom, justice, faith, hope, or love to act with moral maturity in each situation? Regardless of whether character is a matter of genetics or upbringing — nature or nurture — the primary concern is the development of the moral virtues that are treasured for quality character and conduct.

As a result, the virtue-ethics approach considers rules and principles as never adequate to embody what is right and wrong. Nor are the goals or the results achieved the real issue. Ethical principles and moral goals are secondary. It also rejects egoism, because all the virtues we treasure include some sincere concern for others. Moreover, the virtue-ethics approach distances itself from the divine-command theory, because we should have good character and do what is good whether God commands it or not. Under this theory, we should be good and do the good even if God were to command otherwise.

The concept of "**virtue**" in both Latin and Greek culture was literally an "excellence" in being a model human being. It implies a kind of skill or capacity, as in someone who provides a "virtuoso" or skillful performance — as with a singer or violin player. In particular, a moral virtue includes the personal ability to discern a situation and understand what is the right behavior to follow. However, it is always much more than this ability of discernment — it is also the consistent, personal disposition to act well, to behave in an exemplary way, in every situation.

1. PERSONAL BACKGROUND

The Greek philosopher **Plato** may have been the first to develop a detailed, virtue-ethics theory. Plato, one of the best known of ancient Greek philosophers, had spent years as a student of Socrates — the articulate stone-mason who had felt the call of "the god" courageously to raise the difficult core issues about justice in Greek society, and in Athens in particular. In 399 B.C., when Plato saw the people of democratic Athens choose to execute Socrates for his outspoken commitment to truth and justice, and then witnessed Socrates' own extraordinary courage in the face of death, Plato's life was transformed.

Initially, he left Athens in a search for insight and perspective, traveling to various places, including Egypt, Italy, and Sicily. However, by 387 B.C. he had returned to Athens to establish a school he called the "Academy" — from which we get the word "academic" for educational work. There in Athens for the next 40 years he wrote and taught on a variety of subjects, including an emphasis on virtue-ethics. Although he was inspired primarily by Socrates, Plato lacked his teacher's vivid understanding of the God's personal calling on his own life. Instead, Plato focused on the moral character traits he saw so dramatically exemplified in his teacher. He became convinced these moral virtues were necessary for a life of fulfillment and excellence, and for exemplary leadership in society and government, at any time and place.

The four "classical" virtues that Plato promoted were self-control (or patience), courage, wisdom, and justice or rightness. Self-control has to do with controlling one's appetite, in the broad sense, so that one desires only good things and in the right proportions. Courage expresses one's awareness of what to fear and what not to fear. Wisdom is the rational capacity to govern one's own impulses and feelings. Finally, justice or rightness is the condition of having everything in its proper place in one's character and conduct — "to each its own" — including personally possessing all the three other classic virtues in proper measure. The basic logic for Plato is that to have good people you need the right kind of society to educate and empower them. Furthermore, Plato's logic required that to have the right society we need the right kind of people — especially philosophical leaders who, through their personal virtues, can achieve "healthy souls." Then, these same virtuous leaders will be inspiring teachers and examples to the rest of us. Also, these good leaders should be placed in positions of political power so that the good decisions they make will benefit the rest of society, too.

Unfortunately, Plato seemed often to be puzzled as to how to teach or inculcate the virtues, but his most famous student, *Aristotle* (384–322 B.C.) had a more comprehensive theory of moral virtues development. To him, studying examples of virtuous people helped — along with spending time with people who have exemplary virtues. It was especially important, according to Aristotle, for one to cultivate intentionally the very habits that model the desirable virtuous character and conduct. Aristotle believed that such well-practiced habits would gradually percolate deep into the personalities of those who attend to them, for the development of one's own moral virtues. As a result, when these ethical habits became second nature, the corresponding moral virtues would then be an established part of one's personal character. Someone has said, good character is the unconscious doing of right.

Aristotle thought that each human being has a goal or function, which he called *"eudaimonia"* — traditionally translated as "happiness" (which some modern philosophers now call "flourishing") — and when he elaborates finally on that, he sounds once again rather like the otherwordly disciple of Socrates. But unlike **Plato**, Aristotle does not ignore the purposes that pertain to our physical and cultural existence, and in Aristotle we find strong hints of an ethical view that speaks much more directly to the moral urgencies people typically experience than anything we find in Plato. For one thing, Aristotle (unlike Plato) acknowledges a variety of "goods." This is at least suggested by the opening sentence of the *Nicomachean Ethics* which states that "Every craft and every inquiry, and similarly every action and project, seems to aim at some good." And this brings out the intimate relation between being a "good" and being the object of desire. When we are fully engaged in any activity, we are directed toward a purpose that seems truly desirable, worth pursuing. So the particular "good" for, say, a student

Figure 5. Aristotle. Rome National Museum. Corbis-Bettmann.

might be the knowledge to be gained from doing careful homework (*et cetera*).

"Eudaimonia" is the term Aristotle uses to designate this supreme moral good, but the term alone (or any English equivalent) fails to give us much specific information. Aristotle himself thinks that identifying it further is a relatively simple matter once some general characteristics have been noticed (though ever since then, others have not been so sure of this). He considers it obvious, for example, that happiness is the final goal of a person's life — not something he aims for as a means to anything else. For this reason wealth cannot be that goal, because money is merely a means for conducting other pursuits. He also remarks that happiness is not any kind of momentary state, but can be ascribed only to the entire life of a person; and this means that happiness depends on a pattern of conduct, sustained over time by stable traits of a person's character. Those traits of character that support a happy life are the virtues, so that "happiness" — the good toward which humans naturally aim — is defined in terms of activity conducted in accordance with virtue.

But this does not of course go far in clarifying what Aristotle means by "eudaimonia"; it only transfers the nub of the question back upon the notion of "virtue" itself. And here again Aristotle is an ethical pluralist. There are many specific virtues, says Aristotle, and there is even more than one general kind of virtue. There are the intellectual virtues, and then there are the moral virtues proper. Unfortunately, the connection between them is none too clear. On the one hand, the **"moral virtues"** are those we would probably need in order to conduct well the normal affairs of daily life in the upper echelons of Athenian society — such as self-control, courage, gentleness, even wittiness — and these turn out to exclude a range of virtues that other societies have highly valued.

The **"intellectual virtues,"** on the other hand, are supposed to reflect what is unique and important about human nature across the board — namely, human rationality. And this makes Aristotle only a half-hearted pluralist. For here, in his sweeping vision of human nature, we find the key to "happiness" for Aristotle, and perhaps the most powerful indication of his deep debt to Plato. For despite Aristotle's departure from his teacher's asceticism, their intuitions about what finally makes human life most worthwhile do not greatly diverge. Aristotle notices that humans share much in common with the lower animals; what makes humans distinct is their **power of reason.** From this Aristotle concludes that their peculiar function is to exercise that power. Because Aristotle thinks of philosophical truth as fixed and immutable, happiness becomes characterized as a life of rational contemplation of eternal truths. That view represents one of the persistent pitfalls of moral evaluation — the danger of *generalizing inappropriately,* from our own situation into others that don't really match. Aristotle might have succumbed to this occupational hazard here, in a big way.

But at the same time, even if he had done so, does it really compromise the interest and originality of his work as a whole? Should we be too critical of Aristotle for failing to accommodate essentially different approaches to thinking? He simply may have been unaware of them. Certainly what we have in Aristotle is a model for aiming at self-realization, through the process of asking certain sorts of questions about virtue, with an eye toward discovering the sort of human being we should be if we, as rational beings, are to reach our full potential for living a satisfying life. And insofar as living a satisfying life is important to you, Aristotle might be worth keeping in mind.

A central feature of Aristotle's view is moderation, the **"Golden Mean,"** often illustrated in the life of a soldier who wants neither to be cowardly nor foolhardy in battle. In that setting, a virtuous soldier would be courageous. For Aristotle, in thinking, choosing and behaving, we can develop habits of choosing the right and the best in any situation. In so doing, we will find a happy medium between excessive conduct on the one hand and deficient conduct on the other.

Aristotle emphasized four classic virtues: courage, wisdom, self-control and justice. Affirming these, the Apostle Paul, writer of much of the New Testament, added three more: faith, hope, and love. As with the original classic virtues, these are seen as both the individual ability and the personal propensity to behave with ethical excellence in any time or place.

2. HISTORIC BACKGROUND

Much of the history of ethics is reactive, in some sense. In Plato's time, for example, many affirmed virtue-ethics as the best alternative to the rampant egoism pursued by people in both government and business, and in many people's personal affairs. In our own time, virtue-ethics has emerged as the strongest and best alternative to the substantial power of Nietzsche and other influential egoists. Like egoism, the virtue-ethics approach asks and expects people to express their own character. Unlike egoism, however, it insists that character itself needs to be shaped, developed, and educated — by nature and nurture — so that, when people do express their own character, they intentionally practice and seek what is truly excellent.

Virtue-ethics can also be understood as a kind of reaction against the divine-command approach. Even the divine-command theory has a place for certain virtues, especially the well-ingrained habits of personal responsiveness to a Divine Will. Nevertheless, some of the advocates of virtue-ethics doubt whether divine commands are sufficiently clear and complete enough to build an ethic. Perhaps God, too, some have speculated, would rather that humans not act like children, always needing direct parental advice, but become more mature adults, incorporating the divine moral concerns into their own personal character — as virtues.

In modern time the interest in virtue-ethics has grown for a variety of important reasons in addition to its role as an attractive alternative to both egoism and divine-command ethics. After an era of many failed attempts to change society through political means — whether in totalitarian countries with near complete one-party control, or in democratic countries with political reforms to solve moral issues — there is a growing interest in cultivating people's internal motivations instead of dictating or legislating "good behavior." Even after the passage of laws that prohibit racist conduct and other kinds of immoral behavior, people's real behavior seems to remain about the same. The mere existence of laws that prohibit some actions makes certain kinds of immoral behavior all the more attractive and enticing to some people, because "forbidden fruit always tastes better," as they say. According to virtue-ethics, what we may need instead is to nurture people into the right personal inclinations and motivations, i.e., the right virtues. This would be better than relying on a few people to police everyone else — whether they are democratic, totalitarian or philosophical "police."

3. HOW DOES THIS WORLDVIEW AFFECT PERCEPTION?

a. **Focus:** Virtues-ethics gives primary attention to a person's character — both in consciously seeking one's own character development, and noticing the personal character patterns of others. Of course, people's self-interests and their religious orientations play significant roles in character, as egoism and divine-command theories teach, respectively. But virtue-ethics advocates point out that often the way people approach both their self-interests and their religious commitments depends upon the established moral patterns of their personalities. Therefore, so the thinking goes, these character patterns are the real issue.

On the one hand, one's self-evaluation depends primarily on the patterns of character evident as one examines one's own behavior and observes the comments and behaviors of others. Enduring moral principles, other people's rights, valued goals, divine commands, self-interests, and other factors can all play their important roles. Nevertheless, the crucial question is how these factors are processed through the development and expression of personal character.

Similarly, when one wants to improve one's own personal moral character, any of these factors may be used, too. That is, more attention could be given to moral principles and their rationale, and more time could be spent with advocates of those principles. This could be a fruitful method to shape one's own virtues to give the ethical concerns of these moral principles more weight in one's own consciousness and conduct. Alternatively, in order to have the ethical virtues of one who is more responsive to divine commands, one might then seek the appropriate relationship or experience with God in order to nurture the kind of virtuous character one truly desires.

On the other hand, in evaluating others, virtue-ethics advocates look for and consider the patterns of behavior that may evidence the true character traits of the other person. This is not an easy task. For substantial periods, people can skillfully mimic the behavior patterns of someone with character traits that they themselves actually do not have. Personal hypocrisy and "wolves in sheep's clothing" are not rare moral phenomena, unfortunately; clear examples of such virtual virtues are well known to any mature adult.

It is often only in a critical or strategic situation when a person's true character is shown — such as when a person must choose between telling the truth, perhaps at some significant personal cost, or telling a lie instead, for their own substantial personal benefit. Almost everyone will keep their promises — or even keep secrets — most of the time. **The real question is whether a person will keep promises and protect secrets when there is great personal benefit to break trust or violate confidence.** Sometimes, therefore, it is not the general patterns, but such critical incidents that are the most informative about other people's "moral virtues" — or their lack of them. Does anyone not have a personal experience of a "friend," whom they deemed "trustworthy," but who dramatically violated that trust at a critical moment?

The virtue-ethics approach looks for the big picture when it comes to evaluating another person. Its view of character includes respect for others' rights, as well as their self-interest, goals, and principles. All the relevant personality factors that an accomplished biographer would attend to — other "internal" psychological factors and "external" relationships — are important to watch in the virtue-ethics approach.

b. **Blind spots**: The biggest challenge with this broader view is that it is difficult to know when one has enough of the pieces for the "whole" picture to exist. First, when are sufficient virtues in place for a person to be morally mature, to make good moral decisions? Second, at what point is moral personality so secure that the enforcement of moral rules and principles might become irrelevant? Third, when do we know enough about a person to discern his or her true character, so that we know exactly how much we can trust that person? As evidence of this difficulty, biographers of famous people often differ dramatically in the way they portray that person's moral character and virtues. For similar reasons, many voters completely give up trying to discern the moral character of political candidates.

Also, the virtue-ethics view tends to suffer from a blindness to change. Because of its trust in the role of deep patterns of character — the virtues — this perspective is completely shocked when a consistently moral person may suddenly become a bank-robber or a rapist. Were the virtues of that person's good character overridden by some mental disease or social pressure? Alternatively, were people completely wrong in their evaluations of that person's character, although those perceptions were based upon years of experience? Even seemingly well-established moral patterns can still be overridden, broken, twisted — or incorrectly perceived or evaluated in the first place.

Of course, there are good surprises, too. People who have earned a reputation for unethical character, humans deficient in the moral virtues, can sometimes experience a "sudden change of heart," a moral conversion. This may be rare, but it happens. People holding the virtue-ethics perspective would likely be blind to such a change, or be especially slow to recognize it, because according to the virtue-ethics theory the deep patterns of personality do not change quickly but are the result of acquired habits, repeated until they become second nature.

4. SPAR DIMENSIONS

a. **Substance** — Humans are creatures of habit, so that decisions and actions are expressions of deeply engrained patterns of one's personality.

b. **Principle** — The basic principle is that one ought to cultivate the personal habits and the personality patterns that nurture the right virtues, such as integrity, trustworthiness, self-control, courage, wisdom, justice, faith, hope, and love.

c. **Action** — Virtue-ethics theorists especially praise actions that clearly express the treasured virtues.

d. **Results** — According to virtue-ethics, the result of a virtuous life should be "health of the soul," as Plato explained, including personal wholeness, happiness and flourishing ("eudaimonia") because virtue is its own reward.

5. INDIVIDUAL EXAMPLES

Plato wisely selected his teacher, Socrates, as a prime example of a person of virtuous character. For Plato there were other examples, too, such as Solon, an influential lawmaker and poet in Athens who lived two hundred years earlier than Plato.

Marcus Aurelius (121–180 A.D.) was the Emperor of Rome from 161–180 A.D., a Stoic philosopher, and a devoted representative of the virtue-ethics approach. To him, and to the other Stoics, the good things in life — such as health, property and honor — were the natural fruit of being a good person. Who are good people? Especially those having the right attitudes such as **intelligence** (knowing what is good and bad), **bravery** (knowing what to fear and not to fear), **justice** (knowing what is due everyone) and **self-control** (knowing how to affirm, moderate, or extinguish different impressions and passions). These are similar to Plato's classical virtues: wisdom, courage, self-control and justice.

Benjamin Franklin (1706–1790 A.D.), the famous American statesman, diplomat, scientist, printer, author, and founder of the American Philosophical Society, was also an advocate of the virtue-ethics approach. In his writings he offered aphorisms, practical advice and wise rules for behavior. He wanted his readers to develop good habits. (The Autobiography of Benjamin Franklin)

Franklin believed that there were 13 primary virtues: **temperance, silence, order, resolution, frugality, industry, sincerity, justice, moderation, cleanliness, tranquility, chastity, and humility.** He associated each virtue with a specific principle or precept. For humility, for example, the precept was "Imitate Jesus and

BENJAMIN FRANKLIN'S VIRTUE CHART

Virtue	Sunday	Monday	Tuesday	Wednesday	Thursday	Friday	Saturday
Temperance							
Silence	✳	✳		✳		✳	
Order	✳	✳			✳	✳	✳
Resolution		✳				✳	
Frugality		✳				✳	
Industry			✳				
Sincerity							
Justice							
Moderation							
Cleanliness							
Tranquility							
Chastity							
Humility							

Socrates." (Ever earthy and humorous, however, after listing "chastity," Franklin wrote no comment!) He also developed a practical scheme to help him give proper attention to all these 13 virtues, using a 13 x 7 chart. He would note how he had concentrated every day on cultivating the habits for the particular virtue of the week, and then move on to concentrate on the next virtue the following week. The plan was to go through such a thirteen-week cycle four times a year, so that each virtue would be annually given four complete weeks of special attention. Franklin firmly believed that these 13 virtuous habits would lead to health and prosperity for the individual who faithfully pursued them, and people who had cultivated these virtues would certainly contribute nicely to the quality of society as well.

6. GROUP EXAMPLES

Much has been written recently about the role of **"corporate culture,"** a set of behavior habits that each particular corporation fosters by its hiring practices, management training programs, reward systems, personal examples of executives, ethics policies that are actually practiced, corporate stories, anecdotes and mottoes. That is, sometimes organized groups of people — such as corporations, families, schools, houses of worship, and entire cities — develop "personalities" with embedded "habits." Some of these group habits may be ethical, and others quite unethical. For example, when **Johnson & Johnson** was faced with the problem of someone tampering with its Tylenol pain killer — someone was putting poison in some capsules and then replacing the bottles on the store shelves — they chose to recall all Tylenol capsules. It then replaced them with gelcaps, and marketed them in tamper-resistant containers. This step was costly for the company, but corporate executives insisted that it was virtually an automatic expression of the Johnson & Johnson Credo, its practiced moral policy. The net result was a measurable increase in public trust in that company's products — leading then to increased sales and profits. Although these benefits to the company outweighed the costs of the recall, the Johnson & Johnson executives insisted that they did what they did simply "because it was right." It expressed the corporate habits they had cultivated through the Credo.

Other companies have sought to mimic Johnson & Johnson's behavior, in an effort to increase their own sales and profits, though without the company culture to back it up. However, these efforts have generally met with much less "success," in part because these other companies' responses to crises were slower and more calculating. The Perrier Bottling Company, for example, took days to decide to recall all its bottles of drinking water when some were found to include various levels of a poisonous substance. In spite of the recall, partly because it took days to respond to the crisis, and also because it had to admit later that the poison came from its own flawed cleaning process, Perrier's sales and profits plummeted. In general when corporations take days to decide what to do, the public perceives their policies to be calculated moves, rather than evidence of established corporate virtues or habits.

Adam Smith (1723–1790 A.D.), the father of modern economics, and the father of free-market theory, first established his reputation as an articulate spokesperson for virtue-ethics, although he is perceived by some as an egoist. He believed that personal character included strong "sentiments" that guide behavior, and that when these sentiments are well developed they are oriented to three virtues: justice (proper direction of feelings and actions), prudence (careful pursuit of private interest), and benevolence (care for the happiness of others). Justice and benevolence he considered to be the primary virtues, because one cannot simply be "prudent." Instead, one must be prudent in doing something else. That is, a mature moral person must try to be prudent at either being just or at being benevolent.

Later in his writings in economics, Smith made these three virtues foundational to a successful free market. If there is no justice in society, people are not going to have the personal trust that they need to buy and sell freely. Also, the society needs to nurture among its citizens prudence, or good work habits, so that they will seek their goals effectively and efficiently. Finally, if people do not feel that they are cared for in terms of quality products and services and good government, they will not participate in the economy with the needed energy, intelligence, creativity, and enthusiasm. Therefore, some level of benevolence is necessary within the free market system, even if government regulations are necessary to protect it.

Obviously, it makes a difference what virtues one chooses. In the same way that the good virtues, such as justice and benevolence, can be engrained in an individual or a group, so destructive and detestable patterns can also be engrained in individual and collective behavior. For example, gangs and governments can breed violence, hatred, racism, and greed — such as in Mafia or Nazi culture. These destructive and detestable patterns that may be treated by Mafia and Nazi leaders as "virtues" to be emulated and nurtured. The rest of us consider the same patterns to be *vices,* instead. Habits, even sought-after habits, are not necessarily good or virtuous. Selectivity is necessary.

"Only one principle will give you courage, that is the principle that no evil lasts forever nor indeed for very long."
— Epicurus

7. STRENGTHS

Virtue-ethics involves developing and nurturing a well-formed, active conscience, an internal compass. Good habits can become engrained into a personality, so that people become inclined to do the right things, as a matter of "second nature." But who really walks around with moral rule books in their pockets? What we take to be self-interest, or divine guidance, is filtered through our personalities as we make what we take to be the right decisions. Whatever else one says about ethics, it is people, with their individual personalities, who make the decisions, for better or for worse. Moral virtues are cultivated within people's character, within their personalities, and this is the real locus of decisions, the ultimate crossroads of conduct. What could be more effective, or more important?

8. WEAKNESSES

Perhaps everyone would agree that a person's character, especially one's set of moral virtues, is important. Nevertheless, the chief difficulty lies in knowing whether those virtues are really in place, and if not, how then to teach the moral virtues, or inculcate them in some way. If past behavior and habits are our only evidence, then there is no guarantee of future performance, because one's personality may have changed in the meantime, for better or for worse. If people's behavior often surprises us, how secure or stable can the virtues be?

Moreover, moral education has always been a major problem, especially for the virtue-ethics approach. Plato had severe doubts that virtues could be taught. He seriously considered the "recollection" theory that the moral virtues were naturally inborn, and that we have to address the amnesia that disrupted these perfect virtues in the trauma of the human birth process. It is doubtful that Plato or anyone else took this view seriously for very long.

Plato also developed a theory that the virtues could be successfully taught in an ideal society, what he called a "republic." In such an ideal setting potential leaders would have to endure decades of disciplined study about the virtues before they would be given real political power, displayed as ethical examples, and put in charge of the moral education of the next generation. In his dialogue, *The Republic*, where he defended this theory about an ideal society, he made clear that he thought such an exemplary state could not last long. Later he expressed grave doubts whether such a "republic" could exist at all.

It remained a great puzzle to him that the children of very ethical people sometimes turned out to be incorrigible, violent villains. These people could teach their children music, mathematics, and military science, but not what they cared about most, their morals. How could this be?

In our own time, the challenge remains. Different theories for educating people to be moral are regularly invented, or reinvented, but the proponents of these theories are generally not convincing. If the key element of ethics is the state of moral virtues in people's character, then it is disappointing that we do not know more about detecting and measuring the virtues, or how to introduce or teach them.

9. COUNTER ARGUMENTS

Perhaps, of course, measurement and training are not the main concern. The problems with virtue-ethics are just the problems of approaches to moral reasoning of any sort. The only difference is that virtue-ethics honestly focuses on the root of all ethical issues: personal character, individual human habits, cultural patterns. To make a moral difference, we know that we need at least to find ways of nurturing the right virtues in ourselves, in our children, in other people, and in the social structures and groups in which we participate.

Besides, the study of ethical virtues has helped us to appreciate more fully the complexity of the human personality. We also know more about the risk of trusting people, no matter how much we think we know them.

10. SUMMARY

The virtue-ethics approach to moral reasoning sustains a great interest on the part of many people. Most of us do not want merely good behavior or good consequences, but good people and good societies. Because the focus is on quality human character, some interest in virtue-ethics thinking will always exist.

Nevertheless, it is doubtful that such concentration on human character is ever, within itself, sufficient for a comprehensive moral perspective. When it comes to measurement and education, it seems that moral virtues remain elusive. Consequently, serious additional attention to some other aspect of morals seems necessary — whether it is self-interest (egoism), God's direction (divine command theory), moral rules (deontology), ethical results (consequentialism), or some other source of value.

The Natural-Law Approach emphasizes conduct based upon the order inherent in the universe.

The natural-law approach to moral reasoning looks to natural features or characteristics of rational humans as the basis for ethical reasoning. Unlike the virtue-ethics approach, these **determinative characteristics are ultimately in-born and natural to the human condition,** not habits that require training or nurturing to become "second nature."

In their own way, perhaps, each approach to moral reasoning that we have examined appeals to natural law. Egoists argue that self-interest and the "lust for power" are natural human characteristics that should drive ethics. Similarly, divine-command theorists appeal to a natural human desire to know and obey God, and the virtue-ethics advocates try to draw our attention to the natural human need to shape patterns of personality and behavior in positive ways. In contrast, natural-law theorists tend to point out some aspect of human reasoning itself as the primary reference point for acceptable moral reasoning.

1. PERSONAL BACKGROUND

Pythagoras (c. 550–500 B.C.), was an early Greek mathematician, who is credited by many with the Pythagorean Theorem — the theorem that the square of the hypotenuse of a right triangle is equal to the sum of the square of the other two sides. This mathematical genius was so profoundly moved by the power of numbers that he came to believe that all human relationships should be governed by simple mathematical formulas. As an inspiring model for this enterprise, he pointed out that musical harmonic relationships (e.g., musical major and minor thirds and octaves) are based upon simple mathematical ratios — mathematical-physical fact that was already known. The key to the moral life was to find the correct rational relationships for human behavior, a task that required both reasoning and mystical awareness.

Figure 6. Saint Thomas Aquinas. French Government Tourist Office.

St. Thomas Aquinas (1224/5–1275 A.D.), who based his theories mainly on Aristotle's writings, also believed in natural law and affirmed that human rationality was the key. In particular, what distinguishes human behavior from non-human action is that people act on the basis of reason. Humans attach reasons to actions and thus attribute moral value, because actions can contribute to appropriate human purposes. Therefore, good reasoning will always fine-tune moral choices. In addition, Aquinas believed and proclaimed a fundamental, rational natural-law that affected all human choice: "Good is to be done and pursued, and evil avoided." Aquinas believed that this simple natural-law is built into everyone, and no human being is ignorant of it. That is, the simple desire to know and to do what is good — the very interest in ethics — is an important law of human nature. Aquinas went on to explain that God, who is the creator, builds this natural-law into humans.

In a similar way, **C. S. Lewis** (1898–1963 A.D.), an Oxford teacher and distinguished author, argued in *The Abolition of Man* (1943) that many modern people had allowed technology, science, racism, and nationalism to eviscerate a core aspect of human nature: an elementary concern for the welfare of others. To Lewis, the simple rational ability to comprehend and to be moved by other people's needs and concerns is an essential human trait. Without it, humanity itself is lost. Lewis saw in the Golden Rule — "Do unto others as you would have them do unto you" — the verbal expression of this simple rational ability to draw a benevolent analogy between others and oneself. As evidence that this rational principle is a part of human nature, he uncovers versions of this venerable Golden Rule in the ancient literature of many different cultures.

2. HISTORIC BACKGROUND

At different periods of time, natural-law theories have been proposed to remind people that ethical beliefs are never merely a matter of personal choice and opinion, but they are in some sense dependent upon the structure of human nature itself, including especially some objective human reasoning powers. Natural-law theories have played the role of the first and most elementary defense against the potential dehumanizing effects of mathematical, scientific, or technological discoveries. Pythagoras' theory provided this defense in the ancient world.

Aquinas proposed his natural-law theory just as the earliest impressive stages of modern natural science were developing. He was a contemporary of Roger Bacon (1214–1292 A.D.), a key founder of experimental science and a researcher in the study of optics. Aquinas also wanted to avoid the excessively other-world orientation of some other thinkers. C. S. Lewis's role in the twentieth century as a defender of humanity in the face of the potentially crushing impacts of excessive spirituality, as well as scientism, technologism, racism, and nationalism, can be understood in a similar light.

A modern sequel to Natural-Law theory is *communitarianism* — the assumption that the essentials of human identity are bound up in **social interaction**. It is not insignificant that Aristotle's major work in moral philosophy (the *Nicomachean Ethics*) claimed to be about politics, nor that his major work in social philosophy (the *Politics*) was billed as a companion to the *Ethics*. This interpenetration of two arenas of concern reflects the cultural distance between Aristotle's time and our own — and not just in terms of the particulars of language and custom. Today some say we live in an era of "individualism," where it feels natural for us to prioritize our own perceived needs over and above the good of the society at large, and where it is not unusual for people to take no interest at all in the daily political life of their communities. But Aristotle conducted his political associations in the context of rather tiny city-states where all participants knew each other pretty well, and where the sheer complexity of our modern political system, with its competing interest-groups and social urgencies, would have been unimaginable. In such a setting it was nearly just as unimaginable for any male citizen to shun participation in the political life of his community.

3. How Does This Worldview Affect Perception?

a. **Focus**: Natural-law theorists look for and find common, transcultural, objective aspects of human nature that help shape general human moral awareness and ethical behavior.

b. **Blind spots:** Natural-law theorists tend to emphasize core human similarities, at the cost of fully appreciating real differences. With so much attention given to what is common in human nature, some dimensions of personal choice, moral development, ethics education, and supernatural guidance are given less attention.

4. SPAR Dimensions

a. **Substance** — Natural-law theorists see humans as rational creatures with some important common characteristics, including inborn traces of the knowledge of what is morally right, and the awareness that one should pursue it.

b. **Principles** — The primary principle is that one should live in harmony with the basic laws of rational human nature — such as purposefulness, seeking the good, and following the Golden Rule.

c. **Actions** — Natural-law theorists especially praise actions that model the best of rational human behavior.

d. **Results** — The goal is to strengthen those aspects of human nature that make humanity special, and to achieve the goals of human happiness and self-fulfillment.

5. Individual Examples

Aquinas remains one of the most significant models of natural-law theory. An important goal for him was to demonstrate that there is no conflict between human reason and faith, and so he was especially attentive to evidences of moral value within natural human reasoning. His project did not deny or minimize the role of evil in human behavior, but he was glad to find strains of ethical value within the basic rational human nature that he believed God had designed and developed.

In particular, for the natural-law advocate, however evil a person is, there still remains deep in that person some desire for moral good. That is, the basic principle "Good is to be done and pursued, and evil avoided," is embedded in every human soul, whether good or evil. The very existence of this principle is what makes possible human moral development in the first place. [See Chapter 2.] Over the years, many adults may have denied, twisted, or distorted this principle, but it is still there as part of their nature. In addition, Aquinas believed that there are natural human inclinations that are morally good, provided that they are reasonably pursued. These natural inclinations include:

* protection of one's life and health
* human reproduction and care of children
* consideration of other people's interests
* avoidance of ignorance

For **Aquinas**, natural-law provides a substantial basis for ethics. Nevertheless, he himself believed that a full ethical perspective needed to be enhanced through additional means, such as some version of the divine-command theory. His merger of natural-law theory and divine-command theory makes sense especially if one believes that the God who gives the commands is the same being as the one who created human nature in the first place. By this logic, whoever follows natural-law is obeying what God already commanded as part of that person's human nature, and whoever follows a divine-command approach is doing only what humans were naturally designed to do in the first place.

6. GROUP EXAMPLES

The influence of natural-law thinking abounds. Especially notable is the way the natural-law ethic has had a distinguished influence on America's culture and on its legal tradition. For starters, by his ringing appeal to natural-law, Thomas Jefferson defended the American revolution and independence from Great Britain. The Declaration of Independence, of which Jefferson was the primary author, proclaimed in its preamble that the ultimate justification of American independence was "the Laws of Nature and of Nature's God." This merger of natural-law and divine command thinking is a little reminiscent of Aquinas' explicit understanding.

Harmonious with this theme of the Declaration's preamble, the next paragraph also declared that all people "are created equal, and that they are endowed by their creator with certain unalienable rights, that among these are life, liberty, and the pursuit of happiness." The perspective of natural-law permeates the rest of the Declaration as well, such as in its insistence that government powers must derive "from the consent of the governed." For the Natural Law advocate, government authority must itself be justified on the basis of human reasoning.

Dr. Martin Luther King, Jr. publicly justified civil rights — and his use of civil disobedience to help achieve those rights — also by a strong appeal to natural law. He found and used natural-law themes of the Bible, of the Constitution, and of Jefferson to defend his approach. Dr. King argued that by nature all humans deserve respect. He also explained that wherever there are unjust laws or unreasonable government regulations, these laws and regulations could be broken, because it is more proper for people to obey a higher law.

Dr. King assumed that many people's own rational consciences would show them how wrong some of the discriminatory and racist laws were in America, and what basic human behavior required, instead. He also looked to religious people whom he called upon to obey God. As we have seen, both of these great American leaders — Thomas Jefferson and Dr. Martin Luther King, Jr. — intermixed their personal belief in natural-law theory with commitments to their different versions of divine-command thinking.

Natural-law thinking has also shaped a number of important legal discussions. American legal courts have sought to invoke natural law when the Constitution and other written laws are silent on a subject. For example, the Supreme Court, in *Griswold v. Connecticut* (1965), struck down a law in Connecticut that restricted certain sales of contraceptives. The Court claimed that there was a natural zone of privacy that protects some relationships from government intervention. There was no hint or claim that the justices had based the court decision on the Constitution or any written law, but only upon some natural human awareness.

7. STRENGTHS

Natural-law theory is attractive in many ways. First, it seeks common ground among people of diverse perspectives. Second, it seeks that common ground in an objective reference point in rational human nature — beyond the strongly subjective aspects of individual selfishness (egoism), religious experience (divine-command), or personal character (virtues-ethics). Third, the values that natural-law theory defends are values that are widely affirmed, in the United States and elsewhere, so that the claim of objectivity for this natural-law has a strong appeal.

Fourth, all of the different concepts of moral development that we examined in Chapter 2 already assume the existence of some kind of natural-law. On the one hand, concepts of moral development depend upon the basic natural-law that people have some moral awareness and a desire to do good and avoid evil — as in Aquinas's basic principle of natural-law. On the other hand, the idea of objectively observing and measuring people's personal development in "justice thinking" (Kohlberg) or in "care activity" (Gilligan), wisely presumes that there are objective standards — and, thus, natural-laws — by which any human development in these dimensions can be compared and measured. Sometimes we assume natural-law without consciously thinking about it.

8. WEAKNESSES

Although the claim of objectivity has some merit, awareness of these "objective" natural-law values seems to depend on certain kinds of cultural context and education. For example, this "objectivity" of natural-law seems to be more appreciated in democratic societies than in dictatorships or primitive societies.

Moreover, the standards of natural-law theory are generally vague and imprecise. For example, the principles that are defended by Pythagoras, Aquinas, Jefferson, Lewis or King on the basis natural-law seem rather broad and generic. As a result, these principles are rarely fruitfully invoked to resolve narrow disputes.

9. COUNTER ARGUMENTS

The natural-law perspective is not so culturally limited as its critics claim. Consider, for example, many people in former communist countries believed that their atheistic, totalitarian dictatorships were wrong. And they knew that there was a higher law. Note the international popularity of Jefferson's *Declaration of Independence*. This is one of the most widely translated and published documents in all of history, second only to the Bible. The Declaration's direct appeal to natural-law has rung true in the hearts of countless millions of people, and it has consequently inspired scores of liberation movements all over the world.

Examine also the broad international impact of the teachings of Dr. Martin Luther King, Jr. People from many backgrounds and from all levels of education and literacy understand and affirm Dr. King's appeal to a "higher law." Jefferson and Dr. King were great Americans, and they were well nurtured and educated in American values and culture, but their ideas have measurably moved many peoples in scores of countries.

Keep in mind, too, that "objective" perception usually requires some education and training, anyway. Scientific perception, for example, requires training in the sciences. Untrained adults would not know what to look for on the gauges and instruments in a scientific laboratory. Nevertheless, trained scientists claim objectivity, because their experiments produce comparable results. This "objectivity" is more strictly "inter-subjectivity," because many people have similar observations. Even the ability to read words on a page, such as the words in this book, requires years of concentrated training in language and literacy. This training does not take away from the "objectivity" or "inter-subjectivity" of correct reading of a text. Similarly, therefore, if many trained people from different backgrounds recognize and perceive the same natural-law values, these values are in some sense "objective." It may take training to fully appreciate these natural-laws, but evidence of the moral natural-laws may be in every human's life.

Moreover, the lack of precision is not a problem unique to natural-law theory. To one extent or another, precision can be elusive for all the approaches to moral reasoning. Lack of precision may be a generic characteristic of the ethical dimension of human life. Every one of these eight classic theories will ultimately require some level of wisdom, good sense, creativity, and ingenuity.

10. SUMMARY

Natural-law theory is a venerable approach to moral reasoning, and it has inspired many tremendous achievements. By focusing on some "objective" — or at least inter-subjective — natural human reference points, large groups of people have been united for positive change. Perhaps no other approach to moral reasoning has had such a uniting effect. The tremendous international impacts of Aquinas, Jefferson and King are monumental reminders of this influence.

The Deontology Approach emphasizes basing conduct on an sense of moral duty, with no regard for consequences.

For millennia, many people have sought to discover, apply, and disseminate a key principle or rule — or a key set of principles or rules — to govern moral reasoning and behavior. The thought was that with explicitly formulated rules, a group of people could be brought together with a common set of expectations and understandings. If the rules are stated precisely enough, ambiguity is minimized as well. The term **"deontologism"** comes from the Greek word *deon*, meaning "duty." Deontology seeks to guide moral reasoning by duties to specific principles, regardless of the consequences. Moreover, these duties are unaffected by people's inclinations. Also, some deontologists insist that their moral principles allow for no exceptions.

The differences between this view and the ones we have already studied are dramatic. Unlike egoism, deontological rules are publicly stated and are not self-centered. Unlike divine-command theory, deontologism focuses on the rules rather than the rule-giver. Unlike virtue-ethics, **deontology gives attention to human behavior in conformity to the rules, regardless of what is going on inside people's character.** According to Deontologists, personal inclinations to follow the moral rules count for nothing, and may take away from the stern sense of rule-governed duty that deontologism seeks to foster. Finally, unlike natural-law ethics, deontologism does not need to base its rules on any objective aspects of human nature. The rules themselves create the definitions of what is good for a deontologist.

1. PERSONAL BACKGROUND

Confucius (c. 551–479 B.C.) lived at a time of tremendous social chaos and suffering. Confucius believed that life would be dramatically improved if the leaders of society followed a set of principles to guide both ethics and etiquette. While **Confucius** also firmly believed in the importance of virtues and character development, a set of hundreds of rules called *li* was a centerpiece of his approach.

Confucianists based these hundreds of rules on their application of the Golden Rule, a centerpiece of natural-law thinking, but the primary focus was given to the hundreds of *li* rules themselves. Moreover, Confucianists believed that if these rules were widely taught, they would lead to more cooperation and understanding between people, because those people would then share the same basic patterns of behavior, and they would know what to expect from others. Later Confucianists made *li* even more explicitly the primary focus of their teachings.

In modern times, **Immanuel *Kant*** (1724–1804 A.D.) is an especially well-recognized representative of deontological ethics. He lived and wrote in what is now Germany, at the same time Thomas Jefferson was helping to give America direction, and during an historic period sometimes referred to as the "Enlightenment." Moreover, Kant sought to "protect ethics" in the face of some of the same challenges that measurably affected Jefferson: the strong influence of science on people's thinking in general. However, Kant's own attempt to protect ethics led him to develop a highly influential approach to moral reasoning that was markedly different from Jefferson's.

Kant did no known scientific experiments, but considered science a threat to ethical reasoning. As a result, he insisted that deontological moral thinking have no basis in perceived nature, and that it be free from any of the natural laws found in the world of scientific phenomena.

Kant believed that the world of natural phenomena and sensory perception was totally mechanistic, and that it therefore had no place for personal freedom or human responsibility. Rather, he constructed his ethical reasoning upon the con-

Figure 7. Immanuel Kant. Library of Congress.

cepts of **duty** and **good will**. This sense of duty would direct our decisions in our "practical" non-sensory world, unaffected by the world of science or nature. The good will would derive from an innate human ability to act according to principle, what Kant called "pure reason" and what he considered to be its logical ramifications, detached completely from the world of sensory perception. Kant believed that this detached "practical" world of ethics was unaffected even by human nature, human inclinations, self-interest, perceived divine-commands, virtues of character, or natural-law. The ultimate teaching of Kant's ethics was, therefore, duty itself; not duty to a natural-law, or to a character virtue, or to a divine-command, or even to self-interest. Just detached duty. **Duty, as it sometimes is said, for duty's sake.**

Moreover, **personal "autonomy"** is essential to Kant and modern deontological ethics as well. This autonomy requires that each person's self-will legislates to itself, to create its own rules or maxims of duty. This is necessary because each individual must make his or her own decisions anyway! In this way, Kant's idea of moral duty fit into — and contributed to — modern individualism. Keep in mind that this individualism was foreign to Confucianism and other premodern versions of deontologism.

How did Kant apply this devotion to duty? He designed what he called the **Categorical Imperative**, namely: "Act only on that maxim which you can at the same time will to be a universal law." A "maxim" is an *unconditional* general rule or principle on which a person may choose to act. The point of this version of the Categorical Imperative is this: when considering different choices, one should formulate the general rule related to each choice, and then select the choice whose general rule one could consistently choose to be a universal law, and thus choose to be a true duty.

A corollary of the Categorical Imperative deals with **respect for persons:** "Act so that you treat humanity, whether in your own person or that of another, always as an end and never as a means only." So, by Kant's lights, we must respect rather than exploit people, and this applies to ourselves as well as to others.

As the Categorical Imperative is applied, one quickly realizes that "good will" — literally, the human willingness to do right — will usually result, and Kant included this distinctive good will as an element in his sense of true duty.

2. HISTORIC BACKGROUND

The fact that Kant's writings on ethics have drawn a tremendous amount of attention during the past 200 years, and that so many people quote his ideas, is testimony to the strength of individualism in the area of contemporary ethics. It is also testimony to the deeply embedded need people have for some ethical guidance, even if it seems necessary to keep moral reasoning separated from the ordinary world of phenomena and data.

In the modern world, scientific concepts have had a tremendous influence on our understanding of events around us. Many people have been so impressed by science, that they have consigned their entire world of perception to scientific frameworks. Love is merely sex-appeal, family is merely biological bonding, professional responsibility is merely a learned behavioral response, and there are no miracles. In such a world, an ethic of duty based strictly on the logic of people's internal intentions, completely protected from observation, is appealing, as people's values are protected in the privacy of their own thoughts.

3. HOW DOES THIS WORLDVIEW AFFECT PERCEPTION?

a. **Focus:** In this deontologist perspective, truly only one thing matters: one's commitment to duty and to the implications of duty. That is what ethics is about; ethics refers to what "ought" to be rather than what "is." As a result, deontologists' analysis of the concept of duty is often profound and helpful, even to non-deontologists.

b. **Blind spots:** Deontologists explicitly put on blinders in order to focus only on duty. What they fail to see is that while "ought" is not the same as "is" these two concepts are often related. Consider, for example, these evident connections:

> If something is beneficial to me, it ought to be at least considered.

> If the U.S. Marine Corps demands faithfulness, a Marine ought to be faithful.

> If a particular decision is the most just, one ought to pursue it.

> If natural-law is protective of human life, one ought to protect it.

> If a senator's policy is the most likely to benefit the most people, in the most ways, one ought to be for it.

> If that decision is required by a binding contract, one ought to do it.

> If literacy is a human right, one ought to promote it.

Other than deontologism, all the other classic approaches to moral reasoning do not see duty standing alone, but see it connected in some way with other human dimensions, and with perceivable facts.

4. SPAR DIMENSIONS

   a. Substance — Modern deontologism understands humans as primarily law-followers, even if they are also the law-makers.

   b. Principles — Faithfulness to duty, universality of application, and good will are the basic principles of deontologism.

   c. Actions — Deontological actions should follow one's personal principle duties.

   d. Results — Deontologists claim that one who follows duty purifies his or her own self-will to become a "good will." However, objective results are irrelevant.

5. INDIVIDUAL EXAMPLES

One of Kant's examples might help to make this approach to moral reasoning more clear. Imagine that a person is short on cash and needs money for some bills — a step of imagination that is easy for most of us! In order to avoid incurring further debts, that person considers borrowing money by in some way falsely promising to repay it. As a good Kantian, the person considers the maxim or general rule: "It is permissible to borrow money and lie about any plans to repay it." However, it is immediately clear that this maxim could not be willed to be a universal law, because then the person from whom the money would be borrowed would know already the universal law that there is no longer any obligation to repay it. Consequently, the person would not lend the money in the first place! The maxim would conflict with itself. Since, therefore, this maxim could not logically become a universal law, any action that it guides should be forbidden. Similarly, Kant thought that one should not commit suicide, because one could not will that suicide be generally justified by the sense of despair and disappointment that may lead to suicidal feelings. Such an act of self-will would contradict other things people choose, would demonstrate a failure to respect a person (yourself), and so suicide is always wrong. In these ways Kant sought to apply his key concepts of consistency and duty to develop his model of deontological moral reasoning.

   Jean-Paul Sartre (1905–1980 A.D.), a French existentialist philosopher, political theorist, playwright, and novelist, developed a slightly different deontological view, one that depended on one's duty to be personally authentic. Like Kant, Sartre rejected the notion of divine commands. He affirmed what Dostoyevsky had said, that if there were no God, everything would be permitted. Atheist Sartre asserted that there is no God, and thereby everything is permitted.

Sartre believed that not only must one make choices in life, but also one must create the very values upon which those choices are made. One can, of course, do what most people do — follow the traditions, expectations, self-interests, and peer pressures in a person's environment. This is the choice not to choose, and the net result is that you have made yourself something less than human. On the other hand, one can make real choices for oneself and become an **"authentic person."**

What makes one authentic? Under Sartre, this is not easy. First, there is no God, and thus no divine commands to guide one to authenticity. Second, because there is no God, nature itself has no meaning, provides no guidance, and so there is no moral natural-law. Third, there is no definition of humanity, no objective human nature. Consequently, an authentic person must create or invent a definition of what he or she wants humanity to be, and then courageously act in a way consistent with that definition. This becomes one's authentic duty, and nothing else should distract from pursuing it.

For example, during World War II, many people in France were sorely tempted to cooperate with the Nazis — not because they loved the Nazis, but because they wanted to survive. Usually they harbored hopes, and even prayed, that someone, somewhere would effectively resist the Nazis, but they chose to play it safe themselves. Sartre thought that these people were inauthentic. They wanted some people's humanity to mean one thing (resistance to tyranny), while their own humanity meant something else (self-centered safety).

For Sartre, authenticity requires that a person affirm only one definition of humanity. If you choose to cooperate with the Nazis, then choose to like them. If you sincerely want someone to resist them, you must find ways to help undermine the Nazi regime yourself — by yourself or in league with others. With this understanding of duty to his own authenticity, Sartre himself participated in the French Resistance, at great risk to his own life and safety. The college professor actually practiced what he taught, even though it required a daily dance with death!

6. GROUP EXAMPLES

Such a total commitment to a duty can also be a group experience, although there are complications here. One might think of the armed services — army, navy, air force, marines — although duty in the military is also tied to outcomes. Moreover, it is never nearly so individualistic as Kant's and Sartre's kind of duty and deontologism.

Dictatorial and totalitarian society may be considered, too, although it is unclear to what extent the duties to the state are really internalized by the citizens. There is some evidence that totalitarian education and media control can be very powerful, so that large portions of a population, including those who are highly educated, will believe in the dictator, and they will commit their deontological duties to the state. Generally, however, dictatorial regimes rely upon some mixture of duty and fear of punishment.

Perhaps bureaucratic offices can provide another group example. The regulations that they are assigned to enforce can become so ingrained in the minds of seasoned bureaucrats — or even rookie bureaucrats — that they make dutiful decisions quite unmoved by the personal nuances of the cases before them. Their "duty only" approach is evident when the only responsibility these people recognize is to the specific regulations that govern their positions. And, perhaps, this is what we want bureaucrats to do.

7. STRENGTHS

There is certainly something inspiring — and perhaps heroic — about this "duty only" approach. Also, because of its singular focus on duty, deontologism can develop a more simple and logically coherent perspective. Whatever satisfies the requirements of duty is good; whatever violates the requirements of duty is evil; and all else is morally neutral. Clearly, deontologists can create a system of rules that seems to be complete, covering all kinds of cases, and logically coherent, with all values deductively following from basic principles. The resulting approach to ethical reasoning can be as intellectually impressive and aesthetic as the very mathematics Kant opposed as having philosophical value.

8. WEAKNESSES

First, most people do not find life to be so simple that all ethical duties can be stated in a simple set of rules or regulations. Second, values do seem to be connected with perceivable facts, although there are many different viewpoints on how these connections work. Few would go so far as to say that values are in a whole different world than the world of facts and phenomena. Furthermore, not many people would agree with Sartre that there is no moral purpose or guidance in human nature as it exists. Neither would they agree with Kant's intolerance of exceptions when life is filled with subtle twists and turns.

Third, the strong sense of **"ethical privacy"** that deontologism has fostered is potentially very misleading. Sartre seems to justify a person who lives just as he or she chooses or self-legislates, without considering consequences, and without accountability to others. All that matters is that each person self-legislates, or chooses authentically, in a personally consistent manner, because the only real duty in Sartre's view, is to oneself as self-legislator. This attitude of "ethical privacy" may lead to disasters. For example, for years many people have believed that they could engage in any sexual activity that they

How much alike are Kohlberg's 6th level of awareness and Kant's principle of universality? Who was born first?

pleased, according to their own selection of sexual ethics. The awareness that there would be consequences to their self-chosen behavior — consequences to themselves and others in the form of scores of sexually transmitted diseases — came as a great surprise. And the awareness of serious consequences often came too late. Life is more than duties to oneself.

A fourth potential weakness should not be missed: deontologism can be profoundly rigid. For example, because he thought that your only real duty is to yourself, for your own moral consistency, Kant held to the belief that one should never tell a lie, even if it would save a life — even if it could save many lives! From Kant's perspective, there are no circumstances under which you should taint your own self-will, your own sense of duty, with a lie — not because of the consequences to others, but because of your own personal consistency. Therefore, if a tyrant were hunting down innocent people to kill — perhaps, because he hates people of their race — and some of these innocent people are hiding in your house, you are obligated to tell the truth if the soldiers ask you if they are in your house.

From the Kantian perspective, if the innocent people are captured, and then tortured or killed, their blood is on the hands of the tyrant and the soldiers, while you observed the duty of truth-telling regardless of consequences. Out of the consistency of duty you chose not to pollute your own communication with a falsehood because to do so would diminish the truth for everyone. On the other hand, this commitment of consistent Kantians to *always* tell the truth — at all times and in all situations — dramatically impacted people's lives in Germany, especially those of Jews during the time of the Nazi regime. Contrarily, though still a deontologist, Sartre approved of deception if it led to the fulfillment of one's duty; so he engaged in various schemes — that included untruths — to resist Nazis in his homeland.

If you were fighting in defense of your nation, would you rather have a disciple of Kant or Sartre at your side? Why?

9. COUNTER ARGUMENTS

Since Kant, some major deontologists have sought to remedy the truth-telling dilemma. For example, **William David Ross** (1877–1971 A.D.), an Oxford philosopher and scholar, endeavored to humanize deontologism into something more nuanced. Ross believed that people are often faced with a collection of **"*prima facie* obligations,"** which means those obligations that at first glance seem to have some claim on their behavior. Each of these *prima facie* obligations is a duty that one can recognize as having some "weight," some level of importance. People then can use a variety of considerations — including religious beliefs, benefits to others, promises, and self-interest — to try to determine their actual duty in a particular situation. Ross proposed a process of "weighing" each of the *prima facie* obligations, and discerning which is the "weightiest." This process he saw as not purely deductive. There is no logical "algorithm" for it, unlike

Kant's largely deductive deontological structure. Nevertheless, Ross affirmed that for an ordinary person, who did not take the abstract moral theories too seriously, this was not a problem.

A version of one of Ross's examples would help illustrate his nuanced deontologism. Consider a situation where a person promises to lend money to a friend in need, money she has been saving for a new dress. However, before the money is transferred, the same person discovers that her daughter is charged with a crime of which she believes her to be innocent. Now the mother has at least three conflicting duties, all competing for the same cash: the duty to help herself, the duty to fulfill a promise to a friend, and the duty to help her daughter pay a good attorney. All are clearly *prima facie* obligations. What is a good person/friend/parent to do? Only one of these duties is the actual duty, but Ross believed we could have differing opinions as to which one it is.

Ross's deontologism seeks to address each of the four potential weaknesses of Kant's and Sartre's deontologism — it is more nuanced, more connected to other dimensions of life, less committed to "ethical privacy," and less rigid. Similarly, Confucianism is largely able to handle these four potential criticisms, too. From the beginning, Confucius' view had a more wholistic, humanistic vision than Kant or Sartre advocated. Nevertheless, Confucianism did run the risk of some rigidity and insensitivity to the particular case to be decided. These are potential weaknesses of any deontological approach to moral reasoning.

10. SUMMARY

Deontologism is an impressive intellectual perspective that has made a huge impact on ethical discussions in the twentieth century. Nevertheless, without the reforms of Ross or the humanism of Confucius, it can be too simplistic, detached, privatized, and rigid.

In this chapter we have introduced the role of ethical approaches to moral reasoning, and we have compared its role to that of other theories, such as scientific theories. We have also examined the perspectives of the five main classical theories to moral reasoning, looking at some chief examples and basic structures.

In the next chapter we will examine four more contemporary perspectives, including your own.

THE BIG PICTURE
A COMPARISON OF CLASSICAL APPROACHES TO MORAL REASONING

Approach:

Thinkers	Substance of the Person	Principles that Matter	Actions that Fit the Model	Results that Are Sought
1. Egoism	Center of power; Exploiter.	Make your own decisions; Be authentic.	Self-centered; Individuality or fear of punishment.	Personal authenticity and freedom.
2. Divine Command	Person endowed by the Creator with a purpose.	Fulfill the intentions and commands of the Creator.	Creator-centered; Obedience and honor for the Deity.	Positive relationship and peace with the Creator.
3. Virtues	Individual with developing habits and personality.	Cultivate behaviors that improve human flourishing.	Concordant with intended and helpful habits.	Healthy, balanced, and flourishing character.
4. Natural Law	Personality with built-in needs, instincts, and goals.	Live harmoniously with your true essence.	Expressive of the natural qualities and needs.	Fulfillment of intrinsic patterns and potential.
5. Deontologism	Law-maker and law follower.	Follow (deductively) the imperatives that you accept.	Consistent with selected general imperatives.	A good will, one that acts according to chosen principles.

FOR FURTHER INQUIRY

DISCUSSION QUESTIONS

1. So far, which perspective seems the most right to you?
2. What do you take to be the major strengths and weaknesses of each approach?
3. Could you write or dramatize a dialogue or debate between representatives of two of these perspectives — as they might address a contemporary moral issue?

ENDNOTE

1. Liddell and Scott, *Greek-English Lexicon*, Clarendon Press, 1963, p. 317.

CHAPTER 5

CONTEMPORARY APPROACHES TO MORAL REASONING

"Never create by law what can be accomplished by morality."
— **Charles-Louis deSecondat, the Baron de Montestquieu**

"Life can only be understood backwards, but it must be lived forwards."

— **Soren Kierkegaard**

It has not been for lack of classic resources that some contemporary thinkers have introduced additional alternative approaches. The classical approaches are very strong options in the present world. There is nothing "old-fashioned" about any of them. Egoism seems always to be in style, for better or for worse, and the Divine Command for many is an eternal reference point. The virtues of virtue-ethics are abiding values, too, and so are the sweeping principles of natural-law and its claims on ethics. Moreover, most of the rules that the deontologists have framed as ultimate principles are enduring as well.

Nevertheless, in the modern era with increasing influence from quantitative science, from democratic individualism, and from secular perspectives, some new emphases on moral reasoning have emerged. These new focal points that contemporary moral theories have developed include:

CHIEF LEARNING OUTCOME

I am familiar with these contemporary approaches to moral reasoning and I am developing my own particular worldview as a result.

---

* measurable consequences,
* individual human rights, and
* negotiated contracts.

Paul De Vries, M.A. and Ph.D. University of Virginia, is the president of NYES Fund Inc., an educational program, and a partner in Leadership Excellence Inc. He also is president of the International Research Institute on Values Changes, based in New York and Moscow.

KEY CONCEPTS

The *Consequential* Approach emphasizes conduct determined by assessing the moral quality of the *results* likely to follow from various possible courses of actions.

The *Utilitarian* Approach emphasizes always acting in order to produce the most amount of satisfaction (pleasure or happiness) and the least amount of dissatisfaction (pain or unhappiness) for the greatest number of people.

The *Contractarian* Approach emphasizes that all ethical obligation is based exclusively upon contracts and promises.

The *Natural Rights* Approach emphasizes the exclusive protection of and reliance upon common human personal rights.

We will examine three of these contemporary views before we investigate an approach based upon a composition of multiple themes.

Consequentialism seeks to correct a perceived defect of deontologism, and it does this by encompassing a broader range of factors. The central feature underlying consequentialism is the idea that we are morally responsible not just for our actions, but for their forseeable consequences as well.

The modern method of trying to limit one's focus in order to produce a simple ethical theory is evidenced in consequentialism, too, just as much as it is evidenced in the very focused deontologism of Kant and Sartre. It seems that for some people, the logical simplicity of a theory has been an overriding concern. That is, theories based simply on one core idea — such as duty or results — have more appeal to some.

In the case of **consequentialism**, moved by the legitimate importance of achieving good results, some philosophers have developed approaches to moral reasoning that make the consequences of people's decisions and behavior the only real ethical issue. From this perspective, **nothing else truly matters except results — especially measurable results.** That is, selfishness is acceptable if the net results are good for society in general, and divine commands are important only if they benefit human welfare. Religious consequentialists talk primarily about how their spiritual wisdom should be followed because it leads to happier, healthier, or more prosperous living. Similarly, even personal virtues, natural laws, and moral principles have their place in the consequentialist world — but only if these moral "instruments" help produce good results.

The Consequential Approach emphasizes conduct determined by assessing the moral quality of the *results* likely to follow from various possible courses of actions.

While a person could evaluate all decisions and behavior in terms of consequences only to oneself, or merely to one's own business or family, that should still be classified as a kind of egoism. In contrast, **consequentialism always considers as the dominant concern what are the consequences to all the people affected by a decision or an action,** egoism notwithstanding. The target result is to minimize the total pain and maximize the total pleasure that results in the lives of each of the people that are in any way affected in the given case. People's pains and pleasures are relevant, and the pains and pleasures are measured by whether they are **substantial, direct, immediate, enduring, intense, or lead to additional painful or pleasurable consequences** — all these and possibly other dimensions of measure of results are to be taken into account. After all, this is what really matters, because consequentialists perceive people as primarily creatures of pleasure and pain.

For example, when consequentialism is used as the structure for a business decision concerning expanding a factory or other industrial facility, the total impact on the pain and pleasure of everyone affected is taken into account. This consideration includes the effects on stockholders, managers, employees, customers, neighbors, displaced people, besides all people who would be affected by the additional industrial pollution, and so forth. Each group's pain or suffering would be weighed — actually calculated, or at least considered — along with their pleasure and benefit, as the focus in the decision process.

In short, consequentialism is a kind of **altruism**, for it always pays attention to the resulting pain and pleasure of those involved. In contrast, for a business to look only at the impact of a decision on the pain and pleasure of the executives, the managers, or the stockholders. It would be using a version of egoism.

UTILITARIANISM

The most well-known modern version of consequentialism is utilitarianism. In some writings, you might find these treated as equivalent terms, but they are not. Some consequentialists are not utilitarians, especially those who look toward spiritual, emotional, or other less measurable consequences. Does a strategy, plan, system, method, idea, or approach demonstrably work better than alternative strategies, plans, *et cetera*? Does it measurably perform successfully for the most good and most of the time, regardless of any occasional negative, immoral or unethical consequences? This heavy reliance on demonstrable, measurable results is the chief feature of utilitarianism.

Modern utilitarianism, a form of consequentialism, is a little like egoism except at the most important point: In utility, all other people matter as much as self. Whereas, in egoism everything is measured ultimately by its effect solely on self.

Since the early part of the 19th century, *utilitarianism* has been the standard version and widely accepted view of the consequentialist position.

> The Utilitarian approach emphasizes always acting in order to promote the greatest amount of satisfaction (pleasure or happiness) and the least amount of dissatisfaction (pain or unhappiness) for the greatest number of people.

Utilitarianism, in other words, has written into it more than just a formulation of the typical consequentialist insistence that to judge an act's moral worth, we have to estimate an act's effects: It contains as well a general stipulation as to just what those effects should look like.

Endnote 1

There have been a number of different interpretations of the Utility Principle, especially regarding that vague word "satisfaction." What, shall we say, constitutes being "satisfied"? **Jeremy Bentham** (1748–1832 A.D.), who invented the word **"utilitarianism"** and became its first influential proponent, took the view that **"satisfaction"** is nothing but pleasure. In this regard, says Bentham, there is no reason to suppose that the pleasures experienced by animals are any different in kind from the human pleasures. Perhaps humans simply have the capacity for more intense pleasures and more varied pleasurable activities. Nevertheless, he believed that all pleasures and pains of all human beings can be compared on one mathematical scale — with one uniform measuring stick. The total pleasure-and-pain results of the various choices people might make can then be compared through Bentham's **"hedonistic calculus."** That is, moral decisions should be made on the basis of empirical measurement and mathematical calculation.

Bentham's view does have the obvious advantage of offering just what many consequentialists wanted: A seemingly scientific, *empirical basis* for objectively deciding when a moral rule should be applied. To say that a belief is based "empirically" is to say that it is accepted because we have public, measurable evidence from our experience in favor of it. Bentham could not concur with Kant's conclusion, based on the logic of duty, that lying is always wrong. (See Chapter 4.) For Bentham each case of lying would have to be examined for its real results.

Endnote 2

Bentham's most famous disciple, **John Stuart Mill** (1806–1873 A.D.), treated the lying case as an opportunity to examine what level of truth, if any, produces the best results in each situation. This examination would be an empirical test. In other words, what we need to do in each specific situation is *mathematically* to calculate the amount of satisfaction which, from past experience, we have learned is likely to result from each of our various options in this case. These considered options would include (1) telling the whole truth, (2) withholding some information, (3) telling a "little" lie, (4) telling a "huge" lie, and a whole variety of other options in between. **The greater the estimated "total utility" — the sum of satisfaction over dis-**

satisfaction — the more justified we are in acting in that particular manner.

Over time, some of Bentham's own followers — John Stuart Mill in particular — found it troubling that Bentham had failed to include certain powerful aspects of life in his calculation, leaving it peculiarly shallow. For starters, Bentham makes no significant mention of "the deeper feelings" that have traditionally been associated with the notion of human dignity and spirituality. There is little in Bentham to suggest, for example, that the appreciation of beauty is to be preferred to an equally intense satiation of a glutton's appetite. Mill, then, amends Bentham's Utility Principle to include the notion that what is to be maximized in moral conduct is human **"happiness"** — a *qualitatively* more inclusive word than mere "pleasure." Is being moved by the tragic plot of the Titanic not more humanly satisfying than winning a game of *Uno*? Some pains are more satisfying than some pleasures.

Is Socrates' unhappiness more meaningful than a pig's pleasure?

Does Mill's revision introduce new problems? Can it cope with a qualitatively wide range of kinds of human happiness? Can it do so and retain empirical testability? Can it do so and also include the "hedonistic calculus" of Bentham's program, which we will discuss below?

Notice what happens if we accept Mill's revision: The objective criterion Bentham defended — that is, to compare total measurable amounts of pleasure and pain — now gets complicated by the addition of qualitatively different dimensions of human happiness. We know fairly well how to *measure* quantity. But how do we measure the qualitative difference between dignified and crass pleasure-experiences? How in fact do we even empirically define the distinctions between them? Mill relied on the intuitions of educated and cultured people, but this takes Bentham's method out of a "hedonistic calculus" and into subjective comparisons.

Mill's answer to this last question is, like Aristotle, to rely on the convictions of the most cultured in our social group. But then, does this not return us directly to the very problem utilitarianism was designed to avert, the reliance on the mere intuition behind those convictions?

RULE VS. ACT UTILITARIANISM

At first glance it might seem as if consequentialism involves a significant demotion for the status of moral rules, since all that seems to matter is producing good results by whatever means. However, there is one roundabout way of maintaining the importance of rules within the utilitarian-consequentialist framework, and that is the position known as Rule-Utilitarianism. **A Rule-Utilitarian asks: Will the act fall under the rule requiring choices that produce the greatest happiness for the greatest number?** In other words: What would the world be like if the rule were generally disregarded? Also, what would happen if the rule were quite regularly obeyed?

The genius of rule-utilitarianism is this: Even if we cannot know the likely outcome in every specific case, that does not mean we have no idea about the likely result if a particular kind of action were taken by a great many people. We can still discern certain behaviors as generally good or bad. Besides, people cannot conduct complete hedonistic calculations before making every decision. People would be spending perhaps 90% of their time making hedonistic calculations for a few decisions, while most of their moral decision opportunities would slip past them while they were too busy hedonistically calculating! There is a paradox here somewhere.

Rule-utilitarianism, therefore, has a place: restoring a role for moral rules and greatly simplifying hedonistic calculations. It also allows utilitarianism to address general social policies, and not just individual decisions. It allows utilitarians to ask: What if embezzling was accepted practice? For suppose you are a clerk in a bank whose child is in need of expensive medical attention that your insurance won't cover. Let's say you have a chance to "borrow" the needed funds without your employer's knowledge. If you were a devoted rule-utilitarian you might find yourself asking: What would be the result if everybody decided to use their jobs to appropriate funds that are not theirs to use?

Rule-utilitarianism is not without its problems, however. What if you are convinced that this one case in front of you is unique? Unlike the general cases, you can embezzle money from the bank and help your child without anyone finding out, and without hurting the bank very much. What should you do? Rule-utilitarians would still say, "Do not embezzle." However, Bentham and the many other utilitarians hold that the net results of each decision should be calculated individually. They might well advise you to check your calculations carefully, and then do whatever produces the best results. Because consequences are all that matter for some utilitarians, no general rules — neither "Do not embezzle" nor "Always look out for your child any way you can" — are secure.

Act Utilitarianism **is the view that any act should be assessed based upon the greatest happiness for the greatest number produced in its own actual context, rather than upon the results of general adherence to a rule.** And, from the utilitarian perspective, this makes all the sense in the world just as long as we have enough information to guide us reliably. In the case of the bank clerk once again: Maybe she knows for sure that the bank would not be hurt by her use of spare funds; maybe she knows of a way to avoid detection, so her own life would not be ruined as a result (or, on the other hand, maybe she has determined that the welfare of her child is more important than her own future); and maybe she has exhausted all other possibilities open to her. In that case, based on the greatest total utility, an act utilitarian *might* conclude that, it would make sense to take the money.

Words stir

art moves

people think

life turns

Love it !

And God said
"Let their be light—
And there was light

Abraham Rattner (1893–1978), *Temptations of St. Anthony,* study, undated, watercolor, gouache, ink and charcoal on paper, 17 $^{13}/_{16}$ x 13 $^{7}/_{16}$ in. Leepa-Rattner Collection, St. Petersburg

Silk-screen reproduction of Abraham Rattner's India ink and watercolor *Window Cleaner,* 1952, 30 x 25 in., by Esther Gentle (1900–1991). Leepa-Rattner Collection, St. Petersburg

The Ten

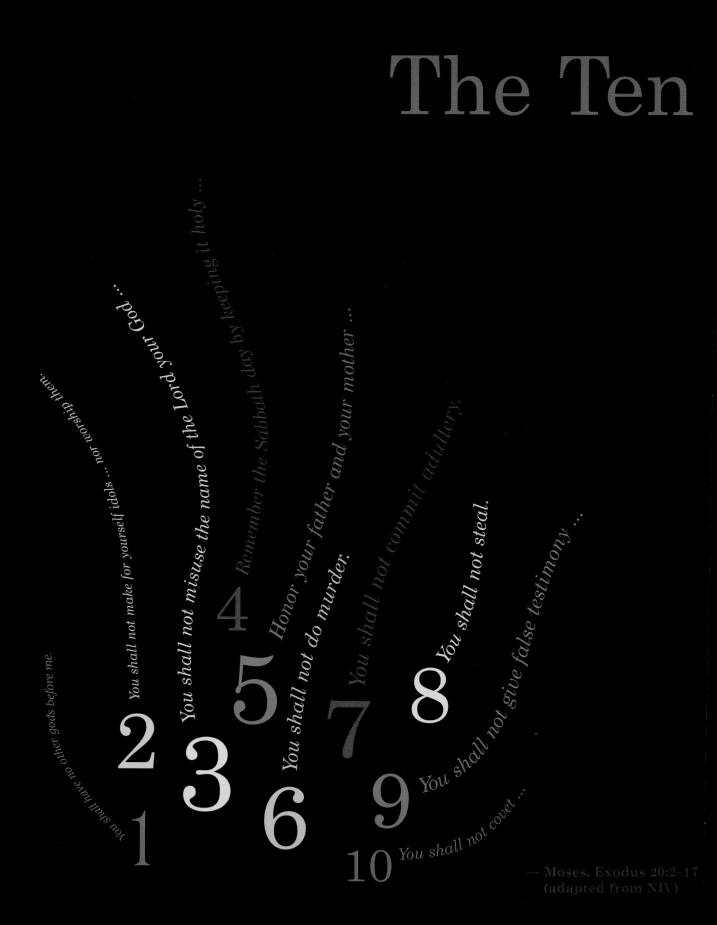

1 You shall have no other gods before me.

2 You shall not make for yourself idols … nor worship them …

3 You shall not misuse the name of the Lord your God …

4 Remember the Sabbath day by keeping it holy …

5 Honor your father and your mother …

6 You shall not do murder.

7 You shall not commit adultery.

8 You shall not steal.

9 You shall not give false testimony …

10 You shall not covet …

— Moses, Exodus 20:2–17
(adapted from NIV)

Commandments

HC/50/60

Abraham Rattner (1893–1978), *In the Beginning: Moses and the Tables of Stone*, 1972, lithograph, edition HC 50/60, 25 $^1/_2$ x 19 $^3/_4$ in. Leepa-Rattner Collection, St. Petersburg

History's Golden

"Do to the doer in order to cause him to do for thee. That is thanking him for what he may do; that is parrying

"Is there one maxim which ought to be acted upon throughout one's whole life? Surely it is the maxim of loving

"This is the sum of all true righteousness—treat others, as thou wouldst thyself be treated. Do nothing

"No one of you is a believer until he desires for his brother that which he desires for himself."

"A man is good only when he is willing not to do to another whatever is not

"All things whatsoever ye would that men should do to you, do ye even so

"This is the sum of duty: do naught unto others which would cause

"What is hateful to you, do not to your fellow man. That is the entire

"Regard your neighbor's gain as your own gain, and your neigh-

"Hurt not others in ways that you yourself would

"LOVE YOUR NEIGHBOR

Rules

something before it is shot. " — Egyptian wisdom literature, taken from Before Philosophy, Frankfurt and Others.

- kindness: do not do unto others what you would not have them do unto you. " — Confucianism: Analects 15:23

to thy neighbor, which hereafter thou wouldst not have thy neighbor do to thee. " — Hinduism

— Islam, Sunan, taken from Reader's Digest, excerpt from The World's Great Scriptures, Lewis Browne

good for himself. " — Zoroastrianism, Marcus Bach - Major Religions of the World

to them: for this is the law and the prophets. " — Christianity: Matthew 7:12

you to pay if done to you. " — Brahmanism, Mahabarata 5:1417

law: all the rest is commentary. " — Judaism, Talmud, Shabbat 31a

bor's loss as your own loss. " — Taoism: T'ai-shang Kan-ying P'ien

find hurtful. " — Buddhism, Udanavarga 5:18

AS YOURSELF."

adapted from the New Testament

Silk-screen reproduction of Abraham Rattner's oil on canvas painting *April Showers*, 1939. 32 x 39 ½ in., by Esther Gentle (1900–1991). Leepa-Rattner Collection, St. Petersburg

Abraham Rattner (1893–1978),
*The Beggar's Opera: Untitled
(Shut Not Your Eyes to the Needy)*,
1971, lithograph, 25/150 Artist's
Proof, 20 x 26 in. Leepa-Rattner
Collection, St. Petersburg

"I have done what people speak of,

What the gods are pleased with,

I have contented a god

with what he wishes.

I have given bread to the hungry,

Water to the thirsty,

Clothes to the naked,

A ferryboat to the boatless.

I have given divine offerings to the gods,

Invocation-offerings to the dead.

Rescue me, protect me,

Do not accuse me before the great god!"

– *Egyptian Book of the Dead*

"Be the change

you want to see in the world."

— *Mahatma Gandhi*

Abraham Rattner (1893-1978), *La Plage (The Beach),* 1938, oil on board
11 x 14 in. Leepa-Rattner Collection, St. Petersburg

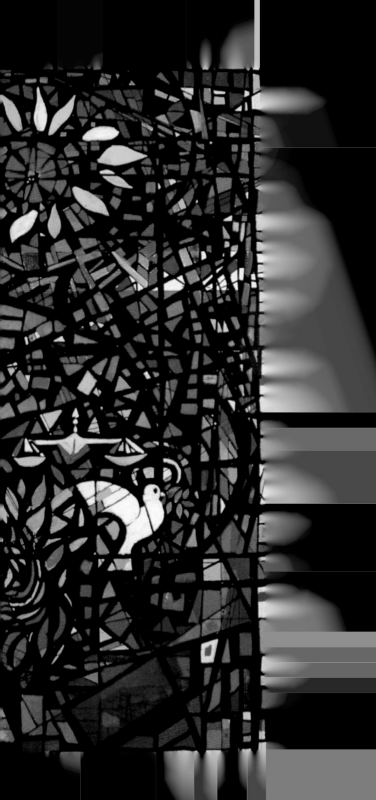

The Blind Men and the

John Godfrey Saxe's (1816–1887) version 1

It was six men of Indostan
To learning much inclined,
Who went to see the Elephant
(Though all of them were blind).
That each by observation
Might satisfy his mind.

The FIRST approached the Elephant
And happening to fall
Against his broad and sturdy side
At once began to bawl:
'God bless me, but the Elephant
Is very like a wall!'

The SECOND, feeling of the tusk,
Cried, 'Ho! What have we here
So very round and smooth and sharp?
To me 'tis mighty clear

The THIRD approached th
And happening to take
The squirming trunk with
Thus boldly up and spake
'I see,' quoth he, 'the Elep
Is very like a snake!'

The FOURTH reached ou
And felt about the knee.
'What most this wondrous
Is mighty plain,' quoth he:
'Tis clear enough the Elep
Is very like a tree!'

The FIFTH, who chanced
Said: 'E'evn the blindest
Can tell what this resemb
Deny the fact who can,

Allen Leepa (1919–) *Glorious Crucifixion,* 1969, acrylic on canvas, 48 1/2 x 36 in. Leepa-Rattner Collection, St. Petersburg

Abraham Rattner (American, 1893–1978) was born in Poughkeepsie, New York of Russian immigrant parents. He received training as an artist at prestigious schools like the Corcoran School of Art in Washington, DC and the Pennsylvania Academy of Fine Arts in Philadelphia. During World War I, Rattner served as a military camouflage artist and while in Europe became enamored with French avant-garde art. After the war, he returned to the United States and in 1920 received a Cresson Fellowship to study art in France. Rattner maintained a residence and studio in Paris for the rest of his life, except for the period of World War II.

Always considering himself an American, Rattner became part of the expatriated lost generation community in Paris. He developed a wide circle of art associates including Picasso, Matisse, Chagall, LeCorbusier and other leaders of the modernist movement. By the 1930s Rattner evolved a distinctive figurative painting style characterized by brilliant colors and sinuous contours. His work reflected some of the trends of futurism, cubism, and expressionism, but imbued with a quality of human drama.

When World War II broke out, Rattner returned to New York with friend and writer Henry Miller. They traveled the eastern United States together trying to re-acquaint themselves with America. The result was the publication of Miller's seminal book *The Air-Conditioned Nightmare* and an extensive portfolio of drawings by Rattner. In the 1950s Rattner began to gain financial security through the sale of his works and became recognized as an important figurative expressionist. In addition to his reputation as a superb colorist, Rattner responded to the oppressive reality of Nazism by focusing on symbolism taken from the Old and New Testaments that promised redemption. His pursuit of prophets' visions and crucifixion imagery, as well as his dedications to the memory of the six million who died in the Holocaust, has earned him the title "painter of the tragic."

"We shall not cease from exploration
And the end of all our exploring
Will be to arrive where we started
And know the place for the first time."

— *T.S. Eliot*

1. PERSONAL BACKGROUND

A strong interest in the social consequences of behavior has had a very long history, dating back to pre-history. Bentham is a highly respected figure in contemporary thought, and his ideas have deeply affected present-day decision-making, especially in business and government in industrial societies. In a more extreme way, some Benthamites revere him personally so much that they have meetings in the presence of his well-preserved body, which University College London displays in a glass case.

Figure 1. Jeremy Bentham's embalmed body. Corbis-Bettmann.

Bentham came from a family of lawyers. However, while pursuing legal studies himself, he became sickened and repelled by the legal structure of his time. He came to believe that the laws and their enforcement often did more harm than good. After all, for him the primary purpose of government — and of all human decision-making — is to achieve *"the greatest happiness of the greatest number."* All other so-called "moral" standards of decision-making were merely disguised egoism or what he termed "nonsense on stilts."

He found this to be especially the case in the area of criminal punishment. As in our own time, prisons were being built and large numbers of people were being locked up with little or no attempt to reform their lives. The *correctional* system was in effect more of a *caging* system, for there was little thought or attempt at improving the character or conduct of the convicts. Bentham made proposals to discover and implement the exact amount of punishment that would deter criminal behavior and reform criminals. For him the pain of punishment of convicts and their families can be justified only on the basis of long-term reduction of pain for the most people. There should be *no place for retribution* because, in Bentham's view, the only measure of value that we can comprehend is the measure of pleasure and pain.

The basic method involves a kind of mathematical procedure — what he called the "hedonistic calculus." **The "utility" is measured for each person affected by each possible decision, and then those *net utility* measures are added together to determine a total for each of the possible choices.** Of the various choices being considered, the one with the highest total utility is the best choice. For Bentham, "utility" is the measure of how strongly a particular choice tends to produce "benefit, advantage, pleasure, good, or happiness," or prevent "mischief, pain, evil, or unhappiness."

In this framework, if it is consistently followed, every individual person's happiness counts as much as anyone else's. Also, no one's unhappiness counts any more than any one else's. As a result, the *un*happiness of an individual or a small group may be the acceptable price for the greatest total happiness or pleasure.

One way to embody this ideal method is to make society more democratic. However benevolent a dictator may be, serious errors and selfishness can distort good judgment. "The greatest happiness of the greatest number" is best chosen by the people that make for the greatest number themselves, even if a minority's needs or wishes are *overridden*, even brutally overridden.

A widespread contemporary concept made popular by Bentham's influence **"cost-benefit analysis," a process of decision-making sometimes used in public policy, government, and business.** It involves numerically calculating the total cost of a possible decision, and its likely benefits, as a way of choosing between alternative decisions. When properly done, from Bentham's point of view, what are often hidden costs should be honestly calculated along with other expenses. For example, the safety risks of new products should be as important as material costs in a business decision. Also, in waste disposal the long-term effects on the environment and on future generations are as important as the immediate costs. Self-conscious exploitation at the expense of others is not acceptable to consequentialism, although it can be to egoism.

Consider an emergency medical situation: You come across a car accident where three people have life-threatening injuries, and you are the only one with the medical training who can help anyone of them. Because of the attention you have to give, you can try to save only two of them. Which two do you save? Which one do you ignore? What if the three include your sister, your father, and your spouse? What if the three are people you recognize to be a lawyer who serves the poor, a chemist who is making progress in advanced cancer

CALCULATING UTILITY

Example: The situation involves what level of quality medical care a couple will decide to provide their ill infant. In this case the only participants in the decision are the infant's parents; the results would vary if there were additional parties to the decision. Let us assume in this case that both of the parents love their child deeply, and that the mother is the one who has to keep track of the budget.

For happiness, rate the choice with a scale of $+1$ to $+5$, with 1 being minimum satisfaction and 5 being maximum satisfaction.

For unhappiness, rate the choice with a scale of -1 to -5, with -1 being least dissatisfaction and -5 being most dissatisfaction.

	Accept Insurance Baby Specialist	Finance Cost of U.S. - Best Specialist
Sue	$+3$	-3
Bob	$+2$	$+4$
Total Utility	$+5$	$+1$

The proper utilitarian decision would be to put to use the baby specialist endorsed by the insurance company, even though both are total positive choices.

research, and a generous millionaire who might reward you handsomely? How do you choose? What scale of comparison will help you? (See a literal calculation using this approach under "Group Examples" below.)

Such techniques as act utility help to uncover what relationships and characteristics a person values most and to enable comparisons among various theories of moral reasoning.

2. HISTORIC BACKGROUND

The extraordinary attention Bentham, Mill and modern consequentialists give to the role of results is in many ways a well-established human concern. What is more human than purposeful action — working for the survival or betterment of one's family, tribe, or nation? And in good utilitarian fashion, individual people have long been willing to sacrifice some of their own benefit or pleasure for the good of a whole group of which they are a part. We may call them involved citizens, police, fire fighters, military personnel, heroes, or saints, but the concern for the benefit of a collection of people is a very strong human motivator.

Consequentialism today has blended this deep human value with a kind of mathematical-scientific methodology that depends on some level of scientific research, and fosters further research. First, there is an explicit mathematical structure to the "hedonistic calculus." Second, the methodology of consequentialism resembles natural scientific methodology in some ways — testing and revising ideas on the basis of measurable results. Third, the purposes of consequentialism have provided an important incentive to the study of many topics in the ranges of psychology and sociology. In turn, consequentialists now also seek to apply the discoveries and theories of psychology and sociology — theories and perspectives that often, in some ways, consequentialist concern helped foster.

The designers and builders of the Titanic *claimed the ship was unsinkable. How much responsibility for the loss of life did they have?*

3. HOW DOES THIS WORLDVIEW AFFECT PERCEPTION?

a. **Focus:** In addition to searching for various measurable results, consequentialism prizes careful observation of any sort. In addition, it gives tremendous encouragement to strategic thinking, since the value of a person's actions depends on the actual consequences that are achieved.

b. **Blind spots:** While results are emphasized, the intentions people have are generally discounted or ignored. Of course, good intentions are no guarantee of good results, and a true utilitarian would have to embrace those good results even if they were produced by decisions and behavior commonly considered unethical or immoral. In addition, individual human rights and enduring moral principles are minimized or ignored, especially in those situations where there is no evident *positive* outcome achieved by honoring those rights or principles.

4. SPAR DIMENSIONS

a. **Substance** — Consequentialists consider humans to be creatures of pleasure and pain, because nothing matters so much in terms of motivation and value.

b. **Principles** — The basic principle: one should always seek the greatest good for the greatest number of people that are touched by this decision. The "hedonistic calculus" is also a principle.

c. **Actions** — Consequentialists especially desire purposeful actions that lead to the desired consequences.

d. **Results** — The desired results are the greatest measurable good (pleasure, benefit, happiness, advantage) and the least amount of measurable bad (pain, mischief, evil, unhappiness) for the greatest number of people touched by this decision.

5. INDIVIDUAL EXAMPLES

In addition to Bentham, many other articulate thinkers have been drawn by the seeming simplicity and objectivity of consequentialist moral reasoning. Of these, John Stuart Mill (1806–1873 A.D.), British government officer and philosopher, and William James (1842–1910 A.D.), American psychologist and philosopher, are especially well-known thinkers that have both defended and further shaped consequentialist perspectives.

John Stuart Mill's father, James Mill, was a devoted follower of Bentham, serving him as publicist and personal assistant. James Mill was so committed to consequentialist thinking that he home-schooled his son in order to protect him from other influences. He started him on Greek when the son was three years old, and Latin when he was eight. He guided him through the Greek and Latin classics as a child, but the underlying perspective for interpreting and understanding everything was Bentham's analytical, results-oriented perspective. Every decision was to be critiqued in terms of measurable consequences. As a result, as a teenager J.S. Mill was a talented and gifted promoter of the consequentialist cause.

However, when he was 20 years old, the young Mill hit a terrible crisis, becoming intensely depressed for months, because the constant quantifying of every result had severely drained his personal capacity for emotion and for other qualitative aspects of life. He had lost the capacity to care for anything at all. Paradoxically, an analytic focus on maximizing results had the consequence of the worst results. When Mill recovered, he composed a far more subtle and *qualitative* consequentialist perspective. Of course, having allowed qualitative judgments, Mill's consequentialism lost most of the elegant simplicity and mathematical precision of Bentham's perspective. The "risk" in valuing qualitative personal judgments is that the deep human respect for divine commands, virtues of character, natural laws, enduring moral principles, and human rights can "sneak into" one's decision-making as qualititive issues — without having to pass through the precise analytical or mathematical filter of Bentham's moral reasoning.

American psychologist **William James** was moved by the example of John Stuart Mill. He recognized Mill as someone who sought to blend mathematical and scientific insights into complex human concerns without eviscerating qualitative thoughts and decisions. James sought to further expand Mill's perspective by evaluating one's choices for belief — including religious belief and political belief — in terms of consequences as well. For example, he argued that there is no objective proof of God's existence, but that it is still a good idea to believe in God because of the real and potential positive consequences. Ultimately, he reasoned, religious faith and following divine commands can make an individual happy and provide a basis for personal purpose and hope. Similarly, James could justify aspects of almost any approach to moral reasoning, as long as the total result is a *happier and more meaningful* life for the individual. Such consequences were his key standard for evaluating both behavior and belief. **Even "truth" was redefined by James to be the expedient in the process of belief.**

"We shall not cease from exploration And the end of all our exploring Will be to arrive where we started And know the place for the first time."
— T.S. Eliot

6. GROUP EXAMPLES

Careful cost-benefit analyses are a standard basis for decision-making in business corporations and in government. The attempt is to **put all values into a common "currency" so that different purposes and priorities can be mathematically compared.** Bentham believed that quantities of happiness could be measured or compared in special utilitarian units. Business corporations and governments pursue their cost-benefit analyses by using the scale of standard currency, such as dollars.

One classic corporate case occurred in the late 1960s when engineers at the Ford Motor Company made an important design decision on the basis of cost-benefit analysis.

Endnote 3

THE PINTO CASE: COST OF DESIGN

Before the new compact model, the Pinto, went into production, test engineers noticed that the gas tank ruptured in every test in which the cars were hit from behind at 25 miles per hour or more. In an accident, any stray spark could ignite the gasoline and cause very serious damage to people and property. The problem was that one of the large bolts holding the back bumper in place appeared to be aimed at the gas tank, and only inches away. **A simple design change would avoid the problem, at the additional cost of $11 per vehicle for what was then a $2,000 car.**

Should the engineers institute the design change? Using utilitarian cost-benefit analysis they made this decision a problem for arithmetic. The total cost of the $11 design change for 12.5 million vehicles that the engineers predicted would be produced in this improved design would involve a total cost of $137.5 million ($11 × 12.5 million = $137.5 million). What would the benefit be? The engineers predicted that the design change would prevent 180 deaths of people, prevent another 180 serious burn injuries, and save 2100 vehicles from burning. Some "exchange rate" had to be used to translate these human benefits into dollars before the cost-benefit analysis would be complete. And the needed "exchange rate" was suggested by the United States Federal Government through its National Highway Traffic Safety Administration. In the late 1960s this bureaucracy estimated that the total social cost of a death was $200,725. The engineers further estimated that on average the value of each prevented burn injury was $67,000 — about one third of a death — and each prevented burn of a crashed vehicle was worth on average $700. The total benefit of the design change would then be 180 saved lives at $36,130,500 (180 × $200,725), 180 saved burn injuries at $12,060,000 (180 × $67,000) and 2100 unburned cars at $1,470,000 (2100 × $700) for a total benefit of $49,660,500. Using these figures the engineers chose not to make the design change.

Was this decision right or wrong? Controversy over these engineers' decision has focused on two perspectives. First, some have claimed that the Ford engineers had the right basic approach, but they simply did a poor job of applying consequentialist ideas. Some argue that their estimates of how many people would die from the less safe design were too low. Others believe the value given to each possibly saved human life should be greater than $200,725, especially considering the excruciating pain of a burn death. Still others point out that Ford engineers **neglected to calculate additional potential benefits of selecting the safer design — such as protecting Ford's *reputation, customer loyalty,* and *integrity.***

Second, others have argued that life and safety issues should not be decided with mere cost-benefit analysis alone. For example, some critics argue that it is always a mistake to put a price on human life. Additional critics allow that such cost-benefit analysis has its place, but only as a limited part of the whole picture. That is, cost-benefit analysis should be considered along side other additional moral considerations, such as divine commands, virtue-ethics of the engineers, corporate moral culture, incalculable aspects of human value, enduring moral principles, or basic human rights.

Government decisions are often approached in terms of cost-benefit analysis. A task-force may be appointed to study the particular costs and benefits of constructing a new park in one of five neighborhoods, the costs and benefits of repairing the old police station verses the costs and benefits of renting or building a new facility for the police. The school board may debate the costs and benefits of expending present schools rather than constructing an additional school building. These decisions based on costs and benefits often attract the same kinds of criticism that surround the Ford Pinto case.

7. STRENGTHS

Consequentialism has great appeal for many reasons, including these three: First, humans are purposeful beings, and we are moved by seeking to achieve goals. We are not only purposeful in selfish ways, but we also seek fruitful goals for the groups with which we are connected, including the human race itself. Consequentialism provides a useful method for being more strategic in our purposeful behavior.

Second, consequentialism embodies some of our well-deserved, modern appreciation for science and the scientific method. In this strategic approach to moral reasoning, we are equipped to consider different beliefs and behaviors, and measure the consequences. Traditions and "the way we have always done things" must stand in line with new and creative ideas to await the evaluation of their subsequent results.

Third, consequentialism suggests a scheme for simple and objective and public evaluation of decisions and choices. This method for moral reasoning seems to circumvent some of the subjectivity and fuzziness that can easily distract from other approaches. In the ideal consequentialist scheme there are no prerequisites — no faith, virtues, traditions, or rights are necessary, but simply unprejudiced, objective measurement of results.

8. WEAKNESSES

There have been numerous criticisms of consequentialism. First, one frequently stated reminder is that the "ends do not justify the means." In other words, the results are never all that matters; other things must be considered in addition to — or instead of —

consequences. The means that are used — means such as principles, nature, virtues, or divine commands — must matter some.

Second, justice and human rights are too easily compromised by a singular focus on results. For starters, promises are potentially neutralized. Other than the risk of creating bad feelings by breaking a promise, the total measurable results are all that matters. Consequently, promise-breaking could be justified rather frequently. Also, standards of justice are easily short-circuited. For example, turning over an accused murderer to an angry mob could possibly make the total happiness of the crowd so great that a consequentialist would have to justify even great pain or death inflicted on the accused. Similarly, such results-based reasoning is often used to defend laws and practices that please a majority, but are unfair to a small minority. After all, "the total happiness is what society is about," some have said.

Third, in consequentialism one cannot knowingly and with certainty make a good decision. This is a weakness of both consequentialism and egoism. On the one hand, one can at best plan and strategize for the desired results, and act accordingly, but the consequentialist evaluation of whether the decision was good must wait until the actual results are in. Even when plans are based upon careful and professional, sociological and psychological studies, mistakes can be made. On the other hand, is there anything more outside our knowledge base than the future? Even when our planning is meticulous, unforeseen factors — and perhaps unforeseeable factors — can dramatically alter actual results, for better or for worse.

"To compose our character is our duty . . . Our great and glorious masterpiece is to live appropriately. All other things, to rule, to lay up treasure, to build are at most but little appendices and props . . .
— Michel De Montaigne

9. COUNTER ARGUMENTS

Consequentialists have created numerous defenses against these criticisms, so we will consider only some of them. First, the very concept of a "mean" depends on an "end" which it serves. No "means" have value unless they at least generally benefit some "end." For example, the virtue of integrity would probably be abandoned if it led us to be unhappy all of the time. Also, people pursue love because they find it fulfilling. Moreover, would anyone treasure divine-commands unless they thought that obeying them would lead to good results, including possibly God's own praise and rewards?

Second, we do not justify treating people unfairly — even if it makes crowds of people happy — because we are rather confident that in the long run they will have serious regrets. For starters, anyone can ask, "What if I were the accused?" and then feel bad. We can also draw for history the lesson that the oppression of a minority is bound to backfire. Again, in the long run, the results demonstrate that respect for people's rights and the pursuit of justice pays back society with the best dividends.

Third, consequentialism can be consistent and honest. Thus, it is okay to admit that even with the best plans and intentions we sometimes fail. When the results turn out badly, it is better to admit mistakes than to mouth the empty rhetoric, "My decisions led to a disaster, but they were right anyway." Hiding behind a "virtuous character" or one's moral principles can be very hypocritical, when selectively ignoring the moral inadequacy of a decision.

10. SUMMARY

Consequentialism has continued to provide creative and objective standards for both planning and evaluating a wide range of individual and group decisions. It could be argued that some consideration of cost and likely success should play a role in any decision. Even courageous and heroic people do not take on just any risk; they take on challenges that seem quite worthy of the possible cost. Nevertheless, it remains true that "the ends do not justify the means;" we do not have to measure the results of each situation to know that people should be treated fairly, enduring principles should be obeyed, character matters, or divine-commands should be followed.

Promises create moral obligation. Many duties we have to other people are not based upon divine-commands, endur-

The Contractarian Approach emphasizes that all ethical obligation is based exclusively upon contracts and promises.

ing principles, or any other foundation, other than that we have actually made a commitment or promise to do something. The world of oral and written language enables us as humans to create new obligations — a distinctively human potentiality.

Inspired by this extraordinary human skill, some have suggested that all **moral obligations are essentially promises stated in contracts or agreements between people — implicit or explicit contracts, written or verbal agreements, indirect or direct, intentional or tacit.** While most people, including even egoists, give some moral value to promises and promise-keeping, **contractarians take the approach that all ethical obligation is based upon contracts and promises, and if we had no such agreements there would be no moral standards.**

1. PERSONAL BACKGROUND

It would be impossible to overestimate the significance of language to human life, as we know it. Someone has said, "Language is the house of being." The concepts supplied by language shape our individual and social "worlds" — including the worlds of *sensory perception, political decision-making and self-awareness*. What we are able to recognize and deal with depends entirely on the resources of language, so that new things that we encounter must be named, in some way.

It is no wonder, then, that so much of moral teaching is found in words. Personal examples are important, too, but even then the desirable behavior can be described. Within this encompassing environment of words, moral obligations often sound like agreements, *whether the contract language is metaphoric or literal*. Even though it is important to distinguish legal duties from moral duties, as we did in Chapter 1, the language of contracts and agreements has been used for centuries to articulate moral duties. In fact, what is literal and what is metaphoric may be hard to distinguish. For example, Socrates refused to accept release from prison and freedom in another city, even though his "criminal" conviction was grossly unjust, he merely awaited the execution of his death penalty, and his friends had already sufficiently bribed the jailer to let him go free. He refused release because he said he had accepted an agreement with the City of Athens to obey its leadership and laws, however, unjust, in order to live a meaningful life in Athens, enjoying its many benefits. Should Socrates have considered that agreement literal or metaphorical? Should this "social contract" be binding or negotiable?

Many authors have developed contractarian approaches to moral reasoning that treat the social contract as more than a literary metaphor. Especially prominent are modern thinkers like Thomas Hobbes, John Locke, and Jean-Jacques Rousseau. Contemporary social and political philosopher ***John Rawls*** (1921– A.D.) has probably developed this contractarian approach to moral reasoning the furthest.

According to Rawls, in his search for the proper and common understanding of fairness, the best model of ethical thinking is an open rational discussion among all parties concerned to reach an ideal, perfect and fair contract, if possible. What helps to define such an open, rational discussion? First, people should be able, ideally, to identify a set of fair and just moral standards without making any reference to their personal stakes. Rawls would have us remove prejudices that come from the personal cost or potential benefit that could ensue for each party to the contract. For example, people should be able to resolve a property dispute fairly without any reference to identifying whether they themselves are the plaintiffs or defendants. In a similar way we can also agree on the ultimate principles of justice, which he defines as fair-

Endnote 4

ness. **This conscious exclusion of personal identification Rawls calls the "veil of ignorance."** By excluding from the discussions of justice and morality the details of personal daily life, Rawls hopes to focus attention especially on the primary principles of value. In this way he attempts to draw on some of the strengths of *deontological* approaches to moral reasoning.

Second, he believes that this formative discussion is best understood and most fairly pursued when we negotiate in an environment of both *total equality and skilled reasoning capacity*. We can then give full attention to the broad and perhaps universal human desires and needs. In this respect, Rawls may be attempting to draw on a few of the strengths of the natural law approaches to moral reasoning.

Would Kant be comfortable with the Rawls 'veil of ignorance'?

Third, this model of moral analysis requires what Rawls calls a *reflective equilibrium*. Nothing should be set in cement, as the saying goes, including moral judgments. Any moral principle or judgment can be applied and examined in real life experiences, and then evaluated and adjusted before it is applied again. As legal contracts can be renegotiated, so the moral-social contract should be written and rewritten over and over again, according to Rawls. The net result is an "equilibrium" between the composition of just and fair moral principles on the one hand, and the understanding of the resulting consequences of applying those principles in the real world on the other hand. This *reflective equilibrium* is Rawls' attempt to draw on some of the consequentialist concerns.

2. HISTORIC BACKGROUND

From the most ancient times, there were frequent covenants and contracts among individual people, their gods and each other, to define responsibilities and rights. When people have solved problems, they have sought to make their agreements explicit, whether these are business contracts or peace treaties. In fact, when people begin a new project, they find it not only useful but also necessary to state concretely their purposes, responsibilities, and the methods

Figure 2. The Magna Carta, 1215, presaged American freedoms. Archive Photos/Carlin.

they will use to work together. Contracts are especially useful for providing legal protections for moral promises — at least from the time of the Magna Carta to the latest business incorporation papers.

Early United States history can be written in terms of the various contracts, including the Mayflower Compact, several colonial charters and constitutions, the Declaration of Independence, Articles of Confederation, and the Constitution. Today every corporation has a contract called the articles of incorporation that permits it to do business under certain circumstances. Non-profit corporations and professional associations also have articles of incorporation, constitutions or charters.

Even the catalogue of a college is considered a contract between the institution and the students, specifying their respective duties. Similarly, in most forms of employment the employees and managers sign contracts that designate everyone's key responsibilities. Even closer to "home," no one gets married without saying "I do" to a series of essential promises. It seems that virtually everything we do as individuals, families, groups, business, or government is evaluated in the context of one or more contracts.

3. HOW DOES THIS WORLDVIEW AFFECT PERCEPTION?

   a. Focus: From the contractarian perspective, the actual wording of agreements and their interpretation is especially important. Since all duties have their basis in contracts, implicit or explicit, attention is focused on clarification of those contracts. Also, since these contracts are made with other people and require their agreement and cooperation, it is essential to listen carefully for others' needs and desires, whether they are primarily leaders or followers.

   b. Blind spots: With contracts at the center, other resources for moral reasoning are either treated as less important or ignored. For example, as we observed with Rawls, moral principles, natural-law, and consequences can have their place in the creation, evaluation, and improvement of the social contract. However, modern contractarian thought gives little or no place to divine-command thinking, or to character and virtue-ethics, because the primary focus is upon reasonable and enforceable agreements between people.

4. SPAR DIMENSIONS

   a. Substance — The contractarian sees people as social problem-solvers — rational, reliable, reflective negotiators.

b. Principles — The ultimate principle is to develop principles and rules and relationships that all can affirm. For Rawls those principles will include the "equal liberty" principle, the "equal opportunity" principle, and the "difference principle." (See below.)

c. Actions — Ideal contractarian actions conform to the agreed upon duties, responsibilities, and behaviors.

d. Results — Individuals and groups should achieve the results for which they entered into the contracts. Moreover, no contract changes should be made unless they are to the benefit of the worst off. Finally, the ultimate purpose of composing and refining contracts is the development of fair relationships and a just society.

5. Individual Examples

The contract process is intriguing. Can a consensus be created for essential moral principles? Rawls draws out three core ethical principles that he is confident rational people, behind the "veil of ignorance," in a state of "natural equality" would define over a process of "reflective equilibrium." The primary one is the **"equal liberty" principle: Each individual is to have a right to the greatest equal liberty compatible with a like liberty for all.**

However, society is bound to have inequalities, so that the second principle protects the **"equal opportunity" principle: Social and economic inequalities are to be attached to offices and positions open to all under conditions of fair equality of opportunity.** However, inequality should be seen as unnatural, and only rare inequalities can be justified at all. For this reason Rawls defended the **"difference" principle: Inequalities are justified only if they *benefit the worst off*.** This latter principle can be seen in the U.S. Supreme Court's struggle with affirmative action employment regulations of the federal government. In particular, to try to rectify years of discrimination that have hurt a minority group, how much affirmative action can be justified before it becomes unfair to the majority?

Business consultants, labor-management negotiators, marriage counselors, and other professions specialize in helping people to listen to one another, and then to come to workable and fair agreements. Real estate and automobile sales people are also supposed to serve their customers in achieving fair purchasing contracts, although they frequently serve primarily the seller's interests. Contracts of various sorts are an essential part of the modern moral landscape, whether they are explicit or implicit. It is reasonable to use them as a crucial tool in the moral reasoning process.

6. GROUP EXAMPLES

Without a doubt, the process of debating, shaping, making, and revising contracts to make them fair is one of the most important activities that goes on in modern society. Much of newspaper coverage concerns local government agreements, congressional debates, legal clashes, business purchases, corporate mergers, cooperative church efforts, club and association activities — all of which involve contracts.

Are we a litigious society because we have so many contracts, or do we rely more and more on contracts because we are a litigious society?

In addition, the news often includes protests against laws that some people think are unfair, as well as lawsuits against unjust prices or unsafe products, pressures to change health insurance regulations, and other efforts for reform — all of which require contract revision. In fact, one of the reasons that the United States has such a disproportionately high percentage of lawyers compared with other nations — for better or for worse — is that so many of our relationships and responsibilities are defined by implicit or explicit contracts. While there seems to be safety and precision in contracts, "misunderstandings" still abound. In the meantime, in most other societies there is a much greater reliance upon trusting human relationships and upon an individual's moral virtues, and less confidence in contracts.

7. STRENGTHS

Negotiating agreements and spelling out some of the details in contracts is a wonderful human enterprise, and a valuable model for ethics. First, because so much of moral reasoning depends upon cooperative efforts with others, contracts are a handy tool for articulating a conception of ethical thought. Second, for people who do not believe in divine-command, or for those for whom virtue-ethics and natural-law seem weak, or for those who otherwise have unclear ethical principles and moral goals, the search for fairness within contracts provides a concrete basis for moral responsibility. Finally, the very process of negotiating agreements can help build other valuable moral resources — such as broad consensus for a way of doing things, at least among those who "sign on" to the "contract," and also a level of precision in defining what is acceptable and ethical behavior.

8. WEAKNESSES

However, there are at least three weaknesses. First, the very process of negotiating, writing, and signing contracts presumes already a level of moral reasoning that the contracts themselves cannot create. Contracts seem to be useful tools for resolving moral issues, but there needs to be non-contractarian standards by which the contracts themselves are *fairly written and enforced*. To appeal ultimately to something else — divine-commands, virtues, natural-laws, deontological principles, or consequences — would make contractarianism merely a branch of the corresponding theory.

Second, contracts only seem to be a concrete basis for ethics, while in fact they are often caught up in fictitious worlds. For example, very frequently a person's real job has very little to do with the duties spelled out in a contract, so that an alert person has to deal with both the business reality and legal unreality. Also, the Constitution and laws of the United States may have relatively little to do with the way decisions are made, even in the Supreme Court. People who seem to give small regard to what it actually says make decisions and policies in the name of the Constitution. Furthermore, Rawls' theory itself relies on such fictions as the "veil of ignorance," which seems to establish an unrealistic starting point for moral reasoning.

Third, contracts themselves are too enticing a model because of their seeming consensus building, objectivity, and precision. However, they lack essential qualities for an approach to moral reasoning. Because contracts can be broken or renegotiated, there is a lack of stability where enduring guidance is needed. Also, contracts are often culturally biased, and they can lead to the justification of grossly unfair policies. For example, the original United States Constitution denied women the right to vote and treated African-Americans as less than human. Clearly, as contracts are negotiated, people can be pushed into immoral compromises and prejudice that they would not otherwise allow. A contract has moral value only if its ethical quality is brought from some other source — such as the moral goals that are achieved or the moral character of those who implement agreements. By themselves contracts are very much like computers: garbage in, garbage out.

9. COUNTER ARGUMENTS

Contractarian thinkers have responses to these criticisms. First, contracts may very well rely on other moral resources — such as virtue-ethics and divine-command, but it is the contract that brings these pieces together and gives them their moral framework. Second, contractarianism does rely on some fictions, like "original equality" and the "veil of ignorance," but these fictions are useful tools to uncover what factually makes human life and society work and work fairly. Third, the flaws of contracts are simply explicit reminders of well-known human conditions — depravity, prejudice, immoral compromises. Contracts not only help make these problems more explicit and clear, they also provide a framework for discovering and designing *resolutions* for these problems. After all, our goal usually is not a holy grail, merely a good approach to moral reasoning.

10. SUMMARY

Contractarianism has offered a useful and powerful model for moral resolution. However, those who participate in discovering and designing the appropriate content of contracts — and their enforcement — will continue to need to look beyond their contracts to other resources for moral reasoning.

 The Natural-Rights Approach emphasizes the exclusive protection of and reliance upon common human personal rights.

The final contemporary perspective we are examining is the **"natural-rights"** approach to moral reasoning. In many respects this theory resembles the "natural-law" approach, as the similarity of their names suggests. Both look to objective aspects of nature — especially human nature — as the basis for ethical value and decision-making. However, there are differences.

First, in a way of speaking, natural-law emphasizes duty. But in **the *natural-rights approach* emphasizes, not the burden of people's duties but the protection of and reliance upon common, human, personal rights.** Of course, duties and rights are often correlated, as many have pointed out. For example, for the very reason that every person has the *duty* to avoid evil, as Aquinas said, others have the *right* not to have evil done to them. The point is the same, although the perspective has changed: "monitor your own behavior" is a theme in natural-law, while "respect others" is a theme in the natural-rights perspective. By the way, this correlation between duties and rights is not complete, because not every duty involves a corresponding right.

Second, the natural-rights approach to moral reasoning is especially focused upon **human interests,** especially **those interests that are so important that they impose duties upon others — at least duties not to damage those interests.** It takes the constructive approach of elevating those valuable interests in the context of people's consciousness and conduct, and instructing people to *act* out of respect for those rights. In contrast, natural-law relies more upon the *language* of responsibility.

Third, although natural-rights thinking was initially based upon divine-command and natural-law theories, defenders of natural-rights rarely appeal to either one now. Instead they appeal to people's intuitions concerning the immense value of every human being. In addition, they also appeal to the practical need to have some generic reference point to counter-balance extraordinary concentrations of political and military power that have become commonplace in the contemporary world. Natural-rights seem more acceptable to secular thinking than the religious sounding divine-commands, or the quasi-religious sounding natural-law.

A different comparison may be helpful: Egoism is also about rights, but there are substantial distinctions. Egoism insists on the individual's rights to do as he or she pleases, but the natural-rights approach emphasizes respect for others' choices. Also, egoism seeks to defend maximum rights for an individual, while the natural-rights perspective seeks to discover and protect basic equal rights for every person.

1. PERSONAL BACKGROUND

The English philosopher whose thinking most influenced Thomas Jefferson and the American Revolution was **John Locke** (1632–1704 A.D.), a medical doctor whose brilliant and creative mind helped focus people's attention on individual human-rights both in England, in English North American Colonies, and elsewhere. Locke himself was a political activist in addition to being a physician and philosopher. His natural-rights ideas were the foundation for England's Glorious Revolution of 1688, when the constitutional monarchy was instituted and William and Mary were elevated as the new king and queen. Locke himself was given the honor of escorting the new Queen Mary from the Netherlands to England. While Locke's ideas are firmly based in both divine-command thinking and natural-law theory, his strong defenses of basic human natural rights — such as life, liberty, and property — are often quoted and utilized by themselves.

Rev. Michael King, Sr. was so deeply inspired by the story of Martin Luther (1483–1546 A.D.), the courageous, German reformer, that he decided to change his legal name, and the legal name of his 6-year-old son, to Martin Luther King. This same father instilled in his son the courage to respect his own human dignity, in a community where fellow African-Americans were often disrespected by others.

His son, Martin Luther King, Jr. (1929–1968 A.D.) came to understand that the human right to such respect was based upon divine-commands, especially in the teachings of the Bible. He saw these rights supported also in natural-law teachings concerning the duty of human respect, and in the social "contracts" that apply to all Americans, such as the **Declaration of Independence.** Dr. King became one of the foremost forces for change to make human rights more a concern for moral and legal protection in the United States, as well as in the many other countries where his extraordinary influence has been felt. While Dr. King based his own thinking upon divine-commands, quotations from his articulate defenses of human natural-rights have a broad appeal, even to secular minds.

Endnote 5

"Be the change you want to see in the world."
— Mahatma Gandhi

2. HISTORIC BACKGROUND

While human rights have been a moral issue for centuries, the moral perspective of natural-rights developed especially during the twentieth century. Three factors contributed to this development. First, in spite of modern advances in science, general human respect for one another did not advance. In fact, new scientific information became the basis for more technologically advanced methods of warfare and torture. As a result, the twentieth century was in some ways the most violent century of human history. For example, although great scientific discoveries were made to heal people, political leaders killed millions: Hitler incinerated more than 6-million persons; Stalin ordered 6-million Ukranians starved to death and killed another 12-million in pogroms; Mao Tse-Tung murdered more than 26-million in his rise to power in China; and Uganda's Idi Amin "merely" killed 1-million in his reign of terror in that tiny nation. So twentieth-century thinkers are attracted to the natural-rights approach as a method to reduce the violence.

Second, contemporary discoveries in the sciences have helped people to be aware of how remarkable and significant human being are — in physical, mental, emotional, creative, and spiritual dimensions. Awe and respect for humanity have found ever more meaningful data to defend its perspective.

Third, the sciences have also increased human choices. Patient rights have become an issue because of a multiplication of health resources. Also, the rights of people affected by pollution have become a concern because of both the increase in our knowledge of the harmful affects of various pollutants, and because contemporary science has opened the door to new types of industry.

Fourth, modern communication has made the reality of terrible abuse to humans a vivid part of the instant, full-color, radio, television, and Internet reporting. Aware of the great abuse of many people's basic rights, the special focus on natural human rights makes all the more sense as a corrective. Moreover, the stunning failures of totalitarian communism, especially in terms of tragic harms to human welfare, have also increased people's interest in the basic natural-rights that are at the foundation of western democracy. People want to understand and affirm those rights, sometimes without knowledge or regard for the context in which they were discovered and defended. For example, some people long for the "unalienable rights" of life, liberty, and the pursuit of happiness, without necessarily affirming the Constitution's claim that these rights were "endowed by their Creator."

Sometimes we think of rights in terms of the employee rights in a particular company, based on the contracts employees have with the management. There are also patient rights that hospitals might post on a plaque on the wall. These are generally not natural-rights but contractual-rights that are special to particular circumstances. The moral reasoning behind these fits contractualism best.

3. How Does This Worldview Affect Perception?

    a. Focus: Unique qualities of human nature are especially recognized, and the ways people are treated in different environments and political systems are given special attention. Specific human interests are identified, as well as ways for individuals and societies to show respect to all people.

    b. Blind spots: For better or for worse, the costs of showing such respect are minimized in favor of the ultimate value of the basic human natural-rights which all people have. Objective human differences are also depreciated in comparison to the importance of the generic human rights.

4. SPAR Dimensions

    a. Substance — Natural-rights approach treats people as inherently valuable and worthy of respect.

    b. Principles — The over-arching principle is that the elementary human rights must always be protected for all human beings.

    c. Actions — Ideal actions protect and respect the rights of all humans, and particularly cause no harm.

    d. Results — The goal is a society — and a world community — where people are truly respectful of all other people and their natural-rights.

5. Individual Examples

The work of **Dr. Martin Luther King, Jr.** has been an inspiration for the contemporary focus on natural-rights, and he is sometimes used as an example. However, he had a more complete approach to moral reasoning, integrating crucial aspects of divine-command, virtues-ethics, natural-law, deontologism, consequentialism, and contractarianism. Often he is made to seem as simply a natural-rights advocate when reputable publishers edit the theological references out of his speeches and articles.

A more profound example of natural-rights thinking is **Ronald Dworkin** (1931 – A.D.), an American philosopher who has taught jurisprudence at Oxford. In his book *Taking Rights Seriously* (1977) he argues that the primary basis for moral thinking for individuals and societies should be natural-rights rather than collective goals (consequentialism) or duties (deontologism). Dworkin believes that the most important priority for modern society should be everyone's right to equality of concern and respect.

6. GROUP EXAMPLES

The Declaration of Independence includes some reference to natural-law. It is probably best understood as a document in the divine-command tradition, because of its orientation to a "Divine Providence," and because the natural-rights perspective did not have much of an audience at that time. The U.S. Constitution, however, is a secular document. Clearly, natural-rights values helped shape the Constitution and the *Bill of Rights*. Another example, Amendment 14, requires that no state "shall deprive any person of life, liberty, or property without due process of law . . . "

The ***United Nations' Universal Declaration of Human Rights*** is another example. Here the primary focus is on natural-rights rather than on the divine or natural-law resources. [We will read and examine this Declaration in Chapter 15.] What is the foundation of the United Nations effort? According to the preamble of the *United Nations Charter,* the organization is based on "faith in fundamental human rights, in the dignity and worth of the human person, in the equal rights of men and women and of nations large and small." The entire project of the United Nations can probably be understood in defense of natural rights, although traces of Judaism and Christianity may be reflected.

7. STRENGTHS

Human rights are a key issue for anyone seeking to survive and thrive in the contemporary world. No one could make enemies defending everyone's basic rights, and paving the way for everyone to receive respect. Besides, this puts a positive focus on the goal of world cooperation. People and nations can work together for human betterment, in addition to stopping the violence.

8. WEAKNESSES

Unfortunately, the world is not simple enough for this approach to work consistently. For one thing, there are competing rights. Two people or two nations can claim the same property and have equally cogent arguments. Someone's right to that property will have to be compromised. For another thing, it is questionable whether a commitment to human natural-rights can sustain its position in the face of the increasing forces of racism and nationalism, unless there is a deeper moral or spiritual understanding to undergird this theory.

9. COUNTER ARGUMENTS

Defenders of natural-rights remind us that all approaches to moral reasoning have to face the challenge of resolving internal conflicts and dilemmas. There are competing claims to people's rights, but there are also competing claims for maximizing results — dilemmas when two moral principles collide. Moreover, even though deep spiritual resources are needed to consistently respect the rights of all humans, each person can find those resources in his or her own conscience and background, while everyone still works together for the natural-rights of all people.

10. SUMMARY

The contemporary world has been shaped especially by the results of violence and disrespect for fellow humans. One cannot work for improvement of our world without giving significant attention to the natural-rights of every human being — child or adult, man or woman. For example, regardless of whether we meet them or not, how does our pollution affect them or their pollution affect us? However, lecturing people on the rights of others does not seem to have much effect on behavior. The resources of other approaches to moral reasoning may be essential for the effective strengthening of the natural-rights perspective.

THE BIG PICTURE

We have now completed our "road tour" of eight approaches to moral reasoning. Although we have devoted only a relatively short amount of time to visit each approach, you should now have some understanding of the perspective each brings.

However, "some understanding" is never the whole picture. To do justice to any of these approaches, a person should at least study some of the primary sources written by the main thinkers and authors. In some ways we have been like tourists in another country or on another continent. Sometimes, for some of us, the language has been familiar, but at other times both the language and customs of some of the approaches to moral reasoning have seemed foreign. In either case, these visits were not long enough for us to become experts. Of course, some places are wonderful to visit, although you would not want to live there — or even stay very long. The same is true of some ethical approaches.

Of necessity, therefore, your understanding of each of these views is at least a bit oversimplified. We have represented each of these views carefully and cogently, so that you should understand the basic ideas, and at the same time you should feel some of their attraction. In developing each of these approaches many people have given a tremendous amount of attention and time, and fellow humans have tried to use these insights in their own decisions.

Now that this part of the road tour is over, please review where we have been. Look again at the eight different perspectives, making note of the strengths or weaknesses you see in each one. To organize your own worldview, please prepare a chart composed of the elements you value most. As a sample of some of the dimensions of these approaches, consider this simple overview:

THE BIG PICTURE
A COMPARISON OF APPROACHES TO MORAL REASONING

Approach:

Thinkers	Substance of the Person	Principles that Matter	Actions that Fit the Model	Results that Are Sought
1. Egoism	Center of power; Exploiter.	Make your own decisions; Be authentic.	Self-centered; Individuality or fear of punishment.	Personal authenticity and freedom.
2. Divine Command	Person endowed by the Creator with a purpose.	Fulfill the intentions and commands of the Creator.	Creator-centered; Obedience and honor for the Deity.	Positive relationship and peace with the Creator.
3. Virtues	Individual with developing habits and personality.	Cultivate behaviors that improve human flourishing.	Concordant with intended and helpful habits.	Healthy, balanced, and flourishing character.
4. Natural Law	Personality with built-in needs, instincts, and goals.	Live harmoniously with your true essence.	Expressive of the natural qualities and needs.	Fulfillment of intrinsic patterns and potential.
5. Deontologism	Law maker and law follower.	Follow (deductively) the imperatives that you accept.	Consistent with selected general imperatives.	A good will, one that acts according to chosen principles.
6. Consequentialism	Maximizer of good consequences, and minimizer of bad.	Produce the greatest happiness of the greatest number.	Prudent and mindful of probable good consequences.	Maximum benefit to the most people that are involved.
7. Contractarianism	Rational, reliable and reflective negotiator.	Develop rules and relationships that all can affirm.	Conforming with agreed interests and rules.	Self-adjusting group of rational rule followers.
8. Natural Right	Somebody worthy of protection and respect.	Never harm the rights of any person involved.	Responsible, protective, and thoughtful.	Complete protection of every person involved.
9. Creative/ Composite	Sensitive, informed, adaptable, creative, rational decision-maker.	Select outstanding insights and blend them into a coherent perspective and commitment.	Perceptive, just, loving, flexible, consistent, sagacious action.	Attentive, fair, caring, and responsible people and community.
10. My Worldview				

As you consider the eight approaches, note the fact that you do not need to choose among these, or to choose between any other set of pre-defined approaches. One of the extraordinary capacities of rational human beings is our ability to *learn, adapt, blend, and create.* For starters, then, each of these approaches is adaptable to your moral needs and priorities as you understand them. Consider also the fact that each of these approaches may emphasize diverse strengths — *some or all of which* are in the range of your own perception and capability, and touch your own humanity.

It would be unfortunate and unnecessary to think that *if* a person were to choose only one of these eight classic approaches, the evident positive insights of the others must be ignored. No one should be required to wear blinders. Also, be aware that all theories have their potential distortions. They are all partial pictures, at best. Even in some of the very wisest human perceptions, something valuable may be missing. That may simply be a fact of human life, whether we like it or not.

Moreover, it is certainly safe to say that some of the truly great moral leaders were not defined by theories. We have already seen this approach of composed perspectives in the examples of Thomas Aquinas, Thomas Jefferson, and Dr. Martin Luther King, Jr. These and others have affirmed a multitude of relevant values as part of the human experience, as part of what makes human decisions good, right, and responsible. Perhaps many moral leaders come to mind, but these great ones in particular defy *precise* labeling.

PERSON	CULTURE
Moses	Middle-eastern
Jesus	Middle-eastern
Augustine	African
Adam Smith	European
Martin Luther King, Jr.	African-American
Gandhi	Asian
Mother Theresa	Asian
Orlando Costas	South-American
Desmond Tutu	African

There is no reason to think that these and other great moral teachers actually did or did not draw from any or all of the eight classic perspectives. Along the way, in their lives they were each certainly exposed to representatives of some of these approaches to ethical reasoning. However, *they were not the kinds of people that could be put into the existing moral boxes* — even spacious and luxurious moral boxes. In short, they had *additional resources that enabled them to see life and its problems from an even more informed and creative perspective.*

Perhaps some of the deeper human resources that these exemplary ones used are broadly available to many or most other humans as well. Therefore, even if you have already decided that one of the eight classic approaches is itself complete and sufficient for your moral reasoning and behavior, it is useful to try to learn from other perspectives.

To do so, you might want to be "cunning." *Cunning* people know their way out of the box, and out of even the nicest "house" of pure theory. They are *creative* and have the ability to *compose* perspective, but not out of some empty claim that values are relative and merely a matter of choice. Rather, they know that *human ethical life is vital, complex and spiritual, and therefore no single human moral theory can quite contain it.* This model of cunning harmlessness was advocated by Jesus of Nazareth. Regardless of religious views about him, he is universally recognized as a great moral teacher. One of the devices he suggested was called "cunning" or "shrewdness." One example: "Be cunning as a snake while you are harmless as a dove." What is required for cunning behavior is not just logic and education, but the ability to select from a big toolbox of different and nuanced logics, multifaceted information, and broad perspective the tools that are most appropriate and useful for each responsibility.

George W. F. Hegel (1770–1831 A.D.) developed a whole theory based on the "cunning of reason." To him we make real progress only when we can merge the best insight of seemingly contrary views. Then we can compose a perspective that has integrity. Dr. Martin Luther King also noticed this cunning aspect of Jesus' teaching, and made it the first lesson of one of his greatest books, *Strength to Love*.

We have been talking about "approaches to moral reasoning," but cunning is more than reasoning. It is *reasoning with an attitude*, reasoning that makes a difference. What attitude? Hopefully in ethics it is **the attitude of discovering and doing what provides for the most attentive, fair, caring, and responsible behavior and character.**

As we have earlier noted, ***Dr. Martin Luther King, Jr.*** himself merged ideas from different moral perspectives — primarily divine-command and natural-law theories. He was especially well-equipped to do this because of his literate background, extraordinary intelligence, superior education, deep passion to make a difference, humility to always learn and grow, and a sincere awareness of his limits in the presence of an infinite God. His leadership was much richer and deeper — much more spiritual and skillful — than he is represented in history books. In particular, it is a caricature of him merely to be portrayed as a political reformer or as a protester. He was so much more. An examination of his published books, articles, and speeches could produce a wealth of comparisons. Consider, for example, the following chart of some of his moral advice:

> *"Human ethical life is so vital, complex and spiritual, that no single moral theory can quite contain it."*
> — Paul de Vries

Endnote 6

Figure 3. Civil rights activist, Martin Luther King, Jr. in Montgomery, Alabama, 1965. UPI/Corbis-Bettmann.

INTEGRATED WORLDVIEW

Dr. Martin Luther King, Jr.	
1. Egoism	"Any true alliance is based upon some self-interest of each component group and a common interest into which they merge. For an alliance to have permanence and loyal commitment from its various elements, each of them must have a goal from which it benefits and none must have an outlook in basic conflict with the others"(*Testament of Hope*, page 309)
2. Divine Command	Dr. King probably never spoke or wrote without quoting the Bible. He also referred to God's authority rather often . . . "God is interested in the freedom of the whole human race and in the creation of a society where all men can live together as brothers, where every man will respect the dignity and the worth of human personality." (*Testament of Hope*, p. 215)
3. Virtue-ethics	"[The method of nonviolence] not only avoids external physical violence, but also internal violence of spirit. At the center of nonviolence stands the principle of love. In struggling for human dignity the oppressed people of the world must not succumb to the temptation of becoming bitter . . . " (*Testament of Hope*, p. 87)
4. Natural-Law	" . . . let us remember that there is a creative force in this universe, working to pull down the gigantic mountains of evil, a power that is able to make a way out of no way and transform dark yesterdays into bright tomorrows. Let us realize the arc of the moral universe is long but it bends toward justice." (*Testament of Hope*, p. 252)
5. Deontologism	" . . . nonviolent resistance breaks with communism and with all those systems which argue that the end justifies the means, because we realize that the end is preexistent in the means. In the long run of history, destructive means cannot bring about constructive ends." (*Testament of Hope*, p. 214)
6. Consequentialism	"And when we allow freedom to ring . . . we will be able to speed up that day when all of God's children — black and white men, Jews and Gentiles, Catholics and Protestants — will be able to join hands and to sing in the words of the old Negro spiritual, "Free At Last," free at last: thank God Almighty, we are free at last'." (*Testament of Hope*, p. 220)
7. Contractarianism	"So we've come here today to dramatize a shameful condition. In a sense we've come to our nation's capital to cash a check. When the architects of our republic wrote the magnificent words of the Constitution and the Declaration of Independence, they were signing a promissory note to which every American was to fall heir." (*Testament of Hope*, p. 217)
8. Natural-Rights	[Continuing from the previous quotation . . .] "This note was the promise that all men, yes, black men as well as white men, would be guaranteed the unalienable rights of life, liberty, and the pursuit of happiness." (*Testament of Hope*, p. 217)
9. Composition perspectives	". . . nonviolent resistance . . . combines being toughminded and tenderhearted and avoids the complacency and apathy of the softminded and the violence and bitterness of the hardhearted." (*Strength to Love*, p. 19)

Endnote 7

DISCOVERIES, DILEMMAS, DEVELOPMENT

Keep in mind that there are two sides to developing one's own ethic — the discovery side and the decision side. The field of ethics includes much that must be discovered. Depending on the point of view, some or all of the following must be discovered or learned: self-interests, divine commands, virtues, natural laws, enduring principles, efficient means to consequences, negotiation points, and natural rights. One cannot simply invent ethics; there are objective patterns and concepts that can and will guide us.

Nevertheless, decision is still an important mode of ethics acquisition. While a command, virtue, behavior, principle, or result may be ethically right, it may still have very little effect on our lives unless we actively choose it. Some level of choice and commitment is necessary for one's moral development, and so mere discovery is not enough. How does the commitment develop? From where does the passion come?

Personal commitment and passion sometimes increase as we work honestly with difficult moral dilemmas, such as the need to choose the lesser of two "evils." Should we save money and buy clothes that were made in sweatshops, or should we pay higher prices to protest these slave-labor arrangements? Should we vote for politician A, who is moral but incompetent, or for politician B, who is a very capable crook? Should we do the difficult research and writing that the professor asked us to do for a term paper, or should we pay a small price and buy a term paper on the internet?

Such dilemmas help remind us that good morals may be costly, and doing the right thing takes commitment.

Commitment and passion also grow through personal moral development — especially in the four dimensions of moral development outlined in Chapter 2. To make good decisions we still must become the right kinds of people who are at least aware, fair, caring, and accountable.

SOME USEFUL DISTINCTIONS

In the context of developing our moral commitments, some distinctions are very useful. Consider the following:

Private vs. Secret: No values are completely private, since they necessarily affect our behavior. We can, however, keep secrets in some circumstances; especially if the values we hold are either rejected or attacked by others.

Ambiguity vs. Neutrality: There are many ambiguous elements to ethical decision-making. Some rules are not clear, and the process of acquiring virtues is slow. Besides, there are moral dilemmas that cannot be easily decided. Nevertheless, neutrality is ultimately impossible, since one must act, decisions need to be made, and sometimes sides must be chosen.

Sincerity vs. Cement: We would hope to sincerely pursue the highest and best goals, virtues, and principles that we can. However, cement is a dangerous home. We should rarely fix our feet in concrete on any issue. We still have much to learn.

Discipline vs. Dogmatism: Any study takes discipline. Critical thinking presumes discipline. Learning moral virtues and principles takes discipline. In fact, many focused learning processes are called disciplines. However, none of this requires the pushy or inflexible mentality of dogmatism. Discipline enables one to be spontaneous — as in mastering a musical instrument or the skills of drama or of a sport. However, dogmatism kills spontaneity.

PUTTING THE MORAL PIECES TOGETHER

No one can study the five classical approaches and the three contemporary approaches to moral reasoning without finding something good in at least two or more approaches. It would be very difficult for an informed person to limit his or her moral reasoning to the *substance, principles, actions, and results* as interpreted by just one of these eight influential approaches. Some composition of diverse parts is necessary for most of us.

What is called for is a creative composition of these diverse ideas into a coherent big picture. A mere mindless mix of positive ideas may sound fine for a Halloween bag of candy, but it is disaster for morality. Because each of us is one person, with one life, one heart, and one brain, we seek to develop moral perspectives that provide us with true and lasting syntheses. In short, we all desire syntheses that are coherent enough for us to pursue and for others to understand. Some of the most important moral exemplars in history have ultimately composed coherent syntheses of two or more approaches. Nevertheless, they have held to themes that have been unifying threads that made their syntheses possible.

Now look again at the different approaches and use your rational and your "cunning" mind to create your own composite worldview. We advocate no particular view or the dominance of any particular approach. The challenge is yours: Act according to what seems most true to you. It may meet the most needs of your life, seem most suitable to you, work best for you alone, work best for you with yourself and others, most help you as you are discovering moral purpose, meaning and ethical applications on your life's journey!

Why not take a few minutes to sketch out what you have discovered to be priorities for moral reasoning and ethical decision-making. Would you say something that would be comparable to some or all of the eight classic and contemporary approaches? Why or why not?

Could you include some positive key insights that you can glean from each of the eight approaches we have now examined?

A mere mindless mix of positive ideas may sound fine for a Halloween bag of candy, but it is disaster for morality. Because each of us is one person, with one life, one heart, and one brain, we seek to develop moral perspectives that provide us with true and lasting syntheses.

INTEGRATED PERSON:
YOU

1. Egoism	
2. Divine Command	
3. Virtue-Ethics	
4. Natural-Law	
5. Denontologism	
6. Consequentialism	
7. Contractarianism	
8. Natural-Rights	
9. Other Approaches	

FINAL COMMENTS

When an electrical appliance is broken, it is wise to turn it off and unplug it before you start opening it up and replacing parts. When a car needs repair, we pull it off the highway and turn it off first. Repairs in our own lives are a little more complicated. Once in a while it might be advised to take time off, reflect on events, revisit our dreams, reconsider our priorities, reformulate our values.

However, some crises in the ethics environment cannot wait for vacation time. Reevaluation of our values may be necessary in the middle of intense personal responsibility and problem-solving. Like an Air Force bomber fueling in flight, or like the Apollo 13 crew repairing their space ship while it is speeding through space, repairs may be necessary with no time off. Again, a crucial tool for coping in this ethics environment is attentiveness — being alert both to circumstances around us and to the value conditions within us as well.

Upon takeoff, with these tools at the ready, we will be prepared to observe and manage the issues we will encounter in the personal, social, business and professional worlds.

FOR FURTHER INQUIRY

REVIEW QUESTIONS

1. Summarize each of the three contemporary approaches to moral reasoning.

2. Which of the contemporary approaches to moral reasoning appeals to you the most? Why?

3. How have the contemporary views influenced major issues of present-day American life?

4. How are the contemporary approaches different from the classic approaches? Should the contemporary approaches displace the classic ones?

APPLICATION QUESTION

Use the hedonistic calculus to evaluate whether your choice to go to college was good. Are all the factors quantifiable? Are you aware of factors now that you did not think about six months ago? Did you make the right decision?

ENDNOTES

1. Bentham, Jeremy, *Introduction to the Principles of Morals and Legislation.*

2. Mill, John Stuart, *On Liberty.*

3. Manuel G. Velasquez, *Business Ethics: Concepts and Cases,* Prentice-Hall, 1982, pp. 94–96.

4. Rawls, John, *Theory of Justice.*

5. Locke, *Two Treatises on Government.*

6. King, Martin Luther, Jr., *Testament of Hope,* Harper, San Francisco, 1986.

7. King, Martin Luther, Jr., *Strength to Love.* Philadelphia, Fortress Press, 1963.

8. de Vries and Gardner, *The Taming of the Shrewd,* Thomas Nelson, Nashville, 1992.

PART II

Major Moral Issues

CHAPTER 6

BIOETHICS

"Whether or not we find what we are seeking is idle, biologically speaking."

— Edna St. Vincent Millay, The Penitent

"Claude Barnard . . . is said to have announced that with a hundred years more of physiological knowledge we would be able to make the organic law ourselves — to manufacture human life, in competition with the Creator. We did not raise any objection . . . but we do believe that at that particular stage of development the good Lord . . . will say to humanity, just as they do at the Art Gallery at five o'clock, "Gentlemen, it's closing time."

— Edmond de Goncourt and Jules de Goncourt, Journals, April 7, 1869

As we enter the 21st century, we are in the midst of one of the most radical projects in the history of the human species — what can be called the biological revolution. We now can create an exact genetic duplicate of a sheep, remove the human heart and keep someone alive entirely mechanically for days or even months. We are well into the amazing project of identifying every gene that makes up the human genetic code. We are starting to learn how to insert new genes hoping to cure gene-caused diseases. Someday soon we may begin to use the same technology to try to improve on the species, making people with different physical and psychological makeups.

We have experimented on human subjects to overcome some feared diseases and, in the case of smallpox, actually to eliminate one. New technologies permit us to use pills to control fertility, end unwanted pregnancies, and snuff out lives that people no longer want to live. Now a woman who wants to become pregnant but is unable to carry the fetus can have egg cells removed so that they can be fertilized with her husband's sperm in a dish and then have the newly created life implanted in another woman — a surrogate — to carry the fetus to term. The same technology can be used to permit unmarried couples to produce children with at least part of their natural genetic makeup.

Robert Marlin Veatch, B.S. Purdue, B.D. Harvard, M.S. California at San Francisco, M.A. and Ph.D. Harvard University, is professor of medical ethics at Georgetown University and former director of the Kennedy Institute of Ethics at Georgetown.

In the process we may be changing the nature of the human species. It has been argued that the great mysteries of life are being replaced by manufacturing children, inserting spare body parts from left-over "brain dead" corpses, and redesigning the nature of the human. Some are beginning to ask whether we have turned what once were deep religious mysteries into engineering projects.

Bioethics is the field of ethics that looks at these controversial uses of new biomedical technology. As a part of ethics it is closely related to the law, but not identical to it. Not everything that is legal is ethical; not everything ethical, legal. The law specifies what a particular state will enforce with *public sanction*; ethics deals with a more personal, but at the same time more overriding, standard of human conduct. It is not enforced by public sanction. It is more a matter of personal conscience, framed within religious communities or schools of philosophical thought.

CHIEF LEARNING OUTCOME

I can recognize bioethical issues and am able to discuss them according to sound theories of moral reasoning.

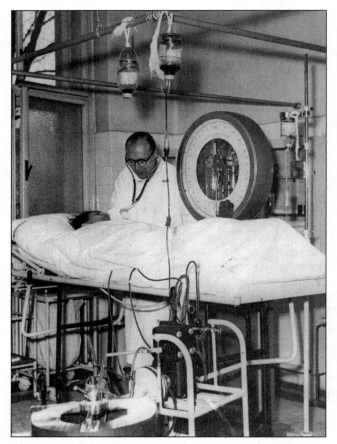

Figure 1. A patient receives life-saving artificial kidney. Hulton Getty.

This chapter focuses on bioethics. It covers the issues that arise within the practice of medicine — what might be called medical ethics, but it also covers certain issues of the biological revolution that extend beyond the practice of medicine: ethical issues of biological research and genetics.

Certain of the issues usually covered in bioethics are taken up in other chapters in this volume including abortion, death and dying, and sexual ethics. But others, including **informed consent for medical treatment, confidentiality, human subjects research, transplantation of organs, allocation of scarce medical resources, and genetic engineering**, will be explored here.

Although it is quite crude, all of bioethics can be reduced to three critical ethical questions. First, for any ethic we have to decide **who is a member of the moral community** to whom our ethical duties apply. For example, the ethical imperative not to kill is central to many ethical traditions, but it only applies to certain creatures. Many believe it does not apply to nonhuman animals, but others extend it to at least some animals as well. Even when applied to humans, it is controversial. Clearly we cannot be guilty of killing someone who is already dead, but it is not always obvious to anyone exactly when a human is dead. The definition of death debate, discussed in Chapter 8, is really nothing more than a debate over who is a member of the human moral community, who should be treated as having the same rights as other humans (including perhaps the right not to be killed). Likewise, the abortion debate, discussed in Chapter 7, is really a debate over whether certain fetuses are to be included in the community of humans who bear the moral and legal rights of other humans. Even the controversy over animal rights, discussed in Chapter 12, is in large part a debate over the moral standing of nonhuman creatures.

The first major issue in biomedical ethics is to determine the **moral standing** of various creatures and exactly who is to be included when we make moral claims about rights and responsibilities. Because these issues are taken up in other chapters of this volume, we will assume that one way or another we are dealing here with moral questions pertaining to humans who are bearers of human rights; that is, humans to whom certain duties are owed. The developments of the biological revolution force us as never before to determine exactly what those rights are and what duties are owed.

The second question raised by the biological revolution is **what should happen when someone believes that benefiting someone will conflict with certain rights** that that person possesses. Classical medical ethics focuses on the individual patient. The single most well-known code of ethics in medicine is the **Hippocratic Oath**, a document written in ancient Greece probably dating from the fourth century B.C. As summarized by its core ethical principle, it insists that the health professional should do what, according to the physician, is necessary to benefit the patient. That sounds plat-

KEY CONCEPTS

Hippocratic ethics: The ethics often seen in traditional health professional groups that holds that the morally right course for the health professional is the one that maximizes the good for the individual patient (not taking into account the affects on other parties and not considering other ethical deontological ethical principles)

Medical informed consent: The moral and legal doctrine that patients and research subjects are entitled to give their permission (or refuse their permission) for involvement in treatments or research after being provided adequate information and substantial voluntariness of choice

Justice: The quality of fairness among persons or societies or acts including: administration of justice (as in fair procedures and due process), distributive justice (as in apportioning advantages and rewards), retributive justice (as in punishing the wrong conduct of wrongdoers) and remedial justice (as in setting right of wrongs)

Autonomy: When applied to persons, the state of being capable of living one's life according to one's own life plan. When applied to actions, those actions chosen based on one's own life plan. As a moral principle, autonomy holds that actions tend to be morally right insofar as they respect the freedom of persons to make their own choices according to their own life plans

Endnote 1

itudinous, but it can be surprisingly controversial. It has been interpreted to support treating patients against their will, failing to inform them of bad news, and breaking confidences when the physician believes it will benefit the patient to do so. After looking at the historical context of this debate, we will examine the conflict between patient benefit and patient's rights.

The third major question arising in bioethics is **how do we relate the interests and rights of the individual to those of other individuals or the society as a whole.** We are beginning to discover that when the patient is the sole focus of medicine — whether the benefit of the patient or the rights of the patient — this can come at the expense of the interests of others. Doing research on human subjects, transplanting organs from one human to another, allocating scarce health resources and doing genetic engineering all raise these issues.

Consider a deceptively complicated case that arose in England several years ago. It became the focus of a major debate leading to a change in our medical ethic when the interests of the patient may conflict with the patient's rights as well as when they conflict with the interests of others in the society.

Is the Pill Dangerous?

Dr. Robert Browne

A 16-year-old young English woman had reached the age at which she thought she needed counseling for birth control. She feared her family physician, Dr. Robert Browne, would not approve, so she went to a clinic that provided contraceptive counseling.

Endnote 2

After suitable history and physical examination, the clinic physician prescribed oral contraceptives for her. In the process, the physician learned the name of the family physician and, believing that Dr. Browne should know of the medication in case of a side effect, he notified him. The young woman, perhaps not realizing the implications, agreed that her doctor could be informed.

One can imagine Dr. Browne receiving the unsolicited advice. After struggling with his options he took it upon himself to inform the young woman's father.

Charges of violating confidentiality were brought against Dr. Browne. When pressed he stated that he had two motives for disclosing. First, he was concerned about the physical hazards of the pill. Second, he was also concerned about the psychological hazards. He claimed that his interests were for the patient and for her alone. He wanted to do what was best for her. The review committee, after considering Dr. Browne's reasoning, concluded that it did not find Dr. Browne's action improper.

While the question of keeping medical information confidential may seem old-fashioned or even trivial, cases like Dr. Browne's — as well as those involving AIDS patients — force us to deal with the classical ethic of medicine. Dr. Browne appealed to the ethic of Hippocrates, which states that the physician should not divulge that "which ought not to be spoken abroad." This, of course, implies that some information can be "spread abroad." Many like Dr. Browne, who work in the older, more paternalistic framework, have claimed that we can tell what information can ethically be spread abroad by asking the physician what he or she believes will benefit the patient. There seems little doubt that Dr. Browne sincerely believed that telling the girl's father would benefit her. That many who hear about the case disagree with Dr. Browne does not

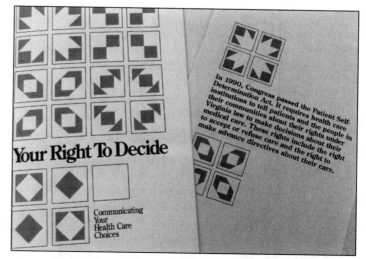

In 1990, Congress passed the Patient Self-Determination Act. It requires health care institutions to tell patients and the people in their communities about their rights under Virginia law to make decisions about their medical care. These rights include the right to accept or refuse care and the right to make advance directives about their care.

Your Right To Decide

Communicating Your Health Care Choices

Figure 2. Advanced directive book for health care. Hulton Getty.

count in the old Hippocratic tradition. The case not only raises questions about whether Dr. Browne determined correctly what would be beneficial to his patient; it also raises questions about whether patients have rights even in cases where the physician believes he or she is acting beneficially.

Invoking the old Hippocratic, patient-benefiting principle to deal with questions of **confidentiality** also presents problems when others might need to know about a patient's medical condition. If a physician learns he or she is caring for an HIV-infected patient who remains sexually active, it is the welfare of others that makes the physician consider disclosing. The classical focus on patient benefit not only may violate the rights of patients, it also may jeopardize the interests and rights of others.

THE HISTORICAL CONTEXT

Dr. Browne's appeal to the Hippocratic Oath makes us ask why a 20th-century English physician would turn to this old medical ethical document. **The Hippocratic Oath** stems from one school of medical practice in ancient Greece. It is part of a large group of writings associated with the physician, Hippocrates. He probably lived in the fifth century B.C. Almost certainly he did not write all the documents, but they have come to be identified with him. Some dealt with matters of medical science and healing; others with matters of ethics.

The Oath itself probably dates from the fourth century, perhaps from the Island of Cos where an enormous Aesclepion, a Greek healing temple, existed. The ruins are still present today. The Hippocratic Oath has great similarities with Pythagoreanism, that strange school of Greek thought that grew out of a scientific, philosophical,

Figure 3. Hippocrates. International Museum of Surgical Science. Copyright © Brian Warling

religious cult — the same group that gave us the Pythagorean theorem in geometry.

The Oath appears to have been used to symbolize the adoption of the medical student into the family of the physician. It contains two major parts: the oath of initiation itself and a code of conduct.

The Oath of Initiation The oath contains a pledge of loyalty to the teacher. It even requires the student to come to the financial aid of the teacher in times of need. It contains other elements alien to 20th century Western thinking, but compatible with the practice of a Greek cult of the day. The one taking the Oath swears by the Greek gods and goddesses, by Apollo, Aesclepius, Hygiea, and Panaceia. Although it is strangely incompatible with our modern emphasis on educating patients, the Oath contains a pledge not to reveal secret medical knowledge. The Oath expresses the idea that knowledge can be dangerous when it is in the hands of the uninitiated layperson.

The Hippocratic Code of Conduct One reason we believe the Oath is Pythagorean is that it divides medicine into three parts: diet, pharmaceuticals, and surgery. It includes some apparently religiously based prohibitions. The Hippocratic physician is expected to refrain from giving patients deadly drugs or performing abortions and, rather oddly, forbids practicing surgery — all provisions compatible with the Pythagorean cult. The prohibition on surgery is not because they believed surgery to be too dangerous. Rather they seemed to believe that surgery would "contaminate" the physician. Many ancient cultures feared that contact with blood would make one impure. The Oath wants Hippocratic physicians to remain "pure and holy," leaving surgery to others more suited to the task.

The core principle of the Hippocratic Oath is the most important element carried forward into modern medicine. It requires the physician to pledge that he will "benefit the patient according to his ability and judgment and keep the patient from harm." This summarizes the commitment of the physician to benefit the patient, but paternalistically bases the benefit on the individual physician's own judgment.

Although many modern physicians might consider themselves as standing in the Judeo-Christian tradition, the relation of the Hippocratic ethic to the major Western religions is controversial. We know that early Christianity was in conflict with Greek ideas. It wasn't until the fourth century A.D. that Christianity finally was accepted in the Greco-Roman world. It challenged the tradition of the Greek healing system. It is not clear why the **Hippocratic Oath** survived. Some claim it, of all Greek medical systems, was most compatible with Christian ethics, but others see them as very different. A Christian form of the oath from the middle ages shows significant changes including an abandonment of the secrecy requirement and the prohibition on surgery as well as the more obvious dropping of the reference to the Greek deities. Given the radical changes in medical ethics in the past decade or two, a case can be made that Hippocratic ethics is in many ways different from that of the Jewish and Christian thought and the secular liberal philosophy that grew out of them.

Endnotes 4, 5

Endnote 6

MODERN PROFESSIONAL ETHICAL CODES

This ambiguity between Hippocratic and other forms of ethics has continued into modern times. Professional ethics of medicine in the Anglo-American world dates from the work of **John Gregory**, a medical professor at the University of Edinburgh in the 1770s, who lectured his students and wrote the first book on medical ethics. In the 1790s, a dispute arose at the Manchester Infirmary in England. An epidemic taxed the capacity of the infirmary and feuds erupted among the physicians, surgeons, and apothecaries over their responsibilities. **Thomas Percival**, a physician who had studied under Gregory, was asked to mediate. He produced a **"scheme of professional conduct"** that eventually became the basis for modern medical ethics in the United States. Percival's ethics is for the most part Hippocratic. The main focus is on benefiting the patient, but he also deals much more with institutional ethical questions of the hospital and takes into account the duties of the professional to society in a way that is totally absent in Hippocratic ethics.

Endnote 7

The American Medical Association Code of 1847 In the 19th century American medicine was in a period of ferment with different schools of thought feuding over what should constitute proper practice. In 1847 the American Medical Association was founded. Among its purposes was to separate what we now think of as orthodox medical practitioners from quacks and charlatans. One of the ways that a profession can gain credibility is to write a code of ethics. The AMA wrote such a code taking sections of Percival's writing verbatim. It also borrowed from the physician/statesman, Benjamin Rush, a signer of the Declaration of Independence who had also studied medicine under Gregory. Like its predecessors, it was essentially Hippocratic, but included sections on the more social dimensions of medical ethics. That code has been revised many times, major changes coming in 1903, 1912, 1947, and 1957.

Endnote 8

The World Medical Association's Declaration of Geneva After World War II, the World Medical Association, the international

Endnote 9

association made up of the national physicians' organizations, was seeking a modern code of ethics for physicians as a response to the association of some German physicians with the Nazi atrocities. Convinced that the Hippocratic Oath remained the basis for the ethical duties of physicians, it set out to provide a modern revision. What emerged was the Declaration of Geneva. First adopted in 1948 and revised in 1968, it follows closely the key moral commitments of the Oath, including the principle that "The health of my patient will be my first consideration."

COLLAPSE OF THE HIPPOCRATIC TRADITION — THE 1970S

The case of Dr. Browne was a key challenge to Hippocratic paternalistic commitment to the welfare of the patient. We began to realize that we really do not always want physicians to do what they think will benefit the patient. One of those times may be when the patient prefers not being benefited. At the same time cases were beginning to emerge of patients being forced to undergo terribly painful efforts to prolong life when they were dying of advanced cancer. Physicians were claiming that the Hippocratic Oath required them to withhold the truth — about cancer diagnoses and many other medical problems — from patients if the physician believed disclosure would harm the patient by upsetting them or causing them to act irrationally.

In the United States the society had just come through a period of active, militant defense of individual rights: racial rights, women's rights, students' rights. Could patients' rights be far behind? The anti-war movement had led to a challenging of scientific and technological authority. Just as war was found to be too important to be left to the generals, so life-and-death medical decisions were now seen as too important to be left to physicians. People began to challenge the Hippocratic ideal.

THREE CHALLENGES TO THE HIPPOCRATIC TRADITION

Just as war was found to be too important to be left to the generals, so life-and-death medical decisions were now seen as too important to be left to physicians.

Problems with Assessing Benefits The Hippocratic Oath was called into question in three ways. First, there are problems in the way benefits are assessed. Some versions of the Hippocratic principle commit the physician to benefit the patient in general while others, such as the Declaration of Geneva, commit the physician only to pursuing the patient's health. We began to realize people could be benefited in many ways other than by promoting their health. We also pursue well-being in other spheres: the aesthetics, the family, our occupation, education, the law, and so forth. The physician cannot possibly be expected to be an expert in promoting all forms of welfare. It is unrealistic to expect physicians to make choices that will promote the total well-being of patients.

On the other hand, if they follow the Declaration of Geneva and pursue only the patient's health, equally serious problems arise. For one thing, health itself is a complex goal. It includes preserving life, curing disease, relieving suffering, and preserving and promoting health. Sometimes these conflict among themselves as when preserving life can only be done by inflicting terrible suffering in a cancer patient. There is no reason to expect the physician to be able to make these trade-offs in the way that will really promote the overall health of the patient without learning from the patient what mix of these health goals is appropriate.

Moreover, in a world of finite resources no one will be able to satisfy fully the goals of health and those of the other spheres of well-being at the same time. In fact, sometimes we purposely fail to pursue our health in order to pursue other aspects of our welfare. Those who smoke, eat a good steak, or spend time reading when they could be exercising understand this notion. Probably no rational person would want to totally maximize his or her health at the expense of these other goods. If this is so, then if the physician single-mindedly pursues the health of the patient, sometimes the patient's total well-being really won't be maximized.

Because the physician cannot be expected to know how to trade off health benefits with benefits in other spheres, the goal of expecting the physician to promote the well-being of the patient is unrealistic whether that goal is interpreted narrowly to refer only to health or more broadly to refer to total well-being.

Problems When Benefits Conflict with Other Moral Duties
Second, many ethical systems hold to the idea that sometimes we have duties other than simply maximizing good outcomes. Jewish ethics requires certain practices such as avoiding killing simply because killing is believed to be a violation of divine law. Hypothetically, patients might be so miserable that they would actually benefit from being killed. Jewish ethics holds that, even if that were true, it is still wrong to kill. Other ethics, such as Kantianism, hold that it is wrong to tell lies — even if the results are better if the lie is told. Kantians also claim it is wrong to break promises — even if breaking them produces better results. These ethics all share the view that some behaviors can be morally wrong even if they produce the best consequences. Collectively, these positions are sometimes called deontological ethics. (See Chapter 4 for a fuller discussion of these views.)

Some of these deontological ethics may be quite sophisticated so that they avoid being applied rigidly and legalistically. In fact, some of them may be more flexible than some forms of ethics that focus exclusively on consequences. The key common feature, however, is that they all hold that sometimes something other than consequences determines an action's rightness.

Problems of Conflict Between the Interests of the Individual Patient and Those of the Society The third major problem with the ethic of benefiting the patient is that increasingly we are discovering that sometimes benefiting the patient comes at the expense of the welfare of others. Benefiting the HIV patient by keeping information confidential may harm others. A physician who remains steadfastly loyal to one patient may, in the process, avoid helping other people whose needs are greater. While considering societal interests poses great risks, equally great dangers results from avoiding all of the social implications of medicine today. Many newer medical ethical codes address questions of the conflict between the interests of the patient and those of the society.

CODES BREAKING WITH THE HIPPOCRATIC TRADITION

Several of the 20th century codes and oaths for medical ethics break with the Hippocratic tradition because of these problems.

The Nuremberg Code (1946) One of the most important problems with having the health professional focus exclusively on benefiting the individual patient is that, taken literally, no research using human subjects could ever be attempted (unless doing so could be justified by the potential benefits to the individual subject). The atrocities of the Nazi medical experiments in World War II led to a crisis in medicine. The Nazi physicians abandoned the portion of the Hippocratic ethic that required always focusing on the welfare of the individual patient. For example, they did studies designed to understand the effects of long exposures to freezing temperatures or high altitudes. Ignoring basic morality, they simply took concentration camp prisoners and exposed them to freezing water or high altitudes until they died.

At the trials at Nuremberg when these abuses were confronted, the international community had two options. They could have retreated to the Hippocratic ethic, insisting that every study be justified solely on the basis of benefit to the individual studied. That would, of course, have ended much important medical research. The other option was to figure out some way to permit the use of subjects without exposing them to terrible abuses. The writers of the Nuremberg Code decided to renounce the Hippocratic answer, turning instead to a rule that humans could be used as subjects provided that they gave their informed consent and met other conditions. This is the first time that informed consent appears in any formal medical ethical document. That it comes not from within the medical profession but from a secular proceedings in international law is significant. Informed consent is alien to Hippocratic professional ethical thinking but easily understood within a framework of liberal political philosophy that focuses on self-determination. In fact, in American legal cases States had acknowledged the patient's right to self-determination since 1914.

This is the first time that informed consent appears in any formal medical ethical document.

The American Hospital Association's Patients' Bill of Rights (1972) Another important event in the shift from the Hippocratic ethic to liberal philosophy is the American Hospital Association's Patients' Bill of Rights. A group organized by the association put forward a bill of rights for patients that included a limited right of patients to consent to treatment. It backtracked, however, by providing an escape clause in cases in which the physician believed the patient would be harmed. With this proviso, however, it acknowledges a right of the patient to information, considerate and respectful care, and to refuse treatment.

Endnote 9a

The American Nurses' Association Code for Nurses (1976) Although the hospital association had referred to rights in the early 1970s, the first association of health professionals to do so was the American Nurses' Association. In 1976 it revised its code, making it begin with the self-determination of clients. It explicitly acknowledged the moral and legal rights of all clients, a notion that signals the shift from the old Greek Hippocratic goal of benefiting patients to a more liberal notion of respecting their self-determination. Later, that code also affirms the duty of the nurse to safeguard the client and to protect the public as well, leaving nurses struggling with cases in which one cannot do all of these at the same time. This was typical of the early days in this generation of health professional ethics in which we still felt the older commitments to promoting patient welfare while simultaneously feeling the newer pull toward respecting patient rights and serving societal interests as well.

Endnote 9b

The AMA Principles of 1980 In 1980 the American Medical Association shifted dramatically away from the Hippocratic focus. It now spoke of the rights of patients, of colleagues, and other health professionals. Here was the clear confrontation between the older, more paternalistic concern with benefits and harms, and the newer concern with rights influenced not by the Hippocratic tradition but by secular liberal political philosophy. This was the first time that the word **rights** had appeared in any formal code of ethics for physicians.

Endnote 9c

Medical Ethics from Non-professional Sources Ethics written by health professional and hospital groups has never been the only source of medical ethics. Ethics is, after all, part of an overall cultural world view that has traditionally been expressed in religious as well as secular understandings of the world.

Medical Ethics in the Religious Traditions Most religious traditions have in one form or another what could be called a medical ethic. They have a set of beliefs and value commitments that express the way physicians, other health professionals, and lay people ought to behave on medical matters. Talmudic ethics in Judaism provides such a framework governing not only dietary laws, but prohibiting abortion and mercy killing, severely limiting autopsy, and generally providing a framework for Jews to approach medical decisions. Likewise, Roman Catholic moral theology has, since the 13th century,

Endnote 10

worked with a framework of "natural law" that distinguishes acceptable from unacceptable omissions of treatment. It proscribes active mercy killing, but permits killing in certain special cases. (See Chapter 8 for more details.) It has been interpreted as prohibiting intentional efforts to limit pregnancy using artificial means (including birth control pills, IUDs, condoms, and diaphragms). But it also presents an entire ethical system for making medical decisions. It provides an understanding of the goal or end of life, as well as a set of standards for shaping daily behavior.

Endnote 11

Protestant religious groups have a much less well-developed medical ethical system, but most denominations by now have adopted positions supporting the right to refuse medical treatment. Sometimes they cautiously accept the legitimacy of abortion. In general, they provide a system of beliefs and values upon which medical decisions are based.

Endnote 12

Eastern religious groups also have medical ethical positions ranging from the ancient *Caraca Samhita* (a Hindu religious writing from the first century) and ancient Buddhist and Confucian writings to the 1981 *Islamic Code of Medical Ethics* prepared at a meeting in Kuwait by the International Organization of Islamic Medicine.

Endnote 13

Medical Ethics in Secular Philosophical Systems Secular philosophical systems also provide a basis for addressing medical ethical questions. Liberal political philosophy, as we noted, is a major contributor, significantly challenging Hippocratic ethics. The United States Constitution's Bill of Rights provides a basis for addressing many ethical questions in medicine as does the United Nations Declaration of Human Rights. In some secular societies state documents have replaced, at least temporarily, professionally generated codes. *The Soviet Oath for Physicians* (1971) was written by the Soviet Government, not the medical profession. It acknowledges "high responsibility . . . to my people and to the Soviet Government." On November 19, 1996, the Council of Ministers of the Council of Europe approved a Convention on Human Rights and Biomedicine. The process of national ratification has begun. It will provide the first legally binding international treaty governing a broad range of bioethical issues.

Endnote 14

Endnote 14a

Any system of belief and value — religious or secular — ought to contain within it an ethic for medical decision-making. There is no reason why the elements of that ethic should match those in the Hippocratic Oath. The Hippocratic ethic can be viewed as one system of belief and value about the ends and purposes of medicine. It might be seen as a kind of "quasi-religion" competing with other religious and philosophical systems for loyalty of health providers. When a provider is a member of one of the other traditions — whether one is a Catholic, a Muslim, or a subscriber to the basic liberal beliefs of America's Founding Fathers — these systems may sometimes conflict with the Hippocratic tradition. When patient and physician stand in different traditions, the conflicts may also arise. In this context, it is easy to see why it is controversial for physicians to hold to the Hippocratic principle.

THE PATIENTS' RIGHTS MOVEMENT

As we have seen, one major conflict with the Hippocratic ethic has been with the view that sometimes duties exist that require health professionals to act in ways that do not maximally benefit the patient. These duties are often expressed in rights-language. Rights are, after all, closely related to moral duties. If one person has a duty to act in a certain way, often someone else can be said to have a right to have the person act that way. Given the American propensity to express ethical claims in rights language, a major challenge to Hippocratism has come in the patients' rights movement that began in the 1970s.

Three major rights claims have received the most attention. Each represents a moral principle that is sometimes seen as standing against the duty simply to benefit the patient. These are the principles of **veracity, autonomy, and fidelity,** which give rise to the rights to the truth, informed consent, and to have promises kept.

The Right to the Truth and the Principle of Veracity One of the first controversies that arose in the contemporary era of health care ethics was the debate over whether physicians owed the truth to their patients. The typical case involved a patient diagnosed by a physician as having terminal cancer. The physician believed that disclosing this diagnosis to the patient would be very upsetting and that, in order to spare the patient the misery, the physician felt justified in withholding the information.

Endnote 15

Empirical Studies As we have seen in the older Hippocratic ethic, physicians were told that they not only could, but should, withhold bad news when they believed it would harm their patients. In a study of physician attitudes, Donald Oken in 1962 found that 88 percent of physicians would tend to withhold a diagnosis of cancer. In 1979, just 17 years later, Dennis Novak repeated essentially the same study finding that 98% of physicians would tend to disclose. What accounts for this dramatic shift?

Endnote 16

Endnote 17

THE MORAL REASONS FOR AND AGAINST TRUTH-TELLING

Hippocratic Therapeutic Privilege Bernard C. Meyer, a New York psychiatrist writing in 1968, held the old view based on Hippocratic reasoning: the physician is morally bound to do whatever will benefit the patient even if that means lying or withholding information. This is now sometimes referred to as the physician's **"therapeutic privilege,"** the belief that the physician has the "privilege" of distorting the truth when he or she believes it will benefit the patient.

Endnote 18

Pro-truth Consequentialism This ethic can be called "patient-centered consequentialism." It bases decisions on the consequences to the patient. But this view can also be used to defend disclosing bad

Endnote 19

news. Medical Ethicist Joseph Fletcher, until his death, was firmly committed to an ethic of maximizing good consequences. Yet he tended to believe that withholding a diagnosis would tend do more harm than good. He imagined patients with unexplained painful growths agonizing as they imagined the worst. Added to that would be the further worry of feeling that people were hiding things from you. He believed that usually more harm than good would be done by following Bernard Meyer's strategy. He was a pro-truth consequentialist. Some people may have shifted into a pro-truth position because they have reassessed the consequences and come to the conclusion that telling is better for the patient. In a world of high-tech bureaucratic medicine, sometimes the private physician may not be able to control information completely. In the worst of cases, a patient learns of a terminal illness when a nurse or consulting physician lets the bad news slip out.

Veracity **as an Inherent Duty** The major reason for the shift in favor of disclosing may be ethically quite different. We have seen that many in the liberal tradition simply believe that in order to respect persons, we owe them the truth. They cannot be treated as mature, responsible decision-makers able to consent or refuse consent to treatment unless they know what their condition is.

Some ethical theories hold that it is inherently wrong to lie to patients regardless of the consequences. Immanuel Kant once wrote a remarkable essay entitled "On the Supposed Right to Tell Lies from Benevolent Motives." In it he argues that deciding whether to be truthful to a patient would not be a matter of calculating the consequences; it would be an unconditional duty.

Endnote 20

One major problem with Kantian ethics is that it is possible that two or more of these duties may come into conflict. Imagine, for instance, that you had promised a patient's relatives that you would lie to her. Kant held it was your unconditional duty to tell the truth, but that it was also your unconditional duty to keep promises. You would be in a bind. You couldn't do both simultaneously.

British philosopher W. D. Ross proposed a strategy of treating such duties as *prima facie*, that is as "binding other things being equal." These would be one's duties if there were no competing considerations. When two of these duties came into conflict he believed

Endnote 21

Endnote 22

one simply had to balance them. More recently, medical ethicist Baruch Brody has advocated using a "judgment" among what he calls "conflicting appeals." One must simply exercise case-by-case judgment. But the conflict, according to Ross or Brody, cannot be settled simply by figuring out which course would produce the best consequences.

Endnote 23

The American Medical Association was long committed to the Hippocratic notion of resolving such conflicts doing precisely this: seeing what would produce the best results for the patient. But in 1980 its members made a dramatic shift in the direction of Kantian, duty-based ethics. At that point they said simply that "a physician shall deal honestly with patients and colleagues. . . ."

That the AMA is not completely firm in its conversion can be seen by the fine print that eventually emerged in the more detailed opinions of their Council on Ethical and Judicial Affairs, the group that is responsible for interpreting the Principles of Ethics adopted by their House of Delegates, their national legislative assembly. The Council saw fit to add a Hippocratic exception not in the House of Delegates' position. They added, "when risk-disclosure poses such a serious psychological threat of detriment to the patient as to be medically contraindicated," then the AMA physician need not inform the patient.

Current bioethics is left with a controversy. The only important case is the one in which a physician might be tempted to invoke the therapeutic privilege, withholding information because it will upset the patient. Those who are committed to the patients' rights perspective tend to reject this exception added by the AMA Council. Those who remain Hippocratic and paternalistic are willing to consider it. Even they, however, must be satisfied that the patient is really better off not knowing.

Endnote 24

Informed Consent and the Principle of Automony

One of the major problems with the therapeutic privilege position is that it makes truly informed consent impossible. Informed consent is the product of the transition to the ethic based on rights and duties to patients. It is totally absent from the traditional Hippocratic ethic. It emerges from the ethical principle of autonomy, which, along with veracity, has become the centerpiece of the ethic of liberal philosophy.

The Place of Autonomy in Medical Ethics Autonomy can be understood as the state of making choices according to individually chosen life plans. Just as autonomy is foreign to Hippocratic ethics, it played no role in early Judeo-Christian ethics. In early Christianity, however, individuals were expected to convert to the new religion, leaving family, former religion, and community, if necessary, to do so. By the time of the Protestant Reformation in the 16th century, the individual was beginning to emerge as a more important figure. Luther, Calvin, and especially the figures of the Left-Wing of the Protestant Reformation provided a context for questioning of authority and affirmation of individual choice. Many claim that these events were the precursors to the full-blown emergence of liberalism in the 18th century. Immanuel Kant, one of the principal advocates of the ethic of this tradition, and the philosophy of Locke, Hobbes, Rousseau, and the Founding Fathers of the American Constitutional system provided a foundation for elevating autonomy to a central place in ethics, a phenomenon not felt fully in medical ethics until the 1970s.

Other medical ethics are more like Hippocratism in down-playing autonomy. Marxism, Buddhism, Hinduism, Confucianism, and Islam all have little room for the choices of the individual based on self-

The physician may even give the patient a choice among the options, but only when, in the physician's opinion, it will serve to benefit the patient.

selected life plans. This is a phenomenon primarily of the modern, liberal West, even though it is beginning to have impact in other cultures as well. For example, modern Japan, which traditionally gave no role to autonomy, has an active patient's rights movement influenced by physicians, lawyers, philosophers, and others who have interacted with Western thought and adapted portions of it that they believe fit their culture.

For bioethics, the most direct implication for bioethics of the principle of autonomy is in the doctrine of informed consent. Different ethics handle the notion of consenting to medical treatment very differently.

Consent in Hippocratic Ethics A truly Hippocratic physician may, of course, from time to time tell patients about treatment alternatives and their risks and benefits. The physician may even give the patient a choice among the options, but only when, in the physician's opinion, it will serve to benefit the patient. Thus, the risk of driving will probably be mentioned when a drug may cause drowsiness. But if the physician believed that the patient might be irrationally persuaded not to accept the treatment if certain risks were mentioned, those risks would not be disclosed. The Hippocratic physician like Bernard Meyer would omit the consent when he believed consent would not benefit the patient and especially when he thought it would cause harm.

Consent with the Principle of Autonomy If consent is grounded in the principle of autonomy, it gets much greater weight. Information must be presented and consent must be obtained whenever it would be necessary to facilitate autonomous choice. Two legal cases show how autonomy has reshaped the consent doctrine in the past generation. In 1955 Irma Natanson suffered from breast cancer for which she had a radical left mastectomy performed. She also underwent cobalt radiation treatment performed by Dr. John R. Kline.

She claimed to suffer injury from the radiation and sued, charging Dr. Kline failed to warn her of the risks. Dr. Kline did not claim to have explained the risks; he simply used his medical judgment that the treatment was appropriate. The issue in the case was whether Dr. Kline should have explained the risks — including the possibility of radiation damage — so that she could consent (or refuse consent) for the treatment.

When the case finally reached the Kansas Supreme Court in 1960, the chief justice ruled that "Anglo-American law starts with the premise of a thoroughgoing self-determination. It follows that each man is considered to be master of his own body, and he may, if he be of sound mind, expressly prohibit the performance of life-saving surgery, or other medical treatment."

The question further arose as to exactly what the physician must say to the patient. On this subject the justice stated, "So long as the disclosure is sufficient to assure an informed consent, the physician's choice of plausible courses of action should not be called into question if it appears, all circumstances considered, that the physician was motivated by the patient's best therapeutic interests and he proceeded as competent medical men would have done in a similar situation."

Endnote 25

By 1960 an explicit appeal to patient self-determination has entered the thinking of the judge in the court. The court reflects the rights-oriented liberal political philosophy. But at the same time the judge still reflects Hippocratic elements in holding to a standard based on the commitment of the physician to the patient's best interest. He assesses this by an appeal to what competent physicians similarly situated would have done in a similar situation, assuming that they would be the authority. This is what has come to be called the *professional standard* of consent. Within the next decade this standard would change, as we can see in the next case.

In 1972 a case was heard in a United States Court of Appeals involving a 19-year-old youth named Canterbury. He had suffered severe back pain and had submitted to an operation performed by a neurosurgeon, one Dr. Spence, without being informed of a risk of paralysis. He suffered a fall from his hospital bed the day after the surgery and was left paralyzed.

One of the critical questions in the case was whether Dr. Spence had to disclose risks such as paralysis in order to have an adequate consent. Canterbury's lawyers challenged the professional standard that had been used in earlier cases.

The court rejected the professional standard as being inconsistent with the patient's right to decide, claiming, "Any definition of scope in terms purely of a professional standard is at odds with the patient's prerogative to decide on projected therapy himself. . . . In our view, the patient's right of self-decision shapes the boundaries of the duty to reveal."

Endnote 26

STANDARDS FOR DISCLOSURE

When deciding what must be disclosed, we might at first be tempted to say that the consent should be "fully informed," but that turns out to be impossible. There are thousands of things that the physician could say about any given treatment, more than any reasonable patient would want to hear. It could take hours to cover all possible risks.

The Professional Standard was often used by Hippocratic physicians: The patient had to be told what a competent physician similarly situated would have disclosed. The idea was that it was a matter of "professional judgment," not only whether the information was correct, but also whether its disclosure would do more good or harm.

The Reasonable Person Standard While that might work in a paternalistic era, it does not make much sense for someone trying to facilitate autonomy. It is quite possible that a patient would find a piece of information important even though neither the physician nor his colleagues would disclose it. Certain side effects of medication might be beyond what most physicians usually discuss with their patients, even though that information could be very important to the patient. Whether physicians tend to disclose does not seem relevant to the question of whether the patient would want access to the information.

Critics of the old professional standard prefer what is now called the *reasonable person standard*. Under it, the physician must disclose what the reasonable person in the patient's situation would want to be told to make an informed choice. That does not mean telling everything, but it may mean considerably more than what was called for under the professional standard.

The Subjective Standard Even the reasonable person standard may not perfectly satisfy the requirements of the principle of autonomy. Imagine a patient who wants more or less information than the hypothetical reasonable person. If this person wants less information about some subject, surely in the name of autonomy the patient should be able to decline further discussion of a topic. But, what if the patient wants more information than the reasonable person would?

Imagine a pianist who tells the physician that he was more worried about injuries to his fingers than most people. If playing the piano is an important part of his life plan, then he would need to know more about the risks of injuries to his fingers than most ordinary reasonable people.

For such situations the *subjective standard* is now usually proposed. Under it the physician must tell what this particular patient would want to know, based on his or her subjective values and goals.

This presents a problem, though. How can the physician be expected to know all the special topics of interest to the patient? The answer has been that the physician must disclose only what the reasonable person would want to know plus anything else that the physician should reasonably be expected to deduce would be of special interest to the patient.

The legal implications are important. Under the professional standard, a physician accused of not getting an adequately informed consent would bring colleagues into the courtroom to testify whether they would have acted the same way. Under the reasonable person standard, it will be up to a jury — a group selected to be reasonable typical citizens — to decide whether they would want the information. Under the subjective standard the jury would have to try to put themselves in the patient's shoes imagining what the patient would want to be told based on what the patient has revealed to the physician about the patient's special interests.

PROMISES, CONFIDENTIALITY, AND THE PRINCIPLE OF FIDELITY

In addition to truth-telling and autonomy, a third principle raises issues that challenge the idea that health professionals should simply try to benefit patients. It is sometimes referred to as the principle of fidelity or promise-keeping. The general idea is that if a commitment is made, other things being equal, it should be kept, even if the consequences might be better if it were not. According to those who hold this principle to be morally important, we can show respect for people not only by dealing honestly with them and respecting their autonomous choices, but also by showing fidelity to commitments made.

Fidelity in Contracts and Covenants The general idea is that if a commitment is made it should be kept. This arises not only in specific commitments such as business contracts, but also in implied promises that are often conveyed when a patient/physician relation is established. When patients are asked what they dislike about relations with their physicians, they often point to what appear to be small things: that the physician doesn't listen and show undivided attention, that the physician won't return phone calls and keeps them waiting for appointments. These episodes raise questions about the fidelity of the physician to the patient.

Sometimes the word **contract** is used to describe the patient/physician relation. It conveys that certain commitments made. In an earlier era the main focus was on the duties of the health professional to remain loyal to the patient. This was in part because it was assumed that only the health provider was an active decision-maker in the relationship. Increasingly, however, that view is being rejected. The contract is being interpreted as involving an active partnership with both parties playing an active role, each having obligations that ought to be fulfilled. If the provider has the duty to give the patient his or her attention, show respect, keep appointments, explain charges and bill accurately, and so forth, the patient also has a set of obligations: to show up on time, disclose potentially meaningful information, pay agreed-upon charges, and the like.

Endnote 27

Among the duties of fidelity is the duty to keep the promise of confidentiality. Correspondingly, the contract between the patient and the physician may imply that the patient has a duty to respect the integrity of the health professional's practice, possibly even refraining from discussing some information learned in the doctor's office.

Some people bristle at the use of the term contract to describe these mutual commitments. They see the term as too much of a business or legal notion. They object to the idea that the commitments made are binding and enforceable. They particularly resist the implication that the obligations of the physician and patient are limited to legalistically fulfilling the agreed-upon terms. These critics sometimes prefer to the use the term *covenant* to describe the commitments that establish the patient/physician relation.

Endnote 28

The defenders of the covenant language need to keep in mind, however, that sometimes in philosophy the term contract is used to describe fundamental social relations having nothing to do with legalistic business deals. The philosophers who influenced the founding of the United States — John Locke, Thomas Hobbes, and Jean-Jacques Rousseau as well as Thomas Jefferson and the writers of the Constitution — spoke of a social compact or contract as the basic hypothetical agreement that establishes the fundamental moral bonds that link a people together.

Sometimes we speak of a marriage "contract" and mean by that something much deeper than a legally binding set of agreements. Some would argue that covenants have certain similarities with contracts, perhaps even should be thought of as a kind of contract. At least they share the notion of commitments of fidelity that generate obligations of loyalty. Holders of the principle of fidelity believe that the relation between health provider and patient involves such commitments — explicit and implied — that obligate the parties over and above any calculation of the consequences of keeping those commitments. Duties are created that are binding, at least if there are not overwhelming reasons to the contrary.

Confidentiality: **An Example of Fidelity to Promises** The first case in this chapter, the case of the kindly old Dr. Browne who believed he could benefit his young patient by telling her father she was on the pill, poses the problem of why the physician has a duty to keep confidences and under what conditions disclosures can be made. It is important to realize that only under certain circumstances do we feel we have a duty not to disclose information we learn about other people. If we see some famous person on the street acting strangely, we do not feel obliged to keep the information secret; if it is a figure with public responsibilities, we may even feel obliged to call the newspaper or local radio station and report it. But in some cases we feel a duty exists to keep what we learn about others confidential.

This is particularly true in lay-professional relations in the physician's office or in conversations with lawyers or with priests. We expect these people to keep what is said confidential. One explanation of this is that we believe there is a promise made — implied or explicit — that what is disclosed will not be revealed to others. To the extent that a promise is made, then there is a duty (other things being equal) to keep it. Thus, when the American Medical Association announces that one of its principles of ethics includes the statement that the physician "shall safeguard patient confidences within the constraints of the law" patients have a right to expect that they will be, at least if their physician is a member of the Association. It turns out, however, that not all physician codes of ethics make exactly the same promise.

Endnote 29

Hippocratic Codes on Confidentiality The Hippocratic Oath itself promises that the physician should not disclose "that which ought not to be spread abroad." That of course simply begs the question of what ought to be spread abroad. The usual answer in the Hippocratic framework is that the physician should disclose only when he or she believes it will be for the benefit of the patient. The core Hippocratic principle provides a basis for determining what ought to be "spread abroad."

In Dr. Browne's case, which occurred in 1970, the British Medical Association's code seemed relevant. It held that exceptions can be made to the duty to keep confidences. "Always, however, the overriding consideration must be adoption of a line of conduct that will benefit the patient, or protect his interests." The American Medical Association at the time held essentially the same position. It said that confidences cannot be broken "unless it becomes necessary in order to protect the welfare of the individual or of the society." Both the BMA and the AMA seem to support Dr. Browne. On that basis he was acquitted of any violation of the duty of confidentiality.

Codes Prohibiting Disclosure Partly as a result of this case, both the British and the American medical associations abandoned their Hippocratic paternalism in favor of a more rigorous promise of confidentiality. In 1980, the American association, as we have seen, switched from the Hippocratic paternalistic exception to confidentiality to a flat requirement of keeping confidences. Here they took a position similar to that of the World Medical Association's Declaration of Geneva, which provides a flat promise to "hold in confidence all that my patient confides in me."

Endnote 30

The Problem of Third Party Interests While these anti-Hippocratic changes in the professional medical groups' views on confidentiality provide protection to patients like Dr. Browne's, they may actually be promises that are too inclusive. The all-inclusive promise of confidentiality covers not only cases in which the physician would like to disclose in order to protect what he or she believes is the interest of the patient, but also cases in which the physician believes the interests of others is at stake.

The World Medical Association's Declaration of Geneva makes what could be considered a blank-check promise of confidentiality: Whatever is disclosed will be kept confidential no matter what. But should a health professional make such a promise? The patient may be about to confess a plan to commit mass murder or some other horrendous crime jeopardizing the welfare of others.

Most physicians as well as lay people believe that the interests of third parties may sometimes require a limit on the confidentiality promise.

Both the British and the American Medical Associations have revised their codes of ethics to conform to this view. They first specify that confidences may be broken when required by law. This almost always applies to cases where there are serious threats to the interests of third parties. Laws require reporting gunshot wounds, venereal diseases, and infectious diseases, all because of the concern for the risks to others. Now our society is debating whether reporting of

HIV infection should also be reported in order to protect others. States have differed in their interpretation, perhaps because HIV is not an airborne disease easily transmitted to innocent third parties, but requires either sexual or blood contact for transmission. Still, some innocent parties — for example, spouses of infected people — may be at real risk if the diagnosis is not disclosed. The reporting of HIV is a test case of how we trade off the duty of confidentiality against the interests of protecting third parties from medical risk.

The American Medical Association's Council on Ethical and Judicial Affairs has gone beyond the general notion of making an exception to the confidentiality promise when disclosure is required by law. It says that, for its members:

> When a patient threatens to inflict serious bodily harm to another person and there is a reasonable probability that the patient may carry out the threat, the physician should take reasonable precautions for the protection of the intended victim, including notification of law enforcement authorities.

Endnote 31

Of course, the fact that the AMA offers this promise does not automatically make it either what ethics or the law requires. But the AMA's view does appear to be emerging as a reasonable compromise between the rights of the patient to confidentiality and the interests of the society in protecting innocent third parties. The duty generated by a promise of confidentiality may be quite different when it is the serious interests of others that are at stake. The Hippocratic ethic focused on benefiting the patient (sometimes even when the patient wasn't interested in the benefit). Hippocratic ethics did not address breaking confidences to benefit others. Now, however, the paternalistic exception seems to have given way to an ethic that respects the right of people to have confidences kept. The controversial cases now are the ones in which the interests of others in the society conflict with the rights of the patient.

THE PATIENT VS. SOCIETAL INTERESTS

This brings us to the third major issue in biomedical ethics: the relation of the individual patient to the interests of others in the society. While the major controversies of the 1970s and early 1980s in bioethics focused on the rights of the individual — to be told the truth, to consent or refuse consent to treatment, and to have confidential information kept secret — the biggest bioethical problems as we move into the 21st century appear to be those posing conflicts between the individual and others in the society. Even if we can resolve the conflict between the rights of the individual and the physician's opinion of what will benefit the individual, we still will be left with cases in which doing what will serve the interests and rights of the individual will come at the expense of others. The most dramatic controversies at this level have involved the use of human subjects in medical research, the transplantation of organs, the allocation of medical resources, and genetics and birth technologies.

SCIENTIFIC AND MEDICAL RESEARCH

Many physicians are shocked to realize that the Hippocratic ethic, taken literally, prohibits all medical **research**. We can define research as the effort to produce what can be called "generalizable knowledge," that is, knowledge for the purpose of general understanding to be applied to the world generally rather than for the benefit of a specific individual. The Hippocratic mandate to act only so as to benefit the individual patient makes all research unethical.

Distinguishing Research from Innovative Therapy Since the time of Thomas Percival in the 18th century we have recognized that sometimes when a patient has a disease incurable with the available standard therapies, the physician is forced to try some innovation. While sometimes this is loosely called experimenting or research, it is actually just doing whatever the physician feels is best for the patient. The options available are not attractive, but sometimes it is rationally the best thing for the patient to try something out. This is not really research in the technical sense. It is not done to produce generalizable knowledge. In fact, researchers tell us that what is learned from such innovative trials cannot produce definitive knowledge.

Real research needs more systematic design, carefully formulated hypotheses, careful statistical methods, and what is called controlled trials; that is, arrangements whereby some patients chosen randomly are given the experimental agent to be tested and others with the same condition are given some other treatment, either a placebo (a sugar pill) or a "standard" treatment that is not believed to be effective enough. In the best trials the assignment of the treatments is "double blind"; that is, both the patient and the investigator are kept ignorant of which treatment the individual subjects are receiving. That way any differences noted must really be differences resulting from the treatments rather than biases based on the expectations of the parties involved. Only when mathematical tests show that the difference could not likely have occurred by chance are investigators justified in concluding that a real difference exists.

The Historical Realization that Medicine Is Social In the 18th and 19th centuries ethicists began to realize a medical ethic that focused exclusively on the welfare of the individual posed serious problems. For some situations even the notion of disease was called into question. By the end of the 18th century people were realizing that there was a **social dimension** to disease, that infection could be spread by contact with others. Medicine began challenging the notions that disease was strictly a problem of the individual and that the physician's duty could be thought of entirely in terms of the isolated patient.

By the middle of the 19th century **Claude Bernard**, often called the father of medical research, began articulating what were to become the basic methods and strategies of scientific medical investigation. He realized that the old patient-benefiting ethic was not going to be acceptable to the research enterprise, saying, "Christian morals forbid only one thing, doing ill to one's neighbor. So, among the experiments that may be tried on man, those that can only harm are forbidden, those that are innocent are permissible, and those that may do good are obligatory."

Endnote 32

In this he surely went too far in saying if the experiment may do good, it is morally required. Many things in life may do good. They may do harm as well. And even if they may do only good, we are not necessarily required to engage in them, so he probably also went wrong in his reading of what Christian morals require. Doing good is surely one element of that ethic, but some interpreters of that tradition recognize other moral limits as well. For example, many theological interpreters now accept the duties of telling the truth, respecting autonomy, and keeping promises as discussed in the previous section of this chapter. As we saw in the Nazi concentration camps, there may be other important moral issues in medical research beyond whether the experiments can do good. There may be issues of consent and fairness that should limit the researcher's right to try to do good.

There may be issues of consent and fairness that should limit the researcher's right to try to do good.

We have seen that the events at Nuremberg were the watershed for the ethics of research on human subjects. Those sitting in judgment at Nuremberg could have retreated to the Hippocratic individualism and banned all research designed to benefit society. They did not. Instead, they specifically authorized research provided several conditions were met. One of those conditions was the social form of the ethic of producing benefits. It is variously called a social benefits ethic or the ethic of utilitarianism. We can think of it as **social utilitarianism** to distinguish it from the Hippocratic ethic of utility that limits its attention to benefits and harms related to the individual patient. The **second principle of Nuremberg** requires that for research to be ethical it must "be such as to yield fruitful results for the good of society, unprocurable by other methods or means of study, and not random and unnecessary in nature." This is essentially the criterion of social utility — doing the greatest good possible, taking into account not only the welfare of the individual, but of all affected.

Endnote 33

This ethic, utilitarianism, is one of the most powerful answers to the question of how we can make medical ethics social. It is one of the dominant ethical principles in contemporary social thought. It has been used to justify not only research on human subjects, but also cost-benefit analysis in allocating scarce medical resources, the allocation of scarce hearts for transplant, and the policies related to the new technologies of genetic engineering. But it is also controversial.

It raises serious ethical problems not only of violating individual rights, but of fairness in social relations.

The American Revolution in Research Ethics Some people resist the Nazi comparison, claiming that such gross abuses could never happen in the United States or in other contemporary societies. The following case gives us pause:

THE TUSKEGEE SYPHILIS STUDY
NO CONSENT, NO INFORMATION

In 1932 researchers wanted to understand the natural history of untreated syphilis. In order to do this, they recruited 400 black men with syphilis and another group of 200 to serve as controls. They followed them continually until 1972 when the study was stopped. During that time they offered no treatment, wanting to see what would happen if treatment were withheld. The men, many of them poorly educated, did not consent to be in the study and were not informed that treatments were available.

In the early days the available treatments were not very effective. They included administration of arsenic and bismuth, but as early as the 1940s penicillin became available that was known to be effective in treating syphilis, and still the drug was withheld.

Figure 4. Herman Shaw, a 94-year-old survivor of the Tuskegee Syphilis Study. Copyright © Paul J. Richards-Agence France Presse/Corbis-Bettmann.

Endnote 34

No one can deny that syphilis was an important social medical problem. Conducting research to learn the long-term effects of untreated syphilis was something worth doing. A carefully controlled trial designed to eliminate the biases of subjects by keeping them ignorant might even be justified, if one appeals solely to the social benefits. Admittedly, a group of men would be at serious risk, but if the rest of the world could benefit (and the rest of humankind into endless future generations), then it could be argued that the total amount of good done by experimenting exceeded the harm done to this group of unfortunate men.

That, however, is reasoning strangely similar to the Nazi concentration camp experiments. Critics of a pure calculation of the total consequences for the future of humanity claim that even if the benefit/harm claims are true, there is still something ethically wrong with the Tuskegee experiment. They claim that the rights of the subjects were violated.

Endnote 35

A similar conclusion was reached in the Nuremberg trial. Before acknowledging what we have called the utilitarian criterion (that there must be good envisioned, and unachievable by other means), the writers of the Nuremberg Code insisted that "the voluntary consent of the human subject is absolutely essential."

Even if one can argue that this notion of consent was not part of the standard ethics of medicine in the 1930s when this study was begun, it surely was by the late 1940s, and the trial continued without the consent of the subjects until it was stopped. The Nuremberg consent principle was argued for by the American representatives at the trial.

It was not until about 1970 that the real conflict between the interests of the individual and those of the society became apparent in medical research. Slowly, a series of controversial medical experiments became known to the public. Live cancer cells were injected into human patients to study the development of cancer; whole-body radiation was administered to unconsenting subjects for research purposes; LSD was administered to military personnel to study the effects; placebos were given to a group of Mexican-American women in place of birth control pills to study the psychological effects of the pill. That last study produced at least seven undesired pregnancies. Distinguished Harvard pharmacologist Henry Beecher could stand it no longer. In 1966 he published an article in the prestigious *New England Journal of Medicine* summarizing the methods of some 22 medical studies, raising serious ethical questions of the sort mentioned here. His exposé led to public outcry.

Endnote 36

In December of 1971 the U.S. government's major research center, the National Institutes of Health, published a little yellow booklet on "Policy on Protection of Human Subjects." It set out the first guidelines for protecting human subjects from medical research. It required the consent of the subjects to enter them into clinical trials, initial review of research protocols to see that the rights and welfare of subjects were adequately protected, and that the risks be justified by potential benefits.

Endnote 37

Soon after the appearance of these initial guidelines, the Tuskegee story broke. Senator Edward Kennedy, outraged by the events, held Senate hearings that led to a law establishing a National Commission for the Protection of Human Subjects and eventually to a new set of federal regulations. The Commission issued what is called the **Belmont Report**, the first federal document formally providing an ethical framework for assessing government activity. It called for federally funded research to conform to three ethical principles: not only maximizing benefit, but also respect for persons (including their autonomy) and for justice. Eventually federal regulations appeared in 1981 that now, in their revised form, structure all federally funded research involving human subjects. Almost all institutions conducting such research apply these same regulations to their work whether it is federally funded or not.

Endnote 38

Endnote 38a

The Moral Conflict These documents all apply what can be called the utilitarian ethic as the minimal condition for acceptable medical research. The benefit expected has to exceed the expected harms. But that is not the only moral principle that must be satisfied. There are also constraints that can be grouped under the general rubric of respect for the individual person: requirements for respecting autonomy, providing for adequate disclosure of relevant information, and keeping the promise of confidentiality. These are what can be called *deontological principles*; they identify characteristics of actions that are simply one's duty, that tend to make them right regardless of consequences. Much of the debate over the ethics of medical research today can be seen as focusing on the conflict between these rights of the individual and the interests of the society. One conclusion seems clear: **Benefits to society alone, even major benefits, do not justify using human subjects in medical research unless additional moral criteria are met.**

In addition to the criteria designed to respect the rights of individuals to consent, to be informed, and to have confidences kept, the Belmont Report introduced the moral principle of justice to the equation. Justice is an ethical principle concerned with giving people their due. It focuses on the distribution of benefits and harms, distributing both punishment and reward in a fair or equitable manner.

The **principle of justice** first was applied to the issue of **subject selection**. The subjects in the Tuskegee experiment do not seem to have been picked at random. They were largely black, poorly educated people with few alternative resources available. Likewise, the Mexican-American women given the fake birth control pills were low-income women who did not understand their alternatives. Similar questions have arisen about the use of prisoners, welfare patients in charity hospitals, and other subjects unable to defend their rights.

Now the formal criteria for approving research protocols require that there be equity in the selection of subjects and that the use of vulnerable populations such as children, the retarded, prisoners, and other confined groups be justified. Normally, using them in research is acceptable only if the study cannot be done on other populations.

This may just be the beginning in the use of the criterion of justice in assessing medical research. Some are suggesting that justice also has to be applied in the design and use of the research. In designing the research, some compromises may have to be made between the interests of the researchers in having ideally designed studies and the interests of the subjects. If the subjects are already among the worst off in the society because of severe illness, they should not be made even worse off by being asked to undergo extensive marginal tests.

Justice also has emerged as a criterion in the use of the findings of the research. If, for example, subjects are put at significant risk or inconvenience, they should also have special claims to be the first to get access to the products of the research should it turn out to produce valuable results.

NEW PROBLEMS IN HUMAN SUBJECTS RESEARCH

Endnote 38b

Fetal Research Recently controversy has erupted over the use of fetuses as research subjects. Increasingly, fetuses who are the products of planned abortions are potentially available. Researchers have realized the potential benefits of testing drugs on pregnant women to see the effects on their fetuses. They have also contemplated new ways of producing abortions and new therapies that could be administered prenatally. With a million or more abortions now performed each year in the United States (See Chapter 7) researchers have sought to conduct research on these fetuses.

Critics have vociferously protested pointing out that the fetuses themselves obviously cannot consent to these procedures that, for the most part, are not for the fetuses' benefit. Moreover, they object to the practice of asking the pregnant woman to give proxy consent, claiming that these women are not in a position to serve the fetuses' interest, having already decided to abort them. Those opposed to abortion have almost uniformly opposed research on purposely aborted fetuses believing that this practice relies on a procedure they consider immoral and tends to put those abortions in an unjustifiably favorable light. They usually would not object to similar research on spontaneously aborted fetuses, but, for scientific reasons, these fetuses are often not acceptable.

During the Reagan and Bush administrations, a moratorium was in place prohibiting the use of federal funds for such research. It remained in place in spite of the fact that a federal advisory panel recommended by a vote of 18 to 3 that it be lifted. One of the first acts of the Clinton administration was to lift the moratorium, but opposition remains to using fetuses as research subjects.

The Right to Be a Subject Another new controversy surrounding **human subjects** research is the right to be a subject. In an earlier time, it was assumed that becoming a subject was a dangerous action requiring altruism. Increasingly, however, studies are being conducted in which intervention is presumed to be beneficial, but the research question is to determine just how beneficial. Experimenting with special, high-quality health care services is an example. People would all like to be subjects. Many are demanding the right to be become one.

Women were long excluded from research, partly out of a fear that they might be pregnant and that the experimental agents would harm the fetuses. The result was that as we realized that many treatments have different effects on women than men, we knew more about those effects on males, who had been studied, than females, who had not been. They began demanding the right to be included in research designs in numbers adequate to produce data useful in understanding the treatment effects in their group.

Endnote 38c

The same claims were made for racial minorities and age groups. The demand to be a research subject became more acute when new drugs were emerging that had the potential to benefit patients with hopeless conditions such as cancer and AIDS, for which no known treatments were successful. They claimed they had nothing to lose and perhaps a great deal to gain by trying the drugs. They were less interested in the adequacy of the research than in the potential benefit to themselves. Several programs are now in place — variously called compassionate use exemptions, treatment INDs (investigational new drug permits), or parallel track protocols (permitting some patients to get new drugs on a nonrandomized basis). These new programs pose in a novel way the conflict between the interests of sick individuals and the society as a whole. Those who emphasize the moral principle of justice interpreted as giving special consideration to the least well off) are likely to handle these conflicts differently from those who strive to maximize aggregate social benefit.

Endnote 38d

TRANSPLANTATION OF ORGANS

Research involving human subjects is not the only controversy in medical ethics raising issues about the relation of the rights of the individual to the interests of the society. One of the major breakthroughs in biomedical technology of the past 30 years has been our new-found capacity to take organs from one human being and transplant them into another.

Thousands of people today are walking around, carrying on normal human functions, with other people's hearts, livers, kidneys, lungs, and pancreases in them. We have even attempted to remove organs from other species — hearts from baboons and chimpanzees, and even livers from pigs — trying to get them to function as human substitutes.

These efforts have raised some questions related to the first major issue we identified as arising in bioethics. Some people have objected that moving organs from one human to another and from one species to another produces monstrosities, that it violates God's plan for human life. It raises questions about who is a member of the human moral community and whether there are some beings that we now have the capacity to create that we should not create.

For the most part, however, these basic religious and philosophical questions have been set aside. Most of the major religions clearly approve of the transplantation of organs (even if some animal welfare activists have protested efforts to obtain organs from other species). The real questions have focused on the matter of the reaction of the rights of the individual to the interests of society.

The Ethics of Procuring Organs The biotechnology of transplant has been so successful in saving life that today there is an enormous demand for organs. Today more 50,000 people in the United States alone are on waiting lists for an organ, hoping to get one before they die. In the 1970s a debate began over the way organs would be procured and who should control the body parts of the deceased. The issue was whether society should consider valuable body parts to belong to the society, to be its for the taking when the organs can do enormous good for the living, or whether they should continue to be thought of as belonging to the individual so that they would have to be given as a gift before they could be used to help others.

Endnote 39

Routine Salvaging One group proposed what was called routine salvaging of organs. The idea was that once a person dies, the body parts can no longer be of use to the individual. If the parts could help others, then society should be able simply to take them and use them as a public resource to save other lives. This method would have been efficient, cost-effective, and simple. However, it also raised critical moral questions about the relation of the individual to society. In the Western world the individual has been seen as having an autonomy over-against the society. The body has not been seen as belonging to the state. Critics of routine salvaging proposed the alternative of having the individual (or the next of kin) donate the organs provided that did not violate any deeply held personal beliefs and values.

Endnote 40

Donation In the United States and most other countries throughout the world the gift-model was endorsed (with limited exceptions in some states where corneas can be taken without permission unless an objection is recorded). The United States developed a Uniform Anatomical Gift Act that was passed in all states providing for the possibility of donating organs. An individual could express such a desire while alive or, if no wishes had been expressed while alive, the next of kin would have the right to do so. On this basis the family of deceased patients who are potential organ donors are asked whether they wish to donate and their wishes are respected. Legally, if the individual has executed a donor card (or marked a driver's license making a donation) the family has no legal authority to veto. Someday transplant surgeons may take such organs even against the wishes of the next-of-kin, but most today fear the wrath of the family even though organ procurement organizations are clearly legally entitled to the organs. Some patients militantly favoring organ transplant are letting it be known that they believe surgeons have a moral duty to take such organs even if family members object. They claim the primary driving moral consideration must be respect for the wishes of the patient. The gift mode has prevailed in most countries, but we are increasingly realizing

that it is not entirely successful. The waiting lists for organs are growing and many people who we know would be willing to donate simply have not taken the initiative to fill out the necessary donor card. Alternative strategies are beginning to be proposed.

Presumed Consent Several people have begun advocating something called presumed consent. Society would presume consent for organ procurement unless someone had executed a document to the contrary. This is sometimes called "opting out" as opposed to "opting in." It is rather like routine salvaging, especially when one realizes that most routine salvaging proposals permitted people to opt out. The one key difference may be conceptual. The language of presumed consent recognizes that Western culture feels very strongly about the sacredness of the individual and wants to hold onto something that looks like gift-giving rather than openly affirming that the body belongs to the state. Calling this opting-out strategy "presumed consent" makes it sound as if we are remaining in the donation mode while, in fact, there may be no reason to believe presumed consent would actually be obtained. We know that, depending on the community and the population group, there is about a 50% chance that an individual would be willing to donate organs. So, presuming consent once someone has died is somewhat of a fiction. There would be a 1 in 2 chance that the presumption would be wrong, hardly a sound basis for presuming agreement. Some have said that if we feel we really need the organs from people who have not explicitly donated, it would be better to simply say we are taking them without permission.

Endnote 41

Required Request Another strategy that has been widely adopted has been to pass a law requiring that hospital personnel ask the relatives of all appropriate deceased patients whether they are willing to donate the organs for transplant. Called *required request*, these laws simply increase the chance that the question will be asked. Whether they have increased the number of organs made available is controversial. One major problem with required request is that, rather than going to the individuals themselves and relying on their personal decisions, society is relying on a backup decision-maker whose views may not be in accord with those of the individual. The search goes on for other ways of getting donations directly from the one whose organs eventually would be used.

Endnote 42

Markets in Organs and Rewarded Gifting One well-tested capitalist method of motivating behavior is to pay people. Some have proposed a free-market in organs that would permit any willing buyer to sell his or her organs to any willing seller, either while the seller is alive (presumably limited to non-life-prolonging organs such as kidneys or, now, liver and lung lobes) or for procurement should the individual die in a way permitting procurement.

The resistance to a market in organs has been strong. It is said to put coercive pressure on the poor and, in a pure market system, would deliver those organs obtained from the poor to those who could

Endnote 43

Endnote 44

afford to pay. Straight markets in human organs are illegal in the U.S. A variant on this scheme has emerged recently, however. Called *rewarded gifting*, it is a desperate effort to hold on to the idea of the gift mode. It would give some gift to individuals who donate in exchange for their donation. The gift could be a small life insurance policy, payment of funeral expenses, or some other gift that might serve as an incentive to donation. Critics have argued that this is little more than payment in disguise. For example, if $2,000 were given toward funeral expenses normally paid by the estate of the deceased, the estate would just be that much larger and the effect would be the same as paying the beneficiaries of the estate the $2,000.

Endnotes 45, 45a

Required Response One final scheme has been called *required response* or *mandated choice*. At some critical point, either upon admission to a hospital, during a routine physical exam, or upon renewal of a driver's license, all persons would be asked if they wish to donate organs and would be required to respond. They could answer either way, but they would have to answer. This might increase the response from those willing to give while still retaining the donation model.

Endnote 46

The Ethics of Allocating Organs Once the organs are obtained, the question of how they will be allocated to those waiting for the life-saving operation is equally controversial. While selling them to the highest bidder has been considered, the real debate is between those who believe they should go where the organs will do the most good and those who believe that justice requires that all people equally needy should have an equal shot regardless of the likelihood of success. These could be called the efficiency and equity views respectively. Consider the following problem.

THE UNOS FORMULA: ALLOCATION BY CALCULATION

The United Network for Organ Sharing is the national quasi-governmental body responsible for allocating organs for transplant. Because there is much greater demand than supply, it must develop some basis for allocating.

For kidneys, a point system has been devised that takes into account several factors thought relevant to claims on available kidneys. Points have been considered for degree of tissue-matching, time on the waiting list, medical urgency, geographical proximity, age, and so forth. The critical moral question is how much each of these factors should count and why.

One group favors maximizing the likelihood of benefit with the scarce supply of organs. They would give the points to those things, such as tissue-matching, that predict successful outcome. Others, concerned more about the fairness of the system, would give the points for reasons, such as time on the waiting list, that try to give people an equal chance of getting an organ.

It gradually became apparent that not all people on the waiting list were equally easy to match with the pool of available kidneys. In particular, Blacks and Hispanics were harder to match than Caucasians. To a lesser degree, males do somewhat better than females, younger people slightly better than older people, and middle-class patients better than lower-class ones. Now if we still want to get the best aggregate outcome, we would give the points for tissue-matching and these other factors that predict good outcome, while if we wanted to give all people an equal shot at an organ we would purposely downplay or exclude them. What percentage of the total points should go to factors that predict successful outcome, what percentage to those that try to make the allocation more equitable?

The UNOS Ethics Committee has an allocation subcommittee that dealt with this issue. It realized it was divided between those wanting to emphasize good medical outcome and those who wanted to emphasize fairness. The committee consciously made a compromise and has proposed that in the future the formula give half its total points to measures of good outcome and half to factors included to try to make the allocation more equitable.

Endnote 47

Underlying the entire debate about procuring and allocating organs is a larger question: Should the limited resources available for health care be spent on high-tech interventions such as transplants that, at considerable expense, will give a chance at life to a small number of people who are among the sickest and worst off in the society? Or should the resources be spent to provide benefits in a maximally efficient manner, targeting preventive and low-tech basic care that will produce greater aggregate benefit?

Some Special Organ Allocation Problems Although the primary issue in the allocation of organs for transplant is the conflict between efficiency and equity, three new issues have arisen recently that raise intriguing moral questions. One is whether alcoholics who develop liver disease deserve the same priority as other persons who need liver transplants for other reasons. No one supports giving livers to active alcoholics who will simply do in their new liver the same way they damaged their original one. Almost no one believes that alcoholism should be an automatic exclusions either. The real conflict in the UNOS Ethics Committee came between two more nuanced positions. One group held that, once one had shown evidence of abstaining from drinking, the same right of access should exist as for persons with other causes of their disease. the other group believed that justice requires **an equal *opportunity*** for health, but that those who were voluntarily risking their health had had that opportunity and therefore deserved a slightly lower standing, which they translated into a proposal for a small number of negative points in the allocation formula. This view relies on the conviction that alcoholism is, at least to some extent, a voluntarily controllable behavior. The conflict between these two views has never been resolved.

A second new conflict has to do with **the role of age** in allocating organs. Should the elderly, who will predictably get fewer years of life out of an organ and who may be somewhat harder to treat successfully, get lower consideration? That was the original policy, but that policy has changed. Presently, children get extra consideration for kidneys. That is perhaps because both efficiency and equity arguments can be made on their behalf. It is efficient to give kidneys to children both because they will predictably get more years of benefit from the organ and because they are at greater risk for neurological damage if they must be sustained on dialysis. The equity argument is more complex. While some people would claim that equity requires giving all persons who are equally sick at a moment in time equal consideration for an organ regardless of age, from another perspective young age deserves a special claim of equity as well as efficiency. Viewed from an over-a-lifetime perspective, one could say that one who has a need for an organ at a young age is much worse off than one who does not need it until a greater portion of life has been completed. It makes a big difference whether one is asking who is worst off at the moment the organ is allocated or one takes the perspective of the whole life.

A third new issue involves **directed donation**, the question of **whether persons or their families may agree to donate organs with the proviso that they be used only for recipients of a certain race, religion, gender, or sexual orientation.** This practice was brought to the public's attention when a Florida man, a victim of a mugging, was left brain-dead. When his family was approached about donating his organs, they pointed out he was a participant in the Ku Klux Klan and that he would want his organs to go only to Caucasians. Now most organ procurement organizations prohibit this practice and most believe it violates civil rights laws even though it is currently legal to direct donation of organs to named individuals or institutions.

ALLOCATION OF SCARCE MEDICAL RESOURCES

This same problem — of choosing between arrangements that do the most good in aggregate and those that will likely benefit the worst — off arises not only in transplant, but in the full range of health-care allocation decisions. Each day in the United States more than $3-billion is spent on health care. Still, the health of Americans is not as great as it could be. Americans are far from the top in life expectancy at birth. Infant mortality is 70% greater than in Sweden. Even more dramatically, about 40-million Americans are without health insurance and another 10% of the population is under-insured. There are dreadful differences based on income, education, and race.

Rationing of scarce medical resources in one way or another is inevitable. Americans are spending upward of $2-billion per year on end-stage renal disease for about 8,000 people a year who come down with the disease, $6-billion for bypass surgery, another $1-billion for Caesarean sections, many of which may not even be needed. Dementias in the elderly cost as much as $50-billion a year, and addictions cost perhaps $60-billion. And that is without even considering obligations to those in other parts of the world. **The costs of doing everything that patients would like done could easily exceed the entire gross domestic product.** It is inevitable that some limits will have to be placed on health expenditures. Any future health care plan will have to include some limits on access to some kinds of care. The ethical question is on what basis the rationing will be done. Consider the preliminary plan being developed in the state of Oregon.

Medicaid is a nationally funded plan for health care for the poor. Each state, however, runs its own program. Oregon was spending its entire Medicaid budget providing a rather extensive range of services for the poorest of the poor — those below 50% of the poverty level.

A Health Services Commission was established with a mandate to reassess the program and create a new arrangement that would fund everyone up to 100% of the poverty level by dividing all health services into a group of 709 diagnosis/treatment combinations. Through a series of public meetings and surveys of health professionals and lay people, officials attempted to rank these from highest to lowest priority.

Endnote 48

THE MORAL PRINCIPLES

They attempted to determine the amount of benefit per dollar of cost through an elaborate scheme that assessed the benefit in terms of the amount of benefit and the number of years of benefit each treatment would provide. The Commission used an elaborate scheme that tried to take into account how badly off people were that were being treated for various conditions as well as the likelihood of success from the treatment. For example, surgery for appendicitis and antibiotics for pneumonia ranked near the top while treating extremely low birth weight babies and uncomplicated hemorrhoids ranked near the bottom. Those things that produced dramatic results cheaply scored high, while both minor problems and serious ones where success was very unlikely did poorly.

Exercises such as this will become more and more common through the years. Each member of the Oregon Commission finally had to vote to rank the diseases in order, knowing that they would fund down the list only as far as the money would go. Imagine you were a member of the Oregon Health Commission. On what basis would you do your ranking?

Maximizing the Aggregate Good Done One criterion would be to maximize the total amount of good done for those in the program. That seems to have been the dominant instinct of the Commissioners. They were attracted to efficient, basic services that did a great deal of good for a low cost. There are real problems with that criterion, however.

First, we have already seen that there are enormous disputes over what counts as a good outcome. Should they have considered total good for the society, giving higher priority to those people who were more productive or to younger people who would get more years of benefit simply because they could be expected to live longer? If so, they would have to end up choosing between treatments for productive business people, housewives, or poets — just as the original group that tried to ration kidney machines did at the University of Washington in the early 1960s when that technology was new and scarce. Or should they have looked only at what can be called "medical benefit," focusing on changes in life expectancy and quality of life? If they were to limit their attention to the medical sphere, they would have to assign values to the various medical goods: saving life, curing disease, relieving suffering, and promoting health.

Distributing the Benefits Equitably It is the nature of the project of trying to maximize the medical good that often those who are sickest are the hardest and least efficient to treat. If the goal is to get as much good as possible, whether the good is limited to the medical sphere or extended to all kinds of good, then directing the resources to those who are relatively well-off may be the more efficient approach. Targeting those who are sickest may require more resources for each unit of benefit achieved. Critics say this is inequitable in rationing health care generally just as it is in allocating organs. Some mix between equity and efficiency seems inevitable, just as rationing itself is. There is no reason why we must choose to produce the greatest possible good. That is what utilitarians would pick, but not the choice of the egalitarians who give greater emphasis to equity. The choice will depend on what social ethic for health care is chosen and how the principle of justice gets played off against the principle of utility.

Some believe, for example, that there is a gene that is partly responsible for alcoholism. Smoking, a cause of many serious medical problems, often begins in early adolescence before we believe people are substantially autonomous agents.

The Role of Voluntary, Life-Style Choices Although efficiency and equity are the primary considerations in allocating scarce health care resources, there is a third dimension that is sometimes included. In the discussion of allocation of organs for transplant we saw that voluntary lifestyle choices have been considered as relevant by some people in conjunction with the discussion over allocation of livers to alcoholics. More generally, some people believe that all justice requires is an opportunity for health so that, in principle, people do not deserve health care services if they have consciously chosen to lead a lifestyle that risks their health — at least they claim that these people do not deserve health care at the expense of society in the same way that someone does who has a genetic disease or sustains an accident or catches a virus that they could not have prevented.

As we learn more and more about the causes of disease, we must face the question of whether those who knew how to prevent a medical problem and chose not to do so have the same kind of moral claim to our health insurance dollars as other people do. Those who are raised this question recognize the complexities involved. For one thing, it is often very difficult to determine just which behaviors are truly voluntary. Some believe, for example, that there is a gene that is partly responsible for alcoholism. Smoking, a cause of many serious medical problems, often begins in early adolescence before we believe people are substantially autonomous agents. There may be substantial nonvoluntary components in many health-risky behaviors.

Nevertheless, people still believe that many lifestyle choices have enough of a voluntary component to them that it is worth considering the moral implications for choosing them. Some argue that when we allocate health care resources some consideration should be given to whether one voluntarily brought on the medical condition needing treatment.

There are good reasons why we would probably not want to respond with a flat-out exclusion of persons from our health insurance plans. Not only is it hard to determine voluntariness, but also we like to think of our society as a compassionate one. We would all find it hard to see the smoker barred at the hospital door because of what it would do to our self-image as compassionate people. Still, there may be ways we can expect people to reimburse our common insurance system for some voluntary health-risky behaviors. For example, some have proposed putting a health fee on tobacco or alcohol that would be earmarked for reimbursing the health insurance system for the predicted added costs. Economists could calculate the expected added costs to the health care system of each package of tobacco and a fee of that amount could be added. Similar taxes could be added to certain other health-risky behaviors.

Critics resist such proposals, pointing out that not all health-risky behaviors are public enough to permit charging such a fee and that it would be unfair to tax some behaviors and not others. Some behaviors may be risky only to those with certain genetic or other confounding conditions, which would make the fee unfair to those who choose to engage in the behavior that, for them, is not risky.

The issue of whether to incorporate consideration of voluntariness along with efficiency and equity in deciding what counts as a fair allocation of our health care resources is an enormous one that will only become more controversial as we learn more and more about what causes medical problems and can increasingly predict who will become ill from their chosen behaviors.

GENETICS AND BIRTH TECHNOLOGIES

One final example of the conflict between the more individual focus of the Hippocratic ethic and a newer, more social ethic is the rapidly emerging possibility of understanding and intervening to change the human genetic code in the process of giving birth.

Endnote 48a

Genetic Engineering Patients with genetic diseases increasingly will have the opportunity to have their defective genetic material supplemented or replaced with genes that overcome problems that, until now, have often only meant a slow death. Attempting the re-engineering of the **human genetic code** was the stuff of science fiction only a few years ago. Now such experiments have been attempted on several diseases and more will certainly follow rapidly. For example, a condition known as ADA deficiency results from a defective gene. It causes a collapse of the body's immune system, making it impossible for it to fight infections. Infants born with ADA deficiency have been kept in a totally sterile environment, in a bubble completely cut off from direct human physical contact, for years. As long as they are not contaminated they thrive, but, once infected, they run a high risk of dying. Their life expectancy is short.

The National Institutes of Health Recombinant DNA Advisory Committee approved an experiment to insert the missing gene into such patients. It is, in this case, done by removing some bone marrow and exposing the marrow to a virus that has the capacity to insert the needed gene into the marrow cells. Then the marrow is re-injected into the patient.

Other **gene therapy** experiments are under way to deal with some forms of cancer, HIV, cystic fibrosis, rheumatoid arthritis, and many other conditions. Still others are sure to be attempted soon. A multi-billion dollar project to map the entire human genetic code, the so-called human genome project, will make a rapid increase in such experiments possible.

Endnote 49

But the ethical questions will remain. The first and most obvious are perhaps once again at the level of whether tampering with the genetic code is "playing God." Is it something that humans ought to refrain from? **Does the desire to change the human species by producing entirely new kinds of beings make such efforts unethical?** Or is it something that follows naturally from the human capacity to learn about and modify nature, attempting to improve on life as we know it. While some fear that, like the splitting of the atom, this is going too far, others are convinced that we finally have the beginnings of the capacity to truly cure diseases that up until now could only be treated symptomatically.

In addition to these fundamental questions about the nature of the species and our role in modifying our very existence, these genetic engineering projects pose serious questions about the relation of the individual to society. New genes are conveyed into patients — like those with ADA deficiency — by modified viruses called vectors. They supposedly have been modified so they cannot escape into the environment and accidentally infect other people, but things can go wrong. Skeptics fear that attempting these therapies will inevitably lead to mistakes exposing the entire species to some catastrophe. Once again, the entire future of the species could be hurt while the benefits will accrue to relatively small numbers. Still, in this case it is not only the patients on whom the experiments are initially tried who stand to benefit, but also all future sufferers from ADA deficiency and other diseases that can be changed genetically.

Somatic vs. Reproductive Cell Engineering Ethicists have tried to make distinctions among types of genetic engineering, hoping to differentiate acceptable from unacceptable types. For example, most gene changes attempted thus far are referred to as *somatic*. They will produce their effects in the somatic (body) cells of the individual who receives the genes, but not enter the sperm and egg cells. We also envision the day when we can change the genes of these *reproductive* cells. Once that can be done, the change will be passed to future offspring, potentially eliminating the genetic defect being treated for all future generations. On the other hand, if a mistake is made and the new genes cause an unanticipated problem, that also could be passed on to future generations. Many people consider the more conservative somatic cell changes safer and therefore more responsible, leaving to the future to decide whether the change should be repeated again in the succeeding generations.

Therapy vs. Enhancement A second distinction that is attempted is between changes that correct defective or missing genes, adding the proper genes in order to provide a **therapy** for a genetic disease and changes that attempt to improve on an already normal genetic endowment providing *enhancement*. Correcting a genetic defect that made one's muscles unusually weak would be therapy; adding a gene that made muscles super-strong would be enhancement. There is much greater support for therapy than for enhancement.

Artificial Insemination and In Vitro Fertilization Genetic engineering is not the only birth technology receiving attention. We now have the capacity to take egg and sperm cells and combine them artificially to produce designer babies.

Artificial Insemination The manipulation of sperm cells is not a new technology. We have had artificial insemination for generations. It can be done with a husband's sperm to provide more concentrated, controlled male reproductive cells. Manipulation of these cells has been attempted to control the sex of the offspring, but without great success. More controversy arises with donor sperm, in which a third-party (often a paid source rather than a true donor) provides the male cells. New moral problems are arising when computerized data-bases are used to permit future parents to select desired characteristics in their donor and when offspring attempt to demand a right to track the identity of what was presumed to be an anonymous donor. Such tracing is increasingly important not only for psychological reasons, but for genetic reasons as well. One fertility expert was accused of providing his own sperm for perhaps thousands of inseminations, raising serious questions about genetics as well as his deceptive practice.

In Vitro Fertilization In July of 1973 Louise Brown was born becoming the first human being ever conceived in vitro, that is through artificial, laboratory methods outside the human body. By surgically removing the mother's egg cells, we could now manipulate externally female reproductive cells just as well as those from the male. The era of artificial reproduction was in full-swing, and the ethical problems were soon to mushroom.

The first in vitro fertilizations were strictly between married couples for whom some medical problem prohibited more traditional conceptions. The moral controversy resembled those involving organ transplants and earlier human subjects research: was this human artificial manipulation an unethical attempt to play God, reducing to human planning and control a process that had throughout history been mysterious, random, and natural?

Soon we realized that, once this technology was in place, there was no real reason why it had to be limited to infertile married couples. Single women could become pregnant using the same technique (provided they could find a donor or a laboratory willing to provide sperm). Lesbian couples could conceive and bear a child that was genetically and gestationally the offspring of one of them. In fact, one could supply the genetic material while the other would provide the gestation. The very same technology that seemed to many people to meet a legitimate need of a traditional, married couple could be used for much more controversial and nontraditional births. Once an egg cell was removed and fertilized, there was no reason why it had to be gestated in the woman who supplied the egg. **Surrogate motherhood** became possible and has eventually led to legal and moral controversies.

Endnote 50

These same technologies make possible endless variations on the theme. A woman who was incapable of providing egg cells could borrow one to be fertilized by her husband's (or someone else's semen); a couple could agree to have the man artificially inseminate another woman who had agreed to turn the offspring over to them (the scenario that became famous when one such surrogate, Mary Beth Whitehead, refused to relinquish the baby as she had agreed); a family member, even one past menopause, not only could but actually has carried a child for a woman incapable or unwilling to do so. **Pressing these technologies to their limits, a five-parent child is conceivable.** Sperm from a donor could be used to fertilize an egg from a donor. Together they would be the genetic parents. The fertilized egg would then be implanted into a host surrogate, who would serve as the gestational parent. At birth, the infant could be transferred to two others serving in the role as social or nurturing parents.

Endnote 51

While all of these new birth technologies are possible, the real moral issue is whether they ought to be used. The social implications are enormous not only for the psychosocial development of the child, but also for the society's understanding of its basic institutions: the family, education, economics, and law. Some have argued that all the parties are not truly free in these transactions, but even if they were, profound questions about the fate of the traditional family relationship and the structure of the society would remain.

Cloning Closely related to these genetics and birth technologies is the emergence of cloning as a bioethical issue. We have known for decades that it was theoretically possible to remove the chromosomes of the cell of an animal, insert them in a single isolated cell, and produce a new individual that was an exact genetic copy of the one from whom the chromosomes were taken. We had actually done such experiments some years ago, but only in small animals. In 1997 the news broke that scientists in Scotland had produced a clone of a sheep. The now-famous Dolly controversy was born. The technique, which involves both manipulation of genetic material and in vitro beginning of a new being, has practical uses in agriculture and animal husbandry reproduction of animals with prized qualities, for instance, as well as medical uses of great value to humans, such as inserting genes that would produce rare chemicals that could be used as medicines.

In vitro fertilization technology was first developed for the plausible purpose of responding to infertile married couples, but, once the technology was in place, it could also be used for far more controversial cases, hardly envisioned by the technology's inventors. A similar problem arises with cloning. There seems to be little technical barrier to attempting cloning of humans. The first case is likely to be a compassionate response to a couple, perhaps now infertile for some reason, whose only child is terminally injured in an accident. If they plead for a chance to reproduce an exact genetic copy, claiming they can never again have a child that is genetically their own, some clinicians would find cooperation plausible. But once again, once the technology is developed for the plausible cases, others will be tempted to use it for other, more controversial cases such as producing armies, athletes, or intellects. In contrast to more complex technologies of atomic physics and space

Figure 5. Dolly, the cloned sheep. Edinburgh, Scotland. AP/Wide World Photos.

exploration, these reproductive technologies are sufficiently cheap and easy to manipulate that, once they are developed, they are likely to be used.

FINAL COMMENTS

In these dramatic new technological possibilities in the world of biology and medicine, we have before us some of the most fundamental and crucial questions in philosophy. They cluster around the three overarching questions presented in this chapter: who is a member of the human moral community; what is the relationship between benefiting patients and protecting their rights; and, finally, what is the relationship between the rights of the individual and the interests of society? It is clear now, as never before, that what once may have sounded like abstract philosophical questions actually have immediate practical payoffs of enormous importance. It is also clear that different philosophical and religious views give significantly different answers to these questions.

FOR FURTHER INQUIRY

REVIEW QUESTIONS

1. A physician challenged by a patient with engaging in unethical conduct points to the Hippocratic Oath on his office wall as the basis for his actions. On what basis might the patient object to this appeal? What three problems have led to the collapse of the Hippocratic tradition? What are some of the codes of ethics that break with the Hippocratic tradition and how do they differ from the that tradition?

2. What moral principle provides the foundation for the doctrine of informed consent? Consider a physician who appeals to therapeutic privilege as his reason for not disclosing the risks of a treatment to his patient. How would someone standing in the tradition of liberal political philosophy respond?

3. The manager of a health maintenance organization (HMO) insists that the organization does not have enough resources to provide every treatment that every physician believes will be beneficial to patients. How should the physician respond? If resources must be allocated what is the difference between allocating on the basis of maximizing aggregate benefit and allocating on the basis of justice to the worst off patients?

4. A researcher proposes to conduct a study on human subjects in order to attempt to produce useful knowledge for future patients. How would the following ethical traditions decide whether to permit the experiment: the Hippocratic tradition, the utilitarian tradition, the rights-oriented tradition that gives priority to autonomy?

APPLICATION QUESTION

1. Locate the text of the Hippocratic Oath and one other code of medical ethics (such as the Ethical and Religious Directives for Catholic Health Facilities, the Patient's Bill of Rights, or the AMA Principles). Analyze the differences between the Hippocratic Oath and the code you have chosen. Write an account of what problems you see in each of the codes you have selected.

ENDNOTES

1. Edelstein, Ludwig. "The Hippocratic Oath: Text, Translation and Interpretation." *Ancient Medicine: Selected Papers of Ludwig Edelstein.* Temkin, Owsei, and C. Lilian Temkin, editors. Baltimore, Maryland: The Johns Hopkins Press, 1967, pp. 3–64.

2. Based on "General Medical Council: Disciplinary Committee." *British Medical Journal Supplement,* no. 3442, March 20, 1971, pp. 79–80.

3. Edelstein, pp. 3–64; Veatch, Robert M., ed. *Medical Ethics.* Boston: Jones and Bartlett, 1989, pp. 1–26.

4. Edelstein, p. 62.

5. Veatch, Robert M., and Carol G. Mason. "Hippocratic vs. Judeo-Christian Medical Ethics: Principles in Conflict." *The Journal of Religious Ethics 15* (Spring 1987):86–105; see also Temkin, Owsei. *Hippocrates in a World of Pagans and Christians.* Baltimore: Johns Hopkins University Press, 1991, for a complex account of the many tensions as well as some compatibilities between Christian and Hippocratic thought.

6. Jones, W. H. S. *The Doctor's Oath: An Essay in the History of Medicine.* Cambridge: At The University Press, 1924.

7. Percival, Thomas. *Percival's Medical Ethics,* 1803. Reprint. Edited by Chauncey D. Leake. Baltimore: Williams and Wilkins, 1927.

8. American Medical Association. *Code of Medical Ethics*: Adopted by the American Medical Association at Philadelphia, May, 1847, and by the New York Academy of Medicine in October, 1847. New York: H. Ludwig and Company, 1848.

9. World Medical Association. "Declaration of Geneva." *World Medical Journal 3* (1956), supplement, pp. 10–12. Reprinted in *Encyclopedia of Bioethics,* Vol. 4. Warren T. Reich, editor. New York: The Free Press, 1978, p. 1749.

9a. American Hospital Association. "A Patient's Bill of Rights." *Encyclopedia of Bioethics,* Vol. 4. Edited by Warren T. Reich. New York: The Free Press, 1978, pp. 1782–1783.

9b. American Nurses' Association. "Code for Nurses with Interpretive Statements." Kansas City: American Nurses' Association, 1976.

9c. American Medical Association. *Current Opinions of the Judicial Council of the American Medical Association.* Chicago: American Medical Association, 1981.

10. Rosner, Fred, and J. David Bleich, editors. *Jewish Bioethics.* New York: Sanhedrin Press, 1979.

11. National Conference of Catholic Bishops. *Ethical and Religious Directives for Catholic Health Care Services.* Washington, DC: United States Catholic Conference; 1995.

12. Verhey, Allen. "Protestantism." *Encyclopedia of Bioethics*, Second Edition. Edited by Warren T. Reich. New York: Macmillan, Vol. 4, 1995, pp. 2117–2126.

13. For compendia of these medical ethical writings see the appendix in volume five of *Encyclopedia of Bioethics,* Revised Edition. Edited by Warren T. Reich. New York: Macmillan, 1995; also International Organization of Islamic Medicine. Islamic Code of Medical Ethics. [Kuwait]: International Organization of Islamic Medicine, 1981.

14. "The Oath of Soviet Physicians." Zenonas Danilevicius, trans. *Journal of the American Medical Association 217* (1971):834.

14a. Council of Europe. "Convention for Protection of Human Rights and Biomedicine." *Kennedy Institute of Ethics Journal* 7 (1997):277–90.

15. For an example of such a case see "The Dying Cancer Patient," in Veatch, Robert M. *Case Studies in Medical Ethics.* Cambridge, Mass.: Harvard University Press, 1977, pp. 141–43.

16. Oken, Donald. "What to Tell Cancer Patients: A Study of Medical Attitudes." *Journal of the American Medical Association* 175 (April 1, 1961):1120–1128.

17. Novack, Dennis H., Robin Plumer, Raymond L. Smith, Herbert Ochitill, Gary R. Morrow, and John M. Bennett. "Changes in Physicians' Attitudes Toward Telling the Cancer Patient." *Journal of the American Medical Association 241* (March 2, 1979):897–900.

18. Meyer, Bernard. "Truth and the Physician." *Ethical Issues in Medicine*. Edited by E. Fuller Torrey. Boston: Little Brown, 1968, p. 172 (159–177).

19. Fletcher, Joseph. *Morals and Medicine*. Boston: Beacon Press, 1954, pp. 34–64.

20. Kant, Immanuel. "On the Supposed Right to Tell Lies from Benevolent Motives." Translated by Thomas Kingsmill Abbott and reprinted in *Kant's Critique of Practical Reason and Other Works on the Theory of Ethics*. London: Longmans, 1909 [1797], pp. 361–365.

21. Ross, W.D. *The Right and the Good*. Oxford: Oxford University Press, 1939.

22. Brody, Baruch. *Life and Death Decision Making*. New York: Oxford University Press, 1988.

23. Their new principles were published the following year in American Medical Association. Current Opinions of the Judicial Council of the American Medical Association. Chicago: American Medical Association, 1981, p. ix.

24. Ibid., p. 25.

25. *Natanson v. Kline* 186 Kan. 393, 350 P. 2d 1093 (1960).

26. *Canterbury v. Spence*, 464 F. 2d 772 (D.C. Cir. 1972).

27. Veatch, Robert M. *The Patient as Partner — A Theory of Human-Experimentation Ethics*. Bloomington, Indiana: Indiana University Press, 1987; Veatch, Robert M.

The Patient-Physician Relation: The Patient as Partner, Part 2. Bloomington, IN: Indiana University Press, 1991.

28. May, William F. "Code, Covenant, Contract, or Philanthropy?" Hastings Center Report 5 (December 1975):29–38.

29. American Medical Association. Current Opinions of the Council on Ethical and Judicial Affairs of the American Medical Association: Including the Principles of Medical Ethics and Rules of the Council on Ethical and Judicial Affairs. Chicago: American Medical Association, 1989, p. ix.

30. "Central Ethical Committee." *British Medical Journal Supplement* (May 1, 1971), p. 30.

31. American Medical Association. Current Opinions of the Council on Ethical and Judicial Affairs of the American Medical Association: Including the Principles of Medical Ethics and Rules of the Council on Ethical and Judicial Affairs. Chicago: American Medical Association, 1989, p. 21.

32. Bernard, Claude. *An Introduction to the Study of Experimental Medicine*. Henry Copley Greene, A.M. (translator), New York: Dover Publications, Inc., 1957 [1865], p. 102.

33. "Nuremberg Code, 1946." In *Encyclopedia of Bioethics, Vol. 4*. Edited by Warren T. Reich. New York: The Free Press, 1978, pp. 1764–1765.

34. Levine, Robert J. *Ethics and Regulation of Clinical Research,* second edition. New Haven: Yale University Press, 1988, pp. 69–70.

35. Ibid.

36. Beecher, H.K. "Ethics and Clinical Research," *New England Journal of Medicine 274* (1966):1353–1360.

37. U.S. Department of Health, Education, and Welfare. *The Institutional Guide to DHEW Policy on Protection of Human Subjects*. Washington, D.C.: U.S. Government Printing Office, 1971.

38. National Commission for the Protection of Human Subjects of Biomedical and Behavioral Research. *The Belmont Report: Ethical Principles and Guidelines for the Protection of Human Subjects of Research*. Washington, D.C.: U.S. Government Printing Office, 1978.

38a. U.S. Department of Health and Human Services. "Federal Policy for the Protection of Human Subjects." *Code of Federal Regulations* 45 Part 46, Revised June 18, 1991, reprinted March 15, 1994.

38b. Walters,-LeRoy. "Fetus: III. Fetal Research." In: Reich, Warren Thomas, ed. *Encyclopedia of Bioethics*. Revised Edition. New York, NY: Simon and Schuster Macmillan, 1995, pp. 857–864.

38c. Mastroianni, Anna; Faden, Ruth; Federman, Daniel. "Women and Health Research: a Report from the Institute of Medicine." *Kennedy Institute of Ethics Journal* 4 (1)(1994 Mar):55–62.

38d. U.S. Public Health Service. "Expanded Availability of Investigational New Drugs Through a Parallel Track Mechanism for People with AIDS and Other HIV-related Disease; Notice Final Policy Statement." *Federal Register* 57 (73)(1992 Apr 15):13250–13259.

39. Dukeminier, Jesse, and David Sanders. "Organ Transplantation: A Proposal for Routine Salvaging of Cadaver Organs." *New England Journal of Medicine 279* (1968):413–19.

40. Sadler, A. M., B. L. Sadler, and E. Blythe Stason. "The Uniform Anatomical Gift Act." *Journal of the American Medical Association* 206 (Dec. 9, 1968):2501–06.

41. Caplan, Arthur L. "Organ Transplants: The Costs of Success, An Argument for Presumed Consent and Oversight." *Hastings Center Report 13* (December 1983):23–32; Matas, Arthur J., and Frank J. Veith. "Presumed Consent — A More Humane Approach to Cadaver Organ Donation." *Positive Approaches to Living with. End-Stage Renal Disease: Psychosocial and Thanatological Aspects.* Edited by Mark A. Hardy, et al. New York: Praeger, 1986, pp. 37–51.

42. New York State Task Force on Life and the Law. The Required Request Law: Recommendations of the New York State Task Force on Life and the Law. March 1986.

43. Peters, David A. "Marketing Organs for Transplantation." *Dialysis & Transplantation* 13 (January 1984):40–41.

44. Public Law 98-507, October 19, 1984. National Organ Transplant Act 98 Stat. 2339.

45. Veatch, Robert M. *Death, Dying, and the Biological Revolution*, Revised Edition. New Haven, Connecticut: Yale University Press, 1989, p. 216.

45a. Spital, Aaron. "Mandated Choice: The Preferred Solution to the Organ Shortage?" *Arch Intern Med* 152 (December, 1992) 2421–2424.

46. They probably should be permitted to give an "I don't know" response in order to avoid pressuring them into refusing to donate. If they gave this response, then their next-of-kin would be asked for permission just as is presently the case.

47. Burdick, James F., Jeremiah G. Turcotte, and Robert M. Veatch. "General Principles for Allocating Human Organs and Tissues." *Transplantation Proceedings* 24 (October 1992, No. 5):2226–35.

48. Oregon Health Services Commission. *Prioritization of Health Services: A Report to the Governor and Legislature.* n.p.: Oregon Health Services Commission, 1991.

48a. Murray, Thomas H, Mark A. Rothstein, and Robert F. Murray, Jr. *The Human Genome Project and the Future of Health Care.* Bloomington, IN: Indiana University Press, 1996.

49. Walters, LeRoy, and Julie Gage Palmer. *The Ethics of Human Gene Therapy.* New York: Oxford University Press, 1997.

50. Gostin, Larry, ed. *Surrogate Motherhood: Politics and Privacy.* Bloomington, In.: Indiana University Press, 1990; Robertson, John A. *Children of Choice: Freedom and the New Reproductive Technologies.* Princeton, NJ: Princeton University Press, 1994; Cohen, Cynthia B., Ed. *New Ways of Making Babies: The Case of Egg Donation.* Bloomington, IN: Indiana University Press, 1996.

51. Whitehead, Mary Beth, with Loretta Schwartz-Nobel. *A Mother's Story: The Truth About the Baby M Case.* New York: St. Martin's Press, 1989.

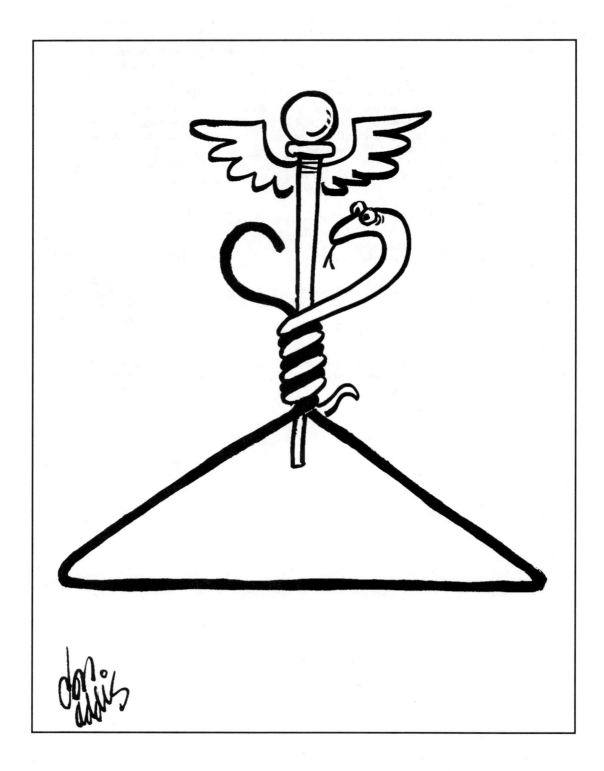

CHAPTER 7

ABORTION

"The pregnant woman cannot be isolated in her privacy. She carries an embryo and, later, a fetus . . . it is reasonable and appropriate for a State to decide that at some point in time another interest . . . becomes significantly involved. The woman's privacy is no longer sole and any right of privacy she possesses must be measured accordingly."

— ***Justice Harry A. Blackmun,*** **Roe vs. Wade**

"By restricting the right to terminate pregnancies, the State conscripts women's bodies into its service, forcing women to continue their pregnancies, suffer the pains of childbirth, and in most instances, provide years of maternal care. The State does not compensate women for their services; instead, it assumes that they owe this duty as a matter of course."

— ***Justices Anthony Kennedy, Sandra Day O'Connor, David Souter,*** **Casey vs. Planned Parenthood**

The range of issues we will address in this chapter can be viewed usefully at four distinct levels. A first level concerns the **fetus's moral status as an individual being.** At this first level we will consider what qualities any being must possess for us to think of that being as having moral interests and rights of its own. While our chief concern will be the moral standing of human beings at the early stages of human development, the general questions the chapter poses are potentially relevant to human beings at other stages of life and to animals who belong to other species. (See Chapter 12 for further discussion of the moral standing of animals.)

A second level broadens our initial focus on the individual and places **the fetus in the context of a unique relationship with another human being,** namely a pregnant woman. We will ask what ethical significance we should attribute to the fact that the fetus depends for its survival on inhabiting another human being's body. We will also consider how the fetus's moral status and rights may alter later in the course of fetal development as the fetus becomes viable and eventually could continue to survive on its own.

Nancy S. Jecker, M.A. Philosophy Stanford University, M.A. and Ph.D. University of Washington, is assistant professor at the University of Washington School of Medicine, Department of Medical History and Ethics. Contributor Robert M Veatch.

An important question at this level of discussion will be the following: If we assume that a fetus has the same ethical rights and interests as a pregnant woman (obviously, a controversial assumption), how, ethically, should we resolve conflicts between the fetus and pregnant woman?

CHIEF LEARNING OUTCOME

I understand and can discuss rationally the moral aspects of abortion.

A third level of the abortion debate is broader still, and situates the predicament of **fetus and pregnant woman in the context of a family or future family.** A future family may include another parent and other offspring. One question the chapter will raise is: Does it make any ethical difference if a woman knows in advance that a particular fetus would be born with a serious genetic condition? A related question concerns the situation of a pregnant woman who already has a large family and cannot afford financially to support an additional child. What role, if any, should such considerations play in a decision about whether to bring a pregnancy to term?

A final level of debate situates *abortion* in **the wider circle of the society and addresses law and social policies** regarding the practice of abortion. This section will review the 1973 U.S. Supreme Court decision, *Roe vs. Wade*, that decriminalized abortion, as well as several important legal decisions that occurred subsequent to Roe. Although many people who oppose abortion on ethical grounds also oppose legalizing abortion, it will be critical for us to distinguish between the ethical and legal permissibility of abortion decisions.

(**Editors' Note:** It is recognized that many Americans refer to the conception in the womb as a baby. Sadly, even the use of a single term — baby or fetus — occasionally has been viewed as taking sides in the abortion debate. Some even believe that solely using the word baby or solely the word fetus implies pejorative treatment of one side of the debate. No such use of the language is intended in this chapter. However, the least emotional contexts for discussion of the abortion issue are medical and legal, and because these professions rely on the term **fetus**, so will this chapter. Also, although various medical terms — zygote, conceptus, embryo and fetus — are used to refer to the developing human being in the womb, the author will use the term fetus globally to refer to all these stages, while respectfully realizing that many persons would describe all such stages with the term baby.)

THE INDIVIDUAL: WHAT IS THE MORAL STATUS OF THE FETUS?

Imagine that you are traveling to a distant planet in the solar system. The vessel on which you are traveling lands. There you discover a new form of life that is nothing like life on earth. While observing these creatures and trying to understand their form of life, several colleagues on board your space craft report that this planet has abundant supplies of various natural resources that have become exceedingly scarce on earth. Your colleagues begin to discuss the potential for harvesting these vast resources and transporting them back to earth. Listening to the conversation, you begin to wonder what implications such a plan might carry for the new form of life that exists on this planet. You raise this concern with others. Together all of you begin to ask yourselves what is the right thing to do. You wonder, Do the strange creatures you have found here have any moral standing? In other words, should they be subjects of moral concern in their own right? Do these creatures possess moral rights? If so, do they have a right to life? One among you asks whether these strange forms of life have the same moral standing as adult human beings. Another person suggests that perhaps these alien creatures have greater moral importance than human beings and possess more significant moral interests.

These are difficult questions. You and your shipmates are not altogether comfortable with them. Your discomfort only grows when you realize that if these creatures have moral claims against you, this may well conflict with your own interests in using the planet's resources to benefit yourselves and other people on Earth. The moral questions you have raised persist and continue to nag at your consciences.

KEY CONCEPTS

Personhood

1. A being, potentially belonging to any species, who is a subject of moral concern and who possesses, in particular, a moral right to life. Used in this way, in theory, an embryo, a fetus, or an unconscious adult could be considered a person.

2. In other literature, some people use the word *person* in a quite different way to refer to a being who possesses certain nonmoral characteristics such as consciousness, awareness, self-consciousness, or self-awareness. Used in this way, in theory, some who are called persons theoretically may not be subjects of moral concern and may not possess a moral right to life and while some who are not persons may be subjects of such concern. This chapter uses the word *person* only in the first sense.

Moral Status or Standing

Living beings who are the subject of moral concern or who have legitimate moral claims are said to have moral status or standing. Not all beings necessarily have the same degree of this moral status, but many believe there is such a thing as "full" or maximal moral standing and that living human beings have such status either from the moment of conception (the conservative position) or after they acquire certain characteristics such as self-awareness (the liberal position). Some believe that embryos and fetuses gradually develop greater moral status until they reach a certain maximal amount, usually late in pregnancy or at birth (the moderate position).

Roe's Trimester Approach

Rulings of the U.S. Supreme Court imply that during the first trimester of pregnancy the public or state interest is limited to that of the pregnant woman; in the second trimester states may regulate abortion but only for purposes of the health of the woman, and in the third trimester the state's interest includes prohibition of abortion to protect a viable fetus but not to interfere with abortions necessary to protect the health of the pregnant woman.

Answers to such questions are not readily found. You and your companions settle upon the following procedure for framing the problem, and you agree among yourselves to use the following language to discuss it.

The Definition of "Person"

A "Person" as One with Full Moral Standing or a Right to Life

You and your fellow travelers agree to use the term "person" to refer to a being, potentially belonging to any species, who is a subject of moral concern and who possesses, in particular, a moral right to life. In your experiences, the most obvious examples of persons are normal adult human beings. But other examples might include certain non-human animals, such as dolphins or chimpanzees; God and angels, if they exist; and extraterrestrial beings, such as the ones you have discovered.

Next, you and your companions agree that you cannot dismiss the possibility that the form of life you have discovered is a person just because it is not human. Your reasoning here is that to assume that only instances of human life could count as persons would be similar to claiming that only members of favored racial groups possess certain rights or are full-fledged persons. The latter mistake is one you are (all too well) acquainted with: Racism. The former mistake, you suppose, might be dubbed, "speciesism." Speciesism shows the folly of thinking that a being must look like a human being to be a person. Although having human facial features or human fingers and toes may elicit certain emotional responses in us, possessing such features is not necessary for being a moral person.

Endnote 1

Finally, you and other members in the group set yourselves the explicit task of deciding what qualities a being must possess in order to qualify as a person. As you and the rest of the Earth crew are contemplating an excavation of the planet's natural resources, with potentially devastating consequences for the planet, you need to know not only whether this alien life form is a source of moral concern, but whether these creatures are persons with a right to life. If the sole moral claim these creatures had was not to be tortured or caused pain, you are confident that painless extinction would be feasible. Your concern, then, focuses on the question: Are these strange beings moral persons, possessing as all persons do a right to life?

Alternative Criteria for Personhood

Having framed the question in this manner, the debate soon heats up and reaches a boiling point. Among the initial criteria you debate as central to personhood are the following:

1. Some Kind of Mental Capacity

Some of those involved in the debate quickly identify some mental capacity as the critical feature that give personhood or a special moral status so that they have a right to life. They seem, however, to disagree among themselves over exactly what capacity that might be.

a. *Consciousness*

Consciousness is the capacity to have states of awareness, such as states of thinking or feeling. Someone suggests that consciousness is the key feature of personhood because it serves to distinguish beings that merit special treatment in their own right from mere objects that can be used as mere means to accomplish others' purposes. For example, flowers, rocks, and pieces of paper are not consciously aware of anything and so can serve simply as a means to serve the purposes of conscious beings.

b. *Self-consciousness*

Someone suggests that what matters is not just having a conscious flow of experiences but also having a concept of one's self, being aware of one's self as a separate being that exists over time. Self-consciousness presupposes not only consciousness, but also a conscious sense of one's self.

c. *Sentience*

Someone else offers the idea that the hallmark of personhood is sentience or the ability to have certain kinds of conscious experiences, such as pleasure and pain, enjoying and suffering, forming wants and aims, having desires and tastes. More sophisticated forms of sentience would include more complex feelings, such as sympathy, honor, religious awe, love, or moral conscience. These capacities certainly make human beings morally special. So perhaps other creatures who have such capacities are special in the same way.

d. *The capacity to communicate*

Others propose that what makes someone a subject of a moral community is the capacity to communicate with at least one other being. Communication includes not just using words and language, but also entirely nonverbal modes of interacting. For example, nods or gestures or giggles can function as means of communicating feelings or plans or intentions. So too, loud noises can be used to convey thoughts without ever forming words.

e. *Reasoning*

Another possible criterion for personhood is the capacity to reason. The point here is not that individuals must be able to perform complex mathematical computations in order to merit moral consideration. Instead, reasoning may occur only at a very rudimentary level. A being reasons merely by formulating goals and identifying behaviors that are instrumental to achieving these goals. At a minimum, reasoning entails a conscience and deliberate thinking process. Reasoning may be evidenced, for example, by the capacity to solve novel puzzles, such as spell new words or find a new way of getting to a familiar location. Reasoning also may be apparent when someone engages in purposeful behaviors, such as using a tool.

f. Social visibility
Another shipmate advances the idea that someone qualifies as a person if that individual is part of a larger social group. This seems initially quite sensible because someone who existed on an island all alone could not be a subject of moral rights at all, because moral rights presuppose having certain claims against other people.

g. The capacity for self-motivated activity
Someone proposes that what makes a creature a person is that the creature is alive and capable of self-directed movement. For example, a rock is not a person because it is motionless. By contrast, creatures that can move at their own will sometimes qualify as persons.

h. The capacity for moral agency
Finally, someone among this group that is focusing on some mental capacity suggests that a being should not be considered to be a full-fledged member of the moral community unless that being can potentially assume moral responsibilities toward others. The reasoning here is that a moral community will not survive long, or at all, if its members have rights and claims against others but no one has any duty to respect the rights or meet the claims of other people.

2. Some biological feature

Others reject the whole idea that it is some mental capacity that is critical for being considered a person. They believe that it may be some biological feature, but, again, this group disagrees among themselves about exactly what that feature is.

a. Capacity for respiration and cardiac function
Some, remembering notions such as "the breath of life," suggest that one very critical aspect of being considered alive is the basic biological capacities of respiration and circulation. They think that any being that breathes and carries on circulatory function might be considered alive and suggest that these features by themselves might be

considered sufficient to have a right to life. They know some Orthodox Jews who seem to hold a similar position. They acknowledge that taken by itself this could mean that all animals, at least those high enough in the orders of evolution that carry on these functions, would be considered to have a right to life. They know animal rights activists who hold such a view.

b. *The possession of a fixed genetic code*

Others among those who focus on basic biological characteristics believe that what is critical is the position of a unique genetic identity. They recognize that many species reproduce sexually and that sperm and egg cells exist in great numbers, but that the uniqueness of an individual occurs only when the genetic material from both sperm and egg combine in a permanent, fixed way, creating a genetically unique individual who will possess that genetic information in all his cells throughout his or her life. They believe that that genetic uniqueness is what is morally critical for personhood and what gives individuals a right to life. They may also recognize that this could occur in all animal species; in fact, it could occur in plants as well.

c. *Membership in a specific species*

In order to address the counterintuitive implications of granting personhood status to all creatures with respiration and circulation or all creatures with a fixed genetic code, some attempt to limit the class of persons in addition to members of certain species: humans, primates, or perhaps some other higher animal species. This, of course, would categorically exclude any creatures we might encounter on other planets who are not included on our list of accepted species.

Potentiality:
In the context of abortion, some believe that it is not the actual possession of certain capacities but the potential for development of those capacities that gives moral status or standing. Fetuses with a high probability of developing these capacities are said to have potentiality.

Mental Capacities Associated with Normal Humans Many, especially liberals, believe that moral standing is associated with the development of some particular mental capacity or some cluster of such capacities. These capacities often include consciousness, awareness, self-consciousness, or self-awareness.

3. Combining biological and mental characteristics

Finally, when trying to determine whether those we encounter are persons, that is beings with a moral status that gives them a claim to a right to life, some might try to combine some mental characteristic, such as consciousness, with some biological characteristics. This could be done in several ways picking one or more of the mental characteristics and combining them with some biological characteristic.

a. *Combining a biological characteristic with the existence of a potential in the individual to develop a mental capacity* Our group might believe that personhood exists in all who are alive who have the capacity to eventually develop one or more of the mental characteristics already identified. This would rule out embryos, fetuses, and even children and adults who have no capacity for the relevant mental function. For example, anencephalic fetuses (who have not potential for mental function), according to this view, would not be persons even though normal fetuses and infants would.

b. *Combining a biological characteristic with membership is a species that normally can develop a mental capacity* Instead of giving personhood to all respiring beings with a fixed genetic code who actually have the capacity to develop mental function, one could grant it to all who are members of species that normally develop this capacity. This would include in the category of persons, human anencephalic fetuses (because humans normally develop mental capacities, even while those with anencephaly do not).

Everyone acknowledges that the various qualities under consideration could, in principle, be realized through a vast array of different physical materials. For example, reasoning might take place without a being possessing the gray brain matter we humans do. Likewise, consciousness could, in principle, exist in someone who did not possess a cerebral cortex of the sort with which we are familiar. Everyone also recognizes that the problem of how to treat the unfamiliar creatures on this planet is only the tip of the iceberg. It carries important implications for life forms generally, including human and non-human life forms on Earth.

Finally, everyone agrees that a systematic approach to evaluating standards for personhood is necessary. One approach would be to identify a single feature or set of features that a being must have in order to be a person. If it were possible to identify a necessary condition for personhood, it would be possible to exclude any creatures that lack that essential feature. For example, the group wonders whether any being that is permanently non-conscious could ever be a person. Perhaps, the capacity for consciousness is an absolute necessity for personhood.

Another approach would be to try to agree upon what quality or qualities are sufficient for personhood. A creature need not have this quality, but any creature that did would automatically qualify as a person. Whereas necessary conditions for personhood function as standards for excluding creatures from the category of personhood, sufficient conditions function as standards for including creatures. You wonder, for example, whether reasoning is sufficient to show personhood. Or are some other qualities also required to demonstrate personhood, such as the capacity to feel certain emotions?

PERSONHOOD: THREE POSITIONS

The above exercise shows that in order to understand more fully what moral personhood means, we need first to figure out what the necessary and sufficient conditions for personhood might include. This is a very large and difficult task. It is perhaps reassuring to know that you are not the first to embark on such an inquiry, at least with respect to the abortion question (aliens are another matter).

Generally speaking, there are three quite different positions people take with respect to when, in the course of development, a human being becomes a person. In order to give you a general sense of the personhood debate, this section describes each of the three views in a general way and then describes, in more detail, one particular version of each view.

The Conservative Position

A first position, often referred to as the conservative position on personhood, holds that a human being is a person from the moment of conception onward. The underlying criterion that supports this view does not refer to any of the eight criteria mental capacities listed above. Instead, conservatives maintain that it is sufficient for personhood that a being has either genetic uniqueness or the potential of developing the morally significant mental capacities. From the moment of conception, a healthy human being has the capacity, for example, to develop consciousness, reasoning, and sentience simply by virtue of having the complete set of human chromosomes. A well-known advocate of the conservative position, **John Noonan**, presents the following arguments in support of this position stated in terms of developing certain critical mental capacities.

Endnote 2

The Probability of Developing the Mental Capacities Normally Associated with Humans

1. It is seriously wrong to destroy any organism that has a significant probability of developing the mental capacities we associate with human beings.

2. If a spermatozoa is destroyed, one destroys an organism that has a chance of less than 1 in 200 million of developing the mental capacities we normally associate with humans.

3. If an oocyte (egg) is destroyed, one destroys an organism that has a chance of less than 390 in 100,000 of developing the mental capacities we normally associate with humans.

4. If a zygote (fertilized egg) is destroyed, one destroys a being that has an 80 per cent chance of developing the mental capacities we normally associate with humans.

5. Therefore, it is seriously wrong to destroy a fetus (from zygote on), although it is not seriously wrong to destroy sperms and eggs.

The Potentiality of Developing the Mental Capacities Normally Associated with Humans

1. Any organism that will, in the normal course of its development, come to have whatever mental capacities we normally associate with humans is itself a moral being with a right to life.

2. Beginning at conception, homo sapiens (who do not have gross abnormalities) will, in the normal course of development, come to have the properties that we associate with humans.

3. Therefore, beginning at conception, homo sapiens (except those with gross abnormalities) have a right to life.

The Moderate Position

Endnote 3

A second position, often referred to as the moderate position, holds that a human being becomes a person sometimes after conception but prior to birth. This position is held, for example, by the philosopher Wayne Sumner. Sumner maintains that sentience is both a necessary and a sufficient condition for being a person. There is no doubt that a human being lacks sentience at the moment of conception; hence Sumner rejects the conservative position. Sumner instead locates the threshold of personhood during the second trimester of pregnancy. This is when the fetus's forebrain has developed, and in particular when the cerebral cortex, which is thought to be the seat of consciousness, and sentience has developed.

In the course of elaborating and defending what often is termed a moderate position, Sumner makes the following observations. He notes, first, that sentience admits of degrees. In its simplest form, sentience includes only the capacity to feel pain or pleasure. More complex forms of sentience include more subtle and complex emotions, such as feeling moral guilt or pride, feeling detachment or empathy toward others' suffering, feeling confidence or insecurity, feeling grief or joy. Because sentience admits of degree, using it as a standard for personhood enables us to think of moral standing as falling along a continuum, rather than being an all-or-nothing phenomenon. For example, we can think of creatures with the most basic kinds of sentience as having only a minimal right to life, and those with more complex capacities as having correspondingly greater moral standing.

One argument supporting this particular version of a moderate position is its explanatory power. That is, it has the apparent advantage of matching people's considered judgments about particular cases beyond the abortion question. Thus, if one believes that higher vertebrates, such as mammals, deserve greater moral protection of life than lower vertebrates, such as fish and reptiles, then this account of personhood can explain these beliefs. Sumner's position also can account for the belief that higher mammals, such as primates, are due greater protection of life than lower mammals, such as dogs and cats, because they have more sophisticated forms of sentience. By contrast, those positions that associate personhood with possessing certain all-or-nothing properties, such as potentiality, cannot explain such judgments. "Crude as this division may be," says Sumner, "it seems to accord reasonably well with most people's intuitions that in our moral reasoning paramecia and horseflies count for things, dogs and cats count for something, chimpanzees and dolphins count for more, and human beings count for most of all."

Endnote 4

One potential problem with this position is that we recognize that just as different animal species have different levels or forms of sentience, so also do human beings. Even among adults some may have more richly developed capacities for sentience than others. This could lead to the conclusion that some humans are more persons than others or that some have more of a right to life than others. For example, it might imply that if one has to be sacrificed for the good of others, the one with the least personhood (least sentience) would be the one to be sacrificed. To overcome this view, some people hold that there is a cut-off point such that all who have capacities beyond that limit are taken to be "fully persons" or to have "full moral standing."

The Liberal Position

A final position, usually referred to as the liberal position, locates personhood as occurring at birth or shortly thereafter. For example, Mary Anne Warren maintains that the traits that are most central to being a person include qualities such as consciousness, reasoning, self-motivated activity, the capacity to communicate, and self-awareness. Thus she associates personhood with the mental capacities we have discussed. She maintains further that it is not necessary to have all of these qualities to qualify as a person; however, any being that lacks all of these person-like features is not a person.

Endnote 5

In support of a liberal position, Warren argues that the conservative position is deeply flawed on the following grounds:

An Argument Against the Conservative Position

1. Any being that has none of the mental capacities we associate with personhood (consciousness, reasoning, self-motivated activity, the capacity to communicate, self-awareness) cannot possibly be a person.

2. At the moment of conception, a human being does not have any of the mental capacities we associate with personhood.

3. Therefore a human being cannot possibly be a person at the moment of conception.

On this analysis, the potential to develop these mental capacities by virtue of having the human genetic code does not confer personhood, as the conservatives suggest. For the human genetic code does not actually impart any of the mental capacities the liberal associates with personhood. Thus, at the moment of conception a human being is still a tiny microscopic organism, and lacks the brain and other physical bases that humans require to support capacities such as consciousness and reasoning. Warren concludes that a human being who has the potential to develop these mental capacities is a **potential person**. Such a being has potential and future, rather than actual, moral rights.

She goes on to point out that a small infant is not very much more person-like than a late stage fetus. A newborn infant, then, is not properly regarded as a person in its own right. However, Warren is also quick to note that there are many, many reasons why we should nonetheless protect the lives of newborn babies. Babies are valued by and give pleasure to persons. They cause parents delight and joy and are loved very much by their family members. Even strangers have strong responses to babies and would prefer, for example, paying taxes to care for infants who are not wanted, rather than allowing such infants to be killed or allowed to die. Warren draws the conclusion that so long as people feel this way about babies, killing babies is morally objectionable. It conflicts with the interests and rights of those who are persons.

A Problem with the Liberal Position Stated as an Argument

Although many who are liberal on abortion agree with Warren's conclusion, here first premise poses a problem. As long as the concept of person is defined in terms of one who has a right to life and not in terms of the possession of these mental capacities, it is not obvious that everyone who agrees that anyone who lacked all the critical mental capacities was not a person. She seems to assume that to be true, but does not prove that having at least some of these mental capacities is necessary to have a right to life, i.e., to be a person. Surely, many conservatives would reject her assumption here.

THE MATERNAL-FETAL RELATIONSHIP: HOW SHOULD A CONFLICT OF INTEREST BE RESOLVED?

Let us return briefly to the space story with which this chapter began. However, this time assume that you and your fellow spaceship travelers have reached some agreement about what the criteria for personhood are and have determined that the creatures in question are persons. Operating on these assumption, it is important to see that there are other vital ethical questions that your group must address before you can know how you ought to act toward the extraterrestrial creatures. For example, even assuming that these creatures possess a moral right to life, this right may conflict with the rights and interests of other persons. One way this might occur is if the creatures in question require special chemicals to stay alive and these are in short supply on their planet. We might suppose that the chemicals these creatures need occur in abundance in the blood of human beings. What if the alien creatures figure this out and indicate their intention to keep you on the planet for nine months so that they can draw your blood and replenish their supply of the vital chemicals?

This may be inconvenient. Perhaps you and your shipmates had other plans and goals. Perhaps giving blood on a regular basis would make you feel weak and sick most of the time. It could even require long periods of bedrest or hospitalization. The amounts they require could even kill you. What's more, perhaps you have no desire whatsoever to be of service to these creatures. Although you believe that they are persons, perhaps you insist that you are a person too, and you possess moral rights and interests of your own that must be taken into account. Perhaps your space travel is part of an important scientific project, and you are simply not free to put this project on hold and stay on the planet while these creatures harvest your blood. Or perhaps you are a mother or father and staying on this planet for nine months would irritate the babysitter, not to mention your spouse and children. Or perhaps you just started a new job. In short, you may begin to wonder why the interests and rights of extra-terrestrial life should automatically take precedence over your own rights.

Needless to say, in the actual world this kind of added moral complexity is present. Persons do not exist in isolation, but exist instead in the context of relationships and moral communities with other creatures. Persons depend on other persons in vital ways and require various things of each other. Although all persons by definition possess a right to life, this right is not always or necessarily absolute. It can conflict with the rights and interests of other persons and must be weighed against these in particular cases.

CONFLICTING INTERESTS

Returning to the abortion question, let us suppose for the purposes of argument that the fetus is indeed a person, that is, has a right to life. Indeed, let us suppose that from the moment of conception onward all human beings are full-fledged persons. In other words, suppose that they are accorded the same moral standing that normal adult human beings are. The adventure of the spaceship travelers should make it abundantly clear that knowing that someone is a person hardly settles the question of how we are ethically required to treat that person. Thus, assuming that a fetus is a person does yet not decide the matter of whether abortion of the fetus is ever morally permissible. For the fetus exists in a moral community with other persons, and the fetus's rights and interests may be at odds with the moral rights and interests of others. These reflections suggest rather strongly that to know whether the fetus's assumed right to life overrides the rights and interests of others, we need to think more carefully about what implications upholding this right can have for the life and welfare of other persons.

It should be immediately clear that the fetus is in a special moral situation. Not only does the fetus exist in a community with other persons but the fetus also exists inside another person's body. Whereas the extra-terrestrial creatures described above needed other people's blood, the fetus needs to inhabit another person's physical being and grow inside it. This certainly involves a much more profound dependency between persons. When this relationship with another person is not wanted by the pregnant woman whose body is inhabited, she is likely to feel that a much more fundamental intrusion is occurring. Not only is another being drawing her blood, it is growing inside her and making use of her body for sustenance. Furthermore, whereas the extra-terrestrial creatures in the previous example wanted to treat people in ways that might make them weak or sick, supporting a fetus requires enduring various other burdens. Thus, during a normal pregnancy a woman not uncommonly experiences a range of uncomfortable symptoms, such as constipation, hemorrhoids, heartburn, pica (craving to eat substances other than foods, such as clay or coal), swollen ankles, varicose veins, leg cramps, backache, breathlessness, urinary tract infections, and lethargy. In addition, hormonal effects on the brain not uncommonly make pregnant women's moods more changeable, produce bouts of depression and crying, or cause them to be more easily angered or annoyed. Pregnant women are also at risk for various complications of pregnancy, some of which are life threatening.

It is important to remember that in most cases a pregnancy involves both a physical and an emotional bond between a pregnant woman and fetus; or, as some would say, between mother and her child. In the usual situation, then, the rights of the pregnant woman are not at odds with the rights of the fetus. Yet when conflict does arise, we need to ask how it can be ethically resolved. Assuming the fetus is a person, we need to ask what is most fair to the two persons who are most intimately involved in an abortion decision.

There are several kinds of conflicts that abortion can reflect and the differences here may prove ethically significant:

1. **The fetus's assumed right to life conflicts with the pregnant woman's right to life**

   In the most dramatic, and least common, example the fetus's continued development threatens the life of the pregnant woman. Here the fetus's right to life is in direct conflict with the same right of the pregnant woman. For example, when a women has an ectopic pregnancy (a pregnancy that implants outside the uterus) her own life is threatened if the pregnancy is allowed to continue.

2. **The fetus's assumed right to life conflicts with the pregnant woman's physical or emotional health**

   A somewhat different situation arises when the pregnant woman's physical or emotional health is placed in jeopardy by a continued pregnancy. For example, a woman who is known to have an underlying chronic condition, such as chronic hypertension (high blood pressure) or multiple sclerosis may wish to avoid pregnancy out of concern that it will adversely affect her health.

3. **The fetus's assumed right to life conflicts with the pregnant woman's right to pursue important projects by imposing serious obstacles and hardships**

In many cases harboring a fetus will not seriously harm a pregnant woman's life or health, but will impose other kinds of hardships. For example, continuing with a pregnancy may require dropping out of high school or college. Or when a pregnant woman decides to bring a fetus to term and then give the child up for adoption, the decision to sever relations permanently with one's child is an emotionally wrenching choice. By contrast, women who continue unwanted pregnancies and then go on to rear their children to maturity may face other hardships. For example, a single parent who lacks access to affordable child care may be forced to quit her job to care for her children. The result may be impoverishment and long-term dependence on public assistance. Generally speaking, pregnant women who lack adequate social and economic support following pregnancy encounter serious obstacles to pursuing whatever educational or career aspirations they envisioned for themselves.

4. **The fetus's assumed right to life conflicts with a woman's right to decide**

In virtually all situations in which a woman prefers an abortion, there exists a conflict between the fetus's right to life, on the one hand, and the pregnant woman's right to decide what will happen in and to her body, on the other hand.

A Moral Analysis of These Conflicts of Interest

In reviewing these potential conflicts between fetus and pregnant woman, it might at first glance be thought that only the first instance of conflict could conceivably be decided in favor of the pregnant woman. Thus, some might suppose that a person's right to life should always take precedence over other, less "vital," rights, — such as a right to have one's health, projects, or preferences protected.

In response to this suggestion, several objections can be made. First, in many other cases we do not think that a person's right to life takes precedence over interests and considerations that do not involve protection of life. For example, persons routinely refuse to take steps to protect the lives of other persons simply because taking these steps would be inconvenient. Thus, most individuals do not donate significant amounts of their income to charitable organizations that protect human life, such as famine relief organizations. Instead, most people spend their earnings on whatever they want, including non-essential items such as movies, alcohol, automobiles, or dinner out. Even though contributing money to charitable organizations could save lives, we usually think that people are justified in giving higher priority to pursuing their own interests.

The Analysis of Judith Jarvis Thomson

Endnote 6

The philosopher Judith Jarvis Thomson takes this point one step further. Thomson argues that it is not only incorrect, but absurd, to suppose that rights to life have automatic priority over other rights. To show that this is so she first imagines a situation where she is "sick unto death, and the only thing that will save my life is the touch of Henry Fonda's cool hand on my fevered brow." In such a situation, Thomson reasons:

Endnote 7

> I have no right to be given the touch of Henry Fonda's cool hand on my fevered brow. It would be frightfully nice of him to fly in from the West Coast to provide it. It would be less nice, though no doubt well meant, if my friends flew out to the West Coast and carried Henry Fonda back with them. But I have no right at all against anybody that he should do this for me.

Endnote 8

Next Thomson makes a similar point by imagining a situation where the Society of Music Lovers kidnaps someone and plugs into that person a famous violinist, who must remain plugged in to that person's body for nine months in order to remain alive. Thomson reasons that it is absurd to suppose that the famous violinist has a right to remain plugged in; instead the kidnaped party is ethically free to unplug this person. The suggestion is that the predicament of the kidnaped person is analogous to that of the pregnant woman who discovers that she is pregnant. Assuming the fetus is a person, even a future famous violinist, Thomson reasons that the pregnant woman is ethically free to refuse to harbor the fetus.

Thomson's argument can be usefully summarized along the lines that follow. First, in the abortion case, Thomson considers the following proposal:

An Argument for Granting Priority to the Fetus's Right to Life

1. The fetus is a person with a right to life.
2. The pregnant woman has a right to decide what happens in and to her body.
3. Yet a person's right to life is always stronger than a person's right to decide what happens in and to her body.
4. Therefore, abortion is never permissible.

The Problems with This Argument

Thomson then proceeds to show the downfall of this initial argument by showing that the reasoning (in premise three) leads to absurd results.

1. A violinist is a person with a right to life.
2. A person has a right to determine what happens in and to her body.
3. A violinist's right to life is always stronger than a person's right to decide what happens in and to her body.
4. Therefore, if the Society of Music Lovers kidnaps a person and plugs into her a famous violinist that needs to use her body for life support for nine months, it is not permissible to unplug the violinist.

In response to this argument it can be noted that there are several important differences between the initial argument and the analogy Thomson seeks to establish. First, the pregnant woman and her partner might be morally accountable for pregnancy occurring. For example, they may have omitted to take precautions, such as using contraceptive devices, to prevent pregnancy from occurring. Or even if precautions of this sort were taken and pregnancy occurred despite this, a pregnant woman and her partner might be considered responsible for bringing pregnancy about if they knew in advance of engaging in sexual intercourse that no method of birth control is 100% effective and that the risk of pregnancy occurring is therefore always present. Unlike the kidnaped person who was dragged unwillingly into a "plugged in" situation, when two people voluntarily engage in sexual behaviors that can lead to pregnancy they voluntarily undertake the risk of pregnancy.

Understood in this light, the violinist example is perhaps most analogous to a situation where a woman is raped and subsequently becomes pregnant. In this case, like the violinist case, a pregnant woman finds a fetus growing inside her that needs to rely on her body for nine months to survive. Like the person who is kidnaped and connected with a violinist, a woman who is raped and subsequently becomes pregnant is forcibly put in a situation where a fetus is developing inside her.

THE MODIFIED VIOLINIST CASE

In situations other than rape it might be useful to alter Thomson's original story. For example, in the case of failed contraception, a better analogy might be as follows.

Imagine that you purchase tickets to see a concert performance put on by the Society of Music Lovers. You love this kind of performance and are very much looking forward to an entertaining evening. Before purchasing a ticket, you are informed that a certain percentage of ticket holders, say 5%, will be kidnaped by the Society of Music Lovers and connected with famous violinists. The violinists will need to use the ticket holders' bodies for nine months. You decide to buy the ticket and go to the concert despite this risk, because you are so fond of the music and looking forward to the event. Suppose, however, that you are in the unlucky 5% of

Figure 1. The Good Samaritan assists a beaten man. Copyright © Drawing by Marion Eldridge.

people who are kidnaped and plugged into a violinist. What are your obligations to the violinist?

In this case, unlike Thomson's original example, the kidnaped persons who attended the concert knew they were taking a risk and they freely decided to do so. This is analogous to the situation of a woman and man engaging in sexual relations and using contraception who are aware that contraception is not 100% effective. The couple chooses to assume the risk of an unwanted pregnancy and therefore is responsible for finding the woman "connected with" a fetus. What are the responsibilities of the couple to the fetus under these conditions? Assuming, as we are, that the fetus is a person, must a pregnant woman sacrifice her own interests to support the fetus? Must she sacrifice her health and welfare? Must she sacrifice her life?

One response to these questions holds that requiring pregnant women in this situation to continue with unwanted pregnancies is expecting too much. After all, we do not expect that men who father unwanted offspring will make similar kinds of sacrifices.

For example:

Men who engage in heterosexual intercourse do not lose (their) right (to defend their physical integrity). Nor should they. A father cannot legally be forced to donate a kidney, or even some easily replaceable blood, in order to save the life of his child. If men are not stripped of that right because of their sexual activity, then it is doubly unjust that women should be.

Endnote 9

Another response argues that a person who risks an unwanted pregnancy by having intercourse does incur certain obligations toward the fetus, but distinguishes between the minimal obligations a person is ethically required to meet and more generous acts of sacrifice and heroism that are not ethically mandatory. In making this distinction, this response invokes the parable of the ***Good Samaritan.***

Endnote 10

The actual Samaritan in this parable has become paradigmatic of "the Good Samaritan," a type of person who will go to unusual lengths to help someone in need. We might contrast the Good Samaritan with a "Splendid Samaritan," a person who not only goes to unusual lengths for another person but also sacrifices his or her own welfare in the course of doing so. For example, we might regard the Samaritan in the parable as Splendid if the money he gave to the innkeeper was all the money he had at the time to feed and care for himself.

Both the Good Samaritan and the Splendid Samaritan stand in sharp contrast to what we might call the "Minimally Decent Samaritan," someone who meets minimal obligations but does nothing over and above this to help a person in need. Such a person lacks the heroic qualities that both the Good and Splendid Samaritans show. However, strictly speaking, a Minimally Decent Samaritan does not act wrongly or violate any moral obligations one is required to meet. In the parable, the Levite and priest were not even Minimally Decent Samaritans, because they failed to meet standards of minimally decent morality. Minimally Decent Samaritans in their situation may have called for someone else to help the injured man, and after help arrived gone on along their way.

LEVELS OF OBLIGATION DURING PREGNANCY

What relevance do these distinctions bear on the abortion situation? They suggest the usefulness of speaking not only in the vocabulary of rights or conflicts of rights, but also in the language of character and virtue. Assuming again that the fetus is a person, we might understand a woman's response to an unwanted pregnancy as falling along a continuum. At one end, perhaps, is a woman who cannot carry a fetus to term without placing her own life in peril. Here the sacrifice to help another is the ultimate sacrifice. A lesser, but still major, sacrifice involves a woman who places her own health at grave peril in order to sustain the life of the fetus. A still significant, but less grave, sacrifice might involve a woman who accepts serious and lasting hardships in order to sustain a fetus. These may be in the form of financial, educational, career, or other interests. As noted above, every woman who continues an unwanted pregnancy to term makes a substantial sacrifice, because pregnancy always places physical limitations on what one is able to do; it involves significant discomfort for an extended period of time and culminates in painful labor.

In reflecting on the situation of a pregnant woman and fetus, Thomson concludes that "no person is morally required to make large sacrifices to sustain the life of another who has no right to demand them and thus even where the sacrifices do not include life itself; we are not morally required to be good Samaritans." In other words, according to Thomson, it is praiseworthy, even heroic, to sacrifice selflessly for others. However, no one is ethically required do this. Instead, people are ethically free to do less.

Endnote 11

Although Thomson's analysis provides a general framework for weighing the interests of the woman and fetus, it does not yet settle the question of what responses specific situations merit. In other words, even assuming we accept the general distinctions between

Endnote 12

Splendid, Good, and Minimally Decent Samaritanism, we still need to determine what actions and situations fall under each of these headings. We also need to attend to the further question of what interests and responsibilities persons other than the fetus and pregnant woman have in abortion decisions.

THE FAMILY

WHAT DO WE OWE FUTURE FAMILY MEMBERS?

Having explored both the moral status of the fetus as an individual and the moral relationship between the fetus and pregnant woman, our discussion now moves to a new level. This third level locates the problem of abortion in the wider context of the future family that the woman and fetus may belong to and live within.

Abortion is frequently pictured as if it involved a woman and fetus exclusively. However, even those who think that an abortion decision should rest entirely with the pregnant woman, nonetheless admit that women often choose to include others in abortion decisions, and often consider the potential impact that their decisions have on family members. In a study of pregnant women contemplating abortion decisions, Carol Gilligan found that women tend to construct and resolve abortion decisions by thinking in terms of relationship and interconnection with others. Thus, the women in Gilligan's study identified a responsibility to care for and avoid hurting others and based their decisions about having an abortion on "a growing comprehension of the dynamics of social interaction . . . and a central insight, that self and others are interdependent." Rather than conceptualizing abortion as a conflict of individual rights, these women tended to see abortion as a problem of how best to care for and avoid harming people affected by their choices. Rather than thinking exclusively in terms of their own health or interests, these women revealed a concern for others and for safeguarding special relationships.

Considered in this light, it is important to think carefully about the consequences that having or aborting a fetus may produce, not only for the women and fetus, but for family relationships and other persons who are most intimately affected. Studies suggest that most women disclose an abortion decision to the fetus's biological father and many women arrive at an abortion decision in tandem with the biological father. Certainly, any decision to have or not to have a child has potentially important and longlasting effects on a couple's relationship. For example, an unmarried couple that brings a child into the world may decide to get married and rear the child together; the same couple may have postponed or avoided marriage altogether had

Endnote 13

Endnote 14

Endnote 15

the child been aborted. Any couple that has and raises a child (or an additional child) may find their relationship profoundly altered. Having and raising a child may bring a couple closer together, but it may also draw them apart by reducing the time and energy they have to devote exclusively to each other and to important goals and projects in their lives.

In addition to impacting a couple's relationship, abortion impacts the wider family circle. For example, a woman who has no children may consider whether she wants to have a family at all, or whether she is ready to begin a family now. Someone who already has children may think in other terms: Can she, or she and her partner, responsibly care for another child, or would an additional child spread family resources too thin? How large should the existing family become? In making a decision about whether to carry or abort a fetus, a woman's perception of family interests may loom especially large when the fetus's interests appear to be strongly at odds with the interests of other family members. Thus, a decision to abort a fetus with a serious genetic disease may rest largely on a woman's or a couple's perception of the financial and emotional stress a sick child would place on other family members. If Gilligan's description of the moral reasoning of women considering abortion is correct, then it is not abstract values, such as "life," that influence women's personal abortion choices. Instead, it is concrete persons and relationships that most affect her decision.

These reflections bring to light that abortion carries profound implications for other people. It also has the potential to alter the nature of relationships that have traditionally been central to women's lives. As others have noted, "When birth control and abortion provide women with effective means for controlling their fertility . . . the relationships that have traditionally defined women's identities . . . no longer flow inevitably from their reproductive capacity but become matters of decision."

Endnote 16

Biological Fathers

Let us begin the ethical consideration of the family by thinking first about the interests and rights of the fetus's biological father. One basis for supporting a role for biological fathers in abortion decisions is the observation that during the latter half of the 20th century men have played an increasingly larger role in many aspects of pregnancy and child care. Thus, young men are much more likely than men of their fathers' generation to attend child birth classes; be present during labor and delivery; and participate in feeding, bathing, diapering, and caring for offspring. It might be thought that men's involvement in these areas is a good thing; for example, such involvement enhances equality between the sexes. Further, it might be thought that a natural extension of men's heightened involvement in these areas should be to increase men's involvement in reproductive decisions generally, including decisions about having or aborting a fetus. According to this perspective, including men in reproductive decisions is part and parcel of fostering men's increased involvement in family life. Although only women can become pregnant and only they can bear the burdens (as well as the pleasures) associated with pregnancy, there are many other aspects of child care where greater involvement and responsibility are possible for men.

From a quite different perspective, abortion opponents might also support greater involvement of boyfriends or spouses in abortion decisions (as well as greater involvement of parents and others). The reasoning here might be that all reasonable avenues for preventing abortion should be pursued. In many instances, including others in an abortion decision serves as an effective barrier to abortion. For instance, involving spouses or boyfriends invites the possibility that they may oppose, and try to stop, enactment of a woman's decision to terminate her pregnancy.

The position that biological fathers should have a role in abortion decisions still leaves wide open the question of what, more specifically, their role should involve.

1. Informing the father

One position holds that the fetus's biological father should be involved in the decision at least to the point of being informed about the pregnancy and informed about a decision to terminate it. One consideration that lends support to such an approach is that both of the fetus's biological parents played a role in bringing the fetus into existence, so both have a right to be informed of the ultimate consequences that ensue from their procreative acts.

2. Finding out what the father's preferences are

A second view agrees with the first — that the fetus's biological father has a right to be told about the abortion decision. In addition, it states that the biological father's preferences must be solicited so that the pregnant woman is aware of what they are. Presumably a pregnant woman remains free to decide whether or not to consider her partner's preferences, and, if she does consider them, how much weight to assign to them. One basis for such a stance is that women contemplating abortion should consider the consequences of abortion for all parties affected by their decisions, and the biological father may be profoundly affected.

3. Regarding the father as having an equal voice in making an abortion decision

A still stronger view maintains that the biological father should have an equal voice with the biological mother in any decision to terminate a pregnancy. One reason that might justify this view is that even though he will not endure the consequences of nine months of pregnancy, the biological father will feel the long-term effects of having or losing a future child.

4. Regarding the father as having veto power over a woman's decision to have an abortion

A final account holds that the father should not only have an equal voice, but should have a potentially stronger voice by having the power to override a women's decision to have an abortion. The general idea is that an abortion should not take place if either partner objects, because both parties have a vital stake in the welfare of their future offspring.

To explore further how the interests of family members can impinge upon abortion decisions, let us focus in more detail on two distinct scenarios. A first scenario involves the decision to terminate a pregnancy when a fetus carries a genetic defect. A second scenario concerns a decision to terminate a pregnancy because a fetus is not of the desired sex.

Two Controversial Reasons for Abortion

Fetuses with Genetic Defects — There are a variety of tests that detect fetal abnormalities in utero. These include amniocentesis, ultrasound, alpha-fetoprotein screening, and chorionic villus sampling (CVS), among others. These tests can tell a pregnant woman whether her fetus has defects in body structure, such as missing limbs or heart malformations; genetic diseases, such as cystic fibrosis or Down's syndrome; or whether other risk factors are present, such as poor fetal development, heart rhythm disturbances, or abnormalities of the placenta.

Many pregnant women use prenatal testing for the explicit purpose of screening for fetal abnormalities. They intend to abort a fetus who has **significant abnormalities**. For example, women over 35 and women who have a family history of genetic disease are at greater risk of having a child with genetic abnormalities and frequently seek prenatal testing for this purpose. Other women pursue certain prenatal tests, such as ultrasound, as part of their routine prenatal health care. In this way, a woman may learn that a fetus has a certain defect or disease which was not anticipated.

Many people who personally oppose abortion identify certain exceptional circumstances as ethically warranting it, including the circumstance of a fetus with a genetic defect or other health problem. Thus some people hold that a prospective parent should not knowingly bring a child into the world who will suffer from a serious, painful, and life shortening illness. Others hold that a pregnant women is justified in aborting a fetus who has a less serious, but still significant, abnormality. For example, a missing limb is a significant disability that will in the future impair the fetus's ability to walk and be viewed as physically unattractive, even though it will not shorten or otherwise threaten life. As suggested already, in evaluating the ethical aspects of such cases, it is often not just the effect that an impairment portends for the fetus, but also the impact that it will have on others. Prospective parents may be poorly equipped to cope with a seriously ill child, lacking the emotional maturity, economic resources, social support, or desire to devote the added time and energy that this is likely to entail. In other cases, a more minor defect may simply be undesirable because it carries a stigma in the society. Any child with a physical disability is likely to have a harder time "fitting in," finding friends, getting a job, and pursuing other goals, because our society tends to discriminate against persons with disabilities.

The two cases described below represent different points along a continuum. In the first case, a couple has conceived a child with a serious genetic disease; in the second, a fetus has a comparatively **minor structural abnormality**.

CASE 1: A SERIOUS GENETIC DEFECT

Maria is a 21-year-old woman who is pregnant with her second child. Her first child was born with cystic fibrosis (CF), a common life-shortening disorder. Persons with CF have a tendency to chronic lung infection and an inability to absorb fats and nutrients from foods.

As CF carriers, Maria and her husband, Ramon, have a one-in-four chance of having a child with CF with each pregnancy. They have decided they are not emotionally or financially able to care for a second child with CF and will abort an affected fetus.

They also want to find out as early as possible in Maria's pregnancy whether the fetus is affected with the disease. During her eighth week of pregnancy, Maria requests CVS to determine the fetus's health status. CVS involves removing a small piece of the chorionic villi (tissue pieces that attach the pregnancy sac to the wall of the uterus) from the pregnant woman. Because the genetic and biochemical makeup of these cells is identical to the genetic and biochemical makeup of the fetus's own cells, DNA tests can be applied to determine whether the fetus is affected with various genetic abnormalities, including cystic fibrosis. The test comes back positive, and the couple feels distraught. Even though they had planned for this, they are devastated.

In thinking about abortion, Maria's physician informed her that although her first child has a severe case of CF, the disease is variably expressed, meaning that different people are affected differently. The physician encouraged Maria and Ramon to take some solace in the fact that although CF sufferers used to die in early childhood, the outlook has improved considerably. Most people with CF now survive into adult life. Still, CF remains a potentially serious and fatal disorder.

Case No. 2: A Minor Structural Anomaly

Leah and Samuel are excitedly expecting their first child. During the course of her pregnancy, Leah has had several ultrasounds to check on fetal status. Ultrasound is a technique that emits sound waves and bounces them off the developing fetus. The waves are then converted into a picture on a TV monitor. During a routine ultrasound, Leah's physician notices a structural malformation in the fetus. Upon closer inspection, the physician determines that the fetus has a cleft palate.

Cleft palate is a gap in the roof of the mouth that runs from the behind the teeth to the nasal cavity. People affected with cleft palate sometimes have other birth defects, including partial deafness. Babies born with cleft palate must be bottle fed, and usually undergo surgery to repair the palate at about one year of age. Following surgery, further operations and speech therapy may be necessary.

Leah and her husband had imagined and hoped for a perfect baby. Because they are young and seem to be in excellent health, they are inclined to feel that the odds of having a healthy baby are in their favor. Although both of them feel attached to the fetus they have conceived, neither opposes abortion. They decide to have an abortion and try for a baby that does not have physical defects. Their reasoning is that a baby without cleft palate would probably be happier than a baby with this condition. As new parents, their job would be made easier if their child did not have to undergo surgeries and other therapies and suffer from ridicule and scorn from other children.

In thinking about these cases, you may wish to consider the following questions.

* What might it be like if you had CF or cleft palate when you were growing up?

* Do you think you would have the friends you have now?

* Do you think people would have treated you differently?

* What impact might having either one of these conditions have had on your parents?

* If you had required surgery when you were very small, for example, would family members have to make certain sacrifices to care for you?

* What impact would the extra time and attention they might devote to you have on your siblings?

✳ In short, how would your family be different than it now is?

✳ On the other hand, what positive understandings or character traits do you imagine you and others might gain through dealing with these conditions?

✳ Do you think you would have become a more compassionate and caring person if you had received the special care and compassion of others?

✳ Finally, what guidance is available to you by way of some of the approaches to moral reasoning discussed in Chapters 4 and 5?

✳ And from Chapter 2, at what level of caring (Gilligan) or of moral development (Kohlberg) will your answers to the questions above place you?

SEX SELECTION

Having considered the problem of selective termination of pregnancy for the purpose of preventing birth defects, let us next turn to a different issue that also involves the selective termination of pregnancy. **Sex selection** refers to selective termination of pregnancies for the purpose of having a child of a particular sex, male or female. The sex of a human being is determined at conception when an ovum (egg) is fertilized by a male-producing or female-producing sperm. There are various techniques for detecting fetal sex in utero, including amniocentesis, ultrasonic scanning, and chorion biopsy. These techniques were not originally developed for the purpose of detecting sex, but rather for the purpose of detecting fetal abnormalities.

The desire to have a child of a certain sex may spring from a variety of reasons. In societies where women are abused and devalued, couples may prefer to have sons in order that their children have a better quality of life and are not subject to abuse and devaluation. Or prospective parents may prefer a son because men on average have higher incomes than women and so are better able to support their parents financially when they become old. Others prefer a child of a particular sex because they think (either consciously or unconsciously) that persons of that sex are more valuable. Concerns about the composition of a future family also play a central role in sex-selective abortions. Thus, many couples who use abortion as a means of selecting the sex of offspring have as their goal producing a family with a certain gender mix or balance. For example, a couple that already has one or more daughters may desire to have a son. Or a family that already includes two sons and one daughter may prefer a second daughter to a third son. Unlike most other abortion decisions, in sex-selective abortion a pregnant woman generally wants to become pregnant, but wants to continue with pregnancy only if the fetus that is conceived meets certain standards. Sex-selective abortion is in this respect analogous to abortions of fetuses with genetic or other defects. In both cases, a woman or couple desire to have a child, but want a certain kind of future child.

It is important to note that in most societies, prospective parents do have preferences about the sex of their future off-spring, and they prefer having a son to having a daughter. Moreover, there exists a definite relation-ship between women's social, legal, and economic status and the tendency of

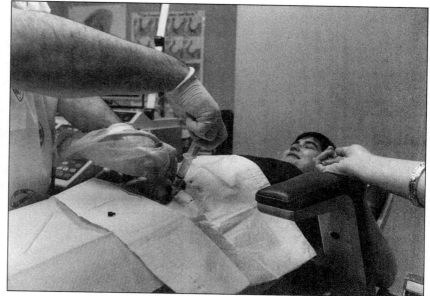

Figure 2. A pregnant woman undergoes amniocentesis. Copyright © 1995 by Robert Ullmann.

both women and men to prefer sons. In general, son-preference increases as woman's social status declines. Some argue that permit-ting sex selection only serves to perpetuate a sexist society in which women are devalued. Others, however, claim that parents cannot be blamed for wanting the best for their future child.

Endnote 17

Endnote 18
Endnote 19

The two cases described below illustrate different circumstances in which parents desire to have an abortion because they prefer a child of a certain sex. In both cases, the personal situation of the cou-ple is pivotal to the decision.

Case 3: Abortion to Select a Boy

Cecile and Frank had never had a child, but they had decided in advance that they wanted only boys. Frank felt that he would be a better parent to a son than a daughter. He had grown up with four brothers and had enjoyed the closeness that same-sex relationships had involved in his family of origin. He hoped to recreate these same strong bonds in his own family. Cecile had other reasons for preferring sons. As a child she had been molested by her father and she felt threatened by the prospect of a daughter being vulnerable to sexual abuse, either by Cecile's own father or by other men. Although she had been through counseling, Cecile continued to feel that she would be inclined to act in an over-protective way with a daughter and that her daughter would sense this and feel anxieties and fears.

Cecile and Frank clearly wanted to be the best parents they could be; both felt better equipped to parent boys than girls.

* Although their intentions are well-meaning, should we as a society support sex selection?

* Perhaps, if we do, other couples will abuse this option and selectively terminate fetuses for less laudable grounds. To what extent should a woman's or couple's personal reasons for wanting an abortion influence public policies?

* In answering this question, consider the following further questions. If a woman is ethically entitled to have an abortion during the early stages of her pregnancy, do others have a right to determine what the reasons for that decision may be?

* Alternatively, if we suppose that the right to choose abortion is not absolute and that only some reasons are sufficient to justify this choice, how do we implement a public policy that distinguishes "legitimate" from "illegitimate" reasons?

* If there are as many reasons for abortion as there are women contemplating abortions, is it possible to define general categories of acceptable and unacceptable reasons?

But if we fail to even attempt to render such distinctions, perhaps many unethical choices will be allowed.

CASE 4: BALANCING THE GENDER MIX IN THE FAMILY

Stacey and Mohammed had four healthy girls. Now they wanted a boy. Although they were financially comfortable, they had decided that five children would have to be their limit. Thus, although they had taken "pot luck" so far, they did not want to continue in this manner. When Stacey became pregnant for the fifth time, the couple expressed their preferences for a son to Stacey's obstetrician and requested that the doctor perform ultrasonic scanning to determine the sex of the fetus. They indicated to the physician that they intended to abort a fetus of the "wrong" sex as early as possible in the course of pregnancy and then to try again.

Unlike the previous example, this example turns on a couple's desire to parent offspring of both sexes. Whereas the previous couple feared they could not parent well, or as well, children who were female, this couple wants to experience the distinct pleasures of parenting boys as well as girls. In reflecting on this case, consider the following issues.

The effects of allowing this one couple to act on their preferences may not be terribly significant for the society. But the effects of a policy that permits such a practice on a larger scale could be quite significant.

* Should Stacey and Mohammed simply be grateful to have healthy children and forget about what sex the children are?

* Or should they be permitted to execute their preferences to have a son, as well as daughters?

* What are some advantages and disadvantages of such a policy?

* Do you think the ethical arguments for it are stronger or weaker than the ethical arguments against it?

ARGUMENTS FOR AND AGAINST 'CHOOSING OUR CHILDREN'

Now that you have reflected independently about possible ethical bases for selective abortion, look briefly at some of the arguments that have been put forward by others. Summarized below are arguments frequently heard on both sides.

Arguments Against

First Argument Against Selecting the Sex or Health of the Fetus

One argument against allowing abortion for purposes of sex selection or screening for genetic defects is based upon the implication this carries for how we may come to view our future children and our future families.

Endnote 20

1. Honoring parents' desires to have children of a particular kind leads to viewing children as products or commodities that can be ordered in accordance with parental specifications.

2. Viewing children in this manner devalues them. It is at odds with regarding children as beings who possess an inherent dignity and worth.

3. Therefore parents should not be permitted to pick the kind of children they want to have, including the sex or health of their child.

In response to this argument it can be noted that it is an empirical (factual) question whether or not the consequences the argument describes will occur. Until there is some evidence to support the claim that selective abortion will depersonalize our attitudes toward children and families, the argument's premises are more speculative than factually based.

Second Argument Against Selecting the Sex or Health of the Fetus

1. If parents are allowed to abort fetuses who are the "wrong sex" or have the "wrong" genetic features, this will lead society down a perilous slippery slope.

2. The next step along this slope will be that parents will want to abort fetuses who do not possess certain positive qualities, such as a certain hair or eye color, a high level of intelligence, or natural talents for music, mathematics or other areas.

3. Producing children according to parental specifications is unethical; it reinforces the tendency (noted above) to view children as objects to be produced.

4. Therefore, society should not allow the first step along this slippery slope to take place.

Once again, making the argument work would require showing that the consequences it predicts are likely to occur.

Third Argument Against Selecting the Sex or Health of the Fetus

A final argument against choosing future children on the basis of their sexual or genetic qualities holds that such a practice necessarily involves wrongful discrimination. There are two versions this argument might take the first dealing with selection based on sex, the second, with selection based on handicap.

Version One

1. Sexism is wrong.

2. It is inherently sexist to prefer one child over another child solely on the basis of that child's sex.

3. Selectively aborting fetuses of a certain sex is sexist in precisely this way.

4. Therefore, abortion for the purpose of sex selection is wrong.

Version Two

1. Discrimination against handicapped individuals is wrong.

2. It is inherently discriminatory to prefer a healthy child over a handicapped child solely on the basis of the child's handicap.

3. Selectively aborting handicapped fetuses is discriminatory in precisely this way.

4. Therefore, abortion for the purpose of choosing healthy children over unhealthy children is wrong.

Arguments For

In addition to the above arguments, the following arguments might be advanced in support of permitting selective abortion. First, it might be argued that granting prospective parents this option increases their happiness.

Endnote 21

First Argument Supporting Selective Abortion: Increasing Parental Happiness

1. For many parents, the desire to have a child of a certain sex or a child who is healthy and free of handicaps is very strongly held.
2. Satisfying these preferences is therefore likely to increase parents' happiness significantly, whereas frustrating these preferences is likely to increase parents' misery.
3. Therefore selective abortion should be permitted.

As with the previous arguments that appealed to the negative consequences of allowing abortion, this argument turns on the strength of its empirical (factual) premise (premise two). We may discover that selective abortion for the purposes under consideration does not make parents happier, but only makes them guilty or miserable. Parents who select fetuses through aborting unwanted offspring may become miserable, for example, if they must make repeated efforts to become pregnant and go through repeated abortions when pregnancy does not bring the desired result.

Second Argument Supporting Selective Abortion: The Value of Freedom

A somewhat different basis for defending the right to abort a fetus in order to choose the sex or genetic health of a future child refers to the more general value of freedom of choice and action.

Endnotes 22, 23

1. A democratic society, such as the United States, places a supreme value on freedom of conscience and action. In particular, we grant citizens basic liberties such as freedom of speech, assembly, and conscience.
2. Reproduction is as basic as these other freedoms and should therefore be included among them.
3. Then denying women the freedom to choose abortion is at odds with the basic ethical tenets of our society.

Against this argument it can be said that even basic liberties are not unlimited. Thus, freedom of speech is not absolute and can be limited when it incites people to violence. Freedom of religion is not tolerated indiscriminately or in ways that infringe upon the welfare of others. So too, it might be claimed that if the fetus is a person at some time prior to birth, then the liberties of the fetus's parents can be ethically constrained.

Clearly, none of the above arguments establishes conclusively that abortion for the purposes of sex selection or the avoidance of genetic defects is ethically permissible or impermissible. Yet, taken together, these arguments make evident the wide range of difficult issues that are at stake. Both the consequences of individual choices and public practices must be considered. In addition, certain non-consequentialist considerations, including liberty and respect for persons, are at issue. Any position regarding the permissibility of abortion must weigh carefully these and other ethical factors.

THE SOCIETY: WHAT DO CURRENT LAWS AND POLICIES ALLOW?

Having discussed the ethical implications of abortion for the individual fetus, the pregnant woman, the biological parents, and the family, it is now time to cast our net still wider and view abortion from the perspective of the larger society, the context in which fetus, woman, and family are themselves situated. The purpose of this section is to review existing laws and regulations pertaining to abortion. Importantly, the emphasis here will not be on the ethical permissibility of abortion. Instead, the point of this section is to describe, in a summary fashion, the laws and policies that provide the framework within which personal ethical choices are currently made.

The Decriminalization of Abortion: *Roe vs. Wade*
Let us begin with the following case, which has played a pivotal role in shaping American abortion law.

CASE 5: THE CASE OF NORMA McCORVEY

Norma McCorvey was an unmarried pregnant woman living in Dallas, Texas. She wanted an abortion but Texas law treated abortion as a criminal offense unless abortion was necessary in order to save the woman's life. Ms. McCorvey had hoped to travel to California, because she had heard that abortion laws were less restrictive there and thought she could obtain an abortion. However, her poverty precluded her from raising the money she needed to pay for the trip. Her pregnancy continued and a baby was later born and put up for adoption.

Some time after this occurred an attorney approached Ms. McCorvey and asked her if she was willing to participate in a class-action suit (a law suit in which a group of people together make a common legal complaint against an opposing party) against the District Attorney of Dallas County. The suit would challenge the constitutionality of the Texas abortion law. Ms. McCorvey agreed, and the law suit proceeded, with the Federal Court ruling in Ms. McCorvey's favor and declaring the Texas abortion law void.

But the matter was hardly over. Instead, an appeal was made to the highest court in the land, the United States Supreme Court, which heard the case. To protect her identity, Ms. McCorvey adopted the pseudonym, Roe, and the person against whom the case was brought, the District Attorney of Dallas County, was Mr. Henry Wade.

Norma McCorvey's story became the well-known 1973 U.S. Supreme Court case, *Roe vs. Wade*. In a 7-2 decision, the Justices of the U.S. Supreme Court found the Texas law criminalizing abortion to be in violation of the United States Constitution. In doing so, the court rendered void laws in many other states that resembled Texas's law in making abortion a criminal offense. Before Roe, very few states had legalized abortion for any purpose other than to save the pregnant woman's life. After Roe, states were allowed to restrict abortion practices in some ways; however, they could no longer criminalize abortion as the Texas statute had done. Instead, Roe established that a woman's right to have an abortion was part of a fundamental "right of privacy."

Endnote 24

The Roe decision, written by Justice Harry A. Blackmun, established a trimester approach (a "trimester" is a period of three months, or one-third of the length of a full-term pregnancy). This approach allows states to place increasing restrictions on abortion as the time period of pregnancy lengthens, so long as those restrictions reflect legitimate state interests. Specifically, the following restrictions are permitted under Roe.

Roe's Trimester Approach

First Trimester — During the first 14 weeks of pregnancy, the abortion decision is treated as a private decision of the individual woman in consultation with her health care provider.

Second Trimester — During the 15th through the 28th week of pregnancy, states may regulate abortion, but only for the purpose of promoting the health of the pregnant woman.

Third Trimester — During the 29th through 42nd week of pregnancy, states may prohibit abortion to protect a viable fetus. Even in the third trimester, however, states are not permitted to interfere with abortions necessary to protect the health of the pregnant woman.

Although all states are required to follow these guidelines, they are also free to differ in ways not covered by these guidelines. Thus, abortion laws differ from one state to the next with respect to the use of state funds to fund abortion. Thirty states and the District of Columbia prohibit the use of state funds to pay for an abortion unless the woman's life is in danger; eight other states allow public funding to be used in limited circumstances, such as pregnancy resulting from rape or incest.

Abortion Law After *Roe vs. Wade*

Subsequent to the *Roe vs. Wade* decision, the U.S. Supreme Court has ruled on several other abortion cases. Although the court's ruling in

Roe has not been overturned, the effect of subsequent decisions has been to narrow and modify the abortion rights that Roe established.

Webster vs. Reproductive Health

Endnote 25

In a 1989 decision, *Webster vs. Reproductive Health Services*, the U.S. Supreme Court upheld by a 5–4 vote a Missouri statue that placed various restrictions on abortion. The Webster decision, written by Chief Justice William Rehnquist, allowed Missouri (and therefore other states) to favor childbirth over abortion and to prohibit state employees and facilities from assisting with abortion. In addition, the decision allowed states to impose regulations that require physicians to test for the viability of the fetus if they suspect that a fetus is at least 20 weeks old prior to performing an abortion. Despite these restrictions, a woman's constitutional right to have an abortion remained intact, and states were not allowed to prohibit abortions of nonviable fetuses.

By upholding Missouri's viability test requirement, the Supreme Court appeared to erode the trimester framework established in Roe. The Roe framework allowed state regulations during the second trimester only if they were for the purpose of protecting the health of the pregnant woman. However, the Webster decision allows state regulations during the second trimester that are not for the purpose of protecting the health of the pregnant woman. In Webster, the majority opinion (the opinion representing the vote of the majority of the nine Supreme Court Justices) criticized "the rigid trimester analysis of the course of a pregnancy enunciated in Roe" on the grounds that the court did "not see why the state's interest in protecting potential human life should come into existence only at the point of viability, and that there should therefore be a rigid line allowing state regulation after viability but prohibiting it before viability." The viability

Endnote 26

tests that are currently available, such as ultrasound and amniocentesis, were not designed for the purpose of determining fetal viability and cannot pinpoint the exact age of the fetus. In addition, these tests add to the cost of abortion and therefore make it more difficult for many women to obtain an abortion.

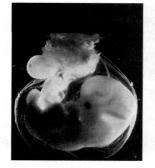

Fetus, 6 Weeks. Copyright © Photo-Researchers, Inc.

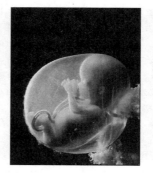

Fetus, 16 Weeks. Copyright © Lennart Nilsson (Bonnierforlagen AB).

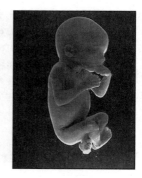

Fetus, 26 Weeks. Copyright © Photo-Researchers, Inc.

Planned Parenthood vs. Casey

Three years after Webster, in 1992, the U.S. Supreme Court ruled in another abortion case, *Planned Parenthood vs. Casey*. In Casey, the court reviewed and upheld certain portions of a Pennsylvania statue that placed restrictions on abortion. Among the restrictions that the Pennsylvania statue imposed were the following:

Endnote 27

1. **Twenty-four hour waiting period** — A pregnant woman was required to give informed consent to an abortion. In addition, at least 24 hours had to pass between her informed consent and the performance of an abortion. "Informed consent" was defined as including informing a pregnant woman about the nature and risks of the abortion procedure and its alternatives, the probable gestational age of the fetus, and the medical risks of carrying the fetus to term.

2. **Parental consent to abortion** — When the woman seeking an abortion was legally a minor, Pennsylvania law required her either to obtain the consent of a parent or guardian, or to have a judge's certification that either she was mature or that abortion was in her best interests.

3. **Spousal notification** — A married woman seeking an abortion was required to notify her husband of her intention. Exceptions to this requirement included situations in which a pregnant woman's husband was not the fetus's biological father, could not be located, or had criminally assaulted her or she feared that he would assault her if he were notified about her intention to have an abortion.

4. **Mandatory reporting** — Pennsylvania law also made it mandatory that health providers report to the Health Department after performing an abortion and include facts, such as the name of the physician performing the abortion, the woman's age, the county or state where she resided, the number of previous pregnancies and abortions she had had, and the probable gestational age and weight of the fetus.

In reviewing Pennsylvania's restrictions, the Supreme Court upheld, by a 5–4 vote, all restrictions except spousal notification. The majority opinion held that "a state may not give to a man the kind of dominion over his wife that parents exercise over their children . . . Women do not lose their constitutionally protected liberty when they marry." It is important to note that none of these restrictions challenges the basic idea established in Roe, that a woman has a constitutional right to have an abortion. Rather, the restrictions upheld in Casey chip away at aspects of this right and make it easier for states to impose restrictions on women seeking abortions.

Endnote 28

The Casey decision departed from Roe in two key respects. First, like Webster, the Casey decision rejected Roe's trimester approach to

Endnote 29

regulating abortion. Second, Casey changed the standard applied to evaluate the constitutionality of state restrictions. Whereas Roe had held that the right to have an abortion was fundamental and could not be overridden unless a state had a compelling interest, Casey established that states could restrict abortion so long as restrictions do not impose an undue burden on women seeking abortions.

REQUIREMENTS IN OTHER JURISDICTIONS

Since the Webster and Casey decisions, many other legal challenges have been mounted to Roe. A State of Utah statute attempted to impose a restrictive set of regulations for pregnancies of twenty weeks duration or less and an even more restrictive set for those over twenty weeks, but that law was struck down in 1996 because the federal court of appeals ruled that the state could not substitute a statutory determination of viability for the judgement of a physician.

Endnote 32

Several states including Louisiana have passed laws severely limiting what is called **"judicial by-pass,"** a provision whereby parental notification or permission is waived by a judge who determines that it is in a minor's best interest not to involve her parents. The Louisiana law was struck down in 1997 because it gave the judge too much latitude even when the minor was mature. A Montana law that required that a minor give a parent 48 hours notice before having an abortion was recently upheld by the U.S. Supreme Court.

Endnote 33

Endnote 34

In 1997 controversy erupted over so-called **"partial-birth" abortions** in which the life of the fetus or infant is terminated during the birth process. Normally this is reserved for extreme cases in which the life of the pregnant woman is in jeopardy, but cases have been reported in which the method was used in less extreme circumstances. Several states have adopted prohibitions on such abortions and several others have defeated bans. The United States Congress attempted unsuccessfully to pass a national ban on the procedure.

THE FUTURE OF ABORTION LAW

Future Supreme Court decisions will be profoundly affected by how the membership of the court changes in the years ahead, as several Justices are nearing retirement age. Some legal experts predict that efforts to overturn Roe are likely to continue. Other scholars discern in the language of more recent abortion decisions a heightened appreciation of the "uniquely female burdens of unwanted pregnancy," and predict that the constitutional right to have an abortion is not itself in serious jeopardy.

Endnote 30

Endnote 31

The entire debate about abortion will be profoundly altered in the event that RU 486, the so-called **"abortion pill,"** becomes available in the United States. RU 486 induces abortion in early pregnancy by blocking the action of progesterone, a hormone that stimulates changes in the wall of the uterus necessary for implementation of a fertilized egg. The drug was developed by the French pharmaceutical company, Roussel Uclaf, and has been used in France since 1989. The drug is now undergoing bureaucratic scrutiny, regulatory testing and legal review in America.

In the event RU 486 becomes widely available in the United States, state laws restricting abortion may pose less significant obstacles to woman seeking abortion. Because RU 486 acts before a fertilized egg becomes implanted in the uterus, it terminates pregnancy before a fetus proper has developed. Thus, state laws restricting abortion of viable fetuses would not apply to RU 486. Furthermore, certain ethical objections to abortion based on the status of the fetus would carry less weight when abortion is performed so early during the course of pregnancy.

FINAL COMMENTS

Abortion is a complex problem for individuals, families, and the society. Even if we could reach an agreement about what ethical criteria should be applied to assess the fetus's moral status, this hardly settles the abortion controversy. Other considerations that must be addressed include the unique relationship of the fetus to another human being, the interests prospective parents may have in forming certain kinds of families, the interests of other family members, the welfare of the society in which abortion decisions occur, and the implications of abortion for other ethical choices, such as our treatment of human beings at the end of life and our treatment of non-human animals. The law governing abortion is in a period of transition; however, a woman's basic legal right to have an abortion remains intact. New technologies, such as RU 486, will have a profound impact on future ethical and legal debates.

FOR FURTHER INQUIRY

REVIEW QUESTIONS

1. What is the significance of the words "person" and "personhood" for the abortion debate? Is it possible, under various definitions of "person" for there to exist human living nonpersons? If so, do they have the same moral standing as persons or are they, by definition, in a lesser moral status?

2. What mental capacities have been considered significant for deciding when a being has moral standing? What difference does it make which of these capacities is critical?

3. The conservative position on abortion does not recognize mental capacity as decisive for moral standing. What features of a being are considered critical for holders of the conservative view?

4. In the era since the *Roe vs. Wade* court decision, states have attempted to place several restrictions on abortion. What are those limits and which have survived legal challenge?

APPLICATION QUESTION

Would you classify the abortion law in your state as conservative, moderate or liberal?

Explain your reasons.

ENDNOTES

1. Peter Singer, *Practical Ethics*, Cambridge University Press, New York, 1982, Chapter 3.

2. John Noonan, "An almost absolute value in history," In Noonan, *The Morality of Abortion: Legal and Historical Perspectives*, Harvard University Press, Cambridge, MA, 1970: 51–59.

3. L.W. Sumner, "A third way," In *Abortion and Moral Theory*, Princeton University Press, Princeton, NJ, 1981, Chapter 4, pp. 124–160.

4. Sumner, "A third way," p. 84.

5. Mary Anne Warren, "On the moral and legal status of abortion," *The Monist* 57, 1973.

6. Judith Jarvis Thomson, "A defense of abortion," *Philos Public Aff*, 1, 1971. Reprinted in Joel Feinberg, ed., *The Problem of Abortion*, Wadsworth Publishing Company, Belmont, CA, 1984, pp. 173–187.

7. Thomson, "A defense of abortion," p. 179.

8. Thomson, "A defense of abortion," p. 179.

9. Mary Anne Warren, *Gendercide*, Rowman and Allanheld, Totowa, NJ, 1985, p. 89.

10. The Gospel of Luke 10:30–35.

11. Thomson, "A defense of abortion."

12. Thomson, "A defense of abortion," pp. 184 ff.

13. Carol Gilligan, *In a Different Voice*, Harvard University Press, Cambridge, MA, 1982.

14. Gilligan, *In a Different Voice*, p. 74.

15. Theodora Ooms, "A family perspective on abortion," In Sidney Callahan, Daniel Callahan, eds., *Abortion: Understanding Differences*, Plenum Press, New York, 1984, pp. 81–108, at p. 94.

16. Gilligan, *In a Different Voice*, p. 70.

17. Warren, *Gendercide*, p. 13.

18. Christine Overall, *Ethics and Human Reproduction*, Allen and Unwin, Boston, 1987, pp. 22 ff.

19. Warren, *Gendercide*, p. 105.

20. Maura A. Ryan, "The argument for unlimited procreative liberty: A feminist critique," *Hastings Cent Rep* 20, 1990: 6–12.

21. Warren, *Gendercide*, pp. 172–173.

22. Warren, *Gendercide*, pp. 179 ff.

23. Jean Bethke Elshtain, "Reflections on abortion, values and the family," In Sidney Callahan, Daniel Callahan, eds., *Abortion: Understanding Differences*, Plenum Press, New York, 1984, pp. 47–72.

24. *Roe vs. Wade*, 410 U.S. 113, 93 S. Ct. 705, January 22, 1973.

25. *Webster vs. Reproductive Health Services*, U.S. 109, S.Ct. 3040, 1989, reprinted in Ronald Munson, ed., *Intervention and Reflection: Basic Issues in Medical Ethics*, Fourth Ed., Wadsworth Publishing Company, Belmont, CA, 1992: pp. 92–94.

26. *Webster vs. Reproductive Health Services*, p. 94.

27. *Casey vs. Planned Parenthood of Southeastern Pennsylvania*, 112 S. Ct. 2791, 1992.

28. *Casey vs. Planned Parenthood of Southeastern Pennsylvania*.

29. John Robertson, "Casey and the resuscitation of *Roe vs. Wade*," *Hastings Cent Rep* 22, 1992: 24–28.

30. George J. Annas, "The Supreme Court, liberty, and abortion," *New Engl J Med* 327, 1992: 651–654.

31. Robertson, "Casey and the resuscitation of *Roe vs. Wade*."

32. *Jane L. v. Bangerter*, 102 F.3d 1112—1996.

33. *Causeway Medical Suite v. Ieyooub*, CA 5, No. 95-31178, 14 April 1997.

34. *Lambert v. Wicklund*, 117 S.Ct. 1169—1997.

CHAPTER 8

DEATH AND DYING

"Of all the wonders that I have yet heard, it seems to me most strange that men should fear seeing that death, a necessary end, will come when it will come."

— ***Shakespeare,*** **Julius Caesar**

"It has been often said, that it is not death, but dying which is terrible."

— ***Henry Fielding***

While death, like taxes, may still be one of the few certainties of life, the new technologies of the biological revolution have literally given humans the power to control the timing and conditions of their own deaths. Unfortunately, sometimes we are able to keep patients alive, but not able to cure their diseases or restore them to normal health. Sometimes we can actually suspend patients in an ambiguous state in which we literally do not know whether they are alive or dead.

Endnote 1

YOSEF CAMP:

HIS BRAIN IS GONE
BUT IS HE DEAD?

Nine-year-old Yosef Camp was playing on the streets of inner-city Washington, D.C., one day when he bought a pickle from a street vendor. Soon after eating the pickle he went into convulsions and collapsed. The rescue squad brought him to the emergency room unconscious. His heart had stopped beating; he was not breathing. When they pumped his stomach they found traces of marijuana and PCP. Someone had apparently spiked the pickle as a practical joke.

The boy had been without oxygen so long that serious, irreversible brain damage had occurred leaving him permanently unconscious. In fact, some tests indicated that his brain had been without oxygen so long that it was destroyed. The physicians claimed there was nothing more

---

Robert Marlin Veatch, B.S. Purdue, B.D. Harvard, M.S. California at San Francisco, M.A. and Ph.D. Harvard University, is professor of medical ethics at Georgetown University and former director of the Kennedy Institute of Ethics.

they could do to restore its function. He was left permanently unconscious, breathing on a ventilator, with organ functions maintained by aggressive support from a team of nurses and other care givers.

Some claimed he should be declared dead based on the evidence that his brain was dead. Others claimed he was still alive because his heart was still beating and he was breathing (albeit on a ventilator). They thought they should ask the parents for permission to withdraw the ventilator and let him die.

When the parents were asked, they turned to their religious tradition. They were Muslims and believed that Allah should be given a chance to intervene. They demanded that the physicians do everything possible to maintain Yosef's life and give Allah a chance. The nurses were required to devote substantial attention to maintaining Yosef while the parents' physicians, lawyers, and courts tried to sort out the case. The intensive life-support cost more than $1,000 per day until the boy died a hundred days later while decision-makers were still trying to sort out what to do.

Endnote 2

THE MAJOR DEFINITIONS OF DEATH

The first issue of debate in such cases is what it means for someone to be dead. Until the last part of the 20th century we all knew more or less what it meant to be dead. We would listen for a heartbeat, feel a pulse, or look for signs of breathing. But in the 1960s we began to question whether these were the only signs of death. With the invention of ventilators, we now had the capacity to maintain heartbeat and blood flow mechanically. If these are maintained, along with nutrition basics and blood pressure regulations, respiration will continue spontaneously — even if brain function was totally and permanently destroyed.

CHIEF LEARNING OUTCOME

I know the major definitions of death and the essential decisions surrounding the process of dying.

In the 1960s most Americans began to realize there could be great social benefits if these patients without brain function could be treated as dead. In some cases they were ideal sources of organs for transplant. It cannot be denied that some of those who began advocating a new, brain-based definition of death were also interested in procuring organs for transplant. Three major definitions of death have emerged from this controversy.

KEY CONCEPTS

DEATH — the cessation of human, physical life; as medically determined:

- **Cardiac-oriented definition** of death holds that individuals are dead when they have irreversibly lost cardiac and respiratory function

- **Whole-brain-oriented definition** of death holds that individuals are dead when they have irreversibly lost all functions of the entire brain (including the respiratory and reflex functions of the brain stem)

- **Higher-brain-oriented definition** of death holds that individuals are dead when they have irreversibly lost all higher functions of the brain (usually defined as all capacity for consciousness)

KILLING — behavior that causes death:

- **Active** killing causes death by an active intervention into the causal chain leading to death (cf. Passive killing)

- **Passive** killing causes death only by omission of actions that could have prevented a death (cf. Active killing)

- **Direct** killing causes death by intention (cf. Indirect killing)

- **Indirect** killing causes death by unintended action, though perhaps action in which death is foreseen (cf. Direct killing)

- **Forgoing life-support** involves withholding or withdrawing of medical interventions that, if provided, are expected to prolong life.

TREATMENT — medical care expected to produce benefits:

- **Ordinary means** of treatment are expected to produce benefit that exceeds the harms (formerly determined by how common or complex the treatment was, but now generally believed to be based solely on benefits and harms expected and usually based on the patient's own quantification of the benefits and harms) (cf. Extraordinary means)

- **Extraordinary means** of treatment are expected to produce benefits that are less than harms or no greater than harms (formerly determined by how common or complex the treatment was, but now generally believed to be based solely on benefits and harms expected and usually based on the patient's own quantification of the benefits and harms) (cf. Ordinary means)

THE CARDIAC-ORIENTED DEFINITION

Those who believe patients like Yosef Camp are alive even if their brain function is permanently destroyed believe in the traditional definition of death. An individual is dead, according to this traditional view, **when there is irreversible cessation of circulatory and respiratory function.** This is often referred to as the "heart definition." When the heart is gone, the patient is gone. But at the University of Utah in December 1992, a critically ill patient named Barney Clark had his own heart removed because of irreversible heart disease. He was the first person ever placed on a mechanical artificial heart that was intended to be a permanent replacement for his heart. For 112 days the mechanical device continued to pump blood through his body with the regularity of a human heart. For much of that time Barney Clark was conscious, capable of carrying on conversations, and debating the wisdom of his new-found place in history. Later, patients given artificial hearts were actually able to get up out of bed and leave the hospital, pushing their mechanical pumps around in a shopping-cart-like basket. Surely, these people were still alive even though their hearts had long since stopped beating and had decayed into a formless mass. It is not the heart per se that the defenders of the traditional definition of death consider critical, but rather the bodily functions normally associated with the beating heart: circulation and respiration. Holders of this view — probably including Yosef Camp's parents — believe one is dead when there is irreversible loss of these functions.

It is critical that the loss of function be irreversible. We do not believe someone really dies if the stoppage is only temporary and reversible. Thus someone who has a heart attack and is immediately rescued by someone competent in CPR, so that the heart begins functioning again, is not properly said ever to have "died." He had a cardiac arrest all right — and would surely have died had not the heart stoppage been reversed in time — but if we are careful with language, no one can suffer "clinical death" and recover. Deaths occur exactly one per person, at least in this world.

In the late 1960s some people began to criticize the cardiac-based definition of death. On a practical level, if these people with irreversible loss of brain function whose hearts continue to beat are considered alive, there would be terrible consequences — not only for potential transplant recipients, but also for many others who could benefit from other important uses for these arguably dead bodies. Critics of the heart-based definition claim these bodies are in reality nothing more than "respiring cadavers" (that is, dead bodies which continue to have heartbeats and respire because of ventilator support). With proper permission, they can be used by medical scientists not only for transplant, but also for research, teaching, and other therapeutic purposes. Great good is at stake in getting the definition of death right.

Still, even if these bodies are valuable, this alone cannot justify calling someone dead unless there are good reasons for doing so. Many people, however, have now accepted the belief that the essence of the human being is not mere flowing of blood and breath. They believe there is something more important, something more essential to being alive than just having a pump moving blood around the body. They see this view as too animalistic; unduly reducing the human too much to a mere biological organism.

THE "WHOLE-BRAIN" ORIENTED DEFINITION

In 1968 the Harvard Ad Hoc Committee on Definition of Death adopted a key report claiming that we should start treating people as dead **when brain function is totally and irreversibly lost.** The committee proposed a set of four criteria for measuring this irreversible loss of brain function.

Endnote 3

It is widely accepted that once one meets these four criteria, one will lose heart and respiratory function soon, but that is not the basis for the new definition of death. In fact, someday scientists may be able to keep a heart beating in such patients indefinitely. The holders of this view believe that the essence of the human is its ability to integrate bodily functions so that one functions "as a whole." They believe, with good reason, that this integration is done by the brain so that when the brain irreversibly loses its capacity to function, then the individual as a whole is dead.

> ### HARVARD AD HOC COMMITTEE CRITERIA FOR MEASURING THE DEATH OF THE BRAIN
>
> 1) **unreceptivity and unresponsivity**
>
> 2) **no movements or breathing**
>
> 3) **no reflexes**
>
> 4) **flat EEG**
>
> **Repeat tests 24 hours later**
>
> **Exclusions:**
>
> — **Hypothermia (low body temperature)**
>
> — **Central nervous system depressants**

The first law establishing a brain-oriented basis for pronouncing death was passed in 1970 in Kansas. Now all U.S. jurisdictions have such a law and the prestigious **U.S. President's Commission for the Study of Ethical Problems in Medicine and Biomedical and Behavioral Research** has endorsed pronouncing death based on irreversible loss of all brain function. Almost all countries throughout the world have such laws as well. Only a few Southeast Asian countries resist adopting a brain-based definition. They do so in part based on traditional religious beliefs regarding the presence of a life force (a "soul") throughout the body. Japan, which has strongly resisted adoption of a brain-oriented definition has recently changed its position.

Endnote 4

Endnote 5

Recently New Jersey has become the first state to modify its definition so that an individual has the right to present a document stating that on religious grounds he or she prefers the use of the traditional heart-based definition.

Endnote 6

Not only Asians, but some Orthodox Jews continue to insist that life is present as long as the heart beats. This **"conscience clause"** gives people the right to choose their own definitions of death. The reasoning offered for this discretion is that choosing a definition of death is essentially a matter of religious or philosophical or public policy choice. Deciding when to treat someone as dead is not something resolvable by medical science. People must choose based on their beliefs about when an individual ceases to be part of the human moral and political community. We generally agree that on such matters of religious and philosophical choice, individuals should be given maximum possible discretion. Hence New Jersey has chosen to give that discretion. Whether the people of that state were justified in giving it only on religious grounds rather than secular philosophical preferences is a matter of continuing controversy.

THE "HIGHER BRAIN" DEFINITION

Under this view, an individual is dead **when the cerebrum (the "thinking part of the brain") ceases function, even though the brain stem (the body regulating part) still functions.** While a whole-brain definition of death is now widely accepted by the general public and the medical community, many philosophers are not yet satisfied. In particular, they have been questioning whether literally all of the brain must have ceased functioning in order for someone to be dead. We know that some parts of the brain perform rather elementary reflex functions. The cerebrum, the highest portion of the brain, is responsible for consciousness, thinking, feeling, memory, and voluntary muscle control, but the lower portions of the brain are responsible for such functions as the cough reflex, eye blink, and control of respiration.

Endnote 7

In 1971 J.B. Brierley published a report on two patients who had lost all cerebral function but continued to breathe on their own for several weeks because their lower brain tissues were still alive. It is widely agreed that such patients can never again regain consciousness. They are in what is now called a permanent or persistent vegetative state. By the whole-brain definition of death they are clearly still alive because the lower brain is still functioning.

Endnote 8

A number of philosophers have for several years been arguing that these people should no more be considered alive than those who have totally lost brain function. They hold that what is really important for being considered alive and part of the human community is some capacity for consciousness or ability to interact socially with other humans. This is what some people have in mind when they refer to the human as a social animal. They believe that one is dead — that is, no longer part of the human community for social purposes — if one has irreversibly lost consciousness. They acknowledge that this would make Yosef Camp, permanently vegetative patients, and others who are permanently unconscious dead by definition. They believe this is acceptable. That means their bodies must be treated with respect, but it also means we can treat them the way we treat other deceased people.

The defenders of the whole-brain-oriented position offer several criticisms of this position. They claim that it is a more radical break from tradition than the whole-brain position; that it relies on a concept of personhood about which there is no social agreement; and that treating people who have some purportedly unimportant brain functions remaining places us on a "slippery slope" that could lead to treating those with some limited remaining cerebral functions (such as the Alzheimer's patient or the severely retarded) as dead also. They ask, "Would you really bury someone who is still breathing?"

Defenders of the higher-brain position say that what is really the break from tradition came with the movement from a definition of death based on circulatory function to one based on neurological function. They believe the whole-brain defenders are just as guilty of risking a new definition as those defending the higher-brain position. They deny that their position is based on any view of personhood or personal identity, claiming that whatever personhood means it has nothing to do with the definition of death. They even deny that they are risking a slide down a slippery slope. They claim that the decisive difference between being alive and being dead is whether there is the presence of any mental function. (The Alzheimer's patient and the retarded clearly are alive by this criterion.) They even have accused the defenders of the whole-brain position of being on their own slippery slope because they try to draw a line between the top of the spinal cord and the base of the brain and there are no principled differences between the reflexes at the top of the spine and those at the base of the brain. They claim that there is a real qualitative difference between the presence and absence of any mental function that is much more significant.

Some defenders of the higher-brain position acknowledge that there are people who, for religious or other reasons, will not accept this position. They offer the proposal to extend the policy permitting conscientious choice among plausible alternatives, as people now have in New Jersey, but they would extend the range of choices for a definition to include complete loss of consciousness. They would propose that a society pick one of the three positions (based on circulatory, whole-brain, or higher-brain positions), whichever has the greatest support, as the default position and then let those who dissent opt for one of the other positions. If the whole-brain position were chosen, then some could exercise a choice in favor of the cardiac view and others could choose the higher-brain alternative.

They claim that the decisive difference between being alive and being dead is whether there is the presence of any mental function.

MENTALLY COMPETENT PATIENTS

Yosef Camp might already be dead, at least if the higher brain position were the default and perhaps if the whole-brain position were. However, if parents were also given the right to exercise conscientious dissent in favor of a reasonable alternative (at least if the patient had never been competent to express a position), then Yosef's parents might have chosen to have Yosef treated as alive until his heart stopped. What actually happened was that the neurologists could not agree that his brain was completely dead. Moreover, the District of Columbia at the time did not legally recognize a brain-based definition of death. Yosef was legally alive. The real moral question was whether he had to be treated to be kept alive or whether the physicians could cease life support and let him die, even against his parents' wishes.

Often the definition of death gets undue attention when the real issue at stake, especially for patients who retain some brain function, is how they should be treated and what decisions are ethically acceptable.

ELIZABETH BOUVIA:
THE WOMAN WHO
REFUSED MEDICAL FEEDING

Elizabeth Bouvia was born with severe cerebral palsy that left her a bedridden quadriplegic. She was totally dependent on others for her care. She suffered from continual painful arthritis for which she received morphine through a tube implanted in her chest. She suffered muscle contractures that left her unable to change her position. Still she was intelligent, having completed a master's degree in social work from San Diego State University. Her problems became so severe that her parents were no longer able to care for her. She was left without financial means.

In 1983 she reached the decision that she would refuse feeding while she starved herself to death. Because she needed the morphine infusion to control her pain, however, she asked to be cared for in Riverside General Hospital while she did this. When the physicians insisted that she would have to have a feeding tube if she stayed in the hospital, she sought a court order. A lower court ruled that she was mentally competent to refuse the feeding tube and had a legal right to do so, but appealed to concerns about the effect on other patients and the integrity of the physicians in ruling that, if she wanted to stay in the hospital, she would have to accept feeding. Others could not be forced to assist her in her plan to end her life.

Later at another hospital, physicians, relying on the earlier court decision, inserted a feeding tube. But the California Court of Appeals intervened, insisting that she had the

right of self-determination to decline the treatment. The court ordered that the tube be removed.

Endnote 9

In cases such as that of Elizabeth Bouvia, major questions have been debated.

SUICIDE/ASSISTED SUICIDE/HOMICIDE ON REQUEST

Many people, debating Elizabeth Bouvia's demand, claim that **refusal of nutrition and hydration** in her situation is tantamount to committing suicide. Others claim she is not committing suicide at all, but merely refusing life-sustaining medical treatment. The difference is controversial. Those who make the distinction focus on one of two dimensions: (1) her intention and (2) whether there is an active effort made to kill or simply an omission that allows the death to take place.

There is a strong tendency in contemporary discussion to describe active interventions with the intention of producing death as **killing**. Sometimes the term is extended to active efforts that accidentally cause death. Giving a patient a drug that unintentionally causes death would still be killing, according to this usage. Sometimes the term killing is extended to cover omissions that result in death, especially if death was the intention. The fight over whether the behavior is called killing is probably based on the widely held belief that killing is, by definition, morally wrong, while letting a patient die may not be in certain circumstances. If we could agree to make the moral assessment of each of these independent of whether we call it killing, the fight over the label would probably subside.

Let us first limit our attention to active interventions that intentionally result in death. If the individual who ends up dying is the one who acts — who points a gun to her own head or intentionally swallows a large dose of phenobarbital hoping to end her life — we call the behavior *suicide.* If someone assists by bringing the gun to the patient, helping her aim it or loading the gun for her, that would be called **assisted suicide** as long as the patient actually pulls the trigger. But what if the patient is too weak or otherwise incapable of pulling the trigger? If she begs someone else to shoot her or to administer the lethal drug, we could say that the person who does so is committing **homicide on request.**

JANET ADKINS
'DOCTOR DEATH'

In June of 1990, 54-year-old Portland, Oregon resident Janet Adkins had reached a decision that she should kill herself. She had been told she had the early stages of Alzheimer's disease. She feared that the disease, which leads to progressive loss of mental capacity, would take over. She wanted to act before she lost control of the decision.

She flew to Michigan to meet a pathologist named Jack Kevorkian, a physician committed to assisting people in ending their lives when they suffer form incurable diseases. After a dinner meeting, he took her to a van parked in a parking lot and attached her to a "suicide" machine he had invented. As originally attached, an intravenous line permitted the flow of a harmless saline into her vein, but the machine was equipped with a valve that permitted her to switch the line to a lethal drug, which caused her death.

Since then, Dr. Kevorkian has assisted in at least a hundred other deaths, using both the suicide machine and other methods of bringing about death. But his license to practice medicine has been suspended both in Michigan and in California.

By our definition Jack Kevorkian has been engaging in assisting suicide. Were he to actually push the button that starts the lethal mixture flowing into the patient, he would then be committing homicide on request. Homicide on request is clearly illegal in all U.S. jurisdictions. The request on the part of a patient, even one who is suffering, does not make the killing legal. Assisting suicide is also illegal in most jurisdictions. When Kevorkian began his project, it was not illegal in Michigan, but the legislature rapidly enacted emergency legislation declaring it so. Suicide itself is generally not viewed as a criminal act in American law.

STATE LAWS PROHIBITING PHYSICIAN ASSISTANCE

Unlike the situation in Michigan when Jack Kevorkian began his campaign for physician-assisted dying, most states clearly make such assistance illegal. That state law was challenged by two actions designed to have the state laws declared in violation of the United States Constitution. These efforts were clearly limited to physician assistance in suicide rather than homicide on request; they were designed to further only cases involving terminally ill patients who were mentally competent and had made repeated requests for assistance in ending their own lives.

The following case was one of the ones involved:

JANE ROE:

FOR PHYSICIAN-ASSISTED SUICIDE

A woman the court called Jane Roe was a 69-year-old retired pediatrician. She had cancer that had metastasized throughout her skeleton. She had tried hospice care, but it was not fully successful in alleviating her pain. Now she suffered from swollen legs, bedsores, poor appetite, nausea and vomiting, impaired vision, incontinence of bowel, and general weakness. She was fundamentally competent.

But she wished to hasten her death by taking prescribed drugs with the help of Compassion in Dying, an organization led by a clergyman in Seattle devoted to helping terminally-ill persons end their lives comfortably. Following the organization's policies, she had made three requests for aid and had received counseling and emotional support. Her physician was willing to help but for the fact that the law made such help illegal. Compassion in Dying brought suit on behalf of three patients including Jane Roe and their physicians attempting to have the court declare the state law prohibiting physician assistance in these circumstances illegal.

The Arguments in the Law

A similar suit was brought in the state of New York. Those two cases eventually reached the United States Supreme Court, which rejected the arguments, leaving the law prohibiting physician assistance in effect. The two cases involved different reasons why the state law might be challenged. It is worth brief examination of each.

The Argument from Liberty

The Washington law was challenged on the ground of the patient's **right to liberty** under the due process clause of the U.S. Constitution. They tried, unsuccessfully, to get the court to hold that prohibiting access to a physician for the purpose of getting a prescription to end one's life deprived these patients of liberty without due process. The Supreme Court would eventually point out that states have always had the right to prohibit assistance in a suicide. It could be argued that what was happening here was no different from many other limits on individual liberty that keep patients from buying dangerous pharmaceuticals. If anyone's liberty is being constrained here, it seems it is the physicians', the ones who are prohibited from prescribing the lethal agents. But physicians — health professionals licensed by the state — have their liberty constrained in many ways. They cannot prescribe heroin or marihuana, for example, and cannot perform abortions in their offices. The Court found that we accept certain constraints on liberty of both lay people and physicians and rejected this argument from liberty.

The Argument from Equal Protection

Meanwhile in New York another group of physicians was arguing that the state prohibition on physician assistance in suicide violated the Constitutional requirement of **equal protection**. Before the Supreme Court eventually rejected this argument, a federal Court of Appeals accepted the claim argument that if a state was going to permit certain people to choose to refuse life-sustaining medical treatment even though doing so would lead to their deaths, then it should grant equal protection to those who choose to die by means of taking a medication prescribed by their physician for this purpose. The point was not that they necessarily had the liberty to do this, but that, if the group who wanted to die by refusing treatment could be protect-

Endnote 9a

Endnote 9b

"No single thing abides."
—Roman philospher-poet Lucretius

Endnote 9c

ed by the law in choosing their preferred method of dying, then the group preferring more active physician assistance should also be protected.

The problem with this argument is that it would also seem to apply to other groups who had other methods of death they preferred. For example, some persons due to paralysis or weakness may not be physically capable of taking the medication. Others may prefer to die in some more public way as a means of political protest. If the group who wanted to die by taking a prescription had a right to equal protection, then these other groups would appear to have that right as well. The U.S. Supreme Court rejected the equal protection argument just as it had rejected the liberty argument.

Endnote 9d

The Current State of the Law

The United States: The net effect of these court actions was to acknowledge that a state could prohibit physician assistance in suicide if it wanted to. That does not mean that a state must prohibit it. In the state of Oregon, a referendum was passed in 1994 that legalized such physician assistance. The opponents of such assistance attempted to argue that legalization would be unfair to those lacking economic or other resources who would be forced to choose assisted suicide as their only option. In 1997 the U.S. Supreme Court refused to take their case, so the Oregon law is now in effect. It is the only jurisdiction in the United States that has clearly legalized physician assistance although several other states appear to have no law either prohibiting it and might thus be said to permit it.

International: **Active killing for mercy** — either through assisted suicide or homicide on request, is being debated throughout the world. While once it was not considered to be realistic to press for legalization, now it must be taken as a serious proposal. It is technically not legal in the Netherlands, but there is an informal agreement between the medical profession and prosecutors that physicians will not be prosecuted if they follow a set of rules. This agreement permits physicians to perform what they call "euthanasia" by which they mean voluntary killing of persons upon request. They do not limit this arrangement to assisted suicide, but include cases in which the physician actually does the killing as well.

THE CLASSICAL APPROACHES

The question of ethics, however, is not whether any of these actions is legal, but rather whether one ought, morally, to engage in them. The classical ethical case against suicide is offered from within the Judeo-Christian tradition by the 13th century Catholic theologian, **St. Thomas Aquinas**. He offered three arguments. First, insofar as the natural end of the human is to seek life, taking our lives thwarts that end and therefore violates the moral natural law. Second, insofar as our lives provide a service to the community, taking our lives deprives

Endnote 10

the community society of our services. And third, our lives belong to God and, therefore, taking our lives is taking something that does not properly belong to us. **David Hume** responds point by point, claiming that suicide need not be a violation of our duty to ourselves, the community, or to God. First, suicide for Hume can violate our duty to ourselves only if it violates our interests, and Hume believes that it is obvious when sickness or misfortune render our lives a burden, it is not contrary to our interest to end them. He claims some people are not useful to the community and their existence may actually be detrimental to it. Thus suicide is not always a violation of the community's interest. Finally, Hume addresses the claim that suicide is a transgression against God. He takes the natural law to refer to physical laws of nature, which cannot be violated, rather than moral laws, which morally ought not to be violated even though we are physically capable of doing so. Thus Hume, misunderstanding what Aquinas means, argues that if humans are capable of committing suicide, it cannot be a violation of God's law.

Secular philosophers have divided over the ethics of suicide. **Libertarians** tend to side with Hume, claiming that our bodies belong to ourselves and that as long as we are substantially autonomous agents we can do what we want with them — including ending them. **Immanuel Kant**, however, sides with Aquinas, arguing that reason requires we must treat all persons as if they were ends in themselves. He believes that, logically, this means it is unethical to kill, and that this includes killing of the self.

Whether suicide itself is considered unethical, assisting suicide and homicide upon request are more likely to be. This is because, in addition to the principled arguments against these involvements in the deaths of others, there are serious practical problems with any social policy that would accept assistance in suicide or homicide upon request. Because the one acted upon ends up dead (if the action is successful) it is difficult to make sure that the individual really was making the request and that he or she was mentally competent if there was one. Since the risk of abuse is grave, there is greater moral reservation against either assisting in suicide or in homicide upon request. At the very least, even if the principled objections to killing can be overcome, procedural safeguards would seem necessary. These might include having a public agency such as a court review the request to determine that it is authentic. Even then, most seem to believe the moral problems with such deaths are great.

However, even if suicide, assistance in suicide, and homicide on request are considered unethical, many would claim it is not obvious that someone like Elizabeth Bouvia is really involved in any of these. Common usage reserves these terms to cases in which the patient is not terminally or critically ill. If the decision to actively end a life is motivated out of a desire to escape intractable suffering caused by an organic medical problem, we tend to label the intervention not as a suicide or homicide on request, but as a mercy killing.

Endnote 11

He claims some people are not useful to the community and their existence may actually be detrimental to it. Thus suicide is not always a violation of the community's interest.

Endnote 12

Endnote 13

Active Killing vs. Allowing to Die

The second major question that confronts us when we debate how to treat terminally or critically ill patients who are still alive is whether there is any significant moral difference between actively killing them and simply allowing them to die by forgoing medical life support. Elizabeth Bouvia, whatever we think of her request, was clearly motivated by the apparently inescapable misery caused by her desperate medical condition.

Because she should clearly have understood that stopping her feeding would result in her death, would it not have been simpler and faster to simply kill her with an injection? Is there a difference morally between that and what she was demanding? The distinction, sometimes called the commission/omission distinction, leads to one of the oldest and most heated debates in medical ethics.

Intuitively There Is a Difference

Some rather lame arguments have been given in support of the difference. One is that, intuitively, it feels as though there is a difference between injecting someone in order to kill them and simply withholding life support. It is probably true that most of us feel the intuitive difference, but that may simply be because we have always been taught there is such a difference. We cannot reasonably rely on our teachers' beliefs to prove that the difference is real. They may simply have been confused. The argument is circular.

Active Killing Is Illegal

Another weak argument sometimes offered in favor of the difference, is that active killing is illegal in all jurisdictions, while forgoing medical treatment, even life-sustaining treatment, is generally legal. It is true that active killing of another person for mercy is illegal in all jurisdictions. The Netherlands has recently been experimenting with an arrangement that makes active killing for mercy "quasi-legal" for patients who make a persistent and voluntary request to be killed after they are diagnosed as suffering from an incurable condition. Medical professionals and public officials have an agreement that medical professionals will not be prosecuted provided the mercy killing meets certain guidelines. These provide that the patient must, after careful consideration, make a voluntary request to be killed. The physician must inform the patient about his or her condition and about measures that could be taken to alleviate the suffering. At least one other physician must be consulted and there must be a written record of the proceedings. The **euthanasia** must be reported on the death certificate. Nevertheless, even in the Netherlands, mercy killing remains against the law. In all other jurisdictions it is more straightforwardly illegal; mercy is not a defense against the crime and one who is proved to have killed for mercy will be convicted. Sometimes judges and juries will take the extenuating circumstances into account in sentencing, but there is no question that mercy killing is a crime whether committed by a physician or a lay person.

The fact that it is illegal does not, however, settle the matter of whether it is ethical. It could be that our law is simply wrong here. Or it could be that even though it is ethical to kill for mercy, for practical reasons it should remain a crime in order to prevent abuses.

PHYSICIANS HAVE RESERVATIONS ABOUT MERCY KILLING

A final poor argument for the difference is that physicians feel strong moral objections. In fact, the **American Medical Association's Council on Ethical and Judicial Affairs** declares that its members should not "intentionally cause death," but the fact that physician groups believe it is unethical for physicians to kill doesn't necessarily make it so. They cannot be the final authority for deciding what constitutes ethical conduct for physicians. Moreover, even if the society believes that physician participation in killing for mercy is wrong, society could create a new role for doing the job. It could be performed by former licensed physicians like Jack Kevorkian or by others trained to do so. If there is really something morally different between active killing for mercy and forgoing medical treatment, there must be some better arguments.

Endnote 14

Three Primary Arguments

Two arguments for retaining the distinction between active killing and forgoing treatment may be more plausible. The first, by appealing to the consequences, uses the same form of argument as those who would treat them as the same, but reaches the opposite conclusion. Whereas the defenders of the moral similarity of **active killing** and **forgoing treatment** believe that they are the same because the consequences are the same — either way, the person dies — some of the defenders of the moral difference claim they are not so sure the consequences are really the same.

Some years ago, a psychologist wanting to test the issue posted a notice to recruit American college students for what was supposed to be an experiment. The notice claimed this was an experiment to study the best way to solve a future serious social problem of either overcrowding or genetic disease. The investigator presented the idea claiming that she simply wanted to understand which "final solution" to these problems would be the most humane. She made clear that the "final solution" would be to "humanely kill" the excess population or the genetically afflicted. What she did not make clear was that "final solution" was precisely the term used by the Nazis in their mass exterminations during World War II. She wanted to see how many people might be open to active killing not for the purpose of relieving suffering but to serve society's purposes. She found that 326 of 570 students more than 57% approved of the project. When the final solution was to be applied to minorities, the acceptance rate was even higher.

Endnote 15

The implication was that if we were to legalize certain killings for mercy, we would be at risk of losing control of our social practices so that other killings would be more likely to occur. In the Netherlands, there are preliminary data suggesting that those who are worrying about the slippery slope have something to be concerned about. In the first study of physician-killings in the Netherlands, the investigators' best estimate was that about 2,300 patients were killed in accord with the agreement in a 12 month period, but an additional 1,030 were killed by physicians where there had not been such requests. More information would be needed to conclude that tolerating active mercy killing after a persistent and voluntary request causes an increase in other killings, but the Netherlands data are a cause for concern. If tolerating active killing were to have worse consequences than simply permitting forgoing of treatment, that would be one reason to hold on to the belief in the difference. This could lead to the conclusion that the rule distinguishing active killing from foregoing life-support leads to better consequences than one that treats them the same.

Endnote 16

Some Hold That Active Killing Is Simply Wrong

Secondly, even if it cannot be proved that the consequences of a rule permitting active killing are worse than one permitting forgoing treatment, some simply believe that active killing is immoral. Just as violating people's autonomy, lying to them, and breaking promises are believed by many to be inherently wrong-making characteristics of actions, so killing may be also, even if there are no bad consequences. People who believe some or all of these are wrong may believe they can produce rational arguments for their position. Immanuel Kant held that ethics requires that people be treated as ends in themselves and that one cannot simultaneously will that they be so treated and that they be killed. This applies even to killing oneself. Others hold that they know by intuition, revelation, or by moral traditions they take to be authoritative — that it is wrong to kill.

If we were to legalize certain killings for mercy, we would be at risk of losing control of our social practices so that other killings would be more likely to occur.

Autonomy Requires Forgoing Life-Support

A third and final argument for the moral difference between active killing and simply letting die is based on the moral **principle of autonomy.** At least as far as physicians, nurses, and other health professionals are concerned, the principle of autonomy requires that when a competent patient refuses to consent to treatment, the provider of health services cannot touch the patient. That means life-sustaining treatment must be omitted. But patient autonomy can never justify or require that the health provider actively kill; at most it could give permission. The health provider can be compelled by patient autonomy to forgo; he or she cannot be obliged to intervene. This, of course, does not establish that, for the patients themselves, there is a difference. If there is a difference for them, it must be for one of the other reasons.

Stopping vs. Not Starting

The term forgoing includes both decisions to **withdraw treatment** and to **refrain from starting** it in the first place. The third major question confronting someone who is attempting to decide about the morality of treatments for the terminally ill is whether the decision to stop a life-sustaining treatment is morally more like active killing or more like not starting it. Withdrawing a treatment is surely an active intervention. Psychologically, to a physician or a nurse, it must feel like injecting an air bubble or otherwise doing something that will kill the patient.

But the argument regarding patient autonomy is revealing. One reason why health care personnel cannot start treatment is if patients have not consented to it. The patient has the autonomy to refuse it. But just as she can exercise her autonomy by refusing to let it start, so she can exercise it by refusing to let it continue. Refusal to consent requires that the clinician refrain from treating. Rational patients would not give consent without restriction. If they think about it they would always limit consents with the phrase: "until I no longer agree that you can continue." Consents can be revoked, and when they are, the moral and legal requirements of autonomy demand that the clinician withdraw.

Another way of arguing that withdrawing is morally like withholding is to look at the intention of the one making the decision. While actions designed to kill necessarily involve the intention to kill, decisions not to treat may be rooted in the intention merely to avoid a treatment that is not going to serve a worthwhile purpose. Defenders of this view claim this may be true even if one knows full-well that the patient will die if the treatment is not provided. Likewise, the decision to withdraw consent may be based on the intention to avoid a treatment that is not serving any purpose any longer. These notions suggest two final distinctions that are relevant to deciding about treatments for terminally ill patients: deciding whether killing is direct or indirect, and whether the means provided are ordinary or extraordinary.

Direct vs. Indirect Killing

If intention is morally important in deciding whether forgoing a treatment is ethical, then it will be necessary to understand the difference between direct and indirect effects that leave people dead. An effect is said to be **direct** if it results from a behavior (an action or omission) in which the intention of the perpetrator is the effect that is produced. If the effect is a death, then someone kills directly if one directly intends the death. For many of those who believe that killing is morally wrong, it is direct killing that they primarily have in mind.

For example, the Catholic Church has historically condemned all direct killing of innocent people. Its adherents make limited allowance for killing of aggressors and killing in wars they consider morally justified. They also make allowance for other killings — even active killings — in which the death is not intended. Anesthesia

These notions suggest two final distinctions that are relevant to deciding about treatments for terminally ill patients: deciding whether killing is direct or indirect, and whether the means provided are ordinary or extraordinary.

STOP

accidents and overdoses of pain-relieving narcotics kill and they do so by active intervention, but the deaths are not intended. Likewise, some omissions that lead to death may be chosen with only the direct intention of removing a burdensome treatment.

By contrast, some deaths are said to be indirect effects of morally justifiable actions. This gives rise to what is sometimes called the **principle of double effect** or **indirect effect.** An effect is indirect if it is not intended and is not a means to a desired effect. Behaviors that produce evil indirect effects are considered ethical when four conditions are met: (1) the behavior itself must not be intrinsically immoral, (2) the evil effect must not be intended (even if one can foresee it will occur), (3) it must not be a means to the intended effect, and — critically — (4) the intended good effect must be proportional to the unintended evil effect; that is, the amount of good must exceed the amount of harm.

The most well-known case of a double effect in medicine is the administration of narcotic pain relievers for the purpose of relieving pain even though one knows that they cause respiratory depression and even risk death. While death might always be viewed as an unfortunate outcome, it is not, according to many, an ultimate evil. While some, such as Orthodox Jews, could consider even the modest hastening of her death unacceptable, others, such as many Catholics, would not consider it an ultimate evil in these circumstances. Both U.S. law and the AMA, as well as many secular groups such as the President's Commission for the Study of Ethical Problems in Medicine and Biomedical and Behavioral Research, essentially adopt positions reflecting this notion of the potential legality of such unintended or indirect killings. Whether these killings are acceptable depends on the final variable — proportionality — which is critical in understanding the ethics of decisions about the terminally ill.

ORDINARY AND EXTRAORDINARY MEANS OF TREATMENT

Deciding which treatments are morally required and which are expendable is one of the most controversial but important aspects of the ethics of caring for the terminally ill. Some older confusing language is now being replaced by new, clearer terms. We used to speak of treatments that were ordinary and those that were extraordinary. Ordinary treatments were morally required while extraordinary ones were not. While those terms are still used, they are often misleading.

Older, Largely Rejected Meanings

These terms were often taken by clinicians to carry their normal English language meanings. **Ordinary treatments were thought to be common ones; extraordinary treatments, uncommon.** That, however, is never what the theologians and philosophers meant by these words. It makes little sense to hold that just because a treatment is uncommon it is extraordinary. Someone with an unusual illness may get great benefit from some very unusual procedure. On the other hand some treatments that are used routinely, day-in and day-out, may still be doing no good. In fact they may be doing harm. Trying to figure out what is morally required by determining what is common makes no sense, and that is never what the terms "ordinary" and "extraordinary" meant.

Likewise, it is not plausible to determine what is morally required and what is expendable by determining how simple or complex a procedure is. Some treatments that are very complex — high-technology gadgets, such as ventilators or kidney machines — may do great good for patients while some simple procedures such as IV fluids and antibiotics may do no good at all. Figuring out how complex or how simple a treatment is does not help in determining whether it is morally imperative.

Today when we still use these terms, we use them only to convey a moral judgment about their importance. **Ordinary simply means "morally required,"** even if the treatment is very unusual and/or high-tech. **Extraordinary simply means "morally expendable,"** even if it is very common and/or technologically simple.

CRITERIA FOR MORALLY EXPENDABLE TREATMENT

That still leaves us with the question of what criteria should be used for determining that a treatment is morally optional. The classical answer generally has been based on the expected benefits and burdens of the proposed procedure. It is just common sense that medical treatments should not be provided if they are likely to do more harm than good for the patient. In fact, if the expected harms equal the expected benefits — if there is a tie, so to speak — there is still no reason to provide the treatment.

Catholic moral theologians have for centuries addressed the problem of the criteria for morally expendable treatments. Two criteria are usually mentioned. First, a treatment is expendable if it is useless. If it will do no good, then there is no reason for providing it. Second, even if it serves some useful purpose, such as prolonging life, it is still considered morally expendable if it is gravely burdensome. Pope Pius XII in 1957 said that treatments are extraordinary — that is, expendable — if they "do not involve a grave burden for oneself or another." Secular commentators have generally accepted these same criteria.

Endnote 17

Proportionality
More recently there has been a movement to replace these older, more ambiguous terms with the term proportionality. It **incorporates into one concept both the notions of uselessness and of grave burden**. If a treatment is useless, it offers no benefit; the numerator of the fraction expressing the ratio of benefits to burdens would be zero. On the other hand if a treatment is gravely burdensome, that is a way of saying that the denominator of that fraction

would be very large, implying a high likelihood that the burdens would be disproportional to the benefits.

Notice, however, that there are still some ambiguities. For example, Pius XII said that according to Catholic thought, a treatment must be gravely burdensome before it is expendable. Older Catholic thinking held that so-called extraordinary treatments are not morally required, but accepting them was nevertheless considered good or noble. These were of such a level of burden that we could not expect a human to endure them, but it would nevertheless be good if they were accepted. They would be "beyond the call of duty."

Recent secular thought and more recent Catholic thought seem to have abandoned this notion of burdensome life-prolonging treatments being noble even if they are not morally required. Secular thinkers might consider it rather foolish to accept a treatment that prolongs life, but prolongs it at a level of burden that exceeds the benefit. One area of lingering doubt is what should happen when the burdens are rather small, but are nevertheless greater than the benefits. Is such a treatment expendable as disproportionally burdensome, or is it still required because it imposes only a small burden?

The critical test case is the hypothetical situation of **a treatment that offers no burdens but no benefits.** A permanently unconscious patient such as Yosef Camp, assuming he really is irreversibly unconscious, might be an example. Do we say of such a case that because the burden is not grave — there is actually no burden at all — the treatment is required if it will prolong his life? Or do we say that because the benefits are not greater than the burdens, there is no reason to provide such treatment? According to some uses of the concept of proportionality, a medical treatment is morally expendable if the expected benefits do not exceed the expected burdens.

The New-Found Subjectivity of Benefits and Burdens

A major new development in this discussion has been a new-found discovery that these judgments of benefit and harm are inherently grounded in something more than medical fact. The questions at stake include: **How valuable is unconscious life? How bad is it to be in pain? Is living extra days of bed-ridden life worth special efforts?** Consider the various cases presented thus far in this chapter. In order to know whether the benefits of treatment outweigh the harms, Yosef Camp's parents need to decide how valuable it is to give Allah a chance to intervene as well as whether there is value in unconscious life. Elizabeth Bouvia must decide whether it is better to die or live a painful life as a cerebral palsy victim unable to get out of bed. Jack Kevorkian and his patients must decide whether life is worth living as Alzheimer's disease and other critical conditions progress. The patients contemplating physician-assisted suicide must decide whether it is wrong to actively end their lives as well as whether the potential harms to others from their actions should count morally. None of these is a question that medical science can answer.

Some might claim that these questions are nevertheless capable of some kind of objective answer. If there is an objective answer, however, it is objective in a different sense than questions of medical science are. It is objective only in the sense that basic religious or evaluative questions are objective. Some would claim that there are no objective answers to such questions; that they are nothing more than matters of personal preference or taste. Others hold to the view that God or reason or some other objective standard can provide truly objective answers.

Either way, from the point of view of the finite human observer, these are questions totally beyond the capacity of medical science to answer. If physicians have no special expertise in answering them, we generally must rely on individuals — perhaps

Figure 1. Benefits and burdens weighed in medical decisions. Corbis Bettmann.

guided by the religious and philosophical sources — to provide answers. This means that different patients with medically identical conditions are, based on their religious and philosophical convictions, going to give different answers to the question of what the benefits and the harms of various treatments are likely to be. Grave burden clearly involves these apparently subjective dimensions. The pain of cancer can be bad for one patient, but tolerable; while for a patient with an identical tumor and perhaps even the same objective level of pain, the burden can be intolerable.

Likewise, deciding whether a treatment is useless involves evaluative judgments. Consider, for example, a ventilator for a persistently vegetative patient. It is utterly useless for restoring consciousness. If that is the goal, it is useless. But it is very effective in some cases for keeping the unconscious patient's heart beating. If that is the goal, it is very useful.

Because these judgments of usefulness and burden involve these apparently subjective dimensions, many people hold that the decisions about them should rest with the patient, if the patient is conscious and capable of communicating. Then the only way for a physician to know the benefit or burden of a treatment, is to ask the patient. That the treatment produces an effect is essentially a matter of medical science; that the effect is a benefit cannot be. If it is a "fact" at all, its nature would not be objective but religious or "normative."

CAN SIMPLE, BASIC TREATMENTS BE EXPENDABLE?

Throughout the 1970s the reasoning discussed here was applied to cases involving decisions to forgo ventilators, kidney machines, cancer surgery, and organ replacement — all major interventions that plausibly extend life, but that have also raised doubts about the benefits of the procedures. Generally, they were technologically complex, expensive procedures.

'You think you're old? I've lived through six presidents, three wars and both health department inspections.'

But once the reasoning based on proportionality was fully in place, people naturally began to apply it to other, more routine treatments. Elizabeth Bouvia's effort to refuse nutrition supplied through a nasogastric tube is an example of a procedure long considered "basic" or "fundamental" eventually being subjected to the proportionality reasoning. Other simple treatments that have been questioned on these grounds include supplying fluids through an IV line, doing cardio-pulmonary resuscitation, administering antibiotics for infection, and, in nursing, routine turning of the patient to prevent bedsores.

In nursing it is standard practice to turn a bed-ridden patient every two hours or so to prevent serious skin eruptions. These practices are governed by standard protocols that every nurse learns. For almost every patient, it is obviously in the patient's interest to follow such procedures.

But what of a patient with hours to live? Suppose such a patient has brittle bone disease, a condition that makes bones so brittle they might simply snap upon movement. If the patient has such a risk of broken bones and has hours to live, does the standard nursing protocol have to be followed?

One approach is to ask what the risks and benefits are. If the risks are great and the benefits negligible, then the proposed turning of the patient would fail the proportionality test. Because the only purpose of turning the patient is to prevent skin problems that will take days to develop, if the patient does not have days, then it seems reasonable to claim that there is no benefit. There clearly seems to be serious risk of pain. If that fact is combined with the lack of potential benefit, then many would conclude that turning the patient fails the proportionality test.

Likewise, some would argue there is little to be gained and a great deal of suffering to be risked if CPR is attempted on a patient who clearly is terminally ill. If the patient has made the assessment of the benefits and harms and finds CPR to come up wanting, then the patient might plausibly decide against resuscitation.

Similarly, if providing fluids will only prolong the agony of death, then medical hydration using intravenous feeding may offer greater risk of harm than benefit.

THREE ARGUMENTS ON FOOD AND FLUIDS ALWAYS REQUIRED

Three arguments have been put forward in defense of the traditional practice of providing food and fluids to all patients regardless of their condition.

Basic Care

First, people such as **Gilbert Meilaender**, an ethicist from Oberlin College, have argued that supplying food and fluids are not medical tasks at all; they are not treatments, but simply basic care. He has argued they should always be provided even if the patient is declining other life-prolonging treatments.

Endnote 18

Critics of his position claim it really doesn't matter whether one calls these procedures medical or not. If the intervention does more harm than good, it should not be provided. To hold otherwise seems to commit one to the strange position that useless and burdensome medical procedures are morally expendable, but that useless and burdensome non-medical procedures are imperative even though, on balance, they do no good.

Symbol of Societal Commitment to the Hungry and Thirsty

The second argument in favor of making nutrition and hydration mandatory are that they should always be provided as a symbol of our commitment to the hungry and thirsty. Providing nutrition and hydration are therefore **"symbolic acts"** conveying our societal sense of the crucial importance of feeding the hungry and providing drink for the thirsty.

Endnote 19

It is a matter of empirical fact whether these patients are actually hungry or thirsty. For mentally competent patients, we can simply ask. Sometimes they say they are not hungry or thirsty; in fact, they claim that providing food or fluids makes them more uncomfortable. It would be odd to act symbolically in the name of the hungry and thirsty by forcing food and fluid on people for whom it simply makes them more uncomfortable. Many patients for whom nutrition and

Endnote 20

hydration are debated are actually unconscious. (We will take up their cases in the next section of this chapter.) It seems impossible, however, to say that unconscious patients are either hungry or thirsty.

Hunger and thirst are fundamentally psychological categories. Surely, we should do everything in our power to prevent the feelings of hunger and thirst. But unconscious people, by definition, do not have those feelings (because they do not have any feelings). The critics of the "symbolic acts" argument believe it would be odd to force food and fluids on people who are not hungry or thirsty in the name of symbolizing our commitment to make some other people more comfortable.

Withholding Care Could Cause Too Many Deaths

The final argument against permitting patients to refuse medically supplied nutrition and hydration is that doing so may make it more difficult to keep separate active mercy killing and decisions to forgo treatment. One of the practical arguments for a rule supporting the distinction between active killing and forgoing treatment was that it may be harder to prevent abuses if we accept the legitimacy of active killing for mercy. Everyone could end up dead if someone claimed that they would be better off killed. It would be difficult to document whether the patient actually requested the killing, especially if decisions were simply made in physician's offices rather than with formal due process judicial reviews. By contrast, permitting decisions to forgo treatment would result in death in only a relatively small number of people, those with certain medical conditions that will result in death if they are not treated. This is part of the rule-utilitarian argument for the sharp distinction between active killing and simply letting die.

However, if supplying nutrition and hydration is included among the treatments that may be forgone, the practical calculations change considerably. Many more patients would be at risk for abusive decisions to forgo treatment. If oral feeding is included as well as naso-gastric tubes and intravenous feedings, **all of us could be made dead by someone's decision to let us die by forgoing intervention.** If this practical consequentialist argument is the basis for distinguishing those things we can do to patients from those we cannot, then perhaps forgoing nutrition and hydration should be treated more like active killing.

Of course, if one of the other arguments for the action/omission distinction is used, then this conclusion would not apply. For example, if there is something that is just intrinsically immoral about active killing that does not extend to letting nature take its course, then the fact that more people are at risk for being allowed to die than we first realized would not make a decisive difference. Likewise, for those who reject the idea that there is a difference between active killing and letting die in the first place, none of this would be terribly important.

The conclusions about forgoing nutrition, hydration, CPR, medications, and protocols to turn patients are not yet clear. Some people hold that, because these are very simple, they are required. Others hold that physicians can somehow know that they are objectively useless and therefore the physician can unilaterally omit them. Still others take a middle position: that their usefulness is a subjective matter, so the decision should rest with the patient or the patient's surrogate.

THE INCOMPETENT PATIENT

These choices are made by the patient himself or herself when the patient is mentally competent as were the patients in the cases in the previous section. But many of the most controversial cases involve patients who are not mentally competent. Yosef Camp, the boy who ate the pickle, was 9 years old. He was never able to form a position while competent.

The controversies over decisions made on behalf of incompetent patients are heated, in part, because there are at least three different kinds of incompetent patients, and each of these involves different ethical principles and decision-making procedures. Some incompetent patients were formerly competent and formulated opinions about the kind of care they wanted to receive when they became terminally ill. Others have never been competent or, what amounts to the same thing, never left any record of their wishes. Among those who have never been competent, there is a further subdivision. Some have family or relatives who are able to participate as surrogates on behalf of the patient; others have no one who knew them while they were competent to be their agent for decision-making.

THE FORMERLY COMPETENT PATIENT

BROTHER FOX:
AN UNWRITTEN
ADVANCE DIRECTIVE

In 1979, Brother Joseph Fox, an 83-year-old member of the Catholic Order of the Society of Mary, underwent minor surgery. Something went wrong, and he suffered a cardiac arrest and was left in a permanent vegetative state.

Rev. Philip Eichner, S.M., the superior in his religious community and president of the Chaminade High School where Brother Fox had lived since his retirement, stepped forward to function as Brother Fox's surrogate. They had known each other for more than 25 years. Brother Fox's relatives (several nieces and nephews) agreed that Rev. Eichner was the appropriate agent for Brother Fox, but when he asked for the life-supporting ventilator to be disconnected, the care givers at the hospital refused to comply.

Rev. Eichner sought judicial approval for the stopping of the ventilator based on the claim that it was Brother Fox's view that he would not want his life prolonged in that condition. Brother Fox had led discussions in the Chaminade community during the public controversy over the Karen Quinlan case and had reaffirmed his views two months prior to his surgery. He was quoted as saying, with regard to patients like Karen Quinlan, "Why don't they just let us go? I want to go."

After a lower court had authorized the withdrawal of the ventilator, the next higher court reversed the judgment before New York's highest court finally authorized the stopping in cases where the patient's previously expressed wishes are clearly known. Brother Fox died while the court deliberations were still in progress.

Endnote 21

The key to Brother Fox's case is that he left a clear record of his wishes expressed while he was competent. He not only led a discussion group on the issues surrounding the Karen Quinlan case, he also reaffirmed his position only two months before his surgery and unexpected, tragic accident. Moreover, he expressed views quite consistent with the religious tradition in which he was a life-long and deeply committed member.

He did not have a formal, written advance directive (or what is sometimes called a "living will"). That is not necessary. What is critical is that there is a clear expression of the patient's wishes, the authenticity of which was beyond dispute. Oral directives are plenty good enough as long as there is no controversy over what the person actually said. However, since one never knows how clearly one's words will be remembered, putting the **advance directive** in writing is generally best.

TYPES OF ADVANCE DIRECTIVES

There are two major types of advance directives: substantive and proxy. **Substantive directives specify a patient's substantive wishes.** They tell what treatments the individual wants or does not want. In an earlier era they were used almost exclusively to specify refusals of treatment, but increasingly today it is becoming standard to assume patients do not want ventilators, CPR, and other life-prolonging technologies once they have become terminally ill and have lost mental competence. Now, as never before, it is crucial if one wants treatments to be continued that that fact be clearly specified in an advance directive.

Instead of trying to spell out exactly which treatments are desired, some people write **a proxy directive, which names the individual whom the patient would like to serve as a surrogate decision-maker.** The writer can name anyone — a spouse, other family member, or friend. The one named should normally be someone who knows the writer's wishes or at least understands his or her general values. It is especially critical to name someone if the next of kin is not the person the writer wants to make these decisions. It is also important if there is more than one person who is equally close. An elderly person may want to spare an infirm spouse the task, naming instead a son or daughter. Or a widow may have three children, one of whom she wants to name as her surrogate.

Surrogate Decisions for Formerly Competent Patients

The task of making a life-and-death surrogacy decision is awesome. It is generally held that the first principle guiding such decisions is that the choice should be the one the patient would have made had he or she been competent to do so. Based on the advance directive or what is known about the individual's beliefs and values, the surrogate should choose what the individual would have chosen. Ethically, this notion is rooted in the moral principle of autonomy. Autonomy can still be morally relevant to a person who is no longer autonomous. It is what might be called **autonomy extended** — that is, extended into the period of incompetency.

Recently, some commentators have been arguing that there are cases in which the patient's formerly expressed beliefs and values should not prevail. They have in mind advanced Alzheimer's disease or severe head trauma patients, in which the individual appears to permanently and completely forget the former self. They claim that if the patient has so lost competence that there is a complete discontinuity of personal identity, then the "old person" who expressed wishes "in a former life" no longer should dictate to the "new person" who has no memory of the former individual. Lawyers Rebecca Dresser and John Robertson and philosophers Allen Buchanan and Dan Brock have all argued this position.

Endnotes 22, 23

They have generated considerable controversy, however. Their critics doubt that the discontinuity between the old and new persons is as great as they imply. The critics believe there may be moral and social links remaining even if the "new" individual cannot express any memory of the old self. Most people seem to believe that they would want such decisions made on the basis of the views they held when they were competent. One who does not want his or her old views to dominate always has the right to designate some proxy and instruct the proxy to try to determine what would be best for the "new" person, but, barring such an instruction, the general pattern is that the decision should be guided by the last clear instruction of the competent individual.

Legally, this is known as **substituted judgment**. The term is a bit confusing. It does not refer to substituting the beliefs and values of the surrogate. It is the patient's values that take precedence when substituted judgment is used. All states in the U.S. now have statutes or case law (judge-made law) authorizing the use of advanced directives under at least some circumstances.

DECISIONS NOT COVERED BY LAW

The limits in the statutes governing advance directives can be quite severe. For example, most apply only when the patient is terminally ill. While this might seem to be the only time one would want a decision to forgo treatment made, the definition of terminal illness is usually quite narrow. It refers only to cases in which one is inevitably declining toward death in a relatively brief period of time regardless of medical interventions. Actually, if death is coming soon regardless, the decision to forgo may not be too critical. Other cases, not terminal under this definition, may be more the kinds of cases in which the individual wants to have treatment stopped: stable but persistent vegetative state (the condition of Karen Quinlan and Nancy Cruzan), advanced Alzheimer's disease, and other chronic, debilitating, but not terminal illnesses. Moreover, even if one has a certifiable terminal illness, some state statutes permit forgoing life support only when "death is imminent." That, of course, is when forgoing treatment becomes academic.

While all U.S. jurisdictions have some form of law granting the right to forgo treatment, other countries may not. Both these settings, as well as cases involving critical but nonterminal illness, press the question of what the legal and moral situation is when specific law does not apply.

In jurisdictions that have laws requiring **informed consent** for medical treatment (including all U.S. jurisdictions), more general common law would apply. It requires that a physician cannot treat without an adequately informed consent. As we have seen, if the treatment has begun, it cannot continue if consent is withdrawn. In the case of a competent patient, consent is grounded in the moral principle of autonomy. The patient cannot be touched without consent. To do so would constitute an assault (or in some situations medical negligence). The doctrine of informed consent is crucial in affirming the patient's right to refuse treatment, especially in cases such as non terminal illness — a condition in which many "living will" statutes do not apply. Even then, the patient cannot be treated without adequately informed consent. In the case of the formerly competent patient, generally the wishes expressed while competent should prevail and a substituted judgment will be made by the patient's surrogate if the patient lapses into incompetency.

MECHANISMS FOR EXPRESSING WISHES

Several different mechanisms are available for expressing one's wishes about terminal and critical care.

The **advance directives** we have been examining constitute the most widely discussed mechanism. A group called the Euthanasia Educational Council in the 1970s introduced the most famous. Called the *"Living Will,"* **it permitted people to indicate they did not want "artificial" or "heroic" means,** terms now largely abandoned because they lack precision. The group, now called Choice in Dying, still circulates copies of a revised form of its Living Will, which has been brought into the form called for by various state laws.

Several criticisms have been made of the original Living Will. For one thing, as originally written it merely gave permission to stop; it did not require it. Some patients have wanted to write such advance directives precisely because they feared that physicians would not stop treatment. Giving mere permission to stop would not provide adequate assurance. Most forms today do not merely give permission; they order that specified treatments be withheld or withdrawn.

Another significant problem with substantive advance directives is that they express wishes when one is mentally competent, perhaps many years from the time of crisis and when one's values may be quite different. Using a proxy directive helps alleviate some of these problems. The designated surrogate, guided by what he or she knows to be recently held views, can fine-tune the advance directive to the specifics of the patient's condition.

Another significant problem of the standard advance directive forms is that they appear to assume that all persons will have the same choices in mind. It is one-decision-fits-all. But in a world of great diversity and increasing medical complexity, there may be as many different views as there are people. Some may want to refuse medically supplied nutrition and hydration, others not; some may want to refuse only when permanently unconscious, others while still conscious and in pain. Some may want to refuse only high-tech machines, others simple devices as well. Most critically, some may want to use an advance directive to demand that certain life-supporting care continue. Clearly, no one standard form will work any longer.

Other groups have prepared sample forms that attempt to reflect the beliefs of their group. The U.S. Catholic Health Association has prepared a "Christian affirmation of Life" that uses the language of "no extraordinary means." It excludes actions with the intention of causing death, although, as we have noted, that should not be taken as excluding all decisions in which death is foreseen but not directly intended.

The President's Commission for the Study of Ethical Problems in Medicine and Biomedical and Behavioral Research endorsed a

Several criticisms have been made of the original Living Will. For one thing, as originally written it merely gave permission to stop; it did not require it. Some patients have wanted to write such advance directives precisely because they feared that physicians would not stop treatment.

Endnote 24

combined substantive and proxy directive, a proposal that has existed since the mid-1970s.

Endnotes 25, 26

Directives by Law

In addition to individually crafted advance directives, many jurisdictions have laws governing decisions about the care of the terminally ill. Several places have considered laws that would legalize
active killing for mercy, beginning in 1937 in Great Britain and then
in New York in 1947 and in other states in later years. None of these
got very far until citizen initiatives got proposals — that would have
legalized active killing upon the request of competent, terminally ill
patients — placed on the ballots of the state of Washington in 1991
and California in 1992. Both received substantial minority votes, but
neither passed.

Endnote 27

Endnote 28

Most legislation, beginning with the *California Natural Death Act
of 1976,* focused only on decisions to forgo life-prolonging interventions for the terminally ill. The legislation varies from state to state,
but generally permits forgoing treatment when the patient is terminally ill and death is imminent. Some state legislation prohibits
refusal of nutrition and hydration under the statutory law. That, however, leaves open the possibility that one can still refuse under
informed consent law. (Some states, including Maryland and Colorado, have either advisory opinions or case law that still permit forgoing nutrition and hydration, in spite of these limits, in cases in
which an individual has a specific advance directive refusing these
treatments.)

Issues to Be Addressed in an Advance Directive

Given the great variety of beliefs and values about terminal illness treatments, advance directives will come in many forms and
styles. Among the issues that almost certainly should be included are
these:

* What treatments are being refused
* What treatments are desired
* When the directive should take effect
* Whether a durable power of attorney (proxy) is to be
  appointed

Some advance directives will also include other more specific
information that could be of concern to specific writers of such directives. This could include:

* What hospital (or jurisdiction) should be used
* What physician should be consulted
* What lawyer should be consulted
* What ethics consultants or religious counselor should
  be involved
* Whether refusal is under statutory or common law

Avoiding Ineffective Advance Directives

An important study (called the Study to Understand Prognoses and Preferences for Outcomes and Risks of Treatments — or SUPPORT for short) has recently been completed that examines the impact of advance directives on decisions about terminal care. This study involving over 4300 patients is the most thorough to date. It found, "Advanced directives had no clinically important effect of decision making concerning resuscitation among the seriously ill patients in SUPPORT." The reasons included a failure to get the directive into the hands of the physician providing terminal care, excessively vague language, and failure to specify precisely when treatments should be removed. Often the physician simply does not understand the patient's preferences. Family members and nurses do slightly better at understanding them, but still do not do well. The critical factor seems to be the adequacy of the communication between the patient and others. A proxy directive designating someone who understands the patient's wishes seems to be the most reliable technique for getting the patient's wishes followed.

Endnote 28a

Endnote 28b

NEVER-COMPETENT PATIENTS WITHOUT FAMILY SURROGATES

Advance directives grounded in the moral principle of autonomy may be the answer for patients who were formerly competent patients and who have expressed their wishes while competent. But they are hardly helpful for the more tragic cases of infants and children or others who have never expressed their wishes while competent. For these patients someone else will have to decide. This group can be further divided into those who have family or others with whom they have a pre-existing relationship who can function as surrogates; and those who are utterly alone, without family to make the choices about medical care.

JOSEPH SAIKEWICZ:
IS IT IN THE INTEREST OF A DYING, MENTALLY RETARDED MAN TO HAVE HIS LIFE PROLONGED?

Sixty-seven-year-old Joseph Saikewicz was a resident of the Belchertown State School in Massachusetts, a facility that cared for the mentally retarded. He had been there since the age of 5. He was described as having an IQ of 10 and a mental age of approximately 2 years and 8 months. He was not able to communicate verbally, resorting to grunts and gestures, but he was physically strong and generally was in good health until it was discovered that he was suffering from acute leukemia.

His physicians were considering chemotherapy and blood transfusions. The physicians had doubts about providing the treatment because it appeared that Mr. Saikewicz could not understand their purpose; i.e., he would perceive

Endnote 29

that his care givers were turning on him and hurting him for no understandable reason. It was agreed that with the treatment there would be a 30–50% chance of remission, but that the remission would probably last only 2–13 months. All agreed that they should do what was best for Mr. Saikewicz, but could not agree on what was best.

The only members of the family who could be located were two sisters who, when notified, said they would prefer not to become involved. All agreed that Mr. Saikewicz could not make the choice himself whether to receive the treatment and that no family were available to take on the decision-making role. The superintendent of the school was unclear whether the physician's opinion about what was in Mr. Saikewicz's best interest should prevail or whether they should err on the side of life — preferring to treat when the treatment could extend life, even though the life would involve the appearance of his care givers turning on him and inflicting suffering for reasons he could not understand.

Some might argue that patients like Joseph Saikewicz are not worth saving. That raises the terrible question of whether there are social and economic reasons why it might sometimes be acceptable to limit care to the terminally ill. The court, when it reviewed the case, however, rejected the idea that the decision should be based how others would evaluate the quality of Mr. Saikewicz's life. While there may be cases in which societal judgments must intervene, before tackling that most difficult of ethical issues, it may be possible to make some choices in a more traditional ethical framework. There has been significant doubt raised about the patient-benefiting ethic that has sometimes been used to force benefits on patients against their will. It has now largely been replaced by an ethic focusing on the ethical principle of autonomy. As we saw earlier in this chapter, patients are expected to evaluate the evidence about the benefits and harms and choose a course that they believe fits their life plan, regardless of the clinician's personal opinion about whether it is the best plan.

Who should make the decision for Joseph Saikewicz?

But Joseph Saikewicz is unable to speak for himself. He left no clear record of his wishes about medical care. Someone must step into the role of decision-maker. He has no family or friends capable of playing that role. He is alone, dying, and out of control; among the most vulnerable of patients. And someone, in this case a physician, apparently believes he would be better off dead.

It is probably true that some patients who were mentally competent and in Mr. Saikewicz's position would forgo the treatment being offered. Some might even contemplate ending their lives. But in this case, if a decision is to be made to forgo treatment it will have to be made by a stranger.

THE PRINCIPLE FOR DECIDING: OBJECTIVE BENEFICENCE

Morally, if autonomy is ruled out, the decision-making principle, by default, must revert to the ethical **principle of beneficence — the decision must be the one that will produce the most good.** Before considering the possibility that the good of others should be factored into the decision, it is worth asking whether, as the physician apparently surmised, it could possibly be in Mr. Saikewicz's interest to have the treatment stopped.

Recalling that judgments of benefit and burden are necessarily subjective, it is crucial not to reduce the question to that of whether competent patients suffering from leukemia similar to Mr. Saikewicz's would accept the treatment. Mr. Saikewicz's situation is somewhat different. The chemotherapy and blood transfusion that would be understandable to competent patients appear to Mr. Saikewicz to be torture imposed by the people he has grown over many years to rely on for the basics of life. Arguably, the burden of these treatments will be much greater for him than for someone who could understand the reason for the apparently painful treatment.

We know that competent patients facing a choice about a burdensome treatment have sometimes concluded that, for their cases, forgoing treatment is justified when the benefits of treatment do not exceed the burdens. It is theoretically possible that a similar conclusion could be reached in the case of the patient who never expressed his wishes while competent.

But this is literally a life-and-death decision. We have seen that these judgments can be very subjective. A patient such as Mr. Saikewicz is at the mercy of the idiosyncratic judgments of the person who happens to assume the decision-making role. For this reason, we insist that the standard should be to do what is best, relying on the most objective assessment possible. The personal religious beliefs or preferences of the decision-maker cannot be imposed on the patient. There is no reason why a stranger's personal value system should be relevant. The legal standard in such cases is the **best interest standard: The decision-maker must do what is best.**

WHO SHOULD THE DECISION-MAKER BE?

The Attending Physician

The key, then, is who should be the decision-maker. Historically that role has been assumed by the attending physician. In the day when the rule of thumb was to do everything possible, that was not terribly critical, but now that we are seriously entertaining the possibility that some life-prolonging treatments are not in the patient's interest, it can literally be a matter of life and death which physician happens to be on duty when the patient is brought to the hospital. It can make enormous difference which hospital is chosen by the emergency rescue squad. It seems odd that Mr. Saikewicz's life would be dependent on which physician he draws.

Hospital Ethics Committee

Endnote 30

Some of the random variation could be eliminated if these key decisions to forgo treatment were referred to committees at the hospital made up of an interdisciplinary group of physicians, nurses, social workers, and chaplains, supplemented by a cross-section of other perspectives such as those of philosophers, business people, lawyers, former patients, and families of patients. This committee would permit many different perspectives to be presented, neutralizing the individual biases of any one decision-maker. Perhaps only with the approval of a hospital ethics committee could life-prolonging treatment be forgone for patients who were never able to express their own views while competent.

But there is a serious problem with this strategy. The hospital's ethics committee as a whole may have certain moral inclinations. We would expect a committee appointed by the administrators or trustees of a local hospital to reflect the value commitments of the institution. An orthodox Jewish hospital ought to have an ethics committee whose consensus opinions are different from those of a secular hospital or a Catholic hospital. Turning the decisions over to the ethics committee may simply be a way of making the decision based on the value system of the institution where the patient happened to reside. Unless the patient has chosen the hospital for its value system, that does not make much sense.

Turning the decisions over to the ethics committee may simply be a way of making the decision based on the value system of the institution where the patient happened to reside. Unless the patient has chosen the hospital for its value system, that does not make much sense.

A Court-Appointed Guardian

The other alternative is to have some more public process for making this one special group of decisions. We have no idea what the wishes of these patients are. Without treatment they will die; with it they will live. Someone who is a stranger to the patient believes the patient would be better off dead. Because these patients are so vulnerable, some people believe it might be wise to bend over backward to protect their lives and permit withdrawal of treatment only after there has been a formal review with the protection of legal due process. If we are talking about a relatively small number of patients, perhaps the extra burden of review is worth it. Right now there is no clearly designated guardian for such patients. This limits not only decisions to forgo treatment, but decisions to authorize treatment as well. There is no one who can give consent to treatment in such cases anymore than there is someone who can authorize non-treatment.

Another Approach: Judicial Hearing of Affected Parties

Yet another method for deciding involves a structured hearing in which all of the alternatives mentioned are represented. By legal precedent (Quinlan case and others), a process has evolved in which a court hears family or family surrogates, physician(s), hospital committee and, perhaps, a state official with standing (in the case of a public prisoner or public official). This method, formally or informally, has the intent of attempting to understand the interests of the patient most fully and to balance interests of others (the state, the hospital, et cetera).

NEVER-COMPETENT PATIENTS WITH FAMILY SURROGATE

Fortunately, relatively few patients are in precisely this predicament. The more usual case of patients who have never been competent involves those who have family ready, willing, and able to step into the surrogacy role. That was the position Yosef Camp, the nine-year-old boy who ate the pickle, was in. It was also the situation of Karen Quinlan, Nancy Cruzan, and many other patients whose families have had to make the tragic choices for or against life support.

Cases such as Yosef Camp's raise the critical issue of whether family can ever make a choice to forgo life-prolonging interventions and, if so, on what basis. It is increasingly clear that the next of kin should be the presumed decision-maker in such cases. The current law in Florida, Iowa, Virginia, and other states specifically authorizes the next of kin to assume this role. Elsewhere, courts have generally accepted this procedure. As long as they make uncontroversial choices, their role as surrogates has been accepted.

Endnote 31

Controversial Family Choices

What happens, however, when the choice is controversial? Some families have made the controversial choice of deciding to forgo treatments such as ventilation, antibiotics or nutrition medically supplied through a gastrostomy.

Likewise, Yosef Camp's parents made a controversial choice, although theirs was problematic in insisting that life support continue. When there is disagreement about whether the next of kin has made the best choice, it is not yet clear what should be done.

Following the ethical framework developed for once-competent patients without familial surrogates, we generally insist that family members should try to do what they believe would be best for the patient. But what happens when there is dispute among the family, or when outside observers believe that the family has not made the best choice?

We could insist that they make the best possible choice regarding what is in their loved one's interest, but many are beginning to conclude we should not. That would, in effect, be telling them they are free to choose, but that they must make only the single best choice. Because deciding what is best is inherently subjective and controversial in such cases, we can assume there will sometimes be disagreements about what is best and no clear standards for making the choice.

Endnote 32

An alternative that seems to be emerging is to instruct the family that they must do what they think is best, but then give them some limited range of discretion in picking among plausible options. It is often the case in medicine that there are many treatment options available and no clearly best choice. In such cases, it would be extremely difficult to insist that the family make only the one best choice. Instead they are increasingly being given discretion to choose among those options that are within what can be called the limits of reasonable standard.

With this approach, several treatment options may be acceptable. Only in the extreme case would family choices be challenged. The family would be taken to court, much as is now done with Jehovah's Witness parents who try to refuse life-saving blood transfusions for their minor children. In those cases we know that the courts will temporarily take custody for purposes of consenting to treatment. We could in like manner seek court orders either to approve of treatment or get it stopped in other terminal illness treatment decisions.

We have not so far had a case in which the courts took custody of a patient for purposes of overruling an unreasonable judgment of a family surrogate when the parental decision was to preserve the life. In theory that could happen. Someday there will be a patient who is so burdened by life-prolonging treatment; a case in which the prolongation will in any case be only temporary. If family members persist in inflicting severe pain or discomfort on such a patient in a fruitless effort to prolong life, some court may have to intervene and overrule.

In such a case as Yosef Camp's, the court would face a difficult, perhaps insurmountable task, if it were to attempt to overrule the parents. Yosef Camp was permanently unconscious. He could not feel pain. The chances of his parents being overruled on the grounds that they were inflicting burden on him were therefore remote.

The Principle for Surrogate Decision-Makers

The moral principle permitting parents to have discretion in such cases is not yet fully established. Clearly, the surrogate must attempt to do what he or she thinks is best for the patient, but what of these special cases where the decision is controversial? It is becoming increasingly clear that doing what is literally best is not going to be what is required. If we are not going to insist that the family do what is the absolute best, then there must be some moral basis for familial discretion. We could call this the **principle of limited familial autonomy.** Under such a principle the family decision-makers would have the discretion to draw on family beliefs and values to exercise discretion as long as they did not exceed the limits of reasonableness. If they were to exceed what society can tolerate, then the state would have to step in and overrule. But it would do so, not when the family decision-makers made a modestly unexpected choice, but only when that choice was beyond reason.

FINAL COMMENTS

If this is the direction the society is headed, Yosef Camp's case will be instructive. We will not be able to resolve the problem his case presents simply by defining him as dead. He probably was not dead, at least by whole-brain criteria. Unless a state adopts a higher-brain definition of death, he will probably have to be treated as alive.

The clinicians cannot make a case in which they know, based on medical science, that the treatment is serving no useful purpose. Judgments of benefit and harm are essentially not matters of medical science. Once it is conceded that the ventilator will prolong the bodily functions, the key question is whether it serves any worthwhile purpose to do so. That is not a question medical science can answer. We could try to overrule his parents, claiming that the burdens of the treatment are too great. That probably would work in the case of some conscious, terminally ill patient, but not in the case of a permanently unconscious patient. If the treatment cannot be withdrawn on any of these grounds, there is only one other possibility. That would be to argue that it is the burden to the hospital staff, to patients, or to others in the society that justifies stopping treatment. That is a move that should be made only with fear and trembling. Up to now civilized society has been reluctant to do so. It may be the medical ethical question of the future. Unfortunately, it is a question that is beyond the scope of this chapter to address.

FOR FURTHER INQUIRY

REVIEW QUESTIONS

1. Why is a brain-oriented definition important for organ transplantation? Is there any reason to use such a definition for a patient who has indicated he is not an organ donor?

2. Jack Kevorkian began his efforts to involve himself in the voluntary deaths of patients by inventing an intravenous injection machine by which a patient could turn a switch to change from a harmless fluid to a lethal one. What would we call the death that results, a homicide or a suicide?

3. What is meant by proportionality in the context of decisions about terminally ill patients?

4. It is sometimes said that families have a duty to do what is best for their incompetent members. Why, then, are some families permitted to choose less than the best possible course for their dying members?

APPLICATION QUESTION

1. When Karen Ann Quinlan's father was given the authority to decide about whether to continue her ventilator, he chose not to do so, but she continued living for the next ten years. If Mr. Quinlan had concluded that the ventilator was an "extraordinary means" that he should refuse, should he also have concluded that antibiotics for infections that she got from time to time over the following years were also "extraordinary"? In the period before an infection set in, she was doing well medically except that she had to be fed medically through a tube. Should Mr. Quinlan have concluded that the medical means of feeding her were extraordinary? Does the fact that we all need food and fluids make them morally required for all patients, even those like Karen Quinlan who are permanently unconscious?

ENDNOTES

1. Ramsey, Paul. *Ethics at the Edges of Life*. New Haven: Yale University Press, 1978; Cantor, Norman. *Legal Frontiers of Death and Dying*. Bloomington, Indiana: Indiana University Press, 1987. Weir, Robert F., ed. *Ethical Issues in Death and Dying*, 2d ed. New York: Columbia University Press, 1986. Veatch, Robert M. *Death, Dying, and the Biological Revolution*, Revised Edition. New Haven: Yale University Press, 1989. President's Commission for the Study of Ethical Problems in Medicine and Biomedical and Behavioral Research. *Deciding to Forgo Life-Sustaining Treatment: Ethical, Medical, and Legal Issues in Treatment Decisions*. Washington, D.C.: U.S. Government Printing Office, 1983.

2. Sager, Mike. "City Seeks Court Order to End Life Support of Brain-Dead Boy." *Washington Post*, August 27, 1980, pp. A1, A12; Weiser, Benjamin. "Boy, 9, May Not Be 'Brain Dead,' New Medical Examination Shows." *Washington Post*, Sect. B (September 5, 1980), p. 1; Sager, Mike. "Nine-Year-Old Dies after Four Months in Coma." *Washington Post*, Sect. B, Col 1 (September 17, 1980), p. 6.

3. Harvard Medical School. "A Definition of Irreversible Coma. Report of the Ad Hoc Committee of the Harvard Medical School to Examine the Definition of Brain Death." *Journal of the American Medical Association* 205 (1968):337–340.

4. President's Commission for the Study of Ethical Problems in Medicine and Biomedical and Behavioral Research. *Defining Death: Medical, Legal and Ethical Issues in the Definition of Death*. Washington, D.C.: U.S. Government Printing Office, 1981.

5. Kimura, Rihito. "Japan's Dilemma with the Definition of Death." *Kennedy Institute of Ethics Journal* 1 (1991):123–31.

6. Olick, Robert S. "Brain Death, Religious Freedom, and Public Policy." *Kennedy Institute of Ethics Journal* 1 (Dec. 1991):275–288; New Jersey Declaration of Death Act (1991). *New Jersey Statutes Annotated*. Title 26, 6A-1 to 6A-8.

7. Brierley, J.B., J.A.H. Adam, D.I. Graham, and J.A. Simpson. "Neocortical Death after Cardiac Arrest." *Lancet* 2 (September 11, 1971):560–565.

8. Veatch, Robert M. "The Whole-Brain-Oriented Concept of Death: An Outmoded Philosophical Formulation." *Journal of Thanatology* 3 (1975):13–30; Green, Michael B., and Daniel Wikler. "Brain Death and Personal Identity." *Philosophy and Public Affairs* 9 (No. 2, Winter 1980):105–133; Gervais, Karen Grandstand. *Redefining Death*. New Haven: Yale University Press, 1986.

9. *Bouvia v. County of Riverside*, No. 159780 (Cal. Super. Ct. Dec. 16, 1983); *Bouvia v. Superior Court of Los Angeles County*. California Court of Appeal, Second District, 1986. 179 Cal. App. 3d 1127, 225 Cal. Rptr. 297, (Ct. App.), *review denied* (June 5, 1986).

9a. *Compassion in Dying v. State of Washington*, No. C94-119R, United States District Court, W.D. Washington, at Seattle, May 3, 1994; *Compassion in Dying v. Wash-*

ington No. 94-35534 D.C. No. CV-94-119-BJR, United States Court of Appeals for the Ninth Circuit.

9b. *Quill et al v. Vacco* et al. Docket No. 95-7028, United States Court of Appeals for the Second Circuit.

9c. *Washington et al v. Glucksberg et al.* Supreme Court of the United States No. 96-110, June 27, 1997.

9d. *Vacco v. Quill,* Supreme Court of the United States, No. 95-1858, June 26, 1997.

10. Thomas Aquinas. *Summa Theologica.* Ed. by Fathers of the English Dominican Province. London: R & T Washbourne, Ltd. 1915, 2a 2ae q.64a.

11. Hume, David. *On Suicide.* Edinburgh, Scotland, 1777.

12. Engelhardt, H. Tristram. *The Foundations of Bioethics.* New York: Oxford University Press, 1986.

13. Kant, Immanuel. *Groundwork of the Metaphysic of Morals.* Trans. by H.J. Paton. New York: Harper and Row, 1964.

14. American Medical Association. *Current Opinions of the Council on Ethical and Judicial Affairs of the American Medical Association: Including the Principles of Medical Ethics and Rules of the Council on Ethical and Judicial Affairs.* Chicago: American Medical Association, 1989.

15. Mansson, Helge Hilding. "Justifying the Final Solution." *Omega* 3:79–87.

16. Van der Maas, Paul J.; Van Delden, Johannes J. M.; Pijnenborg, Loes; and Looman, Casper W. N. "Euthanasia and Other Medical Decisions Concerned the End of Life." *The Lancet* 338 (September 14, 1991):669–74.

17. Pope Pius XII. "The Prolongation of Life: An Address of Pope Pius XII to an International Congress of Anesthesiologists." *The Pope Speaks* 4 (Spring 1958): 393–398.

18. Meilaender, Gilbert. "On Removing Food and Water: Against the Stream." *The Hastings Center Report* 14 (No. 6, 1984):11–13.

19. Callahan, Daniel. "On Feeding the Dying." *The Hastings Center Report* 13 (No. 5, 1983):22.

20. Lynn, Joanne. *The Choice to Forgo Life-Sustaining Food and Water: Medical, Ethical, and Legal Considerations.* Bloomington, Indiana: Indiana University Press, 1986.

21. *In the Matter of Eichner vs. Dillon.* 426: NYS 2d 517; *Eichner vs. Dillon,* 52 N.Y. 2d 363, 438 N.Y.S. 2d 266.420 N.E. 2d 64 (1981).

22. Dresser, Rebecca S., and Robertson, John A. "Quality of Life and Non-Treatment Decisions for Incompetent Patients: A Critique of the Orthodox Approach." *Law, Medicine, & Health Care* 17 (1989):234–44.

23. Buchanan, Allen E., and Dan W. Brock. *Deciding for Others: The Ethics of Surrogate Decision-making.* Cambridge: Cambridge University Press, 1989.

24. The Catholic Health Association of the United States. "Christian Affirmation of Life: A Statement on Terminal Illness." St. Louis: The Catholic Health Association of the United States, 1982.

25. President's Commission for the Study of Ethical Problems in Medicine and Biomedical and Behavioral Research. *Deciding to Forgo Life-Sustaining Treatment: Ethical, Medical, and Legal Issues in Treatment Decisions.* Washington, D.C.: U.S. Government Printing Office, 1983, p. 153.

26. Veatch, Robert M. *Death, Dying, and the Biological Revolution.* New Haven, Connecticut: Yale University Press, 1976, p. 184–85.

27. *California "Natural Death" Act.* Ca. Stat. Chapter 1439, Code, Health and Safety, sections 7185–95.

28. Society for the Right to Die. *Refusal of Treatment Legislation: A State by State Compilation of Enacted and Model Statutes.* New York: Society for the Right to Die, 1991.

28a. Teno, J., Licks, S., Lynn, J., N. et al. "Do Advance Directives Provide Instructions that Direct Care?" *Journal of the American Geriatrics Society* 45 (April, 1997): 508–12.

28b. Uhlmann, Richard F., Robert A. Pearlman, and Kevin C. Cain. "Physicians' and Spouses' Predictions of Elderly Patients' Resuscitation Preferences," *Journal of Gerontology: Medical Sciences* 43 (No. 8, 1988): M1115–121.

29. *Superintendent of Belchertown State School vs. Saikewicz,* 373 Mass. 728, 370 NE 2d 417 (1977).

30. Weinstein, Bruce, D., editor. *Ethics in the Hospital Setting: Proceedings of the West Virginia Conference on Hospital Ethics Committees.* Morgantown, WV: The West Virginia University Press, (1986); Cranford, Ronald E., and A. Edward Doudera, editors. *Institutional Ethics Committees and Health Care Decision-making.* Ann Arbor, MI: American Society of Law & Medicine, 1984.

31. Areen, Judith. "The Legal Status of Consent Obtained from Families of Adult Patients to Withhold or Withdraw Treatment." *Journal of the American Medical Association* 258 (No. 2, July 10, 1987):229–235.

32. Veatch, Robert M. "Limits of Guardian Treatment Refusal: A Reasonableness Standard." *American Journal of Law and Medicine* 9 (4, Winter 1984):427–68.

CHAPTER 9

SEXUAL RESPONSIBILITY

"The omnipresent process of sex, as it is woven into the whole texture of our man's or woman's body, is the pattern of all the process of our life."

—Havelock Ellis

"I consider promiscuity immoral. Not because sex is evil, but because sex is good and too important."

—Ayn Rand

It's easy to pass judgment on someone else's sexual behavior and character, but upholding our own sexual standards or finding suitable ones in the first place is a formidable challenge in our society.

Today, talk show guests reveal the most intimate details of their sex lives, while schools offer curricula that would have made Sigmund Freud and Havelock Ellis blush. Sex scandals rock politicians from their roosts, and explicit scenes of sex entertain millions of movie voyeurs. In fact, few can escape the barrage of sexual messages in modern America.

Socrates advised that an unexamined life is not worth living. While many people might argue that an unexamined sex life can still bring enormous pleasure, taking stock of your moral standards can help place you in the moral driver's seat and give you control over an important area of your life.

Hebrew and pagan views: The ancient Hebrews perceived the issue as one of **fecundity**. Make lots of babies; make sure you know whose babies you are making; and don't stray from home to make them. A pretty clear recipe. In contrast to Hebrew law, certain types of pagan worship encouraged non-marital sex. Temple prostitutes served the gods by sexually serving the men who attended temple. And in Rome and Greece alike, though marital sex was the norm, both prostitution and same-sex relations were acceptable, often serving as a form of male bonding in military settings.

Classical Greek philosophers, in particular Plato, expounded on the subject of sexual ethics and took a more restrained view. Reasoning that body and sexuality have no connection to mind and reason, Plato concluded that mindful contemplation of life and love without sex (Platonic love) is superior to erotic love (with sex).

Early Christianity

Drawing on both a cultural and a religious heritage, two monks, **Augustine** and **Aquinas**, born nearly a thousand years apart, shaped the unique sexual ethic of Roman Catholicism. Augustine, following the teaching of the early church, taught that when Adam and Eve disobeyed instructions and ate of the Tree of Knowledge, the danger, uncontrollability, and sinfulness of sex were released for all humans to follow.

CHIEF LEARNING OUTCOME

I understand sexual responsibility to myself and others and can discuss sexual issues within frameworks of ethical reasoning.

As a result, for the devout Catholic, sex must be controlled, either through celibacy or by limiting it to procreation within marriage.

Thomas Aquinas developed a rational theory of sexuality, based on what he called "natural law." Aquinas illuminated this natural law with Divine revelation and the Will of God.

Aquinas concluded any sex act that does not deposit sperm inside a vagina is unnatural and sinful. This included all erotic or pleasurable sex that is not for the primary purpose of procreation. Catholics reach this conclusion by reflecting on what they take to be the **natural purposes of sexuality.** They identify two such ends, called the procreative and unitive ends. By unitive they mean an act that unites a husband and wife in emotional and spiritual bonds. The most rigorous interpretations within the Catholic tradition insist that each sexual act must be open to fulfilling both of these functions, hence, making these sexual practices that do not include intercourse (as well as contraception) unnatural in the sense of not fulfilling these natural ends of marriage.

Moreover, according to Aquinas, parents should provide whatever is necessary to rear any offspring they do have. Both sex and child rearing, he concluded, are only moral in the context of monogamous marriage. This Thomistic concept of sexual morality has strongly influenced Western Culture.

Endnote 8

Judaism

Jewish and Protestant views on sexuality took a separate course. While Jewish scholars also emphasized fertility in marriage and the control of bodily passion, they interpreted the story of Adam and Eve quite differently. According to David Biale, author of an historic account of Jewish sexual ethics, *Eros and the Jews*, the rabbis interpreted the fall of Adam and Eve as punishment for their disobedience to God, and not for the discovery of sexuality itself.

Endnote 9

Endnote 10

Furthermore, although humans act with a tendency toward sexual abandon at times, rabbinical thought stresses that sexual **moder-**

ation and modesty can control such lack of restraint. It is God's commandment and a blessing for every Jewish man to marry and have children, and the right of every Jewish woman to receive sexual pleasure from her husband, even when she is pregnant, menopausal, and otherwise infertile (although masturbation and sex during menstruation are violations of Orthodox Jewish law).

Protestantism

After 1517, the year in which **Martin Luther** nailed his theses to the door of All Souls Church, the Catholic monopoly on Christian thought ended and new Christian denominations, under the general umbrella of Protestantism, were formed that were apart from the Vatican. While many of these new churches clung to St. Augustine's theory of original sin, based on the fall in the Garden of Eden, other churches reinterpreted Biblical texts and started their own theological dialectics, which produced even newer theories of sexual morality. Like Jewish sexual ethics, many of the Protestant theologians believed that the purpose of sex is not only procreative, but also unitive. They, like some more liberal Catholics, accept the idea that not all sexual acts must fulfill both functions. Thus, in this view, even sex for pleasure (within the context of marriage) further sanctifies the holy state of matrimony and helps "the two become one flesh."

Opening to Sexual Freedom

After the French and American Revolutions, when basic human rights became central to political morality, various philosophers, feminists, and humanists discovered the concept of women's equality in marriage and sex. Others lessened the emphasis on fertility and stressed the idea of **eroticism** and pleasure in sexuality. Valuing sexual freedom and sexual gratification, they remained out of sync with most societal views on sexuality until the 20th century. The Victorians, with their propensity for sexual repression and restraint, saw to that.

The Emergence of Romantic Love

One of the most significant influences on our sexual ethics, besides philosophy and religious teachings, is romantic love, a universal behavior that, for Western civilization, became more prominent in the Middle Ages among nobility. Knights and troubadours

KEY CONCEPTS

Right of privacy: the notion, explicit in some state constitutions, that each individual has a legal right prohibiting invasion of a person's home or personal life

- **Informational privacy:** the state of not having personal information about oneself made public

- **Observational privacy:** the state of not being observed by others

Confidentiality: the notion that private information that one possesses about another ought not to be disclosed without that person's approval

Endnote 11

Endnote 12

Endnote 13

were allowed to "court" and love a married woman. Although our knight in shining armor was permitted to tuck "m'lady" into bed at nightfall, he was expected to bid adieu and leave her chaste by morning.

Endnote 14

Over several hundred years, the notion of sexual purity in romantic love changed to one of sex for love. By this time, our knight pursued a single lady, so that when he found his true love, and she found him, they married. In fact, the quest for true love reached nearly everyone, including members of the middle and working classes, who wholeheartedly embraced the notion.

Endnote 15

During the Industrial Revolution, the dominant pattern was that everyone married for love, and, ironically, during the 1960s, falling out of love became moral justification for scrambling out of a marriage.

By contemporary times, Cupid romped with Eros. Sex for love, unchaperoned dating, the automobile and the privacy it ensured — all these lured many couples into extramarital and premarital trysts, where they engaged in heavy petting and sexual activity. Ultimately they created a radical change in our sexual standards and sexual conduct, as well as loosening orthodox religion's grip on our sexual moral conscience.

Figure 1. Ray Coutura kisses his bride, Laurie, during their hippie wedding ceremony on 9/7/1963 in Berkeley, CA. Corbis-Bettmann.

Endnote 16

Medical Concerns about Sexual Repression and Excess

Endnote 17

During the 1800s, physicians started blaming sexual repression and sexual excess for certain disorders, including hysteria and depression. By the turn of the century, Freud began espousing his novel theories on childhood sexuality and the nature of our sex drive, while a few decades later Havelock Ellis researched and published volumes on the biology of sex and reproduction, including his more liberal viewpoints on sexual ethics.

The Sexual Revolution

Endnote 18

In 1948 and 1953 respectively, **Alfred Kinsey** issued two landmark reports on the sexual behavior of American men and women, which documented the enormous gap between our sexual ideals and our actual behavior. From his reports, Americans learned that many of them masturbated regularly, had premarital coitus, committed adultery, and engaged in heavy petting. And others reckoned that because many were behaving this way, maybe their behaving that way wasn't so abnormal or even immoral.

The National Organization of Women, founded in 1965, heralded a second wave of feminism, while the 1969 riot at Stonewall, a gay bar where homosexuals began the struggle for gay rights, marshaled many activists to a new quest for equality and sexual freedom.

By 1973, we had reliable birth control, medical cures for syphilis and gonorrhea, and legalized abortion. All these factors, together with a general social malaise, stemming in part from cynicism over the Vietnam War, inaugurated the most liberal sexual standards of any period in American history, and an unprecedented interest in sexual ethics.

"Sexuality is the lyricism of the masses."
— Charles Baudelaire

Old stereotypes and myths were rapidly replaced by new ones: Sex and the single girl. The New Age man. Swinging singles. The joy of sex.

Not everyone participated in the Sexual Revolution. Nor did everyone consider it social progress. As Lillian Rubin, author of *The Erotic Wars*, observes, "The revolution, which had freed women to say yes, also disabled them from saying no."

Endnote 23

By the discovery of **AIDS** in 1981, the Sexual Revolution was in high gear. And more than a decade later, according to many experts, there are few signs of its waning or of a rewinding of the clock of history.

Endnote 24

No empirical description of what practices are taking place can provide an answer to the ethical question of whether these practices ought to occur. That requires a different kind of analysis, to which we now turn.

FOUR GENERAL VALUE ORIENTATIONS

The challenge facing anyone committed to assessing sexual morality is how to determine which sexual standards are best and what is the right way to behave.

Because of its diversity, American society includes a wide range of sexual standards, from conservative to liberal. Philosophical reasoning — be it a utilitarian, contract, Kant's Categorical Imperative, the Golden Rule, or any of several other life views — can be used to evaluate these standards and determine right conduct. Most people, however, do not apply such reasoning to their behavior (though perhaps they should). Instead, they inherit sexual guidelines from their parents, religions, peers, and what life itself teaches them. Four such standards are worth considering.

1. Reserving Sex for Marriage

Although some religious traditions, in both Eastern and Western culture, have supported what can only be described as very liberal attitudes about sex, many of the **most conservative moral standards are rooted in religious traditions,** namely the theme that sex is a blessing intended by God within the context of marriage. Of course, many non-religious people also hold the view that sex must be restricted to marriage. According to this view, marital sex is morally good, but only when it is channeled into responsible behavior, which for most holders of this view means heterosexual vaginal intercourse and foreplay leading up to it. This view excludes non-conventional behavior such as homosexuality and anal sex. And for the most traditional denominations, such as Roman Catholicism and Orthodox Judaism, it excludes masturbation as well.

Within such life-views, sexual virginity for both bride and groom is a virtue; fidelity afterward an obligation. An essential purpose of sex is procreative, though for most who hold this view, it also has the function of creating a spiritual union combining two personalities in one new expression — selfless, married love.

Not all theologians interpret religious law so strictly. Instead, with a more liberal outlook that stresses a person's right to sexual gratification and the loving, pleasurable purpose of sex, more liberal theologians and philosophers who take this position allow modern methods of birth control and fertilization, abortion, and a variety of sexual behavior that includes oral sex and masturbation.

Because of the restraints placed on sexuality among certain religious traditions, sex and sin have a strong association that does not necessarily dissipate with a marriage license, and certainly causes a lot of guilt when a person fails to live up to the ideal.

On the other hand, there are rewards for a conscience guided by this general ethical perspective. These include moral certainty, because there is little to dispute or confuse about what is acceptable sexual conduct. By saving sexual intimacy for marriage, people are protected against sexual jealousy, transmission of AIDS and a wide array of venereal disease, sexual scandal, and the like. According to Orthodox Rabbi Manis Freidman, author of *Doesn't Anyone Blush Anymore?*, conservative sexual behavior actually preserves and strengthens a person's sexuality and the marital bond two people share. For some who believe in this ethical perspective, it can be a question of practicality. For most, trusting God's law or an analogous secular moral rule is the only morally decent way to live.

2. 'Boys Will Be Boys' — The Double Standard

In this set of standards, men abide by a different set of moral rules than women. Basically, they are permitted to be more sexually active, more sexually assertive, and more sexually adventuresome than women.

Originally, the double standard woman was a virgin when she married — or at least when she became engaged to be married — while men were allowed and even encouraged to acquire sexual experience long before marriage. Some men believed that later, it was all right to "have a little on the side" outside marriage, either by visiting prostitutes for the type of sex their wife would not consent to have, or via affairs with single women.

The historic rationalization for the double standard is twofold: first, to ensure paternity, and secondly, to reinforce the idea that men need to and can live by a freer set of rules. "Boys will be boys," after all.

Sociologist Ira Reiss believes that such reasoning is based on erroneous assumptions that men cannot repress their sexual urges without dire consequences and that women have an inferior sex drive to men. According to author and feminist Naomi Wolf, exploding the myth that women have inferior sex drives (or that women are entitled to less sexual fulfillment) is the crux of feminism and society's uneasiness with it. "The basic principle of social organization," explains Wolf, "is not just who gets power, but who gets pleasure."

Endnote 29

Endnote 30

There are other problems with this particular moral compass. As Reiss observes, men are encouraged to exploit women and use them as a means to an end. Once they have "scored," they are prone to disrespect and even feel disgusted with their partner. Furthermore, double standard men show little empathy for women who are promiscuous, regardless of the myriad of social, economic, or emotional reasons why women become that way.

Besides exploiting women, Reiss contends the **double standard encourages self-centered sexuality that is devoid of commitment and affection, an experience that hardly prepares men for the give-and-take that an emotionally-rich, satisfying sexual relationship requires.** Trying to live a double standard has adverse effects on women, too. Those women who "fail" the test of sexual purity earn a reputation for being "easy" and are saddled with labels from men, such as "whore," "slut," and the like. To avoid a bad reputation and maintain their desirability as wives, many women become sexual teases or hide their true desire to initiate sex with a man.

Compelled to send out only subtle cues about their sexual desires, they often send out unclear signals, which men easily misread. Many women feign sexual innocence and lie about the sexual experience they do have. Putting up such facades may require painfully harboring secrets about infants given up for adoption, abortions, and sexual abuse or assault. Finally, **treating women as inferior, the way the double sexual standard does, encourages their devaluation in the rest of society, be it in the workplace, academia, home, or elsewhere.** Worse, as Reiss also points out, in both *Journey into Sexuality* and *An End to Shame*, by holding women to an inferior status, while simultaneously validating machismo conquestial attitudes in men, "the double standard can actually contribute to the cause of rape."

Endnote 31

3. Gender Equality in Sanctioning Non-marital Sex

The third general value orientation toward sexuality holds that men and women have equal sexual rights and responsibilities. This view sanctions non-marital sex. Although, according to this general view, sexual intimacy requires no wedding vows, people are expected to have affection toward their sexual partners, and to make an emotional investment in a relationship. How much emotional commitment is required varies, from the belief that two people should have a long term commitment such as marriage or be in love to the belief that they at least ought to mutually respect one another.

Endnote 32

Within this broadly defined standard is also a wide spectrum of thought on *monogamy* and *fidelity*. Some people believe that all sexual relationships should be monogamous, if only for practical reasons, while others believe that as long as there is affection, openness, and mutual consent including fidelity and faithfulness to the relationship itself, then secondary sexual relationships are acceptable. Many famous people have lived and loved by this rule, including Jean-Paul Sartre and Simone de Beauvoir, French philosophers who laid the moral groundwork for other couples who are sometimes called *sexually-liberated*.

Many homosexual men have sex without love. However, some of them — about one in four gay men and a much higher proportion of lesbians — subscribe to the idea that affection should be the basis for a sexual relationship. (Paradoxically, they refer to themselves as "straight" gays.)

Endnote 33

Endnote 34

Holders of this view put less emphasis on sexual coitus and more on the whole context of sexuality and feelings. **General ethical principles, rather than traditional rules of sexual conduct, are the yardstick for making decisions about sexual behavior: Do not harm, exploit, use, or deceive another person during or after sexual encounters.** Among at least some who hold this view, as long as you abide by these basic principles, then increasingly unconventional sexual behavior between two consenting people is acceptable.

Advocates of such a liberal standard argue that it is the emotionally healthiest preparation for marriage and the best way to live the single life. On the other hand, unless people take precautions, non-marital pregnancy and sexually transmitted disease are a risk, as well as the emotional deception of people who profess to live by this moral compass but really don't. As the familiar adage goes, "Women give sex for love and men give love for sex." Moreover, many are left with the sense that there are really moral limits on sexual relations that call this view into question.

4. Permissiveness Without Affection

This last moral compass is what Reiss calls "permissiveness without affection," because sex here is devoid of emotional commitment. "In" with this crowd are free love, swinging singles, swinging couples, cruising, and more. Ranging from recreational sex between two partners unready for any emotional commitment to totally anonymous sex among multiple strangers, this compass covers 360 degrees of sexual freedom to the max, although some of those who use it may choose to impose occasional limitations.

Besides having sex without affection, some in this crowd will have sex with anyone, including bisexuals. A few individuals condone only conventional behavior and refuse to do anything else. But in any case, those who lead the most nonconforming, adventuresome (and even reckless) sex lives subscribe to this view.

Good sex. No strings attached. Whatever turns you on. Devoid of emotion or commitment. . . . Can such sex really be "good"?

While they may still adhere to such moral principles as refraining from harm, deceit or coercion, given the seemingly total freedom of this compass, it is tempting to selectively ignore such principles. Flight from responsibility, cynicism about relationships, and burnout over sex are other pitfalls. So is the empty or degenerate feeling one can get from having sex with hundreds or even thousands of sexual partners who care little or nothing about you afterward, or from sex that is degrading or painful. And what effect does such behavior have on children who are conceived during such casual, perhaps anonymous, encounters?

In addition to the **emotional risks, and the danger of getting abused by strangers, disease lurks eerily behind the veneer of "safer sex." That sex can be dangerous at all, though, powers its very appeal to some people. Even the threat of dying cannot scare them into abandoning their sexually-free, no-strings-attached lifestyle.**

For many people, **recreational sex** is a temporary choice; they are willing to have just physical sex, but they prefer sex with affection. Or, exercising their own double standard, they are unable or unwilling to have affection for some of their partners, but quite willing to have it for others.

Critics of this compass claim that it has no morality at all — that by putting sex in the same category as "eating a good meal, listening to music, or getting a pleasant back rub," we deny its moral richness, and shortchange ourselves.

Endnote 35

Its proponents, on the other hand, believe that by isolating the physical context of sexuality from all its emotional layers, people can actually be more honest in their relationships and thereby avoid the game playing and deception that go with other sexual standards. Their attitude might be characterized this way: Risky sex without affection or commitment is better than no sex at all.

WHICH GENERAL VALUE ORIENTATION TO CHOOSE?

Being True to Your Own Standards

"Be true to yourself and stick by your own moral compass" is a constant theme in moral education. Yet sex nearly always involves at least two people, often with different sexual moral standards. How can we be tolerant of a radically different moral viewpoint than our own? And when people whose respect we want pressure us to change, how can we maintain our own standards? Most of all, how can we make wise, informed choices about our sexual behavior?

"Selling out" on your sexual standards causes not only guilt, but also regret, according to Dr. Pam Bruboker, former professor of sexual ethics at Cleveland State University. She observes that students who profess the most regrets about their sexual past are the ones who have changed their standards in order to accommodate themselves to someone else's expectations.

Endnote 36

Besides exposing your sexual standards to a thorough philosophical analysis, Bruboker suggests the "mirror approach": If you were to do what you have decided was right to do, could you still look yourself in the mirror and respect yourself?

Going Beyond Being True to Yourself

The real question of moral philosophy is whether there is something more to morality than merely being true to yourself and recognizing the freedom of people to develop their own personal sexual lifestyle. Certainly, those who hold either of the first two positions discussed above believe that there are moral rights and wrongs in the area of sexual relations that go beyond mere personal preferences and style. **They hold that morality lends itself to reason, to**

systematic philosophical analysis, or to moral rules that are not merely subjective. They hold that there are features of sexual relationships that will tend to make them morally right or wrong that can be discerned through careful reflection that can lead to the conclusion that certain behaviors are pleasurable. The following features have been suggested as morally relevant.

MORAL THEMES IN ASSESSING SEXUAL RELATIONS

The Subtleties of Free and Informed Choice

Ethics requires an ability to make rational decisions, an ability called moral agency. It also requires the free will to make them, which is called moral autonomy. In sexual ethics, both moral agency and autonomy are sometimes framed as consent: that one party has a right to consent implies that the other party has the obligation to ask for, not demand, sex and the willingness to accept no for an answer. It also requires that the one giving consent be true to himself or herself when deciding whether to consent to any sexual behavior.

In 1991, Naval pilots convened in Las Vegas for a weekend of fraternizing at their annual Tailhook Convention. Although the female pilots attending **Tailhook** knew of its reputation for hard partying and loose sex, many believed they were immune from harm — until they walked through a gauntlet of rowdy pilots who tore at their clothes, fondled, and sexually molested them. The full consequences of those acts and judgments included psychological damage, military penalties, loss of reputation and loss of employment.

Even the most libertarian view of sexual ethics recognizes that coercing persons into having any kind of sex against their will is wrong because it denies them autonomy over their own moral behavior. (Interestingly, denying people their free will also removes their moral responsibility for what occurs. Hence, a person who has been raped should not be morally blamed for the rape.)

In an ideal world, we could trust everyone to respect our sexual rights. As long as society has members who fall short of the ideal, though, why volunteer for situations where forced sex is more likely to occur, or give away your right to choose by getting too drunk to resist sex or give an informed consent to it?

Ironically, many college women don't realize that their being forced into sex is rape, and many college men fail to realize that forcing a woman to have sex is rape. In a survey of college students sponsored by *Ms.* magazine in 1985, 15% of the coeds had experienced forced sex, while another 12% had resisted it. Yet, three out of four women forced to have sex failed to label themselves as a rape victim, and nearly 9 out of 10 men who admitted to forced sex failed to understand they had committed rape.

Many of the women thought that what had occurred to them was just part of a relationship, and somewhat their fault, while their male offenders stated that the women they had forced into having sex had

In an ideal world, we could trust everyone to respect our sexual rights. As long as society has members who fall short of the ideal, though, why volunteer for situations where forced sex is more likely to occur, or give away your right to choose by getting too drunk to resist sex or give an informed consent to it?

Endnote 40

been ambivalent about what they wanted or had pretended not to want sex (or the men had misread their cues).

This study is controversial and open to many interpretations. Another study, one by Louis Harris, found that only 2 percent of females responded affirmatively to the question, In the past five years have you been a victim of a rape or sexual assault? With either set of findings, however, the problem of forced sexual relations and misunderstandings about whether sex is desired is a significant one.

In his book *An End to Shame*, sociologist **Ira Reiss** says the fault for such misunderstandings, and for much of the date rape that is occurring, lies with our adversarial script for dating, which casts women in sexually reluctant roles, and men as persuaders. Such scripting works against honest communication. Women give unclear cues about their desires and men misread the cues. **"Both men and women must stop playing this dangerous sexual guessing game,"** advises Reiss, "and sit down and tell each other how they feel about the relationship and about having sex with each other."

Endnote 41

For many reasons (they can range from mental disability to illness, depression, or insanity) some persons actually lack the ability to make a rational decision about their behavior. In 1989, a young woman with an IQ of only 64 and an "almost insatiable need to satisfy herself through sex" also gave satisfaction to four teenage boys in Glen Ridge, N.J. Despite her desire to please them, because she had a questionable ability to make a decision and rationally consent to sex, three of the teenagers were charged with rape.

Ethics is about choice, choosing the best alternative. Some situations occur in which people feel as though they face a Hobson's choice — they seem to lose either way. A woman at gunpoint may consent to being raped in order to save her life. A wife may voice approval to spousal rape, believing that giving in to her abusive husband's demands will spare herself and her children a worse fate. Or a young man may run away from a terrible home life and resort to prostitution because he feels he has no better choice at the time. While these are extremely difficult moral dilemmas, they are, unfortunately, not uncommon ones. It must be clear that not all voiced approvals constitute adequately **free and informed consent.** Some may be based on inadequate information; others on choice that is inadequately free.

The critical moral issue is whether these circumstances significantly change the degree to which one is morally autonomous and free to choose whether to consent to the proposed sexual encounter. There is a sense in which some psychological and social experience can be said to lessen the degree of responsibility for one's actions. Certainly, anyone who takes advantage of these factors to manipulate a consent is compromising the quality of the consent. Except in extreme cases, however, they probably do not lessen autonomy to the extent that the one agreeing to sexual relations can be said to be totally lacking in responsibility.

Consenting to Immoral Behavior

Many people erroneously believe that mutual consent is a moral green light, that anything two consenting adults do in the privacy of their home is right. But consent, however important, only completes part of the moral picture.

True, without consent, no sexual conduct can be moral. Yet two people can consent to behavior that is wrong. For instance, a professor can hold out high marks to students who consent to have sex with him or her. The consent is there, but for the wrong reason. Similarly, a psychiatrist who has sex with a patient and believes that the patient's consent puts a moral stamp of approval on the experience is rationalizing his or her behavior.

One of the legacies of the double standard was the game people learned to play about signals. Women coyly said "no" when they meant "maybe" or "yes." Some men learned never to take "no" for an answer. That sex requires consent in order to be moral is consistent with nearly all of our ethical approaches. That we must choose our behavior is consistent with moral agency. But as we can see by the examples in this section (and by our laws against sex crimes), consent requires good communication skills. This means learning to be fair about the questions, and honest and wise about the answers.

PROTECTING AGAINST PREGNANCY AND DISEASE

The Risks of Unprotected Sexual Relations

More than 1 million Americans are reportedly infected with HIV, and nearly 170,000 have died from AIDS. Many of these people unknowingly or knowingly spread the infection to others, by failing to take precautions against spreading it to their partners, and keeping their condition a secret. Often, they have multiple partners. Although they are not always life-threatening, other venereal diseases have also reached epidemic proportions.

Endnote 44

Endnote 45

The Roles of Men and Women

Whose **responsibility** is protection from pregnancy and disease? Are all women responsible for protecting themselves from pregnancy? Do their partners have any responsibility, too? What responsibility does a person have to protect himself or herself from sexually transmitted diseases (STDs), and to protect their partners as well?

The Interests of Other Parties

It is easy to believe that we are private citizens and that our sexuality is beyond and apart from the state; even from members of our immediate family. But then we realize that other people share the responsibility for our children, for educating them and footing their bills for housing, health, and other needs when we cannot or do not provide for them. What responsibility do we have to these family members and to the public at large for our sexual conduct? And what responsibility, in turn, do they have to us?

Many experts advocate abstinence as the only responsible protection against pregnancy and disease, and the only safe and moral behavior for single persons. Their argument has logic: If you don't have sex, you probably won't contract an STD. But, given the relative effectiveness of condoms and the strong desire of many for sexual relationships, is abstinence an effective option?

The Role of the Public

Who is responsible for supplying condoms? Is it a private responsibility or should schools or public health clinics freely dispense condoms, Norplant, and other kinds of sexual protection? Do the news media have a responsibility to advertise and promote condom use? What responsibility does the government have to fund research for new methods of birth control? The former U.S. Surgeon General, Dr. C. Everett Koop, believes that government is responsible in many of those areas. **"We know that one person's behavior can be dangerous to another person's life and health,"** Koop told an audience in Minneapolis, "and that the ethics of the state can, in fact, intrude into the deepest corners of one's house."

Endnote 52

Others, especially from the conservative sectors of our society, disagree, claiming that the government has no moral authority to be involved in our personal sexual lives; that doing so undermines parents' right to impart their personal morals to their children.

LEGISLATING PROHIBITIONS ON SEXUAL PRACTICES

Besides laws against forced sex, it has been the public policy pattern in America to pass laws against other sexual behavior regarded as immoral and indecent. Adultery, homosexual relations, oral and anal sex, and fornication, for example, are illegal in many states. Prostitution is legal in Nevada, but only where there is a local ordinance allowing it. And a few states have recently enacted laws against marital rape and against knowingly transmitting venereal disease to an uninformed sexual partner.

Masturbation

In all states, masturbation is legal in private, but mutual masturbation is a crime in some states and masturbation in public in nearly all states is regarded as indecent exposure. Certainly, sexual behavior that seriously harms people, such as rape, incest, and sexual harassment, belong within the sphere of the law. Should other behavior, though, particularly the private sexual behavior between two consenting adults, also be prohibited by law? Indeed, how much right does the law have in our bedrooms?

Endnote 53

Sodomy

At one time, sodomy was considered so "detestable and abominable (a) Vice . . . committed by mankind or beast," that it was a felony punishable by death, no exceptions allowed. When our Bill of

Endnote 54

Rights was written and adopted, the death penalty for sodomy remained. Penal reform and the humanitarian effort to abolish cruel and unusual punishment ultimately eroded such harsh sentencing, until punishment for sodomy was limited to a few years in prison and/or a fine.

Because sodomy was considered such a degrading crime, its legal description was often vague language such as "crime against nature" or "buggery." Moreover, it contained a number of meanings, ranging from homosexual acts and oral and anal sex, to bestiality and necrophilia (acts with corpses). By 1961, all 50 states still outlawed sodomy and The Sexual Offenses Act of 1967 ensured that all homosexual acts, sodomy, gross indecency, and procurement remained criminal.

MICHAEL HARDWICK:
SODOMY NOT A RIGHT

Michael Hardwick is making love to a man in the bedroom of his home. A police officer enters his home and, through a partially open bedroom door, sees Hardwick having sex with another man. The officer arrests him on charges of sodomy. Hardwick now faces a minimum prison sentence of 20 years.

Hardwick challenges the constitutionality of his state's statute against sodomy. After losing his case in a federal district court, he appeals to a higher court. Eventually his case reaches the Supreme Court, as Bowers vs. Hardwick 478 U.S. 186, 194 (1986). In a 5–4 vote, Hardwick loses.

Both Justice Byron R. White, who wrote the majority opinion, and Justice Lewis Powell, who cast the pivotal vote, reason that **conduct that has been condemned for hundreds of years, as sodomy has been, cannot now become a fundamental right.** As a result of their legal reasoning, it remains a crime even though many millions of Americans practice it and believe that it is right.

There are other sexual practices condemned by law that have led to controversial prosecutions. During his trial for allegedly raping his estranged wife, Jim Mosely admitted to engaging in oral sex with her on previous occasions. He was acquitted of the rape charges, but because oral sex is a crime in Georgia, Mosely was convicted of oral sex and given a five-year sentence, two of which he spent in jail before becoming eligible for parole.

Making a behavior illegal, as we know from our civil rights past, does not automatically make it immoral. Nor, as we have learned from the front line of the abortion debate, can legalizing it resolve moral debate. Yet, if laws and their punishments are seriously out of line with our society's ethical standards, we risk having respect for law collapse.

Our right to privacy competes with the moral claims of those who share responsibility for the consequences of our sexual behavior, including both the people who know us well and the public at large as well as those who believe that the state has the responsibility for placing legal limits on some such practices.

Confidentiality and Sexual Secrets

People sometimes find themselves with significant information about the sexual behavior of others. They may learn this because they have had sexual relations with the other individual or because they have observed it or been told about it. In professional relations, such as those between physician and patient or lawyer and client, the rule of confidentiality applies. Even then exceptions exist where disclosure is permitted or even required. Traditionally disclosure of confidential information was acceptable to benefit the individual patient himself or herself, but increasing that is rejected as too paternalistic. However, disclosures are still considered appropriate if they are likely to benefit third parties. Disclosure of information about sexual behavior of friends, lovers, or acquaintances raises more complicated problems, however. In the following scenarios, people consider whether they have the moral right to make such disclosures for various reasons.

To tell or not to tell vexes nearly each of us at some time or another. Harboring secrets such as incest or rape can interfere with our healing process. Secrets can also distance us from people with whom we are trying hardest to be close. On the other hand, candor and confessions, while cleansing your conscience, can be painful to the person whom you tell.

Disclosures of Other's Infidelity

Sometimes we are in a position to know that someone has cheated on a friend or acquaintance. We may feel morally loyal to the one upon whom the cheating was done and feel duty-bound to share the information. On the other hand, we may also feel loyalty to the one doing the cheating. There can first be a conflict of loyalties. Moreover, in some cases, such as one in which a young woman has an attraction to her best friend's boy friend, the burden or embarrassment of sharing the information may make us inclined not to say anything.

Disclosures of Publicly Observed Behavior

In addition to the issues of conflict of loyalty and the discomfort of having to make the disclosure, some would claim that it makes a difference morally whether the information one possesses is private based on information that cannot be known to the public or behavior that in a setting in which the parties could reasonably presume privacy or whether it occurred in a public area where the one observed could not presume privacy.

Sharing One's Own Private Information

While the previous examples involve information private or public about some other person, which might be important to a third party, sometimes the moral conflict involves whether there is a duty to share one's own private sexually relevant information. Here the nature of the relationship with the other person may be particularly

On the other hand, candor and confessions, while cleansing your conscience, can be painful to the person whom you tell.

critical. Strangers surely have no claim on this information while spouses and those contemplating long-term commitments surely do; e.g., whether a woman should disclose to a date that she is sterile.

Or, to consider other situations raising this question, does someone whose treatment for childhood cancer left him sterile, have any obligation to tell anyone he dates about his condition? If so, at what point does that obligation begin? Does a woman have an obligation to tell someone she has had breast augmentation or reduction? Must a person reveal that they have a problem having orgasms? What about fetishes, cross-dressing, the need for dominance, excessive or underactive sex drives? What features of these would give potential partners an interest in this information? Would these features give one a relevant claim to the information? Similar questions arise when one has a history of sexually transmitted diseases, as in the following case.

Disclosing to Protect Another Person

The situation that most closely resembles traditional paternalistic disclosures is one in which one believes that the sexual practices of another may be dangerous to that individual himself or herself. This might involve a minor who was getting herself into a situation that she might not be able to handle or someone who is risking exposure to serious disease. Or it might even involve risk to life.

Vindictive or Self-Serving Disclosures

"Against every claim to secrecy stands the awareness of its dangers," warns ethicist **Sissela Bok**, author of *Secrets*. In the 1980s, a coed at a large university in Texas was talked into having intercourse and was secretly videotaped during it. When the tape was distributed all over campus, she experienced so much emotional trauma that she had to leave school over the incident. Did the students who plotted the scheme deserve the blame? And did those who merely watched the tape have any responsibility for causing her pain? What about telling a secret for the sole purpose of getting even? Can that ever be fair? Sometimes though, while the telling of a secret may feel vindicatory to the person who has been snitched on, the person telling the secret in fact may have a legitimate moral claim. What of a child who was a victim of sexual abuse and now, as an adult, considers whether to confront the abuser?

Endnote 55

A utilitarian would argue that the victim of the abuse should decide by assessing the consequences of the alternatives of confronting the abuser or letting it go, claiming that the end justifies the means. But does it?

Traditionally, the names of women who were sexually promiscuous or easily seduced (or who weren't, but someone wanted to say they were) were scrawled on the men's room walls, where the women had no way to refute the claims or clean up their reputations, literally. Now women on several campuses have begun to emulate the tradition. Only this time, the names of suspected or known campus rapists get top billing. Assuming that the fellows are guilty, does such vigilantism stand up to moral scrutiny? From a deontological perspective in which morality is assessed based on rights and duties rather than consequences, this question would be answered by considering whether the perpetrators have a right to confidentiality, whether any promises were made or implied to them about keeping their conduct private, and perhaps whether justice requires that they suffer punishment for their actions. From a utilitarian perspective the moral concern would focus more on what the consequences of disclosing or not disclosing would be such things as whether other victims might be protected if the disclosure were made.

The Right of Others to Know Someone's Sexual History

The cases involving disclosing confidential information about sexual behaviors considered thus far all involve situations in which people feel inclined to tell about their own or someone else's past behavior. At least the one contemplating the disclosure is not actively invoking a right to privacy. But sometimes we would very much like to keep our own sexual histories private, but we must consider whether someone else has a right to that information. According to Marty Klein, therapist and author of *Our Sexual Secrets*, most of us have sexual secrets we intend to keep forever, or at least from our current sexual partners. The most common of these secrets are sexual fantasies, fears, past sexual involvements, and the like. Which of these secrets are we entitled to keep?

Endnote 56

If we have fathered a child or given birth to a child out of wedlock who was placed in adoption, do we have the right to keep this information secret? Nearly half of all states have some kind of notification laws compelling pregnant women to inform their sexual partner (or those minors who are pregnant to inform their parents). Even in the absence of such laws, what prerogative does a pregnant woman have to keep her condition secret? Does your present partner have any right to find out about your sexual history or go further in investigating besides what they tell you? Candor has an important place in sexual relationships. But according to both Klein and Bok, secrets have a rightful place, too.

Endnote 57

"Secrecy may be used to guard intimacy or invade," says Bok, "to nurture or consume it." How much right do we have to remain silent about our fetishes and sexual orientation? Do we have a right to keep silent about an STD that has been already cured or is under control? The answer will depend, in part, on whether others have a need to know. If we are about to expose others to a significant risk of an infectious disease, of paternity, or even of embarrassment then that person is often seen as having a right to be informed of that risk. Somewhat more controversial is the claim that people entering significant relations have a right to know major elements of the other's past criminal record or previous identities as well as significant sexual history such as having fathered a child who could re-enter the person's life at some point. On the other hand, even intimate, long-term relations plausibly includes zones of privacy about which the other has no claim to a right to be informed.

The Duty to Keep the Secrets of Others

Closely related to the question of our right to keep our own history secret is the question of whether we have a right to demand that others who have learned about that history keep it secret. How much of a right do we have to demand that others keep our secrets? For example, if a sibling tells you he or she is gay, do you have an obligation to guard the information from your parents or the rest of the family? What about a pregnancy, or merely having sex with someone of whom the family disapproves?

Do you have any duty to keep secret about someone's abortion, children out of wedlock, promiscuity, or sexual abuse, even when you think the information will help that person's partner understand him or her better?

Many adoptees search for their natural parents, wanting to know the truth about their conception and who their parents really are. Do these adoptees have any moral claim to know of the circumstances of their conception — whether it occurred during a rape, say, or a casual or paid sexual encounter? Whether it was with a blood relative of the natural mother, perhaps — her father, a brother, an uncle, or grandfather? Does a person have the right to know if he was conceived before his parents' betrothal? If he is the child of an adulterous liaison? If he was fathered by a sperm donor or mothered by a surrogate?

All of these situations involve circumstances when someone knows sensitive information about another that is, in some sense, private. Deciding whether one has a duty to keep that information private will depend a great deal on the nature of the relation between the two parties. The easiest case would be one in which permission is given to share the information. Sometimes when private information is shared with another it is transmitted with an implied or explicit promise of confidentiality. In a medical setting patients disclose with an implied promise. Sometimes friends may share their sexual escapades only after an explicit promise. **Other things being equal, promises ought to be kept.**

Such promises pose serious ethical problems, however, if, after learning the secret, one realizes that others may have a strong interest in being informed. It is widely recognized that third parties have a right to know information, even confidential information, that could be crucial in protecting them from harm. Even psychiatrists have a duty, for example, to warn potential victims if a patient is making a credible threat of serious harm to others. Would that same principle apply if you knew that a friend was about to marry someone without telling his partner that he already has dependent children? The issue here is whether one should make a blank-check promise not to reveal information before learning whether it could be of crucial interest to other parties.

The problem is even more complex if the one learning the secret had no opportunity to consider whether to promise confidentiality. While potential adoptive parents may make an explicit promise not to reveal the identities of natural parents, those who learn of another's sexual orientation or fetishes may not have.

Adultery — The Promise of Marital Fidelity

"I promise to love, honor, cherish, and hold thee only unto me until death do us part." Most people marry and commit to monogamy. Contemporary surveys reveal that adultery is widespread and spreading (women are catching up to men). Even the most conservative findings indicate that at least a third of all men and a fourth of all women admit to having an extramarital sexual experience at least once. Of course, most moral exemplars declare statistics are no basis for morality.

Philosopher Michael Wreen argues that adultery is wrong because it is so inconsistent with our basic definition of **marriage** — the agreement to make an emotional commitment to another person, have a sexual relationship with them, and have it be exclusive of anyone else. In his opinion, the very value of marriage makes monogamy a worthwhile sacrifice.

According to both the law and our major religions, marriage, as Wreen suggests, is based on monogamy, and adultery is acceptable grounds for divorce. What about societies that are polygamous or polyandrous or where adultery, in the form of prostitution or mistresses, is encouraged? Do the values of those societies make the issue a morally relative one in ours?

Christian theologian Stanley Grenz, author of *Sexual Ethics: A Biblical Perspective*, agrees that personal fulfillment may require outside influences. But instead of seeking it from an affair, he suggests that the morally appropriate place to augment your fulfillment is through religion and belief in God. Even those who reject religious claims can find personal fulfillment through deep friendships, careers, creativity, charity, and leisure pursuits of an asexual nature.

Love and Commitment

What does love have to do with it anyway? If people choose to love only one person, does that preclude them from having extramarital sex with persons to whom they will not get emotionally attached, whether prostitutes, casual acquaintances, or an entire group that shares the same perspective? Indeed, can adultery ever be right?

Philosopher Bonnie Steinbock believes that if a person is in a loveless marriage, there is reason to turn elsewhere for affection and sex. Is there, though? Aren't there better ways of solving a marital problem, such as counseling and therapy? Should such marriages be salvaged?

Some philosophers believe the issue pivots on consent. In this view, if two people consent to extramarital sex, or agree to tolerate it in their spouse, then it is not wrong. Others hold that the real issue is commitment. They hold that marriage involves a promise of fidelity and that, since there is a duty to keep promises, spouses owe fidelity to each other. What of mutual consent to abrogate such a promise, however. Many seem to hold that mere mutual agreement is not suf-

Endnote 59

Endnote 60

Endnote 61

Endnote 62

Endnote 63

Endnote 64

Endnote 65

ficient to justify extramarital sex. Secular people may explain this by suggesting that the promise involves other parties as well as the couple's children or other family members, for instance. Religious people may understand the marital promise to be made not just between the couple, but to their deity. Still others, especially those who understand duty to involve more than promise-keeping, may hold that monogamy is simply morally required, regardless of agreement of the parties to permit outside relations.

Making the World Go Away

If adultery is so common, why is it viewed as so wrong? Peggy Vaughan, author of *The Monogamy Myth*, suggests that we ought to take adultery out of the moral realm altogether, and treat it as an amoral (morally neutral) issue entirely. Writes Vaughan, whose marriage survived years of her husband's philandering: "We need to reject the Monogamy Myth, not to excuse those who have affairs, but to relieve the sense of shame and inadequacy felt by their mates." Her critics would claim that this entirely misses the moral point, that it confuses psychology with morality. They would say that what is needed for the spouse of a philanderer is a realistic understanding of who broke the rules and a recognition that those rules, based on the ethics of fidelity to promises, make good moral sense.

Endnote 70

Is Sex Ever a Duty?

"Just say 'no'" may be the hallmark of sexual responsibility in the shadow of AIDS. How responsible, though, is saying no in the context of marriage or deeply committed relationships? Many people would argue that a spouse should be free to refrain from sex, that sex is something you do only when you are in the mood for it. Others disagree, and claim that for the sake of the relationship, spouses ought to have sex, at least when their partner desires it.

Relationships involve two people, each with the potential for a different sex drive, different attitudes toward sex, and a different set of sexual moral standards. How much right do we have to expect our partner to engage in lovemaking when that individual doesn't feel like having sex? Is sex so exclusive from these other activities that it should stand alone and be reserved for only those times when the "mood" is right?

What about societies that are polygamous or polyandrous or where adultery, in the form of prostitution or mistresses, is encouraged? Do the values of those societies make the issue a morally relative one in ours?

Although a person has a legal right to end an unconsummated marriage, do they have a moral right to maintain the marriage with or without seeking sexual satisfaction outside the relationship? The place many start on this issue is **abstinence** (voluntarily refraining from sexual intercourse) and **celibacy** (refraining from all sexuality, including masturbation and even thinking about having sex).

Whether it is temporary or permanent, nearly one fifth of all marriages are celibate, and four percent of all men and 10% of all women have chosen to be celibate. Historically, and in most societies, celibacy, whose Latin root means single, is actually the expected norm for all unwed people. It was the price one was expected to pay for remaining single. But it wasn't always simply a case of doing without. In

Endnote 71

Endnote 72

ancient Greece, for example, despite the Platonic ideal, celibacy was a crime. In Sparta, celibate men were barred from voting. On the other hand, throughout history, especially in religious life, chastity has long been regarded as virtuous moral behavior.

For Mahatma Gandhi, father of India's struggle for independence, chastity was part of a spiritual quest. After more than three decades of marriage, Gandhi asked his wife Kasturba, who had married him when they were both only 13 years old, to take a vow of brahmacharya (Hindu vow of celibacy) in order for him to create peace within himself.

Ironically, temporary celibacy is often prescribed as an antidote for sexual problems. Other couples find themselves drifting into celibacy as sex becomes less frequent, more routine, and unimportant compared to other focuses in their lives. Others abruptly stop having sexual relations after a breech in the relationship, such as an affair, while fear of AIDS has caused still others to choose celibacy or abstention from intercourse.

No one ever died from a lack of sex. But a lack of sexual interest from one's partner can diminish a person's self-esteem and destroy a relationship, as well as create a host of emotional problems in between. As one woman said of her husband's unwillingness to have sex with her, "It feels terrible . . . I feel like I'm not beautiful enough, that I'm not attractive to him, that I don't turn him on . . . it feels pretty bad."

Obviously, if two people freely choose celibacy in their relationship — and some couples report great satisfaction with this choice even though they may be going against the norm — they are neither harming each other nor treating each other deceitfully or unfairly. If sexual ethics can be reduced to mutual consent and avoiding harm, this would seem to settle the matter. On the other hand, some traditions, both religious and secular, hold that being sexually active, at least during the years of reproduction, is an essential part of marriage. Some Jews hold such a view as do those in cultures that fear declining population.

Gabrielle Brown, therapist and author of the book *The New Celibacy*, suggests that celibacy chosen for negative reasons — to punish, control, or withdraw love — does nothing to benefit a relationship, and in fact, only weakens it. Nor is celibacy beneficial that is initiated by only one partner. "Either both partners should decide to be sexual," advises Brown, "or both decide to be celibate in the service of love and positive commitment to their marriage."

Endnote 73

SEXUAL STANDARDS FOR PUBLIC FIGURES

What private sexual standards of conduct should we expect our civil servants, teachers, clergy, and other role models and leaders to hold? Do we have any right to hold them to only the highest of moral standards or to conform to our own sexual moral compass?

Do their private lives interfere with their duties to the public or the people they serve? What responsibility do they have to avoid scandal that may bring shame and ill repute to their families or their profession? Is their private sexual behavior any of our business? And finally, what rights and obligations do writers and reporters have to expose those lives or shield them from our public view?

Some public figures may be in positions in which their private sexual activities could impact on their public responsibilities. For example, knowledge of one's private activities could lead to blackmail. It could reveal a duplicitous character, advocating one position publicly while practicing another in private. Is this a basis for linking private and public lives?

What private sexual standards of conduct should we expect our civil servants, teachers, clergy, and other role models and leaders to hold?

Public Figures Whose Practices Have Been Exposed

Some of the very people teaching us morality may miss the moral mark themselves, shrinking from the ideals they are supposed to inspire in us. In fact, when Jimmy Swaggart and James Bakker, wealthy television evangelists who had mesmerized millions of followers with their family values and spiritual intonements, were literally caught with their pants down — Swaggart with a prostitute, Bakker with the seduction of a former secretary — the public's respect for the television clergy in general diminished significantly.

Endnote 75

Besides the sting of betrayal and hypocrisy, there is also a real threat. Don't people who have the trust of others have a duty to uphold that trust? Reading from a roster of notable presidents that includes George Washington, Thomas Jefferson, Franklin D. Roosevelt, and John F. Kennedy, adultery and sexual dalliance appear commonplace. When U.S. Senator Gary Hart, a Colorado Democrat, ran for the nation's highest office, he challenged reporters on the question of his marital fidelity. It was a challenge that felled Hart from his lofty plateau when they caught him spending the night with model Donna Rice. Both Hart and Rice denied any sexual misconduct, but the political damage had already occurred. As Hart withdrew from the 1988 presidential race, he accused the media of unfair treatment, though when asked point-blank if he had ever committed adultery, he refused to answer.

Endnote 76

The relevancy of a candidate's sexual conduct has surfaced again with President **Bill Clinton.** The controversy began when, as governor of Arkansas, he was accused by one Gennifer Flowers of a 12-year liaison with her. Like Hart, Clinton initially evaded the question of whether or not he had committed adultery with Flowers. He was also accused of an illicit attempt to obtain sexual favors from an Arkansas employee, Paula Jones, who was later to accuse him of sexual harassment. A similar controversy emerged in 1998 when he was accused of an illicit relation with White House intern Monica Lewinsky. And like Hart, Clinton also failed to completely quell suspicions that he had ever committed adultery.

Do journalists have the right to inform us about our candidates' or leaders' private lives? And what right do we, the public, have to that information? In her book *Secrets,* Bok argues that the right to tell and

Endnote 77

Endnote 78

What if the Clinton-Lewinsky behavior occurred between the President of a College and an intern? Or between a corporate CEO and an intern? Or between a general and a sergeant? Should the president be held to an equal, lesser or higher standard?

our right to know is a "patently inadequate rationale," and that while journalists can satisfy our curiosity, they must still "pay special attention to individual privacy." **But what if marital indiscretions interfere with leadership?** If politicians lie to a spouse, what real proof do we have that they will lie to their public?

The 1990s was full of sexual exposés involving public figures. These scandals required more careful analysis to determine exactly what ethical issues are raised and whether public figures are to be held to any standard higher than that for ordinary private citizens. It is currently clear that President Clinton has raised ethical questions. For purposes of an ethical analysis we need presume neither guilt nor innocence. Rather, it is worth asking what should our ethical conclusion be if any of the behaviors Clinton and other public figures have been accused of turn out to be true.

First, the behaviors would be ethically controversial even for private citizens. For those who view extramarital relations for anyone as a violation of a covenant of marriage, they will probably reach the same conclusion in the case of public figures. It is striking to note that, in the case of Clinton, his wife consistently stated her belief in his innocence. Independent of that faith in her husband, however, is the question of whether a spouse's agreement to an extramarital affair would be sufficient to justify it.

Also, some of the behaviors of which Clinton has been accused go beyond extramarital affairs. Paula Jones accused him of sexual harassment. Although the legal charge, as of this writing, has been dismissed, the underlying moral issue is whether a head of an organization — a government, a university, or a corporation — can ever engage in sexual relations with a subordinate of that organization. In Paula Jones's case, it was purportedly without her agreement. In the case of Monica Lewinsky, the accusers imply the relation may have been consensual. In either case, however, if such relations were to occur, one might ask whether the subordinate could freely choose to enter such a relation. This suggests that some of the accusations of recent public controversy raise issues that go beyond mere private relations.

It is striking, however, that many of the public seem to profess indifference to these matters of private sexual conduct on the part of public figures. They seem to be saying that, even if some of these behaviors of which Clinton and others are accused did take place, they are not decisive for evaluating the official's behavior in his or her public role. Perhaps this is symbolic of the enormous changes the ethics of sexual responsibility have undergone in recent years.

This raises a second kind of moral analysis of the sexual conduct of public figures. One might argue that, even if behaviors such as extramarital affairs and relations between supervisor and subordinate in the private world were acceptable, people in public roles may have to meet higher standards. This double-standard-view of sexual morality for public officials might be related to two kinds of concerns.

First, some might hold that **public officials should live lives that are exemplary.** But more than that, public officials might be held to a higher standard because they could come under undue influence from such controversial behaviors. It has been suggested that public officials might be pressured — blackmailed — by their partners in illicit relations to obtain special favors such as job promotions or influence of public policy. All of this suggests that even if such behaviors are morally acceptable for the private citizen and even if the citizen is willing to withhold judgment on such behaviors on the part of public officials, still a complex set of ethical questions is raised by such behaviors in public officials.

Forcing People Out of the Closet

An estimated 3 to 5 million homosexual men, and another 1 million lesbians, reside in America. Many gay activists believe these numbers are even higher, because most homosexuals choose, albeit painfully, to "stay in the closet" and keep their homosexual orientation a secret in order to protect themselves from job discrimination, social condemnation, social ostracism, gay bashing, and the like.

After police raided the Stonewall, a gay bar in New York City's Greenwich Village, on June 28, 1969, many homosexual activists voluntarily "came out" and revealed their homosexual or bisexual orientation. Soon, though, homosexuals were being **"outed"** (their sexual orientation revealed) against their will, usually by other homosexuals.

Michaelangelo Signorile, homosexual author of the now-defunct magazine *Outweek*, who began the practice of outing, claimed that by turning the light of publicity on celebrities and politicians who were actually gay, he was providing role models for the gay community. Another rationale decried the hypocrisy of homosexuals who are "anti-gay" in public, but not in private.

Endnote 82

According to Richard Mohr, professor of philosophy and author of *Gay Ideas: Outing and Other Controversies*, outing is both a permissible and an expected consequence of living morally, but not for the sake of providing role models, exposing political hypocrisy, or being vindictive. As Mohr explains, "Either being gay is okay or it isn't. To accept the closet is to have absorbed society's view of gays, to accept insult so that one avoids harm. **Life in the closet is morally debased and morally debasing.** It frequently requires lying, but it always requires much more. Allowing homosexuality to take its place as a normal part of the human sexual spectrum requires ceasing to treat it as a dirty little secret."

Endnote 84

FINAL COMMENTS

In a pluralistic society such as ours, during an era of such permissiveness, keeping your sexual standards or even knowing the right thing to do is often difficult. For many reasons, people do not follow their consciences when their sexual libido calls. Determining what counts as morally correct sexual conduct is more complex than it may appear. Ethical themes of fidelity to promises, avoiding harm, veracity, and respect for the freedom of others all come into play.

Certain to enliven the 21st century subject of sex in America will be homosexuality: Genetic determination or chosen lifestyle? Homosexual behavior as civil right or criminal wrong? One study suggested homosexual practice may be as low as 1% of the U.S. population, or 2.5 million persons. Meanwhile, the American Psychological Association and other parts of the medical community for years have debated whether homosexuality is a genetic course or a lifestyle choice. Often, the results of that debate have split the association. Related issues are whether homosexuality is a civil *right,* or an orientational matter, or a personal preference.

Other studies show as much as 10%.

Central to these debates is the test of the African-American experience and struggle for civil rights, although one asks: How many formerly black Americans are there? Yet there are cases in medical and psychological history of persons who stopped living a homosexual lifestyle (Exodus International, an organization of persons who formerly practiced a homosexual lifestyle, records 10,000 such changes, including 500 in Washington D.C. alone since 1990.) The Kinsey report on sex said it was easier to come out of the homosexual lifestyle than to recover from alcoholism. Science has not established that homosexual behavior is a *predetermined* behavior. In October 1997 at Harvard Law School's Society for Law, Life and Religion, a polarized debate occurred on the subject of persons reverting from homosexual to celibate or heterosexual lifestyles. "It is indeed possible," noted a reporter present in recounting a Harvard panelist that day.

Dr. Nathaniel S. Lehrman, former clinical director of Kingsboro Psychiatric Center in Brooklyn, New York summarizes epochal history on sexual practice this way: "Three thousand years ago, the Hebrews defined marital sexuality as sacred and banned adultery, incest, homosexuality, promiscuity and bestiality. Christianity and Islam retained these views. The Jews perceived these activities as undermining family stability — thus prohibiting them, despite their worldwide acceptance: Eskimos had traditionally lent their wives to visitors, Egyptian kings married their sisters, and homosexuality was accepted and even elevated in ancient Greece . . . In contrast, the Jews elevated sexual passion into the faithful, conjugal love which cements families, within which children are best nurtured and upon which civilization rests."

Not unrelatedly, the Congress of the United States in 1997 passed the Defense of Marriage Act declaring that the law recognizes a marriage as a union between a man and a woman, and several states have followed suit. These laws were violently opposed by some homosexual groups.

FOR FURTHER INQUIRY

REVIEW QUESTIONS

1. This chapter describes four basic value orientations pertaining to sexuality. What are they? Is there any moral reason why one of these is to be preferred over the others or should we take the position that people can choose whichever orientation suits them?

2. What was the ancient Hebrew view of sexuality?

3. Who is famous for conducting studies of sexual attitudes of Americans in the middle of the twentieth century?

4. What is meant by outing? What ethical problems does it raise?

APPLICATION QUESTION

1. Research the laws governing sexual relations in your state. What practices, if any, are illegal? Discuss what should happen if the law prohibits a practice you believe should be considered ethical.

ENDNOTES

1. Samuel S. Janus and Cynthia L. Janus, *The Janus Report on Sexual Behavior*, John Wiley & Sons, New York, p. 25.

2. Ira L. Reiss, *An End to Shame: Shaping Our Next Sexual Revolution*, Prometheus Books, Buffalo, New York, 1990, p. 121.

3. Janus and Janus, *The Janus Report*, p. 176.

4. About 25% of adult men and 12% of adult women routinely masturbate, though the majority of adults have tried it. Janus and Janus, *The Janus Report,* pp. 30–31; Five to 10% of all Americans are gay or bisexual, Morton Hunt, *Gay,* Farrar, Straus, Giroux, New York, 1987, pp. 105–6.

5. In a 1988 national sample of 18 to 24-year-olds, 40% of the men and 15% of the women had 3 or more partners within the past 12 months; over 80% had at least one partner, Reiss, *An End to Shame*, p. 121.

6. Leslee Welch, *The Complete Book of Sexual Trivia*, Carol Publishing Group, New York, 1992, p. 76.

7. Quoted in Lillian B. Rubin, *Erotic Wars,* Harper Collins, New York, 1990, p. 13.

8. For a brief discussion of Catholic sexual ethics, see James P. Hanigan, *What Are They Saying About Sexual Morality?*, Paulist Press, New York, 1982, pp. 18–20. For a discussion about Jewish sexual ethics, see David Biale, *Eros and the Jews*, Basic Books, New York, 1992. And for a source that briefly summarizes all religious viewpoints on sexuality, see Geoffrey Parrinder, *Sex in the World's Religions*, Oxford University Press, New York, 1980.

9. Hanigan, *What Are They Saying?*

10. Baile, *Eros and the Jews,* pp. 41–59.

11. For a very brief overview of the entire history of sexual ethics, see Robert Baker and Frederick Elliston,

"Introduction," *Philosophy and Sex,* Robert Baker and Frederick Elliston, eds., Prometheus Books, Buffalo, New York, 1984, pp. 11–36.

12. Ira L. Reiss, *Premarital Sexual Standards in America,* The Free Press, New York, 1960, pp. 53–8.

13. Helen E. Fisher, *Anatomy of Love,* W.W. Norton and Co., New York, 1992, pp. 49–51.

14. Reiss, *Premarital Sexual Standards,* p. 56.

15. Ibid., p. 57.

16. An excellent account of religion and sexual behavior in the 19th century is in Peter Garella, *Innocent Ecstasy: How Christianity Gave Ameria an Ethics of Sexual Pleasure,* Oxford University Press, New York, 1985.

17. Garell, *Innocent Ecstasy;* and G.J. Barker-Benfield, *The Horrors of the Half-Known Life: Male Attitudes Toward Women and Sexuality in Nineteenth-Century America,* Harper & Row, New York, 1976.

18. Janus and Janus, *The Janus Report,* pp. 11–12.

19. Ibid., pp. 172–3.

20. Reiss, *An End to Shame,* p. 84.

21. Hunt, *Gay,* pp. 105–6.

22. Kristin Luker, *Abortion & the Politics of Motherhood,* University of California Press, Berkely, California, 1984, p. 94.

23. Rubin, *Erotic Wars,* p. 93.

24. People are more fearful about AIDS and a substantial number are using condoms as a result (80% among homosexual men having anal intercourse, for example). Still, fear of AIDS has not slowed down actual sexual activity in mainstream America, Janus, p. 18; Rubin, p. 79, personal conversation with Jean Burns, Ph.D., Kent State University, Department of Health Education, April 2, 1993, personal interview with Ira Reiss, Ph.D., University of Minnesota, Department of Sociology, April 2, 1993.

25. Hanigan, *What Are They Saying?,* p. 11.

26. Many contemporary theologians are rejecting traditional sexual ethics, including Charles E. Curran, James P. Hanigan, James B. Nelson, Carter Heyward, to name just a few of those prominent on the cutting edge of reform.

27. Findings from the *Girl Scouts Survey on the Beliefs and Moral Vaues of America's Children in 1989* indicate a significant correlation between religiosity and moral certainty and a reverse correlation among adolescents who are not religious.

28. Manis Friedman, *Doesn't Anyone Blush Anymore?* HarperCollins, San Francisco, 1990.

29. For two good discussions on the double standard, see Reiss, *Premarital Sex Standards in America,* pp. 107–116; Rubin, *Erotic Wars,* pp. 23–29; and Reiss, *An End to Shame,* pp. 151–168.

30. Naomi Wolf, "Feminist Fatale," *The New Republic,* March 26, 1992, p. 24.

31. Ira L. Reiss, *Journey into Sexuality,* Prentice-Hall, Englewood Cliffs, New Jersey, 1986, p. 190–193.

32. Albert D. Klassen, Colin J. Williams, and Eugene E. Levitt, *Sex and Morality in the U.S.,* Wesleyan University Press, Middletown, Connecticut, pp. 137–164; *Erotic Wars,* pp. 60–87.

33. Hunt, *Gay,* p. 195.

34. Hunt, *Gay,* see his chapter on "Straight Gays," pp. 187–220.

35. Richard Wasserstrom, "Is Adultery Immoral?" *Philosophy and Sex,* Robert Baker and Frederick Elliston, eds., Prometheus Books, Buffalo, New York, 1984, p. 97.

36. Personal interview, March 26, 1993.

37. Reiss, *An End to Shame,* pp. 218–19; personal interview with Reiss, April 2, 1993.

38. Reiss, *An End to Shame,* pp. 219–20.

39. Ibid., p. 219.

40. Ibid., pp. 157–8.

41. Ibid., p. 158–161.

42. Cited in Gabrielle Brown, *The New Celibacy,* McGraw-Hill, New York, 1989, p. 10; and Norman Hearst and Steven Hully, "Preventing the Heterosexual Spread of AIDS," cited in Reiss, *An End to Shame,* p. 124.

43. Reiss, *An End to Shame,* p. 124.

44. Center for Disease Control Statistics, Atanta, Georgia, telephone interview, March 23, 1993.

45. *New England Journal of Medicine,* May 1990.

46. The Alan Guttmacher Institute Report, November 8, 1990. Available on request from the Institute. Some of the findings also reprinted in Felicity Barringer, "Report Finds 1 in 5 Infected by Viruses Spread Sexually," *New York Times,* April 1, 1993.

47. Ibid.

48. Ibid.

49. Reiss, *An End to Shame,* p. 116.

50. Guttmacher Report.

51. Reiss, *An End to Shame,* p. 125.

52. C. Everett Koop, M.D., "Public Health and Private Ethics," lecture, Minneapolis, October 17, 1986.

53. For a brief overview of medical, legal, ethical, and psychological facts on sexual behavior, see Neville Blakemore & Neville Blakemore, Jr., eds., *The Serious Sides of Sex,* The Nevbet Company, Louisville, Kentucky, 1991, p. 21.

54. For a good account of the history of sodomy laws in the U.S., see Wayne C. Bartee and Alice Fleetwood Bartee, *Litigating Morality,* Praeger, New York, 1992, pp.

31–55; and Richard D. Mohr, *Gay Ideas*, Beacon Press, Boston, 1992, pp. 54–86.

55. Sissela Bok, *Secrets: On the Ethics of Concealment and Revelation,* Vintage Books, New York, 1989, p. 25.

56. Marty Klein, *Your Sexual Secrets,* E.P. Dutton, New York, 1988, p. 56.

57. Bok, *Secrets,* p. 18.

58. U.S. Bureau of the Census, 1993.

59. Janus and Janus, *The Janus Report,* p. 169; Rubin, *Erotic Wars,* p. 179.

60. Flanigan, *What Are They Saying about Sexual Morality?,* p. 13.

61. Michael J. Wreen, "What's Really Wrong with Adultery," *The Philosophy of Sex,* 2nd Ed., Alan Soble, ed., Rowman & Littlefield Publishers; *Savage,* Maryland, 1991, pp. 179–186.

62. Stanley Grenz, *Sexual Ethics*, Word Publishing, Dallas, 1990, p. 87.

63. Bonnie Steinbock, "Adultery," *The Philosophy of Sex,* pp. 191.

64. Rubin, pp. 182–183; Klassen, et. al. *Sex and Morality in the U.S.*, p. 391.

65. Janus and Janus, *The Janus Report*, p. 169.

66. Wreen, *"What's Really Wrong with Adultery?,"* p. 186.

67. Baker and Elliston, pp. 15–16.

68. That Richard Taylor finds a "just" way to conduct a love affair sounds light-hearted at first; his theory is published in a well-respected anthology of philosophical essays Richard Taylor, "The Ethics of Having Love Affairs," *Philosophy and Sex,* Robert Baker and Frederick Elliston, eds., pp. 71–92.

69. Ibid., p. 92.

70. Peggy Vaughan, *The Monogamy Myth,* Newmarket Press, New York, 1989, p. 7.

71. Brown, *The New Celibacy,* pp. 6–7. Among homosexuals, 10% may be celibate today.

72. For an overview of celibacy through history, see Brown, pp. 41–66.

73. Ibid., p. 152.

74. Joan Avan and Diana Walty, *Celibate Wives,* Contemporary Books, Chicago, 1992, pp. 12–13.

75. Gallup Poll, 1989.

76. Dennis Prager, "Faithful Unto Office," *National Review,* July 6, 1992, pp. 47.

77. Bok, *Secrets,* pp. 284, 287.

78. "Take an Honest Look," pamphlet (Columbus Commission on Ethics and Values, Columbus, Ohio, 1989, cited in Susan Terkel, *Ethics,* Lodestar, New York, 1992, p. 89.

79. Katha Politt, "Clinton's Affair?" *The Nation,* February 24, 1992, p. 221.

80. Hunt, *Gay,* pp. 12–13. Some gay activists claim that there are more than two to three times the number of gay people. Furthermore, more Americans have reported homosexual experience. In the Janus survey, respondents were asked whether they had at least one homosexual experience. 22% of the men and 17% of the women said yes, *Janus Report*, p. 53.

81. Estimates vary regarding the number of gays who keep their homosexuality a secret, but they usually vary between two-thirds to nine-tenths, according to Hunt, *Gay,* p. 90; For an excellent discussion of the ethics of outing, see Mohr, Gay Ideas, pp. 11–48.

82. Reported by Alexander Cockburn, "Beat the Devil: The Old In/Out," *The Nation,* August 26/Sept. 2, 1991, p. 220.

83. "Schlafly's Son: Out of the GOP Closet," *Newsweek,* Sept. 28, 1992, p. 18.

84. Mohr, *Gay Ideas,* p. 12

85. Ibid., p. 11.

86. Andrew Sullivan, "Washington Diarist: Sleeping with the Enemy," *The New Republic,* Sept. 9, 1991, p. 43.

87. Mohr, *Gay Ideas,* p. 12.

88. Paul Monette, "The Politics of Silence," *New York Times,* March 7, 1993, Op-Ed.

89. Quoted in Nancy Gibbs, "Marching Out of the Closet," *Time,* Aug. 9, 1991, p. 14.

90. *New York Times,* January 29, 1993, p. A7 (National).

91. Janus and Janus, p. 227.

92. Twenty-five year study by former priest, Richard Sipe.

93. Welch, *Sexual Trivia*, p. 71.

CHAPTER 10

PORNOGRAPHY

"So far, about morality, I know only that what is moral is what you feel good after, and what is immoral is what you feel bad after."

— Ernest Hemingway

"Seven sins . . . (The second is) pleasure without conscience."
— Mahatma Gandhi

Why discuss the subject of pornography? To some, all pornography is obscene and should be banned; to others, pornography is okay as long as it is available only to "consenting adults"; to still others, the only limitations should be those set by individuals governing their own conduct. Some find aspects of the subject too embarrassing even for open discussion; for a few the subject may open old wounds and be painful. Whatever your view, the subject has hounded society for many years. It has been central to a number of criminal cases, and the topic of two national commissions, numerous U.S. Supreme Court cases and congressional proposals. All this suggests it would be quite an omission not to discuss a subject so rich in public moral discourse.

Is pornography harmful or just distasteful? To some, pornography is harmless and should be protected by the First Amendment's "freedom of expression"; to others, it is both harmful and distasteful, degrading to women, and dangerous to society. What are your views about pornography? Is it wrong? Is it right? Should it be banned, censored, regulated, or left alone?

(Editors' Note: Is it necessary to view pornography to discuss it? Certainly not. A person need not have gone to Vietnam to know it was a dubious war. We are able to study thousands of subjects without actually experiencing the presence of them. There is ample information in this chapter to gain knowledge of pornography, and no one should infer from the existence of this chapter that use of pornography is suggested or implied as a necessary part of its study.)

"What is essential is invisible to the eye."
— Saint-Exupery,
The Little Prince

Cynthia A. Stark, Ph.D., University of North Carolina, is assistant professor of philosophy at the University of Utah. Her publications on pornography are: "Pornography, Verbal Acts and Viewpoint Discrimination," *Public Affairs Quarterly*, October, 1998 and "Is Pornography an Action?: The Causal vs. the Conceptual View of Pornography's Harm," *Social Theory and Practice*, Summer 1997. Contributor was **Emily Baker**, former Mississippi Judge and Director of the Applied Ethics Institute at St. Petersburg Junior College.

For some, if one is to give credence to studies such as that of Dr. James McGough from the University of California-Irvine, there is a danger of pornography users becoming addicted to pornography. This comes about, it is thought, because the body produces a chemical, epinephrine, which locks into the brain the experiences one has when one is sexually aroused; these remain and we continue to feed these experiences into the mind, creating a need for additional activity. Users of pornography then move from casual use, to addiction, to acting out their fantasy through anti-social behavior.

Endnote 1

The study concludes that just as one does not know when the first drink is taken, if there is within oneself a predisposition to alcoholism leading to life as an alcoholic, so too does one not know if he is among those persons whose viewing of pornography will lead to addiction, unusual sexual behavior, perhaps even to sexual molestation. Sex is everywhere in today's society and pornography is sex in raw depiction. The U.S. Supreme Court recognized society's interest when it stated that sex is "a great and mysterious motive force in human life that has indisputably been a subject of absorbing interest to mankind throughout the ages; it is one of the vital problems of human interest and public concern."

Endnote 2

Here we will explain the history of pornography as it relates to freedom of expression, report results of studies (including those of two national commissions), consider the views of feminist and other groups, and ponder information both pro and con, so that you may use your critical thinking skills to reach your own moral/ethical decisions on this contemporary subject.

CHIEF LEARNING OUTCOME

I understand the impact of pornography on the individual and society in the light of legal and ethical reasoning.

A note of caution: Words not normally used in polite society are workaday terms of the pornography industry and those who must deal with it. While they may not be terms you would wish to use in conversation, they reflect the content of pornography and the way it is described by law enforcement, the courts, and medicine.

"Congress shall make no law . . . abridging the freedom of speech or of the press . . ." These words, found in the **First Amendment** to our United States Constitution, create "freedom of expression" as one of the basic tenets of our democratic form of government.

Endnote 3

Is this concept of "freedom of expression" an absolute? Is the phrase "Congress shall make no law" to be taken literally? Those who speak in defense of pornography often emphasize that they are defending First Amendment rights rather than pornographic content; therefore, the issue of "freedom of expression" must be examined in any meaningful discussion of pornography.

"Pornography" can be defined as the depiction of erotic behavior intended to cause or causing sexual desire or excitement — deriving from Greek words meaning "writing about whores." *The World Book Dictionary* defines pornography as "obscene writings, or pictures." **Obscenity** has Latin roots meaning "offending modesty or decency; impure; filthy; vile."

Endnote 12

HISTORY OF PORNOGRAPHY AND ITS CENSORSHIP

Pornography has been present in society throughout recorded history. Drawings reflecting sexual activity were discovered on the excavated walls of the ancient city of Pompeii. Early Greek and Roman writings and art objects depicted then-current sexual practices including the use by adult males of young males for sexual pleasure. Oriental art was renowned for its sexually explicit depictions of the various positions of intercourse, particularly in pictures and delicate jade carvings.

THE ORIGIN OF CENSORSHIP

Censorship — the official restriction of speech, writings or visual expression — comes into play when such forms of expression are thought to harm the public morals or public good. Its roots date back to ancient China and Egypt where official views were usually enforced in the name of politics and religion.

In the West, people have put great weight upon the authority

KEY CONCEPTS

Censorship — The official restriction of speech, writings or visual expression

Obscenity — Filthy or foul language or depiction characterized by immodesty and indecency; compare with U.S. Supreme Court rulings noted in this chapter.

Communications Decency Act (1996) — A law passed by the U.S. Congress that made it a crime to use a telecommunications device or an interactive computer service to transmit knowingly to persons under 18, or display in a manner that is available to persons under 18, obscene, indecent or patently offensive materials, where "patently offensive" is judged by contemporary community standards. The law was declared unconstitutional by the U.S. Supreme Court in 1997.

Pornography — The depiction of erotic behavior intended to cause or causing sexual desire or excitement

The Hicklin Test — Whether the tendency of the matter charged as obscenity is to deprave and corrupt those whose minds are open to such immoral influences, and into whose hands a publication of this sort may fall

The Roth Test — Whether to the average person, applying contemporary community standards, the dominant theme of the material, taken as a whole, appeals to the prurient (wanton) interest

The Miller Test — The basic guidelines for the trier of fact must be: (a) whether 'the average person, applying contemporary community standards,' would find that the work, taken as a whole, appeals to the prurient interest; (b) whether the work depicts or describes, in a patently offensive way, sexual conduct specifically defined by the applicable state law; and (c) whether the work, taken as a whole, lacks serious literary, artistic, political, or scientific value.

Endnote 4

of the written word. The British writer Chaucer said in 1380, "What people cannot know from experience, they assume on the basis of authority." In Europe, books were costly, rare, and available primarily to the literate and wealthy. This exclusivity went hand in hand with considerable freedom of expression. However, in 15th century Europe, with the advent of the printing press, books became more readily available and this medium was used to exploit what aristocrats might call the baser side of life — the lower appetites of humankind.

As more people learned to read, both the Roman Church and the government began to be concerned about literary content and its effects on the new class of readers. As a result, there were often two publications of a writing — one an original uncut edition, expensive and available for the aristocrats, while the other was a more delicately worded, less expensive version for mass production.

Just what is obscenity? What forms of expression resulted in censorship in Europe and the United States? How was and is obscenity defined? Can it be defined? How have the courts expanded or restricted the definitions as they apply to pornography? What interest groups have advanced their beliefs regarding pornography and why? Answering these questions charts our path through this chapter.

Yet, to this day, pornography raises moral and ethical issues in society and continues to be a frequently litigated issue. Through the years the rulings of the United States Supreme Court have changed, though perhaps not as drastically as views in the general society.

Your own perspective may be colored by the way in which you were first introduced to pornography. Was it presented as exciting — something adults got to see but children didn't, something "macho" to do, a movie viewed from an adult collection without its owner's knowledge? Was it presented as something lacking good taste, a terrible act of sin, causing you to feel uncomfortable and guilty?

Each of us is a product of our own environment and experience which influence our perspective. We then are responsible for the moral environment we pass on to our children. What will be that moral environment as it pertains to pornography? What perspective will pass on to them?

Justice Potter Stewart once addressed perspectives when he said, "A book worthless to me may convey something of value to my neighbor, and so it is with pornography, for what is abhorrent to me may well be exciting to my neighbor."

Endnote 14

BRITISH LEGAL HISTORY

Our own country has perspectives and roots deeply embedded in the British environment of our forefathers. The history of pornography in our own society can best be tracked through the manner in which the courts have acted. Because our law has its roots in English law, it is necessary to examine the background of pornography within the English system.

Queen vs. Hicklin (1868) is the landmark English obscenity case. Henry Scott, a respectable citizen and member of the Protestant Electoral Union, an organization active in an attack upon the Jesuits, had seized from him 250 copies of a booklet. The booklets were ordered destroyed by a local Justice as authorized under Lord Campbell's Act. However, an appeal was taken and Benjamin Hicklin, the Recorder, directed the booklets be returned pending an opinion from the Queen's Bench, the high Court of England. Hicklin determined the booklet's purpose was not to "corrupt the morals of youth" but was instead an attack upon the Roman Catholic Church. The High Court disagreed with Hicklin and denied the appeal: "It is quite certain that it would suggest to the minds of the young of either sex, or even to persons of more advanced years, thoughts of impure and libidinous character . . . the work itself is, in every sense of the term, an obscene publication, . . . as the law of England does not allow for any obscene publication, such publication is indictable."

The Hicklin Test was then set forth by the Queen's Bench: "The test of obscenity is this, whether the tendency of the matter charged as obscenity is to deprave and corrupt those whose minds are open to such immoral influences, and into whose hands a publication of this sort may fall."

Endnotes 18, 19, 20

American Legal History

The American colonies were not without their own restrictions. There had been a ban on all obscene materials in Massachusetts since 1712. The City of Boston was to become well known for its censorship efforts. After the Revolution, the Constitution separated Church and State (1788) and the Bill of Rights came into being with its First Amendment Protection (1791).

Endnote 21

Erosion of Hicklin

Hicklin had reflected a "class" distinction that was apparent when it was applied in the case of *United States vs. Clarke* (1889). Dr. Clarke wrote a pamphlet allegedly covering "venereal, sexual, nervous, and special diseases." He was indicted and was brought before the court for sending this "scientific" treatise through the mail.

Endnote 25

The judge gave the Hicklin test to the jury in his charge: "You must consider carefully the contents . . . and then the effect that the reading of such contents would naturally have on the class of persons in to whose hands this publication might fall, whose thoughts, emotions, or desires are liable to be influenced or directed by reading matter such as the publication contained. There is to be found in every community a class of people . . . so intelligent . . . that their minds are not liable to be affected . . . . There is another large class to be found in every community — the young and immature, the ignorant, and those who are sensually inclined — those who are liable to be influenced to their harm . . . ." The jury using the Hicklin test found Dr. Clarke guilty, so justice was determined not using the general "aver-

Endnote 26

age man" standard but on a standard set by "youth, immaturity and ignorance."

In the *United States vs. Kennerley* (1913) decision, Judge Learned Hand challenged the "Hicklin Test," saying: "I scarcely think that they would forbid all which might corrupt the most corruptible, or that society is prepared to accept as its own limitations those which may perhaps be necessary to the weakest of its members."

Endnotes 27, 28

THE ROTH TEST

Endnote 34

In 1957 the Supreme Court had the opportunity to resolve the issue and establish its own "test" for obscenity in *Roth vs. United States* (1957). A certain Mr. Roth ran a publication and sales office in New York City using mail circulars to advertise and sell his products. Roth was convicted on four counts of a 26-count indictment for "mailing obscene literature." His conviction was affirmed by the United State Circuit Court of Appeals, and he then appealed directly to the United State Supreme Court.

Endnote 35

The Constitutional question presented to the court was "Whether the Federal Obscenity Statute violated the provision of the First Amendment." Here, for the first time, the Supreme Court specifically held that "Obscenity is not within the area of constitutionally protected speech." "Obscenity," then, seems to lie outside the protection of the First Amendment and is, therefore, an area where Congress or — through application of the Fourteenth Amendment — any of the states, can enforce regulations.

The new test established in Roth is stated as follows: "Whether to the average person, applying contemporary community standards, the dominant theme of the material, taken as a whole, appeals to the prurient (wanton) interest." The material should continue to be utterly without any redeeming social importance in order to be excluded from First Amendment protection. Little did the court realize that pornographers would seize this phrase and include "moral" lessons, quotes from great literary works, or medical information in order to qualify as having "redeeming social importance."

Endnotes 36, 37

The community standard was considered to be a "national" standard. The Supreme Court was fearful that unless a national standard was maintained, we would have in each state a separate interpretation of the First Amendment. However, not all Justices were pleased with the new test. Justice Harlan in writing a separate opinion in this case said, "the court merely assimilates the various tests into one indiscriminate potpourri."

Endnote 38

As the 1960s brought increased interest in civil rights and relaxation of many social mores, the court attempted to keep the "Roth" test, and not further define obscenity. In *Jacobelles vs. Ohio*, a 1964 case, Justice Potter Stewart admitted, "I shall not today attempt to define the kind of material . . . embraced . . . but, I know it when I see it."

Endnote 39

The Supreme Court under Chief Justice Earl Warren was reputed to be liberal in its views, to be concerned with extending basic fairness to all, and it was under this court that many of these decisions concerning obscenity had been rendered. The court itself was to undergo changes beginning with the appointment by President Nixon in 1969 of conservative Warren Burger as Chief Justice of the Supreme Court, the first of Nixon's four appointments. The make-up of the new court would result in a more conservative and restrictive view of pornography.

The "new" Supreme Court continued to struggle with obscenity cases and with their failure to arrive at a clear definition of obscenity. In 1981's *The Brethren*, authors Bob Woodward and Scott Armstrong noted that each Justice seemed to have his own view of material to be prohibited and his own definition of what was "obscene."

Here are the individual views on pornography and obscenity of the then-members of the U.S. Supreme Court as reported in *The Brethren*:

In Jacobelles vs. Ohio, *a 1964 case, Justice Potter Stewart admitted, "I shall not today attempt to define the kind of material . . . embraced . . . but, I know it when I see it."*

Endnote 48

Justice Black — An absolutist who thought there should be no exception to the First Amendment. Found it impossible to define.

Justice Blackmun — Loathed it, found it distasteful and degrading to women.

Justice Brennan — Thought obscenity the one type of expression that should not be protected. Children and unwilling viewers should be protected. Was obscene if there were erections — penetration and oral sex were all right only if there were no erections.

Justice Burger — Loathed it, thought local standards should apply. Thought states could regulate obscene acts: normal or perverted sex acts (actual or simulated), masturbation, excretion, and display of genitals.

Justice Douglas — Said it was impossible to define and should never have been declared an exception.

Justice Harlan — Uncertain. During many of the cases, portrayed actions had to be described for his comments due to his sight problems.

Justice Marshall — Thought it primarily a question of personal privacy. More amused than shocked.

Justice Powell — Shocked at films, favored expansion of the privacy doctrine.

Justice Rehnquist — His opinion did not go so far as to say "any books without pictures could not be ruled obscene," although others seem to be willing to go that far.

Justice Stewart — Could not define it but said he knew it when he saw it. Had his own "Casablanca" test. Thought only "hard core" should be defined obscene.

Justice White — Should be able to define obscene acts so long as the acts were "hard core" and appealed to "prurient interest;" he allowed no erections, penetration, anal or oral sex.

In 1973, the court was scheduled to hear a number of pornography cases. Within the court there was a split in reasoning as to obscenity. Should the standard of "utterly without redeeming social value" remain? Should the absolutist (no laws) view prevail? Should there be no restrictions except for juvenile and unconsenting adults? Should the "right to privacy doctrine" prevail?

THE MILLER CASE: NASTY MAIL BAN

Endnote 56

In the landmark decision of Miller vs. California (1973), a 5–4 decision, Miller was convicted of violations of obscenity laws for mailing unsolicited and sexually explicit brochures, which included group pictures with two or more men and women (some with aroused genitalia), engaged in actual sex acts, all in order to advertise an adult film and adult books.

His conviction was affirmed by California's appellate court, and Chief Justice Warren Burger of the United States Supreme Court, in writing the majority opinion of the court announced: "Apart from the initial formulation in the Roth case . . . no majority of the court has at any given time been able to agree on a standard to determine what constitutes obscene, pornographic material subject to regulation under the States' police power . . . We have seen 'a variety of views among the members of the court unmatched in any other course of constitutional adjudication' . . . This is not remarkable, for in the area of freedom of speech and press the courts must always remain sensitive to any infringement . . . This much has been categorically settled by the court, that obscene material is unprotected by the First Amendment . . . The First and Fourteenth Amendments have never been treated as absolutes."

Endnote 57

THE MILLER TEST

Endnote 58

The court recognized the danger in regulating all expression and so limited regulations to those works that depicted and/or described sexual conduct. The new "Miller Test" is then set forth: "The basic guidelines for the trier of fact must be: (a) whether 'the average person, applying contemporary community standards,' would find that the work, taken as a whole, appeals to the prurient interest; (b) whether the work depicts or describes, in a patently offensive way, sexual conduct specifically defined by the applicable state law; and (c) whether the work, taken as a whole, lacks serious literary, artistic, political, or scientific value."

The court would no longer consider the "utterly without redeeming social value" standard but did go on to give to the states guidelines for activity that could be regulated, including: (a) "Patently offensive representations or descriptions of ultimate sexual acts, normal or perverted, actual or simulated. (b) Patently offensive representations or descriptions of masturbation, excretory functions, and lewd exhibition of the genitals." The court went on to say: "Sex and nudity may not be exploited without limit by films or pictures exhibited or sold in places of public accommodation any more than live sex and nudity. . . ."

So we see Miller reflecting "Contemporary Community Standards" — local standards, rather than one national standard — and a "lack of serious literary, artistic, political or scientific" value used rather than the "utterly without redeeming social value" as put forth in Memoirs. The court changed the "Community Standards" stating: "People in different States vary in their tastes and attitudes, and this diversity is not to be strangled by the absolutism of imposed uniformity. . . ."

Burger denounced the attitude of the dissenting justices: "The protection given speech and press was fashioned to assure unfettered interchange of ideas for bringing about the political and social changes designed by the people . . . But the public portrayal of hard core sexual conduct for its own sake, and for the ensuing commercial gain, is a different matter."

Justice Douglas in his dissenting opinion stated: "There are no constitutional guidelines for deciding what is and what is not 'obscene'. . . ." He added that "any regime of censorship should only be adopted by a constitutional amendment and not by court decisions . . ." Under Miller we see the court move from the early Hicklin test to the present contemporary test that gives more power to the states.

Endnotes 59–63

That the framers of our Constitution intended "freedom of expression" to exist in order to allow for exchange of ideas and even for political debate goes without question. However, at the time of the Constitution's framing, the camera had not been invented, much less the movie camera or home video. Not in their wildest dreams could those men have envisioned pornography as it is today, so the question remains: Just how far should freedom of expression be extended? Should there be special protections for special classes of people?

SPECIAL PROTECTION OF MINORS

By the late 1970s, states that continued to pass statutes regulating pornography were now following the Supreme Court Guidelines set forth in Miller. In their efforts to prevent pornography from reaching unconsenting adults and minors, many states, counties, or cities passed "behind the counter laws," requiring stores to place "adult" publications in a location where they could not be viewed by minors and where they were not available for purchase without a specific request from an adult.

New York vs. Ferber (1982)

Endnote 66

The Supreme Court, for the first time, directly addressed the issue of child pornography in the case of *New York vs. Ferber* (1982). Ferber, a New York bookstore owner, was convicted for selling films depicting male minors under the age of 16 masturbating, in violation of a law prohibiting "knowingly promoting a sexual performance by a child . . . by distributing material which depicts such a performance." The New York Court of Appeals reversed the lower court decision based on the statute's failure to include a clear obscenity standard.

The Supreme Court held that the statute did not violate the First Amendment as applied to the states through the Fourteenth Amendment and recognized that the exploitation of children through child pornography was a serious national problem, and there was compelling interest to protect children, therefore states were entitled to more leeway in the regulation of child pornography.

The court stated: "The state's interest in 'safeguarding the physical and psychological well-being of a minor is compelling' . . . (courts) have sustained legislation aimed at protecting the physical and emotional well-being of youth even when the laws have operated in the sensitive area of constitutionally protected rights . . . virtually, all of the States and the United States have passed legislation proscribing the production of or otherwise combating 'child pornography.'" The court found that states could go further than Miller in order to protect children, saying: **"Recognizing and classifying child pornography as a category of material outside the protection of the First Amendment is not incompatible with our earlier decision."**

Endnotes 67, 68

Information Providers' Coalition vs. FCC (1991)

The United States Supreme Court made clear in Ferber that children should be protected and gave states the power to do so. New technology brought a new avenue of pornography, and a new temptation to children — "Dial-A-Porn." In *Information Providers' Coalition vs. FCC* (1991), a petition for review of a FCC order regulating access to "Dial-A-Porn" was filed. The petition was denied by the Ninth Court of Appeals where the Circuit Judge held that "an effective means of limiting minors' access to Dial-A-Porn services must be instituted," and the Supreme Court denied the Petition for review, thereby adding additional protections for minors. One study of children ages 10–15 who were involved with Dial-A-Porn showed that the children, both male and female, became hooked on phone sex and continued calling until parents were finally made aware through large bills. Several cases reflected more than 300 calls and even though the study was conducted some 18 months to two years later, the children were still ashamed, felt guilty and were able to recall the content of the messages. The degree of harm to these children, if any, cannot be determined fully for some years.

Endnote 69

One study of children ages 10–15 who were involved with Dial-A-Porn showed that the children, both male and female, became hooked on phone sex and continued calling until parents were finally made aware through large bills.

Endnotes 70, 71

Reno vs. American Civil Liberties Union (1997)

In June of 1997, the United States Supreme Court, in the case of *Reno v. American Civil Liberties Union*, considered the constitutionality of the provisions of the Telecommunications Act of 1996 known as the **Communications Decency Act (CDA).** The CDA made it a crime to use a telecommunications device or an interactive computer service to transmit knowingly to persons under 18, or display in a manner that is available to persons under 18, obscene, indecent or patently offensive materials, where "patently offensive" is judged by contemporary community standards. Violations of the Act were punishable by a maximum fine of $250,000 and a maximum jail term of two years. The intent of this legislation was to curb minors' access to pornography on the Internet.

Pornography on the Internet

The Internet is an interlinked set of computer networks that are able to communicate with one another. This large network is divided into various areas defined by the way in which information is organized, displayed, and accessed. These areas include, among others, the Usenet, bulletin board systems (BBS's), on-line chat groups and the World Wide Web. In the 1990s, the Internet grew at an astounding rate.

A wide variety of sexually explicit materials is available on the Internet, including pornographic photos and films, sexually-oriented chat rooms and news groups, X-rated video games, and erotic on-line stories. How much sexually explicit material is present, and how accessible it is to minors, is a matter of controversy. In 1995, Marty Rimm conducted a study at Carnegie Mellon University of the availability and nature of sexually explicit materials on the Usenet and BBS portions of the Internet. He found that there were 1000 adult-oriented BBS's and that 50 per cent of the nearly 6-million images downloaded from these had pedophilic or paraphilic themes. Moreover, he found that two of the ten most popular newsgroups on the Usenet dealt with sexually explicit topics. Of the digitized images stored on the Usenet, 83.5% of the pictures are pornographic. In 1997, two years after the Rimm study was completed, there were over 4,000 sexually oriented Websites.

The CDA was introduced by Senator James Exon (D-Nebraska) in response to the extensive presence of pornography on the Internet. It was passed by Congress and signed into law by President Clinton in 1996. As soon as the CDA became law, a group of twenty plaintiffs led by the ACLU filed suit in a U.S. federal court in Pennsylvania. The plaintiffs alleged that the CDA was in violation of the First Amendment. The district court found in favor of the plaintiffs. The case was appealed by the government and the Supreme Court held, in a 7–2 vote, that the CDA was unconstitutional.

Historically courts have assigned to the state an interest in protecting children. So, for example, as we saw above, the high court upheld the conviction of a man who distributed child pornography,

In 1997, two years after the Rimm study was completed, there were over 4,000 sexually oriented Websites.

Endnote 71a

Endnote 71b

Endnote 71c

Endnote 71d

Endnote 71e

Endnotes 71f–i

Endnotes 71j, k

and it approved the FCC's regulation of minors' access to **"Dial-A-Porn."** Moreover, the courts have also recognized parents' interest in controlling the upbringing of their children, including what expression their children might be exposed to. Advocates of the CDA regarded the legislation as falling within the state's right to regulate speech that might be harmful to minors or to aid parents in their legitimate efforts to protect their children from speech they regard unsuitable. Their specific concerns included worries that children are not emotionally prepared to handle sexually explicit images, especially those that have proven the most popular, i.e., images of "deviant" sexual behaviors such as sado-masochism, bestiality, and activities involving excrement or urination. Those who favored the CDA were also concerned about the exploitation of children through the production of *child pornography* circulated via the Internet. And, they were concerned about the abduction of children by on-line pedophiles.

Some who opposed the CDA held that the amount of sexually explicit material on the Internet was highly exaggerated, and they called into question the validity of the Rimm study. Others claimed that sexually explicit images, while perhaps abundant on the Internet, are not easily accessible by children. This is largely because private BBS's require proof of age such as a driver's license or credit card number and because the images available are contained in binary files which cannot be converted into full-color images without a certain understanding of Unix programming. (Graphic images on the World Wide Web are less widespread and less extreme than those found on BBS's or the Usenet.) Some opponents claimed that since obscenity, child pornography, and kidnaping are already illegal, no further laws are necessary to combat illegal activities on the Internet. And others maintained that the CDA would criminalize expression that should be protected, such as information available on the Planned Parenthood Web site about how to obtain an abortion or information about safe sex found on the Critical Path Aids Project Web site. Finally, some who objected to the CDA argued that sexually explicit discussion should be encouraged on the Internet because it offers an opportunity for people anonymously to get badly needed information about sex and an opportunity to reclaim public discourse on sexuality from pornographers who spread misinformation and play upon people's anxieties about sex.

The main argument against the CDA, however, was that it violated a citizen's First Amendment right to freedom of speech. The ACLU, in its suit against the government, claimed that the law was unconstitutional since it, among other things, criminalized speech that is protected by the First Amendment, and was impermissibly overbroad and vague. The Supreme Court concurred with the ACLU's contentions. First, the majority opinion noted that indecent speech is protected by the First Amendment. It is true, it acknowledged, that the court upheld a restriction on indecent speech when that speech

Endnote 71l

Endnotes 71m–n

Endnotes 71o–t

Endnote 71u

was broadcast on the radio at a time when it could easily be heard accidentally by children. However, the risk of children accidentally encountering indecent expression on the Internet is small since one must take affirmative steps to access that material. Hence the rationale for prohibiting indecent broadcasts at certain times of the day does not support the restrictions contained in the CDA. Second, the court maintained that the terms "indecent" and "patently offensive" were not sufficiently defined. Hence the law would have a chilling effect on expression since people would not know exactly what types speech would be considered criminal.

Endnote 71v

While many disapprove of governmental regulation of expression on the Internet, most agree that the presence of "hard-core" pornography poses a problem given the number of minors who go on-line. The most promising solution on this front is the use of Internet screening products, which would enable parents (and perhaps schools and other institutions populated by minors) to limit children's access to sexually explicit materials.

Endnote 71w

ADDITIONAL APPLICATIONS

Freedom of expression continues to be an issue. In the past few years, there have been attempts to close an exhibit of photographer Robert Mapplethorpe because it was "obscene"; and to challenge the National Endowment of the Arts for refusing grants to controversial artists such as Karen Finley (who, as part of her performance, spreads excrement over her body), claiming that such rejection violated NEA's guidelines and reflected a "political rather than artistic" basis for rejection. In addition, there have been successful efforts to secure labeling for musical lyrics (led, in part, by Tipper Gore, wife of Vice-President Al Gore) in order for parents to monitor recordings available to children and to themselves ban obscene recordings.

Cable TV has allowed more persons to view pornography — particularly children and adolescent viewers, causing them to be exposed to all types of sexual attitudes, to actual or simulated sexual performances, and certainly to explicit sexual practices on television — sexual practices that they might otherwise never encounter. Many of these films are unrated and while many appear in late evening hours, they are being viewed by children. Special adult video stores, adult sections in regular video stores, adult sections of book stores, and adult movie houses can all be easily located. So, in spite of the long history of court cases, the pornography business flourishes.

How extensive is pornography? How harmful is pornography to society? Does the explicit sex shown on TV influence societal attitudes? Does the sexually explicit material desensitize a person's view of sexuality? Who, if anyone, benefits from pornography? What do studies about pornography reveal?

GOVERNMENTAL STUDIES

The President's Commission on Obscenity and Pornography, 1967–70

The United States Congress, concerned over the national problem of pornography, established in October 1967 a Commission on Obscenity & Pornography to study the causal relationship between pornographic/obscene materials and antisocial behavior, including juvenile delinquency. The Commission, appointed by President Lyndon Johnson, was to report its findings and recommendations to Congress as to how the nation should deal with pornography.

Endnote 73

After two years of intensive work at a cost of approximately $2-million, a multi-volume report was completed and forwarded to Congress in 1970. L. Kupperstein and W.C. Wilson in their 1970 study, *Erotica and Antisocial Behavior: An Analysis of Selected Social Indicator Statistics*, reported that, for the period from 1960–69, even though there was more sex-related materials available, adult sex crimes did not increase any more than did other offences. These conclusions were bolstered by the Denmark data which showed that sex crimes actually decreased after the Danes legalized pornography in the 1960s.

Endnote 74

Endnote 77

Endnote 78

The President's Commission Findings

The President's Commission rendered its findings, saying that studies have "found no evidence to date that exposure to explicit sexual materials plays a significant role in the causation of delinquent or criminal behavior among youth or adults. The Commission cannot conclude that exposure to erotic materials is a factor in the causation of sex crimes or sex delinquency."

Endnote 79

The Commission recommended that "all federal, state and local laws prohibiting the sale of any erotic material to consenting adults be repealed" since it found "no evidence" to link exposure to pornographic materials either to criminal behavior or to juvenile delinquency, nor did it find that pornography would adversely affect the moral attitudes of our country even though there were findings that exposure to pornography was very likely where sexual deviance was concerned.

Endnote 80

The Commission reported that the majority of Americans resisted the idea of any restrictions on their freedom of expression rights and that Americans felt strongly about the First Amendment.

The report was not well received in Congress. Senate resolution was adopted, rejecting the Commission findings, and President Nixon declared the report to be "completely unsatisfactory."

Endnote 81

Commission Recommendations to Congress

Among those recommendations the Congress did act upon was the one to restrict distribution of unsolicited sexually explicit materials through the mail and one to strengthen the laws concerning distribution of sexually explicit materials to minors that included limitations on public displays of pornographic materials. These decisions, in

Endnote 82

part, were affected by the work of **Dr. Victor Cline**, clinical psychologist at the University of Utah, who had been involved in research and treatment of sex offenders and had determined that where there had been intensive exposure to "hard-core" pornography, he had been able to isolate a **"near universal four-step pattern"** in the effect pornography had on sex offenders.

Cline reported: "First, there is an addictive effect. The man gets hooked on obscene materials, which seem to provide him with a powerful and exciting aphrodisiac. So he keeps coming back for more to get his sexual "turn-ons." Second, there is an escalation in his need for rougher and more sexually shocking materials in order to get the same sexual stimulation as before. He prods his wife or partner into increasingly bizarre sexual activities. When the woman finally resists, the relationship crumbles. Third, there occurs over time a desensitization to the material's effect. What was at first gross, taboo, repulsive, or immoral — though still sexually arousing — in time becomes acceptable, commonplace, and, in a sense, legitimized. The person begins to believe that everyone does it. And fourth, there is an increased tendency to start acting out the sexual activities seen in the pornography. What was at first fantasy has become reality.

Endnote 83

THE ATTORNEY GENERAL'S COMMISSION, 1985–86

Dissatisfaction prevailed as a result of the President's Commission report. Because there was no clear national policy concerning pornography, a second commission was formally announced by Attorney General Edwin Meese III in May of 1985. Its mission was to "determine the nature, extent, and impact on society of pornography in the United States, and to make specific recommendations . . . concerning more effective ways in which the spread of pornography could be contained, consistent with constitutional guarantees."

Endnote 85

The Attorney General's Commission was given far less time and money to do its investigation. The Commission's two-volume report was issued in July 1986, wherein the Commission, after receiving testimony and reviewing research in the field, reported a radical change in pornography since the study completed in 1970. Pornography had not only become more violent and more degrading; it now contained depictions of force and torture, and extreme violence including disfigurement and murder. In addition, both its production and distribution were found to be dominated by "Organized Crime."

Endnote 86

A total of 92 recommendations for curtailing pornography and its resulting harm were suggested in the report to the Attorney General.

Pornography and Anti-Social Behavior

In the matter of the causal relationship between pornography and anti-social behavior, the Commission found it necessary to establish categories of pornography in order to better relate its findings:

Class 1) Sexually Violent Pornography: That pornography featuring actual/simulated sexually explicit violence, some involving sadomasochistic themes, complete with whips, chains, et cetera; and rape and violent force, with the woman eventually begging for more; even extreme violence including disfigurement or murder, the "slasher" type used in snuff films. In this category the Commission found: "That the available evidence strongly supports the hypothesis that substantial exposure to sexually violent material as described here bears a causal relationship to antisocial acts of sexual violence and, . . . possibly, to unlawful acts of sexual violence."

Endnote 88

Class 2) Non-Violent but with Degradation, Domination, Subordination or Humiliation: That which makes up a great amount of the available pornography. As to this type of pornography, the Commission points to women being shown as "sex objects" and concludes: "Substantial exposure to materials of this type bears some causal relationship to the level of sexual violence, sexual coercion, or unwanted sexual aggression."

Endnote 89

Class 3) Non-Violent and Non-Degrading: A small amount of material, with the participants appearing to be equal and willing participants. The Commission concluded: "We are persuaded that material of this type does not bear a causal relationship to rape and other acts of sexual violence."

Endnote 90

Class 4) Nudity: The Commission addressed nudity and concluded: "By and large we do not find nudity that does not fit within any of the previous categories to be much cause for concern."

Endnote 93

Class 5) Child Pornography: defined as the sexual abuse of a child and as such violates state and federal laws. The great bulk of child pornography is produced by child abusers themselves in largely a "cottage industry" fashion. The Commission concluded: "Child pornography is extraordinarily harmful both to the children involved and to society . . . dealing with child pornography in all of its forms ought to be treated as a governmental priority of the greatest urgency."

Endnote 94

The Commission noted that, while some laws could be strengthened, the problem did not seem to be "the law" or "the courts," but rather the "lack of enforcement" of the existing laws.

THE TWO REPORTS COMPARED

The 1986 Report bolstered some of the conclusions of the 1970 Commission based on Dr. Cline's earlier findings by citing the testimony

Statements:	Per Cent Saying Statement True	
PUBLIC OPINION AT THE TIME OF THE TWO REPORTS	1970	1985
Pornographic materials provide information about sex	61%	52%
They lead some to commit rape or sexual violence	**49%**	**73%**
They offer a safe outlet for those with sexual problems	27%	34%
They lead some people to lose respect for women	**43%**	**76%**
They can help improve sex lives of some couples	47%	47%
They provide entertainment	48%	61%
They lead to a breakdown of morals	**56%**	**67%**
Source: 1986 Attorney General's Commission (Base)	(2,485)	(1,020)

of convicted Florida murderer Theodore Bundy, who was implicated in the deaths of as many as 28 females. Bundy revealed that at about age 13, he discovered "girlie-magazines" and moved on to detective story pornography and then on to "hard-core" pornography, with violence displayed toward women. He continued to watch this violent pornography, and after two years began acting violently, beginning his killing spree.

Endnote 84

In comparing the 1970 Presidential Commission Report with the 1986 Attorney General's Report, it is interesting to consider an attitude survey comparing approximately the same periods of time. It was conducted through a national "person to person" survey concerning the general public's perceptions and attitudes about pornography. Notice the comparison between the 1970 findings and those of a 1985 Gallup-Newsweek poll as set forth in the 1986 Final Report of the Attorney General's Commission on Pornography and reflected on the next page:

Endnote 75

MORAL VIEWS ABOUT PORNOGRAPHY

What has been presented thus far has focused primarily on how the law treats pornography. Independent of how the law views this material, there are at least three different ethical perspectives worth considering.

THE CONSERVATIVE VIEW

Some, perhaps influenced by early Christian views about sexuality (see Chapter 9 for a discussion), are distinctly distressed with any

Endnote 132

sex, at least any sex outside marriage. Sexuality is for them, at best, necessary to provide for unity and procreation within marriage. The Vatican, said in its pastoral response: "While no one can consider himself or herself immune to the corrupting effects of pornography and violence or safe from injury at the hands of those acting under their influence, the young and the immature are especially vulnerable and the most likely to be victimized. Pornography and sadistic violence debase sexuality, corrode human relationships, exploit individuals — especially women and young people — undermine marriage and family life, foster anti-social behavior and weaken the moral fibre of society itself . . ." It continued, "Thus, one of the clear effects of pornography is sin. Willing participation in the production or dissemination of these noxious products can only be judged a serious moral evil . . ."

Any other sexual expression, even in verbal or photographic form is, in principle, morally tainted. Since pornographic materials almost always would involve sexual representation of the human figure for purposes of sexual gratification outside marriage, it would be condemned. It is not the consequences of pornography — any acting out that produces violence, degradation, and the like — that are the problem. Even the Class 3 non-violent, non-degrading material poses a problem of immorality. Pornographic representations involving "deviant" sexual practices would be so much the worse.

THE CIVIL LIBERTARIAN VIEW

Occasionally, those with more liberal attitudes actually attempt to defend the value (or at least the innocence) of pornography. For example, Fred R. Berger, who supports pornography and the "pleasure" theory, says: "It seems to me, however, that we have yet to make the most important response. . . . The more important issue turns on the fact that a great many people like and enjoy pornography and want it as part of their lives. . . . For a society that accepts freedom and self-determination as centrally significant values cannot allow interferences with freedom on such grounds as these. . . ."

Endnote 131

Most traditional liberals, however, have tended not to endorse or praise pornography, but to tolerate it. For holders of these views, respect for autonomy for competent adults is key as long as it does not lead to harm to others. This position, sometimes called the "harm-to-others" view, would limit pornography only when it produced effects on those who were incompetent (children) or those who had not consented. Liberals are acutely aware of the subtle distinctions required to separate pornography from artistic expression. They recognize that some of the greatest art and literary expressions include elements that some would consider pornographic. It is not that pornography can never be distinguished from great art, but that sometimes the lines are hard to draw. For liberals, as long as those involved consent and no one is harmed, pornography will be tolerated. It will not be the most dominant moral concern.

A DIVIDED FEMINIST VIEW

Recently, a new moral voice has emerged on the subject providing a new perspective. This voice is complex and rich, drawing on an emerging perspective often called feminism — a view which is endorsed by a number of male ethicists as well. Two quite different perspectives are seen.

Pornography as Exploitation

Many feminists have been concerned about the increase in pornography, especially the increase in violence toward women depicted in today's pornography. Feminists note the increasing number of rapes, especially "date rapes," and the fact that rapes are happening at ever younger ages.

Both Helen E. Longino and Ann Gary in their writings about pornography from the "feminist" point of view, add to the conception of pornography that "the role and status of women is degraded," and, further, that women are treated as "mere sex objects" to be "exploited and manipulated." Yet there are some feminists who object to any curtailment of freedom of expression, despite these overwhelming feminist concerns. That women feel strongly about pornography and its effects on them is certainly illustrated by this excerpt from the impassioned testimony of Andrea Dworkin, an attorney and author active for years in the fight against pornography, as given before the Attorney General's Commission:

Endnotes 97, 98

> In the country where I live as a citizen, there is a pornography of the humiliation of women where every single way of humiliating a human being is taken to be a form of sexual pleasure for the viewer and for the victim . . . where women are murdered for the sexual pleasure of murdering women . . . Pornography is used in rape — to plan it, to execute it, to choreograph it, to engender the excitement to commit the act. . . . When your rape is entertainment, your worthlessness is absolute. You have reached the nadir (the lowest point) of social worthlessness. The civil impact of pornography on women is staggering. It keeps us socially silent, it keeps us socially compliant, it keeps us afraid in neighborhoods; and it creates a vast hopelessness for women, a vast despair. One lives inside a nightmare of sexual abuse that is both actual and potential, and you have the great joy of knowing that your nightmare is someone else's freedom and someone else's fun . . .

Endnote 99

Lorenne M.G. Clark, another feminist, does not lash out as strongly as Dworkin. Nevertheless in *Liberalism and Pornography*, she points out that pornography is "hate literature" and "relies on depicting women in . . . degrading . . . situations" and participating in such

Endnote 100

degradation "willingly." But she espouses a broader view by pointing out that the harmful effects of pornography apply to both men and women and that the use of pornography will actually prevent equality between the sexes from becoming a reality.

Philosophy professor Ann Gary, in her *Pornography and Respect for Women*, points out that the content of pornography generally treats women as sexual objects, as a "means to an end." By doing so, pornography violates the moral principles of Immanuel Kant and his "respect for persons." Gary goes on to raise questions about "censorship as a control mechanism" and the possibility of creating pornography that is both non-sexist and morally acceptable.

Endnote 102

Gary's position is that even if pornography is immoral she is still not sure that censorship would be the correct way to handle regulation. What about her position that pornography is "here to stay"? Is it possible to change pornography? Would pornography as Gary envisioned it be a marketable item in today's society?

ANOTHER TACK ENTIRELY:
PORNOGRAPHY AS SEXUAL DISCRIMINATION

Endnote 104

Taking a totally different tack on pornography, feminist author Catherine MacKinnon claims that pornography is in fact "sexual discrimination." MacKinnon has been active along with Andrea Dworkin in the drafting of pornography laws using a "civil rights" theory and attempting to hold "those who profit from and benefit from the injury accountable to those who are injured." These laws are not based on censorship, but rather on the theory that pornography can be legally defined as a form of sexual discrimination against women and would, therefore, be a violation of women's civil rights and, as a result, such laws would be enforceable under civil rights legislation and allow for damages.

Gary's position is that even if pornography is immoral she is still not sure that censorship would be the correct way to handle regulation.

An earlier ordinance, drawn for the City of Minneapolis, was vetoed by its mayor. The idea, however, caught on and has now been used as a basis for laws in other areas of the country. A similar Indianapolis ordinance was challenged and declared "unconstitutional" by the Seventh Circuit of the United States Court of Appeals. In this case the city admitted that it sought to restrict pornography that would not be "obscene" under the Miller test, but insisted that they were not regulating speech but conduct — the "unacceptable subordination of women."

Endnote 105

The court found that even though the ordinance was drafted as civil rights legislation, the very wording of the law illustrated that the city was attempting to regulate speech, including speech that went beyond that which would be considered legally obscene under the Miller test set out by the U.S. Supreme Court and thereby protected speech under the First Amendment. The ordinance was ruled unconstitutional.

So we see, then, many feminists objecting to pornography and supporting regulation under one theory or another, yet all women do not support the suppression of pornography, either under the afore-mentioned "freedom of expression" restrictions or as "civil rights violations." Betty Friedan, an ardent feminist, has this to say.

Endnote 106

> I want to express my view, on behalf of a great many women in this country, feminists and believers in human rights, that this current move to introduce censorship in the United States in the guise of suppressing pornography is extremely dangerous to women. It is extremely dangerous to the rights of women as well as men to speak and think freely and to fight for our basic rights, to control our lives, or bodies, and have some degree of economic and political equality . . . There is a dangerous attempt to use a feminist smokescreen and even to claim that this anti-pornography suppression legislation is a weapon against sex discrimination and a weapon to liberate women from the degradation of pornography. Now I speak as someone who has no particular liking for pornography. . . .
>
> You know, some pornography certainly does degrade women. It also degrades men and it degrades sex. The pornography that pushes violence is particularly deplorable. But the forces that want to suppress pornography are not in favor of suppressing guns. They are not in favor of legislation — they would undo legislation — protecting women and children from actual violence. What are they up to? . . .
>
> Underneath the sideshow, they are trying to excite the passions of the people against ideas — sexually titillating or repulsive sexually — but ideas, not actual deeds, not violence, not the obscenity of poverty — to take our attention away while we are being manipulated in this country, being manipulated, and our rights are being threatened . . .
>
> I deplore that even a very few feminists have been diverted by the issues of pornography from the basic protection of all our rights. Now, I urge all women to have their eyes opened to the dangers to our basic rights by the pushing of anti-pornography legislation.

Feminists, then, while they dislike pornography and agree to its "degrading connotations" to women and may agree to its "immorality," differ in their view as to regulation.

Endnote 107

Then, there is the challenge to the sexual discrimination view by feminists Lisa Duggan, Nan Hunter, and Carole Vance. They express concern for the scope of materials that might be reached by legislation of this type, believing that far-right elements could use these ordinances to "enforce their sexually conservative world view." Their article points out that this type of legislation is more likely to "impede, rather than advance, feminist goals" and could indeed be a "useful tool in antifeminist moral crusades." They claim "the argument that pornography itself plays a major role in the general oppression of women contradicts the evidence of history."

Endnotes 108, 109

Feminists, then, while they dislike pornography and agree to its "degrading connotations" to women and may agree to its "immorality," differ in their view as to regulation. Among feminists who do believe in curtailment, there are differences in views as to how that regulation should be accomplished.

SPECIAL PROBLEMS OF PORNOGRAPHY

Child Pornography

The visual depiction of a child taking part in explicit sexual conduct is, in essence, the picture of an ongoing crime and is prohibited by law, as is all sexual activity of adults with minors. State and federal laws have prohibited child pornography and the Supreme Court has upheld in *Ferber* its prohibition and declared it to be outside the protection of the First Amendment, even without a finding of obscenity.

Commercial child pornography is not openly produced or sold in the U.S., although customs officials regularly confiscate such pornography being smuggled into the United States. Most child pornography today is produced by and/or for pedophiles, often with the very children they molest. Pedophiles — adults whose sexual preference is to have sex with children — place great value in their collections of child pornography. According to law enforcement authorities and court cases, they take their own pictures, save them, and swap them with other pedophiles. It is not unusual for some of their pictures to be traded about and eventually reach commercial producers in Europe, where they are added to publications, and then find their way back into America in a public form.

One American child, according to an Alabama customs agent, was able to be followed through foreign magazines for several years. Early editions reflected only her nudity, while later ones portrayed her in explicit sexual actions. Finally, in the last edition in which she was to be seen, she was pictured involved in an action depicted as unmistakably "hard-core" while her glassy-eyed expression seemed to indicate she was in a drugged state, unlike her appearance in the earlier editions.

Searches of future magazines failed to show any further trace of this child whose pictures seemed to span a time from approximately age 10 to age 15. The agent shared his frustrations at never being able to locate this child and his concerns over her failure to reappear.

What happens to these children? Can they ever hope to enter a "normal world," to lead a "normal life"?

What happens to these children? Can they ever hope to enter a "normal world," to lead a "normal life"? If they do get away from that life, do they live in fear of being "found out"? What about "guilt feelings" and "embarrassment"? Can they ever trust or enjoy true love? What if this child was your daughter?

Child pornography is used to lower the inhibitions of children, to convince them that other children have engaged in this activity — and in doing so, had fun, thus encouraging children to cooperate with

Endnote 114

their molester. "Regular" pornography as well as pornographic "comics" are also used to condition children, to arouse their curiosity, and to entice them to participate in sexual activity.

Many pedophiles apparently maintain an extensive picture library. Their pictures and tapes are often very carefully hidden in order to be used for their own personal satisfaction, especially when they are without child victims. Police report that pictures of children can also be used by the pedophile in blackmailing them not to tell, or to continue with the activity, and/or to coerce them to bring in other children to "play."

There are people who support the idea of sex with children, and these persons, including pedophiles, have a way of locating each other and of working together. The advent of the computer and of computer bulletin boards have made locating each other and keeping in touch easier. There are actual organizations that openly support sex between adults and children and who actively lobby to have "the age of consent" lowered so as to have more children legally available for sexual activity.

These organizations publish newsletters that are circulated among their memberships, covering stories referring to sexual activity with children and featuring pictures of young children. One such publication exploits what it calls "man/boy" love.

The Austin Pedophile Study Group II originally published a pamphlet entitled *How to Have Sex with Kids* and another, *Women Pedophiles*? Other organizations that support and advocate child/adult consensual sexual activity include the Rene Guyon Society, the Child Sensuality Circle, the Pedo-Alert Network (PAN), and the National Diaper Pail Foundation.

That child pornography is of great importance to child molesters is illustrated by the testimony of Joe Henry, a pedophile, before the U.S. Senate on February 15, 1985, testifying about the content of one of his letters to another pedophile: "If it were not for all the pictures . . . I would think it was all just a fantastic dream. I will always be grateful to you for . . . giving me a brief taste of heaven. . . . Pedophiles survive through explicit letters and the purchase and trading of child pornography, because live victims are not always available."

A 1986 study by Abel, as reported by the National Coalition Against Pornography, showed that the 240 pedophiles studied averaged 30–60 victims each before even being caught, and on the average, eventually will abuse about 380 children.

Sexually abused children experience guilt and blame. "The use of children as subjects of pornographic materials is harmful to the physiological, emotional, and mental health of a child," said the court in Ferber. If they are involved in the sex acts over a period of time they assume even more blame because they view themselves as having allowed it to continue; yet they are fearful, feel helpless and often are too ashamed to tell anyone of the abuse. Their self-esteem is low to non-existent, so these children generally possess poor social skills. Sociologists suggest the anger they carry within is directed not only

Pedophiles survive through explicit letters and the purchase and trading of child pornography, because live victims are not always available. —Joe Henry, a pedophile

Endnote 115

Endnote 116

Endnote 118

at the abuser but at the adults who have allowed this to happen by failing to afford them protection. But most of all their anger is directed at themselves, which often results in emotional problems.

The 1970 Commission Report did not reflect any real focus on child pornography, but as sexual exploitation of children became more apparent, Congress in 1977 conducted its own investigation. The Senate Judiciary Committee in its report had this to say: "Child pornography and child prostitution have become highly organized, multimillion-dollar industries that operate on a nationwide scale."

Endnote 120

A permanent subcommittee dealing with the Investigation on Child Pornography and Pedophilia was established by Congress. It cited a 1986 Report of the Los Angeles Police Department, showing that of 700 child molesters, more than one-half had child pornography in their possession and 80 percent owned some type of pornography.

Endnote 121

Unfortunately, while laws restricting children being portrayed in pornography are on the books, child pornography continues to flourish in the United States. This occurs even though each depiction of child pornography is actually a crime in action.

PORNOGRAPHY AS BIG BUSINESS AND CRIME

The 1986 Attorney General's Commission found that the pornography industry had not only grown at an alarming rate but had reached out to new markets, and was now primarily a California-based industry of multibillion-dollar scope. Performers themselves earn little in the overall scheme of pornography production. There are some 12–24 major companies. These producers, in addition to wholesalers and retailers, all receive sizeable profit, so much so that organized crime was attracted to the industry and now plays a substantial role in this deplorable business where the "gain far outreaches the risk."

Endnote 122

Endnote 123

A 1978 FBI report stated: "Information received from sources of this Bureau indicates that pornography is (a major) income-maker for La Cosa Nostra (a major U.S. criminal organization sometimes, incorrectly, synonymous with 'the Mafia') in the United States behind gambling and narcotics. Although La Cosa Nostra does not physically oversee the day-to-day workings of the majority of pornography business in the United States, it is apparent they have 'agreements' with those involved in the pornography business, allowing these people to operate independently by paying off members of organized crime for the privilege of being allowed to operate in certain geographical areas."

By 1975, organized crime controlled 80% of the industry and it is estimated that this figure is between 85 and 90% today.

Endnote 124

The overwhelming bulk of obscene and pornographic materials is produced in the Los Angeles area. Organized crime families from Chicago, New York, New Jersey, and Florida are openly controlling and directing the major pornography operations in Los Angeles. According to then-Chief Daryl F. Gates of the Los Angeles Police Department, **"organized crime"** infiltrated the pornography industry in Los Angeles in 1969 due to its lucrative financial benefits. By 1975, organized crime controlled 80% of the industry and it is estimated that this figure is between 85 and 90% today.

Endnote 125

To illustrate the profit margin, consider one film, "Deep Throat." This was produced in Florida through the "Columbo organized crime family" at a cost of only $25,000. By the year 1982, it was estimated to have grossed an estimated $50-million, making its producers wealthy.

Endnote 126

Publishers of magazines and books fall into the "high-profit" category. The market for sexually explicit magazines has expanded, and represents some of the most widely distributed magazines in the country. Adult theater profits have declined due to the now highly profitable home video market. Movies for cable television and "Dial-A-Porn" are recent additions to this profitable pornography industry.

Endnote 127

With a moneymaking base totaling millions of dollars annually, those involved take a strong stand against any restrictions on freedom of expression. They are willing not only to fight court battles but to make large contributions to organizations that support First Amendment freedoms.

"(Pornography is) a clear and present danger to American public health."
—*C. Everett Kopp, M.D.*

ORGANIZATIONAL STANDS

The Defenders of Freedom of Expression

The American Civil Liberties Union (ACLU) founded in 1920 has been a longtime defender of pornography and takes a strong stand against any erosion of the First Amendment. The ACLU has made its presence known in recent fights to support absolute "freedom of expression" in the Arts. It has been involved in an Arts Censorship Project to ensure such freedom. The ACLU is joined in its stand by other organizations including the National Coalition Against Censorship (NCAC), People for the American Way, and the Boston Coalition for Freedom of Expression.

Endnote 128

The Movement Opposing Pornography

On the other side, there are organizations working diligently for the removal of obscenity and pornography. Reverend Donald Wildmon of the American Family Association attempted to block a documentary about censorship because of certain scenes in the television film, "Damned in the USA." Two organizations, the National Coalition against Pornography and Focus on the Family, have founded grass roots coalitions to halt the spread of pornography. The Religious Alliance Against Pornography holds an annual conference featuring well-known religious leaders as speakers, all as part of its battle-plan to restrict pornography.

Endnote 129

Dr. C. Everett Koop, M.D., and former U.S. Surgeon General, called pornography a "crushing public health problem" posing a "clear and present danger to American public health." He issued a call to physicians to "stem the tide" of pornography adding, "This material is

Endnote 130

blatantly anti-human. Its appeal is to a dark and anti-human impulse. We must oppose it as we oppose all violence and prejudice."

FINAL COMMENTS

Pornography in all forms has been reviewed. Different views have been put forth. We have studied concerns for preserving our inherent right of freedom of expression; for preserving our First Amendment rights against all regulation of "freedom of speech"; for the need to limit that freedom due to the harm that pornography is said to cause, or because of the need to respect persons. We have heard arguments that autonomy would allow consenting adults to decide what they should see or read; listened to the concerns that because of the harm to both men and women, society would be best served by limitation; and heard the more paternalistic view that the state should protect its citizens. We have considered a range of views: that pornography should be completely banned because it is immoral; that it is wrong because it circumvents the natural end of marriage; and finally that pornography should be balanced against the right to privacy — which many think should extend beyond the home.

What are your views now? Should pornography be restricted? If so, then to what degree? Under what method should it be restricted? Can you support your view with sound moral/ethical reasoning? Which approach best illustrates your own view?

FOR FURTHER INQUIRY

REVIEW QUESTIONS

1. Explain the difference between pornography and obscenity.
2. What is the Miller test? Is all pornography restricted under Miller?
3. Do you believe that consenting adults should have the right to buy/see/read whatever they wish, including pornography, and why or why not?
4. Using each of the approaches to moral reasoning covered in class, discuss whether or not pornography would be allowed and why or why not?

ENDNOTES

1. Cline, Victor. "The current status of research on pornography's effects on human behavior," *Pornography: A Report*. American Family Association, Tupelo, MS. 1989.

2. *Roth v. U.S.*, 354 U.S. 476 (1957).

3. United States Constitution, Amendment I.

4. Chaucer, Geoffrey (1380), quoted from *The Bonfire of Liberties*, Censorship of the Humanities, produced by Texas Humanities Resource Center, for a traveling exhibition sponsored by the Florida Center for the Book, 1992.

5. Perrin, Noel. *Dr. Bowdler's Legacy, A History of Expurgated Books in England and America*. New York: Atheneum,1969.

6. Ibid., p. 115

7. Quoted in *Queen v. Hicklin*, (*ANA Regina v. Hicklin*) L.E. 3 Q.B. (1868). Lord Campbell's Act, 20 + 21 Viet., c83.

8. Perrin, Ibid., p. 60

9. Ibid., p. 127

10. Ibid., p. 167

11. Hoyt, Olga G. and Edwin P. *Censorship in America*. New York: The Seabury Press, 1970, p. 25.

12. Barnhart, Clarence L., ed., *World Book Dictionary*, Field Enterprise Educational Corp., 1971.

13. Ibid.

14. *Ginsburg v. U.S.*, 383 U.S. 463 (1966).

15. *Dominos Rex (Crown) v. Edmund Curl*, 2 Str. 788, 93 English Rept. 849 (1727).

16. Ibid.

17. Lord Campbell's Act, op. cit.

18. *Queen v. Hicklin*, (*ANA Regina v. Hicklin*) L.E. 3 Q.B. (1868).

19. Ibid., p. 371

20. Ibid.

21. Acts and Laws of the Province of Massachusetts Bay Coloney, CV, § 8.

22. *Commonwealth of Penn. v. Jesse Sharpless*, 2 Serq and Rawle 91. (1815).

23. Ibid.

24. Ibid.

25. *U.S. v. Clarke*, 38 F. 732 (1889).

26. Ibid., p. 734

27. *U.S. v. Kennerley*. 209 F. 119 (1913).

28. Ibid., p. 121

29. *Halsey v. New York Society for Suppression of Vice*, 136 N.E. 219 (1922).

30. Ibid.

31. *U.S. v. One Book Entitled Ulysses*, 5 F.Supp. 182, (SDNY, 1933), 72 F.2d 705 (1934).

32. Ibid.

33. Ibid.

34. Roth, op. cit.

35. 18 USC § 1461.

36. Roth, op. cit., p. 485

37. Ibid., p. 490

38. Ibid., p. 500

39. *Jacobellis v. Ohio*, 378 U.S. 184 (1964).

40. *A Book Named "John Cleland's Memoirs of a Woman of Pleasure", et. al. v. Attorney General of Massachusetts*, 383 U.S. 413 (1966).

41. Ibid., p. 419 (349 Mass. at 73).

42. Ibid.

43. Ginsberg, op. cit.

44. Ibid., pp. 465–68

45. *Redrupt v. New York*, 386 U.S. 767 (1967).

46. *Stanley v. Georgia*, 394 U.S. 557 (1969).

47. Ibid., p. 565.

48. Woodward, Bob, and Scott Armstrong. *The Brethren*. New York: Avon Books, The Hearst Corporation, 1981.

49. Ibid., pp. 290–300

50. *Paris Adult Theater I v. Salton*, D.A. et al., 413 U.S. 49 (1973).

51. Ibid., p. 53

52. Ibid., p. 53

53. Ibid., p. 69

54. Ibid., p. 72

55. Ibid., pp. 112–13

56. *Miller v. California*, 413 U.S. 15 (1973).

57. Ibid., pp. 22–23

58. Ibid., p. 24

59. Ibid., p. 25

60. Ibid., p. 25

61. Ibid., p. 33

62. Ibid., pp. 34–35

63. Ibid., p. 40

64. *Federal Communication Corporation v. Pacifica Foundation, et al.*, 438 U.S. 726 (1978).

65. Ibid., p. 727

66. *New York v. Ferber*, 458 U.S. 747 (1982).

67. Ibid., pp. 756–58

68. Ibid., p. 763

69. *Information Providers Coalition for the Defense of the First Amendment et. al. v. F.C.C.*, 928 F. 2d 866 (9th, 1991).

70. Ibid.

71. Cline, op. cit.

71a. Excerpts from the "High Court's Decision on the Communications Decency Act," Ibid., A22.

71b. Blake T. Bilstad, "Obscenity and Indecency in a Digital Age: The Legal and Political Implications of Cybersmut, Virtual Pornography, and the Communications Decency Act of 1996," *Santa Clara Computer and High Technology Law Journal* 13 (1997):373.

71c. Ibid., 337.

71d. Ibid., 331. See also, Laura J. McKay, "The Communications Decency Act: Protecting Children from On-Line Indecency" *Seton Hall Legislative Journal* 20(1996):470–71.

71e. Marty Rimm, "Marketing Pornography on the Information Superhighway: A Survey of 917,410 Images, Descriptions, Short-Stories, and Animations Downloaded 8.5 Million Times by Consumers in Over 2000 Cities in Forty Countries, Provinces and Territories," *Georgetown Law Journal*, 83 (1995):1849. See also, Anne Wells-Branscombe, "Internet Babylon? Does the Carnegie Mellon Study of Pornography on the Information Super-Highway Reveal a Threat to the Stability of Society?," *Georgetown Law Journal* 83 (June 1995):1935; Catharine A. MacKinnon, "Vindication and Resistance: A Response to the Carnegie Mellon Study of Pornography in Cyberspace," *Georgetown Law Journal* 83 (June 1995):1959; and Carlin Meyer, "Reclaiming Sex from the Pornographers: Cybersexual Possibilities," *Georgetown Law Journal* 83 (June 1995):1969.

71f. Bilstad, 339.

71g. Ibid.

71h. Philip, Elmer-DeWitt, "On a Screen Near You: Cyberporn—It's Popular, Pervasive and Surprisingly Perverse, According to the First Survey of Online Erotica," *Time*, 146/1 (July 3, 1995): 38.

71i. Ibid., 341.

71j. Bilstad, 380.

71k. Lawrence Biemiller and Goldie Blumenstyk, "Supreme Court Strikes Down Law on Internet Decency," *The Chronicle of Higher Education* 43/43 (July 3, 1997), A21.

71l. C. Edwin Baker, "First Amendment and the Internet: Will Free Speech Principles Applied to the Media Apply Here?," *St. John's Journal of Legal Commentary* 11 (Summer 1996):713.

71m. Elmer-DeWitt, 38.

71n. McKay, 47–75; Bilstad, 351–55. See also, Janet M. La Rue, "The Communications Decency Act of 1996: Sensible, Not Censorship," *St. John's Journal of Legal Commentary* 11 (Summer 1996):721.

71o. See Barry Steinhardt, "The Communications Decency Act: Morally Necessary or Politics as Usual?," *St. John's Journal of Legal Commentary* 11 (Summer 1996):727. See also, Bilstad, 331, n. 45.

71p. Elmer-DeWitt, 38; Bilstad 348.

71q. Bilstad, 349–50.

71r. Ibid., 383.

71s. Steinhardt, 728–29.

71t. See Meyer, *passim*.

71u. Bilstad, 379

71v. See *FCC v. Pacifica Foundation*, 438 U.S. 726, 748-50 (1978) (holding that an afternoon broadcast of George Carlin's famous Filthy Words monologue was unprotected indecent speech because of the pervasive presence of radio broadcasts and the unique accessibility of afternoon broadcasts by children).

71w. Bilstad, 382.

72. *Luke Records Inc. v. Navarro* (1992) as reported in *St. Petersburg Times*, June 7, 1990.

73. Public Law 90-100 (1967).

74. Report of the Commission on Obscenity and Pornography, New York: Bantam, 1970. (Here-in-after referred to as "Report").

75. Abelson, H., R. Cohen, E. Heaton, and C. Suder (1970), Technical Report of the Commission on Obscenity and Pornography, Vol. 6, Washington, D.C.: Government Printing Office, 1-255.

76. Final Report of the Attorney General's Commission on Pornography, with Introduction by Michael J. McManus. Nashville, Tenn: Rutledge Press, 1986, p. 257. (Here-in-after referred to as "Final Report").

77. Ibid., pp. 311–324

78. Ibid., p. 259

79. Ibid., p. 223

80. Report, op. cit., p. 80

81. Senate Resolution 477, 91st Congress, 116 Cong. Rec. 36478 (1970).

82. 39 U.S.C. § 3008 et. sec.

83. Kirk, Jerry R. Dr., *The Power of the Picture: How Pornography Harms*. Pomona, Calif.: Focus on the Family, 1989.

84. Dobson, James, and Gary L. Bauer, *Children at Risk, The Battle for the Hearts and Minds of Our Kids*. Dallas: Ward Publishing, 1990.

85. Attorney General's Commission on Pornography, Final Report Vol. I and II. Washington, D.C.: Government Printing Office, 1986.

86. Ibid.

87. Final Report, op. cit., p. 290.

88. Ibid., pp. 38–40.

89. Ibid., pp. 41–42.

90. Ibid., pp. 43–45.

91. Ibid., p. 40.

92. Ibid., p. 42.

93. Ibid., p. 47.

94. Ibid., p. 70.

95. *Standing Together*. Vol. 6:1, Feb.–March, 1992: Cincinnati, OH. The National Coalition Against Pornography.

96. ACLU Arts Censorship Project, "Above the Law; the Justice Department's War Against the First Amendment." New York: ACLU, 1991.

97. Longino, Helen E., "Pornography, Oppression, and Freedom: A Closer Look," in Marilyn Pearsall, ed. *Woman and Values*. Belmont, CA: Wadsworth Publishing Co., 1986.

98. Gary, Ann, "Pornography & Respect for Women." *Social Theory and Practice*. Vol. 4:4. Tallahassee, FL: F.S.U., Dept. of Philosophy, 1978: pp. 395–421.

99. Dworkin, Andrea, testimony before the Attorney General's Commission on Pornography, New York, NY, Jan. 22, 1986 as reported in Resources for Concerned Citizens from the National Coalition Against Pornography, Cincinnati, Ohio.

100. Clark, Lorenne M.G. "Liberalism and Pornography," *Pornography and Censorship*, ed. D.Copp and S. Wendell, Buffalo, N. Y.: Prometheus Books, 1983. rpt. in *Ethical Theory and Social Issues*. David Theo Goldberg. New York: Holt Reinhart and Winston, Inc., 1989. First published under the title "Sexual Equality and the Program of an Adequate Moral Theory, The Poverty of Liberalism," Resources for Feminist Research, Special Publication 5, Toronto: Ontario Institute for Studies in Education, 1979, pp. 302–306.

102. Gary, op. cit. See pp. 395–421.

104. MacKinnon, Catherine. *Feminism Unmodified*. Cambridge, Mass.: Harvard Community Press, 1987. Reprinted as "Pornography, Civil Rights & Speech" in *Morality & Practice*. 3rd ed, James P. Sterba. Belmont, Ca.: Wadsworth Pub. Co.

105. *American Booksellers Association, Inc. v. William H. Hudnut III*, 598 F. Supp. 1316, 105 S.Ct. 1172 (1984).

106. Friedan, Betty, speaking at a Public Information Briefing on the Attorney General's Commission on Pornography, the proceedings of a National Coalition Against Censorship, Jan. 16, 1986 and published in *The Meese Commission Exposed*, New York: NCAC, 1987.

107. Ibid., p. 24

108. Duggan, Lisa, Nan Hunter, and Carole Vance, "Feminist Antipornography Legislation" from *Women Against Censorship*, ed. Varda Bernstein, Groundwood Books/Douglas & McIntyre, 1985 and reprinted in *Morality in Practice*, 3rd ed. James P. Sterba. Belmont, Ca.: Wadsworth.

109. Ibid., p. 326

110. Senate Bill 1521, 102d Congress, 2d Session.

111. Ibid., Sec. 2 (1) ,(2) [Report No. 102-372]

112. Heins, Marjorie. "Crime & Punishment American Style," a paper distributed by The Arts Censorship Project, ACLU, NY.

113. Ibid.

114. Lanning, Kenneth V. Child Molesters: A Behavioral Analysis for Law Enforcement Officers Investigating Cases of Child Sexual Exploitation. National Center for Missing & Exploitation of Children. Washington, D.C., 1986.

115. Henry, Joe. Testimony of a Child Molester, United States Senate: 15 February 1985. rptd. R. P. "Toby" Tyler, San Bernardino County Sheriff's Department. San Bernardino, Calif.

116. "Research on Pornography: The Evidence of Harm, Pornography's Relationship to Child Sexual Exploitation and Abuse." National Coalition Against Pornography, Cincinnati, Ohio. 1989.

117. Child Abuse Conference. Pascagoula, MS: March 13, 1985.

118. Ferber, op. cit., p. 758

119. Addis, Don. *St. Petersburg Times*. Jan. 7, 1993.

120. Senate Report 438, 95th Congress, 1st Session. 5(1977) as quoted in Report, op. cit., p. 132

121. Research, op. ct., (LAPD) p. 3

122. Final Report, op. cit., p. 341

123. Ibid.

124. Ibid., p. 293.

125. Ibid., p. 294.

126. Ibid., p. 295.

127. "Executive Summary: Images of Children, Crime and Violence in Playboy, Penthouse, and Hustler Magazines," 1986, issued by the United States Department of Justice, National Center for Missing and Exploited Children, Washington, D.C., noted: pg. 3, "*Playboy* reaches 15,584,000 people per issue, *Penthouse* 7,673,000 and *Hustler* 4,303,000. This compares to *Psychology Today* with 4,704,000 readers, *Sports Illustrated* with 13,034,000, and *Ms.* with 1,635,000."

128. Heins, Marjorie, op. cit., p. 101

129. ACLU, op. cit.

130. *American Medical News*, October 10, 1986.

131. Berger, Fred R. "Pornography, Sex, and Censorship," *Social Theory and Practice*. Vol. 4:2, Tallahassee, FL: F. S. U. Dept. of Philosophy. 1977.

132. "Pornography and Violence in the Communication Media," A Pastoral Response, Pontifical Council for Social Communication, Vatican City, Office for Publishing and Promotion Services, United States Catholic Conference, Washington, D.C., 1989.

133. Ibid., pp. 5–6

THE CONQUEROR

CHAPTER 11

ETHICS AND THE ENVIRONMENT

"To see the Earth as we now see it, small and blue and beautiful, in that eternal silence where it floats, is to see ourselves as riders on the Earth together . . . brothers who do not see they are truly brothers."

— Archibald MacLeish,
after the first landing on the moon

"Man has lost the capacity to foresee and to forestall. He will end by destroying the Earth."

— Albert Schweitzer

Environmental ethics is theory and practice about appropriate concern for, values in, and duties to the natural world. Environmental ethics as a separate field of study was unknown in Western philosophy until the mid-1970s. That was to change rapidly. Today, thousands of works have been published, by policymakers, lawyers, environmental professionals, foresters, conservation biologists, ecologists, philosophers, economists, sociologists, historians, developers, business persons, citizens — all with an ethical concern about human uses of and relations to the natural environment.

Endnote 1

For example, if **global warming** is occurring, then sea level is likely to continue to rise, and changes in weather patterns are also likely to occur. Many scientists think that global change has already occurred due to anthropogenic forces. While it is not arguable that humans can exert global-scale influence on the planet, it is not known whether changes induced by humans are equal to or greater than (or complementary to) natural changes. Scientific research must continue in order to address these questions.

Change is a key component of climate. It has been shown that human migrations due to climate change are not unprecedented in the Earth's history. But are the changes that have been induced by

---

Holmes Rolston III, Ph.D., University of Edinburgh, 1958, is University Distinguished Professor at Colorado State University where he is especially known as a leading scholar in environmental ethics having published *Philosophy Gone Wild* (1986), *Environmental Ethics* (1988) and *Conserving Natural Value* (1994).

humans causing such rapid changes that humans cannot adapt? Will the depletion of the ozone layer cause death to many species and disease for humans? Will desertification render large areas of arable land useless? The answers to these questions are controversial and probably lie somewhere between the extreme positions. The seriousness of the problems has not been quantified. Some think it unwise to institute expensive changes when the problems and consequences are uncertain. Alternatively, the wait-and-see approach can have disastrous consequences. Tougher laws seem necessary.

Because the actions of humanity may have far-reaching effects, many environmental problems must be considered global in scope. The actions of people residing in mid-latitude areas of the Earth may affect people living in high latitudes and vice versa. Solutions to major problems (e.g., ozone-layer depletion) cannot be devised without attention to global concerns. People must work together on both a global and an individual level in order to solve many of the Earth's myriad environmental problems. The proposed solution to the ozone-layer depletion problem is an excellent example of an international effort to solve a global-scale problem.

CHIEF LEARNING OUTCOME

I recognize the kinds and nature of environmental issues and can apply approaches to moral reasoning to those problems.

Human power to affect nature has dramatically escalated, for example, with species loss or global warming. Industrialization, advanced technologies, global capitalism, consumerism, and exploding populations raise the profound question: **Are humans in a sustainable relationship with their environment?** Have they distributed the benefits derived from natural resources equitably? Have they been sensitive enough to the values present in and the welfare of the myriads of other species that inhabit the same biosphere?

Philosophers have thought about nature for millennia, since ancient Greece and Asia. There is an ethic implicit in many of these worldviews, but it was hardly developed as an environmental ethics. Following the Enlightenment and the scientific revolution, nature in Western philosophy came to be regarded as a value-free realm, governed by causal forces. Scientists like Isaac Newton and philosophers like René Descartes held that two fundamentally different metaphysical entities existed, mind and matter. Values in nature arose only with the interests and preferences of conscious minds. Animal bodies and plant organisms were more or less biological machines. So for four centuries, Western philosophy was dominantly humanistic or, to use a more recent term, anthropocentric (human-centered). People were what counted and all that counted in ethics.

Vigorous interest in nature and human responsibilities toward it is one of the unexpected changes of perspective in philosophy in recent centuries. Somewhat ironically, in the century when humans, with their increasing industry and technology, seemed further and further from nature, having more knowledge about natural processes and more power to manage them, just when they were more and more rebuilding their environments, the natural world emerges as a focus of ethical concern. Such environmental ethics is still novel, and developing. There are 12 primary areas.

1. HUMANISTIC AND NATURALISTIC ETHICS

That there ought to be some ethic concerning the environment can be doubted only by those who believe in no ethics at all. Humans are evidently helped or hurt by the condition of their environment. Environmental quality is necessary, though not sufficient, for quality of human life. Humans dramatically rebuild their environments; still, their lives, filled with artifacts, are lived in a natural ecology where resources — soil, air, water, photosynthesis, climate — are matters of life and death. All that we have and are was grown, dug, and gathered out of nature. Culture and nature have entwined destinies, similar to (and related to) the way minds are inseparable from bodies. So ethics needs to be applied to the environment. That requires an *anthropocentric* or

KEY CONCEPTS

- *Sustainable development* — Human habitation and activity that meets the needs of the present without compromising the ability of future generations to meet their own needs; according to J. Ronald Engel, "the kind of human activity that nourishes and perpetuates the historical fulfillment of the whole community of life on Earth."

- *Environmental ethics* — Theory and practice about appropriate concern for, values in, and duties to the natural world.

- *Naturalistic ethics* — An ethic in which humans are concerned about appropriate respect and duty toward those who are other than human (Cf. humanistic ethics).

- *Humanistic ethics* — An ethic in which humans care about the environment because of the impact it has on human beings rather than out of intrinsic respect for nature (Cf. naturalistic ethics).

- *Biocentrism* — An ethic that respects life, with the focus on any and all living beings.

- *Deep ecology* — An ethic that holds that humans, like all other species, are what they are only in their connections with their natural environment, that there is no division in reality between the human and the non-human realms.

- *Axiological environmental ethics* — An ethic that focuses on questions of what is intrinsically valuable in nature and how these elements can be sustained and increased.

- *Bioregionalism* — A view that emphasizes living on regional landscapes. The most workable ethic is one in which persons identify with their geography.

- *Ecofeminism* — According to Karen Warren, "the position that there are important connections — historical, experiential, symbolic, theoretical — between the domination of women and the domination of nature, an understanding of which is crucial to both feminism and environmental ethics."

Endnote 2

humanistic ethics. Many, such as Bryan Norton, maintain that environmental ethics must be largely, if not entirely, of this kind. Holders of this ethic are concerned about the environment because they believe it will serve human ends.

THE HUMANISTIC ETHIC

That there ought be this deeper ethic will be doubted by those entrenched in the prevailing anthropocentric, personalistic ethics. According to holders of the humanistic perspective, humans can have no duties to rocks, rivers, or ecosystems, and almost none to birds or bears; humans have serious duties only to each other, with nature often instrumental in such duties; the environment is the wrong kind of primary target for an ethic; nature is a means, not an end in itself; nothing there counts morally; and nature has no intrinsic value. A naturalistic environmental ethics has been steadily challenging precisely those claims.

THE NATURALISTIC ETHIC

Nevertheless, others insist, environmental ethics goes further than an ethics of prudential resource use, human benefits and costs, and their just distribution, further than concern about risks, pollution levels, rights and torts, needs of future generations, and so on, although these figure large within it. A *naturalistic ethics* is one in which humans are concerned about appropriate respect and duty toward those who are other than human. Environmental ethics does require that ethics be applied to the environment, analogously to business, medicine, engineering, law, and technology. Yet it is more radical than such humanist application; it revises traditional ideas about what is of moral concern to include animals, plants, endangered species, ecosystems, and even Earth as a whole — at least occasionally. For a proponent of naturalistic ethics, whales slaughtered, ancient forests cut, Earth disrupted by global warming — these also count morally and directly. Such environmental ethics is unique in moving outside the sector of human interests.

Once the mark of an educated person could be summed up as *civitas*, the privileges, rights, responsibilities of **citizenship.** People ought to be good citizens, upright and moral, productive in their communities, leaders in business, the professions, government, church, education. That was the responsibility that went with one's rights. But the mark of an educated person today, increasingly, is something more. It is not enough to be a good "citizen," for that is only half the truth about who we are; we are "residents" dwelling on landscapes.

Our responsibilities to Earth, to ecosystems, species, animals and plants, might be thought vague beside our concrete responsibilities to our children or next door neighbors. But not so. A century ago, a call for community was typically phrased as the brotherhood of man and the fatherhood of God. Now such a call must be more ecological, less paternalistic, a call for appropriate respect for the non-human species with which we co-inhabit this planet.

Nature has equipped **homo sapiens,** the wise species, with a conscience to direct the fearful power of the brain and hand. Only the human species contains moral agents, but perhaps conscience is less wisely used than it ought to be when, in an anthropocentric ethics, it exempts the global community of life from consideration, with the resulting paradox that the sole moral species acts only in its collective self-interest toward all the rest. We ought to develop an environmental ethics that optimizes values in nature, complementary to human values. In this sense, these more radical ethicists insist that being a naturalist is more important than being a humanist. This is the biology of ultimate concern.

Nature has equipped homo sapiens, the wise species, with a conscience to direct the fearful power of the brain and hand.

2. HUMANS, ANIMALS, AND A LAND ETHIC

J. Baird Callicott finds a three-way division. On one corner of a triangle is **ethical humanism,** with its anthropocentric focus. But now the naturalists divide two ways. On a second corner is **animal welfare or rights,** a humane moralism that extends ethical consideration to the higher animals (See Chapter 12). Jeremy Bentham, a classical utilitarian philosopher, asked famously, "The question is not, Can they *reason?* nor, Can they *talk?* but, Can they *suffer?*" Perhaps people can use animals for their legitimate needs, but they ought to be humane about it, caring for their domestic animals. Decent hunters track wounded deer; humane trappers check their lines daily. The rancher who lets his horses starve is prosecuted in court. An ox in the ditch is to be rescued, even on the sabbath. "A righteous man has regard for the life of his beast" (Proverbs 12.10).

Many of these humane moralists have misgivings, however, about ways in which humans regularly do use animals. Peter Singer and Tom Regan have been especially vocal. Is it right to hunt recreationally, even if one is a humane hunter? Eating domestic food animals, cows and chickens, might not be justified, since humans (at least those in modern societies) can be quite adequately nourished on a vegetarian diet. Using animals for medical experiments will have to be justified; using them for testing cosmetics is not justified at all. (These issues are explored in more depth in Chapter 12.)

Endnote 3

Endnote 4

Endnote 5

Endnote 6

On a third corner of the triangle is a ***"land ethic,"*** advocated by Aldo Leopold, a forester-ecologist and one of the prophets of environmental ethics. "A thing is right when it tends to preserve the integrity, stability, and beauty of the biotic community. It is wrong when it tends otherwise." "That land is a community is the basic concept of ecology, but that land is to be loved and respected is an extension of ethics." Leopold's ethic is more than mutually recognized obligations within the human community. Animal rights moralists want also to extend morality, but only as far as animals. Leopold claims that ***ecosystems*** can count morally.

Wild animals are *what* they are only *where* they are, adapted creatures fitting in niches in ecosystems. They ought be respected for what they are in themselves, but such an ethic has also to enlarge to consider the ecology of animal life. A wolf caged in a zoo really isn't a wolf anymore. It used to be a wolf, but is now torn from the ecological matrix in which it could behave like a wolf. In the whole picture, in a holistic ethic, this ecosystemic level in which all organisms are embedded is what really counts morally — in some respects more than any of the component organisms, because the systemic processes have generated, continue to support, and integrate tens of thousands of member organisms. The ecosystem is as wonderful as anything it contains.

Endnote 6

A wolf caged in a zoo really isn't a wolf anymore. It used to be a wolf, but is now torn from the ecological matrix in which it could behave like a wolf.

We want to love "the land," as Leopold terms it, "the natural processes by which the land and the living things upon it have achieved their characteristic form and by which they maintain their existence," that is, evolution and ecology. The appropriate unit for moral concern, according to a proponent of the "land ethic," is the fundamental unit of development and survival.

One might first think there will be no conflict between these two types of naturalistic ethic: humane concern for animal welfare and ecological concern for biotic community. Doubtless this is often so, but it is clearly not always so. Animal moralists may forbid hunting or recommend rescuing injured wild animals; a proponent of a land ethic may recommend culling to control populations or letting nature take its course. Land ethic advocates killed tens of thousands of feral goats on San Clemente Island, off the California coast, to protect endangered species of plants and preserve biotic communities.

3. BIOCENTRISM AND RESPECT FOR LIFE

Endnote 7

Biocentrism respects life, with the focus on any and all living beings. The question is not, "Can it suffer?" but "Is it alive?" Albert Schweitzer said: "A man is truly ethical only when he obeys the compulsion to help all life which he is able to assist, and shrinks from injuring anything that lives. . . . Life as such is sacred to him. He tears no leaf from a tree, plucks no flower, and takes care to crush no insect." More recently, Paul Taylor argues: "The relevant characteristic for having the status of a moral patient is not the capacity for pleasure or suffering but the fact that the being has a good of its own which can be furthered or damaged by moral agents."

Endnote 8

Peter Singer objects, claiming that ethical concern stops "somewhere between a shrimp and an oyster"; after that "there is nothing to be taken into account." Below sufficient neural capacity to suffer pains or enjoy pleasures, ethics is over. In fact, however, most of the biological world has yet to be taken into account: lower animals, insects, microbes, plants, species. Animals with developed nervous systems are only a fraction of the described species. Over 96% of species are invertebrates or plants, only a tiny fraction of individual organisms are sentient animals. An animal-based ethics can value everything else only instrumentally. This is little better than humans valuing everything, higher animals included, as their own resources. A deeper respect for life must value directly all living things.

Endnote 9

Fishermen in Atlantic coastal bays toss beer bottles overboard, to dispose of trash. Small crabs, attracted by the residual beer, make their way inside the bottles and become trapped, unable to get enough foothold on the slick glass neck to work their way out. They starve slowly. Then one dead crab becomes bait for the next victim, an indefinitely resetting trap! Are those bottle traps of ethical concern? Or is the whole thing out of sight, out of mind, with crabs too mindless to care about? Biocentrists argue that crabs count morally, because they are alive and put in jeopardy by human carelessness, regardless of whether they can suffer much. True, one crab may not count very much, but, according to the biocentrist, it is a mistake to say it does not count at all.

Considering plants makes the biocentrist's differences with an animal rights ethic even clearer. A plant is a spontaneous life system, self-maintaining with a controlling program (though with no controlling center, no brain). Plants do not have ends-in-view. They are not subjects of a life, and in that familiar sense, they do not have goals. Yet the plant grows, reproduces, repairs its wounds, and resists death, maintaining a botanical identity. An acorn becomes an oak; the oak stands on its own.

An objector can say, "The plants don't care, so why should I?" But plants do care — using botanical standards, the only form of caring available to them. The biocentrist asks, why should I take no account of that form of caring because it is not my form of caring? The plant life *per se* is defended — an intrinsic value. Though things do not matter *to* trees, a great deal matters *for* them. We ask, What's the matter *with* that tree? If it is lacking sunshine and soil nutrients, we arrange for these, and the tree goes to work and recovers its health. Such organisms do "take account" of themselves; and we should take account of them.

Figure 1. Giant sequoia. Archive Photos.

In the 1880s a tunnel was cut through a giant sequoia in what is now Yosemite National Park. Driving through the Wawona tree amused millions. The tree was perhaps the most photographed in the world. The giant blew over in snowstorms in 1968–69, weakened by the tunnel. Some proposed that the Park Service cut another. The rangers refused, because this is an indignity to a majestic sequoia. The comedy of drive-through sequoias perverts the best in persons, who ought to be elevated to a richer experience of the sequoias. But there is a deeper conviction. Using trees for serious human needs is justified, but not this. *Sequoia sempervirens*, the species line, has been around several million years, with each of its individual sequoia trees defending a good of its kind. This tree ought to be respected for what it is in itself.

Ordinary trees can count, especially when aggregated. Newspapers are a good thing, up to a point; but, since the Sunday paper is mostly ads and much of it is only glanced at, one might argue that Americans having their Sunday papers does not warrant sacrificing half a million trees a week, as it does. Imposing a return tax so that half the papers are recycled would save a quarter of a million trees a week.

For classical ethicists, all this seems odd. Plants are not valuers with preferences that can be satisfied or frustrated. It seems curious to say that wildflowers have rights, or moral standing, or need our sympathy, or that we should consider their point of view. We would not say that the needless destruction of a plant species was cruel, but we might say that it was callous. We would not be concerned about what the plants did feel, but about what the destroyers did not feel. We would not be valuing sensitivity in plants, but censuring insensitivity in persons. Still that does not end the question, because we at once ask what are the properties in plants to which a person should be sensitive. Biocentrists claim that environmental ethics is not merely an affair of psychology, but of biology. Man is the only measurer of things (an often quoted claim of Protagoras, a Greek philosopher), but man does not have to make himself the only measure he uses. Life is a better measure.

4. DEEP ECOLOGY

Deep ecologists argue that ecology, deeply understood, teaches that humans, like all other species, are what they are only in their connections with their natural environment. The human "self" is not something just found from the skin-in, an atomistic individual set over against other individuals and the rest of nature. Rather the "self" is what it is with its connections; the self takes up its identity in these interrelationships with the biotic community, which is true self-realization. So argue Arne Naess, George Sessions, Bill Devall, Freya Mathews, and Warwick Fox. An animal ethic, biocentrism, and a land ethic must figure in a comprehensive world view that contrasts with the shallow, humanistic ethics, resulting from the Western legacy of a dualism between humans and the natural world.

Deep ecology emphasizes the ways in which humans, although individual selves, can and ought to extend such selves through a web-work of connections, taking a model from ecology. On this view, humans have such entwined destinies with the natural world that their richest quality of life involves a larger identification with these communities. Such transformation of the personal self will result in an appropriate care for the environment.

In human society one's personal identity is bound up with human relationships; one is a father, a mother, a brother, a sister, also a citizen of a community, a state, a nation, perhaps a member of a church or synagogue, a club or interest group, an owner or employee in a business, a teacher, or a physician. A person is educated into a heritage, critically interiorizes it, invests his or her life in this civic community. But personal identity is just as much bound up with nature, the air we breathe, the sunshine and the rain, the food we eat, the landscapes on which we reside. **Environmental health is as necessary as bodily health.**

Ecology dissolves any firm boundary between humans and the natural world. Ecology does not know an encapsulated ego over or against his or her environment. Ecological thinking is a kind of vision across boundaries. The skin is like a pond surface or a forest soil, life is making connections across boundaries, constant interpenetration. So the self is ennobled and extended, rather than threatened by nature, because the beauty and complexity of nature are continuous with ourselves. The human vascular system includes arteries, veins, rivers, oceans, air currents. Cleaning a dump is not that different from filling a tooth. The self metabolically, and so metaphorically, interpenetrates the ecosystem. Paul Shepard puts it forcefully: "We must affirm that the world is . . . a part of our own body." Human life is always incarnate spirit in flesh and blood intricately linked with the environment in which one lives, moves, and has one's being.

Man is a complex being: he makes deserts bloom— and lakes die.
—Gil Stern

Endnote 11

Endnote 12

Endnote 13

"When we try to pick out anything by itself, we find it hitched to everything else in the universe."
—John Muir,
American Naturalist

Warwick Fox puts it this way: "The *central* intuition of deep ecology . . . is the idea that there is no firm ontological divide in the field of existence. In other words, the world simply is not divided up into independently existing subjects and objects, nor is there any bifurcation in reality between the human and the non-human realms. . . . To the extent that we perceive boundaries, we fall short of deep ecological consciousness." J. Baird Callicott says, "Nature is one and continuous with the self. . . . Nature is the self fully extended and diffused."

With that conviction, one is oriented to act. Here is the **deep ecology platform:**

1. The well-being and flourishing of human and nonhuman life on Earth have value in themselves (synonyms: intrinsic value, inherent value). These values are independent of the usefulness of the nonhuman world for human purposes.

2. Richness and diversity of life forms contribute to the realization of these values and are also value in themselves.

3. Humans have no right to reduce this richness and diversity except to satisfy *vital* needs.

4. The flourishing of human life and cultures is compatible with a substantial decrease of the human population. The flourishing of human life requires such a decrease.

5. Present human interference with the nonhuman world is excessive, and the situation is rapidly worsening.

6. Policies must therefore be changed. These policies affect basic economic, technological, and ideological structures. The resulting state of affairs will be deeply different from the present.

7. The ideological change is mainly that of appreciating *life quality* (dwelling in situations of inherent value) rather than adhering to an increasingly higher standard of living. There will be a profound awareness of the difference between big and great.

8. Those who subscribe to the foregoing points have an obligation directly or indirectly to try to implement the necessary changes.

Deep ecologists are thus radical environmentalists, leaving many at once stimulated and puzzled by these claims, which lift ecology into a metaphysics, almost like a religion, also wondering whether people — many of them at least — can or must go this "deep" for an adequate environmental ethics.

5. THEOLOGY AND THE ENVIRONMENT

STEWARDSHIP, CARING FOR CREATION AND NATURE SPIRITUALITY

A theological environmental ethics sees the natural world as God's creation, pronounced "very good" in the opening chapters of

Genesis. Humans are and ought to be trustees or stewards of this creation. The aboriginal human couple is invited to "have dominion over," to "till and keep," or, better, to "till and serve" this creation. "Conquering nature" although widespread in Christianity, perverts this stewardship. Respect for life, sought by the biocentrists, leads to something deeper, reverence for life.

Endnote 14

The brooding Spirit of God animates the Earth, and Earth gives birth. "The earth was without form and void, and darkness was upon the face of the deep; and the Spirit of God was moving over the face of the waters. And God said, 'Let there be . . .'" "Let the earth put forth vegetation." "Let the earth bring forth living things according to their kinds." "Let the waters bring forth swarms of living creatures" (Genesis 1). "Swarms" is the prescientific word for biodiversity. Earth speciates, teeming with life. The creation is a series of divine imperatives that empower Earth with vitality.

What is required for an ethic that can genuinely motivate people, however, is not just an admiration of creation. There must be disciplining, reformation of human life. The creation can be enjoyed and preserved only if there is justice and love in the land. How *nature* works is the province of physics, geology, biology. How *human nature* works and ought to work requires also theology, philosophy, and ethics. What it means to be blessed and what it means to be wicked are theological questions. Humans must repair their broken wills, curb innate self-interest, and reform corrupt social forces. One is not going to get much help here from ecology. There really is no scientific guidance of life. After four centuries during which science has progressively illuminated us about the facts of nature, the value questions are as sharp and as painful as ever.

The Hebrews long ago knew enough to trust that there is in every seed and root a promise. Sowers sow, the seed grows secretly, and sowers return to reap their harvests. God sends rain on the just and unjust, and this is cause enough for praise. But, take care. The supporting ecology is not enough. There must be obedience to commandments (*Torah*, Instruction) by which people can flourish in the land. Lands do not flow with milk and honey for all unless and until justice rolls down like waters. That is human ecology with a focus on ethics, not science. A theological environmental ethics insists that justice, love, and caring for creation are necessary parts of the answer. Monotheistic religions, such as Christianity, Judaism, and Islam, urge the *stewardship of creation*; or they may prefer to speak of *caring* or *reverence* for a sacred creation. A *creation spirituality* has a strong sense of the divine presence in nature.

Others argue that Eastern religions have something to offer, such as the *yang* and *yin* of Taoism in harmonious balance, or the *ahimsa*, non-injury and respect for life traditions in Hinduism and Buddhism. Native Americans and indigenous peoples in Africa, Australia, and South America have claimed that their traditions respect the natural world better than either traditional monotheism or the modern West. These views, however, are not easy to import into the secular West.

Ecclesiastes 3:19–21

"Man's fate is like that of the animals; the same fate awaits them both: As one dies, so dies the other. All have the same breath; man has no advantage over the animal. Everything is meaningless.

All go to the same place; all come from dust, and to dust all return.

Who knows if the spirit of man rises upward and if the spirit of the animal goes down into the earth?"

—Solomon

Endnote 15

What they have to say can perhaps be recovered by the monotheist's listening to them, using them to correct their own tendencies to anthropocentrism and to forge a better ethic.

Biology and theology are not always easy disciplines to join. One conviction they do share is that the ecosystemic Earth is prolific. Biology and religion have increasingly joined in recent years in admiration for this marvelous planet. No other species can be either responsible for or religious toward the creation, but *Homo sapiens* is given a responsibility to oversee the creativity within the natural system humans inherit.

For monotheists, such as Christians and Jews, this experience of creation, detects God, the Creator, in, with, and under the spectacular natural history. But for others, less sure about the monotheism, there can still be a kind of "ecological spirituality," one which, though unwilling to venture the language of creation-Creator, finds the natural history on Earth evoking a sense of the numinous. Perhaps there is no *super*natural; but, then again, the natural is *super*, superb. One can doubt whether there is any God, Ground of all Being. But one can hardly doubt that there is nature, the fundamental ground in which we live and move and have our being. Encountering this Nature, one detects something sublime in the awe-inspiring sense because there is something sublime in the etymological sense of that word, something that takes us to the limits of our understanding, and mysteriously beyond.

Endnote 16

Viewing Earthrise from the moon, the astronaut Edgar Mitchell, was entranced: "Suddenly from behind the rim of the moon, in long, slow-motion moments of immense majesty, there emerges a sparkling blue and white jewel, a light, delicate sky-blue sphere laced with slowly swirling veils of white, rising gradually like a small pearl in a thick sea of black mystery. It takes more than a moment to fully realize this is Earth . . . home." Mitchell continued, "My view of our planet was a glimpse of divinity." If there is any holy ground, any land of promise, this promising Earth is it. One needs, by this argument, to go at least that deep for an adequate ethics.

6. EXPANDING COMMUNITIES

Endnote 17

By another account, environmental ethics involves a series of *expanding communities*. Peter Wenz calls this **"the concentric circle theory."** Richard Sylvan and Val Plumwood use a tree-ring analogy:

"What emerges is an *annular picture* of types of objects of moral relevance . . . with nested zones of moral obligation." J. Baird Callicott uses a "tree ring" model with "inner social circles," then animal, plants, and a "land ethic" in circles further out. "The charmed circle of moral considerability expands to take in more and more beings." Ethics has a "ballooning circumference," following "the image of annual tree rings in which social structures and their correlative ethics are nested in a graded, differential system." Environmental ethics finds "the newly discovered existence of a global biotic community and its land ethic," with the "land ethic" the most comprehensive circle.

Endnote 18

Endnote 19

Endnote 20

Lawrence Johnson calls this "a morally deep world." Not just humans and animals, but also plants, and species, a hive of bees, wildernesses, and ecosystems can have interests or well-being that we ought to consider. "Man sees the circle of his responsibilities widening"; we gain "a wider moral awareness and sense of values." "Thereby we may better live deep and worthwhile lives in a deep and valuable world."

Endnote 21

In the moral self's most immediate circle are duties to one's family and nearby neighbors. After that come duties to one's local community, to one's nation, heritage, or religious communities, to those with whom one shares values and commitments. More globally, one has duties to humans transnationally, to persons whom we affect by our business or foreign policies, the broad duties of human rights. Here duties of non-maleficence are stronger than duties of beneficence. We ought not to harm the Mexicans by exploiting their poverty for cheap labor. But we also have duties to help the starving Ethiopians.

Tree with concentric rings. Copyright © PhotoDisc, Inc.

Another circle includes claims made by future generations. "People are thought of as existing in concentric circles around me. Generally speaking relatively few people exist in the closest circle, more people in the next circle, and so forth. My obligations toward a person increase with the proximity to me of the circle on which the person exists." So far this is inter-human ethics.

Endnote 22

Environmental ethics adds circles of duty to the natural world, first to domestic animals, such as livestock or pets, to animals used in medical research, or kept in zoos. Beyond, there are duties to wild animals. If one hunts, hunt humanely. If one develops natural areas, one has a duty to minimize and mitigate the loss of habitat to wildlife. "From the concentric circle perspective, nonhuman subjects-of-a-life 'exist,' for the most part on one or more of the concentric circles outside those 'inhabited' by human beings. Expanding the circle of our moral concern to include these animals is equivalent to acknowledging their 'presence' on such concentric circles."

Endnote 22

In a still outer circle, one passes to the flora, to the sequoia trees for example, as claimed earlier, or to the old growth forests. Another circle is that of endangered species, with duties not so much to individuals as to species lines, as when we recently returned wolves to the Greater Yellowstone Ecosystem. The next to outermost circle is the land ethic — urging land health on the modified rural landscapes, and ecological integrity in remnant wild lands, setting aside wilderness areas, where these remain. This requires restoring degraded areas, such as cleaning up rivers and riparian ecosystems, or restoring tall-grass prairies.

The outermost circle is a planetary ethic, an Earth ethics with a concern for the whole system of life. "Ecocentric Holism can be integrated within the theory by thinking of evolutionary processes as 'inhabiting' a relatively remote circle of moral concern." But this circle is rapidly growing less remote. Previously, persons did not have much power to affect planetary processes, but now we do, as with global warming. In this circle we operate with the "principle of process-harm," which forbids us to harm evolutionary and ecosystemic processes.

Endnote 22

The individual self is at the center of the series of circles. Others of moral concern are located on radiating circles by their closeness to the moral agent at the focus. However, critics may ask, does such closeness really follow these concentric circles all that well? For instance, the outmost human-inhabited circle is that of future generations, and yet I might feel stronger ties to grandchildren yet unborn than to persons now living on the other side of the world. Within the animals circle, there is little guidance for what animals get located where. If fish are less intensively subjects-of-a-life than are seals, fishing might be recommended over seal hunting.

The strengths of obligations within the human circles is determined by biographical details; one has stronger obligations to a brother than he does to a distant Ethiopian. Is there any analogue with animals? Does one have more obligations to endangered grizzlies in one's home state than to elephants in Kenya? Rarity might make more difference in an environmental ethic than closeness. We might prefer plants at the species level to sentient animals at the individual level, as when we shot the San Clemente goats.

Since my Self is at the center of my concentric circles, her Self at her center, and his Self at his, and since we have different careers, locations in the world, and family ties, the strengths of pull will differ. Each carries about a personal set of concentric circles. My judgments will not be your judgments. Could this mean that at the same event in Earth history, intersected differently by our concentric frameworks, I operate pulled by strong obligations while you feel no such pull but operate with weak obligations. To some extent our personal ethical obligations, though perhaps not our ethical criteria, differ with our biographies. But when the concentric circles are simultaneously biographically and biologically formed, some boundaries determined by natural kinds, some boundaries determined by personal histories, the result is no clear decision rules for persons jointly making contested decisions, and rather much muddling through.

7. AXIOLOGICAL ENVIRONMENTAL ETHICS

Intrinsic, Instrumental, and Ecosystemic Values: An **axiological environmental ethics** identifies multiple values in nature. (Axiology is value theory, from the Greek *axios*, "worthy," "valuable," also in "axiom," "axle" or "axis," the pivot about which everything turns.) A better approach than concentric circles, or biocentrism, or animal rights, or a land ethic, is to locate domains of value. Though my son is close to me, provided he is reasonably well off, I might devote my energies to saving a whale species on the brink of extinction. Although the land ethic is an outermost circle, I might have more obligation to keep ecosystems healthy, or preserve wilderness or old growth forests, than I do to care for my pets or zoo animals, in closer circles. One ought critically to assess values at stake, sometimes in culture, sometimes in nature, appraise outcomes, and act to optimize value.

According to this view, value is present on Earth at multiple, interwoven levels — "intrinsic, instrumental, and systemic." Humans value nature as their life-support system (economically, recreationally, scientifically, aesthetically) as a repository for genetic diversity, as cultural symbols, and so on. Such values may be assigned to natural things by humans or they may come into existence in human interactions with nature.

Defenders of this position hold that beyond and before this placing of value by humans, many intrinsically valuable things are found in nature that are present independently of human valuations. Such values are discovered, not placed, not generated in interaction. Examples of such intrinsically valued goods are seen in certain facts of nature. Plants and animals alike defend their own lives; they are members of species lineages perpetuated over millennia. Ecosystems are the sources and systems of life, having generated myriads of species over evolutionary time. An adequate ethics will need to optimize all of these relevant values, humanistic and naturalistic. Moral concern needs to focus on the relevant survival unit, not always the individual, often the species, the ecosystem, and ultimately the planet Earth.

Do not humans sometimes value Earth's life-supporting systems because they are intrinsically valuable, and not always simply because they are useful to humans? When Astronaut Mitchell marveled over the Earth, is the value he sees just a matter of late-coming human interests? Or is Earth not historically a remarkable and valuable place whose intrinsic qualities provide bases for the wise human uses of it? It seems parochial to say that our part alone in the drama establishes all its worth. The production of value over the millennia of natural history is not something subjective that goes on in the human mind. The creativity within the natural system we

Endnote 23

inherit, and the values this generates, are the ground of our being, not just the ground under our feet.

True, humans are the only evaluators who can reflect about what is going on in animals, plants, and species lines over evolutionary history, or on a global scale, or who can deliberate about what they ought to do to conserve it. When humans do this, they must set up the scales. Humans are the measurers of things. Animals, organisms, species, ecosystems, Earth cannot teach us how to do this evaluating. But they can display what it is that is to be valued. The axiological scales we construct do not constitute the value, any more than the scientific scales we erect create what we thereby measure. Humans are not so much lighting up value in a merely potentially valuable world, as they are psychologically joining ongoing planetary natural history in which there is value wherever there is positive creativity.

From this more objective viewpoint, there is something subjective, philosophically naive, and even hazardous about living in a reference frame where one species takes itself as absolute and values every thing else in nature only because of its potential to produce value for that species.

Well, the protest will come, saying: All this is theoretically very interesting, but in practice there will be conflicts of value. Here humans will need to win while nature loses. Certainly, culture is the peculiar human excellence, and advanced culture is not possible except as superimposed on nature in such way that it captures things intrinsically valuable in nature and redirects them to cultural uses. When Columbus set foot in the Americas in 1492, there was no way that modern America could have been built without damage to the integrity of the then-existing natural ecosystems. America could, however, have been built with much less damage to nature; we might have preserved ecosystem health where we could not preserve pristine ecosystem integrity.

But that is looking past. What now? **Must we further harm nature to develop culture?** No. A satisfactory culture is quite possible without further degrading nature; and, indeed, further degrading nature is likely to make culture less satisfactory. We do not need further development at cost to fauna, flora, endangered species, ecosystem health. Nor will humans be harmed if we do not get that development. We win when there is no more degrading development. And our win is simultaneously nature's win.

The protest may continue that there is no way to quantify all these values in our decision making, so the theory is no help in practice. But there is seldom any calculus for any kind of ethics. When ethicists and citizens debate permitting euthanasia or capital punishment, abolishing child labor or slavery, whether a war is just, or what the minimum wage should be, figures may be relevant, but they are never decisive. What a democratic society has to do is lay out the values at stake in public debate and hope that with sufficient education and reflection, the wise course — the value-optimizing course — can be found. That is what Americans did, for instance, when we

Man is now, whether he likes it or not, and indeed whether he knows it or not . . .the sole agent for the evolutionary process on earth. He is responsible for the future of the planet.
—Sir Julian Hurley

We win when there is no more degrading development. And our win is simultaneously nature's win.

passed the Clean Air Act, the National Forest Management Act, the Wilderness Acts, or the Endangered Species Act. Environmental ethics can dramatically alter our sense of values at stake in the conservation of nature.

8. POLITICAL ECOLOGY

Another ethics puts the emphasis on economic, political, and educational forces and institutions. Social systems make humans behave as they do toward their environment, and this is where any effective reformation will have to be worked out. Environmental ethics must be corporate; action must be taken in concert — in **political ecology**, which has been popularly dubbed *"green politics."* The natural environment is crucially a "commons," a public good. No ethics is going to be effective unless it shapes environmental policy.

Policies will need to relate such a commons to capitalism, ownership of the means of production, market forces, the concerns of labor, real estate development policies, the property rights of individuals, population control, equitable distribution of the products made from natural resources. The forces of capitalism and individualism do not attend to the public good automatically. There is no "invisible hand" that guarantees an optimal harmony between a people and their landscape, or that the right things are done in encounter with fauna, flora, ecosystems, or regarding future generations.

Humans are mostly moved to act in their self-interest, and they will do so to the degradation of the environment — unless environmental policy gives them an incentive to do otherwise. Short-term self-interest will get out of hand, especially when coupled with social power. Thus, there is a need for laws to regulate private and business use of things in nature. These regulations are imposed in the public interest by the forces of democracy.

At depth, such an ethics asks whether the European Enlightenment is compatible with the emerging ecological movement, both theoretically and practically. Science, technology, industry, democracy, human rights, freedom, preference satisfaction, maximizing benefits over costs, consumerism — all these are outcomes of the Enlightenment worldview. And they are all seriously implicated as causes of the environmental crisis. According to proponents of political ecology and green politics much of the enthusiastic humanism that the Enlightenment stood for needs to be ecologically chastened.

A test of a democracy is whether its citizens can learn to practice enlightened restraint, developing an ethic about the environment, as Americans have been doing in the last quarter century. But this is still largely a civil ethics. A further test, one for the 21st century, is whether a people can see the whole commonwealth of a human soci-

Endnote 24

A test of a democracy is whether its citizens can learn to practice enlightened restraint, developing an ethic about the environment, as Americans have been doing in the last quarter century.

ety set in its ecosystems, developing an environmental ethics in the primary sense. It is not simply what a society does to its slaves, women, blacks, minorities, handicapped, children, or future generations, but what it does to its fauna, flora, species, ecosystems, and landscapes that reveals the character of that society.

Environmental ethics, one can say, leaves ethics among humans and moves to other concentric circles; it must evaluate nonhuman levels of value. Still, what is really going to make the difference is the legislation we can get passed. Though there is a long tradition about rights and restrictions of access to public goods such as water, grazing, and timber, as well as a history of regulation in the public interest and of multiple uses of public lands, "ecological values" had little history in policy until about 1960. In the last quarter century, however, there has been steady enactment of environmentally oriented legislation. This includes over a hundred acts of the U.S. Congress. States, counties, and municipalities have passed hundreds more.

The U. S. Environmental Protection Agency, the Forest Service, the Bureau of Land Management, the Fish and Wildlife Service, and other agencies promulgate various environmental standards. The tone of these acts and regulations differs from earlier ones. They are now phrased as a concern about environmental quality and values, endangered species, biotic diversity, wilderness, unimpaired productivity or diversity of the land, retaining a natural or primeval character of wildlands, or preservation as well as conservation.

The National Environmental Policy Act requires for major federal projects a detailed statement of expected environmental impacts and of alternatives to the proposed action. There has been greatly increased environmental regulation and litigation and much controversy over agency decisions about public land use. People are increasingly persuaded that the national treasures include natural givens, both amenities and necessities, which are not always merely commodities.

Some ethical choices are made by individuals, but in other cases we must choose together. Government and business are large influences in our lives; both have vast amounts of power to affect the environment for good or ill. In setting policy, we can by "mutual coercion, mutually agreed upon," do in concert what no individual, interest group, or business can successfully do alone. We sometimes "legislate morality," at least in common denominator areas. There must be a management ethic for soil, air, water, pollution, the ozone layer, mutagens, wildlife, the eagle as a national symbol, endangered species, and future generations. This ethic will be voluntary in the sense that it is an enlightened, democratically achieved consensus. No laws can be enforced without the widespread voluntary compliance of citizens. Still, compliance cannot be entirely voluntary. Even if 99 percent of citizens are glad to behave in a certain way, provided that all others do, one percent of the citizens will persist in freeloading, and this will trigger bad faith. One rotten apple spoils a bushel.

Endnote 25

Endnote 26

This does not mean that large-scale social institutions can have moral commitments in the robust way in which individuals and small groups can. Still, a nation needs collective choices producing a public land ethic. Michel Serres argues that "the old social contract ought to be joined by a natural contract."

Endnote 27

9. SUSTAINABLE DEVELOPMENT AND SUSTAINABLE BIOSPHERE

At the United Nations Conference on Environment and Development (UNCED) in Rio de Janeiro, June 1992, the norm of **sustainable development** was crucial. Environmental ethics is inextricably coupled with development ethics. The *Rio Declaration* begins: "Human beings are at the centre of concerns for sustainable development. They are entitled to a healthy and productive life in harmony with nature." Sustainable development has proved an umbrella idea, permitting various interpretations.

Endnote 28

The U.N. World Commission on Environment and Development declares, "Sustainable development is development that meets the needs of the present without compromising the ability of future generations to meet their own needs." The idea was first applied to agriculture, also forestry, but later to water use, allowable pollution levels, industry, urbanization, and national policies and strategies.

Endnote 29

The terms "sustainable" coupled with "development" conveys continued growth but not such as degrades opportunities and environments for the future. Within ecological limits, we still retain the optimistic idea of progress. The Commission continues, "All human beings have the fundamental right to an environment adequate for their health and well-being."

Endnote 30

Endnote 31

The Commission pleads that we must have development because most people do not have anywhere near enough resources to sustain life. Not enough is produced; what is produced is not equitably shared. Five to tenfold development is needed to fulfill human needs in generations to come. "Humanity has the ability to make development sustainable. . . . Meeting essential needs requires not only a new era of economic growth for nations in which the majority are poor, but an assurance that those poor get their fair share of the resources required to sustain that growth."

Endnote 32

Now it seems that "sustainable" also means "fair" or "just," an ethics of **ecojustice.** There are two major blocs of nations, the developed Group of 7 (the industrial nations of North America, Europe, and Japan), and the underdeveloped G-77 nations, once 77 but now including some 128 nations, often south of the industrial North. The G-7 nations hold about one-fifth of the world's five-billion persons, and they produce and consume about four-fifths of all goods and services. The G-77 nations, with four-fifths of the world's people, produce and consume one-fifth. Of the 90-million new people on Earth each year, 85-million appear in the Third World, the countries least able to support them. The result is poverty and environmental degradation in a feedback loop. Meanwhile, the five-million new people in the industrial countries will put as much strain on the environment as the 85 million new poor.

Development in the West has been based on the Enlightenment myth of endless growth, bringing several hundred years of explosive development. But across the United States, whether one considers agricultural land developed, forests cut, rivers dammed and diverted for water, ranges fenced, minerals extracted, or highways and subdivisions built, the next hundred years cannot be like the last hundred. Americans have not yet settled into a sustainable culture on their landscape.

"Sustainable development" has become a key term both in international treaties and covenants and in domestic planning. The overconsumption problem in the G-7 nations is linked with the underconsumption problem in the G-77 nations, and this results in increasing environmental degradation in the G-77 nations. Sustainable development must close the gap between the rich and the poor, between and also within nations. Even if there were an equitable distribution of wealth, the human population cannot go on escalating without people becoming more and more poor, because the pie has to be constantly divided into smaller pieces. Even if there were no future population growth, consumption patterns could not go on escalating on a finite Earth. There are three problems: overpopulation, overconsumption, and maldistribution.

Such an ethic is humane and appealing, but critics ask whether there is enough concern for the integrity of ecosystems, for biodiversity? According to the political ecology view, the Earth is regarded as a natural resource; what really counts is meeting people's needs. The goal is to sustain things humans value: GNP or GDP, profits, trade opportunities, natural or manmade capital, substitutable resources, per capita income, and adequate food. Nature is not ultimately important, but is (in the literal sense) provisionally important. Any condition of nature that supplies such opportunities will be acceptable.

Is there a way of defining sustainability that gives nature a more central place? "Sustainable development," J. Ronald Engel tells us, "may be defined as *the kind of human activity that nourishes and perpetuates the historical fulfillment of the whole community of life on Earth.*" That puts human and biotic communities together comprehensively, a more promising outlook. But the problem is that everything cannot equally flourish; some things have to be sacrificed for other things. When Iowa is plowed to plant corn, it can hardly be said that the grasslands of Iowa reach their historical fulfillment. The most we can say is that Iowans can and ought to sustain their agriculture within the hydrology, soil chemistries, nutrient recycling processes, and so on, that operate on the Iowa landscape. Humans

Even if there were an equitable distribution of wealth, the human population cannot go on escalating without people becoming more and more poor, because the pie has to be constantly divided into smaller pieces.

Endnote 33

should build sustainable cultures that fit in with the ecological carrying capacities. The bottom line, transcultural and non-negotiable, is a sustainable biosphere, and, at least in one sense, this makes environmental ethics prior after all.

10. BIOREGIONALISM

Living on regional landscapes is emphasis of **bioregionalism.** The most workable ethic is one in which persons identify with their geography. A planetary ethic is remote; the Earth is too big. Concern for sustainable development in the Amazon, though a laudable goal, is less likely to motivate someone than what that person has at stake on his or her home landscape. Redistributing first and third world resources more equitably, though desirable, is not politically possible. True, one ought to have concern for endangered species, vanishing wildlife, intrinsic natural values, or wilderness conservation; but that too is not what orients day-to-day behavior. What is politically possible is concern about the countryside of everyday experience. After all, ecology is about living at home (Greek: "*oikos*," house). That is where the land ethic really operates. That is where people can act, where they vote, and pay taxes. They need to be "natives," as much as "citizens."

Endnote 34

Myriads of peoples live on thousands of kinds of landscapes. Communities need to define sustainable development and environmental ethics for themselves. In the United States, persons can identify with the Everglades, the Adirondacks, the Appalachians, the Rocky Mountains, the Desert Southwest, the Pacific Northwest, or the Chesapeake Bay. People who live in the Greater Yellowstone Ecosystem have as much at stake in the condition of their forests and rivers as they do in whether their towns are prospering. Similarly for those on the prairies, or in the Ozarks, the Sierra Nevadas, the Great Lakes, along the Mississippi River, or on the Georgia or Florida coasts. Africa contains environments from the Sahara to rain forests; Australia has its eastern rain forests and desert interiors; England its moors, Scotland its highlands, Russia its steppes.

A bioregion, says Kirkpatrick Sale, is "a place defined by its life forms, its topography, and its biota, rather than by human dictates; a region governed by nature, not legislature." A focus on bioregions permits "ecosystem management," a much lauded goal. Bioregionalism appeals to geographers, landscape architects, developers, state legislators, county commissioners — all those charged with decisions about a quality environment. Humans need to learn to "reinhabit" their landscapes. This is environmental ethics on a human scale.

Endnote 35

We do live on one Earth, with some planetary concerns, like global warming. But the modern world is becoming a global monoculture, with international markets, free trade, World Bank loans, transnational corporations, electronic communications, satellite TV, websites and e-mail, jet planes, and people living in giant cities. The average bite of food eaten in the United States has traveled 1,200 miles. Watching Western advertising, people want the same thing everywhere — not just blue jeans and Coca-Cola, but refrigerators and automobiles. When people become captive to these global forces, they lose their independence. This reduces local color and diversity, the distinctive cultural patterns worked out in response to the particulars of landscapes.

People lose control over their resident environments. Nebraska wheat is no longer grown on family farms, where four generations have loved the land. That has been replaced by big agriculture, owned by absentee investors; the way in which wheat is now raised is dictated by world markets. Environmental ethics requires a feeling of identity with local place, and globalization corrupts this.

On closer analysis, however, one needs to ask to what extent the regional landscape processes do constrain policy, which would seem to require ecological science. By contrast, to what extent are there numerous options available on any landscape, which would seem to require policy and social decision? American Indians and Europeans have both lived in Colorado, with very different lifestyles. Twentieth-century Coloradoans have different lifestyles from nineteenth-century Coloradoans. Can one really say that the Rocky Mountain bioregion does or ought to constrain the lifestyle of Coloradoans for the twenty-first century? Geography is no longer the principal determinant of human society. Global connections are here to stay, they are the wave of the future.

Bioregions vary widely and are not all that easy to identify. Does one look for watersheds, mountain ranges, rainfall, grasslands, forests, or what? Are political boundaries of any significance, such as the U.S.-Canadian border in the Great Lakes region? Are there bioregions nested within larger bioregions? The Pacific Northwest has rain forests, but also, not that far away, semi-arid deserts. How big is a bioregion? The Great Lakes region is larger than Great Britain and France combined. Are the British Isles one bioregion or many? Doesn't a U.S. citizen living in Virginia need a continental sense of place? Does that person need to be concerned about the wolves in Yellowstone or preserving what wilderness remains in Montana? Doesn't the Grand Canyon belong to Pennsylvanians?

Despite these puzzles, bioregionalism does recognize that life is incarnate in place. The passage of consciousness through nature in time takes narrative form, a "storied residence." Henry David Thoreau's views were those of Walden Pond; and John Muir loved the high Sierras. John James Audubon saw birds and Rachel Carson the sea. Wendell Berry loves Kentucky and Barry Lopez the arctic. Leopold concludes with a land ethic that he recommends around the world. It is essential that the earlier pages of his *Sand County (Wisconsin) Almanac* remember a January thaw, the spring flowering of *Draba*, the April mating dance of the woodcock. Leopold's biographi-

Nebraska wheat is no longer grown on family farms, where four generations have loved the land. That has been replaced by big agriculture, owned by absentee investors; the way in which wheat is now raised is dictated by world markets.

Endnote 36

cal residence is the personal backing to his ethic. An environmental ethic needs roots in locality.

11. ECOFEMINISM

An **ecofeminist ethics** finds a caring for nature present among women, contrasting with an attitude of dominion among men. Such dominion is doubly expressed in an alliance between the forces that exploit nature and those that exploit women. This patriarchal bias has been present in many societies, but has especially characterized the modern West. Karen Warren explains: "Ecological feminism is the position that there are important connections — historical, experiential, symbolic, theoretical — between the domination of women and the domination of nature, an understanding of which is crucial to both feminism and environmental ethics."

Endnote 37

The environmental crisis arises, significantly, from a male-gender bias that elevates human reason, resulting in a neglect of the complementary feminine virtues. Reason is thought to be impartial, objective, analytic, abstract, and universalizable. It seeks understanding, control, and dominion. The complementary feminine virtues that are thereby neglected include individual, person, and particular concern, involving participation, sharing, and nurturing. Women have often been supposed less rational, more emotional, closer to nature, devoting more time to giving birth, nursing, feeding and taking care of children, subject to and inferior to men. Women need domestication by the dominant sex, their men ruling the family and the farm, running the business, and confronting the outside world. This male-gender bias is dualistic: man/woman; mind/body, reason/emotion, culture/nature, self/other, where the first in the pair is hierarchically superior to the second.

When men think ethically they prescribe duties, claim rights, distribute justice, and optimize utility, and do these from a humanistic perspective that leaves them disinclined to be appropriately concerned for animals, much less plants, endangered species, or ecosystems. Men want to be stewards, trustees, managers, always in control. They may argue about their effectiveness here; but none of this really addresses the question of male privilege.

In fact, claim the ecofeminists, in many cultures women have been the primary managers of households. As gatherers of food women were more important than the hunting men. As growers of food, gatherers of fuel, or carriers of water, women are both more important providers than men, and more sensitive to the human/nature interconnections. Men build grand theories and dream of universal knowledge and the power it brings; but women live narrative stories in their particular communities, times, and places.

Nature is often thought of as "Mother Nature." The etymological root of "nature" is "giving birth." Ecofeminists are of mixed minds as to whether to develop this imagery or to set it aside as too problematic in its historical associations. They more likely agree that ecofeminism offers a corrective perspective, not gender-biased, that can enable the development of a better environmental ethics complementary with a development policy. Marti Kheel says, "It is the androcentric worldview that deserves primary blame."

Endnote 38

The androcentric (male-centered) view is quite as problematic as any anthropocentric (human-centered) view. Male values must yield to empowered women, who can correct this bias, a prerequisite for solving environmental problems. Warren concludes: "Ecofeminism provides the framework for a distinctively feminist and environmental ethics. It is a feminism that critiques male bias wherever it occurs in ethics (including environmental ethics) and aims at providing an ethic (including environmental ethics) which is not male-biased — and it does so in a way that satisfies the preliminary boundary conditions of a feminist ethic."

Endnote 39

Critics worry that ecofeminism has become too much a single-issue ethics. Endangered species policy, biodiversity conservation, pollution levels in streams, wilderness conservation, global warming, North-South inequities, or sustainable development are not especially feminist issues. Women are as apt to be willing consumers as men, whether of feathers for hats, timber for their houses, or of gasoline in their automobiles. They generate waste just as quickly as men. Women are quite capable of being anthropocentric. Previous promises that the influence of women would redeem society (as were made when women gained the vote) have failed to be fulfilled. Logical argument about equity, rights, duties, optimizing benefits, and minimizing costs are as relevant for women as for men.

Tendencies to exploit and oppress are a problem in human nature, not just male nature. The critics of exaggerated human dominion have as readily been men (Aldo Leopold, John Muir, Paul Taylor) as women (Rachel Carson, Carolyn Merchant). Humans in their cultures are, indeed, radically different from animals and plants in wild nature, and one does need to be discriminating (if not dualistic) about this, before any adequate environmental ethic can be formed — although this may also require storied residence, bioregional identity, social ecology, ecosystem management, and stewardship.

12. PLURALISM, POSTMODERNISM, AND A SENSE OF PLACE

A **postmodern environmental ethics** doubts whether humans can know nature independently of the cultural schemes we use to interpret nature. A worldview is a social construction, more than it is a realist account of nature in itself. These views can be judged better or worse by their sustainability, equitable distribution of resources, or quality of life as understood from within that culture; and that is all that is needed. We do not have to have absolute, final, or even true accounts of what nonhuman nature is like to form *an ethics of place.* Ecology, once again, is a logic of one's home place. Our "environment" is as much of nature as comes within our horizon. Such ethics may differ with various peoples, a **pluralist environmental ethics.**

Endnote 40

Endnote 41

Educated persons in the West tend to think that the "modern" view is the right one. This comes out of the Enlightenment philosophy coupled with the sciences. This outlook is quite successful in enabling humans to be literate and free, and to pursue their happiness, make progress, learn more about nature and how to use it resourcefully, and gain higher standards of living. More than this — so we think — this modern view is so successful because it is the true one; other views are outmoded. In culture, democracy and human rights are the best form of government. Totalitarian kings and slavery are wrong because they are social institutions based on a false view of humans, their nature, and their possibilities. In nature, Darwin discovered natural selection and evolutionary natural history. The fixity of species and the six-day creation were wrong. Indigenous peoples populated nature with spirits; but these do not exist. The enlightened, scientific view is the correct one.

Postmodernism argues that this is arrogant and naive. We need to be post-enlightened! Even in the West, we know nature only provisionally, operationally or pragmatically, and such knowledge is much more limited than we realize — not much more than a sketch or a cartoon of nature. Don Cupitt puts this bluntly:

> Science is at no point privileged. It is itself just another cultural activity. Interpretation reaches all the way down, and we have no 'pure' and extra-historical access to Nature. We have no basis for distinguishing between Nature itself and our own changing historically-produced representations of nature. . . . Nature is a cultural product.

Endnote 42

Australian aborigines, who live in intimate contact with their arid landscape, drawing their living from it, may in fact know more about nature there than Western ecologists, who get their groceries at the supermarket.

"Nature" is a loaded word, as is revealed by the metaphors used to describe it: the creation of God, the Great Chain of Being, a clockwork machine, chaos, an evolutionary ecosystem, Mother Nature, Gaia, a cosmic egg, *maya* (appearance, illusion) spun over *Brahman,* or *samsara* (a flow, a turning) which is also *sunyata,* the great Emptiness, or *yang* and *yin* ever recomposing the *Tao.* Neil Evernden concludes, "What we know as nature is what we have *constituted* as nature"; that is we only have access to "the social creation of nature."

Endnote 43

Endnote 44

These pictures of nature have to be recognized as power struggles between different social forces. The environmentalists returning wolves to Yellowstone talk a lot about the integrity of the ecosystem or the wolf as a majestic animal. What really drives them is their sense that the social forces that, earlier in this century, eliminated the wolf were mistaken and that we now ought to choose for Yellowstone to be a different kind of place. Ranchers who oppose the wolf's reintroduction have a different vision of what they want northwest Wyoming to be. They paint the wolf in a different light. At stake is not so much what the wolf really is, but two social groups choosing different futures. The whole future of Earth is always a contest of social forces, constructing first in ideal and then in reality what kind of nature we wish to have.

Figure 2. A coyote in Yellowstone National Park in Wyoming. Animals/Earth Scenes.

Endnote 45

But, the critics reply, we humans are not on Earth alone, and we must be mindful of what and who else is here. We have to know this much to know what else counts in forming our ethics. We do need to know about intrinsic values in nature, if such there are, as we decide what to make of this place we inhabit, what relationship to take up toward these places. On Earth, nature is natural history, and no one has any doubt that there are trees and tigers, mountains and rivers. Any knowing of the various things in nature will be relational. We cannot think about anything without language, but this does not mean that we cannot think with words about the world. This does not mean that that we must avoid claiming these thoughts are right or wrong, or less and more true to what really exists in the external world.

Endnote 46

Environmental ethics is lived on a geographical landscape. So why not accept that in such encounter, nature always wears a human face? Why all this insistence on otherness out there? Because the appropriate behavior for humans, faced with ethical decisions, often involves knowing what good is there in other lives and remains there when humans face in other directions. Environmental ethics is about being native to a place, so why not think of it as choosing our human story? Because there is more story to consider, solidarity with larger biotic communities with whom we share this planet, about whom we must gain truth enough to know something of their places before we can rightly choose ours.

FINAL COMMENTS

Environmental ethics, as we have seen, come in many different forms. There are important differences among the types of environmental ethics we have traced. Nevertheless, variously constructed kinds of environmental ethics need to join as all humans see themselves as Earthlings, with their home planet as a responsibility.

FOR FURTHER INQUIRY

REVIEW QUESTIONS

1. Which of the types of environmental ethics appeals to you most? Which least?

2. Are all the types compatible with each other? Or are there irreconcilable differences among them?

3. Can you think of further types of environmental ethics not sketched here?

4. Are there so many different types of environmental ethics that a person is left confused and hesitant about what he or she ought to think or do?

5. Environmental ethics is sometimes thought to be marginal, less important than medical, business, or development ethics, than concerns for peace or justice, learning the ten commandments or the golden rule? What do you think?

ENDNOTES

1. Lists on the ISEE website bibliography, under "Anthologies" and "Systematic Works." See also under "Introductory Articles."

2. Bryan Norton, *Toward Unity Among Environmentalists*. (New York: Oxford University Press, 1991).

3. J. Baird Callicott, "Animal Liberation: A Triangular Affair," *Environmental Ethics* 2(1980):311–338.

4. Jeremy Bentham, *The Principles of Morals and Legislation* (1789) (New York: Hafner, 1948), ch. 17, sec. 4, p. 311.

5. Peter Singer, *Animal Liberation*, 2nd ed. (New York: A New York Review Book, Random House, 1990); Tom Regan, *The Case for Animal Rights* (Berkeley, CA: University of California Press, 1982).

6. Aldo Leopold, *A Sand County Almanac* (New York: Oxford University Press, 1949, 1969), pp. 224–225, pp. viii–ix, p. 290.

7. Albert Schweitzer, *The Philosophy of Civilization* (New York: Macmillan, 1949), p. 310.

8. Paul Taylor, "Frankena on Environmental Ethics," *Monist* 64(1981):313–324, citation on p. 314; Taylor, *Respect for Nature*; Kenneth E. Goodpaster, "On Being Morally Considerable," *Journal of Philosophy* 75(1978):308–325.

9. Singer, *Animal Liberation*, p. 174, p. 8; W. K. Frankena, "Ethics and the Environment," in K. E. Goodpaster and K. M. Sayre, eds., *Ethics and Problems of the 21st Century* (Notre Dame, IN: University of Notre Dame Press, 1979), pp. 3–20.

10. Paul Shepard, "Ecology and Man — A Viewpoint," in Paul Shepard and Daniel McKinley, eds., *The Subversive Science* (Boston: Houghton Mifflin, 1969), pp. 1–10, citation on p. 3.

11. Warwick Fox, "Deep Ecology: A New Philosophy of Our Time?" *The Ecologist* 14 (nos. 5–6, 1984):194–200, citation on p. 196.

12. Callicott, *In Defense of the Land Ethic*, pp. 173–174.

13. Devall and Sessions, *Deep Ecology*, p. 70.

14. James Nash, *Loving Nature: Ecological Integrity and Christian Responsibility* (Nashville: Abingdon Cokesbury, 1991); Calvin DeWitt, *Earth-Wise: Reclaiming God's Creation* (Grand Rapids, MI: CRC Publications, 1994); Michael S. Northcott, *The Environment and Christian Ethics* (Cambridge: Cambridge University Press, 1996).

15. J. Baird Callicott, *Earth's Insights: A Survey of Ecological Ethics from the Mediterranean Basis to the Australian Outback* (Berkeley: University of California, 1994).

16. Edgar Mitchell, quoted in Kevin W. Kelley, ed., *The Home Planet* (Reading, MA: Addison-Wesley, 1988), at photographs 42–45.

17. Wenz, *Environmental Justice,* pp. 310–335.

18. Richard Routley and Val Routley (later, Richard Sylvan and Val Plumwood), "Human Chauvinism and Environmental Ethics," in Don Mannison, Michael McRobbie, and Richard Routley, eds., *Environmental Philosophy* (Canberra: Department of Philosophy, Research School of Social Sciences, Australian National University, 1980), pp. 96–189, citation on p. 107.

19. J. Baird Callicott, "The Conceptual Foundations of the Land Ethic," in *Companion to a Sand County Almanac*, ed. Callicott (Madison: University of Wisconsin Press, 1987), pp. 186–217, on pp. 207–208.

20. J. Baird Callicott, "The Search for an Environmental Ethic," in Tom Regan, ed., *Matters of Life and Death*, 3rd ed. (New York: McGraw-Hill, 1993), pp. 322–382, citations on pp. 366–367.

21. Johnson, *A Morally Deep World*, p. 134, p. 162, p. 211, p. 217, p. 230, p. 288, and passim.

22. Wenz, *Environmental Justice*, pp. 317, 325, 329, 330.

23. Holmes Rolston, III, *Environmental Ethics*, p. 216–217; Rolston, *Conserving Natural Value*; Rolston, "Value in Nature and the Nature of Value," in Robin Attfield and Andrew Belsey, eds., *Philosophy and the Natural Environment* (Cambridge: Cambridge University Press, 1994), pp. 13–30. Lawrence Johnson makes much the same claims under the vocabulary of "interests" at stake.

24. Tim Hayward, *Ecological Thought: An Introduction* (Oxford: Polity Press, 1995); John O'Neill, *Ecology, Policy, and Politics* (London: Routledge, 1993); Andrew Dobson, ed., *The Green Reader* (London: André Deutsch, 1991); Herman E. Daly and John B. Cobb, Jr., *For the Common Good: Redirecting the Economy toward Community, the Environment, and a Sustainable Future*, rev. ed. (Boston: Beacon Press, 1994).

25. A list is in Rolston, *Environmental Ethics*, pp. 249–253.

26. Garrett Hardin, "The Tragedy of the Commons," *Science* 162 (1968): 1243–1248.

27. Michel Serres, *The Natural Contract* (Ann Arbor: University of Michigan Press, 1995), p. 20.

28. UN Conference on Environment and Development, The Rio Declaration. UNCED Document A/CONF.151/5/Rev. 1, 13 June 1992.

29. Michael Redclift, *Sustainable Development: Exploring the Contradictions* (London: Methuen, 1987); Ronald J. Engel and Joan Gibb Engel, eds., *Ethics of Environment and Development* (Tucson: University of Arizona Press, 1990); John Cobb, Jr., *Sustainability: Economics, Ecology, and Justice* (Maryknoll, NY: Orbis Books, 1992).

30. UN World Commission on Environment and Development, Our Common Future (Oxford: Oxford University Press, 1987), p. 43.

31. United Nations World Commission on Environment and Development, Environmental Protection and Sustainable Development: Legal Principles and Recommendations (London/ Dordrecht, Netherlands: Graham and Trotman/ Martinus Nijhoff Publishers, 1987), p. 9. Also: Our Common Future, pp. 348–351.

32. Our Common Future, p. 8.

33. Engel and Engel, *Ethics of Environment and Development*, pp. 10–11.

34. Kirkpatrick Sale, *Dwellers in the Land: The Bioregional Vision* (San Francisco: The Sierra Club, 1985); Jim Cheney, "Postmodern Environmental Ethics: Ethics as Bioregional Narrative," *Environmental Ethics* 11(1989):117–134; Van Andruss, Christopher Plant, Judith Plant, and Eleanor Wright, eds., *Home! A Bioregional Reader* (Philadelphia: New Society Publishers, 1990); Daly and Cobb, For the Common Good.

35. Sale, *Dwellers in the Land*, p. 43.

36. Rolston, *Environmental Ethics*, pp. 341–354.

37. Karen Warren, "The Power and the Promise of Ecological Feminism," *Environmental Ethics* 12(1990): 125–146, citation on p. 126; Warren, ed., *Ecological Feminism* (London: Routledge, 1994); Irene Diamond and Gloria Feman Orenstein, eds., *Reweaving the World: The Emergence of Ecofeminism* (San Francisco: Sierra Club Books, 1990); Val Plumwood, *Feminism and the Mastery of Nature* (London: Routledge, 1993); Carolyn Merchant, *Earthcare: Women and the Environment* (London: Routledge, 1995).

38. Marti Kheel, in Diamond and Orenstein, "Reweaving the World," p. 129.

39. Warren, "Power and Promise . . . ," p. 141.

40. Neil Evernden, *The Social Creation of Nature* (Baltimore: The Johns Hopkins University Press, 1992); Arran E. Gare, *Postmodernism and the Environmental Crisis* (London: Routledge, 1995); Kate Soper, *What Is Nature?* (Oxford: Blackwell, 1995); Max Oelschlaeger, ed., *Postmodern Environmental Ethics* (Albany: State University of New York Press, 1995).

41. Bryan G. Norton and Bruce Hannon, "Environmental Values: A Place-Based Approach," *Environmental Ethics* 19(1997):227–245; Mark Sagoff, "Settling America or The Concept of Place in Environmental Ethics," *Journal of Energy, Natural Resources and Environmental Law* 12(1992):349–418.

42. Don Cupitt, "Nature and Culture," pages 33–45 in Neil Spurway, ed., *Humanity, Environment and God* (Oxford: Blackwell Publishers, 1993), citation on p. 35.

43. Evernden, *The Social Creation of Nature*, p. 30.

44. Michael E. Zimmerman, *Contesting Earth's Future: Radical Ecology and Postmodernity* (Berkeley, University of California Press, 1994); John A. Hannigan, *Environmental Sociology: A Social Constructivist Perspective* (London: Routledge, 1995).

45. Holmes Rolston, III, "Nature for Real: Is Nature a Social Construct?" in Chappell, ed., *Respecting Nature*, pages 38–64.

46. Elizabeth M. Harlow, "The Human Face of Nature: Environmental Values and the Limits of Nonanthropocentrism," *Environmental Ethics* 14(1992):27–42.

CHAPTER 12

ANIMAL WELL-BEING

"We need a boundless ethics which will include animals also."
—Albert Schweitzer, missionary and statesman

"In studying the traits and dispositions of the so-called lower animals, and contrasting them with man's, I find the result humiliating to me."

—Mark Twain, author

There are a myriad ways in which animals may be treated for human benefit. These include food, clothes, transportation, entertainment, sport, education, research, and — as companions. Although these uses enjoy wide public acceptance, most people would agree that there are limits to the ways we can justifiably interact with animals. We should not torture them because that is cruel and inhumane. But what about situations where hurting or killing animals brings some benefit to human beings?

The quick answer is that animals should not be harmed unless there is good reason, but what is sufficient "good reason"? Is there reason enough to justify harming animals to test cosmetic products? Is animal experimentation that seeks to improve the treatment of human diseases acceptable? Is intensive factory

CHIEF LEARNING OUTCOME

I understand the range of views as to the moral standing of animals and can apply ethical reasoning to the issue.

farming an acceptable way to increase production of food? Are frog dissections, zoos, marine mammal exhibits, greyhound racing, and bull fights justified? The purpose of this chapter is to analyze the ethical reasoning that goes into deciding just where you stand on some of these controversial issues.

F. Barbara Orlans, Ph.D., is a Senior Research Fellow at the Kennedy Institute of Ethics, Georgetown University. A physiologist, she is the author of *In the Name of Science: Issues in Responsible Animal Experimentation*, published in 1993 by Oxford University Press.

MORAL REASONING ABOUT ANIMALS

Four approaches to moral reasoning will be used throughout this discussion to help in decision-making. The concepts are explained below and will be elucidated later when they are applied. The first is the **utilitarian** approach of making a cost/benefit assessment whenever there are conflicting moral choices. This is a mainstream view in which a decision is made by weighing the likely benefits (or pleasures, or good outcomes) against the costs (such as the likely animal pain, deprivation, suffering, or death, etc). A second is the **amount of pain or suffering** the animal experiences as a result of being used by humans for certain purposes. Is it none, or is there minor, moderate, or severe levels of animal pain? There are ways of assessing the degree of animal pain and suffering in terms of severity and duration, and this information is essential before any assessment can be made to justify a particular action. A third concept is a **test of necessity**. What human activities that inflict pain, suffering, or death of an animal can pass this test? A fourth concept, related to necessity, is called the **Three R alternatives — replacement, refinement, and reduction.** Can the same or a similar human objective be achieved without harming an animal at all by *replacing* it with a non-animal method? Can the degree of animal pain or suffering be alleviated by *refining* the methodology? Can the numbers of animals used be *reduced*? By applying the Three R principles, the moral acceptability of a human endeavor can be systematically analyzed and probably be enhanced. These concepts have been gaining greater acceptance over the years in response to the changing public attitudes to animals.

FIVE VIEWS OF HUMAN INTERACTION WITH ANIMALS

<_Exploitation____Use____Welfare____Rights____Liberation_>

Opinions about human relations with animals range across a spectrum of five positions.

Five Positions Regarding Nonhuman Animals: As seen in the figure above, five viewpoints will be presented to reflect varying levels of concern about animals. These views will be described in turn. At the far left is **animal exploitation** which is the view that humans have absolute dominion over animals to use or abuse them for any purpose without restriction. Examples of such activities include blood sports such as bull fighting and dog fighting, and for-profit exploitation such as poaching and trading in exotic and endangered species. There is no concern about the method of killing an animal, however painful or protracted, nor about complying with animal protection laws.

The second view is **animal use** which holds that animals can be used to meet human needs for food, biomedical research, educational purposes, entertainment (such as rodeos, greyhound racing), clothes (such as furs and leather), zoos and marine mammal exhibits. Some of these activities involve holding animals captive against their will, or harming them in other ways or killing them. This treatment is considered justified because humans derive some pleasure or benefit. Persons who hold these views usually believe they can police themselves and don't need animal protection laws. Proposals to enact or strengthen current legislation aimed at improving animal welfare are invariably opposed. Some people with this viewpoint believe that humane shelters should mandatorily hand over one-time companion animals such as dogs and cats to become laboratory animals.

Animal welfare, the third view, holds that animals should be protected from harm, and limits should be placed on animal use for human purposes in order to achieve socially acceptable standards. Groups such as certain animal welfare organizations, animal shelters, and wildlife conservation and environmental protection groups share this view. Animal welfarists believe killing an animal, when needed, must always be fast and painless. Primary activities of welfarists include educating the public about their responsibilities to animals and promoting legislative oversight, legal enforcement, and public scrutiny of the use of animals in many contexts.

The fourth viewpoint, **animal rights,** holds that animals have intrinsic rights that should be guaranteed in the same way as are those of human beings. These rights include not being eaten, used for sport or research, abused, or killed for human purposes. They oppose the killing of animals except to reduce animal suffering. They speak out against use of animals for experimentation, hunting, factory farming, exhibition of wild animals, and wearing fur and leather. They urge public demonstrations, peaceful confrontation, and civil

KEY CONCEPTS

animal exploitation — humans have absolute dominion over animals to use or abuse them for any purpose without restriction

animal use — animals can be used to meet human needs for food, biomedical research, educational purposes, entertainment clothing, zoos and marine mammal exhibits

animal welfare — animals should be protected from harm, and limits should be placed on animal use for human purposes in order to achieve socially acceptable standards. Killing an animal, when needed, must always be fast and painless

animal rights — animals have intrinsic rights that should be guaranteed in the same way as those of human beings are

animal liberation — animals should not either be put to work or used to produce for human benefit in any way

Figure 1. Anti-fur protesters demonstrate. Photo Edit.

Compare Kohlberg's stages of moral development with human treatment of animals.

disobedience, usually working within the law. Animal rights groups and anti-vivisection societies fall within this group.

The fifth view is **animal liberation** which holds that animals should not either be put to work or used to produce for our benefit in any way. Liberationists tend to live a moral life that avoids encroaching on animals and avoids killing animals. Many are vegetarians, and some will not keep companion animals, considering it a form of enslavement. Some hold that their cause is so noble that it justifies breaking the law, as in the laboratory raids of the 1980s in which animals were stolen and equipment vandalized.

These five viewpoints represent a philosophical spectrum; individuals may demonstrate many inconsistencies between the categories. Certain professional groups span a wide spectrum, such as veterinarians, who usually show a great kinship with animals and whose life's work is to look after them. Although the views of some official professional veterinary associations fall squarely in the animal use category, opposing every reform, some veterinarians are among both the animal welfarists and animal rights activists.

RECENT CHANGES IN ATTITUDES

With the rise of the animal rights movement, public attitudes have become more sympathetic toward animals. There has been a shift toward animal welfare, animal rights, and animal liberation. Membership of People for the Ethical Treatment of Animals (PETA), the most well-known animal rights organization, has grown from 60,000 in 1985 to more than 500,000 in 1996. Some people are now more concerned about animal pain, and public opinion polls have documented this concern. For instance, over many years the National Science Board in the United States has asked survey participants to express their level of agreement or disagreement with the following statement: "Scientists should be allowed to do research that causes pain and injury to animals like dogs and chimpanzees if it produces new information about human health problems." The level of agreement with this statement has dropped about ten percentage points (from

63 percent agreeing to 53 percent agreeing) from 1985 to 1992, and continues to drop.

A 1991 Gallup poll of teenagers showed that two-thirds of them supported animal rights. That age is related to attitude was demonstrated in the results of well-designed surveys conducted in 1996 of mental health workers who are members of the American Psychological Association, along with a companion study of undergraduate psychology students. The percentage of students who described themselves as strong supporters of animal research was less than half the corresponding percentage for psychologists (14% versus 31%). There was also a gender difference: female psychologists were significantly less supportive of animal research than were male psychologists (21% of women strongly favored animal research versus 39% of men). A primary and striking result of this survey showed that 92% of these mental health professionals reported that they had rarely or never used findings from psychological research on animals in their clinical practice. Nearly 95% of these psychologists indicated they would not be seriously hampered by a ban on animal research.

Considerable change has taken place. Activities that once were thought to be socially acceptable, such as blinding rabbits in order to test the safety of cosmetics, have now become socially unacceptable and abandoned by some manufacturers. Some highly invasive laboratory animal procedures, such as swimming animals to death as a stress test, have now stopped. More laws have been passed to ensure oversight of animal experimentation and to provide for more humane transportation and killing of food animals. Zoos and animal breeders are subject to government inspections, and tuna fishermen are required to use special nets so that dolphins are not trapped and killed as they were before.

REASONS FOR THE CHANGES

The shift in public attitudes is attributable to two major factors. One is the rise in the animal rights movement, which was sparked by the publication of Peter Singer's book *Animal Liberation* in 1975. The Australian philosopher made a compelling argument about the moral significance of animal pain. He documented many morally unacceptable human uses of animals. Singer's message that we should treat animals more humanely resonated throughout the world. The second major influence on public attitudes emerged from the scientific findings about animal behavior and animal intelligence. From the work of people like Jane Goodall, Donald Griffin, and Jeffrey Masson we learned that chimpanzees use tools (once thought to be a uniquely human ability) and have complex social lives, that animals think, make decisions, and have considerable cognitive abilities. Their work also revealed that many species of animals possess a wide range of emotions such as joy, sadness, grief, fear, rage, shame, compassion, and altruism. Particularly revealing were the scientific insights into

Endnote 1

the considerable mental capacities of non-human primates like chimpanzees, baboons, and gorillas, and of elephants and marine mammals. Scholarly books by animal behaviorists and primatologists include *Almost Human*, *So Like Us*, *When Elephants Weep*, *Animal Thinking*, and *Animal Minds*. With the increasing appreciation of how similar some other species of animals are to humans, the question is raised, just what distinguishes human beings from other creatures as to moral considerations?

Endnotes 2–5

MORAL STANDING OF ANIMALS

The traditional Judeo-Christian view is that there is a great divide between human beings and other animals. Typical are the views of St. Thomas Aquinas, a 13th century philosopher, who held that while humans have rights, animals do not. Humans, he said, are the center of the universe, and animals are here to serve us. Aquinas's views are the official doctrine of the Roman Catholic church today and are reflected in the 1995 edition of the catechism which states: "They [animals] may be used to serve the just satisfaction of man's needs." Only humans have moral standing, that is, are a full part of the moral community.

Over the years, many characteristics have been identified as being uniquely human. Aquinas believed that only humans are capable of abstract thought, while animals lack this capacity. An 18th century French philosopher, Réne Descartes, separated humans from other animals on the grounds that only humans are capable of experiencing pain and suffering. He held that animals are like machines and the cries of animals are like the ticking of a clock, no more. He wrote, "The greatest of all prejudices we have retained from our infancy is that of believing that the beasts think." These views, that animals are incapable of perceiving pain, have persisted into the twentieth century.

Endnote 6

Jeremy Bentham (1748–1832), the English philosopher, disagreed. In his most widely quoted passage, he wrote: "The question is not, can they reason? Nor can they talk? But can they suffer?" These views about the evil of pain have been sympathetically received by the modern animal rights movement.

THE BASIS FOR ANIMAL MORAL STANDING

The Utilitarian Case

Peter Singer's *Animal Liberation* reinvigorated Bentham's view about the significance of animal pain and changed the way many of us view animals. It was published on the heels of the civil rights movement of the 1960s and of the women's rights movement of the 1970s. Another major influence was a sense of outrage over medical experimentation on vulnerable groups, starting with the shocking revelations of the Nazi experiments on concentration camp victims in the Second World War. Prisoners, most of them Jews, were used to test the length of time a human being can survive either in freezing water or in high altitudes which lack suf-

Figure 2. Cats immobilized in laboratory test boxes. Hulton Getty.

ficient oxygen to support life. As a result, victims died painful and lingering deaths. Later came revelations about unacceptable American experiments on syphilitic patients, those terminally ill with cancer, and the mentally disabled. A new field of bioethics emerged, led by philosophers and ethicists who developed arguments and guidelines to protect the rights of vulnerable humans used as subjects of experiments. Most recently, within the past decade, the view has emerged that not only non-Caucasian races, women, prisoners, and indeed all human beings merit moral concern, but that the compass of concern should be extended to non-human animals as well.

Singer rejected Descartes' view that we can treat animals as we like because they are without sensation. Singer argued that animals have feelings, desires, and preferences and that their moral status should be based on their capacity to suffer or experience pleasure. He observed that stimuli causing pain to humans (such as hitting, burning, and so on) also appear to cause pain to animals. However, the capacity to experience pain and to suffer varies. Animals with more complex nervous systems, at least those higher on the phylogenetic scale than mollusks, are capable of perceiving pain, he thought. He argued that these species (cephalopods, fish, amphibians, reptiles, birds, and mammals), like humans, share an interest in not being subjected to pain.

His position is not, as is often mistakenly supposed, that animals are equal in *moral* status to humans. It is that equal harms should be counted equally and not downgraded for animals. As an example, if you slap a horse on its rump, it may start but presumably feels little pain because it has a skin thick enough to protect it. If a baby is slapped with the same force, the baby will cry and presumably does feel pain for its skin is more sensitive. So it is worse to hit a baby than a horse. But there must be some kind of blow, perhaps with a heavy stick, that would cause the horse as much pain as we cause a baby by slapping it with our hand. This is what he means by the "same amount of pain." If we consider it wrong to inflict that much pain on a baby for no reason then, unless we are *speciesists,* it is equally wrong to inflict the same amount of pain on a horse for no good reason. This is a simple point, but nevertheless a part of a far-reaching ethical revolution.

The word speciesism is like racism and sexism, says Singer. Species membership — considered solely as such — is as morally irrelevant as race or gender. Racism and sexism fail to accord equal consideration to equally significant interests and are morally wrong. By similar reasoning, human undervaluation or disregard of the central interests of other species is as morally unjustified as discrimination on the basis or race of sex.

Singer tolerates the need for limited animal research — provided that the likely human benefits that derive from the research outweigh the known animal harms. He is a vegetarian and opposes factory farming. He holds a Utilitarian view that makes pain and pleasure the main criteria for morality. Singer's contribution comes from emphasizing the moral significance of the animal harms in the utilitarian comparison.

The Natural Rights Argument

Endnote 7

Another type of argument, this time based on rights, is made by Tom Regan, professor of philosophy at North Carolina State University. Unlike Singer, he holds that all animal experimentation is wrong, irrespective of how much humans may benefit from the results. He believes that animals have a basic moral right to respectful treatment. Animals have preferences, goals, and desires; they have mental states that enter into the explanation of their behavior. Animals are "subjects of a life" just as humans are, and a subject of a life has intrinsic value. Regan thinks that a sound way to proceed is, for instance, to develop alternative ways of testing toxic substances that will not infringe on animal rights, perhaps using cell and tissue cultures.

THE CASE AGAINST MORAL CONSIDERATION OF ANIMALS

The opposing view claims moral justification for animal experimentation and other human uses of animals that cause the animals harm or death. This view is supported in a number of ways.

Animals Have No Moral Claims

One is to deny that harming and killing animals raise any moral issues at all. This is not a widely held view, but two modern-day proponents are the Nobel Prize winner David Baltimore, a microbiologist, and Robert J. White, a professor of surgery at Case Western Reserve University. Baltimore appeared on public television in 1974 in a panel discussion of a controversial documentary that had been made about primate research. The scientists present were asked if the fact that an experiment would kill hundreds of animals is ever regarded by them as a reason for not performing it. Baltimore responded by saying that he did not think that experimenting on animals raises a moral issue at all. White, in 1990, sharply criticized a 32-page report that had appeared in the highly respected journal of biomedical ethics, the *Hastings Center Report*, that had explored the "middle ground," which holds that some but not all animal experimentation is justified. White, in a letter to the editor, expressed his "extreme disappointment" at this series of articles which "quite frankly, has no right to be published. Animal usage is not a moral or ethical issue and elevating the problems of animal rights to such a plane is a disservice to medical research and the farm and dairy industry." Some years before, White's own research of grafting a second head onto a live dog had come under severe criticism from the humane movement.

The Defense of Speciesism

Another approach is taken by a much-heralded supporter of animal research, Carl Cohen, a professor of philosophy at the University of Michigan. In 1986, in a brief article in the *New England Journal of Medicine* he defended speciesism in which only humans have moral worth. He maintained that speciesism is "essential for right conduct" and more, not less, animal experimentation should be done. Cohen's view is that animal experimentation is justified virtually without restriction. He holds that animals lack certain capacities and therefore have no rights. The essential ingredients that are lacking in animals are the ability to respond to moral claims, the capacity to comprehend rules of duty, and the capacity to recognize certain conflicts between what is in their own interest and what is just. For animals, membership in the moral community "remains impossible."

Cohen believes that we should load the scale of weighing benefits against harms with the "terrible" human pains that would have resulted had animals not been used in research. His defense of increasing animal experimentation is based on the premise that we should avoid when feasible the use of humans as experimental subjects. He does not address the possibility that non-harmful human experimentation could replace some injurious animal experiments — as in the substitution of human clinical research instead of producing animal models of head injury studies. He denies that non-animal alternatives (cell cultures and computer modeling) have been extensively developed in recent years. The argument goes that humane, generous treatment of animals is a matter of charity and compassion. It stems from human benevolence, not from the animal's moral claim.

A Challenge to Utilitarianism

In justifying human uses of animals that cause harm and death, the utilitarian viewpoint is not altogether satisfactory. As we have seen, Singer suggests weighing the utilitarian scales by taking more account of the animal pain, and Cohen urges taking more account of the human benefits. But critics claim that a fundamental flaw exists in this equation: We are trying to compare two incommensurables. Virtually all the harms fall on the animals and virtually all the benefits fall on the humans. Some critics of utilitarian thinking believe that there is more to ethics than merely the net amount of benefit. They believe it also matters morally how the harm is *distributed*. So, there is a movement to reject this utilitarian view in favor of a stronger claim for the animals on the basis that they are part of the moral community. Therefore, they should not be harmed just as humans should not be.

According to the view that gives priority to humans over animals, human interests rank higher and have more value, and count for more whenever they are in conflict with the interests of animals. These people hold (in a manner similar to those discussed in Chapter 7 who defend abortion) that one has full moral standing if and only if one possesses certain distinctive cognitive properties. Among the conditions that have been suggested are a list similar to the one considered in Chapter 7 including such features as:

* capacity to make moral judgments
* self-consciousness (of oneself as existing over time)
* capacity to appreciate reasons for acting
* capacity to communicate with other persons using a language
* rationality

But this view is challenged. Since Charles Darwin's day in the 19th century, the similarities of humans with other animals have been increasingly documented. Darwin's important scientific work demonstrated a continuum of life. Within the compass of living organisms there are generalizations that apply broadly. There is a unity in biology that is seen in the universality of cell theory and of other common features in biological structure and function. A prime example is that the genetic code exists from the simplest virus all the way to humans.

Universality is seen in the development of all vertebrate embryos (those with a backbone) consisting of a common program of blastula formation — a program that is characteristic also of most creatures who lack backbones (such as insects and snails). Indeed, it can be hard for the naked eye to distinguish between developing embryos of certain species; a bird embryo looks very much like a human embryo. In some respects certain animals have innate capacities of the sort relevant to the above list that exceed those of humans. To mention only a few, dogs and several other species have a better sense of smell and range of hearing than humans; hawks and other birds can see better; mice can see ultraviolet light; bats have innate ability to use radar and to orient themselves to the sun's rays; bees with their waggle dance can convey information about the direction, distance, and desirability of a food source; and whales can communicate with each other over hundreds of miles. Whales have complex language in their "singing" which humans are only now beginning to study and appreciate. Of course all species are different from each other but the superiority of humans in every function, aspect or behavior is not absolute.

In some ways, other species are very similar to humans. Differences sometimes seem to be more a matter of degree than of kind. For instance, the cognitive and behavioral abilities

Figure 3. Is pain suffered by animals in laboratory tests justified by pain relieved in humans as a result of such experiments? PhotoDisc, Inc.

of chimpanzees are thought to be very much like those of humans. They live and hunt in communities, they form strong family bonds, and they make tools. They can suffer emotional and physical pain in similar ways and often for the same reasons as humans. Chimpanzees, like many other species, have an ability to communicate with each other; they tell each other about specific dangers and the location of food sources.

Tom Beauchamp, a professor of philosophy at Georgetown University, has argued that so long as one requires a high level of cognitive criteria, animals may not be able to qualify for significant moral standing. But if one appeals to less demanding cognitive capacities, such as intention, understanding, desire, preferences, suffering, and having beliefs, animals will likely acquire a significant range of moral protections. For example, if a high-level qualifying condition such as the capacity to make moral judgments is eliminated and conditions like intention and understanding are substituted, then it becomes plausible to find the cognitive capacities needed for moral standing in at least some animals.

In this light, a group of animal behaviorists, philosophers, and other scholars has recently argued the case for a widening of the moral community. They note that some women and racial groups who once were thought to have no moral rights have recently attained some equality with white males, and urge that now it is time to extend the moral community still further. In a 1993 Declaration on Great Apes, they declare: "We demand the extension of the community of equals to include all great apes: human beings, chimpanzees, gorillas and orangutans. The Community of Equals is the moral community within which we accept certain basic moral principles or rights as governing our relations with each other and enforceable at law." The principles are the right to life, the protection of individual liberty, and the prohibition of torture. The supporting argument is that the great apes are *persons* just as humans are *apes*. This Declaration was agreed upon by such animal rights advocates as Jane Goodall, Tom Regan, and primatologists Roger and Deborah Fouts, and Francine Patterson. A worldwide campaign is in progress for additional signatories to this Declaration.

With this overview of philosophical positions regarding moral treatment of animals, we now turn to some specific cases of human use of animals to examine how various approaches to moral reasoning can be applied.

USE OF ANIMALS IN EDUCATION

In recent decades, biology education has relied extensively on killing animals for dissection and often also involves harming sentient animals in experiments. Questions are now being raised about the widespread use of frogs, cats, dogs and pigs for dissection. Much valuable laboratory time is spent in dissection that nowadays often starts in elementary schools and continues through high school and college so that a student may conduct many animal dissections. Furthermore, high school projects are being questioned that include cutting open turtles to watch their hearts beat, feeding rats and mice diets deprived of essential nutrients or injecting animals with known toxic substances.

A reason for this unfettered animal experimentation has been the total lack of any formal review process for animal use in biology education. Only recently, since 1985, have classroom projects for some undergraduate programs been subject to formal review by an institutional oversight committee to determine compliance with the Animal Welfare Act. Only certain educational institutions that are registered under the Animal Welfare Act are subject to these provisions. As a result of this review by Institutional Animal Care and Use Committees, some student labs, for instance, those in which toxic substances have been administered to rabbits or guinea pigs, have been disapproved in some institutions. However, a great many colleges, including most community colleges, fall outside the Animal Welfare Act because they only use rats, mice, or birds, species excluded from the Animal Welfare Act.

In medical schools, students are protesting "dog labs" in which normal healthy animals are tested for drug reactions or used for practice surgery before being killed. Veterinary students have been in the forefront of demanding that they graduate without ever having harmed an animal unnecessarily. They have joined this profession, they say, because they love animals. They want to learn animal surgery by doing only needed therapeutic operations, for instance spay and neuter surgeries in local shelters, or working as apprentices in a veterinary clinical practice. Alternative methods to learn the practice of the veterinary profession are being developed.

One rationale for not harming vertebrate animals in biology education is that harming or killing them is unnecessary. A wide range of educational alternatives is available, and there is a moral imperative to use these methods wherever possible. Some people hold that it is morally indefensible to hurt or kill sentient animals unless original contributions that will advance human health and welfare can be expected. Emotionally immature youth, especially in this age of violence, can become desensitized and their attitudes toward animals can be hardened if they are required to harm or kill an animal.

Arguments in favor of having young students do dissections, live-animal surgery, and cancer studies are based on the view that students will be attracted to careers in science because of these activities. Some have defended dissection as an "essential" part of education.

Official policies and voluntary guidelines governing the use of animals in education are in their infancy. Codes of practice have been slow to develop and have lagged behind those concerning the use of animals in research and testing. Indeed, often no distinction is made between what a student is allowed to do and what a fully-trained scientist feels justified in doing. But this does not make sense because beginning students lack the competency of fully-trained persons and are more likely to produce botched work and greater animal suffering. Also, student experiments can be of a trivial nature, and the results are highly unlikely to make a contribution to original knowledge, as can well-planned experiments by skilled professionals.

An important ethical consideration is that alternatives are available that do not harm or kill sentient animals. The types of suitable alternatives vary with educational level. A common, social view is biology education would be enhanced by an increased study of living organisms. At the grade school and undergraduate college level, useful studies can include plants, protozoa, invertebrates, free-living animals in their natural habitats, companion and zoo animals. The use of invertebrates, protozoa, and plants have the advantage of ready availability in large numbers and little expense. Use of these living creatures carries less ethical cost than using vertebrate animals because living organisms lower on the phylogenetic scale do not have such complex nervous systems and therefore are less able to perceive pain than those "higher" up. Some states and school districts have either adopted official policies allowing student rights to conscientious objection or have specifically outlawed dissection.

Alternatives for veterinary, medical, and nursing schools include high-tech, life-like patient simulators complete with pulses, heart and breath sounds, EKG, and pulmonary pressure reading that respond to simulated administration of dozens of different drugs.

These allow trainees to learn, make mistakes, and start over in a realistic context. Also, videos and inter-active computer programs are available for demonstrating drug reactions for basic pharmacology, and to learn anesthesiology, physiology, and clinical medicine.

A number of organizations are involved in fostering use of Three R alternatives in education. These include The Humane Society of the United States, which has a web site to help students and teachers. The Association of Veterinarians for Animal Rights has also been active in this area. They survey veterinary schools and publish information on which schools offer alternative programs that allow students to qualify without harming or killing healthy animals. The Physicians Committee for Responsible Medicine serves a similar role for medical schools. In 1996, 34 out of 128 U.S. medical schools (or about 27% of the total) had no dog or other animal labs. Harvard University offers an alternative program that does not require participation in harming animals.

Use of these living creatures carries less ethical cost than using vertebrate animals because living organisms lower on the phylogenetic scale do not have such complex nervous systems and therefore are less able to perceive pain than those "higher" up.

Although there is no absolute consensus in the U.S. about just what students should or should not be allowed to do, this is not true of some other countries. Nationally mandated policies of several European countries (including Germany and The Netherlands) relate the student's educational level (which is related to competency level) to justification for experimentation that causes animal pain or death. High school and undergraduate students are not permitted to conduct experiments *that cause vertebrate animals pain or death*. Students must have completed university degree studies in the natural sciences before they can start such work.

To understand the basis for these policies, application of the pain scale concept can be useful. Beginners (elementary, high school, and college undergraduates) start with projects that do not involve ethical costs, so studies of plants, protozoa, invertebrates such as insects and worms, and non-harmful investigations of vertebrates including human subjects are selected. Non-harmful student observation projects include study of normal living functions such as food intake, growth, behavior, communication, and the study of normal living patterns of companion animals or wild animals in their natural habitats or in zoological parks or aquaria. As the student's commitment to a career in the sciences matures, then non-harmful vertebrate studies or those involving only minor pain — such as blood sampling, taking X-rays, and terminal experiments under anesthesia are permitted. Later, the goal of the experiment shifts from being solely educational to the search for new, significant knowledge. Most commonly, this occurs at the graduate school level so, at this point, minor and moderate levels of pain infliction may be considered permissible. The severe band of pain infliction would be restricted to fully-qualified persons who use minimal numbers of animals in exceedingly well-designed experiments that have been subjected to careful peer review. In this way, only those seriously committed to a career in the sciences receive public sanction to harm animals.

BIOMEDICAL RESEARCH

For the past 20 years, the largely unproductive debate over the use of animals for biomedical research has been intensive but views are highly polarized. Much of the discourse has been clouded by propaganda of simple assertions with little attempt to achieve a productive discussion. At the core of the dispute is the value judgment of how far is it permissible to use animals as a means to an end. Those who believe that animals are here in this world to serve human ends are pitted against those who do not share this view and have a qualified (limited) view of what animal research is acceptable.

The Human-Benefit Justification

Those who support animal experiments argue that the "ends justify the means": great improvements have been made in human health as a result of animal research. The argument is that animals have played a crucial role in the development of modern Western medicine. Knowledge has been gained about the diagnosis, treatment, natural history, and prevention of diseases. Research continues to be needed not only to alleviate existing human ailments but to respond to the emergence of new diseases such as AIDS. Many past examples are cited including the development of vaccines, antibiotics and insulin, treatments for kidney failure, heart disease, cancer, and infertility, and many life-saving surgical procedures. Animal research also contributes basic knowledge. Without animal research, utilitarians argue the development of new treatments for human diseases would be seriously impaired.

The Opposition

Those who oppose this view claim that this approach is wasteful, misleading, and morally wrong. They believe that animal research is poorly suited to address urgent health problems of our era. Methods such as epidemiological studies, human clinical studies, patient studies, study of autopsies and biopsies, computer and mathematical modeling, and tissue culture work yield more reliable information. According to this view, improvements in human health and longevity during the 20th century are not attributable to animal experimentation, as some claim, but to improvements in sanitation and better living conditions. Some animal experiments have given false data that are not applicable to the human condition. An oft-cited example is the Thalidomide tragedy of 1961 in which the drug (used for suppression of morning sickness in pregnant women) had passed safety testing in animals in Europe but resulted in severe abnormalities of missing arms and legs in children born to many of these women. Finally, the opposition contends, animals have integral worth of their own which should be respected and certain species of animals (especially chimpanzees and other non-human primates) are part of the moral community.

Oddly enough, both pro-animal researchers and those opposed to animal research may argue their case from a Utilitarian approach of weighing harms against benefits. Those, like Cohen, emphasize the weight of human benefits and others, like Singer, emphasize the weight of animal harms. So, with the same data, using a harms and benefits calculus, people can arrive at opposite views.

Primate Research — A Special Case

Special problems are faced when considering experimentation on non-human primates such as chimpanzees, baboons, and rhesus monkeys, common laboratory species. The easily recognized similarities of these species to humans and their well-developed cognitive abilities and capacities to experience pain and suffering have aroused public sympathy. Furthermore, these species were, up until recently typically single-housed in barren laboratory cages and therefore lived in deprived conditions.

In 1987, Jane Goodall, the world-renowned primatologist, wept when she saw chimpanzees being used for hepatitis research at Sema, a laboratory under contract with the National Institutes of Health, housed in "isolette" cages. She graphically described the suffering of these chimps who were maintained in conditions of severe sensory and social deprivation that caused aberrant behaviors that would make them become insane. She wrote that they were "far gone in depression and despair . . . crammed into tiny cages."

Dogs and Cats for Research

A highly contentious issue is whether or not one-time companion animals should be mandatorily relinquished from humane shelters and used for research. The biomedical community seems pitted against the humane movement on this issue. In the rising affluence after the second world war, the United States embarked on an accelerated program of biomedical research and the demand for laboratory dogs and cats increased. A ready source of cheap animals appeared to be from city pounds where unwanted and abandoned animals were being euthanized. In the 1940s and thereafter, national lobbying organizations for the biomedical community have worked for the passage of state laws requiring that shelters, pounds, and animal control agencies relinquish unadopted dogs and cats for use in laboratories. On the other hand, the animal protection movement has pressed for laws that prohibit this practice. Currently, of the states that have laws at all, they are about evenly divided between these opposing viewpoints.

The pet overpopulation has aggravated this problem. Over recent decades, many dogs and cats unfortunately are kept by irresponsible owners who allow their animals unrestricted breeding. The resultant pet overpopulation has been hard to control. Humane shelters, who adopt out abandoned and unwanted animals, run vigorous campaigns to persuade the public to spay or neuter their pets. But even so, shelters have to euthanize about 6-million dogs and cats each year because no homes can be found for them. It is some of these animals that the scientists want.

Researchers argue that since these shelter animals are unwanted and doomed to die anyhow, why not use them for a socially useful purpose? Also the animals are less expensive than animals bred specially for the purpose of research, thus saving research dollars. The animal welfare/rights view is that human beings have a profound moral responsibility to domesticated animals, and this cannot be forsaken at any point in those animals' lives. Shelters should be sanctuaries for animals, and not a supply line for biomedical researchers. Animals for research should be a different population of animals than those that were one-time pets. From a dog's viewpoint, a humane death may be a better choice than a longer life being a subject of a painful experiment.

At one time, virtually all dogs and cats used in research came from animal shelters. But since the mid 1980s, this clash of viewpoints has been somewhat lessened by the fact that commercial breeders for laboratory dogs have become established. It is a profitable business. Commercial breeders can supply animals who are healthy, of known age and genetic make-up, and who are more reliable experimental subjects than so-called "random source dogs" from shelters.

U.S. Animal Welfare Act Amendments

Some improvements have occurred because of an amendment to the United States Animal Welfare Act which now requires that the "psychological well-being" of primates must be considered. As a result, efforts are now made to double cage or group house primates and also to provide them branches, perches, toys, and more varied food.

In the 1980s when laboratory raids were a major activity of the animal rights movement, primate research was a major target. Activists produced evidence of ill treatment of animals, poor housing conditions, and some serious infractions of the Animal Welfare Act. This law requires certain minimum standards of housing involving cage size and sanitation, use of anesthetics and pain-relieving drugs during and after surgery, veterinary care, and other provisions. The unacceptable conditions uncovered by these raids aroused worldwide public concern. In the United States, infractions of the law found during the 1984 raid on the baboon head-injury laboratory of the prestigious University of Pennsylvania was a key factor in the enactment of more stringent legal federal requirements in 1985 which, for the first time, required prior committee approval of research protocols. At the same time, personal threats to researchers and destruction of their property and research data caused anger in the scientific community.

Animal Care and Use Committees

The 1985 amendment to the Animal Welfare Act requires that Institutional Animal Care and Use Committees be established to oversee animal experiments. Their responsibilities include approving all research protocols and inspecting the animal facilities. Typically such a committee consists, at a minimum, of an animal researcher, a

Researchers argue that since these shelter animals are unwanted and doomed to die anyhow, why not use them for a socially useful purpose?

veterinarian, and a person not affiliated with the institution (who could be a retired researcher, a high school science teacher, an ethicist, a non-scientist, a banker, etc.) At first, these committees were little more than rubber stamps, but they have improved over time. Although the law requires that the Three R alternatives be "considered," in the early days investigators would state that this was not applicable to their research. However, the US Department of Agriculture, the administering government agency, now requires specific documentation that alternatives have been considered. Mainly the committees check for adequacy of anesthetics and humaneness of euthanasia method.

Problems with Public Representation on the Committees

There are still problems. Committee appointments are made by the institution giving them complete control on membership and there is not a strong public involvement in decision-making. Congress had wanted to make clear that scientists are not free to do whatever they want to animals and decision-making should not rest solely in their hands. But the letter and not the spirit of the law seems to apply, and the voice of the public remains muted in most cases.

Problems with Assessment of Pain

Another problem is that in the US there is no formal requirement of these committees to assess the degree (severity and duration) of animal pain. It is essential that this be done in each individual case for three reasons. First, it is necessary to determine that the upper level of permissible pain is not exceeded, and only when it has been established that the experimental procedures fall within an acceptable range is the *second* judgment made of balancing the level of pain against potential human benefit. Without establishing an upper limit, potentially extreme levels of animal pain and suffering can be justified by high levels of perceived potential human benefit. The second judgment involves balancing the level of pain against the potential human benefit to see if the experiment is justified at all. The third judgment is to see if any alternatives can be applied. This involves seeing if non-animal models could be substituted, or if the level of pain reduced by modifying the experimental procedure or if the numbers of animals could be reduced. Then, when the level of animal pain or harm has been either eliminated or reduced, the second judgment can be reassessed of balancing the final level of pain against the potential human benefit.

Regarding the first point, a number of countries have banned specific procedures. For instance, in 1997, the Swiss Academy of Medical Sciences announced a long list of procedures that are no longer permitted. Examples include social deprivation of young animals, the use of pain for negative enforcement (i.e. as punishment), the induction of convulsions that do not cause immediate loss of consciousness, and many others.

As to the second point, it is a legal requirement in several countries that investigators assess their projected animal experiments according to the level of likely animal pain, suffering, or other harms. The justification for using a pain classification is that without knowledge of how much animal pain is involved, any assessment of the justification of an animal experiment cannot even begin to be made. This rating system establishes various categories of animal pain as minor, moderate, or severe. This system is variously called a "pain scale," severity banding, or an invasiveness scale. As examples, minor procedures include simple blood sampling, taking X-rays of unanesthetized animals, and force feeding innocuous substances; moderately painful procedures include insertion of indwelling catheters, skin transplantation, and cesarean section; severe procedures include prolonged deprivation of food, water, or sleep, total bleeding without anesthesia, application of painful stimulation and induction of convulsions. The national policies of Canada, United Kingdom, The Netherlands, New Zealand, and Switzerland require use of such a pain scale. Although a few US research facilities voluntarily use this system in their review process, efforts to make this a national policy have repeatedly failed.

Research Involving New Technologies

Complex ethical issues already surround biomedical research but with new advances in biotechnology, they are increasing. Efforts have been made to transplant livers from baboons to humans, and there has been talk of farming baboons or pigs to provide a ready supply of organs for humans. Little is known about the ways in which diseases can be spread from one species to another, so this tissue transfer raises concerns for both humans and other animals. Genetic manipulation in which genes are transferred from humans to other animals raises serious issues of species identity (a problem considered further in Chapter 11). Genetic engineering adversely affects animal welfare, as happens when animals are intentionally created with diseases that cause intense suffering. Examples include laboratory animals that have cancer, cystic fibrosis, Huntington's disease, Alzheimer's disease, and some rare but severe neurological conditions. With cloning of agricultural animals which is likely to become more widespread, genetic diversity is threatened. While biotechnology is revolutionizing science, public debate over the moral, ethical, and physical effects of this research has been lacking and societal rules have yet to be developed.

ANIMALS AS FOOD

Traditions of using animals as food are long-established in the U.S. and many other cultures. But this is not universal: Hindus are vegetarians and other religions put restrictions on eating certain animal species. According to official U.S. data, in 1997 there were 9.3 billion animals killed for food consumption, a number overwhelmingly greater than the approximately 13 million animals used for biomedical research. The numbers of animals eaten in America has remained fairly constant over recent years, but there has been a decline in eating beef and an increase in eating chicken. In 1992, the U.S. per capita consumption of broiler chickens was 66.8 lbs., which surpassed both beef (66.5) and pork (53.1).

The Emergence of Automated Mass Production of Animals

In American and European cultures, farming practices have changed radically over the last few decades. The image of Old McDonald's farm of nursery-rhyme fame, where the benevolent farmer individually tended his free-roaming cattle, sheep, pigs, and chickens is a thing of the past. Current "factory farming" practices involve mass production of animals in heavily engineered and automated systems. The animals are reared indoors in huge numbers, closely confined in artificially lit spaces, mechanically supplied with food, and treated with drugs and hormones to prevent disease and to speed growth. These systems pay little regard for animal welfare. The animal protection movement has been strongly opposed to these farming methods ever since they started. But profits for farmers are considerably increased. An ethical question that arises for the chicken, veal, dairy, beef, and hog farmers and others associated with the meat trade, is under what conditions, if any, should farmers be permitted to sacrifice animal welfare for personal gain?

The Broiler Chicken Industry

As an example of this factory farming, the broiler chicken industry will be described. Day-old chicks are reared as a single batch on an all in/all out system. They have been intensively bred for rapid growth, high appetites, and breast muscle volume. Throughout their short six-week lives they live in vast overcrowded sheds that typically house from 10,000 to 50,000 chicks. Near-continuous low-level lighting is provided for 23 or even 24 hours a day so that aggression resulting in cannibalism and feather pecking is reduced. In the past, this was a significant problem but flocks have now been bred to be less aggressive. The bed of wood shavings on the floor is gradually replaced with feces, and the shed can become smelly. Birds are provided with a high-protein diet which contains growth promoters, antibiotics, and antiparasite drugs to prevent infections. Food and water are always available. The maximum recommended stocking density is around seven pounds of bird mass for every square foot, which is equivalent to a single sheet of legal-size paper for each fully-grown bird.

A major health problem for these birds is leg weakness. In some extreme cases, birds have been bred to the point that they have so much body weight that they cannot stand at all; their legs are not strong enough. But some degree of leg weakness is common among all flocks of factory-farmed broiler chickens. A 1992 survey in four flocks of broilers comprising 1127 birds at slaughter weight raised under factory farming conditions found that only one-tenth of the birds walked normally. All the others (90%) had some abnormalities of which 26% were severe enough so that the birds limped, had unsteady strut or severe splaying of the legs. Other health problems are lung infections, heart disease and blisters that develop because of the close contact with the damp litter as they squat. Approximately 6% die before reaching the slaughterhouse.

All the birds are killed at the same time. Teams of catchers collect the birds, load them into crates, and drive them to the processing factory. The birds are shackled by their legs onto a moving conveyer belt. Hanging upside down, they are stunned instantaneously with an electric current and a mechanical cutter slits their throats so that they bleed to death. If insufficient current is used, the birds may recover consciousness before being bled out. To make plucking more easy, the birds first pass into a tank of boiling water. They are then eviscerated, inspected, and packed for the retail trade. Sheds are then cleaned and disinfected, and the process starts again.

Balanced against the poor welfare of these animals are some benefits for some people. Farmers make greater profits than previously and some members of the public are provided with a food that they like. Production costs for the farmer are relatively low because the systems are efficient and intense automation significantly reduces labor costs. In the retail market place, chicken is considered to be an inexpensive, palatable source of healthful protein. Twenty-five years ago, chicken meat cost $3.75/lb; in 1998 it cost approximately $1.30/lb. The public has welcomed this trend by relying more and more on eating chicken. On the other hand, the public has become more desensitized to food production methods and pays little heed to the animals' well-being.

The Vegetarian and Other Alternatives

Despite these problems, meat eating continues both because of tradition and because some people find it adds to life's pleasures. Meat is not a dietary necessity. Indeed, environmentally, it is an inefficient source of human dietary protein. Meat substitutes, such as soybean, nuts, and other plant products are more environmentally friendly. Considering the poor nutrition standards of many countries, some people consider that the level of meat-eating in Western countries is environmentally unsound and unjustified. People most sensitive to animal issues will not eat meat at all or at least they cut back on meat-eating. This seems to be particularly true among younger populations.

What other alternatives are being pursued? Some members of the public willingly pay more for their meat, eggs, and dairy products in order to gain more welfare-friendly products. Some beginning efforts are being made to label food products to provide information on system of production, thus giving the public a choice. National laws could be changed. In some U.S. states, poultry are exempt from the cruelty statutes because they are not considered "animals." The animal protection movement is working to achieve mandatory codes of practice for farmers that restrict stocking densities and improved standards of animal housing and maintenance. Animal welfare standards (such as acceptable levels of mortality and disease) could be established and farmers who fail to achieve these standards could be penalized.

ANIMAL TESTING FOR COSMETIC PRODUCT SAFETY

Products such as cosmetics, toiletries, and vanity products have been routinely tested on animals to check for safety before they are marketed. The rationale is that what is harmful to animals is likely to be harmful to humans. Two widely-used tests — the Draize and the Lethal Dose (LD) 50 — have been the focus of a largely successful campaign to make animal testing more humane. The LD50 is the dose that causes death of 50 percent of the animals. As used in the past, the Draize, in which irritants and toxic substances were applied directly to the eye, could cause blindness in rabbits.

Because of efforts by animal rights' activists, many reforms have taken place. By 1980, Revlon announced that it would donate $750,000 to Rockefeller University to research possible alternatives. By 1988, Revlon announced a moratorium on animal tests conducted in their own facilities. By 1998, a number of companies have announced that they have completely stopped using animals in product testing. These include Amway, Mary Kay Cosmetics, Charles of the Ritz, Elizabeth Arden, Estée Lauder, and others.

Many Three R alternatives have been developed for both the Draize and LD50 tests and other toxicity tests that cause animal pain. Non-animal methods have been developed and substituted. Methods that reduce animal pain and numbers of animals used are now common. Among the many modern, widely-used ways of testing eye irritation is the "low-volume eye test" which was developed by scientists at Procter and Gamble. Only one tenth of the previously used dose volume is now applied, and only dilute substances are tested. Similar improvements have been made for testing skin, and inhalation irritation. By now, the test results are not only more humane but are a more accurate predictor of irritation. Similarly, more humane methods that use either no animals or fewer animals, and cause less pain and suffering have been substituted for the old fashioned LD50. Many new tests have been developed that rely on use of tissue cultures, use of computers, and *in vitro* assays on protein reagents. Another alternative now widely used in the cosmetic industry is to test new products on human volunteers.

Many people are of the view that animal testing for cosmetics should be banned because it fails the necessity test. Not only does the animal suffering far outweigh the likely human benefits, but many alternative ways of achieving the goal of assuring consumer safety are available. The European Community has banned the use of Draize and LD50 tests. In some nations (but not the U.S.) any animal use in cosmetic testing is banned. For instance, both Germany and the United Kingdom have enacted national bans on use of animals in product development and testing of cosmetics, alcohol, and tobacco products.

The impact of these reforms, although concentrated on the cosmetic and household product manufacturers, has had a broad effect. There has been intensive work by toxicologists in the development of Three R alternatives applicable to all areas of consumer safety testing. Acute toxicity tests, as described more than 50 years ago, involved large numbers of animals and required death as the endpoint. These tests have now been superseded. The tests normally performed in the late '90s accept estimated data on lethality, and in some countries regulatory authorities accept signs of toxicity rather than death as a valid endpoint. The LD50 test has been further refined so that a maximum dose level is laid down, the so called Limit Test, in which a maximum single dose rate is given. If the substance shows no toxicity at that level (interpreted as one or no animal(s) dying out of 10 dosed after fourteen days) the substance is classified as nontoxic. If two or more animals die, then a second group will be tested using a lower dose. The complete test normally requires ten to twenty rats instead of hundreds. It is likely that even further humane refinements will be possible in the future.

The advances in applying the Three Rs in the field of cosmetics testing have been influential in other areas of animal testing, research, and the use of animals in education. The science of new tests using tissue cultures, computer modeling, and other less animal-harming methods has demonstrated the practicality of the Three Rs approach. Toxicologists, those scientists who are involved in investigating poisonous effects of substances, are among those most committed to the Three Rs. Many toxicology journals are now devoted to Three R publications. Academic institutions have established professorial chairs in animal welfare, and in several countries, including the U.S., there are government-funded centers devoted to providing information to scientists and the public about the Three Rs.

Of course, live animal testing continues to be used for many purposes other than cosmetics, for instance, to check the environmental safety of persons working in factories producing toxic chemicals, to protect the users of pesticides in agriculture, and to protect children who might swallow a toxic substance. These other purposes do not so readily fail the necessity test as does cosmetic manufacture. So live animal testing is not likely to die out completely for a long time, but application of the Three Rs in these other fields will contribute significantly to reducing the degree of harms inflicted on animals.

BLOOD SPORTS

Blood sports are those in which the purpose or outcome of the activity is the maiming or killing of an animal. They include cockfighting, dogfighting, bullfighting, and also hunting wild animals to death such as deer or fox. In some blood sports animals are pitted to fight either against each other (as in cock or dog fighting), or against humans (as in bullfighting). The entertainment value for humans comes from enjoying the spectacle of fierce and often deadly combat, which some people find thrilling, and admiring the skills of the protagonists. According to one view, people should be entirely free to choose their recreational activities. In some countries these sports can be a major national recreation and part of their cultural heritage.

Indeed, there are specific "cultures" that accompany these sports. They require rituals and strictly followed routines of how the combat should proceed. For the human participants specific clothing may be required, sometimes colorful and extravagant. Complicated rules of combat apply that only the fully initiated know. In bullfighting, for instance, there is a sequence of rituals: cape waving is followed by lancing of the bulls, the banderilleros plant stinging barbed sticks into the animals' withers, and finally the matador comes with cape and sword and kills the bull. To be involved in these activities provides camaraderie and "membership in a club."

Cockfighting

"Animals are my friends . . . and I don't eat my friends."
—George Bernard Shaw

Cockfighting is a centuries-old blood sport in which two or more specially bred roosters (called gamecocks) are placed in an enclosed space of 15 to 20 feet diameter to fight. A cockfight usually results in the death of one of the birds; sometimes it ends in the death of both. Before the fight, steel "gaffs" (knives) are attached to the roosters' legs and bound into place with leather straps in order to increase their ability to harm. A typical cockfight can last from anywhere from several minutes to more than half an hour.

A mature gamecock resembles a rooster whose comb and earlobes have been surgically removed. Serious cockfighters subject their birds to intensive programs of training before a fight which include such activities as running, flying, resistance pulling, and sparring. Vitamins, strychnine (used as a stimulant), hormones, and drugs are often given to the birds. The bird's "gameness," or ability to withstand fighting, is much admired. In 1998 cockfighting was illegal in 45 of the 50 U.S. states and the District of Columbia. Current efforts are being made by humane organizations in both Missouri and Arizona to pass state laws to prohibit these activities. In South Carolina, a magazine for cockfighters with ads on where to obtain supplies is published openly and distributed to other states. Cockfighting is generally not recognized as a form of sport by the Latin American countries, and it has been prohibited for years in some countries including Cuba, Paraguay, and Costa Rica.

Cockfighting has existed for thousands of years in many parts of the world. It is believed to have been a popular diversion in ancient times in parts of India, China, Persia, and other eastern countries. Cockfighting was introduced to Greece in about 500 BC, and it spread throughout Asia Minor and Sicily. The Romans were responsible for the first artificial gaffs and the introduction of cockfighting to Britain.

Dogfighting

Dogfighting, although more recent in origin, has a number of similarities to cockfighting. This is a contest in which two dogs, specially bred and trained to fight, are placed in a pit for the purpose of attacking each other to earn money for their owners and to entertain spectators. Fights average nearly an hour in length and often last more than two hours. Dogfights end when one of the dogs is no longer willing or able to continue. Injuries sustained by dogs in these fights are frequently severe, even fatal. A commonly used breed is the American pit bull terrier, which has been specially bred and trained for fighting. These animals have extremely powerful jaw muscles that are able to take hold with their front teeth and produce severe bruising, deep puncture wounds, and broken bones. In a contest, dogs can die from blood loss, shock, exhaustion, or infection. Owners often train their dogs for fights by using smaller animals such as cats, rabbits, or small dogs. These "bait" animals are often stolen pets or animals obtained through "free to a good home" advertisements. Organized dog fights continue despite the fact that they are illegal in all 50 states of the Union, and interstate transportation of dogs for fighting purposes is prohibited by the federal Animal Welfare Act. Humane societies and the police are active in bringing such activities to light.

Historically, U.S. pit bull terriers trace their ancestry to the bulldogs of the 19th century. By the time of the U.S. civil war, American fighting dogs had also become popular. Although the fighting dogs of the 19th century generally posed little threat to people, this is not true today. Law enforcement and animal control agencies around the country have recently reported an escalation of street fighting, an activity that has dramatic negative impact on neighborhoods. A number of city ordinances now exist that forbid pit bull dogs being kept in city housing because these violent dogs are seen as a safety threat to the residents.

The Ethical Arguments

As for ethical standards, one could argue the necessity argument to the conclusion that no essential purpose is served by this combat or apply the concept of an upper limit of permissible pain to come to the conclusion that these sports go beyond an acceptable limit of pain and suffering and are therefore unjustified. However, if these concepts are not used and only a cost/benefit assessment is made, then the weakness of using only a Utilitarian approach becomes apparent. Since in some cultures millions of people derive pleasure from bull fighting, then the sum of these pleasures might be judged to outweigh the costs to the relatively few bulls that are gored and suffer lingering deaths — few, that is compared with the numbers of spectators. So the sum total of their happiness could outweigh the animals' pain.

Are alternatives available? Well, yes, replacement alternatives abound. There are myriad sports and entertaining spectacles available that could be enjoyed even more than blood sports. There would be some economic repercussions if these blood sports declined in popularity; some people would have to learn new skills for continued employment, and some people would lament the loss of a rich heritage associated with that sport. Certainly the enactment of laws prohibiting some blood sports substantially reduces the numbers of animals harmed.

What about refinements? The rules of the sport could be modified so that fighting continued only to a certain point without the animal's death, and then stopped. Indeed, a few veterinarians participate in some of these sports to oversee drug administration at the contest for stimulating aggression, relieving pain, and body-building during the training. What are the ethical responsibilities of veterinarians? Should they refuse to participate, or should they do their best to alleviate the pain of the animals and bring some influence to make the sports more humane?

An argument can be made that, where the animal has no chance of escape, the ethical costs are increased. In cock, bull, and dog fighting the animals are captive and have no way of escaping from their fate. They are under the complete control of their owners. So is the sport unfair? The lack of opportunity to escape distinguishes these blood sports from hunting and fishing where the free-living wild animals may have at least some chance to remain alive. For hunting and fishing, the playing field is still uneven, but not *so* uneven. An exception to this is "canned hunting" in which hunters often pay large sums of money to visit at a ranch for the purpose of killing animals. Here, wild animals, often purchased from zoos and including exotic game, are kept caged and then let out a short distance from the hunters who are waiting with their guns. This takes place in an enclosed, fenced-off area. These animals are of course ready prey to the bullets. The hunters go home satisfied with their trophies of heads of exotic animals. What are the arguments for trying to close down such sports? Who should decide whether blood sports should continue? One could assume that the vast majority of Americans consider dogfighting and cockfighting unethical, and protests have been made about hunting, but should the majority view prevail to the exclusion of all other views? What are the conditions that must be met to establish protection of minority activities? What are the limits of rights that are protected?

GREYHOUND RACING

Far removed from blood sports is another type of sport where animals are pitted against each other: animals are kept and trained to race against each other, and the public are invited to bet on which animal will win. Greyhound racing started in America in the late nineteenth century and the number of racetracks spread so that as of December, 1997, 48 operating greyhound tracks were conducting racing in five

U.S. states. With fifteen tracks, Florida has by far the greatest number followed by Colorado which has five. Six states have banned greyhound racing in the last five years (ME, VA, VT, ID, WA, and NE) and in others, the sport does not exist. Greyhound racetracks are inextricably linked with organized crime because the enormous cash flow provides a fertile setting for dispersal of counterfeit money and laundering of profits from drug operations. Proponents of the sport claim that it is a fun, harmless activity and the animals, which are athletes, receive the best of care. Logic dictates, they say, that racing greyhounds must be well treated well so they can win races.

Dogs are kept caged for up to 22 out of every 24 hours a day, and for most their racing days are over at 2 to 3 years of age. As soon as they cannot race fast enough for their owners and trainers, they are put to death by veterinarians. Few live more than 4 years, yet the normal life span of a greyhound is 12 to 14 years. More than 500 dogs racing at the Pensacola Greyhound Track are killed every year and the annual national total is more than 28,000. A small number of greyhounds end up their days either in research laboratories or adopted as pets.

Opponents to this sport deplore the conditions in which the animals are maintained and their early deaths. They claim that the animals are fed cheap, raw low-grade meat from diseased livestock and that greyhound placement groups nationwide routinely receive racing dogs riddled with both external and internal parasites, sores, and broken bones. Gambling of course is part and parcel of this sport, and brings with it certain social problems. According to *International Gaming and Wagering Business* magazine, the popularity of greyhound racing is declining: the amount of money wagered in this sport dropped 47 percent from 1993 to 1996. Competing casinos have taken over some of the profits previously made from greyhounds.

Personal decisions on whether or not greyhound racing is acceptable depends on how much weight one places on the harms to the animals or, conversely, to the perceived human benefits of enjoyment, thrill, and gaming, and the consideration of what alternative sports that cause less harm to animals are available.

ZOOS, MARINE MAMMAL EXHIBITS

The final case to be discussed is zoos. In a 1995 Roper survey of public attitudes toward zoos, aquariums, and animal parks, (hereinafter called zoos) 69% said they feel either very or somewhat strongly about the treatment of animals in these facilities. Essential functions of zoos were considered to be education (listed by 50% of respondents) and entertainment (20%). Another survey showed that the top three reasons for a trip to the zoo were to "bring children," "see the zoo and/or animals," and enjoy a "nice day." In the U.S., more than 100 million people visit zoos each year.

Recently, marine mammal exhibits have gained popularity, especially in Florida. There is the Seaquarium in Miami and Sea World Park in Orlando, among others. Whales and dolphins number about 450 in all the institutions throughout America but numerous other species such as seals, sea lions, and manatees are captured from the sea for public display. Usually these animals are maintained in fairly small tanks, a far cry from their natural habitat. Some of these animals are trained to perform tricks (jumping through hoops, tossing balls, and swimming in patterns) for public amusement.

Loss of Freedom

A primary concern of zoo critics is the animals' loss of freedom. In a noted 1986 essay entitled "Against Zoos," Dale Jamieson, a professor of philosophy at Carlton College, argues against keeping wild animals in captivity. He reasons that, for the most part, animals in zoos are prevented from gathering their own food, developing their own social orders, and generally behaving in ways that are natural to them. If we are justified in keeping animals in zoos, then there must be some important benefits to be obtained by doing so. Jamieson does not consider there is sufficient reason to have zoos.

The Purpose of a Zoo

Most zoo curators reject the idea that the primary purpose of zoos is to entertain the public, although this is of course true of some zoos, especially roadside zoos that exhibit dancing bears and chimps dressed up in clothes eating at a table. They hold that entertainment is not a sufficient reason for capturing and holding wild animals. As for education, many people learn from visiting zoos. Not all zoos attempt to carry an educational message, however. But in a first-rate zoo much public education can take place about natural habitats, animal species, environmental protection, and so on. Both children and adults are delighted to see animals for the first time. Zoos may promote sympathetic attitudes toward animals. Zookeepers are admired because of their caring attitudes to animals. Members of the public volunteer as "friends of the zoo" and undertake activities to help in caring for the animals and other duties.

Criticism of Zoos

Critics charge that scientific research and conservation efforts are of little account in the objectives of zookeepers. Indeed, very few zoos support scientific research, fewer still have staff scientists with full-time research appointments. The anatomy and pathology studies do not constitute adequate reason to maintain zoos. Also, according to critics, attempts to preserve endangered species that would otherwise become extinct have, with few exceptions (such as the Mongolian wild horse and the European bison), been a failure. Zoo breeding results in lack of genetic diversity among the few remaining endangered species. Another problem is the creation of many unwanted male animals (since a few males can service a whole herd of lions, tigers, and zebras, for instance). Surviving animals can end up with very different traits from their relatives in the wild. Critics charge that the usual result of these programs is a dwindling population of captive animals that exist a few years longer than those who have already died out in the wild. Reintroduction of captive-bred animals into the wild is, with rare exception, a failure. A better approach, critics claim, would be to work on preserving the animals' natural habitats, an activity engaged in by only a few zoos.

The American Zoological and Aquarium Association has been active in promoting conservation among its members who represent the best of American zoos. Wildlife specialists work in areas where species are threatened to help protect the animals. Funding for protecting habitats of endangered species is now available from a few zoos and is being promoted.

The treatment and welfare of zoo animals is also an issue. Zoos can be depressing, unnatural environments that create false stereotypes of animals. There may be no connection between the animal exhibit and the animal's natural habitat. In some poor quality zoos, animals are housed in cages or concrete enclosures that lack space or opportunity for the animals to pursue normal behaviors, such as foraging, running, jumping, and social interaction. The high occurrence of stereotypic animal behavior, (repeated, non-functional movements), such as tigers pacing to and fro or lions twirling continuously on one spot, are indications of stressful animal husbandry. Similar abnormal behaviors are found in factory-farmed species.

There is a conspicuous difference between illegal, roadside zoos and the best zoos in the country, which have made important advances in providing at least some of the most important interests of wild animals in captivity. Zookeepers have been among the leaders in promoting environmental enrichment of captive animals. Lessons learned in zoos have been transferred to the primates and other species kept as laboratory animals. Improvements have been forthcoming. A better understanding of the behavior and ecology of animals in the wild makes it possible to construct better zoo exhibits and holding facilities. Behavioral enrichment programs have been initiated for some species along with better nutrition, and the provision of veterinary care. San Diego Wild Animal Park is renowned for its high standards which provides natural habitats for groups of animals in conditions that attempt to replicate the wild condition. Visitors go round the zoo on a monorail, and it is compared to a safari.

Efforts have been made in recent decades to require zoos to maintain acceptable humane standards. Regular inspections are needed. In 1966, the Animal Welfare Act provided for government licensing and inspection of "animal exhibitors." Usually inspections take place only at the behest of a complaint from the public.

Also helpful in establishing standards is the American Zoological and Aquarium Association, which has established an accreditation program designed to evaluate zoos in order to bolster public confidence by certifying that an institution meets certain standards.

Also helpful in establishing standards is the American Zoological and Aquarium Association, which has established an accreditation program designed to evaluate zoos in order to bolster public confidence by certifying that an institution meets certain standards. The maintenance of accreditation includes an inspection every five years.

However, of the 2,098 licensed USDA exhibitors, only 185 are accredited, a poor representation.

Further ethical problems are raised by the widespread trading in surplus and exotic animals from zoos. Surplus males (not needed for breeding) are traded to roadside zoos, canned hunts (discussed under blood sports), and individuals who regard their pets as status symbols. Some two thousand tigers are kept by individuals in Texas alone.

Ethical questions arise also about the source of non-endangered species for zoos. Should animals be constantly taken from the wild to fill the zoos or should zoos breed their own captive animals wherever possible? Should zoos accept retired circus animals, animals whose life-styles are far different from what they can expect in a zoo but neither life is natural to the animal?

Zoos, although a 19th century invention, have now become something of a tradition in many countries but it may be a tradition that calls for reexamination. Are zoos harmless enough and useful enough to be socially and ethically acceptable? If so, then what social policies are needed to refine the standard by providing naturalistic environments according to species needs so that the facilities become ethically acceptable? Should the number of zoos be reduced to eliminate those with least-acceptable standards?

FINAL COMMENTS

These seven areas of applied ethics related to animals — the use of animals in education, biomedical research, food, animal testing for cosmetic product safety, blood sports, greyhound racing and zoos — raise remarkably similar questions. All of them reflect traditional uses of animals that in many cultures have been viewed as innocuous and useful or entertaining. All arguably bring some satisfaction to humans. In an earlier era, most people, perhaps encouraged by the Judeo-Christian view of the human's superiority to animals, seem not to have worried any further about animal treatment. The needless torture of animals has always troubled us. That is perhaps a nagging sign that there is a moral issue beneath the surface. Both utilitarians and rights-based theorists are expressing their concerns about the status of animals much more openly — the utilitarians because of the needless pain and suffering that for them counts morally, regardless of species, and the rights-based theorists because of the belief that non-human animals, like humans, have a moral standing that should protect them from even useful appropriation of the animal for human uses. The moral status of animals is destined to continue as a controversy.

FOR FURTHER INQUIRY

REVIEW QUESTIONS

1. Apply the utilitarian view to the issue of animal moral standing. Should animals be spared pain and suffering just as humans provided that their kind and quality are the same?

2. Apply the rights-based view to the issue of animal moral standing. Do animals have moral claims grounded in rights (such as the right to life) that cannot be overcome by appeals to good consequences?

ENDNOTES

1. Singer, Peter. *Animal Liberation: A New Ethics for Our Treatment of Animals.* New York: Avon Books, 1975.

2. Strum, Shirley C., and George B. Schaller. *Almost Human: A Journey into the World of Baboons.* W. W. Norton & Company, 1990.

3. Masson, Jeffrey M., and McCarthy, Susan. *When Elephants Weep: The Emotional Lives of Animals.* New York: Bantam Doubleday Dell Publishing Group, Inc., 1995.

4. Griffin, Donald R. *Animal Thinking.* Cambridge: Harvard University Press, 1984.

5. Griffin, Donald R. *Animal Minds.* Chicago: University of Chicago Press, 1992.

6. Bentham, Jeremy. *The Principles of Morals and Legislation* (1789). New York: Hafner, 1948, ch. 17, sec. 4, p. 311.

7. Regan, Tom. "The Case for Animal Rights." In Regan, Tom, and Peter Singer, eds. *Animal Rights and Human Obligations*, second edition. Englewood Cliffs, NJ: Prentice Hall, 1989, pp. 105–11.

CHAPTER 13

PUNISHMENT

"The broad effects which can be obtained by punishment in man and beast are the increase of fear, the sharpening of the sense of cunning, the mastery of the desires; so it is that punishment tames the man, but does not make him 'better.'"

— Frederick Wilhelm Nietzsche

"The generality of men are naturally apt to be swayed by fear rather than by reverence, and to refrain from evil rather because of the punishment that it brings, than because of its own foulness."

— Aristotle

Punishment is a philosophical problem. Should we punish someone for what they have done or, as is often the case, for what we only think they have done? What degree of punishment should we use? Or should we punish, ever? And how do we decide? As we approach these issues in this chapter, we will see that there is more than one broad position we could take on the matter of punishment and that each possible viewpoint involves asking its own questions and making its own use of relevant facts.

CONSIDER JACK'S CASE

In any event, punishment is clearly both a legal and a moral matter, and that fact allows us to give particular thought to the following kind of case:

> Jack, 18 years old, never completed even a sixth-grade education, was reared in a series of temporary foster-care arrangements, and has been in legal difficulties ever since the age of 12 (when he began serving time in juvenile detention centers). Since then, and up until his release six months ago, he has been free on parole for a total of only two months. He is now under arraignment for passing bad checks.

David L. Seiple, M.A. and Ph.D. Columbia University, M.T.S. magna cum laude, Drew University Theological School, is Adjunct Lecturer of Humanities at New York University.

Jack, though legally speaking now an adult, is obviously a kid very much in trouble. What is to be done with him — or, perhaps, *for* him? In most states people such as Jack, if convicted, are likely to be imprisoned. But the first question we might want to ask is a moral question: *Should* he be punished at all?

When we ask this question, we are of course searching for some *moral justification* for punishment, and at one level this might simply mean: Will punishing Jack really do any good? But there is a deeper question lurking in the background here, which is this: Even if punishment might "do some good" in this case, is that enough to warrant someone imposing it on Jack? At first, this might seem to be a far-fetched matter to raise. After all, few of us suppose that society can suddenly, magically be transformed into a Utopian abode of universal family affection. It is hard to imagine a society where parents don't discipline their children, or where criminals are indulgently tolerated by those who have suffered at their hands. Isn't punishment simply one of the requirements for society to function at all? In that case, seriously questioning the justifiability of punishment might seem boringly academic.

CHIEF LEARNING OUTCOME

I can develop my own view of the role of punishment in a society and contrast it with classical and contemporary ethical approaches to this issue.

But let's look again. What is "punishment," philosophically speaking? When we ask this kind of question, we are really asking for an analysis of the word itself — its definitional essence. Whenever we venture into philosophy we need to do analysis again and again, because analysis can very often help to unmask our own misunderstandings. And that's how it would seem in this case, for once we define "punishment" it becomes much more clear why we need to justify it. Let's define "punishment" as the intended infliction of pain or loss upon a person by a duly constituted authority, as a result of some apparent misdeed the person has committed.

Obviously, one cannot be punished sensibly for something unless at least two conditions hold true: (1) the crime in question has been identified, and (2) the socially approved punishment has been determined. But aren't there other necessary conditions as well? For example, it is widely (though not universally) supposed that it is unfair to punish someone *retroactively* — that is, by declaring an act to be a crime only *after* the defendant has committed the act. And similarly, punishment is not commonly sanctioned (at least not in Western civilization) unless the defendants foresaw the likely consequences of what they did, or at least were aware of the legal status of their actions. If that sort of mental fact can be proven, then a court takes that as proof of **intention on** the part of the defendants. They knew

Endnote 1

what they were doing, legally speaking, when they did it, so they must have actually intended to break the law.

This last condition, however, can become the source of all kinds of complications. One of these concerns the question about how we really know what someone's mental state really is. No doubt people sometimes commit crimes when they are not, as the court later says, **"mentally competent"** — which means that they don't really "know" the difference between right and wrong. But when assessing the punishment to be imposed on a criminal, how can we reliably determine exactly what a person's mental state was when the crime was committed? What usually happens is that various psychiatric experts testify during the legal proceeding, and not all of them always agree.

Related to, but separate from, assessment of intent is the question of the mental state of the one accused of the crime. No doubt people sometimes commit crimes when they are not, as the court later says, "mentally competent" — which means that they don't really "know" the difference between right and wrong. But when assessing the punishment to be imposed on a criminal, how can we reliably determine exactly what a person's mental state was when the crime was committed? What usually happens is that various psychiatric experts testify during the legal proceeding, and not all of them always agree.

Authority — Take the case of an adult disciplining a child by inflicting a spanking or the loss of playtime. This would not be justi-

KEY CONCEPTS

Crime — Behavior that a society has judged to be intolerable against which it has devised codified sanction.

Punishment — from the Latin, *poine*, meaning "penalty;" the intended infliction of non-pleasurable feelings or activity upon a person, by an appropriate authority, sometimes including acts of pain, the denial of liberty and even the taking of life (capital punishment) — as a result of an act that violated a law, code or other set of standards.

Abolitionism/Rehabilitationism — A group of views holding that punishment is not justified because of appeals to charity, lack of blame, or lack of effectiveness. Often this view is combined with the claim that the goal of social policy should be rehabilitation.

Retentionism — A group of views holding that punishment is justified usually based on appeals to consequences (general or specific deterrence) or deontological concerns (retribution).

Deterrence — The consequentialist argument in favor of punishment based on the claim that it will prevent the individual from committing further crime (specific deterrence) or produce an effect that will prevent others from engaging in such activity (general deterrence).

Retributivism — another name for deontological retentionism. Retributivists do not base their defense on considerations of beneficial results. Retributivists focus on the belief that people who do evil deserve to be punished (and those who do good deserve reward). They hold this belief independent of whether the punishment will produce good consequences.

fied if that adult had no jurisdiction, such as a parent or a guardian. Or what if the child had not really done something wrong? These are the kinds of intuitions which that definition is meant to capture.

Intrusion — On the other hand, the analogy with the child may only go so far. Some philosophers would point out that the child is not yet an adult, and adulthood brings not only certain responsibilities but also certain rights. And this suggests the important idea of **intrusion**. Take imprisonment as an example of punishment. Just as a person who breaks into one's house and steals some item of property has intruded upon the owner's personal space, so, too, someone who deprives another of liberty of movement intrudes into that life. Incarceration is intrusive in just this way.

In other words, we all suppose that we are entitled to continued life, a reasonable degree of liberty, and some gainfully attained property; and we'd all agree that anyone who would deny us of these had better have an extremely good reason for it. Punishment denies us some of these basic human goods. **Punishment is characterized by intrusion and needs some kind of authority.**

THE ARGUMENTS FOR AND AGAINST PUNISHMENT

The Abolitionist or Rehabilitationist Position

So let's return to Jack's case. Here we have a young person who is an adult only in a technical sense. He has passed the age of 18, but in any other respect he would probably not qualify as one. He certainly lacks an adult education, and he may lack all means of landing a stable job, especially since he seems likely to lack the social skills needed to function appropriately in adult society. Many people hearing such a story would insist that the very last thing society should do is "punish" Jack for being in the circumstance he is in.

Those who look at Jack's case and find grounds for doubting the general appropriateness of punishment are abolitionists with respect to punishment. **Abolitionists** (also called **rehabilitationists)** hold that the general problem of anti-social behavior presents us with a story very much like the one we'd give in Jack's case, and toward cases such as Jack's, there are three general kinds of appeals that the abolitionist can make. (These correspond to the various approaches to ethics that we addressed in Chapters 4 and 5.)

The Appeal to Charity

The first of these is often, though not always, espoused by Christianity, and is based on some notion of human virtue — some quality of character "agape" (self-denying love) or "charity" or benevolence that is thought incompatible with the act of punishing someone. This kind of Christian position is typically founded on the belief that Jesus abjured for Himself and discountenanced for His followers all use of militant methods against their fellow human beings. In all its forms the will to hurt is, therefore, a wrongful and un-Christian will. Anger, and the conduct it inspires, is always misdirected and wasted energy. It is also wrong in principle, for it contradicts a fundamental Christian rule, which is to act with a good will to all people whatever the provocation. However it may be disguised, the desire for retaliation still belongs to the unlovely and unregenerate side of human nature.

Endnote 2

Such an argument is based upon the idea that when deliberating about the issue of punishment, we must pay primary attention to the qualities of one's own character. Concern for the well-being of the offender or of society at large might derive from that, but only through the spiritual or psychological state of the one who would impose the punishment. As it stands, however, this does not really address some of the important questions raised by the issue of punishment. What would happen, for example, if government officials really took their own primary role to be that of acting lovingly toward whomever is affected by their policy decisions? It is not clear, at least not in any significant detail, just how the specific operations of an entire society are supposed to be based on such virtues, and some philosophers have thought that there is an inherent tension between the demands social roles impose and the demands of religiously based personal ethics. If such a tension existed, then religiously inspired virtues might not be expected to ground the ways social institutions operate. On the other hand, others might argue that the inherent tension is natural and even constitutes a creative co-existence, whereby sociologists and religionists produce dialogue from which society may enrich its laws.

The Appeal to Fairness

But even if the Christian tenets seem unworkable for an entire society, does any of that prohibit Christians, for example, from making use of different strategies that work in favor of the same result? For in public discussion at least, Christian abolitionists are likely to appeal to either or both of the other general approaches discussed in Chapters 4 and 5 — duty-based approaches (deontology) or consequence-based ones (utilitarianism). The first is a deontologically based strategy that takes as primary some fundamental notions about rights, duties, or other moral attributes a person is supposed to possess. For example: We normally suppose, as a fundamental notion, that it would be unfair to blame someone for an act he could not avoid. We may get angry at the person — let's say, for example, that you find out that your kid brother spilled a soft drink all over your homework. But then you also learn that even after he had taken great pains to be careful, your pet Great Dane had become overly friendly at the crucial moment, and caused his hand to slip. Blame means responsibility, and your brother wasn't really responsible for what the dog did. So your anger would really be misplaced.

This same kind of deontological consideration is prominent among some abolitionists. Consider the following argument:

Many would agree that it is wrong to punish persons for something they could not help. An analogy to punishing someone for being sick reveals how inappropriate it is to punish for conditions that are not one's fault. At least if we think about traditional illnesses caused by germs or genes that are beyond human control no one can help

Endnote 3

being sick. Therefore, no one ought ever be punished for being sick. In the words of the Supreme Court of the United States: "Even one day in prison would be cruel and unusual punishment for the 'crime' of having a common cold." Some abolitionists believe that it just so happens to be the case that everyone who commits a crime has a kind of sickness. Hence, it is morally wrong to punish anyone who commits a crime.

When we isolate the main assumptions here, we notice two:

(1) First, the obvious point that illness is generally not something we have much control over. Of course, I might get a cold if I foolishly stay outside in bad weather, and I have a choice about that; but the kind of "illness" that criminals are supposed to suffer is not of this sort at all. The illness in question would be mental; its origins would have to lie in medical history of the person, the family life and social circumstance of the individual, and these are not things we really choose for ourselves. The criminal, in other words, would not even be derivatively responsible for his conduct, and this points to a second basic assumption that really provides the key to the deontological view. (2) There are moral truths or principles underlying our ordinary understandings of such notions as blame, duty, and responsibility.

For example, one kind of deontological argument would go like this: Anything over which I have no control is not something I am responsible for, and if I am not responsible for something, I can't properly be held to account and be punished for it. For the deontologist, this is the kind of fundamental, fixed principle that moral deliberation requires. It is an appeal to fairness. Moral responsibility, he would say, is not attributed under certain moral conditions, and then abandoned if doing so might suit our purposes. Either we are morally responsible for what we do or we're not; and if we are not, we should not be held accountable. In that case, persons suffering from certifiable mental illness or otherwise acting out of forces beyond their control at the time of the commission of the crimes should not be punished.

The Appeal to Consequentialism

However, not all recent opponents of punishment have taken this approach. There is another general strategy open to somebody who opposes the practice of punishing offenders, and it rejects the idea that punishment should be decided purely by notions like moral responsibility. This view bases assessment of punishment on the benefits or the harm that result. These considerations extend far beyond the act a person commits. Consequentialist abolitionists are likely to insist that punishment simply does not usually produce the results we would like.

In 1901, in his lectures at the University of Naples, the criminologist **Enrico Ferri** claimed that punishment was ineffective for doing what society really needs to be concerned with, which is the prevention of crime:

We have but to look about us in the realities of contemporaneous life in order to see that the criminal code is far from being a remedy against crime, that it remedies nothing, because either premeditation or passion in the person of the criminal deprive the criminal law of all prohibitory power. The deceptive faith in the efficacy of criminal law still lives in the public mind, because every normal man feels that the thought of imprisonment would stand in his way, if he contemplated tomorrow committing a theft, a rape, or a murder . . . But even if the criminal code did not exist, he would not commit a crime, so long as his physical and social environment would not urge him in that direction. The criminal code . . . prevents the criminal for a while from repeating his criminal deed. But it is evident that the punishment is not imposed until after the deed has been done. It is a remedy against effects, but it does not touch the causes, the roots, of evil.

Endnote 3

Notice the main assumptions contained in this passage. Ferri claims first that punishment ought to be a "remedy" against crime (and in a later passage he too goes on to an explicit comparison between criminality and disease). He then makes the claim that the enforcement of punitive sanctions against criminals has done little to cure the social malady. In other words, he is making both a value-statement and a factual statement: (1) punishment should be evaluated with regard to its beneficial consequences, and (2) punishment does not produce the benefits that its defense requires.

This kind of abolitionist would foresee a sad pattern in the case of Jack. What is to be gained by placing him, as a young adult, back once again in the same kind of hostile environment that produced his anti-social behavior to begin with? Is incarceration alone, with no effort at rehabilitation, really effectual as a long-run social expedient? In the present system, we send an offender to jail, straight into the company of those who are likely to harden his attitudes and sharpen his criminal skills. If he stays there for a very long time, society must bear the very high cost of confinement. And then, whenever he is finally released, he returns (probably poor) to the street, a product of a society of prisoners who have very badly prepared him for ordinary life. If I were in circumstances like that, I'd probably think of a return to prison as an improvement. (At least, I'd get three square meals and a roof overhead!) Imprisonment, which in that case was supposed to serve as a deterrent, actually acted as a magnet instead.

THE RETENTIONIST POSITION

We have just seen that if your intuitions on this question of punishment lean toward abolitionism, in addition to appealing to the virtue of charity, there are two general kinds of approaches you can take. You can argue (as we saw in Chapters 4 and 5) that, for example, it is not morally right to punish someone if they are not responsible for their actions. That is a deontological approach. On the other hand, you might be led to believe that punishment is not likely to improve the situation: Too many criminals are only embittered and alienated by a system that really ought to be treating them as dysfunctional human beings in need of psychological help. That would be a consequentialist approach.

But what if your intuitions lie in another direction entirely? In Chapters 4 and 5 we noticed that neither of these two bases for moral claims (the deontological and the consequentialist) always provides us with the same conclusions each time it is applied. An abolitionist might appeal to either strategy to support his position; but other philosophers, also arguing in either a deontological or consequentialist style, might arrive at very different conclusions from his. This time let's consider the consequentialist approach first.

The Consequentialist Case in Favor of Punishment

Some philosophers have noted that rehabilitation looks only toward the interests of the individual offender, whereas other consequences might be every bit as compelling.

For one thing, since rehabilitation occurs only after an offense is committed, the need to prevent the initial crime is left unaddressed. And here one needs to ask: Isn't Ferri being too quick to assume that the threat of punishment does not really prevent others from committing similar crimes? In other words, doesn't the rehabilitationist ignore the **general deterrence** achieved by the institution of punishment?

Other consequentialist defenders of punishment might appeal to what is called **specific deterrence** or deterrence of the punished individual. They point out that, at least, incarceration prevents the criminal from engaging in more crimes while he or she is in prison. Moreover, even though imprisonment may teach the incarcerated more bad attitudes and techniques, it may also leave a fear of being incarcerated again, thus deferring the criminal even after release.

Others, arguing along similar lines, would recommend an even more sophisticated view of the goal of punishment. Just as long as we think of punitive threats on a par with brute intimidation (they would say), we miss its important **educative function**. Respect for legal authority is more than just a response to coercive power. Legal authority is a vehicle and symbol of the cultural values that any society must convey to its members, and for that reason punishment has a ritualistic aspect. Here punishment is viewed as a means of expressing social disapproval, which not only purges lingering resentment but also reinforces norms, as the evil of the wrongdoer is dramatized through a publicly shared event.

Thus we have examples of (a) retentionist arguments regarding punishment, which are (b) based on consequentialist assumptions. So we see that in addition to two main versions of abolitionism (the deontological and the consequentialist), we are also presented with two varieties of consequentialism (abolitionist and retentionist) which produce two very different conclusions — the one consequentialist insisting that punishment is socially regressive, the other insisting that punishment is socially indispensable. And it turns out that philosophers in this last group would agree with one statement made by an abolitionist like Ferri: When we ask whether or not punishment is justified, we need to look for the beneficial consequences of applying it. The difference with someone like Ferri lies with what kind of factual evidence is cited and how it is assessed.

A consequentialist, remember, is going to look at results, to see if the consequences are beneficial or not. But unfortunately this is not a simple, straightforward matter. Conflicting evidence seems to exist in favor of each point of view. For Ferri, the evidence suggests that punishment is at best only a temporary preventative that "does not touch the causes, the roots, of evil." Others, such as Walter Berns, dispute the evidence on which this kind of claim is made. Disagreements like this show how much more work is still needed in the social sciences.

Endnote 4

In the meantime, however, we should not allow ourselves to be thrown off by the mere appearance of a paradox. There are some strategies we can use for looking more closely at the nature of the evidence. One key here is to be alert to the limits of merely anecdotal evidence. "Anecdotes" are accounts of events that may give us a vivid picture of a circumstance, and provide us with a handy fix on our first intuitions about an issue. There is nothing wrong with considering anecdotes: Indeed, they typically provide us with our entry into the complexities of a problem. The description of Jack's situation toward the beginning of this chapter is an anecdote. But until we bear down on the complexities embedded in it — and so treat it as more than just an anecdote — we only glide along the surface of a problem, and we are left only with prior prejudice, or else with undispelled perplexity.

In other words, we need to concern ourselves with the appropriate evidential assessment. This comes into play early on in any dispute among consequentialists. For example, few if any abolitionists suppose that punitive measures never, ever have any appropriate application. Ferri himself admitted that "if a crime manifests itself, repression may be employed as one of the remedies of criminology;" his point simply was that "it should be the very last remedy, not the exclusively dominating one . . ." And, likewise, consequentialist defenders of punishment have to admit that rehabilitation does sometimes work. So there is conflicting evidence that needs to be assessed, and the place to begin doing that is by identifying which piece of evidence should be treated as exceptional, and which should be treated as paradigmatic.

A paradigm is a related series of events described in a way that illustrates a general point we want to make. It can be used, as we did in Jack's case, to orient us toward a problem we want to discuss. But it can also be used to confirm an interpretation or theory we happen to favor. Thus, a defender of punishment might use the story of Jack as a paradigm in both ways.

On the other hand, a defender of abolitionism might not want to regard this story about Jack as paradigmatic in the least. Maybe Jack is some kind of exception. On the other hand, the abolitionist should admit that Jack's kind of case does actually happen, and it's not even all that uncommon. In the end, both abolitionists and defenders of punishment may have to admit that the consequences of punishment are more complex than they originally claimed. Moreover, even if it can be established that punishment in some instances serves a useful purpose, there remains the difficult questions of the form that punishment should take and how much of it should be administered in order to accomplish the good ends while minimizing the negative effects Ferri and others fear.

So a consequentialist on this issue is going to approach a situation and look at what is likely to happen as a result of punishing someone. Is the offender going to be deterred from further crime? Are others going to be deterred by his example? Punishment, in other words, is evaluated in light of its causal influence. Here we need to take account of a whole complex of factors, including the offender's own assessment of the likelihood of a sentence actually being imposed and the degree of its severity.

This raises the issue of **determinate sentencing**. For some crimes, the judge or jury has wide latitude as to what sentence to prescribe for a guilty offender, whereas for other crimes (such as drunk driving, typically) there is far less leeway. The fact that all crimes are not treated as strictly as, say, drunken driving has been criticized by some, who claim that this leniency dilutes punishment's full deterrence. This issue, as we'll see later in this chapter, has had a significant impact on recent legal developments concerning capital punishment.

But here we might want to ask a very basic question. What really causes somebody to act morally rather than anti-socially? Might it not be the case that a good part of our capacity to act conscientiously is either innate or else so well fixed in character by an early age, that rehabilitating a badly deformed conscience is usually a hopeless enterprise? As we shall now see, this clears the way for a deontological strategy for the defense of punishment known as retributivism.

The Deontological Case for Punishment: Retribution

Retributivism is another name for deontological retentionism. All retentionists want to defend the moral value of retaining punishment as a social practice, but retributivists do not base their defense on considerations of beneficial results. Many retributivists, for example, tend to be rather skeptical about the deterrent value of punishment. They would acknowledge that, with some people anyway, deterrence does not work. People drive the highways at unsafe speeds all the time, despite the obvious threat to their own and others' lives. And even in the case of many other ("more serious") crimes, ones that carry a more severe punitive threat than a speeding ticket, clever people probably realize that the chances of getting caught can be minimized with some careful planning.

Giving People What They Deserve — A retributivist is going to insist that the feelings of blame a person has over some misdeed are altogether appropriate, regardless of the social consequences. Blame is the flip side of responsibility. To base a theory of punishment upon the fact that criminals are underprivileged, disturbed, or diseased (as the abolitionist does) is to turn the scope of blame away from the individual offender, and to place responsibility upon surrounding circumstances. And this is unacceptable because people really are responsible for what they do. Retributivists focus on the belief that people who do evil deserve to be punished and those who do good deserve reward. They hold this belief independent of whether the punishment will produce good consequences.

Compare, for example, the consequentialist discussion above with a recent deontological justification of punishment by the *Newsweek* columnist **George F. Will**:

> "In 1952 (U.S. Supreme Court) Justice Thurgood Marshall wrote that 'punishment for the sake of retribution is not permissible under the Eighth Amendment.' That is absurd. The element of retribution — vengeance, if you will — does not make punishment cruel and unusual. It makes punishment intelligible. It distinguishes punishment from therapy. Rehabilitation may be an ancillary result of punishment, but we punish to serve justice, by giving people what they deserve."

Endnote 6

Will's fundamental intuition is a deontological one, which does not essentially have to do with the actual consequences of taking one or the other moral point of view. As we saw in Chapter 4, a deontologist believes that a person enjoys basic rights that cannot normally be violated — even if doing so would bring a greater benefit to a greater number of people. Likewise, Will is suggesting here that a person might be said to deserve moral censure and even retaliation on account of some terrible deed he or she has committed; that this dessert is not in itself affected by the actual results of society's imposing blame upon the offender.

For the retributivist, the issue of punishment proper enters right at this point. In some cases, what an offender actually deserves is not just blame: He is the proper recipient of the appropriately harsh social response. In those cases some institutionalized form of punishment would be the natural vehicle for that blame, so that the offender actually deserves punishment as well.

CONSEQUENTIALISM AND DEONTOLOGY COMPARED

What do these illustrations of different types of moral disagreements reveal about the process of moral deliberation? Here we find quite a difference in procedure between consequentialists and deontologists, one that is based on the possibility of distinguishing empirical fact-statements from value-statements.

Consequentialists tend to treat a value-statement as a kind of fact-statement. Let's regard "fact-statements" as statements that we can test out by checking our experience, especially ones that can be established by scientific observation. This means that not just any run-of-the-mill account of someone's experience will suffice. If, for example, someone claims that punishment makes offenders better human beings (because it may "teach them a lesson"), we need to ask what reliable evidence exists for such an opinion. And evidence is not scientifically "reliable" unless it is based on a fair sampling of cases. One or two anecdotes won't decide the matter for us.

Does holding people accountable for their actions by imposing punitive sanctions really make them better individuals? Does it benefit society as a whole? And do these two considerations ever conflict?

Consequentialists, as we have seen here, believe that moral categories should be applied to people only if there are empirically observable benefits to doing so. The "value" of doing so, in other words, depends upon the likely "factual" consequences.

Most consequentialists these days are utilitarians; and (as we saw in Chapter 5) utilitarians believe that basic moral questions can be decided by looking to see which moral decision is likely to improve the general well-being — the greatest good for the greatest number. So current disputes among consequentialists typically take the form of a disagreement about which social course of action will bring about that benefit. Of course, consequentialists will still face questions that cannot be resolved by empirical observation. They may disagree not over what the requests will be, but rather over whether the results are good or bad or over how good or bad they are. These are fundamentally not matters that can be resolved by scientific observation.

DEONTOLOGISTS

For two disagreeing deontologists, on the other hand, matters are different. What separates them is a basic conflict of fundamental ethical norms that is not really open to arbitration by the observable facts. Does a criminal deserve humane treatment due to his stature as a member of the human race, or does he deserve suffering due to his standing as a moral reprobate? If we pose the question in those terms, the answer is not apparent just from looking at the facts. Different people, after all, may have different evaluative responses to identical facts. The facts about Jack, whose story opened up our discussion in this chapter, are likely to draw a different set of responses, depending upon what set of ethical norms govern a person's judgment. (And if you yourself are confused about what you really do think about Jack's case, that may be because you are sensitive to a range of conflicting norms!)

There are major difficulties with both the deontological and the consequentialist strategies.

Difficulties for Deontologists

The problem with deontologism is rather apparent. There is no way of proving scientifically whether, in principle, an offender "deserves" to be punished. This is not to say that a court of law cannot determine one's guilt or innocence. That is a different matter — a legal, as opposed to a moral, question. The moral question here has to do with what society ought to do once guilt is already determined. Should an offender be punished? And if the fundamental question is a deontological matter, all we can do is appeal to each others' moral judgments about right, wrong, blameworthiness, and so forth.

Difficulties for Consequentialists

Now consequentialism is supposed to have the advantage of offering a scientific basis for assessing just this sort of question, so that our answers to it need not rest on personal intuition. A consequentialist appeals to the evidence, to predict what the effects of punishment are likely to be. But there are two different sorts of difficulties here.

Difficulties in Assessing What the Consequences Are

First, as we have begun to see, this is easier said than done. The consequentialist abolitionist position assumes, for example, that criminals as a class of people really can be rehabilitated, and admittedly there are cases where attempts at rehabilitation do appear to have succeeded. On the other hand, consequentialist retentionists are more convinced that evidence exists that punishment is an effective deterrent. Moreover, even if we could reach agreement on the empirical claims about what the consequences are, we would still have to face the nonscientific question of whether they are good or bad and how good or bad they are.

Difficulties When Punishing the Innocent Produces Good Consequences

But there is another kind of difficulty with consequentialism — especially in its utilitarian form — which does not have to do with the infancy of social research. The problem is that, if a utilitarian is concerned with the greatest good for the greatest number of people, might that not mean punishing someone who is really innocent of a crime?

For example: Suppose a prosecutor, who was concerned about rampant crime in his district, had in custody a person widely believed to be guilty of many of the crimes. What ought he to do if he comes to know that this person must be innocent but that, by keeping this fact secret, he can surely win a conviction that will send a strong message to the community that those who engage in these crimes are caught and dealt with severely. A utilitarian holds that he should decide whether to prosecute and punish based on a judgment of the consequences. This means that, if he believes that prosecuting the innocent will do more good than letting him off, the innocent should be prosecuted, a conclusion a deontologist finds unfair and unreasonable.

The conflict between consequential and deontological reasons to decide about punishment raises complicated issues, and it may be that the only way to handle them is to adopt a "mixed" (integrative) approach to punishment. It may be, for example, that rehabilitation is possible in some cases but not in others, and that it should be attempted only in promising circumstances. Or it may be that there are socially beneficial consequences to holding people blameworthy and (at the same time) that they really deserve to be held blameworthy as well.

In any case, you will need to think these matters through carefully for yourself.

THE ULTIMATE APPLICATION: CAPITAL PUNISHMENT

Few debates in recent years have evoked more public venom in the United States than debates over whether or not the death penalty is an acceptable form of punishment. Here some previously discussed issues re-emerge.

Legal History

The Eighth Amendment of the U.S. Constitution prohibits "cruel and unusual punishment," and the Fourteenth Amendment guarantees equal protection under the law. A number of U.S. Supreme Court decisions involving African-American defendants sentenced to death — most prominently, *Furman vs. Georgia* (1972) and *Gregg vs. Georgia* (1976) — have attempted to address the question as to how those Constitutional provisions affect that practice. Sometimes the issue has been dealt with broadly and unequivocally, as when Justice Thurgood Marshall declared, at the time of *Furman*, that the death penalty itself was "morally unacceptable" and did indeed fail the cruel-and-unusual test. But at the time, the majority of the court was not able to agree on such a sweeping determination and restricted the scope of the decision to invalidate due to the arbitrary and capricious manner in which the death penalty was applied, the lack of due process by states in the selection of those who receive the death penalty.

Endnote 7

Since then, the legal ground has shifted out from under the abolitionists, who had so welcomed the *Furman* result. Since the mid-1970s, attention has centered not so much upon the possibility of outright mistake in determining guilt, nor on the morality involved in sanctioning execution. The more pressing matter has seemed to be the issue of fairness. It is a matter of record, for example, that most juries do not sentence a guilty defendant to death, even when the crime is first-degree murder. Why is this, and what factors go into a jury's considerations? Are these factors always legally relevant?

In view of the history of racial inequity in the U.S., it is worth noting that, in the period 1930–1967, 50% of the inmates executed for murder were African-Americans, even though blacks comprised about 13% of the total population. And one study has indicated that offenders charged with killing a white person were 4.3 times more likely to be sentenced to death in Georgia as someone charged with killing a black person. This has led many to claim not just that capital punishment is "cruel," but that it is "unusual," in the sense of being too often applied capriciously.

Endnote 8

However, in the *Gregg* case, the court has held that the discriminatory aspect of death sentencing could be addressed if the wide latitude previously exercised by juries in Georgia and elsewhere was curtailed. Many states redrafted their statutes to call either for mandatory capital sentencing, or else for "guided" direction that spelled out sentencing parameters for aggravating and mitigating circumstances. Under Florida law, for example, trials of capital crimes have a bifurcated structure: The first is determination of guilt by the jury, while the second is a jury's option to recommend or not to recommend the death penalty (*Proffitt vs. Florida,* 1976). The judge may impose the jury's recommendation or is required to explain at length another sentence. If the jury fails to recommend the death penalty, the judge may still impose it with certain explanations.

Endnote 9

Eventually, the Supreme Court majority decided that the punishment of death does not invariably violate the Constitution. In the Furman case, the court majority, even while lacking detailed empirical evidence, invalidated some existing state death-sentencing statutes on the ground that the laws were applied disproportionately to minorities. Yet, after exhaustive evidence was made available, the court determined that the actual "risk" of such discrimination was acceptably small and defendants would have the opportunity to show evidence of discrimination in their specific cases.

Meanwhile, the prospect of "mandatory life sentences without parole" has become a campaign of some abolitionists who argue that the certainty of such a sentence would be a more likely deterrent on the one hand, and on the other would still pass the test of not being "cruel and unusual." Capital punishment advocates argue that the social costs of mandatory life sentences make them unacceptable, but some admit the effect of certain imposition of any punishment as likely to increase deterrence of crime.

FINAL COMMENTS

Moral analysis has involved both consequential and deontological appeals. Consequentialists, for example, ask if the death penalty really deters capital crimes. Once again, the evidence is not conclusive.

Endnote 7

The murder rate in the U.S. doubled in the 14 years preceding 1974, but the number of executions declined to zero during that period. Does that imply their deterrent value? Even retentionists on this question are hesitant to make such a claim, because so many other factors might have come into play.

Even if capital punishment does not deter, does it not at least provide retribution ? Is there not, some would ask, a rather compelling appeal in the equation of "an eye for an eye"? Here there are even more complicated matters involved than in cases of ordinary punishment. One of these is the fact that death is irrevocable, and this puts into dramatic light the problem of mistaken sentences. Certainly if a person is only incarcerated over some years for a crime he did not commit, that part of his life has been irrevocably and unjustifiably lost to him; but at least he has some time left, and hopefully some chance to redeem meaning and value in what remains to him. But that is singularly impossible in the case of the death sentence, and it seems institutionally impossible to avoid some cases of mistaken executions. Some would say that even one innocent person legally executed invalidates the entire practice of capital punishment. They often go on to say that we should impose mandatory life sentence rather than execution.

Endnote 8

But then what about the case (had he lived long enough) of Lee Harvey Oswald (the person judged by a special Commission to have been the assassin of President John F. Kennedy)? Do perpetrators of especially heinous crimes not deserve the retribution that follows justified public outrage? Consider here once again a claim by George Will: "Increasingly, a life sentence is seen as a fraud that mocks the dead and jeopardizes the living by trivializing the crime of murder and diluting the indignation society needs for self-defense."

FOR FURTHER INQUIRY

REVIEW QUESTIONS

1. Some attempt to resolve the question of whether punishment is justified by appealing to the consequences. What consequences are cited that could lead to conclusion that punishment, on balance, produces bad results? What consequences would support punishment as producing good results?

2. If good consequences justify punishment, would it be immoral to knowingly punish someone you (but not others) knew was innocent in order to impress on others that crime does not pay? Why or why not?

3. Critics of capital punishment point out that it is inevitable that occasionally an innocent person is punished. They claim that death, the ultimate punishment, is irreversible and that, as long as we cannot guarantee certainty of guilt, such an ultimate, irreversible punishment is unacceptable. What is the best rebuttal to this position?

ENDNOTES

1. Sir Walter Moberly, *The Ethics of Punishment* (Hamden, Ct: Archon Books, 1968), p. 38.

2. Richard Wasserstrom, "Why Punish the Guilty," in Gertrude Ezorsky, *Philosophical Perspectives on Punishment* (State University of New York, 1972), p. 330.

3. Enrico Ferri, "The Positive School of Criminology" in Stanley E. Grupp, ed., *Theories of Punishment* (Indiana University Press, 1971), p. 231.

4. Walter Berns, *For Capital Punishment* (Basic Books, 1979), pp. 83–152.

5. Ferri, "The Positive School of Criminology," p. 233.

6. George F. Will, "The Value of Punishment," *Newsweek* (May 24, 1982), p. 92.

7. Raymond Paternoster, *Capital Punishment in America* (Macmillan, 1991), p. 156.

8. D.C. Baldus, C. Pulaski, and G.G. Woolworth, *Equal Justice and the Death Penalty* (Boston: Northeastern University Press, 1990).

9. *McCleskey vs. Kemp* (1987).

CHAPTER 14

WAR

"Older men declare war. But it is youth that must fight and die. And it is youth who must inherit the tribulation, the sorrow, and the triumphs that are the aftermath of war."

— ***Herbert Hoover, 1928 GOP National Convention***

"War hath no fury like a non-combatant."

— ***Charles Edward Montague**, Disenchantment 1922*

When peoples go to war against one another, we might think of it in various ways: As a test of will for titanic personalities (George Bush and Bill Clinton vs. Saddam Hussein); as an indication of the strength or weakness of national character (Vietnam?); or as the culmination of centuries of ethnic rivalry (Serbs vs. Croats vs. Bosnian Muslims). But do we ever think of going to war as the failure or success of a clearly articulated and carefully pursued process of moral deliberation? The Gulf War of 1991, according to its proponents, was waged based on the principle of the sovereignty of nations mainly to restore a small nation (Kuwait) from bullying and brutal annexation by its much larger neighbor, Iraq. (It may not have been that simple, as we shall see later.) More often, war is the result of conflicting policy agendas between nations, which surely are formed out of some perception of national goals and circumstances. To what extent do those goals, and the strategies a government is willing to use to attain them, reflect morally acceptable principles? And should policymakers care about this?

In this chapter we will look at the relation between moral deliberation and warmaking. We will discuss what "war" is, how war has often been glorified, and how some have refused to participate in war of any kind and why. We will explore the possibilities for formulating some restrictions on when war can be deemed morally acceptable, what is sometimes called "justified" or "just." We will show how complex the issue has become in the nuclear age, and we will indicate how international law takes on a new importance as a result.

David I. Seiple, M.A. and Ph.D. Columbia University, M.T.S. magna cum laude, Drew University Theological School, is Adjunct Lecturer of Humanities at New York University.

WAR AS A PHILOSOPHICAL TOPIC

"War," just as other terms we have been discussing, is a word used in various ways, and it will help us right off to see how differently it can be used. It is common to think of a **"war" as an officially sanctioned state of affairs, legally declared by the parties involved (such as The Spanish-American War or World War II).** That is the definition often given by military theorists. But what about Korea or Vietnam? Each was a "war" — armed aggression between two or more nations — that was never officially declared. Do all conflicts that lack an explicit national government declaration necessarily lack the traits of warfare?

CHIEF LEARNING OUTCOME

I recognize the ethical implications of war and can apply certain moral theories in a debate about a "just war."

War is a state of affairs in which its participants are protected by international agreements. When captured in battle, for example, they are required to reveal only name, rank, and serial number, and they are released through negotiation between captor and home country. Looters, on the other hand, can be convicted and sentenced purely at the behest of the captor's court system. That system holds them responsible for their acts of violence. So, in this important sense, riots could not really be considered "wars." Writers on military history have influenced standard usage by restricting the term "war" to a situation in which two organized, hostile parties enjoy, at least for a short time, some measure of military parity. The looters in Los Angeles obviously enjoyed no such status, and we'll be using the term "war" here in this restricted way.

Should we (as moral agents) ever sanction an act of war? And if so, under what conditions should we do so? What is our own moral responsibility when questions of war and peace are at stake? The changing face of society over the past several centuries has made these live questions. Can we afford to ignore them?

Not so long ago, wars might have been waged at the behest of a feudal sovereign on behalf of his own very personal interest to avenge a perceived insult, for example. This is probably how we think of King Arthur and the Knights of the Round Table. In those days armies were small professional units who owed allegiance to their lord and whose personal motives may not have reached far beyond the promise of glory and bounty. Combatants undoubtedly thought very little about their responsibility as participants. But for us, participation in war is likely to raise deep questions.

With the French Revolution in 1789, the constitution of armies began to change. Ordinary citizens were conscripted into a scene of combat they would much rather have avoided. With the expansion of voting rights, mothers and fathers and prospective inductees could all have some direct, democratic say in the governmental decisions that could bring that about.

Offensive or Defensive?

The central focus of our discussion here will concern the possible **justification of war**. There are a number of specific questions worth keeping in mind. One, for example, trades on the purpose behind the waging. A war might be primarily offensive (as it was in the case of Germany's invasion of Poland in 1939 or the American invasion of Grenada). In that case war is an instrument of a national policy that did not succeed, as anyone might naturally hope it would have, by diplomacy alone. On the other hand, a war can be undertaken in self-defense (as it was by the new French Republic after 1789, when it was threatened by invasion from royalist forces, or by the Americans against the Japanese after Pearl Harbor). To what extent then does this difference affect the strength of the justification behind the decision to conduct war?

Gravity of the Consequences

A second issue worth considering here concerns the **gravity of war's effects**. All of us have lived for much of our lives under the threat of nuclear annihilation, and we need to consider what impact that possibility has upon the moral matters before us here. War is an organized *violent* intrusion upon the personal lives of human beings. We normally think of it as that. But one wonders about **terrorism**. Might that not be seen broadly as a kind of warfare? Palestinian airplane hijackers have claimed that. Or do we say the same thing about terrorism as we just have about armed rebellion against a government?

In the post-Cold War period, the U.S. Central Intelligence Agency, no longer tracking a "Red menace," identified international terrorism, nuclear proliferation and international narcotics traffic as the targets of

KEY CONCEPTS

War — a formal declaration of armed conflict by a sovereign nation against another nation; also, a condition of aggression between populations in which disputed claims, usually of territory, are pursued by systematic and violent means

Holy War — An ancient moral doctrine holding that some wars are fought to accomplish an ultimate good of establishing religious control or eliminating infidels subjecting a territory to religious authority. In some cases, the deity is considered to be directly in command providing reason to believe that the cause cannot fail regardless of human assessment of chances of success. Often members of the religious group are believed to be obligated to participate and to be destined to immediate divine reward should they die while participating in a holy war. Although there are differences from Jewish and Christian doctrine, Islamic *jihad* (as applied to war) has many of these characteristics

'Just war' theory — the notion that war may be justified by certain moral conditions having been met — such as the war is a last resort, formally authorized by civil authority; its motive is just including the vindication of justice; it has a reasonable probability of success; good consequences can be expected to outweigh the evils; only the force necessary to prevail is exercised; targets are only those under arms.

Militarism — a philosophy of governing in which a nation relies upon aggressive military power, including war, as its chief instrument of foreign policy

Pacifism — a moral principle renouncing war; a philosophy of governing in which a nation rejects the use of military power as its chief instrument of foreign policy, relying exclusively on negotiation

Realpolitik — the view that substantive moral principles simply cannot be applied to disputes between nations

destabilization in the coming decade. Bombings at the World Trade Center in New York, U.S. embassies in Kenya and Tanzania, U.S. personnel quarters in Saudi Arabia, a nightclub frequented by American servicemen in Germany — not to mention the downing of a Pan Am 747 over England — all have evidenced that America faces terrorists as if it were at war. Indeed, the Arab plotter believed to be behind the Kenya and Tanzanian bombings had declared in 1997 that he was leading a movement that was "at war" with the United States. Is it a war when only one group declares it?

Finally, think about the fact that in a democracy, despite the ideal of representing the will of the people, no one group has its way all the time. When the decision to go to war is made, there will be objectors. What is their status, morally speaking? Do they owe more than they are willing to give to their society? Or does society owe them more personal latitude than the majority, at such occasions of national stress, is typically eager to grant?

Militarism

This philosophy of governing a nation relies upon aggressive military power, including war, as its chief instrument of foreign policy. War, as we all know, has been a part of human civilization for a very long time, and during much of that time the excitement and drama of war have appealed to many people from the fans of John Wayne to the followers of Adolf Hitler. Supporters of armed conflict exalt such values as loyalty to country, defense of life and property, military efficiency, physical discipline, valor, and hatred of the enemy. They do not exalt such values as individual autonomy, humanitarian conduct toward others, or international cooperation. Taken together, their values define *militarism.*

The militarist mentality is a cultural descendant of an era when war could be conducted more or less in isolation from other aspects of society. Insulating innocents from war's effects was never perfectly achieved: We have only to think of the fall of Troy in Homer's *Iliad* to see that some innocents are always likely to suffer in war. But during much of human history it was sometimes possible even for thinking people to minimize this, because armies were often arrayed against each other in underpopulated areas so that accounts of the Battle of Waterloo in 1815 (unlike, say, the military operations of the Vietnam conflict) do not include any high civilian casualty figures.

But World War I (1914–1918) put all this in a very different light. This saw the introduction of total war into human history. By that war's end, entire populations had been mobilized, more than 10 million Europeans had perished, and the economies of victor and vanquished alike were too enfeebled to enable restoration of prewar prosperity. And yet the exhausted armies persisted in a brutal war of attrition long after the glories of promised victory had faded from popular memory.

Is it not intriguing that wars of this kind could never be conducted unless the home population were actually willing to participate in all this? You might well wonder why a population would ever support such a disastrous arrangement. There are complex reasons. Ancient border disputes flare. At other times, what drives a nation to battle might be a fierce sense of national pride. Trade battles break out over tariffs. Most frequently, wars erupt when a tyrannical leader uses fear of "enemies" and other inflammatory rhetoric to preserve national control and has some egomaniacal agenda to rule all or part of the world. His people harken to his ranting, to martial music and the flash of helmets. In "defense," the nation declares war with some palpable sense of grand purpose. Soon, however, the troops embark and the death notices begin to appear. Here's an account of the results of that process from World War I, according to *The Columbia History of the World*:

> Governments did their best to whip up ever fresh enthusiasm for the killing, and in the process received ample help from the established classes. The chauvinistic cant that poured from press and pulpit was meant to rouse flagging spirits to new sacrifices. The techniques of propaganda, borrowed from prewar modes of advertising, became so important in the hands of governments that one English wit spoke of "propagandocracy" as the new type of rule. Wartime propaganda became ever cruder and uglier: It started with the theme "love your country and defend it" and gradually turned to "hate your enemy and kill him."

Endnote 1

So it is no secret why "militarism" has become such a term of disapproval among so many since then. For it was the susceptibility of entire populations to the appeals of militarism, it is argued, that allowed World War I to continue.

On the other hand, do we need to infer from this that qualities such as loyalty, discipline, courage, self-defense, and efficiency have no legitimate place in human society, or that those who esteem them are necessarily "militarists"? Militarism is the value that places those qualities above others that most of us want preserved. The difficulty comes in attempting to reach a feasible balance.

Realpolitik

But before we consider the ethical justification for using force as an instrument of national policy, we should consider whether ethics even has a place in this discussion. Realpolitik is the view that substantive moral principles simply cannot be applied to disputes between nations.

The idea that war is a moral topic is often based upon an analogy between individual persons and entire countries. For example, one factor we evaluate as a moral agent is the intention that lies behind an act: If someone kills a person he instead meant to save, we don't regard him as morally responsible for murder. And in the case of nations, we could look at the national aims that inspire foreign conduct. We say that World War II, from the perspective of the Allies, was justified because its aim was to thwart German aggression. But proponents of Realpolitik hesitate to make this kind of moral assessment. One of the most prominent of these is Henry Kissinger, the U.S. Secretary of State under President Richard Nixon, who was the architect of opening trade with mainland China, *detente* with the Soviet Union and the end of the Vietnam war. He is reported to have declined to speculate at all about the motives of the North Vietnamese. He said, "I have too much difficulty understanding our own."

Endnote 5

Claims about moral principles then become nothing more than rhetorical exercises, designed to bowl people over into agreeing with one's own point of view.

Wouldn't this mean that policymakers are left with little moral basis for assessing their own policy options? For in a situation that involves more than one party, is it not necessary to accommodate more than just one's own particular point of view? Lacking either the will or the ability to understand the other side leaves only one's own aims and interests as motivating considerations.

Realpolitik aims to be "realistic," by appealing for policy justification only to one's own national interests, at least as those policymakers perceive them. Why would anyone think this? Different groups of people in different societies have different moral codes. Doesn't that make morality "culture-specific"? That would mean that moral disputes might be resolved rationally within a particular society but that conflicts between them cannot be morally decided. If all morality is relative to some particular society, how can we try to assume a moral stance beyond our own restricted cultural perspective? And why not think that everybody is limited in similar ways by perspectives of their own? Claims about moral principles then become nothing more than rhetorical exercises, designed to bowl people over into agreeing with one's own point of view. Moral "truth" becomes nothing but conversational power. Realpolitik could use this argument to bolster its claim that a nation's only rational perspective is viewed from its own self-interest.

Or we might want to put this same point in a slightly different way. Maybe the only universal moral code is ethical egoism as applied to nations. Ethical egoism (see Chapter 4) is the view that says that people should care most about what only directly concerns themselves, and Realpolitik applies this to the conduct of nations. But this still seeks to deny the applicability of moral categories to the collective sphere, just as ethical egoism does to the personal. On this view, just as individuals ought to pursue their own self-interest, so too with nations. And this would mean that no nation, in war or in anything else, is constrained by any principle but the principle of self-interest.

This need not mean that other countries' interests are never accommodated. Any nation needs countries around it to be economically viable, to prevent the infection of political unrest from spreading. This puts certain constraints upon the conduct of war, doesn't it? Could any enlightened nation today so cripple the economy of its neighbor that it would put itself at an economic disadvantage? Of course not. It needs that neighbor as an export market. And that (so says Realpolitik) is just a rational, self-interested recognition of the need to maximize the benefits for oneself in whatever one does.

Of course, in the extreme case, as during the era of Western hegemony before the late 20th century, the competition for international position is heavily weighted toward one culture at the expense of another. At that point, some would argue, the need for the dominant power to have a neighborly export market turns into the need for a parasite to have a host; and this was the real basis for Western colonialism in the years before World War II. During those years, European powers established an economic base in foreign lands, for the cheap extraction of natural resources for use at home and, eventually, special rights for private industrialists to invest abroad. This was theoretically supported by the idea that other cultures were inferior to the European and those natives lived in underprivileged conditions because of their bad luck and partly because of their laziness or stupidity.

Now what do the wars in the 20th century tell us about this? What, after all, is the logical result of ethical egoism? Any action, any at all, is permissible just as long as it suits one's own best interest? If an entire population had no value to the ascendant culture, then that population would become expendable. And now we have the technology to do it. The Nazis used a sophisticated system of gas chambers to dispose of its unwanted humans.

This is trouble for Realpolitik. Almost no one who is not alienated from the entire international community is willing to justify the Nazis. And why not? Because, they would have to say, the Nazi conduct was morally wrong. It is plainly wrong to murder six-million Jews and many thousands of homosexuals and gypsies. But Realpolitik refuses to consider anything but perceived self-interest as a basis for foreign policy. Does Realpolitik actually provide an argument in favor of Nazism?

THREE MORAL VIEWS ABOUT WAR

Three general moral views about the ethics of war can be identified. The first, often called *holy war*, usually grounds the imperative to engage in certain wars in divine command or some other form of religious authority. The second, *pacifism*, opposes all war in principle, based on moral objections to violence. The third, the most complex, is called *just war theory*. It attempts to differentiate between moral and immoral wars by the application of a set of moral criteria.

Holy War Theory (The *Jihad*)

The holy war view has its origins in traditional religion. It is prominent in the history of ancient Judaism and Catholicism, which at various times, including the Crusades of the Middle Ages, had members who believed they had a divine imperative to eliminate infidels or capture sacred land. A somewhat similar view has occurred in the thought of Shiite sect of Muslims. Islam refers to wars based on religious authority as the *jihad*. Since holy wars are fought in a religious framework, the stakes are believed by the participants to be high: often to eliminate evil, infidelity, or offense against a deity. They are pursued as if ultimate matters were at stake, as if failure would make life not worth living and success would be accompanied with ultimate reward.

Islam commands a spiritual struggle against evil. This can be fulfilled in a number of ways, one of which is by the sword. Some Muslims believe all nations must surrender to Islamic rule. According to these interpretations, adult males are expected to take part in wars or *jihads* against non-Muslim lands. Those who are killed during such wars are made martyrs who are given an immediate and special place in heaven. It is often believed that since such wars are under divine command, normal reasoning about such matters as likelihood of success (a criterion in the just war theory discussed below) need not govern decisionmaking about entering such a war. Many actions in contemporary near-Eastern conflict can be understood in the context of the ethics of the *jihad*.

Pacifism — Strategic vs. Principled Pacifism

Some people, when confronted with the contrast between the requirements and purposes of military conduct, on the one hand, and the moral values of individual rights, human freedom, and social cooperation, on the other, will insist that there is indeed a fundamental incompatibility. Those who refuse to sanction or participate in war, on the grounds of moral principle, are called *pacifists*.

Pacifism is more than just a concern for bringing about peace. By the end of the 19th century, many in Europe and the U.S. had joined peace advocacy groups, which were formed to give intellectual and political opposition to the prevailing militarist interests. But in World War I most peace advocates actually supported their own national war effort, in the hope that military victory would reshape the political landscape along more peaceable lines. That hope was perhaps the most heralded rationale for the American entry into the War.

And pacifism is not just the refusal to participate in war. In the days of the military draft, a young man might find serving in the military to be personally inconvenient or temperamentally distasteful, without necessarily adopting the stance of the pacifist. This is because those kinds of **"self-regarding" considerations** are probably not moral considerations. Likewise, someone might follow nonviolence as a kind of lifestyle choice, but insist that such views are only "true for him" and not to be imposed on others. Neither of these individuals is really a pacifist.

Strategic pacifists are those who decline to be involved in war because they think war is a morally wrong thing to be involved in. This is not a choice of lifestyle; it is the declaration of what that person takes to be morally true for everyone, whether they know it or not. And a real pacifist refuses participation in war, even if doing so might provoke severe legal reprisal. A great many pacifists have been convinced that merely avoiding active participation in war is not morally sufficient. They believe war is such an evil that they feel called upon not only to become **conscientious objectors,** but also to engage in nonviolent resistance. The personal consequences of that are likely to be highly unwelcome. During the Vietnam conflict, for example, an estimated 5,000 inductees made a public show of turning in their draft cards. In all,

Figure 1. Smaller non-nuclear missiles such as this one have been used in the Middle East. U.S. Military Academy.

more than 200,000 men were accused of draft-related offenses. Most must have been painfully aware of the social cost of doing so, and 4,000 of them were eventually imprisoned and many more went into hiding. For them, such a decision apparently was not motivated simply by personal convenience.

But all this is not to say that what they did was necessarily *justified.* For this, pacifists appeal to a wide range of considerations. Those with Christian commitments cite Biblical passages such as the Sermon on the Mount. Others appeal to the teachings of the 20th-century Hindu sage Mahatma Gandhi, whose popular following made a successful political strategy out of nonviolent resistance to British rule over India. Others cite the moral arguments of the German philosopher Immanuel Kant, whose Categorical Imperative directs us to avoid acting in any way we could not willingly universalize for others as well. In other words, they ask what would the world be like if everyone were to resort to violence?

Endnote 2

Endnote 3

Endnote 4

Pacifism as Opposition to War and as a Total Life-Style

But then what about those cases of individual conduct? Is violence never, ever justified in one person's dealings with another? What about self-defense? Many people have admired leaders such as Mahatma Gandhi, who can turn the other cheek if insulted or assaulted. But though this may be admirable, are we morally required to be saints? If you believe that there are certain circumstances when it is permissible for an individual to use violence, then it is only natural to consider seriously the possibility that there are circumstances when a nation as a whole is justified in using violence.

And what about the possibility that the taking of some lives may be necessary for the saving of others? World War II is the classic example: It gradually became obvious that Hitler was pursuing a policy of genocide against the Jews, and that only military intervention could have saved them.

Principled pacifists believe that their commitment to nonviolence must extend to all phases of life, including a commitment not to resist an assault by a thief or a madman. They will commit to avoiding any violent retaliation. Others limit their pacifism to a moral commitment for conduct of international relations among nations. They hold that pacifism is a morality for public social institutions such as the state, while acknowledging that in their personal lives and in domestic relations sometimes physical resistance and police action may be necessary, even actions that involve physical violence.

'JUST WAR' THEORY

Questions about war and peace are not idle items of academic interest: They are matters of deep concern to citizens of a democracy, who have the responsibility to play a role in determining national priorities. Unless we want to cede the political decision-making entirely to the specialists in the field, we need to have some basis for assessing our leaders and their policies. But doesn't this create a grave crisis for the democratic system? Notice how, at this point in history, culture has evolved to such a level of complexity that the factors to be considered are too diverse for the expertise of the average citizen.

For example, what do you think really are the chances that Star Wars technology can be used, as its proponents claim, to protect American cities against a missile attack? On what basis could you possibly claim to know? Unless subject to the sway of mere media appeal, the average voter is likely to be able to decide about certain complex issues only on moral grounds.

Do we have moral standards for our leaders? Of course, we do. And not just in matters of private conduct. Look at domestic policy. At present, could any U.S. President who systematically sought to place blacks in concentration camps avoid impeachment? So we really have to wonder: Is it true that there are no international moral standards for us to use in our moral assessment of the President's foreign policy? Think again about what Realpolitik claims. Is it true, as Henry Kissinger insisted, that "the security of free peoples depend(s) on whether the United States could develop a concept of national interest that we would defend regardless of the guise that challenges to it might take"? What if the "guise" were a moral principle against hoarding an unfair share of the world's industrial goods? Or a moral principle against harming innocents during a jungle bombing?

There are certainly international standards, and these have been encoded in the Geneva agreements and the United Nations Charter. Many countries recognize the authority of the 1950 European Con-

Endnote 6

vention on Human Rights, which mandates moral standards for the conduct of military trials. Wouldn't this mean that military conduct is not exempt from moral evaluation? And what is the significance of the harsh international war crimes judgment at Nuremberg, against Nazi conduct in World War II? Leading Nazis were sentenced to death for what they did during the War. So is any political leader really exempt from moral responsibility? There is general international agreement about the acceptable limits of conduct during wartime, and this has received refined philosophical expression in what is known as the **Just War Theory.**

"Just War" in Historical Context

Just war theory has ancient roots. While much justification of war in ancient Israel had the quality of holy war commanded by God other wars were fought constrained by moral limits. Early Christianity had elements of pacifism, but as early as the second century participation in war was morally tolerable within limits. The just war tradition as known in modern times is often traced to Augustine and his mentor, Ambrose, in the fourth and fifth centuries, who supported limited intervention to protect a victim against an assailant. It was Augustine who is credited with introducing the standard of a just intention or motivation as well as other criteria described below. The doctrine of the just war was refined by the 13th century theologian, Thomas Aquinas, and debate over it continues to this day.

Definition of "Just War"

The Just War Theory was formulated to state the conditions of when and how to fight a "morally acceptable" war. But, as we began to see earlier, we cannot determine what those conditions might be unless we can agree as to what a "war" is. We already saw that we should not assume just any kind of violence qualifies as "war," and whether acts of violence in situations besides war can be justified would be a separate question, not even addressed by the Just War Theory. During the 1960s, the radical group known as the Weathermen was engaged in a series of terrorist actions that at one point included blowing up New York police headquarters. But these were not acts of "war," at least not as defined by the Just War Theory. Today militant terrorists in Islam claim to be conducting a "holy war" against the West by various bombings. Are these acts of war simply because the terrorists say so?

War Narrowly Defined

Does it take a formal decision by an internationally recognized government to establish a legal war? What is the advantage of such a narrow definition? First, we need a way of simplifying our discussion. Conceivably, there might be justification for some spontaneous uprisings, and we should not simply exclude the possibility that even terrorism might be justifiable under some conditions. But we would need to examine those issues separately, not as instances of "war." Secondly, prisoners of war are generally supposed to deserve treatment not awarded to outlaws or murderers. Soldiers, after all, are not

Endnote 6a

Soldiers, after all, are not responsible agents, in the way we often think of criminals as being responsible for their acts of violence. Soldiers are often conscripted against their will and do most of what they do under orders from others. The distinction between these two groups would not be possible unless we understood how war differs from ordinary crime.

responsible agents, in the way we often think of criminals as being responsible for their acts of violence. Soldiers are often conscripted against their will and do most of what they do under orders from others. The distinction between these two groups would not be possible unless we understood how war differs from ordinary crime.

So we need at least a working definition. War, according to traditional proponents of the Just War Theory, is a controlled use of force, undertaken by persons organized in a functioning chain of command under a competent authority, conducted against an opponent who enjoys some measure of military parity.

Endnote 7

Ambiguous Cases

Unfortunately, this is not as clear and adequate a definition as one might hope for. It excludes, as it should, marginal cases such as food riots and mass shootings by deranged people. But it also leaves unclear exactly how we determine what a **"competent authority"** is. In a civil war, which side qualifies as the "competent authority"? It also leaves unsettled how we should classify cases of armed insurrection, where the rebellion is effective against a government not out of military might, but owing to other factors. Some people might, for example, think of the violent response of the Chinese government to the 1989 demonstrations by its own people in Tiananmen Square as an act of war.

Nonetheless, it does open the discussion to those agreeing with St. Augustine (354–430), who held that (1) the use of violence on the part of private individuals is immoral, but that (2) there are occasions when governments have a right (and even perhaps an obligation) to go to war. Certain stages of World War II, the later stages of the Vietnam conflict and the invasion of Panama are occasions where this definition is not really an issue. Others, such as sending U.S. troops into Somalia on humanitarian grounds (to help distribute food in an impoverished nation that lacked political stability) might be considered "borderline cases."

What Makes Wars "Just"

We should probably be concerned less with the definition of "war" and more with the definition of **"justice."** According to this theory (as its name implies) only just wars are morally permissible. So how do we decide what makes a war "just"? The traditional strategy has been to regard acts of war as one would regard actions of individual persons. Generally speaking, actors have intentions and their actions have consequences, both foreseen and unforeseen. And though consequences cannot always be foreseen with certainty, it is often possible to gauge which possible consequences are the more probable to occur. Likewise, actions can be seen as conforming (or not) to some given standard or rule. Traditionally, **Just War Theory proposes to use**

Endnote 7a

several criteria in assessing the moral quality of a nation's conduct, including legitimate authority, right intention and just cause.

* **Legitimate Authority:** Thomas Aquinas argued that a just war must be declared by a legitimate public authority, not by a private individual. Some discussions of this criterion include the requirement that the authority must formally declare the war rather than leaving the situation ambiguous.

* **Right Intention:** Second, a just war must be carried out with "right intention." If the Just War Theory could be plausibly grounded on the right intention condition, it would provide a powerful (though very selective) defense of some wars. According to the traditional Just War Theory, war is unacceptable if the intention behind it is not morally right. To say that one's action proceeds from "a right intention" is to say one's motives are good, and it is easy to find accounts of bad motives that have brought war about which would mean that those wars were unjustified. Historians usually cite Hitler's desire for domination of Europe as one major cause of World War II, and it is plausible to suppose that the war was prolonged due to the desire of the German command to spare themselves the punishment for their own genocide towards Jews, homosexuals, gypsies, et cetera. Even if pacifists are wrong, even if the general rule against killing and irreparably disrupting the lives of countless human beings can be overridden under certain extraordinary conditions, would a leader's desire for power, or for exemption from justifiable punishment, qualify as that sort of condition? Quite a few people will answer "no" to that last question.

But still, how do we really discover the motive behind national policy? This is a difficulty that does not face us as much when we are considering only the conduct of individual persons. Surely the U.S. is a multicultural land with many diverse and competing interests. For such a nation to act cohesively, shouldn't many of those diverse interests be reflected in national policy? So even if oil interests played a part in fighting the Gulf War, others would undoubtedly appeal to other motivations.

It may be difficult to imagine what it could mean for an entire nation to act out of right or wrong intention. As long as a multiethnic nation, such as the U.S., is really democratic, its national policy can never be a reflection of only one interest group: It would become politically fatal for a leader to push a policy as serious as war without many diverse groups recognizing crucial self-interested advantages of doing so. At those moments, there would need to be many social "intentions" that coalesce, for a time, into the harrowing national policy of war. There would be individual intentions as well, some of which may be morally justified (helping others in need) or morally unjustified (benefitting personally from the probable deaths of hundreds, maybe millions, of human beings).

At the national level, who is even supposed to "have" that good intention, anyway? The President of the United States, who usually plays the role of proposing a war to the nation? The Congress of the United States, which, according to the Constitution, must declare war for the nation officially to be at war? The determination of intention in war will necessarily involve many different actors with complex, mixed motivations.

> * **Just Cause:** The third criterion of the Just War Theory is that it must have a just cause. We become clear about that by asking ourselves what the facts are, what we value (and, perhaps, what we think the probable results of our conduct might be), and why we want to bring about any particular outcome. At the national level, where policy decisions are made, this means that defenders of a war would have to make clear the probable consequences of a proposed policy. But we do need to concern ourselves with the standards for deciding matters of public policy. That means we need to see what the probable consequences of a proposed policy would be, and decide whether those consequences are justified.

Factor — The American Invasion of Panama

What would it mean to be able to apply moral considerations to the evaluation of war policy? In the planning stages, at least, it would involve deciding what the results of waging war, and its advantages or disadvantages, are likely to be. For the Panama invasion, American conduct even aspired to the stature of the morally justified act, with the Bush Administration calling it "Operation Just Cause." That is an invitation for any student of contemporary history to think about whether the conditions for correctly calling it that have really been fulfilled.

One formulation of a just cause is that war is in response to overt aggression. Sections of the Charter of the United Nations do not, except perhaps in the vaguest way, establish a criterion for what a "right" national policy would be. They talk instead about the kinds of things a nation should not do, which is summarized under a term such as **"acts of aggression."** However, though a nation should not act aggressively, it is permitted to respond in **self-defense** to aggression committed against it. And here the important point is that acts of aggression are defined only in terms of the unilateral, unprovoked, and threatening use of force against another country.

Was there any serious military threat to the United States from the armed forces of Panama? If not, one could argue that the invasion itself was a violation of international law. Of course, there might conceivably be other criteria for "justice" besides the very minimal one set forth by the U.N. In that case, we might want to look into the truth and the significance of the drug-smuggling charges against Panamanian strongman Manuel Noriega, and consider whether that kind of act could justify what the U.S. did.

Factor — First-Strike Theory

Other possible considerations need to be taken as well, besides the question of whether a war is launched in response to overt aggression. For example, can a nation justifiably go to war in anticipation of a hostile military threat without, in other words, waiting for it to actually happen? That is what occurred in the weeks leading up to World War I, where millions of men throughout Europe were mobilized, as instruments of what has been called "gunboat" diplomacy. There the idea was: The louder the threat, the greater the chance your opponent will capitulate. Unfortunately, this was a strategy pursued with equal bravado on both sides, and it escalated out of hand when both sides decided they could not suddenly back down from the threats they had been broadcasting. This is exactly the kind of situation that the U.N. Charter was written to avert. The idea was that if no one went to war unless actually attacked, no one would ever be attacked.

But what if not all parties agree to that principle? In 1967 the state of Israel was actually faced with hostile Arab armies who did not recognize its very status as a nation, and at that point (some would argue) the legitimate state interest of self-preservation sanctioned the strategic first strike by the Israelis. Of course, this assumes that Israel really did enjoy statehood, a claim endorsed by the United Nations when it admitted Israel to membership. A further question concerns the logical implications of such a justification. For even if adequate, does this justification of the Israeli action mean that the Arabs did not have legitimate interests, or that either side is blameless for the hostile conditions?

And what happens in the case when **military intervention** is recommended for clearly **humanitarian purposes**, such as distributing food in Somalia or saving the beleaguered Bosnian citizens of Sarajevo? The difficulties with deciding this kind of borderline case have often led involved parties to seek international consensus on the action to be taken. Thus, for example, starting in 1992, both the European Community and the United Nations began trying to negotiate a settlement in Bosnia.

Factor — International Approval

The Gulf War and the Bosnian intervention raise another question. Does the mere fact that an international body approves of an action in itself make the action morally just? The War in the Persian Gulf, conducted only after a favorable vote in the United Nations

Security Council, was criticized by some on moral grounds, despite its international sanction.

And there is another complication with restricting a "just" war to include only the response to acts of overt aggression. What about a continuing violation of a nation's rights? Let's suppose a country's neighbor has exercised hostile control over that country's economy, perhaps by controlling the international market so that the disadvantaged country could not get the imports it needs for political stability. This is not an armed intervention. But isn't it an act of war "by attrition"? That is the sort of charge that Saddam Hussein's government was making against Kuwait, as one pretext for the Iraqi invasion. Or what if a colonial power is exercising painful economic domination over its colonies? That was the rationale offered by the Viet Cong against the Americans, by Indian nationalists joining Mahatma Gandhi against the British, and it was the same rationale as given by American revolutionaries at the time of the Boston Tea Party in 1773. We need to look very carefully, in each case, to assess the political rhetoric that attempts to portray a "just cause."

But what about the way that cause is actually pursued? This leads to another question: Even if the cause is just, does that always mean that the war is just?

Factor — Proportionality

Most proponents of the Just War Theory will insist that for a war to be just, its actual conduct must conform to a rule of **proportionality.** In international matters, just as in the conduct of an individual's personal life, there are always tradeoffs: Results of any extended endeavor always bring benefits and costs alike, and we need to weigh the one against the other in decisions of public policy, in order to decide if the proportion of good to bad consequences is acceptable.

Any such assessment is a complicated matter, requiring the testimony of "experts" who may or may not be knowledgeable or reliable in their advice as well as quantifying complex value judgments deciding how bad it is to risk destroying families and lives as well as how important the good consequences are.

This, however, raises troubling questions indeed: is it moral to consider the factor of a potential or actual "body count" to evaluate whether a war is or may be just?

This, however, raises troubling questions indeed: is it moral to consider the factor of a potential or actual "body count" to evaluate whether a war is or may be just? Is it inherently dehumanizing to make such assessments as part of a justification for or argument against war? What sort of consideration should be paid to the lives lost on the other side? The Iraqis may have lost up to 243,000 people. To what extent were those deaths really only a tragic moral necessity for achieving our own just military cause?

Endnote 8

This raises the question of the **collateral effects of war.** What weight do we give to the destruction of nonmilitary property and the killing of innocent bystanders? Many proponents of the Just War Theory would reject the strategy of total war and recognize some commanding moral scruples against destruction that is purely arbitrary or vengeful.

This concern over collateral effects would probably invalidate Union General Sherman's "scorched-earth policy" during his Civil War march through Georgia, but that would still depend upon what sorts of action we take to be merely "vengeful." If a commander's aim is to prevent the current generation of inhabitants from ever again being in an economic position to wage war, then almost any conceivable property destruction would seem justified. But why would people think such drastic measures necessary? Do they reject the chances of securing a reliable agreement safeguarding the rights of all parties? When that sort of agreement exists, what remaining reason or enthusiasm for war could there be?

The need to preserve noncombatant immunity (the protection of innocent bystanders) would place a high moral burden on military commanders. Destruction, if it is not to be arbitrary or vengeful, must be limited to, or at least aimed at, military targets alone. Under this rule, commanders would need to discriminate between military and civilian targets and then decide which targets are really necessary for the war aims. In 1940 and 1941, for example, the British kept only military objectives targeted, despite the indiscriminate German bombing of London. But it became clear that the German war effort remained intact as long as its heavily populated industrial base remained untouched. At that point British Prime Minister Winston Churchill policy shifted to permit bombing of cities by treating widespread civilian casualties as only a byproduct of necessary military conduct. During the Gulf War, on the other hand, it was stated American policy to avoid civilian targets.

Factor — Reasonable Hope of Success
Next, even if all the previous criteria have been satisfied, a war is not considered morally acceptable if it has no hope of success. Lives cannot be put in jeopardy if the effort is doomed to fail. Here just war theory differs substantially from holy war theory, which relies on the belief that the war is being fought for a cause of ultimate importance and under the command of the deity to eliminate the need to assessment of likely result.

Factor — The Notion of "Last Resort"
Finally, all possible peaceful means of resolving the conflict must have been exhausted before war becomes a legitimate possibility. War must be the "last resort." Only when all of these criteria are satisfied is a war considered justified.

APPLICATION OF JUST WAR THEORY TO NUCLEAR WAR

This raises the question of the claim of noncombatant immunity in the nuclear age. It took an immense effort on February 12, 1945, for the Allies to pull off the bombing of the German city of Dresden. Scores of planes were orchestrated to drop thousands of rather small bombs. But six months later, the nuclear bombing by a single Ameri-

Figure 2. Marxist doctrines of Lenin (pictured on banner) fueled the military state of the Soviet Union. Corbis-Bettman.

can aircraft killed 100,000 people in Hiroshima and five times that in Nagasaki. How does this affect the argument?

For American President Harry Truman, the convincing military argument had been that more casualties might well have resulted if the Americans had been forced into a conventional invasion of the Japanese homeland. This was a utilitarian argument, one which many have questioned, and since the improvement of nuclear technology one wonders how valid such justification would be today. When the U.S. and the Soviet Union faced each other as two armed camps, with enough nuclear strength to destroy every living thing, and faced as well the likelihood of a cataclysmic escalation after any first strike, what could possibly justify the use of nuclear weapons?

Until the end of the **"Cold War"** — the polarized struggle between the Soviet Union and the U.S. from 1946 to 1991 — it was U.S. policy to threaten the use of nuclear weapons, on the assumption (then called the theory of **Mutual Assured Destruction**) that neither side would be stupid enough to start a nuclear war under such conditions. That assumes the leadership on both sides would allow sane, rational considerations to direct military policy. But what if another Hitler came to power? This nuclear policy also meant actually having the intention to use nuclear weapons if the other side were that stupid or lost control of its own arsenal, by accident or through the unilateral action of rogue commanders. What can we say, morally, about that? The issue never received a full public discussion, so one could not claim that the policy was truly democratic. But that alone might not invalidate such a policy. For we have already admitted that there are cases such as Pearl Harbor, and other emergencies that make full consultation impossible. Would this be one of them?

The question really comes down to this: Would the American population ever agree, if asked, to regard itself as expendable? Perhaps. Maybe patriotism would make martyrs of them. On the other hand, maybe people really would rather be "Red than dead" (as the signs of early antiwar protesters used to say). In any case, imagine you are the President, or a Strategic Air Commander, and you don't have the time to find out. The moral burden is all yours. How do you decide? Do you surrender your sovereignty to the threat, or do you capitulate (for the sake of your people's very lives)?

Until the collapse of the Soviet Union, the American leadership was in exactly this position. American plans were governed by what was called the Countervailing Strategy, under which even an ordinary, massive Soviet land attack, using only conventional, nonnuclear, weapons, would elicit an American nuclear strike, and this was because the Soviet conventional force was generally thought to be superior even to the strength of our allies in Europe combined under terms of the North Atlantic Treaty Organization (NATO). This bleak choice would be forced upon any American leader who loses confidence in the power of international agreements, agreements which would be secure only when all parties feel sufficiently protected by their provisions. At the desperate moment we are imagining here, as Soviet troops begin pouring into West Germany, such confidence might have worn pretty thin. What does this say about the wisdom of collectively securing the legitimate interests of all powerful potential adversaries?

The Countervailing Strategy was accepted by both sides during much of the Cold War. With the antiballistic missile (ABM) treaty in 1972, both agreed not to construct the antiballistic missile systems that would protect home cities, because if one side achieved that aim before the other, it might remove the main military impediment against a policy of first nuclear strike.

However, the Soviets violated the ABM treaty and in response U. S. President Ronald Reagan proposed a drastic overhaul of military policy with his introduction of the Strategic Defense Initiative (**"Star Wars"**). American cities would be protected against Soviet missiles. And the reason the Soviets were so bitterly opposed to that was the fact that Americans could then launch a first nuclear strike, if they eventually chose not to share their technology, without fear of massive Soviet retaliation. This would mean that only American adherence to moral principle might stand in the way of millions of Soviet deaths. Would the moral caliber of the American leadership stand such a test? The Soviets, at least, doubted that it would. But, apparently, faced with a failed economic system that could not muster a continuing military juggernaut, the Soviets virtually capitulated to the United States as the strongest power in the world. Did Reagan's Star Wars Initiative speed that decision? Or was the decision taken in spite of any American initiative?

Obviously, the predominance of nuclear technology has presented the world with unappealing choices, and it puts traditional discussions about "just war" in a new light. But are these any longer serious matters for us? Isn't it obviously tempting to breathe more easily today, simply because there is no more Soviet Union? Tempting, yes. But it is also just as obvious that political realities are ever changing, and as long as there are nuclear weapons around, these questions will remain very much with us. By the mid-1990s, for example, the political health of Russian President Boris Yeltsin was becoming increasingly precarious, and the possibility of some future change in Russian policy could no longer be ignored. So it is worth asking: When should national debate over these matters occur when an immediate crisis is looming, or when we have enough cool distance to assess the alternatives calmly and thoughtfully? Consider what the alternatives fairly clearly seem to be:

Countervailing Strategy targets massive retaliation against enemy arsenals, and gambles on the deterrent force of this kind of threat to prevent the enemy from ever launching an attack. But what about the chance of a tragic accidental launch? With perhaps insufficient time for the defenders to identify the accident as such, the intention of military policy would be to proceed with the nuclear option. And in the event of a ground attack upon our European allies, American intention was for a measured, tit-for-tat nuclear response against those forces which would almost certainly obliterate thousands, maybe millions of people in the countries we are supposed to be protecting! Given the human costs of that, is it moral for any country's leadership to have such an intention?

Strategic Defense, on the other hand, would seek to prevent those missiles from ever hitting their target, because technology would provide a nuclear shield of protection for the homeland. Yet the technology remains in its infancy, and there is no assurance as to how successful its development will turn out to be. What if it were 80% effective? A 20% failure rate is a pretty good return in some endeavors, but in this case it would still annihilate millions of people and jeopardize the ecological state of the entire planet. And because Strategic Defense would be enormously expensive as well, what social needs would have to be ignored in order to pay for it?

Finite Deterrence prohibits the *use* of nuclear weapons in any battlefield situation. But the military would retain a sufficient nuclear capability, stored in highly protected areas such as patrolling submarines, so that an eventual, searing second strike would surely be possible. And that, the theory insists, should be enough to deter an intentional enemy attack, while at the same time allowing the military to determine whether first-strike enemy missiles were mistakenly launched. This is akin to what actually happened in World War II when the U.S. responded, eventually, to the attack on Pearl Harbor by detonating atomic bombs on Nagasaki and Hiroshima bringing the war to an end. President Nixon would maintain that his controversial bombings of Haiphong brought the fierce North Vietnamese generals to the table to negotiate U.S. extrication from South Vietnam. But would deterrence really work today? Might the enemy leadership decide that they could absorb a limited **second-strike response,** and the costs of that, however terrible, would be outweighed by the benefits of total victory? (The Soviets, after all, suffered an estimated 20-million dead during World War II but they helped stop Hitler!) And could even that second-strike response by "our" side ever be morally justified, in view of the terrible costs that it would inflict on millions of innocent human beings? Wouldn't this still amount to mass murder?

Nuclear Disarmament Perhaps the prevailing pressures in favor of launching a first nuclear strike stem from the fear that the other side will do so. If one of the adversaries no longer possessed that capability, that motive would be eliminated. This is the central argument often presented by advocates of unilateral disarmament the idea that we should abolish nuclear weapons without first gaining the assurance of similar action by the other side. But the other side would no longer fear a crippling reprisal. So might this not instead increase the chance of attack? Not, of course, if we could be certain that its leadership took seriously its moral responsibilities, for surely there could be no moral justification for them to commit such an act. But can we be sure they would take these responsibilities seriously? Most Americans, throughout the Cold War, were unwilling to trust the Kremlin on that.

What **unilateral nuclear disarmament** might actually mean is that the chances of a massive nuclear attack would be lessened. For it may be a little hard to imagine even Joseph Stalin calling arbitrarily for the annihilation of an entire population. In any event we know that a massive nuclear holocaust, even if it did not directly touch the perpetrator's home base, would still have devastating ecological effects that no country on earth could avoid. But even so, how would unilateral disarmament affect the possibility of national self-determination? A healthy national life surely requires that important policy decisions not be held hostage to coercive stipulations by unfriendly forces, and wouldn't a nation that lacked a nuclear capacity find it difficult to withstand unscrupulous hostile demands of a foreign nuclear power?

This leaves open the avenue of **bilateral nuclear disarmament** — a negotiated arrangement, with sufficient safeguards, where two adversaries agree to a gradual, eventual elimination of all nuclear weapons in their possession. Conceivably, this might be the actual result of the kind of arms control policy followed by both major powers after the Reagan-Gorbachev summit in 1987. But difficulties have persisted even under such favorable conditions. Without the total elimination of nuclear weaponry from both sides, the situation remains at best one of Finite Deterrence. How do we finally get down to zero on this? Isn't there a tremendous, self-interest for either side to retain a few nuclear devices, fully hidden in some cave somewhere, as a threatening instrument of last resort?

Nuclear Proliferation

As the planet moves into the 21st Century, the "nuclear club" of nations possessing such devastating power expands, with both India and Pakistan detonating devices in 1998. Meanwhile, the foremost target of American and European intelligence agencies has been a cadre of "rogue" nations — Libya, Iran, Iraq, Syria — who seek to have nuclear-armed missiles to use as part of their campaigns of terrorism against the free world. Some multinational treaties have been drawn to try to restrict the proliferation of nuclear weapons, but not every nation signs them. Meanwhile, the United Nations attempts to enforce regulations against the spread of nuclear weapons by imposing embargoes on "nuclear wanna-be" countries, with mixed and unclear results.

FINAL COMMENTS

These questions about war are unresolved, but nevertheless inescapable for each of us. They touch on many more issues than we can pursue here. One of the most important of these is the place of international arbitration. If disputes between nations could be settled under the framework of international law, would there be any further need for war of any kind? This in turn illustrates the need to ask why a nation would ever resort to the drastic expedient of war. Surely, only under the most dire circumstances would an entire people agree to the kind of sacrifice a prolonged conflict requires. What kind of circumstances would do that? In our culture, after all, we normally think that it is wrong to kill innocent people or to destroy others' property or to arbitrarily prevent them from attaining the quality of life we aspire to ourselves.

FOR FURTHER INQUIRY

REVIEW QUESTIONS

1. What sorts of reasons would make you willing to support a war, see your spouse embark in uniform, fight in it yourself? What sorts of reasons do you think appealed to the North Vietnamese or the Iraqis? Would they be basically much different from yours? In other words, what would the nature of an international threat have to look like to a people who go to war? If war is to be a last resort, do we not need to turn our attention, as a global community, to diminishing those kinds of perceived threats?

2. The evolution of an all-volunteer military, a Nixon stratagem, may have altered public support of recent military initiatives. How much of a difference does it make, in finding moral justification for war, if a nation's fighting forces are paid volunteers? Did it affect popular support for the Gulf War?

3. It seems natural, from our discussion of nuclear war, to view war as a moral issue, and not simply a matter for the strategists of Realpolitik. The very possible consequences of war

endanger life on this planet, and one could hardly hope for a better entry for moral theory. In any event, we do need some way of deciding on national policy and in the Western democracies at this point, no one but the very marginalized seems willing to reject the idea of a fair ballot system for universal electoral participation. So it is useful to remind ourselves of the role of voters in a representative democracy. Let's say that an American President decides that a brutally conducted series of air and ground strikes against an uncooperative country serves our own national interest. What should our response be? Does anyone really want to say that there are no moral standards for national leaders? And even if there were no "objective" moral standpoint for deciding international behavior (as some versions of Realpolitik might insist), does that mean that our leaders are not subject to the standards of morality espoused in our own culture?

ENDNOTES

1. John A. Garraty and Peter Gay, ed., *The Columbia History of the World* (Harper & Row, 1972), p. 9878.

2. Todd Gitlin, *The Sixties: Years of Hope, Days of Rage* (Bantam, 1987), p. 291.

3. In Matthew 5 we read: "Ye have heard it said, thou shalt love thy neighbor, and hate thine enemy. But I say unto you, Love your enemies, bless them that curse you, do good to them that hate you. . . ." Of course, in Matthew 10 the following saying of Jesus also appears: "Think not that I am come to send peace on earth; I came not to send peace, but a sword." (Obviously, the context of any authority figure's remarks must be studied to gain full understanding of the statements.)

4. See Chapter 4 (Kant).

5. Quoted by Lackey, *The Ethics of War and Peace*, p. 32.

6. Henry Kissinger, *Years of Upheaval* (Little, Brown and Company, 1982), p. 168.

6a. Johnson, James Turner. "Historical Roots and Sources of the Just War Tradition in Western Culture" *Just War and Jihad,* edited by John Kelsey and J. T. Johnson. (Westport, CT: Greenwood Press, 1991), pp. 3–30.

7. This definition is suggested by the discussion in Douglas P. Lackey, *The Ethics of War and Peace*, pp. 29ff.

7a. Childress, James F. *Moral Responsibility in Conflicts: Essays on Nonviolence, War, and Conscience*. Baton Rouge: Louisiana State University Press, 1982, chapter 3, especially pp. 64–65; and DeCew, Judith Wagner. "Warfare, Codes of," *Encyclopedia of Applied Ethics*, Volume 4. San Diego: Academic Press, 1998, pp. 499–505.

8. Douglas Kellner, *The Persian Gulf TV War* (Westview, 1992), pp. 89–92.

9. Lackey, *The Ethics of War and Peace*, pp. 734.

FREEDOM IS:

— CREATIVITY'S BATTERY MATE.
Share it with love. Someone gave you some.

What freedom means to me is My business.

THE PROMISE OF FREEDOM IS NOBLE, BUT GET IT IN WRITING.

—choosing—

absolute freedom is absolutely exhausting

Like a garden, it has to be cultivated.

Freedom is spelled any darn way I want to

FREEDOM WORKS BETTER IF YOU THINK OF IT AS OURS, NOT YOURS.

— TELLING THE GOVT. WHERE TO GET OFF

freedom is toating the load off your pillow

— having a party, not obeying one.

Freedom is tax exemption for the National Atheist Foundation

— telling a cop you disagree with him

Freedom is having the power to do harm and not using it.

— Visiting Georgia without a visa.

— walking in the hills without a permission slip
—WHAT JOHN MUIR'S CHEST IS STUFFED WITH

— A ROUND-TRIP TICKET TO SIBERIA
— The substance eagles breathe at 1,000 feet.

— coming home and finding it there.

— The most desirable form of turmoil.
—WHAT DOESN'T SEPARATE THE RICH FROM THE POOR.

— staying up with the grownups?

— LEGALIZED HUMAN DIGNITY

— THE RIGHT TO HATE APPLE PIE IF YOU WANT TO.

— anarchy with a brain

— INTELLECTUAL ELBOW ROOM

NEVER HAVING TO SAY "YOUR MAJESTY"

— THE ANTIDOTE FOR FEAR.

— Responsible Disorder

— JUST ACROSS THE YARD AND OVER THE WALL

FREEDOM IS ALIVE & WELL ABOARD THE CONSTITUTION

— a jealous lover — it's own reward
—COMMON SENSE

free's a crowd.

FREEDOM? I'M INSANE TO IT!

Freedom's just another word for nothing left to be.

Keep your freedom out of my freedom

Is freedom ready for self-government?

Freedom is HABIT-FORMING

FREEDOM MAKES YOUR POOR OPINION AS GOOD AS MY INSPIRED WISDOM

freedom is wearing a Canadian cap while all around you are in hard hats
LET FREEDOM ZING!

FREEDOM IS CONTAINING ABOUT NOT HAVING ENOUGH FREEDOM

Freedom is only for those with the guts to line with it.

Freedom is being at liberty to say

FREEDOM IS EASIER SAID THAN DONE

FREEDOM IS MORE IMPORTANT THAN ORDER

Freedom is not a product but a tool.

"freedom" & "communism" in communism

CHAPTER 15

HUMAN RIGHTS

"Be not intimidated, therefore, by any terrors, from publishing with utmost freedom whatever can be warranted by the laws of your country, nor suffer yourselves to be wheedled out of your liberty by any pretenses of politeness, delicacy or decency."

— **John Adams, 1765**

"All men are created equal . . . they are endowed by their Creator with certain unalienable rights, and among these are life, liberty and the pursuit of happiness."

— **The Declaration of Independence, 64 signers, 1776**

One day the police stop you on the street, check your identity, and take you directly to jail. You have no idea why you were arrested — you don't think you've done anything criminal — and once you are in jail nothing happens. Somebody puts food in your cell once a day, but no charges are mentioned or filed, no lawyer appears, no trial is scheduled. Your requests to make a phone call are ignored. One day a prison official is passing by the small hole in your cell door, and you are about to cry out.

But what should you say? Perhaps you should just beg like a dog who wants out of a cage. "Please, please, let me out of here, let me make a phone call, let me talk to a lawyer." You worry, though, that this will seem too pathetic.

Another possibility is reminding the official that you have rights. If your arrest occurred in the United States and you know something about American law, perhaps you'll remind the official that as an American you have constitutional rights to due process of law and to a speedy and public trial.

Or perhaps you'll appeal to your human rights as found in the Universal Declaration of Human Rights (1948) and other contemporary human rights documents. You might demand compliance with your internationally-recognized rights against arbitrary detention, to a fair and public trial, and to a presumption of innocence (Universal Declaration Articles 9–11). And perhaps you'll suggest that your friends have probably already contacted Amnesty International.

James W. Nickel is Professor of Philosophy at the University of Colorado, Boulder. He is the author of *Making Sense of Human Rights* (Berkeley: University of California Press, 1987)

Of course appeals to rights don't work like magic. Your indignant appeal to your rights may just irritate the official. Nevertheless, many of us think that appeals to people's rights are a powerful and important part of political discourse and persuasion. People have rights, and those rights constrain what governments can do to them.

When appeals to rights are made fully explicit, they have several parts. First, it identifies some person, group, or agency as the **rightholder**(s), the one(s) who benefit from or are protected by the right. Second, an appeal to rights identifies some persons or parties as the **addressees** of the right, the ones upon whom the right imposes obligations or duties. And third, an appeal to rights has some content that specifies what the rightholders are entitled to and what actions the addressees must take or refrain from taking.

CHIEF LEARNING OUTCOME

I understand six kinds of rights that can be universally applied to all humankind and can discuss them in terms of moral reasoning.

Complaining about the misconduct of governments is nothing new. Throughout the ages people have complained about their bad treatment by saying that under a better (or more civilized, or more rational) legal system such treatment would be prohibited. In the last few centuries the language of rights has become widely used for this sort of complaint. Instead of saying that arbitrary imprisonment is bad, crazy, or unjust, people have come to say that it violates their rights — thereby emphasizing the harm or wrong that such imprisonment does to its victims. And in the last fifty years ideas about universal human rights have become widespread. Massacres, or cases of torture, are now described not just as atrocities or injustices, but also as violations of human rights. Journalists, politicians, and ordinary people all around the world now commonly use the idea of human rights.

Appeals to human rights have been made easier and more plausible in the last fifty years by the creation of international human rights standards. To the jailor's or torturer's contemptuous question, "What human rights?", the victim can now respond by saying "The human rights recognized in the Universal Declaration of Human Rights" or even "The human rights found in interna-

Figure 1. Tienanmen Square. Associated Press/Wide World Photos.

tional human rights law — which this nation is bound to by its ratification of human rights treaties."

Efforts to create and promote international human rights have not succeeded in eliminating human rights violations. Severe violations of **human rights** continue to occur in most parts of the world. For example:

In Algeria thousands of civilians have been killed or disappeared in the struggle between the government and its radical Islamic opponents. Killings, kidnappings, and torture are committed by both sides. These actions violate rights to life, rights against arbitrary arrest, and rights to freedom from torture. Government security forces are responsible for many serious human rights abuses.

In China, rights of political participation are severely limited. Political dissidents are often jailed for expressing their views. Violations of due process rights, including detention without trial, are also common. In the Tiananmen Square massacre, pro-democracy demonstrators were brutally killed, beaten, and arrested.

Was This a Good Samaritan Argument?

The map of the world changed dramatically in February 1999, when the United States and allies in the North Atlantic Treaty Organization (NATO) decided to overturn the tyrannical rule of a tiny province of Yugoslavia known as Kosovo. Serbian masters of Kosovo, led by "President" Slobodan Milosevic, had

KEY CONCEPTS

Human rights — morally authorized claims applying to all people solely on the basis of their being human individuals; particularly those formulated or expressed in multinational treaties, enforced by national courts, and/or by significant international institutions, applicable in six areas

- **security rights** protect people against murder, injury, and torture.

- **due process rights** protect people against arbitrary and excessively harsh punishments and require fair and public trials for those accused of crimes.

- **liberty rights** protect people's freedoms in areas such as belief, expression, association, and movement.

- **political rights** protect people's liberty to participate in politics by assembling, protesting, voting, and serving in public office.

- **equality rights** guarantee equal citizenship, equality before the law, and freedom from discrimination.

- **welfare rights** require that people be provided with education and protected against starvation and severe poverty.

engaged in "ethnic cleansing" — systematic murders, rapes and purges of mainly Albanian Muslim neighborhoods throughout Kosovo. The U.S. deployed an array of air forces similar to those used in the Gulf War in defense of tiny Kuwait when it was invaded by Iraq's Saddam Hussein in 1990. The Kosovo situation was different from Kuwait in at least one distinctive respect — Kosovo is a part of the federal republic of Yugoslavia as much as Rhode Island is of the United States. Opponents of the NATO bombing and invasion of Yugoslavia argued that the matter was essentially a civil war within a sovereign nation and that no "vital U.S. interest" was at stake there.

Figure 2. Mao Tse-Tung ruled China with an iron fist. Corbis-Bettman.

Secretary of State Madeline Albright pressed the case that the free world could not sit idly by as thousands of persons were systematically killed because of their ethnicity. Allusions to the Holocaust of Hitler's Germany were made, suggesting that mass murders could not be ignored. Ironically, Serbian interest in Kosovo had been popularized because of one small area there where 500 years earlier Serbian defenders had held off Muslim marauders. This was a struggle whose outcome was not unlike "the Alamo" in U.S. history or Masada in Israeli history — the defenders actually lost at the time but the site became a shrine of nationalistic pride. Milosevic in 1988 had gone to the Kosovo shrine and pledged to protect it forever. Meanwhile, as the NATO bombs fell in the spring of 1999, leaders of the Orthodox Church in Yugoslavia began to express opposition to Milosevic's policies.

Others argued that the "proportionality" of the Kosovo murders did not approach the horrors of the Holocaust. On the other hand, if the U.S. and NATO were to serve as the planet's Police Force, they noted equally appalling conditions in other parts of the world, such as the pre-existing situation in the Sudan, where 2 million persons in the south of that nation had been killed by the dominant Muslim regime, based on their own non-Muslim tribal and religious heritage.

While the philosophies collided, the bombs dropped. NATO forces, mainly U.S. war planes, unleashed an historic assault. Many more Kosovar refugees fled their homeland as the bombing increased. Tiny neighboring nations were overrun with fleeing families. Global humanitarian aid efforts were slow to respond and inadequate. NATO bombings persisted with the goal that Milosevic was to pull his forces out of Kosovo and allow an international presence there to establish a peace and allow the Kosovars to return to their homes unmolested.

Meanwhile, Russia, not a member of NATO, indicated it lamented the Serbian purges of Kosovars but supported the Milosevic regime. After four months of the air campaign, which included hundreds of civilian casualties in the Yugoslav capital of Belgrade and the striking of the Chinese embassy in an apparent accident based on old maps, Milosevic yielded. NATO had amassed "peacekeeping" forces on Kosovo's borders, and they soon entered the sub-state to discover mass graves and fields laden with land mines left by the departing Serbian forces. Various diplomats and heads of NATO nations made visits to Kosovo to emphasize its new freedom from fear. There were talks of an independent government, but autonomy was the thrust of the NATO plan. Meantime, throughout the remainder of Yugoslavia

Milosevic struggled to fend off democratic forces seeking his ouster. He was indicted in the World Court for alleged crimes against humanity but seemed to enjoy safe haven in Serbian Yugoslavia.

Amazingly, during the air campaign NATO forces experienced no combat loss of life. One pilot was downed and promptly rescued. Two U.S. helicopter pilots were killed in a training exercise. Historic precedents were set, but they were not synthesized into a new U.S. or NATO or United Nations policy. Apparently, crimes against humanity would continue to be dealt with on a case-by-case basis, leaving it to the U.N.

Figure 3. Saddam Hussein, right, deals with Yasser Arafat, center. Associated Press/Wide World Photos.

and/or other bodies such as NATO to decide which cultures would be defended and which would not, and which territories with ethnic atrocities would be viewed as candidates for autonomy and which would not.

Sadly, history is replete with human rights atrocities. Large-scale, historic human rights violations include:

* The Holocaust, in which Adolph Hitler's Nazi Germany massacred millions of Jews, Gypsies, homosexuals, and handicapped people.

* Stalin's slaughter of millions in his efforts to impose communism in the former Soviet Union, including the forced famine that starved 6-million Ukrainians.

* Mao Tse-Tung's pogrom that killed tens of millions in China in the late 1940s, eliminated intellectuals and religion-based opponents of his communism.

* The enslavement of Africans and the imposition of slavery in most nations of North and South America, 1500–1870.

* America's civil war over slavery and ongoing violations of civil liberties due to official racism and segregation (or apartheid) as in the United States and South Africa.

* The killing and oppression of indigenous peoples in most nations of the Americas and the Pacific.

* The murder, "disappearance," torture, imprisonment, and exile of hundreds of thousands of leftists and sus-

pected leftists during the 1970s by military regimes in Chile, Argentina, and Brazil.

❊ Idi Amin's pogrom killing an estimated 1-million Ugandans as he gained power in the '70s.

❊ The nearly 2-million deaths in the Cambodian "killing fields" during the reign of Pol Pot.

History suggests that much blood-letting is often required before peoples choose peace and the mutual respect of others. This chapter discusses some ethical and philosophical issues about people's rights. An applied ethics course is a good place to consider people's rights because to arrive at plausible lists of rights we have to engage in the application of ethical ideas. In formulating international rights norms we have to decide which of the many bad things that governments do are so bad that they ought to be condemned internationally. In this chapter we will consider the sources of rights, analyze some philosophical issues about rights, and discuss racism as a human rights issue.

MAJOR TERMS

Other significant terms to know in discussing human rights issues include:

❊ **Addressees** of rights are the persons or parties that bear duties or responsibilities under a right

❊ **Civil rights** are conferred by a national legal system, such as rights in the area of racial justice

❊ **Constitutional rights** are conferred by a national constitution or bill of rights

❊ **Cultural diversity**, for this discussion, is the fact of significant difference among nations and cultures in values and norms

❊ **Cultural relativism** occurs when a person or policy holds that the idea of international human rights is undermined by cultural and religious differences

❊ **Discrimination** involves disadvantaging or excluding people from benefits such as education, housing, and jobs on the basis of race, ethnicity, religion, sex, or sexual orientation

❊ **Feasibility of rights** is a test of whether a nation has the resources to respect and implement a right

❊ **Importance** of rights is the test of whether a claim is sufficiently important to be a human right

* **Inalienable rights** cannot be taken away by governments; described as "unalienable" in the U.S. Declaration of Independence
* **Natural rights** somehow exist naturally, apart from human conventions and laws; related to inalienable rights
* **Rightholder** is a person or party who has a right
* **Universal Declaration of Human Rights** provides a list of specific human rights

SOURCES OF RIGHTS

How is it that people have rights? Are they somehow born with them? Do they get their rights from their nation's legal system? Or do they get them from international human rights law? I'll discuss all three possibilities.

Born with Rights

Many have suggested that people have rights because basic rights are somehow innate or inherent in human beings. How to interpret and make plausible this idea is a matter of some difficulty. It isn't very plausible to suggest that rights are part of standard human equipment, such as noses or needs for food and water. "People have a right to a fair trial when arrested for a crime" is not a simple factual statement like "People have noses." It is a statement about how people ought to be treated, and such evaluative or normative statements have to be established in ways that are more complicated than just taking a look. Further, specific rights such as a right to a fair trial or to vote in free elections presuppose circumstances and institutions that have only come into existence recently in human history.

One familiar interpretation of this idea is that people's rights are God-given. For example, the Declaration of Independence (1776) speaks of people as being "endowed by their Creator" with **natural rights** to life, liberty, and the pursuit of happiness. It was a bold act for the American revolutionaries not only to rebel against the reigning king but to assert for themselves and others explicit rights that no one had conferred upon them. This sort of view suggests that people have rights because God decreed that they should have them. God is the supreme lawmaker, and moral rights are created by God's legislative acts. Presumably the rights that God conferred on people are quite general since they have to apply to all of human history. But if people have abstract rights to life, liberty, and fair treatment, then perhaps we can figure out what this means today for things such as criminal trials and the treatment of minorities.

The idea that people are born with rights, or have God-given rights, is often combined with the assertion that rights are **inalienable**. This means, most obviously, that these rights can't be taken away by governments. It may also mean that these rights can't be bargained away by the rightholders.

In a diverse society, or a pluralistic world, appeals to God's commands as a source of human rights will often be unsuccessful in persuading others. If they don't believe in God, or in your kind of God, then you've got to persuade them of your preferred theological view — a task likely to involve a long detour. And even when the existence of God is recognized, one may still need to persuade people that God has commanded respect for all people's rights, rather than, say, the extermination of unbelievers.

A more attractive view, suggests that under favorable circumstances humans generally develop moral capacities which, when combined with experience and relevant information, allow them to see the wisdom in contemporary circumstances of giving all people rights within social morality and positive law.

RIGHTS DERIVED FROM NATIONAL LAW

An obvious source of people's rights is law. If the legal system of one's nation recognizes and implements a right to a fair trial, then one can appeal to that right if one is arrested. Legal rights are often referred to as "civil" rights, because they are part of national law, and as "constitutional rights" because the most general rights of citizens are often set out in national constitutions.

Liberty rights include freedom of thought and religion, freedom of speech and press, freedom of association, freedom of movement. **Political rights** include freedom to participate in politics by voting, campaigning, and running for office. **Equality rights** include freedom from slavery, the right to equal citizenship and protection of the laws. **Due process rights** include speedy and public trials with assistance of counsel in serious criminal matters. Not all important civil rights are found in the Constitution; ordinary legislation is also an important source of rights. The Civil Rights Act of 1964, for example, gives people rights against discrimination in housing and public accommodations (equality rights).

If every nation gave people an adequate and effectively enforced set of civil (or constitutional) rights, then little would need to be done at the international level. A nice alignment would exist between people's civil rights and their human rights. But we are a long way from enjoying this happy state of affairs. Many nations grant their citizens few rights, and the rights that are granted often fail to be effectively implemented. If people's rights are limited to those that their nations confer on them, billions of people will have very limited rights.

RIGHTS DERIVED FROM INTERNATIONAL AGREEMENTS

The history of human rights from an international perspective traces easily to **The Magna Carta** of England, 1215. It represented a synthesis and affirmative declaration of decades of decisions made by judges appointed by kings of England and by the kings themselves. It was a codification of ways to settle property and person rights issues that had grown out of human disputes taken before a judge. It is quite lengthy but worth review (on-line) by searching the "www.nara.gov/exhall/charters/" and selecting "Magna Carta" in the "Charters of Freedom" section of the Library of Congress Archives. In a sentence, the Magna Carta was, in effect, this planet's first widely circulated official document asserting human rights in the resolution of human problems. It took an approach to moral reasoning about problems of person and property that, one could say, blended Divine-Command, deontological and natural-law approaches to moral reasoning about problems of person and property. That is, England's government was based on a "divine right" of kings to rule and the kings' duty to rule fairly, while serfs (those with no property) were subject to an economic slavery sanctified by the rule of kings and their henchmen, also known as knights and nobles.

Fast-forward to the 20th century, and, with various wars and treaties in hand and in mind, American President **Woodrow Wilson** (1856–1924) is trying to settle the First World War, then described as "the war to end all wars." He frequently used shorthand to record his first thoughts on topics. In 1918 he outlined his famous Fourteen Points, the terms which he believed should be used as the basis for the peace treaty settling the First World War, which the United States had entered in April 1917 on the side of the Allies — Great Britain, France, Italy, and Russia. Wilson was challenged how to give the American people a clear set of war aims, which both appealed to their idealism and expressed his view that the nation had entered the conflict as "a war for freedom and justice and self-government."

Wilson's declarations contributed to the settlement of World War I but his concept of "a League of Nations" was not widely embraced for 30 more years after World War II.

Organizing International Rights: The United Nations
Beginning after World War II attempts were made in the **United Nations** to formulate international human rights law. These international norms were intended to promote respect for human rights and to encourage nations to enact analogous norms within domestic law. In this period immediately after the Holocaust it took no stretch of the imagination to see Hitler's disrespect for people's rights as one of the causes of the war. The founders of the United Nations believed that reducing the likelihood of war required preventing large-scale violations of human rights, and they committed the United Nations to this goal.

Soon after the first manned moon landing, Archibald MacLeish wrote: To see the Earth as we now see it, small and blue and beautiful, in that eternal silence where it floats, is to see ourselves as riders on the Earth together . . . brothers who do not see they are truly brothers.

WILSON'S FOURTEEN POINTS

1. Open agreements openly arrived at.

2. Freedom of the seas.

3. The removal of economic barriers and equality of trade conditions among nations.

4. Reduction of national armaments.

5. A readjustment of colonial claims in which the interests of the colonial populations must be given equal weight with the claims of the governing power.

6. The evacuation of Russian territory by non-Russian forces and Russia left to determine its own political destiny.

7. Removal of foreign forces from Belgium and restoration of its national independence.

8. Removal of foreign forces from France and the return of Alsace-Lorraine to France.

9. Readjustment of the frontiers of Italy along national lines.

10. Self-determination for the peoples of the Austro-Hungarian empire.

11. A redrawing of the boundaries of the Balkan states along historically established lines of nationality.

12. Self-determination of the peoples under rule of the Turkish empire and freedom of navigation of the Dardanelles under international guarantees.

13. National independence for Poland and its free access to the sea guaranteed by international treaty.

14. Formation of a league of nations for the purpose of affording mutual guarantees of political independence and territorial integrity to great and small states alike.

Source: John E. Haynes, The Woodrow Wilson Papers, Manuscript Division, Library of Congress.

In December 1948, the General Assembly of the United Nations approved the **Universal Declaration of Human Rights.** This groundbreaking international bill of rights was not binding as law, but it set the pattern for the legal documents that followed. It prescribed promotion of human rights through "teaching and education" and "measures, national and international, to secure their universal and effective recognition and observance." The Universal Declaration contains all six of the types of rights listed in the Key Concepts above (security rights, due process rights, liberty rights, political rights, equality rights, and welfare rights).

Many advocates of an international bill of rights in the United Nations wanted not a mere declaration but international laws backed by enforcement procedures capable of applying strong, international pressure to governments engaged in large-scale violations of human rights. The establishment of such law had to be done through the creation and approval of international treaties. These included the International Covenant on Civil and Political Rights and the International Covenant on Economic, Social, and Cultural Rights. These treaties were approved by the General Assembly in 1966, and had been signed by enough nations to come into force in 1976. Strangely, the United States has not ratified these treaties, even though it has been generally supportive of the international human rights movement.

FRANKLIN DELANO ROOSEVELT'S IDEA

The idea for the United Nations was elaborated in declarations signed at the wartime Allied conferences in Moscow and Tehran in 1943. The name "United Nations" was suggested by President Franklin Roosevelt. From August to October 1944, representatives of the United States, United Kingdom, France, Russia, and China met to elaborate the plans at the Dumbarton Oaks Estate in Washington, D.C. Those and later talks produced proposals outlining the purposes of the organization, its membership and organs, as well as arrangements to maintain international peace and security and international economic and social cooperation. These proposals were discussed and debated by governments and private citizens worldwide.

On April 25, 1945, the United Nations Conference on International Organizations began in San Francisco. The 50 nations represented at the conference signed the Charter of the United Nations two months later on June 26. The United Nations was born on October 24, 1945, after the Charter had been ratified by the five permanent members of the Security Council — China, France, U.S.S.R., U.K., and U.S. — and by a majority of the other 46 signatories.

The U.S. Senate, by a vote of 89 to 2, gave its consent to the ratification of the U.N. Charter on July 28, 1945. In December 1945, the Senate and the House of Representatives, by unanimous votes, requested that the U.N. make its headquarters in the U.S. The offer was accepted and the U.N. headquarters building was constructed in New York City. U.N. membership is open to all "peace-loving states" that accept the obligations of the U.N. Charter and, in the judgment of the organization, are able and willing to fulfill these obligations. Admission is determined by the General Assembly upon recommendation of the Security Council. With the admission of Palau in December 1994, 185 nations are members of the U.N.

Figure 4. U.S. Secretary of State, Edward R. Stettinius, Jr., signs the United Nations Charter at the Conference of the United Nations in San Francisco, April 1945. Library of Congress.

The multilateral system provides a powerful platform for advancing human rights, free trade, labor standards, and public health. U.N. programs also try to meet humanitarian needs for those disadvantaged by circumstances beyond their control. Private charitable agencies rely on the multiple capacities of the U.N. system to develop the infrastructure and political climate required for the success of such programs. U.N. activities such as UNICEF, the U.N. High Commissioner for Refugees, and the World Food Program have made a remarkable impact on the lives of those most at risk around the globe: children, women, and refugees.

Important treaties in the development of international human rights law are the Genocide Convention (1948), the European Convention on Human Rights (1950), the American Convention on Human Rights (1969), and the African Charter on Human and Peoples' Rights (1986). **International human rights norms are now recognized — sometimes with qualifications — in most nations of the world.**

Human rights treaties are often enforced or implemented by allowing governments and individuals to complain about human rights abuses to some sort of human rights commission established as part of a human rights treaty. Typically the human rights commission investigates these complaints and, if they are determined to be well-founded, attempts to pressure the offending government to change its policies and compensate the victim(s). International pressure of this support, particularly when it is supported by many nations, has often been effective in getting nations to stop or diminish their violations of human rights.

The U.N. Charter obliges all member nations to promote "universal respect for, and observance of, human rights" and to take "joint and separate action" to that end. The Universal Declaration of Human Rights, though not legally binding, was adopted by the General Assembly in 1948 as a common standard of achievement for all. The General Assembly regularly takes up human rights issues.

On December 10, 1948 the General Assembly of the United Nations adopted and proclaimed resolution 217 A (III), the Universal Declaration of Human Rights. Following this historic act the Assembly called upon all member nations to publicize the text of the Declaration and "to cause it to be disseminated, displayed, read and expounded principally in schools and other educational institutions."

Since the end of the Cold War, the number of peacekeeping operations has risen dramatically. More operations were mounted between 1991 and 1998 than in the previous 46 years. During 1991–92, peacekeeping activities were established in the Mideast, Africa, Cambodia, and the former Yugoslavia. Since 1992, 10 more peacekeeping, observer, and assistance operations have been authorized: Chad, Mozambique, Rwanda, Somalia, El Salvador, Liberia, Georgia, Haiti, Tajikistan and Angola.

MORAL REASONING ABOUT PEOPLE'S RIGHTS

Justifying Rights

To assert that all governments are obligated to respect the human rights of each and every one of their citizens is to make a strong claim. Universal human rights presuppose that people everywhere are equal in their basic moral status and rights, and that governments have duties to behave in ways that respect the lives, liberty, and dignity of their citizens.

Because these claims are strong, demands for justification are sure to be heard. People will ask why anyone should assume that all people have basic rights, and why we should accept the specific rights in some human rights document as an authoritative list. Perhaps the first question will seem perverse. Isn't it obvious that all humans are created equal in dignity and basic rights? It may seem obvious to us, but it hasn't seemed obvious to many peoples. Racists, past and present, deny that some groups of people are equal in dignity and basic moral claims.

"No (one) is an island."
— John Donne

Because the belief in **equal dignity** and rights is such a deep and pervasive belief, it is hard to defend without begging the question (assuming what one is trying to prove). But there are two broad ways of defending this belief. Negative ways attack the grounds for saying that some individuals or groups lack equal dignity and rights. Here, for example, one might try to criticize racist views as unscientific, lacking plausible supporting grounds, or leading to terrible consequences. Positive approaches, on the other hand, offer substantive reasons for believing in equal dignity and rights. These arguments may appeal to:

* religious beliefs; e.g., God created all humans equal.
* shared human characteristics; e.g., consciousness, rationality, or the ability to choose.

Note that these same sorts of arguments can be used to try to establish that non-human animals have rights (see Chapter 12 here-

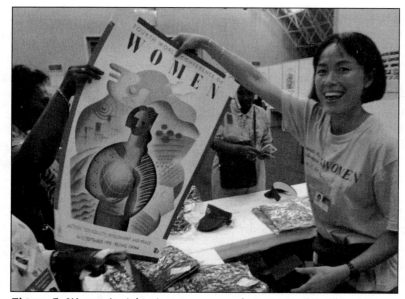

Figure 5. Women's rights issues are now being raised in China. Associated Press/Wide World Photos.

in on Animal Well-Being for further discussion of whether animals have rights).

Although it is theoretically difficult to provide good defenses of our deepest moral beliefs, we shouldn't forget that the general idea of human rights is an attractive one. This idea is that all people have claims against their political institutions and fellow citizens to fair and decent treatment, liberty in key areas of choice, opportunities to survive and flourish, and assistance when necessary in meeting basic needs.

Questions may be directed not merely to the general idea of human rights, but also to claims about specific human rights — such as the claim that there is a human right to a fair trial when one is charged with a crime. Defending a specific right can be done by: (1) showing that it blocks serious threats to very important human interests; (2) does not impose duties that are unreasonable; and (3) is feasible in most nations today. Let's examine these three steps in more detail.

FIRST: ABUSES AND IMPORTANT INTERESTS

The specific rights found in historic and contemporary bills of rights were declared in response to perceived abuses by governments. Some bills of rights actually begin with a list of complaints against the government, or the previous government. The right to a fair trial, for example, responds to the fact that governments have often used their legal systems to kill, imprison, and disadvantage their political opponents. This linkage between abuses and specific rights suggests that the sorts of specific rights we find in human rights documents are partially determined by the sorts of abuses people have experienced or know about from history or the recent experience of other nations.

But these abuses must be to fundamental interests of persons. Suppose that someone said that her human rights were being violated because her government hadn't provided her with public swimming pools to use during hot summer days. We'd probably respond that while swimming pools are good things, the interest in having them isn't so important or fundamental that a failure to provide them is morally wrong. It would be good if swimming pools were available, but it wouldn't be an injustice or violation of rights if they weren't provided. In contrast, if someone complained of being literally tortured for an extended period, we wouldn't doubt that a fundamental interest was at stake. The importance of what is protected supports the high priority that genuine human rights have.

Different ethical theories such as utilitarianism and Kantianism offer different accounts of fundamental interests and of how human rights are binding. Utilitarians will interpret fundamental interests as the most imperative requirements of well-being and will presuppose a general obligation of persons and states to promote human happiness or well-being. Kantians will interpret fundamental interests as key requirements of human dignity or autonomy and will presuppose a general obligation to respect such dignity or autonomy.

Figure 6. In China national law limits couples to bearing only two children, and the state may require abortion to enforce the policy. Corbis-Bettman.

SECOND: REASONABLE ASSOCIATED DUTIES

Human rights don't just say that fair trials or freedom of religion are high-priority goals; they go on to say that these are rights imposing duties of compliance and protection on individuals and governments. **To justify a specific right we have to show that the duties it imposes are reasonable.** A number of considerations are relevant to reasonableness including whether the important claim can be satisfied without imposing duties, whether the addressees are the appropriate ones to bear these duties, whether there is a fair distribution of burdens, and whether the duties are excessively burdensome.

Suppose we are considering the justification of a right against torture. As we consider the imposition of duties (e.g., not to torture) we might ask whether we can treat the elimination of torture as a goal rather than as a matter of duty (surely not), who should be forbidden to torture (all persons and agencies, including governments), how to fairly share the burdens of combating torture (probably through taxes to pay for the costs of government protection against torture), and whether the burdens imposed by this right on individuals and governments are excessively burdensome (surely not).

A right against torture blocks individuals and governments from using torture to promote their ends and requires governments to provide effective protections against and remedies for torture. Refraining from torture will sometimes be costly to governments (e.g., in quickly getting information needed to arrest a terrorist group). The same is true of providing protection against torture. This will require laws and law enforcement, as well as monitoring the actions of police and other security forces. Nevertheless, these costs are bearable and not unreasonable. Similar points could be made about the provision of fair trials.

THIRD: FEASIBILITY

As we have seen, rights impose duties (or other mandatory normative burdens) on their addressees. But for these duties to be justified, they must be **feasible** — i.e., they must only require things that can be done and that most of the addressees are actually capable of doing. Because of the great variations between nations in wealth, and in human and institutional capacities, the authors of the Universal Declaration faced great difficulties in formulating norms for the entire world. They wanted to formulate rights that were specific enough to provide clear guidance, but they also had to somehow address all of the world's governments.

The approach they took was to formulate relatively high standards. The Declaration's list of human rights presupposes that nations have, or will soon have, the financial and other resources needed to construct democratic political institutions, operate a humane and procedurally fair legal system that protects important liberties and rights, and provide a comprehensive welfare state. This list of demands is appropriate to the world's richer nations, but is perhaps excessively demanding for poorer nations. Compliance with and implementation of human rights is not, however, an all-or-nothing matter. A reasonable suggestion for the establishment of such rights would be that international human rights standards are sufficiently feasible if most nations in the world are able to respect and at least partially implement them.

ARE WELFARE RIGHTS REALLY HUMAN RIGHTS?

Welfare rights were the most controversial category of rights included in the Universal Declaration. The Declaration broke new ground by including welfare rights (also called economic and social rights) that addressed matters such as education, food, and employment. The first 21 articles of the Universal Declaration declared rights similar to those found in historic bills of rights. These **"political rights"** included rights to personal liberties, due process of law, and political participation. But articles 22 through 27 declared rights to free public education; a standard of living adequate for health and well-being; social security during sickness, disability, and old age; free choice of employment and protections against unemployment; fair pay, including equal pay for equal work; and rest and leisure.

Opponents of welfare rights often deny that they are really human rights. They restrict that status to civil and political rights. Objections to welfare rights correspond to the three steps in the justification of a specific right that we just discussed. These objections are that welfare rights: (1) don't have the importance of civil and political rights; (2) are too burdensome on governments and taxpayers (this burden-bearing may extend to violating other, more important rights); and (3) are not feasible in less-developed nations.

The Importance of Welfare Rights

As we just saw, human rights, such as rights to freedom from torture, or to fair trials in criminal and civil cases, set out minimal but extremely important standards that governments everywhere should meet. One might object that welfare rights don't meet this standard of great importance. Perhaps they identify valuable goods, but not extremely valuable goods. To discuss the issue of importance let's use two welfare rights as examples: (1) the right to an adequate standard of living, and (2) the right to free public education. These rights require governments to try to remedy widespread and serious evils such as hunger and ignorance. The importance of food and other basic material conditions of life is easy to show. These goods are essential to people's ability to live, function, and flourish. Without adequate access to these goods, interests in life, health, and liberty are endangered and serious illness and death are probable. The connection between having the goods the right guarantees and having a minimally good life is direct and obvious — something that isn't always true with other human rights.

In the contemporary world, lack of *access* to educational opportunities typically limits (both absolutely and in comparison to other people) people's abilities to participate fully and effectively in the political and economic life of their nation. Contemporary economies have few jobs available for people who lack literacy and numeracy, and hence lack of education increases the likelihood of unemployment.

Another way to support the importance of welfare rights is to show their importance to the full implementation of civil and political rights. If a government succeeds in eliminating hunger and providing education to everyone, this promotes people's abilities to know, use, and enjoy their liberties, due process rights, and rights of political participation. This is easiest to see in the area of education. Ignorance is a barrier to the realization of civil and political rights because uneducated people often don't know what rights they have and what they can do to use and defend them. It is also easy to see in the area of democratic participation. Education and a minimum income make it easier for people at the bottom economically to follow politics, participate in political campaigns, and to spend the time and money needed to go to the polls and vote.

Are the Duties Imposed by Welfare Rights Reasonable?

Questions that arise under this heading are whether people's welfare needs can be dealt with as a matter of social goals rather than as rights, who should provide welfare benefits, how to share the costs of welfare rights, and whether the burdens imposed on individuals and governments by welfare rights are excessively burdensome.

Let's look at two of these questions, beginning with the issue of who should provide welfare benefits. Historically, such benefits have been provided to people by their families, communities, and employers. But welfare rights place this burden on national governments, requiring them to ensure that all residents have access to food, housing, education, health care, and employment. But unless governments have enormous oil wealth, or something of that sort, they will have to pass the costs of providing these guarantees on to their citizens in the form of taxes or reduced wages.

It is only in the last century that governments have taken over a substantial part of the burden of providing for the needy. The taxes associated with welfare rights are replacements for other burdensome duties, namely the duties of families and communities to provide adequate care for the unemployed, sick, disabled, and aged. Deciding whether to implement welfare rights is not a matter of deciding whether to bear such burdens, but rather of deciding whether to continue with total reliance on a system of informal provision that distributes benefits in a very spotty way and whose costs fall very unevenly on families, friends, and communities.

Once we recognize that liberty rights are burdensome, that intelligent systems of provision for welfare rights supply the requisite goods to people in only a small minority of cases, and that these systems are substitutes for other, more local ways of providing for the needy, the difference between the burdensomeness of liberty rights and the burdensomeness of welfare rights doesn't seem to be a large one.

Feasibility

Real rights aren't ideals or goals. They impose duties (or other mandatory normative burdens) on their addressees. But for these duties to be justified, they must require things that most of the addressees are actually capable of doing. Since welfare rights are expensive, perhaps they fail this test. And one might conclude that since welfare rights are not in fact feasible to implement everywhere today, they can be ideals or high-priority goals but not real rights.

Burden-bearing

Let's also look at the issue of **burden-bearing.** It is very expensive to guarantee to everyone the basic material conditions of life, along with education and health care. Perhaps welfare rights are too expensive or burdensome to be justified, especially in a world in which many nations are poor. Frequently the claim that welfare rights are too burdensome uses other, less controversial human rights as a standard of comparison, and suggests that welfare rights are substantially more burdensome or expensive than liberty rights. Suppose that we used as a basis of comparison **liberty rights** such as freedom of communication, association, and movement. These rights are claims not just to respect for people's freedoms to speak,

*"Those who profess to favour free-
dom, and yet deprecate agitation,
are people who want rain without
thunder and lightning. They want
ocean without the roar of its many
waters. Power concedes nothing
without a demand. It never did and
it never will."*
— *Frederick Douglass, abolitionist*

Figure 7. Frederick Douglass, 1817–1895. Library of
Congress.

associate, and move, but also to government protection for those freedoms. And people can't be adequately protected in their liberties
unless they also have **security** and **due process rights.** The costs
of liberty, as it were, include the costs of law and criminal justice.

Once we see this, liberties start to look a lot more costly. To provide effective liberties to communicate, associate, and move, it isn't
enough for a society to make a prohibition of interference with these
activities part of its accepted morality. An effective system of provision for these liberties will require a legal scheme that defines personal and property rights and protects these rights against invasions
while ensuring due process to those accused of crimes. Providing such
legal protection in the form of legislatures, police, courts, and prisons
is extremely expensive.

We shouldn't think of welfare rights as simply giving everyone a
free supply of the goods these rights protect. Guarantees of things
like food and housing will be intolerably expensive and will undermine productivity if everyone simply receives a free supply. A viable
system of welfare rights will require most people to provide these
goods for themselves and their families through work as long as they
are given the necessary opportunities, education, and infrastructure.
Government-implemented welfare rights provide guarantees of availability, but governments should have to supply the requisite goods in

Figure 8. Former British Prime Minister Margaret Thatcher and Russian author Aleksandr Solzhenitsyn helped shape Russian human rights in the decade of the '80s. Hulton Getty.

only a small fraction of cases. Note that primary education is often an exception to this since many nations provide free public education irrespective of ability to pay.

Nations that don't accept and implement welfare rights still have to bear somehow the costs of providing for the needy since these nations — particularly if they recognize democratic rights of political participation — are unlikely to find it tolerable to allow sizeable parts of the population to starve and be homeless. If government doesn't supply food, clothing, and shelter to those unable to provide for themselves, then families, friends, and communities will have to shoulder this burden.

UNIVERSAL RIGHTS AND CULTURAL DIVERSITY

A third philosophical issue about human rights stems from cultural diversity. Among the earth's peoples we find enormous diversity in customs, languages, religions, moral norms, and political practices. Let's call this the "Fact of Diversity." The existence of so much diversity and disagreement leads many to ask whether it is realistic to hope to formulate and justify a single set of human rights standards for the entire world. A person who holds that the validity of international human rights is refuted by the existence of cultural and religious differences might be called a **"cultural relativist."** Does the fact of diversity imply cultural relativism?

We must begin by trying to interpret the cultural and religious diversity that exists. How deep does it go? There are obvious differences among the moralities of different groups around the world, but it is not obvious how deep these differences are. We know, for example, that the moralities of some circumpolar groups allow (or allowed at one time) the killing of very old people when they became a heavy burden on the group. The key question here is whether this killing involves the absence of respect for human life, or is merely an exception to general prohibitions of killing people based on economic necessity or cosmological beliefs

It is clearly possible to find deeper agreement beneath many surface differences in moral norms, but it is far from certain that such deeper agreement always exists. For example, if a group justified killing incapacitated elderly people by arguing that this was regrettably necessary during some periods of extreme scarcity to protect the survival of the group, but should never be practiced otherwise, this would not show a lack of respect for human life. However, many anthropologists have concluded that we can't safely say that deeper agreement is always present in cases where groups have practices that violate familiar moral norms.

It is possible, of course, to dismiss moral disagreement by simply saying that one of the groups is wrong. If a group recognizes no prohibition of killing and torturing humans, it is just wrong about what morality requires. Its morality requires not accommodation but improvement through persuasion and education. In regard to the most fundamental norms, this is the position taken by the human rights movement. It holds that people in all cultures have the capacity, given relevant information and opportunities for thought and reflection, to recognize the validity or reasonableness of fundamental moral norms.

This said, we should emphasize, first, that human rights, as formulated in contemporary documents and treaties, are few and broad. Hence they can coexist with a lot of variation in cultural practices and norms. Because human rights norms are few in number, they leave most areas of life alone. Second, the terms used in formulating human rights are often broad enough to allow some latitude to local interpretation. For example, rights against "arbitrary arrest" and to "fair trials" allow for a lot of flexibility in interpretation. Third, most human rights documents explicitly provide for suspending some human rights in emergency situations. Finally, the human rights movement has supported cultural diversity within a structure of basic principles by endorsing the principle of self-determination and by limiting the circumstances in which one state may intervene in the affairs of another.

PREJUDICE AND CIVIL RIGHTS

Most people have the ethnocentric belief that their own group or nation is superior to other groups (and consequently that other peoples are inferior to some degree). Mild ethnocentrism seems to be normal among humans everywhere — if not particularly rational. But extreme ethnocentrism, of which racism is a species, involves the belief that the members of some human groups are greatly inferior and hence are not entitled to full moral consideration and fair treatment.

Prejudice and ethnic hostility, and the **discrimination** and other forms of bad treatment that they generate, are found in all parts of the world and often lead to violence. Civil wars often occur along ethnic lines, as they recently did in Rwanda and in the former

Yugoslavia. Prejudice typically involves a negative attitude towards a group because its members are believed to be somehow inferior or deficient. Prejudices are often based on stereotypes — simplified and negatively slanted conceptions of groups.

Racism is a form of prejudice (or extreme ethnocentrism) in which the boundaries between groups are drawn along racial lines. Race is a very messy concept. People who use the concept of race often focus on physical differences such as type of hair and color of skin, or on the place of ancestral origin (typically Africa or Asia). Other species of prejudice include religious bigotry, sexism, extreme nationalism, and homophobia.

Severe prejudice often expresses itself in discrimination, segregation, and bad treatment. Discrimination involves disadvantaging or excluding people from benefits such as education, housing, and jobs on the basis of race, ethnicity, religion, sex, or sexual orientation.

Many ethnic groups have been subjected to discrimination in the United States and other nations. These groups include American Indians, African-Americans, Chinese-Americans, Jews, and Mexican-Americans. African-Americans have been most severely handicapped by racial prejudice, and I will use their history as my focus here.

From the 16th century on, people of African ancestry were subjected to slavery in most nations of the Americas. Apart from extermination or genocide, slavery is the most severe form of racism or ethnic prejudice. Slaves were the captives of their owners, their labor was exploited, and they had almost no legal rights — not even rights to marry and hold property. The Civil War was fought to end slavery in the United States. Then the 13th, 14th, and 15th Amendments to the U.S. Constitution gave African-Americans legal rights to citizenship, equal protection of the law, and political participation. But the system of segregation that emerged within a few decades after the Civil War denied African-Americans the enjoyment of their constitutional rights to political participation and kept them in separate neighborhoods and schools.

In 1940, for example, blacks living anywhere in the U.S. south of a line going from Washington, D.C., to El Paso, Texas, were subject to formal segregation. They were required to attend separate schools, use separate water fountains, restrooms, parks, and swimming pools, live in separate neighborhoods, and attend separate churches.

Serious legal challenges to segregation began in the 1940s, but formal segregation existed in many parts of the nation until the mid-sixties. Informal segregation, and the legacy of formal segregation in areas such as housing, education, and employment, continues into the present in all parts of the United States.

American law has historically licensed and enforced slavery and segregation, but in recent decades it has helped to oppose and limit racist practices. In a landmark decision in 1954, the Supreme Court held that segregated schools were unconstitutional (*Brown v. Board of Education*). It subsequently extended its ruling to segregation in other public facilities such as parks and post offices, and went on to require mandatory busing as a means of dismantling segregated school systems. In 1964 the U.S. Congress finally began enacting civil rights legislation, eventually prohibiting racial discrimination in public accommodations, education, employment, and housing. African-Americans and other minorities can now appeal to their legal rights against discrimination.

The international human rights movement has played an active role in the struggle against racial apartheid and discrimination. It was particularly active in condemning apartheid in South Africa and in organizing international pressure against the South African government.

As an issue in applied ethics we can ask, "What is it about racial discrimination that makes it wrong?" Suppose that we have a clear instance of discrimination, as when the owner of a plumbing company refuses to hire African-Americans under any circumstances. What's wrong with this policy? First, discrimination is often irrational. It frequently relies on unjustified beliefs and stereotypes, and rejects or disadvantages people on irrelevant and arbitrary grounds. Second, it insults African-Americans through its underlying premise that they are generally bad employees. Third, when discrimination is widely practiced it harms African-Americans by reducing self-esteem and producing a sense of inferiority. It also deprives them of opportunities that would have allowed them to live better lives and make greater contributions to the community. Finally, the most important reason why discrimination is wrong is that it is unfair. Its unfairness lies in treating some people worse than others without adequate grounds for doing so.

Figure 9. Ronald Reagan implored Mikhail Gorbachev to tear down the Berlin Wall, and East German students did dismantle the barrier which separated free Germany from communist Germany for four decades. Corbis-Bettmann.

SUMMARY: HUMAN RIGHTS

This chapter has explained and defended the idea that people have rights. Different sorts of rights (legal, constitutional, civil, human) were distinguished, and some philosophical questions about rights were explored. People do have morally important rights, and these include security rights, due process rights, rights to important liberties, rights to participate in politics and elections, equality rights that guarantee equality before the law and prohibit racial and other forms of discrimination, and welfare rights.

FOR FURTHER INQUIRY

REVIEW QUESTIONS

1. What was the Universal Declaration of Human Rights and why is it important?

2. What are the six areas covered by contemporary human rights?

3. What are some contemporary and historic abuses of people's rights?

ENDNOTES

1. Alexander, Larry, "What Makes Wrongful Discrimination Wrong?: Biases, Preferences, Stereotypes, and Proxies," *University of Pennsylvania Law Review* 141 (1992): 149–219.

2. Brownlie, Ian (ed). *Basic Documents on Human Rights* (Oxford: Clarendon Press, 3rd edition, 1992).

3. Buergenthal, Thomas. *International Human Rights in a Nutshell* (St. Paul, Minn.: West Publishing Company, 2nd edition, 1995).

4. Boxill, Bernard. *Blacks and Social Justice* (Totowa, N.J.: Rowman and Allenheld, 1984).

5. Ezorsky, Gertrude. *Racism and Justice: The Case for Affirmative Action* (Ithaca, N.Y.: Cornell University Press, 1991).

6. Franklin, John Hope. *From Slavery to Freedom: A History of Negro Americans* (New York: Alfred A. Knopf, third edition, 1967).

7. King, Jr., Martin Luther. "Letter from the Birmingham City Jail," in H. Bedau, (ed.), *Civil Disobedience* (New York: Pegasus, 1969) — see Appendix.

8. Kluger, Richard. *Simple Justice* (New York: Vintage, 1977).

9. Nickel, James W. *Making Sense of Human Rights* (Berkeley: University of California Press, 1987).

10. Shue, Henry. *Basic Rights* (Princeton: Princeton University Press, 1980).

11. Wellman, Carl. *Welfare Rights* (Totowa, NJ: Rowman and Littlefield, 1982).

CHAPTER 16

ECONOMIC JUSTICE

"To give aid to every poor man is far beyond the reach and power of every man . . . Care of the poor is incumbent upon society as a whole."

— Benedict (Baruch) Spinoza, Ethics 1677

"It is preoccupation with possession, more than anything else, that prevents men from living freely and nobly."

**— Bertrand Russell,
Principles of Social Reconstruction 1916**

In a nation where millions are rich yet thousands go to sleep each night hungry and without a roof over their head, the question must be asked: Is this fair?

Some would say that any government which allows some of its citizens to be malnourished and without even a simple home while others are able to live a life of luxury without even having to work is fundamentally unjust. Others would say that the only way a nation becomes as rich as ours is to provide economic incentives for hard work, brilliant inventions, and entrepreneurial skill. If individuals were not allowed to keep the fruit of their labors, then the United States would not be nearly as rich as it is today. Thus, the only way a government can make its citizens' income more equal is for it to make all its citizens poorer. These basic philosophical approaches will be the focus of the first part of this chapter.

CHIEF LEARNING OUTCOME:

I understand the concept of economic justice and am able to discuss various moral theories as they apply to a nation's economy.

These are not new issues. The ancient Greek philosophers Plato and Aristotle addressed them in many of their works. In fact, it was Aristotle who first noticed that there are two fundamentally different meanings of the word "justice." On the one hand, there is the justice

---

Ric S. Maschuga, M.A. Philosophy, University of Oregon, M.A. History, California State University, Chico, is a tenured professor of philosophy, ethics and history at Butte College in Oroville, Calif. and is currently the President of the Academic Senate.

which fairly and appropriately punishes some prior wrongdoing. Aristotle called this **"retributive justice."** On the other hand, there is the justice which fairly and appropriately distributes everything from economic goods and services to public honors and awards. He called this **"distributive justice."** It will be the kind of justice examined throughout this chapter.

While the issue of distributive justice is not new, many of the problems associated with it have been greatly exacerbated, or even created, by the Industrial Revolution of the 18th and 19th centuries. It is during these centuries that the idea of capitalism develops, and the first great "Captains of Industry"—Carnegie, Rockefeller, Gould and others—become household names. It is also in these centuries that many people begin to refer to the super rich as "Robber Barons," and philosophers begin to speak of **socialism** as an alternative to **capitalism.** These economic theories and systems will be specially discussed in the second section of this chapter.

In the third section the implications of these theories for national policies pertaining to income and taxes will be examined. Policies pertaining to **welfare** will reflect these theories. They will be discussed here as well as the American Supreme Court's shifts in attitudes about these issues.

KEY CONCEPTS

Retributive Justice — A system which fairly and appropriately punishes some prior wrongdoing.

Distributive Justice — A system which fairly and appropriately distributes everything from economic goods and services to public honors and awards.

Entitlement Theory — The theory of distributive justice seen in John Locke and characterized by Robert Nozick by three premises:

1) All people are entitled to that which they acquire justly.

2) All people are entitled to that which is justly transferred to them from someone else who justly acquired that which was transferred.

3) No person is entitled to anything except by (repeated) applications of (1) and (2).

Patterned Principle of Distribution — Any principle of distribution of resources that holds out some pattern according to which the good should be allocated such as one in which all people have the same amount of good (egalitarianism) or in which the worst of people have as much as possible (sometimes called the *maximum*

(continued)

pattern because the person with the minimum has the maximum that he or she can have). Patterned principles of distribution are contrasted with principles such as those in entitlement in which no particular pattern is held out as the right one, but rather the right distribution is simply whatever arises from free acquisition and transfer.

Egalitarianism — The patterned theory of distribution in which the goal is to arrange resources so that people have equal amounts. Some principles may be relatively egalitarian, such as Rawls's difference principle, which justifies inequalities provided they serve to benefit the worst off, while others may be more radically egalitarian, rejecting even inequalities that benefit the worst off.

The Difference Principle — The principle of John Rawls that holds that differences in the amount of primary social goods are justified provided the differences improve the position of the worst off compared to what they would have if there were more equality.

Classical Republicanism — The political philosophy having its roots in Aristotle and Thomas Aquinas that holds the human has an essential nature that includes rationality, sociability, and membership in the animal kingdom. This essential nature permits distinction between human needs and mere human wants. A just distribution of resources is one that uses resources to meet needs rather than desires.

Communitarianism — The view of contemporary philosophers who emphasize the importance of the human as a social being who is part of a community rather than primarily an isolated individual. Communitarians generally favor the Classical Republican theory of justice and communal decisions about the use of resources rather than leaving such choices up to the individual.

A "Thin" Conception of the Good — A conception of what is good for which there is agreement on only the most primary or general and abstract goods such as liberty, political and economic opportunities, secure and adequate income, wealth, and self-respect. These are goods that any person would desire no matter what his or her more specific desires. This view is generally held by liberals, both Entitlement theorists and egalitarians. It contrasts with the "thick" conception of the good usually held by Classical Republicans and communitarians.

Capitalism — An economic system where all property (including factories and other "means of production") is privately owned and operated for individual profit as determined by a free market.

Socialism — An economic system in which all the means of production are socially owned and operated for the good of the public as a whole.

Mixed Economic System — An economic system in which some of the means of production are privately owned while others are publicly owned.

The final issue will turn to the **international dimensions of economic justice.** It is here that population, food supplies, and world hunger will be discussed. While there have always been famines, up until quite recently there didn't seem to be much that could be done. Famine was a simple fact of nature, no more in humans' control than the weather. However, it now seems to many people that the situation is essentially different. Though we still cannot control the weather that is often a contributing cause of a famine, we now live in a world where food is always abundant somewhere. Furthermore, the means are readily available for transporting it to those parts of the world where it is desperately needed.

Do these two facts create new moral obligations? Are we who live in affluent societies morally obligated to help those who are starving to death in less developed countries? Some philosophers argue that from the moral point of view, letting someone starve to death when the means to save them are readily available is really no different than murder. Others argue that while there may be enough food to feed those who are currently malnourished, it is simply impossible for us to feed them indefinitely, especially because the countries in need are typically the countries which have the highest growth rates. The only choice, these people would say, is whether we let thousands starve now or millions starve later.

JOHN LOCKE'S VIEW OF PRIVATE PROPERTY

In his Second Treatise on Government, **John Locke** assumed that all people have a self-evident right to their own life and liberty. No person or government can justly deprive another person of life or liberty, unless that other person has committed some crime for which he deserves to be punished. More significantly for our purposes, Locke went on to argue that these first two rights logically imply a third fundamental right, namely, the right to private property.

Locke's defense of private property is simple and almost absolute. He begins by imagining a number of people living as a tribe of hunters and gatherers. The fact that these people are living without a formal government and written constitution does not, he thinks, mean that they are also living without the right to life and liberty. These are self-evident rights because they are rights guaranteed by nature.

Americans' right to trial by a jury of one's peers is guaranteed by the Constitution. This sort of right is often termed a positive or politically created right because its existence depends on a decision which is explicitly laid down by the legislative arm of the government. It is not self-evident that in a society of hunters and gatherers these same rights would also exist. However, natural rights are different. The right to life and liberty are bestowed by God and/or nature on every person who ever has or will have lived on this Earth. These rights do not depend upon any government's action or decision.

Now suppose, says Locke, that an individual in this tribe of hunters and gatherers goes out and collects a basket full of acorns. They become, so to speak, the fruit of his own labor. Because this person's labor flows from his liberty, it too is protected by a fundamental natural right. This means that any other person who forcefully or coercively takes this person's acorns from him violates his natural rights. Thus, according to Locke, the self-evident right to life and liberty naturally creates a right to private property over which no other person has a rightful say.

ROBERT NOZICK'S DEFENSE

John Locke's theory of property has been articulated and championed by the contemporary Harvard philosopher, **Robert Nozick,** in an important book, *Anarchy, State and Utopia.* According to Nozick, the only legitimate role for any government is the protection of its citizens' free exercise of their rights to life, liberty, and property. To do this, a government must tax individuals

Figure 1. John Locke. National Library of Medicine.

enough to provide for a police force to protect citizens from criminals within and a military force to protect them from enemies without. However, any other use of the government's power of taxation — for example, the taxation of the well-to-do to help the less fortunate — is a violation of fundamental rights because it deprives the well-to-do of money and property to which they are entitled.

In his defense of what is now termed the **entitlement theory,** Nozick says that an exhaustive understanding of all true principles of distributive justice follows straightaway from three simple premises:

1) All people are entitled to that which they acquire justly.

2) All people are entitled to that which is justly transferred to them from someone else who justly acquired that which was transferred.

3) No person is entitled to anything except by (repeated) applications of (1) and (2).

The crucial terms in the above definitions are **"acquire justly"** and **"justly transfer."** Much of Nozick's book is spent clarifying these notions. Not surprisingly, Nozick turns to Locke for help. Locke said that all land and its resources were originally held in common by all people. This meant that all people had an equal right to use or appropriate any land or resource that was not already being used or had already been appropriated by others.

The Lockean Two-Part Proviso

He also believed that "the earth and all that is therein" are meant by nature to be used for the support and comfort of human beings. However, Locke did not believe that individuals had an absolute right to do with unappropriated land or resources anything they wished. While he believed that all people would consent to other people's limited use of unappropriated land and resources, no one would consent to their unlimited appropriation. More specifically, when people acquire property by appropriating previously unused land and resources, they must ensure (1) that "there is enough, and as good left in common for others" and (2) that they use what is appropriated before it spoils or is wasted. These two qualifications on the right to acquire property, Nozick calls the **"Lockean proviso."**

1. **Leaving Enough and As Good for Others:** The point of the first qualification is fairly evident. A person cannot, says Nozick, rightfully acquire, or purchase from someone who originally acquired, "all the drinkable water in the world" and then sell it to others for whatever the market will bear. This first aspect of the Lockean proviso is meant to ensure "that the situation of others is not worsened."

2. **The Non-waste Qualification:** The point of the non-waste qualification is less clear. Nozick suggests that it is necessary to stave off a problem that may arise with the limitation implicit in the qualification "that the situation of others is not worsened." Nozick writes:

> Consider the first person Z for whom there is not enough and no goods left to appropriate. The last person Y to appropriate left Z without his previous liberty to act on an object, and so worsened Z's situation. So Y's appropriation is not allowed under Locke's proviso. Therefore, the next to the last person X to appropriate left Y in a worse position, for X's appropriation wasn't permissible. But the appropriator two from last, W, ended permissible appropriation and so, because it worsened X's position, W's appropriation wasn't permissible. And so on back to the first person A to appropriate a permanent property right.

Nozick then says that perhaps Locke "meant the non-waste condition to delay the end point from which the argument zips back." Locke himself describes the deliberate waste of natural resources as a kind of "robbery" and a frustration of the Divine intent in creation which was "to give us all things richly to enjoy." Because that which is wasted isn't enjoyed by anyone, waste frustrates God's intention for his creation. But whatever Locke's own intentions were in the second qualification, it is clear that no person can justly acquire so much land, or so many natural resources, so as to make those who come after him significantly worse off.

How much can people justly acquire before they make the position of those who come after them significantly worse off? Obviously such a question cannot be answered with mathematical precision. Of course, very few important questions can be answered with such precision, so that in itself should not be construed as a criticism of the entitlement theory. Furthermore, Nozick believes the issue is not very pressing because "as an upper limit" no more than five percent of our nation's wealth is from "rental income representing the unimproved value of land, and the price of raw materials."

Nozick's argument is this: If land and other natural resources constitute a great percentage of any community's wealth, then any appropriation of unheld land would significantly worsen the position of everyone else because they would no longer be able to appropriate a major source of wealth. However, if land and natural resources constitute only a small percentage of a community's wealth, then the appropriation of land would not significantly worsen the position of anyone else because the vast majority of potential earnings lie elsewhere.

In order to more fully understand how Nozick's appeal to the "facts of the matter" affects his understanding of the entitlement theory let us examine a situation in which there is clearly "enough and as good left." Suppose gold were as common as ordinary sand. In that case, the market value of gold jewelry would depend primarily on the skill, effort, and talent (in Nozick's words, "upon human actions") of the jeweler who formed, shaped, and designed the objects in question. Now it has already been granted that people have rights and among them is the right to expend their time and effort in lawful pursuits. Because it is not unlawful to make jewelry, any individual has the right to do so. Let us also assume that all individuals have the right to engage in wholly voluntary contractual relations. This means that the jeweler in our example has the right to sell his jewelry for whatever other people are willing to pay. Moreover, because the value of the raw materials used to make the jewelry is, by hypothesis, negligible, there is no concern that the jeweler may have violated the "Lockean proviso." It follows that the jeweler has a right to the full market value of his product.

Difficulties with Nozick's Position

Most philosophers have little problem with Nozick's argument thus far. Difficulties begin to arise only when we consider a world in which gold is scarce. Suppose a person, living in a world like our own in which gold is quite rare, purchased a piece of farm land, fully intending to farm it, but then discovered that his land sat on top of a rich and easy-to-mine vein of gold. With little effort, and no talent, this person could live a life of luxury and leisure. His neighbors, working long days in sweltering temperatures, might naturally be expected to feel a little jealous, and to mutter under their breath, "It isn't fair."

Nozick would dismiss these mutterings as no more than an expression of petty human jealousy. "After all," he might say to the mutterers, "your neighbor's good fortune in no way worsened your condition. He didn't become wealthy by taking something from you. How, then, can it be rightfully suggested that you have some claim on what he found?" (In fact, it is possible that the neighbor's discovery of gold might actually improve the position of the rest of the farmers by increasing the money supply and thereby lowering the interest rates farmers must pay. During the 1890s, the discovery of gold in Alaska seems to have had this very effect for the American farmer.)

Yet not every complaint about the good fortune of others is the product of mere jealousy. Let us begin with the least problematic example.

Only the most callous among us would say that a person living in luxury has no obligation to help those who are living in absolute poverty. Nozick himself describes it as "an essential element" of Locke's theory that every person has (and now he quotes Locke) "title to so much out of others' plenty, as will keep him from extreme want, where he has no means to subsist otherwise."

Endnotes 2a–8

To see how this admission might affect Nozick's argument, let us imagine a whole community living in **"extreme want"**; let this include inadequate clothing and housing, malnutrition, and a total lack of medical care. Now suppose several members of this community, solely as the result of good fortune, strike it rich. If these people kept all of their newly found wealth to themselves, or even if they resisted efforts by the rest of the community to tax their riches for the benefit of others, Locke and Nozick would both agree that it is more than petty jealousy for those in "extreme want" to mutter, "It isn't fair." And note: Those who struck it rich cannot be said to have violated the Lockean proviso and thus to be without clear title to their possessions. They have not worsened the material condition of others. The only thing they could possibly have worsened would be the relative position of those in extreme want.

Sometimes social scientists say an individual or group is living in poverty even when they are not malnourished, not lacking in shelter, not without medical care.

"Extreme want" is admittedly a slippery notion. It becomes even more slippery when we introduce the social scientist's distinction between absolute poverty and relative poverty. Sometimes social scientists say an individual or group is living in poverty even when they are not malnourished, not lacking in shelter, not without medical care. Their poverty, it is said, is due only to the disparity between their station in life and that of others in their community. If 95% of your community drove Mercedes Benzes and lived in million-dollar houses while you drove a 1980 Ford Pinto and lived in a one-room apartment, there would undoubtedly be times when you felt like you lived in "extreme want." Is this feeling justified, or again, is it really another instance of petty jealousy?

Certainly few of us would feel much sympathy with the plight of the five percent who drove Pintos and lived in apartments if we ourselves had no car and lived under a bridge on a local interstate highway. But suppose that within the community in question everyone owned at least a Pinto and a two-room apartment. Would we then feel more sympathy for the plight of the bottom five percent? Perhaps. But even if we did, what would that tell us about the justice of the situation? Suppose the 95% who drove a Mercedes and lived in million-dollar houses gained their wealth purely by good fortune and did so in a way that involved no great skill, talent, or effort on their part. Could those at the bottom claim that their "extreme want" entitled them to a portion of the good fortune of the 95%?

Some people might feel that it does, but personal idiosyncrasies, says Nozick, don't establish individual rights. Even if they did, Nozick would argue that the sort of hypothetical example we just considered is totally unrealistic because, as a matter of fact, "95% of the income and wealth of Americans is not solely the result of 'good fortune.' Instead, it is based upon individual effort, talent, and skill, and clearly one has earned, and thus has the right to keep, that which is so based."

Just Transfers in Entitlement Theory

We have now summarized Locke's and Nozick's theory of just acquisition. The rest of the entitlement theory follows fairly simply. We have already alluded to the idea of **"just transfers."** By this Nozick only means that if a person is justly entitled to a basket of acorns because he gathers them himself while leaving plenty for other people, then he is free to transfer that basket of acorns to another person either as a free gift or as an exchange for something in return, for example, a pair of sandals.

The Injustice of All Other Bases of Acquisition

The third part of Nozick's definition of distributive justice simply says that there is no other way to justly acquire some good other than that specified by the first two principles. The point of the third principle is to exclude principles of need, equality, or utility from consideration in determining a just distribution of economic goods and services.

Nozick's primary concern here is to make it clear that according to the entitlement theory, no government has the right to use its power of taxation and coercion to redistribute its citizens' income and wealth in accordance with some pattern of need, equality, or utility that it deems to be more fair or just. Some philosophers have thought it is blatantly unfair or intrinsically harmful that some people live in luxury while others live in poverty. Plato, for example, argued in *The Laws* that no government should allow any of its citizens to become more than four times as wealthy as its poor citizens. We will discuss more fully Plato's reason later on in this section, but for now, let us take Plato's proposal as a prime example of a **patterned principle of redistribution.**

The problem with Plato's proposal, and all other government plans for redistribution of income, according to the entitlement theory, is that they necessarily violate a person's natural right to liberty. Noz-

Endnote 9

Figure 2. Wilt Chamberlain. Associated Press/Wide World Photos.

ick attempts to show that this is the case in his widely discussed "Wilt Chamberlain example." (Wilt Chamberlain was an outstandingly talented basketball center who might today be compared with Shaquille O'Neal.)

Suppose you are made "Dictator for the Day" so that you have the freedom and power to impose upon a nation what you deem to be the most just pattern for the redistribution of all income and wealth. Let's suppose, just for the sake of the argument, that you favor Plato's proposal. Therefore, you change Shaquille O'Neal's contract so that during the next year they will pay him no more than four times as much as the average full-time minimum wage employee at McDonald's earns in a year. As "Dictator for the Day" you have that power.

But now suppose O'Neal and a few other star players get together during the off season, rent a gymnasium with their own money, and begin playing games. Word gets out, and soon people want to come watch O'Neal and other NBA stars practice. O'Neal and the others have no objection, but they do ask all who come to drop a dollar bill in the box before they enter to help pay the cost of renting the gym. Pretty soon so many of McDonald's employees are taking every opportunity to watch O'Neal play basketball, that now he and the other NBA stars have far more than four times the income as the minimum wage McDonald's employee.

Thus, what by hypothesis began as a just pattern of distribution is soon turned into something else so long as O'Neal's freedom is not violated. As Nozick says, "Any distributional pattern with any egalitarian component is overturnable by the voluntary actions of individual persons over time."

Endnote 10

The alternative to all patterned principles of distribution is a historical principle that looks not at the current pattern of distribution but, instead, considers only how the currently existing pattern of distribution arose. If it arose solely in accordance with the principles of just acquisition and just transfers, then no matter how unequal the present distribution, it is nonetheless a just distribution and any government that used its coercive powers to change it would necessarily be violating individuals' natural rights.

Distinguishing Justice and Charity

Finally, while the entitlement theory has strict requirements as far as **justice** is concerned, and while these requirements may permit some to live in luxury when others are living in poverty, it says nothing about what well-to-do individuals might voluntarily decide to do to help their less well-off neighbors. There is, in other words, a strict distinction between matters of justice and matters of **charity**, according to the entitlement theory. In fact, entitlement theorists are free to argue that principles of morality should encourage the rich to help the poor whenever possible. All the entitlement theory forbids is that laws be framed that allow governments to use their power of coercion to require the rich to help the poor.

Figure 3. Shaquille O'Neil. Reebok International.

EGALITARIANISM

The Theory of John Rawls

Another Harvard philosopher, **John Rawls,** wrote a book in 1971, *A Theory of Justice,* which may well turn out to be one of the most important philosophical books written in the 20th century. In it Rawls develops in great detail and defends with powerful arguments a much more egalitarian theory than the entitlement theory. According to Rawls, justice does require that a certain pattern of distribution be maintained.

Rawls recognizes the debt his theory owes to the **social contract theories** of Rousseau and Immanuel Kant. But in this case, Rawls' own development of what he calls "justice as fairness" is so clear and powerful that we won't bother to discuss its historical antecedents. The fundamental assumption of Rawls' theory is that for any economic system to be just it must allocate both **burdens and benefits** fairly. The bulk of his book is an attempt to flesh out in some detail what constitutes a fair distribution of social goods such as jobs, income, and wealth.

Often we rely on the judgment of impartial observers to establish a fair distribution of burdens and benefits. However, there are two

Endnote 11

problems with such a solution when applied to fundamental questions. First, there are no impartial judges of such fundamental issues as which principles a society is going to adopt for distribution of jobs, income, and wealth. Any decision the judge makes is necessarily interested, i.e., all possible decisions will affect the judge's own job, income, and wealth. Second, even if we could find a wholly altruistic judge without the slightest tendency to make a judgment benefiting his own situation, it is unlikely that everyone else would willingly abide by his decision, especially if it appeared that their interests were adversely affected.

The Hypothetical Agreement from Behind the "Veil of Ignorance" Rawls circumvents these problems by relying, as much as possible, on a purely procedural understanding of justice. Here is an example of a purely procedural solution to a problem: You are hosting a birthday party for 6-year-olds and two of them have been arguing with each other from the start. It is time to cut the birthday cake, and it is obvious that no matter how carefully it is cut, one of the boys will surely complain that he received the smaller piece. A purely procedural solution would be to have one of the boys cut the cake while the other boy is given the first choice. That way, no matter how the cake was actually distributed, neither boy would have a rational complaint. While Rawls does not pretend to have discovered so neat a solution to all the complex issues surrounding distributive justice, he does believe there is a procedural solution to many of the enduring problems.

The guiding idea behind Rawls' conception of **justice as fairness** is that the fundamental principles regulating social and economic intercourse ought to be principles to which free and rational persons would all consent if they were starting from a position of initial equality. To determine what these principles would be, Rawls performs a kind of "thought experiment," which he refers to as the **"original position."** Suppose, he said, that we imagine all members of society (or representative members from all classes) coming together in a kind of constitutional convention where the fundamental principles of justice are to be decided. If the outcome is to be fair, it is essential that the people making these crucial decisions start from a position of initial equality. So, to insure fairness, Rawls says we must imagine that all agreements are made from behind a "veil of ignorance," a strictly fictional notion that the ones making the decision don't know their own position in the society or their own unique characteristics.

The reason for the veil of ignorance is clear. People born with physical strength would be tempted to formulate principles that would reward the physically strong; those born with mental gifts would be tempted to formulate principles that would favor the intellectually gifted; and those born with musical talent would be tempted to favor a society whose fundamental principles richly rewarded great musicians, et cetera. Only a community of saints could reach an agreement with such temptations.

Because very few, if any, of us are really saints, Rawls says we must imagine that the parties in the original position do not know their "fortune in the distribution of natural assets and abilities, intelligence, strength, and the like." Thus, Rawls concludes that this veil of ignorance "ensures that no one is advantaged or disadvantaged in the choice of principle by the outcome of natural chance or the contingency of social circumstance. Because all are similarly situated and no one is able to design principles to favor his particular condition, the principles of justice are the result of a fair agreement or bargain."

Before we examine the principles of justice that Rawls thinks people would adopt in such a situation, a couple of assumptions and implications about the original position should be made clear. First, Rawls assumes that while parties to the original position are not saints, they are nonetheless rational sinners. And by **"rational"** he means no more than "taking the most effective means to given ends." Now because all people, says Rawls, want certain primary goods such as liberty, political and economic opportunities, secure and adequate income, wealth, and self-respect, a rational person can be defined as a person whose decisions maximize the acquisition of these **primary goods.**

Second, Rawls' theory implies that justice ought to nullify "the accidents of natural endowment and the contingencies of social circumstance as counters in the quest for political and economic advantage." Because no one deserves the genes they are born with, and because no one chooses the family, community, and nation into which he or she is born, Rawls thinks that it will be simply obvious to any person willing to take a moral point of view that no just society would reward or punish people for factors that are completely outside their control. (While there is much to be said for Rawls' point of view, it should be noted that a philosopher like Nozick would not be willing to make such assumptions. For Nozick, the only morally relevant issue is a person's rights, and while a handsome person does not deserve his good looks, he nonetheless has a right not to unjustly be deprived of his good looks.)

Endnote 11a

RAWLS'S TWO PRINCIPLES OF JUSTICE

And what are the fundamental principles of justice that Rawls believes would be adopted by those in the original position behind a veil of ignorance?

First: Each person is to have an equal right to the most extensive basic liberty compatible with a similar liberty for others.

Second: Social and economic inequalities are to be arranged so that they are both (a) reasonably expected to be to everyone's advantage, and (b) attached to positions and offices open to all.

Justifying Equal Liberty

The meaning and justification of the first principle is fairly obvious. Because **liberty** is assumed to be a primary good that all people desire, it follows that all people would argue for social and economic institutions that would maximize their own freedom. However, because no one knows, for example, whether she will be born physically strong or weak, she would not be willing to formulate laws that would permit a person the freedom to punch another person in the nose whenever she wanted. Thus, the liberty they would choose would be a "liberty compatible with a similar liberty for others."

Justifying the Difference Principle

Rawls' second fundamental principle is often referred to as the **difference principle.** It can best be understood and justified if we picture the total economic output of a society as composing a single pie that is then cut into different-size pieces for distribution to each member of the society. Suppose 10 persons work together in a simple society. In this society work is looked upon as a burden that is only freely chosen if it is rewarded with a pay check. If the economic pie is divided equally among all 10 members of society, it would undoubtedly be smaller than it would be if the more productive members were given a larger share of the pie. With these assumptions, consider the table on the following page.

In society A, the economic pie is divided equally and each member of society receives 3 PUs (pie units). In society B, the economic pie is not divided equally. The two poorest members receive only 4 PUs each, while the two richest members receive 8 PUs each. In societies C and D there is even more economic inequality, and, given our assumptions, greater rewards for skill, talent, and effort bring forth even greater total productivity.

Now, according to Rawls, no rational person would choose to live in society A if given a choice between A and B. This is because all people want to maximize their primary goods (for the sake of simplicity we are here ignoring primary goods other than income). Even if they end up being the poorest members of society B, they are better off than if they end up being the richest member of society A. In this case, though there are inequalities in society B, they are justifiable according to the difference principle because they work to the advantage of the least favored members of society.

The choice between B and either C or D is not as simple. If a party in the original position opts for either C or D then that party is making a big gamble. Whether he wins big will only be known after the veil of ignorance is removed. Would rational people be willing to make such a gamble? Rawls thinks not. His reasons are twofold. First, he emphasizes the fact that the choices made in the original position are absolutely binding for all of one's own life and perhaps even for one's posterity. Given the importance of a steady and secure income, Rawls

	Total GDP	Lowest 1/5	Middle 3/5	Top 1/5
A	30	3	3	3
B	60	4	6	8
C	120	2.5	10	27.5
D	150	1	6	56

thinks it is unlikely that one would gamble about such fundamental issues. This is especially true if it turned out, as it very well may, that the 1 PU the two poorest members of society D receive is not even enough on which to survive.

If this first argument leaves one unconvinced, Rawls strengthens the procedural element in the theory. In our original example of a purely procedural solution to a problem, we imagined that the boy who cut the cake was forced to select his own piece last. This insures that he will cut the cake fairly by exercising the greatest possible care in cutting equal-size pieces. Likewise, Rawls' second argument requires that all parties to the original position assume that it is their own worst enemy who will assign them at birth their actual talents, skills, and educational opportunities. Given this stronger procedural assumption, it seems clear that all rational people would agree to the difference principle when selecting the fundamental principles by which their society was going to be ordered.

Rawls's Method for Implementing Reform

All that remains to discuss is Rawls' method for implementing his reform. Though Rawls lays down no specific political requirements for a just society, he does say that the first and second principles of justice are *lexically ordered*. That is, they are arranged like a dictionary or a "lexicon." One can't move on to the second principle until the first principle is fully satisfied. In other words, Rawls doesn't believe that people in the original position would be willing to sacrifice their political freedoms for improved economic conditions, except in the most severe situations. If a group of people are literally starving to death, then they may be willing to trade in their right to vote for improved economic conditions. Short of that, however, Rawls believes that people's sense of self-worth as expressed by their participation in self-government is more important to them than mere economic advantages such as driving a late-model car or taking a vacation in Europe. Though Rawls provides few specific details about the actual political organization of a just society, it is clear that it will be democratic in the broadest sense.

RADICAL OR PURE EGALITARIANISM

While Rawls's two principles strive toward an end-state pattern of distribution that tends to produce equality, it should be clear that his second principle, the "difference principle," *explicitly justifies certain inequalities,* i.e., those that make the worst off better off than they would be with greater equality. Thus, although it is common to call Rawls's view egalitarian, there are special situations in which it actually justifies inequalities. The key is that it is not just acquisition or trades that justifies the inequalities (as it does in entitlement theory) and it is not the sum total of all the good that justifies them (as it does in utilitarian theory). It is only the improving of the lot of the worst off that provides a legitimate reason for unequal distributions.

Some egalitarians go even further. Rawls believes that rational people would have no reason at all to choose a more equal world with lesser goods for the worst off over a less equal world with greater goods. In Figure 14.1 Rawls is convinced they would choose world B. But others still are interested in world A, in which there is greater equality albeit with everyone at a somewhat lower level of well-being. The choice may depend on one's moral psychology. Rawls thinks there is no reason to be attracted to equality per se. It is attractive, but will rationally be abandoned in order to improve the position of the worst off. By contrast, some people believe that there is something intrinsically offensive about the fact that, even though all are equally deserving, some have more than others. They psychologically appreciate the solidarity that comes with everyone who exerts equal effort receiving the same. Some would go so far as to choose world A in Figure 14.1 rather than world B. We could call these people "radical" or "pure" egalitarians. Some religious communities, such as some in more sectarian Christianity, adopt this view over the Rawlsian Difference Principle.

CLASSICAL REPUBLICANISM

This theory began with the attempts of Plato and Aristotle to make philosophical sense of the Greek city-state and to determine its ideal form. It was carried on and refined by Thomas Aquinas in the Middle Ages and has been picked up by such modern philosophers as Alasdair MacIntyre, Charles Taylor, and Michael Sandel. The core of this conception of justice is a theory of human nature which emphasizes the fact that all people are rational, social animals.

Differences from the Earlier Theories: By speaking of a **"theory of human nature"** Classical Republicans mean to deny the now prevalent view that people are what they choose to be. Conventional wisdom emphasizes the variety of goods that different people choose to pursue. Some people enjoy intricate intellectual problems; other people enjoy physical and athletic challenges; still other people enjoy social interaction, the pursuit of political power, or simply helping other people in distress. There are probably even a few people who, as Rawls says, would enjoy nothing more than "to count blades of grass in various geometrically shaped areas such as park squares and well-trimmed lawns."

Endnotes 12–14

Which of these pursuits is better or more worthy of people's essential natures? According to both of the previous philosophies we have examined, these questions have no answer because humans do not have anything called an essential "nature." Thus, a just state must be neutral with respect to various conceptions of the "good life" and allow its citizens maximum freedom to choose the life they prefer. The only limit a state may properly impose on its citizens' free choice is that they cannot impinge upon the freedom of other people to act as they choose to act. This conception of freedom is captured well by the cliche: "The freedom to move one's fist ends at everyone else's nose." Because both Nozick and Rawls heartily endorse this conception of freedom, both the Entitlement theory and the Egalitarian theory are correctly called **liberal theories of justice.**

There is, of course, an important difference in these two liberal views of freedom. The Entitlement theory emphasizes **negative freedom** — freedom from all forms of restraint, especially restraint from the coercive arm of the state and its taxes. The Egalitarian theory emphasizes **positive freedom** — the freedom to act as one chooses because the state or someone else has a positive duty to provide the money or other means needed to act.

The difference between these two forms of freedom is clear if we imagine a person shipwrecked on an uninhabited desert island. Such a person would have complete negative freedom because there are absolutely no restraints on his actions. But obviously, such a person is not in an enviable position because he lacks the means to satisfy many of his desires. Without these enabling means (e.g., access to food and water) a person's negative freedom isn't worth much. Because in most modern societies the most important enabling means is money, egalitarians are willing to permit the state to use its powers of taxation to equalize the positive freedom of its citizens.

While Classical Republicans acknowledge the value of both negative and positive freedom, their conception of a just and well-ordered society requires an additional kind of freedom. A contemporary Aristotelian, Mortimer Adler, calls it **moral freedom,** and he describes it this way:

> Moral freedom consists in our having a will that is habitually disposed by virtue to will as it ought. Virtue . . . is the habitual disposition to desire aright, which means choosing what one needs — the real goods one ought to desire. The obstacles or impediments to right desire stem from appetites or wants that tempt or solicit us to make the wrong rather than the right choices.

Endnote 15

According to Classical Republicans, a just society — and, hence, a just system of distributive justice — is defined as one that maximizes the moral freedom of its citizens. Classical Republicanism stands or falls on the distinction between wants and needs. If people are no more than individual wants, desires, and preferences, then it makes no sense to speak of virtuous citizens whose "habitual disposition (is) to desire aright (correctly)." The notion of a **right desire** presupposes that not all desires are equally worthy. Thus, Classical Republicans must deny the prevalent conception of human nature as being infinitely malleable and constituted wholly by the equally worthy choices individuals make. Some choices naturally lead to a full and flourishing life, while other choices lead to a life buffeted and burdened by conflicting and insatiable desires.

According to Classical Republicans, human nature is not infinitely malleable, but instead, is such that humans are by nature rational, social animals. It therefore follows that those desires which are in accordance with one's nature are more worthy than those which reflect desires which are in fundamental opposition to human nature. In other words, the more worthy desires are in accordance with real needs, whereas the less worthy desires only reflect individual preferences.

The Classical Republican View of the Human's Essential Nature

Though it is impossible to fully flesh out a picture of humans' essential nature as conceived by Classical Republicans in this chapter, we must at least draw a quick sketch. We will do this by focusing on the three essential elements of human nature: rationality, sociability, and membership in the animal kingdom.

Rationality

The fact that humans are rational animals means that they are born with capabilities and potentialities which other members of the animal kingdom lack. Perhaps the most important of these is the ability to communicate with other members of their species using an infinitely complex set of symbols. This ability to use language gives humans an ability to learn, and in turn teach, an incredible variety of important survival skills. It also gives humans the ability to formulate abstractions which allows them to ask not only technical questions about how things work, but also, philosophical questions about why they work as they do.

For example, people have not only figured out how to raise crops by determining the spring and fall equinoxes of the sun, but they also want to know why the sun and stars move the way they do. Human rationality entails infinite curiosity. As Aristotle says in the opening lines of the *Metaphysics,* "All men by nature desire to have knowledge." And that which we desire by nature constitutes a real need.

Sociability

Humans' social nature is a natural outgrowth of their rationality and their use of language. Hermits have no use for language. And the converse is also true: Those who have a use for language must live in societies with other members of their species. But beyond the fact that humans' social nature is implied by their rationality, we need only to look around at others and at ourselves to observe that humans derive much enjoyment from social relations. Aristotle devoted a fifth of his *Nicomachean Ethics* to a discussion of friendship. So again, the fact that we are social by nature means that the desire for friendships and other forms of social interaction constitute a real need.

One of those other forms of social interactions which is important to contemporary Aristotelians is participation in the political process.

All societies require some form of government. Because a society's political organization affects all other social interactions, this means that all people have an interest in their society's form of government. Thus, all people have a real need to have some say in the laws that govern their social relations.

Membership in the Animal Kingdom

Finally, Classical Republicans do not ignore the fact that humans are all members of the animal kingdom. This simple fact means that in addition to the real needs of knowledge, friendship, and some form of political freedom, all human beings have real needs of a purely material nature, e.g., food, drink, shelter, medical attention, etc.

Earlier we said Classical Republicans define a just society as one which maximizes the moral freedom of all its citizens. We can now understand their justification for such a definition. If these philosophers are correct, people can only flourish if their real needs are being met, and people's real needs can only be met if they live in a society which distinguishes between wants and needs. Furthermore, a just society will insist on meeting all its citizens' needs before attempting to satisfy individual wants. Only then will the common good of all its citizens be met.

The Just Distribution of Goods
According to Classical Republicans

Classical Republicans have no particular formula for distributing economic goods and services. What is best in one time and situation may not be best in another time and situation. However, for the modern societies of the West, there are certain safe generalizations that most Classical Republicans are willing to make. First, no society can be considered just that does not meet the fundamental material needs of all its citizens. This entails a certain minimum standard of living for everyone.

And where is that line to be drawn? Again, it is impossible to say with mathematical precision. As Aristotle noted long ago, one of the marks of an educated person is that a person "searches for that degree of precision in each kind of study which the nature of the subject at hand admits." Nonetheless, this much can be said without fear of contradiction: The limits of justifiable inequalities in any society lie somewhere in between the 4-to-1 ratio permitted in Plato's Laws and the 93-to-1 ratio that currently exists in the United States. And only those who are blinded by greed would argue that our current practice is closer to the truth than Plato's legislation.

Classical Republicans are not only concerned with how much an economy produces and how it is distributed, they are also concerned with what an economy produces. A society that richly provided for all its citizens' material needs, yet ignored their need for knowledge and friendship, may be a fair society, but it would not be a good society. Thus, Classical Republicans would insist that a society's economy makes ample provision for the education of all its citizens, and, of course, education is not conceived of as mere training that allows its

As Aristotle noted long ago, one of the marks of an educated person is that a person "searches for that degree of precision in each kind of study which the nature of the subject at hand admits."

Endnotes 16,17

citizens to compete better on the world market. Instead, it is conceived of as a liberal education which leads to a flourishing of all the human arts and sciences, irrespective of their economic value.

Finally, a just economic system does not ignore the social and even spiritual values of its citizens when making economic decisions. Such a society, for example, willingly forgoes economic advantages in order to make ample provision for its citizens to gather together and enjoy each other's fellowship. This may include everything from parks to "blue laws" which provide for a common day of rest.

Implementing Classical Republicanism

Having sketched in outline the principles of a just economy as conceived of by Classical Republicans, it is necessary to say something about its implementation in today's society. Contemporary philosophers who favor such a theory of justice are usually called **communitarians**. They are fully aware that their position is a radical departure from **modern liberalism.** Liberals inevitably ask: "Who makes all these crucial decisions? And how can one person, or group of people, decide what is best for someone else?"

Such questions cannot be adequately answered without considering the Aristotelian system of ethics in its entirety (see also Chapter 3). All that can be said here is that all totalitarian or dictatorial regimes are categorically rejected because they are inconsistent with humans' social nature, which requires political freedom. Thus, according to communitarians, all social and economic change must begin by changing the conventional wisdom of the age and convincing people of the truth of this conception of justice.

Of course, it is no small task to form a new consensus on such fundamental ethical issues. But in response to the liberal cliche — "Who's going to decide?" — communitarians offer another cliche: "We'll do it one step at a time." Robert Bellah, a sociologist at the University of California, says: "That happiness is to be attained through the limitless material acquisition is denied by every religion and philosophy known to man, but is preached incessantly by every American television set."

Endnote 18

However, even when there is widespread agreement, the liberal's conception of individual rights as a card that trumps all other concerns makes it virtually impossible for us to act for the common good of society. Thus, a necessary second step, according to communitarians, is to persuade people of the truth of Article 15 of the Virginia Bill of Rights:

> No free government, or the blessing of liberty, can be preserved to any people, but a firm adherence to justice, moderation, temperance, frugality and virtue and by frequent recurrence to fundamental principles.

A liberal conception of individual rights, even when there is such widespread agreement, makes it virtually impossible for us to act as a society on such a truth because a person's rights are viewed as a card that trumps all other concerns. Communitarians argue that this absolutist conception of individual rights will slowly, but surely, lead to our own self-destruction.

COMPARISON AND CONTRAST

These theories of distributive justice are distinct, yet they each share some common characteristics. Entitlement and Egalitarian theories both emphasize individual rights. Though they are usually founded on a Kantian conception of the dignity of each individual, sometimes they are founded on a utilitarian concern to maximize the general welfare. Only free people are happy, say utilitarians. As John Stuart Mill writes in *On Liberty*, "The only freedom which deserves the name is that of pursuing our own good in our own way, so long as we do not attempt to deprive others of theirs, or impede their efforts to obtain it."

Nonetheless, according to both these theories, whether based on a Kantian or utilitarian theory of ethics, all people have a right to as much freedom as is consistent with equal freedom to others. And though the Entitlement theory emphasizes negative freedom while Egalitarianism emphasizes positive freedom, both understand freedom in terms of persons doing what they want to do.

Classical Republicans and contemporary communitarians emphasize the common good. While a person's needs are never inconsistent with the good of the whole society, a person's wants often are. When this occurs, both these philosophies subordinate individual preferences to the good of the larger whole. But in doing so, they argue that they are not restricting freedom, properly conceived, but only restricting license. Of course, none of this makes sense apart from an Aristotelian conception of human nature and the whole ethical system that grows out of it.

The Entitlement theory and Egalitarianism are both based on a "thin" conception of the good and thus can tolerate a society in which citizens have widely varying conceptions of what is good. Classical Republicanism and contemporary communitarianism are based on a "thick" theory of the good which presupposes that on certain fundamental issues a shared conception of the good is possible. Such a theory of justice cannot tolerate widespread viciousness in its citizens and, thus, presupposes that all just governments must actively encourage the development of virtuous citizens.

Modern liberalism, of which the Entitlement theory and Egalitarianism are two different versions, leads to an atomistic conception of persons. That is, liberalism conceives of people as essentially autonomous and independent agents. Classical Republicanism and contemporary communitarianism lead to a more social conception of person that emphasizes both socially shared responsibilities and individual privileges.

Thus, the Entitlement theory favors a minimalist state; Egalitarianism favors an interventionist state; Classical Republicans and contemporary communitarians favor an activist state.

ECONOMIC SYSTEMS

Capitalism

The seminal work of modern capitalism is *The Wealth of Nations*. It was written in 1776 by the English philosopher, **Adam Smith**. In this long book (over 700 pages) Smith argues against the current mercantilist definition of a nation's wealth.

Mercantilism

According to mercantilism, a nation's wealth consists solely of the sum total of its gold and silver bullion. This meant that for a nation like England, which has no gold or silver mines of its own, the only way to become wealthy was to maintain a positive balance of trade. If a nation consistently sold more abroad than it purchased, then it would increase its stores of bullion and would, according to the mercantilist's definition, be wealthy. Because all nations want to become wealthy, the standard practice of governments was to actively regulate their nation's economy with a large number of laws designed to encourage exports and discourage imports. For example, it might pass a law that allowed only a certain number of cobblers to purchase leather from other nations, and forbid all shopkeepers to purchase cheap wine from another country.

SMITH'S CRITICISM OF MERCANTILISM

Smith argued that the mercantilist's understanding of wealth was fundamentally misguided. The true measure of a nation's wealth was the sum total of the market value of all the goods and services that its people produced. A nation of manufacturers and merchants like England, according to Smith, would inevitably become wealthy if government would simply allow its citizens the economic freedom to do as they pleased. Cobblers who were good at making shoes should be free to purchase raw materials from wherever they pleased and to make as many shoes as they could. Furthermore, they should be free to sell them for as much as they could get on the free market. Similarly, shopkeepers who were good at buying cheaply from other countries should be free to do so, and they should also be free to sell their merchandise for as much as they could.

To many people, this seemed to entail certain fundamental problems: If cobblers were free to sell shoes for as much as they liked and if shopkeepers were free to sell their goods as dearly as they could, then what is to stop them from selling shoes at an unfair price or making an unfair profit on the exchange of goods? That is, what is to prevent some particular individual from becoming rich at the expense of the nation as a whole? Smith's great insight was that a free and unregulated market is guided by an "invisible hand" that would ensure no cobbler or shopkeeper was making an unfair profit. If governments stopped issuing licenses that determined who could be a cobbler and where shopkeepers could purchase goods, then all cobblers and shopkeepers would automatically have to sell their goods for a fair price.

For example, if cobblers started selling shoes for too high a price, then shopkeepers would start making and selling shoes and that would drive down the cost of shoes. Conversely, if shopkeepers began to make unfair profits on imported wines, then cobblers would stop making shoes and start keeping shop. All this would work without a hitch just as long as government did not pass laws regulating who could make shoes and sell wine. By individuals actively and rationally pursuing their own respective self-interests, Smith argued, the nation as a whole would prosper because it would have the most efficient system of production and distribution.

Adam Smith was not only the great defender of free markets, he also sang the praises of the Industrial Revolution, which was just beginning in England. The heart of industrialization is the division of labor. It takes a considerable amount of skill and training to turn untanned leather, glue and thread into a good-fitting and handsome pair of shoes. However, if the manufacturing of shoes is broken down into its individual operations so that one person tans the leather, another person cuts out the sole, a third person attaches the heel, et cetera, then a collection of relatively unskilled laborers can produce goods that would require a large amount of skill if a single individual were to make the entire shoe by himself. Furthermore, by dividing the manufacturing of goods into relatively simple and mundane procedures, it is possible to house a large number of workers in a single factory and take advantage of water- or steam-powered machines.

THE IMPORTANCE OF PRIVATE CONTROL OF PRODUCTION

A natural question then arises: Who should organize and control these new factories — private individuals or the government? Once again, Smith argued that government ought to keep clear of a nation's economy. While the actual work of making a pair of shoes can be broken down into individual operations that require no particular skill, knowing how to most efficiently organize workers — and to ensure that the whole operation runs smoothly — is a job that requires a great deal of skill.

Figure 4. Karl Marx. The Granger Collection.

It also requires a good deal of capital, i.e., saved-up resources that allow a person to purchase the land, buildings, and machines which go into making a modern factory. Rather than having government determine who has such skills and capital, it is more efficient to allow anyone the freedom to raise the capital, build the factory, purchase the machinery, and organize the workers in any way they choose. If government adopts such a laissez-faire position, all these complex decisions will be made in accordance with the highest degree of efficiency by the invisible hand of the market. However, it should be noted that, unlike his followers, Smith never said laissez-faire economics was in all ways superior to government intervention.

In sum, capitalism can be defined as an economic system where all property (including factories and other "means of production") is privately owned and operated for individual profit as determined by a free market. The principal advantage of capitalism is economic efficiency and the fact that it preserves individual freedom.

Socialism

The great theorist of socialism is **Karl Marx.** Marx produced his major work on economics almost a century after Smith. In that three-volume work called simply *Capital*, Marx did not argue that Smith was wrong about the virtues of the free market, the division of labor, and industrialization. His fundamental objection was that Smith's picture of industrial capitalism was incomplete. The final stage of economic development had yet to be reached.

Marx himself believed that a socialist economy is only possible after an economy has obtained a high degree of industrialization. Socialism presupposes capitalism, according to Marx. Only given a highly developed industrial base is it possible for a nation's economy to produce the wealth of goods necessary to supply all its citizens' needs. It is therefore a mistake to view Marx as a totally unsympathetic critic of capitalism.

The Social Costs of Capitalist Production

According to Marx, capitalists tend to view industrialization as nothing more than the most efficient means of production. Again, Marx was not blind to these efficiencies. However, he argued that they carried with them great social costs. A single skilled cobbler making shoes in pre-industrial Europe may not be able to produce as many shoes as unskilled laborers in large 19th century factories, but the shoes that he did produce were his. And this is true not only in the sense that whatever profit he could make selling them was his, but also in the sense that he could take pride in his own creation and the craftsmanship it reflected. In pre-industrial economies, work carried with it its own intrinsic rewards.

Alienation

In an industrialized economy, the worker owns nothing except his own labor. Everything a factory worker produces is owned by someone else. But even more important, the way it is produced requires little skill on the worker's part. This leads to a state of alienation between the worker and his work, according to Marx. A person's work is no longer significantly connected to her own creative abilities. Work in a factory is nothing but an economic necessity that no person would freely endure were it not for the wages it paid. Rather than being a natural and joyful expression of a person's own skill and talent, factory work becomes an activity whose only reward is wages, often extremely meager.

Exploitation of the Worker

The second social cost of industrial capitalism is the exploitation of the worker. Marx's theory is based on the "Labor Theory of Value." On this theory the value of everything is determined by the amount of labor it takes to produce the good in question. Of course, the work of a doctor is more valuable than the work of a garbage collector. However, that is only because it takes a tremendous amount of labor to train a doctor, whereas it takes very little labor to train a garbage collector. Though skilled labor is more costly than unskilled labor, all labor is nonetheless a commodity and its value is the cost of producing a single unskilled laborer.

And what is that cost? Defenders of the labor theory of value said that the cost of producing an unskilled laborer is nothing other than a subsistence wage. Pay laborers less than a subsistence wage and they will not be able to reproduce themselves. And if unskilled laborers are not able to reproduce themselves then there are not enough workers. This will in turn cause individual factory owners to have to increase their wages. If they don't, then they won't be able to attract workers to enable them to keep their mills and furnaces operating.

Of course, this all sounds very condescending and cruel to the unskilled laborer. But we must remember that at this time, the extreme poverty of the masses and harshness of factory work seemed to fit well with such a theory of value.

Profit as Surplus Value

All this leads Marx to ask an interesting theoretical question: If the value of everything is the amount of labor it takes to produce the item in question, and if all items sell for their true value in a free market, then how can factory owners ever make a profit? As Adam Smith demonstrated, factory owners must pay laborers their actual value and sell their products for actual value. So whence the profit?

Marx's answer is found in his notion of surplus value. Though the laws of the free market demand that workers be paid their true value (i.e., subsistence wages), factory owners are free to work their employees 12–14 hours a day, even if it takes only six hours' work to produce a subsistence wage. This six- to eight-hour-a-day difference is what creates the profit for the capitalist. Surplus value, which is the source of all profit, is thus a result of the exploitation of workers.

But how is such exploitation possible in a free market? After all, in a capitalist economy, no person has the right to force another person to work for them. Marx found the answer in the fact that the worker needs the wages of the factory owner more than the factory owner needs the labor of the worker. This inequality of needs is created by the fact that in capitalist economies there exists, in Marx's term, an "Industrial Reserve Army," or in modern terms, unemployment. If an individual laborer chooses not to work in a factory, the factory owner can typically find some other worker who is willing to take his place. However, the laborer cannot typically find another factory that is willing to pay his wages.

Instability
A final problem with free market capitalism according to Marx is its inherent instability. For reasons that we won't lay out in detail here, Marx predicted that as capitalist economies developed, there would be a natural tendency for the number of individual firms to decrease while their size increased. However, this trend toward a few, very large companies will not come about in a gradual and orderly manner. Instead, it will be characterized by fits of rapid expansion followed by a collapse, which will then start another cycle. Though many economists disagree with the explanation that Marx gave for these business cycles, Marx's prediction that they would arise clearly came true. And while government intervention in the economy has made these cycles much less severe than they used to be, they still remain as a source of significant social problems.

Modern socialists distance themselves from Marx's revolutionary politics and a number of his specific economic explanations of the interworkings of capitalism. However, they typically begin with Marx's analysis of capitalism, and define socialism as an economic system in which all the means of production are socially owned and operated for the good of the public as a whole.

Now it is important to understand that neither Marx nor modern socialists want to eliminate all private property. Houses, automobiles, boats, et cetera, are still going to be bought and sold on the free market and owned by private individuals. The only forms of private property that socialists wish to eliminate are those forms of property that allow individuals to profit from the work of other people. For example, socialists do not wish to eliminate the family farm where a husband and wife grow food to sell on the free market. They do, however, wish to eliminate the corporately owned farm where laborers work for wages while the owners receive all the profit.

Secondly, to say that large-scale means of production are socially owned and operated is not inconsistent with democracy. In fact, one philosopher has said, "Socialism is democracy extended to the world of work and money." Social ownership of the means of production simply means that all people, or at least all the people who work in a par-

Endnote 19

ticular factory, have an equal say in how the factory is going to be organized and run.

Finally, to say that all means of production will be run for the good of the whole public simply means that issues of alienation, exploitation, and instability will be addressed like all other political issues. For example, if the majority of a nation's citizens or their elected representatives decide that closing a large automobile plant in Detroit would cause too much social dislocation, then it would not be closed, even if a purely economic analysis showed that the plant was not profitable. And the reason is simple: According to socialists, economic efficiency is not the only goal of a just economy. Worker satisfaction, fairness of wages, and reasonable job security are all factors that a just economic system will take into consideration when allocating goods and resources.

ARGUMENTS PRO AND CON

Having defined two alternative economic systems, let us examine, in a fairly cursory manner, seven arguments for and against capitalism and socialism. (Specific details and examples will be discussed in the next section.)

1. Personal Freedom

Capitalism maximizes individual freedom. Only under a capitalist system are people fully free to employ their specific skills, talents, and efforts in any lawful manner that they see fit.

Socialism would say that while individual freedom from governmental coercion is valuable, such negative freedom is only a single element in any adequate understanding of freedom. True freedom includes not only being unconstrained by laws and regulations, but it also includes the enabling means to carry out one's wishes. Without a job or some other source of income, a person will not be able (i.e., free) to purchase food for his family even if there is no law forbidding such a purchase.

2. Production/Efficiency

Capitalism argues that by providing material incentives, the free enterprise system produces far more than competing economic systems. There is no better motivation to work both hard and efficiently than personal profit.

Socialism argues that it is not obvious that the free enterprise system is economically the most efficient. Such countries as Sweden, Germany, and Japan all have governments that take an active role in regulating their economies, and these countries all have economies that are doing as well as or better than that of the U.S. But even if a free enterprise system were shown to be the most efficient, that would not make it a just system.

3. *Private Property*

Capitalism looks at the bottom line of all socialist systems as the "Robin Hood" principle of robbing the rich to help the poor. And just as Robin Hood violated the rights of the rich, all socialist systems that tax the rich to support the poor violate the rights of the rich, even if those taxes are written into a country's legal system.

Socialism argues, as Thomas Aquinas said, "It is not theft, properly speaking, to take secretly and use another's property in cases of extreme need; because that which he takes for the support of his life becomes his own property by reason of the need."

Endnote 20

4. *Poverty*

Capitalism argues that except in cases of absolute poverty, the "Robin Hood" principle violates individuals' natural rights.

Socialism argues that material goods and services have not historically been distributed solely, or even primarily, by a system of free markets and uncoerced contracts. Fraud and brute force have historically been of much greater significance than free and fair trade. Furthermore, the politically powerful have always had the ability to get laws passed that promote their own interests, e.g., hat manufacturers who get a high tariff passed on imported hats or large farm corporations that get governments to build huge dams and then "sell" the water back to them at a highly subsidized rate. Therefore, for a government to suddenly insist that all economic exchanges will take place according to the dictates of free markets only institutionalizes and freezes in place past injustices.

5. *Taxation*

Capitalism argues that all people have a natural right to the fruit of their own labor. For government to tax individuals for any reason other than providing for the common defense (against criminals from within or aggressors from without) is no different than a system of forced labor.

Socialism says that luck, nature's bounty, and the existing social order contribute at least as much to any individual's productivity as does her own talent and effort. As R. H. Tawney wrote, "Few tricks of the unsophisticated intellect are more curious than the naive psychology of the businessman, who ascribes his achievements to his own unaided efforts, in bland unconsciousness of a social order without whose continuous support and vigilant protection he would be as a lamb bleating in the desert."

Endnote 21

6. *Redistribution*

Capitalism says that people who work hard and save their resources ought to be rewarded for their effort and their willingness to delay gratification of their own desires.

Socialism counters that perhaps this is true for the actual generation that did the work and saved the capital, however, no such effort is expended by the next generation. That is, the first generation of Rockefellers and DuPonts may in some sense have earned their wealth, but this is not true of succeeding generations of Rockefellers and DuPonts. They receive large incomes from their inheritances without any effort on their own part.

7. *Experience*

Capitalism says we know from recent experience that socialism doesn't work — just look at Eastern Europe and the former Soviet Union.

Socialism argues that the ideal was no more real in countries such as East Germany and the Soviet Union than the capitalist ideal was in such countries as Peron's Chile and Marcos's Philippines. To judge the virtues of socialism by looking at the former countries is to set up a straw man.

MIXED SYSTEMS

Thus far we have been treating capitalism and socialism as if they were two distinct economic systems. In fact, the vast majority of actually existing economic systems are combinations of both systems. We defined capitalism as a system where all the means of production are privately owned, and socialism as the system where none of the means of production is privately owned. A **mixed economic system** is one where some of the means of production are privately owned while others are publicly owned. The United States, for example, clearly has a mixed system. Here automobile factories, steel mills, and resort hotels are all privately owned; the postal system, air traffic control system, and all large water projects are publicly owned.

The principal advantage of a mixed system is its ability to balance competing principles in a manner politically acceptable to the majority of its citizens. In the United States, as in most modern industrial countries, both economic efficiency and social justice are believed to be significant. Thus, when these two principles conflict, there is no need in a mixed system to choose one or the other. Instead, a workable political compromise is sought.

COMPATIBILITY OF THEORIES AND ECONOMIC SYSTEMS

The entitlement theory requires a capitalist system because only in a free market system are free and enforceable contracts the sole method for distributing economic goods and services. Egalitarian theories tend to favor a socialist system because socialism gives the largest consideration to economic equality. However, because a system like

Rawls' also has an important place for considerations of personal freedom, such a theory is also compatible with some mixed systems.

Finally, Classical Republicanism tends to prefer a mixed system, though it is conceivable that in a very simple agrarian society, it might favor a capitalist system, and in a highly developed industrial system, it might favor socialism. The important point to note is that Aristotle and Aquinas made it clear in all their political writings that the best way to achieve a just society will vary from place to place and from age to age.

DOMESTIC PERSPECTIVES

Three Standards for Determining Income

Philosophers and economists are not the only people who ask questions about distributive justice. Almost all people — politicians, taxpayers, soon-to-be politicians, and soon-to-be taxpayers — have asked whether their taxes are too high or whether their employers are paying them as much as they deserve. Serious thought about either of these questions involves important issues of distributive justice.

When ordinary people ask whether they or a friend are being paid what they are really worth for their work, they almost always have one or more of the following standards in mind: (1) need/equality, (2) contribution/productivity, (3) moral worth/effort.

Need

If a young widow is working two jobs just to support her three pre-teenage children and her combined take-home pay is insufficient to provide her family with a modest apartment, simple clothes, and nutritious meals, then almost all would agree that she should be paid more.

Now it is important to understand that by invoking need as a criterion we are implicitly assuming equality of moral worth. We believe that such a person ought to be paid a living wage because we believe that all people who work hard are equally worthy of a living wage. Thus "equality of personhood" is the presupposition that supports our conviction that this young widow deserves better treatment.

Contribution

If two people are performing the sort of work where it is fairly easy to determine their productivity — say, foresters planting trees or maids cleaning hotel rooms — and one person is doing twice as much as the other, then it seems reasonable to suppose that the first should get paid twice as much.

When we start thinking about many other kinds of work it is often more difficult to measure productivity, but we nonetheless make the same sorts of judgments. If one person is making important purchasing decisions for a large company and another person is doing janitorial work for the same company, it is difficult to directly compare their "productivity." Instead, we typically think in terms of comparative contribution. The person making important purchasing decisions usually makes a larger contribution to the profitability of the company than does the janitor. And one of the reasons we say this is that it is typically more difficult to replace a purchasing agent than it is a janitor. Many people can perform janitorial work; only specially trained and talented people can perform well the tasks of purchasing agents. In short, while it is often impossible to make a direct comparison between two very different kinds of work, we do make judgments about their relative "difficulty" and then equate the more difficult with the more productive.

Moral Worth or Effort

This standard is really more of a judgment about the person than the work. Students, for example, will sometimes approach their instructor after receiving a grade and say something like this: "I know this paper isn't especially good, but I really put a lot of time and effort into writing it so I would really appreciate it if you gave me a 'B.'" Though it doesn't happen all that often, some instructors will sometimes honor the student's request, and oftentimes they do so for good reasons. But in saying that there were good reasons, we do not mean to imply that a "C" paper magically turns into a "B," or even that the instructor was wrong about her original judgment. Essays are graded on what is written, not how long it took to write them or how many drops of sweat dripped from the brow of the author. Yet, rewarding effort is sometimes justifiable. It often motivates a student to continue trying to improve her writing skills which, in the end, usually has the desired results.

Thus, while most of us believe that effort should not be the sole criterion of an essay's worth, it is one of the relevant factors. Furthermore, this principle seems to apply just as well to some jobs as it does to some graded essays. It seems not only fair but also useful in some situations to reward the employee who is obviously trying harder than one who is not even trying to work up to his full potential.

How Much Inequality Actually Exists?

How can these standards be applied in the United States? When we consider the standard of equality, it is natural to begin by asking how much equality or inequality actually exists. How many young widows really are working two jobs and are still not able to adequately support their families? While no one knows how many people meeting this description actually exist in the United States today, some useful conclusions can be drawn from what we do know about income distributions. The most widely used measure of equality/inequality is

Endnote 22

Endnote 23

Endnote 24

Endnote 25

Endnote 26

in terms of quintiles, i.e., dividing people into five groups from richest to poorest and then comparing the top and bottom fifths.

The most recent figures (1990) show the top fifth earning 43.5% of the GDP while the bottom fifth earned only 5.1%. (These figures include all welfare payments to the poor and subtract all taxes paid by the rich.) And while all figures show that **inequality** increased during the 1980s, it has nonetheless remained relatively constant throughout this century. A historical view of personal income in the United States between 1910 and 1970 shows this: The top fifth received between 40 and 45% of all family income.

Thus, we can say with a high degree of confidence that in the United States over the long run, the average person in the top fifth earns between six to 10 times as much as the average person in the bottom fifth.

Comparing actual incomes of the top and bottom fifths has one advantage and one disadvantage. The advantage is that income figures are relatively easy to come by and their accuracy is quite high.

Another advantage is that this method facilitates international comparisons. In Japan and West Germany the bottom fifth earned 9% and 8% respectively, while the top fifth earned 37% and 40% (Lester R. Brown, *State of the World 1990* p. 138). Thus, two of our chief economic competitors have equity ratios of between 4 and 5, while we have an (after taxes) equity ratio of 8.5.

The disadvantage is that they tend to strongly understate the inequalities that actually exist. The reason is simple: The poor's total wealth is almost completely based on current income, whereas the rich's wealth is typically based to a large degree on what they own, not what they earn. A poor person cannot by definition have either a large income or a large estate; but many rich people have very large estates without having a very large income.

Government estimates of the distribution of wealth in the United States in 1972 show that the top fifth owned 76% of the total wealth, the middle three-fifths 23%, while the bottom fifth owned only 0.2%. More recently, it was estimated by the Joint Economic Committee of Congress that the top one-half of one percent of the United States households owned 26.9% of the nation's total wealth. While these figures are only estimates, they cannot be ignored. And even if they are a little inaccurate, it is clear that the inequality of wealth is skewed far more in favor of the rich than the inequality of income.

So how many people in the United States are unable to afford modest housing, simple clothes, and nourishing food? To get an accurate picture about these matters we need to look at poverty rates in the United States. In 1996 the official poverty income for a family of four was $17,227. This is hardly a liberal amount with which to house, clothe, and nourish a family of four when one considers that rents for modest housing for such a family in metropolitan areas of the United States average between $800 and $1,000 per month (or between $9,600 to $12,000 per year).

According to the U.S. Census Bureau, by the late '90s, unlike in other boom cycles of American economic history, **living standards** were not going up. The average hourly wage increased 3.7% from 1996 to 1997 — but the **purchasing power** of those wages actually *declined* 11%. Meanwhile, corporate profits were up 7.3% in 1996, while average big-company compensation rose, shamelessly, by 35%. [This huge executive pay hike was attributed in large measure (55%) to the stock options that are in executive contracts and the stock market as a whole grew by 28% in 1997 over 1996.]

Meanwhile, "ordinary folks" got deeper in debt: Household indebtedness was more than 30% higher than in the '60s, '70s or early '80s, and a record 1.3-million persons filed for bankruptcy protection in 1997. While we will never know how many industrious and hardworking young widows can't support their families, we do know that a sizable number of Americans are living with essential needs unmet through no fault of their own.

THREE KINDS OF TAXES

While most Americans — Republican, Democrat, or Independent — will agree that this sort of inequality presents a serious problem; there is no agreed-upon solution. But one thing is clear: Whether a person favors "enterprise zones," a cut in the capital gains tax to create new jobs, or fully funding "Head Start" and other government programs to help the poor, all of these ultimately require government spending. And there are only two sources of revenue for government spending: taxes and borrowing. Because borrowing is really no more than a tax on future generations, we need to consider only taxes here.

With respect to issues of distributive justice, all taxes fall into one of three categories:

A Proportional or Flat Tax is one that taxes each unit of income, wealth, or expenditure at the same percentage rate. Most states, for example, have sales taxes that meet this definition.

A Progressive Tax is one that taxes additional units of income, wealth, or expenditure at an increased rate. The federal income tax is an example of a tax that is (at least) designed to be minimally progressive. In 1998, *for single individuals:*

* up to $25,350 is taxed at 15%;
* from $25,351 to $61,400, the tax due is $3,802.50 plus 28% over $25,350;
* from 61,400 to $128,100, the tax due is $13,896.50 plus $31% of the excess over $61,400.
* from $128,100 to $278,450, the tax due is $34,573.50 plus 36% of the amount over $128,100.

* the final bracket is over $278,450, the tax is $88,699.50 plus 39.6% over $278,450.

A Regressive Tax is one that taxes additional units of income, wealth or expenditure at a decreasing rate. The Federal Social Security tax is regressive in this sense. All people pay a flat rate (i.e., proportional) on the first $50,000 of income, while additional income is not taxed at all.

Entitlement theorists, Libertarians, and conservative Republicans view all taxes as at best a necessary evil. If these people had their way, there would be no taxes except those necessary to provide for the common defense against criminals at home and aggressors from abroad. Taxes for any other purpose, according to Nozick, are no better than "involuntary servitude."

However, in the real world of political give-and-take it is extremely unlikely that these ideals ever could be fully implemented. Most people believe that money spent for schools, roads, and even some kinds of welfare are legitimate expenditures for a government. Moreover, it is often difficult to separate defense from non-defense expenditures. Is the money spent on street lights a form of defense spending because it makes it easier for police to capture criminals? Is the money spent by publicly supported colleges and universities to train engineers a form of defense spending because without qualified engineers we couldn't sustain our defense industries? Was the National Defense Highway Fund, which paid for our interstate highway system in the 1950s and '60s, really a military expenditure?

Given these political realities it seems likely that government expenditures for such purposes will continue for the foreseeable future. The most conservatives can reasonably expect to accomplish is to restrict the kind of taxes imposed. Though they believe all taxes for non-defense expenditures are wrong, a "flat" or proportional tax is the least evil. First, it doesn't place an unequal and additional burden on the rich, and second, it doesn't create a disincentive for the hard-working and creative businessperson.

Contemporary communications, socialists, and liberal Democrats take a different position. They often harken back to the idea of noblesse oblige, i.e., wealth brings with it not only privileges but also obligations. These people therefore favor some form of progressive taxation. And in doing so, they implicitly deny the claim that a progressive tax places an unequal burden on the rich. While it is true that progressive taxes require an additional monetary contribution from the wealthy, the justification for doing this is to equalize the real burden. The widow's mite proportionally costs her much more than the same amount from the rich man. Therefore, because the rich can afford to pay more, the idea of "equal burden" favors a progressive tax system.

The second argument against a progressive tax is that it creates a disincentive to hard work and creativity. If this is in fact true, then even even someone whose views are relatively egalitarian like Rawls would argue against such a tax. Suppose a progressive tax reduces the total productivity of a nation to such a degree that even though the poor are receiving a larger percentage of the national product as a result of government transfer payments, in actual dollar totals they are receiving less because there is so much less to distribute. If this ever happens, then the difference principle has been violated, and Rawls would say that the tax structure should be made less progressive.

It is extremely difficult to determine exactly how much less productive a progressive tax system makes an economy. Some people have argued that European countries (e.g., Germany) have more progressive tax structures yet are just as productive. Others argue that the large tax cut on upper incomes in the early 1980s produced a growth in the economy that improved everyone's position. Though the economy certainly expanded, it is less clear that it produced a tide that lifted all boats. What in the '80s was proudly termed "supply side" economics is now derisively referred to as "trickle-down" economics.

Whichever of these is a more accurate description of our recent past, there has been some interesting work done on the relation of taxation and productivity by contemporary philosophers and economists which combines both liberal and conservative points of view.

FLAT-TAX DANGERS

Let us grant the conservative's contention that a tax on income is an incentive not to work and a tax on wealth is an incentive not to save. Because both work and saving are important elements of economic prosperity, progressive taxation of either work or saving is prima facie a mistake, from at least an economic point of view. The only other source of revenue is a tax on consumption. However, the traditional sales tax, even though it is in name "flat" or strictly proportional, in fact turns out to be quite regressive. The poor must spend almost all of their income to live while the rich only spend a fraction of their income. This causes the poor to pay a much higher percentage of their income in taxes than the rich which, from the liberal point of view, is morally objectionable.

A proposed solution to this dilemma is to use the existing tax system to determine, first, people's taxable income and, second, their actual savings or capital investments. By subtracting the latter from the former, a person's consumption would be determined. Once this figure is determined, tax tables on consumption could be made as progressive as is politically desirable. The first $15,000 of consumption, for example, might be tax free for a family of four; the next $15,000 of consumption might be taxed at a 20% rate; the next $15,000 at a 30% rate, et cetera. The advantage of such a taxing system is that it would equalize real burdens on families without creating a disincentive to work — and in fact creating an incentive to save and invest.

ANALYZING CONTRIBUTION AND PAY

Economic justice has been mentioned, from different perspectives, in the last two chapters, and will not be taken up independently here. It should be mentioned only because wide disparities of income surely *feel*, to a worker, like any other of the **"disparate results"** mentioned by the Supreme Court in some of the racial discrimination cases. Most recently, Philip Purcell, the top executive of Morgan Stanley/Dean Witter Discover, cashed in on stock options worth $36.4-million in the 12 months ended November 30, 1997. That was *in addition to* $14.4-million in salary, bonuses and restricted stock. Graef Crystal, a "compensation expert" from San Diego, pointed out that Purcell "could have taken an additional $43.2-million of exercisable options, but he chose not to. That would have given him $94-million. That's a staggering amount." Yes. If workers of all races should be treated equally, should all levels of workers be treated equally? Is there some rule of proportionality that would say what relation the highest salary in the company should bear to the lowest, or what sacrifices the top ranking executives should be prepared to make before serious layoffs begin?

At the outset, there is no real evidence that CEO salaries are related to shareholder wealth — recall that while corporate profits fell 4.2% in 1989, for instance, CEO salaries went up 8% (see Chapter 14). And when CEO bonuses are pegged to increases in the price of the stock, the result can be considerably worse for the employee: the quickest way to boost the price of the stock is to "downsize" the company, laying off labor, the highest of the cost factors, while the income still rolls in. With the ratio of income to cost radically changed, the profit soars, the quarterly report looks terrific, the stock leaps upward, and the CEO may find himself dandling a bonus in the tens of millions. (The knowledgeable investors depart at that point, it may be noted.) Surely this must be unjust? But there is nothing in that scenario that is illegal, and everything in it that increases the wealth of the shareholders — the first responsibility of the CEO. This question will remain to be addressed in the future.

In 1960, the average chief executive officer (CEO) in a major corporation was making 41 times as much as the average factory worker. In 1988, it was up to 93 times as much. As recently as 1980 the average of the two top executives in the top 354 corporations was a little more than $600,000 per year. By 1988 it had risen to more than $2-million per year. It is hard to believe that their productivity more than tripled in these eight years. Workers, on the other hand, increased their productivity 13% during these years, yet in real terms, their income only increased seven percent. With figures like these it seems understandable that *Business Week* (May 1, 1989) would conclude that workers are not getting rewarded in proportion to their contribution and that top management is "skimming" profits off the top.

Is there some rule of proportionality that would say what relation the highest salary in the company should bear to the lowest, or what sacrifices the top ranking executives should be prepared to make before serious layoffs begin?

How are we to evaluate such a charge? First, it is worth noting that these sorts of complaints are not new. As early as the end of the 19th century, such social critics as Edward Bellamy were arguing that there is no particular correlation between a person's output and his earnings:

Endnote 28

> All that a man produces today (over and above) his cave-dwelling ancestor, he produces by virtue of the accumulated achievements, inventions, and improvements of the intervening generations, together with the social and industrial machinery which is their legacy . . . Nine hundred and ninety-nine parts out of the thousand of every man's produce are the result of his social inheritance and environment. The remaining part would probably be a liberal estimate of what by "sacred justice" could be allotted him as "his product, his entire product, and nothing but his product."

Endnote 29

George C. Lodge has recently argued that "labor increasingly means skill, knowledge, education and organization." He goes on to conclude that this makes Lockean individualist thought obsolete because these factors are intangible and not obviously owned by individuals the way a person "owns" his body and its labor.

Endnote 30

Classical economists and entitlement theorists tend to reject these claims. They argue that in a free market all people, from the farmer laborer to the CEO, are paid according to their "marginal product." It is both impossible and unnecessary to consider here the intricacies of marginal product theory. In essence it is no more than a sophisticated working out of the implications (in an ideal world) of the intuitively plausible notion that we hinted at earlier: The reason purchasing agents earn more than janitors is that if both the purchasing agent and janitor quit their jobs, it is easier to find another janitor than it is to find another purchasing agent. Therefore purchasing agents are paid more than janitors. How much more? According to marginal product theory, companies will pay both their purchasing agents and janitors just enough to keep them from quitting.

These critics point to studies by *The Wall Street Journal* (April 18, 1990) and *Business Week* (May 7, 1990), two relatively conservative publications, which strongly suggest that there is little actual connection between executives' total compensation and the profitability of their companies. While the corporate profits for the top 325 companies fell by 4.2% in 1989, the pay of CEOs increased by 8.0%. Looking at the performance of individual CEOs reveals similar discrepancies between marginal product theory and the real world. Between the years 1987 and 1989, Lee Iacocca, chairman of Chrysler Corporation, earned more than $25-million even though the return on investment by Chrysler's owners went down 10%. During those same years, Albert Ueltschi was paid a little over $700,000 by Flight Safety International. But their owners received more than a 200% return on their investment!

What accounts for such a wide discrepancy between theory and actuality? Many critics have argued that the problem ultimately stems from the separation between the ownership of a corporation (the stockholders) and the control of a corporation (the management).

On paper the way a modern corporation works is like this: Top management is hired and controlled by the board of directors and the directors are elected by the shareholders. Thus, the owners of the company have theoretical control over their investment. But in point of fact, boards of directors have neither the time nor access to the information necessary to exercise effective review of managements' actions, and thus boards are typically no more than a rubber stamp of management's decisions.

The problem is exacerbated by the fact that most shareholders in all modern corporations are not individual investors carefully choosing the best directors to watch over their investment. Instead, most stock in a large corporation is controlled by groups of investors (mutual funds) or insurance companies, and this removes management from ownership by yet another step.

When one considers that 80% of all employment in the United States is in corporations with 20 or more employees, the discrepancy between contribution and compensation that seems to exist in corporate America is certainly of more than academic interest.

IS WELFARE A RIGHT OR A PRIVILEGE?

Welfare is another place where questions of distributive justice touch real people. Those receiving public assistance are touched directly; those paying taxes are touched indirectly.

And how hard are these respective groups touched? Many people believe that welfare payments make up a significant portion of the federal budget and, thus, that taxpayers would be significantly affected by any reduction of these payments. While nearly half of the federal budget is spent on transfer payments from the federal government to individuals or corporations, only 15% of those payments are *Endnote 31* made to the poor. Most of the rest is spent on non-needy seniors, both retirees and Medicare claimants. Thus, any changes made in transfer payments to the poor are going to directly affect them much more than they will indirectly affect taxpayers.

One way to get at philosophically important issues in this case is by asking: Is welfare a right or a privilege? (See discussion in Chapter 15.) If it is a "right," then it can be nothing other than a person's need which has created that right. A person does not lose his right to a fair trial if he is lazy or unwilling to work up to his full potential. Likewise, if a certain minimal income is everyone's right, then it cannot legitimately be withheld because a person is deemed morally unworthy.

However, if welfare is a privilege or a form of charity, then the moral worth and behavior of the person on welfare becomes a legitimate criterion for withholding welfare payments. Is the person making a reasonable effort to support herself and her family? And does the person make good use of the funds she receives? If so, then public assistance seems a legitimate use of public funds; if not, then it is not a legitimate use of such funds.

If the history of American jurisprudence on this issue is any indication of public opinion, then our view of welfare has evolved over the last century, but it has yet to reach a stage of clarity and coherence.

Welfare a Privilege

At the beginning of this century, any attempt by legislators to pass laws protecting the health and welfare of even the working poor was looked on by the courts as a violation of property rights and the "due process" clause of the Fourteenth Amendment. In 1905, for example, the U.S. Supreme Court considered legislation passed by the State of New York designed to protect the health and safety of employees by limiting the number of hours (in this case, to 60) they could be obligated to work by contract. Lochner, a bakery owner, filed suit charging that the law had infringed upon the freedom of individuals to freely make and enter enforceable contracts. The majority in *Lochner vs. New York* agreed and struck down the New York law, writing: "The general right to make a contract in relation to his business is part of the liberty of the individual protected by the 14th Amendment to the Federal Constitution." In one of his famous dissenting opinions, Justice Holmes retorted that "the Constitution is not intended to embody a particular economic theory, whether of paternalism and the organic relation of the citizen to the state or of laissez faire."

Welfare a Right

By the 1970s, the court's and public's attitude had changed considerably. Not only had laws protecting the health and welfare of the working poor become generally accepted, but largely as a result of President Roosevelt's "New Deal" and President Johnson's "Great Society," government-funded programs to help the non-working poor became common.

In 1970 the Supreme Court once again considered a New York case. The issue this time was whether the state could terminate Aid to Families with Dependent Children (AFDC) payments without a full legal hearing. The administrators of New York's program argued that they could because welfare was a privilege, not a right.

The Supreme Court disagreed with New York, saying that welfare payments were entitlements more like "property than a gratuity" and therefore protected by the "due process" clause of the 14th Amendment. Furthermore, the court argued on sociological grounds that "we have come to recognize that forces not within the control of the poor contribute to their poverty" and on moral grounds that "public assistance, then, is not mere charity, but a means to 'promote the general Welfare, and secure the Blessing of Liberty to ourselves and our Posterity.'"

Endnote 32

Recent Ambiguity Over Right or Privilege

In *Wyman vs. James* the court wrote: "One who dispenses purely private charity naturally has an interest in and expects to know how his charitable funds are utilized and put to work. The public, when it is the provider, rightly expects the same." Given the court's indecision on this question, it is not surprising that the public at large has been unclear about the nature of welfare.

Endnote 33

INTERNATIONAL PERSPECTIVES

Though poverty is clearly a problem in the United States, only a tiny percentage of Americans are living in absolute poverty, i.e., poverty that constitutes an immediate and direct threat to a person's life. However, when considering the problem of poverty in lesser developed countries, those percentages change significantly. Every year throughout the past decade 18–20 million people died as a direct result of insufficient food and lack of clean water. That is more than twice the number of persons who died in all of World War II. As one person put it, "This death toll is equivalent to the number killed instantly by a Hiroshima bomb every two days."

Endnote 34

Of course, the fact that many people die from malnutrition does not by itself constitute a moral problem. A large number of people die each year from cancer and other untreatable diseases. But cancer deaths (as a whole) constitute a scientific problem, not a moral problem, because, based on our present knowledge, most forms of cancer are neither preventable nor treatable. However, given the huge surplus of grain around the world, not to mention the millions of Americans who are suffering from "overnutrition," the death of millions from malnutrition does seem to be preventable and, hence, a fit topic to be morally explored.

WORLD POVERTY:
THE MALTHUSIANS VS. THE DEVELOPMENTALISTS

Malthus's Essay on Population

Yet, appearances are sometimes deceptive. Shortly after Adam Smith sang the praises of industrial capitalism in the *Wealth of Nations*, Thomas Malthus (1766–1834) played a dirge in his *Essay on Population*. In that book, Malthus argued that no matter how productive and efficient an economy became, there would always be a significant number of deaths from starvation and malnutrition given the lack of sexual restraint by the lower classes.

The problem, said Malthus, is that agricultural output at best increases at an arithmetic ratio, but population tends naturally to double after each generation and, hence, increases at a geometric ratio. "Taking the population of the world at any number . . . the human species would increase in the ratio of 1, 2, 4, 8, 16, 32, 64, 128, 256, 512, etc. and subsistence as 1, 2, 3, 4, 5, 6, 7, 8, 9, 10, etc. In two centuries and a quarter the population would be to the means of subsistence as 512 to 10; in three centuries as 4,096 to 13, and in 2,000 years the difference would be incalculable."

Endnote 35

Malthus concluded: "The power of population is so superior to the power of the Earth to provide subsistence, that premature death must in some shape or other visit the human race." Maybe those deaths would be caused by war or maybe by disease. But if we should ever succeed in eliminating these, then "gigantic inevitable famine stalks in the rear, and with one mighty blow, levels the population with the food of the world."

Endnote 36

The Neo-Malthusians — Garrett Hardin

Malthus's perspective on population and world hunger has been adopted and defended by contemporary thinkers. One of the most clearly identifiable neo-Malthusians is Garrett Hardin. Trained as a biologist, Hardin has argued both in the popular press and in more scholarly essays and books that the unchecked growth human population constitutes a serious threat to the Earth's fragile ecosystem.

Many people have likened the Earth to a giant spaceship. Because we all live on the same Earth, unless we take care of it and all its passengers, all of us will inevitably suffer the consequences. Hardin argues that this metaphor is quite misleading and even dangerous. Spaceships have a captain with coercive powers to insure that all aboard the spaceship act in a responsible fashion. The Earth has no such captain.

Rather than being like a spaceship, Hardin says, the Earth is more like a lifeboat — both have a limited carrying capacity. It is self-defeating to let more people on board a lifeboat than it can safely carry. To allow 110 to climb aboard a boat that is made for 100 persons is not being generous to the last 10 persons. Now, all aboard are likely to die. Similarly, it is self-defeating for affluent countries to continue to send food to nations that are chronically suffering from hunger. There is nothing generous, says Hardin, about affluent countries shipping food relief to countries with chronic food shortages. Such charity and foreign aid only encourages these countries to continue their irresponsible population growth. Sooner or latter, population will exceed Earth's carrying capacity and the empirical evidence, says Hardin, demonstrates that we are fast approaching that point.

The problem with foreign aid and private famine relief is that it ends in "the tragedy of the commons." "A farmer," Hardin writes, "will allow no more cattle in a pasture than its carrying capacity justifies. If he overloads it, erosion sets in, weeds take over, and he loses the use of the pasture. If a pasture becomes a commons open to all, the right of each to use it may not be matched by a corresponding responsibility to protect it." To treat the agricultural resources of the affluent nations as resources to be shared equally by all people will

Endnote 37

inevitability lead to tragedy. Once the ecological balance of the Earth is destroyed by the scourge of overpopulation, we will all perish.

The only solution, according to Hardin and other neo-Malthusians, is to adopt a "triage policy." Those countries which will survive without our aid don't need it; those countries that are perennially poverty stricken should be allowed to perish — to provide aid will only prolong their suffering or destroy the whole Earth. Only those countries suffering the temporary effects of some natural disaster should receive our charity or foreign aid.

CRITIQUE OF MALTHUS: THE DEVELOPMENTALISTS

Neo-Malthusians emphasize overpopulation as the primary cause of world hunger. Their critics are often called developmentalists. According to developmentalists, the primary cause of world hunger is injustice. While Hardin says that the empirical data show that the Earth is fast approaching its "carrying capacity," developmentalists like Lappe and Collins dispute such data. They write:

> The world today produces enough grain alone to provide every human being on the planet with 3,600 calories a day. That's enough to make most people fat! And this estimate does not even count the many other commonly eaten foods — vegetables, beans, nuts, root crops, fruits, grass-fed meats, and fish. Abundance, not scarcity, best describes the supply of food in the world today. Rarely has the world seen such a glut of food looking for buyers. Increases in food production during the past 25 years have outstripped the world's unprecedented population growth by about 16%. Indeed, mountains of unsold grain on world markets have pushed prices downward over the past three decades.

Endnote 38

The reason people are dying of malnutrition, say developmentalists, is the gross inequality in the distribution of food produced by our planet. In 1989 the world had 157 billionaires, perhaps 2-million millionaires, and 100-million homeless. Moreover, the inequality has been increasing during the past decade. World Bank figures suggest that the global poverty rate declined steadily up to 1980 when it reached its low point of 22.3% of the global population. That trend was reversed in the mid-80s and has now climbed up to 23.4%.

Endnote 39

Developmentalists are also quick to point out that the industrialized countries of the West are not nearly as generous and self-sufficient as we like to believe. The United States, for example, allocates a mere fifth of one percent of its gross development product (GDP) to developmental assistance. Furthermore, the vast majority of that money is distributed for wholly political reasons. Less than five percent of all bilateral economic assistance in fiscal year 1985 went to the world's two poorest countries. And during the past three decades the industrialized countries of the West have consistently imported more food from the less-developed countries than it has exported to them.

Endnote 40
Endnote 41

Though there are no longer any colonial empires, developmentalists argue that the West has continued to exploit the resources of the Third World with little concern for the well-being of the people living there. The island of Mindanao in the Philippines constitutes a single case in point. Prior to the mid-1960s, small farms produced a large variety of crops on the island for consumption by the local farmers. That changed radically when Del Monte, Dole, and other multinational corporations began offering contracts to the area's largest landowners to grow bananas for export to Japan. The Japanese are now able to purchase cheap produce, the large corporations have improved their earnings ratio, and those who labor in the fields earn less than a dollar a day and are regularly exposed to pesticides.

Endnote 42

COMPARING MALTHUSIAN AND DEVELOPMENTALIST VIEWS

Even though neo-Malthusians and developmentalists approach the problem of world hunger from quite different perspectives, they nonetheless agree on a couple of points. First, they both support increased developmental assistance to help underdeveloped countries raise capital and improve agricultural techniques because both appreciate the truth of the Chinese proverb: Give a man a fish and you'll feed him for a day; teach him to fish and you'll feed him for a lifetime. Furthermore, both understand the care with which such aid needs to be distributed. Too often in the past it ended up in the hands of corrupt governments and the ruling oligarchy instead of helping to alleviate hunger.

Second, neo-Malthusians and developmentalists both agree on the appropriateness of emergency famine or disaster relief to help less-developed countries meet a particular problem. The fundamental disagreement concerns the chronically malnourished countries. Neo-Malthusians argue that foreign aid should be withheld unless coercive measures are introduced to bring about reduced population growth. Aid for such countries only makes the problem worse and will in fact increase suffering in the long run.

Developmentalists resist coercive measures. Instead, they argue that history demonstrates that as food supplies increase and become more secure, population growth naturally decreases. When Western countries industrialized there was a "demographic transition" during which birth rates fell sharply without any coercive restraints being imposed. The reasons are manifold. In a pre-industrial farm economy even young children are an economic asset because they produce more than they consume. Children are also the only support parents have in their old age. Finally, a "lottery mentality" is associated with poverty everywhere. No matter how long the odds, the hope is that the next child will be the one who is clever and bright enough to get an education, land a job in the city, and be able to support the entire family.

FINAL COMMENTS

What are we obligated to do? While everyone thus agrees that there is much that can be done, there remains a further question: What are we in the West morally required to do? In recent years, this question has been addressed from both a utilitarian and Kantian point of view.

The Utilitarian View of Peter Singer

A contemporary defender of utilitarianism, Singer has summarized his argument like this:

* First premise: If we can prevent something bad without sacrificing anything of comparable moral significance, we ought to do it.
* Second premise: Absolute poverty is bad.
* Third premise: There is some absolute poverty we can prevent without sacrificing anything of comparable moral significance.
* Conclusion: We ought to prevent some absolute poverty.

The justification of the first premise is implicit, says Singer, in the following sort of example: Suppose I am walking to class in a new pair of wingtip shoes. Along the path I see a small child face down in the middle of a two-foot deep pond struggling to catch a breath. It would be easy for me to walk out and save the child's life, yet it would undoubtedly ruin my new shoes. However, only the most morally corrupt would contend that I am not obligated to sacrifice my shoes to save the child's life.

Endnote 43

The second premise Singer takes to be virtually self-evident.

Some people might object to the third premise on the ground that there will always be poor people and thus it is impossible to eliminate poverty. However, the third premise doesn't require that absolute poverty be totally eliminated. It only requires that as long as some absolute poverty is preventable without sacrificing something else of comparable moral significance, then our obligation to help the poor remains.

Given these premises, the conclusion is logically inescapable. However, a neo-Malthusian objection remains. Hardin, for example, would argue that in many cases helping those in absolute poverty does cost something of comparable moral significance, namely, the future death of even more people. Such an objection clearly presupposes a utilitarian ethical theory, and Singer is happy to meet it on those grounds. All calculations of the consequences of action necessarily concern probabilities. Says Singer: "Better one certain unit of benefit than a 10% chance of 5 units; but better a 50% chance of 3 units than a single certain unit. The same principle applies when we are trying to avoid evils."

The slow and painful death by famine and disease of millions this year is a certain evil if we do nothing. But the future growth of populations a generation from now to an absolutely unmanageable size is based on forecasts that are notoriously fallible. In the early 1970s, for example, the population of mainland China was 830-million. Population experts were then predicting that by 1990 it would top 1.3-billion. In fact, it only reached 1.1-billion. That's an error of 57% in less than 20 years. For reasons like these, and because Singer believes there is strong evidence to support the "demographic transition" theory mentioned above, he believes that Hardin's prediction of worldwide disaster in the future is at best uncertain. Therefore, it is argued, a 10% chance of future disaster ought not to deter us from acting to prevent the certain death of millions this year.

Endnote 44

Kant and Shue

Henry Shue argues from an essentially Kantian perspective that we all have a fundamental moral obligation to alleviate world hunger. Shue defines a basic right as any right that would be self-defeating to sacrifice for the enjoyment of some other right. For example, if a soldier is caught behind enemy lines during a war, he may willingly forego a desire to sing "The Battle Hymn of the Republic." His basic right to physical security is obviously more important than his right to free speech. Furthermore, it would be no violation of anyone else's right if one soldier forcefully prevented another soldier from exercising his right to free speech in similar situations. Without physical security, no other rights are of any value.

Thus, the right to physical security is more basic than the right to free speech because the right to free speech requires physical security. It makes no sense to sacrifice physical security to obtain a right to free speech. If a person's right to physical security is not guaranteed, then everyone else is free to shoot him the moment he chooses to exercise his right to free speech. Obviously, placing free speech before physical security on any list of rights is self-defeating.

Shue then argues that "the same considerations that support the conclusion that physical security is a basic right support the conclusion that subsistence (minimal economic security) is a basic right." If a person is so emaciated from lack of food that he hasn't the strength to speak, then his right to free speech is defeated. Therefore, if there are any rights, then there must be the basic right to minimal economic security.

Endnote 45

Finally, Shue argues that all rights attach to human beings as humans, and not to members of a particular racial group or national state. This means that if any person has a right, then all persons have the same right. Combining these two conditional statements, Shue concludes that if any person has any rights, then all people have a basic right to minimal economic security. Because every right carries with it a corresponding duty for others not to infringe upon that right, Shue believes we all have an obligation to

1) *avoid* depriving the poor of the means of obtaining subsistence through structural injustices;

2) *protect* the poor from others who would deprive people of the only available means of subsistence, and

Endnote 46

3) *aid* those who are unable to provide for their own subsistence.

There is nothing in the United States Constitution or Bill of Rights which guarantees basic rights as Shue conceives of them. "The United Nations Universal Declaration of Human Rights" is much broader. When it was adopted by the General Assembly of the United Nations in 1948, it called upon all member countries to publicize the rest of the Declaration and "to cause it to be disseminated, displayed, read and expounded principally in schools and other educational institutions." It thus seems appropriate to close with selections from this document:

ARTICLE 23

1. Everyone has the right to work, to free choice of employment, to just and favorable conditions of work and to protection against unemployment . . .

3. Everyone who works has the right to just and favorable remuneration ensuring for himself and his family an existence worthy of human dignity . . .

ARTICLE 25

1. Everyone has the right to a standard of living adequate for the health and well-being of himself and of his family, including food, clothing, housing and medical care and necessary social services. . . .

FOR FURTHER INQUIRY

REVIEW QUESTIONS

---

1. Assume for purposes of discussion that we lived in a society committed to redistributing resources so as to make the worst off in the society as well off as possible. Once this is done, we discover that certain people — for reasons that may be genetic, psychological, or physical — are inclined to work much harder than the average while others work much less than the average. Would the inequalities that then result be

considered fair or would society have to continually readjust to make those who are worst off do better?

2. Read the following case and respond to the questions below:

YORK INTERNATIONAL: TRADING LIVES

The economic pressure on York International was great. Foreign imports had significantly reduced their share of the domestic automobile market to the point where York's survival as a corporation depended on the success of the newly designed Jupiter. The normal three years it took from the initial concept to the finished product had been squeezed to 18 months. Market tests indicated that the Jupiter had successfully anticipated new consumer preferences, and York International was eight months to a year ahead of its foreign competitors. In fact, production had already begun and the first Jupiters would be in the showrooms in a couple of months.

It was under these circumstances that the CEO of York and a handful of top executives were faced with an agonizing decision: A memo from the chief design engineer of the Jupiter revealed that a design flaw would cause the air bags to fail in approximately one out of every 250 head-on crashes. The mistake could be corrected, but it would cost millions to retool and would delay sales for at least six months.

After the top legal and marketing executives were consulted, the options were quickly reduced to two: First, continue production, re-establish market share and the profitability of the company, and then pay generous settlements if (when?) suits are brought against the company. Second, recall the Jupiter, discontinue production during retooling and almost certainly face the demise of York International. The CEO of York chose the former.

Three years later, after York had re-established itself as a viable company, the CEO of York read the following statement at a news conference prior to beginning his five- to 10-year sentence at the federal penitentiary:

"While I have broken the law, my conscience is clear. The livelihood of thousands of employees was on the line three years ago. Life is tragic. Either option was sure to cause great pain. My critics will retort: Human life is priceless; no purely economic advantage will ever outweigh the loss of even a single life. But that is simply not true. First, there is no such thing as a purely economic advantage. When 10,000 employees lose their jobs, it is statistically certain that there will be one or two suicides, hundreds of divorces, and the neglect or abuse of thousands of children. Second, our economic system continually engages in cost-benefit analysis. We trade tobacco subsidies for cancer deaths; the reduction of air traffic controllers for airline accidents; and political expediency for the lives of famine-stricken children in foreign countries when their governments vote against us in the United Nations. My decision was no more immoral than any of these and the countless others that all politicians and business executives make at least once in their lives."

a. Was the CEO of York International correct when he said that there is no such thing as a purely economic advantage? Is he correct to suggest that all major economic decisions inevitably involve matters of life and death?

b. The CEO's second argument seems to be open to the objection that "two wrongs don't make a right." But if we make such an objection, does moral consistency demand that we also become actively involved in correcting the other abuses of economic power mentioned above?

c. If the CEO of York were a conscientious utilitarian, how might he have acted? A conscientious Kantian? A conscientious communitarian?

ENDNOTES

1. U.S. Bureau of the Census, Statistical Abstract of the United States: 1992 (112th edition). Washington, DC, 1992. p. 454.

2. Robert Nozick, *Anarchy, State and Utopia*. (New York: Basic Books), 1974.

2a. Nozick, p. 151.

3. Nozick, p. 175–176.

4. Nozick, p. 179, 178.

5. Nozick, p. 176.

6. Nozick, p. 176.

7. Nozick, p. 177.

8. Nozick, p. 288.

9. Plato, *Laws* (Bk. 5). Penguin Classics, 1970. p. 215.

10. Nozick, p. 164.

11. John Rawls, *A Theory of Justice*. (Cambridge: Harvard University Press, 1971).

11a. Rawls, p. 12.

12. Rawls, p. 15.

13. Rawls, p. 60.

14. Rawls, p. 432.

15. Mortimer J. Adler, *Six Great Ideas*. (New York: Macmillan, 1981). p. 141.

16. Aristotle, *Nicomachean Ethics* (Book 1, sec. 3. line 1094b 23–27). Martin Ostwald, translator. Library of Liberal Arts, (New York: Bobbs-Merrill, 1962). p. 5.

17. For Plato, cf. note 9; for current figures cf. *Business Week* (May 1, 1989), p. 146.

18. Robert N. Bellah, *The Broken Covenant*. (New York: Seabury Press, 1975). p. 134.

19. Carl Cohen, *Four Systems*. (New York: Random House, 1982). p. 42.

20. Thomas Aquinas, *Summa Theologica*. (II–II, Question 66, Art. 7)

21. R. H. Tawney, *Religion and the Rise of Capitalism*. (New York: Penguin, 1947). p. 221.

22. Statistical Abstract, p. 462. Before welfare and taxes the numbers are: 1.1% for the bottom fifth and 50.7% for the top fifth.

23. Milton Fisk, *Ethics and Society*. (New York: New York University Press, 1980). pp. 224–225.

24. Another advantage is that this method facilitates international comparisons. In Japan and West Germany the bottom fifth earned 9% and 8% respectively, while the top fifth earned 37% and 40% (Lester R. Brown, *State of the World 1990*, p. 138). Thus, two of our chief economic competitors have equity ratios of between 4 and 5, while we have an (after taxes) equity ratio of 8.5.

25. Kevin Phillips, *The Politics of Rich and Poor*. (New York: Random House, 1990). Appendix B.

26. U.S. Department of Labor, 1998.

27. Statistical Abstract, p. 458.

28. *Business Week* (May 1, 1989) p. 146.

29. Joseph Dorfman, *The Economic Mind in American Civilization: 1895–1981 vol. 3*. (New York: Viking Press, 1949). pp. 151–152.

30. George C. Lodge, *The New American Ideology* (New York: New York University Press, 1986). p. 204.

31. *U.S. News and World Report* (Oct. 31, 1988) p. 55.

32. *Goldberg vs. Kelly United States Supreme Court*. 397 U.S. 254 (1970).

33. *Wyman vs. James United States Supreme Court*. 400 U.S. 309 (1971).

34. Frances M. Lappe and Joseph Collins, *World Hunger: Twelve Myths*. (New York: Grove Press, 1986). p. 3.

35. Thomas Robert Malthus, *Population: The First Essay* (Ann Arbor: University of Michigan Press, 1959). p. 9 (chap. 2).

36. Malthus, p. 49 (chap. 7)

37. Garrett Hardin, "Lifeboat Ethics: The Case Against Helping the Poor." *Psychology Today* (1974) vol. 8.

38. Lappe, p. 9.

39. Alan B. Durning, "Ending Poverty." *State of the World: 1990*, Lester R. Brown, et. al. p. 135, 139.

40. Lappe, p. 106.

41. Ronald J. Sider, *Rich Christians in an Age of Hunger*. (Downers Grove: Inter-Varsity Press, 1984). p. 145. Cf. Lappe, p. 86ff.

42. Lappe, p. 89.

43. Peter Singer, *Practical Ethics*. (New York: Cambridge University Press, 1979). pp. 169–170.

44. Susan Greenhalgh, "Socialism and Fertility in China." *The Annals of the American Academy of Political and Social Science*. vol. 510, July 1990. p. 74.

45. Henry Shue, *Basic Rights: Subsistence, Affluence, and U.S. Foreign Policy*. (Princeton: Princeton University Press, 1980). p. 24.

46. Shue, p. 60.

Mores in the Marketplace

INTRODUCTION TO PART III:

ETHICS IN BUSINESS, THE PROFESSIONS, AND TECHNOLOGY
THE RESPONSIBILITY PERSPECTIVE

The first objective of this section is to cover the field of business, professional and government ethics, including all the major areas where ethical controversies arise in business practice; the second objective is to sketch the outlines of a vision, an ideal of practice that would be completely compatible with the moral maturity of all the individuals involved with the economic and governmental institutions with which we must deal. The extent to which this ideal might be realizable in an increasingly complex world will be the subject of the last part of the section.

Every time you pick up a piece of merchandise these days, the first thing you see is a label that says "Warning!" and another one that says "Disclaimer: . . ." and a third that says "Caution: This product is not intended to . . ." Then it is appropriate for a section on the ethics of business, the professions, and government — three of the most distrusted areas of American life — to start off with disclaimers and warning labels, for the benefit of all consumers of this volume.

First disclaimer: we will not repeat the theoretical ethics material of the first section of the book; you're just going to have to remember it. The theories we are most likely to refer to are the **Utilitarianism** of Jeremy Bentham and John Stuart Mill, the **deontology** of Immanuel Kant, and occasionally the theory of **justice** of John Rawls. Beyond that, we will refer on occasion to the principled duties of beneficence, of justice, and of respect for persons; of the imperative to cultivate virtues appropriate to one's occupations; and of the general relational duties of **care** and compassion. So that you may be forewarned, the thread of ethical theory that this account of business, professional and government ethics is most likely to follow is the centrality of human **autonomy, choice, freedom and responsibility**, foreshadowed by Immanuel Kant.

"Responsibility" may mean many things: it may designate an assigned task ("He is *responsible* for cleaning the third floor of the building"), a hierarchy of authority ("He is *responsible* to the building janitor"), accountability for some event ("He is *responsible* for the cleaning fluid getting into the third floor smoke alarm"), culpability ("and the janitor intends to hold him *responsible* for that,"), and liability ("and make him pay for the Fire Department's answering a false alarm"). To "assume responsibility" means to acknowledge any or all of those. "Responsibility" also refers to a trait of character, combining **prudence** (the tendency to think ahead, to foresee any bad outcomes of your actions, and to act to avoid them), **reliability** (the disposition to keep your word and to do what is expected of you), **concern and compassion** for others (the ability, and willingness, to imagine the consequences for others of any of your actions), and the **integrity and courage** to make your actions, with all their consequences, your own (despite any pain or embarrassment it may cause you). A "responsible" person is one who recognizes and assumes responsibility for those areas of activity within his or her power and right.

2-19

CHAPTER 17

DOING RIGHT IN BUSINESS

"We demand that big business give the people a square deal; in return we must insist that when anyone engaged in big business honestly endeavors to do right, he shall himself be given a square deal."

— ***Theodore Roosevelt***

"You can tell the ideals of a nation by its advertisements."

— ***Norman Douglas***

Why is it so much fun to describe "business ethics" as an oxymoron (a contradiction in terms), and pretend that all business persons are greedy graspers who will gladly sell their own grandmothers to improve **the bottom line**? (Literally, the final line on the quarterly income statement; figuratively, the net profit or loss in dollar terms for any person or company.) There is little evidence that those who make a living in the business world are any better or worse than those of us who, for instance, teach in college; so why the prejudice? In this section we will try to set out the moral configuration of business as a whole, as conceived by philosophers and economists who have tried to understand it as a whole. We will try to see why we might be disposed to view business as somehow fundamentally good or otherwise, and if business turns out to be a moral enterprise, we will look for the central moral principles on which its goodness rests. In later sections we will try to understand the moral dimensions of business from the perspective of those who practice it.

BUSINESS AS MORAL ENTERPRISE

We will conduct this exploration in several steps. The first series of steps will trace the roots of the inherited moral opposition to business enterprise, the nature of work and the growth of the work ethic, the growth of the city and of commerce, the establishment of the rights of private property and contract, the discovery of the potential of the

Lisa H. Newton, Ph.D., is Professor of Philosophy and Director of the Program in Applied Ethics at Fairfield University in Fairfield, Connecticut. She is author or co-author of several textbooks in the fields of Ethics and Environmental Studies, and has a faculty appointment in the Department of Medicine at Yale Medical School for the teaching of medical ethics.

free market, and the emergence of business as a critical arena of moral growth and accomplishment, a place for the exercise of autonomy, prudence and responsibility. The second series will trace the birth of the modern corporation, the effects of the factory system, the separation of ownership and control, and the foundations of the moral dilemmas that confront business now.

Aristotle and the Ancient World's Class System

If there may be a prejudice against the possibility of morality in business bred in our bones, it may be useful first to find out where that prejudice came from (and therefore what of it we should retain in our contemporary critiques of business). The Greek philosopher Aristotle (4th century B.C.) was the first to attack the foundations of the marketplace. In the first book of the *Politics*, where he discusses the laws of the household (*OEconomica*), he distinguishes the worthy occupations by which a man may support his family from the unworthy ones. Hunting in all its varieties is worthy; fighting is worthy; farming and animal husbandry are worthy; ruling is worthy, and certain kinds of crafts will qualify. All forms of commerce are unworthy, with retail trade and banking catching the worst opprobrium. Why banking? Because in the practice of usury (collecting interest on loans) it allows money to make more money, "as if cold metal could breed!" Why retail trade? Because it focused a man's mind on money, and petty gain, and hoarding, and getting more, and all that was thoroughly bad for the character. Crafts, which focused on beauty, were acceptable; farming and herding, which produced necessary food in cooperation with nature, were good; and hunting, with the contest of skill and strength between hunter and prey, was positively ennobling, as was any military endeavor. As a final insult, Aristotle classifies piracy — freebooting — as a form of hunting, and therefore a worthy occupation, as if the merchant, along with all his goods and employees, were just another prey animal to be slaughtered for the hunter's enrichment.

Why was Aristotle so intolerant of business folk? It has been said that he was just a man of his time: The landed aristocracy, to which he belonged (or whom he served), had total contempt for the Athenian merchants, whom they regarded as an alien and inferior race given to taking advantage of honest farmers even as they traded the Athenian crops; misunderstanding and mistrust between rural areas and urban, farmers and bankers, continues to this day, often with good cause. Actually, Aristotle was a man well past his time; even as he wrote, Athens was a cosmopolitan city with a bustling worldwide trade, carried on by some of the most astute merchants the world has

CHIEF LEARNING OUTCOME

I understand the concept of corporations and professions and am able to discuss various moral theories as they apply to business decisions.

ever known. Aristotle was not describing the society in which he lived, but one that he preferred. Yet his inherited prejudice, against any occupation that dealt not with natural goods but with the institutions that traded in them, carried the day: The Roman Church adopted the prohibition on usury, and by doing that, significantly slowed the growth of commerce in the Middle Ages.

The Monastic Movement and the Work Ethic

At the end of what we know as the Ancient Period in Western History, about 500 A.D., the two social classes that Aristotle knew were firmly in place: there was a horseback aristocracy, ruling and fighting and playing and living on the labor of slaves and hired labor, and there was everyone else: merchants, craftsmen, farmers, and all manner of workers. Some of the merchants were very rich; but money could not get them out of the disgrace of working for a living. Then, in 529 A.D., **St. Benedict** founded a Christian monastery at Montecassino. It wasn't the first celibate colony founded for the purpose of religious retreat and enlightenment (many religious sects had those), but it was one of the first Christian ones, and it made a difference: Benedict's idea was that instead of merely begging to support a life of prayer and meditation, his monks should work in the fields and at other tasks, to teach them humility. His model was the arresting figure of Jesus, towel wrapped around his waist, washing the feet of his disciples — the task assigned to the lowest of the servants in the Judean household. As a rule for Benedict's monks, the work assignments made sense: At first, most of them were from the ruling class, and working in the fields was the most humiliating thing they could think of. To leap forward almost a millennium, most of the monasteries that were formed in the first 1500 years of

KEY CONCEPTS

Corporation — for profit, is a venture financed by investors (the people who put their money into the venture, at the outset or later on) for the purpose of making more money, getting a return on investment (ROI) as great or greater than they could get in any other allotment of their money.

Contract — is an agreement — a *quid pro quo*, mutual promising of something in exchange for something else — to mutual performance of some specific commitments.

Trade — is the willing exchange with another for the purpose of advancing one's own interests; it is the fundamental "capitalist act."

Categorical Imperatives — are rules that always define appropriate conduct; e.g., "Don't kill anyone, ever."

Hypothetical Imperatives — are rules for what to do in order to achieve certain goals; e.g., "Eat an apple a day to stay healthy."

A Profession — briefly, an occupational group distinguished from others by possession of a constellation of standards, more or less central to its operations.

A Fiduciary Obligation — is a duty that professionals have toward their clients to make each decision for the client's best interests and welfare, not the professional's own.

Christendom taught their novices that for the sake of service to the Lord, it was appropriate to imitate Jesus in the cheerful performance of all useful menial tasks — in short, to work. They did this work as part of their **vocation** (literally, "calling," the life that they felt the Lord wanted them to live), and so the work became noble and good. This ethic, that embraced hard work in the world as something ennobling and even holy, played a vital part in the growth of the industrial civilization that followed.

Guilds and Burghers

Deprived during the Dark Ages of Medieval Europe of the rich urban patrons of the ancient world, skilled craftsmen — builders, carpenters, metalworkers, weavers, tailors, candlemakers, glassblowers and the like — had gathered into guilds (associations formed for mutual protection and the increased prosperity of the craft, rather along the lines of early trade unions). When prosperity began to return to Europe, toward the end of the 12th century, it created among the wealthier nobles and their families a market for the goods of the far East — silks and spices, ivory and aromatic woods. A new class of merchants and traders arose, to finance expeditions, by land and water, to the East and to sell the goods when they arrived in Europe.

Part of the history of the European Jews begins at this point: Unconstrained by the Aristotelian limits of the Roman Church, Jews could lend money at interest, and were essential as financial backers of these expeditions. The merchants, agents and beneficiaries of that prosperity, soon formed a new class, a "middle" class between the feudal knights and the serfs who worked the land as tenant farmers. The merchants set up their headquarters on the trade routes, and the craftsmen joined them. Where trade was heavy, gold was sure to be found, and bandits became interested; it was necessary to put strong walls around these towns to keep the bandits out, and the burg (walled town) became the center of business enterprise. Hence the common name for the middle class, the owners of banks and manufacturing establishments: the ***bourgeoisie,*** or "burghers."

Contract: A Voluntary Commitment

What did these merchants have to guarantee that the ship they sent off to Heaven knows where off in the East would return to them, at least if it survived the ocean's storms, and that they would get the profit from the goods brought back? Very little, actually, except the power of the word — the captain's *promise* that in return for a salary, or a share of the profit, he would not run off with the goods and sell them somewhere else. The agreement made — *quid pro quo,* mutual promising, an agreement to mutual performance of some specific agreement — was a **contract**.

Endnote 5

There had been contracts in the ancient world, of course, but through the intervening ages, Europe had relied entirely on authority, of Church or Feudal Lord, or tradition, to command performance. But there was no tradition for the commercial class; they had to make up their own ways of cooperating. So a series of contracts bound together the banker, who put up the funds for the voyage, the merchant who ordered the goods, the captain who set sail with European products in trade, and the distant merchants in storied lands who supplied the riches of the East for transport. The contract then was a chancy thing at best, with so much time and distance between agreement and performance. But enough of them worked so that the practice, of contract and performance, became an established way to conduct the business of business; by now, it is second nature, and one of the strongest moral obligations we acknowledge, in or out of business.

Private Property

Come to think of it, a contract is indeed a powerful thing. We all know about moral obligations — thou shalt do no murder, thou shalt not steal, *et cetera*. **Moral obligations are non-optional** (you don't have any choice about being bound by them), and everlasting: As long as families exist, there will be an obligation to take care of the children and honor the father and mother. **But a contract is optional**. You don't have to agree to a contract. But if you do agree, then you are under a very strong moral obligation to fulfill it — all the stronger because it was of your own free will that you made it. In a world whose major ancient institutions were dying or paralyzed in the throes of change, a world flooded with new possibilities, Europe suddenly discovered a moral principle capable of handling all novel circumstances, one that could engage human reason to decide the patterns of human conduct. Europe emerged into the modern age convinced that this notion of "contract" could underlie all moral obligation and political theory.

Accordingly, when the major political thinkers of our immediate tradition — the political thinkers of the modern age — undertook to challenge the sacred authority of the Church and the Divine Right of Kings, they imported the commercial notion of contract to justify the political authority of the state over the citizen. **Thomas Hobbes** (1588–1679) was among the first to propose that Society (all organized human life) should be seen as the product of an agreement among freely contracting parties, to get them out of a chaotic and violent "state of nature," characterized by Hobbes as "the war of all against all." Once humans realize that it is not in their interest to spend all day in lethal competition for the bare necessities of life, they will agree to recognize a Sovereign, the State (or King), who will set the rules and whom they will obey. Never mind if the Sovereign's laws be just! Peace is the point, and any rule is better than the anarchy from which they came.

John Locke (1632–1704), whom we met in Chapter 16, held a view of human nature much more optimistic than that of his earlier countryman. Locke allowed that people could live in peace with only natural reason to guide them. Most of us seem to live under the *Natural Law* (regarding it as a fixed order of eternal laws, proceeding from an understanding of God's Mind and binding on all humans forever, but accessible to human reason) and can figure out our major duties from that. Of course, the Natural Law will not protect property or civil rights. The boundaries of a parcel of land are arbitrary from God's perspective, as are the rights of neighbors along a riverbank or claimants of air rights in New York City. To provide for settled laws on these subjects, to establish impartial judges, and to create a fair and efficient enforcement procedure, Civil Government is essential; so Locke argues in his *Second Treatise from Two Treatises of Government*). But because we certainly don't want to give up any of the primary rights we had in Nature — the right to life, the right to liberty, e.g. — the government Locke wants to establish will be a very limited government, possessed only of those powers that the people elect to give it. It will be a republic, electing representatives to a common parliament or other decision-making body, making decisions by majority rule. It sounds very like the English government after the Glorious Revolution of 1688; Locke's treatises appeared in 1690, and are generally supposed to be his attempt to defend that Revolution.

Endnote 6

How may people acquire property in the State of Nature? For Hobbes, people seize what they can, but the Sovereign can overrule them if he wants it himself, or by extension to today, the state can overrule if it can establish an overriding interest of all citizens. In Locke there is no such sovereign (or governmental right). People acquire property by using it, by "mixing their labor" with it, and they are free to take from the common stock of unowned land as much as they can use (and no more), as long as they leave "enough and as good" for the next person who comes along. Once it's theirs, it's theirs by **entitlement** (right); no one may take it from them without their consent.

There are a host of exceptions to that rule — the state may levy taxes and take a portion of the property, the state may occupy land by eminent domain as long as it compensates the owner, and so forth. But the property owner gets to vote on any laws by which he may be deprived of property, and the law will protect him in the safe enjoyment of the rest of it, and protect his right to transfer it by gift, sale, or bequest, any time he wants to do that. As Locke saw it, the rights he defended as Natural were part and parcel of each other: the rights to Life and Liberty were fundamental (no other rights made sense without these), and the right to Property, Contract, and Limited Government protected the first two. Property (primarily, in the 17th century, property in land) protected a person's right to make a living and simultaneously a person's right to privacy: "A man's home is his castle," an early court had ruled, and no one could come on a man's property to spy him out without his permission. Contract protected his right to change his status — buy or sell land or a business, take a new job or hire new workers, move from one place to another — without calling on the Officers of the State to approve or veto. And Limited Government, formed only for the purpose of protecting rights, was a government that would not try to limit these rights for some imagined Public Good.

The Wealth of Nations

Most of the elements of an ethic of business had come together in the Protestant Reformation: **Martin Luther**, an ex-monk, preached that *every* person had a vocation from God, to work honestly, to produce excellent products, to earn a living by the sweat of his brow in the way for which he was best fitted. Add to that teaching the release from the Roman Church's prohibition of usury, so that bankers could now join their Jewish brethren in making commercial loans, and Protestantism dignifies the entirety of the commercial enterprise. A practical, middle-class religion, Lutheranism made enormous strides in the cities. Freed from the domain of the prevailing Church, philosophers also tried to capture the new spirit of Renaissance, Reason, and Enlightenment, and one of the best of them echoed perfectly the practical calculations of the merchants. This was **Jeremy Bentham** (1748–1832), the founder of *Utilitarianism*. [See the section on Bentham in Chapter 5.]

Writing about half a century after Locke had established Property and Representative Government on a foundation of Natural Rights, Bentham started afresh. His definitions cut through two thousand years of ethical theorizing, echoing the ethical teaching of Epicurus [See Chapter 4]. This teaching is called **hedonism**; from *'edoni*, pleasure: the belief that pleasure is the only good and pain the only evil. He needed no Divine Command or Natural Law to discern what was right: if people were made happy, enjoyed pleasure, from something, then it was good. If it caused pain, it was bad. No agonies of doubt were necessary: people are their own best judges on what is pleasurable or not, so all you have to do is ask them what they like and what they don't like and you'll know what's right and wrong. By "the Common Good" we mean no more than the sum of individual goods. To see if a proposed piece of legislation will serve the Common Good, then, all you need to do is adopt a single unit of pleasurableness (say, one hour of pleasurable consciousness for one citizen). Next you apply **utilitarian calculus** (a technique of adding units of pleasure and subtracting units of pain to come up with a Happiness bottom line, or "total utility" as we studied in Chapter 5). This leads you to achieve the total utility that will tell you not only whether, on balance, the legislation will serve the common good, but also if it will do so better than any alternative.

The moral philosopher and economist **Adam Smith** (1723–1790) proceeded to apply Bentham's assumptions to the marketplace. Let us assume, said Smith, that Bentham is right; that apart from short and rarely significant bursts of **altruism** (the motivation to help others, with no thought for oneself), people are selfish. Most people,

"Without some dissimulation, no business can be carried on at all."
— Philip Dormer Stanhope, the Earl of Chesterfield

Endnote 1

Endnote 4

most of the time, want to find pleasure and avoid pain for themselves. In the marketplace, that disposition translates into a determined effort to advance one's own interests — to become wealthier, in terms of money, goods, and enjoyments. **The fundamental "capitalist act," on this assumption is the self-interested voluntary exchange** (the willing trade with another for the purpose of advancing one's own interests).

For example, two adults, of sound mind and clear purposes, meet in the marketplace, to satisfy some felt need. They discover that each has that which will satisfy the other's need: The housewife needs flour, the miller needs cash; and they exchange, at a price such that the exchange furthers the interest of each. The *total utility* (the increase in wealth brought about by this exchange) to the participant in the free market of the thing acquired must exceed that of the thing traded, or else why would he make the deal? So each party to the voluntary exchange walks away from it richer.

Adding to the value of the exchange is the *competition of dealers and buyers*. Because there are many purveyors of each good, the customer is not forced to pay exorbitant prices for things needed. It is a sad fact of economics, that to the starving man, the marginal value of a loaf of bread is very large, and a single merchant could become unjustly rich. Conversely, *competition among the customers* (typified by an auction) makes sure that the available goods end in the hands of those to whom they are worth the most. So at the end of the market day, not only does everyone go home richer, in real terms, than when he came, the voluntary nature of the exchange ensures his success, because he had available all possible options of goods or services to buy and all possible purchasers of his goods or services for sale.

Sellers and buyers win the competition through high efficiency (ratio of quantity and quality of production to the costs of production; i.e., "the bang for the buck"). This is accomplished through producing the best quality goods at the lowest possible price, or through allotting their scarce resources toward the most valuable of the choices presented to them. It is to the advantage of all participants in the market, then, to strive for high efficiency; i.e., to keep the cost of goods for sale as low as possible while keeping the quality as high as possible. Adam Smith's most memorable accomplishment was to recognize that the general effect of all this self-interested scrambling would be to make the most possible goods of the best possible quality available at the lowest possible price. Meanwhile, sellers and buyers alike must keep an eye on the market as a whole, adjusting production and purchasing to take advantage of fluctuations in **supply and demand**. Short supply will make goods more valuable, raising the price, so the producers will make money; and that will bring more suppliers into the market, whose competition will lower the price, to just above the cost of manufacture for the most efficient producers. Increased demand for any reason will have the same effect. Should demand exceed supply, the price will rise until only as many buyers as there are products will be able to afford them. Should supply exceed demand, the price will fall to a point where the goods will be bought. Putting this all together, Smith realized that in a system of **free enterprise** (recall the term in Chapter 16?), you have demonstrably the best possible chance of finding for sale what you want, in good quantity and quality, at a reasonable price. Forget benevolent monarchs ordering things for our good, he suggested; in this system we are led as by an **"invisible hand"** to serve the common good even as we think we are being most selfish.

Smith pointed out that certain *virtues* are presupposed by the operations of the free market. These excellences include traits of character that enhance an individual's ability to perform his duties, live well and serve the public good; see Chapter 4. The whole system will not work at all unless the participants are *honest* in word and deed — that is, they tell the *truth*, especially about the invisible properties of their products for sale, they *pay their debts and honor their contracts*. The capitalism that he describes will not, in fact, work for very long unless the participants are *rational* (for these purposes, just that they know what their own interests are and are not often subject to emotional outbursts that interfere with acting on them), *prudent* (foresighted, able to set aside present gratification for long term profit), *industrious* (hard-working, not lazy), *temperate* (moderate in their demands, not greedy), *thrifty* (strongly disposed to save money; a kind of prudence), and for the most part in possession of some saleable skill that they can use to make a living. Above all they must be *responsible* (willing to follow up on their commitments and keep their contracts, making sure that their goods are as described and do no harm to anyone, and taking a full and active part to protect the community that underlies their own and their neighbors' business endeavors).

Benjamin Franklin and the Bourgeois Tradesman

Adam Smith's theory of economic enterprise and the "wealth of nations" came from a combination of the Natural Law tradition of the 17th and 18th century (exemplified by John Locke) and the empirical tradition represented by Jeremy Bentham. Locke was needed to establish the sanctity of Property and Contract; Bentham to establish the priority of self-interest in human relations. Smith translated the conclusions as so many elaborations of the Natural Law; for example, the Law of Supply and Demand that links supply, demand, and price; or the law that links efficiency with success; and ultimately, the laws that link the absolute freedom of the market with the absolute growth of the wealth of the free market country.

The point of it all was **liberty**, or freedom: the natural liberty that every human had from God and Nature, and the liberty of exchange in the free market that would increase the wealth of the nation without limits. The theorists of the Free Market were prepared to argue for the primacy of liberty on deontological and utilitarian grounds; see Chapter 4. It is no accident that the currents of liberty, political and economic, came together in the English colonies in the New World. The colonies had been settled first as a *business enterprise* (the

*Above all they must be **responsible** (willing to follow up on their commitments and keep their contracts, making sure that their goods are as described and do no harm to anyone, and taking a full and active part to protect the community that underlies their own and their neighbors' business endeavors).*

companies that colonized Virginia and Massachusetts Bay expected to make a profit trading the products of the New World), then become a *refuge for Protestant burghers of various traditions* (English Separatists, French Huguenots), and rapidly came to see themselves as an experiment in freedom. The ferment of freedom came to a head simultaneously in several ways: Recall that the year 1776 saw the publication of Bentham's *Theory of Morals and Legislation*, Adam Smith's *The Wealth of Nations*, and the American *Declaration of Independence*.

Endnote 3

The American colonists who agitated most for independence were the wealthy businessmen (like John Hancock) who found British taxation cutting severely into their profits. But the ethic of American business had been laid down 40 years previously, in the widely read issues of *Poor Richard's Almanack* by **Benjamin Franklin** (1706–1790). The Almanacks contain some tracking of the stars, predictions of eclipses, and remarks on the weather; but in the "vacancies" between the stars, Franklin provides a strong restatement of the work ethic, along with assurances that work will provide prosperity.

Franklin's Business Credo

He advised: "Keep thy shop, and thy shop will keep thee."

He had no use for laziness and was sure that honest toil would always yield prosperity: "Employ thy time well, if thou meanest to gain leisure," "Be always asham'd to catch thy self idle."

Time invested in apprenticeship was well worth it: "He that hath a Trade, hath an Estate."

Don't forget: "Haste makes waste," and "Early to bed, early to rise, makes a man healthy, and wealthy, and wise."

In such proverbs, aphorisms, and sage advice on a multitude of subjects, Franklin addresses the small farmer and businessman who is assumed to make up the population of America, urging prudence, industriousness, honesty, and lapsing repeatedly into simple praise for profitable trade. (Please see the Selections following this Chapter for excerpts from Franklin on business, and the virtues that business teaches.) Aristotle is repaid to the full: Franklin matches his boundless admiration for the small businessman with profound contempt for the foppish "gentlemen" who put on airs around the working folk.

SUMMARY: BUSINESS AS MORAL ENTERPRISE

So the business system in America certainly started out as a moral enterprise: It embodied that "pursuit of happiness" to which Thomas Jefferson, in the Declaration of Independence, assured us we had a right. It seemed to be the best way to promote the general prosperity, one of the purposes (according to the Preamble to the American Constitution) of the founding of this country; and it served as its own teacher of virtue, as Benjamin Franklin would have it.

The virtue that sums up Franklin's tradesman of the 1700s is **responsibility**: He owns and is in full charge of his farm or shop; he freely exercises rational choice in the decisions for the expenditure of resources (including his own time and effort) in accordance with the dictates of prudence; he makes commitments appropriate to the flourishing of the business and his family; he follows up on the commitments, making sure that all work that he does is done right, representing it truthfully and billing only for what was done. With the highest stake in the continuing good order of the community, this tradesman is also the best candidate for holding office in its government, and is the basis for democracy. [Editor's Note: Today, of course, *she* might do a better job!]

Jefferson's letters suggest that he, at least, believed that *only* the small tradesmen and farmers could be relied on to run the country properly: Their property, he believed, gave them a stake in the stability and laws of the country, in contrast to the urban working class that he had encountered in Paris, and most definitely in contrast to the lazy and functionless "nobility" left over from pre-modern civilization. With Franklin, he saw that managing their own property for a profit taught them responsibility and prudence, surely qualities needed to run the state as well.

All of this is good news, for a nation that needed responsible management in both the economic and the political domains. As Adam Smith had insisted, the very natural self-interested struggle to get a living will teach those virtues that are necessary to ensure not only prosperity and wise administration throughout the land, but mature and adaptable citizens who can be relied on to take responsibility for the government of a state with the same sober industry as they apply to their own business.

Contrast Jefferson and Franklin's view about the role of the tradesman with Plato's contention that only philosophers should run the nation.

BUSINESS AS ARENAS OF MORAL DILEMMAS

Then whence the images of business as a cruel exploiter of its employees, the purveyor of cheap goods of which the buyer should beware? Business was not perceived as a villain in the United States until the 19th century — the age of the limited liability corporation, the industrial revolution, and the civilization of the factory. To the corporation and the ethical dilemmas that surround its operations we now turn.

The Nature of the For-profit Corporation

A for-profit corporation, the kind with which this chapter is primarily concerned, is a venture financed by investors (the people who put their money into the venture, at the outset or later on) for the purpose of making more money, getting a **return on investment (ROI)** as great or greater than they could get in any other allotment of their money. Once launched in business, a corporation is legally a fictional person — as Chief Justice of the Supreme Court John Marshall put it in 1819, "an artificial being, invisible, intangible, and existing only in the contemplation of the law." Intangible or not, it is a real thing, that outlives all its members, that can sue and be sued and make contracts like any individual. It is the status as a legal individual of Exxon or Pepsico or General Motors that has us assuming that they can have moral rights and obligations like any one of us.

It is the status as a legal individual of Exxon or Pepsico or General Motors that has us assuming that they can have moral rights and obligations like any one of us.

Any individual or group can carry on business; why would one form a corporation to do that? The answer lies in a curious point of legal history. Historically, corporations have been chartered by the state, and granted by the state the privilege of **limited liability**; which means that the members of the corporation (the investors) are financially liable for corporate debts only to the extent of their investments. They can lose the money they put in, but the creditors of the corporation can't come after their personal funds to satisfy the corporation's debts. Such enterprises created international trade. You can see why commercial corporations were formed: Each trip to the East put the investors terribly in debt, and if the boat were to be lost, as many were, the creditors could come after the owners' personal funds, houses, and possibly their persons (remember that the Merchant of Venice, in Shakespeare's play of that name, nearly lost a pound of flesh nearest the heart!) The East India Company, established in 1600 by Queen Elizabeth I explicitly to undertake the commercial exploitation of Asia, was one of the earliest and largest corporations. The Massachusetts Bay Company, formed to undertake the similar exploitation of the American Colonies, was another.

The Corporation in the Free Market

The nations of early modern Europe were **mercantilist**; i.e., they assumed that all economic dealings within their borders (or across them) should be monitored for the public good, and that it was part of the prerogative and duty of the state to charter only those corporations that would serve the national interest. Naturally, the officers of the state in charge of deciding who deserved a corporate charter and who did not tended to favor friends and party members, and the entire approval process became cumbersome and corrupt. After Adam Smith, the defenders of free enterprise pointed out that it was also entirely unnecessary. Let people make their own economic arrangements, they argued, and the public good will be served. Furthermore, in the name of liberty, especially liberty of association, there should be no reason why any group of persons should not be able to form a corporation if that is what they wanted to do. So in the 19th century the process was streamlined; now all it takes to form a corporation is a form that any lawyer can supply, a fee for the state, and a few signatures. You and a classmate could form one.

Not all corporations are formed for the purpose of making a profit. Charities, hospitals and universities are also incorporated. For the moment, however, let us leave the non-profit sector alone and concentrate on the *"private sector"* **corporation**, formed for the sole purpose of returning money to its investors — to take advantage of corporate freedom to carry on business and the limitations of investor liability to maximize the chances of personal profits while minimizing personal risks. Corporations enjoy most of the freedoms available to humans (including free speech and participation in political campaigns). Then can they be held morally responsible? Must they honor moral duties of (for example) helping the poor or supporting the arts? Should they be required to control harmful emissions from the factories even beyond the level required by law? Should they be urged not to fire those who really need the jobs? Here a real problem arises. To understand the structure of the problem, let us look for a moment at the structure of the corporation.

Ownership and Agency

When a corporation is started, it is wholly *owned* by the investors; its name and all its assets and all the product of its activity are property, and it is theirs. They can do what they (collectively) like with it and with the return it yields — save it, reinvest it, give it away. Let's suppose a company was started by ten investors; each would have a one-tenth share in the company (or one-tenth of the **stock** of the company), and presumably all decisions about what the company should do would be made by a majority vote among those ten. If the local fishermen asked the corporation to install some extra equipment so their toxic waste water wouldn't flow into the creek (equipment not required by law), or the local opera needed money and came to the corporation asking for a corporate contribution, the ten could take a vote among themselves on whether to install the equipment or contribute to the opera. If they decided to spend the money, no problem — that's their right. It's theirs.

Now, if they want to be about their other business, and so hire a manager to run the corporation in their absence, the manager has none of the rights of ownership. The owners are the *principals* in this engagement (strictly speaking, the owners collectively *are* the corporation, and the corporation is the principal), the manager is the *agent* of the corporation, and in this *agency* relationship the manager has a *fiduciary* obligation to the corporation to advance its interests. (The principal is the decision maker and initiator of the relationship; the agent is one who acts on behalf of another, not for himself; and a fiduciary relationship, [from *fides*, faith or trust] obligates the fiduciary to act for the interests of the *beneficiary*, the persons or institution for which he is the agent.) He can do only what he is instructed to do by the owners, and the owners have told him to run the business profitably, deduct his costs and salary, and send them the profits (the higher the better) as *dividends*, as a return on their investment. The owners have also, of course, told him to run the business in strict compliance with the law, because going afoul of the law can be very expensive; in the worst case, the whole business might be shut down and all the investment lost. So he'll spend the money needed for compliance. But if the town asks for control of runoff into the creek beyond the letter of the law, or the opera asks him for money for the next production, he really should do nothing until he's had the opportunity to ask the owners. If they are far away, that may be difficult to do. If he cannot consult them, he may just have to continue doing what he was told, which is to increase the shareholders' wealth. After all, it's not his money.

The situation gets worse (for the creek and the opera) if the original owners decide not only to sell their shares to other parties, splitting them several ways as they do so, but also to issue more stock, selling it to the public at large, in order to raise capital. (Their small factory has been doing so well that they decide to build two more, and need a lot of money, more than they could borrow from a bank, to start building.) By this time the corporation will have assumed its contemporary form, run not by the shareholders directly but by a **Board of Directors**, elected by them, whose charge it is to further shareholder interests — in short, to increase their wealth by directing the managers to follow policies that will raise the value of the stock in the market for stock, the Stock Exchange. By the time several new issues of stock have been sold, there will be many thousands, ultimately millions, of shares of company stock outstanding, owned by the public, and the manager is never going to be able to get hold of all the owners. Since on the Stock Exchange the shares can be traded (ownership can change) every day, the idea of contacting the shareholders for advice about the pipe or the opera rapidly becomes absurd.

Can the manager assume that the shareholders might want to clean up the creek or contribute to the opera? He might be wrong, but for most of the corporation's history, he could certainly try. The shareholders, however many and anonymous they were, were at least individual human beings who could be presumed to want the community fishermen and opera patrons to think well of the company, and to possess at least a passing interest in the natural environment and the arts. Throughout most of the twentieth century, corporations could assume at least some responsibility for community support and protection beyond the letter of the law. More recently, even that presumption has been defeated. (For a further discussion of the social responsibility of corporations, see Chapter 18.)

Funds, Buyouts, and Takeovers: The Corporate Dilemma

In the latest transformation of the corporation, the whole structure of ownership has changed. Since the 1920s we have had **mutual funds**, investment pools, which give the small investor with neither the time nor the skill to manage his own investments the

Throughout most of the twentieth century, corporations could assume at least some responsibility for community support and protection beyond the letter of the law.

opportunity to participate in the stock market with an experienced manager to make the investment decisions. Since the 1930s, college endowments, workers' pensions and many other projects have been provided for by similar funds, money pooled and saved for special purposes, run by fund managers whose job it to make sure that the fund is properly administered — invested in ways that will make sure that it is there when it is needed and that it will grow, as much as possible. For most of this century, such public funds stayed out of stocks — they bought corporate or municipal **bonds** (loans to corporations or cities), because they seemed so much safer. Once the fund managers of these large public funds, endowment and pension funds, realized that the Stock Market was not going to crash again, and that the return on stocks was much higher than that on bonds, they started putting their funds into shares of the corporations publicly traded on the Stock Exchanges. By now, up to 80% of our large corporations may be owned by these funds.

When there are 50-million shares of stock outstanding, the corporation's manager cannot poll the shareholders to find out if they want to give up some of their ROI to donate to the opera or cut back on emissions. But at least in theory, that might be what individual shareholders want to do, and if the cause is very good, he may be justified in assuming that they are. With the funds as the owners, the corporation manager's freedom disappears. The fund managers have no more right than the corporate managers to authorize charity, or public-spirited expenses beyond the letter of the law. They were appointed to run their pension fund, or endowment fund, in such a way as to increase its monetary value for the sake of the retirees or the college. They cannot give to charity from the fund's money, and it is difficult to see how they could authorize one of the companies in which the fund is invested to give the money due the fund in dividends away as charity, or spend it unnecessarily on community benefits.

Let's review that structure. Who owns the corporation? To illustrate: All of the public school teachers in a state pool their pension money and hire an administrator to manage that money for their benefit. The teachers collectively, from whose salary the pension money came, are the principal, the fund manager is the agent, with a fiduciary obligation to the teachers, to increase the amount of money they'll have to retire on. The fund buys stock in a major U.S. company. Now the fund owns part of the company, and it becomes an owner/principal of the corporation. The corporate manager is now essentially the agent of the teachers' pension fund and all the other funds. *No one in this picture* has any right to install environmental equipment, contribute to the opera, or undertake any action at all beyond the requirements of law in the name of the corporation; in this bizarre limiting case in the history of private property, no one who knows whose money that is has any power to spend it, while the actual principals — the group of schoolteachers — have no idea that

Figure 1. Bill Gates. Associated Press/Wide World Photos.

they are owners of that or any corporation. The money does not belong to anyone who can do anything with it; it is its own; it has developed an engine of its own, and a single direction — to make more money. Cold metal has learned to breed.

This transformation of ownership has led to some sad and confusing developments in U.S. corporations. Starting in the 1980s, a relatively small number of bankers, stock brokers, lawyers and other financial officers discovered that whole businesses could be bought and sold in a matter of days. Since the mutual fund managers watched the price of the stock minute by minute, and could buy stock, or sell all the thousands of their shares of a single company's stock, on a moment's notice, all a **broker** ("raider") had to do was borrow a large amount of money, make a tender offer (an offer of a certain price per share in return for the owner "tendering," giving over, the stock in the corporation) on the open market to buy out a controlling share of a company for a price per share a few dollars at most over the going price, and the mutual funds would take him up on the deal immediately. Mutual managers were compelled to: they had no choice but to advance the interest of the fund, and a few dollars per share is a huge amount of money when you own hundreds of thousands of shares. So to the extent that U.S. corporations were publicly owned, and actually owned by the big mutual funds, they became very vulnerable to these sudden "unsolicited" sales — the "leveraged buyouts" and "hostile takeovers" of the last decades of the twentieth century.

SUMMARY OF BUSINESS DILEMMAS

Generally, being "taken over" in this kind of "raid" did not work out to the advantage of the managers and workers of the "target" company (the company taken over) in the long run, because the only way the raider could pay back his loan was by selling off parts of the company and laying off large numbers of employees. The usual denouement (outcome) of the affair was that the target company, weakened by loss of its assets and experienced employees, ended up a small part of some other company — and the original business enterprise, product of the collective efforts of many people, often over many generations, died.

Yet doubts about the goodness of the consequences of these mergers cast no shadow on the clear rights of the major actors in these dramas. After all, the corporation is no more than a piece of paper; ownership of it may change at any time; and it is the owners' right to do what they want with it. This chapter of the history of American business is still being written. **One of the enduring problems for business ethics concerns the fate of corporations and employees in a time when capital moves with the speed of light across all time zones and all national boundaries.** We will return to this problem in later chapters.

THE FACTORY AND THE WORKER

Thomas Malthus, David Ricardo, & the Iron Law of Wages

Adam Smith had predicted prosperity for the nation. Soon enough Thomas Malthus (1766–1834) outlined prosperity's dark side. In his *Essay on Population* Malthus argued that every species increases until it outruns its food supply, at which time starvation brings its numbers down to the carrying capacity of its environment. Humans are no different. The undisciplined sexual behavior of humans inevitably produces more babies than the region can feed. Should Smith's predictions of increasing wealth actually come true, then, the inevitable result would be that more babies would survive infancy, and proceed to adulthood, eating more every year, until they had consumed the available food supply and people started to starve again. The famine will continue until it has brought down the number of potential parents to a point of reproduction low enough to live within the food supply. This must mean that human life is one long cycle of prosperity and famine, and that all people, despite temporary flashes of good living, will generally live a mouthful away from starvation.

How did Malthus' grim demographics influence the conduct of business? Benjamin Franklin knew business enterprise as an affair of small family farms and small shops, in small towns and small cities. It didn't stay that way. Adam Smith was the first to sing the praises of **division of labor**, which means the fragmentation of each task in production into a series of simple steps, so that even unskilled laborers can perform them, and consequently of the new industrial revolution, then starting.

Consider this example:

> People need shoes. At the time Smith wrote, making shoes was a highly skilled affair. You needed experienced cobblers to fit and make shoes, and that meant that the pay for a cobbler had to be high enough to attract a skilled person from all other enterprises that might tempt him. The cobblers could charge what they liked (constrained by competition with other cobblers); if you did not want to pay what they charged, you could go without shoes. If you hired the cobblers for your shoe manufactury, and they did not like what they were being paid, they could walk off and they could not practicably be replaced. No one could become a cobbler

"Here are all sorts of employers wanting all sorts of servants, and all sorts of servants wanting all kinds of employers, and they never seem to come together."
— *Charles Dickens, in* Martin Chuzzlewit

overnight; and in practice, anyone who wanted to become a cobbler first had to persuade an existing cobbler to take him as an apprentice for several years. Employer and craftsman had approximately equal power in any wages negotiation.

Endnote 1

Then division of labor was introduced. Now, if you wanted to make shoes, you could feed all the leather in at one end of a very long moving platform along which your workers stood. The first would cut the leather into shoe-size squares. The second, working from a mechanical pattern (a different one for each size and style) would cut the leather into shape — or three workers did that, each making one simple cut. The fifth punched holes for laces. The sixth inserted grommets. By the time the heel is nailed on and the laces inserted, upwards of sixty workers may have had a hand in the making of the shoe, each one performing repetitively a task that it took him only half an hour to learn. If one of the workers wants more wages or better working conditions, he can be fired on the spot. There are plenty more where he came from. That's what Malthus showed us.

David Ricardo (1772–1823), one of the first real economists, fed Smith's law of supply and demand — interpreted here as the **law of labor supply and wages** — into the projections as given by Malthus, and rapidly concluded that workers would always live within a meal of starvation. The factory owners must pay workers enough to get food to live; dead people don't show up to work in the morning. But there is no point paying them any more than that. There are more workers than jobs; all workers must work or starve; if any worker wants more than subsistence wages, there's another beside him willing to work for subsistence. This condition only holds true, of course, as long as all jobs are unskilled, so the worker cannot profit by developing a rare and necessary saleable skill and charging more money for it.

So in the end, by the theory, the owners and investors in the factories will plow their profits back into profitable enterprises, building more plants and using capital equipment to substitute for human skill; that way they will make sure that all jobs in their factories can be performed by people without skills. As each worker increases **productivity**: the ability to produce more of the product per period of time or labor, because of the aid of the factory's machines, the owner's profit increases. At the same time, the worker's wages become more firmly fixed at the subsistence level. Increasingly, the society is divided into two classes — the fabulously rich owners of the factories and the desperately poor workers.

Charles Dickens and Karl Marx — Moral Response

The industrial revolution of the late 18th and 19th centuries followed much the same path in England and in the United States. In both places it resulted in a good deal of human misery — 16-hour days of grinding toil, filth, and poverty for the workers, the blackening of the skies with smoke from the coal-fired machines, the noise and grime of the factories. The industrial revolution did exactly what

Adam Smith said it should — increased the wealth of the nations that experienced it — and exactly what his contemporaries had feared. The factories could make goods more quickly and much more cheaply than the village craftsman could, and usually, though everyone hated to admit it, of better quality in many ways: parts were genuinely interchangeable (so the product could be easily repaired by its owner), manufacture was uniform and predictable, and for the making of heavy machinery, factories were capable of feats of strength beyond the capability of any craftsman.

The move from shop to factory was irreversible for all but the most marginal goods. Yet in the process, all that Franklin and Jefferson had valued in business was lost: the contact with land and raw materials, the direct service to the customer, the whole nexus of reward for hard work (in the factory, it hardly mattered how hard you worked — you got paid no more), and above all, the opportunity to exercise prudence and responsibility by running a business owned by the craftsman. All that had taught virtue in the farm and shop had been stripped out of the factory. The life of the worker was poor in that his work was poorly compensated; but in terms of opportunities to govern his own life and exercise responsibility in his life choices, his life was impoverished indeed.

The human misery caused by the Industrial Revolution, widely recognized precisely because it was concentrated in the towns and cities where everyone could see it, provoked moral outrage among a wide variety of educated citizens. The Romantic poets praised the farm, and nature, and the small shops in the small village, and condemned the ugliness of the factories on simple **aesthetic** grounds (reasons having to do with art and beauty). Faced with the drab consequences of greater efficiency in production, they created a whole new ethic — some would say a religion — of nature, and of earlier, simpler times, and of the whole escape to country life. Moral reformers tended to condemn the degradation of human life implicit in factory conditions.

Charles Dickens, a Victorian novelist, wrote an influential tract called *Hard Times*, with no particular plot but an abundance of outrage. In it he condemned absolutely every aspect of industrial society — the dangerous machinery that took workers' hands and arms, the practice of employing helpless children, the filth of land, sky and water created by the factory's emissions, the relentless toil and exhaustion, the slave wages, the unimaginative industry-oriented educational system, the factory's unhealthy effect on the character and morals of worker and owner alike, the factory owners for maintaining such conditions, the government for tolerating them, the economists for justifying them, and the Utilitarian philosophers for providing the underlying ethical structure! All this criticism laid the basis for reform, which ultimately came in the form of wages-and-hours laws, the prohibition of child labor, environmental protection laws, and, ultimately, government agencies to enforce those laws and otherwise provide for safe and non-polluting worksites. But all this was in the future.

The human misery caused by the Industrial Revolution, widely recognized precisely because it was concentrated in the towns and cities where everyone could see it, provoked moral outrage among a wide variety of educated citizens.

Endnote 2

Meanwhile, reform would not satisfy one critic of the industrial revolution and the factory system. Karl Marx (1818–1883), an economist and political philosopher, was a follower in his youth of the German political philosopher **G. W. F. Hegel**, who saw the history of the world as a series of ideal ages, or stages. Each stage was called, as it took shape, a **thesis** (statement, or proposition) and each successive idea governed all events during the period of its ascendancy. No thesis lasted forever: as soon as it reached its flowering, it generated its own **antithesis** (a stage whose ruling idea was a direct contradiction to the idea of the thesis). Then, in a third stage, both previous stages were swallowed up in a **synthesis** (an idea which combined the best of both thesis and antithesis in something totally new). Marx found this three-part succession very persuasive, and had been toying with ways to show how it applied to the 19th century society in which he lived. Eventually he concluded from his study of economics that Hegel had to be wrong: the phases of history were ruled not by ideal stages, but by the *material conditions* of life (food, furniture, housing, and other products and evidences of wealth or poverty), and their evolution one from another came about as the ruling class of each age generated its own revolutionary overthrow.

Marx's theory, especially as it applies to the evolution of capitalism, is enormously complex; for the purposes of this unit, it can be summarized simply. According to Marx, the **ruling class** in every age is the group that owns the means of production of the age's product. Through the seventeenth century, the product was almost exclusively agricultural, and the means of production was almost exclusively agricultural land: landowners were the aristocrats and rulers. With the coming of commerce and industry, the means of production became money itself: the capital invested by the merchants in their ventures. It was a short step to turn that capital to investment in the factories of the industrial revolution, and in that step, the old "middle class" merchants and manufacturers became the ruling class.

Life was not good for the workers, Marx observed; and by the laws that had brought the economy to this point, the situation could only get worse. It was in the nature of capital-intensive industry to concentrate within itself more capital: its greater efficiency would, as Adam Smith had proved, drive all smaller labor-intensive industry (the shops of the craftsmen) out of business, and its enormous income would be put to work as more capital, expanding the domain of the factory and the machine indefinitely (at the expense of the cottage and the human being). Thus would the wealth of society concentrate in fewer and fewer hands, as the owners of the factories expanded their enterprises without limit into mighty industrial empires, dominated by machines and by the greed of their owners.

Meanwhile, Marx went on to argue, all this wealth was being produced by a new class of workers, the unskilled factory workers. Taken from the ranks of the obsolete peasantry, artisans and craftsmen, this new working class, the "**proletariat**," expanded in numbers with the gigantic mills, whose "hands" they were. So Marx took from Ricardo the vision of ultimate division of Western society under capitalism: into a tiny group of fabulously wealthy capitalists and a huge mass of paupers, mostly factory workers. The minority would keep the majority in strict control by its hired thugs (the state — the army and the police), control rendered easier by thought control (the schools and the churches). According to Marx, the purpose of the "ideology" taught by the schools and the churches — the value structure of Capitalism — was to show both classes that the capitalists had a right to their wealth (through the sham of Liberty, Free Enterprise, and the utilitarian benefits of the Free Market) and a perfect right to govern everyone else (through the sham of Democracy and Equal Justice). Thus the capitalists could enjoy their wealth in good conscience and the poor would understand their moral obligation to accept the oppression of the ruling class with good cheer.

Marx foresaw, and in his writings attempted to help bring about, the disillusionment of the workers: There will come a point when they will suddenly ask, *why* should we accept oppression all our lives? and the search for answers to this question will show them the history of their situation, expose the falsehood of the ideology and the false consciousness of those who believe it, show them their own strength, and lead them directly to the solution which will usher in the new age of socialism — the revolutionary overthrow of the capitalist regime. Why, after all, should they not undertake such a revolution? People are restrained from violence against oppression only by the prospect of losing something valuable, and the industrialized workers of the world had nothing to lose but their chains.

As feudalism had been swept away, then, by the "iron broom" of the French Revolution, so capitalism would be swept away by the revolt of the masses, the irresistible uprising of the vast majority of the people against the tiny minority of industrial overlords and their terrified minions — the armed forces, the State and the Church. After the first rebellions, Marx foresaw no lengthy problem of divided loyalties in the industrialized countries of the world. Once the scales had fallen from their eyes, the working class hirelings of army and police would quickly turn their guns on their masters, and join their natural allies in the proletariat in the task of creating the new world.

After the revolution, Marx predicted, there would be a temporary "dictatorship of the proletariat," during which the last vestiges of capitalism would be eradicated and the authority to run the industrial establishment returned to the workers of each industry. Once the economy had been decentralized, to turn each factory into an industrial commune run by its own workers and each landed estate into an agricultural commune run by its farmers, the State as such would simply wither away. Some central authority would certainly continue to exist, to coordinate and facilitate the exchange of goods within the country (one imagines a giant computer, taking note of where goods are demanded, where goods are available, and where the railroad cars are, to take the goods from one place to the other). But with no ruling class to serve, no oppression to carry out, there will be no need of state to rule people; what is left will be confined to the administration of things.

Even as he wrote, just in time for the Revolution of 1848, Marx expected the end of capitalism as a system. Not that capitalism was evil in itself; Marx did not presume to make moral judgments on history. Indeed, capitalism was necessary as an economic system, to concentrate the wealth of the country into the industries of the modern age. So capitalism had a respectable past, and would still be necessary, for awhile, in the developing countries, to launch their industries. But that task completed, it had no further role in history, and the longer it stayed around, the more the workers would suffer and the more violent the revolution would be when it came. The sooner the revolution, the better; the future belonged to **communism**.

SUMMARY OF BUSINESS, FACTORY AND WORKER

Let us review the theoretical conclusions to this point. There is a possible world — Benjamin Franklin, Thomas Jefferson, and Adam Smith thought they lived in it, as a matter of fact — where the practice of business teaches virtue, provides wealth and comfort for individuals, families, towns and nations, and provides ultimate human fulfillment in the exercise of autonomy and responsibility in the conduct of one's life. Presupposed in this world is a system of *small businesses* — small farms, shops, crafts — competing for repeat customers in a place where everyone knows everyone and word gets around fast if a product or service doesn't measure up. But the actual world, from the end of the eighteenth century onward to the present moment, has not matched that system.

Instead, we seem to have a world of publicly owned *corporations* (see previous section) impressed with their use of mechanization. By their nature, they are unable to be anything but profit-maximizing machines. They feature two primary types of enterprises: (1) *heavily capitalized manufacturing*, especially in heavy industries (iron and steel, automobiles, mining, building materials) in which entry into the business is limited to those with access to large amounts of money; (2) *mass production*, wiping out the skills of craftsmanship and the responsibility of the craftsman for his product.

As a result of all this, according to the theory, the creation of a new class of worker, unskilled, dulled by repetitive work, living in abject poverty, ultimately only an appendage of a machine until he dies or is brutally cut off from his brutish livelihood. It would be nice if he could get his government to pass laws to protect him, or at least get the police and the courts to enforce the laws that are in place now, but these institutions are supported by the rich corporations and really work only for the rich corporations — and the corporations are bound, like it or not, to seek only greater wealth. So, Marx concluded, reform within traditional societies won't happen. For him, the worker's only hope is to beat his screwdriver into a bayonet and join a violent revolution which will overthrow the government and put in place a benevolent dictatorship of comrades who have his best interest at heart and will make sure to run the society for his benefit, maybe. That is where the theory leaves us.

Why the Bad News Is Wrong

We are not at the point where the theory leaves us, of course. The society triumphantly deduced by Karl Marx has no resemblance to our own, fortunately, when compared to the sad state of those nations who embraced Marxian theory fully. Something got off the track between theory and practice. What?

Ordinarily we distinguish carefully among some terms: *Empirical laws* are those laws of science. *Descriptions* are generalizations about what, in fact, happens, most or all of the time; e.g., "If it rains, the streets get wet." *Normative laws* are moral rules. *Prescriptions* are general precepts about what to do. **Categorical imperatives** are rules that always define appropriate conduct; e.g., "Don't kill anyone, ever." **Hypothetical imperatives** are rules for what to do in order to achieve certain goals; e.g., "Eat an apple a day to stay healthy." Many of these can be shown to be false if the hypothesis fails to hold. If apples make us sick, it is no longer *true* that we should eat an apple a day to stay healthy.

Business theory also has laws, but sometimes it is hard to tell whether they are meant to be empirical or normative, and if normative, what kind. For example, the "law" according to which the prosperity of the nation will be increased without limit if only "the government" will stay out of the economy, appears to be an empirical law, which means that we could make observations that would tell us whether it is true or false. As a matter of fact, once the industrial revolution happened, the more "government" stayed out of the economy the poorer the workers got, suggesting that the law was not true. But then why would business theorists continue to pretend that it is true, except that it was in their personal interest to do so (and they wanted the rest of us to believe it so that their interest would continue to be served)? Or do they mean it to be normative — insisting on the desirability of non-interference even when it obviously fails to maximize happiness?

When we argue that because of Smith, and Malthus, and Ricardo, workers' wages must remain at the subsistence level, how do the theorists handle the fact that wages are not, in fact, at subsistence level? Often enough, the theorists argue that the reason we are losing out to the Pacific Rim nations in manufacturing is merely because our wages are "too high," and we should lower them. In short, the Iron Law of Wages was normative, not empirical — never mind the way the world turned out, the theorists seem to be arguing, all those workers *should* be living at subsistence level!

So when pointing out that the Laws of Economics adduced to govern business in the modern world are really a poor fit with the actuality of business practice, we don't know whether we have disproved the laws empirically, because they turn out not to apply in the very late 20th century, or whether we are disregarding the normative laws

As a matter of fact, once the industrial revolution happened, the more "government" stayed out of the economy the poorer the workers got, suggesting that the law was not true.

because they seem to us not to be very good laws much of the time. If the Iron Law of Wages decrees subsistence living for much of the nation while the few rich owners feast, who needs the Iron Law of Wages?

The Human Factor: Legislation and Labor Unions

What, in fact, happened? Contrary to theory, government did intervene on behalf of the factory worker, limiting the hours that an adult worker could work and abolishing child labor altogether. Minimum wages were set and safety measures required in the workplace. Contrary to theory, *labor unions* were allowed to form in the 19th century, gained strength in the first half of the twentieth, and after World War II became very powerful; the combined power of owners, managers, police and Pinkerton men was insufficient to stop them. They in their turn negotiated a fine middle class lifestyle that became part of what we know as the "American Dream"; wages were sufficient to allow the worker's spouse to drop out of the workforce altogether. Communities began to hold their corporate establishments accountable for the damage done to the environment of the town, and the corporations often found ways to contribute to that opera. Why? In the name of the careful definitions we have laid out, how could they?

The short answer is that the most rational corporation is still run by human beings who have to get along with their neighbors in town. The long answer will be found in the following two chapters, on the Internal and the External Constituencies of Business, tracking the ways that Business finds to be a moral agent and a responsible citizen in the community despite a business theory that says it should not. We will not be surprised to find that there is an ongoing tension between the profit-seeking theory and the real need to be responsive to the community, even at the expense of profits. In fact, the rest of business ethics tracks an uneasy compromise between a single-minded pursuit of profit (the bottom line, the increase in shareholder wealth, whatever we choose to call it) and a conscientious adjustment to the expectations of the surrounding community, present and future, local and global, human and otherwise.

A Business Ethic for Our Time

Business in the 18th century was a moral enterprise in ways best described by Jefferson and Franklin. Business in the late 20th century is a moral enterprise in very different ways. In the course of the next two chapters we will track ways in which a fundamentally impersonal enterprise can be moral: 10 imperatives, or, if you like, commandments, for business in our time.

BUSINESS IMPERATIVES

In Chapter 18: The corporation satisfies its obligations to its **internal constituencies** by treating its employees fairly in all respects, respecting their rights to privacy, dignity, and integrity, protecting their health and safety, and adhering to fairness and justice in all decisions having to do with hiring, firing, promoting and disciplining.

I. Non-discrimination: The corporation shall adhere to fair laws in hiring and promoting, with no discrimination among workers that is not clearly related to the job.

II. Employee rights: The corporation shall respect the employee's public and private rights, especially the right to privacy.

III. Employee welfare: The corporation shall protect the health and safety of the employees, and maintain a healthy and accident-free workplace.

IV. Employee dignity: The corporation shall maintain a workplace that protects and nurtures dignity, free from physical or psychological harassment, free from degrading stereotypes.

V. Employee integrity: The corporation shall provide channels through which employees may question and criticize company decisions and policy.

In Chapter 19: The corporation satisfies its duties to its **external constituencies** — customers, suppliers, local communities, national and international audiences, and the natural world itself — by providing excellent goods and services, by representing itself and its products honestly, by cooperating with civil authorities at all levels and in all places, and by cherishing the natural world as the condition for all human enterprises.

LOOKING AHEAD

The factors above will be discussed in Chapter 19 along with four others: A comparison of stockholder/stakeholder models; the "real" — unofficial but workaday — culture of an enterprise; the concept of a "social audit" whereby the values of a larger global marketplace are applied to a given business; and an actual "ethics program" with its strengths and weaknesses as may be applied to a business.

VI. Quality of the product: The corporation shall do its work well, make safe and functional products and stand behind them.

VII. Veracity: The corporation shall be truthful in all of its marketing and advertising, and direct its campaigns to audiences that can understand them.

VIII. Citizenship: At the local and the national level, the corporation shall carry on all of its transactions in compliance with the law and for the common good, with special sensitivity to local communities that rely on corporate payrolls to survive.

IX. Consistency: The multinational corporation shall, to the extent possible, carry its ethical procedures abroad and try to follow them there.

X. Stewardship: The corporation shall protect and preserve the natural environment, defending the biosphere against its own actions and the actions of others.

PROFESSIONALISM: BENEVOLENT EXPERTISE

A **profession** is, briefly, an occupational group distinguished from others by possession of a constellation of standards, more or less central to its operations. Professionals claim:

a. The possession of *knowledge* of an art, or esoteric body of knowledge, scientific or otherwise, not easily acquired, imparted by a lengthy course of *professional education*, governed and evaluated by the professionals, through which the professionals exercise *control over entry* into the profession.

b. A certain dedication to service to *clients*, persons who benefit directly from professional work, with whom the professional has a fiduciary relationship, which is protected by some form of *professional-client privilege* that ensures the maintenance of *confidentiality* of all dealings between professional and client.

c. A certain dedication to service to *the public*, or the common good, from whose politics the professional is protected by professional *autonomy*, which entails that only *peer review* (review by other professionals) shall be used to evaluate professional conduct.

d. A professional creed or *code of ethics* that binds the professionals to a certain standard of behavior.

e. The intention to *make a living* at what they do (as distinct from amateurs in the field).

Every profession claims all of those, although each profession would put them in a different order of priority. Medicine, for instance, which has evolved as a consulting profession since the days of Hippocrates of Cos (500 B.C.) would put duty to the client, or patient, first, and others beneath it; but physicians also acknowledge the duty to do research and advance medical knowledge, to help run the medical schools, to contribute to public health, and to maintain the peer review system that protects professional autonomy. All physicians will subscribe to the short American Medical Association Code of Ethics. The structure of the legal profession is much the same, with the difference that their Code of Professional Conduct is not nine sentences long, but a whole volume — and it has the force of law.

Scholars, university professors, may put service to the body of knowledge in their field first among their obligations; yet they will protect and serve their students as clients, acknowledge an unwritten code of professional ethics, help to educate their graduate students, and protect their academic freedom, which guarantees professional autonomy. Journalists may see the public at large as their primary client; policy analysts may serve government as its client, with the public (as distinct from the government) a distant second in its thoughts.

In all professions, an ideal of service with integrity informs the professional practice of most of the practitioners. It is helpful to remember that the notion of "profession," like "vocation," came originally from those who chose to dedicate their lives to service in a religious order; some professions originated in religious orders (the Hippocratic Oath describes a religious order of physicians) or, like the priesthood, retain the relationship to this day. Professionals regard themselves, and are generally regarded, as a privileged group of initiates into private wisdom, bound to special laws and obligations that the lay public cannot understand, let alone enforce.

Whatever element each profession may place first in the constellation, the elements of a profession are tied together in a logically coherent pattern which is the same for all. Because the *expertise* of the professional field is esoteric, difficult and time-consuming to obtain, there is no point in putting *laymen* (non-professionals) in charge of evaluating professional practice; they simply won't understand it, and will not be able to tell whether or not it is being done well. Hence *professional autonomy* is a natural necessity, not some kind of dispensable privilege. Since professionals must operate autonomously, they are bound to a system of *peer review* according to a *code of ethics*, because otherwise there would be no standard at all by which their performance could be judged. And since only professionals can say what a professional ought to know, only professionals can run the *professional educational system* and determine which of its graduates are fit to practice the profession. A profession serves the *common good*, by participating in town committees and engaging in community education activities, but its primary service is through service to its clients, governed by *fiduciary obligation* including the protection of *confidentiality*.

By way of example: it is in the public interest that people who are sick should seek medical care, and that people who have violated the law should come forward and make restitution. But people who are frightened by the social implications of their disease or legal trouble may be unwilling to step forward unless they know that the information they give will not be shared with anyone, at least until they have agreed that it is in their interest to share it. Hence we protect confidentiality between doctor and patient, lawyer and client, and by extension, priest and penitent, teacher and student. Again, to protect the public interest, there are limits on the privilege of confidentiality: The client must be of age (limiting teachers in protecting information), must not be currently engaged in fraud or other crime (which would activate a "duty to warn" for the professional), and certain conditions may not be kept private no matter who the clients may be (venereal disease, gunshot wounds, and child abuse, for instance).

The professional of any kind is committed to quality and integrity: he or she is obliged to practice the art at its most advanced state, defend the honor of the profession (in part by helping to weed out the dishonorable members) and to advance the state of the art through research, writing and teaching. All this takes time, which is why a "professional" is one who works at the profession full time; no profession worthy of the name can be done half-heartedly or half-time.

Professional Ethics and Business Ethics

The professional ethic is anchored by the **fiduciary** obligation that the professional has toward his client — **the obligation to make each decision for the client's interests and welfare, not the professional's own**. Without this ethic, the very notion of professional practice is impossible. By definition, the central characteristic of the profession is esoteric knowledge, beyond the ken of any layman. The client comes to the professional because of needs that the client cannot satisfy on his own because he, as a layman, lacks that knowledge: the patient comes to the doctor because he does not know why he feels sick, the client comes to the lawyer because he does not know enough of the law to know if he has a case against his neighbor, or is in some kind of trouble with the law, or has the right to carry on business as he plans. He must *trust* the professional to use that esoteric knowledge to help him out. If the professional decides to use it to advance his own interests at the expense of the client's (by telling a perfectly healthy woman that she has a dangerous illness that will require expensive medicine made by the physician, for instance; by telling the client that he's got a wonderful case against his neighbor which the lawyer will be glad to pursue for a retainer of several thousand dollars, when no such case can be successful), every client would leave the professional's office worse off than when he went in. By definition, the layman has no way of evaluating the quality of the professional's advice; to know enough to do that, he would have to be a professional himself. Were that the common experience, the custom of consulting professionals would rapidly pass out of existence.

The professional ethic, then, stands in distinct contradiction to the **market ethic** for which Adam Smith argued. Smith believed that in the open market, if each party looked after his own interests and his own interest only, the result would be the advancement of the common good. Therefore when dealing on the market, it is not only the right but the duty of merchant and customer alike to seek his own advantage, limited only by the requirements of honesty in representation of the goods, abstention from physical or psychological coercion, and fulfillment of contract. The **professional ethic** is just the opposite:

Dealing with the client, the professional's first duty is to find out if the client needs professional services at all, and if not, to bid him farewell without taking a penny. His second duty is to arrange to serve a client who needs his service in such a way as to maximize the client's profit from the service while minimizing its cost. Again, the client will be unable to verify any of this, so if the professional decides to cheat the client, there is little likelihood of being found out — unless the cheating becomes habitual and the professional gets careless.

To an astoundingly large extent, the viability of professional practice in the United States, for all professions, rests on the integrity of the individual practitioners, unmonitored by any but their peers. The professional's third duty is to protect the client in the profit from that service by maintaining the strictest confidentiality concerning the identity of his clients and the nature of the services provided, despite temptations to serve his own advantage (financial or social) by revealing them.

Professionals in Business

Professions intersect with the larger business world in several ways. First, each professional is in business, in that as above, he expects to make a living practicing his profession. In Franklin's time, the professional carried on a solo or partnership practice in towns and city neighborhoods, serving clients as they came in the door, billing them individually for services rendered. Medicine and law, the flagship professions, worked that way until very recently. In such cases, the determination of a fair fee was in part an individual matter, in part a community agreement that would probably, today, not pass anti-trust scrutiny. Professionals had always to resist the temptation to convince clients that more services were necessary than really were, and they were not always successful. But in the confines of town or neighborhood, it was difficult for professional greed to get out of hand; most of the restraints on small businesses worked for the professionals.

Some professions, like nursing and engineering, were composed from their beginning primarily of practitioners employed in larger institutions, hospitals or corporations, who had to hammer out their claims to professional autonomy against the claims of their employers. As colleges and universities joined the scientific and commercial growth of post-War America, college professors joined the ranks of professionals worrying about autonomy while collecting significant paychecks. These "employed professionals" have had to negotiate the narrow channels of professional responsibility among the rocks of employer demands, and the negotiations are not always successful.

Should nurses, for instance, join *unions* (organizations of employees formed to protect their material interests — wages, benefits, and job security — vis-a-vis the employers)? How does protection of nurse salaries fit with protection of the patient's interests? The same question applies to the college professors. On the other hand, should engineers leave the status of employee by joining *management* (corporate officers charged with protecting shareholder interests, in part by

As colleges and universities joined the scientific and commercial growth of post-War America, college professors joined the ranks of professionals worrying about autonomy while collecting significant paychecks.

keeping employee demands to a minimum)? By doing that, do they not abandon the engineer's commitment to a quality product in favor of the management goal of cost-cutting?

More recently yet, even the flagship professions have found themselves caught up in corporate objectives. The "storefront law firms" have turned members of the legal profession into underpaid and overworked clerks with specialized knowledge, monitored by corporate managers for productivity and deprived of the autonomy to run each case as they see fit. The "HMOs" (Health Maintenance Organizations), through which so many of the American population are now insured for health care services, have turned physicians into employees without protections: If a physician costs the HMO too much in a given year, he or she can be dropped from its list and lose his or her entire practice. The conflict of interest built into this and similar arrangements is excruciating for physician and patient alike. To eliminate it, should we encourage physicians to join unions?

Developments in American society since the early 1960s have accelerated the commercialization of the professions. The professional's clients — patients and students included — were encouraged to become informed consumers. They were encouraged and where possible empowered to ask questions, make demands, take charge of their treatment or education, to, in effect, shop around and get the deal they really wanted for themselves. As autonomous consumers, they no longer took "doctor's orders"; they negotiated contracts. Increasingly, the clients demanded that the professional-client transaction become a market transaction instead of a fiduciary one. Where client power was insufficient, the consumer purchasing organization — the HMO — intervened to specify the type of interventions that were considered advisable (and reimbursable). At this point professionals find themselves presented with insoluble dilemmas resulting from the incongruity between their traditional, protective, fiduciary ethic and the contemporary trend to reduce all relationships to the cash nexus, the market transaction where each party must look out for his own interests.

FINAL COMMENTS

At this moment, both business and the professions stand at crossroads in American society. Both have strong and readily available traditions as fundamentally ethical enterprises — activities guided by clear moral principles, such that the work redounds to the prosperity and virtue of the practitioner and of the society as a whole. But both are under a great deal of pressure now, as the small town society that they presuppose fades into a distant past, and the social controls upon which they relied disappear. Business is under pressure to take the general mandate to seek profit for oneself and increased wealth for the shareholder as an exclusive command, ruling out all other options and obligations; professions are finding themselves increasingly commercialized, in part by the very client autonomy that they helped to foster. The most immediate result of this pressure is the profound distrust of the public for *all* institutions — professions, corporations, and government alike — all of whom seem to be vast and impersonal machines for corruption and profit seeking.

Over the course of the next several chapters, we will be considering how businesses and the professions might protect the moral core that defined them while surviving in an increasingly complex financial environment. After the next two chapters on Business, we will return to the professions and see if their traditional ethics can help the business person make ethical decisions.

FOR FURTHER INQUIRY

REVIEW QUESTIONS

1. What values are maximized by the operations of the free market, unlimited by any public order or decision? What values are threatened?

2. What values are maximized by a democratic socialist system? What values are threatened?

3. In the effort to develop personal responsibility among its citizens, what advantages does a society of small tradesmen have over a society of large corporations?

4. What does the author mean by the statement, "Cold metal has learned to breed"?

ENDNOTES

1. Adam Smith, from *The Wealth of Nations.*

2. Karl Marx and Friedrich Engels, from *The Communist Manifesto.*

3. Benjamin Franklin, from *Poor Richard's Almanac.*

4. Milton Friedman, "The Social Responsibility of Business Is to Increase Its Profits," *New York Times Magazine*, September 13, 1970, 33, 126.

5. Melvin Anshen, "Changing the Social Contract: A Role for Business," *Columbia Journal of World Business* 5 (November–December 1970).

6. Kenneth Goodpaster and John B. Matthews, Jr., "Can a Corporation Have a Conscience?" *Harvard Business Review* 60 (January–February 1982) 132–141.

7. John Ladd, "Morality and the Ideal of Rationality in Formal Organizations," in Thomas Donaldson and Patricia Werhane, eds, *Ethical Issues in Business: A Philosophical Approach* 2nd ed. (Englewood Cliffs, N.J.: Prentice-Hall, 1983).

8. Milton Friedman, *Capitalism and Freedom,* Chicago: Univ. of Chicago Press, 1962.

9. Keith Davis, "Five Propositions for Social Responsibility," *Business Horizons* 18 (June 1975):20. Theodore Levitt, "The Dangers of Social Responsibility," *Harvard Business Review* 36 (September–October 1958).

10. Manuel G. Velasquez, "Why Corporations Are Not Morally Responsible for Anything They Do," *Business and Professional Ethics Journal* 2 (Spring 1983):8.

11. Christopher McMahon, "The Political Theory of Organizations and Business Ethics," *Philosophy and Public Affairs* 24 (Fall 1995):303. Edward Stevens, *Business Ethics,* New York, Paulist Press, 1979.

12. E.F. Schumacher, *Small Is Beautiful*, New York: Harper and Row, 1975.

13. Robert Heilbroner, *The Worldly Philosophers.*

14. Lisa Newton and David Schmidt, *Wake-Up Calls: Classic Cases in Business Ethics*, Belmont, CA: Wadsworth, 1996.

CHAPTER 18

EMPLOYEE RIGHTS AND RESPONSIBILITIES

"Measure not the work until the day's out and the labor's done."
— **Elizabeth Barrett Browning, Aurora Leigh**

"The world works only for today, as the world worked twelve thousand years ago, and our children's children will still have to toil and slave for the bare necessities of life."
— **Richard Jefferies, 1883**

What are employees entitled to? A "fair day's wages for a fair day's work," to begin with. They have a contract, written or implied, that indicates their wages and when they are to be paid, their benefits and what they have to do to qualify for them. The worker is worth his wages, and his employer is enjoined by law and by the holy scriptures not to keep them back overnight.

But beyond contract, the employee has a spectrum of rights proceeding from general social and legal understandings of his position *vis-a-vis* an employer. We may summarize those clusters of rights under five headings or ethical imperatives: justice, privacy, workplace health and safety, dignity and integrity. Each of these headings specifies a condition worth preserving in the workplace, so that the worker may thrive and flourish as an individual and a responsible citizen.

Dilemmas for the employer — and for the employee and the larger society — arise when the efficient and profitable conduct of business is made more difficult either by honoring the ethical imperatives or by providing the bureaucratic enforcement mechanism to implement them. Difficulties also arise, as we shall see, when our values for the workplace compete against each other. Let us consider these rights-clusters in sequence.

Lisa H. Newton, Ph.D., is Professor of Philosophy and Director of the Program in Applied Ethics at Fairfield University in Fairfield, Connecticut. She is author or co-author of several textbooks in the fields of Ethics and Environmental Studies, and has a faculty appointment in the Department of Medicine at Yale Medical School for the teaching of medical ethics.

WORKPLACE JUSTICE

Non-discrimination in hiring and promoting

The law is very clear. If you are an employer, you will not decide who among your applicants is to get the job, or who among your employees is to get the promotion, bonus, preferment, educational benefit, or more desirable corner office, on the basis of criteria irrelevant to the job that is to be performed. There are two categories of decision on the basis of irrelevance, both of which can be called **prejudice** (a disposition to judge before knowing the facts, a bias that works in favor of some and against others regardless of the objective features and facts of the situation). First, less troublesomely, there is the ancient prejudice *in favor of* your relatives and your friends. Second, more seriously, there is the ingrained prejudice *against* certain power minorities (groups which, while not necessarily numerically a minority in the employment situation or region, have traditionally not held decision-making power. Incidentally, that makes the ones that have dominated the field — usually but not always white males — serve as the standard "majority.") We will take these on in order.

A pattern of hiring your relatives is called **nepotism** (from the Greek word for "nephew." Presumably, your brother has put pressure on you to hire his son). Many relatives are perfectly well qualified for the job, of course, and not every one you hire has to be a relative. But in a nepotistic system, it is well known that family members (including spouses) will always control the business and no non-family member can ever be preferred to a family member. Nepotism is very widely practiced in some societies (India, for instance) where it is accepted as a matter of course. In certain kinds of small "family" businesses, it is common everywhere. But in larger enterprises in modern European and American societies, nepotism is frowned upon, on two moral grounds. First, it raises serious questions of trust and competence, since it creates the presumption that the relative did not have to meet the same tests as a non-relative; and second, it destroys the hope, and often the morale, of any non-relatives who had been faithful to the company for a long term. **Cronyism** (systematic hiring and retaining and promoting friends who can be counted on for loyal support) is a variant of the same practice. Both are also contrary to the free-market criterion of efficiency, which requires that an objective decision procedure pick out the best qualified candidate for any function in the corporation. Any publicly held company will be required by law to maintain fair standards in hiring, so that the shareholders will not be cheated by corporate officers doing favors for their families.

CHIEF LEARNING OUTCOME

I understand employee and employer responsibilities in both legal and ethical dimensions.

"A fair day's-wages for a fair day's-work.' It is as just a demand as governed men ever made of governing. It is the everlasting right of man."
— *Thomas Carlyle, 1843*

Discrimination is an act or pattern of acts that *irrationally* deny opportunities or benefits to persons solely based, for example, on their race, religion or sex; denying a person due rights and opportunities without considering the person's abilities or character. The more serious form of discrimination excludes or otherwise negatively impacts power minorities. Such discrimination is illegal. Following the Equal Protection Act of 1963 (which referred specifically to equal opportunity for women), Title VII of the Civil Rights Act of 1964 made it illegal "to fail or refuse to hire or to discharge any individual, or otherwise to discriminate against any individual with respect to his compensation, terms, conditions, or privileges of employment, because of such individual's race, color, religion, sex, or national origin."

The amendment of the Act by the 1972 Equal Employment Opportunity Act kept this language. The Age Discrimination in Employment Act (ADEA) of 1967 and the Americans with Disabilities Act (ADA) of 1990 extended protection to those over forty years of age and to those suffering from disabling handicaps. In some places, protected groups include those who have chosen alternative lifestyles and sexual orientation (gays and lesbians). But for the most part, non-discrimination laws cover only traits that are in no way chosen and cannot be concealed, like color and sex.

Occasionally courts have ordered companies with a history of discrimination not just to abstain from discrimination from that point on, but also to take **affirmative action** to compensate for that history; that is, actively to seek out qualified candidates of the group that has been discriminated against, to hire them and to promote them. Sometimes, companies have been asked to hire up to a certain **quota** or percentage of their workforce of the minority in question. Affirmative action by now has

KEY CONCEPTS

Non-Discrimination: The corporation shall adhere to fair laws in hiring and promoting, with no discrimination among workers that is not clearly related to the job.

Employee Rights: The corporation shall respect the employee's public and private rights, especially the right to privacy.

Employee Welfare: The corporation shall protect the health and safety of the employees, and maintain a healthy and accident-free workplace.

Employee Dignity: The corporation shall maintain a workplace that protects and nurtures dignity, free from physical or psychological harassment, free from degrading stereotypes.

Employee Integrity: The corporation shall provide channels through which employees may question and criticize company decisions and policy.

Mutual Responsibility: The corporation must exercise responsibility over the areas which it controls (the physical conditions of the workspace, the monitoring devices and policies in place), while the employees must take responsibility for that portion of the work that is within their control.

acquired another meaning. It encompasses any social programs, in the public or private sectors, intended to ensure that minorities enjoy all of the opportunities that any member of the power majorities might have, whether or not in compensation for past discrimination. During the late 1960s and early 1970s, all corporations contracting with the federal government were required to have such programs.

The Equal Employment Opportunity Commission, established in 1972, required that all companies doing business with the United States had to issue a written equal employment policy and an affirmative action commitment, appoint a high-ranking officer in the company to implement it and to publicize it, and must keep careful track of the actual number of minority employees by department, job classification, and compensation, in order to flag any pattern of under representation and discrimination. If any such be found, specific programs with specific hiring and promoting "goals" had to be developed, implemented, monitored and audited for progress. Court decisions disagreed on whether a real "quota" could be adopted.

Certain glaring forms of discrimination can be identified and punished under this legislation. In November, 1996, for instance, Texaco, Inc., was forced to settle for $176.1 million (the largest such settlement in history to date) a racial discrimination lawsuit brought by employees. The case involved an executive suite in which executives had been heard to express contempt for African-American customs and an intention to conceal the evidence of discrimination against black employees. Often, however, discrimination is much more difficult to detect and fair treatment difficult to enforce. Based on the ideal of universal equality, non-discrimination may be adopted as a policy in pursuit of the value of a truly diverse workforce. If so, serious ethical issues arise in the attempt to balance that diversity with other values that seem equally important. Some of these issues will be covered in the next sections.

Often the only way to judge a policy, or an industry, or a nation, is by the results. How do black and white families fare in a country dedicated to racial equality? Very unequally, it seems. According to the White House's Council of Economic Advisors, in 1996 black and Hispanic families were further behind whites than they had been twenty years ago.

Endnote 1

> The typical white family earned about $47,000 in 1996, almost twice that of blacks. Worse, the typical black household had a net worth of only about $45,000, a tenth of the white figure. . . . About 95 percent of black families own no stock or pension funds.
>
> . . . Unemployment among black men fell last year to 8.6 percent, the lowest in 23 years, but nevertheless twice the jobless rate of white men.
>
> Since 1972 black family incomes have risen less than 10 percent, at a time when white family incomes have risen 15 percent. . . .

Meanwhile, back on the distaff side, while here too there has been progress, women do not earn the salaries that men do for the same work. Diane Harris, a business writer, argues that for executive women at least, the situation is improving. "In the 28 fields for which salary information was available by gender, women typically earn 85% to 95% of what men in similar jobs take home. . . ." That is better than the Bureau of Labor Statistics average on all jobs (blue-collar and white), which has women earning 74 cents to every dollar a man takes home.

Endnote 2

Clearly whatever the laws say, our society keeps blacks and whites, men and women, in different jobs, somehow, and on different pay scales. Three cases demonstrate how unjust discrimination lodges in common business practices and attitudes: in setting job qualifications, in collective bargaining agreements, and as inadvertent sex stereotyping in hiring and promotion decisions.

THREE CASES OF BIAS

DUKE POWER
JOB TESTING

Endnote 3

Prior to 1970, Duke Power Company of North Carolina required a standardized general education (aptitude or "intelligence") test of every job applicant for any department other than their Labor Department. The wages of the Labor Department were the lowest, and transfer out of Labor was difficult. Eventually a group of black employees sued the company, arguing that the test was unfairly keeping them out of good jobs. The case was difficult to make. No one doubted that prior to 1964, when the Civil Rights Act was passed, Duke Power had openly discriminated against black applicants, routinely consigning them to low-paying jobs. But since 1964, all applicants had been subjected to the same requirements, a high school diploma or passing the test for any department but Labor; all applicants were graded fairly and assigned to jobs accordingly. It just so happened that Blacks always ended up not employed or in the lowest paying jobs.

Justice Warren Burger wrote the majority opinion. The test was unjust, he argued, on two grounds. First, the new requirement did not change the status of all the whites who had previously been hired without having to take it, who had obtained their jobs simply because they were white, and under the Act, practices, procedures, or tests *neutral upon their face, and even neutral in terms of intent*, cannot be maintained if they operate to "freeze" the status quo of prior discriminatory employment practices.

Endnote 4

Second, the blacks who took the test were at a significant disadvantage because they came from a school system still substantially segregated, and the black schools were known to be vastly inferior to the white schools. *But unjust or not*, he argued, if Duke could show a clear correlation between what the test was about and qualifications for the job, the test would pass Constitutional muster.

Nothing in the Act precludes the use of testing or measuring procedures; obviously they are useful. What Congress has forbidden is giving those devices and mechanisms controlling force unless they are demonstrably a reasonable measure of job performance. . . . Far from disparaging job qualifications as such, Congress has made such qualifications the controlling factor, so that race, religion, nationality, and sex become irrelevant. What Congress has commanded is that *any test used must measure the person for the job and not the person in the abstract.*

Endnote 5

The burden of proving that connection Duke could not meet; you did not need a high school diploma or the skills tested for on the aptitude test to do most of the jobs at Duke Power. On those grounds the test was ruled in violation of Title VII, and Duke Power Company was ordered to remedy the situation by hiring more blacks in all positions.

Endnote 6

TEAMSTERS VS. U.S.
VALUE OF SENIORITY

This lawsuit was initially brought by a group of African-American and Hispanic truck drivers, arguing that their company and their union discriminated against them. They were largely correct; instance after instance was cited where their requests for transfer or promotion were ignored or denied, or where they were simply lied to about qualifications, application procedures, or the existence of jobs. Since the passage of the Civil Rights Act, most of that had stopped, yet few minority drivers had been hired or transferred to better positions.

This lack of progress, the employer argued, stemmed not from discrimination but from "low turnover." More accurately, it was a result of collective bargaining agreements that put disincentives in the way of the kinds of transfer the minority drivers wanted. Of course the disincentives now worked against white new hires and transfers as well as against minorities, but all the senior positions in a system that (by union preference) strongly favored **seniority** (years accumulated on the job, either with the company or in the present job) were already occupied by whites because of past discrimination. The situation was in many ways analogous to that in Duke Power Company, except in this case the company could claim that it was bound by the union contract.

In the decision, handed down in 1977, Justice Potter Stewart stopped short of dismantling the seniority system as a method of controlling employment decisions, but made it clear that collective bargaining agreements would be subjected to the same scrutiny as employer's policies in the Court's efforts to end employment discrimination.

PRICE WATERHOUSE
SEX STEREOTYPING

Endnote 7

According to many of her co-workers, Ann Hopkins was one of the best partnership candidates that Price Waterhouse had seen for years. She had secured a $25-million State Department contract after working on it for two years, and had run it herself. No one else who went up for partner in her year had anything like her track record. She apparently had no difficulty dealing with, and pleasing, the firm's clients; she was a competent project leader, she worked long hours and pushed herself and her staff very hard to meet deadlines; in short, she did everything her male colleagues did to make partner. So why was her candidacy put "on hold" for a year?

There was a suggestion that perhaps the partners who voted against her disliked her approach and behavior because she was a woman. It was not that they objected to women, and not that they objected to her behavior, her competitive drive and aggressiveness, salted occasionally with strong language — they liked those qualities in a man — but that they perceived those qualities as inappropriate *in a woman*. That kind of perception is known as **stereotyping**, in this case **sex stereotyping**. This means basing your judgment of a person on his or her skills or some stereotype you happen to have of persons of that type, kind, group, race or sex. When the partner delegated to explain the Policy Board's decision to Hopkins advised her, to improve her chances next year, to "walk more femininely, talk more femininely, wear make-up, have her hair styled, and wear jewelry," she took the case to court, and eventually won.

"The business of America is business."
— President Calvin Coolidge to American Society of Newspaper Editors, 1925

Endnote 8

The point here was not that the policies by which partners were chosen was invalid, nor yet that Price Waterhouse did not have the right to demand good "interpersonal skills" (Hopkins' weak point) of their partners, but that it was clear that in this decision of the Board, sex stereotyping had taken place, and that made the decision discriminatory.

Job discrimination, in brief, is seriously wrong and illegal, and not only the blatant sort of job discrimination that characterized this country's history, which included:

* Signs in store windows at the start of the century reading "Irish need not apply"

* Jewish quotas and exclusions of the 1930s and 1940s

* Blatant discouragement of blacks in all except agricultural and service categories of employment up through the 1950s

✳ Various practices even today that lock in the results
   of previous discrimination

All these are seriously flawed, and all practices that stem from
such unwarranted stereotypes of power minorities are subject to
review and reversal. The object of the law is to make sure that hiring,
promotion, transfer and compensation decisions are made on objective and job-related criteria only. The history of subsequent court
decisions indicates a national intention to enforce the spirit and letter of anti-discrimination laws.

AFFIRMATIVE ACTION AND JUSTICE

What do we do if a decision like the ones tracked above seems to create as much injustice as it ends? Let's continue the story of Duke
Power, and look at one case where an allegation of "reverse discrimination" went as high as the Supreme Court.

Employment in the construction sector of the power industry is
cyclical. When times are good, plants expand and new ones are built,
and the companies hire workers. When times are bad, they lay them
off, keeping their names for recall when times get better; the workers
are used to this. By 1974, three years after the Supreme Court decision in *Griggs v. Duke Power Co.,* Duke Power Company, with plants
throughout the South, was faced with the necessity of laying off some
thousands of construction workers. But there was a complication.
When the Supreme Court decided that Duke Power had unfairly discriminated against black construction workers by imposing that aptitude test, it had instructed Duke Power to hire black workers in all
departments until the proportion of blacks to whites in the workforce
was equal to the proportion in the general population in the regions in
which they operated. Duke had complied with the order, and for several years had hired a large proportion of black workers, who were generally doing very well and beginning to be promoted to supervisory
positions. All these affirmative action gains would be lost if the company laid off workers according to its usual formula, which respected
seniority — that the last hired would be the first to be laid off.

The vice president who had to make the decision, Bill Lee, was
faced with three demands. (1) Management wanted to lay off all the
worst performers and keep the best, of whatever seniority or race
(*reward for merit*); (2) Senior workers wanted to lay off in reverse
order of hiring, by straight seniority (*reward for service*); (3) Court
decision and newer laws called for preserving the proportion of black
workers in the company (*diversity*). He could satisfy everyone to some
extent. He began by laying off the worst performers, as far as the
foremen could document; he went on to discharge all workers, of
whatever race or competence, who had been hired during the last six
months. But that didn't begin to reach the number he needed to lay

off. For the rest, he would have to choose straight seniority or choose to keep the black workers.

In the end, he chose to keep the black workers, going to the work-sites to explain his decision personally to the discharged white work-ers. His explanation appealed to justice, to the fact that those who had gone before him in the company, and the region, had indeed dis-criminated against blacks, and that it was their duty to try to provide some compensation for that now. The decision was accepted by the workers, and worked out better than he had anticipated. As a result of that choice, he told an interviewer ten years later, the black work-ers were able to build up some seniority themselves, and the next time the company had to lay off workers, he could make up the lists on the basis of straight seniority while keeping the legal proportion of black workers.

Bill Lee's white employees understood his position and did not protest that their rights had been violated by a policy that essentially gave jobs to black workers that they might have expected to be theirs.

Endnote 9

BRIAN WEBER
REVERSE DISCRIMINATION

Endnote 10

> Brian Weber, a semiskilled worker at Kaiser Aluminum's plant in Gramercy, Louisiana, was denied admission to a skilled craft training program due to a policy that essen-tially gave jobs to black workers that current white workers might have expected to be theirs. Weber saw the matter dif-ferently. He sued for admission. His application had been denied in accordance with a collective bargaining agree-ment that Kaiser had made with United Steelworkers "to eliminate conspicuous racial imbalances" in the skilled craft positions; so although his scores on the qualifying test were higher than the scores of the senior black applicant (a friend of his named Kernell Goudia), the black applicant was accepted and he was turned down. He figured he was being cheated, so he brought his case to the law.
>
> Five years later, Justice William Brennan delivered the opinion of the Court, upholding affirmative action plans against this kind of protest. He wrote. "We need not today define in detail the line of demarcation between permissible and impermissible affirmative action plans. It suffices to hold that the challenged Kaiser-USWA affirmative action plan falls on the permissible side of the line. The purposes of the plan mirror those of the statute. Both were designed to break down old patterns of racial segregation and hierarchy. Both were structured to "open employment opportunities for Negroes in occupations which have been traditionally closed to them."

Endnote 11

So Weber lost his case. Brennan went on to note that the plan did not entirely shut down opportunities for whites, and was in any case a temporary measure.

AFFIRMATIVE ACTION, PRO AND CONTRA

When all is said and done, is "affirmative action" really justified? Does a society require a program of increasing minority representation in places where minorities are underrepresented, even if that means passing over members of the majority who would otherwise have gotten the job, raise or promotion? America as a whole is badly divided on the subject. The federal government has largely abandoned the strict affirmative action requirement of the 1970s. Some state legislatures adopted that federal affirmative action program, requiring all contractors to show efforts to recruit minorities; more recently (1996) California passed an anti-affirmative action initiative, Proposition 209, by a very narrow margin. It provides in part:

> "Neither the State of California nor any of its political subdivisions or agents shall use race, sex, color, ethnicity or national origin as a criterion for either discriminating against, or granting preferential treatment to, any individual or group in the operation of the State's system of public employment, public education or public contracting."

Endnote 12

The Supreme Court, as noted in the decision on *Weber*, had been willing to defend some, but not all, affirmative action programs as Constitutional; in *Memphis Firefighters v. Stotts* the Court faced a situation identical to the one Bill Lee faced in the Duke Power layoffs, and came down on the other side. Straight seniority won, and the affirmative gains were lost. The results-oriented "disparate impact" theory articulated by the Court in *Griggs v. Duke Power* above, justifying affirmative action programs by citing the inequality of the *result* of policies, rather than their intent, was contradicted eighteen years afterwards, in *Wards Cove v. Atonio*, where the Court held that Title VII aimed only to remedy *intentional* discrimination.

Endnote 13
Endnote 14

Meanwhile, affirmative action is one of the most hotly debated topics in politics; like the abortion issue, it has become a conservative/liberal litmus test for any candidate for public office. Among political philosophers and ethicists, the battle rages just as furiously, if less publicly. Some defend it as a proper form of compensation for centuries of wrong, and certainly no worse than the other forms of preferential treatment we accept. A smaller number attack it as unjust to those of the majority who are excluded from deserved benefits, and certain to stigmatize its beneficiaries as less-than-qualified in the public eye. They also see it as a source of resentment that will follow anyone favored by the policy throughout his or her career. Finally, it is seen as improperly turning an area of law and justice into a political football.

BEYOND JUSTICE TO CELEBRATION

Possibly the best hope of agreement is to treat the whole issue of the hiring and promotion of minorities not as a matter of justice, but in a utilitarian framework, as a social and political ideal to be attained as far as possible. Homogeneity is easy; nothing is more soothing than working, playing, marrying, and living in a group of people exactly like ourselves. But diversity — simply the presence in the workplace (at least) of many different types of people — has enough advantages to make it worth working toward. Among them:

a. It salts the enterprise with genuinely different points of view, many of which will not have occurred to the majority members of the group, and therefore expands the number of insights and options available to the decision makers.

b. It supports, by providing breadwinners for, a series of different communities, each of which can learn and contribute to its own culture, enriching the nation and preserving its pluralist heritage.

c. In an increasingly multinational business atmosphere, it provides links and ambassadors to many nations with which American business is cultivating economic ties.

d. Minority coworkers may enrich and expand the minds of their majority colleagues, perhaps making them more curious, tolerant of differences, and interesting to be with.

The matter is infinitely complex, and those four reasons provide the merest beginning of a discussion of diversity beyond the scope of this work. Consider this: Until recently, the U.S. was the only place in the world committed to the "melting pot" concept of nationality, where people of all ethnic backgrounds are supposed to become good Americans through assimilation into our culture. Until very recently, it has been the only nation in the world reluctantly committed to such an "orchestra" or "mulligan stew" concept of nationality, where people of all ethnic backgrounds retain their cultural identity while participating in the civic life of an open society. Diversity as an ideal is very new to all of us, and its consequences may take much of the next millennium to work themselves out.

PRIVACY AND CIVIL RIGHTS

The Rubber Hits the Road — Testing and Monitoring

Employees usually work within sight of many other workers, and generally do not mind being informally watched. This is good, because corporate employers have a legitimate interest in keeping track of what happens at the workplace, and in making sure that employees are spending their time on the company's business and not, with rare exceptions, on their own personal business. Further, the employers have a duty to keep track of the workplace to make sure that the law is obeyed, that there are no hazards to health or safety, and that all employees are being treated with respect. Monitoring is also necessary to find out if training is effective. The employer is supposed to measure efficiency and effectiveness, to make sure customers are being treated in accordance with policy, to gather the data needed for objective evaluations and, in general, to control the quality of the performance. But is the employer actually doing it? "Supervision," oversight, then, is part of any workplace that distinguishes clearly between employers and employees, and employees generally do not object to having their work overseen, directed, inspected, and occasionally rejected. That's the boss's job and prerogative. (Universities, except for limited purposes, are not among these.)

But **supervision** of work respects a boundary around the *person* of the employee, a personal "space" that ought not to be entered by the boss without clear invitation, or at least permission, from the employee. The right to this space of noninterference is part of a **right of privacy**, generally understood, in the words of Justice Louis Brandeis, to mean "the right to be left alone," and identified as one of the most valued rights of the citizen in a free country. What kinds of monitoring might be held to violate this boundary? When does "overseeing" become "spying," and supervision become intrusion? We will take on three current issues. Electronic monitoring, drug testing, and genetic testing among other health inquiries.

Electronic and Video Monitoring

The technology of monitoring continues its relentless advance. We can now store the data from computerized performance monitoring to review the number of keystrokes in an employee's day, to watch his or her computer screens, track the destination and length of telephone calls. There are computerized location badges that can tell the employer precisely where an employee is at any time. These allow precise measurement of time spent in the restrooms or at the water cooler (do they still have water coolers?). The problems with all this electronic monitoring, according to employees subject to it, are that it is dehumanizing to be judged by a machine, that the machine cannot measure good work as opposed to much work, and that the devices regularly permit employers to read e-mail and notes stored on the computer for personal reference only. Video monitoring can be conducted with miniaturized cameras beamed through pinholes. It can spy on employees in unguarded moments — scratching, yawning, slumping, squirming. Then, a composite tape could easily be made from the product of the videos that would reflect very unfavorably on the employees, even if they were doing absolutely nothing wrong.

The issue of overly intrusive monitoring is really a matter of **trust**, and of restraint of idle curiosity. To what extent *must* the

"The foundation of morality is to have done, once and for all, with lying."
— *T.H. Huxley*

Endnote 16

employer watch an employee, or arrange to have the employee watched, as part of an implied contract with the shareholders and the public, to ensure that law is being respected and the company's interests are being served? To what extent beyond that minimum may an employer monitor, without sending the signal that the employees are simply not trusted? In a typically enormous corporate setting, is there any way for an employee to *earn* the employer's trust? If there is not, can we say that, in the absence of bad behavior, it is a matter of *right* for an employee to be trusted? In this context a pervasive question begins to make sense. Is there something in the human mind that really wants to know too much?

From the fact that technologically, the employer *can* know his secretary's number of keystrokes, does it follow that he should want to know that, that that information is of any use to him? The answer is probably not, and further, that the secretary will probably find out about the keystroke counting, and that it will decrease his or her efficiency slightly and his or her morale significantly; the probability, however, is that the employer will have that monitoring device installed.

The issue of trust has a more general form. **What may employers ask, and how may they ask it?** What kinds of questions can show up on pre-employment questionnaires? Some states prohibit questions about religion or sexual orientation; others about encounters with the police that did not end in conviction for crime; others about marital status. With employee theft estimated at $10-billion annually, may an employer require that an employee take a **lie detector test** — on penalty of firing if he or she refuses? It's a reasonable way to find the thief. Everyone knows that physiological changes accompany the kind of emotional stress that comes from stealing and lying about it, and the polygraph is a quick and cheap way to verify information and catch thieves.

But the use of such tests raises very serious problems. First, they test for nervousness, not crime, and cannot catch calm criminals even as they incriminate nervous innocents; and second, they are humiliating and degrading, associated with a criminal element and law enforcement rather than a supportive workplace. For this reason, the legislatures of several states have passed laws restricting private use of polygraphs. These acts join the Federal Employee Polygraph Protection Act (1992) which prohibits private employers (except security firms and drug companies) from using polygraphs in pre-employment testing. It also requires that if they are to be used when there has been a pattern of thefts from the company; for instance, the employee must have the test explained to him or her, along with the reason why the testing is being done and why this particular employee has been chosen for testing.

Perhaps the best way to approach the difficult questions of monitoring and testing is by a **three-way test**.

1. Are there really good job-related reasons for using them, or could the information be obtained other ways? **Always use**

the least intrusive methods to gather information. While normal supervision is necessary and welcome, concealed monitoring, electronic or visual, and testing (especially by mechanisms such as the polygraph), are inherently repugnant.

2. Is the collected information strictly job-related or does it include a fair amount of personal prying for information that just might come in handy some day? **Collect and store no information that is not directly relevant to the way the employee is doing the job for which he or she was hired.**

3. Who has access to this collected information? Only those on the job who "need to know" it to do their work of protecting the customer, the shareholder and the public, or anyone with access to the computer or to the boss? **No one should have access to employee information except those in the appropriate departments who really need to know it.**

DRUGS AND DRINKING

Substance abuse is a national problem, a problem of any affluent society, especially when, as in the developed world in the 20th century, primary structures of family and community have been seriously eroded. The problem of **substance abuse** is not a problem created by business or the market. But corporations have to deal with the problem, for substance abuse creates intolerable conditions in any workplace. (1) The behavior of the abuser is often beyond his or her control, and may be injurious to co-workers, for whose safety in the workplace the employer is responsible; (2) Job performance is predictably substandard, a recipe for actionable errors if the employee is manufacturing automobiles and a recipe for indefinitely extensive loss of life and property if the employee is driving one; (3) Even when the employee is not operating machinery, or responsible for public health and safety, the substandard performance drags down the productivity, and morale, of the abuser's co-workers, who have to carry the abuser's job as well as their own.

It should be noted that substance abuse damages job performance in any position requiring judgment; the oil tanker captain on alcohol and the subway operator on marijuana may get more publicity, but bond traders on cocaine can do just as much damage to the financial position of their clients as oil spills can do to Alaskan fisheries.

For all these reasons, corporations and public services like police, firefighters, and transit operators have adopted a variety of policies to test for drug use in the workplace. These are not simple policies to draft or enforce. It is worth looking at some of the difficulties.

Testing — Methods and Mores

The usual method is to test some body part or substance, usually urine, for the presence of the breakdown products of known controlled substances. First, this method does not distinguish between workplace use and weekend recreational use of drugs. To be sure, the unauthorized use of controlled substances is illegal any time; but is it the employer's responsibility to crack down on weekend use of drugs, even though behavioral effects *may* have worn off by the time the worker arrives in the workplace?

Secondly, the method is not always *valid* — that is, it does not always accurately signal the presence of drugs. If the test yields a false negative, the employee continues unidentified and dangerous. If the test yields a false positive, the employee is unfairly plunged into very bad trouble. Of course the test can be repeated, but repeating increases the chance of the false positive. Suppose there were only one false positive in a hundred tests. A record of 99% accuracy is excellent, better, in fact, than we can actually achieve. In a workforce of 20,000, that's 200 false positives. A repeat test, also 99% accurate, will still yield two false positives, and that's two totally innocent employees accused, tried, convicted, fired and probably unable to find another job. The actual statistics for the validity of the tests are much worse. Is this kind of error tolerable for the sake of the safety of the whole?

Finally, the method by which the urine must be obtained is notoriously intrusive. The employee must urinate into a cup *under the direct observation* of a supervisor; if a female employee is allowed to use a stall in the restroom, the door must remain open. Nowhere else in business practice, or indeed in the practice of any other institution, is the taboo against non-voluntary, overt or covert, observation of a person eliminating bodily wastes violated for any person of sound mind and good health past the age of four. The fact that drug testing by this method is accepted anywhere indicates the importance that has been attached to the problem of substance abuse.

Monitoring for alcohol abuse raises many of the same dilemmas as monitoring for drug abuse, but at a lower level. The reasons why alcohol abuse cannot be tolerated in the workplace are the same, but the tests are far less intrusive. Most able supervisors can spot containers of alcohol when vials of drugs would be invisible. They can identify drinking on the job much more quickly than drug abuse. If testing is required, a much less intrusive (and often more accurate) breath analysis can be performed. Alcohol abuse becomes problematic for corporations when all supervisors are absolutely certain that an employee is abusing alcohol, and someone has to decide what to do about it.

Before the passage of the **Americans with Disabilities Act**, an alcoholic employee would be given a chance to reform, and if that did not work, the employee was out. But alcoholism is now classified as a disabling disease, and no employee can be separated from the company until a series of efforts have been made to rehabilitate him. The employee may not be fired just because of a history of alcohol abuse. That is the effect of the ADA. There must be careful documentation of failure of performance on the job. If ultimately the employee cannot perform the job for which he or she has been hired, separation is possible. But the documentation of that performance, as well as documentation of the efforts at rehabilitation, must be thorough.

In the new legal climate, most large corporations have found it advisable to institute Employee Assistance Programs. Based in the Human Resources Division, these programs assign skilled counselors to help employees with a variety of problems that are interfering with work — personal, emotional, and sometimes practical (housing and personal finance, for instance). The workplace supervisor may send the employee to the program, and require the employee to keep the appointment. Thereafter, the advice to the employee is confidential, and unless the employee consents to more extensive sharing of information, the supervisor may only know whether or not the employee has kept the appointment and whether or not the advice is being followed. If either of those is negative, given a clear record of substandard performance, a procedure may be set in motion to dismiss the employee. (This usually includes a set of steps, such as suspension without pay, short of firing.)

Health and Gene Testing

Endnote 17

In light of the intrusiveness of the standard drug test, alternatives to body fluid testing have been suggested. One obvious alternative is **hair sampling**. It costs an employee nothing to pluck a single hair and give it to a supervisor. It will grow back! Observation to make sure it is the employee's own hair can be accomplished without direct viewing of the private parts or their functions, and traces of drugs can be detected in hair strands for up to 90 days after the employee has used them. Yet in 1996, two employees of Global Access Telecommunications in Boston, who had cheerfully submitted to urine tests, were dismissed for refusing to give hair samples. They argued that hair could be used to determine not only drug use but also a wide range of **genetic data**, including predispositions to disease or disabling conditions. These predispositions range from BRCA1, the gene for breast cancer, with a small but significant ability to predict onset of the disease, to the Huntington's Disease gene,

Endnote 18

which is 100% predictive of Huntington's Disease. Identification of them could lead to refusal of insurance benefits in the future. Possession of the gene would allow the company to call the disease, if it were to materialize, a "pre-existing condition," treatment for which is non-reimbursable.

In an era when health insurance is becoming increasingly cost-conscious, employee fears about employer awareness of health conditions are justified. An employee in New Jersey was fired from her small company because at her age (52), and with her history of arthritis, the company's health insurance would be higher than it could afford as long as she was on the payroll. Without her working there, the insurers were willing to offer a much lower price to cover the other employees, whose average age was 32. When she protested that her work record was excellent and that she was, in effect, being dismissed because of age and because of non-work related disability, both of which are illegal, she was informed that it was not the employer discriminating, but the insurance company. She was told that it is perfectly legal for insurers to charge more for older people with established medical conditions. She had to find another job.

To be sure, such practices seem to contradict the original purpose of insurance, which was to spread the risk over a large pool of the older, younger, sicker and healthier employees, so that all could afford to be covered in case of catastrophic health emergency. But it occurred to the insurance companies long ago that they could earn higher profits in their health insurance business if they covered only those persons who would not get sick. At least, they could improve profits relative to their competition if they made sure that their client pool was healthier than the competition's. If they could pay out significantly less in reimbursements to the insured, they would be favored with an agreeable choice: To increase the return to shareholders, to keep back a portion of profits to increase investments, or to increase market share by underselling the competition.

Since this line of reasoning struck every player in the insurance market at once, the result was a strong effort at **creaming** — discovering, through careful research, which groups of potential customers enjoyed the best health, and arranging to insure only those. And any information that the company can legally obtain can be used in the calculations. All these became barriers to insurance for the poorer workers, inner city residents, older workers, and any with a history of or predisposition to disease.

Occasionally, legislation is required to counter the determined quest for information on health and other conditions. It is now illegal to require a person to undergo a test for the presence of the Human Immunodeficiency Virus (HIV) that leads to Acquired Immunodeficiency Disease Syndrome (AIDS), a serious collapse of the immune system that is often ultimately fatal. There are two reasons. First, because the victims of the disease tended to be male homosexuals (who acquired the virus from unprotected intercourse) or intravenous drug users (who got it from sharing contaminated needles), both groups become subjects of fear and contempt from the larger population. Second, because for a long time the disease was inevitably lethal, the means of transmission were known only in part, and co-workers were terrified of infection. In the light of the inevitable stigmatization of an identified HIV carrier (in which the immediate loss of his or her health insurance would be only one of many worries), even before he or she became ill with AIDS, many states have ruled that no test for HIV may be required unless someone other than the suspected HIV carrier is at risk. Also material to that decision was the fact that no treatment was effective in curing the disease, so it could not be argued that its detection was of benefit to the individual or society in the procuring of timely treatment. As with other disabilities, any job deci-

It is now illegal to require a person to undergo a test for the presence of the Human Immunodeficiency Virus (HIV) that leads to Acquired Immunodeficiency Disease Syndrome (AIDS), a serious collapse of the immune system that is often ultimately fatal.

sion for the affected employee must depend on work performance and nothing else; until the HIV positive employee is simply unable to do the job, the employer may not dismiss him.

With genetic research progressing rapidly — the current flap about "cloning" is only a symptom of a much wider sophistication of technique and genetic theory — the problem with health insurance probably is only going to worsen. With full genetic information available, soon any insurance examiner will be able to predict which of the applicants will develop expensive chronic diseases, since asthma, arthritis, sickle cell disease, cancer, lupus, multiple sclerosis, Alzheimer's Disease, ALS (Lou Gehrig's Disease), and most disabling heart, lung and back diseases have genetic components. The ultimate invasion of privacy — determination of precisely that molecular code that determines our individuality — may soon be within the capability of those most likely to abuse it for their own profit. This may be one of the areas that market solutions only make worse; we may have to rely on very complex regulation and legislation to retain privacy in these matters.

EMPLOYMENT AT WILL?

Adam Smith's model makes every employment agreement a free and voluntary contract between worker and employer. From this model it follows that, absent contractual restrictions, the employee can leave at any time and the employer can separate the employee at any time. It all sounds very fair, and of course, it is not. The employer does not need any individual employee anywhere near as much as the employee needs the job. The only way to create a modicum of fairness in the workplace is to protect the worker in his or her employment, at least from arbitrary and discriminatory firing. That, fundamentally, is what this chapter is about. Workers may not be fired or kept in positions beneath their ability on grounds of disfavored minority status. Workers may not be deprived of rights of privacy they have earned elsewhere in the society except as absolutely necessary to protect the workplace — and the definition of that absolutely necessity is under continuing negotiation.

But that, naturally, is only half the story. We have laws in place now that protect minorities in the workplace from the discrimination which history proves will likely occur. Citizens with disabilities are appropriately included in this protection. Yet one part of the result of that protection is that employers have a long, difficult, and expensive battle in front of them if they try to dismiss an alcoholic or emotionally disturbed employee who not only is not doing his or her job, but is making it impossible for co-workers to do theirs. What is the employer to do? Probably, seek some *other* form of legal protection — new judicial rulings, new legislation — that will protect the workplace from the *intolerably disruptive employee*. At the end, we settle for the knowledge that there is a pendulum swinging in employer/employee relations; the beauty of a free system is that it swings freely, and that common justice has the potential to correct whatever imbalances common justice has created.

PROTECTION OF HEALTH AND SAFETY

Hazards in the Workplace

For most of the human experience, we have accepted the fact that injuries occur in the course of making a living. In many of our older industries, whole regional cultures grew around the shared risks of the dominant occupation. The "Widow's Walk" and community support for the families of seagoing merchant-ship crews and fishermen who were lost at sea; the coal-mining towns where a man's status as seasoned miner was set by the tone of his black-lung cough, the cattle and logging towns where every family had lost at least one man to accident on the range or in the woods; and of course, the military installations around the world, where one of the oldest occupations led most predictably to death. Tracking the growth of health and safety provisions in the United States is, essentially, tracking the decreasing social tolerance for physical risk of any kind, just as we shall see in the next chapter's discussion of consumer risk and manufactured products.

The first century of modern industrialization, from about 1830 to 1930, saw man-made workplaces as dangerous as the seas, mines, plains and forests of our early industries. Exposed machinery amputated fingers and hands, massive steam explosions were common, and all the hatters in Danbury, Connecticut, ended their careers insane, with lethal brain damage from the fumes of the mercury used to process the felt for the hats — hence, "mad as a hatter."

Contributing to a high accident rate and widespread health problems was the brutal pace expected of factory workers. Sixteen-hour days were the rule, Saturday work was often expected, and workers could be counted on to show up for overtime opportunities because wages were so low — the factory owners, if no one else, read David Ricardo (see Chapter 17). Early in this century several states passed wages-and-hours laws limiting the hours that women, at least, could work during a given day, and specifying a minimum wage. After several bouts with a Supreme Court that seemed determined to protect Adam Smith and Freedom of Contract in the face of impossibility, these laws were declared Constitutional and were followed by federal legislation on minimum wage and working conditions.

Endnote 19

By the 1930s further progress had been made. Workers' compensation laws, awarding insurance payments to workers injured on the job, thereby incidentally preventing them from suing their employers for damages, at least provided support for the families of workers hurt on the job. Meanwhile, labor unions had taken over the job of negotiating wages and working conditions, with the federal government setting only the barest minimums.

By the late 1960s, however, it was clear that leaving the matter of protection of health and safety in the workplace to the private parties to work out and to insurance to pay for would provide insufficient protection; not enough workers were unionized, compensation schemes required waivers of legal rights and did nothing to make the workplace safer, while public tolerance for workplace risk had fallen below the point where unions could be permitted, for instance, to bargain protection away in return for higher wages.

FEDERAL WORKPLACE REGULATION

So the Federal Government stepped in to create its own superagency to monitor the protections, and the **Occupational Safety and Health Administration (OSHA)** was born in 1970. It assigns the primary responsibility for protecting workplace health and safety to the federal government, rather than to the states or private parties. Its intention is to ensure "so far as possible every working man and woman in the nation safe and healthful working conditions," and it creates mechanisms to implement it. Every workplace must be kept free of recognized hazards that are likely to cause serious injury or death. The implications of that general purpose are spelled out in specific provisions for each industry. Machinery must be designed to shield fingers and hands from sharp surfaces or moving parts; where deleterious toxins are known or suspected, frequent inspection by sampling of the air must take place to ensure that the amount is not high enough to cause harm.

Changes in the law have not prevented industrial accidents, especially in industries working with substances whose lethal potential is not entirely known, and OSHA does not always protect the employee. The chemicals that are used in the manufacture of computer chips, for example, are known to be toxic, and often a safe level of such contaminants is difficult to determine. The composite plastics used in the skin of the Stealth bomber sickened some of the workers involved in its manufacture in the late 1980s and 1990s. A worker whose job was stirring tanks of chemicals at a Film Recovery Services plant in Illinois suddenly became dizzy from the toxic fumes, went into convulsions and died. Was this a freak accident or a case of company negligence? OSHA and the local courts disagreed; OSHA fined the plant a few thousand dollars, while the state attorney general for Cook County sought, and obtained, convictions of three of the company's officers for murder and reckless conduct. Fires and explosions continue to claim lives in industrial accidents; are these all preventable? Is it OSHA's job to prevent them?

Reviews of OSHA's work are mixed. On the one hand, its critics assert that its regulations multiply like rabbits and significantly raise the cost of doing business by rapidly changing rules on trivialities — the size of toilet seats, for instance. Further, OSHA regulations can conflict with those of other agencies, as they did for awhile in meat packing plants. OSHA wanted the often bloody floors corrugated so workers would be less likely to fall, while the Food and Drug Administration (FDA) wanted them smooth so that they could be hosed clean to prevent infection. Overzealous enforcement of OSHA provisions has been blamed for the closure of small companies that could not afford compliance. (Commonly, when the political shoe changes feet, the opposite criticism can be heard. During the administrations of industry-friendly presidents, enforcement funds and personnel are slashed, and the agency is accused of neglect and ineffectiveness.)

"Carpe diem . . . seize today, and put as little trust as you can in tomorrow."
— Horace

On the other hand, there is no doubt that the agency's existence, and the ever-present threat of unannounced inspections, have helped to keep the workplace safer. And OSHA seeks to guarantee workers' rights that were unenforceable or "waived" under previous law. Among these are the right to know what hazards await them in the workplace, the right to refuse to accept risky assignments, the right to know the extent of their exposure to toxins, the right to petition for higher safety standards, the right to file complaints against their employers and request federal inspections of the workplace. Backing up all of these is the right to immunity from discharge or other retaliation for exercising these rights.

OSHA shares the drawback of most attempts to manage business enterprises by federal legislation. OSHA is behind the times, working only on the information that has survived the political process, and cannot weigh its own values against competing values in any particular situation. We can illustrate these drawbacks with three typical workplace-injury situations: lung damage from the inhalation of asbestos fibers, reproductive anomalies from exposure to lead and other chemicals, and "repetitive stress injuries."

REPRESENTATIVE DILEMMAS IN WORKPLACE HEALTH AND SAFETY

Asbestos: "Outrageous Misconduct" or War Effort?

Asbestos was thought to be a miracle fiber when it was discovered. A mineral that could be spun like cloth, light, durable, and absolutely fireproof, it rapidly became the standard of safety where protection from fire was concerned. As early as the 1930s, doubts about possible harm from breathing asbestos fibers had begun to surface, and a condition of "asbestosis," mild lung scarring from asbestos fibers, had been identified; but at industry request, these doubts were set aside in the interests of keeping the work moving and the people employed. The country's major exposure to asbestos occurred during the second World War, when the U.S. Navy needed ships built quickly to replace those lost at Pearl Harbor. All the ships had to be insulated by asbestos, which was applied inside the confined spaces of holds and compartments in the ship. Because of the warnings from the early studies of asbestos, the workers were usually issued masks to protect them from inhaling the fibers; but the workers found them uncomfortable and inconvenient, no one required them to wear them (especially when they cut into productivity), and they were generally ignored. Speed of production was essential.

About 30 years later, physicians noted the first cases of mesothelioma, a cancer of the lining of the chest attributable almost entirely to fibrosis — the scarring of the lungs by some durable fibers. After the first round of cases, it was clear that mesothelioma was significantly associated with former employment in one of several industries, especially defense industries, that had used asbestos. It was clear to the lawyers contacted by some of the first victims that these sick individuals merited some sort of compensation for being put at risk for this deadly and painful disease. But who should pay? The workers could not sue the federal government, which had ordered those ships, because there had been no law protecting them from asbestos exposure and therefore no negligence on the part of the government for not enforcing it. Also, the government cannot be sued without its consent. Most importantly, the workers were not employed by the federal government, but by private contractors who had agreed to do the work to prepare the ships. Many of these were by this time out of business, and besides, any injury suffered on the job had to be compensated through workers' compensation laws, and no further suits against the employer could be brought.

Whom to sue? The lawyers rapidly came up with an answer. The manufacturers of the asbestos, who knew or should have known that the stuff was dangerous and who did not sufficiently warn their customers to make sure that the workers applying it should be protected from inhaling it. The theory was wildly successful, and some excellent accounts of the ensuing asbestos battles supply the details. But the bankrupting of Johns Manville, the major asbestos contractor, and the subsequent class action suits and settlements, do not address the ethical dimensions of the asbestos incident.

The principle of law for holding someone liable for putting someone else at risk, is that the risk was unknown to the victim and therefore not accepted *voluntarily* by the victim. Had the victim known about the risk ahead of time, the victim would never have consented to the exposure. But, first, can we take seriously the worker claims that "had they been informed about the hazards of asbestos, they would not have continued to work in those settings"? For if they cannot substantiate that claim, involuntary exposure is not an issue. Second, to what extent is the judgment of praise or blame for the industry due to "concealment" of the data, which showed asbestos to be dangerous? Didn't the workers already know that you shouldn't breathe that stuff? Some testimony suggests they did. Third, the danger of mesothelioma and other forms of lung cancer turns out to be

But the bankrupting of Johns Manville, the major asbestos contractor, and the subsequent class action suits and settlements, do not address the ethical dimensions of the asbestos incident.

Endnote 20

strongly correlated, in these workers, with the habit of smoking tobacco. We know that smoking causes lung disease and predisposes for many different kinds of cancer, asbestos or no asbestos. Should all asbestos workers who smoked be excluded from awards on grounds that we cannot tell if their disease is from asbestos or smoking, or have the awards docked proportionately to their smoking on some ground of contributory negligence? And fourth and most importantly, what kind of risk was involuntarily assumed by those workers — in comparison with the risk assumed by others in their positions?

The United States right after Pearl Harbor was a military camp on a war footing; every young man who was not paralyzed, in another military service, or working in a war industry was drafted into the Army. So the alternative for the asbestos workers was military service, with a moderate risk of violent death within the next two or three years, against an asbestos risk, a mild risk of death by sickness twenty-five years into the future. Which risk would it have made more sense to assume? And just as the soldiers killed in the war did not have their rights violated, so, it could be argued, there was no violation of rights in assigning these workers to spray asbestos. Of course risks could have been minimized, had the workers worn their masks; again, it can be argued that the workers contributed some negligence to the situation and to their ultimate disease. Asbestos obviously continued to be used long after the war was over. But the proportionate risks and the problem of contributory negligence remain, even after the military draft was ended. The debate continues, in and out of court.

Women of Childbearing Years in Chemical Factories

For this issue, one must know the rudiments of ontogeny, which is the developmental course of a fetus from fertilized egg to baby. If a woman is fertile, i.e. at that point in her monthly cycle when she is able to conceive a child, then there is a chance that some 24 hours after intercourse, a sperm will meet up with a fertile egg and conception will take place. If either sperm or egg are mutants (genetically changed by some process), there is a chance that a deformed child will be conceived. Mutation might have taken place in response to a *mutagen,* a substance that causes mutations which is somehow absorbed from the environment. The fertilized egg implants itself into the womb and starts to grow. Within the first month, before the embryo is visible to the naked eye and usually before the mother knows for sure that she is pregnant, all the body's systems start to form; organs, limbs, nervous system. Rapid formation of new systems goes on for the next month or so; after that, the course of growth is set, and the baby finishes the job and gains weight for the next seven months.

During those first two months the embryo is very vulnerable to interference with development by foreign substances that interrupt one or more of the terribly delicate processes of growth and formation. This sets the stage for *teratogens,* literally, "monster-makers," which are substances that harm the embryo by interfering with such growth. For if the embryo is exposed to these teratogens, the result may be major malformations of limbs, loss of kidneys, heart damage, or mild to severe nerve and brain damage. The teratogen in the drug thalidomide, for instance, kept arms and legs from growing normally. Such children used to be called "monsters," and the name stuck.

Clearly, it would be a good thing to keep all adults who may sire or bear children from exposure to mutagens, and all embryos from exposure to teratogens. How does this task become part of the corporation's responsibility? Recall the workplace hazards cited above. Among them were fumes of cyanide compounds, chlorine compounds, arsenic compounds and ambient lead, byproducts of the manufacture of plastics, film, paint, pesticides, airplanes and even computer chips. Some of these substances are deadly, and they are carefully controlled with masks, suits, and special rooms. Some are harmful, and they are regulated. Some don't seem to do any harm at all, at sufficiently low concentrations. But the concentration that will seep into the germ cells and turn out to be mutagens — producing no harm to the adult but creating genetic chaos for the children — is not known. Also unknown is the concentration that will hurt an embryo, if the mother were to be exposed to the substance and if the substance crosses the placenta.

One of the major controversies that arose in the conduct of business in the 1980s was whether a corporation was justified in banning all women, but not men, from a workplace where some low concentration of a harmful substance was in the air. On the one hand, no one wanted a badly damaged baby born — a baby the corporation would probably have to pay for the rest of its life, after a jury heard the tearful mother blame the company and its teratogens for the damage done to her child. On the other hand, women have the same right to work as men; so, what if the mother objected to being forced to leave her job, or prevented from taking one, because of ambient chemicals?

Corporations argued vigorously about this issue, trying several means to reconcile the claims of justice with the safety of the child. Some corporations asked women to pledge that they would not have a baby while working there. When some of them got pregnant, the women claimed that the pledge forced them to seek abortions. That horrified the press, and the practice was dropped. Some plants barred all *fertile* women, women of childbearing age who had not received surgical sterilizations, from entering areas with chemical contaminants in the ambient air; younger women protested that they were being compelled to undergo sterilization on pain of losing their jobs. That did not sit well with the courts. Others required women in such jobs to sign a waiver saying that they understood the risks and would not sue. When a child with birth defects was born of one of those employees, she did not sue, but the child's grandmother did, on behalf of the child, arguing that it was the child who was affected and that the child had not signed anything at all. A woman may waive her rights, but not someone else's. Some reformers argued that any teratogen could also be a mutagen, and just as damaging to men as to women. Finally, the Supreme Court decided the matter, in favor of absolute equality of men and women. **Anywhere a man may work, so may a woman and vice versa**. The effect was to restore peace and end experiments with discrimination; it also, occasionally, resulted in the closing of plants whose ambient air the management could not sufficiently clear of chemicals.

Repetitive Stress Injuries

Like the teratogens, "repetitive stress injury" (RSI) is a twentieth century hazard. It arises from work activities which might seem totally free from stress of any kind apart from the psychological stress of a boss demanding faster and faster work, like operating a word processor or checking out groceries at the supermarket. Some of the machines to blame for any number of very physical ailments are automatic letter sorting machines, cash registers, modern day assembly lines, switchboards, keyboards, all of which require the same motion, swiftly performed. They have been known to cause tendinitis in any joint in the arm, wrist, or fingers, carpal tunnel syndrome, inflammations like arthritis, and a wide assortment of complaints about swelling, numbness, and much, much pain.

This type of injury raises ethical dilemmas of honesty, of remedy, and of compensatory damages. Unlike the industrial injuries of the past — such as mangled limbs or bashed heads, the stress-related injuries are hard for an employer to understand and impossible to verify. A secretary's complaint of "shooting pains up my hand and arm" may be the first step in a case that will cost the employer a fortune. The employee may need surgery, which may or may not work. There may be long-term disability and vocational rehabilitation to pay for, as the employee rests and prepares for another job.

And there is no limit to these cases. According to a 1995 report from the U.S. Bureau of Labor Statistics, RSI accounted for 60 percent of all workplace illness and even then, had cost more that $20-billion in worker's compensation. By that time, IBM was the defendant in 350 RSI lawsuits. Given the uncertainties of the cure, should the rehabilitation even be attempted? Given the uncertainties of the injury, the wide distribution of the complaints, and the likelihood of more in the future, if insurance companies are especially stringent about compensating these cases? How much is real and how much is due to sheer boredom from spending all day cooped up by a machine?

Endnote 21

Meanwhile, office supply designers are doing their best to lower the incidence of these complaints, by redesigning computer keyboards, chairs, desks, every other aspect of the workplace to be more human-body-friendly. Only time will tell if the ergonomic designs now being tried will make the workplace genuinely less stressful for those in it.

Safety and Health as Cultural Problems

Ultimately, health and safety have more to do with the attitude and lifestyle of the employee than they have to do with the stresses of the modern workplace. Some companies have made a fetish of safety consciousness, drilling safety and health protection rules into the employees: "*Never* reach out to brace yourself on a working machine." "*Never* lift with your back, always with your legs." "*Always* wear your safety equipment." These companies reward units that are accident-free and low in absences, posting records of health and safety to encourage employees to remember the rules, and on occasion, even shutting down units found in violation of safety regulations until the violation is fixed. Such shutdowns send a clear message to all units that minor deviations from rules will not be tolerated.

Beyond adherence to good rules on the job, the quest for employee health and safety can expand into a variety of **wellness programs** in the workplace. A wellness center, then, including fitness programs, may be one of the best investments a company can make: exercise rooms available between tasks or meetings, with an exercise plan to go with them and a company physician to recommend individualized programs, such as diet and nutrition programs offered by the company cafeteria, and rewards for employees who agree to stay smoke-free or fat-free. Why might a company undertake these programs, which seem to have so little to do with the company bottom line? The answer lies in the cost to train and prepare workers, especially new, high-level executives for the corporation. It takes a very long time to bring a really good corporate officer on line, with-up-to date expert knowledge in the field, relevant people skills, and a deep understanding of the company's history and culture. If fitness and "wellness" initiatives can keep an executive active 15 more years than he would have been active otherwise, they pay for themselves.

"Integrity is the singleness of life, character and person that informs us at our best, that requires us always to act in accord with our moral principles, and thereby permits us to undertake courses of action that, if we waited for deep analysis, would scare us to death."

MOMMY TRACKS

Since the first stirring of the women's suffrage movement, women have been working for equality with men in the public space and in the workplace. Women have wanted to be hired, compensated and promoted, merely as would a man be with the same work skills. Women with children have asked no more than to be treated as men with children, and that was not an easy task. Expectations were different. Men who had a child were expected to become better workers ("He'll settle down now that he's got the future to work for"). Women were expected to become worse ("With all those responsibilities at home she won't be able to handle responsibility at work"). So the fathers were favored for promotion or challenging assignments while mothers were passed over. It was a major accomplishment when women managed to persuade managers, usually with the help of a friendly judge, that considerations of family status were not relevant to job qualifications and must be ignored in job-related decisions. As with questions about minority status, religion, and sexual preference, questions about family status are now barred by law from the entrance interviews; e.g., how is the prospective employee going to handle the knotty problem of day care?

Even so, new questions seem to arise — specifically those questions we worked so hard to get rid of. Now, it has been argued, it is time for employers to take into account the special needs of women — for pregnancy leave, for maternal leave, for sick children at home. It has been suggested that women be able to opt for a "Mommy Track" at work, that will give them shorter hours, compatible with their children's school schedule, access to childrearing leave when they want it, and generally the freedom to tailor work demands to the home demands. The proposed new standard is that employers *must* be aware of the needs women have to care for children and home, and *must* adjust work demands accordingly.

Proponents of the "Mommy Track" in business argue that women have been forced to set aside their real nature in order to compete with men in a man's world — a macho, sacrifice-all-for-the-company, family-doesn't-count world which tears working mothers apart. To be sure, such a world is as wrong for men as it is for women. But men will stick with it indefinitely, until they can be shown that another, more balanced, approach is possible. The only way to show them that is by living it. So put in the Mommy Track, in every company possible. Let women at least live balanced lives where, as one puts it, "priorities come first, right now." This view concludes: When women have shown that balancing family and work demands is no hindrance to reaching the top posts in the company, maybe men will begin to join them, and the whole corporation will become more humane.

Opponents of "Mommy Track" argue that it is inappropriate in a free market system to have the company responsible to non-company interests of the employee, whether it be to make childrearing easier or to support an employee's outside consulting business. They say that it is unfair to male employees to give women benefits of shorter hours and unscheduled leaves if there are no career penalties attached, and unfair to female employees if there are. They argue that bringing to the fore the image of female employee as mother and helpmate to her husband in dealing with human resources concerns is a sure route to the return of job discrimination against females. This view further argues: "Now that equality is won, why not live it, continue on to CEO, and find a good child care center along the way? It is unlikely, very unlikely, that a Mommy Tracker will ever reach a high post in any company; she lacks the reliability, the dedication, and the willingness to take on unusual challenges that are expected of the employees who will contend for the highest positions."

THE BIG PICTURE

Let's summarize the situation. Women have always worked. As partners in the family farms of agrarian societies, as the craftsman of nomadic herding societies, as the farmers of hunting societies, women have borne an equal share of the economic production. In the 18th and 19th centuries, women and children worked alongside the men, as they always had. Only as the factories became more brutal, the hours longer, and, most importantly, their success more evident, did the wives of the bourgeoisie find it possible to retire to a life of lace-making and chocolates, and a movement arise to exempt first children, then women, from the hardest work of the factory itself. By the turn of the 20th century, an atypical, and probably unrealistic, ideal of "womanhood" held sway, in which the woman was solely the custodian of the Heart, while men had the work of the Head. Women managed the hearth and the home (a haven in a heartless world). Men braved the competitive wars and backbreaking work of the industrial age and the workplace in general. (That ideal never applied to the poor — the Irish and the African-Americans who supplied servants to the rich; their women *always* worked.)

The ideal of stay-at-home women was revived at maximum volume after the second World War, when it became necessary to send women "home" from the factories that had supplied the war effort, in which they had been spectacularly successful, so that returning veterans could have jobs. The ideal prevailed through the 1950s, but by the end of the 1960s it was dead, and the older model prevailed: Women shall work beside men in whatever work the society does. That leaves the home in some disarray, as previous, non-factory, work economies did not. What shall be done about that? As is probably evident from the foregoing, the role of the woman in the modern workplace is not yet settled.

DIGNITY, AND PROTECTION FROM HARASSMENT

As a general principle, the workplace shall nurture dignity, and shall not tolerate assaults upon it. What is dignity? For our purposes, two meanings will suffice. First, empirically, dignity is an understanding of one's own self-worth resting on no external criterion but generated within oneself. Normatively, dignity is a characteristic possessed of every human being according to which he or she deserves respect from others. Putting the two together, we arrive at what we may call a social understanding of dignity: a presence in all persons of a recognition of self-worth, accompanied by an expectation that it will be recognized by others, fostered by respectful treatment by the entire society, individually and institutionally. **For people to *have* dignity, others in general must *acknowledge* dignity; it is a social creation.**

How does this apply to business? The workplace is a space in which the dignity of every employee must be recognized by every other employee, by every supervisor at every level, and by the institutional policies and structures built into the conduct of business. In practice, this means that while at work, no employee will be subjected to ridicule, annoyance, embarrassment or humiliation, in connection with the job or otherwise. This proviso excludes any "embarrassment" felt by an employee in the course of normal instruction or correction of job performance, but it requires that any such instruction or correction be administered in a way minimally embarrassing. This requirement is particularly difficult to implement or enforce in the normal conduct of business because, while the *formal structures* (rules and policies) of the company may insist on correct and respectful behavior at all times from all employees, the *informal structures* (customs and practices of the employees) may be sufficiently offensive to support legal action against the company, should any victimized employee choose to complain. The company's officers are generally held to be responsible for monitoring the "corporate culture," the informal, non-mandated, conduct of the employees toward each other, just to make sure that assaults on dignity are not taking place.

Figure 1. Employee rights to personal workspace include the right not to be sexually harassed. Tony Stone Images (Chicago).

Sexual Harassment

What, in a corporate setting, might count as an assault on dignity? Certain easy examples come to mind. Fraternity-type hazing of new employees by old ones, and the habitual use of racial or ethnic slurs, stereotypes, or derogatory names in the course of the daily routine. The corporate culture is also manifested in logo, publicity, community relations and advertising copy, all of which should be free of stereotype and derogation. Probably the best example of workplace affronts to dignity is sexual harassment, which is the systematic humiliation or degradation by stereotyping a person, exemplified in unwanted sexual attentions bestowed as though they could not be refused, the conditioning by a superior of promotion or job on response to these attentions, or the creation of a workplace environment so sexist, so contemptuous of the talents of a person (most commonly women), as to render the workplace absolutely hostile to the women and their work.

As the Equal Employment Opportunity Commission (EEOC) pointed out in 1990, harasser and harassed do not need to be of different sexes. It is possible for men or women to be harassed in the same way by homosexual supervisors, and for men to have sexual favors demanded of them by a female supervisor. These cases are much less common.

Sexual harassment has been held to fall into two major categories. The first we call *quid pro quo* and arises when an employee is given to understand that the likelihood that he or she will advance in the company or in his or her career is conditional upon a favorable response to sex-laden suggestions by superiors. Classically, the suggestions have been that the woman must engage in sexual intercourse, otherwise undesired on her part, with her superior, or see her job dead-end or disappear. But as we saw in *Price Waterhouse v. Hopkins*, it is just as insulting, and illegal, to condition promotion upon a woman's closer adherence to a "feminine" stereotype in dress, make-up, language and behavior.

Endnote 22

Title VII of the **Civil Rights Act of 1964** forbids discrimination on grounds of gender. In *Meritor Savings Bank v. Vinson,* (1986) the Supreme Court found that the creation of a "hostile environment" through sexual harassment was a violation of Title VII; it was discriminatory even though there were no identifiable employment decisions conditioned on the woman's response to sexual advances. The EEOC went on to define sexual harassment:

> Unwelcome sexual advances, requests for sexual favors, and other verbal or physical conduct of a sexual nature constitute sexual harassment when 1. submission to or rejection of this conduct explicitly or implicitly affects an individual's employment [*quid pro quo*]; 2. unreasonably interferes with an individual's work performance; or 3. creates an intimidating, hostile, or offensive work environment.

Note that the EEOC definition specifies any *one* of those three situations constitutes sexual harassment. Who is to judge whether a workplace is "intimidating, hostile, or offensive"? That question was decided in 1993, in Sandra Day O'Connor's opinion in *Harris vs. Forklift Systems*. It is hostile if a **reasonable person** would see it to be hostile, and if the victim perceives it to be so. It is not necessary to show that severe psychological damage has been inflicted on the victim, who is not required to stay on the job until a nervous breakdown occurs in order to be compensated for damages. Admittedly, the criterion is subjective and difficult to interpret; but it accomplished its objective, which was to put all businesses on notice that the way their employees treat each other at the office is to be taken very seriously.

How many laws could be repealed if everyone merely practiced the Golden Rule in the workplace?

Endnote 23

Fostering Dignity Through Diversity

In general, dignity can best be protected by respecting and accepting differences in the business workplace. Just as the best non-discrimination rule for racial, ethnic and religious differences is the celebration of diversity, so the best rule for the prevention of harassment may be a positive appreciation of different kinds of lives and lifestyles in the corporate world. Women would certainly gain from such appreciation. So would gay and lesbian employees, whose legal protection against discrimination is sporadic at best, and varies from state to state. A corporate culture that incorporates such an attitude of appreciation of differences might also provide protection against very different sorts of harassment — the tendencies to retaliate against employees who manifest their differences publicly by participation in political and social associations outside the workplace, in feminist or gay activism. Political activity on the part of the employee is protected by law, but there are few effective formal safeguards against informal sanctions when an employee is perceived as "different" in a setting where "different" is a pejorative term.

It could be argued that the most effective way to show respect for employees is to invite their participation in workplace decision-making. Including workers in workplace decisions on a democratic basis can be justified, as business scholar **John McCall** argues in *Contemporary Issues in Business Ethics,* in five ways: (1) that the legitimate interests of all in the company are better protected by worker participation than by protective legislation; (2) that only an extensive system of democratic participation recognizes the dignity of persons as moral agents and rational decision makers; (3) that the worker's perception of his or her ability to influence corporate policy will result in higher productivity and a much higher level of responsibility and accountability, and (4) a much lower level of alienation and disaffection; and (5) that workplace democratic participation and responsibility is an essential training ground and reinforcement for civic participation and responsibility, good citizenship in the larger society.

Figure 2. Clarence Thomas objects to sexual harassment charges made against him during his confirmation for the U.S. Supreme Court. Corbis-Bettman.

Endnote 24

There have been some experiments along the lines of workplace democracy. One of the most famous was the **"Bolivar Project,"** started in 1972 by Sidney Harman, then owner and CEO of Harman International Industries, and Irving Bluestone of the United Automobile Workers union. A far-reaching experiment in worker empowerment, it began by encouraging and rewarding workers to invent their own workspace and processes, and to join in creating new opportunities for workers. It caused classes, day-care centers, gospel groups. Morale soared, productivity increased, and absenteeism declined. But by the early 1980s, the company began to get into trouble. One major cause of the trouble was human nature, specifically, laziness. The company had been letting workers decide their own incentive system, and eventually the workers in areas where work could be accelerated were asking to leave work early if they finished their work. That created tensions across the company with workers whose jobs could not be so tailored, lured workers who only wanted to go home early into the company, and tempted workers to cut corners to appear to have their work done. Firm management would have nipped this trend in the bud, but by that time firm management was no longer part of the corporate culture.

The second major cause was the rapid change in the market for their major product, rear-view mirrors; new product materials and directions should have been adopted, but were not, leaving the company by the wayside. Underlying both factors, speculated Harman and Bluestone — both out of the project by 1976 — was the fact that neither the new owners of the company nor the old managers *really* bought the concept of worker democracy, and they were not sad to see the project fail. But the experiment was not entirely a failure. By the time Harman Automotive went out of business on March 1, 1998, it had taught a whole generation of industry how to bring workers into management decisions, saving the GM Tarrytown plant for about 26 years, and making workplace empowerment one of the criteria by which companies can be judged.

Endnote 25

INTEGRITY, AND RESPECT FOR MORAL CHOICES

We begin with a *general principle* and a *general duty*. The general principle is that employees are presumed to be rational moral agents, and the employee does not leave his critical intelligence in the parking lot. It should be respected. More to the point, the employee, consistently with his or her dignity as a moral agent, *cannot* avoid taking responsibility for situations that morally call for action when the employee is the only one in a position to act. If employees see some wrongdoing, and fail to do something to stop it, they incur guilt, the "guilt of silence" that has accompanied so many of the historic atrocities of the 20th century.

The general duty for the corporation, then, is to provide channels through which employees may question and criticize company decisions, policies, and the conduct of company operations in general and on specifics in the areas that they have observed. Failure to provide such channels essentially disregards the critical intelligence and the moral agency of employees, treating them merely as machines, or pieces of office furniture. What is the employee to do when confronted with a serious moral problem in the workplace — a practice that threatens some serious harm to someone, identifiable or not — in a setting that does not allow employee concerns to be voiced, taken into account, or acted upon by the company? If there is no way to act responsibly through company channels, the only responsible course open to the worker is to tell others about it, to try to end the practice by publicity, even if it means bringing the whole corporate enterprise to a screeching halt. This effort to stop the game, to make everyone pay attention to what is going on, is called "blowing the whistle."

Figure 3. When Bendix Corp. official Mary Cunningham resigned, speculation centered on an alleged sexual relationship with William Agee, then president of the company. Corbis-Bettman.

Blowing the Whistle: Definition and Justification

Employees and former employees of corporations often complain that the company is involved in wrongdoing — failing to inform the public about defective products, failing to inform the Nuclear Regulatory Commission about safety problems in nuclear plants, failing to inform the Environmental Protection Agency about environmental problems caused by the corporation's operations. The corporations inevitably reply that the complainer, the "whistle-blower," is exaggerating, wrong, misleading, out for his or her own glory only, and, in the case of former employees, disgruntled. Two questions are raised by such claims and counter-claims. First, how should an employee of a company involved in dubious practices decide whether to bring concerns to some outside agency? Second, how may we determine whether or not such an employee's complaint is valid?

Endnote 26

In his 1982 edition of *Business Ethics*, **Norman Bowie** presents the classic definition and set of criteria for the moral justification of blowing the whistle.

> A whistle-blower is an employee or officer of any institution, profit or nonprofit, private or public, who believes either that he/she has been ordered to perform some act or he/she has obtained knowledge that the institution is engaged in activities which (a) are believed to cause unnecessary harm to third parties, (b) are in violation of human rights, or (c) run counter to the defined purpose of the institution, and who informs the public of this fact.

Endnote 27

Note that it doesn't count as blowing the whistle as long as the complaint stays inside the company or within a small circle of peers in the industry or profession; the public must be involved, so the stakes are high. The presumption of this topic is that a certain amount of harm is going to be done when the whistle blows. The company gets a black eye in the press, the employees involved in the practice on which the whistle is blown are defamed and hurt, no one likes the whistle-blower and his or her job is promptly in danger. Against that harm, the justifiability of blowing the whistle requires an argument, and must bear the burden of proof. Bowie considers that the burden is met when:

a. The whistle is blown from the appropriate moral motive — to save innocent third parties from harm, to expose wrongdoing so that it can be dealt with by the proper authorities, or to restore the agency or firm to its proper course. A desire for attention is not a proper motive, which is why our response to whistle-blowing varies so profoundly when we find that a book contract has already been inked. To be sure, the public can profit from knowledge of wrongdoing no matter what the motive of the informant. But given the ambiguity of findings of wrongdoing, as general poli-

cy, the public will be much better off with a predisposition to ignore tell-all publicity seekers no matter what stories they have to tell.

b. Unless the whistle-blowers know for sure that they will be fired, discredited, and barred from further information if they so much as hint of their concerns to their supervisors — or that some major explosion or other danger is imminent — all internal channels for expressing dissent must be exhausted before the whistle-blowers go public. The officials of the company may honestly not know what is going on; even a minimum of loyalty to the firm requires that they be given a chance to right the situation before the irreversible damage of unfavorable publicity has occurred.

c. The wrongdoing must be carefully documented, the evidence certain.

d. The employee must give the matter careful thought, and be sure that the danger is real, the harm imminent, there is specific misconduct to cite, and there are no alternatives to blowing the whistle that will bring the matter to light and get it remedied.

e. The employee has some chance of success. If the whole matter is doomed to failure, the employee is not obligated to destroy his or her career by blowing the whistle.

Let's be practical. In response to wrongdoing in the workplace, why destroy your career, put yourself and family at risk, distress your friends, infuriate erstwhile co-workers, entertain the press and generally turn your life into a circus for the short attention span of a scandal-hungry society? Unless it is clear that there is little danger to the whistle-blower (and that is rarely the case) there cannot be a strong obligation to blow the whistle. That is why this topic turns on the notion of **integrity**, which is the singleness of life, character and person that informs us at our best, that requires us always to act in accord with our moral principles, and thereby permits us to undertake courses of action that, if we waited for deep analysis, would scare us to death. Therefore, due to the substantial risks involved, there is a presumption that without integrity, an employee will not blow the whistle. The corollary is that without integrity, there's no telling what else the employee will or won't do.

Ultimately, some ready and relatively painless means of upward communication must be found. Employees must know how they can access the highest officers in the company to share their concerns. They must know that the officers are listening and will act on employee concerns one way or another. (By all means try a suggestion box, someone said, but make sure that the employee knows that the suggestions are being read.)

The Corporation and the Whistle

There are several reasons why a corporation might want to institute practices that make it unnecessary for employees to blow whistles.

Any quick consequential analysis will yield the undesirable results of whistle-blowing. The company's operations suffer short-term disruption because of the investigations triggered by the whistle and by the need to devote resources to the confrontation with an angry public and press. The company may be in trouble with the law and face fines or criminal or civil proceedings. Employee morale plummets as the employees take sides with or against the whistle-blower. Other stakeholders (shareholders, vendors, customers) may decide to make other business arrangements and hurt the company's long-term interests. But there are worse consequences.

Figure 4. Members of the Space Shuttle *Challenger* crew, including (left to right, front row) Astronauts Michael J. Smith, Francis R. Scobee, and Ronald E. McNair, and (left to tight, back row), Ellison S. Onizuka, Sharon Christa McAuliffe (representing the Teacher in Space Project), Gregory Jarvis (representing the Hughes Company), and Judith A. Resnik. The crew members lost their lives when the *Challenger* exploded shortly after lift off on January 28, 1986. USA NASA/Corbis.

First, there are the undesirable results of the corporate governance practices that made whistle-blowing seem the only recourse for the employee. If the corporation does not respect the employee's contribution to the ongoing dialogue of company operations, it not only places itself at risk for whistle-blowing, but it loses the value of that contribution. Also, the policies and practices that discouraged the whistle-blower's communication will have discouraged all the other employees from joining the dialogue, and a good portion of their creativity, experience, cultural slants and ideas will have been lost to the company. A second consequence is the loss of employee enthusiasm, or "ownership," regarding the company mission and work, duplicating the morale problems incurred by any exclusion of the employees from the decision-making process.

But the worst consequence of the whistle-blowing scenario is the damage to the employees who confront the corporate evil, whether or not one of them blows the whistle, whatever they decide to do. Consider the case of the spacecraft ***Challenger***:

> On January 28, 1986, the space shuttle *Challenger* lifted off from the launch pad at Cape Kennedy in Florida, flew seven nautical miles down range, and exploded, killing its seven astronauts, including a popular New Hampshire schoolteacher, Christa McAuliffe, chosen from all the nation for the honor of space flight. As it shortly became known, most of the Morton Thiokol engineers responsible for the spacecraft had advised against the flight, on grounds that in the unusually cold morning air (there was still ice on the

launch pad), the O-rings (loops of rubber-like material between the segments of the booster rocket) might be too stiff to seal the joints in the rocket. If that happened, hot gases might blow by the rings and ignite with explosive force, destroying spacecraft, crew, and the entire launching apparatus. The engineers had assumed that the explosion, if it came, would be at the liftoff. They were listened to, but eventually overruled by senior management at Morton Thiokol, who in response to the National Aeronautics and Space Agency (NASA) felt they could tolerate no more embarrassing delays. After the explosion, Congress wanted to know what had gone wrong. Against the advice and pleas of his colleagues, engineer Roger Boisjoly, the first to notice the erosion of the O-rings in previous flights, and the person responsible for the task force working to solve the problem, told the Rogers Commission exactly what had gone wrong. He said he and others had tried to stop the flight but had been overruled.

As a result, Boisjoly was isolated and shunned in his workplace, sent away from the centers of decision, removed from projects in which his expertise would count, deprived of his functions; soon enough, he had to resign. He lost his job, income, security, career, and very nearly his sanity. The fate of the employees who stayed may be worse. Now they knew that their failure of courage — and, in the case of the managers, failure of wisdom — caused the death of the astronauts. But having done nothing about it since, and having done nothing while the one person who did try to do something was persecuted by the company, they must carry that guilt with them forever. It is only compounded by their silent mistreatment of Boisjoly.

Endnote 28

Boisjoly's action, even though taken after the fact of the explosion, still constitutes external whistle-blowing. It is plainly "a disclosure by organizational members of illegal, immoral, or illegitimate organizational acts or omissions to parties who can take action to correct the wrongdoing." There was no correcting the wrongdoing for Christa McAuliffe and her shipmates, but there was much that could be done to make sure that it did not happen again. In the future, NASA could worry less about media embarrassment and more about safety checks. The engineers and the managers could spend more time learning to understand each other's preoccupations. The hierarchically-organized company could figure out some way to empower employees to pursue ethical concerns to the end, instead of being asked to bottle them in the name of corporate (and agency) convenience. A good company will make sure that its employees can follow their consciences, no matter how much delay and disruption those consciences threaten to spawn. Ultimately, when management realizes the inevitability of confronting employee consciences in tight situations, management will learn to have the confrontation much earlier in the decision process, when things are easier to change, and next time the disaster may be averted.

WHAT ARE SOME OTHER EMPLOYEE RESPONSIBILITIES?

Just as an employee has certain rights, so also does an employee have certain responsibilities to the corporation, to coworkers and to the community. Below we will look at employee rights and responsibilities. Business ethicist **Patricia Werhane's** book, *Persons, Rights and Corporations* (Prentice-Hall, Inc., Englewood Cliffs, N.J., 1985), has two lists — one of employee rights, and one of employee obligations:

Employee Rights

1. Every person has an equal right to a job and a right to equal consideration at the job. Employees may not be discriminated against on the basis of religion, sex, ethnic origin, race, color, or economic background.

2. Every person has the right to equal pay for work, where "equal work" is defined by the job description and title.

3. Every employee has rights to his or her job. After a probation period of 3–10 years every employee has the right to his or her job. An employee can be dismissed only under the following conditions:

   a. He or she is not performing satisfactorily the job for which he or she was hired.

   b. He or she is involved in criminal activity either within or outside the corporation.

   c. He or she is drunk or takes drugs on the job.

   d. He or she actively disrupts corporate business activity without a valid reason.

   e. He or she becomes physically or mentally incapacitated or reaches mandatory retirement age.

   f. The employer has publicly verifiable economic reasons for dismissing the employee, e.g., transfer of the company, loss of sales, bankruptcy, et cetera.

   g. Under no circumstances can an employee be dismissed or laid off without the institution of fair due process procedure.

4. Every employee has the right to due process in the workplace. He or she has the right to peer review, to a hearing, and if necessary, to outside arbitration before being demoted or fired.

5. Every employee has the right to free expression in the workplace. This includes the right to object to corporate acts that he or she finds illegal or immoral without retaliation or penalty. The objection may take the form of free speech, whistle-blowing, or conscientious objection. However, any criticism must be documented or proven.

6. The Privacy Act, which protects the privacy and confidentiality of public employees, should be extended to all employees.

7. The polygraph should be outlawed.

8. Employees have the right to engage in outside activities of their choice.

9. Every employee has the right to a safe workplace, including the right to safety information and participation in improving work hazards. Every employee has the right to legal protection that guards against preventable job risks.

10. Every employee has the right to as much information as possible about the corporation, about his or her job, work hazards, possibilities for future employment, and any other information necessary for job enrichment and development.

11. Every employee has the right to participate in the decision-making processes entailed in his or her job, department, or in the corporation as a whole, where appropriate.

12. Every public and private employee has the right to strike when the foregoing demands are not met in the workplace.

Employee Obligations

1A. Any employee found discriminating against another employee or operating in a discriminatory manner against his or her employer is subject to employer reprimand, demotion, or firing.

2A. Any employee not deserving equal pay because of inefficiency should be shifted to another job.

3A. No employee who functions inefficiently, who drinks or takes drugs on the job, commits felonies or acts in ways that prevent carrying out work duties has a right to a job.

4A. Any employee found guilty under a due process procedure should be reprimanded (e.g., demoted or dismissed), and, if appropriate, brought before the law.

5A. No employer must retain employees who slander the corporation or other corporate constituents.

6A. The privacy of employers is as important as the privacy of employees. By written agreement employees may be required not to disclose confidential corporate information or trade secrets unless not doing so is clearly against public interest.

7A. Employers may engage in surveilance of employees at work (but only at work) with their foreknowledge and consent.

8A. No employee may engage in activities that literally harm the employer, nor may an employee have a second job whose business competes with the business of the first employer.

9A. Employees shall be expected to carry out job assignments for which they are hired unless these conflict with common moral standards or unless the employee was not fully informed about these assignments or their dangers before accepting employment. Employers themselves should become fully informed about work dangers.

10A. Employers have rights to personal information about employees or prospective employees adequate to make sound hiring and promotion judgments so long as the employer preserves the confidentiality of such information.

11A. Employers as well as employees have rights. Therefore the right to participation is a correlative obligation on the part of both parties to respect mutual rights. Employers, then, have the right to demand efficiency and productivity from their employees in return for the employee right to participation in the workplace.

12A. Employees who strike for no reason are subject to dismissal. Any employee or employer who feels he or she has been unduly penalized under a bill of rights may appeal to an outside arbitrator.

Now let's look at employee obligations from a *corporation's* point of view. The following statements of employees' obligations to their employer are extracts from a model code of ethics published by the United Technologies Corporation as cited in *A Code of Ethics: Do Cor-*

porate Executives Need It? (Itawamba Community College Press, Fulton, Ms, 1990).

CONFLICT OF INTEREST — Employees must deal with suppliers, customers and others doing business with the firm. The employee is responsible for avoiding even the appearance of conflict between his or her personal interests and those of the business or corporation. This requirement applies equally to business relationships and personal activities relative to the employees' conduct in the areas of

* direct or indirect financial or stock ownership interest in suppliers, customers or competitors;

* seeking or accepting gifts or any form of compensation from suppliers, customers or others doing business, or seeking to do business with the firm; directorships, employment with or voluntary service rendered to another company or organization; or

* the use of confidential or non-public information that may be acquired in the course of employment related activities.

ANTI-TRUST COMPLIANCE — Businesses and corporations must comply with the anti-trust laws of every jurisdiction in which the firm does business, both within and outside the United States. Every employee, no matter what position he or she holds in the firm, is responsible for compliance with the applicable anti-trust laws.

U.S. GOVERNMENT PROCUREMENTS — A corporation expects all employees and any consultants used by the business or corporation to comply with the laws and regulations regarding government procurements. Special care must be taken to comply with the unique and special rules of the U.S. Government procurement process and to ensure the accuracy of all data submitted to the Government.

PRODUCT QUALITY AND SAFETY — All operating employees of the business or corporation have the responsibility to design, manufacture and deliver quality products and services. All required inspection and testing operations should be properly completed by employees. Likewise, all products must be designed, produced and delivered with the safety and health of customers and product users as a primary consideration.

MARKETING AND SELLING — The employee has the responsibility to understand customer require-

ments and to seek to satisfy those requirements by offering quality products and services at competitive prices and terms. Employees must offer to sell products and services honestly, based upon their merits, and will not pursue any sale that requires the firm to act unlawfully or in violation of company policy just to win a sale.

PROTECTION OF PROPRIETARY INFORMATION — Employees must respect the proprietary information and trade secrets of the customers and suppliers of a firm. New employees are not to divulge the proprietary information of their former employers. And, employees of the firm will not disclose any proprietary information of customers or suppliers unless the release or disclosure is properly authorized by the individual or firm owning the information.

SUPPLIERS, VENDORS AND SUBCONTRACTORS — Employees of a firm should follow policy relative to the purchase of all equipment, supplies and services on the basis of merit. Suppliers, vendors and subcontractors must be treated with fairness and integrity and without discrimination.

ERROR RECONCILIATION — Firm policy should be followed to advise customers and suppliers of any clerical or accounting errors, and promptly to effect correction of the error through credits, refunds or other mutually acceptable means.

DRUG AND ALCOHOL ABUSE — The firm expects all employees to abide by applicable laws and regulations relative to the possession or use of alcohol and drugs. Employees should abide by policies which prohibit the illegal use, sale, purchase, transfer, possession or presence in one's system of drugs, other than medically prescribed drugs, while on company premises. Similarly, employees are expected to abide by policy which prohibits the use, sale, purchase, transfer or possession of alcoholic beverages by employees while on company premises, except as authorized by the firm.

PROTECTION OF ASSETS — Every employee of the firm is responsible for the proper use, conservation and protection of corporate assets, including its property, plants and equipment.

INTELLECTUAL PROPERTY — The firm's employees frequently have access to the intellectual property of the business, such as inventions, sensitive business information, and sensitive technical information, including computer programs, product designs, and manufacturing expertise. All employees are charged with the responsibility to use and protect these assets in accordance with the firm's guidelines.

ACCURACY OF COMPANY RECORDS — Firm business transactions must be properly authorized and be completely and accurately recorded on the firm's books and records in accordance with generally accepted accounting practice and established firm financial policy. Budget proposals and economic evaluations must fairly represent all information relevant to the decision being requested or recommended. No secret or unrecorded cash funds or other assets will be established or maintained for any purpose. The retention or proper disposal of company records shall be in accordance with established firm financial policies and applicable statutory requirements.

EMPLOYEE INVOLVEMENT IN THE POLITICAL PROCESS — The firm encourages all employees to be informed voters and to be involved in the political process. Personal participation, including contributions of time or financial support, shall be entirely voluntary. Employees, representatives, consultants or agents who are designated to represent the firm or its entities must comply fully with all applicable laws and corporate policy relevant to participation in political and public affairs.

FOREIGN CORRUPT PRACTICES ACT — Employees involved directly or indirectly in non-U.S. operations must abide by the provisions of the Foreign Corrupt Practice Act of 1977. Business transactions outside the U.S. will be governed by the company's policies regarding payments to foreign representatives and foreign payments reviews.

COMMUNITY SUPPORT — As a good corporate citizen, firm policy is to support the organizations and activities of the communities in which the firm resides. Employees are urged to participate personally in civic affairs.

ANTI-TRUST LAWS — Firm employees never must exchange information with competitors regarding prices, market share, or any other data that could be in violation of U.S. anti-trust law or comparable competition laws that apply to firm operations outside the U.S.

COMPETITIVE INFORMATION — In the highly competitive global marketplace, information about competitors is a necessary element of business. Such information should be accepted by employees only when there is a reasonable belief that both receipt and use of the information is lawful.

MARKETING, SELLING AND ADVERTISING — Firm competition in the global marketplace is on the basis of the merits of firm products and services. Legal and ethical considerations dictate that marketing activities be conducted fairly and honestly. Marketing and selling practices by employees should be based on the superiority of the firm's product offerings. In making comparisons to competitors, care must be taken to avoid disparaging a competitor through inaccurate statements.

COMPLIANCE WITH THE FIRM'S STANDARDS OF CONDUCT — The employee is responsible for complying with the standards of conduct adopted by the firm and implementing policies. Failure to comply with the standards and the associated policies will result in appropriate employee sanctions, to be determined by the cognizant operating manager in conjunction with the business practices office. As with all disciplinary matters, principles of fairness and equity will apply.

REPORTING VIOLATIONS — (All employees have) personal responsibility to bring violations or suspected violations of the standards of conduct to the attention of their supervisor, the legal department of the firm, or to the company ombudsman, as appropriate. Firm policy prohibits any retribution against employees for making such reports.

The following examples of issues that arise from such codes are taken from the United Technologies Corporation's "Questions and Answers About the UTC Code of Ethics."

1. A conflict of interest exists when an employee, or a member of his or her immediate family, receives an unearned, personal benefit as a result of the employee's job or position with the company.

2. Multi-national corporations doing world-wide business must comply with the Foreign Corrupt Practices Act which prohibits employees from paying (bribing) a foreign government official to award business to the firm. How does the law apply if the firm uses a third party, or "agent," to deal with the foreign government? The use of an intermediary, such as an agent or representative, does not relieve the firm from the requirement to comply

with the Foreign Corrupt Practices Act. It is the employee's responsibility to prevent improper payments, whether made directly or indirectly.

3. Many codes talk about possible anti-trust problems in dealing with customers as well as competitors. What is the reason behind anti-trust laws? The U.S. economic system encourages as many companies as wish the freedom to compete for consumer acceptance. The success of this process depends on free and fair competition among suppliers. If the competition is not free and fair, then consumers and the American economy may be subjected to higher prices and inferior goods. The purpose of the U.S. anti-trust laws is simply to ensure that American consumers enjoy the benefits that flow from a free market economy, unrestrained by anti-competitive practices such as price fixing, market allocation or bid rigging.

FINAL COMMENTS

So, in the employer-employee relationship, what are the obligations of the parties? The general duty may be summed up as **mutual responsibility** — the corporation must exercise responsibility over the areas which it controls (the physical conditions of the workspace, the monitoring devices and policies in place), while the employees must take responsibility for that portion of the work that is in their control. Each of the imperatives of this chapter is really a mutual imperative, binding not only on management and Boards of Directors (as is traditional in business ethics), but also on the employees individually and, to a lesser extent, collectively.

For privacy and other individual rights to be honored in the workplace, management must learn to trust the employees. But, *a fortiori* (literally, with convincing force), the employees must be trustworthy, not taking advantage of the hands-off, eyes-off policy for behavior that would hurt the company's interests. For health and safety to be protected, management can only make a start at keeping the workplace safe; workers must learn safety consciousness and create a work atmosphere where protection is taken very seriously. Dignity also is preserved as much by co-workers as by front office policy; the climate of dignity is created not by rules but by thousands of acts of respect among employees of all levels. Integrity must not only be permitted but encouraged; in a world that seems to have forgotten the notion, employees cannot always be expected to know how to live with integrity when they enter employment. In a company that depends on employee integrity to survive, as most companies do, it is imperative to include some lessons on integrity near the beginning of employment.

What would a lesson plan look like, for these integrity lessons? On the assumption that they would be for top managers and every level beneath them, they cannot include the specifics of anyone's job, and they certainly cannot contain how-to material for handling, supervising, outwitting, intimidating, or spying on each other. That's one of the advantages of a course designed for the whole company. Experience suggests a four-item **integrity curriculum**, elaborated in any way that may seem useful to the company.

1. Primarily through the discussion of cases (supplemented by some limited instruction on the terminology of ethics), help each employee acquire the **wisdom** to see ethical problems when they arise — to discern injustice and insult as they happen, to foresee problems from unsafe practices, to know when rights and welfare are being violated.

2. Through empowering policies and direct encouragement, accompanied by some very specific instructions to the first-level managers, help each employee acquire the **courage** to speak out about problems when they are first noticed, and to follow up to make sure something is done about them.

3. That said, and done, continue the lesson, primarily through the relation of stories that trace signal events over time to show both short-and long-term consequences, to help each employee acquire the **patience** (or temperance, for traditionalists) to recognize that in the best of circumstances, while minor changes that avert disaster may certainly be hoped for (let's put off the flight for a few days and maybe it will get warmer), radical changes in corporate structure and practice are not going to happen quickly. Action that continues a controversy beyond reason and beyond effect can only harm the company and therefore everyone who has a stake in it.

4. For **justice** to prevail in the corporation, (1) hiring and promoting practices must reflect non-discrimination, (2) where appropriate, affirmative action plans are required, and (3) the employees must work informally to create an accepting and empowering working situation.

Employees must know, in short, how to take responsibility — how to recognize a problem, how to act effectively to solve it, and how to lay it to rest to minimize harm to others. (Sound familiar to the "critical thinking" of Chapter 3?) The corporation is, after all, a world unto itself; it absorbs the best part of the lives of those who work in it, commanding their obedience, their social support and their individual creativity. Their lives are lived as part of it, and if they are to be truly *human* lives — lives of choice and responsibility — the corporation must be an arena of responsibility for all its human participants.

FOR FURTHER INQUIRY

1. Employers ought not to discriminate against workers solely on the grounds of disability; such discrimination is unfair and contrary to law — specifically, contrary to the Americans with Disabilities Act (ADA). Employers are expected to make rea-

sonable accommodations to make it possible for disabled persons to operate in the workplace — ramps for those in wheelchairs and the like. But what kind of "accommodations" are appropriate for a person who is emotionally disturbed and likely to become disruptive and violent in the workplace? An employer who fires a mentally disabled person risks a lawsuit under ADA; an employer who retains a disruptive person risks lawsuits by co-workers placed at risk by his or her behavior. What should the employer do? How should these conflicts be resolved?

2. The statistics on disparity of wealth and income raise many questions, some of which are beyond the scope of this book. One of them, for instance, is whether we value integration of all professions and work settings to the point where we are willing to override all task organization based on voluntary association. It is one thing to say that states must hire clerical workers regardless of race, religion, age, sex, or ethnic origin. Must we require garden clubs to show that they invite new members on the same criteria? Another question of societal scope has to do with economic equality and empowerment. Does the fact of economic equality, regardless of what it says about the way business is conducted, cry out for remedy simply because it is wrong for some to have so much when others have so little? Did the chapter on Economic Systems deal with this question to your satisfaction? What do you think?

3. Under what conditions is simple observation, simply looking at someone else, a violation of rights? Why? (What do those conditions have in common?)

ENDNOTES

1. *New York Times* editorial, Tuesday, February 17, 1998. See also the article it is commenting on, by Richard W. Stevenson, ironically entitled "Black-White Economic Gap Is Narrowing, White House Says," Tuesday, February 10, 1998, p. A-16.

2. Diane Harris, "How Does Your Pay Stack Up?" *Working Woman,* February 1996 21(2) p. 27 ff.

3. 401 U.S. 424, 91 S.Ct. 849 (1971)

4. Id at 430; emphasis supplied

5. Id at 436

6. 431 U.S. 324, 97 S.Ct. 1843, 52 L. Ed. 2d 396 (1977)

7. 490 U.S. 228, 109 S.Ct. 1775 (1989)

8. Id at 1782

9. Matthews, Goodpaster, and Nash, *Policies and Persons*, McGraw-Hill, 3rd edition 1997. Also, the video of Kenneth Goodpaster's interview with Bill Lee in 1984 (Harvard Business School Series)

10. *United Steelworkers of America, AFL-CIO vs. Weber*, 443 U.S. 193, 99 S. Ct. 2721, 61 L.Ed. 2nd 480 (1979)

11. 443 U.S. 190, 218

12. *Memphis Firefighters v. Stotts*, 104 S. Ct. 2576 (1984)

13. *Wards Cove Packing Co. vs. Atonio*, 490 U.S. 642, 104 L. Ed. 2d 733, 109 S. Ct. 2115 (1989)

14. See Robert Belton, "The Dismantling of the *Griggs* Disparate Impact Theory and the Future of Title VII; The Need for a Third Reconstruction," 8 Yale Law and Policy Review 223.

15. Peter Truell, "Morgan Merger Creates Windfall, at Least for Boss," *The New York Times*, Saturday, February 21, 1998, p. D-1.

16. Charles Pillar, "Bosses with X-Ray Eyes," *MacWorld*, July 1993.

17. "Alternatives to Body Fluid Testing," *HR Magazine,* April 1992, p. 42.

18. David Adams and Edward W. Maine, *Business Ethics for the 21st Century*, Mountain View, Ca: Mayfield Publishing Co. 1998, p. 169.

19. Early Supreme Court decisions.

20. See especially Dennis Brodeur, *Outrageous Misconduct*, also Samuel S. Epstein, "The Asbestos 'Pentagon Papers'", in *Mark Essays on Corporate America*, New York: Pilgrim Press, 1980; most recently, "Asbestos Settlement Tossed," *San Jose Mercury News*, May 11, 1996, p. 1D.

21. David Adams and Edward W. Maine, *Business Ethics for the 21st Century*, Mountain View, Ca: Mayfield Publishing Co., 1998, p. 417, citing *National Law Journal* 2/20/95.

22. 477 U.S. 57 (1986).

23. 114 S.Ct. 367 (1993) for an editorial underscoring this point, see "A Victory on Workplace Harassment," *New York Times* 11 November 1993.

24. John J. McCall, "Participation in Employment," from Joseph R. DesJardins and John J. McCall, eds. *Contemporary Issues in Business Ethics, 3rd Edition*. Belmont, CA: Wadsworth, 1996.

25. Barnaby Feder, "The Little Project That Couldn't," *The New York Times,* Saturday, February 21, 1998, p. D1.

26. See, for example, the cases in Alan F. Westin, including Challenger, Pinto, Vandevier and the Goodrich Brakes.

27. Norman Bowie, *Business Ethics*, Englewood Cliffs, N.J.: Prentice Hall, 1982, pp. 142ff.

28. Marcia Miceli, Janet P. Near, and Charles R. Schwenk, "Who Blows the Whistle and Why?" *Industrial and Labor Relations Review* 45:113 (October 1991).

CHAPTER 19

CUSTOMERS, COMMUNITY, AND WORLD

"Here are all sorts of employers wanting all sorts of servants, and all sorts of servants wanting all kinds of employers, and they never seem to come together."

— *Charles Dickens, in* **Martin Chuzzlewit**

The corporation is a highly specialized social instrument, designed for the explicit purpose of creating wealth. Business, therefore, must operate in its own self-interest. Proponents of the social or moral view rebut these arguments by underscoring the idea of a social contract for business, the corporation's character as servant of the larger society. Because businesses are socially created, they have greater responsibilities to the good of the larger society.

The other half of the corporation's obligations concerns the constituencies beyond the plant walls. Customers, suppliers, local communities, national and international audiences, and ultimately the natural world itself. The duties to the people outside are much the same as the duties to the people inside. They must be treated fairly, with respect for culture and differences, with concern for the health and safety of all who deal with the company. The duties may be summarized under five headings: (1) **quality** of product and service, and the willingness to back up the product with warranty and keep track of it, possibly to the place or manner in which it is finally disposed of; (2) **truth and sensitivity** in the representation of the corporation and its products; (3) **good citizenship** in all the communities in which the corporation functions, including candor and cooperation with the government(s) and governmental agencies with which the corporation must deal; (4) **consistency** in the application of moral

Lisa H. Newton, Ph.D., is Professor of Philosophy and Director of the Program in Applied Ethics at Fairfield University in Fairfield, Connecticut. She is author or co-author of several textbooks in the fields of Ethics and Environmental Studies, and has a faculty appointment in the Department of Medicine at Yale Medical School for the teaching of medical ethics.

codes and standards abroad; and (5) **stewardship** of the natural environment. We will take these on in that order.

QUALITY OF PRODUCT AND SERVICE

The first duty of any association that provides goods or services for sale is to do what it is doing *well*. The products should be safe, durable, and beautiful; the services should be promptly and cheerfully performed; what is done should be done right the first time. At the least, the company should be able to stand behind, guarantee, anything it makes or does.

In simpler times, the entire duty of the company could be summed up in the commitment to quality, or excellence. The quality of the product or service, recognized and appreciated by the customers, would keep the customers satisfied, and keep them coming back, assuring the company's profits. As we recall from Chapter 17, that was why Adam Smith was so sure that competition among suppliers would increase the real wealth of the people indefinitely. He assumed that customers were interested in the highest quality goods for the lowest price, and were able to tell exactly what they were getting. Quality, and the reputation for it, provided the foundation for fulfilling the rest of the obligations to the larger community. With a good product, the advertising can tell the truth, the suppliers and the local community are assured a continuing enterprise to provide support for them, and there is no reason to fudge on compliance with laws. Incidentally, that same commitment and reputation was the best start to fulfilling the company's duties to its employees, for it ensured them adequate resources for wages and benefits, and reason to take pride in their work.

CHIEF LEARNING OUTCOME

I can recognize ethical issues in the modern business world and apply moral reasoning to them.

For purposes of this chapter, a **consumer** is any person who buys and-or uses goods and services marketed and sold by another. In some cases, we have to distinguish between the **customer**, the buyer who chooses and purchases the goods for sale, and the **user**, or ultimate consumer, who actually puts the product to its end use. Parents are often the customers while children are the users of, for instance, sugar-coated cereal. "Consumer" covers both; "ultimate consumer" is the user.

How is the manufacturer of any product accountable to the consumer? The first kind of product guarantee is called a **warranty**.

Essentially, a **warranty** is a promise made by the manufacturer to the consumer, that the product is as it is presented. The most general kind of warranty is the *implied warranty of merchantability,* the universal promise that the product is as it appears to a reasonable person to be, and will do what it is obviously intended to do. A saw will cut wood; a bicycle will not fall apart as soon as someone sits on it; a radio has working parts; if there are light switches in the new house, there is an electrical system to which they are connected. Beyond that, there may be any number of *express warranties,* in which a manufacturer specifically promises a particular level of performance. He will be held to that standard on account of the warranty. Warranties may cover anything that a manufacturer could be held responsible for: the design of a product, its construction, and any or all of its component parts. By law, a manufacturer may also be held responsible for the labels attached to the product and the instructions and warnings that come with it, which must be clear and easy to read.

Our courts have noted that the link between the quality of the product and the fortunes of the company is not as clear as it once was, in part because the product is simply too complex to be examined by the consumer for defects, and in part because our more articulated system of product distribution often places the manufacturer at several removes from the ultimate consumer. The resulting dilemmas have

Key Concepts

Quality of Product and Service — products should be safe, durable, and beautiful; the services should be promptly and cheerfully performed; what is done should be done right the first time. At the least, the company should be able to stand behind anything it makes or does.

Veracity (**truth and sensitivity**) — first, in the representation of the corporation and its product; and second, in the right and duty of the consumer to exercise prudence in making choices of what to buy.

Good Citizenship — in all the communities in which the corporation functions, the corporation is to operate with candor and cooperation with the government(s) and governmental agencies and community organizations.

Consistency — in the application of moral codes and standards, the corporation establishes a pattern of reliability. It is the job of the multinational corporation in the first instance to establish what its position will be regarding everything from bribes to working conditions, and to stick with its position.

Stewardship — in conducting business in the environment, the corporation seeks to reduce or eliminate pollution, preferably by recycling its elements; conserve resources; avoid cost-cutting at the expense of environmental protection and seek always to respect whole biosphere, the entire interlocking system of topsoil, plant life, oceans and ocean life, and the composition of the atmosphere itself, including the ozone layer, seen as one interdependent living system.

made the judgments of product quality, product safety, responsibility for both, and liability for misfortunes that occur in the use of the product, considerably more complicated. Certain principles of responsibility for product quality and safety are ancient and well-known. For instance, we have a moral *duty not to harm* each other, intentionally or otherwise. Intentional harm is clearly wrong, and since the elaboration of duties in the book of *Exodus* it has been a principle of community life that we must be careful not to hurt others unintentionally either. Even colloquially, we recognize a duty to exercise **due care**, the carefulness expected in order to make sure that people don't get hurt. That principle is expressed in our law. The Anglo-American Common Law has held since the 17th century (at least) that if a person acts negligently — carelessly or neglectfully — in such a way as to injure another, that other may recover from the careless one the damage that has been caused. *Negligence,* as a cause of action (reason to sue) with expectation of recovery — includes four elements, each of which must be proved by the plaintiff for the suit to be successful.

1. The defendant must have had a *duty* to the plaintiff.
2. There must have been a *breach* of that duty: the defendant failed to perform the duty or failed to perform it to a required standard.
3. There must have been *harm* to the plaintiff.
4. The *breach* must have been the nearest *cause* of that *harm.*

An infinitely large number of possible breaches of normal duties are included under the umbrella of "negligence": failure to shovel the sidewalk in front of your house, on which the postal worker slips and hurts himself; failure to operate machinery in a safe manner; failure to supervise a nurse who allows a patient to fall out of bed. Since the establishment of this legal category, it has been accepted that "harming" someone through negligence may include giving or selling that person a defective product, which causes damage to the person when used. In fact, there is a positive duty to make a product safe. As can be imagined, the scope of the duty is as wide as the range of human activity, and as problematic. Is the manufacturer under any duty to a burglar who steals the chainsaw and hurts himself with it? Is a homeowner negligent if he allows a rotting tree to stand until it falls in a storm on the neighbor's car?

Amid the confusion, we can track at least one important trend. In vendor-buyer relations, the responsibility for the safety of the consumer has been transferred from the consumer to the company that made the product. For example, consider the family car.

The Safety of the Car
Until the beginning of this century, if a product you bought was defective, you could recover damages under contract law from the person you bought it from, who had promised to sell you a safe prod-

uct in exchange for your payment and then failed to fulfill his promise. That understanding made sense in Benjamin Franklin's day when the person who made the product also sold it. But by the time a wheel fell off Donald MacPherson's Buick, the dealer, who had not made the car, had no way of finding out that the product was defective. Yet the only *contractual relationship* was between MacPherson and the dealer. Could MacPherson hold Buick responsible? Yes, the court in *MacPherson v. Buick Motor Car* (1916) held, not only because the manufacturer would be better able to bear the burden of remedy for defective products than the hapless retailer, but also and primarily because it was possible to bring this case into the category of "negligence" and thus acknowledge another legal duty, that of **due care**, by the manufacturers. In the doctrine of "due care," manufacturers and customers are not Adam Smith's equally knowledgeable bargainers meeting in the marketplace. The manufactured product is assumed to be something of a mystery to the buyer, and therefore the manufacturer has the responsibility to exercise special care to make sure that it is made properly, and will present no hazard to the consumer.

Endnote 1

MacPherson reversed Adam Smith's guiding principle for the free market, **caveat emptor** (let the buyer beware), which had clearly become unrealistic in the days of complex manufactured products. From that point, the maker of the product was responsible for taking care that the product was properly made. But the burden was still on the consumer of the product to show, in case of product failure, that the manufacturer was guilty of negligence. Had the company negligently failed to perform some required operation in the production of the car? Was that failure the most likely cause of the injury to the consumer? This burden was lifted, and placed on the manufacturer, in succeeding cases, most notably *Henningsen v. Bloomfield Motors* (New Jersey, 1960) and *Greenman v. Yuba Power Products* (California, 1963) in which it was established that injured consumers could be awarded damages even if there had been no provable negligence in the manufacture of the product. The courts in effect decided that a consumer has a *right* to expect that the products offered for sale are reasonably safe when used for their intended purpose.

Endnote 2
Endnote 3

So the decisions held that a car must be safe when used by ordinary people in ordinary ways — not just "appropriately safe" within the confines of the market, but *safe*. In 1960, Ralph Nader, an articulate critic of the American automobile companies, wrote *Unsafe at Any Speed*, a critique of the Corvair in particular, but also more generally all automobiles on the road at that time. He showed that features adopted purely for marketing purposes rendered the car more dangerous than the consumer probably expected. At no point did he claim that there had been negligence in the making of any individual car, or that statistics showed a particular car to be alarmingly mis-engineered. It was simply that, under certain circumstances *that motorists could avoid but probably would not*, accidents happened. From that conclusion, it was a short step to the Pinto case.

Endnote 4

PINTO CASE:
CRIMINAL LIABILITY

The Pinto was a small "subcompact" car developed by the Ford Motor Company in 1970; by dint of strong pressure, Ford President Lee Iacocca got the car on the market by 1971. It was developed in response to higher gasoline prices and stronger competition from Japan in the small car market; it was under 2,000 pounds and under $2,000 to buy. At that price, and that gas economy, suitable for four passengers, a generally agreeable car overall, the Pinto sold well, competing well in its class. Then in 1977 Mark Dowie, a freelance journalist, published an expose of the Pinto, "Pinto Madness," in the journal *Mother Jones*, claiming that the gas tank of the Pinto blew up when struck from the rear, and that the inferior construction of the Pinto in this regard had been responsible for "500 burn deaths," although "the figure could be as high as 900." In 1978, three girls — two sisters and a cousin — were killed in Indiana when a speeding van rear-ended their Pinto, stopped on a highway, and it caught fire. Their families sued, and the Elkhart County prosecutor brought the Ford Motor Company up on **criminal charges** of reckless homicide. By then, because of Dowie's article, there was a pile of evidence that Ford may have cut corners and "written off" a certain number of victims in order to get this economical car on the market.

On the other hand, as the defense attorney was quick to point out, the Pinto was very probably "as safe as" the other subcompacts, a kind of car that Americans seemed to like; that the "burn death" figures were squishy at best and probably no worse than others of its class; and that it was somewhat unusual, when a heavy van, neglectfully operated (the driver was clearly responsible for the accident), smashed into a stopped car, to charge the manufacturer of the car, instead of the driver of the van, with **criminal liability** for the injuries. This is not the place for the details of the case. Suffice it to say, that although Ford was acquitted in the **criminal case**, the costly recalls and **civil settlements** to which the company was subjected sent a very clear message.

The civil liability impact of that case has been extended. Ford was again the defendant when a jury awarded two sisters $62-million for injuries

Endnote 5

Endnote 6

Endnote 7

Figure 1. A new Ford Pinto burning, June 14, 1979. UPI/Corbis-Bettmann.

received when the Bronco II in which they were riding as passengers turned over. Who was at fault? Of course, the driver was trying to pass two cars at once by going off the road, an illegal maneuver. But the kind of "sport utility vehicle" (SUV), exemplified by the Bronco, has a high center of gravity and a tendency to flip when going around corners at high speed. The jury found against Ford in this civil case, underlining the trend toward manufacturer liability. Incidentally, this case is part of the most recent chapter in the family-car controversy, which is still being written.

Endnote 9

Those popular sport utility vehicles occasionally harm their drivers and passengers, but are much more likely to cause substantial injuries in any other automobiles they may strike in the course of an accident, simply because they are much heavier than the average car. (One reason for their popularity is the impression among young families that if an accident should happen, the people in the sport utility vehicle, especially the children, will be more likely to emerge from the accident unscathed. On this logic, will we all soon be driving Sherman tanks?) If you drive a standard, medium weight car, and you are injured in an accident where the other vehicle is a heavyweight sport utility vehicle and the other driver is at fault, whom should you sue to compensate you for your injuries? On the older understanding, you should sue the driver of the other car. Based on the Pinto doctrine, you should sue the manufacturer of your own car on grounds that it is negligence to put a medium weight vehicle on the same road with sport utility vehicles. Common sense would suggest that you sue the manufacturer of the sport utility vehicle for putting on the road a car dangerous to others. Insurance companies are beginning to come to that understanding, and the SUVs may soon be very expensive to own.

The family car may be an appropriate platform for the really serious questions about product quality and safety. First, how safe is safe enough for a prudent person to use the product? The requirement of "zero risk" will keep us indoors all our lives, and it is true that we sometimes take enormous risks (rock-climbing) just for the fun of it. But does that mean we have no right to complain about cars that carry risk with their low price tags? Second, how far into the field of consumer choice should government agencies step in order to ensure safety? By government "agencies," we may understand agencies of every branch of government — state legislatures tempted to "protect" constituents by demanding standards of safety, executive-branch regulatory agencies enforcing those standards, or courts that shift the burden of loss from the victims of accidents to the manufacturers of the automobiles involved in them. On the one hand, we want some legal guarantee that the complex product we buy will not cause damage to us, or to our passengers. On the other, we still want to be able to choose our car among competing products on a free market, according to our notion of the optimal balance of safety and economy.

This area of the law is still evolving. As other aspects of our lives become safer (through immunizations and good sanitation, for instance), our tolerance for accidents involving consumer products decreases, approaching zero as a limit. The result of the lowered tolerance has not always been what we would have wanted. Fearing liability, towns have closed playgrounds (children might get hit by swings, or fall off the monkey bars), high diving boards have been taken from swimming pools, churches have closed soup kitchens for the poor, fearing lawsuits if someone should be injured in a fight. It is not so in other nations. In Germany, lawsuits for accidental injury are unusual, and rarely successful. In a typical case, a child accidentally injured in a Koblenz swimming pool was awarded no damages even though supervisors were admittedly away from their posts at the time. The appeals court affirmed the lower court decision not to hold the pool liable, remarking "that children must learn responsibility and that supervisors might hinder development if they watch too closely." Given the rich opportunities for exploration at the German playgrounds and zoos, some American parents might wish the U.S. to move in the direction that Germany has taken. At some point *a balance will have to be reached, between protection of safety and permission to assume responsibility, but it is not apparent from here just where that will be.*

Endnote 10

Strict Liability

As a result of the Pinto doctrine, a new understanding was introduced to the relationship between buyer and manufacturer, approximating *strict product liability*. This doctrine of strict liability requires the maker of a product to compensate the user of that product for injuries sustained because defects in the product made it dangerous, *whether or not* the manufacturer was negligent or deviated from normal process in making the product. Still, strict liability is not *absolute liability,* in which the burden is on the manufacturer to show that the product was not defective if used in the ordinary way, but that burden can be borne, at least in theory, if it can be shown that the user did not exercise ordinary care and prudence in using the product.

In deciding to hold manufacturers responsible for almost all injuries incurred in the use of a product, the courts and some legislatures employed a set of moral calculations worth noting. To be sure, it is not always *fair* to hold a manufacturer responsible for injuries that no one could have foreseen, after the product has been made with all appropriate care. Nevertheless, manufacturers are *in the best position* to modify the product so that such injuries will not occur in the future, and to think out the possibilities for other types of injuries. Let the burden fall, then, on the one most clearly in position to make sure that there will be fewer burdens in the future.

But there can be problems with this approach. Mark Peterson, a college student, was awarded $12.65 million in a suit against Goodyear Tire and Rubber Company, brought because an improperly repaired tire had blown out and caused an accident, rendering him quadriplegic. To be sure, he was probably driving too fast, and the tire had been improperly repaired by a garage nearby; but these portions of responsibility were ignored by the jury. Here's a more famous case:

McDonald's: Hot Coffee!

And most famously, Stella Liebeck brought suit against fast-food restaurant giant McDonald's for serving its coffee too hot. She was burned on legs, thighs and buttocks after balancing a just-bought cup of McDonald's coffee between her legs, while driving to work, while she pried off the top to add cream and sugar; the car hit a bump, the coffee spilled, and the burns were, by all reports, very bad, requiring skin grafts. So she sued McDonald's for not adequately warning her that the coffee was "unreasonably" hot, and recovered $160,000 in compensatory damages and $2.7 million in punitive damages (later reduced to $480,000; the actual final settlement was out of court, for an undisclosed amount).

Those who attempt to put a good face on the verdict insist that it was really McDonald's callous attitude toward Stella Liebeck that was to blame for the enormous sum, and they have a point; it took a very long time for McDonald's lawyers to take seriously a lawsuit brought by a customer who spilled her coffee because she was trying to pry the safety cap off to add cream and sugar to the coffee which was wedged between her legs while she was driving her car.

The point of the jury's award, the jury later explained, was to send a message to fast food establishments that *all* customer complaints were to be taken seriously, and in that, I'll warrant, they succeeded. What has happened in these cases is that the principle above — let the burden fall upon those in the best position to make sure it doesn't happen again — has been modified to, let the burden fall into the "deepest pockets," the party in the best financial condition to insure anyone who gets hurt, no matter whose fault the injury was. After all, there is little a tire company can do to make sure that its tires are always repaired properly, or that MacDonald's can do to make sure the coffee isn't spilled by the customer. It makes a certain amount of sense, it could be argued, to let rich corporations be the insurers of anyone who gets hurt, although surely a more efficient system (involving more taxes and fewer lawyers) could be devised to accomplish this objective. But there is no consensus that there should be such insurance, and in the absence of consensus, these results cast a pall over too many areas of ethics. They weaken our assumption that consumers and intermediaries are responsible adults too, and must share responsibility for the vicissitudes of life. They drive up insurance rates for all of us. They cause the same sort of demoralization that the fantastic CEO bonuses are thought to cause — the generalized belief that these people have won a rigged lottery, and that perverse human decisions are making life a lot less fair than the natural lottery of luck would have it.

Endnote 11

Endnote 12

CORPORATE VS. CONSUMER LIABILITY

The problem of assuring product quality and safety is significantly increased in the area where unproven new technology and luxury products intersect. If a product is a necessity — including in this category a home, food, clothing, and likely the family car. We may be offended when the product fails to perform satisfactorily. So we may seek to recover from the manufacturer the expense we have been put to in repairing the damage it caused, but we can hardly make the most effective argument for compensation for injuries and further damages. The strongest argument would be: "We did not need this product, and had we been warned of the possibility of injury, we would never have bought it." That argument lies at the heart of the most expensive lawsuits. It goes like this: The victim was sold a bill of goods, induced by false promises to make a purchase that he or she would never have made otherwise, and therefore deserves full compensation plus punitive damages from the company that is responsible for the promises as well as the product.

MARIANN HOPKINS:
FAULTY BREAST IMPLANTS

Of all the product controversies that have featured consumer lawsuits, the most distressing to the scientific community, and potentially the most damaging to whatever is left of a purchase on justice in the court system, is the Silicon Breast Implant controversy. Breast "implants" of some sort have been around for awhile, used as prostheses in reconstructive surgery after breast removal (usually as part of treatment for breast cancer). During the 1960s, Dow Corning (a combination company of Dow Chemical and Corning Glass, founded in 1943 to produce silicon products) discovered a way to make silicone gel for mammary prostheses. Over 1-million women have had such prostheses, and not just for reconstruction after breast cancer surgery; by 1990, most of them were for cosmetic purposes only — for "breast augmentation" for healthy clients who had become convinced that larger breasts would advance their social and professional standings.

Then, during the 1980s, complaints began to be heard. Women who had had implants were suffering from unspecified diseases characterized by pain, fatigue, and other vague symptoms. Some of the implants may have been leaking silicon into surrounding tissue. There was concern that silicon breast implants might be implicated in connective tissue disease, one of several auto-immune disorders in which the body's immune system attacks its own connective tissue. Then in 1991, Mariann Hopkins claimed that her breast implants had ruptured and left her suffering from pain, weight loss, and fatigue. The jury awarded her $7.3-million. A litigation industry promptly developed, with groups of lawyers processing large numbers of potential clients (women who had had breast implants) through private clinics staffed by young physicians recruited for the purpose of documenting their symptoms.

What was the evidence of connection between implant and disease? There had been many complaints of "implant-caused" disease, with symptoms so vague and shifting that it was very difficult to find out what really might be the matter. The only real and diagnosable disease specified as possibly connected to the alleged leakage of the implants was "connective tissue disease." A decisive study conducted by the prestigious Mayo Clinic showed that there was no scientific evidence backing up any such connection (i.e. the number of women who had breast implants *and* had connective tissue disease, a not uncommon condition, was about what would be predicted by chance). Yet even as more and more scientific studies, collected in the wake of that initial survey, showed that there was no likely connection between implant and disease of any kind, the plaintiff's lawyers mounted more and more successful campaigns against these findings, or rather, against the decisive weight the defendants wanted them to obtain in court.

Endnote 12

By 1995, when Dow Corning filed for bankruptcy on account of the cases brought against it, at least some parties had taken an unshakable stand against the company and against the literature that supported its position. After Dow Corning filed for bankruptcy, the lawyers turned their attention to Dow Chemical, one of the parent companies, on grounds that Dow Chemical must surely have known what Dow Corning was doing and therefore shared responsibility for it. Their first effort yielded a verdict of $14.1-million against the company, despite (1) the maker of the prostheses was a totally separate company, (2) all the scientific evidence available to the court showed there was no connection between implant and disease, and (3) there was evidence that false data had been cooked up for the plaintiffs' lawyers by disreputable laboratories, rendering it likely that many claims were based on a tissue of lies.

Endnote 11

David Kessler, then head of the **Food and Drug Administration** (which is responsible for the safety of all medical products on the market), in response to the fears voiced by women with implants, reclassified the implants from "Class II" to "Class III" devices. This meant that test data on the safety and effectiveness of the implants had to be submitted to the FDA. He also asked the FDA panel of advisors to reconsider the breast implants. In 1992, he declared a moratorium on the insertion of the implants until entirely new data had been submitted in good order, and the devices had been proven safe. Under the circumstances, Dow simply did not resubmit an application to the FDA; it's out of that market for good, and it may close its whole medical department.

This particular case has spawned a very wide range of secondary effects, probably totally unforeseen by any of the actors in the drama to this point. For instance, there is now a shortage of silicon for medical purposes. Dow had been a major supplier, and along with all the other suppliers, had stopped manufacture of silicon because of the lawsuits. So all the other manufacturers of medical products using silicon — artificial joints, heart valves, catheters, pacemakers — have also had to curtail production while new sources are located. They must price and label their products in future in contemplation of spillover lawsuits, even though no safety problems have arisen with their product line. Promising medical advances using silicon implants have been abandoned as a result of these lawsuits. For example, the long-acting contraceptive Norplant, which promised much greater reproductive control for women in circumstances where ordinary contraceptive protection is difficult, is now virtually off the market, threatened by the same type of lawsuit.

The effects of the breast implant controversy on the operations of our legal system are more devastating than the effects on the medical industries. Consider the evidence of these cases against the traditional elements of "negligence," as set out above. There is no doubt that the defendants were under a duty to the plaintiffs to make a safe product. But despite the virtual absence of substantiating evidence, especially as to Dow Chemical, juries continued to make awards. We seem to have reached a new phase of what used to be called "negligence" law, and it is not clear that our legal system is set up to deal with it.

MAKING POLICY ON SAFETY AND QUALITY

Meanwhile, back at the company, extravagant lawsuits aside, how should a corporation set the scope of its responsibility for its products? The Tylenol case provided an unusual, and inspiring, standard, and bears retelling.

TYLENOL
RIGHT RESPONSE

Tylenol, as most people know, is a harmless painkiller manufactured by Johnson & Johnson, often preferred to competing products because its use is not associated with intestinal bleeding and other problems common to the species. It is freely sold over the counter in all drugstores and supermarkets. Then in 1982, seven people in the Chicago area died from cyanide poisoning; when the substances they had consumed were examined, the cyanide turned out to come from Tylenol capsules. Amid the shock, the company took action. It recalled 31-million bottles of Tylenol, notified 500,000 doctors and hospitals to discontinue use of the capsules, set up a toll-free hotline to answer questions, and asked customers to bring back partly used or unused bottles of capsules to trade for free tablets.

Any information the company got was immediately made public; all employees and retirees were kept informed, interviews were granted to TV talk shows and to the business journals *Fortune* and *The Wall Street Journal*. The whole affair cost the company tens of millions of dollars. It had been perfectly clear to almost everyone from the beginning that the company and its employees were innocent of any connection with the cyanide. The tainted bottles had such diverse origins, and the cases so closely spaced geographically, that the contamination had clearly taken place in the retail stores themselves. Yet Johnson & Johnson executives were unanimous in accepting responsibility for protecting the public from any more poisoning, fault or no fault.

As a business strategy, the company actions worked. The brand name Tylenol was saved, capsules were replaced by caplets (not susceptible to the same adulteration), and the reputation of the company for honesty and responsibility, strongly enhanced by its handling of this crisis, gave new luster and appeal to their products. Observers attribute this triumph to the corporate culture of Johnson & Johnson; the half-century corporate commitment to a one-page statement of values called the "Credo." This credo had been inculcated in every employee throughout the company. Reliance upon it succeeded in overcoming the universal tendency to defend, evade responsibility, and cover up all embarrassing stories for the sake of saving company profits. As a case of responsible action in the field of for-profit enterprise, the company actions are a model for business enterprise from a responsibility perspective.

"Act swiftly, decisively and credibly without a hint of defensiveness or damage control, to protect the public against possible harm."

Some greater benefits came out of the incident. When a copycat crime involved Tylenol some years later, much less had to be done in the way of public relations. A smoothly run police investigation promptly caught the perpetrator, and meanwhile, new universal anticontamination regulations placed plastic wraps and seals over most consumer products, making the crime that much more difficult to repeat. The business community had learned that it is indeed possible for a company to **act swiftly, decisively and credibly, without a hint of defensiveness or damage control, to protect the public against possible harm** from its product. With such a comprehensive response, the company is more likely to be believed and the situation resolved in an ethical manner.

Endnote 13

Is it time for a new kind of **product stewardship** that includes *complete responsibility for a product?* The ideal may be an understanding of product stewardship that takes it from cradle to grave, placing the manufacturer in charge of the product from the moment it leaves the factory door to the moment it is ultimately consumed and its remainders placed in the proper disposal or recycling site. Society would have to do some reordering of priorities and assumptions, but the Chemical Manufacturers Association has promulgated that very ideal for its constituents. Here it is: No chemical has left the domain of manufacturer responsibility until it has finally been consumed or disposed of, until it is nonexistent.

The adoption of this policy would entail a *new kind of product paternalism* (adoption of public rules and policies on exactly who may *buy* what products, made for the protection and benefit of the purchaser). This would be analogous to the laws forbidding the purchase of alcohol and cigarettes by minors. If the manufacturer is to be held liable for what a consumer does with a product once bought, defective or not, the maker surely must be able to keep the product out of the hands of those who would abuse it. In the more cautious manufacturing of the next millennium, this policy may be further explored.

TWO PRACTICAL GUIDES FOR BEHAVIOR

Universal cradle-to-grave product stewardship ultimately may be the standard required by a responsibility perspective, but that standard will need as a foundation some major institutional changes. For the time being, it might make more sense to try to inculcate two clear convictions in corporate executives, corporate employees, and the vast consuming public.

1. We are required by the fundamental ethics of business practice to do our work well, to insist that only top quality merchandise emerge from our manufacturers, and to blow the whistle (see previous chapter) on any practice that frustrates that standard. This requirement is really the **craftsman's ethic**, the work ethic that treats trade as a vocation, a holy calling, into which we may pour all our pride and for which we are entirely willing to be held accountable.

2. "There is a general risk in life," said a German judge, explaining his nation's disinclination to reward product-liability lawsuits, "And if you try to avoid all of life's risks, you avoid its rewards as well." **Consumer patience** is required. We are not living in a safe world. No one gets out of it alive, and the hazards along the way are to be expected and, ultimately, accepted. Accidents happen, including outrageous freak accidents.

Endnote 2

Furthermore, we are not living in a fair world. The freak accidents that happen to us may leave us *unfairly* disadvantaged in comparison with our contemporaries and fellows who suffered no such accident, and often there is no way of really recovering value afterwards. Sometimes, it is not worth the hassle — worth it to us as individuals or worth it to us as a society — to attempt to shift the terrible burden from such accident to broader shoulders, or deeper pockets. Sometimes the blows of fate simply must be endured, as they have been for one global generation after another. A society raised to think it was universally entitled and universally insured must learn otherwise. Beyond the requirement that consumers as well as manufacturers take responsibility for their actions, consumers may have to develop a peculiarly old-fashioned endurance. The requirement of such quiet endurance is really the requirement for **patience**, the ability to suffer outrageous misfortune cheerfully, a virtue for which the current American generation is not famous. It is time to relearn it.

Let these two be combined — adherence to the craftsman's ethic on the part of the manufacturer and the practice of patience on the part of the consumer. In the 21st century, humankind may be able to find a balance of expectation that will not require lawsuits to enforce.

TRUTHFULNESS IN MARKETING

Once a good product is made, how shall we make sure that lots of people buy it? **Marketing** is about the presentation of the product; its purpose is to place the product before the consumer, as attractively as possible, accompanied by a message that will make the consumer want to buy it. The quality of the marketing effort will determine whether or not even a very good product will survive in the open market. It must sell, in sufficient quantity at sufficient price, to cover the costs of manufacture and return a profit to its investors, or it is destined for oblivion. The moral tension in all aspects of product marketing is between the duty of the company to make a fair representation of its product while competing successfully in a market system, and the right and duty of the consumer to exercise prudence in making choices of what to buy in that market.

The standard appropriate to both law and ethics is that of the **"reasonable person,"** the prudent consumer with a normal knowledge of the ways of the world. This person is quite capable of evaluating an honestly presented product in terms of its worth generally and its value, given its price and his circumstances. In a society of imbeciles, there would be no marketing — nor, for that matter, a market. The intelligence of the consumer is essential and is presupposed. Truth, then, is the focus of any discussion of marketing. This involves the company's duty to tell the truth, and the consumer's duty to understand it. We will take on this topic under three heads: (1) the presentation of the product itself, (2) the content of the messages sent about the product, and (3) duty to tailor that presentation to audiences with less experience dealing with the market.

PACKAGING AND LABELING

When a product is designed for sale, it is designed to be attractive to the consumer. Its properties are designed with a known market in mind, and all optional aspects of it — color, shape, decoration — are coordinated to complement the image that that product carries with it to the market. (Toilet soaps, but not hammers, come in pink.) After the design of the product itself, the first message to the consumer is the label that identifies it by name, company logo, size, weight, or quantity, and the like. Historically, the label on a product has been no more than an attractive picture and name, to place a trusted brand before the consumer and to encourage purchase with pictures of smiling faces.

It has become considerably more than that at present. In response to the increased complexity of products of all sorts, a variety of consumer protection legislation has demanded more and more consumer-friendly information on the label. All poisonous substances must be so labeled. If a machine has sharp or moving parts that may cause injury, a stern and clear warning label must be located near those parts. If the product is edible, the label must contain a complete nutrition chart, spelling out calories, fat content, sugar content, salt and vitamins per serving. Such clarity usefully replaces the previous barrage of buzz-words that decorated the supermarket shelves, most of them promising that the product would not damage heart or waistline — "light" (or "lite"), "Low fat/cholesterol," "Sugar-free," and so forth. Over-the-counter pharmaceutical labels must contain an approved statement of what the product is expected to do, as well as warnings against harmful use (that will be infinitely elaborated in the package insert, an extension of the label). Prescription drugs are accompanied by more lengthy statements and explanations.

Similar candor now attaches to packaging. The time-honored practice of putting small amounts of product in a large and colorful box is now rendered useless by the required supermarket shelf information on actual price per unit of weight or volume of product. Those responsible for the packages are still perfectly free to call them "Extra Large Economy Size," not to mention "35% more absolutely free!" but there are ways for intelligent consumers to see what they are buying, and that is all to the good.

Even at this stage of the presentation of the product, ethical questions arise. If a product is being prepared for sale to American consumers under American law in an American supermarket, consumer protection is built into the situation and consumer sophistication may be assumed. But in other conditions, many of the same considerations arise as in the product quality controversies. The manufacturer must exercise care to make sure that the presentation is honest, that the nature of the product is clear from the package, and no misleading claims, explicit or implicit, appear on package or label.

SALES AND ADVERTISING

The Salesman's Lot

Where does the salesman's duty of candor leave off and his duty to sell the product begin (or vice versa)? Long before there was any federal law on the subject, it was generally believed that all products should be presented honestly, and generally conceded that many products were not. Sales practices presumably required little scrutiny when goods were sold personally by the maker or dealer to a customer relied on for repeat business. But in the anonymity of mass markets, where contact with each consumer may be the last, sales personnel may feel that they can afford to move the product at whatever cost in consumer understanding. The "used-car salesman" was famous for persuading unwary customers to buy "as is" automobiles that would barely make it down the street; those who sell roofs and building siding know that a customer will make only one such purchase in 30 years, so repeat business can be ignored. In complex products like computers, the salesperson may be reasonably confident that the customer who asks for advice is in no position to criticize it when he gets it.

"When in Rome, make sure you're dealing with the right Romans."
— Unknown

The consumer faced with a salesperson may not only be ignorant of the product's true features and (for him) true worth, but also at a disadvantage in dealing with the interpersonal situation. The salesperson is highly motivated to get the sale — his job or income may depend on it — and highly skilled in putting a product in a favorable light. The customer arrived in the store in order to buy some such product, so is favorably disposed to being sold. The question often becomes one of price, or features, or terms, and on these matters the customer may have no preconceived boundaries.

The ingredients of the face to face contact between customer and salesperson surely include an exchange of questions and information, but may also include a witches' brew of psychological pressure tactics. Salespersons say: "The sale ends today, there's only one of these left, the new law requires you to have only this kind or risk lawsuit, I've arranged to add several desirable features to this model available at no extra cost and available nowhere else, I've put my job on the line to get you this deal, another customer is looking at it right now, sign here."

Are such tactics justifiable as "part of the game" of salesmanship? Unaccustomed to adversarial bargaining relationships of any kind, the customer may well be overwhelmed by the onslaught. If not, must employers forbid their use, even if it means telling sales personnel to walk away from sales that could be obtained by their use (knowing that the competition has no such scruples)? If they are justifiable up to a point, where does the salesperson's duty not to exploit others dictate an end to such tactics?

We expect that sales personnel will act responsibly in their jobs, balancing their need to succeed in making sales with their disinclination to take advantage of a weak or ignorant person who will really derive very little advantage from the product. But in general, in all situations where customer confronts salesperson, the only protection that consumers may expect from their own ignorance and weakness is their knowledge that they are ignorant and weak. However, there is the general **duty of prudence**. Consumers have a duty to shepherd their own resources, fulfill their responsibilities to themselves, family and others, and help keep the business system honest. In addition, there are practical rules for doing one's consumer duty:

1. Do not decide now. The last day of the sale is very likely to be followed by a new sale tomorrow. And it is really unlikely that that poor young salesgirl will be fired just because you don't buy that computer today.

2. Take every piece of literature you can find on the products available, including price lists.

3. Reconsider your own needs for the product. Use the time gained in postponing a decision to review the literature with someone who has expertise on the subject. Do not ignore the possibility that, given what you have found out about the price, you do not need the product at all, or perhaps a used one would suffice.

But in general, in all situations where customer confronts salesperson, the only protection that consumers may expect from their own ignorance and weakness is their knowledge that they are ignorant and weak.

ADVERTISING TO GROWN-UPS

Advertising is merely salesmanship in print, and takes the moral dilemmas of salesmanship a step further by increasing the anonymity. Interpersonal morality may decrease to zero when no person is in sight, and the advertising copy is broadcast anonymously to a researched or presumed "market" of millions of faceless people. Advertising is very big business, with hundreds of billions of dollars spent annually in all forms of media advertising. Recently, Procter & Gamble spent $1.1-billion on television advertising alone, General Motors with $728-million, and PepsiCo with $611.5-million. Very little of this advertising is designed to convey real detailed information to the consumer. To obtain such information, consumers go to Consumers Union or read the latest edition of *Consumer Reports*. Advertising occasionally does convey real information about new products available; just as the unimaginative weekly fliers from the supermarket do convey real information on the week's prices. But most of those billions of dollars is spent for a more subtle purpose: to portray the product in a certain light, specifically as that, and that alone, which will fill a recognized gap in a consumer's life. Because the whole enterprise of advertising, under that description, treads on dubious ethical ground, it bears examining.

Endnote 14

For purposes of this text, we will pass quickly over obvious offenses that do no harm to anything but our faith in human nature. The transparent use of ambiguity involves not-quite-deceptive advertising, puffery, little visual deceptions and put-ons. Some philosophers have treated advertising ambiguity as a serious moral offense, citing the "danger of misleading" consumers and often calling for stricter regulations. Some, however, find it difficult to believe that a consumer would make serious and permanent consumption decisions on a clever turn of phrase. Visual deceptions are rightfully forbidden — the product must be shown as it is, and as the consumer will buy it.

Endnote 11

The more serious problems of advertising begin when a whole product line is developed and sold to meet needs that are themselves the product of advertising manipulation. We may begin from the unarguable premise that advertising exists to persuade us to buy products that we would not buy otherwise; if we would buy it anyway, why spend the money to advertise? The purchases contemplated by the advertiser are those in which one brand of a necessary product (toothpaste or light bulbs) is chosen from among indistinguishable competitors, where the advertising exists to create a *brand preference,* or those in which an essentially unnecessary product is purchased. For the former case, a brand name must be given an image more favorable than the competitors' images, and that image kept before the public. The task is substantial, but essentially mechanical, by the book. (For a variant, there are cases where a necessary product must be given a positive image to encourage consumer use; adult diapers, for example.) For the latter case, the task is much more challenging and imaginative. A need must be created, either extended from existing needs or created out of whole cloth, and the product shown to satisfy that need.

MARKETING MAYHEM

Possibly some examples will clarify the task at hand. There is an enormous market, approximately $100-million currently, in deodorants of many kinds — soaps for general body odor, mouthwashes to make the breath smell sweet (or minty), the underarm deodorants favored by athletes, and the "feminine" deodorants for odors elsewhere in the body. There's a consensus among consumer advocates that given good health and normal bathing, these products are entirely unnecessary. The advertising preys on terrors of giving social offense, of being rendered at once ridiculous and disgusting by others' perceptions of an unpleasant body odor, and those millions of dollars are spent to protect us from that terror. Such expenditures on such products may be seen as a type of "social insurance." What is troubling about this insurance is that it would not even be contemplated without the artificial creation of social insecurity by the very advertising that sold us the product. This is what economist **John Kenneth Galbraith** has called the **"dependence effect,"** pointing out that we cannot defend production as "satisfying wants and needs" if the production process creates the needs as a by-product. The need for more and ever more consumer products — "autos, appliances, detergents, cosmetics" — is an artifact of a society that has emphasized private goods over public goods, and ended in significant confusion of priorities. At the extreme, there are entire lines of products that are sold only as participants in fantasies — most perfumes or after-shave lotions, for instance, or the clothing in specialized catalogs. Does a fantasy provide a reason to buy?

Endnote 15

Where mature and healthy consumers are concerned, what would a responsibility perspective suggest in the ongoing debate over the morality of advertising? In general, deliberately and unambiguously deceptive advertising should be forbidden. This would include false advertising where complex products like consumer electronics and automobiles are supposed to perform tasks that they cannot perform. Beyond that, according to this argument, advertising should be left alone. It is not the duty of the company to provide Consumer Union information about every virtue and drawback of its products in comparison with all others on the market. The purpose of the advertisement is to get the consumer to try the product, once, and after that, to decide on rational grounds if the purchase should be repeated.

Endnote 16

Advertisements are often artistic and interesting, if only to keep the potential purchaser's attention long enough for the brand name to get across. For the same reason, they are often funny, memorable, musical, and of greater entertainment value than the programs they interrupt. By reason of their repetition, they provide us with a common vocabulary and a set of sayings, much as the Bible once did for our forebears. They also finance our access to network news, sports, and films; and they do, occasionally, tell us about a new product we might enjoy.

Section 5 of the **Federal Trade Commission Act** grants the government broad powers to protect the consumers from "unfair or deceptive acts or practices." How should these powers be applied? Sparingly, as we have seen above. Outside of outright deception that the consumer cannot be assumed to be able to detect and correct, we waste government time and taxpayer money chasing down attempts at manipulation through ambiguity and puffery. For the most part, as consumer products play a large part in our lives, so the fantasies created about them enrich our lives. Advertising belongs. Enjoy it.

"Without some dissimulation, no business can be carried on at all."
— Philip Dormer Stahope, the Earl of Chesterfield

ADVERTISING TO THE UNSOPHISTICATED

We expect adults, at least the adults in our society, to take responsibility for themselves and to shape their own responses to advertising and marketing accordingly. The case is different with *juveniles*. For "children," the under-10 group whose viewing habits can be controlled by their parents, strict regulations have been adopted for advertising. This includes the stipulation that a toy advertised for sale on television may not be shown coming alive, or doing other things it cannot do. Youngsters may not be assumed to be able to distinguish reality from fantasy. But no such regulations would make any sense for *teenagers*, who are exposed to all advertising available to adults. Ought we to be concerned about the content of advertising for the sake of these teenagers, if not for ourselves?

A certain amount of evidence suggests that we should. The body image of young girls is known to be problematic. Unsure about their bodies and their futures as they enter upon the changes of puberty, their self-esteem plummets at the age of 13 or 14. Contributing to this insecurity is the fact that they are likely to begin to gain weight as they reach their mature height. At this point they are assaulted with advertising images of the beauty of slimness, the dangers of ugly fat, and of course, the merits of whatever diet plan is being sold. (Diet products now comprise a multimillion dollar industry all by themselves.) Clothing advertisements reinforce the value of the willowy figure, models and movie stars display the advantages of being thin. Partly as a result of this barrage, alarming numbers of young women develop eating disorders, anorexia and bulimia especially, which compromise their physical health and put them in a cycle of humiliation and desperation that severely warps their ability to attain psychological maturity and moral character. This phenomenon was unheard of until the industrial society replaced work images with leisure images. Similarly, advertising seeks to exploit developmental weaknesses in boys, with claims about strength, appearance, and the ability to control social situations. Should these vulnerable groups be protected from such messages?

Yes, American society seems to be saying as to teenage cigarette smoking. Advertising campaigns influence, and possibly harm, young people of both sexes. For the socially insecure (all teenagers by definition), smoking cigarettes and drinking alcohol have been systematically associated with images of sophistication, maturity, and success — especially but not exclusively success with the opposite sex. "Luckies separate the men from the boys — but not from the girls!" "You've come a long way, baby." Should such advertisements be illegal?

The first answer to both questions is that the advertisements, and the companies that design them and the companies that make the products and pay for the ads, are secondary targets at best. The first priority for action lies outside the field of business entirely, in the worlds of family, school, church and synagogue and community. It has never been easy for young people to grow up to be responsible adults. But every society until the present day has addressed itself vigorously to the problem of escorting children into adulthood. There were rules, rituals, milestones, tests, quests, skills training and other preparation that laid a clear, if difficult, road before the adolescent, leading in understandable steps to adulthood as the society defined it.

Modern Americans seem to have no clear idea of what an adult should be, and no clear idea of how a child should become one. We send our youngsters a truly bewildering array of mixed messages on all the important matters — love, family, sex, work, wisdom, and God. It is hardly surprising that our messages about body image and product consumption are similarly confused. The advertisers seem to be the only ones with confident messages about what will make an adolescent seem, and be "cool," popular, sophisticated, and blissfully happy.

What can we ask of advertiser, besides a promise not to tell outright lies in the process of puffing the product? We can ask that they not target the young people. Not that it is the advertiser's fault, or the fault of the business community as a whole, that our adolescents are so inordinately confused about all aspects of their developing bodies, minds and souls, and hence inordinately vulnerable to the attractions of products that promise to make the transition to adulthood easier. At the least, advertisers have a responsibility not to make matters worse. If they don't accept that duty, they will likely be faced with calls for banning cigarette and alcohol advertisements near schools, banning diet program ads from the teen magazines, even removing these messages from our lives and our children's lives completely. In any case, there would remain unanswered even more fundamental questions: What do we want our children to grow up to be? How do we want them to get there? When we know the answers to *those* questions, it might be a good idea to recruit the best advertisers we have, to help us get the ideas across.

GOOD CITIZENSHIP

Responsiveness to the Local Community

James Bere of Borg-Warner argued in the late 1970s that the corporation is always a "guest" in the community, and must behave itself accordingly. It should be quiet and non-polluting in its habits, obedient to all the local rules, alert to opportunities to help out the hostess and the local charities, and to leave the land and streams as clean and beautiful as they were when it arrived.

Endnote 17

The exact nature of the relationship between corporation and community is not fixed. Much of the debate revolves around to two opposite perspectives of the role of business — the stockholder and stakeholder models of corporate behavior. Throughout most of our history, **the stockholder model** has been the norm. This views the corporation essentially as a piece of private property owned by those who hold its stock. These individuals elect a board of directors whose responsibility is to serve the best interest of the owners. This model assumes that the interactions between business organizations and the different groups affected by their operations (employees, consumers, suppliers) are most effectively structured as buyer/seller relationships. The forces of supply and demand and the pressures of a competitive market will ensure the best use of business and its economic resources. In essence, the board of directors and its appointed managers are fiduciary agents or trustees for the owners. The directors and managers fulfill their social obligations when they operate in the best financial interests of the stockholders. In other words, when they **act to maximize profits.**

Endnote 18

The stakeholder model suggests that corporations are **servants of the larger society.** This approach acknowledges that there are expanding demands being placed on business organizations which include a wider variety of groups not traditionally defined as part of the corporation's immediate self-interest. In a narrow sense, stakeholders are those identifiable groups or individuals on which an organization depends for its survival, sometimes referred to as primary stakeholders, stockholders, employees, customers, suppliers, and key government agencies.

On a broader level, however, a stakeholder is any identifiable group or individual who can affect, or is affected by, organizational performance in terms of its products, policies, and work processes. In this sense, public interest groups, protest groups, local communities, government agencies, trade associations, competitors, unions, and the press also are organizational stakeholders. Stockholders continue to occupy a place of prominence, but profit goals are to be pursued within the broader context of the public interest. Businesses are socially responsible when they consider and act on the needs and demands of these different stakeholders. In addition to the tension created by the stockholder and stakeholder models of corporate performance, arguments about business's social role inevitably include questioning motive: *Should business operate in its own self-interest or should it consider broader social or moral duties?* A number of prominent economists, Milton Friedman for one, argue that the pursuit of profit is and must always remain the most fundamental social responsibility of any business, provided that such activity occurs within accepted moral and legal rules.

Two of the most common concerns of a community are the plant-closing and discount retailer scenarios. In the case of a manufacturer, it could be argued that when the corporation lured families to the area with the promise of jobs, fed a substantial payroll into the community for years, made promises to suppliers and the local retail businesses of continuing patronage, it incurred an obligation not to close down the plant without very good reason. Marginally higher profits elsewhere do not count as a very good reason. The economic impact of plant closings is substantial. From the 1960s to the 1990s, New England and the Middle West have both seen their economic bases suddenly remove themselves, leaving behind the poverty-stricken offspring of the workers who had come to work in the plants, and a wake of urban problems as a permanent inheritance. At first, the industries left for the more congenial sunbelt or the nearby suburbs, raising the hope that the problems left behind could be dealt with by governments — if no longer the local government, then the regional or national government. Now, the corporations go overseas, and those jobs are gone for good, taking with them the economic viability to deal with the problems remaining here.

More recently another scenario of unfavorable local impact has unfolded, created this time by shifts in retailing rather than manufacturing. The large retail establishments (Wal-Mart, for instance), create similar disruptions in the small and mid-sized towns that they prefer. After destroying large areas of undeveloped land to set up their store and adjoining strip mall, their discount businesses rapidly dispossess the traditional small stores of the area, leaving the picturesque downtown areas shuttered and derelict. If the profit margin does not reach expectations in the allotted time, they leave as quick-

Endnote 19

From the 1960s to the 1990s, New England and the Middle West have both seen their economic bases suddenly remove themselves, leaving behind the poverty-stricken offspring of the workers who had come to work in the plants, and a wake of urban problems as a permanent inheritance.

ly as they came, leaving their neighbors on the strip mall similarly orphaned. Downtown does not recover. The small establishments' owners and workers are gone for good, and the customers have already grown accustomed to driving for their shopping — so they stay in the car to the next town, and shop at the mall there. Without an economic base, and after all those leave who can, the small town is reduced to the post-office where the welfare checks come in.

What responsibility does business have for ameliorating these scenarios? Specifically, *what are obligations of those manufacturers heading offshore or of those retailers building their malls?* Given the expectations the manufacturers have promoted in their towns, and the efforts they have made to convince the town fathers of their commitment to the town in the course of seeking zoning waivers or permissions to expand, the nation might require, through federal legislation, that a responsible business will not close a significant plant until four conditions are met:

1. There must be very good reason why this plant is nonviable as it is,
2. Efforts with the workers and with the local community must have been made to make the plant viable again; if those do not work and the plant must be closed,
3. There must be adequate notice, and
4. Everything possible must be done to cushion the blow to the displaced workers and the community.

As for the major retailers, no matter what is asked of them, the fact remains that *the responsibility for the welfare of the town and its citizens lies with the local government,* and it is not beyond the power of that government to set terms for the arrival of the new retail outlets. Terms might include, for instance, (1) that the store locate downtown in culturally appropriate architecture, (2) that it house its cars in multilevel parking garages that can be shared with other merchants, and (3) that the owners or franchisees take an active and responsible part in the civic activities of the town. A responsible retailer may welcome the chance to work with local government to enhance the downtown area and serve the town to more than inexpensive consumer goods; an irresponsible retailer should not be wanted in the town anyway.

What responsibilities does a going business have in its local community? In Chapter 17, we suggested, by way of example, that two requests a business might honor are to keep the local stream free of pollution — specifically, cleaner than the law requires — and to contribute to the local opera. A typical small business, entirely owned and operated locally, is free to invest as much of its income stream as it likes in the local community, on grounds that the building of local good will is crucially important to its success. The plant, or outlet, of a much larger publicly owned company may have a harder time justifying such outlays, for reasons suggested above. The owners, such as they are, must be expected to want higher profits above all, and cannot be assumed to have any interest at all in the local natural or cultural environment. Typically, a responsible corporation, owned by the public or by distant partners, will allot money to the local community anyway. Such a corporation would act to clean up the stream on the rationale that if there is no law protecting that stream now, there might well be soon, and that if a site is found polluted when that law is passed, they will have to clean it up under the watchful eye of the government, and that will be *very* expensive. Such a business would give the money to the opera on grounds that it is something enjoyed by the employees.

In some of the more imaginative community relations plans, the corporation does not necessarily choose the opera, or anything at all; rather, the cultural events in which their employees volunteer their time or make contributions will be chosen for corporate generosity. Such contributions, which "follow the employee," serve to make the employee look good in the community, to encourage the employees to pick volunteer assignments and local charities to seek out company employees as volunteers, and to call attention to the company's generosity — because the employee is likely to mention it in the course of dealings with the charity. Such a policy is more effective in many ways than having a CEO, or a small committee, choose charities on grounds of what *they* would like, or based on what is only in the best interests of the corporation.

Honesty in Financial Transactions

It would seem obvious enough that it is the corporation's duty to carry on financial transactions in compliance with the law and for the common good. In the world of high finance, however, where new ways of making profits come into being much faster than the law can regulate them, the law may be obscure and the common good may be a matter of sharp disagreement.

A case in point is **insider trading**, generally defined as the sale or purchase of a publicly owned company's stock by persons privy to information about company plans or fortunes which is not yet generally available to the public. The assumption is that such sales and purchases advance the interests of the insiders, sometimes substantially. There have been those who argue that insider trading is the swiftest way to get the new information to the market, and that government interference with such transactions is counterproductive. They go on to point out that most countries with stock exchanges do quite well without such interference. But there is a broader spectrum of opinion that holds insider trading to be seriously wrong, on several moral grounds.

Endnote 20

TEXAS GULF SULPHUR:
INSIDER TRADING

In the early Spring of 1963, Texas Gulf performed some test drilling near Timins, Ontario, and found a body of rich ore. Company officials decided to minimize its importance, blandly describing the drilling site as a "prospect" in the initial press release on April 12. Then they got to work buying company stock, and calling selected friends and relatives to tell them to buy stock too. When a more accurate press release came out four days later, describing the drilling site as a "major discovery," then they all reaped handsome profits — made out like bandits, as we say, which indeed they were.

Now, what had they done wrong? First, they had **misappropriated** company property, because that's what company-generated information is. Given the results from the drillings, they were, as officers, under a **fiduciary** obligation to the company to use that information for the company's benefit and not their own, according to the same rules that govern company telephones and computers. That obligation required them to make the information available to the press as soon as it was verified, to allow all investors to bid for the company's stock. Instead, they kept it for themselves for a crucial interval, so that they could make money on it. That's stealing. Second, they had **tipped** others to the news, and thereby made the "tippees" (as they are called), willingly or unwillingly, parties to the theft. On both those grounds, they were in violation of the Securities and Exchange Commission's 1961 ruling, which said corporate insiders (officers and directors of a corporation) in possession of *material* nonpublic information were required to disclose that information to all or to refrain from trading.

Endnote 21

Endnote 22

Accordingly, the SEC charged that all those Texas Gulf officers were in violation of the Securities and Exchange Act of 1934, and the courts backed it up, ruling that the first press release was "misleading to the reasonable investor using due care." The courts then ordered the officers and directors *and all the tippees* to pay into a court-administered fund used to compensate investors who had sold their Texas Gulf Sulphur stock after hearing the disappointing first news. That conclusion identifies the third reason why insider trading is wrong: It tilts the investment playing field, depriving some investors of advantages available to others, unfairly depriving them of an equal chance to make money through investments.

Why do we want the playing field of investments to be as level as possible? Because the economic fortunes of the country, eventually, depend on our faith in the country's businesses and the availability of capital to build and expand them, and also because of a perception that Wall Street is completely rigged in favor of a few malefactors of great wealth will drive capital out of the market, as it did in the 1920s. So insider trading is generally held to be wrong, on the two theories suggested above. According to the **misappropriation theory**, you are guilty of insider trading if:

    a. You trade a corporation's security (shares of stock, for instance)

    b. while in possession of material (important) nonpublic information about that corporation,

    c. that was obtained in breach of fiduciary duty (the duty to put the company's interests before your own.)

According to the "tipper-tippee" liability theory, you are guilty of insider trading if you know or *should have known* that:

Endnote 23

    a. The information on which you trade is material nonpublic information,

    b. and was given to you in the breach of a fiduciary duty owed (to his company) by the tipper.

It is not always easy to sort out what chain of information constitutes that knowledge. Clearly, if a piece of paper with material nonpublic information about a company blows past you on the street, and you act on it to your profit, *that* is not insider trading, since there was no breach of duty in your acquisition of the piece of paper.

The Savings and Loan Collapse

Ethical problems resulting from the intricate relationship among government, financial institutions, and the people who run them are probably best shown in the S&L crisis. Savings and loan institutions (S&Ls — also, ironically, called "thrifts") were set up as single-purpose banks to lend money for mortgages on family homes. The S&Ls got the money to lend from savings accounts, on which they paid a fixed rate of interest (those interest payments were their *costs)*; they lent it out to buy homes, charging a fixed rate of interest on the loans (those mortgage payments were their *income)*. Like any business, they had to keep income higher than costs, and their ability to do that depended on mortgage interest rates exceeding (by a comfortable margin) the interest on savings accounts.

Endnote 24

Running a thrift was supposed to be an easy application of the rule of 3-6-3: Pay three percent on the savings accounts, collect 6 percent on the mortgages, and be on the golf course by 3:00 in the afternoon. The directorships of the S&Ls did not attract the outstanding talent of the financial world. The fact that mortgages were fixed-rate and long-term, while savings accounts could be emptied at any time, points to trouble in store if interest rates generally started going up, which they did in the 1970s. When depositors realized that their money could earn much higher interest elsewhere, they started pulling it out of the S&Ls, who appealed to the government for help.

The government was glad to help. First, it let them raise the interest rates they could pay out for deposits. As soon as that rate exceeded the fixed rates of the mortgages, of course, the S&Ls started to lose money. The new Reagan administration, opposed to regulation as a matter of philosophy, offered further help.

Second, it allowed the S&Ls to diversify investments in order to increase the rate of return. No longer bound to home mortgages, they could invest in commercial real estate, and eventually in futures, options, and high-interest "junk" bonds. The higher the interest, the higher the risk of losing the principal.

Third, it let the S&Ls use a new set of Regulatory Accounting Principles (RAP), concededly less stringent than the traditional Generally Accepted Accounting Principles (GAAP) previously in use by the accountants charged with auditing the S&Ls. Just by presenting their numbers under the new rules, an S&L that was going broke could appear to be in good financial shape.

Fourth, Reagan appointees made it clear to the regulators that too much zeal in auditing would not be rewarded in that administration; supervision became accordingly lax.

Fifth, Congress increased the deposit insurance limit from $40,000 to $100,000 for each account, through the Depository Institutions Deregulation and Monetary Control Act of 1980. That provision assured depositors that they could not lose their money (up to $100,000), rendering unnecessary any prudent evaluation of the solvency of the S&L holding their deposits — which was convenient, because the switch from GAAP to RAP (above) probably made it impossible anyway. Depositors put their money in the S&L promising the highest interest rates, most likely the one taking the greatest risks with the depositors' money, at no risk to themselves.

The System Was Set Up for a Crash

One of the most spectacular implosions was that of Lincoln Savings of California, whose owner, Charles Keating, had indicated only an interest in continuing home mortgages when he took over the bank in 1984. When the Home Loan Bank Board counseled the S&Ls to diversify investments, Keating obligingly diversified into takeover stocks, junk bonds, hotels, financial futures, and high-risk loans, up to 62 percent of Lincoln's assets by 1986. During that time, Lincoln had gone from about $600-million in loans to nearly $6-billion, and had reported profits in every quarter since Keating took it over. Employee morale was kept high with special perks, bonuses, and low-interest mortgages for their own houses. When the Federal Savings and Loan Insurance Corporation finally took over Lincoln Savings in 1989, it found an investment portfolio consisting of vacant land (for which the bank had paid far too much), half-built hotels, disastrously weak junk bonds and large numbers of unsold homes.

Lincoln's failure was one of more than 700 S&L failures, presenting the American taxpayer with a bill amounting to an estimated $220-billion dollars in deposit insurance liabilities. Eventually criminal liability attached to Charles Keating and his officers. But criminal mischief does not account for all the failures. The prime enabler of this financial disaster was a system of interlocking guarantees that ensured that no one could, or would, take responsibility for the prudent management of the thrifts. There is no way the traditional low interest could hold depositors, and the government was not about to make up the difference by funding the mortgages (which might have been cheaper in the long run). By law, the thrifts could not suddenly announce that all those fixed-rate mortgages were really variable rate and start charging higher interest. The search for higher interest loans inevitably meant riskier loans, and the Act of 1980 compounded the problem — by 250 percent, to be exact — by insuring two and a half times the traditional deposits. The thrift officers were not up to the challenges of these new portfolios, and could not see that they had any choice but to scramble for high-interest obligations that, at least on paper, would show the bank bringing in more income than it was paying out in costs.

The only guardians of prudence not caught up in the imperatives of this cycle were the professional accounting firms that were obligated, through their annual audits, to warrant the solvency and sound practices of the banks for the assurance of the government and the investors. When the Lincoln Savings disaster became clear, it was the accountants, Ernst & Young, that the Office of Thrift Supervision (OTS) sought to prosecute. In November, 1992, at the end of extended negotiations, Ernst & Young agreed to pay the U.S. government $400-million to settle claims that it had improperly audited federally insured banks and S&Ls that later failed. At least 300 banks for which Ernst & Young had issued reassuring reports (clean audits) had gone bankrupt. The government's argument was that the accounting firms, which are charged with monitoring the financial health of the nation's businesses, ought to have tumbled to the fact that something was going wrong and said something about it.

Endnote 25

It is, OTS claimed, the traditional task and responsibility of the accounting profession to be the watchdog against just such bungling and crime, and appropriate to hold the accountants answerable for its proper fulfillment. There are those who hold that it was unfair to hold accountants responsible for the crimes of others, when all they were trying to do was serve their clients well. But it could be argued that the judgment, small as it was in comparison to the whole S&L debacle, was a welcome reminder that those set to guard should take the job seriously.

Consider another commentary and examples of this problem of insider mismanagement for personal profit.

MICHAEL MILKEN
JUNK BOND KING

Financier Michael Milken was jailed for his trading in junk bonds and insider deals that provided him a fortune. (He was released from prison after serving less than two years.) According to the *Wall Street Journal,* March 1992, Milken and his former firm, Drexel Burnham Lambert Inc. settled more than 150 lawsuits for a total of $1.3 billion, including fines. After paying a total of $900 million in fines, Milken still had a $125 million fortune and a family estate worth approximately $500-million.

INTERNATIONAL CORPORATE ETHICS

A fourth constituency of the corporation is the world itself. Just at the point that the American corporation had begun to accept the **"new social contract"** of corporate responsibility, including the increasingly fashionable codes of ethics, suddenly business globalized. The framework of globalization of all business transactions had begun in the 1970s, but until the end of the 1980s it operated still in the cold war framework that limited commercial transactions to those that served national purposes — or at least insisted that Cold-War, national-interest rhetoric be used to describe international business transactions. Now that the Cold War is over, we must address business ethics abroad much as we do at home — as no doubt influenced by politics, but not a simple subset of political purposes. From that perspective, the basic premise of international ethics for the corporation is simplicity itself. Don't leave your moral principles in the airport (or the suitcase). *It is the corporation's duty, to the extent possible, to carry ethical procedures abroad* and try to follow them there. The problem comes when the principles seem to be in direct contradiction to the customs of the country. We will consider three representative cases of international dilemmas.

Bribery, Extortion, and Other Irregular Payments

Should a corporation engage in **bribery**, the practice of offering payments to officials in return for new contracts or other favorable treatment? It has been argued that where it is accepted local custom to offer gifts and payments in return for business, it is only good manners to respect that custom — when in Rome, do as the Romans do. Further, it seems pointless to lose business abroad to competing countries that have no such scruples. On the other hand, bribery is wrong, and corrupts both the foreign official and the corporation offering the bribe; and practices illegal in the United States ought not to be taken abroad. Often the facts of the local customs are difficult to discern. Consider the case of Lockheed Aircraft.

The CEO of Lockheed Aircraft Corporation was convinced by his Japanese partners that it was customary and necessary in Japan to make substantial payments in order to persuade Japan's national airline to purchase the Tristar aircraft; mindful of his company's future and the future of its workers' jobs, he eventually paid out $22-million in bribes. Yet when the truth came out, it was his Japanese partners who went to jail, and the government of Japan went into crisis. In The Netherlands, Prince Bernhardt had to resign all government duties after accepting a similar bribe. The implication of these instances? **Make sure you're dealing with the right Romans.**

On the evidence that nearly 400 U.S. companies had made large payments to foreign governments in the mid-1970s, amounting to some $300-million, Congress passed the **Foreign Corrupt Practices Act of 1977**, essentially forbidding all forms of bribery, much to the distress of many experienced cosmopolitan businesspersons.

Amendments permitted the payment of **"grease,"** small payments to lower level officials as fees just to do their jobs. In the anti-regulatory climate of 1988, permissions and immunities from prosecution were expanded. The situation persists in many nations, where government officials expect to support themselves and their families on the proceeds of bribes. Is such payment part of responsible business practice?

The following considerations may be worth bearing in mind. First, the imperative to take business away from unscrupulous competitors grounded on national interest is much less persuasive if the competitors are other U.S. corporations, which they usually are. Second, "respecting local custom" is no benefit to a nation that is struggling, against the current of its own history, to achieve rational and honest government. Third, corruption is a poor respecter of a nation's business persona. No matter the intra-organizational Chinese Walls, what is accepted practice abroad inevitably colors what happens at home. This area of business practice is still evolving, even as are the nations that have customarily been the recipients of the bribes.

Workers' Rights in the Developing Nations

One of the major developments of the post-Cold War world is the rapid increase of the offshore manufacturing platforms, as new entrepreneurs, often in the developing world, discover that they can produce goods for the United States far less expensively than American workers can. Consider the case of Nike, a well-known maker of fashionable athletic equipment and clothing — especially sneakers — after the Winter Olympics at Nagano, the best known in the world. The athletic shoe division accounts for about $3.77-billion in annual sales, and every shoe is made offshore, primarily in Asia, through independent local contractors. Nike plants employ nearly 500,000 workers in Indonesia, China and Vietnam. Nike had 47% of the U.S. market share in 1998. Reebok, with $1.28-billion in sales and 16% of the market, Adidas with $500-million and 6%, along with several others, also have their shoes made abroad.

The Asian subcontractors are famous for the **"sweatshops"** in which the shoes are manufactured. Indonesia alone has more than 25,000 workers employed making athletic shoes for American companies. The employees in China make about $73 a month, and the company provides dormitories and meals; in Vietnam, they can make as little as $40 a month and must buy their own meals. In Indonesia, the workers, mostly young girls, earn as little as 15 cents per hour, work 11 and 12 hours a day in airless factories, and are often abused by the factory supervisors. Labor laws that require better conditions and higher wages are routinely ignored; government and factory posts are often occupied by the same people, and enforcement varies from lax to nonexistent. The yearly $40-million endorsement honoraria that Nike pays to Michael Jordan exceeds the yearly income of the entire Indonesian athletic shoe workforce. The arrangement works for the benefit of

Nike, to its credit, has accepted responsibility for the conditions under which its products are made and is attempting to address the problem; but how much can it do?

Endnote 26

Endnote 27

the American consumer and especially for the benefit of Nike. Shoes that cost $5.60 to produce in Asia retail in the U.S. for more than $70.

Nike, to its credit, has accepted responsibility for the conditions under which its products are made and is attempting to address the problem; but how much can it do? The current situation is not an encouraging prospect. The global free market system draws capital to the least expensive labor market, and simple market calculations can show the futility of protective legislation that would keep high paying jobs in the manufacture of athletic shoes in the United States *or* require the improvement of working conditions abroad. The governments of the less developed countries in which the factories are located are eager to get foreign investment, and compete vigorously with each other for the contracts. The workers are eager for the wretched jobs, which are in many cases better than the abject poverty available to them otherwise. The efforts on the part of one company to set a higher standard for working conditions, on threat of withdrawing from the country, risk offending the nation it is attempting to influence and abandoning workers who have come to depend upon it, thus setting itself at a competitive disadvantage in the sale of its product.

Should the principles that would govern working conditions in the United States be followed to the letter abroad, no matter how unrealistic they may seem? Is it the responsible course of action to allow developing nations to set their own rules on working conditions, even tainted by government corruption? Again, a responsible corporation would have to look not only at the present government of a country in which it contracts for manufactured goods, but at the aspirations of the people. The model of the prosperous middle-class democracy will not be attainable until the nation can put a viable economic floor under its workers. Ideally, a multinational corporation would be able to set an absolute minimum of guarantees for its employees. At least physical security and subsistence must be guaranteed, and fundamental rights to property and education honored. Where the ideal cannot be met, a responsibility persists for improving the workers' conditions wherever possible.

Endnote 28

Sales and Marketing to the Developing Nations

If corporations find it difficult to carry on business without exploitation in the manufacture of their products abroad, we may expect to find difficulties in the sales and marketing of those products. The Nestle case is illustrative of the parallel, with an extra political twist.

Endnote 29

Nestle's Infant
Formula Dilemma

Nestle is a multibillion dollar food company, specializing in milk products, based in Vevey, Switzerland. Beginning in the 1920s, Nestle had marketed worldwide a line of infant formula, a breast milk substitute for women who could not or did not wish to nurse their infants. Efforts to market breast milk substitutes in the developing nations increased in the 1960s, when birthrates in the West generally leveled off. Nestle marketed its formula by all the usual means adopted in the developed world — posters of happy babies sitting beside cans of formula and the like — but also developed some innovative marketing practices adapted to nations without a history of consumer sophistication. Prominent among these was the deployment of "mothercraft nurses," sales personnel placed in hospitals to make themselves useful by teaching new mothers how to bathe and care for their babies, to distribute product samples and to mention the advantages of infant formula to supplement or supplant breast feeding. By the late 1970s, Nestle claimed sales of about $750-million in the developing nations, leaving its competitors to share the other half of the market. Business was booming; the product was just what a newly urbanized middle class woman needed, whose office job did not permit her to nurse an infant every four hours.

Opposition to Nestle's marketing of infant formula began with a U.S. government pamphlet written in 1966 by Dr. Derrick Jelliffe, entitled *Child Nutrition in Developing Countries*. In it Jelliffe argued that breast milk was the best food for the newborn infant (which no one denied), and that the sale of breast-milk substitutes in poor lands did positive damage, according to a scenario which rapidly became a classic. Jelliffe pictured the uneducated and timid mother in the developing nation pressured by the sales personnel to use formula instead of nursing because nursing was "old-fashioned"; then, once the use of formula had begun and the breast milk dried up, unable to resume nursing when she realized that the formula was too expensive for her to afford; then forced to overdilute the formula to save money; with polluted water that she did not know needed to be boiled. The result of the overdilution is malnutrition, the result of the polluted water is diarrhea, and between the two of them they can spell death for a weak child.

His scenario was backed up by anecdotes of pediatric observations of such diarrhea and malnutrition connected to bottle feeding; health workers had dubbed the syndrome "bottle illness." Accordingly, Jelliffe concluded, those who sold formula to mothers in these nations were to blame for the worldwide decrease in breastfeeding, and the resultant disease and death for ten million children in developing nations, by Jelliffe's estimate. His scenario, and resulting condemnation of Nestle for providing the formula, were picked up seven years later by two pediatricians in the U.K. in an article, "The Baby Food Tragedy," in *The New Internationalist*, elaborated upon by groups of activists in the U.K. and in Germany, eventuating in a book *Nestle Totet Babys (Nestle Kills Babies)*. Three years later, on July 4, 1977, a U.S. activist group known as the Infant Formula Action Coalition (INFACT) announced a boycott of all Nestle products.

In its innocence of any factual basis, the Nestle case was an eerie precursor to the breast implant controversy, above. First, there was no evidence that breastfeeding had decreased worldwide, especially in the developing nations. From the 1930s through the 1960s, there had been a sharp decrease of breastfeeding in the U.S., to less than one-fifth of all new mothers choosing to breastfeed; that was followed by an increase to 50 percent in the late 1970s; but there was no evidence at all for the developing nations. There was no evidence that the infant death rate had increased in the developing nations (Jelliffe admitted that his "ten million" was an "estimate," meant to be "symbolic"), and no good data for a baseline to support such evidence.

Further, there was no evidence that the observed cases of "bottle illness" were connected to infant formula; no one knew what was in those bottles, but it was probably powdered cow's milk distributed as part of U.S. AID programs. There was no evidence that the women choosing formula over breastfeeding were uneducated, influenced in their choice by advertising, or pressured into it by sales personnel. There was, in fact, none of the evidence that would be needed to back up any part of the plausible scenario first advanced by Jelliffe. There was no evidence at all that Nestle had done anything but sell a high-quality product at its usual selling price to willing buyers.

And to compound the bewilderment of the observers, the only target of the boycott was Nestle's United States subsidiary, which had nothing to do with the formula. Neither was there evidence that the boycott was or ever could be economically effective against Switzerland-based Nestle S.A., the company that was actually making and marketing the formula. Yet the boycott recruited Dr. Benjamin Spock to its cause, had hundreds of marches and rallies, and persisted until 1984 in the United States, with something of the inevitability of the court decisions in the breast implant case.

Political activism resembles litigation; it has internal motives of its own not susceptible to modification by the facts, it is very expensive, and there seems to be no way to prevent it, confront it, or reason it to a halt. *When engines without brakes start cruising the business scene, we know that there has been a failure of responsibility somewhere.* In the typical case, the scenario, the outrage, and the action taken against the corporation make no sense unless we assume that the consumer of the product, in this case a new mother in a developing nation, is totally incapable of taking responsibility for her own decisions — a proposition that remains to be proved. In the case of product litigation, we have called for responsibility from the lawyers, to recognize their responsibility for the runaway engine. We must also demand such duty from the political activists who would assume the role of conscience to the nation.

Stewardship of the Natural Environment
It is difficult to overstate the importance of the effort to protect the natural environment. In the first half of 20th century, that effort might be understood as an attempt to preserve natural beauty, woods

and songbirds for human enjoyment, and air and water not contaminated with substances that would damage human health. By now the protection of the environment requires the preservation of the good health of the whole **biosphere**, the entire interlocking system of topsoil, plant life, oceans and ocean life, and the composition of the atmosphere itself, including the ozone layer, seen as one interdependent living system. Said another way, between 1900 and 1950, we were worried about keeping Nature's face clean and her hair brushed; now we are worried that continued deterioration of her lungs may lead to general organ failure and death — our death. For instance, when John Muir pleaded for the preservation of the sequoia forests of California in the 1920s, he did it in terms of the majesty of Nature and our spiritual need for wilderness in our lives. Now, seeing the results of the destruction of the forests, and the destruction of the topsoil due to clearcut logging operations, we can anticipate several consequences:

* mudslides on the steep slopes which will wipe out villages in an hour,
* the destruction of the salmon industry,
* the extensive loss of forest-dependent species (of which the spotted owl and the marbled murrelet are only the indicators),
* the permanent desertification of the mountains, resulting in significant loss of oxygen production in that area.

Over the long-term, how can inhabitants of planet earth sustain the living processes that make human life possible? In a world where the number of humans is increasing exponentially and the amount of cropland, forest, and ocean is not, the general duty to protect the natural environment, and the corporation's part in fulfilling that duty, take on a new urgency. Ultimately, we may have to reform the free market's custom of regarding all of the natural world as the "resources" and "raw materials" to be fed into the bottomless maw of the consumer culture, and that will take a conceptual, and moral, revolution.

There is a chapter (11) on the stewardship of the environment *supra* in this volume; accordingly, our treatment of the corporate interface with the dilemmas of the environment, and the corporate share of that duty of stewardship, will be very brief. In this section we will simply note three aspects of that interface.

1. There are ways that corporation and environment can both profit from simple changes of policy (the "win-win" scenarios),

2. There are many more areas where some kind of compromise will have to be reached between company agendas and environmental needs (the "win-lose" scenarios), and

3. There are some areas where the natural tendency of our customs will damage both business and environmental interests (the "lose-lose" scenarios).

We will suggest that the first scenarios should be implemented, the third brought to a swift halt, and the second negotiated in sincerity, good faith, and concern for the 10th generation after us.

The Win-Win Scenarios

There are areas where good business practice is also the best practice for the environment. For instance, the 3M Corporation's "Preventing Pollution Pays" initiative recovered materials that were being flushed away (or sent up the stack) as waste products, and recycled them to save money. In that case a single company adopted practices that brought them into compliance with law, improved community relations (recall the trout stream of Chapter 17), and recovered enough material to make cost-effective the investment in anti-pollution technology. The same logic created our recycling programs. If we can recycle our newsprint, we'll unclog the landfills and save money on pulp; if we can recycle our aluminum cans, we'll get them off the highway and save money (in this case, a lot of money) on processing. If we can recycle our plastics, which are for all intents and purposes immortal in any landfill, we work a tremendous waste disposal saving and create new products at the same time. Town recycling programs are much less efficient than the one-company recycling. They require many transactions and substantial monetary incentives. Next, consumer demand for the recycled product has to be created, firms have to be started up that will buy the waste and turn it into products to meet that consumer demand, and collection and transfer programs have to be put in place. Sometimes, it is very hard to demonstrate that these programs will pay for themselves in the short run. Patience is necessary, for the long run is usually not only cleaner but profitable.

The big win-win scenario for the corporation and the environment begins with the recognition that people really do value a clean and beautiful natural world, and for a variety of reasons. Health is usually the strongest one. Since the publication of Rachel Carson's *Silent Spring*, fear of the effect of "chemicals" in the environment has been a powerful motivation for environmental protection. In the long run the strongest motive is the simple desire to live in a beautiful setting. As the industry of America turns away from smokestack manufacturing and toward pure information, there is less need to build facilities that pollute the surrounding streams and air, and much more need to preserve pleasant places for people to build their homes, because in all likelihood that's where they'll be working in a few years.

The Win-Lose Scenarios

Much more common on the interface of corporation and environment is the trade-off. There is no way to paint the options such that both parties win. There are only better and worse ways to negotiate between the economic imperatives and the environmental imperatives, to make sure that as much as possible is preserved for both sides. Some trades are not difficult. Toward the second quarter of this century, for instance, the oil industry discovered that if they added ethylated lead to gasoline, the automobiles performed better. Then we started getting incidents of lead poisoning from the automobile emissions. Solution: Ban all lead from gasoline, as required by the Clean Air Act of 1970. The result was an immediate drop in the ambient lead, followed by a drop in lead poisoning events. For a relatively small cost in performance, we got an enormous gain for the environment.

That is what is called "picking the low-hanging fruit." The first 50% of the pollution is usually very easy to control. After that, it gets harder, and stopping the last 5% of the pollution may be astronomically costly. For instance, we discovered that DDT, an all-purpose insecticide, was harming birds in the U.S. It was banned, along with closely related chemicals used for the same purpose. The birds recovered. But where are we willing to say, that the pesticide must be tolerated for the sake of its value? DDT all but wiped out malaria worldwide in the years following World War II; it increased the yield of crops worldwide, especially in tropical developing nations, substantially contributing to the world's human food supply; and some form of insecticide is absolutely required to combat the pests that attend the large monoculture crops of agribusiness. We can diminish the use of pesticides, but we cannot stop it, unless we are willing to see the world food supply drop significantly. On the other hand, the pesticide sprayed on the crops runs off into the stream and kills the fish. The same fishermen who objected to the factory's pollution will object to the farmers' use of pesticides, for the same reason. We can ask only that the parties to each dispute negotiate in good faith for the solution appropriate to each area.

The Lose-Lose Scenarios

The worst cases play themselves out where business imperatives, imperfectly understood, destroy the natural environment and natural resources mindlessly, and business is unable or unwilling to place restraints on what they are doing to nature. These scenarios are among the "engines out of control" mentioned in Chapter 17. These are areas that would be described by their participants as compelled by law or economics, where no one seems to be in a position to think about, or take responsibility for what's happening — even when what's happening is horrible. *Most of these scenarios build for years and erupt in a moment.* For instance, consider the 1984 explosion of the pesticide plant in Bhopal, India, which released large amounts of methyl isocyanate into the air, killing thousands of local residents. While started by a single employee, it was made possible by years of cost-cutting on safety devices. Each cut was justified as a savings *at the time,* backed up by complacency. All together, they added up to disaster.

Exactly the same scenario played out in Prince William Sound five years later, when the *Exxon Valdez*, led by an impaired captain, an unqualified helmsman, and a crew under strength by reason of cost-cutting, fetched up on Bligh Reef and spilled about 11-million gallons of oil in the pristine waters of the Sound. The same cost-cutters had, year by year, reduced the safety equipment and ready crews to handle an oil spill, so none of the promised spill-containment measures actually took place. *Again, who controls the cost-cutters, when safety is at stake?* The events ended up costing Union Carbide India and Exxon much more than they would have spent had they kept their safety provisions in good shape.

Sometimes the scenarios of loss begin and continue with corporate action, even as the public howls its protests. Such a scene is the work of Pacific Lumber, captured in a hostile takeover by Charles Hurwitz's MAXXAM Inc. in 1985, who immediately set to work in the systematic stripping of the slopes of Humboldt County of all their *sequoia sempervirens*, the tallest of trees, some of which were 2,000 years old. There was immediate protest. After the company had violated several court orders to desist from cutting the oldest trees, the company even had its license to conduct logging operations suspended for awhile. Yet it continues to destroy the trees, with the free market as its justification, and a state and a forest service dependent on the industry do not appear to be able to stop it.

ASSUMING STEWARDSHIP

It is possible for a corporation to be responsible in its stewardship of the environment. An instructive example is found in the contrast between the chemicals manufacturing industry's reaction to the Bhopal disaster and the oil industry's non-reaction to the *Exxon Valdez* disaster. Exxon agreed to pick up the oil that had been spilled and washed ashore on the beaches of Prince William Sound This was an apparent acceptance of responsibility. But, to the dismay of Alaska and the volunteers who had arrived to help with the cleanup, Exxon did its best *not* to find oil to clean up. Instead, it chose to *play down* the need for cleaning (by not bringing in very much cleaned up oil), to bring the whole operation to a halt and, incredibly quickly, to forget it. Exxon had a better model to work from, had its leaders chosen to use it. Five years earlier, at Bhopal, the Chemical Manufacturers Association (CMA) had announced a turnaround for the industry. They affirmed their intention to make the entire industry safe. They started out with low-hanging fruit — a provision that if there was a chemicals spill, the nearest chemicals plant would respond with the specialized equipment and neutralizers to handle the crisis, *regardless of whose chemicals those were or how the spill came about.* That provision saved hours in responding to a crisis, ended bickering, and reassured the neighborhoods that they were sincere in trying to protect the land and the humans in it. They went on to promise to recruit a local advisory committee for every one of their plants, to alert all police and fire departments in the area of their plants as to the nature of the chemicals stored there, and to help them with a yearly drill to combat the worst-case scenario for that plant. These initia-

Endnote 30

tives, collectively known as the Community Awareness and Emergency Response Program (CAER), were adopted and made compulsory for all members of the CMA. The Canadian members eventually generalized the ethical thinking of CAER to all other issues for the industry — *truth in advertising, health for the employees, product stewardship and environmental concerns.* They called it **"Responsible Care,"** and U.S. and Canadian chemical makers operate on its principles to this day.

There are direct and indirect means of effecting good stewardship within an organization. Indirectly, the culture of the organization, born of a thousand decisions and discussions, on- and off-duty, eventually enforces ethical behavior. A direct approach usually involves the formal adoption of certain values, "mission statements," "standards" or as we will see in Chapter 22, formal codes of ethics.

FINAL COMMENTS

In Chapter 18, we considered what a responsibility perspective would make of the relationship between employers and employees in a corporation. We suggested a model of **mutual responsibility**, dividing responsibility between management and employees within the corporation. From the inside, the corporation appears to be multiple — directors, managers, accountants, consultants, supervisors, workers. But for this chapter, **the corporation is a single individual, with a personal philosophy, engaging the external world on the basis of responsibility**. It interacts with external stakeholders whose welfare depends in some way upon the responsible operation of the corporation. How does a responsible corporation do that well?

For the corporation to maintain the **quality** of its product or service, it will do its work well, to a standard of excellence, and maintain strong communication channels with its customers to make sure that its standards are being met. The search for **honesty** should be a continuous process of examining all corporate communications in marketing, advertising, and public relations, to make sure that the corporation is as it presents itself, and that it preserves its transparency in all its operations. **Citizenship** will present dilemmas; the corporation has a duty to the shareholders to maintain profits and to increase the value of the stock, and if it serves these objectives to pull out of a New England town and head to Indonesia, how can the corporation decide not to move its plant? And while cooperation with one's government is certainly desirable, it may be very unclear what kinds of trades of stock are ruled out by law, and very difficult to operate for the benefit of one's clients in the pea-soup fog of government regulation and deregulation. Being a good citizen, beyond mere compliance with clear law, will never be simple for the corporation. **Consistency** abroad is like the law of contract. It depends upon reliance. It is the job of the multinational corporation in the first instance to establish what its position will be regarding everything from bribes to working conditions, and to stick with its position (save as improving governmental conditions in the LDC's make it possible to meet a higher standard of working conditions). The duty of **stewardship** of the environment is difficult and evolving, more nebulous than even multinational obligation. Certain obligations are clear: reduce or eliminate pollution, preferably by recycling its elements; conserve resources; do not, next time you're looking to increase profits, do it by cutting costs in your environmental protection area. The rest is changing. Does the corporation have a positive duty to preserve wilderness, the Eastern forests, the ozone layer, the spotted owl?

There is no easy answer; if the corporation is to deal honestly with its external constituencies, it should reach some conclusion on all of these matters and publish them in a mission statement or in company ethical standards. How will we write these? Let us make the controlling concept the notion of **responsibility**, consistent with the rest of the text, and then formulate, in general terms, the content of a responsibility perspective for this purpose. It should turn on three general propositions.

1. **Warranty**. The corporation is, exists, makes things, provides services, and takes responsibility for its decisions and its work.
2. **Community**. The corporation exists in community, and recognizes its obligations to all stakeholders, with special attention to obligations created by law and obligations within a large circle of community members.
3. **Foresight**. With respect to all dealings abroad, and all dealings at home or abroad with regard to the natural environment, the corporation will maintain contact with all research on these sites, to the extent possible, and will try to make all decisions in accordance with the best interests, not only of the present stakeholders, but of the those ten generations in the future.

The exact wording of the standards or mission statement, of course, will have to be tailored to the individual company. But the theme of concern for the long-term consequences of all its policies, practices, and acts, and the willingness to own those consequences, will be central to the corporation's understanding of itself and to its relations with its world.

FOR FURTHER INQUIRY

REVIEW QUESTIONS

1. If we are trying to ensure quality in our manufactured products, it is hard to imagine a less efficient, or more corrosive, mechanism than civil liability for negligence. It requires huge public expenditure as cases drag through the public courts; it consumes the time, energy, minds and souls of the people involved, who can think of nothing but the fate of their lawsuit for years at a stretch; and in the end, whatever money is transferred from the manufacturer to pay the judgment of the court goes largely for costs and fees for the lawyers on both sides.

   a. Can we think of a better policy?

   b. How about a government agency in charge of Setting Things Right (or some such title) that heard all cases of alleged negligence and decided on the basis of general common sense and the advice of a few ethicists? No lawyers allowed! The agency might be considerably less costly than the court system, and the results couldn't be any less systematically just than the present system. Or could they?

   c. What would be wrong with such an agency? Would it, with all its drawbacks, be better than the present system?

2. Should tobacco advertising be banned? Present arguments pro and con.

ENDNOTES

1. *MacPherson v. Buick Motor Car* [New York Court of Appeals].

2. *Henningsen v. Bloomfield Motors.*

3. *Greenman v. Yuba Power Products.*

4. Ralph Nader, *Unsafe at Any Speed.*

5. Mark Dowie, "Pinto Madness," *Mother Jones,* September/October 1977.

6. *State of Indiana v. Ford Motor Company*, U.S. District Court, South Bend, Indiana, 15 January 1980, 75–138.

7. See Lisa H. Newton and David P. Schmidt, *Wake Up Calls* (Belmont, CA: Wadsworth Publishing, 1996), Chapter 2, "The Case of the Ford Pinto," pp. 47–60, 66–81.

8. Reginald Stuart, "Ford Won in *Pinto* Case, but the Memory Will Linger On," *New York Times*, 16 March 1980, sec. 4 p. 20.

9. Edmund L. Andrews, "Where a Lawsuit Can't Get Any Respect," *The New York Times*, Section WK, p. 3, Sunday, March 15, 1998.

10. Adams and Maine, citing *National Law Journal* 2/5/96.

11. William H. Shaw and Vincent Barry, *Moral Issues in Business*, 7th edition (Belmont, CA: Wadsworth, 1998) pp. 486–487.

12. Marcia Angell, backed up by an article (later a book) by Marcia Angell, Editor-in-Chief of the *New England Journal of Medicine* and a first-rate scientist.

13. For Tylenol story see *Economist,* April 8, 1995, 57, and August 19, 1995, 56.

14. *Business and Society Review* 93 (Spring 1995) p. 77.

15. John Kenneth Galbraith, *The New Industrial State* (New York: Signet, 1967), p. 219. See John Kenneth Galbraith, *The Affluent Society*, 3rd ed. (New York: Houghton Mifflin, 1976), p. 131.

16. Vance Packard's *The Hidden Persuaders*, the first edition of Galbraith's *The Affluent Society*, Samm Sinclair Baker, *The Permissible Lie* (New York: World Publishing, 1968), and Theodore Levitt, "The Morality (?) of Advertising," *Harvard Business Review* 48 (July–August 1970):84–92.

17. R. E. Freeman, *Strategic Management: A Stakeholder Approach,* (Pitman, Inc., Boston, 1984), p. 88.

18. R. E. Freeman and D. L. Reed, "Stockholders and Stakeholders: A New Perspective on Corporate Governance," *California Management Review*, vol. 25, Spring, 1983, pp. 88–106.

19. Keith Davis, "Five Propositions for Social Responsibility," *Business Horizons*, June, 1975, pp. 19–24.

20. Henry Manne, for instance. See "SEC Professor Split on Insider Trades," *Wall Street Journal*, March 2, 1984, p. 8.

21. *In re Cady, Roberts,* 40 SEC 907 (1961).

22. "Texas Gulf Ruled to Lack Diligence in Minerals Case," *Wall Street Journal* (Midwest Edition), February 9, 1970, p. 1.

23. Newton and Schmidt, *Wake Up Calls*, Belmont, CA: Wadsworth, 1996, pp. 83–101. See Gary L. Tidwell and Abdul Aziz, "Insider Trading: How Well Do You Understand the Current Status of the Law?" *California Management Review* 30:115–123 (Summer 1988).

24. Newton and Schmidt, op. cit., pp. 109–115. See also L. William Seidman, *Full Faith and Credit* (New York: Random House, 1993); Martin Lowry, *High Rollers: Inside the Savings and Loan Debacle* (New York: Praeger, 1991).

25. Kenneth H. Bacon and Lee Berton, "Ernst to Pay $400 Million Over Audit of 4 Big Thrifts," *Wall Street Journal* 24 November 1992, A1, A16.

26. *Time*, March 30, 1998, p. 51, 52.

27. John R. Boatright, *Ethics and the Conduct of Business*, 2d edition (Englewood Cliffs, NJ: Prentice Hall, 1997). p. 390.

28. Thomas Donaldson, *The Ethics of International Business.*

29. Newton and Schmidt, *Wakeup Calls*, op. cit.

30. Lisa H. Newton and Catherine K. Dillingham, *Watersheds 2: Ten Cases in Environmental Ethics* (Belmont, CA: Wadsworth Publishing Co., 1997).

CHAPTER 20

COMMUNICATIONS
IN COMMERCE

"The trouble with lying and deceiving is that their efficiency depends entirely upon a clear notion of the truth that the liar and deceiver wish to hide. In this sense, truth, even if it does not prevail in public, possesses an ineradicable primacy over all falsehoods."

**— Hannah Arendt, "Lying in Politics,"
Crises of the Republic**

"Euphemisms, like fashions, have their day and pass, perhaps to return at another time. Like the guests at a masquerade ball, they enjoy social approval only so long as they retain the capacity for deception."

— Freda Adler, Sisters in Crime

The world of commerce spins on the integrity of communications — statements and propositions represented as accurate and truthful. Each business communicator presumably is bound by whatever ethical standard governs his or her general business behavior. Communication as a business activity takes on another dimension when it is *institutional* or **"official" communication**; i.e., statements binding upon the corporation and its communicator. Usually, it is the province of professional communicators.

Those are the persons whose ethical choices and conflicts are the subject of this chapter. The people who work in *advertising, journalism and public relations* practice separate professions and may subscribe to different codes of professional ethics. But all three have as their prime mission the communication of messages binding upon the individuals or corporations declaring these messages. Nevertheless, they share the attribute of shouldering the responsibility for conveying messages that may not be primarily of their own choosing.

Lisa H. Newton, Ph.D., is Professor of Philosophy and Director of the Program in Applied Ethics at Fairfield University in Fairfield, Connecticut. She is author or co-author of several textbooks in the fields of Ethics and Environmental Studies, and has a faculty appointment in the Department of Medicine at Yale Medical School for the teaching of medical ethics. Contributor was **Joanna DeCarlo Wragg**, B.A. Florida State University, a Pulitzer Prize-winning editorial writer and former associate editor of the Miami Herald, is a partner in Wragg and Casas, a communications and advertising firm in Miami. Past president of the National Conference of Editorial Writers, she also served as chair of the Professional Standards Committee.

Lawyers, physicians and accountants, among other professionals, also sometimes fit the definition of professional communicator, but because their professions each have a different prime mission than that of communications, they will not be detailed here.

The nature of the communicator's work is to be an intermediary — a messenger. As such, he or she lives a professional life on the fault line of potential conflict between the interests of the people who send the message and the interests of the people who receive it. Those groups' interests may be in serious opposition as buyers or sellers, as readers or public figures, as editors or advertisers, or as executives or employees.

CHIEF LEARNING OUTCOME

I can recognize ethical issues in communications in the technology era and apply moral reasoning to them.

Conflict is the norm in the communications environment. Communicators have obligations to their employers, and those duties may conflict with the interest of the client or, in the case of a journalist, with the interests of the readers. As citizens, communicators also have obligations to the community at large and to other practitioners of their profession.

The pen may or may not be mightier than the sword, but it certainly shares the sword's capacity to be double-edged and therefore dangerous to user and target alike. In order to remain sane and effective, communicators need a clear sense of ethical balance to guide them in making the myriad decisions that present themselves in every working day.

As they use this chapter, students may be tempted to give up the exercise as an impossible task. If they succumb, they will be joining the legions of burnt-out, embittered cynics and hacks who already wreak so much havoc in the communication professions. These are the thoughtless or cruel practitioners who have given rise to such pejoratives as journalism's "mad dog reporter" and "hack," public relations' "flack," and advertising's "Madison Avenue" as a synonym for untruthfulness.

The real-life versions of those cliches exist, certainly. So do the professional outlaws who believe and practice a doctrine that "anything goes" if it serves their purposes. For these individuals, there are no rules except the rule of not getting caught.

Happily, this type is more prevalent in fiction than in the mainstream world of successful journalists and commercial communicators. The practical fact is that **communicators who shade the truth put their employer or client at risk** — of lawsuits, of damage to their credibility, or of disrepute among their peers. Consequently, communicators who gain a reputation for sleaziness systematically are weeded out of their various trades.

Even in the hardball realm of political campaigns, the "spin doctor" (a communicator who attempts to influence the *public interpretation* of facts and events) must maintain the trust of the candidate. No campaign rhetorician operates for long outside the boundaries that mark the comfort zone of the candidate. Campaign communicators who go too far inevitably go all the way — out the door and off the payroll — because they made their candidate look bad.

Voters rightly hold candidates responsible for the tone of their campaign literature and rhetoric. Dirty or racist campaigns, for example, reflect the principles of candidates who choose the campaign operatives that specialize in such appeals. The professional communicators in such campaigns are not operating as free agents. The truly renegade political operative, like the rebel reporter, publicist, or ad writer, doesn't last long.

When professional communicators gather, whether they are journalists or business communicators, they discuss this outlaw phenomenon and the danger that young, entry-level professionals might glamorize and imitate it. The experienced practitioners make reference to "kids who believe what they see in the movies," or who "watch too much television."

Knowing the damage that a no-holds-barred attitude can do when paired with an immature

KEY CONCEPTS

Truth — objectively accurate statements, always applicable.

Lying — not telling the truth, including verbal and non-verbal expressions; one of the acts forbidden by the Ten Commandments and The Koran and by every court of law.

Plagiarism — the action whereby one appropriates another's writings or works or art and makes use of them as one's own; implied is the notion that by so doing one is "stealing" original work produced by another.

Private Property — goods, land, structures and intellectual assets (music, books, computer software) owned by private individuals or corporations.

Professional Ethics — the standards or codes of conduct adopted formally by a group of persons practicing the same vocation.

Right of Privacy — the notion, explicit in some state constitutions, that each individual has a legal right prohibiting invasion of home or personal life.

Situational Ethics — determining what is right or good solely on the basis of the momentary context; implying that what is right or good today in this situation may not be right tomorrow in another set of circumstances.

Times v. Sullivan — a landmark U.S. Supreme Court ruling involving libel law in which the private lives of public persons fell under the concept of the general public's right to know and the news media's right to obtain information.

judgment, supervisors watch carefully for telltale signs of a cavalier attitude toward the facts, for example. Or a cynical view that "everybody lies." Everybody does not lie, but people who make that claim usually do. Mainstream executives in journalism, advertising and

Figure 1. Urban centers suffer visual pollution. New York Convention & Visitors Bureau.

public relations know that **dishonesty is the fundamental problem in communications.**

The goal of this chapter, then, is to help and encourage today's students to avoid those pitfalls, to think through the issues, and thus to become part of the solution. In the quotation at the beginning of this chapter Hannah Arendt identifies the starting point of any model for ethical communicating. Because truthfulness is the central issue, the communicator must first identify the facts of the matter. Decisions about which facts to use and how to characterize them must come second. The communicator's first obligation is to learn What Is.

Next comes the need to define the **purpose of the communication.**

 ❈ Is it to inform? Whom? Why?

 ❈ To persuade? Whom? Why?

 ❈ To entertain? Whom? Why?

 ❈ To deceive? Whom? Why?

Once these questions are expressed in plain language, the ethical requirements of the situation should be clear. If not, there is one **final test** that may be useful: **Is there any person I admire whom I would not want to learn about my *actions* and my *motives* here?**

If there is, then either the admiration is misplaced or the action is unjustifiable. The communicator who answers that questions has resolved the ethical dilemma.

Uncertainty can be reduced only by thinking through the issues and making certain decisions *in advance* of the situation that requires them. Thus, when students confront an ethical question in their work place, they will have sound reasons and techniques to guide them to a quick decision instead of wallowing in moral crisis.

IS IT AGAINST THE LAW?

The history of professional communication in the United States is itself a history of tension between two inherently conflicting ideals. One is the law — common and statutory — prohibitions against hurting other people through falsehood in the form of fraud and libel. The other is the First Amendment to the Constitution, which guarantees the rights of free speech and freedom of the press.

As a result of these two ideals, Americans are free to say or publish what they wish, without prior restraint by government censors. However, they also are responsible for what they say or write. They can be sued in civil court, or even prosecuted in criminal court, if their communication is sufficiently damaging or deceitful, or if it invades the privacy of a private person.

(The major exception to First Amendment rights is National Security, and the debate over what restrictions are legitimate in order to protect the nation's security is a robust one. That debate is not covered here because the national security concern is far removed from most business communications and arises rarely even for journalists. This chapter attempts to focus on ethical choices that confront communicators regularly.)

The line that separates personal privacy from First-Amendment freedom is a constant battleground and one mined with real conflicts as well as widespread misunderstanding. The advent of the Internet and the entire "cyber world" of virtual reality and actual legality challenges the best philosophical and legal minds.

MORAL USE OF THE COMPUTER

In the lead article of the 1996 edition of *Media Ethics*, Adam Clayton Powell III reflects on "the inexorable march of computer technology," which is making it "ever easier and ever more tempting to be unethical." His catalog of assaults on the ethical barriers from the new technologies marches through the dilemmas we have surveyed in this chapter. The deadlines and sensationalist expectations of the journalist, the commercial and political motivations of public relations, and the irresistible urge to use high technology to its furthest capability typical of — well, of all of us. "Not that long ago," he points out, "changing the reality captured by photography required skill and time." Not many were proficient enough with film and chemicals to fake a picture to say what they wanted it to say. "Today, however, with the computerized digital darkroom becoming the industry standard, changing the reality captured by photography is fast, easy, and difficult to detect."

Endnote 1

Not only is the technology better than it used to be, it's a lot cheaper. Any one can own a photo shop. As a result, the computer has spawned a brave new world of **altered images.** "This democratization of the digital darkroom means that anyone with a low-end PC can play with photographic reality to create the photo — excuse me, image — needed to illustrate the story. And if the image is slightly retouched or wholly rearranged, the computer-executed collage is so seamless that detection, even by experts, is quite difficult or, in practice, impossible." Video tapes have gone through the same democratization. He cites Andrew Grove, President of Intel. "Processing power is going to

Ibid.

Endnote 2

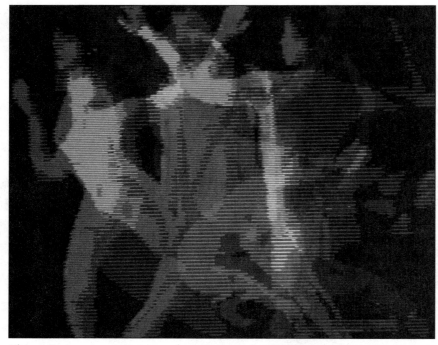

Figure 2. A computer picture depicting overlapping human figures in motion. Copyright © Photo Researchers, Inc.

be practically free and practically infinite," he claimed, "This will allow us to turn automatic 3-D photo-realistic animation into ubiquitous reality within two to three years." What that means is that "tens of millions of people around the world will have the tools to create the television — excuse me, video images — needed to tell a story by the end of this century." Soon reporters will be able to get rid of bystanders mugging for the camera behind their shot from the accident scene, and still bring the shot "live;" for that matter, any citizen will be able to "air-brush" out former spouses from family vacation pictures! And the whole change will be "so seamless that detection will be impossible."

Given the American interest in glitch-free fast-paced entertaining television, Powell thinks that

Endnote 1

> [t]his may also be the end of ethics and television. Within a few years, it will be so fast, easy and inexpensive, even on deadline, that the temptation will become an imperative: clean up those shots, make them beautiful, grab those eyeballs. Pseudoreality will beat dull old unprocessed reality every time.

He looks forward to a "new" ethic, in which unretouched reality, rather like antique barber shop signs, will reacquire value just because of its quaint originality.

Computer ethics is an embryonic discipline in which moral standards are applied to the use of computers. This involves all ethical questions of the rightness or wrongness of "using," "borrowing," or "stealing" software and shareware, as well as the use of computers for moral or immoral purposes — such as the collection of information on persons by big business or government to impose certain behavior on those persons.

Intellectual property and the theft of software. Unauthorized copying of software — taking someone else's disk and feeding its programs into your machine, without paying a royalty to the person who wrote the programs — is illegal, as most of us know. **Copyright law** protects software authors and publishers, just as patent law protects inventors. Unlawfully copying software can wreck a professional's business and reputation. Illegal copying and use of software deprives publishers and developers of a fair return for their work (in short, it is a violation of justice). It also damages the long run interests of every party to the practice. It increases prices, reduces the level of future support, and can inhibit the development of new software since the inventors will get discouraged if they don't get any return on their investment of time and ingenuity. The law reads as follows.

PUBLIC LAW 102-561 — OCT. 28, 1992 106 STAT. 4233
102d Congress
An Act

To amend title 18, United States Code, with respect to the criminal penalties for copyright infringement. Oct. 28, 1992 (S. 893)

Be it enacted by the Senate and House of Representatives of the United States of America in Congress assembled,

SECTION 1. CRIMINAL PENALTIES FOR COPYRIGHT INFRINGEMENT.

Section 2319(b) of title 18, United States Code, is amended to read as follows:

"(1) shall be imprisoned not more than 5 years, or fined in the amount set forth in this title, or both, if the offense consists of the reproduction or distribution, during any 180-day period, of at least 10 copies or phonorecords, of 1 or more copyrighted works, with a retail value of more than $2,500;

"(2) shall be imprisoned not more than 10 years, or fined in the amount set forth in this title, or both, if the offense is a second or subsequent offense under paragraph (1); and

"(3) shall be imprisoned not more than 1 year, or fined in the amount set forth in this title, or both, in any other case."

EDUCOM is a consortium formed to get this message delivered. It urges "respect for the intellectual work of others." This respect traditionally has been essential to most professions. Just as professions do not tolerate plagiarism, ethical computer users do not condone the unauthorized copying of software, including programs, applications, data bases and code. Here are excerpts from the **EDUCOM Code**:

SOFTWARE AND INTELLECTUAL RIGHTS

Respect for intellectual labor and creativity is vital to academic discourse and enterprise. This principle applies to works of all authors and publishers in all media. It encompasses respect for the right to acknowledgment, right to privacy, and right to determine the form, manner, and terms of publication and distribution.

Because electronic information is volatile and easily reproduced, respect for the work and personal expression of others is especially critical in computer environments. Violations of authorial integrity, including plagiarism, invasion of privacy, unauthorized access, and trade secret and copyright violations, may be grounds for sanctions against members of the academic community.

EDUCOM's Educational Uses of Information Technology (EUIT) Program encourages the broadest possible adoption of this statement of principle. The EDUCOM code is intended for adaptation and use by individuals and educational institutions at all levels.

CLASSIFICATION OF SOFTWARE

In terms of copyright, there are four broad classifications of software, i.e., Commercial, Shareware, Freeware, and Public Domain. The restrictions and limitations regarding each classification are different.

• COMMERCIAL software represents the majority of software purchased from software publishers, commercial computer stores, etc. When you buy software, you are actually acquiring a license to use it, not own it. You acquire the license from the company that owns the copyright. The conditions and restrictions of the license agreement vary from program to program and should be read carefully. In general, commercial software licenses stipulate that (1) the software is covered by copyright, (2) although one archival copy of the software can be made, the backup copy cannot be used except when the original package fails or is destroyed, (3) modifications to the software are not allowed, (4) decompiling (i.e., reverse engineering) of the program code is not allowed without the permission of the copyright holder, and (5) development of new works built upon the package (derivative works) is not allowed without the permission of the copyright holder.

• SHAREWARE software is covered by copyright, as well. When you acquire software under a shareware arrangement, you are actually acquiring a license to use it, not own it. You acquire the license from the individual or company that owns the copyright. The conditions and restrictions of the license agreement vary from program to program and should be read carefully. The copyright holders for **Shareware** allow purchasers to make and distribute copies of the software, but demand that if, after testing the software, you adopt it for use, you must pay for it. In general, **Shareware**

software licenses stipulate that (1) the software is covered by copyright, (2) although one archival copy of the software can be made, the backup copy cannot be used except when the original package fails or is destroyed, (3) modifications to the software are not allowed, (4) decompiling (i.e., reverse engineering) of the program code is not allowed without the permission of the copyright holder, and (5) development of new works built upon the package (derivative works) is not allowed without the permission of the copyright holder. Selling software as **Shareware** is a marketing decision; it does not change the legal requirements with respect to copyright. That means that you can make a single archival copy, but you are obliged to pay for all copies adopted for use.

• FREEWARE also is covered by copyright and subject to the conditions defined by the holder of the copyright. The conditions for **Freeware** are in direct opposition to normal copyright restrictions. In general, **Freeware** software licenses stipulate that (1) the software is covered by copyright, (2) copies of the software can be made for both archival and distribution purposes, but that distribution cannot be for profit, (3) modifications to the software are allowed and encouraged, (4) decompiling (i.e., reverse engineering) of the program code is allowed without the explicit permission of the copyright holder, and (5) development of new works built upon the package (derivative works) is allowed and encouraged with the condition that derivative works must also be designated as **Freeware**. That means that you cannot take **Freeware**, modify or extend it, and then sell it as **Commercial** or **Shareware** software.

• PUBLIC DOMAIN software comes into being when the original copyright holder explicitly relinquishes all rights to the software. Since under current copyright law, all intellectual works (including software) are protected as soon as they are committed to a medium, for something to be **Public Domain** it must be clearly marked as such. Before March 1, 1989, it was assumed that intellectual works were NOT covered by copyright unless the copyright symbol and declaration appeared on the work. With the U.S. adherence to the Berne Convention this presumption has been reversed. Now all works assume copyright protection unless the **Public Domain** notification is stated. This means that for **Public Domain** software (1) copyright rights have been relinquished, (2) software copies can be made for both archival and distribution purposes with no restrictions as to distribution, (3) modifications to the software are allowed, (4) decompiling (i.e., reverse engineering) of the program code is allowed, and (5) development of new works built upon the package (derivative works) is allowed without conditions on the distribution or use of the derivative work.

QUESTIONS YOU MAY HAVE ABOUT USING SOFTWARE

1. What do I need to know about software and the U.S. Copyright Act? It's really very simple. The Copyright Law recognizes that all intellectual works (programs, data, pictures, articles, books, etc.) are automatically covered by copyright unless it is explicitly noted to the contrary. That means that the owner of a copyright holds the exclusive right to reproduce and distribute his or her work. For software this means it is illegal to copy or distribute software, or its documentation, without the permission of the copyright holder.

If you have a legal copy of software, you are allowed to make a single archival copy of the software for backup purposes. However, the copy can only be used if the original software is destroyed or fails to work. When the original is given away, the backup copy must also be given with the original or destroyed.

2. If software is not copy-protected, do I have the right to copy it? Lack of copy-protection does NOT constitute permission to copy software without authorization of the software copyright owner. "Non-copy-protected" software enables you to make a backup copy. In offering non-copy-protected software to you, the developer or publisher has demonstrated significant trust in your integrity.

3. May I copy software that is available through facilities on my campus, so that I can use it more conveniently in my own office or room? Software acquired by colleges and universities is usually covered by licenses. The licenses should clearly state how and where the software may be legally used by members of the relevant campus communities (faculty, staff, and students). Such licenses cover software whether installed on stand-alone or networked systems, whether in private offices and rooms, or in public clusters and laboratories. Some institutional licenses permit copying for certain purposes. The license may limit copying, as well.

4. May I loan software? The 1990 modification to the Copyright Law makes it illegal to "loan, lease or rent software" for purposes of direct or indirect commercial advantage without the specific permission of the copyright holder. Non-profit educational institutions are exempted from the 1990 modification, so institutional software may be loaned. Some licenses may even restrict the use of a copy to a specific machine, even if you own more than one system. In general, licenses usually do NOT allow the software to be installed or resident on more than a single machine, or to run the software simultaneously on two or more machines.

5. Isn't it legally "fair use" to copy software if the purpose in sharing it is purely educational?

Historically, the Copyright Law was modified to permit certain educational uses of copyrighted materials without the usual copyright restrictions. However, "fair use" of computer software is still a cloudy issue. The "fair use" amendments to the Copyright Law are intended to allow educational use of legally protected products, but it is limited (for paper-based products) to small portions of full works. For most software it is clearly illegal to make and distribute unauthorized, fully functional copies to class members for their individual use. Making copies of a small section of code from a program in order to illustrate a programming technique might not be a violation. The best alternative is to clear any such use with the copyright owner or consult the appropriate authorities at the college.

ALTERNATIVES TO EXPLORE

Software can be expensive. You may think that you cannot afford to purchase certain programs that you need. Site-licensed and bulk-purchased software are legal alternatives that make multiple copies of software more affordable. Many educational institutions negotiate special prices for software used and purchased by faculty, staff and students. Consult your campus computing office for information. As with other software, site-licensed or bulk-purchased software is still covered by copyright, although the price per copy may be significantly lower than the normal commercial price. A usual condition of site-licensing or bulk-purchasing is that copying and distribution of the software is limited to a central office which must maintain inventories of who received it. When you leave the college by graduation, retirement, or resignation you may no longer be covered by the institutional agreement and may be required to return or destroy your copies of the software licensed to the institution.

Many colleges sell software through a campus store at "educational discounts." If you purchase software for yourself through such an outlet, the software is yours and need not be destroyed or surrendered when you leave the institution. It is, however, still covered by normal copyright protection and covered by the specific conditions of the licensing agreement.

A FINAL NOTE

Restrictions on the use of software are far from uniform. You should check carefully each piece of software and the accompanying documentation yourself. In general, you do not have the right to:

- Receive and use unauthorized copies of software, or

- Make unauthorized copies of soft ware for others.

If you have questions not answered by this brochure about the proper use and distribution of a software product, seek help from your computing office, the software developer or publisher, or other appropriate authorities at your institution.

This brochure has been produced as a service to the academic community by the Educational Uses of Information Technology Program (EUIT) of EDUCOM and the Information Technology Association of America (ITAA). EDUCOM is a non-profit consortium of colleges and universities committed to the use and management of information technology in higher education. ITAA is an industry association providing issues management and advocacy, public affairs, business-to-business networking, education and other member services to companies which create and market products and services associated with computers, communications and data.

(Although this brochure is copyrighted, you are authorized and encouraged to make and distribute copies of it, in whole or in part, providing the source is acknowledged.)

COMPUTERS AS A TOOL OF ABUSE

Computer Monitoring of Employees

Technology now permits any employer to access the computers of all his employees in incredibly detailed ways. He can read everyone's e-mail. He can survey all the websites and everything that is posted in them. He can even count the keystrokes of his secretaries, finding out in that way which ones are staying at their desks and working and which ones are spending too much time in the Ladies' Room. Should he do that? There is no evidence at all that employee efficiency is improved by such careful monitoring of bathroom breaks and keyboard diligence (see Chapter 18), but employers have tended to place great store on the ability to acquire this kind of knowledge, and have contracted to receive it, even if it can be shown that it will do them no good. Somehow the computer provides not only delusions of power, but imperatives of power. What I can know, control, monitor, that I *must* know and control and monitor. Presumably the information the employer may now acquire could be of use to him someday — for instance, if he wanted to confront an employee with the time spent away from her desk. And because of that presumption, many employers feel that they cannot be without it.

Again, is this new? Of course not. The employer before the computer was free to stand over his secretaries, if that's what he wanted to do, time their bathroom breaks and keep a log of their mistakes. But now the information is literally at his fingertips and he does not have to invite disapproval by his physical presence in the room. The ethical balance has not changed. It is the employer's duty to make sure that each employee is pulling his load and that the job is getting done, and it is the employer's duty to respect the employees' privacy (and in his interests not to damage morale by constant criticism). All the computer does is change the location of the supervision, and raise the temptation to monitor closely.

The Circulation of Information

What kinds of information can the computer collect and put to use? My supermarket has a little coupon machine at the checkout that emits useful coupons good for price reductions at your next shopping trip. I was surprised to see that the little machine always gave me a coupon for some product I had just bought! What a coincidence! Of course it was no such thing; the little machine was not just rolling out pre-printed coupons, as I had assumed, but printing them up as they came out, choosing the coupon from a menu in the computer matched to my checkout receipt, which had just gone through the same computer. That means, for those who still need these things spelled out, that there is a computer somewhere in that store with a total list of everyone's shopping, and if you use the convenient store card that gets you special discounts, as I always do, all the shopping you have done for the last year or so can be filed under your name. Should you worry about this? I worry sometimes that the Health Maintenance Organization that covers my health insurance knows about any genetic testing that may have been done on blood samples I release at my annual physical exam. Suppose it turns out that I have the gene for an expensive disease? Knowing that before I do, they can figure out ways to drop me from the plan before I get sick. But suppose they want to know if I am really a non-smoker, as I claim to be? All they need is the supermarket record showing me buying a carton or so of cigarettes every week, and I can lose my health insurance.

Even worse, or at least more immediate, problems arise when it is the *credit rating,* rather than the health records, that are in question. Exactly what kinds of information need to be known, and by whom, and on what justification? Just as information about ourselves becomes more available, it becomes more precious, because of the serious consequences incurred if it falls into the wrong hands. In the end, we are going to have to require consent forms for the release of information, and notification to the person whose information it is of what information is released, and when. For the online journalist, the dilemma is the same as always. "Between the duty to provide information of public importance and the duty to respect others' privacy,"

"Measure not the work until the day's out and the labor's done," — *Elizabeth Barrett Browning, Aurora Leigh*

Endnote 3

as Voakes puts it. As Voakes goes on to point out, we have not begun to address the new kinds of violation of privacy made possible by the rapid growth of technological innovation.

Endnote 4

The Vulnerability of Our Record-keeping Systems

The acknowledged masters of the violation of privacy are the infamous **"hackers,"** computer experts, usually young, who from the anonymous safety of their home computers carry out unauthorized invasions of the files of others. All computers with links to the outside world, apparently, are vulnerable. The purposes of the invasions vary: amusement, money (from the banks), vandalism for fun or for revenge, or just for that feeling of power that comes from a use of expertise that no one can oppose.

Where do hackers fit in our moral institutions? The damage they can do is tremendous. When the movie *War Games* hypothesized that a youngster trying to steal a computer game from its manufacturer accidentally broke into the Pentagon's War Room computers and came within a hair of starting World War III, its viewers took it seriously. Downsized employees, understandably disgruntled, probably know enough about their ex-employer's computers to destroy a substantial number of the programs and files it needs to carry on its business. And most of the files that you and I need to live — our health insurance, our bank accounts, our employment records — are kept in computers that are vulnerable to hacking. What would I do if a vengeful hacker in one night sent me a phone bill for $2,000, cancelled my health insurance, canceled my credit cards and put two bankruptcies on my credit record, fired me from my job, and foreclosed my mortgage? It can happen. Laws now forbid any unauthorized tampering or visiting of files not one's own, and prosecutors take violations very seriously. Yet there is something in the American temperament that harbors a fondness for the smart young outlaw, whose image the hacker has appropriated. His crime, like all computer crime, is not new; criminals have been breaking and entering, stealing, destroying and vandalizing since locks have been on houses, and if he used the older methods, he would have no sympathy. But somehow his persistence, and his expertise in a technology few of us can understand, retains more of our sympathy than he deserves or we should bestow. The moral understanding to deal with this crime is one of the computer-wise developments we expect to see emerge in the next century.

New Medium: Internet; Old Moral Issue: Integrity

What is new in the eloquent appeals for respect for intellectual property spawned in the computer generation? Not much. **Intellectual property is property.** Unauthorized use of property is stealing. Stealing is wrong. There is little here that is new. The ethical imperatives have not changed, but because the theft of intellectual property is much harder to detect than, say, the theft of a car — the owner literally does not know that it is gone — the crime is much harder to prosecute. And since, in case of the theft of software, we have no material evidence (plagiarized books or articles, for instance), detection is that much more difficult. The note sounded here will ring with increasing frequency in the "computer" and "Internet" discussions that follow. The technology has not raised new ethical problems in the information and communications fields, not in the same way, for instance, that the discovery of *in vitro* fertilization raised new problems in the medical field. Instead, it has made old problems more difficult to cope with by lowering the probability that ethical violations will be seen and publicly condemned, and therefore by raising the level of temptation to commit them. The technology has not raised new ethical challenges, chal-

Figure 3. On the information highway, access is easy but ethical hazards abound. PhotoDisc, Inc.

lenges for the intellect; it has raised new moral challenges, tests for the will. We are weak, and we are entering an age when new temptations will prey on our weakness; we must learn, not new levels of analysis, but new ways to be strong.

DEFINING THE INTERNET

To help the world understand the telecommunications technology known as "the Internet," the Federal Networking Council (FNC) on October 24, 1995 unanimously passed a resolution defining the term. The FNR said: "This definition was developed in consultation with the leadership of the Internet and Intellectual Property Rights (IPR) Communities." Here is the resolution and its definition:

Endnote 6

"The Federal Networking Council (FNC) agrees that the following language reflects our definition of the term **"Internet."**

"Internet" refers to the global information system that

    (i)   is logically linked together by a globally unique address space based on the Internet Protocol (IP) or its subsequent extensions/follow-ons;

    (ii) is able to support communications using the Transmission Control Protocol/Internet Protocol (TCP/IP) suite or its subsequent extensions/follow-ons, and/or other IP-compatible protocols; and

    (iii) provides, uses or makes accessible, either publicly or privately, high level services layered on the communications and related infrastructure described herein."

ETHICS ON THE INTERNET

Intellectual Property revisited

Just when we thought we knew what could and could not be done under the regular copyright laws, along came the Internet and the possibility of unlimited anonymous downloading. Yet the law and the ethic that applies elsewhere applies here as well. What is available for the taking may be gratefully taken; what is clearly proprietary must be respected as such, and what is in doubt, must be inquired about and permission must be asked. Nothing here is new, but in the new convenience and anonymity of the taking, the temptation is high to ignore the property rights.

FRANCIS JOHN KUFROVICH:
INTERNET DATING AND HARASSMENT

On June 10, 1998, Francis John Kufrovich, a wealthy California financier, was sentenced to 18 months in federal prison and fined $25,000 because he "plotted to seduce a New Canaan honor student over the Internet." Seems that in September 1995, Kufrovich, posing as a teenager (he is 43), introduced himself as "Valley Guy" in a teenage "chat room." When he met his 13-year-old victim, he "invited the girl to enter a private chat room where only they could talk." How do you do that? Over the next several months, the two exchanged nightly e-mails and many telephone calls, as the girl became more and more enamored of the so-called boy, as she thought. The whole relationship came crashing down when he showed up at her hotel in March 1996, "kissed and fondled her" before her mother returned to the room and put a stop to his actions.

Endnote 5

The incident was surely reprehensible from the perspective of any century — 43-year-olds should know better than to lust after 13-year-olds. What seemed to catch the court's attention was that this particular lusting had taken place on the computer, in a frightening midnight atmosphere of high-tech anonymity, contact outside of the time and space of any life we understand. In Internet communications, all the visible and audible cues we use to find out about each other — appearance (which usually reveals age), posture and carriage, attributes (choice of clothing, for instance), tone of voice (revealing mood), dialect (which locates home and family) — are hidden; misrepresentation is child's play, and exploitation much more difficult to prevent. But is it that much worse than the ordinarily objectionable, street-level, sexual pursuit of minor child?

Sexual harassment also takes on new dimensions on the Web, in the form of personal sexual questions from anonymous respondents and unsolicited interruptions while surfing or using a "chatroom." Such behavior should be reported immediately to the system administrator.

Endnote 6

Both types of sexual pursuit illustrated by these cases are clearly wrong. Are they more wrong for occurring in cyberspace? As above, we would argue that they are not. To be sure, the Internet's anonymity raises the level of temptation — it is always more tempting to commit crime if you are very unlikely to be caught — but the moral status of the crime, and the criminal, does not change at all. (Anonymity works both ways, of course. How did the Net-based stalker know that his "13-year old" wasn't a sex-starved obese 50-year old divorcee? *That* would have been an interesting meeting.)

Accuracy, Fairness and Verification

As many of us have discovered, posting a "search" on the Internet can yield an enormous storehouse of information, not much of it really useful, but some of it invaluable. For those of us who write books and articles, as well as for the professional journalist, the question becomes how do you check up on information off the Internet, when the sources are anonymous and absolutely anyone can post information? It is very, very tempting to let your search engine do the walking and download everything you need all in one place. "Steele and Cochrane (1995), in an excellent summary of online ethical challenges, caution journalists that by succumbing to the convenience of online information gathering they may sacrifice certain other aspects of accurate reporting."

Endnote 3

The problem really arises because of the casual, everyday nature of Internet posting. On the one hand, it is passing, spontaneous, like lunch table conversation — if you feel like gossiping about your boss, or your best friend, you go ahead and do it. On the other hand, it is widely available, and in some sense, published; so you feel confident taking it down as information for your next story or article (as you would not with the lunch table conversation), and it is forwardable and downloadable and otherwise circulatable, and if it should come to the attention of your boss or your best friend, as the lunchtable conversation would not, you could be sued for libel. Libel has not changed, nor the moral obligations that lead to its prohibition, but the Internet is in a category that straddles our distinctions. It is not the casual untrackable conversation it feels like, it is not the sober, verified, peer-reviewed exposition it looks like, it is somewhere in between and creates a mightily gray area for all who use it.

FOIA: How Much Should We Know?

According to the **Freedom of Information Act,** we ought to be able to find out what our government is doing for (to) us, and that means that we ought to have access to government records. Does that include computer records — e-mail notes, for instance — that have never been printed out and do not exist in hard copy at all? Early in 1994, after almost four years of legal wrangling, Judge Charles R. Richey announced that all government back-up tapes, computerized records of any kind, including hard drives and floppy disks, and even all e-mail logs and directories, even though they had no existence in material form at all, were discoverable public records under the 1966 Freedom of Information Act. There was a reason for this.

Endnote 7

> As NSA researcher and co-plaintiff [in the Iran-contra investigation] Eddie Becker has noted, it was the flexibility of the computer network system that allowed Lieutenant Colonel Oliver L. North to coordinate all the government agencies necessary to "run a covert war on three continents" without leaving a paper trail.

Endnote 8

There are epistemological, not to mention metaphysical, problems with ensuring access to something which has no material form; but the decision, and the circumstances that gave rise to it, underscore the importance of electronic operations and communications.

THE WIRED AND THE UNWIRED: REFLECTIONS ON JUSTICE

Ours is an age increasingly dominated by the computer, and we have yet to figure out the implications of that fact. Let us conclude this section by suggesting a research agenda for those who come after us.

The North and West, Interface of Machine and User

That we now, in these developed countries, spend much of our days staring at a Cathode Ray Tube while tapping at a keyboard, when thirty years ago that would not have been the way anyone spent their days, has had an inestimable effect on the civilization we call our own. It is changing the workplace, the home, and the school, in ways that we will not be able to evaluate in this millennium, and possibly not in the next. What does it mean, for a species that evolved outdoors, to live its worklife indoors? What does it mean, for a species that is highly social and has accomplished all its work for the last 50,000 years in highly interactive groups, to isolate its members before a CRT? **"Interactive software"** refers to programs that you can talk to, and that will give you built-in reinforcements when you get the answers right ("Good going, Jack!"). Should these developments be viewed as terrifying? If not, why not?

The South and East, the Unwired

There is an increasing gap between those who live by the computer, carrying on their business in front of the CRT, and those who simply have no access to the potentials of computer, Internet, and all the problems associated with them. The world is dividing quickly into a new standoff, replacing East and West. We are dividing into the Wired and the Unwired classes within the developed world — the "fast" societies and the "slow" societies. Soon enough, Alvin Toffler has predicted, unless the wired societies find some way to bring the unwired societies up to speed, there will be no possible commerce among them. He may be wrong about that. Without direct aid, the commercial interests of the developed world seem to be discovering ways to initiate cooperation with the developing nations to create new havens of contemporary technology, if only for the purpose of maximizing profits in their investments. Technology, once introduced, will spread rapidly through the wealthier sector of the country. The problem in the less developed nations, as with our own, is spreading the technology to all classes, making sure that the children of disadvantage get the same computer literacy as the children of advantage. Such social problems are the center of social ethics, and will always be with us in one form or another.

EVERYONE'S A PUBLISHER AND EVERYONE IS LIABLE

The information age has now dawned, borne by technologies that allow each individual to be a publisher; literally, publishing abroad on electronic impulses words and thoughts and ideas that for all of previously recorded history was a province of privilege. It took wealth to own a printing press and more money still to distribute the printed page. One need not even own a computer to use one and the Internet to deliver a message to the entire planet. To wrestle with some of the implications of this new era, let's review briefly major tenets of three professions as they are practiced in the United States of America (trying to act on these principles in other parts of the world has cost the lives of the naive).

Libel essentially is the publication of a false and damaging report. If the report is false but not damaging, as in a parody that no one takes seriously, then there is no libel. For example, television viewers who are offended by an interview taped in the home of a tearful crime victim may not realize that the victim's consent was required for the reporter and camera crew to enter the home. Likewise, photographs and broadcasts of funeral services often are criticized in ignorance of the fact that families and churches can and do bar cameras when they wish. The First Amendment does not give reporters a license to trespass on private property.

Modern American press behavior has been influenced greatly by the 1964 Supreme Court decision in *Times v. Sullivan*. Traditionally, people who sued news media for libel tried to prove that the published report was false and had damaged their reputation. Truth was the press's usual defense.

This case involving *The New York Times* set a new standard for public figures, including public officials. Under *Sullivan*, such persons can no longer win a libel suit merely because the published report was false. The Sullivan decision said that a public figure also must prove that the false report was the result of "actual malice" on the part of the news organization. **"Actual malice"** means that the journalists knew that they were publishing a false report or that they published the false story "with reckless disregard of whether it was false or not." The title of the movie "Absence of Malice," starring Sally Fields as a reporter and Paul Newman as a controversial business-man, turns on the Supreme Court's phrase.

In the three decades since *Sullivan*, however, the decision has turned out to be more complex than most news people had thought. The notion of malice, after all, refers to a state of mind. If an injured celebrity is required to prove malice in order to win libel suits, then clearly the lawyers for those celebrities are bound to inquire about the attitudes of reporters and editors. In the 1979 case of *Herbert v. Lando*, the Supreme Court ruled that plaintiffs in libel cases indeed have the right to seek testimony about how the writers and editors did their jobs, and what their attitudes were.

The First Amendment says: Congress shall make no law respecting an establishment of religion, or prohibiting the free exercise thereof; or abridging the freedom of speech, or of the press; or the right of the people peaceably to assemble; and to petition the Government for a redress of grievances.

The First Amendment does not single out major media corporations for special protection. There were none in colonial America. Indeed, it does not even mention newspapers, and for good reason: The general circulation newspaper that is an institution in America today did not emerge until 100 years after the adoption of the Bill of Rights. The "press" of the First Amendment consisted primarily of pamphlets full of essays advocating the opinion of the editor, who usually was the man who owned or rented the local printing press.

Thus, the "new" concept of "advertorials," or purchased space used to advocate a company's positions rather than sell its product, has deep historical roots. For example, the business press in Florida was surprised in 1992 when United States Sugar Corporation purchased a months-long series of multi-page spaces in *Florida Trend* magazine to explain its position on the controversy over allegations that agribusiness was harming the Everglades. The Founding Fathers would not have batted an eye.

While there is little dispute about the right of a business to publish its opinion on public issues, there is considerable debate over restraints on "commercial speech" in the form of spoken or written language that is part of a sales message. The Constitution does allow for the regulation of commerce, though not of speech or of the press.

Fraud is a crime, and fraud is intrinsically an act of speech or print — an act of communication. Thus the notions of free speech and regulation of commerce have been on a collision course since the birth of the republic.

This historic tension surfaces regularly in debates over certain kinds of advertising, such as for tobacco or unconventional medical treatments, abortion clinics or crude entertainment. It also is involved in debates over "political correctness" and other controversial political expressions such as bigotry, anti-democratic theories or the defense of either communism or unfettered capitalism.

PROFOUND QUESTIONS SPUR ETHICAL BEHAVIOR

Those are large ethical issues. Sometimes more troubling are the more narrow and local conflicts that the typical communicator faces every day, and some of these will be discussed later. However, the first question for the communicator — as for any other person in business or the professions — is this:

Q: Is it ever ethical to do things in your role as a businessperson/professional that would be unethical/immoral in your personal life?

If your answer is Yes, then other questions demand answers:

1) Which of your usual rules can you break at the office? Misleading someone? Lying? Cheating? Stealing? Intimidation? Physical violence?

2) What office goals are sufficient to justify breaking your personal code? Getting a raise? Winning a Pulitzer Prize? Saving your business from bankruptcy? Satisfying your client? Easing public hysteria? Avoiding an unjust tax burden? Contributing to community harmony? Beating an unscrupulous competitor? Serving the public's "right to know"?

In other words, Does the end justify the means? If so, which ends justify which means?

If your answer is No, then life may be simpler because you will need only one ethical formula. However, that formula will have to be complete — it will have to cover every eventuality.

The notion of a special license to break the normal rules arises subtly throughout business and the professions, but it is overt in journalism. Professional and otherwise law-abiding news people routinely engage in serious discussion over whether to break the law, to infringe on an individual's privacy, or take an action that they know will be hurtful to an innocent party.

JOURNALISTIC VIEWS

Endnote 9

Professor Philip Meyer's analysis of the 1982 ethics survey of the American Society of Newspaper Editors (ASNE) is telling. Meyer notes that journalists uniformly reject the idea of any right to violate laws or rules in order to pursue personal gain. (1) The ASNE Code of Ethics is specific on this point. (2) However, when they are acting in their role as journalist, many take a different view.

From the ASNE data, Meyer identifies 20 percent or more of the U.S. newspaper industry as "First Amendment fundamentalists" who will violate norms, such as an individual's privacy or the secrecy of a Grand Jury, if the material at issue is "newsworthy." Another 57 percent adopt a "situation ethics" approach and will violate rules selectively, for example if they believe "the importance of the material revealed outweighs the damage to the system from the breaching of its security." (3) Modern technology is stretching the issue of means and ends even further. The 1992 case of NBC News and General Motors illustrates the point.

"MAKING NEWS" — NBC AND THE WASHINGTON POST

* To illustrate a report that claimed that GM trucks were more likely than other makes to catch fire on impact, NBC News attached fireworks to a GM truck used as an example in order to make the fire sufficiently eye-catching. GM sued. At first the network defended its action as merely cosmetic, but subsequently retracted the position, apologized and fired several producers and reporters.

* The NBC doctoring of the visual image "for effect" has echoes of the 1981 incident involving Washington Post reporter Janet Cooke. Writing about the real horror of drugs in the inner city, Cooke won a Pulitzer Prize for her gripping story about "Jimmy," an 8-year-old heroin addict. Only in the glare of publicity about the Pulitzer was it discovered that Jimmy was not a real child at all, but a sensationalized composite of many ghetto residents. The Post fired Cooke and returned the Pulitzer Prize.

That hardly settles the issue, however. While Cooke was a classic liar who deceived her own editors, and NBC News applied its "cosmetics" the old-fashioned way, with actual explosives, new technology is posing new challenges. NBC could have achieved exactly the same effect with computer imaging. The same techniques that allow the crime-stopper programs to artificially "age" a missing child or a fugitive can produce footage of nearly anyone doing nearly anything. NBC was not the only violator of ethical standards. In 1996, ABC got into the act of manufacturing news.

THE CASE OF THE TAINTED MEAT

ABC sent employees undercover to check on the cleanliness of practices at the Food Lion supermarket chain. Employees of ABC falsified job application forms, carried concealed cameras, lied about what they were doing to the other Food Lion employees, and managed to gather some arresting footage on how our meat is really treated in the stores. At three Food Lion stores in the Carolinas, they found food-handling practices that were surely dangerous to customers, and aired a powerful accusation on *PrimeTIME Live*, ABC's newsmagazine. Food Lion did not like what it saw on its television set, and sued for libel. After listening to arguments pro and con, the jury came back with a verdict of $5.5 million against ABC.

Now what was the jury thinking, to award that amount of money to a plaintiff who had been caught red-handed — caught "on tape" —

using unlawful and dangerous procedures to avoid having to throw out past date, unsafe, products? And to demand that amount of the heroic journalists who had put themselves at risk (and their employers to a great deal of expense) in order to expose that crime to the public? Those were the questions that tormented veteran journalist Louis Hodges, who concluded that "their moral calculus seems to be that it is better for people to eat rotten meat than for journalists to lie on job applications." But for other journalists, the American public was sending a message. In effect, Food Lion jurors told ABC: **News organizations cannot break the law to get a story; nor can they lie their way into an establishment to get a story.** Other commentaries on the verdict acknowledged that whatever the United States may have thought of investigative reporting at an earlier time, by now reporters were at the rank of trust of used car salesmen, and could hope for no mercy from the public.

Endnote 10

Endnote 11

Endnote 12

For the moment, no verdict seems safe. How such decisions are made depends far too much on details of the individual case, skillfully presented, of which we know nothing, and on the particular combination of the personalities of attorneys for both sides, plaintiffs, defendants, jury and judge, also imponderable. But some of this has to do with the cheapening of the image of the press, with a popular conviction that journalism, at least TV journalism, is one more business trying to make money by purveying shock. If we are to avoid the real and perceived descent of journalism into entertainment and titillation — and who would need an amendment to the Constitution to protect that? — we are going to have to reaffirm the faith of Thomas Jefferson and Fred Friendly, that an informed and active citizenry is an empowered electorate and the best, ultimately the only, guarantee of a healthy democracy, and that the major job of the press is to get the information to the people.

*"The world works only for today, as the world worked twelve thousand years ago, and our children's children will still have to toil and slave for the bare necessities of life."
— Thomas Jefferies, 1983*

The new generation of professional communicators will face the challenge: Just when does an altered image stop being a factual representation and become a work of fictionalized computer art? At what point is the communicator obliged to disclose the doctoring of the image, and to whom?

Likewise, traditional copyright law is being tested by the ease of copying computer software, and the concept of "public records" is expanding to include the e-mail of public employees. No doubt libel lawyers soon will discover the computer billboard and push the courts to rule that a notice on such an electronic device constitutes "publishing." Hacking clearly presses the definitions of trespass, privacy, and property rights.

Today's students will need clear ethical standards that they can apply to the rapidly changing communications technology.

Endnote 13

ADVERTISING APPROACHES

Because it consists of paid-for space or air time, advertising is the most "commercial" of the communications disciplines and the one least protected by the First Amendment. **Commercial speech** — that is, speech that is part of a sales effort — does not enjoy the same protection as political speech or even as general business speech. There is a clear legal consensus that representations that are related to sales may be scrutinized for fraud as part of the implied contract of a transaction.

The Federal Trade Commission Act and other specific laws attempt to define what is "fair" or "deceptive" in the field of advertising. States commonly provide penalties for **"bait-and-switch"** advertising (in which the bargain item is used as bait and stocked in small quantities if at all, in a planned effort to "switch" the buyer to a higher priced product.) States even govern the manner in which the prices of individual items may be displayed in a store or outside a gas station.

While people in business may make reference to the old ***caveat emptor*** (let the buyer beware) attitude as a justification for blatantly deceptive practices, American courts have rendered that position largely moot. The 1993 federal fraud convictions of several former executives of Miami-based General Development Corp. strongly reinforced the responsibility of advertisers and promoters to represent their products honestly. The jury found that the company executives conspired to misrepresent the value of houses it sold to out-of-state buyers. *Miami Herald* Business Columnist James Russell saw in those convictions a lesson that the "caveat emptor" theory does not excuse "fraud and deception."

As a consequence of this long and growing body of law, advertising seems even further removed than public relations from any theory of immunity from ordinary morality such as the one that many journalists claim.

The Communicator as Conscience

Take, for example, the issue of advertising standards set by publications. Publishers devote considerable attention to standards by which advertising will be judged as to suitability for their publication. Advertising standards rarely attract public attention, and when they do it typically is because a major product is pushing conventional boundaries in its new ad campaign. This is most likely to happen when sexier-than-usual images are injected into ads for consumer items, such as perfume or blue jeans. When the public learns that a major magazine, for example, has rejected a new perfume ad, the reader can be sure that the advertiser expects to benefit from the resulting notoriety. Controversy itself is sometimes an effective means of communicating a message of unconventionality.

Most discussions of ad standards, however, take place within the organization. Newspapers, magazines, television stations and networks all have guidelines that set limits on what they choose to convey as paid advertising. Most reject hard profanity, for example, even though they have a legal right to publish it. Many also refuse advertising for pornographic movies or books, or severely restrict the content of ads for those products.

Though the public may not be aware of them, such rules actually are quite common. For many years, the *Los Angeles Times* refused ads for "triple-X" movies or liquor. The *St. Petersburg Times* refused liquor ads during the lifetime of its legendary publisher, Nelson Poynter. Later executives relaxed those rules at both newspapers. The *Miami Herald* and other newspapers still require evidence in support of claims made by candidates in political ads in the paper.

TRUTHFULNESS IS THE PIVOTAL IDEA

Once the issue of special professional privilege has been settled, communicators face the basic demand of their role, which is how, and how much, to serve the principle of truthfulness. Issues of *accuracy, completeness, disclosure* and *good faith* punctuate every ethical case study involving professional communications. It is inherent in the concept of communicating that listeners and readers expect not to be lied to.

Distortions and sensationalizing will instill a sense of betrayal whether or not the practitioner intended to betray. Professional communicators, after all, cannot hide behind the excuse, "I didn't mean it that way." If they didn't mean it the way it was taken, then they are incompetent as communicators. Granted, incompetence is a defense of sorts against the charge of unethical or immoral behavior, but it is a poor argument for keeping one's job or professional reputation. Communicators are hired precisely because they are supposed to be better than most people at getting the message across the way they intend it to be received.

© 1988 Creators Syndicate, Inc.

That skill imposes a serious burden that business and news organizations alike tend to recognize. It is that the communicator assumes some responsibility for the content of the message and for the policy implications inherent in the message. The ethical complexity of that role can hardly be exaggerated.

What role does **truth** — simple truth, the accurate depiction of what really happens — play in our understanding of the role of the media and our evaluation of its place in our lives? (The question presumes, of course, that we are not all post-modernists who believe there is no such thing as what really happens!) From the "infotainment" accusations leveled against "the media" from all sides, you'd have thought that "truth" was a quaint idea long since abandoned in the search for riveting images and shocking scenes. Yet the popular reaction to recent episodes of investigative reporting, and the presentation of its results, yields some food for serious thought, especially in contrast to popular reaction to previous episodes.

PUBLIC RELATIONS' APPROACHES

There is no comprehensive survey comparable to the ASNE study that compiles the attitudes of public relations professionals, in part because this relatively young industry lacks the organizational structure of the news business. While the general circulation newspaper dates from the Nineteenth Century, **public relations** as a profession is an outgrowth of the rapid social changes of post-World War II America. Those changes include urbanization, increases in mobility and a multiplication of the media of mass communication.

While more than 200,000 persons in the United States identify themselves as "public relations professionals," only 14,000 are members of the Public Relations Society of America (PRSA), the largest organization in the field. As with journalists, there is no licensing mechanism and no disciplinary body. The First Amendment umbrella prevents government from licensing communicators the way it regulates lawyers, physicians and accountants.

A significant survey of practitioner ethics, Cornelius Pratt's 1991 compilation of the existing data on public relations ethics, found a correlation between age and ethical standards in public relations. Older practitioners reported stronger moral values in their business conduct. Indeed, the sum of the surveys of the successful seasoned professionals who make up the membership of PRSA is an emphasis on the importance of ethics education. *These practitioners ranked the need for more and better ethics study as their top priority.*

This survey supports the observation that *young professionals frequently underestimate the importance of sound ethics within their chosen profession.* Students thus may be encouraged that the exercise in which they are engaged here is not an idle or a futile one. The ability to recognize ethical problems and to discuss them intelligently is an important value to in-house corporate communicators and to the owners and executives of most of the nation's best known and most profitable public relations firms. There is wide acceptance within the field of the view that "The success of public relations in the 1990s and beyond will depend to a large degree on how the field responds to the issue of ethical conduct."

On the specific question of whether the practitioner possesses a license to suspend his personal morality in pursuit of his profession, there is no parallel in mainstream public relations to the extreme First Amendment fundamentalist of the newspaper world. There is, however, considerable overlap with journalism's situation ethics and subjectivism as a major tendency within public relations. Public relations professionals agree that it is important to behave ethically, but there are disagreements among practitioners about what is ethical and what is not.

It is important to note, however, that "responsibility to society was perceived as more important than the practitioner's responsibility to an employer or client." The PRSA Code of Ethics flatly asserts that "a member shall conduct his or her professional life in accord with the public interest." Thus, there is no widely accepted theory within the profession, as there is in journalism, that permits practitioners to view themselves as above the rules of ordinary society.

Seasoned public relations professionals know that even clients may not understand the practitioner's role. It is common, in an early interview with a new public relations counselor, for the client to say something like, "This situation is making our company look terrible. What are you going to do to improve our image?"

The professional's answer may be, "We'll get to the image later. First, let's find out what the reality is. Let's start at the beginning. We have to see clearly what caused this situation that is making you look bad and what you can do to correct it. When we have those answers, then we can develop a message for your employees, customers and stockholders."

THE ETHICS OF PUBLIC RELATIONS

The Public Relations Officer, by definition, speaks for others, not for himself; it is essentially an adjunct position, joined to something else for which it is the outreach function. What sort of profession is this? Several analogies have been suggested.

The Analogy of the Attorney

The profession of advocate, or attorney, has generally been left to the lawyers, for it is before the law, especially in its public aspect, that we feel most in need of someone to speak for us. In Mafia lore, the lawyer is often referred to as "the mouthpiece," signifying that his speech was not his own, and that he served primarily the role of shaping and amplifying the speech of others; this description suits the Public Relations Director to a T. The speech is that of the client, principal, or employer, a private-sector corporation, a university or other non-profit organization, or God help him, a Government agency or individual, up to and including the White House. It has a message. The Public Relations officer, as professional, agent, and employee, has the task of shaping that message so that it serves the interest of that

"A fair day's-wages for a fair day's-work': it is as just a demand as governed men ever made of governing. It is the everlasting right of man."
— Thomas Carlyle, 1843

which he serves. Like the attorney, extending the analogy, the PR person is expected to take his client's part and point of view, fight for him, acquire and use professional skills in the interest of the client. The image of the Public Relations officer as defending and championing the interests of another, just as does an attorney, suggests the most urgent job of Public Relations: to be the official face of the corporate client in times of trouble and accusation, allegations of wrongdoing and picket lines of protesters around the block. At these junctures, all too common in corporate and government life, it is PR's work first, to inspire trust and confidence in press and public by whatever means suggest themselves, then, to release to press and public just as much truth as will serve the interests of the client, and to give the facts a subtle but indelible spin in the client's direction. (It is not a good idea to lie.) If the first job is well done, the remaining two should not be overly difficult.

But it is essential that the mission statement be found and formulated, and it is part of the PR officer's job to make sure that it happens if it has not already at the time that he was hired. For as we saw in the Tylenol case earlier in the book, the possession of a strong mission and ample practice in articulating it and living by it can make all the difference when the accusations and allegations begin, especially when the accusations are totally unprovoked, unforeseeable and unjust. If the public already has a firm positive image of the client, it will be slow to believe accusations and quick to believe explanations. If the public has no image at all of the client, or a muddy or mixed one, the opposite applies.

Problems of Personal Identity and Integrity

One of the saintlier of our religious orders has designated its members as Men (or Women) for Others: dedicated people whose sole satisfaction lies in caring for other people or building organizations, finally totally consumed in a life of selfless service. Selflessness may describe a saint; but the profession of Public Relations rarely aspires to sainthood, and the "loss of self" for one whose sole job description is as *agent for a principal* is not at all a noble outcome. What comes out of a person's mouth is generally held to be the best evidence of the state of his heart and the criterion of judgment of his life and character. How are we to evaluate and judge a person out of whose mouth come not his own words, but always another's? How does the Public Relations officer preserve his own identity and integrity in a life spent delivering a spin not his own for a product not of his choosing? We can expect the same type of moral dilemmas to arise in the practice of Public Relations as arise in law and in salesmanship, **dilemmas of truth** and **dilemmas of zeal.** A dilemma of truth (or dilemma of sincerity) arises either (1) when the officer, unsure of the truth, must present it as pure and beyond question, by his attitude of transparent sincerity; or (2) when the officer, knowing the truth all too well, must select just that part which is favorable to the client while appearing to deliver the whole.

The Dilemma of Truth

A typical (all too typical!) dilemma of truth is generally known as the "cover-up." The client has suddenly come to public attention in some way which is (a) serious, (b) unfavorable, and (c) a total surprise to the client (if the client is collective, all the senior officers of the client). Suddenly it is discovered that the former Governor of New York has died in his New York city apartment, news of the death phoned in from the apartment by an attractive young woman, or that the apple juice made by the baby food company is really only colored sugar water, or that a major U.S. company's factory has just blown up, killing 4000 citizens of India, or that a freshman at the university has just given birth to a stillborn child in the dormitory bathroom. The daily newspaper's reporter is halfway in the door, the evening news' cameras on the front lawn, and it's the Public Relations Department's job to put a good face on whatever happened, show all the client's actions (or the actions of all its senior officers) in a sympathetic light, and above all, make sure that the press understands that the whole matter is over, has been taken care of, is being dealt with by the appropriate authorities, and so there's nothing more to say and they can all *go home*.

A man's name should appear in the newspaper three times in his life, President George Bush used to say: "When he's born, when he is married, and when he dies." All the client wants is for the press to go away, but the matter is serious, and the public has a right to know. To know what? *When is withholding information tantamount to lying?* The Public Relations officer has a very short time to make a series of very subtle distinctions. The public has a right to know about the Governor's death, at least to know that foul play was not involved, but has no need for speculation on what the Governor was doing when he died; the baby food company can best get rid of the press by owning up to everything, apologizing, recalling product, making refunds where appropriate and not trying to blame others; the major corporation has the job of seeking out the facts, but the public has no right to profuse apologies until a lot more is known; the University should be able to show that it takes reasonable care of the health of its students without going into the details of how, when, why, this particular student became pregnant and how much her parents know about all this. If the press does not already have her name, the university need not reveal it.

The Public Relations officer is required by his job to reveal some information while concealing other information. Some things, for instance, *should* be "covered up," if only, as with an attractive body, for the sake of decency, or for the sake of the protection of individual rights and privacy. Professional confidentiality must be protected, for instance, strictly limiting the amount of information hospitals can release on patients or universities on students. The downside of this clear moral obligation is that, in the corporate mind, these restrictions can devolve quickly into protecting the collective client's "right" to preserve the privacy, i.e., the good name, of the institution — and

A man's name should appear in the newspaper three times in his life, President George Bush used to say: "When he's born, when he is married, and when he dies."

that "duty" has been evoked to justify any amount of lying. At this point the integrity of the Public Relations officer is tested. The job requires serving the best long-term interests of the client, and if the panicked client is in error about where those interests lie, the PR officer must politely disagree and, if necessary, put his job on the line for the sake of his profession.

Events that may not be covered up include any that legitimately cast doubt on the institution's ability to do its job, when its job is a public service or where its goods are publicly sold; any that show that a corporation's processes may put people at risk (like the gas explosion at an insecticide plant in Bhopal, India — from a factory substantially identical with many in the United States); and in general, any situations knowledge of which would be necessary or useful to the public *in order to make their own responsible choices in their life and work.* The **responsibility perspective,** from which we are working in these chapters, requires that any information relevant to a responsible choice in personal life or work is information that all people deserve to have. Idle curiosity, morbid curiosity, prurient curiosity, do not create such a right. The cases presented as examples, above, contain interesting admixtures of subjects on which the Public Relations officer must be entirely candid, and subjects on which he can, or must, be mute. But the lines are not clear and bright, and the choice can be very difficult.

The dilemma of zeal is different, arising not over how much of the client's information should be revealed, but over the formation and limitation of the professional-client relationship. Are there clients that do not deserve an advocate, whose speech does not deserve shaping and amplifying by a mouthpiece? Should a professional accept a job representing the Ku Klux Klan? (Should an attorney accept a retainer from the Mafia? Many do.)

The Personal Mission
Ultimately, the task of finding a personal ethic in the work will not be easy for the Public Relations professional. There is an unmistakable, even thrilling, challenge to such a job. Can we spin the story *that* much, to make even *this* look like just one more Good Old American Boys' club, warm and fun as apple pie at a picnic? Or is the whole premise of its existence so repellent, so irredeemably evil in its narrow ignorance and mindless violence, that it must corrupt the soul of any person who could, even hypothetically and professionally, take its part? Again, only the professional himself can decide whether there are tasks that are so corrupting that professional integrity cannot stand such employment.

The Analogy of the Salesman
In balmier times, the Public Relations job better approximates the work of the sales force of a typical company, but a sales force with only one product, the *image* of the company, no matter what kind of company the client may be. Image is a highly subjective notion, approximating the "picture" of the client that a member of the public

may be supposed to have. Here the real creative work of Public Relations takes place. If the client is clear on its mission, what it is trying to do in the world and how it intends to do it, the formation of an "image" should be a simple matter of fitting that mission into the expectations of the public and the needs and symbols of the times, and giving it a bit of a polish to attract attention; a good creative Public Relations Department should be expert at that. In these cases, no opportunity should be lost to place that image firmly in the public's mind, to spur sales (or contributions, or applicants, depending on what kind of client it is), to facilitate work in the community (plant expansions and other permits, for instance), and to be the first wall of defense when the client is under attack. If, on the other hand (as is often the case), the client is mightily unclear on what it is that it might be trying to do, the creativity goes beyond fitting and polishing. It is the job then of the PR experts to engage the client in dialogue on the central core of the client's activities, a dialogue that may not initially be welcomed by the client,

Figure 4. NBA star Patrick Ewing depicts the magnetism of print advertising. Modern Curriculum Press.

in order to elicit enough commitments, norms, or values, to translate into a mission statement. At this point the Public Relations officer becomes a philosopher, engaging, like Socrates, in inquiry after the truth within the client, to bring it out into the light and make it shine forth to the public in the bright rays of the sun. The client may not be enthusiastic about this exercise, either because it really has no idea what it is trying to do beyond (say) fool people into buying a worthless product to facilitate a quick profit for the client, or because it is terrified of any publicity at all. Sometimes the PR officer is required to be part psychiatrist, too.

"If you wait until wind and the weather is just right, you will never sow anything and never harvest anything."
— Solomon, Ecclesiastes 11:4

Does Everything Deserve to Be Sold?

When he is not acting as a public forum defense attorney, a Public Relations officer is his client's salesman. Are there products that should not be advertised or sold? There are products on the worldwide market right now — alcohol for drinking purposes, tobacco, and firearms — which are known to cause damage wherever they are sold and used, and which cause disproportionate damage when available to children. Their purveyors solemnly promise to cooperate in all efforts to restrict their use to responsible adults, efforts that are inevitably worthless, since any product normally kept about the house cannot be kept from curious younger members of a family. Nor can a plausible case be made that the purveyors really intend such restriction, since in the case of alcohol and tobacco, the recruitment of the next generation of customers is essential to their future, and in the case of firearms, the youngsters treated to hunting expeditions, not to mention the street fighters of the inner city, provide one of their largest markets. The Public Relations officer (or lobbyist) for such products is in a different position from that of his colleague employed by the chemicals or baby food company that has just incurred some unexpected human tragedy. Human tragedy is stock in trade, business as usual, for these products. The choice to represent one of these industries, or one or several companies within them, turns entirely upon the individual professional's sense of moral integrity. Some professionals can serve the industry without qualms, others simply cannot. There is no right answer.

Ultimately, the Public Relations professional must reconcile his personal values with the job at hand, or fail both the job and himself. The ideal is to perfect and hone the skills of public relations until representing Satan himself would be easy, then to find a cause, or organization, which rightfully claims the full loyalty of any good person, and to spend a life representing that cause or organization. Learning to live with compromises is part of any professional life; knowing that there is an ideal may help to live that life as ideally as possible.

ONWARD, WITH TREPIDATION

All of the abuses attributed to high technology, as we have seen, are variants of abuses elsewhere in the society that do not change when translated into computer language. Sexual harassment, stealing, cheating, plagiarizing, laziness, libel, are not rendered any better or any worse by occurring electronically.

Any one of the many approaches to formal ethics may be applied to the practice of communications in commerce. Whether the approach is through Utilitarianism or Kant, Natural Law or Contractarianism, problems in communications ethics are accessible to the student of formal ethics. If students by this time in this course of study have chosen a favorite ethical approach, they would do well to reread this chapter from that point of view, testing their approach against these real life questions.

As they do so, students are likely to confront the centrality of the obligation of truthfulness in their chosen philosophy of ethics, for communication problems invariably touch that question. Whether to tell the truth, Whether to tell the whole truth, and Whether to tell anything that is not the truth are inescapable issues for the professional communicator.

That fact should come as no surprise, for the assumption of honesty is the basis for all communication, whether personal or professional. No society could function unless people could assume that most others tell the truth most of the time. Whether asking directions from a stranger, inquiring about merchandise in a store or chatting idly with a neighbor, we tend to assume that we are being told the truth and will take offense if we discover otherwise. Honesty thus is a central issue in any discussion of ethics.

As the issue of truth is explored, the notion of passive and active deception arises: Is there a moral difference between speaking an untruth and merely standing mute in the knowledge that the person in front of you believes an untruth?

The next question is likely to be that of differing levels of obligation: Is the requirement of truth-telling or disclosure always the same, or does it vary depending on the nature of the relationship in whose context the communication occurs? Are we required to tell our bosses everything that we would tell our mothers? And vice versa?

If the requirements are variable, then by what principles do we apply them to different situations? How do we decide when it is all right just to keep quiet when we know something that others don't? Conversely, how do we decide when an obligation of confidence to someone else *requires* us to keep quiet?

These are not simple questions, but neither are they impossible ones for the student to answer. To the contrary, the issues of communication ethics are no more — and no less — complex than the ordinary issues of family life and general citizenship. If you are certain that it is always wrong to lie to your parent or spouse, many other decisions fall into place automatically.

Likewise, if you are certain that it is permissible always to lie to them, other decisions are clarified. It is uncertainty about the morality of an action or about the strength of the obligation involved that makes ethics — and life — complex.

FINAL COMMENTS

In another context, Shakespeare observed, "Cowards die many times before their death; the valiant only taste of death but once." A similar efficiency accrues to successful students of ethics: Once they reach a decision about a basic principle of ethical behavior, they will not have to worry much about it in the future. In a complex world that demands constant relearning and readjusting, that steady "moral compass" provides a benefit that is as practical as it is admirable.

Will we survive this kind of life as psychologically sound persons? More importantly, will we be able to maintain a moral community, a public space where conformity to rule can be compelled at a minimum, and where policy for the common good can be discussed and enacted? How can a community enforce moral rules on people it can't see and who may not be there anyway? What counts as a "common good" for people who cannot be immediately aware of each other's needs and interests and who cannot realistically share each other's lives? These questions form more than a research agenda for the next millennium. They are a tocsin, a warning bell, sounding in the night as we move with incredible speed into completely uncharted waters. Let's keep our eyes open.

FOR FURTHER INQUIRY

REVIEW QUESTIONS

1. Take the example of the "exploding truck," given above. Would there have been any way of making this dramatic point without deceptive effect? What is the line between "hypothesizing" and deceiving? Where would *you* draw it?

2. What is it that makes a story "newsworthy"? Consider some definitions from the literature and try your hand at making up one.

ENDNOTES

---

1. Adam Clayton Powell, III. "Technology and the Death of Ethics (And the Possible Rise of the New Ethics)," *Media Ethics* Fall, 1996, pp. 1, 14.

2. Andrew S. Grove, president of Intel, interviewed in *Newsweek,* Sept. 2, 1996.

3. Paul S. Voakes, "Ethics for the Online Journalist," *Media Ethics 1996*, 8(1):5 (Fall 1996) p. 4.

4. Ibid. See also R. Reddick and E. King, *The Online Journalist: Using the Internet and Other Electronic Resources* (New York: Harcourt Brace, 1995).

5. Michael Mayko, "Net Seducer of Girl Gets 18 Months," *Connecticut Post* (Bridgeport, Conn.) June 11, 1998.

6. Ronald Doctor, "Justice and Social Equity in Cyberspace," in *Ethics Information and Technology: Readings,* ed. Richard N. Stichler and Robert Hauptman (Jefferson N.C.: McFarland & Company, 1998). pp. 231–240.

7. Grant Kester, "Access Denied: Information Policy and the Limits of Liberalism," *in Ethics, Information and Technology Readings*, ed. Richard N. Stichler and Robert Hauptman (Jefferson N.C.: McFarland and Company, 1998).

8. Grant Kester, "All the President's Memory: Federal Record-Keeping and the Politics of Information Management," *Afterimage* 20 (8): 8–10 (March 1993), cited in Kester, supra, p. 219.

9. Philip Meyer, *Ethical Journalism* (New York. Longman Publishers, 1987).

10. Louis W. Hodges, "The Real Issue Is Tainted Food," *Media Ethics 1997*, Spring 1997, volume 8 number 2, p. 4.

11. Tom Pfeifer, "We're Better Than That," *Media Ethics 1997*, Spring 1997 Vol. 8 (2), p. 5.

12. John Michael Kittross, "Food Lion vs. ABC: Leo and Mickey at the Divide," *Media Ethics 1997*, Spring 1997, Vol. 8 (2).

13. *Philosophical Issues in Journalism*, ed. Elliot D. Cohen, (New York. Oxford University Press, 1992).

14. *Ethics, Information and Technology Readings* ed. Richard N. Stichler and Robert Hauptman (Jefferson, NC. McFarland & Co., 1998).

15. *Responsible Journalism*, ed. Deni Elliott (Beverly Hills, CA. Sage Publications, Inc. 1986).

16. D. Bartlett, "The Soul of a News Machine. Electronic Journalism in the Twenty-first Century," *Federal Communications Law Journal* 47(1).1–23 (1994).

17. Sissela Bok, *Lying. Moral Choice in Public Life* (New York. Vintage Press, 1979).

18. Clifford Christians, "Enforcing Media Codes," *Journal of Mass Media Ethics*, 1(1).14–21 (1985–1986).

19. Franklin Donnell, "What Can Philosophy Do for a Journalist?" *The International Journal of Applied Philosophy*, 4(3) (Spring 1989).

20. Frederick A. Elliston, "Whistleblowing: The Reporter's Role," *International Journal of Applied Philosophy* 3(2).25–36 (Fall 1986).

21. C. Hausman, "Information Age Ethics. Privacy Ground Rules for Navigating in Cyberspace," *Journal of Mass Media Ethics* 9(3).135–144 (1994).

22. L. P. Husselbee, "Respecting Privacy in an Information Society. A Journalist's Dilemma," *Journal of Mass Media Ethics* 9 (3).145–156 (1994).

23. Robert A. Hutchins, *A Free and Responsible Press. . . .* (Chicago. University of Chicago Press, 1947).

24. Stephen Klaidman and Tom L. Beauchamp, *The Virtuous Journalist* (New York. Oxford University Press, 1987).

25. Roy L. Moore, *Mass Communication Law and Ethics* (Hillsdale, NJ. Lawrence Erlbaum Associates, 1995).

CHAPTER 21

DECISION-MAKING IN PUBLIC SERVICE

"My basic principle is that you don't make decisions because they are easy, you don't make them because they are cheap, you don't make them because they are popular; you make them because they are right. Not distinguishing between rightness and wrongness is where administrators get into trouble."

— Father Theodore Hesburgh, former president, University of Notre Dame

"That's why we hold our political leaders to such a high standard — not because we expect them to be perfect, but because we know there has to be an image projected, an expectation aroused, a standard raised."

— William Moyers, journalist, former press secretary to President Johnson

A lone chapter can barely scratch the surface of the complexities of official decision-making within an ethical context. But we can see that (1) public officials do have ethical and moral responsibilities beyond merely obeying the law, (2) there are core values that contribute to effective and honorable public service, (3) processes and systems exist for ethical official decision-making, and (4) there, indeed, are individuals who have taken seriously the "calling" of public service and have performed honorably. In a democracy, however, a key component of "successful government" is the informed voter, the vigilant news medium and healthy skepticism of the power of government itself. That's why the framers of the American Constitution divided power into three branches of government and assumed public interest and publishing interest.

Public service in American political life once was considered a **"high calling,"** in the classical sense of a noble profession uplifting all persons. "Public service is a sacred trust," were words heard as the

---

Donald Pride, former press secretary for two-time Florida Governor and U.S. Senate candidate Reubin Askew, was director of investigations for the Chief Inspector General, Office of the Govenor, State of Florida. **Michael Richardson**, retired editor of editorials from St. Petersburg Times and Evening Independent, is past predsident of the National Conference of Editorial Writers Foundation and former chairman of the NCEW Professional Standards Committee. He is director of government relations and Executive Assistant to the President of St. Petersburg Junior College.

American democratic experiment was being launched. Parents encouraged children to think of it as a career of high purpose serving humanity, equated with such service professions as the clergy, medicine, and the law. Becoming president of the United States was a noble childhood goal, and William Jefferson Clinton of Hope, Arkansas had that goal as a youth, realizing it in 1992.

CHIEF LEARNING OUTCOME

I can apply theories of moral reasoning to evaluate public decisions and those who make them.

In the nation's second hundred years, families cited the inspiring example of Abraham Lincoln, who never won an election until his first try for President. Holding public office commanded respect with the stations of university faculty, judgeships, medical doctors. By the 1990s the image of those professions also had been tarnished as the robes of secrecy and privilege had been lifted to reveal incidents of scandal, ethical lapse, abuse of trust, and moral failure. **But perhaps no other American profession's image has fallen as fast and as far as that of the public servant,** both elected and appointed. American opinion surveys in recent years show the public holds members of Congress, for example, at the bottom of any listing of professions; dogcatchers fare better in the perceptions of ordinary citizens.

It has been argued that the modern technology-driven information explosion, scandal-seeking media and the human bent for juicy gossip distort the perception of public service. "I am not a crook," an American president felt compelled to disclaim in the spring of 1975. Within weeks, Richard Nixon became the first American president to resign from office, driven by the catastrophic moral failures uncovered by the Watergate affair of 1974–75. Nixon in 1972 had received an overwhelming vote of the American people for re-election — a modern record plebiscite. Historians suggested his quest for power, his desire to wreak retribution on an "enemies list," and his unrelenting attempt to "cover up" the breaches of public trust and the law within his Committee to Re-Elect the President (CREEP) were vain abuses of power. Indeed, CREEP had gone so far as to plot a campaign of "dirty tricks" to embarrass, discredit and taint supporters of Democratic presidential candidate George McGovern.

Nixon had extricated the nation from the divisive and demoralizing Vietnam War, but his personal and political tactics prevented him from retaining the power he so zealously had won. By August 1975 he

Figure 1. Richard Nixon. Bryn Campbell/*The Observer* (London, UK).

was gone from the White House, and the nation groped for its moral foundations. It was not mere public cynicism that drove him out. A cadre of young persons involved in his campaign, directed by their political elders (all Nixon cronies), had lied, violated criminal laws, abandoned virtually any sense of ethical standard, and operated not by the *Golden Rule* but a perverse corollary: Do unto others before they do unto you.

What did Nixon do wrong? Beneath the legal mumbo jumbo, (1) he simply did not tell the whole truth when asked and (2) he tried to cover up the sins of his friends who ostensibly were acting in his interest when they broke laws, (3) and, as a result, he broke an unwritten contract between a president and the people of the United States by breaking his oath to uphold the Constitution and laws of the United States. He could have "ridden out" an ugly impeachment process, perhaps, but to his credit he recognized his misdeed and resigned before any more damage to American credibility, especially in international circles, could be done.

In those same '70s, Wilbur Mills, who was one of the powerful Americans of his time as chairman of the U.S. House Ways and Means Committee — the man who decided whether you could deduct your donations to the Red Cross or the United Way — fell from power. His downfall was not over some of the special tax breaks he had given industries who had favored him with cash for his campaigns; rather it was fueled by his escapades with Fanne Foxe, a female Washington dancer who engaged in alcohol-laced soirees with Mills and others. Over the ensuing years, his career drew sad parallels: U.S. Senator John Tower of Texas, a brilliant defense policymaker and presidential adviser, retired due to his lack of control of alcohol. U.S. Senator Gary Hart abandoned a dynamic campaign for president because his marital fidelity, or lack thereof, became an ongoing campaign topic.

Americans, hypocritically perhaps, embraced soap operas laden with moral failure where ethical factors never prevailed over hormonal impulse, and then scoffed at politicians whose soap-opera values propelled them into the spot-

"Always do right. This will gratify some people, and astonish the rest."
—Mark Twain

KEY CONCEPTS

Competing Values and Interests: Official decisions involve the **Constitution** of the United States and, where applicable, the Constitution of a state, the **laws** of the land, certain **regulations or rules,** prescribed **guidelines** within the regulations, **precedents** and **procedures,** including those involved in an official **audit,** as well as specific **codes of ethics** and any prevailing **court rulings** of the U.S. Supreme Court or the federal appeals court in a given region of the nation, and finally, the **governing culture** of the office — the dominant values around which most decisions are made.

Duties of Sound Governance:

Prudence — the wise management of resources for the benefit of the whole including the virtues of foresight and frugality.

Courage of Conscience — the quality of character recognizes compromises and does not hesitate to act on a balance of idealism and realism.

Truth-telling — official telling of the *whole truth* to appropriate authority.

Moral Foundations of Public Administration: Honor, Benevolence, Justice.

light. Meanwhile, in Europe, America's political antecedents wondered why the U.S. took such matters so seriously. Europe's social critics, however, had to admit that from the British Profumo scandal in the 1950s to more recent events, public officials did lose their jobs and their influence as a result of immoral behavior.

A New Generation

But the late '70s also saw American resilience in ethical public service emerge. Across the nation, Jimmy Carter's politics of hope — of restoring public confidence in government, of repudiating the corruption within the Washington beltway — made him the nation's first president from the so-called Deep South. His campaign rhetoric included a reference from George Washington: "If, to please the people, we offer what we ourselves disapprove, how can we afterward defend our work? Let us raise a standard to which the wise and honest can repair."

In this chapter we will consider such standards, the ethical decision-making principles and processes of a range of public officials. In public service, is it enough for officials merely to obey the law, or **does the oath of office demand a higher standard, one of avoiding the appearance as well as the actuality of unethical behavior?**

We are told that no one trusts the government any more. How much of that is due to perceptions, some of them distorted, flowing from media frenzy? Consider the evidence from only a few months in 1998:

* An alleged murderer released by a runaway jury brings the cheers of a grateful crowd, we may conclude that the public prosecutors have lost credibility.

* America's major tax-gathering agency is humiliated and punished by outraged taxpayers, again to roars of approval.

* Federal agents tracking thieves and murderers adopt a painfully cautious, almost delicate, approach to their barricaded quarry, for fear of disturbing the neighbors.

* A sitting President of the United States (Clinton) is subjected to year after year of harassment, not over high crimes and misdemeanors, but over some possible financial misdealings *prior* to assuming office, some possibly inappropriate sexual conduct with consenting adults, and the possibility he may not have told *the whole truth when asked*!

The greater question is: In the mind of the American people, if its leaders appear to be immoral, is the government itself legitimate?

That, of course, is one form of a very serious problem, which we may put as follows: If my moral agency — my capacity to define my own life according to my discernment of what is right, the faculty through which I place my actions subject to deliberation and choice

— defines my humanity, how can I ever give my governance up to another? This is the fundamental problem of political philosophy, and as such it is beyond the scope of this chapter. The problems of ethics in governance start from the presupposition that government in general is legitimate, and then asks what duties bind the government official. To that topic we now turn.

THE GENERAL DUTIES OF SOUND GOVERNANCE

1. ***Phronesis,* or Prudence:** the wise management of resources for the benefit of the whole. All officials, at whatever level, are required to exercise responsible stewardship over the domain to which they are assigned. The virtue of **prudence** divides into two dispositional duties, or subordinate virtues: *foresight and frugality.*

    It does not matter what role a given person plays in governing — elected legislator, appointed tax assessor, President of the United States or 34th level bureaucrat in the Department of Commerce. The general duty of Prudence applies, over just as much of the public weal as he or she exercises *power* and *stewardship.* This duty defines a "public sector" task.

2. **The Courage of One's Conscience:** For the governor seeking re-election, courage is complex. It is not simply charging forward with what the governor knows to be right. That's just likely to alienate people that cannot be alienated if governing is to continue. The kind of **courage** needed here recognizes compromises, makes them on occasion, yet proceeds to govern as effectively as possible. Only when continuing to govern becomes impossible does courage require resignation. It analyzes, then, into a combination of *idealism* and *realism.*

3. **Truth-telling:** In the case of officials, acting with powers derived from and in the name of all the people, there is a greater responsibility: It is **telling the whole truth** — not necessarily volunteered

Figure 2. Abraham Lincoln. Library of Congress.

except in reply to responsible, authoritative inquiry. Example: In the Watergate affair, very incriminating tape recordings of presidential conversations existed, but virtually no one knew of them until a public servant was asked by a Senate Committee whether he knew of any "records." His complete response included reference to the tape recordings, and from that moment of official truth-telling, the Watergate burglary became a matter of mammoth, historic proportions.

In the case of President Bill Clinton's untruthful description of his "inappropriate" behavior with White House Intern Monica Lewinsky, the existence of various tape recordings again contributed to a president's public admission of moral failure. Clinton admitted in August 1998 after seven months of scrutiny that "I misled people" including the American people, members of Congress and his family. Also, his testimony before a federal Grand Jury, though provided by videotape from the White House with his attorney present, was unprecedented. The degree of his contrition became a matter of public debate when his initial August admissions included an attack on the federal prosecutor involved.

WHEN OFFICIALS COVER UP

In the Watergate affair, historians noted two distinct decisions that Nixon made: (1) to " stonewall," or not disclose or respond to public and official inquiries; and (2) to participate in a "coverup" of illegal activity. In 1974 Nixon resigned as impeachment articles were being prepared by a House Committee. At bottom of the Nixon scandal was the **coverup** and his own deceptions about his role in that coverup. In 1998 there apparently were similar decisions to delay and deceive taken by President Clinton, when he was asked questions about the Lewinsky affair.

His August admissions via video before a Grand Jury floored members of his family and the Cabinet, who had openly defended him and then realized they, too, had been misled by the President. He admitted he had "misled" the American people. Nevertheless, Mrs. Hillary Rodham Clinton and the entire Cabinet did not desert the President. There were no resignations as impeachment proceedings were unfolding.

On September 11, 1998 the U.S. House of Representatives was presented a report by the Office of Independent Counsel (OIC) Kenneth Starr. (See Internet URL: **http://icreport.loc.gov/icreport/7grounds.htm9/11/98**) The constitutional grounds for impeachment are "high crimes and misdemeanors." Because impeachment had only occurred once before (President Andrew Johnson was acquitted by the margin of one vote by the U.S. Senate in 1868), legal scholars disagreed on the exact meaning of "high crimes and misdemeanors," some holding that it means whatever Congress determines it to mean at the time of impeachment decision and trial.

In November the U.S. House of Representatives voted to impeach President Clinton primarily on charges of perjury and obstruction of justice. Meanwhile, that same month Clinton paid $850,000 to Paula Jones to settle the sexual harassment suit she had filed against him. She received $200,000 and the remainder went to her attorneys. She

"No people were ever found who were better than their laws, though many have been known to be worse."
— William Goodell, 19th-century Abolitionist

declared she had won a victory for women in the workplace, although the primary harassment she said she had experienced was with Clinton in a Little Rock hotel while he was governor of Arkansas.

The impeachment alleged that Clinton violated his constitutional oath to faithfully execute the laws of the land, that he committed perjury in lying to the civil jury in the Paula Jones lawsuit, and that he obstructed justice in misleading and misdirecting officials of the government to aid his coverup of sexual activity with Monica Lewinsky. There were seven counts of alleged obstruction of justice: "(1) On or about December 17, 1997, William Jefferson Clinton corruptly encouraged a witness in a Federal civil rights action brought against him to execute a sworn affidavit in that proceeding that he knew to be perjurious, false and misleading. (2) On or about December 17, 1997, William Jefferson Clinton corruptly encouraged a witness in a Federal civil rights action brought against him to give perjurious, false and misleading testimony if and when called to testify personally in that proceeding. (3) On or about December 28, 1997, William Jefferson Clinton corruptly engaged in, encouraged, or supported a scheme to conceal evidence that had been subpoenaed in a Federal civil rights action brought against him. (4) Beginning on or about December 7, 1997, and continuing through and including January 14, 1998, William Jefferson Clinton intensified and succeeded in an effort to secure job assistance to a witness in a Federal civil rights action brought against him in order to corruptly prevent the truthful testimony of that witness in that proceeding at a time when the truthful testimony of that witness would have been harmful to him. (5) On January 17, 1998, at his deposition in a Federal civil rights action brought against him, William Jefferson Clinton corruptly allowed his attorney to make false and misleading statements to a Federal judge characterizing an affidavit, in order to prevent questioning deemed relevant by the judge. Such false and misleading statements were subsequently acknowledged by his attorney in a communication to that judge. (6) On or about January 18 and January 20–21, 1998, William Jefferson Clinton related a false and misleading account of events relevant to a Federal civil rights action brought against him to a potential witness in that proceeding, in order to corruptly influence the testimony of that witness. (7) On or about January 21, 23 and 26, 1998, William Jefferson Clinton made false and misleading statements to potential witnesses in a Federal grand jury proceeding in order to corruptly influence the testimony of those witnesses. The false and misleading statements made by William Jefferson Clinton were repeated by the witnesses to the grand jury, causing the grand jury to receive false and misleading information."

But in the ensuing trial in the U.S. Senate, not even a majority of the senators voted to convict the President (a two-thirds vote of the 100 senators was required to convict). By February 12, the trial was over, summarized by Democratic Senator Bob Kerrey of Nebraska to *ABC News:* "He was willing to risk her going to jail to protect himself," Kerrey said. "Remove him because he's a pig? That's not on the list [of impeachable offenses]."

By March of 1999, federal judge Susan Webber Wright ruled that Jones' experience did not constitute legal sexual harassment. Then, in July 1999, Judge Wright found the President in contempt of federal court for not telling the truth. The judge fined him $90,686, payable to Jones' lawyers. She said he lied when he denied "having sex with Monica Lewinsky in his testimony in the Paula Jones sexual harassment lawsuit." Judge Wright ruled that Clinton gave "false, misleading and evasive answers that were designed to obstruct the judicial process." Managers of the House impeachment process declared that Judge Wright's decision vindicated their findings that the President had lied. They also admitted that the Senate's decision seemed to reflect a majority of public opinion that Clinton's wrongdoing did not reach a threshold worthy of removing him from office.

OFFICIAL DECISION-MAKING: YOUR VIEW

When a report such as that of the OIC in 1998 goes to the House, three official points of decision loom for those elected by the people to run the national government:

"Oh the tangled web we weave when first we seek to deceive" is an adage about truthtelling. How does it apply to the Clinton-Lewinsky scandal?

1. If you were a member of the House Judiciary Committee in the fall of 1998, and were presented with the report cited here, would you have voted to send an impeachment motion to be considered by the full House of Representatives? Why or why not?

2. If you were a member of the House of Representatives and the Judiciary Committee presented a motion for impeachment based on the information mentioned above, would you have voted for impeachment of the President? Why or why not?

3. If you were a member of the U.S. Senate and impeachment proceedings were instituted by the House, based on the report above, would you have voted for conviction of the president on any of the counts cited? Which ones? Why or why not?

How much of your decisions was based on the ethical theory of deontology? How much on divine command? How much on egoism? How much on another ethical theory?

PRESIDENT CLINTON'S CONFLICTS OF INTEREST

As President Clinton made decisions about what he would tell under oath and what he would tell to the public, he was torn among at least three interests: (1) His individual interest to keep secret his affair; (2) His family interest in his reputation and that of his wife and daughter, and (3) His official or presidential interest as an officeholder sworn to uphold the Constitution of the United States. Think about how these interests were in perpetual conflict once he decided in January 1998 NOT to tell the truth publicly or officially about his affair. Did he place his individual interest ahead of his family interest? Ahead of his official interest and sworn duty?

What might have happened if President Clinton had told the whole truth in January 1998 to the American public? What if he had said THEN what he said on September 11 at a National Prayer Breakfast? Among his remarks: "I have sinned . . . I have asked for forgiveness . . . I must always keep this as a caution light in my life."

Figure 3. Benjamin Franklin. Associated Press/Wide World Photos.

MAKING DECISIONS IN PUBLIC SERVICE

As each scandal comes to officials, they face essentially the same moral dilemma. They can: (1) act promptly on the serious information before them and call upon the appropriate investigators and prosecutorial authorities to act immediately; (2) delay decision, buying time to consider every ramification but also providing helpful time for the parties involved; or (3) ignore the information as incomplete and not sufficient to warrant action. The highest and best pattern seems to choose the first course without hesitation.

APPROACHING DECISIONS

As public officials approach decision-making, they are faced with an array of **competing values and interests.** Fundamentally, they are sworn to uphold respectively the *Constitution* of the United States and, where applicable, the Constitution of their state. Next they are sworn to uphold the *laws* of the land. Pursuant to the laws are official *regulations or rules* that detail how and when certain actions may be taken.

Then there are suggested *guidelines* within the regulations, and then a board or agency has *precedents and procedures* for conducting the public's business that must be followed — not the least of which is a maze of requirements subject to *audit* by other branches of the government. Overarching all those responsibilities is an awareness that both federal and state governments have "inspectors general" who may investigate operations of a given agency at any time.

That's not all. Specific **codes of ethics** exist for federal employees and most state and local officials, and the provisions of these codes have the force of law. Then there are prevailing **court rulings** of the U.S. Supreme Court or the federal appeals court in their region of the nation — and these then supersede any other official edicts that might exist. Sometimes transcending this multitude of requirements in public decision-making are moral concerns, commonly held beliefs, and values of the public officials involved. These become part of a *governing culture* — the dominant values around which most decisions are made in any particular office or agency of government. (Indeed, it was part of the culture of the Nixon presidency that "leaks" of information to the media were despised. This eventually led the Nixon White House to establish a "Plumbers" operation that turned the nation's foreign intelligence capacities on America's own people, raising moral and ethical questions as well as violating U.S. laws.)

Ibid.

Not surprisingly, as all these competing laws, codes, cultures, personal values and procedures intersect and compete, public officials often find themselves in a quagmire from which it seems difficult simply to "do the right thing."

APPLYING VALUES

Endnote 1

Peter Madsen of the Center for the Advancement of Applied Ethics at Carnegie-Mellon University suggests that public officials, as they approach decisions, first must distinguish between "management mischief" and "moral mazes." This is not unlike the notion of "cardinal" and "venial" sins in Roman Catholic tradition. The attempt is to recognize that some decisions have greater moral stakes and more significant impact on society than others. "Management mischief" at the national level might include the use of official aircraft for personal and-or partisan use by the White House Chief. A "moral maze" surely was involved in the decision to enter the Persian Gulf War with its competing and conflicting vales.

It should be noted, for example, that under the conception of management mischief a public employee's home use of an office computer to produce personal work is not morally less deficient than a White House official using federal airplanes for personal or political use. **Money isn't the standard; morality is.** In like thinking, the Josephson Institute of Ethics emphasizes that the amount of money involved does not determine the morality or immorality of a decision. For 30 pieces of silver, it may be remembered, Judas Iscariot betrayed a 33-year-old Jewish teacher whose subsequent death gave rise to an entirely new religion. For less than $10,000 Americans have sold national secrets involving billions of dollars worth of defense materiel and thousands of lives to avowed enemies of the U.S. In this view, then, the amount of money, though a seeming preoccupation of many in the 1980s in the U.S., does not establish the moral value of a decision.

"GOLDEN KANTIAN CONSEQUENTIALISM"

In developing a decision-making model that avoids the shortcomings of each traditional theory and that can be practically applied to common problems, the Josephson Institute has combined features of each and added the stakeholder concept. Josephson terms its theory "Golden Kantian Consequentialism" — a combination of the Golden Rule, Kant's categorical imperative and a healthy dose of consequentialist doctrine. There are three steps:

   I. All decisions must take into account and reflect a concern for the interest and well being of all stakeholders.

  II. Ethical values and principles *always* take precedence over nonethical ones.

 III. It is ethically proper to violate an ethical principle only when it is *clearly necessary* to advance another *true ethical principle* which, according to the decision maker's conscience, will produce the greatest balance of good in the long run.

Five steps to principled reasoning. Josephson offers his formula for sound reasoning, although his approach is occasionally criticized as oversimplification:

Endnote 2

1. **CLARIFY — Determine precisely what must be decided.** Formulate and devise the full range of alternatives (i.e., things you could do). Eliminate patently impractical, illegal and improper alternatives. Force yourself to develop at least three ethically justifiable options. Examine each option to determine which ethical principles and values are involved.

2. **EVALUATE — If any of the options require the sacrifice of any ethical principle, evaluate the facts and assumptions carefully.** Distinguish solid facts from beliefs, desires, theories, suppositions, unsupported conclusions, and opinions which might generate rationalizations. Take into account the credibility of the sources of information and the fact that self-interest, bias, and ideological commitments tend to obscure objectivity and affect perceptions about what is true. With regard to each alternative, carefully consider the benefits, burdens and risks to each stakeholder.

3. **DECIDE — After evaluating the information available, make a judgment about what is or is not true, and about what consequences are most likely to occur.** If there is not an ethical dilemma, evaluate the viable alternatives according to personal conscience, prioritize the values so that you can choose which values to advance and which to subordinate, and determine who will

be helped the most and harmed the least. It is sometimes helpful to consider the *worst case scenario* — what is the worst outcome possible if things go wrong. In addition, consider whether ethically questionable conduct can be avoided by modifying goals or methods or by consulting with affected people to get their input or consent. Finally, you may want to resort to three *"ethics warning systems."*

A) **Golden Rule** — Are you treating others as you would want to be treated?

B) **Publicity** — Would you be comfortable if your reasoning and decision were to be publicized (i.e., how would it look on the front page of tomorrow's papers)?

C) **Kid-on-Your-Shoulder** — Would you be comfortable if your children were observing you? Are you setting the example you preach?

4. **IMPLEMENT — Once a decision is made on *what* to do, develop a plan of *how* to implement the decision in a way that maximizes the benefits and minimizes the costs and risks.** Remember, any decision or act — no matter how intrinsically ethical — that is accompanied by a sanctimonious, pious, judgmental or self-righteous attitude, is bound to be less effective, if not counterproductive.

5. **MONITOR AND MODIFY — An ethical decision-maker should monitor the effects of decisions and be prepared and willing to revise a plan, or take a different course of action, based on new information.** Since most decisions are based on imperfect information and the "best efforts" predictions, it is inevitable that some of them will be wrong. Those decisions will either fail to produce the consequences anticipated or they will produce unintended and/or unforeseen consequences. The ethical decision-maker is willing to adjust to new information.

Ibid.

SEEKING OFFICIAL MORAL ARCHITECTURE

Searching to establish sets of values as a base for official decisions can be a useful but challenging exercise, as you learned in Chapter 5 in developing your own integrated worldview. Consensus on official values seems a rare commodity at first glance. Consider some of these summations of what constitute the most important official virtues, as researched by Kathryn G. Denhardt in *Ethical Frontiers in Public Management* (Jossey-Bass, 1991, p. 101):

Endnote 3

* Charles Goodsell (1989) says: "One can argue persuasively that government must be based not only on democratic responsiveness but also on the moral

foundations provided by natural law, the Judeo-Christian ethic, or the founding fathers. Values such as equality, justice, honesty, fairness, and the protection of individual rights must prevail, despite election returns, the wording of statutes or the orders of elected officials."

* Worthley and Grumet (1983) cite the roots of public service as being "the rule of law, accountability, efficiency, responsiveness, competence, objectivity, and fairness." Frederickson and Hart advocate a "patriotism of benevolence" that comprises "a combination of patriotism (the love of regime values) with benevolence (the love of others)."

* Terry Cooper (1987) asserts that justice is the main "internal good" (an Alasdair MacIntyre distinction), and Cooper speaks of just practice as being accompanied by popular sovereignty, accountability, due process and the enhancement of excellence. His keys for achieving these goals include benevolence, courage, rationality, fairmindedness, prudence, respect for law, honesty, self-discipline, civility, trustworthiness, respect for colleagues, responsibility for the practices and independence.

* York Wilbern (1984) proposes "six types, or levels, of morality for public officials." These are "basic honesty and conformity to law, conflict of interest, service orientation and procedural fairness, an ethics of democratic responsibility, an ethics of public policy determination and an ethics of compromise and social integration.

* Stephen Bailey (1965) says such basic virtues as honesty and loyalty are relevant for public service but should be presumed and not require explanation. But he adds that a useful list of moral qualities in public servants "begins beyond the obvious and ends where essentiality ends," including "optimism, courage and fairness tempered by charity."

Endnote 4

THE DENHARDT DESIGN

Studying these and other paradigms of public service virtue, Kathryn Denhardt arrived at her own triad of values: **honor, benevolence, justice.** Her treatise serves as an excellent synthesis of the values that have been the foundation for the vast majority of public service in American history.

UNEARTHING THE MORAL FOUNDATION OF PUBLIC ADMINISTRATION: HONOR, BENEVOLENCE, AND JUSTICE
KATHRYN DENHARDT

Honor. Honor is adherence to the highest standards of responsibility, integrity, and principle. It is a term often used to mean being held in public esteem or being well thought of — in other words, a desirable by-product of virtue (MacIntyre, 1966, p. 60). But as interpreted here, rather than being a by-product of virtue, honor is the preeminent virtue in that it is understood as magnanimity or greatmindedness, presupposing excellence in all of the virtues (McNamee, 1960, pp. 1–7). Honor denotes a quality of character in which the individual exhibits a high sense of duty, pursuing good deeds as ends in themselves, not because of the deeds.[1] It is these high standards of personal integrity and this commitment to principled and responsible conduct that characterize the ideal of public service. Public service is often described as an honor, a privilege, even a calling. In recent times these words have been used most often to involve a revival of this view of public service after years marked by scandal and widespread criticism of public servants. But public service as an honorable calling has remained the ideal, even during difficult times. It challenges public servants to exhibit honor as a most fundamental dimension of that calling.

Why are virtues, or qualities of character, associated with honor so essential to the moral foundations of public administration? For societies to function adequately, social interaction must be based on an assumption of honesty, truth, and the keeping of promises or commitments. This is particularly true of the relationship between members of society and their powerful institutions (especially government but also other institutions and professions). Therefore, the highest standards of honesty and integrity must be the cornerstone of any ethics of public service. Stephen Bailey (1965) argues that honesty is so obviously fundamental that it needs no explanation. Sissela Bok (1978) discusses honesty in detail in *Lying*. It is the basis on which public confidence rests. Without a fundamental commitment to honesty, public administration will have no legitimacy in the eyes

of the public and will find its capacity to serve that public severely restricted.

But basic honesty does not sufficiently define what the public administration profession stands for. Beyond honesty, the highest standards of integrity, sincerity, and principle are demanded of us. To be *honorable* is to be known for exhibiting those high standards consistently. It is to put principle before self-interest. It is a standard to which few others are held, certainly a higher standard than usually expected of business executives. But it nevertheless defines in part the moral foundation of public administration.

Honor involves truth telling, avoidance of deception, acknowledging the decisions and actions to which one was a partner, the fulfillment of duty, and holding oneself to a standard higher than self-interest. It requires a commitment to something beyond oneself. In the case of public administration this commitment is to the public interest, to the principles of democratic governance, and to the moral principles that define the commitments of our social contract.

Honor is a broadly encompassing tenet. It calls public servants to exhibit excellence in virtue. It is the failure to be honorable that raises the "character question" in the eyes of the public. The frequency with which the question of character has arisen in recent years (most often among elected officials and high-level appointees) testifies to the powerful presence of honor as a defining characteristic of the public service ideal. This ideal applies no less to career public servants. And while it might be claimed that it is an impossibly high standard, it nevertheless helps define the moral foundation on which the *ideal* of public service has been built.

Benevolence. In benevolence is found the other-regarding essence of public service. It is the disposition to do good and to promote the welfare of others. The very foundation of public administration is commitment to service (both to the public and the elected representatives of that public). But service is itself but an expression of the more fundamental moral principle of benevolence. Based on the Latin words *bene* (well) and *volens* (wishing), benevolence implies not only *actions* that promote good and the welfare of others but also *motivation* to pursue those ends. This point is important. Beneficence (performing acts of kindness and charity) is a somewhat lower standard in that the acts need only be kind and charitable, but no such motivation or concern is demanded of the individual responsible for the act. Benevolence, in contrast, requires not just doing good but also a driving motivation to do good *for the sake of others*.

It seems clear that in terms of acting on behalf of the welfare of others, public officials are held to a higher standard than those in private life. Private sector managers are expected by many to adhere to a standard of beneficence — expected to act in a socially responsible manner, doing things that provide some benefit to (or at least do not harm) the society. But few would argue that social responsibility should be the primary purpose or motivation for businesses. It is generally accepted that the socially responsible actions of businesses will be motivated by the value placed on good public relations or profit maximization rather than benevolence, but from those in the public sector more is expected.

A recent Hasting Center report discusses the "public duties" of professions, counting public administration among those professions with an explicit public service orientation. Public duties, or "the obligations and responsibilities owed in service to the public as a whole" (Jennings, Callahan, and Wolf, 1987, p. 3), encompass an orientation toward both the *common good* ("that which constitutes the well-being of the community") and the *public interest* ("the aggregation of the private interests of individuals") (Jennings, Callahan, and Wolf, 1987, p. 6).

Benevolence is a moral principle that encompasses the public duties of the profession and also prescribes the motivation that should guide the pursuit of these public duties. Benevolence implies both sympathy and enthusiasm (regard for others and purposeful intent to help) — characteristics that Thompson (1975) suggests the public demands of bureaucracies but cannot get. Clearly it is a standard to which not all public officials adhere, but it nevertheless defines the moral foundation on which the profession rests and on

the basis of which the public determines its level of trust in the profession.

Codes of ethics directed towards public administrators regularly invoke these notions of the public interest and the common good, describing a public service ideal dedicated to these public duties. The codes of ethics for the American Society for Public Administration and the International City Management Association both make references to the public interest, the good of all, and regard for the interests of others being more important than personal interests (Chandler, 1989). These aspects of the codes are often seen as cautions to avoid conflict-of-interest situations. However, it is important to understand that the fundamental moral principle reflected in these codes is benevolence as a moral imperative. Benevolence clearly requires avoidance of conflicts of interest, but more important, it enjoins public servants to act affirmatively on behalf of others, holding the public in highest regard.

Benevolence, then, encompasses the service orientation and the other-regardingness, of public administration and as a moral standard will help administrators recognize and balance obligations to various (and sometimes competing) groups. For example, benevolence requires that public administrators act as advocates on behalf of certain policies and proposals, not merely a technician carrying out the instructions of elected officials.

But "service" in public administration also means to serve the particular administration in which one finds oneself, and a moral standard of benevolence provides support of that kind of service as well. By grounding a service orientation on the standard of benevolence rather than on institutional obligations to particular officials, however, the profession will be better able to discern the appropriate course of action on those occasions when service obligations to various groups come into conflict with one another. When serving the interests of a particular elected official coincides with acting benevolently to pursue the public interest, no conflict exists. But when service to the elected official comes in conflict with the interests of the public, the moral standard of benevolence should provide some guidance for the administrator in discerning the acceptable limits to serving either group.

Justice. Justice signifies fairness and regard for the rights of others. The rights of others include, most fundamentally, respect for the dignity and worth of each individual. This is the foundation of democratic morality as Redford (1969) has described it, but it is also the foundation of Kant's "categorical imperative" and Rawls's (1971) theory of justice.

Attendant to basic respect for the dignity and worth of individuals is a commitment to developing and preserving rights for individuals that will ensure that their dignity and worth will not be violated by others in the society. Such rights are essential to a just society. As Aristotle argues, "Political justice is manifested between persons who share a common way of life which has for its object a state of affairs in which they will have all they need for an independent existence as free and equal members of the society," and, "Justice can exist only among those whose relations to one another are governed by law" (1953, p. 156).

For public administration, then, a commitment to justice demands that public servants be committed to respecting the dignity and worth of every member of the society, to promoting a government of laws that protects the rights of those free and equal members of the society. Even though the role of the public administrator is not to make laws or to define rights for individuals, even applying and implementing the law properly are possible only for someone committed to the principle of justice.

Because justice can only be ensured through the virtuous acts of public servants *and* through a set of laws and other institutions that protect the rights of individuals, one can see the strong connection between the moral foundations of public administration and the institutions of democratic governance. Democracy, the Constitution, laws, and "regime values," then, are institutional means of achieving justice and are thus to be respected and upheld. But it is important to recognize that these institutions are means and not ends in themselves. *Justice* is a fundamental moral principle helping form the moral foundation of public administration. It is because they rest on this principle of justice that the law and regime values are to be respected and upheld. Only by putting justice first, followed by laws and regime values, will public administrators be able to identify and oppose

unjust laws, interpretations of regime values that are unfair or inequitable, and other forms of injustice that are inevitable in any society. In contrast, if obedience to the law is identified as the primary moral imperative, then it is implied that even unjust laws are to be actively upheld by public administrators.

In the fundamental moral principle of justice we find the foundation needed to support public administration's commitment to democracy, individual rights, regime values, laws and the constitutional democracy, individual rights, regime values, law and the constitutional order. Justice requires that public administrators permit and promote informed participation in the governing process. It requires commitment to equality and fairness as rights that individuals can claim. It requires that administrators act to improve the decision-making process in their area of responsibility, giving full consideration to how current policies affect future structure of rights and legitimacy of institutions (Moore, 1981).

An argument for identifying justice as an essential element of the *ethos* of public administration is not new. For example, justice was the cornerstone of the ethics advanced by the new public administration (Hart, 1974; Henry, 1975). Where the argument of this chapter differs from earlier arguments is that justice is seen as one of three fundamental values — neither the single most important moral imperative nor only one of a long list of principles and virtues.

Honor, benevolence, and justice together delineate the moral foundations of public administration ethics. They offer the essence of the many ideals that characterize public service ethics and do so in a way that permits a ready answer to the question: What does public administration really stand for? Few of us could identify many of the components of commonly referred to codes of ethics because the codes are relatively long and detailed. Honor, benevolence, and justice capture the essence of these longer codes, but with the advantage of providing a more easily articulated identity and moral focus to the enterprise of public administration.

Identifying a core of fundamental values (as opposed to a single most important principle) creates a situation whereby excessive zeal for any one of the moral principles will be tempered by the other two. As Aristotle argues, "It is the nature of moral qualities that they can be destroyed by deficiency on the one hand and excess on the other" (1953, p. 58). Thus defining the essence of public administration ethics as justice, or equality, or any other single moral principle opens up the possibility that the unbridled pursuit of that single moral good will result in unacceptable excesses that would then erode the very foundation on which public administration ethics rests.

A definition of the moral foundations of public administration that balances the complementary and competing values of honor, benevolence, and justice will lead to striking the mean in each. For example, benevolence in excess implies paternalism. Justice, in contrast, demands self-determination. Any tendency toward paternalism, therefore, could be "checked" by the principle of justice. Because justice tends to focus on individual rights, taken to the extreme it might stand in the way of working toward the common good. Benevolence, as it is oriented toward doing good for others, could be a check on excessive individualism. Whereas honesty associated with honor would appear to require telling the truth regardless of any harm that might result (as in some national security areas), both benevolence and justice would permit otherwise. Where benevolence requires extraordinary efforts to help others, justice offers a mitigating influence, as it compels consideration of the burden borne by those who must pay for the helping services (that is, taxpayers). Finally, while benevolence and justice articulate moral principles, it is honor that defines the virtue, or quality of character, necessary to put principle into action.

Conclusion

All three imperatives — honor, benevolence, and justice — make up the moral foundation of public administration, and this foundation should have a central place in the education of students of public affairs and administration. Teaching these moral imperatives is not moral indoctrination. It is instead the obligation and prerogative of a profession to impart its values to those seeking to enter the profession. Articulating, studying, and internalizing these moral commitments are essential steps in becoming a true professional.

Students of public administration can develop an awareness of these guiding principles and can be assisted in cultivating these principles and virtues in their own lives and actions. The educa-

tion process can help students equip themselves with the skills needed to act virtuously. For example, Stephen K. Bailey suggested that there are three essential mental attitudes: "(1) a recognition of the moral ambiguity of all men and of all public policies, (2) a recognition of the contextual forces which condition moral priorities in the public service, and (3) a recognition of the paradoxes of procedures" (1965, p. 285). By helping students to develop these and other awarenesses and attitudes, educators help them to act in a principled and virtuous manner without being rigid, absolutist, or dogmatic.

For practitioners, the identification of the moral foundations of public administration ethics would help restore a meaningful identity to a discipline that has experienced an identity crisis during the past three decades. A strong foundation provides an anchor for resisting unreasonable demands felt during shifting political winds. It also helps practitioners readily articulate the meaning of public service, thus serving both as an essential guide to action and as a defense of the legitimacy of public administration when questioned by other entities.

A case has been made for honor, benevolence, and justice as the moral foundations of public administration ethics. Perhaps this can serve as a springboard to the next step of engaging in dialogue about these moral foundations, a dialogue involving critique, elaboration, and adjustment. Research in the discipline has already begun to examine the role of virtue in public administration ethics, and the continuation of this line of research will illuminate the meaning of honor in public service. Justice, as a central principle of public administration ethics, has been explored in some detail over the past 20 years, but the principle of benevolence has not. Discouraged about the possibility of defining "the public interest," scholars have generally abandoned the effort. By recasting the public interest question in terms of benevolence, perhaps the line of research could be resurrected — not in terms of defining the specific content of the public interest but in terms of the duty and motivation to be other-regarding — and could *pursue* the public interest and the common good. Finally, research on the *interaction among and balancing of* multiple public service values might prove very fruitful. Arguments for any single moral principle serving as the focus of public administration ethics will be met with numerous examples of potential abuses. A response to this problem might be finding a combination of core principles with the potential of creating an equilibrium.

The desired outcome is building a broad consensus in the profession around a clear, concise moral identity. With such a consensus, the profession can address more powerfully the issue of professional ethics, both in educational programs and in the workplace. A reinvigorated public service ethics based on this moral identity can also help rebuild confidence in government. This challenging new frontier for the profession holds great promise for supplanting an era of chaos and crisis in public administration, with an era of renewed moral understanding, commitment, and action.

NOTE

McNamee (1960) explores the changing concept of honor over the centuries. He describes a shift from the exaggerated individualism of the concept of honor among ancient Greeks to periods of exaggerated statism. He also describes "an attempt on the part of Christianity to check, elevate, and transform both exaggerations with the new virtues of humility and charity" (1960, p. 181). It is this latter concept of honor — one characterized by humility and charity — that influenced 19th century liberalism and the birth of public administration as a profession.

Endnote 3

COMPARING ETHICAL SYSTEMS

Now when you see a public official making a decision, you might ask which of the above sets of values were dominant in the decision. Further, you can evaluate these decision models according to the dominant "ethical system" in each, as propounded by William Hitt in *Ethics and Leadership* (Battelle Press, Columbus, Ohio, pp. 66–67)

END-RESULT ETHICS — John Stuart Mill (1806–1873) — The moral rightness of an action is determined by considering its consequences. "I would make the decision on the basis of *expected results*, what would give us the greatest return on investment."

RULE ETHICS — Immanuel Kant (1724–1804) — The moral rightness of an action is determined by laws and standards. "I would make the decision on the basis of *what the law says*, on the legality of the matter."

SOCIAL CONTRACT ETHICS — Jean-Jacques Rousseau (1712–1778) — The moral rightness of an action is determined by the customs and norms of a particular community. "I would make the decision on the basis of the *strategy and values* of my organization."

PERSONALISTIC ETHICS — Martin Buber (1878–1965) — The moral rightness of an action is determined by one's conscience. "I would make the decision on the basis of my *personal convictions* and what my conscience told me to do."

Endnote 5

For the *elected* official, there apparently is a significant difference between the kinds of decision-dilemmas faced as a candidate and those faced as a politician in office. Walter Lippman, longtime Washington-based journalist and political critic, said: "The role of the leader would be easier to define if it were agreed to give separate meanings to two very common words . . . **'politician' and 'statesman.'"**

For Lippman, the politician says: "I will give you what you want." But the statesman says: "What you think you want is this. What it is possible for you to get is that. What you really want, therefore, is the following . . . " Lippman concludes: "The politician stirs up a following; the statesman leads it."

Further contrasting the two roles, Lippman adds: "The politician, in brief, accepts unregenerate desire at its face value and either fulfills it or perpetrates a fraud; the statesman reeducates desire by confronting it with the reality, and so makes possible an enduring adjustment of interests within the community."

Where can such leadership be found? "It requires courage, which is possible only in a mind that is detached from the agitations of the moment," Lippman postulates. "It requires insight, which comes only from an objective and discerning knowledge of the facts, and a high and imperturbable disinterestedness."

Endnote 6

THE COMMON BUGABOO: CONFLICTS OF INTEREST

A focus of ethical concern that seems to be perpetually challenging includes conflicts of interest, real and apparent. Discussed broadly among professions, business and government earlier in this book, the discussion here focuses on actual cases wherein **conflicts of interest** officially were ruled upon by the **Florida Commission on Ethics.**

In reviewing these case rulings, identify the ethical dilemmas and the various conflicting interests. In public acts, obviously, the democratic society itself is one interest, the public official another, and then various other interests of a personal, professional or agency nature compete for the official's primary allegiance.

Endnote 7

> **Case One:** No prohibited conflict of interest would exist were a circuit court clerk to attend an annual conference for the Florida Association of Court Clerks where some of the meals and activities are sponsored by entities doing business with county governments. The purpose of the conference is to provide continuing education and training for the clerks attending. As stated in earlier Commission opinions, the Code of Ethics does not absolutely prohibit a public officer from accepting a gift or other thing of value from a business entity which may be doing business with his agency, and it does not prohibit a public officer from accepting hospitality within reasonable limits. Rather, whether an official may accept such a gift depends on the intent of the donor and on the circumstances under which it is given. Here, the fact that some meals and social hours are sponsored by entities doing business with county governments does not create a prohibited conflict of interest.

The commission raises the notion that a public official should consider "the intent of the donor" and "the circumstances" under which the gift is given. The official will rely heavily on documents related to the event to substantiate claims of sufficient disinterest by the giver and the official.

Endnote 8

Case Two: Section 112.313(2)(a), F.S. 1975, prohibiting a public officer or employee from accepting any gift which would cause a reasonably prudent person to be influenced in the discharge of his public duty, was declared to be unconstitutionally vague by the Florida Supreme Court. Anderson vs. D'Alemberte, S.Ct. Case No. 49,851. Paragraph (b) prohibits a public employee from accepting a gift that is based upon any understanding that the official action or judgment of the employee would be influenced thereby. In the absence of any such understanding, the provision would not be violated were employees of a municipal building department to accept a box of candy from a general contractor or were an official of the department to accept a magnum of whiskey from an aluminum contractor.

However, s. 112.313(4) further prohibits a public employee from accepting anything of value which the employee knows, or with the exercise of reasonable care should know, was given to influence his official action. This provision similarly requires knowledge on the part of the public employee, or circumstances which strongly suggest, that a particular gift is being given with the intent that the employee's future official action will be influenced. In the absence of any testimony to this effect, we can only offer the language of the provision for guidance. Also, please note that a person required to file financial disclosure by s. 112.3145. F.S., must disclose gifts of $100 in value received during the disclosure period.

This case, among other things, demonstrates the public official's burden of trying to interpret vaguely drawn laws and how something as seemingly insignificant as a box of candy can spell ethical trouble.

Endnote 9

"While statutes usually speak falsely as to actual behavior, they afford probably the best single means of ascertaining what a society thinks behavior ought to be; they sweep up the felt necessities of the day and indirectly expound the social norm of the legislators."
— *Winthrop D. Jordan,* White Over Black

Case Three: A prohibited conflict of interest is created where a city councilwoman owns a material interest in a wrecker business which accepts wrecker rotation list calls from the police department for the towing of impounded vehicles, at city expense, as a public officer is prohibited from acting in a probate capacity to sell services to any agency of his political subdivision, Fla Stat. s. 112.313(3)(1975). Although Florida Statues s. 112.316 provides that it is not the intention of the Code of Ethics to preclude private pursuits which do not interfere with the discharge of public duty, this provision is inapplicable in the instant case, as the rotation list does not contain the names of all licensed wreckers in the city. Rather, the chief of police has the authority to establish requirements for wrecker services appearing on the list. Inasmuch as the police chief is employed by and is subject to the supervision of the city council, the potential for interference with public duty is not precluded. However, calls may be accepted for the towing of disabled vehicles for which service the vehicle owner pays.

Some cases are easier than others. When a public official's authority can affect a decision that directly benefits a business interest of that public official, no Socratic debate is needed; that *is* a conflict of interest.

> **Case Four:** Section 112.313(7)(a), Florida Statues, prohibits a public officer from having any employment or contractual relationship with a business entity which is doing business with his agency. CEO's 74-82, 78-55, 84-112, 82-28, 88-19, and 81-76 are referenced.

Endnote 10

An even less subtle conflict surfaces when a public official fails to recognize the conflict of interest in serving for compensation with two entities who enter into a contractual relationship.

> **Case Five:** An alternate member of the city board of adjustment is prohibited by Section 112.3143, Florida Statutes, from voting on variance petitions of persons who are clients of his surveying and engineering firm at the time of the vote and from voting on variance petitions where the client is expected to require further surveying or engineering work as a result of the decision on the variance. CEO's 78-59 and 84-1 are referenced.

Endnote 11

How easy it is, in selecting an "alternate" appointed official, to name "someone who really knows this business" — someone actually *in* that business. How easy, and how clearly creating a conflict of interest. (At the end of this chapter consider five other case rulings.)

WHEN PRUDENCE, COURAGE AND TRUTH DO NOT PREVAIL

In November of 1992, Bill Clinton was elected President of the United States, running on a platform of change. A month after the election, the office of the President-Elect issued this statement about ethics in government:

> "Last month, the American people voted for change. They made it clear that they want to take their government back, and that they want to end business as usual in Washington. In recent years, too many former top officials began to sell their access and influence almost the day after they left office. That saps public confidence in our political process.
> "During his Presidential campaign, Governor Clinton promised the American people that he would seek to 'stop the revolving door' by requiring his top appointees to refrain from lobbying their agencies for five years. Today, we are announcing rules that keep that promise to the American people. Top officials will be required to sign a pledge agree-

Figure 4. President Bill Clinton. Associated Press/ Wide World Photos.

ing to these new standards. These rules seek to change the climate in Washington, and usher in a new era of public service."

Political commentators Jack Germond and Jules Witcover described the most significant of these new ethical standards: "The Clinton code prohibits 1,100 appointees from lobbying their former agencies for five years and from lobbying for foreign governments at any time. That should put a damper on those ex-officials profiting from retainers of $500,000 a year or more from big interests, domestic or foreign, from the day they leave the government."

From the first days of the Clinton administrations, these new rules became easier to promulgate than to enforce. A *New York Times* editorial (Jan. 8, 1993) declared that "Twelve days before the inauguration, we may be able to predict the fate of Bill Clinton's promise to free American government from the grip of special interests: Broken from Day One."

The irony was this: the new ethical rules shone a bright light on the possible conflicts of the president-elect's own appointees, some who seemed unwilling to play by the new rules. As the Times concluded: "Bill Clinton needs to give new instructions to his Cabinet appointees before these (confirmation) hearings continue. If necessary, he should find new appointees to replace those who demonstrate greater allegiance to their private trades than to the president-elect's promise to the people."

It didn't take long before criticism mounted:

BREAKING CLINTON'S PROMISES

Twelve days before the inauguration, we may be able to predict the fate of Bill Clinton's promise to free American government from the grip of special interests: Broken from Day One.

The questioning of Ron Brown by the senators reviewing his fitness to be secretary of commerce was a bipartisan disgrace. The Republicans on the committee joined with Brown, the chairman of the Democratic Party, in a public compact to make Washington safe for Brown's law firm, Patton, Boggs & Blow.

Many Democrats have accused Washington reporters of pulling punches when it came to influence-peddling in the Reagan and Bush administrations. Let the record show that the press did a fine job of penetrating this Senate hoax.

Keith Bradsher of the *New York Times* reported Brown's refusal to recuse himself from the full range of matters involving the Japanese companies that have retained Patton, Boggs & Blow to lobby for them in Washington. Brad-sher also documented the recent hiring of Brown's son, Michael, by a lobbying firm that represents Japanese clients, and Brown's failure to say how he would resolve family conflicts of interest.

Throughout the Reagan and Bush years, Democrats were upset when businesses and lobbying firms hired the relatives of high-ranking Republicans. Do they now think it is unreasonable to ask how a Cabinet secretary will handle potential professional and family conflicts? To ask the question does not insult the integrity of father or son. It simply says that Clinton promised a stricter standard and this is not it.

Bob Davis of the *Wall Street Journal* reported on the veil of secrecy that Brown has dropped over his activities. The nominee seemed surprised by a committee request for a copy of his partnership agreement from Patton, Boggs & Blow. Brown indicated the agreement might show that the firm owes him a $1-million golden handshake when he resigns on Jan. 20.

Yet Brown proposes to recuse himself for only one year from dealing with the firm's clients. Any recusal that does not last his full tenure at Commerce insults every voter who believed Clinton's pledge to reverse both the appearance and the reality of special dealing.

Brown's presentation was, potentially, a critical moment in the ethical history of the Clinton administration. It amounted to an open declaration that companies with strong Democratic connections reserve the right to continue the attitude of greed that prevails in Washington. Only this time it will be the Democrats eating the fat.

Ron Brown told the Senate an astonishing thing Wednesday. He will adhere, he said, to conflict-of-interest rules that are more lax than those voluntarily adopted by Bush administration officials. Bill Clinton needs to give new instructions to his Cabinet appointees before these hearings continue. If necessary, he should find new appointees to replace those who demonstrate greater allegiance to their private trades than to the president-elect's promise to the people.

Editorial
New York Times News Service

Ethical problems are not restricted to American government:

TRUCKLOADS OF SCANDAL

In the fourth major scandal to hit Japan in the last three years, a trucking company called Tokyo Sagawa Kyubin allegedly made payoffs amounting to $80 million to politicians and Yakuza to help it get access to new routes and service areas. The scandal is unusual in that it has illuminated the back alleys of the Japanese system, showing how huge sums of money flowed from legitimate financial insti-

Endnote 11

tutions through a major trucking company and into the hands of politicians and organized crime. — NYT, 3/1/92; LAT 2/24/92

Ethics: Easier Said Than Done

CORRUPTION SPREADS IN RUSSIA

It seems that Russian officials have become even greedier under the newly semi-democratic system than they were under Communism. State officials are grabbing former state property as they build their private portfolios. Bribery has become the cost of doing business, and more than ever, part of every day life as people struggle to find food and grease the wheels of the Kafkaesque bureaucracy. — NYT, 3/14/92; WPNW, 3/23-29/92; LAT 3/1/92

Ethics: Easier Said Than Done

Meanwhile, back in America, the lack of ethical sensitivity plagued Washington, D.C. Enjoy scandals? Pick your poison, as there was plenty for everyone:

Unethical Income

In May of 1989, Democrat Jim Wright of Texas was forced to resign, becoming the first speaker of the House ever to be forced to resign from office in midterm. His scandal revolved around his acceptance of gifts and outside income, specifically proceeds from a book he wrote. It was found by the House Ethics Committee that he had 69 violations of House restrictions concerning such income. He received uncommonly high royalties from a modest book of his speeches and various opinions.

Senatorial Misconduct

In February 1991, the U.S. Senate Ethics Committee issued reprimands in the "Keating Five" case. This included five senators charged with lobbying bank regulators on behalf of Charles H. Keating, Jr., who owned defunct California-based Lincoln Savings and Loan Association. Keating was among a group that raised $1.5-million for those five senators' election campaigns. He was eventually convicted of securities fraud and imprisoned. But the Senate Committee only found "substantial credible evidence" of misconduct against one senator, Democrat Alan Cranston, who merely retired the next year.

Floating Checks at Public Expense

In April 1992, the House Ethics Committee reported 325 current and former members of Congress who had written checks at the private House bank against accounts that had no funds. The so-called "overdraft privilege," in and of itself was not illegal, but as a perquisite of office it smacked of elitism and quickly drew public wrath. The Committee's releasing of names had its effect on some re-election campaigns, and later that fall, Americans voted the first Republican majority of the House of Representatives in six decades. House postmaster, Robert V. Rota, resigned in March 1992 after it was established that he let House postal employees cash checks for House members and also redeem stamps for cash. The House post office probe led to one of the most influential members of Congress, Democratic Representative Dan Rostenkowski of Illinois, chairman of the powerful Ways and Means Committee.

Taking Public Money for Personal Use

Rostenkowski later was indicted for embezzling $50,000 from the House post office. He lost his re-election bid in 1994, then pleaded guilty in 1996 to two counts of mail fraud and was sentenced to 17 months in prison and fined $100,000.

Sexual Misconduct

In September 1995, both Senator Bob Packwood of Oregon and Democratic Representative Mel Reynolds of Illinois resigned due to charges of sexual misconduct.

Spousal Embezzlement of Campaign Funds

Meanwhile, the husband of GOP Representative Enid Greene of Utah embezzled funds from her campaign treasury and used them for his purposes. She chose not to seek re-election in 1996.

Tax-Deductible Income for College Course Funding

For the first time in history, in January 1997, the House of Representatives reprimanded a sitting Speaker of the House, Newt Gingrich of Georgia. He was ordered to pay a $300,000 fine. He had been a strident critic of former speaker Jim Wright about ethics; now he was charged with various ethical concerns including improper use of tax-deductible donations. He used the money to fund a college course promoting himself and his partisan political agenda. Worse, he later admitted not giving the whole truth — i.e. false information — to the House Ethics Committee.

Figure 5. Thomas Jefferson. Frick Art Reference Library.

REFORMING WASHINGTON ETHICS

"A public office is a public trust. The people shall have the right to secure and sustain that trust against abuse."
— Sunshine Amendment, Florida Constitution, 1976

If public officials are to be accountable to the people they serve, they must be willing to let the people see and judge their actions. As Thomas Jefferson once said, "When a man assumes a public trust, he should consider himself as public property." Of course, all candidates for public office say they want to serve the people. On the campaign trail, they're ready and willing to be held accountable. But some begin acting as if they own the office once they achieve it. From City

I DUNNO... I JUST DON'T TRUST ANY CANDIDATE WHO WEARS A BOW TIE!

Endnote 12

Hall to the White House, American politics is rife with examples of politicians who not only forgot they were public property, but assumed that the *public's* property — or money — was their own.

The governor of what is now America's fourth largest state, Florida, bluntly expressed that attitude in 1966, as an era of rural and often secretive control of state government neared its end. A reporter for the *St. Petersburg Times* had discovered the State Road Department was paying the costly upkeep on a 17-passenger executive airplane provided by one of the South's largest grocery chains for the political and other travels of Governor Haydon Burns. When confronted with this finding, Burns accused the reporter of prying into his personal business "and that of my friends."

The governor angrily threatened to deny the reporter access to state government news. "As governor," he growled, "I don't have to account to you or anybody else."

More than a decade later, after reforming much of Florida government, Reubin Askew in an address to the National Council on Governmental Ethics Laws said: ". . . The important work of our democracy must be conducted in an atmosphere in which people have confidence that those in positions of power within the government perceive the public interest as paramount and are committed to keeping the public trust.

"There is no single or simple way to create such an atmosphere of confidence. But whatever else it may take to inspire the confidence we need, surely an indispensable prerequisite is an ethical framework for government. For how the people view public officials, how they perceive their priorities, and how they discern their values is intimately and inevitable related to governmental ethics . . . **Ethics laws alone obviously are not and will not be enough. But they are essential.**"

Endnote 13

This notion of ethical public service, of "raising a standard," spread and eventually hit a couple of years later Washington D.C. An **Office of Government Ethics** (OGE) was created within the executive of the federal government. It is responsible for overseeing and providing guidance on Government ethics for the executive branch, including the ethics programs of executive departments and agencies. OGE first was created by the Ethics in Government Act ("the Act") of 1978, Public Law No. 95-521, as amended but was not a separate agency until Oct. 1, 1989. The Act created OGE to provide overall direction for executive branch policies designed to prevent conflicts of interest and to help insure high ethical standards on the part of agency officers and employees. Pursuant to the Ethics Reform Act of 1989 (Public Law No. 101-194), as revised by the technical amendments of May 4, 1990 (Public Law No. 101-280), OGE is the "**supervising ethics office**" **for the executive branch for various**

purposes, including public and confidential financial disclosure reporting by executive agency officials.

OGE also has various Government ethics guidance responsibilities under President George Bush's Executive Order 12674 of April 12, 1989, "Principles of Ethical Conduct for Government Officers and Employees." The OGE is divided into the following functions: administration, legal, monitoring and compliance. The Director is appointed by the President and confirmed by the Senate. That person's duties include:

> ***advising*** the White House and executive branch Presidential appointees on Government ethics matters;
>
> ***maintaining*** ethics liaison with and providing guidance on ethics to executive branch departments and agencies;
>
> ***providing*** ethics liaison to the Congress;
>
> ***responding*** to public and press inquiries on ethics;
>
> ***overseeing*** and coordinating all OGE rules, regulations, formal advisory opinions and major policy decisions.

The OGE Deputy Director is also attached to this office and assists the Director in carrying out OGE's responsibilities, including serving as Acting Director in the absence of the Director. Any federal agency quickly can become a sweeping power entity. Consider the duties of The Office of the General Counsel, who is supposed to develop regulations and approve executive agency implementation under conflict of interest laws, administrative standards of conduct, post-Government employment restrictions, and public and confidential financial disclosure reporting; to initiate executive branch administrative ethics corrective actions; to review public financial disclosure statements of advise-and-consent on Presidential executive branch nominees; to identify and resolve conflicts; to advising the OGE Director about ongoing administration of executive branch Ethics in Government Act qualified trusts; to issue certificates of divestiture; to provide informal ethics advisory opinions/advice; to participate in training and public forums on ethics; to monitor and provide technical assistance on legislative Government ethics initiatives; to make Freedom of Information Act and Privacy Act determinations for OGE; to facilitate executive agency referrals of criminal conflict of interest violations to the Department of Justice; and to advise on executive agency exemptions and designations under relevant sections of federal law.

Such an extensive and exhaustive array of duties merely demonstrates the difficulty of trying to legislate and enforce moral and ethical behavior. If everyone had Kant's belief in truth-telling and respect for people, would such legislation be necessary?

CAMPAIGN FINANCE

A Federal Case

In 1992 the Washington bureau for the Knight-Ridder newspapers examined an exclusive group of campaign supporters known inside the Bush White House as the **"Team of 100."** The team's wealthy business leaders, real-estate developers, financiers, ranchers and racetrack owners — actually some 250 in all — had each contributed $100,000 through the Republican Party to George Bush's 1988 election. (Funneling huge corporate and large individual contributions, or so-called **soft money,** through state party organizations circumvents federal restrictions on contributions made directly to the candidates. This scheme has been utilized by both Democrats and Republicans in recent presidential elections.) The Knight-Ridder reporters found that Team 100 members had received a variety of special benefits, appointments and favorable policy decisions during Bush's four-year term.

Case in point: Cable television executive Bill Daniels was a $100,000 contributor. In 1990 he became alarmed over proposals to curb soaring cable TV rates and wrote to the President urging that the administration "take a strong stand now against re-regulation." The White House did.

A Florida Case

Endnote 13

When the president of the Florida Senate decided to seek an elective state Cabinet seat in 1988, he wanted his friends to be the first to know. So he summoned the special-interest lobbyists to his Capitol office to break the news. Then, with the Legislature about to decide the state budget and other key issues, more than 100 lobbyists with a huge stake in those decisions attended a fund-raising reception to hand-deliver their contributions to the senator's campaign.

Although he lost his bid for state insurance commissioner, he was hardly the first to engage in what the Common Cause public interest lobby calls **"legalized extortion."** Powerful state and federal officials are constantly putting the arm on special interests and their **political action committees** (PACs) to help finance increasingly costly campaigns for re-election or higher office.

Is there anything wrong with any of this? Isn't a candidate's fund-raising ability one sign of his or her ability to build the support needed to govern? Is the money not needed to reach today's busy voters via costly television advertisements? Don't wealthy contributors, or powerful special interests, have a right to be heard — just like everyone else? Isn't this the American way?

Public disgust with such irregularities created a new wave of campaign finance reform efforts in the states and the nation's capital during the 1990s. The outcome was by no means clear. Because they benefit from the status quo, members of the Congress and state Legislatures have been slow over the years to correct abuses of the American political system. But scandals, from time to time, have virtually forced reluctant lawmakers to enact election reforms — sometimes with unintended consequences. A look at past and recent efforts follows.

CAMPAIGN FINANCE REFORM

The Watergate scandals precipitated a spate of campaign finance reforms at federal and state levels during the 1970s. In all, 21 corporations and/or their executives were indicted in 1973 and 1974 for secretly and illegally contributing millions of dollars to Richard Nixon and other candidates. Congress, alarmed by the abuses, expanded campaign finance laws first enacted in 1971, requiring **uniform disclosure** of campaign receipts and expenditures and offering future presidential candidates public funds in exchange for limits on private contributions and overall spending. But the Supreme Court, in its 1976 *Buckley vs. Valeo* decision, struck down other parts of these reforms, invalidating overall expenditure ceilings not tied to public financing and limitations on independent expenditures and candidate expenditures from personal funds. The court's landmark finding that such restrictions violated freedom of speech effectively erased spending caps in state as well as federal campaigns.

Ironically, the reforms of the 1970s, coupled with the Buckley ruling, led to a proliferation of special-interest expenditures that critics say are "independent" of candidate campaign organizations in name only. And they've encouraged even greater reliance on political action committees, known as PACs, as a means of funneling corporate, union and other special-interest money into political campaigns.

Moreover, the reforms left several loopholes through which individuals may raise and spend money to influence elections in ways unintended by Congress. The law allows, for example, separate campaign contributions to be **"bundled"** for a particular candidate by a lobbyist or other intermediate, thus raising money from interest groups far in excess of what its individual members could contribute. And, as mentioned above, it permits candidates and their political parties to skirt federal restrictions by channeling unlimited amounts of "soft money" into state and local party organizations for spending on the candidates' campaigns. In 1992, more than $60-million in soft money was raised by the two major parties, circumventing the spending limits that Bill Clinton and George Bush had accepted in exchange for $46-million each in public funds.

On becoming President in 1993, Clinton began work on new reform proposals expected to include measures designed to restrict soft money donations, reduce from $5,000 to perhaps $1,000 the limit on individual PAC contributions, and provide additional ways to voluntarily limit overall campaign spending. But that reform never became reality, and by 1998, Washington was engulfed in one congressional investigation after another aimed at the influence of "soft

Endnote 14

"The trouble with lying and deceiving is that their efficiency depends entirely upon a clear notion of the truth that the liar and deceiver wish to hide. In this sense, truth, even if it does not prevail in public, possesses an ineradicable primacy over all falsehoods."
— Hannah Arendt, "Lying in Politics," Crises of the Republic

money" — especially foreign money. There were appearances that Chinese nationals sent hundreds of thousands of dollars through the Democratic National Committee in an attempt to influence President Clinton's foreign policy toward China. Hefty foreign donations also went for the benefit of George Bush's 1996 campaign. These independent organizations — party national committees as well as issue-based, separate entities — had complicated spending reform. In following the money, it becomes painfully clear that the major costs of campaigning are those for television airtime. But few would advocate the unspeakable: A requirement that federally-chartered broadcasters provide free access or dramatically reduced advertising rates for presidential and congressional candidates.

Who Gave It, Who Got It

Endnote 15

Among the 50 states and the federal government, Florida pioneered the development of laws to publicly disclose the giving and spending of campaign money. Its original "Who Gave It, Who Got It" disclosure law was enacted in 1951, three years after three rich power brokers had secretly put up $450,000 to elect Fuller Warren governor.

The law has been improved over the years in the wake of periodic newspaper revelations on how various candidates disguised the real source of their campaign money (for example, listing among contributors people who happened to be dead). A *St. Petersburg Times* examination of Governor Burns' $1.4-million re-election fund in 1966 revealed that not only did the money largely come from interests benefiting from state contracts but much of it did *not* come from average citizens listed as $1,000 contributors on the governor's campaign reports. "There must be some mistake," said one young man on the list who had just had been graduated from college and turned out to be the son-in-law of Burns' campaign coordinator.

'People of Virtue'

Endnote 16

"Public leaders face a crisis of confidence," U.S. Rep. Lee H. Hamilton, D-Indiana, wrote in 1988. "There are significant social costs when the public trust is violated. Opinion polls indicate that a lack of confidence in the integrity of elected officials is a major reason for the low voter turnout in recent elections. **Without trust, democratic government just does not work."**

Hamilton, who chaired the House hearings on the Iran-Contra affair, recalled the testimony of witnesses who claimed that the ends justified the means and that lying to Congress and the American people was an acceptable practice. "So often during the hearings I was reminded of President Jefferson's statement: 'The whole art of government consists in the art of being honest,'" Hamilton continued.

"Our Founding Fathers recognized that no matter how well-structured government is, it will not work unless its offices are held by people of virtue."

The question, of course, is this: How do you ensure that the occupants of public office indeed are "people of virtue?" Many have argued that morality cannot be legislated, and their assertions have proved at least partly correct. Recurring scandals have afflicted every level of government, regardless of the laws enacted to prevent them. In the case at hand, for example, the flurry of reform legislation that followed the Watergate coverup didn't deter the Reagan administration from illegally funding the Nicaraguan Contras with profits from a secret arms sale to Iran.

But if campaign finance reforms and formal ethics codes and rules are no cure-all, they nevertheless can provide a helpful framework and guideline for cleaner politics and government. The 1978 Ethics in Government Act, part of Watergate's legacy, required financial disclosures by officials in the federal executive and judicial branches, restrained the **"revolving door"** between public and private sector employment, and created an **independent counsel** to investigate wrong-doing in the executive branch. Many of the states have enacted or strengthened their own codes of ethics to guard against conflicts of interest and other abuses, restricted gifts, required greater disclosure by officials and lobbyists, and created ethics commissions and elections commissions to enforce the higher standards.

Ethics and elections codes are always subject to adjustment and improvement. Some officeholders may not like them, but it's difficult to argue that the public would be better off without them. It's even more difficult to make a case against requirements for **open meetings,** public records and financial disclosure. For, while public disclosure is no guarantee of virtuous behavior in public office, it provides constituents with the information they need to judge official behavior. Another look at the Florida experience is instructive.

"Euphemisms, like fashions, have their day and pass, perhaps to return at another time. Like the guests at a masquerade ball, they enjoy social approval only so long as they retain the capacity for deception."
—*Freda Adler,*
Sisters in Crime

Endnote 17

SUNSHINE GOVERNMENT

In their 1976 book, *The Transformation of Southern Politics*, Jack Bass and Walter DeVries wrote: "No state matches Florida in experience with openness in government, and political leaders there understand that secrecy breeds suspicion and that public confidence derives from trust. **The sunshine law** is considered by many to have had 'the single biggest good effect upon government since I have been in politics.'"

The state already had a strong public records law on its books when in early 1967 four reporters balked at leaving the Senate chamber so the senators could meet in secret, ostensibly to discuss

Endnote 18

executive appointments or suspensions. Reapportionment was the hot issue of the day, and the press had become increasingly skeptical when the Senate kept closing its doors on the public.

Although the reporters' sit-in was brief, the adverse publicity over their forcible removal had an impact. Within a few months, the Legislature enacted legislation stipulating that all meetings of public officials must be open. The Sunshine Law has been strengthened over the years by attorney general opinions, far-reaching court rulings and, finally in the 1990s, constitutional amendments clarifying that requirements for open meetings and records apply to state legislators as well as to members of the executive branch and local governments.

What Is 'Open'?

Florida's courts have concluded, understandably, that it is not only the *final decisions* that the people have a right to know, but *how* and *why* their elected officials reach those decisions. "Every thought, as well as every affirmative act, of a public official as it relates to and is within the scope of his officials duties, is a matter of public concern," the Second District Court of Appeal ruled in *Times Publishing Company vs. Williams* in 1969; "and it is the entire decision-making process that the Legislature intended to affect by the enactment of the statute before us. This act is a declaration of public policy, the frustration of which constitutes irreparable injury to the public interest. Every step in the decision-making process, including the decision itself, is a necessary preliminary to formal action. It follows that each such step constitutes an 'official act,' an indispensable requisite to 'formal action,' within the meaning of the act."

Endnote 19

Askew believed the people's right to know went beyond the official actions and records of their representatives in government. He believed the people had a right to know the sources of their representatives' income, and whether their representatives profit from public service. Beginning with his initial gubernatorial bid in 1970, he voluntarily filed annual statements revealing his personal finances to the public. In the eight years of his governorship, his net worth increased from $72,700 to $126,066, largely due to the normal increase in the value of his life insurance and a home he purchased for his mother in Pensacola.

If a few of Askew's executive branch colleagues had followed his example and handled their own finances scrupulously and openly, they might have spared themselves and their state the embarrassments that plagued Florida in the mid-1970s. Instead, the state's elected education commissioner, insurance commissioner and comptroller were each indicted on unrelated charges involving financial matters. Across from the Capitol in the Florida Supreme Court, two justices were forced to resign for other forms of ethical misconduct.

Askew's only role in any of these cases was to assign a special prosecutor, when and where the circumstances warranted such action. The governor wasted no time doing his duty. He appointed Duval County State Attorney Ed Austin to investigate in 1974, even when the target was Education Commissioner Floyd Christian, a state Cabinet ally toward whom Askew felt great empathy. When Christian one day sought the governor's advice, Askew's sincere response was: "Pray." Christian later admitted in effect that he took $29,000 in kickbacks from a longtime friend doing business with the Department of Education, and committed perjury in lying about it. He paid $43,000 in fines and restitution, and served several months in prison for federal income tax evasion.

Scandal had hit closer to the governor's office a year earlier when the *Fort Lauderdale News* and Tampa television station *WTVT* revealed that Lieutenant Governor Tom Adams, whom Askew had assigned to run the Department of Commerce, was using a state employee to work, while on state time, on a cattle farm that Adams had quietly leased in Gadsden County west of Tallahassee. Askew ordered the state personnel director to investigate, uncovering other improper work that Adams had assigned to the employee. Adams was fired as commerce secretary, dropped from Askew's 1974 re-election ticket and forced to repay the state $1,736 for the employee's time and travel expenses. "I cannot condone the practices followed in this situation," Askew told a news conference.

Endnote 20

In the wake of the Adams and Cabinet scandals, Askew tried to persuade the Legislature to require full financial disclosure from major officeholders in the state and local governments. When the Legislature balked, Askew led Florida's first successful petition campaign to place the issue on the November 1976 general election ballot. The voters overwhelmingly adopted Askew's "Sunshine Amendment," writing both personal financial disclosure and campaign finance disclosure into the Florida Constitution.

In addition to its disclosure requirements, the Amendment prohibits members of the Legislature and statewide officials from lobbying their former government body or agency for two years after leaving office, prohibits incumbent legislators from representing clients before any state agency, and makes public officials and employees financially liable to the state for breaches of the public trust.

FINAL COMMENTS

We have seen that there are ethical and moral responsibilities for public officials beyond obeying the law. We have identified some core values that contribute to effective and honorable public service. We have reviewed several of the processes and systems that do exist for ethical official decision-making,. And we have noted that there, in fact, are individuals who take seriously the "calling" of public service and have performed honorably. Meanwhile, voters still need a healthy skepticism of a campaigner's promises and a well-founded respect for the checks and balances of the three branches of government and for the role the media play in uncovering dishonorable public service.

No single law or code will guarantee ethical public service, but reformers hope that the raising of standards and the discussion of new laws, modified codes and ethical decision-making processes ultimately will contribute to government in which the people's trust can be more justifiably placed.

FOR FURTHER INQUIRY

REVIEW QUESTIONS

"Always do right. This will gratify some people, and astonish the rest."
— Mark Twain

1. Name at least five of the factors a public official must ponder in making an official decision.
2. Discuss which of the duties of governance (prudence, courage of conscience, truth-telling) is most difficult to perform and state your reasons.
3. Name the three fundamentals of public administration.
4. Following are two rulings of the Florida Commission on Ethics as to conflicts of interests involving public officials. Using one of the "decision models" described in the chapter, identify the stage of the decision-making process where the conflict should have been identified and determine upon what basis a decision should have been made to avoid the conflict.

> **Case A:** An attorney for the Florida Real Estate Commission is prohibited by s. 112.313(7), F. S. 1975, from holding outside employment as a real estate salesman or broker, as he would be employed by a business entity subject to the regulation of his public agency, the Real Estate Commission, and would hold employment which creates a continuing conflict between his private interests and the performance of his public duties and potentially would interfere with the full and faithful discharge of his public duties. His public responsibility is to advise and interpret state laws pertaining to real estate licensing, to prepare rules, and to prosecute or defend matters as directed by the Commission. Such duties would not necessarily coincide with his private real estate interests. The Ethics Commis-

sion is unable to advise whether or not conflicts might exist in such attorney engaging in the private practice of law, as opinions must be issued within a particular factual context [see s. 112.322(3)(a)] rather than offering general guidelines.

Case B: A prohibited conflict of interest is created where an elected mayor of a municipality is employed within that city as the designated fire and rescue employee. Although said employee is compensated by the county pursuant to an interlocal agreement, he would be subject to the supervision of the municipal fire chief administrative officer of the city. He therefore would hold employment with an agency in violation of s. 112.313(7)(a), F.S. 1975.

ENDNOTES

1. Peter Madsen, *Ethical Issues in Professional Life: A Multimedia Course* (unpublished), Carnegie-Mellon University, Pittsburgh, Penn. Copyright 1992.

2. Michael Josephson, *Making Ethical Decisions,* pp. 20–26. The Josephson Institute of Ethics, Marina Del Rey, Calif. 1991.

3. Kathryn Denhardt, "Unearthing the Moral Foundations of Public Administration: Honor, Benevolence, Justice," *Ethical Frontiers in Public Management,* pp. 101–111, Jossey-Bass. 1991.

4. James S. Bowman, Editor, *Ethical Frontiers in Public Management,* Jossey-Bass Inc., Publishers, San Francisco, Calif. 1991.

5. William D. Hitt, *Ethics and Leadership*, pp. 98, 100–101. Battelle Press, Columbus, Ohio.

6. Walter Lippmann, *A Preface to Morals,* pp. 279–81, 83, Transaction Publishers.

7. Florida Commission on Ethics, CEO 86-73 — September 17, 1986.

8. Ibid. CEO-77-96 — July 21, 1977.

9. Ibid. CEO 76-148A — October 25, 1976 (CEO 76-148 revoked).

10. Ibid. CEO 88-25 — April 28, 1988.

11. Ibid. CEO 86-9 — February 20, 1986.

12. Pride. Interview with Askew.

13. Frank Trippett, *The States: United They Fell,* World Publishing Company, Cleveland, Ohio. 1967.

14. Congressional Research Service, Jan. 29, 1993, *CRS Issue Brief on Campaign Financing.*

15. Pride, personal interview.

16. Neal R. Peirce, *The Megastates of America*, W.W. Norton & Co. New York, N.Y. 1972.

17. Anne Marie Donahue, editor, *Ethics in Politics and Government*, H. W. Wilson Co. 1989.

18. Jack Bass and Walter de Vries, *The Transformation of Southern Politics*, 1976, Basic Books.

19. Office of Attorney General of Florida, *Government in the Sunshine Manual,* 1993, First Amendment Foundation.

20. Pride.

21. Josephson.

22. Bonnie Williams, executive director, Florida Commission on Ethics, an unpublished speech.

CHAPTER 22

CODES OF ETHICS

"Seven sins: Wealth without work. Pleasure without conscience. Knowledge without character. Commerce without morality. Science without humility. Worship without sacrifice. Politics without principle."

*— **Mahatma Gandhi***

"The Japanese recognize that there are really only two demands of leadership: One is to accept that rank does not confer privileges, it entails responsibilities. The other is to acknowledge that leaders in an organization need to impose on themselves that congruence between deeds and actions, between behavior and professed beliefs and values, that we call 'personal integrity'."

*— **Peter Drucker***

A young accountant in New York City is offered an "incentive bonus" of 15% of the amount he saves a corporation on its state and federal taxes this year. Should he accept the deal? In Dallas, a buyer for a major department store chain opens his mail one morning to find a rather expensive gift from a supplier with a note thanking him for placing such a large order. Should he keep it? A California state senator is told by a lobbyist for a powerful special interest group that strings can be pulled to get the politician's underachieving son into a prestigious Ivy League university if the senator will vote against an upcoming bill. Should she do so?

What do these scenarios have in common? Of course, they represent situations requiring ethical decisions. More than that, they are examples of dilemmas in which individuals are not simply left alone to wrestle with their own consciences and principles, hoping that their decision will be able to withstand the scrutiny of peers or superiors. In each of these cases, the person in question has an additional form of guidance; a corporate, professional, or governmental code of ethics.

Keith Goree, B.A. Harding University, M.A. Abilene Christian University, is professor of Applied Ethics and Honors Applied Ethics at St. Petersburg Junior College and author of an ethics text for secondary students.

WHAT IS A CODE OF ETHICS?

A code of ethics is a written set of principles and rules intended to serve as a guideline for determining appropriate ethical behavior for those individuals under its authority. It is "a formal statement of good intentions" from a corporation or profession. An ethics code delineates in behavioral terms "a system of value-based principles or practices and a definition of right and wrong." It represents a bridge spanning the chasm between the idealistic and ethereal principles of moral philosophy and the cold, hard realities of business.

Endnote 1

Endnote 2

However, a code of ethics is not the same as a **moral code**. A moral code is a definitive statement of right and wrong. As **Richard DeGeorge** states, "No individual or group can make actions moral or immoral by fiat. Every code, therefore, can and should appropriately be evaluated from a moral point of view." In other words, while a typical code of ethics contains rules and principles of behavior based on moral principles, these are not moral principles in themselves, and should not be treated as such. To do so invites the dangerous practice of "code worship" — i.e., assuming that anything the code allows must be moral and anything it forbids must be immoral. A profession or corporation that falls into this trap will be unlikely to be able to make the kinds of genuine changes and adaptations in the code that are necessary to keep it relevant and useful.

Endnote 3

CHIEF LEARNING OUTCOME

I understand the role and development of codes of ethics in business, professions and government.

ARE CODES NECESSARY?

Why not just pass laws? Indeed, some states and the federal government have enacted laws embodying codes of ethics. Both codes of ethics and laws are frequently based on ethical principles, but laws have limits. They often are only passed and enforced after the damage has been done (e.g., environmental protection statutes, airline safety regulations). Codes of ethics tend to be more preventative in nature. Also, because the politicians who write the laws cannot possibly have expertise in all the complexities of business, industry, and the professions, formulating appropriate laws and designing effective regulations are difficult. In addition, basing all corporate and professional behavior on the letter of the law invites a "loophole mentality," in which individuals seem to expend more energy in trying to get around the law than in obeying it.

Endnote 4

Because taking legal action against corporations is so expensive and these cases can spend so many years tied up in litigation, it seems wiser to find another approach. **William Shaw** in *Business Ethics* (Wadsworth) says, "We do not want a system in which business people believe that their only obligation is to obey the law and that it is morally permissible for them to do anything not (yet) illegal. With that attitude, disaster is just around the corner."

Endnote 5

HOW DO CODES OF ETHICS VARY?

Business and professional codes of ethics can vary widely in several important ways. First, the **purposes** of the codes are not all the same. Some corporate codes are written primarily to give administrators a tool for controlling employees, or even as an excuse for firing them. Some professional codes are purely ceremonial. They are read at initiations or graduations with great pomp, but the principles are antiquated and irrelevant to modern issues in the field. Other codes are constructed with the central goal of improving public relations. The words are comforting, the principles reassuring, but the code does not seem to have much impact on the behavior of those who are supposed to be following it. On the other hand, there are also many effective codes of ethics. Their purposes are to create and maintain a sense of professionalism, to offer some guidance to those facing thorny ethical dilemmas, and to give the public a standard to which it can hold a corporation or profession.

Codes also vary according to **authorship**. Corporate codes are often written at a management or administrative level and, unfortunately, sometimes with little contribution from the employees who are to follow it. There-

KEY CONCEPTS

A code of ethics is a written set of principles and rules intended to serve as a guideline for determining appropriate ethical behavior for those individuals under its authority.

Categories of codes of ethics include corporate, professional and government/public service.

fore, these codes can seem authoritarian and heavy-handed, geared more toward increasing company profits than fulfilling social responsibilities. In contrast, codes of professional organizations are often constructed at the peer level because many of the individuals in the professions are self-employed (or at least are granted more autonomy than corporate employees). For instance, the American Dental Association code of ethics was written by dentists, the American Bar Association code by lawyers, and the American Institute of Certified Public Accountants code by accountants. There are strengths and weaknesses in peer-level codes which will be discussed later in this chapter, but one important step in critiquing any code is considering the identity and motives of who wrote it.

Figure 1. Code of Hammurabi. Corbis-Bettman.

Finally, codes can vary in their **ethical level** — the degree of ethical behavior to which they call their subjects. Some codes seem to be little more than a collection of lofty ideals to which everyone should aspire, but which no one is realistically expected to practice consistently. These codes sound nice but are unenforceable, and thus have little effect on people's behavior. They come across as shallow and insincere. At the opposite end of the spectrum are the minimum standard codes. These consist of little more than lengthy lists of rules that must be followed to keep one's job or license to practice. Each rule has a corresponding penalty for its violation, and ethical behavior is generally seen as not violating the letter of the code. This approach spawns searches for loopholes, as mentioned above, and, ironically, may actually lower the ethical level of behavior of some individuals who might otherwise have followed higher personal principles. The most relevant and useful codes of ethics, whether for corporations or professions, have their roots somewhere between these extremes. They are the blended codes; combining the noble principles of lofty ideals with clearly stated, enforceable rules that can be monitored for compliance.

For purposes of this study, codes of ethics are divided into three main categories: corporate, professional and governmental/public service codes. This is not the only possible approach to such a study, and there will be instances where a code may overlap categories, but this approach can effectively demonstrate how the factors of purpose, authorship, and ethical level can impact the ability of a code of ethics to uplift the ethical behavior of its subjects.

In the Tylenol Case cited in Chapter 19, Johnson & Johnson's leaders turned to their code of ethics, which they refer to as "Our Credo." Its first sentence states, "We believe our first responsibility is to the doctors, nurses, and patients, to mothers and all others who use our products and services." *Endnote 6* They chose to pull the product off the shelves. In referring to the role played by the code of ethics in this decision, James Burke, the corporation's chairman, said, "This document spells out our responsibilities to all our constituencies: consumers, employees, community, and stockholders. It served to guide all of us during the crisis, when hard decisions had to be made in what were often excruciatingly brief periods of time. All of our employees worldwide were able to watch the process of the Tylenol withdrawal and subsequent reintroduction in tamper-resistant packaging, confident of the way in which the decisions would be made. There was a great sense of shared pride in the knowledge that the *Endnote 7* Credo was being tested . . . and it worked!"

The premise that a corporate code of ethics can make a significant impact on the behavior of individuals within the company is not universally accepted. As will be seen further in the chapter, a few critics have even argued that such codes can never amount to more than publicity ploys, capable only of making a corporation appear ethical to a gullible public. On the other hand, there are many more voices in the business arena who argue that, while we must be realistic about the scope of what a code should be expected to accomplish, it can indeed make a substantive difference in the ethical behavior of the people within a company.

Figure 2. On Wall Street, looking up is often followed by having to look out. Tony Stone Images.

How Pervasive Are Corporate Codes of Ethics?

Surveys have not reported identical findings, but there does seem to be an overall consensus that many American businesses have constructed such codes and rely on them for guidance. Raiborn and Payne discuss this issue in *Taking Sides: Clashing Views on Controversial Issues in Business Ethics and Society,* (2nd edition, Lisa H. Newton and Maureen M. Ford (eds.), The Dushkin Publishing Group, Inc., Guilford, Conn., 1992). They report on a study of 300 major companies by the Conference Board showing that more than 75% of the corporations responding had adopted written codes of conduct for their employees. Catherine Fredman found that in the period between 1984 and 1987, the number of American companies among the Fortune 500 who had a stated code of ethics increased by 12%. Patrick Murphy reports that approximately 90% of the Fortune 500 firms and almost half of all companies in America currently have codes of ethics in place.

One of the most ambitious studies to date on corporate codes of ethics was done by the Ethics Resource Center in Washington, D. C. This 1987 survey of 2,000 American companies found, among other things, that 85% of the corporations responding said that they had "a code, policy statement, or other written guidelines on ethics." This figure varied widely, however, with different types and sizes of corporations. Bigger corporations were more likely to have developed codes than smaller ones. The practice of distributing the code to all company employees ranged from 72% among defense contractors, and 71% in the finance/insurance industry, to only 36% in construction, and only 30% of retail sales firms. But it is interesting to note that only 2% of defense contractors, 4% of finance/insurance industry firms, and only 3% of very large firms (more than 50,000 employees) said that they had no code and no plans to implement one. Also revealing is that fact that these codes are not just gathering dust on a shelf. But 76% of firms with a written code were currently revising it or had done so within the previous five years. Only 15% of firms who had a code reported that theirs had never been revised.

"The last temptation is the greatest treason: To do the right deed for the wrong reason." — *T.S. Eliot*

Endnote 1

Endnote 8

Endnote 9

Why Would a Corporation Want to Develop a Code of Ethics? There are many reasons why companies see the development and maintenance of a code as a worthwhile endeavor. Of course, it is in the corporation's best interests to be perceived as ethical by the public. In a survey by Touche Ross, most of the respondents believed that businesses actually strengthen their competitive positions by maintaining high ethical standards. Codes can help a firm to do that. In the same study, 39% of those responding cited adoption of a code of ethics as the best way to inspire ethical behavior in a corporation. The industries rated by the respondents as having the best reputations for ethical behavior were commercial banking, utilities, pharmaceuticals, and cosmetics. The main reason given for their prestige was the existence of strong industry standards, which would be directly related to the development of strong codes of ethics.

Another reason for developing a corporate ethical code stems from the great pressure upon employees to increase profits for the company, tempting them to act unethically to do so. Wartzman reports a survey from the early 1980s that found more than 70% of the executives interviewed felt the pressure to conform to organizational standards and often had to compromise personal principles. Obviously, unethical employees are often more expensive for the company due to more frequent litigation, damage to the corporation's public image, decreased morale, employee theft, abuse of sick time, and so forth. Shaw states, "If those inside the corporation are to behave morally, they need clearly stated and communicated ethical standards that are equitable and enforced." He adds that codes "encourage members to take moral responsibilities seriously." Raiborn and Payne note, "Companies want to communicate management's concern for high-level ethical standards of behavior and corporate social responsibility." These corporations suggest that it would not be fair to hold employees to a standard of ethical conduct that had not been clearly spelled out to them in advance.

Richard DeGeorge lists six reasons why a corporation would want to develop, implement and maintain a company code of ethics:

1. The exercise is in itself worthwhile. The company receives inherent benefits simply from discussing these ethical issues.

2. Once adopted, the code generates continuing, open discussion of ethical issues.

3. The code helps instill proper ethical attitudes in employees at all levels.

4. The code provides employees with a reference when asked to do something contrary to the code.

5. The code helps reassure customers and the public; giving them a "touchstone" for measuring the corporation.

6. The code gives workers and managers a way to evaluate in moral terms the goals and practices of the firm to ensure that the corporation as a whole is acting in accordance with the code.

Endnote 10

Endnote 11

Endnote 12

Endnote 2

Endnote 3

Jack Behrman adds a different light. He states, "Regardless of why codes of ethics are being established, one of the major benefits of establishing (such codes) is the process of discovery and harmonization of interests that occurs from the participation of many different managers in the formulation of the code."

Endnote 13

What Kinds of Behaviors Are Included in Corporate Codes? Obviously, because codes of ethics are written for a variety of different purposes, the content of the codes will vary widely as well. Each company will develop a code tailored to meet its own specific needs. For instance, a corporation that has had a problem with sexual harassment is likely to put a rule prohibiting such acts in its code of ethics. Since each company's history and value system is different, each code will be unique.

There are, however, some common threads among corporate codes. In the Ethics Resource Center study previously cited, an attempt was made to determine which ethical issues were addressed the most often. Companies were asked (1) to rank the ethical issues they considered to be the most important, (2) to report issues covered by their own code of ethics, and (3) to further report issues also covered in employee ethics training sessions.

A cursory analysis of these results produces some interesting conclusions. It is obvious that many of the ethical issues that corporate leaders consider to be important are not reflected as such in company codes of ethics or employee training. Therefore, many companies are probably failing to communicate the importance of those issues to their employees. Drug and alcohol abuse is ranked as the most important issue facing American businesses, yet only 64% of the companies that have written codes of ethics include anything about substance abuse. Only 36% of the corporations responding include drug and alcohol abuse as part of employee training. Are corporate leaders effectively communicating their values to the employees? How are those employees to understand that this issue is considered crucial to the well-being of the company? Is it fair to discipline a worker harshly for actions for which he has been given little guidance by the company? William Shaw warns, "If management does not make explicit the values and behaviors it desires, the culture will typically develop its own norms, usually based on the types of behavior that lead to success within the organization."

Drug and alcohol abuse is ranked as the most important issue facing American businesses, yet only 64% of the companies that have written codes of ethics include anything about substance abuse.

Endnote 14

Are Codes of Ethics Effective? Do they upgrade the behavior of employees? Not always. There are several factors that may make codes less likely to be effective. First, they will obviously not achieve much when written "just for show." "Codes of conduct continue to be criticized as . . . serving purely as public relations ploys, or being designed strictly to avoid legal problems." If anything, such codes might actually work to lower the ethical behavior of employees. Because the corporation itself appears insincere or intellectually dishonest, the employees may tend to treat the codes lightly.

Endnote 8

Endnote 15

Codes of ethics also lose effectiveness when the expectations of the code are unrealistically high. Kenneth Arrow, in his award-winning business essay states, "One must not expect miraculous transformations in human behavior. Ethical codes, if they are to be viable, should be limited in their scope."

Most business ethicists maintain that a code of ethics is doomed to failure if its principles appear to be inconsistent with the actual corporate culture. The corporate culture is something akin to Jean-Jacques Rousseau's "social contract" — that mutual understanding of expected values and behaviors among the members of a society. The corporate culture represents the real attitudes of the company; the understood expectations of how individuals within the company should act. It is "the pattern of shared values and beliefs that give members of an institution meaning and provide them with rules for behavior in their organization." For instance, an automotive repair company could put dozens of rules in its code of ethics concerning the importance of "treating the customer right" and "upholding honesty and integrity." But if that same company pays its mechanics commissions or bonuses based on the amount that customers end up paying for their repair work, which would tend to encourage them to do unnecessary repairs, then the code loses its integrity and relevance.

Endnote 16

There is a principle of interpersonal communications which says that if there is a **"mixed message"** between what a person says (verbally) and how that person acts (non-verbally), then others will tend to disregard the verbal message and believe the non-verbal one to be the truth. For example, when a person's eyes and facial expressions have an angry look, others will assume he feels that way, even if he denies having those emotions. A code of ethics can be seen as a verbal message to the public and the employees from the top management of a corporation. But it is only one of many different types of messages the company sends. Employees, for example, may read company policies, contracts, job descriptions, corporate guidelines and memos. Where does the company's code of ethics fit into this hierarchy? If an employee notices discrepancies between the code and memos from his boss, which should take priority?

A corporate code of ethics will only be accepted, believed, and effective, when the actions and expectations of those administrators are consistent with the message of the code. For example, one study found, in studying corporate codes of ethics, that "codes give more attention to unethical conduct likely to decrease the firm's profits than to conduct that might increase profits." This assertion is supported by the findings of the Ethics Resource Center study. Protecting the company's proprietary information was ranked third among issues addressed in company policies, while ethical policies regarding gathering that same information from competitors was ranked last. When these kinds of inconsistencies exist between what a corporation says it believes and what it actually emphasizes in daily operation, then the code's effectiveness in upgrading the ethical behavior of the employees is weakened.

Endnote 17

One inherent defect of codes of ethics is based upon the diverse interests to whom corporations have obligations. LaRue Hosmer in *Taking Sides: Clashing Views on Controversial Issues in Business Ethics and Society,* 2nd edition, Lisa H. Newton and Maureen M. Ford (eds.), Dushkin Publishing Group, Inc., Guilford, Conn. 1992) observes: "The problem is that it is not possible to state the norms and beliefs of an organization relative to the various constituent groups (employees, customers, suppliers, distributors, stockholders, and the general public) clearly and explicitly, without offending at least one of those groups . . . The basic difficulty . . . is that they do not establish priorities (among those groups). The code does not tell us how to choose between our distributors, our customers, and ourselves." Hosmer cites the Johnson & Johnson Credo as an example of the problem, noting that it contains an inherent contradiction. The first sentence states, "We believe our first responsibility is to the doctors, nurses and patients, to mothers and all others who use our products and services." This is the principle that the company claimed guided it through the Tylenol-tampering crisis. But Hosmer points out that there are other competing statements, such as, "We are responsible to our employees, the men and women who work with us throughout the world," and, "Our final responsibility is to our stockholders." Which one of these groups should take priority? Does the code of ethics offer more guidance or confusion? Hosmer concludes, "I think that we can agree that the employees of Johnson & Johnson should be proud of the response of their firm, which put consumer safety ahead of company profits, but we also have to agree that that response, and that priority ranking, is not unequivocally indicated in the Credo of the company."

Endnote 7

Endnote 7

While there is some honest disagreement as to how effective codes of ethics can be, there is relative consensus regarding the conditions necessary for increasing their effectiveness. This consensus holds that a code with the capacity to have a substantive impact on the behavior of the members of a corporation will have the following characteristics:

QUALITY CODES OF ETHICS

1. **Its expectations are clearly communicated and specific.** There is a place for value statements and principles, but employees need specific guidelines to follow when facing difficult decisions. Is it forbidden to accept any gifts at all from clients, or just gifts worth more than a nominal sum of, say, $25?

   Endnote 15

2. **It is comprehensive, covering virtually all conduct associated with the workplace.** How fair is it to discipline an employee for using unethical methods of gathering information from a competitor if your firm is one of the 72% of the companies that has a code of ethics, but does not offer any guidance in that area?

   Endnote 2

Endnote 8

Endnote 15

Endnote 15

Endnote 8

Endnote 2

3. **It is direct, even blunt and realistic about violations and their consequences.** If there is to be any deterrent effect, it will be because individuals see that unethical behavior has negative consequences.

4. **It is widely accepted. Employee involvement is essential**. If a code is simply handed down to workers from above without their input or participation, then it is not likely to win their allegiance. On the other hand, if the employees can be meaningfully involved in the process of developing a code, then they are more likely to take personal ownership of the code; to think of it and act on it as something important belonging to them.

5. **It is understood to benefit everyone.** Kenneth Arrow states, " . . . above all it must be clearly perceived that the acceptance of these ethical obligations by everybody does involve mutual gain. Ethical codes that lack the latter property are unlikely to be viable."

6. **It is a public document, as opposed to a tool used only for internal employee control**. If the employees believe that the administrators and managers who produced the code are less interested in ethical behavior than in employee control, and especially if the employees believe that those administrators and managers are not acting ethically themselves, the code becomes meaningless and subject to ridicule.

7. **It is written at an appropriate ethical level**. In evaluating codes of ethics, Raiborn and Payne have created a hierarchy of ethical behavior based on the types of standards used in cost accounting. Their four levels of ethical behavior are as follows:

The *theoretical level* represents the ethical ideal. This level is virtually impossible to consistently attain, but represents "the highest potential towards which society should continually strive." For example, the hypothetical Lincoln Construction Company wants to develop a reputation in the community for dealing with its clients honestly. To do so, it could develop a code of ethics requiring absolute honesty and integrity. The company might even begin to advertise that "all of our employees are as honest as ol' Abe ever was"; or "we would walk two miles to return your penny."

The *practical level* represents behavior which can be achieved the majority of the time through diligent effort. In its early days, the J. C. Penney Corporation was known across America as the "Golden Rule Company." The company's foundational principle was that its employees would treat customers like the employees themselves would wish to be treated. Such a policy represents an admirable goal, and it can be argued that most people could conceivably meet this standard most of the time if they tried earnestly.

The *currently attainable level* represents the behavior normally exhibited by individuals. This behavior is socially acceptable, but not particularly praiseworthy, since reaching it does not require much effort. For example, an air conditioner repair company could develop and advertise policies such as, "We will not cheat our customers," "Employees shall not curse at the customers," and "Employees will be expected to work forty hours per week."

The *basic level* represents behavior within the letter of the law. At this level there is no concerted effort to comply

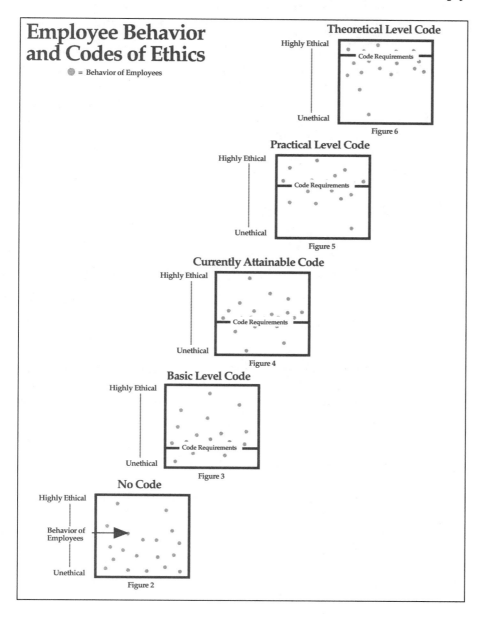

Employee Behavior and Codes of Ethics

⬤ = Behavior of Employees

Theoretical Level Code

Highly Ethical

Code Requirements

Unethical

Figure 6

Practical Level Code

Highly Ethical

Code Requirements

Unethical

Figure 5

Currently Attainable Code

Highly Ethical

Code Requirements

Unethical

Figure 4

Basic Level Code

Highly Ethical

Code Requirements

Unethical

Figure 3

No Code

Highly Ethical

Behavior of Employees

Unethical

Figure 2

with the spirit of the law, thus producing the "loophole mentality," in which the person is more concerned with getting around the rules than in doing the right thing. An example might be a code of ethics for a chemical company stating that its employees will not dump any more than the legal limit of a dangerous pesticide into a nearby river.

This process of analyzing a code of ethics to determine its ethical level is more than just an academic exercise. The level of ethical behavior required by a code impacts the actions of the employees who are to follow it, especially if the corporate ethical climate is consistent with the provisions in the code. **Codes written at the higher levels should motivate the employees to maintain higher ethical standards than would codes written at the basic level.**

Notice that in Figure 1, demonstrating a corporation with no code of ethics, the expected ethical behavior of employees varies widely but is concentrated on the unethical end of the spectrum. This expectation is based on the principle voiced by William Shaw earlier in this chapter. It is important enough that it bears repeating. "If management does not make explicit the values and behaviors it desires, the culture will typically develop its own norms, usually based on the types of behaviors that lead to success within the corporation." What kinds of behaviors typically lead to success within a corporation that has no clearly stated ethical standards for its employees? Commission earnings? Sales? Revenue generated for the company? While these represent the healthy goals of many companies, notice that they are goals or ends, and the means used to accomplish them may more often be unethical if employees are not given ethical guidance.

Notice that the code requirements are relatively low, since they are based on the minimal letter of the law. Most behavior is concentrated around the level called for in the code, which is to be expected. Notice that while there are a few employees maintaining higher personal conduct, the presence of a minimal code has actually lowered the behavior of others. In a company with lower-level ethical expectations, acting on a higher level may go unrewarded or even be actively discouraged. Many highly principled individuals have been demoted or fired for blowing the whistle on unethical corporate policies and practices.

Then there is the expected employee behavior under a code of ethics written at the currently attainable level, or the level normally exhibited by most individuals. As you see, the code requirements have risen somewhat and the behaviors have risen with them. Notice also that as the eth-

Endnote 14

ical expectations rise, the number of individuals failing to meet that standard increase.

Next, there is the ethical behaviors anticipated under a practical level code of ethics. This is the standard which could be achieved the majority of the time through diligent effort. Again, the behavior level should rise to meet the requirements of the code, and more individuals would be expected to fail to meet this higher standard. Such individuals might be dealt with less harshly than at the lower levels since it would be unreasonable to expect people to be able to maintain such lofty behavior all of the time.

Finally, there is the expected employee behavior under a theoretical level code of ethics, or one based on ethical ideals. On the surface this would seem to be the superior type of code, but the lofty nature of its principles presents some practical problems. Only a few individuals would be able to consistently meet these requirements; the failure rate would be much higher. Such a system could tend to produce a certain cynicism toward the code, since no one seems to be expected to achieve it very often. It would seem unfair to punish violators very harshly, thus making enforcement difficult, if not impossible.

Raiborn and Payne argue that codes of ethics should be written at least at the currently attainable level, with incentives for reaching toward higher levels. If the code is written at the theoretical level, then enforcement is impossible because only rarely will individuals reach it. If the code is written at the practical level, then the company is accepting the responsibility of requiring additional efforts of its employees to do the right thing. On the other hand, if the code is written at the currently attainable or basic levels, the punishments for deviations from the code should be harsh, because these are minimal standards. Snoeyenbos and Jewell concur, adding that a code "should not be window dressing, or so general as to be useless. It should set reasonable goals and subgoals, with an eye toward blunting unethical pressures on subordinates."

Endnote 18

8. **It is monitored and enforced**. Even for companies who have spent considerable time and effort developing a viable code, enforcement is often a problem. The Ethics Resource Center (ERC) study found that while 46% of the corporations responding to their survey reported allegations of misconduct occurring at a rate of less than 1 per 1000 employees per year, 27% indicated that their companies had no way to determine even an approximate number of allegations. Nearly 50% were unable to estimate what percentage of allegations in the previous year turned out to be valid. Obviously, if a code of ethics cannot be enforced, then its usefulness is limited.

Endnote 19

The ERC study also noted that the highest ratings on the effectiveness of monitoring and enforcement of the code of ethics were among corporations who shared these important characteristics:

a. The firms distributed the code of ethics to all employees of the corporation.

b. The firms had developed ethics training for all employees.

c. The companies frequently used videotapes, articles, posters and speakers as methods of communicating ethics policies.

d. The firms demonstrated the greatest range of company departments used by employees as sources of advice on applying ethics policies.

e. The companies had corporate ethics committees at the board of director level, where policy decisions are made.

f. The firms used "hot lines" to allow employees to report unethical behavior without risking retaliation by other employees.

g. These companies often established a separate corporate ethics office to monitor and enforce compliance with the code.

Endnote 8

9. **It is revised periodically.** A company's needs, values, and concerns are constantly changing. A code of ethics that is never revised and updated becomes stagnant and irrelevant.

Endnote 19

10. **It is supported by management and employee ethics training.** This may be the area in which businesses need the most improvement. The Ethics Resource Center study found that only 28% of their respondent companies provided employee training on ethical issues in business. Ethics training was the least common in retail and wholesale industries (19%) and most common among defense contractors, who are subject to much more stringent federal ethics laws (52%). This absence of training is puzzling. Perhaps managers believe that giving out the code of ethics will be sufficient in itself. Perhaps the company is writing the code more for the public relations value than for its employees to follow. Perhaps it is related to the common misconception that ethics cannot be taught to adults (in which case, why have a code at all?).

Whatever the reason, a reasonable conclusion is that codes of ethics, in themselves, are inadequate to effect change in the behavior of the members of a corporation, even when written well. The corporate climate, and the factors which go along with it (management/employee communication, commonality of goals and values, sincerity of purpose in the development and implementation of the code, etc.), are often the decisive factors in how effectively or ineffectively a code of ethics will be in motivating and enabling members of the company to act ethically.

Endnote 2

There is an old joke that asks how many psychologists it takes to change a light bulb. The answer is, "Just one, but the bulb really has to want to be changed." One of the primary purposes of a code of ethics is to change people's behavior; an outcome that humans tend to vigorously resist. Writing, developing, and implementing a code is a difficult process, fraught with political obstacles and interpersonal land mines. Even if a company's management is committed to the importance of a code, the feat of getting one implemented is daunting.

Raiborn and Payne point out several problems that typically arise in the process of designing and implementing a corporate code of ethics:

> First, it sometimes gives employees the implication that the administration believes someone is doing something wrong. This may or may not be the case, but an atmosphere of distrust and suspicion can result, making communication about the code even more difficult.
>
> Second, if the top managers themselves are the ones acting unethically, and the code is only intended for image-building, then trying to communicate the value of ethics to all employees will be virtually impossible. As stated previously, it is the unethical (non-verbal) behavior that will be seen as more accurately representing the actual beliefs of those leaders.
>
> Third, there are problems inherent in determining who has violated a code. How much credibility should be given to the information provided by whistle-blowers? How much protection should they be given? When it boils down to one person's word against another's (in sexual harassment cases, for instance), who should be believed?
>
> Fourth, determining the level of specificity in a code can be problematic. At which ethical behavior level should it be written? Theoretical? Practical? Currently attainable? Basic? How can general principles and specific rules be combined?
>
> Finally, Raiborn and Payne point out that a challenge also exists in keeping the tone of the code positive, rather than negative. If the code is too negative, with every other sentence beginning with "Thou shalt not . . . ," then the suspicions of the workers that they are distrusted will be magnified, morale impaired, and the code's effectiveness limited.

But effective codes of ethics exist and more are being written. While the obstacles are formidable, there are company-wide benefits that result from the process of creating and implementing an ethics code. The most valuable goals often involve the biggest challenges. Robert E. Sweeney, Memphis State University professor, has suggested five steps that he believes are necessary in the development of a viable corporate code of ethics:

Endnote 20

Develop the Code

It must be assembled by a company's ownership and top management. It is, after all, the statement of their values, principles, and priorities. The code should provide guidelines for conduct, aid in resolving conflicts, and spell out disciplinary action for violations of the code. To avoid pitfalls already mentioned, it should consist of broad guidelines supported by detail.

Gain Approval

For the code to be effective, everyone needs to buy into it. This can be accomplished by continually seeking workers' input into its content, keeping its tone positive, and pointing out to employees that they will also benefit from having a code of ethics. Unfortunately, many companies do not seem to understand the criticality of employee support in this process. For example, according to the Ethics Resource Center survey, only 50% of the responding companies having codes of ethics in place had guidelines in their codes regarding employee right to privacy. Only 46% of the codes stated support for employees' volunteer community activities, and only 29% contained information concerning administrative policies on plant closings and layoffs. While the ultimate goal of a company's code of ethics should be to maintain high levels of ethical behavior by its employees, getting workers to accept and value the code will be easier if they can see that it has been constructed with their interests in mind.

Endnote 19

Implement the Code

There are a variety of methods that can be used, but management must fix responsibility for getting the code in place and operative. Some corporations have found it worthwhile to set up a separate ethics office to oversee the process. Others have delegated the task to one administrator. How this is done does not seem to be as important as that it is done. Simply passing out copies of the code will not be sufficient.

Communicate the Ethical Message

Each employee should have a copy of the code, but the company must add training sessions including the use of videotapes, seminars with speakers and consultants from outside the firm, and indoctrination workshops for new employees or promotees. Discussions regarding relevant ethical issues should become a regular part of meetings involving management and employees. At one community college in Florida, time is set aside at every meeting of the president's cabinet for some discussion of ethical issues facing the college. This is an important step in developing the *ethical climate* discussed earlier on this chapter. In addition, ethics "hot lines" should be installed for reporting violations of the code. Without them, and the inherent protection which they give to whistle-blowers, monitoring compliance to the code is much more difficult. Also the code should be communicated externally to the public/community. While public relations should not be the solitary goal of developing a code of ethics, publicizing the code gives members of the community an important standard to which they can hold the company's behavior. If the corporation lives up to the good intentions expressed in the code, then there should be a substantially positive public relations effect.

Administer the Code

Compliance to the tenets of the code must be diligently monitored. Disciplinary procedures for violations of the code should be established and consistently followed. Provisions need to be made for whistle-blowing and the investigation of reported violations. The code itself must be revised periodically to keep it current and relevant to the needs of the company.

In summary, when analyzing corporate codes of ethics, consider these questions:

1. How well do these codes effectively communicate the most important ethical issues facing businesses? Are there important issues which are not included?

2. How well do these codes provide employees with appropriate guidance in making difficult decisions?

3. Are enforcement policies explained adequately?

4. At what ethical level is each code written? (See Figure 1)

5. What are the strengths and weaknesses of each? How do you think each could be improved?

In the high-pressure environment in which administrators, managers, engineers, and employees must work, crucial decisions must often be made very quickly and without enough accurate information. The consequences can at times involve life and death. A code of ethics is not a guarantee that all future decisions will be right, or that employees will always do the right thing. It does offer a set of guidelines, based on a clear philosophy of business, which can be invaluable when those tough choices must be made.

U. S. Representative Newt Gingrich of Georgia has been quoted as stating that ethics is "a binary problem; either you is or you isn't." To be sure, there are people at both ends of that spectrum in every company. There are those who would act with integrity and honor with no outside guidance and those who will act unethically regardless of what preventative steps are taken. Corporate codes of ethics are most effective for the majority of employees in the middle who need a little help and encouragement to do the right thing.

Endnote 20

LESSONS LEARNED

Jacqueline Dunckel in her study of successful businesses discovered the following lessons are learned in the process of pursuing ethical standards:

1. If a company sets ethical standards for itself, the company, and its employees, all must live by them.

2. It must have a way to monitor the ethical standards to ensure that they are being met.

3. It must have a means to react if the standards are not adhered to.

4. It must take the initiative to see that the standards are being followed, monitored and action is taken if there is deviation.

5. Most important, the president or chief executive officer must set the example for all other employees. If he or she loses their good reputation, all is lost relative to the ethics program.

6. Although the company is in business to make money, if it becomes greedy its reputation will be compromised and it may be tempted to yield to unethical practices.

PROFESSIONAL CODES OF ETHICS

Should a doctor accept "kickbacks" from pharmaceutical companies in exchange for writing more prescriptions for their drugs than for those of their competitors? Should an engineer obey the insistent demands of his client to disregard minor, or even major, safety violations? Should a psychologist break her promise of confidentiality if she believes doing so would help her client in the long run? Should a dentist refuse to treat any individuals she suspects of being infected with the HIV virus? What if she receives letters from her other patients insisting that she do so or they will find another dentist?

What distinguishes these cases from those mentioned earlier is that the individuals facing these dilemmas do not work for a corporation, and therefore are not subject to any corporate codes of ethics. People identified as "professionals" in our society are often, though not always, self-employed. Thus, they do not have managers or administrators peering over their shoulders. They have much more autonomy and independence than do corporate employees. Yet, professionals face just as many thorny ethical dilemmas, and probably bear even more personal responsibility for their choices. We have already seen that the law, all by itself, is limited in its ability to resolve many of these kinds of dilemmas. What, beyond the law, guides the behavior of these professionals?

Figure 3. Wall Street. Tony Stone Images.

William Shaw states, "Somewhere between etiquette and the law lie professional codes of ethics. Generally speaking, the members of a profession are understood to have agreed to abide by those rules as a condition of their engaging in that profession. Violations of the professional code may result in the disapproval of one's peers and, in serious cases, loss of one's license to practice that profession."

Endnote 21

What is a "profession"? According to the American Heritage Dictionary (2nd edition), a profession is **"an occupation or vocation requiring training in the liberal arts or the sciences and advanced study in a specialized field."** This brings to mind individuals such as doctors, lawyers, dentists, psychiatrists, and engineers. Thus, for many people, the term "professional" has come to be associated with high salaries, social prestige, and independence. As a result, the boundaries surrounding the concept of a "profession" have been blurred in recent years. Attempts have been made, with mixed success, to upgrade many occupations to the status of "profession" which traditionally have not fit the technical definition. These fields include, to name but a few, pest control, journalism, acupuncture, counseling, advertising, physical therapy, teaching, interior decorating, and law enforcement.

Endnote 22

This raises some interesting questions. Is journalism, for instance, a profession? Does it require "advanced study in a specialized field"? What about education? Does teaching at the college/university level fit the technical definition of being a profession? Does doing so at the elementary or high school level? Are there justifiable distinctions? In addition, there are questions of semantics. We speak of "professional athletes," yet understand that they must meet few, if any, educational requirements.

We are left, therefore, with more than a little confusion. Today, the traditional definitions do not always lend themselves to clear distinctions among trades, crafts, and professions. Interestingly, however, many persons in various occupational fields wish to be considered as professionals. Their motivations seem to be increased prestige, income, and especially autonomy. Richard DeGeorge states, "Typically, professions have been self-governing, and society has allowed them a large amount of autonomy . . . Members of a profession set their own standards, regulate entry into the profession, discipline their own members, and function with fewer restraints than others." Can the practice of giving a group this much power over its own affairs be justified?

Endnote 3

The answer is a cautious yes. DeGeorge adds, "In return for such increased autonomy, however, they are properly expected to serve the public good, to set higher standards of conduct for their members than those required of others, and to enforce a higher discipline than others do . . . More is expected of them because of their roles, not less. The argument in favor of allowing a profession to govern itself is based on two claims. The first is that the knowledge that the members of a profession have mastered is specialized, useful to society, and not easily mastered by the layman. The second is that the mem-

Thus, for many people, the term "professional" has come to be associated with high salaries, social prestige, and independence. As a result, the boundaries surrounding the concept of a "profession" have been blurred in recent years.

bers of the profession set higher standards for themselves than society requires of its citizens, of unskilled workers, and of those in the business world."

In the medical profession, for example, it is accepted that doctors have mastered a body of knowledge that fits these criteria. It is highly specialized, extremely useful to society (Can you imagine our trying to survive without it?), and beyond the understanding of average members of society. It is also assumed, but not as widely accepted anymore, that doctors will understand that they have additional responsibilities to the community to use these abilities for the common good. In return, society allows the medical profession to determine, through its medical schools, how many new doctors will be admitted into the field. The profession is allowed to determine what are considered good medical practices and to discipline its own members when they fail to meet those standards.

As long as the members of a profession fulfill these obligations and voluntarily maintain this higher level of ethical behavior, then it is unnecessary for society to burden them with additional regulations. Interestingly, one of the first actions taken by an occupational field to demonstrate that it is capable of meeting this level of responsibility is to develop its own code of ethics.

PROFESSIONAL CODES CONTRASTED WITH CORPORATE CODES?

Professional codes are *written, monitored, and enforced on a peer level, while corporate codes are generally handed down from top management to employees.* Therefore, members of a profession tend to have more individual input into the rules and principles contained in the code, have more of a personal stake in making the code successful, and find more peer support for complying with the code.

Also, professional codes tend to *exhibit more variety* than corporate codes. For instance, they vary widely in purpose. Some are written simply to declare that a group wishes to be thought of as a profession (exterminators, respiratory therapists, etc.). Other codes have been developed (or revised at a lower level) as a substitute for the higher personal moral standards which their members were once expected to maintain. DeGeorge illustrates by pointing out that doctors were once expected to treat patients whether they could pay or not, to keep inconvenient office hours, to make house calls when necessary, and to keep both their personal and professional conduct above reproach. Today's society has less lofty expectations and the American Medical Association code of ethics reflects those changes.

Shaw adds that professional codes vary according to the kinds of behaviors *allowed and disallowed,* whether those behaviors are defined in vague generalities or minute detail, the level of enforcement (if any), and the relevance of the code to the daily operations of those individuals covered. So, while corporate codes of ethics vary in terms of the content of the rules and principles included in them, professional codes are even more diverse. Some are simply ceremonial documents, others are idealistically worded public relations gestures. Some are disciplinary tools, others do not even attempt enforcement.

What makes professional codes effective? DeGeorge has detailed four characteristics of a viable professional code. He states that, first and foremost, it should be *regulative*. Ideals and principles are appropriate, but "unless a code actually regulates the conduct of the members of a profession, the profession has no public statement to which it can be held by the public."

Endnote 3

Second, it should be *protective* of the public interest and the interests of the individuals who are served by that profession. In other words, the code should not exist simply to serve the needs of the profession. Surprisingly, there are codes (or at least parts of codes) which exist to serve the profession at the expense of the public's interests. For instance, there could be regulations unduly restricting the number of new practitioners allowed into the profession. By keeping demand (and therefore salaries) artificially high, costs to the public are inflated. Some professions have tried to restrict advertising by their members, making it more difficult for new members to establish a practice. DeGeorge specifically points out the American Medical Association and the American Bar Association as examples of groups who have been criticized for using their codes of ethics in self-serving manners.

Third, the code should be *specific and honest*. As stated previously, any good code must be more than "window-dressing." DeGeorge adds, "If a code is honest, it deals with those aspects of the profession that pose particular and specialized temptations to its members . . . Unless these are being addressed, the profession is not truly regulating itself."

Finally, the code must be *enforceable and actually policed*. While the code as a whole is more than just a composite of minimum standards, it is essential that some of those minimum standards be present, be monitored, and be diligently enforced. Professional codes, by the nature of the autonomy the profession has been granted by society, should encourage their members to go above and beyond the bare requirements of the law. In corporate codes this is preferred; in professional codes it is mandatory. When a profession has the appearance of giving lip service to ethics but is not attempting to pull its members up to this higher plane, it runs the risk of losing the social trust which it has been granted. Then it will lose the autonomy it cherished and even lose its identity as a profession.

What are the limitations of professional codes? Some limitations already have been indirectly discussed. Some codes are too self-serving to a particular profession, at times even at the expense of those the profession is supposed to be serving. Others are mere collections of "lofty ideals," written primarily with public relations in mind, and thus can seem so vague and general as to be useless. Some codes, and public service codes may be the best example, rely almost exclusively on already established laws for their rules. If a group is going to be respected as a profession, and granted the autonomy discussed earlier, then it must call its members to a standard of behavior higher than the mere letter of the law.

There are some other important limitations. There are situations in which following the precepts of one's professional code of ethics can mean violating other moral principles. For instance, what should a defense attorney do if a client charged with the murder of a child admits, in confidence, that he did indeed commit the crime and reveals the location of the body? Should the confidence be broken and the police informed? Should the grieving family be told of the new information, even if doing so would aid the prosecutors in convicting the client? Assuming that all of the other evidence is circumstantial in nature, should the attorney continue trying to get a "not guilty" verdict? Our society — and that includes members of the Bar Association itself — believes in the principle of justice. Yet the code implies that protecting attorney-client confidentiality has an inherent value as high as, perhaps even higher than, justice itself. Does the attorney follow his or her conscience or the code? Shaw comments, "Adherence to a professional code does not exempt your conduct from scrutiny from the broader perspective of morality." And DeGeorge concurs, adding, "Members of a profession are people first and members of a profession second. Hence, there is no special ethics that allows people in a profession to do as professionals what it is immoral for others to do."

Endnote 23

Endnote 3

DeGeorge also notes that sometimes professional codes can produce conflicts in obligations to the client or patient, the employer, the public, and the profession. He gives a hypothetical example of a company doctor who knows about hazardous working conditions but is instructed not to say anything. This physician may be subject to a corporate code of ethics requiring her to keep such proprietary information confidential, and a professional code which insists that she do whatever is necessary to protect the health and safety of the workers. Which code takes priority? What happens when it boils down to a judgment call?

A final limitation, as DeGeorge also mentions, is that professional codes give little guidance of what actions should be taken when the profession as a whole acts inappropriately. Some fields, such as architecture and engineering, have been criticized for allowing too much "word of mouth" advertising of employment opportunities. This practice can lead to a "good ol' boy" environment in which only people who know someone at the firm have a fair shot at getting a job there. The criticism is that, as a result of this tradition, women and minority members have not had equal access to these professional fields. If these charges are true, is it reasonable to expect that a code of ethics written at a peer level by some of the very individuals who have been participating in this practice could effectively deter the discrimination? Does it not seem more likely that the legislature or courts would have to step in and insist that fair practices by set in place? As stated previously, the autonomy granted to a profession by society could eventually be revoked if the profession does not live up to that expected higher plane of ethical behavior. On the other hand, it is difficult to find an example of a profession that has had that autonomy taken away. It is possible, therefore, that the professions do not consider this to be a serious threat to their welfare.

How can professional codes of ethics be analyzed? The process of evaluating a professional code is very similar to that of evaluating a corporate code. The first thing to note is content. What does the code say? Which principles and rules are spelled out? Are the statements vague and fuzzy, or concrete and clear? The nursing code of ethics, for example, seems to focus primarily on patients' rights and the responsibility of nurses to protect those rights. The American Institute of Certified Public Accounting's code of ethics deals more with avoiding situations that could produce a conflict of interest, or even the appearance of one. The Accreditation Board for Engineering and Technology code of ethics has rules concerning conflicts of interest, but adds important principles regarding public safety. In other words, the code of ethics for a profession can reveal the kinds of issues that individuals within that profession must face. There are some principles, such as avoiding conflicts of interest, that are present in many different professional codes because they are relevant to many occupational areas, but each code has its own unique combination of these rules.

Professional codes can also be evaluated in terms of their ethical level. Remember Raiborn and Payne's **four ethical levels?** Consider whether the code is written at (1) the theoretical level, representing an almost unreachable ethical ideal; (2) the practical level, or behavior which can be achieved the majority of the time through diligent effort; (3) the currently attainable level, representing behavior considered normal for most individuals; or (4) the basic level, or the letter of the law. Since these are professional codes, and one of the qualifications for being considered a profession was that the group would agree to hold itself to higher ethical standards than are expected of society in general, the ethical level should be higher than for corporate codes. Because enforcement is very difficult at the theoretical level, it would seem that most of the rules and principles should be written at the practical level.

Finally, a professional code should be evaluated in terms of its monitoring and enforcement procedures. If a code contains no provisions for enforcement, then it is safe to assume that it was written for public relations value and that the members are not likely to take it seriously. Punishments for violations of a code may range from admonishment or censure, to fines, to suspension of one's license, or even expulsion from the profession or group. Keep in mind that some professions are limited in their abilities to monitor compliance of the code, enforce the rules, and punish offenders because they lack the kind of powerful national organization that makes this possible.

If a code contains no provisions for enforcement, then it is safe to assume that it was written for public relations value and that the members are not likely to take it seriously.

For instance, the American Medical Association would seem to have the power and resources to carefully monitor how well its members follow their code. The American Association of College and University Professors currently does not. And even in the professions generally recognized as having the most elaborate enforcement systems, the effectiveness of those processes continues to be controversial. Can a system designed so that doctors or lawyers decide when fellow doctors or lawyers have erred function objectively? In the words of California State Bar Governor Richard Annotico, a lawyer who violates the code "is generally somebody's friend who is basically a good guy who has 'gone bad' temporarily. And who in hell enjoys being an executioner?"

Endnote 24

Society grants special status to the professions based, in part, on the assumption that higher standards will be self-imposed, monitored for compliance and enforced. Yet, skepticism is mounting regarding how well this arrangement is working. Robert Fellmeth (quoted by Sarah Glazer in "Policing the Professions," *Editorial Research Reports,* May 26, 1989) states that in California 97% of seemingly valid complaints against doctors are never even investigated. He adds: "The attitude of those making these decisions (the disciplinary boards) is openly solicitous of the physician." In a 1987 report of the California state bar's discipline system, Fellmeth called attention to an apparent **conflict of interest**. He noted that a committee dominated by a majority of practicing attorneys was "making a final decision based on a record given to them by another practicing attorney about the discipline of a third practicing attorney." These self-governing professions defend their ability to maintain high ethical standards among their membership and are resistant to governmental interference. But remember that if a profession is not able to adequately maintain a higher level of behavior among its members than is present in society at large, then it risks losing the status of being considered a profession at all. After all, providing enforcement resources is a test of a profession's commitment to ethical behavior, is it not?

Endnote 25

GOVERNMENT/PUBLIC SERVICE CODES

A mayor for a city of 100,000 residents has recently signed an agreement in principle with a large corporation to locate one of their factories in her town. Assuming that the arrangement has not yet been made public, would it be wrong for the mayor to buy stock in the company as a sign of good faith? Across the city, the owner of the local paint store is married to the woman who oversees the purchasing office for the local school system. Should he be able to bid on painting contracts for the schools? Would it be all right as long as the bids are sealed? A secretary in the office that handles building permits discovers that several of her superiors have been accepting illegal gifts from contractors and developers in exchange for speeding up the permit process. Should she blow the whistle, even if it means placing her own job in jeopardy?

Our final category of codes of ethics are the **codes for public officials** — those individuals who work for the government at the federal, state, or local level, and whose salaries are paid by tax dollars.

How are government/public service codes of ethics different?
First, these codes frequently look like corporate codes of ethics in style and function, but are written, and often enforced, at the peer level like professional codes. The government represents an employer and yet the legislators consider themselves to be a part of the profession of public service. The legislators who write the rules of these codes are themselves subject to those rules, and do not necessarily function as managers or bosses to the employees at lower levels of government service, as would normally be seen in a corporate code written by top administrators. The prohibitions and principles contained in these codes are similar to the type found in the corporate codes already examined; however, an important distinction must be understood. **Because of the unique nature of these government/public service codes of ethics, once adopted as part of the code, the rules become laws.**

Thus, the guidelines given in these government/public service codes are, by definition, based on the minimum requirements of the law. This has been referred to as the basic level, or the lowest possible ethical level at which a code can be written. Writing a code of ethics at this level was not preferred in corporate codes because it can lead to the "loophole mentality" discussed previously, and because doing so implies that anything not illegal must be ethical. Such codes were strongly discouraged in the professions, because they hinder the ability a group might have to lift up the behavior of its members to the higher ethical plane required to gain social prestige and autonomy. It is no small coincidence that, with these comparatively weak codes of ethics, American legislators and government workers in recent years have found themselves with declining social prestige and less autonomy than at almost any time in recent history.

A final idiosyncrasy of these government codes of ethics is that they tend to be much *more limited in scope* than corporate or professional codes. For example, the Florida Code of Ethics for Public Officers and Employees deals almost exclusively with the concept of conflicts of interest, and primarily financial ones at that. There is certainly nothing wrong with attempting to prevent conflicts of interest, for they indeed present strong temptations to our elected and appointed government officials. However, limiting the scope of a code of ethics to conflicts of interest alone implies there are no other serious ethical issues that are relevant. What about campaign issues? Should candidates be able to use negative campaign tactics that verge on slander and libel? What if these personal attacks come, not directly from an opposing candidate, but from a third party, as did the "Willie Horton" advertisements which were used effectively against Democratic presidential candidate Michael Dukakis in 1988?

Endnote 26

There are other important ethical issues that fall through the cracks of current ethics codes. The system at times appears to discourage higher-level ethical behavior. For example, a candidate who refuses to accept any large contributions from special interest groups as a matter of principle, may find it difficult to compete with other candidates who feel bound only by the letter of the law. In many states, a judicial candidate is allowed to solicit campaign contributions from the very lawyers who will make arguments before her bench. What implications are present for attorneys who choose not to contribute?

What about the issue of partisanship? Is it an ethical issue if the elected Republicans and Democrats alike are working harder to promote the interests of their respective parties than the interests of the citizenry? Clearly, there are other issues at stake than avoiding financial conflicts of interest. The absence of these and other important issues in most government service codes of ethics weakens the codes themselves and the public's perception of the credibility of the officials who are subject to them.

What are the strengths of government/public service codes? Government codes of ethics serve several important functions. They give the citizenry a public statement of ethical conduct to which public servants can be held. Thus, officials who are found to be in violation of the rules of the code have more difficulty arguing that the issue is just a matter of perception. Also, these codes do at least call public officials to a minimal level of ethical conduct. Compared to governments in other parts of the world, where open corruption, bribery, and even violence seem to be the norm, this would have to be seen as a step in the right direction. From the point of view of the public servants themselves, the codes give them some guidance in regards to what is considered appropriate and inappropriate conduct. In the confusing world of politics, where conflicting values and obligations are almost a daily given, these guidelines are helpful.

What are the weaknesses of government/public service codes? Some have already been noted. Because they are usually written at the basic ethical level, which is based on the minimal requirements of the letter of the law, they invite the abuse of "searching for loopholes." Because the provisions of these codes automatically become laws upon their adoption, it could be argued that they are not technically codes of ethics at all, but simply compilations of laws about ethics. Calling such a collection a "code of ethics" probably leads people to further confuse the legal standard with the very different standard of ethics. Thus, it could be argued that those government "codes of ethics" which are simply listings of laws might be doing as much harm as good.

Second, these public service codes do not typically require of government officials any higher standards than are required of citizens at large. In the earlier section on professional codes of ethics it was noted that it is important for a profession to call its members to a higher ethical plane if it wanted to maintain the respect and admiration of the community. Raiborn and Payne maintain that "a code of ethics should be based at the highest possible moral level in order to have an ultimate standard towards which to strive." A code written at the basic level would not have this effect; in fact, it might act to pull the ethical behavior of some officials down to the letter of the law in order that they might remain competitive with other candidates for office. A possible solution to this problem would be for public officials to organize themselves into an actual profession. If there existed a non-partisan organization named the American Association of Ethical Public Officials, or something similar, the group could write its own code of ethics on a higher level than is allowed by law. Only individuals agreeing to maintain this higher level of ethical behavior would be admitted into fellowship in the group. Compliance with the provisions of the code could be monitored and enforced from within the association. While membership in the organization could not be a requisite for holding elected or appointed office, voters would almost certainly support candidates who represented higher ethical standards than mandated by law.

Endnote 2

Another weakness in government/public service codes of ethics is that, because of the political factors involved in their development, at times the inconsistencies in their rules and principles are indefensible. For example, according to the Florida Code referred to earlier, it is permissible for a legislator to accept a gift, but not a gift intended to influence his or her judgment. But are not all of these gifts intended to influence? Why else would anyone give a legislator a gift? And why would it be ethically acceptable for an appreciative constituent to give a $500 watch to a legislator, but a travesty of justice if an appreciative plaintiff gave a similar gift to a judge? Does it make sense that an attempt to influence the judgment of the person interpreting the law is worse than an attempt to influence the judgment of the person enacting the law?

In a similar vein, consider the laws regarding **"revolving door" lobbying**. Should a government official who leaves office be permitted to immediately return as a paid lobbyist, attempting to influence the decisions of his or her ex-colleagues? Most public service codes of ethics include restrictions on such behavior, often mandating a period of time which must elapse before the individual may begin lobbying where he or she used to work. The Florida code, for example, requires a two-year waiting period applicable to all elected officials, appointed officials, and most bureaucrats. In Washington, D. C., however, an interesting inconsistency exists. Employees in the executive branch of the federal government are required to wait at least one year from the date they leave government service before they may return as a paid lobbyist. This wise law, written by Congress, is designed to prevent the misuse of their influence with those with which they used to work. However, these rules do not apply to legislative members and their staffs, who are permitted to begin lobbying their ex-colleagues for money the day after they leave office. Can a behavior be judged wrong if conducted by a member of the executive branch working in the White House, but judged right if performed by a staff member on Capital Hill? Is there some different ethical issue at stake?

Finally, there are problems in implementing these government/public office codes. The provisions of the codes vary widely and change every year. It can be difficult for public officials to know with certainty whether an action is acceptable or not. In Florida, for example, officials are encouraged to seek advisory opinions from the state Ethics Commission. Adapting and updating a code of ethics regularly helps to keep it viable and relevant, but if the changes are motivated by something other than a sincere desire to improve the ethical climate, they may not always be for the better.

Endnote 27

In the areas of monitoring and enforcement, **whistle-blowing** has not been dealt with adequately in most public service codes. What are an official's obligations when he or she becomes aware of illegal or unethical actions by others within government? When is going public with that information justified? In one of the best-known cases of whistle-blowing by a government employee, A. Ernest Fitzgerald, a former high-level manager in the U.S. Air Force and CEO of Lockheed, told Congress and the press about a systematic practice of unethical bidding conducted by Lockheed and the Air Force in the 1960s. Lockheed would intentionally underbid to ensure that it received a contract, as it did for the C-5A cargo plane, and then bill the Air Force for cost overruns on the projects. Fitzgerald went public with the truth and was fired for his efforts. He fought for 13 years to be reinstated and eventually was, in 1982, at full rank. Nevertheless, his case underscores the lack of protection typically afforded individuals who choose to follow the dictates of conscience. Even codes of ethics that do make provisions for protecting whistle-blowers from retaliation often have loopholes that undercut their effectiveness. Former Morton Thiokol engineer and whistle-blower, Roger Boisjoly, (see Chapter 19) voiced the feelings of many when he said of his decision to inform the public of the shuttle O-ring design flaws, "I stepped into quicksand . . . It was the total destruction of my career."

Endnote 28

FINAL COMMENTS

There often appears to be an inverse relationship between competition and ethical behavior. As competition grows more intense, people become more tempted to bend the rules. The areas of life we have considered in this chapter — corporate America, the professions, and government service — are each fiercely competitive. Too often the path to success is not defined in terms of excellence, but of vanquishing an opponent. It is as if the old cliche had been updated to say, "All's fair in love, war, business, and politics." And yet we know inside that "all isn't fair." We understand that the end of success does not justify all possible means. We realize that fairness and integrity are important, if for no other reason, because that is how we wish to be dealt with by others. And often the most tenacious proponents of this "no holds barred" approach are those who complain the loudest when they perceive that they have been cheated or mistreated.

The appeal for business and professional ethics is a call to make the playing field level and fair. Corporate and professional codes of ethics represent voluntary attempts to do that. However, developing, writing, and distributing a code of ethics is not enough. There must be a solid connection between the rules and principles of the code and the universal ethical principles discussed earlier in this book. Further, the individuals subject to the code must understand that connection. Participating in a conflict of interest is not wrong because the chief executive officer of the company says so, and it is not wrong because a committee of accountants votes that it is; it is wrong because it violates important ethical principles. DeGeorge explains:

"A code should appropriately and helpfully refer to the principles from which the code flows, to principles of justice and fairness . . . An objection might be that this is asking too much of a code. It cannot and should not provide general moral principles because these are assumed to be held by everyone . . . But unless the code is understood in terms of moral principles, it will tend simply to be the expression of rules learned in rote — or even worse, of ideals never to be obtained. If the members of a profession are to internalize the rules of their profession, or if workers are to internalize the rules of their firm, they must understand how the rules are derived, and how they implement moral principles . . . Ideally, each member who is covered by a code should understand its moral principles, as well as the nature of his or her profession or firm. Rather than memorizing a code, each could then derive the same code by thinking clearly and objectively about the moral issues typically faced by those covered by the code."

Endnote 3

FOR FURTHER INQUIRY

REVIEW QUESTIONS

Analyze one or more codes of ethics for effectiveness. These questions may be useful:

1. What types of actions are allowed and disallowed? Are the rules consistent and fair?

2. Are there important ethical issues that have been omitted or avoided?

3. At what ethical level is each code written? Is that level appropriate?

4. What are the strengths of the codes? What changes do you think should be made? Why?

ENDNOTES

1. Catherine Fredman, "Nationwide Examination of Corporate Consciences," *Working Woman* (December 1991), p. 39.

2. Cecily A. Raiborn and Dinah Payne, "Corporate Codes of Conduct: A Collective Conscience and Continuum," in *Taking Sides: Clashing Views on Controversial Issues in Business Ethics and Society*, 2nd edition, Lisa H. Newton and Maureen M. Ford (eds.), The Dushkin Publishing Group, Inc., Guilford, Connecticut, 1992, p. 18, 20, 21, 22, 23, 24

3. Richard T. DeGeorge, *Business Ethics,* 3rd Edition, Macmillan Publishing Company, New York, 1990, p. 381, 385, 387, 389, 382, 390, 391–2,

4. Christopher D. Stone*, Where the Law Ends*, Harper and Row, New York, 1975. (Quoted in William H. Shaw, *Business Ethics,* Wadsworth Publishing Company, Belmont, CA, 1991, p. 172.)

5. William H. Shaw, Ibid, p. 173.

6. Johnson & Johnson Corporate "Credo," Company Annual Report for 1982, p. 5. (Published in Lisa H. Newton and Maureen M. Ford (eds), *Taking Sides: Clashing Views on Controversial Issues in Business and Society,* The Dushkin Publishing Company, Guilford, CT, 1992, p. 29.)

7. Quoted by LaRue T. Hosmer in "Ethical Codes," in Newton and Ford, Ibid, p. 30.

8. Patrick E. Murphy, "Implementing Business Ethics," *Annual Editions: Business Ethics, 1991–2,* John E. Richardson (ed), The Dushkin Publishing Group, Inc., 1991, p. 101, 102.

9. Ethics Policies and Programs in American Business: Report of a Landmark Survey of U. S. Corporations, Ethics Resource Center and Behavioral Research Center, Washington, D. C., 1987, p. 6.

10. Ethics in American Business: A Special Report; Touche Ross and Company, 1988, p. 7.

11. Rick Wartzman, "Nature or Nurture? Study Blames Ethical Lapses on Corporate Goals," *The Wall Street Journal*, (October 9, 1987), p. 21.

12. Shaw, Ibid, p. 174.

13. Jack N. Behrman, *Essays on Ethics in Business and the Professions*, Prentice Hall, Englewood Cliffs, NJ, 1988, p. 156. (Quoted by Raiborn and Payne, Ibid, p. 21.)

14. Shaw, Ibid, p. 175.

15. Kenneth Arrow, "Social Responsibility and Economic Efficiency," Public Policy (21), Summer 1973. (Republished in William Shaw and Vincent Barry, *Moral Issues in Business, 4th Edition*, Wadsworth Publishing Company, Belmont, CA, p. 217.)

16. Alyse Lynn Booth, "Who Are We?," *Public Relations Journal*, July, 1985. (Quoted in Shaw, Ibid, p. 174.)

17. Donald R. Cressy and Charles A. Moore, "Managerial Values and Corporate Codes of Ethics," *California Management Review*, (Summer, 1983), p. 53ff.

18. Milton Snoeyenbos and Donald Jewell, "Morals, Management and Codes," in Milton Snoeyenbos, Robert Ameder and James Humber (eds), *Business Ethics*, Promethus Books, Buffalo, NY, 1983, p. 107. (Quoted in Shaw and Barry, p. 196.)

19. Ethics Resource Center, Ibid, p. 11.

20. Robert E. Sweeney, holder of the Thompson-Hill Chair of Excellence in Accountancy at Memphis State University, in a speech entitled, "Developing an Ethical Climate Within Business" at the University of South Florida, March 9, 1992.

21. Shaw, Ibid, p. 10–11.

22. *The American Heritage Dictionary (2nd College Edition),* Houghton Mifflin Company, Boston, 1985.

23. Shaw, Ibid, p. 11.

24. Annotico, Richard. Quoted by Sarah Glazer in "Policing the Professions," Editorial Research Reports, May 26, 1989, p. 291.

25. Fellmeth, Robert C., Quoted by Sarah Glazer, Ibid, p. 294.

26. Florida Commission on Ethics, Guide to the Sunshine Amendment and Code of Ethics for Public Officers and Employees, 1992.

27. Nielsen, Richard P., "Changing Unethical Organizational Behavior," *Executive*, May 1989, p. 123–130. (Republished in *Annual Editions: Business Ethics,* 1991–92, John E. Richardson (ed), The Dushkin Publishing Group, Inc. 1991, p. 91.)

28. Boisjoly, Roger, in a speech at the University of Tampa, September 23, 1991.

Appendix

Glossary

Index

LETTER FROM THE BIRMINGHAM JAIL
Why We Can't Wait
Martin Luther King Jr.
Harper Collins Publishers, Inc. 1963, 1964

We know through painful experience that freedom is never voluntarily given by the oppressor; it must be demanded by the oppressed. Frankly, I have yet to engage in a direct-action campaign that was "well timed" in the view of those who have not suffered unduly from the disease of segregation. For years now I have heard the word "Wait!" It rings in the ear of every Negro with piercing familiarity. This "Wait" has almost always meant "Never." We must come to see, with one of our distinguished jurists, that "justice too long delayed is justice denied."

We have waited for more than 340 years for our constitutional and God-given rights. The nations of Asia and Africa are moving with jet-like speed toward gaining political independence, but we still creep at horse-and-buggy pace toward gaining a cup of coffee at a lunch counter. Perhaps it is easy for those who have never felt the stinging darts of segregation to say, "Wait." But when you have seen vicious mobs lynch your mothers and fathers at will and drown your sisters and brothers at whim; when you have seen hate-filled policemen curse, kick, and even kill your black brothers and sisters; when you see the vast majority of your twenty million Negro brothers smothering in an airtight cage of poverty in the midst of an affluent society; when you suddenly find your tongue twisted and your speech stammering as you seek to explain to your six-year-old daughter why she can't go to the public amusement park that has just been advertised on television, and see tears welling up in her eyes when she is told that Funtown is closed to colored children, and see ominous clouds of inferiority beginning to form in her little mental sky, and see her beginning to distort her personality by developing an unconscious bitterness toward white people; when you have to concoct an answer for a five-year-old son who is asking, "Daddy, why do white people treat colored people so mean?"; when you take a cross-country drive and find it necessary to sleep night after night in the uncomfortable corners of your automobile because no motel will accept you; when you are humiliated day in and day out by nagging signs reading "white" and "colored"; when your first name becomes "nigger," your middle name becomes "boy" (however old you are) and your last name becomes "John," and your wife and mother are never given the respected title "Mrs."; when you are harried by day and haunted by night by the fact that you are a Negro, living constantly at tiptoe stance, never quite knowing what to expect next, and are plagued with inner fears and outer resentments; when you are forever fighting a degenerating sense of "nobodiness" — then you will understand why we find it difficult to wait. There comes a time when the cup of endurance runs over, and men are no longer willing to be plunged into the abyss of despair. I hope, sirs, you can understand our legitimate and unavoidable impatience.

You express a great deal of anxiety over our willingness to break laws. This is certainly a legitimate concern. Because we so diligently urge people to obey the Supreme Court's decision of 1954 outlawing segregation in the public schools, at first glance it may seem rather paradoxical for us consciously to break laws. One may well ask: "How can you advocate breaking some laws and obeying others?" The answer lies in the fact that there are two types of laws: just and unjust. I would be the first to advocate obeying just laws. One has not only a legal but a moral responsibility to obey just laws. Conversely, one has a moral responsibility to disobey unjust laws. I would agree with St. Augustine that "an unjust law is no law at all."

Now, what is the difference between the two? How does one determine whether a law is just or unjust? A just law is a man-made code that squares with the moral law or the law of God. An unjust law is a code that is out of harmony with the moral law. To put it in the terms of St. Thomas Aquinas: An unjust law is a human law that is not rooted in eternal law and natural law. Any law that uplifts human personality is just. Any law that degrades human personality is unjust. All segregation statutes are unjust because segregation distorts the soul and damages the personality. It gives the segregator a false sense of superiority and the segregated a false sense of inferiority. Segregation, to use the terminology of the Jewish philosopher Martin Buber, substitutes an "I-it" relationship for an "I-thou" relationship and ends up relegating persons to the status of things. Hence segregation is not only politically, economically, and sociologically unsound, it is morally wrong and sinful. Paul Tillich has said that sin is separation. Is not segregation an existential expression of man's tragic separation, his awful estrangement, his terrible sinfulness? Thus it is that I can urge men to obey the 1954 decision of the Supreme Court, for it is morally right; and I can urge them to disobey segregation ordinances, for they are morally wrong.

Let us consider a more concrete example of just and unjust laws. An unjust law is a code that a numerical or power majority group compels a minority group to obey but does not make binding on itself. This is difference made legal. By the same token, a just law is a code that a majority compels a minority to follow and that it is willing to follow itself. This is sameness made legal.

Let me give another explanation. A law is unjust if it is inflicted on a minority that, as a result of being denied the right to vote, had no part in enacting or devising the law. Who can say that the legislature of Alabama which set up that state's segregation laws was democratically elected? Throughout Alabama all sorts of devious methods are used to prevent Negroes from becoming registered voters, and there are some counties in which, even though Negroes constitute a majority of the population, not a single Negro is registered. Can any law enacted under such circumstances be considered democratically structured?

Sometimes a law is just on its face and unjust in its application. For instance, I have been arrested on a charge of parading without a permit. Now, there is nothing wrong in having an ordinance which requires a permit for a parade. But such an ordinance becomes unjust when it is used to maintain segregation and to deny citizens the First-Amendment privilege of peaceful assembly and protest.

I hope you are able to see the distinction I am trying to point out. In no sense do I advocate evading or defying the law, as would the rabid segregationist. That would lead to anarchy. One who breaks an unjust law must do so openly, lovingly, and with a willingness to accept the penalty. I submit that an individual who breaks a law that conscience tells him is unjust, and who willingly accepts the penalty of imprisonment in order to arouse the conscience of the community over its injustice, is in reality expressing the highest respect for law.

Of course, there is nothing new about this kind of civil disobedience. It was evidenced sublimely in the refusal of Shadrach, Meshach and Abednego to obey the laws of Nebuchadnezzar, on the ground that a higher moral law was at stake. It was practiced superbly by the early Christians, who were willing to face hungry lions and the excruciating pain of chopping blocks rather than submit to certain unjust laws of the Roman Empire. To a degree, academic freedom is a reality today because Socrates practiced civil disobedience. In our own nation, the Boston Tea Party represented a massive act of civil disobedience.

We should never forget that everything Adolf Hitler did in Germany was "legal" and everything the Hungarian freedom fighters did in Hungary was "illegal." It was "illegal" to aid and comfort a Jew in Hitler's Germany. Even so, I am sure that, had I lived in Germany at the time, I would have aided and comforted my Jewish brothers. If today I lived in a Communist country where certain principles dear to the Christian faith are suppressed, I would openly advocate disobeying that country's anti-religious laws.

I must make two honest confessions to you, my Christian and Jewish brothers. First, I must confess that over the past few years I have been gravely disappointed with the white moderate. I have almost reached the regrettable conclusion that the Negro's great stumbling block in his stride toward freedom is not the White Citizen's Counciler or the Ku Klux Klanner, but the white moderate, who is more devoted to "order" than to justice; who prefers a negative peace which is the absence of tension to a positive peace which is the presence of justice; who constantly says, "I agree with you in the goal you seek, but I cannot agree with your methods of direct action"; who paternalistically believes he can set the timetable for another man's freedom; who lives by a mythical concept of time and who constantly advises the Negro to wait for a "more convenient season." Shallow understanding from people of good will is more frustrating than absolute misunderstanding from people of ill will. Lukewarm acceptance is much more bewildering than outright rejection.

I had hoped that the white moderate would understand that law and order exist for the purpose of establishing justice and that when they fail in this purpose they become the dangerously structured dams that block the flow of social progress. I had hoped that the white moderate would understand that the present tension in the South is a necessary phase of the transition from an obnoxious negative peace, in which the Negro passively accepted his unjust plight, to a substantive and positive peace, in which all men will respect the dignity and worth of human personality. Actually, we who engage in nonviolent direct action are not the creators of tension. We merely bring to the surface the hidden tension that is already alive. We bring it out in the open, where it can be seen and dealt with. Such as a boil that can never be cured so long as it is covered up but must be opened with all its ugliness to the natural medicines of air and light, injustice must be exposed, with all the tension its exposure creates, to the light of human conscience and the air of national opinion, before it can be cured.

THE ALLEGORY OF THE CAVE
(excerpted from Plato's *"Republic"*)

"Now, Glaucon," I said, "Let me show in a figure how far our nature is enlightened. Behold, human beings living in an underground cave, which has a mouth open toward the light! Here they have been from their childhood, and are chained so that they can only see before them. Above and behind them a fire is blazing, and between the fire and these prisoners there is a raised way. You will see, if you look, a low wall like the screen which marionette players have in front of them, over which they throw their puppets."

"I see."

"And do you see men passing along the wall carrying all sorts of vessels and statues and figures of animals made of various materials, which appear over the wall? Some of them are talking, others silent."

"You have shown me a strange image, Socrates and they are strange prisoners."

"Like ourselves," I replied, "they see only their own shadows, or the shadows of one another, which the fire throws on the opposite wall of the cave."

"True," he said. "How could they see anything but shadows if they were never allowed to move their heads?"

"And of the objects which are being carried, in like manner they would see only the shadows. If they were able to converse with one another, would they not suppose that they were naming what was actually before them?"

"Very true."

"Suppose further that the prison had an echo which came from the other side. Would they not be sure to fancy, when one of the passers-by spoke, that the voice which they heard came from a passing shadow? To them the Truth would be literally nothing but the shadows of the images."

"That is certain."

"Look again! You see what will naturally follow if the prisoners are set free and so come to realize their error. At first when one of them is liberated and suddenly compelled to turn his neck round and look toward the light, he will suffer sharp pains. The glare will distress him. He will be unable to see the realities of which, in his former state, he saw only the shadows. Then conceive someone as saying to him that the shadows and images which he saw before were an illusion. But that now, when his is approaching nearer to Being and his eye is turned toward more real existence, he has a clearer vision. Will he not fancy that the shadows which he formerly saw are truer than the objects which are now shown to him?"

"Far truer, Socrates," he replied.

"He will be required to grow accustomed to the sight of the upper world. At first he will see the the shadows best. Last of all he will be able to see the sun, in its own proper place, and not mere reflections of it. He will then proceed to argue that this is what gives the seasons and in a certain way causes all things which he and his fellows have been accustomed to behold. When he remembers his old habitation and the wisdom of the cave and of this fellow-prisoners, do you not suppose that he will pity them?"

"He most certainly will."

"If the inhabitants of the cave have been in the habit of conferring honors among themselves, he will no longer care for such honors or envy the possessors of them. Will he not endure anything rather than think as they do and live after their manner? If, however, such a one were suddenly to come out of the sun and be placed again in his old situation, he would be certain to have his eyes full of darkness. It would be very bad for him if there were a contest and he had to compete in measuring the shadows with the prisoners who had never moved out of the cave.In such an instance, the men of the cave would say of him that up he went and down he came without his eyes. They will maintain that it is better not even to think of ascending. Hence, if anyone tried to loose another from the cave and lead him up to the light, let them only catch the offender, and they would put him to death."

"No question, Socrates."

"This entire allegory you may now append, dear Glaucon, to the previous argument. The prison-house is the world of sight. The light of the fire is the sun. And the journey upward is the ascent of the soul into the intellectual world. Whether true or false, my opinion is that in the world of knowledge the Idea of Good appears last of all. It is the power upon which he would act rationally either in public or private life must fix his eyes. Moreover, you must not wonder that those who attain to this beatific vision are unwilling to descend to human affairs. Their souls are ever hastening into the upper world where they desire to dwell."

"Yes, this would be natural."

"And is there anything surprising, if one who passes from Divine contemplations to the evil state of man should be guilty of misbehaving? The bewilderments of the eyes arise from two causes — either coming out of the light, or going into the light. They are true of the mind's eye quite as much as of the bodily eye. He who remembers this when he sees anyone with perplexed and weak vision will not be too ready to laugh."

"Very true."

"Therefore, must there not be an art which will effect the conversion from becoming to Being in the easiest and quickest manner?"

"Indeed there must, Socrates."

"By this conversion wisdom is rendered useful and profitable, or, on the other hand, hurtful and useless. Did you never observe the narrow intelligence flashing from the keen eye of a clever rogue? How eager he is. How clearly his paltry soul sees the clever way to his end! He is the reverse of the blind, but his keen eyesight is forced into the service of evil. And he is mischievous in proportion to his cleverness. But what if there had been a circumcision of such natures in the days of their youth? What if they had been severed then from their sensual pleasure? Then the very same faculty in them which is the cause of their evil would now see the Truth. This they would see as keenly as that to which their eyes are now turned."

"Very true," he replied.

"Then, " I said, "the business of us who are the founders of the state will be to compel the best minds to attain that knowledge which we have shown to be the greatest. They must continue to ascend until they arrive at the Good. When they have ascended and seen enough, however, we must now allow them to do as they now do. I mean that they must not be allowed to remain in the upper world, but must descend again among the prisoners in the cave and partake of their labors and honors, whether these are worth having or not."

"But is not this unjust? Ought we to give our best minds a worse life, when they might have a better?"

Taken from *PLATO'S COMPLETE WORKS* (abridged) by Henry Drake, Littlefield, Adams & Co. Paterson, New Jersey, 1959.

THE PROBLEM OF ETHICS
Excerpted from
Vital Speeches of the Day
Charles W. Colson
Harvard University
April 4, 1991

I THINK HARVARD well deserves the reputation that it enjoys of being a very liberal university, liberal in the best sense of that word because you would have as a lecturer in the university today someone who is an ex-convict. But that maybe is not so inappropriate after all, as you look at what is happening on Wall Street in the business community. Perhaps in the business courses here at the business school they should take a little bit of attention to what is happening in prisons. I just spent three hours last week with one of your distinguished alumni, who is headed off for four years of free room and board, courtesy of the United States Government, as I did. I must also say that Harvard deserves the reputation for being a liberal university in the best sense of the word for inviting me to speak, because for the last three or four years I have written articles that here in Harvard could be considered quite impertinent, in which I have described my views at least on why it is impossible to teach ethics at Harvard. I may touch on that briefly today and I hope you will all accept it in good spirit, and I will be prepared for your questions.

I'm no longer in politics. I've done my time, literally and figuratively, but it's awfully hard not to watch what is happening in the political scene with a certain sense of dismay when we see the Keating 5, as you've read about, 5 United States Senators tried in effect by their own tribunal. Just before that another Senator, who happens to be a good friend of mine, Dave Durenberger, who was censured by the Senate. I spent some time recently with Mayor Barry, the former mayor of the District of Columbia, who was of course arrested for drug use. You look at South Carolina and Arizona and you see scams going on in the legislatures that have been now exposed by Federal prosecutors and I saw a press release in which the Department of Justice boasted last year that they had prosecuted and convicted 1,150 public officials, the highest number in the history of the republic. They were boasting about it and I read it with a certain sadness because it seems that that kind of corruption has become epidemic in American politics. We see Congressmen one after another, Coehlo, Wright, Frank, Lukens, both sides of the aisle, either being censured or forced out of office. We see, probably the most cynical of all, was the HUD scandal, where people were ripping off money from the public treasury that was designed to help the poor. And then we've seen more spy scandals in the past 5 years than in all previous 195 years of American history combined — people selling their national honor for sexual favors or for money. Business is not immune. The savings and loan scandals are bad enough on the face of them, but the fact that they're so wide spread, almost a looter's mentality. Mr. Milken, Mr. Boesky, who spoke at UCLA Business School five years ago and said, "Greed is a good thing," and ended up spending 3 years in a Federal prison. Just last week one of the major pharmaceutical firms fined $10-million for covering up, acting, violating criminal statutes. It affects athletics — if you picked up a newspaper this week, you saw that Sugar Ray Leonard was just admitted for drug use. He's been a role model for lots of kids on the street. Pete Rose spent time in prison for gambling. Academia. I don't know how many of you saw Stanford University President Kennedy charged with spending $7,000 to buy a pair of sheets — they must be awfully nice bedsheets, bedlinens — and charging it to the government improperly on government contracts. A Nobel Prize winner one day was exposed for presenting a fraudulent paper and the very next day a professor at Georgetown University was charged with filing a fraudulent application for a grant from the Federal Government, from the National Institutes of Health — this all in the matter of the past two weeks. And probably saddest of all, at least from my perspective, religious leaders. Jim Bakker, whom I've also visited in prison, Jimmy Swaggart prosecuted for violating what should be the most sacred trust of all, to speak for God and to minister to people in their spiritual needs.

Well, the first question that comes to mind is whether this is simply an example of people — rotten apples, or maybe better prosecution, or maybe you can dismiss this by simply saying, well, this is simply the nature of humanity. I think it was Bishop Fulton Sheen in quoting G.K. Chesterton or paraphrasing G.K. Chesterton, who once said that the doctrine of original sin is the only philosophy empirically validated by 3,500 years of human history. And so maybe you sort of dismiss this and say well, this is just the way people are. Or is there something of a pattern here is the question that I would pose to you today.

Time magazine, doing a cover story on ethics, recently said what's wrong: Hypocrisy, betrayal and greed unsettle a nation's soul. *The Washington Post* said that the problem has reached the point where common decency can no longer be described as common. And *The New Republic* magazine said there is a destructive sense that nothing is true and everything is permitted. Now I would submit to you that when *The Washington Post* and *The New Republic* magazine and *Time* magazine, which have never been known as bastions of conservative, biblical morality, begin to talk about some sort of ethical malaise, that a line has been crossed and that this isn't simply isolated instances, but rather there is a pattern emerging in American life. No institution has been more sensitive to that than Harvard. President Bok has given some quite extraordinary

speeches talking about, decrying the loss of ethics in the American business community, and business school students, I think maybe some of you have seen the recent polls, business school students across America by 2 to 1 believe that businesses are generally unethical. It's a very fragile consensus that holds together trust in our institutions, and when 2 to 1 business school students believe there aren't any unethical operations, you begin to have to wonder if something isn't affecting us a lot more broadly than simply isolated instances of misbehavior that have been exposed. In my view I believe we are experiencing in our country today what I choose to call crisis of character, a loss of what traditionally through Western civilization had been considered those inner restraints and inner virtues that prevent us from pandering to our own darker instincts. If you look back through the history of Harvard, you'll see that President Elliott was as concerned about the development of character as he was about education, and classically education. Plato once said if you asked why we should educate someone, we educate them so that they become a good person because good persons behave nobly. And so I come to a place today where we should be deeply concerned about the loss of what Edmund Burke might have called the traditional values of republican citizenship — words that will almost sound quaint when uttered in these surroundings, words such as valor, honor, duty, responsibility, compassion, civility — words which have almost fallen into disuse.

Well, why has this happened? I'm sure many of you studied philosophy in your undergraduate courses and if so, you are well aware that through 23 centuries of Western civilization, we were guided by a consensus, a shared set of assumptions that there was a transcendent value system, not always the Judeo-Christian value system, though I think the Judeo-Christian values were, as Christopher Dawson, the eminent historian, wrote, "sort of the heart and soul of Western civilization." But it goes back to the Greeks. It goes back to Plato saying that if there were no God, there could be no concord and justice and harmony in a society. And there is a strain all through the 23 centuries of the civilization, the history of the West, a strain of belief in a transcendent value system, whether it was the unknown god of the Greeks, whether it was the Christ of the Scriptures revealed to the Christian, whether it was the Yahweh of the Old Testament revealed to the Jews or whether it was as enlightenment thinkers chose to call it, natural law, which I believe to be not inconsistent with Judeo-Christian revelation. Nonetheless that guided our conduct for 23 centuries until a great cultural revolution began in America. A great cultural revolution took place in our country in the 1960s. Some think it goes back further. When I met a historian, Paul Johnson, who happens to be one of my favorites, Paul Johnson wrote the history of Christianity, the history of the Jews, he wrote a classic book called *Modern Times*. If you're not too busy with your business school studies, it's a wonderful history of the 20th century. Paul Johnson said all of this began in 1919 when Einstein's discovery of relativity in the field of physical sciences was confused with the notion of relativism in the field of ideas, and that gradually through the '20s and '30s people began to challenge what had been fixed assumptions by which people lived, a set of fixed and shared common values. In the '60s it exploded. If any of you here were on campuses in the '60s, you will well remember that the writings of Camus and Sartre invaded American campuses and basically what they said was exactly what Camus said when he came to America and spoke at Columbia University in 1947 and to the student body assembled said, "There is nothing." The idea was introduced that there is no God, God is dead, it was on the cover of *Time* magazine. There is no transcendent value; life is utterly meaningless and the only way that we can derive meaning out of life is if we overcome the nothingness of life with heroic individualism and the goal of life is to overcome that nothingness and to find personal peace and meaning through your own autonomous efforts. And most of the people of my generation dismissed what was happening on the campuses as a passing fad, protest, in the '60s. It was *not*. The only people who behaved logically in the '60s were the flower

children. They did exactly what they were taught. If there was no other object in life than to overcome the nothingness, then go out and sniff coke or smoke pot and make love and enjoy personal peace.

Then America came through the great convulsion of Watergate and Vietnam, a dark era, and into the '70s, and we thought we shook off those protest movements of the '60s. We did not, we simply embraced them into the mainstream of American culture. That's what gave rise to the "me" decade. That's why if you look at the bestsellers of the '70s, it's very revealing. The bestselling books of the '70s were *Winning Through Intimidation, Look Out For Number One, I'm Okay, You're Okay*, which is saying, "Don't worry about we." And we emerged into a decade that Tom Wolfe, the social critic, called "the decade of Me." And very logically that graduated into the '80s into what some have cynically called "the golden age of greed." There's a professor at the University of California by the name of Robert Bellah, who wrote a book, a take-off on the title from Tocqueville's classic work on American life entitled, *Habits of the Heart,* and Robert Bellah took a couple hundred of average middle-class Americans and tried to examine really what their values were. He came to the conclusion that the reigning ethos in American life in the '80s was what he called "otological individualism," radical individualism — the idea that the individual is supreme and autonomous, lives for himself or herself. And he found that Americans had two overriding goals: vivid personal feelings and personal success. He tried to find out what people expected from the institutions of society. From business they expected personal advancement. Okay. That's fair enough. From marriage personal development. No wonder marriages are in trouble. And from church personal fulfillment! But the personal became the dominant consideration. Now I would simply say to you today and I'll try to be as brief with this as I possibly can, I would simply say to you that this self-obsession destroys character, it *has* to! All those quaint-sounding virtues I talked about that historically have been considered the elements of character are no match for a society in which the exaltation and gratification of self becomes the overriding goal of life. *Rolling Stone* magazine did a survey of the baby boom generation of which many of you in this room are baby boomers, emerging leaders. Forty percent said there was no cause for which they would fight for their country. If there's nothing worth dying for, there's nothing worth living for. Literally the social contract unravels when that happens and there can be no ethics. How can you have ethical behavior? The crisis of character is totally understandable when there are no absolute values. The word "Ethics" derives from the Greek word "ethos," and "ethos'" literally meant "a cave," a hiding place. It was the one place you could go and find security. There could be rest, there could be something there that you could depend upon, it was unmovable. "Morals" derives from the word "mores," which is "always changing." "Ethics" or "ethos" is the normative, that is what ought to be. "Morals" is what is, and unfortunately in American life today we are totally guided by moral determinations. So we're not even looking at ethical standards. Ethical standards don't change. It's the cave, it's the ethos, it's the environment in which we live. Morals change all the time, and so with shifting morals, if 90% of the people say that it's perfectly all right to do this, well, then, that must be perfectly all right to do it because 90% of the people say it. It's a very democratic notion. Ethics is not, *cannot be*, democratic. Ethics by its very definition is authoritarian, and that's a very nasty word to utter on any campus in America, particularly at Harvard where Arthur Schlesinger has written a magnificently argued assault on the perils of absolutism, and I'll refer to that in just a moment.

In a relativistic environment ethics deteriorates to nothing more than utilitarian or pragmatic considerations, and if you're really honest with yourselves and you look at the ethical questions that you're asked to wrestle with in your courses here at Harvard, you will see that what you are being taught is how you can arrive at certain conclusions yourself and make certain judgments yourself that ultimately are going to be good for the business, and that's fine. You should do that. That's a prudential decision that has to be made and that's being a responsible business leader. It just isn't ethics and shouldn't be confused with ethics. Ethics is the what *ought* to be, not what is or even is prudential. There was a brilliant professor at Duke, Stanley Hauerwas, who writes that moral life cannot be found by each person pursuing his or her options. In relativism all you have then are a set of options. The only way moral life can be produced is by the formation of virtuous people by tradition-formed communities, and that was the accepted wisdom of 23 centuries of Western Civilization.

GLOSSARY

A

abolitionist — a person who supported the legal abolishment of slavery; today, one who seeks abolishment of capital punishment.

abortion — permanently halting the development of a fetus or baby in the womb of its mother, usually by expulsion from the womb.

accountability — the moral relationship whereby a person reports deeds and attitudes, usually to another person or authority; e.g., a student has accountability for class performance to an instructor; a taxpayer has accountability for paying taxes to the Internal Revenue Service; a family member has accountability for actions and attitudes to that family. See Chapter 4.

act utilitarianism — the moral view that any act should be assessed based upon the greatest happiness for the greatest number produced in its own actual context.

affirmative action — in American law, the notion of taking assertive action to redress past discrimination patterns in the workplace by providing opportunities for the class discriminated against.

air pollution — unnatural degradation of the air and its atmospheric gases.

ambiguity – vagueness; see fallacies, Chapter 3.

amphiboly – see fallacies, Chapter 3.

animal well-being — the notion that animals feel pain and pleasure, and the quality care and treatment of them constitutes a moral act.

a posteriori reasoning — from effect to cause; making decisions based on the gathering of knowledge gained from experience.

applied ethics — actual use of moral standards of behavior in making decisions about human problems.

approach to moral reasoning — the manner in which one chooses to resolve human problems by applying a body of moral standards; see **exemplar**.

a priori reasoning — from cause to effect; making determinations based on what is understood to be universally true.

argument to the people — see fallacies, Chapter 3.

autonomy — when applied to persons, the state of being capable of living one's life according to one's own life plan. When applied to actions, those actions chosen based on one's own life plan. As a moral principle, autonomy holds that actions tend to be morally right insofar as they respect the freedom of persons to make their own choices according to their own life plans.

B

bad — not good, nor as it should be; not having positive value, contradictory to one's moral philosophy; usually referring to acts but also to persons and things.

beneficence — quality of kindness and honorable treatment of others including generosity, favor and liberality; the quality of "doing good" and often including the results of so doing.

bestiality — human sexual relations with non-human species.

bioethics — the discipline of assessing the rightness or wrongness of acts taken within the life sciences.

bisexual — referring to a person who has sexual relations with persons of both sexes.

bribe — anything presented to induce illegal activity or favorable treatment that would not otherwise have been produced.

business ethics — standards related to what is good and bad including moral duty and obligation, values and beliefs used in critical thinking about behavior in the marketplace. (In 1959 the Ford Foundation and Carnegie Corporation sponsored a study, "The Education of American Businessmen," that urged training for managers to develop "a personal philosophy or ethical foundation.") It includes such issues as whether to pay bribes, take outside compensation, insider trading and blowing the whistle on improper company behavior.

C

capitalism — an economic system where all property (including factories and other "means of production") is privately owned and operated for individual profit as determined by a free market.

capital punishment — state-sanctioned taking of life to punish a person for being convicted of a capital crime, usually murder or treason.

cardinal virtues — from Christian tradition, those qualities of life to be revered including wisdom or prudence, justice, temperance and fortitude.

care — as a noun in ethical context, it is the quality of giving acts of value to a person or situation; help, improvement of condition; see Gilligan, Chapter 2.

carnal knowledge — a term referring to sexual experience with another person, usually including intercourse.

categorical imperative — a concept put forth by Immanuel Kant (1724–1803) declaring that a person has a moral obligation to perform "duty for duty's sake," as a universally applicable obligation. Therefore, one does not kill or does not lie or steal, for example, out of respect for a moral duty.

censorship — the act of prohibiting certain statements, ideas or depictions from general usage as a result of the value judgment of a few.

character — in human personality, the unconscious doing of right, consistently making honorable decisions according to high moral standards.

cheating — the act of deceiving by any maneuver or trick to gain temporary or permanent advantage over others.

CFC (chloro-fluoro-carbon) — an inert gas developed by man which has the capacity to destroy ozone.

Christianity — one of the world's primary religions based on the life and teachings of Jesus Christ, organized in Protestant and Catholic organizations and emphasizing one true God, the Holy Bible as its sacred scriptures for faith and practice, prayer and acts of love and kindness as evidenced by Christ.

civil disobedience — the conscious breaking by deed of an enactment, statute or ordinance adopted by a government; e.g., Rosa Parks refused to sit in the "Negro section" reserved by local ordinance at the back of a bus in Alabama. See Martin Luther King's "Letter from the Birmingham Jail."

civil rights — fundamental benefits, freedoms and responsibilities afforded to an individual or group by a state.

clarity — in journalism, the fundamental standard for writing; that statements made are expressed plainly for the understanding of the reader.

classical republicanism — a political philosophy having its roots in Aristotle and Thomas Aquinas that holds the human has an essential nature that includes rationality, sociability, and membership in the animal kingdom. This essential nature permits distinction between human needs and mere human wants. A just distribution of resources is one that uses resources to meet needs rather than desires.

codes of ethics — a collection of statements of moral principles for guiding behavior of persons sharing a common interest.

communism — the economic system in which the means for producing and distributing goods is owned and controlled by the state; a prominent communist thinker was Karl Marx.

communitarianism — the view of contemporary philosophers who emphasize the importance of the human as a social being who is part of a community rather than primarily an isolated individual. Communitarians generally favor the Classical Republican theory of justice and communal decisions about the use of resources rather than leaving such choices up to the individual.

competence — fitness, the ability to act according to a set of standards.

computer ethics — an embryonic discipline in which moral standards are applied to the use of computers; involving all ethical questions of the rightness or wrongness of "using," "borrowing," or "stealing" software and shareware, as well as the use of computers for moral or immoral purposes — such as the collection of information on persons by big business or government to impose certain behavior on those persons; see also Chapter 20.

conclusion — statement that can be made as a result of reasoning the effects of propositions and variables and inferences upon each other; see Chapter 3.

confidentiality — the notion that private information that one possesses about another ought not to be disclosed without that person's approval.

conflict of interest — the predicament arising when a person confronts two actions that cannot be ethically reconciled; competing loyalties and concerns with others, self-dealing, outside compensation; divided loyalties among, for example, public and-or professional duties and private and-or personal affairs.

conscience — an internal awareness of right and wrong, otherwise explained by various disciplines such as religion and philosophy; the conscience usually communicates a desire to do right.

consent — expressed or implied agreement with or support for a certain course of action.

consequentialism — an approach to moral reasoning that emphasizes conduct determined by assessing the moral quality of the *results* likely to follow from various possible courses of actions.

contractarianism — an approach to moral reasoning that emphasizes all ethical obligation being based exclusively on contracts and promises.

copyright — a right vested by law to an individual or corporation prohibiting the copying of one's "work" product by others without permission of the copyright-holder; thus enforceable in a court of law.

corporate culture — the atmosphere or environment of an entity as to the values and beliefs that guide its decision-making.

corporate social audit — an accounting of a corporation's assets testing whether they are used in a responsible manner for the benefit of society.

crime — behavior that a society has judged to be intolerable against which it has devised codified sanction.

critical thinking — the informed, reasoned and responsible human thought about human problems.

D

death — the cessation of human, physical life; as medically determined, it may be marked by the cessation of the heart or brain or both and the loss of certain other bodily functions.

decision-maker — a person who makes choices when confronted by sets of circumstances and conflicting or competing interests; **ethical decision-makers** are those who have applied moral values (a philosophical life-view) to reach a conclusion as to the most beneficent way of solving human problems.

deductive reasoning — drawing a specific conclusion from at least two premises that are true.

defeasibility — the potential for overriding one moral prescription when other commanding considerations intersect with that philosophy.

deforestation — the process by which a forest is systematically cut and not allowed to continue its normal growth, thus removing the natural effects of the presence of trees including their absorption of carbon dioxide and their emission of oxygen.

deontology — an approach to moral reasoning in which acts are based on a self-determined, innate sense of moral "duty" with no regard for consequences. Someone who adopts the Divine Command theory, for example, imports the Will of God as "the inner sense of duty." But a deontologist may choose any set of values as the basis for this innate comprehension of duty.

difference principle — the principle of John Rawls that holds that differences in the amount of primary social goods are justified provided the differences improve the position of the worst off compared to what they would have if there were more equality.

disclosure — a revealing; in ethical terms, especially the making public of information about oneself that "puts all the cards on the table" before the fact of a decision; usually referring to real or perceived conflicts of interest and mainly involving knowledge about personal financial dealings affecting the pending decision.

discrimination — an act or pattern of acts that *irrationally* deny opportunities or benefits to persons solely based, for example, on their race, religion or sex; denying a person due rights and opportunities without considering the person's abilities or character.

disinterest — that quality of being or attitude of self-detachment to a situation, without bias; sometimes termed **disinterestedness;** to act with disinterest is to assist without seeking gain for oneself; e.g., the Good Samaritan acted with disinterest.

distributive justice — a system which fairly and appropriately distributes everything from economic goods and services to public honors and awards.

Divine Command — a moral philosophy in which good acts are based on conforming to an understanding of the Will of God, as may be determined from prayer and Holy Scriptures (Bible, Talmud, Koran, et al) and as declared by those speaking for God — ministers, priests, prophets, sages, clerics, mullahs, rabbis; see Kant, Aquinas, Butler, Hobbes et al.

'doing the right thing' — the phrase used in decision-making whereby the intent is to pursue both a decision and an outcome that is moral, ethical and beneficent; most agree it is easier said than done.

due process — in business, those specific and systematic procedures allowed workers for appealing disciplinary and discharge action by employers; in law, those protections of people against arbitrary and excessively harsh punishments and require fair and public trials for those accused of crimes.

duty — any action required by one's position or by moral or legal consideration; often contrasted with personal inclination or pleasure.

E

Earth — the planet inhabited by humanity as we know it, the fifth largest mass in the solar system revolving around the sun that is visible from this mass.

economic justice — the notion that equality of human condition can be attained by the fair distribution of goods and wealth.

egalitarianism — the patterned theory of distribution in which the goal is to arrange resources so that people have equal amounts. Some principles may be relatively egalitarian, such as Rawls's difference principle, which justifies inequalities provided they serve to benefit the worst off, while others may be more radically egalitarian, rejecting even inequalities that benefit the worst off.

egoism — a moral philosophy in which persons are required always to act in their own perceived self-interest, usually in the long-term, even at the expense of the well-being of others.

either-or — see fallacies, Chapter 3.

empirical, empiricism — referring to acts that gather information to verify statements.

employment — performing work for another for compensation.

entitlement theory — the theory of distributive justice seen in John Locke and characterized by Robert Nozick by three premises: (1) All people are entitled to that which they acquire justly. (2) All people are entitled to that which is justly transferred to them from someone else who justly acquired that which was transferred. (3) No person is entitled to anything except by (repeated) applications of 1 and 2.

environmental ethics — theory and practice about appropriate concern for, values in, and duties to the natural world.

equality — a condition in which there is a perceivable identity of value, status, quantity or function between persons or things.

equivocation — not deciding; also see fallacies, Chapter 3.

ethical decision-making — see **decision-makers**

ethical level — a way of assessing the practicality and effect upon human behavior of codes of ethics as applied to persons covered by such codes.

ethics — a discipline related to what is good and bad including moral duty and obligation, values and beliefs used in critical thinking about human problems.

ethics construct — any method of approaching human problems that applies ethical standards to reach conclusions.

eudaimonia — a Greek word for which no single English equivalent exists; a state of satisfaction or fulfillment or happiness as to one's condition in life; life-goal espoused by early philosophers; see Socrates, Plato, Aristotle.

euthanasia — from Greek "good death," whereby persons — whose lives seem to be irreversibly ending without continued use of extraordinary means of life support — choose immediate death or authorize death in anticipation of such an eventuality; see Chapter 8; see also **right to die**.

exemplar — an ideal model or pattern; any of several philosophical life-views and their approaches to moral reasoning to solve human problems; e.g., egoism, Divine Command, utilitarianism, et al; see Chapter 3.

expedience — acting on the basis of what is temporarily useful or resolving, not necessarily on the basis of what is right or wrong; classically seen in the decision of Pontius Pilate to let a crowd decide what to do with the thief Barabbas and Jesus Christ.

F

fallacies — from Latin: to deceive; statements made contrary to logic; formal fallacies are due to the *form* of the argument or statement; informal fallacies are due to the *wording* of the statement or argument.

false appeal to authority — see fallacies, Chapter 3.

faulty causation — see fallacies, Chapter 3.

fetus — the developing human being in the mother's womb, used here to include all the stages of development such as zygote, conceptus and embryo.

fidelity — loyalty, faithfulness, trustworthiness, especially to one's own moral standards.

fiduciary obligation — a duty that professionals have toward their clients to make each decision for the client's best interests and welfare, not the professional's own.

First Amendment — the first amendment to the U.S. Constitution declaring: "Congress shall make no law respecting an establishment of religion, or prohibiting the free exercise thereof; or abridging the freedom of speech, or of the press; or the right of the people peaceably to assemble; and to petition the Government for a redress of grievances."

first-strike theory — the notion, in defense of a nation, that the most effective means of protecting a nation against war is to be first to launch an attack against potential aggressors.

flack — a person working in the public relations field whose work seems devoid of ethical and professional norms.

free will — a concept in philosophy and law whereby an individual has self-inherent authority and moral agency to choose without coercion.

G

gay — homosexual

gene — a unit in a chromosome whereby hereditary traits are passed from one generation to the next.

general moral principle — issuing from a moral philosophy, it is a statement of what should always be done in a certain situation; e.g., the Golden Rule.

genetic defects — abnormalities in the nature or structure of genes.

genetic engineering — changing the makeup of a gene, presumably to improve or enhance the mental or physical health of the being in which it resides.

genetic fallacy — see fallacies, Chapter 3.

gifts — anything given freely with no intent to induce behavior, usually in connection with favorable treatment.

global warming — a phenomenon on the Earth in which atmospheric temperatures are rising.

Golden Rule — attributed to Jesus Christ, the saying: "Do unto others as you would have them do unto you."

good — not bad; not evil; positive, helpful to oneself and-or to others; valuable, honorable, benevolent, just; expressed in personal or societal situations — usually referring to acts but also to people and things.

Good Samaritan — character in a parable told by Jesus Christ who stops travel in order to help an injured person; an exemplar.

greenhouse effect — the phenomenon in which heat, rather than circulating in and out of a structure, is retained in that structure or system, usually referring to a place where plant growth is fostered and more recently referring to heat being retained in the Earth's atmosphere rather than being in circulation.

guilt — the human emotion related to feeling that the person's moral values have been violated.

H

hack — a person working in the communications field whose work evidences compromise and unethical behavior.

happiness — from Greek *eudaimonia* (which see), literally, "goodly demon;" Aristotle called this the *goal* of life, fulfillment, complete life satisfaction. In utilitarianism, however, the *degree* of happiness is measured.

hasty conclusion — see fallacies, Chapter 3.

heterosexual — referring to a person who has sexual relations only with persons of the opposite sex.

Hippocratic Oath — attributed to a Greek physician, Hippocrates (c. 460 – 377 B.C.), this pledge by physicians has as its essential tenet to "do no harm" and has since been revised; see discussion in Chapter 6.

Holy Bible — Book of sacred scriptures relied upon by primarily Catholics and Protestants for faith and practice.

homo sapiens — the most advanced life form on Earth, which has the capacity to adapt and to control other life forms.

homosexual — referring to a person who has sexual relations only with persons of the same sex.

honesty — from Latin *honor*, "a mark of respect," essentially referring to truth-telling and including self-disclosure.

human rights — morally authorized claims applying to all people solely on the basis of their being human individuals.

hypocrisy — pretending to possess qualities which, in fact, are not objectively apparent.

I

ignorance — see fallacies, Chapter 3.

illegal — in violation of a statement of behavior adopted as law by a state or nation's legislative body, and subject to enforcement by that state or nation.

incest — sexual relations with a member of one's own family other than one's spouse.

inconsistency — the quality of not maintaining the same conduct in same circumstances; also see fallacies, Chapter 3.

inductive reasoning — thinking or reasoning from within and applying the conclusion generally, usually based on intuitively measuring the probability of its application.

inference — statements that can be drawn from combining propositions and variables; e.g., "Sometimes, the weather is hot and sometimes it is not."

informal logic — intuitive human processes of critical thinking including the acts of observing, analyzing, developing potential solutions, verbalizing them and evaluating them. See Chapters 1 and 3.

informed consent — a legal term referring to a person, upon having suitable information, granting authority to someone else to take actions affecting that person.

insider trading — purchase or sale of stocks by officers or employees of a company based on information that only certain employees of that company could possess, usually for profit.

intuition — the ability of the mind to perceive data, receive, impressions, and make judgments without formally submitting these factors to a conscious, rational decision-making process.

invincible ignorance — see fallacies, Chapter 3.

Islam — a prominent world religion based on the teaching of the prophet Mohammed and relying upon the Koran as its sacred scriptures and Mecca as its holy city and Allah as its God; adherents are called Moslems.

is - ought — see fallacies, Chapter 3.

J

Judaism — the monotheistic religion of most Jews, based on the teachings of Moses and various prophets as recorded primarily in the Talmud and including books of the Old Testament of the Holy Bible and relying upon Jehovah or Elohim as its God; its holy city is Jerusalem.

justice — the quality of fairness among persons or societies or acts including: administration of justice (as in fair procedures and due process), distributive justice (as in apportioning advantages and rewards), retributive justice (as in punishing the wrong conduct of wrongdoers) and remedial justice (as in setting right of wrongs).

'just war' theory — the notion that war may be justified by certain moral conditions having been met — such as the war is a last resort, formally authorized by civil authority; its motive is just including the vindication of justice; it has a reasonable probability of success; good consequences can be expected to outweigh the evils; only the force necessary to prevail is exercised; targets are only those under arms.

K

kickbacks — giving back part of money received as payment, usually based on favorable treatment.

killing — behavior that causes death.

Koran — sacred scriptures for faith and practice of Moslem adherents; see also **Islam.**

L

legal — behavior that conforms to a law enacted by a state or nation's legislative body and having behind it the enforcement power of that state or nation.

lesbian — a female who has sexual relations only with other females.

Letter from the Birmingham Jail — a classic letter conveying the doctrine of civil disobedience, portraying the conflict between morality and ethics as against civil laws, written by Dr. Martin Luther King Jr. See Chapters 1 and 2 and Appendix.

libel — the tort in law whereby a person's reputation is maliciously damaged by printed or recorded statements in permanent form; while the U.S. Supreme Court in *Times vs. Sullivan* virtually set aside this right to sue as it applies to essentially public persons, it remains a right for most Americans.

lobbyist — a person who represents an interest in seeking to affect legislation pending before a Legislature or Congress; derived from meetings between such persons and those legislators in a lobby near the seat of decision.

logic — a system of evaluating statements or arguments.

lying — not telling the truth, including verbal and non-verbal expressions; one of the acts forbidden by the Ten Commandments and by every court of law.

M

metaethics — a system of assessing moral philosophy emphasizing the meaning of the language used; e.g., what is "love" to one person may not be to another, so the definitional context of the language used becomes the basis for determining the ethical value of the act.

militarism — a philosophy of governing in which a nation relies upon aggressive military power, including war, as its chief instrument of foreign policy.

moral — capable of distinguishing right from wrong with a predilection for right; as an adjective, it describes a person or act or thing that conforms to agreed-upon standards of conduct; as a noun, it is a summation of truth from an incident or parable.

moral development — human growth in awareness of rightness and wrongness of actions, often accompanying maturity but not necessarily; see Kohlberg, Gilligan in Chapter 2.

morality — the inherent right or wrong nature of an action or conduct

moral judgment — a personal conclusion about the rightness or wrongness of an action in a particular set of circumstances based on general moral principle(s).

moral reasoning — any process that applies general moral principle(s) to a situation or human problem and reaches a conclusion or decision; see also Chapter 3.

motive — the basis, reasoned or irrational, for the way a person acts; see Kohlberg, Chapter 2.

N

natural law — an approach to moral reasoning based on the perceived order inherent in the universe; acts that seem to conform to this order are considered good, those not conforming are considered bad.

natural rights — an approach to moral reasoning emphasizes the human protection and reliance upon common human personal rights.

neo-Malthusian argument — the primary cause of world hunger is held to be overpopulation and unjust social policy.

nepotism — favoritism in the workplace toward relatives or close friends.

Nicomachean Ethics — a treatise by Aristotle, especially glorifying the value of human endeavor (work) as ordained by God as valuable and uplifting.

nuclear energy — power derived from the collision and interaction of the nuclei of atoms.

nuclear war — any war in which strategic nuclear weapons of mass destruction are used.

nuclear waste — the residue from the creation of nuclear energy, in the form of substances.

O

obligations — duties or debts to others; constraints on behavior because of a favor granted or received from another.

obscenity — filthy or foul language or depiction characterized by immodesty and indecency; compare with rulings of the U.S. Supreme Court noted in Chapter 10.

ozone-layer — a condition of the upper atmosphere (stratosphere) in which there is present large amounts of ozone, which is developed when the sun's rays strike an oxygen molecule.

P

pacifism — a moral principle renouncing war; a philosophy of governing in which a nation rejects the use of military power as its chief instrument of foreign policy, relying exclusively on negotiation.

Patterned Principle of Distribution — any principle of distribution of resources that holds out some pattern according to which the good should be allocated such as one in which all people have the same amount of good (egalitarianism) or in which the worst of people have as much as possible (sometimes called the *maximum* pattern because the person with the minimum has the maximum that he or she can have). Patterned principles of distribution are contrasted with principles such as those in entitlement in which no particular pattern is held out as the right one, but rather the right distribution is simply whatever arises from free acquisition and transfer.

person — a human being who is a subject of moral concern and who possesses a right to life and certain medically described abilities such as (but not limited to) consciousness, reasoning, and communication; theoretically, medical science could deem a being of a non-human species also as a person. See also definitions in Chapter 6.

personal freedom — individual liberty enabling moral agency in making choices.

philosophy — the study of principles that underlie human conduct and order in the universe.

photosynthesis — the natural process whereby plant life absorbs carbon dioxide and emits oxygen.

plagiarism — the action whereby one appropriates another's writings or works or art and makes use of them as one's own; implied is the notion that by so doing one is "stealing" original work produced by another.

pleasure theory — a moral theory in which acts are deemed good if they bring pleasure.

pornography — from a Greek term meaning "writing about whores;" defining it has stumped modern courts and societies; the visible depiction of erotic behavior intended to cause or causing sexual desire or excitement, often including acts of sexual activity in violation of law; see Chapter 10.

poverty — the condition of being poor due to the absence of possession of certain living standards such as quality housing, goods or money.

prima facie — from Latin, "at first sight," obvious meaning adequate to establish fact unless refuted.

private property — goods, land, structures owned by private individuals or corporations.

production — the process of making things by human action in industry or art; see Chapter 16.

profession — a vocation that has sought to codify its values and enforce them among those who participate in that vocation.

professional ethics — the standards or codes of conduct adopted formally by a group of persons practicing the same vocation.

proposition — a basic thought; see Chapter 3.

proprietary information — information and trade secrets belonging to a person or corporation.

provincialism — see fallacies, Chapter 3.

punishment — from the Latin, *poine,* meaning "penalty;" the intended infliction of non-pleasurable feelings or activity upon a person, by an appropriate authority, sometimes including acts of pain, the denial of liberty and even

the taking of life (capital punishment) — as a result of an act that violated a law, code or other set of standards.

Q

questionable claim — see fallacies, Chapter 3.

R

realpolitik — referring to the view that substantive moral principles cannot be applied to disputes between nations.

recycling — the notion of reusing materials and substances so as not to deplete naturally occurring resources that produce those materials and substances.

red herring — see fallacies, Chapter 3.

redistribution — a system for reallocating wealth among members of a society.

republicanism, classical — the political philosophy having its roots in Aristotle and Thomas Aquinas that holds the human has an essential nature that includes rationality, sociability, and membership in the animal kingdom. This essential nature permits distinction between human needs and mere human wants. A just distribution of resources is one that uses resources to meet needs rather than desires.

retentionist — a person who opposes abolition of capital punishment; also one who supported slavery; see also abolitionist.

retribution — the act of imposing a penalty upon someone convicted of illegal or immoral behavior.

retributive justice — a system which fairly and appropriately punishes some prior wrongdoing.

right — correct moral judgment producing actions that are deemed consistent with a moral philosophy.

right of privacy — the notion, explicit in some state constitutions, that each individual has a legal right prohibiting invasion of a person's home or personal life.

right to die — the notion that persons have state-sanctioned authority to make choices affecting the length of their life.

rules — established guidelines and procedures for guiding human conduct.

rule-utilitarianism — a subset of utilitarianism in which the guiding principle is a rule requiring actions that produce the greatest happiness for the greatest number.

S

self-realization — a moral philosophy in which the goal is acting in ways to develop one's own human potential.

sex — the essential maleness or femaleness of a human being; also, commonly used to refer to sexual intercourse and even to acts of petting and foreplay in anticipation of intercourse.

sexism — discrimination based on whether a person is a male or female.

sexual harassment — acts or pattern of acts in the workplace discriminating against an individual on the basis of sex.

sin — the violation of a Divine Command, an evil or wicked wrongdoing.

situational ethics — determining what is right or good solely on the basis of the momentary context; implying that what is right or good today in this situation may not be right tomorrow in another set of circumstances.

slippery slope — see fallacies, Chapter 3.

socialism — an economic system in which all the means of production are socially owned and operated for the good of the public as a whole.

sodomy — performing oral and-or anal sex with another person.

statistical conclusion — see fallacies, Chapter 3.

strawman — see fallacies, Chapter 3.

suicide — death brought about by one's own actions.

Sunshine Amendment — an amendment to the Florida Constitution causing public officials to disclose personal finances, declaring public meetings and records open to the public, prohibiting certain actions by former officials; when adopted it codified the notion of "open government" in the state.

surrogate — a substitute, usually referring to those who stand in for actions that need to be taken by a member.

sustainable development — human habitation and activity that meets the needs of the present without compromising the ability of future generations to meet their own needs; according to J. Ronald Engel, "the kind of human activity that nourishes and perpetuates the historical fulfillment of the whole community of life on Earth."

syllogism — two statements followed by a third that is conclusionary.

T

Talmud — foremost among sacred scriptures of Judaism.

taxation — fees or charges levied and collection by a government upon residents of a state or nation.

teleological ethics — the notion that moral decisions are constituted by actions those aimed at pleasure, self-realization and happiness.

terrorism — planned violent acts against persons that evoke fear, usually causing death.

Times vs. Sullivan — a landmark U.S. Supreme Court ruling involving libel law; see **libel**.

truth — objectively accurate statements, always applicable.

two wrongs make a right — see fallacies, Chapter 3.

U

Utilitarianism — an approach to moral reasoning emphasizes always acting in order to produce the most satisfaction (pleasure of happiness) and the least amount of dissatisfaction (pain or unhappiness) for the greatest number of people; prime advocates include Jeremy Bentham and John Stuart Mill.

V

veil of ignorance — a philosophical notion assuming that persons can operate morally without understanding all the implications of their actions; cf. Locke.

virginity — the quality of human sexuality prior to ever having sexual intercourse.

virtue — from Latin *virtus,* literally all summarizing "manhood," a single term conveying all the qualities comprising excellence in human beings.

virtue ethics — an approach to moral reasoning that emphasizes the aim of excellence by doing the right thing as a result of focusing on certain character values.

W

war — a formal declaration of armed conflict by a sovereign nation against another nation; also, a condition of aggression between populations in which disputed claims, usually of territory, are pursued by systematic and violent means.

water pollution — the unnatural degradation of water on the Earth.

whistle-blowing — bringing into public view neglectful or abusive practices of an employer that threaten the public interest.

INDEX

A

LIST OF LINKED TERMS

The following words are highlighted in the CD-ROM text as hyperlinks. Where indicated, some of the words may be found under a different heading or term; for example, "computer ethics" and "computer hacking" will point to a Cybercrimes link page. Likewise, the term "sustainable development" will point to an Environmental Ethics link page.

Abortion
Acquired Immune Deficiency Syndrome (AIDS)
Advance directive
Advertising
Affirmative action
Animal rights
Apartheid
Applied ethics
Aristotle
Assisted suicide
Bentham, Jeremy
Bioethics
Biomedical research
Bonds
Brand preference
Campaign finance reform
Capital punishment
Capitalism
Carter, Jimmy
Censorship
Civil rights
Classical Republicanism
Clinton, Bill
Code of ethics
Cold War
Communication
Communitarianism
Computer hacking
Conflict of interest
Consequentialism
Contractarian
Corporate culture
Crime
Critical thinking
Cultural diversity
Death
Decision-making
Declaration of Independence
Deontology

Discrimination
Divine command
Doctrine of informed consent
Egalitarianism
Egoism
Employee obligations
Entitlement theory
Environmental ethics
Environmental Protection Agency
Equal Employment Opportunity Commission
Ethics
Euthanasia
Franklin, Benjamin
Freedom of Information Act
Genetic engineering
Gilligan, Carol
Global warming
Grievances
Hinduism
Hippocratic ethic
Hobbes, Thomas
Holy War
Human genome project
Industrial Revolution
Informal fallacy
Iron Law of Wages
Islam
Judaism
Just distribution of resources
Just war theory
Kant, Immanual
Kierkegaard, Soren
King, Martin Luther, Jr.
Kohlberg, Lawrence
Labor unions
Leadership
Liberty rights

Lincoln, Abraham
Locke, John
Logic
Magna Carta
Malthus, Thomas
Marketing
Marx, Karl
Mass production
Medical informed consent
Mentally incompetent
Mercy killing
Militarism
Mill, John Stuart
Moral development
Moral reasoning
Mutual assured destruction
Mutual funds
Natural law
Natural rights
Nixon, Richard M.
Nozick, Robert
Nuclear disarmament
Obscenity
Occupational Safety and Health Administration (OSHA)
Ozone
Pacifism
Packaging and labeling
Partial-birth abortion
Plagiarism
Plato
Pornography
Principle of utility
Product paternalism
Productivity
Professional ethics
Protection of health and safety
Protestant
Public relations

Racism
Rawls, John
Realpolitik
Rest, James R.
Reverse discrimination
Revolving door lobbying
Right of privacy
Roe vs. Wade
Routine salvaging of organs
Self-defense
Sex stereotyping
Sexual harassment
Shareholders
Smith, Adam
Socialism
Speciesism
Stewardship
Stocks
Suicide
Supply and demand
Taxation
Terrorism
Title VII
Trade
United Nations
Universal Declaration of Human Rights
Utilitarian
Values
Vatican
Virtue-ethics
Wages-and-hours laws
Watergate
Welfare rights
Whistle-blowing
Workers' compensation
Workplace decision making
Workplace safety
World War I
World War II

ADDITIONAL LINKED TERMS

Absenteeism
Acid rain
Antitrust laws
Baby Boomers
Balanced Budget
Branding
Budget deficits
Bureaucracy
Collective bargaining
Company image
Conflict management
Corporate chain of
command
Corporate goals
Corporate planning
Culture in organizations
Customer loyalty
Discipline procedures
Dismissals (pink slips,
etc.)

Distribution of income
Diversity training
Downsizing
Employee recognition
Entrepreneurial
organization
Ethics in the workplace
Feedback
GATT
Generation X'ers
Global economy
Government debt
Group behavior
Hersey and Blanchard's
theory
Inflation
International trade
Interviewing
Job stress
Labeling

Labor-management
relations
Labor market
Laissez-faire
management
Managing change
Marketing strategies
Market research
Market share
Mass marketing
Message content
Media selection
Mediation/arbitration
Mentoring
Monopoly
NAFTA
Need theories
Organizational behavior
Organizational change
Performance appraisals

Pollution permits
Price controls
Price discrimination
Price fixing
Product identity
Product quality
Promotional campaigns
Promotions
Resistance to change
Reward systems
Selection process/hiring
Sensitivity training
Stereotype
Supply curve
Target audience
Turnover of employees
Unemployment
Wages
Worker obsolescence

CD-ROM INSTRUCTIONS

SYSTEMS REQUIREMENTS

Windows PC

— 386, 486, or Pentium processor-based personal computer

— Microsoft Windows 3.1, Windows 95, or Windows NT 3.51 or later

— Minimum RAM: 4 MB for Windows 3.1; 8 MB for Windows 95 and NT

— Available space on hard disk: 4MB for Windows 3.1; 8 MB for Windows 95 and NT

— 2X speed CD-ROM drive or faster

— Browser: Netscape Navigator 3.0 or higher or Internet Explorer 3.0 or higher*

Macintosh

— Macintosh with a 68020 processor or higher, or Power Macintosh

— Apple OS version 7.0 or later

— Minimum RAM: 12 MB for Macintosh

— Available space on hard disk: 6MB for Macintosh

— 2X speed CD-ROM drive or faster

— Browser: Netscape Navigator 3.0 or higher or Internet Explorer 3.0 or higher*

* You can download either of these products using the addresses below:

NetscapeNavigator: *http://www.netscape.com/download/index.html*

Internet Explorer: *http://www.microsoft.com/ie/download*

GETTING STARTED

Insert the CD-ROM into your drive.

— Windows PC users should double click on My Computer, then on the CD drive. Find and double click on the Index.html file.

— Macintosh users should double click on the CD icon on the screen, then find and double click on the Index.html folder (Index.html may come up automatically on the Macintosh).

You will see an opening screen with the book cover and chapter navigation buttons. From this screen, you can click on the First Use button or begin navigating the CD content.

MOVING AROUND

If you have installed one of the required browsers listed previously, you will see two frames on your screen. The frame on the left-hand side contains a navigational toolbar with buttons. From this toolbar you can click on the buttons to link to that portion of the text, which will then appear in the frame on the right-hand side. Note: At any time, you can use the Back button on your browser to return to the previous screen.